THE HUMANITIES IN WESTERN CULTURE

VOLUME 2

THE HUMANITIES IN WESTERN CULTURE

A Search for Human Values

TENTH EDITION

VOLUME 2

ROBERT C. LAMM

ARIZONA STATE UNIVERSITY, RETIRED

Boston, Massachusetts Burr Ridge, Illinois Dubuque, Iowa
Madison, Wisconsin New York, New York San Francisco, California St. Louis, Missouri

McGraw-Hill
A Division of The **McGraw-Hill** *Companies*

THE HUMANITIES IN WESTERN CULTURE: VOLUME 2

This book is printed on acid-free paper.

7 8 9 10 CK/CK 9 0 9 8 7

ISBN 0-697-25429-1

Publisher *Rosemary Bradley*
Senior Developmental Editor *Deborah Daniel*
Associate Marketing Manager *Kirk Moen*
Editor *Ursula Sadie*
Designers *Barbara Mercer and Richard Foenander*
Picture Researcher *Carrie Haines*
Maps by Oxford Illustrators

Library of Congress Catalog Card Number: 95-76177

http://www.mhcollege.com

Front cover Jan Vermeer, *A Lady Writing,* detail. Ca. 1665. Oil on canvas, 17¾ × 15¾" (45 × 39.9 cm). National Gallery of Art, Washington, D.C. (Gift of Harry Waldron Havemeyer and Horace Havemeyer, Jr., in memory of their father, Horace Havemeyer).

Spine Jan van Eyck, *Ghent Altarpiece* (open), detail. Ca. 1425–32. Oil on panel, full altarpiece 11' 3" × 14' 5" (3.43 × 4.39 m). St. Bavo, Ghent, Belgium. Photo: Scala, Florence.

Back cover Paul Gauguin, *Where Do We Come From? What Are We? Where Are We Going?* 1897. Oil on canvas, 4' 6¾" × 12' 3½" (1.39 × 3.75 m). Museum of Fine Arts, Boston (Tompkins Collection).

Half-title Jacob Lawrence, *Harriet Tubman Series, No. 7.* 1939–40. Casein tempera on hardboard, 17⅛ × 12" (43.5 × 30.5 cm). Hampton University Museum, Hampton, Virginia.

Frontispiece Jan Vermeer, *Woman Holding a Balance*, detail. Ca. 1664. Oil on canvas, full painting 16¾ × 15" (42.5 × 38.1 cm). National Gallery of Art, Washington, D.C. (Widener Collection).

Prologue Constance Marie Charpentier, *Mlle. Charlotte du Val d'Ognes,* detail. 1785. Oil on canvas, full painting 5' 3½" × 4' 2⅝" (1.61 × 1.29 m). Formerly attributed to David. Metropolitan Museum of Art, New York (Mr. and Mrs. Isaac D. Fletcher Collection; bequest of Isaac D. Fletcher, 1917.17.120.204).

Unit Opener Illustrations

Unit 6 Giotto, detail of campanile, Florence. 1334–50s. Photo: Scala, Florence.

Unit 7 Louis le Vau and Jules Hardouin Mansart, Palace of Versailles, part of central section of garden facade. 1669–85. Photo: Robert Harding, London.

Unit 8 Pierre Auguste Renoir, *Le Moulin de la Galette,* detail. 1876. Oil on canvas, full painting 4' 3½" × 5' 9" (1.31 × 1.25 m). Musée d'Orsay, Paris. Photo: R.M.N., Paris.

Unit 9 Gerhard Richter, *Vase*, detail. 1984. Oil on canvas, full painting 7' 4½" × 6' 6¾" (2.25 × 2 m). Museum of Fine Arts, Boston (Juliana Cheney Edwards Collection).

Complete Contents

Volume I

Volume II

Expanded Contents

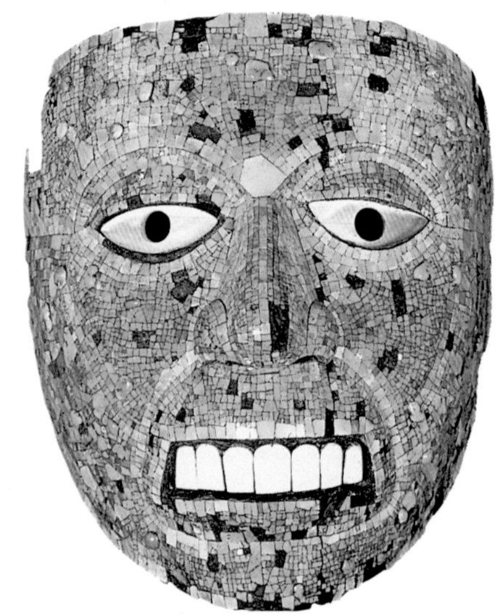

UNIT 6
The Renaissance 7

Maps

Listening Examples

Preface

Welcome to the tenth edition of a text that first appeared over forty years ago with multiple authors and entitled *The Search for Personal Freedom.* The original title continued through the seventh edition, after which the undersigned became the sole author of what is now *The Humanities in Western Culture.*

This is a two-volume text for the integrated humanities: the arts of literature, painting, music, sculpture, photography, architecture, and film, and the discipline of philosophy. Although philosophy is not an "art" in the strictest sense, the major philosophical ideas so consistently permeate each of the arts that they are, of necessity, interwoven throughout the book. The components of the humanities—philosophy and the arts—are presented not as separate technical disciplines but as interrelated manifestations of human creativity. Moreover, they are studied within the context of important developments in science, technology, economics, and politics. This is, in sum, a book about people and about "art's eternal victory over the human condition" (André Malraux).

In order to understand better why we are the way we are, our studies are centered on our cultural legacy—from Mesopotamia, Egypt, Greece, and Rome to the present day. Throughout the book the accomplishments of the past are considered not as museum pieces but as living evidence of enduring responses to the perplexities of life. These achievements have become, in our day, a basic part of our attempts to make sense of the universe.

The text is arranged chronologically and divided into nine major units in two volumes. Because artists naturally respond to the issues of their own time, each unit is prefaced by an overview of the social, scientific, religious, and philosophical climate of the period. Forming the core of this text are the primary sources, the art works themselves—many of them complete works rather than fragments: plays, poetry, short stories, entire sections of large works, hundreds of art illustrations, and numerous musical examples. Introduced with appropriate commentary, the selections are followed by practical exercises and questions. Additionally, there are maps, graphs, time charts, and, at the end of each volume, a glossary of important terms in philosophy and the arts. There is more than enough material for a two-semester course based entirely on the text; alternatively, the book can be used as a central text embellished by additional primary sources.

Because each major culture is distinct and merits its own special study, this is an examination of the evolution of Western civilization and its place in American culture. It is perhaps more multicultural than any other civilization because it has been more open to outside influences and ideas. Western culture—the humanities in particular—derives not just from the Mesopotamian, Egyptian, Graeco-Roman, and Germanic heritage. It has been influenced, altered, and/or enlarged over thousands of years by virtually every culture in the world. With its diverse origins Western humanities is an especially rewarding study in what is undoubtedly the most multicultural nation on earth. From colonial times onward, the United States has been a gathering of immigrants. Whether political refugees or seekers after a better life, people from all parts of the globe have been coming here for over three centuries, and will continue coming. What was once dubbed a "melting pot" culture is actually a rich and unique civilization. Whatever one's ancestry, there is something singular and special about being an American and, to cite only one example, we see it writ large at every session of the Olympic Games.

The presence of numerous non-Western immigrants in a rapidly changing population strongly reinforces the necessity of studying the cultural heritage of the West. Many immigrants are, after all, attracted to Western civilization because of the educational and vocational opportunities and the high standard of living, all of which have derived from the economic, political, and scientific development of Western nations. This does not imply, however, that newer citizens must leave their culture behind: far from it. It is most important to go on to study other major cultures plus what is currently called "global humanities," for global considerations are among the conspicuous realities of the late twentieth century. However, the author is convinced that most students, whether native-born or recent arrivals, would derive greater benefits from studying other cultures after they have acquired a better understanding of the Western heritage. Establishing a frame of reference seems the most practical and efficient way of comprehending cultural developments around the globe, most of which have been influenced by Western civilization.

In this new edition there are many changes in both content and style; a humanities textbook is, or should be, a living document that adjusts to the ever-changing world. New facts about the past are continually emerging, while today's world changes so rapidly as to leave us grasping for comprehension, not to mention gasping for breath.

The biggest change in this book is the addition of many feature boxes that, variously, focus on interesting ideas, other cultural influences, and significant events. There are more and better color illustrations and improved maps. In Volume 1 the chapter on Greek music has been integrated into the chapters on art and philosophy. Added to the art chapters are descriptions and color illustrations of the art and craft of jewelry. Aristophanes' *Lysistrata* is given in a different translation, as is Aristotle's *Poetics*. The unit on the Middle Ages includes additional material on Islamic arts plus a selection from Christine de Pisan, an important writer and early feminist. There is, in fact, increased coverage throughout of some notable contributions of women, especially in art and literature.

The Literary Selections in Volume 2 now include poems and short stories from South Africa, Germany, Greece, Egypt, France, Israel, and Ghana. Other additions include consideration of the religions other than Christianity, Judaism, and Islam that have become increasingly important in American life. These include Hinduism, Buddhism, and Zen Buddhism. The multiplicity of religious beliefs has, of course, added to the multiplicity of American life and culture.

What has not changed is the reading level of the text. After abundant input from users, reviewers, editors, and other interested parties, the author has concluded that writing down to students benefits no one. A watered-down text is manifestly unfair not only to students, but to teachers and higher education in general. Textual clarifications have been added as deemed necessary and the glossary has been substantially enlarged to better support the meaningful utilization of technical terminology. Much of the book has been reorganized with more precise heads and subheads that should contribute to the clarity of the text. The spelling of a number of the Greek proper names has been altered to reflect the most common usage, although a twenty-four-letter alphabet in which thirteen letters differ from the Latin ones can never be totally standardized. Overall, the author has endeavored to compose lucid material that is both accurate and consistently interesting, even entertaining, bearing in mind that the Greeks demanded of their dramas both enlightenment and entertainment. It should surprise no one that much of the content is challenging, for it concerns difficult and abstract concepts. What is most important, however, is that this material represents an essential aspect of what it means to be prepared to live and even flourish in a complex world of ceaseless change.

Robert C. Lamm

ACKNOWLEDGMENTS

This book could not have been written without the expertise and diligence of a reference librarian, photographic associate, and in-house editor, namely Katy Lamm.

I wish to thank the team at Calmann & King for their expertise during production: editor Ursula Sadie, designer Barbara Mercer, and picture researcher Carrie Haines.

I also wish to thank the following professors whose careful reading of the manuscript proved invaluable for this tenth edition: Bernard R. Conroy, Harold Washington College; Rick Davis, Ricks College; Michael G. Davros, Oakton Community College; Connie LaMarca-Frankel, Pasco-Hernando Community College; Stanley J. Kozikowski, Bryant College; Kathryn Kramer, Purdue University; George Rogers, Stonehill College; and Diane M. Snow, Brigham Young University. Thanks to Nanette Kelly of Imperial Valley College for her contributions to the new material on women in the humanities.

SUPPLEMENTS FOR THE INSTRUCTOR

The integrated teaching package of ancillary materials is available to instructors using *The Humanities in Western Culture*. Please contact your Brown & Benchmark sales representative or call 800–338–5371 to obtain these supplements, or to ask for further details.

Instructor's Resource Manual and Test Item File

The Instructor's Resource Manual is designed to assist instructors as they plan and prepare for classes. Included are chapter summaries, learning goals, lists of key terms, discussion topics, essay questions, and ideas for optional activities. The revised test item file appears at the end of the Instructor's Manual and contains chapter specific objective-type test questions that may be photocopied and used for quizzes or tests. Also included is a list of videotapes, recordings, videodiscs, and their suppliers.

MicroTest III

The questions in the test item file are available on MicroTest III, a powerful yet easy-to-use test generating software available for DOS, Windows, and Macintosh. MicroTest III allows instructors to generate tests and quizzes, and customize questions, headings, and instructions.

Call-in/Mail-in/Fax Service

Instructors may use Brown & Benchmark's convenient call-in/mail-in/fax service to generate tests. Select questions from the test item file at the end of the Instructor's Manual. Then call 800–338–5371, or mail your selections to Educational Resources at Brown & Benchmark Publishers,

25 Kessel Ct., Madison, WI 53711, or fax your request to Educational Resources at 608–277–7351. Within two working days of receiving your order, Brown & Benchmark will send by first-class mail (or fax) a test master, a student answer sheet, and an answer key for fast and easy grading.

Three Audiocassettes

Two sixty-minute cassettes (one each for Volumes 1 and 2) and one ninety-minute cassette (for Brief) contain the core Listening Examples from the text, a total of thirty-eight musical selections. Instructors may obtain copies of the cassettes for classroom use by calling 800–338–5371. Individual cassettes may be purchased separately, or, upon request, cassettes can be packaged with corresponding texts.

Instructor's Set of Compact Discs

This is from *Listener's Guide to Musical Understanding*, seventh edition, by Leon Dallin. An instructor's set of four CDs includes thirty-seven of the Listening Examples in the text as well as additional musical selections.

Slides

A set of fifty high-quality color slides correlated to Volumes 1 and 2, or a museum-specific videodisc, is available free to qualifying adopters.

Videos

Qualifying adopters may select video(s) from the Brown & Benchmark video catalog.

Humanities Transparencies Set

A set of seventy-three acetate transparencies is available with *The Humanities in Western Culture*. The set includes illustrations of art elements and principles; architectural styles; media; maps; musical forms, instruments, and selected musical scores.

Technology Products

Culture 2.0

Developed by Cultural Resources, Inc., Culture 2.0 © takes interdisciplinary humanities students on a fascinating journey into humanity's cultural achievements via Hypercard © software. Available for purchase in either IBM PC or MAC formats, this seven-disk program gives students access to essays, almanacs, and visual and musical examples. For each time period, categories include history, politics, religion, philosophy, art, and music, which provides an interactive Socratic method of learning for students. Culture 2.0 also features note-taking capabilities, report capabilities, and a student workbook for more guided learning. Contact your Brown & Benchmark sales representative or call Educational Resources at 800–338–5371 for ordering and purchase information.

Explore the Humanities!

Currently under development by Brown & Benchmark, this CD-ROM series will soon be available for purchase. *Explore the Humanities!* provides you and your students with a fully interactive exploration of many of the arts, ideas, and societies discussed in *The Humanities in Western Culture*. For further details, call your local Brown & Benchmark sales representative.

PROLOGUE

An Introduction to Integrated Humanities

> Each of the [artistic] masterpieces is a purification of the world, but their common message is that of their existence and the victory of each individual artist over his servitude, spreading like ripples on the sea of time, implementing art's eternal victory over the human situation.
>
> André Malraux

Everyone is capable of living a more rewarding life, which is reason enough for studying the humanities. From cave art to the present, the arts and ideas of human beings are beacons of hope, truth, and beauty for a world that needs to pay far more attention to the humanities, to the arts that teach us "nothing except the significance of life," in the words of twentieth-century American author Henry Miller. In our integrated approach to the humanities, we examine literature, painting, music, sculpture, philosophy, and architecture not as separate disciplines but as marvelous varieties of human creativity. Nor do we study the arts and artists in isolation. Artists are individuals, coping with the stress and strain of everyday life and, perhaps more than other people, influenced by the ideas and values of their society. "Artists are," observed composer Ned Rorem, "like everyone else, only more so."

The focus of our study of the humanities is the belief that the quality of life can be enhanced and that this enrichment is available to all. Unlike Middle East oil reserves, the reservoir of Western (or any other) culture is limitless; the more we draw from it the more there is to draw upon. The only deposits necessary are time and effort. The process amounts to addition or even multiplication; no one has to discard a collection of rock records to listen to Beethoven nor exchange Cowboy Art for Rembrandt.

This prologue is an introduction to the significance of the artist as an individual, the necessity of art, and the primacy of human values. Fundamental to cultural development are values such as truth, beauty, love, justice, and faith. Our investigation of how other cultures developed their value systems is chronological, a "return to the past" to see how the Egyptians, Greeks, and later civilizations handled their problems. What questions did they ask? What solutions did they try? We explore earlier cultures from the vantage point of our own world, studying earlier achievements not as museum pieces but as living evidence of enduring responses to life's perplexities. This priceless legacy is central to our attempts to make sense of the world and of our lives. Some will ask why we look to the past to prepare for the future. Where else can we look?

WHY STUDY THE HUMANITIES?

We explore the humanities not just to acquire facts about past eras but to try to understand those cultures: their questions, answers, and values. We can see the qualities they prized in their art and philosophy, and in their social and political institutions. We examine all of these areas to learn what they did; more importantly, we are concerned with why and how their cultures evolved in certain unique ways. Culture can be defined as what remains after a particular society has vanished. What is left behind is much more than artifacts. The creations of other cultures reveal their visions, their hopes, their dreams.

This is a text for the integrated or interdisciplinary humanities, the interrelationships of the arts, philosophy, and social and political ideas and institutions. Life is itself interdisciplinary. Using the interdisciplinary approach we study the "lives" of other civilizations to see how their values are manifested in just about everything they did, made, or thought. Whatever we learn from other cultures leads inevitably to a fuller understanding of civilization in general and of our own culture in particular.

Each of us has the option of accepting value systems from institutions or other persons, or we can generate a personal set of beliefs and values. The acquisition of an informed set of personal values is, of course, a lifelong project. The knowledge and understanding of other cultures and of ourselves are certainly their own reward, but there are additional advantages. If "the unexamined life is not worth living," as Socrates said, then self-knowledge would seem to be an acquired virtue. The greater our understanding of what is going on in our lives, the more likely we are to be aware of our options and thus of opportunities to improve the quality of life.

We can achieve the freedom objectively to examine alternatives and possibly make better choices. This freedom is not conditioned absolutely by political, social, and

economic considerations, although these factors can help or hinder. One can imagine a political prisoner of a totalitarian state whose knowledge and informed personal values allow a free and independent spirit in the most squalid of surroundings. The prisoner's goals, in this case, are not those of going somewhere or of acquiring material things, but of being a particular person. Those who, in the phrase of American essayist and poet Thoreau, "lead lives of quiet desperation" are at the mercy—intellectually and spiritually—of unknown forces over which they have no control. With no knowledge, no understanding, there is no way to determine whether there are one, two, or more viable choices. All of us have to accept the "slings and arrows of outrageous fortune" (Shakespeare) when we have no alternative. The trick is to be so aware of what is going on in our society and in our lives that we can, at least some of the time, select viable options that will help improve the quality of life. It is worth our while—worth our lives in fact—to study cultures of the past and present, and to make conscious cultural choices.

Western Civilization

As proclaimed by the title, this book is primarily—but not exclusively—concerned with Western civilization and its monumental contributions to world culture: its art, literature, performing arts, philosophy, science, and technology. Because it has had great complexity and influence and because it is our very own heritage, Western civilization commands our full attention. Light years from being monolithic, Western civilization is multicultural, having assimilated elements of every advanced culture in the world from ancient Mesopotamia and Egypt to modern India and China.

> All important cultures have ingenuities of their own. They are all marvelous manifestations of the power of the mind. But our own culture—Western civilization—is the most intellectual of all. More than the others, it is the product of systematic thought. The whole world uses its inventions. Its [science and] scientific methods . . . have been adopted by other civilizations and are transforming them.[1]

That the preeminence of Western culture is the result of systematic thought is only part of the equation. By asking, "systematic thought about what?" we can find the key to Western dominance in science.

> Dear Sir
> Development of Western Science is based on two great achievements; the invention of the formal logical system (in Euclidean geometry) by the Greek philosophers, and the discovery of the possibility to find out causal relationship by systematic experiment (Renaissance). In my opinion one has not to be astonished that the Chinese sages have not made these steps. The astonishing thing is that these discoveries were made at all.[2]

Yes, these discoveries are astonishing, for they led to the preeminence of the West in empirical science and technological advances. But there is more. The social and political values of the West have also had worldwide influence, ranging from the thought of Solon, Plato, and Aristotle to Cicero, Dante, Voltaire, John Locke, Thomas Jefferson, and Martin Luther King, Jr. Though immigrants from Asia, and Africa, for example, cannot readily perceive Western culture as "theirs," the fact is that their own cultures have adopted much of Western culture, and only partly because of colonialism. The adoption in various degrees of Western technology, science, political, and economic systems by the rest of the world speaks for itself. The further fact that Western civilization was, in general, created by what some have called "dead white men" alters nothing for we cannot rewrite history. The Greeks invented democracy, speculative philosophy, and formal logic, and Renaissance innovators invented and developed the experimental scientific method. The list of Western inventions is virtually endless: the incandescent light bulb, telephone, automobile, airplane, computer, space flight, and, yes, nuclear fission and fusion. The power eventually attained from nuclear-fusion power plants may even save the world from its manifold excesses.

The Culture-Epoch Theory

One begins to understand a culture by learning how that culture developed and what it means to us. We consider the past using a simplified version of the culture-epoch theory of cultural formation. Except for a smattering of political-military history, many of us are neither concerned nor knowledgeable about our cultural heritage. The culture-epoch theory helps overcome that deficiency: it stresses the critical fact of ceaseless change; it weaves cultural and intellectual history into a historic tapestry; and it emphasizes evolutionary processes in the course of history. The theory is neither more nor less "true" than other concepts of cultural evolution; for our purpose, in an interdisciplinary context, the theory works.

According to the culture-epoch theory, a culture is founded upon whatever conception of reality is held by the great majority of its people over a considerable period of time. Most people may not be aware of any concept of reality or, more likely, take it so much for granted that they don't know it is a human idea, held on faith. Thus, for most people at the time this is written, a typewriter is real, a physical tree is real, and all things that can be seen, heard, smelled, felt, or tasted are real.

1. Gilbert Highet, *Man's Unconquerable Mind* (New York: Columbia University Press, 1954), p.14.
2. Albert Einstein, Letter to J. E. Switzer, 23 April 1953. In D. J. de S. Price, *Science Since Babylon* (New Haven: Yale University Press, 1962), p.15n.

Scientists, philosophers, and theologians have given us different concepts of reality that have, at various times in history, come to be widely held. These thinkers contemplated the millions of forms of life, many of them similar yet each one different; they examined the forms of earth, air, fire, and water; they wondered about the processes of change by which a tree today may, at some time in the future, disintegrate into earth and reappear in some totally alien form. They watched such non-tangible things as sunlight and air becoming leaf and branch. Pondering these things, they came inevitably to the ultimate question: "What is the nature of reality?"

To reach an answer, they usually focus on a few profound inquiries, some of which may be given here. For example, they might say, "We see change all around us. We see grass eaten and turn into cow. We see cow eaten and turn into human. We see humans disintegrate and become earth. If all these changes can take place, what are the universal elements of which all things are composed?" Or they might say, "We see an individual human, Jane Doe, as baby, as youth, as adult, as frail old woman, as corpse. From one moment to the next, she is never the same, yet she is always the same, Jane Doe, a distinct being. Can it be that nothing is permanent, that reality is a process rather than a thing or group of things? If we have change, then, how does the process take place? And more to the point, we know that we live in a world of constant change, but what force directs the process?"

"Nonsense," retorts another group of thinkers. "Anything in a constant state of flux cannot be real. Only that which is permanent and unchanging is real. What, then, in the universe is permanent, unchanging in itself, yet can transform itself, manifest itself, or produce from itself the countless forms we see around us?" The responses to basic questions such as these are various concepts of reality.

Based on the idea of reality accepted as "true," specialized thinkers build different thought-structures that underlie visible institutions. These include a philosophy of justice from which particular forms of law and government spring; a philosophy of education that dictates the nature and curriculum of our schools; a religious philosophy that becomes apparent in churches and creeds, in synagogues, mosques, and temples; and an economic philosophy that is manifested in the production and distribution of goods and services. There are, of course, other philosophies and institutions, but these are some that affect our daily living.

A culture may be said to be "complete" and "balanced" when its underlying philosophies and its institutions are in harmony with its concept of reality, but by the time such a pattern is established, there are new forces already at work to undermine it. The wreckers are new critics who note inconsistencies within the idea of reality itself, who question postulates and detect contradictions.

From these innovative thinkers (philosophers, scientists, theologians) emerges a new idea of reality so convincing that it cannot be brushed aside. Once the new reality is generally accepted, the whole cultural structure finds itself without foundation. Law and justice of the old culture are no longer appropriate; educational philosophies are unsatisfactory; religious beliefs must be adjusted or even discarded; old ways of making and distributing things no longer suffice. Over a stretch of time, the culture is plunged into a period of chaos, the first step in the formation of a new epoch.

Periods of Chaos

A notable example of a chaotic period is the Early Middle Ages (ca. 400–800), once called the Dark Ages. The relative stability of the Graeco-Roman era of 480 BC to AD 180 began to disintegrate following the reign of Marcus Aurelius, though the Greek ideal of the individual as reality was superseded by the Roman view that reality was the state without seriously disturbing the cultural balance. Both the Greek and the Roman were secular societies with a general respect for law and justice, a stable social order, and reasonably effective government. Rome's decline was very gradual. Government, the economy, and the rule of law began to unravel and both the rise of Christianity and the barbarian invasions helped finish off a weary and decadent civilization. Most of western Europe soon found itself deep in a period of chaos. Graeco-Roman civilization was not totally destroyed—as demonstrated by the classically inspired Renaissance—but the stage was set for a new idea of reality through which order would be restored.

Periods of Adjustment

Out of the turmoil and confusion of chaotic periods of past cultures emerge periods of adjustment. At these times innovative artists and thinkers—whether painters, scientists, writers, composers, or philosophers—make important contributions that can suggest innovative lines, shapes, or patterns for a new culture.

No one needs to know all about new ideas of reality. In our own time, for example, artists (in particular) may or may not understand Einstein's theories of relativity. As sensitive persons, they generally feel the tensions caused by Einstein's work and its implications. Because they are creators, artists feel compelled to explore the impact that theories, ideas, and events have on their society and to examine or invent new experiences and relationships.

Many people experience the tension and turmoil in periods of chaos and adjustment, but artists tend actively to respond to the chaos and confusion. They explore conflicts within their culture and create new structures and designs; they synthesize the elements of dissension and give fresh meaning to experience. Some works of art are so outstanding that they become symbols of the new age. The Parthenon, for example (see fig. 7.35), still symbolizes the Golden Age of Athens.

At some point another element of the population—we may call them intellectuals—enters the picture. They are people like ourselves, college students and faculty, government officials, business executives, and others who have been troubled by the tensions and conflicts of the time. Still laboring in the period of adjustment, they become aware of fresh meanings and patterns produced by artists and other innovators. They begin reshaping these designs into new philosophies of government, justice, education, economics, and the like. Through their work, order slowly emerges out of chaos. Based on the idea of the Christian God as the ultimate reality, the period of adjustment of the medieval world saw the expansion of the power of the Church of Rome, the rise of universities, and the growth of cities (plus other factors) that coalesced in the thirteenth century into the period of balance of the High Middle Ages.

Periods of Balance

Order is the hallmark of periods of balance. At this point the idea of reality, the philosophies underlying the basic institutions, and the institutions themselves are all in harmony. Life must be very satisfying early in a period of balance with everything tidy and orderly. But new and challenging ideas are already stirring. Probably no one in thirteenth-century Europe perceived the era as a period of balance. Certainly no one foresaw that the balance would be upended by forces leading to stronger national states, the revival of humanism, and the rediscovery of Greek philosophy.

But change is the only constant. At the beginning of this century, for example, some physicists were convinced that the ultimate discoveries had been made with little left to do but some tidying-up. Yet Albert Einstein was just then formulating theories that would overthrow previous knowledge in physics. Exactly when people become certain of virtually everything during a period of balance, new ideas are already fermenting that will dump the apple cart into a new period of chaos.

A word of caution is needed here. This systematic description of an epoch makes it appear that artists function only in a time of chaos or adjustment, or that philosophers quit philosophizing until their proper time comes around. Of course this is not true. While any epoch can be divided roughly into the three periods described above, all functions occur with greater or lesser impact throughout the entire time period.

A COMMON BASIS FOR UNDERSTANDING THE ARTS

In the humanities we take art seriously. As Aristotle observed, "Art is a higher type of knowledge than experience." As previously indicated in the description of a culture-epoch, eminent artists help to create patterns for a way of life. "The object of art is to give life a shape," said the twentieth-century French dramatist Jean Anouilh. The Parthenon, Chartres cathedral, Augustine's *The City of God*, Beethoven's Ninth Symphony, Michelangelo's *David* and Sistine Chapel ceiling are only a few examples of art works that have affected life in the Western world.

One might ask what area of the universe is the darkest, the most unknown. The universe itself? Einstein once said that the most incomprehensible fact about the universe is that it is so comprehensible. No, the most bewildering portion of the universe is yourself. As a member of the human race you are (or should be) asking yourself such questions as "Who am I?", "What am I?", "Why am I here?" It is the artist who persists in reacting to these questions, who seeks answers from within, and who discovers answers that strike responsive chords in the rest of us. As Henry Miller said, "art teaches nothing, except the significance of life."

A Shakespearean scholar once remarked that Shakespeare, in his plays, had made discoveries as important as those made by a scientist. Such an assertion seems, at first, to be an overreaction to the dominance of science in today's world. Consider, however, the playwright's treatment of love and hate in *Romeo and Juliet*, good and evil in *King Lear*, and murder and revenge in *Macbeth*. As enacted on stage, these aspects of the human condition constitute artistic truths. This idea of discoveries by Shakespeare or any other artist can provide a basis for a better understanding of the arts. In this respect, as the French poet and playwright Jean Cocteau observed, "art is science in the flesh."

The physical world is explored by the sciences; the social sciences make discoveries about the behavior and activities of people in various groups; the arts and humanities probe the inner meaning: humanity's hopes, fears, loves, delights as individuals act and react within a social context. "All art is social," historian James Adams noted, "because it is the result of a relationship between an artist and his time." Art is also exploration, and the discoveries made can be expressed as concepts and percepts. Concepts are intangible ideas such as friendship, beauty, truth, and justice. What we perceive with our senses are percepts: line, taste, color, aroma, volume, pitch, and so forth. Artists express concepts by the unique manner in which they choose to arrange the percepts, that is, the sense-apparent objects and materials. Obviously this kind of vivid creativity can never be done by committee. "Art is the most intense mode of individualism that the world has known," said nineteenth-century Irish writer Oscar Wilde.

Differences and Similarities

Because of variations in media and modes of expression, the arts differ from one another in a variety of ways. Certainly a time-art such as music, which exists only as long as it is heard, differs from a space-art such as painting, which uses visual symbols as its means of expression. Both arts are separated from literature, a word-art that depends upon fully developed literacy. The differences between Beethoven's Fifth Symphony, the *Mona Lisa*, and *Hamlet* are obvious; not so obvious are their similarities. "Painting," wrote nineteenth-century American poet and essayist Emerson, "was called silent poetry, and poetry speaking painting. The laws of each art are convertible into the laws of any other." As early as the fourteenth century Dante called sculpture "visible speech." The common basis of all the arts is the exploration, by means of sensory percepts, of the emotions, mind, and personality of human beings; their common goal is to speak directly to our inner being. As Emerson also wrote: "Raphael paints wisdom; Handel sings it; Pheidias carves it; Shakespeare writes it."

The artist deals subjectively with all materials while drawing upon a singular store of personal experience. Artistic production depends as much on the background and personality of the artist as it does upon the raw material of experience. It therefore follows that each artist is unique and that the artist's production is necessarily unique. To illustrate, let us examine the treatment two literary artists make of the same theme: the emptiness of the life of a woman who, herself, is virtually a complete blank, but who moves from man to man, living only as a reflection of each man. Read Dorothy Parker's "Big Blonde" and Anton Chekhov's "The Darling," both short stories. Though the experience is very similar in the two stories, the end result is quite dissimilar and the reader's experience is also different. The reader might protest: "But one of them must be right about this woman and one must be wrong." Actually, both Parker and Chekhov are right—both stories have the ring of truth—and any other artist treating the same material with a different insight would also be right. The discovery of multiple truths is a personal matter and the corollary is that the realm of truth in personality, that prime area where the arts are focused, is inexhaustible. Anyone who understands any work of art grows with each facet of experience shared with the artist. Our boundaries are expanded as we add the artist's experiences to our own.

> Thanks to art, instead of seeing one world, our own, we see it multiplied and, as many original artists as there are, so many worlds are at our disposal.
>
> André Malraux

SUMMARY

The humanities include, but are not limited to, the arts of literature, painting, music, sculpture, architecture, and dance, and the discipline of philosophy that permeates all the arts and finally unites them all. The arts, taken together, are a separate field of human knowledge with their own area of exploration and discovery, and with a method of their own. So these volumes will concentrate on some of the most significant artistic productions of each of the major periods of Western civilization. Each unit begins with an overview of the social, scientific, religious, and philosophic climate of the period in which the artists were working, for artists usually accept the scientific and social world-picture of their time. Following these introductory discussions, attention turns to the arts themselves to reveal answers to the great questions of humankind—the new patterns, structures, and meaning that artists found for life in their time. This procedure enables the student to trace the development and changes of the problems that plague us so sorely in our own time. Equipped with knowledge of the great answers found in the past that still shape the way we live today, having come to know the exalted expressions of humanity revealed at their fullest, each individual can work to develop an informed set of values and a freedom to be the person he or she would like to be.

Not everyone will derive the same kind or degree of satisfaction from a particular art form, but the educated person is obliged to know that "there is something in it," even if that "something" is not deeply moving. And perhaps, with deeper acquaintance and wider knowledge, that "something" will become clearer and of greater value. "I don't get it" is no refutation of either Einstein or Bach.

We have made the assertion that the artist is an explorer and discoverer in the realm of the human personality. The artist uses the methods of intuition and composition. The artist's raw material lies in the human personality and in human experience, with their vast and unknown reaches, their disrupting conflicts. The artist gives form to the component elements of personality and experience, and in so doing generates an artistic truth. No matter whether we speak of literature, painting, sculpture, music, or any of the other arts, this concept of creating form out of chaos is the common basis and foundation for all aesthetics.

UNIT 6

The Renaissance, 1350–1600

The Renaissance

1350–1600

	People and Events	Art and Architecture	Literature and Music	Philosophy, Science, Discovery
1350	**1305–76** Papacy at Avignon **1348–50** Black Death **1382** Wiclif's Bible	**Limbourg Brothers** fl. 1385–1416 *Très Riches Heures du Duc de Berry*	**Petrarch** 1304–74 sonnets **Boccaccio** 1313–75 *The Decameron*	
1400	**1415** Jan Hus burned at stake; Henry V of England defeats French at Agincourt **1378–1417** Great Schism of church **1428** Joan of Arc defeats English **1436** Dedication of Florence Cathedral **1419–67** Philip the Good of Burgundy **1453** Hundred Years' War ends; Constantinople falls to Turks **1449–92** Lorenzo de' Medici **1456** Gutenberg Bible printed **1469–1504** Reign of Ferdinand and Isabella of Spain **1492–1503** Alexander VI (Borgia pope) **1494** Beginning of French and Spanish invasions of Italy **1498** Savonarola burned at stake; Petrucci obtains printing monopoly in Venice	**Brunelleschi** 1377–1446 Florence Cathedral dome; Pazzi Chapel **Donatello** 1386–1466 *David* **van Eyck** 1390–1441 *Ghent Altarpiece* **Uccello** 1397–1475 *Battle of San Romano* **van der Weyden** 1400–64 *Portrait of a Lady* **Masaccio** 1401–28? *Tribute Money* **Alberti** 1404–72 Santa Maria Novella **Verrocchio** 1435–88 *David* **Memling** 1440–94 *The Presentation in the Temple* **Bramante** 1444–1514 Tempietto **Botticelli** 1445–1510 *Birth of Venus* **Bosch** 1450–1516 *Garden of Delights* **da Vinci** 1452–1519 *The Last Supper*	**Dunstable** 1390–1453 English composer **Dufay** 1400–74 Burgundian composer **Lorenzo Valla** ca. 1407–57 proved *Donation of Constantine* a forgery **Issac** 1450–1517 German composer at Medici court **Josquin** 1450–1521 Franco-Flemish composer **Mirandola** 1463–94 *Oration on the Dignity of Man* **Erasmus** 1466–1536 *The Praise of Folly* **Machiavelli** 1469–1527 *The Prince* **Sir Thomas More** 1478–1535 *Utopia* **Castiglione** 1478–1529 *The Book of the Courtier* **1498** *The Witches' Hammer,* a manual for finding witches	**Prince Henry the Navigator** 1394–1460 improves compass and navigation charts **Ficino** 1433–99 translates Plato for Platonic Academy **1462** Cosimo de' Medici founds Platonic Academy **Copernicus** 1473–1543 heliocentric theory **1486** Diaz sails down African coast **1492** Columbus discovers America **1497** John Cabot lands in America; North America claimed by England **1497–99** Vasco da Gama sails around Africa to India
1500	**1503–13** Julius II (Warrior pope) **1517** Luther posts 95 Theses **1521** Diet of Worms: Luther's formal break with Rome **1509–47** Henry VIII of England **1515–47** Francis I of France **1519** Cortés conquers Aztecs in Mexico **1527** Rome sacked by Charles V **1531–33** Pizarro conquers Incas in Peru **1534** Church of England founded by Henry VIII **1540** Society of Jesus officially sanctioned **1545–64** Council of Trent; Inquisition renewed **1547** Calvin's Bible **1588** English defeat Spanish Armada	**Grünewald** 1483?–1528 *The Small Crucifixion* **Dürer** 1471–1528 *Erasmus of Rotterdam* **Giorgione** 1475–1510 *Adoration of the Shepherds* **Michelangelo** 1475–1564 *David, Pietà,* Sistine Chapel **Raphael** 1483–1520 *School of Athens* **Titian** 1488–1576 *Venus with a Mirror* **Holbein** 1497–1543 *Sir Thomas More* **Parmigianino** 1503–40 *Madonna with the Long Neck* **Tintoretto** 1518–94 *The Last Supper* **Palladio** 1518–80 Villa Rotunda **Bruegel the Elder** 1525–69 *Winter (Return of the Hunters)* **Veronese** 1528–88 *Christ in the House of Levi*	**Rabelais** 1490–1553 *Gargantua and Pantagruel* **Vasari** 1511–74 *Lives of Architects, Painters, Sculptors* **Palestrina** 1524/5–94 Roman composer **Lassus** 1532–94 Flemish composer **Montaigne** 1533–92 *Essays* **Cervantes** 1547–1616 *Don Quixote* **Gabrieli** 1557–1612 Venetian composer **Shakespeare** 1564–1616 *The Tempest* **Farnaby** 1565–1640 English composer **Bennet** 1575–1625 English madrigal composer	**1513** Balboa discovers Pacific **1519–22** Magellan sails around world **Tycho Brahe** 1546–1601 astronomer **Francis Bacon** 1561–1626 empirical science Illustration from Kepler's *Prodromus Dissertationum Cosmographicarum.* Photo: A.K.G., London.
1600	**1558–1603** Elizabeth I of England	**El Greco** 1541–1614 *The Resurrection of Christ*		

CHAPTER 16

A New Way of Looking at the World

A remarkable period of intellectual energy and artistic creativity, the Renaissance (ca. 1350–1600) ushered out the Middle Ages and set the stage for the emergence of the modern world. It was also a turbulent time of social unrest, political turmoil, religious conflict, and, particularly in Italy, constant warfare. Seen by its contemporaries as a "rebirth" of classical civilization, the era was also a period of chaos that followed upon the breakdown of the balanced culture of the High Middle Ages. Graeco-Roman civilization had neither died nor been "lost." Rather, it had been both replaced and partly absorbed by 1,000 years of what humanists designated the "Middle Age" between the fall of Rome and the revival of Graeco-Roman culture.

The emphasis in medieval Christendom on eternal salvation in another world as the sole purpose of human existence gradually gave way to the idea that life on earth had its own worth and that the life of each individual man and woman was unique and valuable. Everyone had worth and dignity and a free will that enabled them to use their God-given capacities to transform the world. They could and should develop their minds by study and reflection, activities advocated by Cicero as worthy of the "dignity of the human race" (*On Duties*, I, 30). Renaissance men and women were often as sanctimonious, superstitious, and naive as their medieval ancestors, but they were also more individualistic, materialistic, and skeptical than almost anyone in that vanished world. The enthusiastic revival of their ancient heritage reinforced their pride in being singular individuals who would create a brave new world.

Glorification of the distant past originated in Italy and spread to France, England, and the Low Countries, none of which even possessed a classical heritage, though all contained Roman ruins. What Italy and the northern countries had in common was vigorous trade, the growth of capitalism, expanding craft guilds, burgeoning industries, growing cities, and a widespread spirit of creative endeavor.

THE RISE OF HUMANISM

On 8 April 1341 the Latin scholar with the Latinized name of Petrarch (Francesco Petrarca; 1304–74) was crowned with a laurel wreath as the first poet laureate of modern times. Symbolizing an intellectual movement called **humanism** that had begun in Verona and Padua a century earlier, the ceremony took place, fittingly, in Rome. Humanists believed in the worth and dignity of the individual and that belief led, in turn, to the rediscovery of the culture of classical antiquity: literature, history, rhetoric, ethics, and politics. Describing his abandoned law studies at Bologna as "the art of selling justice," Petrarch devoted his life to acquiring what he called the "golden wisdom" of the ancients: proper conduct of one's private life; rational governance of the state; the enjoyment of beauty; and the quest for truth. Humanism was a union of love and reason that stressed earthly fulfillment rather than medieval preparations for paradise. The humanists had rediscovered their ancestors, seeing them as real people able to lend assistance in the restatement of human values. Petrarch wrote letters to Cicero, whom he called his father, and to Virgil, who was, he said, his brother.

There had been earlier stirrings of classical revivals in the ninth century at Aachen, where Charlemagne established his famous school, and in the twelfth century at the Cathedral School of Chartres and the Court of Eleanor of Aquitaine; but not until the middle of the fourteenth century did the rediscovery of antiquity become a true cultural movement. Petrarch's friend, the writer Giovanni Boccaccio (bo-KOTCH-yo; 1313–75), was one of the first Westerners to study Greek, but by 1400 nearly all the Greek authors had been recovered and translated into Latin and Italian: Homer, Herodotos, Thucydides, Aeschylus, Sophocles, Euripides, Aristophanes, and all of Plato's dialogues. Human history was divided into three ages, said the humanists: ancient, middle, and their own modern era. The middle was the Middle Ages, deemed a benighted phase between the fall of Rome in 476 and the rebirth of classical cultures. The men and women of the Renaissance were, in effect, discovering themselves as they recovered the past. They were aware that their time was significantly different from the Middle Ages, that they were the spiritual heirs of a distant past that was being reborn through their own efforts. There was no Latin word for rebirth, but Giorgio Vasari (1511–74) invented the word *rinascita* ("renaissance") in his *Lives of the Most Excellent Italian Architects, Painters, and Sculptors from Cimabue to our own Times* (Florence, 1550). Vasari's term was applied to the fine arts that had developed out of early humanism, but the label now describes an era that consciously freed itself from the bondage of medievalism.

Lorenzo Valla (ca. 1407–57), one of the few Renaissance scholars not associated with Florence, confined his activities mainly to Rome and Naples, where he translated Herodotos and Thucydides into Latin. A dedicated scholar of immense learning, he dared to challenge any authority. He criticized Cicero's supposedly flawless Latin, wrote a philological critique of the New Testament and, most notably, exposed the *Donation of Constantine* as a forgery. This was the document that willed Constantine's entire empire to the Church of Rome and on which Rome based its claims to temporal power.[1]

Valla would be called a bookworm today. He was one of the many scholars who devoted their careers to conserving antiquity by copying and translating ancient documents. Other humanists, such as Boccaccio and Rabelais, preferred writing in the vernacular, whereas still others tried to synthesize the classical past with the Christian present. Marsilio Ficino and Pico della Mirandola were two of the most important of the synthesizers, particularly for the Platonists of Florence.

Platonic Academy

A celebrated center of humanistic studies, the Platonic Academy was founded at Florence in 1462 by the banker Cosimo de' Medici (1389–1464), the sire of a family that was to dominate Florence throughout most of the Renaissance. The guiding force of the academy, Marsilio Ficino (fi-CHEE-no; 1433–99), promoted the study of Platonism through his translations into Latin of Plato, Plotinus, and other philosophers. In his major work, the *Theologia Platonica* (1482), Ficino described a universe presided over by a gracious and loving God who sought to bring humankind to him through beauty, one of his attributes. The contemplation of the beauty of nature, of beautiful things, of glorious art became a sort of worship of this God. When beauty was arranged in words or paintings (as in fig. 17.17), these works of art, too, became part of the circle of love by which people reached beyond themselves to a loving God. Ficino's theory of "Platonic love," a spiritual bond between lovers of beauty, had strong repercussions in later English, French, and Italian literature.

Pico della Mirandola (PEA-ko del-la mere-AN-do-luh; 1463–94) was a colleague of Ficino and a major influence on the Florentine humanists. His broadly based classical education in Greek and Latin was enriched by studies in Hebrew and Arabic that brought him into contact with Jewish and Arabic philosophy. Pico's attack on astrology impressed even the astronomer Johannes Kepler. More importantly, his conception of the dignity of the human race and the ideal of the unity of truth were significant contributions to Renaissance thought. His *Oration on the Dignity of Man* has been called "The Manifesto of Humanism." The following excerpts from Pico's ringing affirmation of the nobility of humankind epitomize Renaissance optimism.

1. C. B. Coleman (ed.), *The Treatise of Lorenzo Valla on the Donation of Constantine* (New Haven: Yale University Press, 1922).

LITERARY SELECTION 41

Oration on the Dignity of Man, 1486

Pico della Mirandola

I have read in the records of the Arabians, reverend Fathers, that Abdala the Saracen, when questioned as to what on this stage of the world, as it were, could be seen most worthy of wonder, replied: "There is nothing to be seen more wonderful than man." In agreement with this opinion is the saying of Hermes Trismegistus: "A great miracle, Asclepius, is man." But when I weighed the reason for these maxims, the many grounds for the excellence of human nature reported by many men failed to satisfy me—that man is the intermediary between creatures, the intimate of the gods, the king of the lower beings, by the acuteness of his senses, by the discernment of his reason, and by the light of his intelligence the interpreter of nature, the interval between fixed eternity and fleeting time, and (as the Persians say) the bond, nay, rather, the marriage song of the world, on David's testimony but little lower than the angels. Admittedly great though these reasons be, they are not the principal grounds, that is, those which may rightfully claim for themselves the privilege of the highest admiration. For why should we not admire more the angels themselves and the blessed choirs of heaven? At last it seems to me I have come to understand why man is the most fortunate of creatures and consequently worthy of all admiration and what precisely is that rank which is his lot in the universal chain of Being—a rank to be envied not only by brutes but even by the stars and by minds beyond this world. It is a matter past faith and a wondrous one. Why should it not be? For it is on this very account that man is rightly called and judged a great miracle and a wonderful creature indeed.

But hear, Fathers, exactly what this rank is and, as friendly auditors, conformably to your kindness, do me this favor. God the Father, the supreme Architect, had already built this cosmic home we behold, the most sacred temple of His godhead, by the laws of His mysterious wisdom. The region above the heavens He had adorned with Intelligences, the heavenly spheres He had quickened with eternal souls, and the excrementary and filthy parts of the lower world He had filled with a multitude of animals of every kind. But, when the work was finished, the Craftsman kept wishing that there were someone to ponder the plan of so great a work, to love its beauty, and to wonder at its vastness. Therefore, when everything was done (as Moses and Timaeus bear witness), He finally took thought concerning the creation of man. But there was not among His archetypes that from which He could fashion a new offspring, nor was there in His treasurehouses anything which He might bestow on His new son as an inheritance, nor was there in the seats of all the world a place where the latter might sit to contemplate the universe. All was now complete; all things had been assigned to the highest, the middle, and the lowest orders. But in its final creation it was not the part of the Father's power to fail as though exhausted. It was not the part of His wisdom to waver in a needful matter through poverty of counsel. It was not the part of His kindly love that he who was to praise God's divine generosity in regard to others should be compelled to condemn it in regard to himself.

At last the best of artisans ordained that that creature to whom He had been able to give nothing proper to himself should have joint possession of whatever had been peculiar to each of the different kinds of being. He therefore took man as a creature of indeterminate nature and, assigning him a place in the middle of the world, addressed him thus: "Neither a fixed abode nor a form that is thine alone nor any function peculiar to thyself have we given thee, Adam, to the end that according to thy longing and according to thy judgment thou mayest have and possess what abode, what form, and what functions thou thyself shalt desire. The nature of all other beings is limited and constrained within the bounds of laws prescribed by Us. Thou, constrained by no limits, in accordance with thine own free will, in whose hand We have placed thee, shalt ordain for thyself the limits of thy nature. We have set thee at the world's center that thou mayest from thence more easily observe whatever is in the world. We have made thee neither of heaven nor of earth, neither mortal nor immortal, so that with freedom of choice and with honor, as though the maker and molder of thyself, thou mayest fashion thyself in whatever shape thou shalt prefer. Thou shalt have the power to degenerate into the lower forms of life, which are brutish. Thou shalt have the power, out of thy soul's judgment, to be reborn into the higher forms, which are divine."

O supreme generosity of God the Father, O highest and most marvelous felicity of man! To him it is granted to have whatever he chooses, to be whatever he wills. Beasts as soon as they are born (so says Lucilius) bring with them from their mother's womb all they will ever possess. Spiritual beings, either from the beginning or soon thereafter, become what they are to be for ever and ever. On man when he came into life the Father conferred the seeds of all kinds and the germs of every way of life. Whatever seeds each man cultivates will grow to maturity and bear in him their own fruit. If they be vegetative, he will be like a plant. If sensitive, he will become brutish. If rational, he will grow into a heavenly being. If intellectual, he will be an angel and the son of God. And if, happy in the lot of no created thing, he withdraws into the center of his own unity, his spirit, made one with God, in the solitary darkness of God, who is set above all things, shall surpass them all. Who would not admire this our chameleon? Or who could more greatly admire aught else whatever? It is man who Asclepius of Athens, arguing from his mutability of character and from his self-transforming nature, on just grounds says was symbolized by Proteus in the mysteries. Hence those metamorphoses renowned among the Hebrews and the Pythagoreans.

For the occult theology of the Hebrews sometimes transforms the holy Enoch into an angel of divinity whom they call "Mal'akh Adonay Shebaoth," and sometimes transforms others into other divinities. The Pythagoreans degrade impious men into brutes and, if one is to believe Empedocles, even into plants. Muhammad, in imitation, often had this saying on his tongue: "They who have deviated from divine law become beasts." And surely he spoke justly, for it is not the bark that makes the plant but its senseless and insentient nature; neither is it the hide that makes the beast of burden but its irrational, sensitive soul; neither is it the orbed form that makes the heavens but its undeviating order; nor is it the sundering from body but his spiritual intelligence that makes the angel. For if you see one abandoned to his appetites crawling on the ground, it is a plant and not a man you see; if you see one blinded by the vain illusions of imagery, as it were of Calypso, and softened by their gnawing allurement, delivered over to his senses, it is a beast and not a man you see. If you see a philosopher determining all things by means of right reason, him you shall reverence: he is a heavenly being and not of this earth. If you see a pure contemplator, one unaware of the body and confined to the inner reaches of the mind, he is neither an earthly nor a heavenly being; he is a more reverend divinity vested with human flesh . . . .

Are there any who would not admire man, who is, in the sacred writings of Moses and the Christians, not without reason described sometimes by the name of "all flesh," sometimes by that of "every creature," inasmuch as he himself molds, fashions, and changes himself into the form of all flesh and into the character of every creature? For this reason the Persian Euanthes, in describing the Chaldaean theology, writes that man has no semblance that is inborn and his very own but many that are external and foreign to him. But why do we emphasize this? To the end that after we have been born to this condition—that we can become what we will—we should understand that we ought to have especial care to this, that it should never be said against us that, although born to a privileged position, we failed to recognize it and became like unto wild animals and senseless beasts of burden, but that rather the saying of Asaph the prophet should apply: "Ye are all angels and sons of the Most High," and that we may not, by abusing the most indulgent generosity of the Father, make for ourselves the freedom of choice He has given into something harmful rather than salutary. Let a certain holy ambition invade our souls, so that, not content with the mediocre, we shall pant after the highest and (since we may if we wish) toil with all our strength to obtain it.

Let us disdain earthly things, despise heavenly things, and, finally, esteeming less whatever is of the world, hasten to that court which is beyond the world and nearest to the Godhead. There, as the sacred mysteries relate, Seraphim, Cherubim, and Thrones hold the first places; let us, incapable of yielding to them, and intolerant of a lower place, emulate their dignity and their glory. If we have willed it, we shall be second to them in nothing.

VIRTÙ

Renaissance scholars taught that *virtù* was the highest goal of human existence. *Virtù* is not our word "virtue"; loosely defined, call it "excellence as a person," but with masterful qualities and multiple abilities: exceptional intelligence and creativity, physical courage and daring, and, above all, action that reveals all these characteristics.[2] It occupies the central place in Machiavelli's *The Prince*. *Virtù* became identified with the concept of the "Renaissance man" as exemplified by Leonardo da Vinci. He, like Francis Bacon, could announce "I take all knowledge as my province."

RENAISSANCE SCIENCE AND TECHNOLOGY

The Copernican Revolution

The medieval idea of the universe was based on Ptolemy's geocentric theory, which identified the earth as the center of the universe, with the moon, planets, and stars revolving around it in more or less fixed spheres, or orbits. Around the whole lay the crystalline sphere, beyond which was the realm of God. However, many medieval scientists—particularly the Arabic astronomers—had observed movements of stars and planets that did not fit into this scheme but required additional spheres. Working within the confines of Ptolemaic assumptions, these scientists postulated backward loops of heavenly bodies to account for variations in their rotation periods. By the Renaissance, astronomers had compiled a complicated system of more than seventy spheres surrounding the earth, with each of the heavenly bodies performing an epicycle (little backward rotation of its own) around a central point on its orbit.

The Ptolemaic system was first questioned by the Polish astronomer and mathematician Nicholas Copernicus (1473–1543). Copernicus never advanced the theory that the earth was not the center of the universe; he believed that mathematical calculations would be less complicated if one accepted the sun as a stationary point and based one's computations on a heliocentric system. Though he failed to design a simpler system or to eliminate mistaken assumptions about orbits, his contribution was monumental. Copernicus opened the door to modern astronomy.

> Today we honor Copernicus not because he produced the modern view of the solar system (he didn't) or because his system was simpler than Ptolemy's (it wasn't), but because he was the first person in "modern times" who had the courage and perseverance to carry his idea beyond the realm of philosophical speculation. It was he who pointed out that the emperor's new clothes might be missing. After him everyone came to see geocentrism as just an assumption, one that could be challenged like any other.[3]

Paradoxically, other advances in Renaissance science were made by translating the ancient writings of Galen, Archimedes, Hippocrates, and other Greek scientists into Latin. Additionally, there were improvements in anatomical and geological studies but, on the whole, Renaissance scientific studies were mainly preparation for the scientific revolution of the seventeenth century.

Technology

Printing was invented in China in 756, gunpowder around 1100, and the magnetic compass a decade or two later. Like many Chinese innovations, these were so rigidly controlled by the imperial government that they had no value for the common people. With no equivalent central authority in Europe the impact of just these three inventions was dramatic. Movable type was invented in the 1440s in the Rhine valley of Germany, possibly in Mainz by Johannes Gutenberg (1398?–1468; fig. 16.1). Once the privilege of the few who could afford hand-copied books, learning became available to all. The invention of printing made possible the most rapid expansion of knowledge that we have known prior to the proliferation of computers in our own time. By 1500 there were over 1,000 printshops and millions of volumes in print. The printing press was the key to the success of the Protestant Reformation—Martin Luther's tracts attacking the Church of Rome were rushed into print and spread like wildfire throughout Europe.

The technique of making gunpowder was imported from China and first used during the latter part of the Hundred Years' War (1337–1453) between England and France. Subsequent improvements in firearms and artillery made gunpowder, in effect, a great leveler. One man with a gun was more than a match for a knight on horseback, and even primitive cannons could bombard medieval castles into submission. The feudal age ended abruptly and, one might say, explosively.

2. A comparison can be made with the Greek word *arete,* which was such a crucial concept in ancient Greece. *Arete* translates as "diligence in the pursuit of excellence."
3. James Trefil, *The Dark Side of the Universe; A Scientist Explores the Cosmos* (New York: Macmillan, 1988), p.18.

EXPLORATION AND DISCOVERY

Trade between European cities and the Near and Middle East was an important factor in the evolution of the Renaissance. A few intrepid travelers, the most famous of whom was the Venetian Marco Polo (1254?–1324?), made their way along the great land routes to India and China (map 16.1). Marco Polo returned to Venice after spending many years in China (1271–95), but no one believed any of the wonders that he related. The conquests of the Ottoman Turks, especially the capture of Constantinople in 1453, had cut off the traditional Mediterranean routes.

Limited navigational aids forced sailing vessels to remain within sight of Mediterranean shores, which became unsatisfactory when other routes to the East had to be found. Not until the fifteenth century did European sailors have the capability to circumnavigate Africa to reach China, and the driving force behind this exploration was Prince Henry the Navigator (1394–1460), son of King John I of Portugal. Apparently without referring to Chinese work, a crude magnetic compass had been invented in the twelfth century. Henry improved this crucial device, had accurate maps and tables drawn, improved the design of ships, and

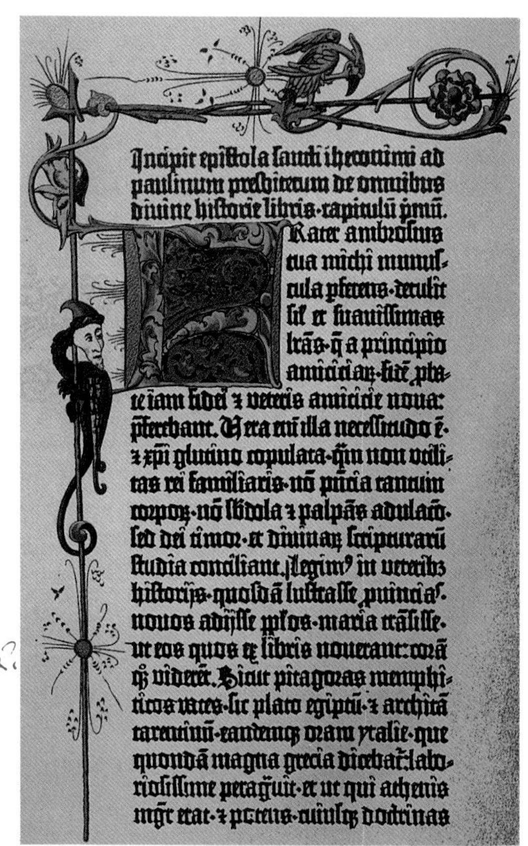

16.1 The Gutenberg Bible, part of page 1 with handpainted initials and decorations. Completed ca. 1455. Book printed using movable type. Photo: A.K.G., London.

Map 16.1 World exploration 1271–95; 1486–1611.

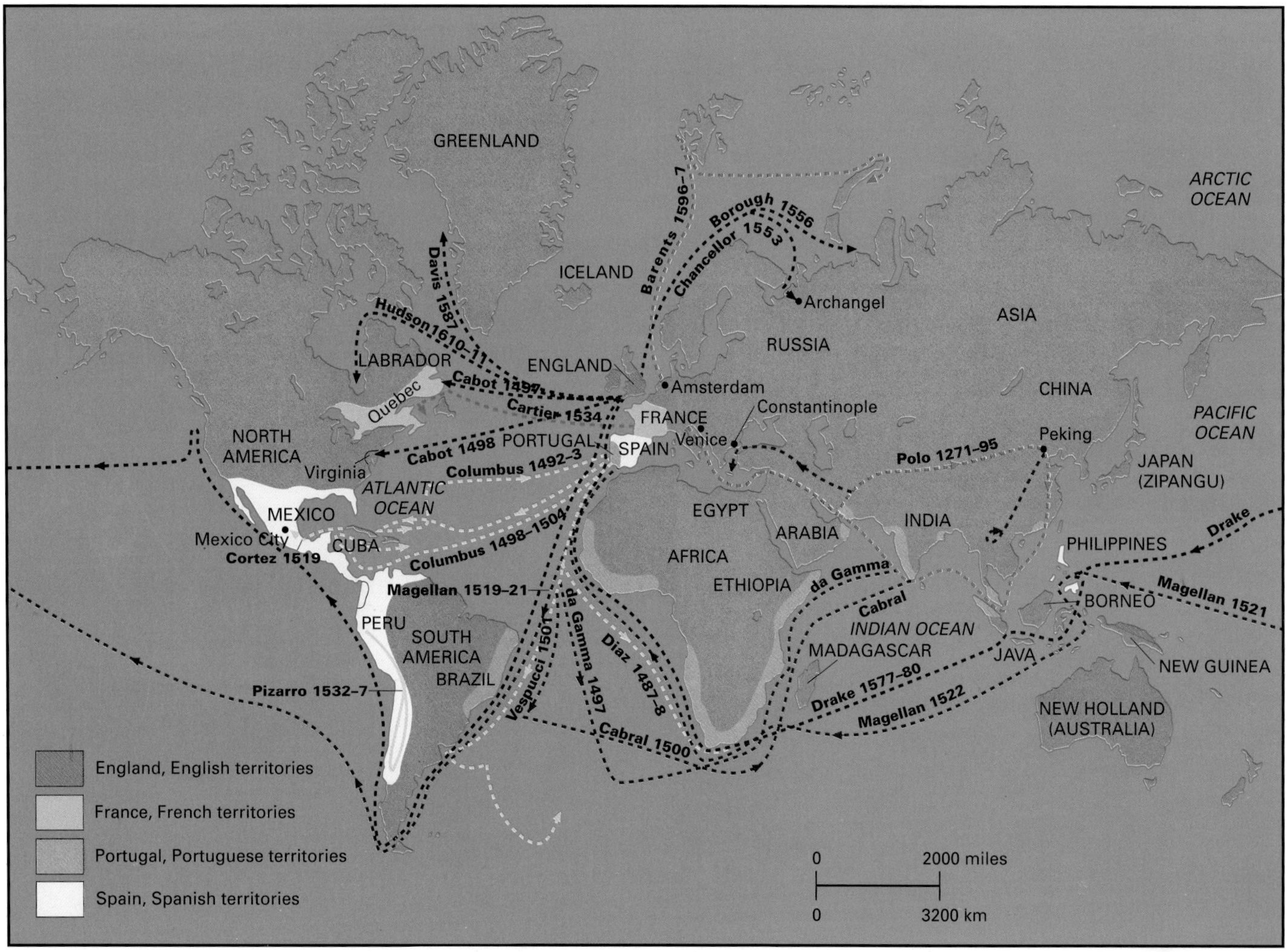

reintroduced the **astrolabe**, an Arab invention. A ship's latitude could be calculated to within about 30 miles (48 km) by using the astrolabe to determine the angle of the sun above the horizon at noon. This figure was then compared with Henry's tables of the sun's declination at known latitudes for each day of the year.

Navigation could not be made more precise until the marine chronometer was invented in 1760 to determine longitude. Nevertheless, navigational aids were adequate for voyages of exploration. In 1497, for example, Vasco da Gama (ca. 1469–1524) sailed southwest and then south from Portugal for ninety-seven days before turning east and sailing directly to the known latitude of his African destination, the Cape of Good Hope. He continued around Africa and on to India, returning to Lisbon in 1499.

Before da Gama's successful voyage, India had been the destination of Christopher Columbus (ca. 1451–1506), who sailed west rather than south and discovered instead a New World—new to Europeans, that is, with the exception of earlier Viking voyages. Columbus claimed the land for Spain, and the claim was confirmed in 1493, when Pope Alexander VI drew a vertical line in the Atlantic and awarded the Americas to Spain and Africa to Portugal. No one knew that the line ran through Brazil until it was accidentally discovered a year later by a Portuguese captain, leading to a treaty confirming Portugal's ownership. It apparently occurred to no one that the Americas and Africa were already inhabited by people who were never consulted by their new "owners." European colonialism had begun.

Vasco de Balboa (1475–1517) marched across the Isthmus of Panama in 1513 to discover a Pacific Ocean that residents of the Pacific Basin had always known was there. Ferdinand Magellan (1480–1521), a Portuguese in the service of Spain, sailed west in 1519 with five ships to find a passage, now called the Straits of Magellan, around South America and across the Pacific to Asia. He was killed in the Philippines, but his crew continued on to circumnavigate the globe and prove empirically that the world was round (fig. 16.2).

Spain and Portugal intended to divide the entire overseas world between them but England and France had other ideas. An Italian mariner whom the English called John Cabot (1450–98) was dispatched in 1497 to find a "northwest passage" to the Indies. The passage did not exist, of course, but Cabot's landings somewhere around Labrador and Newfoundland provided England with an opportunity to claim all of North America. The explorations of Jacques Cartier (1494–1553), plus later discoveries by Samuel de Champlain (1567?–1635), gave France competing claims, and the Dutch joined the competition with the explorations of Henry Hudson (d. 1611), an Englishman who entered Dutch service in 1609.

Maritime explorers were followed by adventurers such as Hernando Cortés (1485–1547) and Francisco Pizarro (1471–1541), who conquered the only two high civilizations of the New World. Cortés took the Aztec empire of Mexico in 1519 with 600 soldiers, and Pizarro conquered the Inca empire of Peru in 1531–3 with only 180 soldiers.

16.2 World map, from P. Apian and G. Frisius, *Cosmographia sive Descriptio Universi Orbis* (Antwerp: J. Withagen). 1584. Woodcut. Photo: A.K.G., London.

16.3 *The God Quetzalcoatl or Tonatiuh.* Aztec. Ca. 1500. Turquoise mosaic set in resinous gum over wood, with eyes of pearl shell and teeth of mussels, height 6⅝" (16.8 cm). Museum of Mankind, London. Photo: A.K.G., London.

There was treasure aplenty in the New World (fig. 16.3), but Europeans found another in their own minds. Accounts of the voyages of explorers inspired Renaissance imaginations much as space exploration fascinates today's world. Renaissance Europe had opened up new frontiers in art, literature, philosophy, and science, and now there was the lure and challenge of new lands as well. America became, for many Europeans, the literal utopia that Sir Thomas More used as the setting for his fictional *Utopia*.

THE REFORMATION: NEW IDEAS ABOUT GOD AND HUMANKIND

Concepts about the world and the universe changed rapidly during the Renaissance, but it was the Reformation that transformed the face of Europe. It not only divided a once monolithic institution but kindled social, political, economic, and intellectual revolutions. There had been earlier challenges to the authority of the Church of Rome, but the Reformation inaugurated by Martin Luther was the first to succeed on a large scale.

Centuries earlier, in 1170, a French merchant named Peter Waldo (d. 1217) founded a puritan sect known as the Waldenses. Preaching apostolic poverty, they rejected Rome and its papal claims. Though excommunicated in 1184 and harassed for centuries, the sect survives today as the Vaudois in the Alps of Italy and France.

In England, John Wiclif (or Wycliffe; ca. 1320–84), an Oxford scholar, revived interest in St. Augustine and openly questioned the need for a priestly hierarchy. Contending that God and the Scriptures were the sole sources of spiritual authority, he translated the Bible from the Vulgate into English and urged everyone to read it for themselves. He was silenced by the church, but the Wiclif Bible was undisputed after 1534, when Henry VIII broke away from the Church of Rome with the Act of Supremacy and confiscated all church property.

Jan Hus (or Huss; 1369–1415) was a Wiclif follower and a priest/professor at Charles University in Prague. His opposition to the sale of indulgences led to charges of the Wiclif heresy, and he was burned at the stake on 6 July 1415. His martyrdom caused bloody riots in Bohemia, followed by an evangelical movement of the Unitas Fratrum (Unity of Brethren). By 1500 the Brethren (later called the Moravian church) had over 200,000 members in 400 parishes. In 1501, the church published the first hymnal in the vernacular and placed it, and the Bible, in the hands of the people.

Martin Luther, 1483–1546

The term "reformation" was used in the late Middle Ages by individuals and groups who protested against the secularization of Christianity and the abuses of power and privilege by the church hierarchy, from parish priests to popes. An unbroken succession of corrupt Renaissance popes, from Sixtus IV (reigned 1471–84) to Leo X (reigned 1513–21), fueled the flames of a revolt that was ignited by Martin Luther when he posted his ninety-five Theses, or statements for public debate, on the door of the castle church at Wittenberg on 31 October 1517. Luther was incensed at what he called the "sale" of indulgences, particularly the fund-raising activities of a monk named Tetzel. Operating under papal authority, the **Dominican** John Tetzel was dealing in indulgences—soliciting contributions to swell the depleted papal treasury and finance the construction of the new St. Peter's in Rome.

Luther intended, at first, a clarification of the teachings of the church. The origins of the Reformation are found primarily in Luther's religion. An **Augustinian** friar and professor of theology at the University of Wittenberg, Luther had experienced a spiritual crisis. Convinced that he was a lost soul and destined for Hell, Luther took the advice of a confessor and plunged with characteristic fervor into intensive study of the Bible. He rediscovered, in the epistles of Paul, a faith in salvation by grace. The central doctrines of the Church Fathers, especially Augustine, confirmed his belief in the authority of the Word of God; faith alone was sufficient for salvation. Church doctrine stipulated that good works and the intercession of priests were also necessary, but Luther was convinced that he expressed the true faith of the church. Faith and the Bible were enough for Luther, making the break with Rome inevitable.

Why was Luther so concerned about indulgences? Indulgences were remissions by the church of temporal punishment on earth or in **purgatory**. The **sacrament** of penance of the Church of Rome consists of contrition, confession, absolution, and satisfaction on the part of the penitent. The penitent must feel contrition for his or her sins, confess to the priest, and be absolved of guilt. The sinner satisfies God's justice by working out the penalties assigned by the priest. Indulgences could be granted for the guilt or punishment in purgatory, according to the church, but the sin remained after confession. According to the doctrine of Thesaurus Meritorum, the church had a treasury of spiritual merits accumulated from the crucifixion of Christ for the sins of the world and the martyrdom of the Saints. Indulgences transferred spiritual merit from this treasury to the penitent. Tetzel, among others, misled the people when he chanted his favorite **refrain**: "As soon as the coin in the coffer rings/A soul from Purgatory springs." The doctrine behind indulgences was too complex for lay persons to understand, many of whom believed that even sins could be absolved if they could buy enough indulgences, which misunderstanding, as Luther observed, "put a grievous instrument in the hands of avarice."

"Therefore those preachers of indulgences err who say that a papal pardon frees a man from all penalty and assures his salvation" was one of Luther's theses. Arguing some of his theses with the theologian John Eck, Luther publicly admitted that his statements attacked an institution that

16.4 Lucas Cranach the Younger, *Martin Luther and the Wittenberg Reformers.* Ca. 1543. Oil on panel, 27⅝ × 15⅝" (70.2 × 39.7 cm). Toledo Museum of Art (Gift of Edward Drummond Libbey).
Luther is at the far left and Ulrich Zwingli to the right of John Frederick the Magnanimous, Elector of Saxony and patron of the reformers and the Lutheran church.

could have him burned alive. When shown that his position was similar to that of Jan Hus, Luther dared to assert that the church was in error in burning Hus. Jan Hus was a condemned heretic, and Luther put his life on the line by openly challenging the authority of the pope and the councils of the church.

In 1521, Emperor Charles V convened the estates of the **Holy Roman Empire** in the town of Worms to compel Luther, already excommunicated by the pope, to retract his writings. "I neither can nor will make any retraction, since it is neither safe nor honorable to act against conscience" was his response. Insisting that "the Church universal is the number of the elect," Luther concluded his defense, according to tradition, with the words, "Here I stand. I cannot do otherwise. God help me. Amen." The Diet of Worms declared Luther an outlaw, but the verdict was academic because Luther had many supporters among the German princes (fig. 16.4). Church corruption and forming a new faith helped promote Luther's church, but a rising tide of nationalism and the desire to end the flow of money to the papal treasury were perhaps even more significant in the rapid spread of the Reformation throughout the Holy Roman Empire and Scandinavia (map 16.2).

The principles of Lutheranism were later formulated by a Lutheran scholar, Philip Melanchthon (1497–1560), who stated them as follows:

1. The only final authority either for conduct or belief is in the Scriptures *(Sola Scriptura).*
2. The one condition of salvation is faith or trust in Divine Love *(Sola Fide).*
3. Faith itself is a gift of God, not a human achievement *(Sola Gratia).*
4. The community of the faithful is the true church whose only head is Christ. The growth of this church is fostered by preaching the gospel and the observance of two sacraments, Baptism and the Lord's Supper. In sum, Lutheran belief stresses individuality; salvation and a knowledge of God are direct processes, needing no church or priestly intercessor.

Calvinism

The Reformation in Germany was closely followed by a notable movement in Switzerland, first led by Ulrich Zwingli (1484–1531; see fig. 16.4), who even more than Luther believed in the individuality of worship and the authority of the Scriptures. Later, this group was led by John Calvin (1509–64), a French Protestant originally educated for the law as well as theology. Persecuted in France, he fled to Geneva, where he established a theocratic republic, that is, a government ruled by elders of the church.

Calvin stated the philosophy of his faith in *The Institutes of the Christian Religion* (final form in 1559). This rests on the unconditional sovereignty of God; whatever transpires is because God wills it so. The assistance of a Saviour is necessary because Calvin believed in humanity's abject helplessness and total depravity. Predestination is rigorous and universal: a few of the elect will be saved through faith in God but many will be forever damned. Finally, he stated that the group of the elect constitutes the church, the preservation of which is the duty of both religious and civil authorities. An infraction of divine law therefore requires civil punishment by officials subject to church authorities. This, as one can see, was a very stern belief; Calvin forbade many of the ordinary pleasures of life in Geneva and vigorously persecuted all who did not follow his faith.

Various forms of Calvinism spread throughout

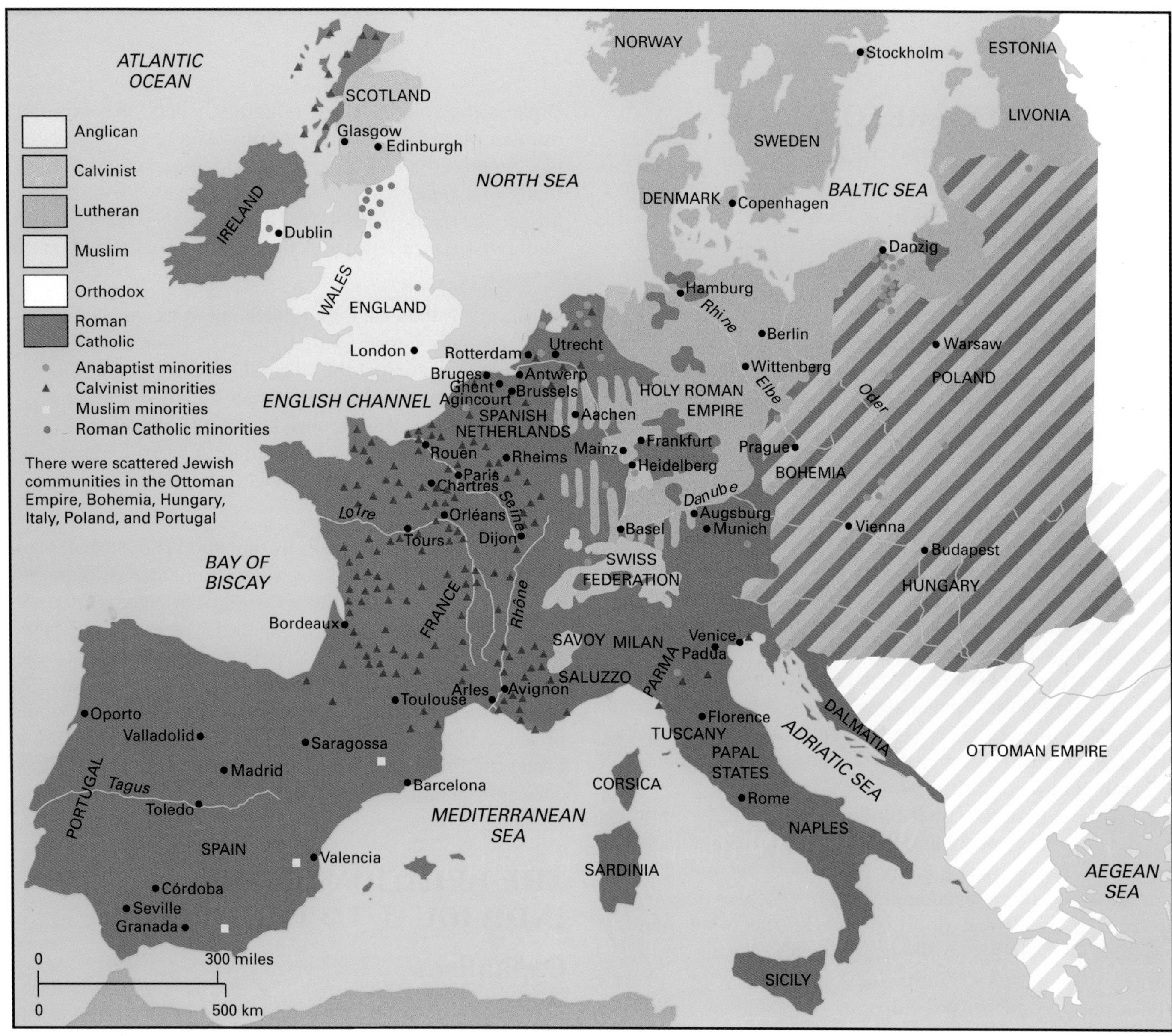

Map 16.2 Religion in Europe, 1565.

Europe. John Knox (1505–72) founded the Presbyterian church in Scotland and England following the principles laid down by the Swiss leader. The English Puritans were Calvinists who emigrated to America to found their own theocratic colony.

Other Sects

The individual's right to interpret the Scriptures—virtually the cornerstone of churches spawned by the Reformation—quite naturally led to the formation of many sects. Lutheranism and Calvinism attracted converts from the growing middle class, but many of the newer sects, for whatever reason, drew their following from the poorer classes. Among these latter were the Anabaptists, who believed in baptism only when the individual had reached adulthood and was able to make a free choice. This concept of rebirth marked by baptism continues today among so-called "born again" Christians. From the Anabaptists came such modern denominations as the Friends (Quakers) and Baptists. The Socinians, who took their name from Faustus Socinus (1539–1604), were antitrinitarians who refused to hold serfs or take part in any war. Persecuted in Poland by the Catholic church led by the Jesuits, they were banished in 1658 on pain of death. The Socinians were the single most important precursors of the Unitarian church. The Arminian church was led by the Dutch theologian Jacobus Arminius (1560–1609). It was an offshoot of Calvinism but asserted that each person was free to choose his or her own way of living, thus denying the doctrine of predestination. Its theology was, in essence, accepted by John Wesley (1703–91), ordained in the Church of England, who founded the movement leading to the Methodist church.

THE COUNTER-REFORMATION

The Catholic Reformation, also called the Counter-Reformation, was the papal response to Luther's revolt. Convened by Pope Paul III (reigned 1534–49), the Council of Trent met from 1545 to 1563 and reaffirmed every element of Roman doctrine attacked by the reformers: original sin, grace, redemption, the sacraments, the sacrifice of the Mass, and purgatory. Every violation of discipline was denounced, reforms were enacted, and observance was demanded under pain of censure. The music of the church was reformed, and there was a strong thrust of Counter-Reformation art and architecture (see p. 187). The Counter-Reformation was given a mighty assist by the Jesuits (Society of Jesus), founded by Ignatius Loyola in 1534 and later approved by Pope Paul III. The Jesuits led the disciplined drive of the movement, but the popes also revived the Inquisition, an old and seasoned mechanism for stamping out heresy. Sitting as medieval courts and employing medieval methods of torture, the papal and Spanish inquisitions sentenced convicted heretics to "purification." The operative term was *auto-da-fé* (Portuguese, "act of the faith"), meaning that secular authorities purified the victims by burning them at the stake (fig. 16.5). Judicial murders failed to stem the Protestant tide but the Spanish Inquisition was not abolished until 1834.

How can we sum up the influence of the Reformation on the lives of people? First, it encouraged national identity, the strongest single force of this period. Second, it had a marked influence on education, in many cases divorcing it from ecclesiastical domination. On the other hand, because of Calvinist influence, education was limited largely to subjects of immediate utilitarian value. The Reformation encouraged religious independence; if the Bible is the sole basis for religious beliefs, there are any number of possible interpretations. As a result, Protestantism generated a host of sects in which one could find virtually any type of religious belief. Finally, Protestantism influenced the growth of capitalism, for the ideal Calvinist, Methodist, or Lutheran took the beginning of the first **psalm** to heart:

> [1]Blessed is the man that walketh not in the counsel of the ungodly, nor standeth in the way of sinners, nor sitteth in the seat of the scornful. [2]But his delight is in the law of the Lord; and in his law doth he meditate day and night. [3]And he shall be like a tree planted by the rivers of water, that bringeth forth his fruit in his season; his leaf also shall not wither; and whatsoever he doeth shall prosper.

Clearly this psalm tells us that good people shall prosper. In a time when making, saving, and spending money became more and more the surest signs of success, men and women concluded that prosperous people were good people. Furthermore, the sober, steady, shoulder-to-the-wheel and nose-to-the-grindstone way of life advocated by most of the new sects was exactly the sort of life that would promote industrious work and prudent spending. And so began the Protestant work ethic, which produces the ideal person for a capitalist system.

16.5 Bernard Picart, *Execution and burning of heretics in Spain*, from *Cérémonies et coutumes religieuses*, vol. 1, *Cérémonies en usage chez les Catholiques* (Amsterdam: J. F. Bernard). 1723. Copperplate engraving. Photo: A.K.G., London.

THE RELATION OF THE INDIVIDUAL TO THE GROUP

Capitalism

The growth of capitalism is but one more example of the trend toward individualism that characterized a transitional period in a European society that was busily rebuilding itself to match the new view of reality. There was considerable mercantile activity in the Middle Ages, especially in the twelfth and thirteenth centuries, but the economic system called mercantile capitalism did not come into full flower until the Renaissance. Before this time economic affairs had been dominated by political or religious concerns, granted that merchants always keep an eye on the bottom line. Just as knowledge of the real world developed into science, so evolved an economic system free of religious or political considerations.

Medieval **guilds** produced solely for human needs, and manufacturing and selling were interrelated processes. A cobbler, for instance, made shoes only to order; with no orders he could close his shop and go on a picnic. His guild regulated the quality of materials and workmanship and set the prices. There was no competition and the business died with the cobbler, unless he had a son yearning to follow in his footsteps.

The rising fortunes of the Fugger family in what is now Germany illustrate the development of Renaissance capitalism. Anton Fugger became a weaver in Augsburg in 1380 and soon began collecting and selling other weavers' products. His son, Jacob Fugger I, continued a business later vastly enlarged under Jacob Fugger II, the leading capitalist of the era. Jacob expanded into metals within the Hapsburg Empire, dealing in silver and copper in Austria and silver and mercury in Spain. Lending huge sums (at high interest) to the Hapsburg emperors, he received, in return, monopolies on the ores he mined. Inevitably, he bought the mines to control all his products from raw materials to market. Fugger set prices at whatever the traffic would bear and no one supervised product quality. Finally, he formed a company that piled up profits far exceeding the needs of the Fuggers or any other family. From this example we can explore the essential attributes of capitalism.

Characteristics of Capitalism

Capitalism creates "companies" that exist separately from the people who form them. The company can conduct business, make contracts, assume debts, distribute and/or reinvest profits, and be subject to litigation. The purpose of the company is to make money with no limit whatever on the amount of money (and power) that can be amassed (fig. 16.6). Capitalism assumes that making money is the goal of economic activity because, after all, no sensible person goes into business to lose money.

A company is a rational organization that must plan and control every step of its operation from raw materials to the marketplace. It must have an accounting system that keeps track of materials, money, and human energies. Capitalism shapes ends to means and the end is making a profit. This is a rational goal with no room for feeling or emotion. The system is pragmatic; whatever works is good and what doesn't is eliminated. An irrational aspect of early capitalism was the lack of safety standards, whether installed by industry itself or imposed by government. Competition between companies could and did exploit the consumer. Moreover, workers were paid as little as possible and worked as long as possible. In the final analysis:

> Profits, no matter how large, can never reach a level sufficiently high to satisfy the economic agent—acquisition therefore becomes unconditional, absolute. Not only does it seize on all phenomena within the economic realm, but it reaches over into other cultural fields and develops a tendency to proclaim the supremacy of business interests over all other values.[4]

Effects of Capitalism

The flourishing of capitalism dramatically increased the possibilities of individualism. Those who made it to the top of the economic heap acquired the power to do whatever they wished. The only limits on individuals lay in their own imagination, creativity, and ability to spot and exploit opportunities. A second effect was the marked increase in available goods. Guilds made goods when people wanted them, but capitalists made more of everything and sold the surplus to ever-expanding markets. The rapid rise of the standard of living in sixteenth-century Europe was due almost entirely to the expanded economic system. In material terms capitalism was a whopping success.

Capitalism transformed cities. Medieval stores, such as they were, had been booths at fairs or traveling wagons with itinerant peddlers. In the guild system the factory was the workshop and living quarters for the craftsman, his apprentices, and his family. But capitalists had to get their merchandise before the public, and this required buildings in which goods were "stored." The impact on Renaissance cities of the expanding industry of retail sales was, of course, remarkable. To appreciate this, try to imagine a city without a single retail store.

16.6 Quentin Matsys, *The Money Lender and His Wife*. 1514. Oil on wood, 28 × 26¾" (71.1 × 67.9 cm). Louvre, Paris. Photo: R.M.N., Paris.
Distracted from reading her Bible, the wife is as fascinated as her husband as he lovingly examines his money.

The Development of Sovereign Power

Perhaps the most striking Renaissance development was the increase of royal power. The beginning of this movement had emerged during the latter part of the Middle Ages, when the inadequacies of feudalism had become obvious. There was no common currency, feudal tariff barriers hindered

4. Edwin R. Seligman (ed.), "Capitalism," in *Encyclopedia of the Social Sciences*, vol. 3 (New York: Macmillan, 1937), p.197.

CROWN VERSUS POPE

England's break with the Church of Rome had little to do with the theology or politics of the Reformation. Henry VIII (fig. 16.7) wanted a male heir to further the Tudor line and his first wife, Catherine of Aragon, was unable to cooperate. When Rome also failed to cooperate by granting an annulment, Henry's chief minister suggested that England break with the papacy so that the Archbishop of Canterbury could grant a divorce. Parliament passed the legislation in 1533, leaving Henry VIII free to marry Anne Boleyn. Now the head of the Church of England, Henry proceeded to confiscate every Roman monastery, nunnery, and church in the land. Later, he executed Anne Boleyn for infidelity and failing to bear a son. Ironically, it was Boleyn's daughter who became the exalted Queen Elizabeth.

16.7 Hans Holbein the Younger, *Portrait of Henry VIII.* 1539–40. Oil on panel, 34¾ × 29½" (88.3 × 74.9 cm). Galleria Nazionale d'Arte Antica, Rome. Photo: Scala, Florence.

trade, justice was inconsistent at best, and competent civil servants didn't exist. Kings drove to new power with their might increasingly keyed to the extravagant stream of treasure from the newly discovered lands across the sea. The Spanish monarch, for example, claimed a fifth of all riches brought to Spain by the *conquistadores.* With seemingly unlimited funds, kings created brilliant courts that attracted the nobles from their muddy country estates and inevitably made them totally dependent on the monarch. Most nobles were willing to exchange their rural independence for the privilege of participating in the rituals, grand balls, and resplendent festivals of the royal courts in England, France, and Spain.

Not only did the nobles pledge their allegiance to the sovereign, but the common people looked to the throne as the single source of order in a world changing so rapidly they could scarcely keep up. Order had been the rule in the Middle Ages but "future shock" was present in the Renaissance as it is today. Protestantism shattered the monolithic authority of Rome, science demolished the unity of the universe, and capitalism dismembered the old economic order controlled by the guilds. The king was the single stabilizing influence in all this chaos. Wherever we turn, we find references to the centrality of the sovereign. In Shakespeare's play *Hamlet,* Rosencrantz speaks of the monarch's importance:

> The cease of majesty
> Dies not alone, but, like a gulf doth draw
> What's near it with it; it is a massy wheel,
> Fix'd on the summit of the highest mount,
> To whose huge spokes ten thousand lesser things
> Are mortis'd and adjoin'd; which, when it falls,
> Each small annexment, petty consequence,
> Attends the boisterous ruin. Never alone
> Did the king sigh, but with a general groan.

Historically, the Renaissance saw the brilliant reigns of the Tudor rulers in England, especially Henry VIII (reigned 1509–47) and Elizabeth I (reigned 1558–1603). These two monarchs understood the rising importance of trade and commerce and the vital role the middle class played in England's growing prosperity. It was under Elizabeth, also, that the English navy defeated the mighty Spanish Armada in 1588, making England mistress of the seas until well into the twentieth century.

In France, Francis I (reigned 1515–47) set a pattern for later kings, such as Louis XIV (reigned 1643–1715), by bringing the best artists to a sumptuously furnished court that became a model for all of Europe. Francis I cemented national feeling by a series of wars fought largely by mercenary soldiers in a helpless and divided Italy. France was later bitterly embroiled in a struggle between the Protestant Huguenots, led by the house of Bourbon, and the Catholics, led by the house of Guise. This struggle came to a head in 1589, when Henry of Navarre took the throne as Henry IV, the first Bourbon king (reigned 1589–1610). Henry professed himself a Catholic, but by the Edict of Nantes (1598) guaranteed certain rights to the Huguenots in selected cities—rights that Louis XIV cancelled in 1685, at which time thousands of Huguenots left the country.

Spain reached its single high point of brilliance at this time, at first under the rule of Ferdinand and Isabella (1469–1504). They and later rulers enjoyed tremendous profits from the Spanish conquests in Central and South America. In fact, the decline of Spain can be attributed to their disinterest in permanent colonies; they preferred instead to plunder their holdings. Later, Spain became one of the countries ruled over by the Hapsburgs, for Charles I of Spain (reigned 1519–56) also held the title of Archduke of Austria. He was, moreover, Charles V, Emperor of the Holy Roman Empire. His holdings included the kingdom of Naples and Sicily, plus the Netherlands. The Spanish Hapsburgs became the leading Catholic monarchs in Europe and had the force of the Church of Rome as a part of their spiritual and secular power.

In 1566 the Netherlands revolted against the Hapsburg kings, a revolt provoked in large part by the importation of the ruthless Inquisition. After a series of bloody wars Holland became an independent nation in 1648, but the area known today as Belgium did not free itself until 1713. Portugal also achieved full independence during the Renaissance and, like Spain, achieved a short-lived glory based on the wealth plundered from its hapless possessions.

Map 16.3 Renaissance Italy.

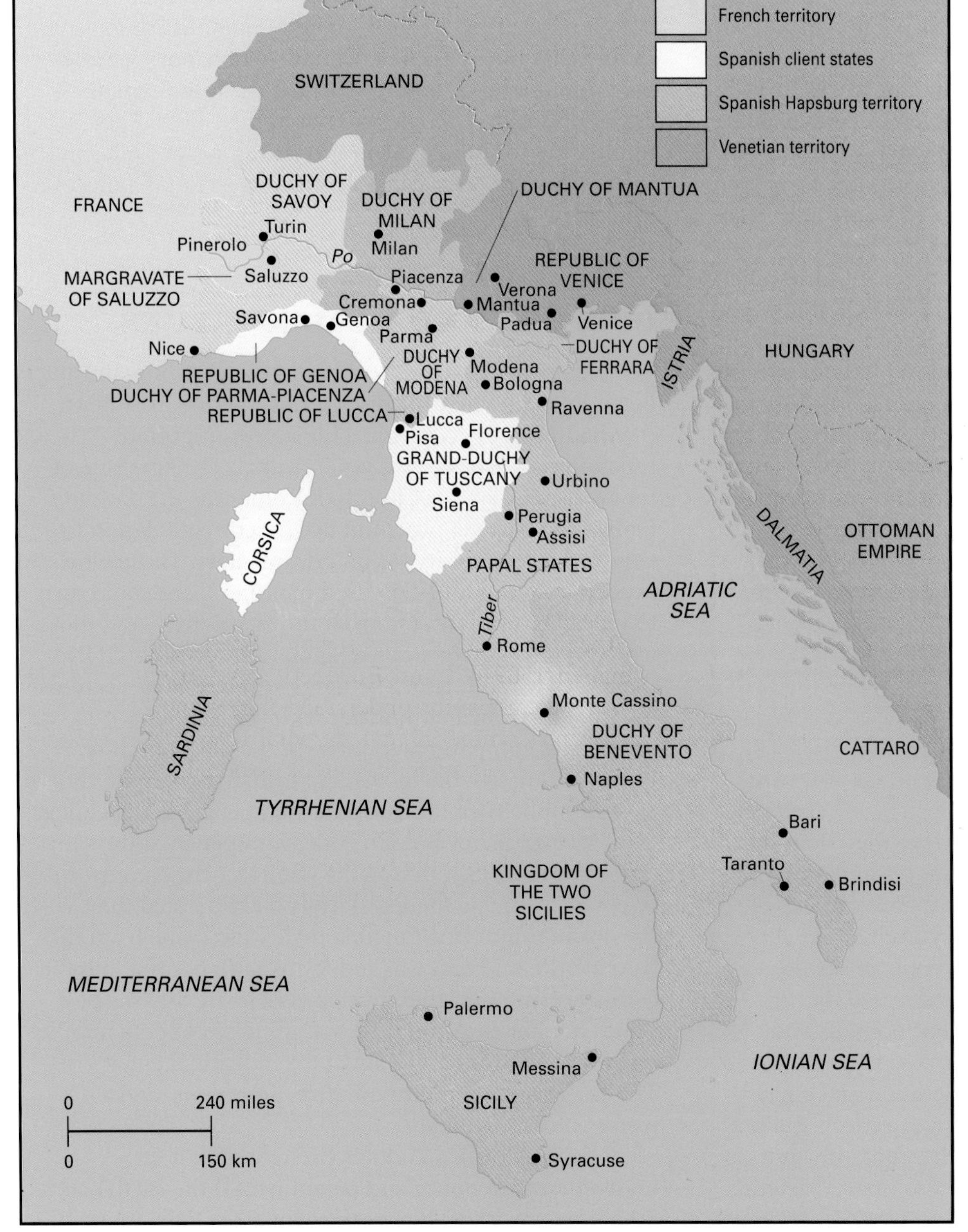

Germany became the battleground of the Thirty Years' War (1618–48), which began as a conflict between Catholics and Protestants and ended as a political struggle against the Hapsburgs by Holland, France, Sweden, and other nations. Germany was devastated as the largest armies since Roman days surged over the countryside. Sweden alone had over 200,000 men in the field. The ferocity of the struggle prompted the writing of the *Law of War and Peace* (1625) by the Dutch jurist Hugo Grotius. Though he recognized war as "legitimate," he did distinguish between just and unjust conflicts and laid down principles for "humane" warfare. Drawing on actual events of the war, he condemned such acts as poisoning wells, mutilating prisoners, massacring hostages, raping, and pillaging. In time, the work of Grotius became the basis of the Geneva Convention. It was this bitter and disastrous war that spurred emigration to America, where there would be a clear separation of church and state and no more religious disagreements fought out on a battlefield.

Italy's fate deserves a special note, for it was in Italy that humanism first appeared, not to mention the inspired creations of artists such as Leonardo da Vinci, Michelangelo, and Raphael. Early mercantile capitalism was made to order for enterprising individuals to exploit in flourishing city-states. As a result, a few powerful families rose to prominence, each controlling one of the important cities. The Visconti family ruled in Milan, and the Sforza family was a power in Lombardy and later in Milan. The most notable of the ruling families was the Medici clan in Florence, whose leading member was the famous Lorenzo the Magnificent (1449–92)—banker, ruler, artist, and patron of the arts. A council of rich merchants took over the Venetian republic. Like the Greek city-states of old, however, the rich and powerful Italian cities could never unite, and went into decline after 1500, when Italy became a battleground for internal squabbles and rampaging foreign armies (map 16.3).

SUMMARY

There has scarcely been a time, except perhaps our own, when people busied themselves so industriously exploring the dark room of their universe. Wherever they went they turned up new facts that upset old balances and archaic institutions. Humanism, as one of the manifestations of the secular spirit, stripped the **allegory** from all manifestations of nature and helped people to see the world as it really was. Humanism also stressed the importance of the individual and the harmonious and complete functioning of the natural person in a rich world guided, the humanists hoped, by moderation and good sense. To a certain extent, humanism was a revolt against the submissive nature of Christian ethics, not only in its turning back to classical sources, but also in its insistence on the reason for leading the good life: it was not the hope of eternal bliss in heaven, but because the good life was its own reward. The view of what constituted the real world was shifting from the medieval idea that God was the ultimate reality to the belief that human existence on earth had its own validity. This shift did not necessarily mean that there was widespread denial of Christianity or the Christian message. Rather, growing resentment over corruption in the church hierarchy led people to question whether this powerful bureaucracy provided the best way to the Kingdom of Heaven. The **Great Schism** certainly forced many to wonder which of the two or three competing popes was the true keeper of the keys of the kingdom. Amidst all the negative factors, humanism served as a positive bridge from the medieval to the modern world.

The new science, especially the heliocentric solar system and the mechanistic theory of the universe, completely shifted the base of all human institutions. Before that time God had been the whole purpose and goal of human life, and it was on these **teleological** assumptions that people had based their lives. That foundation for human aspirations was swept aside, and men and women regarded themselves as inhabitants of a brave new world.

CULTURE AND HUMAN VALUES

Not only was the theoretical foundation for human values invalidated by scientific discoveries, but the institution that had formerly controlled life's most important functions was questioned and rejected. The keystone of the revolt against the Church of Rome was the dazzling realization that people could live in a direct relation to God with no necessity for an intermediary. Those who needed religious authority to direct their lives could turn to the Scriptures and interpret for themselves. And those who did not need or want religious authority could live their lives without fear. The new churches, however, did institute their own authorities with restrictions sometimes comparable to those of the old Church of Rome. Ultimately, the movement from a monolithic church to a multiplicity of faiths meant that people had a choice.

Vast areas for human endeavor opened at the same time. The idea, as much as the reality, of the New World swept aside musty medieval walls and liberated the European mind. One tangible reality did come from the New World, and that was money. Wealth poured into the countries who sent their buccaneers forth, and the new riches bought ease and luxury. Capitalism offered another marvelously stimulating outlet for individual enterprise. The sky was the limit for creative, ambitious, and resourceful individuals.

Each of these freedoms brought with it an undercurrent of doubt and pessimism. If the earth and its inhabitants were no longer the center of God's attention, and God no longer the goal and purpose of men and women, then what were they and what was their purpose, if any, here on earth? If the Bible was to be read and interpreted by each person, where was there any certainty? In a world that ran like a machine, where could people find answers about their relationship to each other and to the Creator of that world? Was the new relationship between people only dog-eat-dog as capitalism suggested? The only answer the Renaissance could suggest for maintaining order and stability was the absolute monarch. In the seventeenth century kings would claim that God ordained them to care for his people and would therefore rule by divine right. As perceptive people observed the actions of their rulers, they had abundant reason to be apprehensive about this basis for an orderly existence.

Another trend, too small and remote as yet to cause alarm, but present nevertheless in the intellectual currents of the time, deserves mention. Science had discovered a rational world that appeared to operate like a machine, and capitalism, though it guaranteed freedom for the captains of commerce and industry, operated "rationally" within the companies that composed it. This meant that the men and women who worked in capitalistic units were not truly free. They had, in effect, traded their heavenly servitude and guild regulations for a new bondage: the clock, production quotas, and the account book. The coming industrial revolution would intensify that servitude.

Renaissance Men and Women: Real and Ideal

> What a piece of work is a man! How noble in reason! how infinite in faculty! in form in moving how express and admirable! in action how like an angel! in apprehension, how like a god! the beauty of the world! the paragon of animals! And yet, to me, what is this quintessence of dust? man delights not me . . . .
>
> William Shakespeare, *Hamlet*, II, ii

When contemplating the Renaissance, one can call to mind the glories of exploration and discovery and names such as Michelangelo, Luther, Copernicus, Shakespeare, Cervantes, and Elizabeth I. We picture the era as a time of radiant optimism and expansion of the human spirit. The possible zones of human action were widened, it seems, in every respect: geographically, with the new discoveries; spiritually, with the Reformation; economically, with the growth of capitalism. This, of course, is true but it is only part of the total picture. Hamlet says, "Man delights not me."

This hints at another aspect of the Renaissance as important as the first exuberant picture. A troubling melancholy strain ran throughout the whole period, a deep-seated pessimism concerning human nature. What is Hamlet saying? Primarily, that in appearances, actions, and potentialities, people are great. Yet somehow in reality they fall short of greatness. Such pessimism usually indicates a failure to reach some ideal.

The Renaissance Problem

What was the problem that confronted the thinkers of the time? On the one hand they had opportunity unlimited with beckoning horizons extending in all directions. Human beings, with their awesome achievements, could at last become godlike creatures.

Yet at the same moment, the very forces that opened these new possibilities undermined the concept of human beings as special among all of God's creations. Matters of the soul and divinity were relegated to an inferior position below material things. Even further, the more the hopes held out for humankind, the more it seemed people's animal nature won out. All too often venality and greed triumphed as people seized opportunities savagely and selfishly. Not only did those of low station show themselves unworthy, but even the best and the wisest, the noblest among men and women stared deeply into their own personalities and found there the same base instincts.

Here, then, is the problem. How can people's animal nature be controlled so they may become the noble creatures they were apparently destined to be? How can the rough, crude, and selfish aspects of human nature be disciplined so that all men and women may achieve fulfillment in the expanding world in which they live? Philosophers, theologians, artists, psychologists, men and women in all walks of life have wrestled with the problem, but the question remains.

STUDY QUESTIONS

1. Give a definition of Renaissance humanism in your own words. What is a humanist in today's world? How does a humanist differ from a humanitarian?
2. The invention of movable type and gunpowder changed history. Which, in your opinion, has had the greater impact? Why?
3. Have nuclear weapons changed history as much as gunpowder?

Renaissance Art: A New Golden Age

THE EARLY RENAISSANCE IN FIFTEENTH-CENTURY ITALY

Florence (from *flora*), the city of flowers, dates back to the Bronze Age (3000 BC). Influenced by the Greeks as early as the eighth century BC, it flourished under Roman rule and even prospered during the difficult centuries following the demise of the empire. As early as 1199 it was a city of bankers and wealthy craft guilds, destined to become a leading financial power and the city most closely identified with the Renaissance (fig. 17.2). Intended to symbolize Florentine

17.1 *Right* Giotto, campanile, Florence. 1334–50s. Photo: Scala, Florence.

Opposite Lorenzo Ghiberti, detail of fig. 17.6.

17.2 View of Florence across the Arno River. From left to right: the Gothic tower of the Palazzo Vecchio, the square white tower of Giotto's campanile and the Cathedral of Sta. Maria del Fiore with its mighty dome. Photo: Scala, Florence.

17.3 Florentine Cathedral group: Romanesque baptistery, 1060–1150, at the left; Giotto's campanile, 1334–50s, left of center; cathedral, 1296–1436. Photo: Alinari, Florence.

influence and wealth, the great cathedral Santa Maria del Fiore (St. Mary of the Flower) was begun by Arnolfo di Cambio in 1296. Work slowed down after Arnolfo's death in 1302 and stopped altogether during the terrible days of the Black Death in 1348 and several subsequent years. Like many cities in Europe, Florence was devastated by the plague, its population falling in just a few summer months from about 130,000 to around 65,000. Recovery was relatively swift, however, and in 1368 the cathedral design was finalized and building resumed, though no one had the faintest idea of how to construct the **dome**.

Filippo Brunelleschi, ca. 1377–1446

In 1417 a special commission announced a competition for the design of the dome, optimistically trusting in Italian ingenuity to solve the problem. The expected genius materialized in the person of Brunelleschi (broo-nuh-LES-key), one of the three founders of the Florentine Renaissance (with Donatello and Masaccio) and the greatest architect of the Renaissance. His design was selected in 1420 and triumphantly completed sixteen years later.

On 25 March 1436 all of Florence was bursting with anticipation. Pope Eugene IV was to preside over the long-awaited consecration of the cathedral. On the day of the Feast of the Annunciation, the pope, accompanied by thirty-seven bishops, seven cardinals, the ruling Signoria, and envoys of foreign powers, began the solemn procession from the doors of the monastery. Moving along the specially constructed passageway (sumptuously carpeted and decorated with tapestries, damask, silk, and fresh flowers), the notables turned into the Via de' Banchi where the major banking houses were located. Passing through the eleventh-century **baptistery**, the dignitaries entered the spacious cathedral **nave**, where a five-hour service celebrated the completion of what was then the largest church in Christendom. The most famous composer of the time, Dufay (doo-FYE; see p. 64), was present to hear the choir sing his **motet** *Nuper Rosarum Flores (Flower of Rose)*, commissioned for the occasion by the Florentine Republic.

Brunelleschi began his artistic career as a sculptor, but after losing the 1401 competition for the north doors of the baptistery to Ghiberti, he turned to architecture. He subsequently made several trips to Rome in the company of the young sculptor Donatello to study and measure the existing buildings of ancient Rome. His design for the largest

17.4 Filippo Brunelleschi, Pazzi Chapel, Cloister of Church of Santa Croce, Florence. Ca. 1441–60. Photo: Angelo Hornak, London.

dome since the Pantheon consisted of eight massive ribs arching upward from an octagonal drum and held in place by a classically inspired **lantern** (fig. 17.3). Within the dome a complex web of smaller ribs and horizontal **buttresses** tied the main ribs firmly together, all done without expensive scaffolding. Brunelleschi's hoisting device was so practical and simple that city authorities had to issue injunctions forbidding children from riding it to the dome. Averaging 140 feet (42 m) in diameter, the dome was 367 feet (136 m) high—the dominant feature of the Florentine skyline from that day to this.

The 269-foot (81-m) **campanile** at the southwest corner of the 508-foot (152-m)-long cathedral was designed by Giotto in 1334 and completed by Talenti in the 1350s (fig. 17.1 and p. 7). Though the design is Gothic, the multicolored marble facing and the lucid proportions of the basically horizontal design reflect Italy's classical heritage. When compared with the dynamic thrust of the south tower of Chartres Cathedral, Giotto's campanile is restrained, poised, and serene.

It was in the Pazzi Chapel (fig. 17.4) that Brunelleschi applied his knowledge of classical designs. A diminutive building measuring only 59 feet 9 inches by 35 feet 8 inches (18.2 × 10.9 m), its Renaissance design is clearly apparent, perhaps because the architect was not preoccupied with complex structural problems. In this beautifully proportioned building the break with the Gothic tradition is total. Gothic arches are replaced with **Corinthian** columns and **pilasters** in even, harmonious spacing. The walls are treated as solid, flat surfaces and, overall, there is a subtle and graceful balance of horizontal and vertical elements.

Rather than dominating the building, the central dome rests effortlessly on its supporting rim. From within (fig. 17.5), it seems to float on the light of the twelve *oculi,* somewhat in the manner of Hagia Sophia. The white stucco is articulated by the *pietra serena* (It., "clear stone") pilasters and moldings of clear gray Tuscan limestone and highlighted by the deep blue backgrounds of the terra-cotta reliefs and the Pazzi coat of arms on the **pendentives**. The harmonious proportions of the facade are confirmed by an interior space that is also shaped into clear geometric units. The Pazzi Chapel is a prototype of the new Renaissance style, which revived the concept of harmonious proportions on a human scale—a point of view even more germane to the work of Renaissance sculptors and metalworkers.

Lorenzo Ghiberti, 1378–1455

Though initially trained in the International Gothic style, Ghiberti (gee-BEAR-tee) later mastered **perspective** and classical motifs to excel as a metalworker of the Early Renaissance. Winner over Brunelleschi of a competition to design the north doors of the Baptistery in 1401, Ghiberti went on to design the east doors that were quickly pronounced (by Michelangelo) as worthy of the Gates of Paradise. Illustrating ten scenes from the Old Testament, the bronze, gilded doors are a classically inspired landmark of the Early Renaissance style (fig. 17.6). Contrary to the International Style, the figures and their settings are perfectly proportioned, creating the illusion that these events are taking place on stage right before our eyes. The *Story of Adam and Eve* (top of the left door; see p. 24) is designed in three receding planes using high, middle, and low **relief**. In the left center foreground is the creation of Adam and Eve. The Garden of Eden appears in the middle ground, with the background representing God and his angels as part of a remote past. Bordering the panels are figures and portrait busts representing Hebrew prophets and sibyls of antiquity who had supposedly foretold the coming of Christ.

17.5 *Opposite* Pazzi Chapel, interior, looking up into the dome. Photo: Scala, Florence.

17.6 Lorenzo Ghiberti, "Gates of Paradise," east doors of Baptistery of S. Giovanni, Florence Cathedral; detail, *Story of Adam and Eve*, on p. 24. Commissioned 1425, executed 1429–52. Gilt on bronze, height 18'6" (5.64 m); detail 31¼ × 31¼ " (79.4 × 79.4 cm). Photo: Scala, Florence; detail A.K.G., London.

17.7 Donatello, *Prophet ("Zuccone")*. Ca. 1423–5. Marble, height 6'5" (1.96 m). Originally on the campanile, Florence; now in the Museo dell'Opera del Duomo, Florence. Photo: Alinari, Florence.

17.8 Donatello, *David*. Ca. 1430–2, but possibly later. Bronze, height 5'2" (1.57 m). Museo Nazionale del Bargello, Florence. Photo: Alinari, Florence.

Donatello (Donato de Niccolò Bardi), 1386?–1466

When Donatello (don-a-TEL-o) completed his statue of a biblical prophet (fig. 17.7), he is said to have commanded it, "Speak, speak or the plague take you." The story may be apocryphal, but Renaissance artists did view themselves as creators, not as mere makers of things. With an assurance that the ancient Greeks would have admired, these artists hacked, hewed, painted, and composed as though they partook of the Divine Spirit. Though still regarded by society as craftsmen engaged in manual labor, they repeatedly proclaimed their preeminence as artists—an elevated status finally accorded Leonardo, Raphael, and Michelangelo in the sixteenth century. Created for a niche in Giotto's campanile, Donatello's biblical prophet displays the rude power of a zealot, a man of God fiercely denouncing wickedness and vice. Known in Donatello's time as Zuccone ("pumpkin head," i.e., baldy), the figure is not a category but a specific individual. Wearing a cloak thrown hurriedly over his body, the prophet is intent on his mission: calling down the wrath of God on the faithless.

After a prolonged stay in Rome studying Roman art, Donatello returned to Florence in the early 1430s, where he created his *David* (fig. 17.8), a favorite image of Republican Florence, which saw itself as a latter-day David, champion of liberty. Representing a second stage in the development of Renaissance art, *David* is more classical than the biblical prophet, standing in a pose reminiscent of Praxiteles' *Hermes*. Though the gracefully flowing lines and the balance of tension and relaxation are classical, this is the body of an adolescent boy, not a Greek warrior. The Tuscan shepherd's cap and warrior boots emphasize what is possibly the first life-size freestanding nude since antiquity. The agony evident in the face of the slain Goliath contrasts sharply with the curiously impassive expression of the shepherd boy. The Middle Ages interpreted David's triumph as symbolic of Christ's victory over death, but Donatello's intentions remain a tantalizing mystery.

Donatello's colossal equestrian statue of the Venetian soldier of fortune (condottiere) Gattamelata (fig. 17.9) was commissioned by the general's family, which led to a ten-year sojourn in Padua. This, in effect, exported the Florentine Renaissance to northern Italy, spawning a whole school of painting and sculpture influenced by Donatello's powerful personality. The statue itself was possibly inspired by the vigor of the equestrian statue of Marcus Aurelius in Rome, then thought to portray Constantine. Donatello's work, however, exceeded the representation of the Roman emperor in the concentrated power of his figure's commanding presence. Apparently guiding his charger by sheer willpower (note the slack reins and spurs), the general is an idealized image of majestic power. Outfitted with a combination of Roman and Venetian armor, the horse and rider have a composition unified by the vigorous diagonals of the general's baton and long sword. Donatello not only solved the technical problems of large-scale bronze casting, but created a masterpiece[1] in the process.

Though no one knows exactly what Donatello meant by his *David*, the intentions of Early Renaissance painters are quite clear—they were concerned with representing the natural world regardless of metaphysical symbols. Artists studied anatomy to determine how the human body was constructed and how it functioned. Using scientific procedures they developed linear and aerial perspectives to create the illusion of actual space. They studied optics, light, and color to add the final touches to the illusion of light and personality. Through keen observation they confidently developed new forms for the new age.

17.9 Donatello, *Equestrian Monument of Gattamelata*, Piazza del Santo, Padua. 1443–53. Bronze, height 12'2" (3.71 m). Photo: Alinari, Florence.

Masaccio (Tommaso di Ser Giovanni di Mone), 1401–28?

Renaissance painting appeared in the 1420s in fully developed form in the work of a single artist, whose nickname of Masaccio ("Slovenly Tom") indicated so much preoccupation with art that personal appearance was neglected. Though only in his mid-twenties, Masaccio (ma-SOT-cho) created a fresh repertory of illusionist techniques avidly studied by later Renaissance painters, especially Leonardo and Michelangelo. Working with his colleague Masolino, Masaccio painted a series of **frescoes** in the Brancacci Chapel, of which his *Tribute Money* (fig. 17.10) is the acknowledged masterpiece. The subject is based on Matthew 17:24–27, in which the Roman tax collector, wearing the short tunic, demands his tribute of Peter. Christ instructs Peter to cast a hook and take the first fish caught. In the fish's mouth Peter will find a shekel that he will give to the tax collector "for me and for yourself." Told in continuous narration in the Roman manner (as on Trajan's Column), Peter appears first in the center, fishing at the left, and finally handing the coin to the tax collector at the right. Masaccio convinces us that we are looking into deep space by using four illusionist devices: linear perspective, visual perspective, atmospheric perspective, and **chiaroscuro** (key-AR-o-SCOOR-o).

1. Some nowadays consider "masterwork," "masterpiece," etc. politically incorrect. However, one cannot change the past. Historically speaking, a masterpiece is a work presented to a guild by a craftsman for admission to the rank of master. The term is probably a translation of the Dutch *meesterstuk* or German *Meisterstück*. It has been used for centuries to describe anything superlative.

Paolo Uccello, 1397–1475

For an age already using crossbows, gunpowder, and cannons, Renaissance warfare was paradoxical, a cultivated legacy from the Age of Chivalry. The system followed the tradition of medieval lists: armored knights in formal combat, complete with code of honor and the pageantry of wheeling and charging with trumpets blowing and banners flying. For the Florentines, the relatively minor fray at San Romano epitomized fifteenth-century concepts of honor and, most especially, *virtù* (see p. 12). Immortalized by Uccello (oo-CHELL-o) in three magnificent panels, the *Battle of San Romano* originally hung in the bedchamber of Lorenzo the Magnificent. The central panel (fig. 17.11) portrays the climax of the battle. Uccello was obsessed with the problems of scientific linear perspective, and thus more concerned with the patterns of lances, armor, trumpets, and crossbows than with the ferocity of warfare. The result is a stylized composition of a bloodless battle, with horses looking like transplants from a merry-go-round. The work is both a study in perspective and a memorial to military honor, Renaissance-style.

17.10 Masaccio, *Tribute Money*, Brancacci Chapel, Sta. Maria del Carmine, Florence. Ca. 1425. Fresco, 8'4" × 19'8" (2.54 × 6 m). Photo: Scala, Florence.

17.11 Paolo Uccello, "The Unhorsing of Bernardino della Carda," *Battle of San Romano*. Ca. 1455. Tempera on wood, 6' × 10'5" (1.83 × 3.18 m). Galleria degli Uffizi, Florence. Photo: A.K.G., London.

Leonbattista Alberti, 1404–72

During the first half of the fifteenth century such classical elements of the Roman past as columns, capitals, and arches were examined by Brunelleschi, Donatello, and others. By mid-century the whole of antiquity was scrutinized, under the leadership of the remarkable humanist Alberti, who adopted the glorious past as a way of life. The first to study in detail the works of the Roman architect Vitruvius (first century BC), Alberti wrote enormously influential scientific treatises on painting, architecture, and sculpture. His design for the facade of a wealthy merchant's townhouse was inspired by Roman architecture but, there being no precedents for such a building in an ancient society in which the rich lived in country villas, Alberti invented for the

17.12 Leonbattista Alberti (designer) and Bernardo Rossellino (architect), Palazzo Rucellai, Florence, facade. Begun 1461. Photo: Alinari, Florence.

17.13 Leonbattista Alberti, Sta. Maria Novella, Florence, facade. 1470. Photo: Scala, Florence.

Palazzo Rucellai (fig. 17.12) a new architecture based on his classically derived system of ideal proportions. Divided into three clearly articulated stories separated by **friezes** and **architraves**, the structure is faced with rusticated blocks of identical patterns in each bay, changing to related patterns in the upper two stories. Alberti adapted the articulation of superimposed pilasters from the Colosseum, but without the deep spaces. He used the **Tuscan** order for the ground floor and the Corinthian for the top floor. In between he invented his own composite order—a layer of acanthus leaves around a palmette—maintaining that a thorough knowledge of classical designs enabled architects to extend the vocabulary, and then proving his point.

Alberti was responsible for two Florentine buildings, the Palazzo Rucellai and the facade of the Church of Santa Maria Novella, neither of which had any noticeable effect on contemporary Florentine artists. Outside of Florence, however, Alberti's classical designs influenced all Renaissance architects, especially Bramante, Michelangelo, and Palladio. His design for the facade of Santa Maria Novella (fig. 17.13) had to cope with the existing Gothic arches on the ground level, a challenge which he met brilliantly by topping them with blind arches and matching their green and white marble with the corner pilasters and the four pilasters on the second story. His masterstroke was the addition of **volutes** on both sides of the narrow upper temple, which

A MATTER OF PERSPECTIVE

Literally meaning "clear-seeing," perspective comprises the techniques giving the illusion of three-dimensional spatial relationships on a two-dimensional surface. Apparently first developed by Brunelleschi, linear perspective is based on the principle of all lines converging on a single **vanishing point** located, in figure 17.10, at the head of Christ. Visual perspective suggests depth of space by overlapping shapes and by the smaller size of distant objects. Perhaps invented in Italy by Masaccio, atmospheric perspective is based on the optical fact that colors become dimmer and outlines hazier as they recede into the distance. Flooding *Tribute Money* from outside the pictorial space, light strikes the figures at an angle, outlining the bodies in a tangible space. With light sculpting the bodies in gradations of light and shadow, called chiaroscuro (literally "clear-dark"), the illusion communicates weight, substance, and bulk. Masaccio's contemporary in northern Europe, Jan van Eyck, also used these perspectives in varying degrees, indicating that naturalistic painting had become, virtually simultaneously, the goal of a number of widely separated artists.

17.14 Andrea del Verrocchio, *David*. Ca. 1465. Bronze, height 4'1⅝" (1.26 m). Museo Nazionale del Bargello, Florence. Photo: Alinari, Florence.

17.15 Andrea del Verrocchio (completed by Leopardi), *Equestrian Monument of Bartolommeo Colleoni*. Ca. 1481–96. Bronze, height 13' (3.96 m). Campo SS Giovanni e Paolo, Venice. Photo: Alinari, Florence.

solved two problems: (1) it supplied needed buttressing for the nave walls, and (2) it beautifully filled the space above the side aisles of a **basilica**-plan church. The harmonious whole of the facade was the result of a rigorous set of proportions. Width and height are identical with a ratio of 1:1. The upper structure can be encased in a square one-fourth the size of the basic square, or a ratio of 1:4. The lower portion is a rectangle of double squares forming a ratio of 1:2. Throughout the facade the proportions can be expressed in whole-number relationships: 1:1, 1:2, 1:3, and so on. Along with Brunelleschi, Alberti was convinced that beauty was inherent in these ratios.

Andrea del Verrocchio, 1435–88

An overriding characteristic of Renaissance artists was their individuality, their compulsion to be uniquely, unmistakably themselves. In Verrocchio (veh-ROE-key-o) we see distinct manifestations of this drive for individuality when treating the same subject. Verrocchio's *David* (fig. 17.14) is totally different from Donatello's conception. Donatello's figure is essentially a composition of sinuous and graceful lines; in his young warrior, Verrocchio emphasizes texture by a delicate rendering in gleaming bronze of skin, underlying veins, muscle, and bone. These are qualities that, unfortunately, can be best appreciated only when walking around the actual work. The tactile qualities are enhanced by clothing the figure in a skintight short skirt designed to look like leather. That Verrocchio used his pupil, Leonardo da Vinci, as a model may or may not be true, but the age and looks are about right.

Donatello's *Equestrian Monument of Gattamelata* (see fig. 17.9) is idealized, but Verrocchio's portrayal of Bartolommeo Colleoni (fig. 17.15) is strikingly realistic, with

17.16 Andrea del Verrocchio, *Lorenzo de' Medici*. Ca. 1480. Terra-cotta, 25⅞ × 23¼ × 12⅞" (65.8 × 59.1 × 32.7 cm). National Gallery of Art, Washington, D.C. (Samuel H. Kress Collection).

the fiercely scowling general readying his mace as he rides boldly into battle. Twisting in his saddle, the powerful figure seems almost too massive for the sprightly horse to carry. The tensions of horse and rider are portrayed at a dynamic moment in time, an instant before the battle.

Also naturalistic is Verrocchio's portrait bust of Lorenzo the Magnificent (fig. 17.16), banker, poet, patron of the arts, and Florentine autocrat. Any accomplished craftsman can reproduce the crooked ski-slope nose, tight lips, and knitted brow. These are details that assist in the communication of a tangible presence: the overpowering personality of a unique human being. Classical portraiture had been revived; here is a masterful portrait of a powerful Renaissance figure.

Sandro Botticelli, 1445–1510

Three of the leading painters of the last quarter of the century—Botticelli, Ghirlandaio, and Perugino—were all vastly different in temperament and style. Botticelli (bot-tee-CHEL-lee), in fact, stands alone as one of the great masters in the use of line. In his celebrated *Birth of Venus* (*Venus Landing on the Shore*; fig. 17.17), Botticelli subordinates perspective and "correct" anatomical proportions and details to the elegant and sensual lines that make his style so delightfully unique. Like many of his generation, especially the elite circle of Lorenzo de' Medici and the Platonic Academy, Botticelli was fascinated with themes from classical mythology. According to an ancient myth, Venus was born from the sea, a legend interpreted by Ficino as an allegory of the birth of beauty. What the Florentine **Neoplatonists** actually did believe is still debated. Much of Plato's work had become available, but there was also a large body of Neoplatonist writings with Christian elements superimposed on Platonic theories.

Whether Botticelli's *Venus* symbolizes non-Christian or Christian ideas, or both, she is certainly lovely. Possibly inspired by a poem by Poliziano, Botticelli has painted her poised lightly on a conch shell, being blown gently to shore by two Zephyrs as one of the Hours hastens to drape her body with a flowered mantle. This is poetry in motion. The sea is flat, marked by upward-thrusting, V-shaped lines and bound by a stylized shoreline to form a serene setting for the sinuous lines of the moving figures. Probably inspired by classical statues in the Medici collection, the body of the goddess of spiritual and intellectual beauty is elongated and exquisitely curved, proportionately larger than the scale of the landscape. The gold-line shading on the trees is a

17.17 Sandro Botticelli, *Birth of Venus (Venus Landing on the Shore)*. After 1482. Tempera on canvas, 5'8" × 9'1" (1.73 × 2.77 m). Galleria degli Uffizi, Florence. Photo: Scala, Florence.

further indication that Botticelli intended no realistic representation of the landscape. It was this sort of stylized treatment of the background that led to his friend Leonardo's wry comment that Botticelli created landscapes by throwing a sponge at the canvas.

Domenico del Ghirlandaio, 1449–94

Botticelli was favored by the intellectual elite of Florence, but the style of Ghirlandaio (gear-lan-DAH-yo) was preferred by the merchants and bankers of the city. Not interested in mythological fantasies, Ghirlandaio was a conservative painter for a commercial clientele and, as might be expected, a very successful artist. His *Old Man with a Child* (fig. 17.18), one of his most endearing works, is a compassionate portrayal of an elderly man holding an adoring child who could be his grandson, though the subjects have never been identified. Perhaps influenced by the naturalism of Flemish painting, which was well known in Italy by this time, the objective treatment of thinning hair and a deformed nose adds to the tender scene of familial love. As was customary in Renaissance portraiture, the human subjects totally dominate a composition that is reinforced by the lovely and distant landscape.

17.18 Domenico del Ghirlandaio, *Old Man with a Child.* Ca. 1480. Panel, 24⅜ × 18" (61.9 × 45.7 cm). Louvre, Paris. Photo: R.M.N., Paris.

Perugino (Pietro Vanucci), ca. 1445–1523

Until about the middle of the fifteenth century, the Early Renaissance was essentially Florentine; the second half of the century saw the dissemination of Renaissance techniques throughout Italy, notably by artists such as Perugino and Bellini. Though his early training is a mystery, Pietro Vanucci was in Florence by 1472, where he acquired his

17.19 Perugino, *The Crucifixion with the Virgin, Saint John, Saint Jerome, and Saint Mary Magdalene*. Ca. 1485. Oil on panel, transferred to canvas: center 39⅞ × 22¼" (101.3 × 56.5 cm); wings each 37½ × 12" (95.2 × 30.5 cm). National Gallery of Art, Washington, D.C. (Andrew W. Mellon Collection).

knowledge of drawing and perspective, probably from Verrocchio. It was in the Umbrian city of Perugia that he established his reputation and acquired the name by which he is known today: Perugino (pay-roo-GEE-no), the "Perugian." In his *Crucifixion with the Virgin, Saint John, Saint Jerome, and Saint Mary Magdalene* (fig. 17.19), Perugino created a wonderful pictorial space that is much more open than Florentine landscapes, with a sky stretching to infinity. As polished and cool as the work of the Flemish painter Hans Memling (see fig. 17.25), and probably influenced by his work, the **altarpiece** shows none of the usual emotions of Florentine crucifixions. Christ is not racked by pain nor do Mary at the left nor John at the right display any grief. In the wings St. Jerome and Mary Magdalene stand serenely in counterbalancing poses. In the vast expanse of the natural setting all is quietude. Whether the absence of emotion reflects Vasari's statement that Perugino was an atheist is a moot point. Though religious convictions were important for many people at that time, Renaissance artists were valued chiefly for their skills, not their spirits.

THE EARLY RENAISSANCE IN THE NORTH

Limbourg Brothers, ca. 1385–1416

A focus of significant new developments in art and in music (see p. 64) was the sumptuous court of the dukes of Burgundy, from which the dukes governed the most prosperous lands in Europe (see map 18.1). Philip the Bold and his brother, the Duke of Berry, sponsored leading artists such as the Limbourg brothers: Paul, Herman, and Jean. Their work in manuscript illumination marked the high point of the International Style (late Gothic), while also moving beyond to a new naturalism. Commissioned by the Duke of Berry, they created for him a personal prayer book, a Book of Hours containing passages of Scripture, prayers, and **Office hours**, all lavishly decorated and illustrated with paintings. Of particular interest are the twelve illuminated calendar pages; ten include peasants and aristocrats and two are devoted solely to peasant **genre** scenes. "February" (fig. 17.20 and p. 72) has, at the top, a zodiac representing the route of the chariot of the sun and including, in this case, the zodiacal signs of Aquarius and Pisces. The scene is an intensely cold, snowy landscape—the first convincing snow scene in Western art. On the upper level a peasant cuts firewood as another herds a donkey laden with faggots toward a distant village. In the tiny farmyard snow caps the beehives and covers the roof of the sheep pen except for the unrepaired hole in the roof. At the right a woman blows on her icy hands and stamps her feet to try to restore circulation. With the front wall removed for our benefit, we see a man and a woman seated before the fire with skirts raised high to gather in the welcome warmth. At the doorway, the lady of the house rather more decorously lifts her skirt; the cat is, of course, cozily warm and comfortable. The

OIL REPLACES EGG YOLK

Until early in the fifteenth century tempera (TEM-pur-uh; Lat., "to mingle or temper") painting was the standard medium. Artists mixed powdered pigments in egg yolk and painted, usually, on a wood panel. They had to paint rapidly and precisely because the paint dried so fast. Capable of details and bright colors, the medium had a narrow range between light and dark; colors too dark became dead while very light ones became chalklike.

Northern artists mixed their pigments in linseed oil and painted on canvas, which held paint better than wood. The surface was prepared as in tempera with gesso (plaster of Paris mixed with glue), and paint then applied in layers. Colors ranged from the lightest to the darkest with no loss of intensity, attaining, in the Flemish school, the rich glow that characterizes their work. With oil, artists could paint minute still-life details and vast landscape vistas; it dried slowly, giving them time to correct, revise, enrich. One wonders which came first: northern artists' obsession with painting everything they saw (leading to the invention of oil painting) or the discovery of a medium that enabled them to paint what they saw.

17.20 Limbourg Brothers, "February" from the *Très Riches Heures du Duc de Berry*. 1413–16. Illuminated manuscript. Musée Condé, Chantilly, France. Photo: Giraudon, Paris.

perspective that gives the illusion of depth is empirical rather than mathematically precise, the way the artists actually perceived the scene. Marking the beginning of the northern tradition of naturalistic art, the overriding concern is with the visible world, with loving care devoted to minute details in all their complexity.

The decisive victory of the English king, Henry V, at Agincourt in 1415 effectively ended, for some forty years, the dominance of the French court and thus royal sponsorship of the courtly International Style. The center for art shifted to the Low Countries, where Philip the Good (reigned 1419–67) maintained his Burgundian court and negotiated hardheaded trade alliances with England. Artists found in the flourishing cities of Flanders—Bruges, Ghent, Louvain, Brussels—new patrons in the bankers and merchants who were the true arbiters of the wealthiest society in Europe. The society was **bourgeois**, but cosmopolitan rather than provincial, with powerful banking and trade connections throughout Europe. This solid middle class wanted art that pictured the real world and, by a strange coincidence, there were several artists of genius available to help fulfill the passion for naturalism.

Jan van Eyck, ca. 1390–1441

The leading painter of the early Flemish school, indeed of any age, van Eyck (van IKE) first served the court of John of Bavaria and later the Burgundian court of Philip the Good. Credited by Vasari with inventing oil painting, van Eyck probably perfected an existing procedure. Using a technique still not fully understood, he probably put a **gesso** coating, or ground, on his panel; then, by applying alternate layers of opaque and translucent color, he enhanced the brilliance of his colors. He made infinitely subtle and smooth gradations between color tones, obtaining a jewellike radiance comparable to medieval stained glass. He undoubtedly learned some of his techniques from manuscript painters such as the Limbourg brothers, but it also seems likely that van Eyck was influenced, possibly inspired, by Gothic stained glass.

Ghent Altarpiece

The greatest work of early Flemish painting and a monumental accomplishment in any age, the *Ghent Altarpiece* (fig. 17.21) is a polyptych, a central painting with two hinged wings. The twenty different panels of the work range from the Annunciation on the outer panels to the Adoration of the Mystic Lamb within. In the lunettes of figure 17.21, the prophet Zechariah (left) with the Erytraean Sibyl, Cumean Sibyl, and prophet Micah symbolize the coming of Christ. The Annunciation figures are placed in a contemporary room containing Romanesque and Gothic elements that probably symbolize the Old and New Testaments. In the center panels below, the simulated sculptural figures of St. John the Baptist and St. John the Evangelist are flanked by the donors Jodoc Vyt and his wife.

In the open altarpiece (fig. 17.22), the lower central panel shows the community of saints, come from the four corners of the world to worship at the altar of the Mystic Lamb, from whose heart blood cascades into a chalice. In the foreground the Fountain of Life pours from spigots into an octagonal basin, running toward the observer as the "river of life" (Revelation 22:1). In the left-hand panel, judges and knights ride to the altar; on the right, hermits, pilgrims, and the giant St. Christopher walk to an altar scene backed by the heavenly Jerusalem in the distance. Forming a continuous view of Paradise, the five lower panels are designed with a rising perspective, another of the artist's innovations. On the upper level, the Lord has Mary as the Queen of Heaven on his right hand and St. John the Baptist on his left. To either side are choirs of angels with St. Cecilia seated at the portative (portable) organ, flanked by Adam and Eve on the outer panels.

The first large nudes in northern panel painting, the figures of Adam and Eve reveal a keen appreciation of the human body and innovative painting techniques in perspective and lighting. Once bowed by shame, the figures stand erect as the First Man and First Woman. The placement of the altarpiece puts the feet of the two nudes at eye level, which accounts for the view of the sole of Adam's foot. This bit of naturalism is typical of a visual reality so precise that botanists can identify dozens of plants in this awesome work.

The *Ghent Altarpiece* was created early in the supremacy of the Duchy of Burgundy but, even as van Eyck worked on it, Joan of Arc (ca. 1412–31) was leading Charles VII and the French army to victory (in 1428) over the English invaders. By 1453 Charles had triumphantly ended the Hundred Years' War with England (1337–1453) and absorbed Burgundy, Picardy, and Flanders.

The Arnolfini Wedding

The meticulous details in a van Eyck painting are fascinating, but the whole of a picture—its unity—is greater than the sum of its parts. In a work commissioned by Giovanni Arnolfini, an Italian merchant, he and his bride, Jeanne Cenami, apparently pose for a portrait as a form of wedding certificate, duly witnessed by the artist (seen in the convex mirror) and notarized on the back wall: "Jan van Eyck was here" (fig. 17.23). The light, space, volume, and the two distinct personalities are all unified, both visually and psychologically. Patron and artist must have been more than acquaintances; two individuals make up this couple, joined in a tender moment without the slightest hint of sentimentality. The texture of cloth, glass, metal, wood, and even the furry little dog are exquisitely detailed.

Though unobtrusive, symbols abound. The single lighted candle is, according to custom, the last to be extinguished on the wedding night, but it may also symbolize Christ as the light of the world. Carved on the post of a bedside chair is the image of St. Margaret, the patron saint of childbirth. (The lady is not pregnant but holding up her

17.21 Jan van Eyck, *Ghent Altarpiece* (closed). Ca. 1425–32. 11' 3" × 7'2" (3.43 × 2.18 m). St. Bavo, Ghent, Belgium. Photo: Paul M. R. Maeyaert, Zelzate, Belgium.

17.22 *Below* Jan van Eyck, *Ghent Altarpiece* (open). 11'3" × 14'5" (3.43 × 4.39 m). Photo: Scala, Florence.

17.23 Jan van Eyck, *The Arnolfini Wedding Portrait*. 1434. Oil on canvas, 32¼ × 23½" (81.9 × 59.7 cm). National Gallery, London.

full-skirted dress in the contemporary fashion.) The dog represents fidelity (Lat. *fides*; hence "Fido"), and the abandoned slippers are a reminder that the couple is standing on holy ground. By uniting the classical concern for naturalism and spatial depth with the Christian idea that every material object has transcendent importance, Flemish painters developed a radically new style of painting. Craftsmanship at this level verges on the superhuman; indeed, nothing like this had ever been done before.

Rogier van der Weyden, ca. 1400–64

Because his paintings were perfect in their own marvelous way, van Eyck had many admirers in northern Europe, Spain, and Italy, but no emulators. There were imitators, of course, but no disciples who could even approach his rare gifts. Adopting a more expressive and emotional style than that of van Eyck, van der Weyden (van dur VYE-den) was the leading Flemish painter of the next generation, becoming City Painter for Brussels in 1435. When he traveled to Italy for the Holy Year of 1450, he influenced Italian art and was, in turn, impressed by what he saw there. As technically accomplished as van Eyck, he painted portraits with a psychological depth then unknown in Flemish painting.

17.24 Rogier van der Weyden, *Portrait of a Lady*. Ca. 1460. Oil on panel, painted surface 13⅜ × 10¹⁄₁₆" (34 × 25.5 cm). National Gallery of Art, Washington, D.C. (Andrew W. Mellon Collection). Photo: Richard Carafelli.

Portrait of a Lady (fig. 17.24) is a study of a young woman tentatively identified as Marie de Valengin, the daughter of Philip the Good, Duke of Burgundy. Her forehead and eyebrows are shaved, a fashionable indication of intellectual acumen. Also high fashion, the high-waisted dress and triangular coif focus attention on the exquisite modeling of the face. The portrait is both beautiful and baffling. The impression of an almost ascetic contemplation is contradicted by the sensuality of the full mouth with its ripe underlip. The overall impression is that of an assertive personality—an intelligent, self-confident, and strong-willed young woman. She certainly looks like a princess. Contrasting curiously with the broad facial planes, the thin fingers are almost Gothic in style. Bewitching and beguiling, this is a great psychological study by one of the first of a long line of Low Country painters leading directly to Hals and Rembrandt.

Hans Memling, ca. 1440–94

Memling served his apprenticeship in his native Germany, but then moved to Flanders (at that time a French province) where he apparently studied with van der Weyden. A contemporary of Ghirlandaio in Italy, his style is similarly genial and rather naive. It appealed to a large clientele of merchants and led ultimately to a considerable fortune. Using extensive studies of earlier Flemish masters, particularly van Eyck, he developed a somewhat melancholy art of extreme refinement. In *The Presentation in the Temple* (fig. 17.25) the figures are immobile, frozen in time, or even outside time. The light falls on people grouped in harmony with their imaginary setting; the overall feeling is unworldly and slightly sad.

Memling's work was in tune with a general feeling of pessimism, an erosion of confidence in the moral authority of the church, an almost prophetic feeling of the impending Reformation. In Italy the pessimism was fully warranted, for it was in 1494—the year of Memling's death—that the Medicis were expelled from Florence, coinciding with the invasion of the French armies of Charles VIII, which launched a tumultuous era in Italy called the Italian Wars.

17.25 Hans Memling, *The Presentation in the Temple*. Photo: Bridgeman, London.

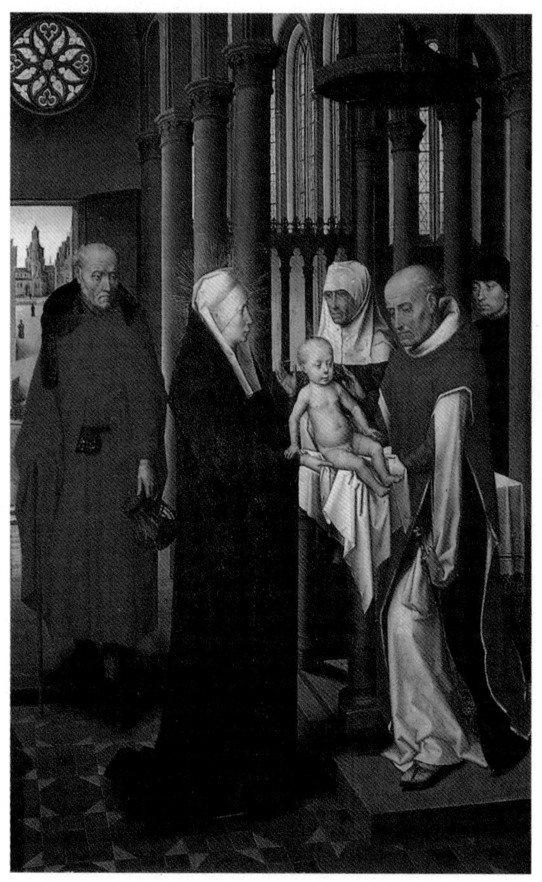

Hieronymus Bosch, ca. 1450–1516

This pessimistic age found its supreme artist in the person of Bosch (bahs), one of history's most enthralling and enigmatic painters. He lived and worked in present-day southern Holland, but little else is known about either his life or his artistic intentions. Art historians have wondered about his bizarre iconography, and so have psychiatrists. This was an age obsessed with death and with an almost pathological fear of the devil and his demons. His work makes it plain that Bosch had a pessimistic view of human nature—though some would call his vision realistic—and he certainly raged against sinfulness.

17.26 Hieronymus Bosch, *Garden of Delights*. Ca. 1505–10. Oil on panel, sides 86 × 36" (218.4 × 91.4 cm); center 86 × 76" (218.4 × 193 cm). Museo del Prado, Madrid.

One of his major and most enigmatic works is the huge triptych entitled *Garden of Delights* (fig. 17.26). The side panels of this incredible work depict an idyllic Garden of Eden and a spectacularly disastrous Hell, both rendered in an unconventional but fairly consistent manner. The central panel is quite another matter. Complex, bizarre, and bewildering, the sparse landscape teems with hundreds of naked men and women and various animals, both real and imaginary—and in all sizes. There are several lakes, a pond, giant strawberries, mussel shells, eggs, and assorted mysterious and grotesque objects. Frail of body and seeming all the same age—about twenty-one—men and women frolic and tease and gambol about the strange arena.

Despite the universal nudity and much pairing off, there is no explicit sexual activity. The general ambiance is certainly erotic, but no one displays any sexual desire except, perhaps, by stroking a giant strawberry. Most are busy with silly activities. One cuddling couple wears an owl for a headdress and someone rides a lion while clutching a giant fish. The foolishness is virtually endless, but apparently harmless. The faces are generally calm and composed; the entire scene appears to resemble a genteel nudist camp.

What does all this mean? In the absence of a universally accepted interpretation, there are several possibilities. Perhaps there are messages hidden behind symbolic acts and objects—a vocabulary taken from non-Christian traditions, Flemish folklore, and medieval bestiaries. Pursuing this line leads one into a quagmire of ambiguities that apparently have no resolution. Too much of the old symbolic vocabularies has been lost over the intervening centuries.

Others take the view that this is a message in code directed to people practicing a secret religion. This kind of activity amounts to heresy and a possible death sentence—hence the code. But can we accept these vapid people as high practitioners of a secret sect? Their actions seem too ridiculous for that. Nothing in this picture has any religious connotation whatsoever, and this at a time when religion pervaded every nook and cranny of life.

We can never know exactly how Bosch's contemporaries viewed this painting but, in our own time, there are startling flashes of recognition. All too familiar is the aimless pursuit of pleasure, the lack of ambition, direction, or purpose, the games people play. Did Bosch anticipate the twentieth century, or has he perhaps indicted all humankind for persistent foolishness and failure?

When considering Bosch's total output, there is no denying his pessimism; his was perhaps the darkest vision in an age of deep pessimism. This painting seems to be, therefore, a despairing depiction of the human condition in which there is no Christ, no Redemption, no Salvation. Humanity is doomed, not because it is vicious or depraved, but because it is vain, vapid, and silly. The Incarnation is useless because folly was present in the Garden of Eden and remains as the dominant characteristic of the human race.[2] This interpretation leaves us no alternative but to see Bosch as the ultimate pessimist: humankind will move endlessly from folly to damnation with no hope of heaven.

Enormously popular in the sixteenth century, Bosch's paintings typify an age that groveled in a sickening undercurrent of fear of the devil, leading to fierce, misdirected religious zeal. In 1484 Pope Innocent VIII declared witchcraft (activities of women possessed by the devil) a prime heresy. During the next two centuries a tidal wave of sadism and misogyny led to the torture, hanging, and burning of some 100,000 to 200,000 women, plus many men (and children) who were enveloped in the madness. Two

2. See also Erasmus, *The Praise of Folly*, pp. 74 and 80–4.
3. Heinrich Kramer and James Sprenger, *Malleus Maleficarum*, trans. Montague Summers (London: Pushkin Press, 1928). Approved by the pope, the book was first published in 1490.

unscrupulous Dominican monks wrote a handbook for self-appointed witch-hunters, *The Witches' Hammer,*[3] a bestseller that ran to thirty editions, a melancholy testimony to the dissemination of printed books.

The career of Hieronymus Bosch marked the end of the Early Northern Renaissance and the beginning of a tormented period of warfare in Italy, of corrupt and dissolute popes, and of spiritually bankrupt religious orders. One year after Bosch's death, Martin Luther published his ninety-five Theses to set in motion the Reformation.

THE HIGH RENAISSANCE IN ITALY, CA. 1495–1520

The relatively peaceful and prosperous existence of Florence ended in two rough jolts in the fateful years of 1492 and 1494. Lorenzo the Magnificent—a strong, moderating force in the fortunes of Florence—died in 1492, the same year in which Ferdinand and Isabella captured Córdoba, the last Moorish stronghold in Spain. Columbus, using a map drawn in Florence, discovered the New World. In Rome, Rodrigo Borgia was crowned as Pope Alexander VI, the embodiment of a decadent and corrupt Renaissance pontiff and a merciless enemy of the Florentine Republic.

In 1494, concerned about the military support of Lorenzo's dim and feckless son Piero, Ludovico Sforza of Milan encouraged Charles VIII of France to invade Italy. Charles, who was spoiling for a fight, willingly did so. For the next thirty-five years French and Spanish armies, the latter freed by the removal of the Moors, fought the Italian Wars against the city-states and, for good measure, each other. Always assuming that each invasion was the last, the Italian city-states never banded together to expel their foreign tormentors. Paradoxically, High Renaissance art flourished against this backdrop of continuous warfare. Exploiting and refining Early Renaissance discoveries in Italy and the North, Leonardo da Vinci, Michelangelo, Raphael, and Bramante created masterworks that crowned the Italian Renaissance.

Leonardo da Vinci, 1452–1519

The illegitimate son of a peasant girl known only as Caterina, and Piero da Vinci, a notary, Leonardo da Vinci (lay-o-NAR-do da VIN-chee) was the acknowledged universal man of the Renaissance, the most astounding genius in an age of giants. Inventor, civil and military engineer, architect, musician, geologist, botanist, physicist, anatomist, sculptor, and painter, Leonardo left untouched only classical scholarship, poetry, and philosophy. Theology was of no interest to him, for he was a lifelong skeptic who recognized no authority higher than the eye, which he called the "window of the soul."

As was customary with bastardy during the Renaissance, Leonardo was acknowledged by his father and, at about age fifteen, apprenticed to Verrocchio in Florence. Though little else is known about the first thirty years of his life, records indicate that Leonardo, like Masaccio and Botticelli before him, was admitted to the guild as a craftsman in painting. Unlike Early Renaissance masters, however, Leonardo, along with Michelangelo, launched a successful campaign to raise the status of artists from mere artisans to members of the highest level of society.

In 1481 Pope Sixtus IV summoned the "best" Tuscan artists to work in the Vatican, including Botticelli, Ghirlandaio, and Perugino, but not Leonardo. Furious at the slight, Leonardo decided to leave Florence, but not before he had completed a commission for the de' Benci family of wealthy bankers. His portrait of *Ginevra de' Benci* (fig. 17.27), the only Leonardo painting in the United States, is an enchanting study of a lovely but strangely tense and wary young woman. She was known to be a very devout person, ill at ease in the fun-loving exuberance of Florence, and sternly disapproving of Lorenzo de' Medici's long-term affair with her aunt. Framing her golden curls in juniper branches (Ginevra means "juniper"), Leonardo has created a melancholy work; the pallid face is set against a thinly misted background, with details deliberately softened and blurred. Though not invented by Leonardo, this **sfumato** (foo-MAH-toh, literally "smoky") technique was one of his significant contributions to the art of painting. The twilight atmosphere is another innovation, contrasting sharply with

17.27 Leonardo da Vinci, *Ginevra de' Benci*. Ca. 1474. Oil on panel, 15¼ × 14½" (38.8 × 36.7 cm). National Gallery of Art, Washington, D.C. (Ailsa Mellon Bruce Fund). Photo: Jose A. Naranjo.

17.28 Leonardo da Vinci, *The Last Supper*. Ca. 1495–8. Mural, oil and tempera on plaster, 14'5" × 28' (4.39 × 8.53 m). Refectory of Sta. Maria delle Grazie, Milan. Photo: Scala, Florence.

the sunlit scenes of other painters. The painting is minus some 6 inches (15.2 cm) at the bottom, which may explain why the lady's hands are not shown.

Seeking a more appreciative patron than the Medici or the pope, Leonardo wrote to Ludovico Sforza, duke of Milan, touting his expertise as a military engineer but mentioning, in just two sentences, that he was also a sculptor and a painter. During his stay in Milan (1482–99) Leonardo produced *The Last Supper* (fig. 17.28), a treatment of the familiar theme unlike anything before or since. The High Renaissance begins with this magnificent composition. After suffering the indignities of Leonardo's experimentation with fresco painting, damp walls, Napoleon's troops, and World War II bombing, the painting has been restored, but only to an approximation of its original condition.

The moment of the painting is not the traditional one of the Eucharist, but Christ's electrifying statement: "One of you shall betray me." Except for Christ, Leonardo used life models for the disciples and had difficulty only in finding a suitable Judas. According to Vasari, when the prior of Santa Maria complained to Sforza that Leonardo was "lazy" in his execution of the painting, Leonardo remarked that locating a Judas was difficult but that the prior would serve nicely. Leonardo's contemporaries would have looked for Judas where other artists had placed him—across the table from Jesus. Instead, we see the villain as part of the first group of three Apostles to the left of Christ, composed in a tight, dark triangle with his face in darkness. Clutching a bag of money, he is in the group but not a part of it. His dark bulk is in sharp contrast to the lighted profile of Peter and the luminous radiance of John. Each Apostle is an individual psychological study, reacting to Christ's startling statement in a manner consistent with his personality.

The design of *The Last Supper* has a mathematical unity, with divisions of groups of threes and fours that add up to seven and multiply into twelve. The three windows place Christ's head in the center window as the second person of the Trinity. The shocked Apostles are grouped into four units of three each, divided in the middle by the isolated triangular design of Christ. Echoing the four groups are the wall panels on either side, and on the ceiling there are seven beams running from both front to back and side to side. Leonardo may have had Christian number symbolism in mind (Holy Trinity, Four Gospels, Seven Cardinal Virtues, Twelve Gates of the New Jerusalem) but three, four, and seven also stand for the *trivium* and *quadrivium* of the **seven liberal arts**. Moreover, Pythagorean number symbolism included the concept of one as unity, three as the most logical number (beginning, middle, end), and four as symbolizing Justice. Given Leonardo's skepticism and explicit anticlerical feelings, something other than Christian symbolism would be an appropriate interpretation.

There is no question, however, about the picture as a whole. Despite the mathematical precision of the perspective, there is no place from which a spectator can view the perspective "correctly"; it exists as a work apart, on an ideal level beyond everyday experience. This is the elevated style of formal design and noble theme that characterizes the Italian High Renaissance.

Leonardo insisted that painters were noble creatures and that painting should be a part of the seven liberal arts. For him, sculptors were craftsmen standing in dust and debris chiseling away at stubborn marble. Michelangelo, on the other hand, claimed that sculpture was as superior to painting as the sun was to the moon.

Michelangelo Buonarroti, 1475–1564

Perhaps the greatest artistic genius who ever lived, Michelangelo (me-kell-AHN-djay-lo) excelled in sculpture, architecture, painting, and poetry. A towering figure even in his own time, he was the "Divine Michelangelo." Words and more words have been written trying to account for such a man, but there is no accounting for him. Born of a vain and mean-spirited father and a dimly pathetic mother to whom he never referred, he appeared with prodigious gifts at a time and place seemingly destined to make him immortal. He learned painting techniques in Ghirlandaio's studio and sculpting both from a pupil of Donatello and from ancient works in the Medici collection.

His first masterpiece, the *Pietà* (fig. 17.29), is more characteristic of the fifteenth century than the sixteenth in style, with elegant lines reminiscent of Botticelli. The triangular composition is fashioned of contradictions. Though Christ is dead, the blood pumps through his veins as if he were asleep. The Virgin is portrayed as younger than her son, her lovely face composed rather than distorted by grief; only her left hand indicates her sorrow. The figure of Christ is life-size but that of the Virgin is elongated. Her head is the same size as Christ's, but in proportion she would be about 7 feet (2.1 m) tall if she were standing. The overall visual effect of these distortions is a super-authenticity beyond earthbound reality.

The *Pietà* was a youthful work but the *David* (fig. 17.30), initiated only a year or so later, was the first monumental statue of the High Renaissance, a product of Michelangelo's already mature genius. Though the Palazzo della Signoria proudly possessed three Davids, two by Donatello (fig. 17.8) and one by Verrocchio (fig. 17.14), one more hero was not too many for a city battling to maintain its power and independence. A Florentine Republic was established after the Medici were expelled in 1494 but it did not last long. While Michelangelo was working on his *David*, the dangerous Alexander VI died, in 1503, and shortly thereafter the incompetent Piero de' Medici, known as Piero the Unfortunate, drowned while fighting with the French in an attempt to gain reentry into the city. By 1504 Florence was finally at peace and the prime civic concern was where to place Michelangelo's mighty *David*. The commission to select the site included Leonardo, Botticelli, and Perugino, attesting to the status the nearly completed work had already acquired. Originally scheduled to be placed high on Florence Cathedral, *David* was triumphantly set in front of the center of government, the Palazzo Vecchio, where it became the symbol of a republic ready to do battle against all enemies. During the nineteenth century the statue was moved indoors to protect it from the weather and replaced by a copy.

17.29 *Above* Michelangelo, *Pietà*. 1498–1499/1500. Marble, height 5'8½" (1.74 m). St. Peter's, Rome. Photo: Anderson-Giraudon, Florence.

17.30 Michelangelo, *David*. 1501–4. Marble, height 13' 5" (4.09 m). Galleria dell'Accademia, Florence. Photo: Alinari, Florence.

idealized Florence → everything florence wanted to be - "idol"

BONFIRE OF THE VANITIES

A Dominican monk, Girolamo Savonarola (1452–98), established a theocracy in Florence after the Medici were expelled and even declared Christ king of the city. A virtual dictator, he imposed rigid reforms while warning of approaching doom. Railing against materialism, he condemned ownership of anything beautiful or valuable as sinful and urged people to burn their "vanities," which many dutifully did. Friends of Botticelli barely managed to keep him from burning his paintings. Inevitably Savonarola came into conflict with the corrupt Alexander VI. When the monk ignored the pope's excommunication, he was arrested, tortured, tried, hanged (and then burned) for heresy and schism.

The Davids of Donatello and Verrocchio were adolescent boys; this is a strapping young man standing alert, every muscle vibrant with power. The head might be that of Apollo and the body that of Herakles, yet this is the portrait of a Platonic ideal as well as David the King. His father was both Hebrew and, collectively, Lorenzo, Ficino, and the Florentine Platonic Academy.

The fame of the *David* was instant, and Michelangelo had more commissions than he could handle, including one to construct a vast tomb for Pope Julius II. The tomb project was never finished as originally planned; instead, Michelangelo somehow found himself in 1508 standing atop the scaffolding in the Sistine Chapel. How all this came about has never been satisfactorily explained, but one plausible theory involves the alleged machinations of Bramante, the recently appointed architect of the new St. Peter's. He was known to be concerned about funds for his project and was also intensely jealous of Michelangelo. Julius had lavished enormous sums on his tomb project—money that Bramante needed for his mighty basilica. If the pope could be encouraged to put Michelangelo to work painting the Sistine Chapel ceiling, a monumental undertaking Bramante felt not even Michelangelo could bring off, then he would have no further financial or artistic competition. Whatever transpired behind the scenes, Michelangelo was, in fact, the only artist who was capable of tackling the project.

With a ceiling proportionately too high (68'; 20.7 m) for its length and width (132 × 44'; 40.2 × 13.4 m), the private chapel of the popes was neither intimate nor monumental. Michelangelo's frescoes made it monumental. In only four years, 1508–12, he filled the entire 700 square yards (630 m^2) of **barrel-vaulted** ceiling with over 300 powerful figures. Relating the Genesis story from the Creation to the Flood, Michelangelo fused Judeo-Christian theology with ancient mythology and Neoplatonic philosophy to create one of the truly awesome works of Western art. In just one detail, the *Creation of Adam* (fig. 17.31), one can perceive some of the majesty of the total work. Embracing an awestruck Eve and with his left hand resting on the shoulder of the Christ child, God the Father extends his finger

17.31 Michelangelo, *Creation of Adam*, Sistine Chapel ceiling, detail. 1511. Fresco. Vatican, Rome. Photo: Nippon Television, Tokyo.
This photograph was taken after the ceiling was cleaned in the 1980s.

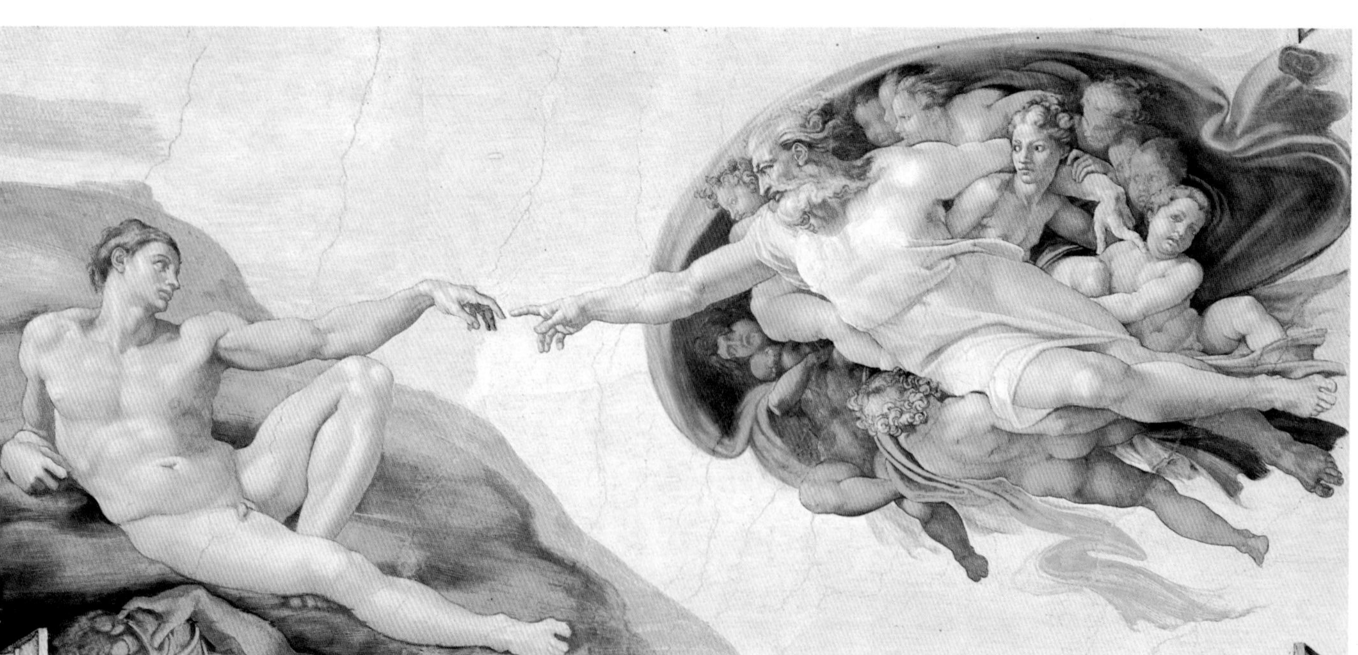

and the spark of life to an inert Adam. Against a background of generations waiting to be born, the twisting, dynamic figure is lovingly paternal, imparting to Adam the soul that will actuate his potential nobility.

After protesting for four years that he was a sculptor, not a painter, Michelangelo proved that he was both; all the figures are sculptural forms, conceived in the mind's eye of a sculptor and executed in paint on wet plaster.[4] A recent cleaning of the entire ceiling has brilliantly revealed the original rich, even dazzling, colors employed. Totally overwhelming the work of many notable artists on the walls, the ceiling frescoes express the optimism of a supreme artist at the peak of his powers.

The following **sonnet**[5] embodies Michelangelo's personal and agonizingly physical reaction to four years of lying on his back and painting over his head:

Sonnet V

To Giovanni da Pistoia
"On the Painting of the Sistine Chapel"
(I' ho gia fatto un gozzo)

I've grown a goitre by dwelling in this den—
As cats from stagnant streams in Lombardy,
Or in what other land they hap to be—
Which drives the belly close beneath the chin:
My beard turns up to heaven; my nape falls in,
Fixed on my spine: my breast-bone visibly
Grows like a harp: a rich embroidery
Bedews my face from brush-drops thick and thin.
My loins into my paunch like levers grind:
My buttock like a crupper bears my weight;
My feet unguided wander to and fro;
In front my skin grows loose and long; behind,
By bending it becomes more taut and strait;
Crosswise I strain me like a Syrian bow:
Whence false and quaint, I know,
Must be the fruit of squinting brain and eye;
For ill can aim the gun that bends awry.
Come then, Giovanni, try
To succour my dead pictures and my fame;
Since foul I fare and painting is my shame.

Donato Bramante, 1444–1514

The dominant political figure and artistic patron of the High Renaissance was Pope Julius II (reigned 1503–13), known as the Warrior Pope. Determined to obliterate the appalling memories of Alexander VI and the Borgia crimes, he refused even to live in the apartment of his decadent predecessor. Julius II restored order to the city of Rome, ruthlessly reconquered papal provinces with the sword, and proceeded energetically to rebuild his beloved Rome. A fortuitous quirk of history put a dynamic pope in power at precisely the time when he could utilize the mature talents of Michelangelo, Raphael, and Bramante. Bramante of Urbino, the foremost architect of the High Renaissance and a close friend of the pope, was entrusted with many building projects, with the new St. Peter's leading the list. Julius II decided, in 1505, that the 1,100-year-old Basilica of St. Peter's was to be replaced by a Renaissance structure worthy of the imperial splendor of the new Rome—a project not completely finished until 1626, some fourteen architects, twenty popes, and one Reformation later.

Though much of Bramante's design can still be seen in St. Peter's, his architectural genius is better illustrated by a circular structure of only modest size but of immense influence in architectural history. Constructed on the spot where St. Peter was supposedly crucified, the Tempietto ("little temple"; fig. 17.32) became the prototype of classical domed architecture in Europe and the United States. The exquisitely proportioned building was placed on a three-step base like a Greek temple and conceived as an articulated work of sculpture in the manner of classical Greek architecture. Influenced by Leonardo's radial designs, the building is distinguished by the severely **Doric** colonnade, above which are classical **triglyphs** and **metopes** topped by a lightly rhythmical **balustrade**. The overall effect of majestic serenity in a small building may have been the decisive factor in Bramante's selection as the papal architect.

17.32 Donato Bramante, Tempietto, S. Pietro in Montorio, Rome. 1502. Height 46' (14 m); external diameter 29' (8.8 m). Photo: Kersting, London.

4. On his first paycheck he pointedly wrote, "I, Michelangelo Buonarroti, sculptor, have received 500 ducats on account . . . for painting the vault of the Sistine chapel." From Peter De Rosa, *Vicars of Christ: The Dark Side of the Papacy* (New York: Macmillan, 1988).
5. John Addington Symonds (trans.), *The Sonnets of Michelangelo Buonarroti and Tommaso Campanella* (London: Smith, Elder & Co., 1878), p.35. See pp.94–5 for other poems by Michelangelo.

17.33 Raphael, *Alba Madonna*. Ca. 1510. Oil on panel, transferred to canvas, diameter 37¼" (94.5 cm). National Gallery of Art, Washington, D.C. (Andrew W. Mellon Collection). Photo: Jose A. Naranjo.

17.34 Raphael, *Baldassare Castiglione*. Ca. 1515. Oil on canvas, 32¼ × 26½" (81.9 × 67.3 cm). Louvre, Paris. Photo: Giraudon, Paris.

Raphael (Raffaello Sanzio), 1483–1520

The third artist working in the Vatican, in addition to Bramante and Michelangelo, was Raphael (RAHF-ee-el), one of the greatest painters in Western art. Born in Urbino like Bramante, Raphael studied first with Perugino and then, as many artists had done before him, moved to Florence, where he studied the works of Leonardo and Michelangelo and painted many famous Madonnas.

Raphael is the most reproduced painter of the Renaissance and his works, especially the Madonnas, are perhaps too familiar. He was an intellectual painter whose works should be studied for both form and content; but viewers tend to see his Madonnas as pretty and sweet, partly because they were intended as sympathetic portrayals of Mother and Child and partly because there have been countless sentimental imitations.

The *Alba Madonna* (fig. 17.33) is a tightly controlled triangular composition derived from Leonardo's style, but designed as a *tondo* (circular painting). Unlike Leonardo and other Madonna painters, Raphael used life models, usually in the nude, sketching the basic figure until he had all elements just right. In this work he was concerned with subtly contrasting the humanity of John the Baptist with the divinity of the Christ child, who is the focal point of the painting. The counterbalancing diagonals of the left arm of the Madonna and the back of the kneeling John form the top of the pyramid. Meanwhile the left leg of Christ echoes the reverse diagonal that extends from the Madonna's left forearm and down her leg. Enclosed within the space between the blue-draped leg and the fur-covered back of John, the figure of the Christ child is essentially vertical. The one horizontal element in the composition is the right arm of Christ, leading our eye to the slender cross so lightly held. Like so many of Raphael's paintings, this work suffers perhaps from too much loving care; it has been so vigorously cleaned that the colors are not as vibrant as they undoubtedly once were.

Characterized as Aristotelian in his approach to art, Raphael was a keen observer of nature and of people. His mastery of his craft, combined with his perceptive examination of the world about him, enabled Raphael to be one of the foremost portrait painters of his age. A member of the circle of Baldassare Castiglione (author of the *Courtier,* a book about courtesy and conduct; see pp. 95–9), Raphael was described by the writer Aretino as having "every virtue and every grace that is appropriate to a gentleman." It was, in fact, Raphael's social graces and material success that lay at the heart of his cold war with the socially inept Michelangelo. In his portrait of Castiglione (fig. 17.34) Raphael depicts his friend in the coolly composed pose of a Renaissance gentleman. The poise and quiet confidence are emphasized by the restrained elegance of his dress, which exemplifies a cultured society reacting against the flamboyant dress of the preceding century.

Raphael was an active member of a philosophical

17.35 Raphael, *School of Athens*. 1501–11. Fresco, 26 × 18' (7.92 × 5.49 m). Stanza della Segnatura, Vatican, Rome. Photo: Scala, Florence.

circle dedicated to reconciling the views of Plato and Aristotle, and when he was commissioned to decorate the papal apartments, he was eager to put his ideas into visual form. The result was four giant wall murals depicting the four branches of human knowledge and wisdom: theology, law, poetry, and philosophy. The last painting, the so-called *School of Athens* (fig. 17.35), is itself a summary of Renaissance humanism. Grouped on the left side of the painting are the Greek philosophers who were mainly concerned with ultimate mysteries, from Plato at the top to Pythagoras writing on a slate at the lower left. Holding the *Timaeus*, Plato (a likeness of Leonardo) points to the heavens as the source of his ideas/forms. Herakleitos sits in the foreground with his elbow on a block, but his face is probably that of Michelangelo. At the upper left we see Socrates in a typical dialogue with some of his students. Aristotle holds his *Ethics* as he indicates the earth as the rightful object of all observations. Diogenes sprawls on the steps, and at the lower right, Euclid bends over a slate, but his face is that of Bramante. Continuing the portraiture, Raphael depicts himself at the extreme right looking at the viewer. The statue of Apollo, patron of poetry, presides at the upper left, whereas Athena, goddess of wisdom, watches over the empirical philosophers and scientists. Though Plato used poetic images and Aristotle utilized rational analysis, Raphael and his circle were convinced that the philosophers agreed in substance even though they disagreed in words. Raphael has here harmonized not only the schools of philosophy but the ancient and Christian worlds as well.

The premature death of the frail Raphael signaled the end of the High Renaissance in Rome.[6] By this time the innovations of Leonardo, Michelangelo, Bramante, and Raphael were being studied and applied throughout Italy, especially in Venice, and northward into Germany, France, and the Netherlands (today's Holland and Belgium).

6. Historical periods in any field (art, music, society, government, whatever) are identified after the fact, usually long after, by historians who look for significant defining events.

HIGH AND LATE RENAISSANCE AND MANNERISM IN SIXTEENTH-CENTURY ITALY

Giorgione da Castelfranco, ca. 1475/7–1510

The High Renaissance style emerged very clearly in the work of a shadowy figure known first as Giorgio and later as the famous Giorgione ("big George"; giorge-o-nay). Very

17.36 Giorgione, *The Adoration of the Shepherds*. 1505–10. Oil on panel, 35¾ × 43½" (90.8 × 110.5 cm). National Gallery of Art, Washington, D.C. (Samuel H. Kress Collection). Photo: Richard Carafelli.

little is known about the man or even his work. He was, according to Vasari, a humanist, musician, and lover of conversation, parties, nature, and women—probably in reverse order.

Though another hand has added some distant figures in the left landscape, Giorgione's *Adoration of the Shepherds* (fig. 17.36) is a superb example of the new pastoral poetic style that he introduced to painting in general and to the Venetian school in particular. One of the most innovative and influential Renaissance painters, Giorgione used his mastery of light and color to paint magical landscapes in which human figures become part of the Arcadian mood. The natural setting is, in fact, so prominent that we can call this a landscape with nativity scene. The setting is depicted not in ideal naturalistic terms, as in the works of van Eyck or Leonardo, but as nature in the raw viewed through the eye of the poet. The figures are not drawn but rather formed of contrasting light and shadow, with the body of the child and the heads of the parents radiating a heavenly light against the gloomy recesses of the cave. The high moral tone and noble values of the Florentine and Roman High Renaissance are utterly foreign to this romantic evocation of mood and feeling.

Giorgione died of the plague at an early age, leaving a number of works unfinished. Though it is known that Titian completed some of the paintings, what may never be known is which paintings were involved and what "completed by Titian" really means. To confuse matters further, Giorgione probably contributed to some of Titian's paintings, but again we have no sure knowledge of which specific paintings were involved.

Michelangelo and Mannerism

The art of the remainder of the century can be considered as two basic stylistic streams: Mannerism and Late Renaissance. The High Renaissance, with the beauty, harmony, and proportions of its paintings, sculpture, and architecture, was seen at this time as a golden age, an era in which Leonardo, Michelangelo, and Raphael had convincingly demonstrated that there was nothing an artist could not do.

What was left for subsequent artists? Vasari used the term *maniera* ("style") of working "in the manner of" supreme artists such as Raphael and Michelangelo. Later artists could either adopt the techniques of the masters or use these techniques as a point of departure, to replace the serenity of the High Renaissance with a Mannerist virtuosity that delighted in twisting, confusing, and distorting human figures. Raphael and Michelangelo studied nature; the Mannerists studied Raphael and Michelangelo, especially Michelangelo.

The so-called Mannerist crisis may also have been a reaction to the momentous events of the 1520s, both local and international, that affected the viewpoints and lives of just about everyone. Florence's power came to an end, as the proud city became a pawn in the hands of the Medici popes, Leo X (reigned 1513–21) and Clement VII (reigned 1523–34). Luther's defiance of Pope Leo X led to the dissolution of unified Christianity, followed by over a century of sectarian warfare. In 1527 the political machinations of Clement VII led to the sack of Rome by the rampaging armies of the Holy Roman Emperor, Charles V of Germany. In 1529 Clement VII refused to annul the marriage of Henry VIII of England and Catherine of Aragon, leading to England's break with Rome. It was a decade of disasters. In the New World, rapidly becoming a significant factor in European culture, the decade was prefaced by Cortés' conquest of the Aztecs in Mexico (1519) and followed by Pizarro's conquest of the Incas in Peru (1533).

Michelangelo's Later Works

During a visit to Rome, Michelangelo discussed the Sistine Chapel with Clement VII. The east, or altar, wall contained the *Assumption of the Virgin* by Perugino, but Clement wanted this replaced with a Resurrection. By the time the new pope, Paul III (reigned 1534–49), had commissioned the artist to paint the entire wall, the subject had become the Last Judgment, though how this came about is not clear. Paul III was a Counter-Reformation pope whose most significant act was the convening of the Council of Trent (1545–64) to reform the church and to counter the challenge of Protestantism. However, nepotism was rampant during Paul's reign and he, along with his illegitimate sons and daughters, lived the lavish life of a Renaissance pontiff. Michelangelo, on the other hand, was deeply religious and was, moreover, sixty-one years old when he accepted the commission.

17.37 Michelangelo, *The Last Judgment*, after restoration. 1536–41. Fresco, 48 × 44' (14.63 × 13.41 m). Altar wall of the Sistine Chapel, Vatican, Rome. Photo: Nippon Television, Tokyo.

Preoccupied with the fate of humanity and that of his own soul, Michelangelo apparently began *The Last Judgment* (fig. 17.37) with the conviction that the world had gone mad. (He began his project in the same year that Henry VIII defied Rome and established the Church of England.) The ideal beauty and optimism of the chapel ceiling had been superseded by a mood of terror and doom, with the gigantic figure of Christ, based on Matthew 24:30–31, come to judge the quick and the dead. Everyone "will see the Son

17.38 Michelangelo, *Rondanini Pietà*. Ca. 1554–64. Marble, height 5'4" (1.63 m). Castello Sforza, Milan. Photo: Alinari, Florence.

17.39 Michelangelo, Dome of St. Peter's, Rome, from the west. 1546–64, completed by della Porta in 1590. Height 452' (138 m). Photo: Alinari, Florence.

of Man coming on clouds of Heaven with power and great glory," his body twisted and his arm raised in a gesture of damnation. In an energetic clockwise motion, the figures at the bottom rise toward Christ and are either gathered in by waiting angels or pulled by demons down into Hell. The resurrected women (always clothed) and men (generally nude) float into the helping arms of angels, who are unencumbered by wings or halos. The scale of the figures is from small in the region of the Damned, close to eye level, to monumental at the distant top section in the region of the Blessed. The nervous energy and the twisting, writhing, elongated figures are techniques adopted by the Mannerists. In this powerful fresco, however, they are manifestations of the unique artistic vision of a master, a natural evolution, given the subject matter, of his mature style.

Only a few days before his death, Michelangelo was reworking his *Rondanini Pietà* (fig. 17.38), cutting the head back into the Virgin's shoulder and making the composition a slender, unified work of infinite pathos. Far removed from the High Renaissance style, the elongated figures are reminiscent of the **jamb** statues of the Royal Portal of Chartres, seeming to symbolize the artist's direct appeal to God. His death in his eighty-eighth year, probably of pneumonia, left this sculpture unfinished and his major project, the dome of St. Peter's, still under construction.

Michelangelo's **apse** and dome of St. Peter's (fig. 17.39) were not a commission but, in his words, done "solely for the love of God." Whether or not Michelangelo's late style can be described as Mannerist—still a moot point—his late architectural style is powerful and confident. The great dome is a huge sculptured shape rising above an apse, distinguished by enormous pilasters. This is Michelangelo's "colossal order"—pilasters that are both decorative and structural. Their upward thrust is repeated and reinforced by the double columns of the drum and carried ever upward by the arching ribs to a climax in the lantern. The vertical stress of classic forms, a new Renaissance procedure, is visible proof that classicism can be as emotional and as transcendental as the High Gothic style of Chartres Cathedral. Though the nave was extended far beyond Michelangelo's **Greek-cross** plan, the dome is still the major landmark of Rome, a fitting symbol for the art and life of Michelangelo.

Parmigianino (Francesco Mazzola), 1503–40

Unquestionably a Mannerist, Parmigianino (par-me-dja-ah-NEE-no) painted in an elaborate, tense, elegant, and artificial style in sharp and deliberate contrast to the harmonious naturalism of the High Renaissance. His *Madonna with the Long Neck* (fig. 17.40) is a marvel of decorative beauty. With a swanlike neck, exceptionally long fingers, and cold, ivory-smooth flesh, the Madonna smiles tenderly on a seemingly lifeless Christ child. The background figure of the biblical prophet is dramatically small, and the rising, uncompleted columns add to the artificiality and strange mood of unreality. Parmigianino planned a complete temple in the background but left it incomplete, further illustrating, perhaps, the perverseness of an artist notorious for flaunting social and artistic conventions.

LATE RENAISSANCE AND MANNERISM IN ITALY AND SPAIN

Titian (Tiziano Vecelli), ca. 1488–1576

With an artistic career spanning sixty-eight years, Titian (TISH-un) was a giant of the High and Late Renaissance, excelling in every aspect of the painter's craft. After Raphael, he was the finest portrait artist of the century, courted by the nobles and royalty of Europe. Titian achieved the social status advocated by Leonardo, acquiring a towering reputation that led to many honors, the title of count, and a princely life. He repeatedly celebrated the goddess of love, and his late painting, *Venus with a Mirror* (fig. 17.42), is permeated by a tangible sensuality that is, however, not erotic, but instead expresses the natural loveliness of woman. The famous color tones are exceptionally rich rather than just brilliant, mellowed by layer on layer of glazes. Titian produced several variations on the Venus-and-mirror theme; this painting he kept for himself and willed to his son. Perhaps more than any other Renaissance artist, Titian understood the spirit of classical art. Drawing on the Greeks, he incorporated High Renaissance techniques and some Mannerist devices in what is best described, in this work, as Late Renaissance style.

Formerly attributed to Giorgione, the *Fête Champêtre* (fig. 17.41) is now known to be by Titian, who may have had

17.40 Parmigianino, *Madonna with the Long Neck*. 1534–40. Oil on panel, 7'1" × 4'4" (2.16 × 1.32 m). Galleria degli Uffizi, Florence. Photo: Scala, Florence.

17.42 Titian, *Venus with a Mirror*. Ca. 1555. Oil on canvas, 4'1" × 3'5½" (1.24 × 1.05 m). National Gallery of Art, Washington, D.C. (Andrew W. Mellon Collection).

17.41 Titian (and Giorgione?), *Fête Champêtre*. Ca. 1505. Oil on canvas, 3'7¼" × 4'6" (1.1 × 1.37 m). Louvre, Paris. Photo: R.M.N., Paris.

some assistance from Giorgione. In the painting we see two opulent nudes painted in the lush Venetian manner. The one on the left is gracefully emptying a crystal pitcher and the other holds a recorder while gazing dreamily into the distance. They may represent Greek muses, thus giving the painting a Neoplatonic cast. The fully clothed men are deep in conversation, but only the man casually playing the lute is fashionably dressed. Having been labeled at various times "Pastoral Symphony," "Fountain of Love," or, as here, "Country Festival," the work has even been called an allegory of poetry. In other words, the subject matter may never be known or even be important. The painting exists as an enchanting combination of forms and shapes in a poetic setting, created by an artist who may have had in mind nothing more than that.

Tintoretto (Jacopo Robusti), 1518–94

Titian's Venetian contemporary, Tintoretto (tin-toe-RET-toe), developed a more fervent style that blended Mannerist devices with the drawing technique of Michelangelo. In *Christ at the Sea of Galilee* (fig. 17.43) we view a turbulent sea with wave edges as sharp as knifeblades, spottily applied white highlights, and deliberately atonal combinations that heighten the emotional content. The curved and elongated figure of Christ dominates an intensely dramatic scene in which the frightened fishermen look to the Savior for deliverance.

A comparison of Tintoretto's *The Last Supper* (fig. 17.44) with that by Leonardo (see fig. 17.28) dramatically illustrates the differences between the High Renaissance style and the Mannerist style of the Late Renaissance. In Tintoretto's version the table is sharply angled and placed at the left. The size of the disciples diminishes from foreground to background, with Christ highlighted only by the brilliant glow of his halo. Almost lost in the agitation, Judas, dressed as a servant, sits on the opposite side of the table, a pathetic, isolated figure. This is the moment of the Eucharist, what Roman Catholics regard as the transubstantiation of consecrated bread and wine into the flesh and blood of Christ. The agitated clutter of servants, hovering angels, flaming lamp, and radiant halo combine to proclaim the emotional spirit of the Counter-Reformation.

17.43 Tintoretto, *Christ at the Sea of Galilee*. Ca. 1575–80. Oil on canvas, 3' 10" × 5' 6¼" (1.17 × 1.69 m). National Gallery of Art, Washington, D.C. (Samuel H. Kress Collection).

17.44 Tintoretto, *The Last Supper*. 1592–4. Oil on canvas, 12' × 18'8" (3.66 × 5.69 m). S. Giorgio Maggiore, Venice. Photo: Scala, Florence.

Palladio (Andrea di Pietro), 1518–80

The intense dramatic style of Tintoretto heralds the coming age of the Baroque, but the architectural designs of Andrea Palladio (pah-LAH-djo) are clearly, lucidly classical. The only north Italian architect comparable to Brunelleschi, Alberti, Bramante, and Michelangelo, Palladio was born Andrea di Pietro but is known to posterity by a name derived from Pallas Athena, goddess of wisdom. An avid student of classical and Renaissance architecture, Palladio designed churches, public buildings, and private homes. His Villa Rotonda (fig. 17.45), one of nineteen Palladian villas still in existence, was built in the countryside near Venice, much in the manner and style of Roman villas. From a central square identical porticoes thrust out from each side, each with a different view and a slightly variable climate at different hours of the day. Palladian designs became popular for English stately homes, and this particular design became a model for southern plantation homes in the American South, where outdoor living was customary for much of the year. In the Villa Rotonda the proportions of length and breadth, height and width, of and between the rooms were based on the Pythagorean ratios of the Greek musical scale.

17.45 Palladio, Villa Rotonda, Vicenza. Begun 1550 and finished by Vencenzo Scamozzi. Photo: Alinari, Florence.

Paolo Veronese, 1528–88

Paradoxically, only the country villas of Palladio were placed in the natural settings that the Venetian painters Giorgione, Titian, Tintoretto, and Veronese celebrated in their richly colored paintings. Venice itself, except for private gardens, was a congested city of marble, brick, stone, and waterways with few plants, flowers, or trees. The fourth of the great Venetian masters, Veronese (vair-oh-NAY-se), like his contemporaries glorified nature in his work, but unlike other artists he concentrated on the sumptuous material world. Pleasure-loving Venetians preferred luxurious paintings that dazzled the eye and soothed the conscience. In *Christ in the House of Levi* (fig. 17.46) Veronese demonstrated his skill in *di sotto in sù* (It., "looking up from below") perspective. A superb example of Veronese's theatrical style, the elaborate perspective opens to the sky like a stage set. Although Christ and his disciples occupy the center, the rest of the painting is crowded with exotic characters totally unrelated to the biblical text. Veronese was called before the Inquisition because the unorthodox details lacked the mandatory seriousness and piety for a Last Supper, and was given three months in which to modify the composition. Rather than wreck his grand design, he simply gave the painting a less exalted title. That this painting caught the attention of the Inquisition is a kind of backhanded testimony to the power of this work.

17.46 Paolo Veronese, *Christ in the House of Levi* (originally *The Last Supper*). 1573. Oil on canvas, 42' × 18'3" (12.8 × 5.56 m). Accademia, Venice. Photo: Scala, Florence.

El Greco (Domenikos Theotokopoulos), 1541–1614

Veronese's style is lavishly and opulently Late Renaissance and basically secular, but that of El Greco is mystical, a fervent expression of the Counter-Reformation spirit. The last and possibly the most gifted of the Mannerists, Domenikos Theotokopoulos, known as El Greco ("the Greek"), was born in Crete, then a Venetian possession, and trained in late Byzantine art and Venetian Mannerism before moving to Spain in 1576. Even before the defeat of the Spanish Armada in 1588 Spain was a fading power, artistically provincial and obsessed with the Counter-Reformation. Yet it was the proper environment for an artist of El Greco's religious convictions. Combining the Byzantine tradition with his thorough knowledge of the Venetian masters, El Greco created a passionately religious art that was the embodiment of Spanish mysticism. In his *Resurrection of Christ* (fig. 17.47) the illusion is of Christ floating upward as the Roman soldiers are afflicted with various contortions indicating their awe and terror. This very shallow space is enlivened by shimmering splashes of light that add to the mystical quality of the work.

A nation supercharged with religious zeal, Spain formed the spearhead of the Counter-Reformation as the birthplace of the Society of Jesus (Jesuits) and the stronghold of the merciless Inquisition. El Greco was its peerless master of religious subjects, an artist who, more than any other, made visible the spiritual content of the Catholic faith. Widely admired in his time, El Greco had a reputation that declined rapidly as most of western Europe (though not

17.47 El Greco, *The Resurrection of Christ*. Ca. 1597–1604. Oil on canvas, 9'4¼" × 4'2" (2.85 × 1.27 m). Prado, Madrid.

Spain) plunged enthusiastically into the scientific and intellectual discoveries of the Enlightenment. It was not until the twentieth century that El Greco's unique and intensely personal art received proper recognition.

HIGH AND LATE RENAISSANCE IN THE NORTH, CA. 1500–1600

For most of the fifteenth century, northern artists and some Italians were influenced by the dazzling naturalism of the Flemish masters. Not until the end of the century did Italian influences begin to beguile northern patrons with their scientific rules and especially a literary tradition that included a vocabulary of art criticism. Noble patrons were delighted with classical examples of "good" and "bad" art. Increasingly, this meant that art based on models from antiquity was good, but the rest, including the entire Flemish tradition, was "wrong" or at best "primitive." With remarkable suddenness, Italian artists were busily engaged with important projects for patrons such as Henry VII of England and the French royal family, whereas northern artists were traveling to Italy to study the masters of the Early and High Renaissance.

During the sixteenth century it became fashionable to view northern culture as backward and its artists as inferior, especially those who had not been blessed with Italian instruction in the rules of perspective and proportion. Speaking, in essence, for the Italian Renaissance, Michelangelo remarked to the Portuguese painter Francesco da Hollanda that Flemish landscape paintings were fit only for "young women, nuns, and certain noble persons with no sense of true harmony." "Furthermore," he observed, "their painting is of stuffs, bricks, mortar, the grass of the fields, the shadows of trees and little figures here and there. And all this," said he, "though it may appear good in some eyes, is in truth done without symmetry or proportion." Consigned to the attic of northern art, the matchless paintings of the Flemish masters were, for over three centuries, derided as primitive or naive. It was not until 1902 that the first international show of fifteenth-century Flemish art opened in Bruges, and only considerably later in this century that the derogatory labels were finally dropped.

Albrecht Dürer, 1471–1528

For reasons still unknown, Italian art caught on first in Germany, where Dürer (DOO-rer) became the founder of the brief but brilliant German High Renaissance. His two trips to Italy (1494–5 and 1505–7) exposed him to all the Italian techniques, but he was never attuned to Italian form, preferring instead the strong lines of the northern tradition. Though Dürer became a master painter, his most significant achievements were in the graphic arts of engraving and woodcuts, which were printed in quantity and sold

17.48 *Above* Albrecht Dürer, *Knight, Death, and the Devil.* 1513. Engraving, 9¾ × 7⅝" (24.8 × 19.4 cm). Metropolitan Museum of Art, New York (Harris Brisbane Dick Fund).

throughout Germany, making the artist a wealthy man.

Northern art retained a Gothic strain—a fascination with the bizarre, the grotesque, and the supernatural—as embodied, for example, in *Knight, Death, and the Devil* (fig. 17.48). The subject was apparently derived from the *Manual of the Christian Soldier* by Erasmus of Rotterdam (1466–1536). With death mounted on a decrepit horse in the background and a hideous devil behind him, the Christian knight rides confidently along the path of faith. Mounted on a superb horse and accompanied by his faithful dog, he fixes his unwavering gaze on his ultimate goal of the Heavenly Kingdom. The drama, control, and incredible detail of this powerful work are highly representative of the vigorous Northern Renaissance, created by an artist who had chosen to follow the faith of Martin Luther.

Dürer was deeply involved in the religious and political movements in Germany and in the Italian humanism that flourished briefly on German soil until the winds of the Reformation swept away what was essentially a Catholic point of view. The leading humanist of sixteenth-century Europe, Erasmus influenced many intellectuals of the period, including artists such as Dürer and Hans Holbein the Younger. In the *Erasmus* portrait by Dürer (see fig. 19.1) the scholar sits in his study surrounded by books, some presumably his own publications, as he drafts a new work. Behind him in Latin is the elaborate title of the print and the name of the artist. At the bottom is Dürer's monogram, above which is the date and above that a Greek inscription that translates as, "His writings portray him even better," meaning that his books were a more accurate measure of the man than Dürer's reverential portrait. The northern passion for detail is, to say the least, clearly evident in this print.

Matthias Grünewald (Mathis Gothardt Neithardt), 1483?–1528

Dürer was internationally famous, but his worthy contemporary Grünewald, though widely known in his own time, was neglected until this century. A highly original artist, Grünewald was familiar with the work of Dürer and possibly that of Bosch, but there is no evidence of Italian classical influence, as one glance at his *Small Crucifixion* (fig. 17.49) immediately reveals.

This is the brutal reality of nailing a man to a cross and leaving him there to die. His body a mass of cuts and suppurating sores, his limbs twisted, his skin gray and speckled with dried blood, Christ is depicted in relentless detail as having died for the sins of all humankind. The grief of John, Mary, and Mary Magdalene is vibrant with intense

17.49 Matthias Grünewald, *The Small Crucifixion.* Ca. 1511–20. Oil on panel, 24⅛ × 18⅛" (61.3 × 46 cm). National Gallery of Art, Washington, D.C. (Samuel H. Kress Collection).

pain and sorrow. Grünewald has elevated the horror of the Passion to the level of universal tragedy, producing a composition as convincing as anything in Western art.

Hans Holbein, 1497–1543

Fully conversant with all that the Italians had to teach, Holbein (HOL-bine) the Younger was the last of the superb painters of the German High Renaissance and one of the finest portrait painters in the history of art. He traveled widely in France, Switzerland, and Italy, then finally settled down in London, where he became the favorite painter of Henry VIII, who furnished a special suite in St. James's Palace for "master Hans." Holbein gained access to the English court through Erasmus, who provided him with a letter of recommendation to Sir Thomas More. His portrait of More (see fig. 19.2) is a noble portrayal of the humanist statesman. Depicted realistically, including a stubble of beard, More wears the luxurious clothes of his rank and the heavy chain of his office as Lord Chancellor of England. With meticulous attention to detail in the manner of van Eyck, Holbein depicts the dignity and determination of a man who was later to be executed for opposing Henry's establishment of the Church of England.

A French Château

The Italian influence in France is epitomized in the chain of elegant châteaux built throughout the scenic Loire valley. Imposing and elaborate as befits the king of a prosperous nation, the Château of Chambord (fig. 17.50) was originally a hunting lodge. It was redesigned for Francis I by an Italian architect who appears to have used many designs and ideas of his nearby neighbor, Leonardo da Vinci. Leonardo definitely designed the magnificent double spiral staircase located in the center of the château. The huge central block is connected by corridors leading outward to sets of apartments designed in the modern manner as self-contained units. Anchored at the four corners by large round towers, the entire complex is surrounded by a moat. The matching of horizontal and vertical features in windows and moldings is taken directly from the Italian palazzos, but the forest of **dormers**, chimneys, and lanterns is straight out of the Gothic tradition and flamboyantly French.

17.50 Château of Chambord, aerial view. Begun 1519. Photo: Viollet, Paris.

Pieter Bruegel the Elder, 1525?–69

Most of the Renaissance art of France was courtly but, as mentioned previously, there was a growing number of middle-class art patrons in the Netherlands, which in the latter sixteenth century became a battleground of religious and political strife. Militantly Protestant, particularly in the north (today's Holland), the Netherlands fought to overthrow a rigid Spanish rule that became even more brutal under the fanatical Philip II and the imported Spanish Inquisition. Nevertheless, the Netherlandish school of painting flourished and produced Bruegel (BRU-gul), the only northern genius to appear between Dürer and Rubens. A highly educated humanist and philosopher, Bruegel studied in Italy from 1551 to 1555, returning home with a love of Italian landscapes and a profound knowledge of Italian control of form and space. In *Landscape with the Fall of Icaros* (fig. 17.51) Bruegel depicts the **myth** of the reckless one who ignored the advice of his father, Daidalos, and flew so near the sun that the wings fashioned by his father melted, and he plunged to his death in the sea. Bruegel emphasizes everything but Icaros, who is just a pair of kicking legs and a splash in the sea in front of the sailing galleon. The plowman and the singing shepherd are oblivious of the fate of a foolish boy who has caused his own destruction. He dies in the sea, but the plowing, the shepherding, the world go serenely on. Bruegel viewed humankind as basically noble, but depicted men and women as faulty individuals who were easily degraded or destroyed by materialism, avarice, or, like Icaros, just plain folly.

In *Winter (Return of the Hunters)* (fig. 17.52) Bruegel demonstrates his mastery of perspective as he details what first appears to be a simple genre scene. Two moods are conveyed: the bleak coldness of nature and the warmth and activity of human beings. Our attention is drawn to the hunters and their dogs as, cold and exhausted, they return to their frosty hamlet. Before them are all sorts of activities from work to play and the promise of a warm fire in a cozy house. Bruegel has presented us with a microcosm, an image of his time and place as he saw it. But there is also the universality that great works have in common. This is not just 1565 in a northern clime but a sensitive portrayal of human activities in a hostile environment: working, playing, coping, surviving.

17.51 *Above* Pieter Bruegel the Elder, *Landscape with the Fall of Icaros*. Ca. 1558. Oil on canvas, 44 × 29" (111.7 × 73.7 cm). Musée Royal des Beaux Arts, Brussels. Photo: Giraudon, Paris/Bridgeman, London.

17.52 *Below* Pieter Bruegel the Elder, *Winter (Return of the Hunters)*. 1565. Oil on panel. 3' 10" × 5' 3¾" (1.2 × 1.6 m). Kunsthistorisches Museum, Vienna. Photo: A.K.G., London (Eric Lessing).

STUDY QUESTIONS

1. Compare and contrast the *David* sculptures of Donatello, Verrocchio, and Michelangelo. Consider first every detail then the overall effect.
2. Compare and contrast the Pazzi Chapel with Sainte-Chapelle in Paris. Then, using the two chapels as representative of their ages, compare and contrast the Gothic era with the Renaissance.

SUMMARY

Symbolized by Brunelleschi's dome and the dedication of Florence Cathedral in 1436, a new age came into being in fifteenth-century Florence. This was a city of bankers and craftsmen whose self-image was personified by the Davids of Donatello, Verrocchio, and Michelangelo. To create the new style, a fresh repertory of illusionist devices was developed by Masaccio and later used by all painters.

By the second half of the century, classical designs had been fully assimilated, leading to the classically based architecture of Alberti and the mythological painting of Botticelli. Florentine innovations spread throughout Italy, promoted by Perugino and by Bellini, the founder of the Venetian school.

The Renaissance in the North took another course. Influenced by the International Style and a long tradition of brilliant craftsmanship in manuscript illumination and stained glass, van Eyck perfected the new technique of oil painting and created matchless works of meticulous naturalism. Rogier van der Weyden and Hans Memling continued in the naturalistic style but, coinciding with the rising pessimism and fear of death and the devil, the bizarre art of Hieronymus Bosch epitomized the religious torment of a society on the brink of the Lutheran Reformation.

The High Renaissance in Italy was a time of constant warfare, but was illuminated by the incredible achievements of Leonardo in scientific investigation, invention, and painting. Excelling in the arts of sculpture, architecture, painting, and poetry, the "divine Michelangelo" created, among other works, the *Pietà*, *David*, and the frescoes of the Sistine Chapel ceiling. Raphael achieved a classic balance of form and content that became the hallmark of the High Renaissance, and Bramante, in his Tempietto, designed the prototype of classical domed structures.

In sixteenth-century Venice, Giorgione was the first of the Venetian colorists, followed by the assured painting of Titian and the luxuriant style of Veronese. Michelangelo influenced such Mannerist painters as Parmigianino, Tintoretto, and the Spanish painter from Crete called El Greco. During the latter stages of his career Michelangelo painted the awesome *Last Judgment* and designed the apse and dome of St. Peter's. Marking the end of the Renaissance in Italy, Palladio's villas became models for eighteenth- and nineteenth-century domestic architecture in England and the United States.

In sixteenth-century Germany Albrecht Dürer, Matthias Grünewald, and Hans Holbein the Younger were the leading painters of the High Renaissance. In France, Italian styles influenced French courtly art and contributed to the designs of elegant châteaux in the Loire valley. Renaissance art in the strife-torn Netherlands culminated in the work of Pieter Bruegel the Elder.

By the end of the sixteenth century the ideals and aspirations of the Renaissance had perished in the wreckage of cultures beset by religious wars—with the worst yet to come. Marking the end of an era, the Renaissance set the stage for the emergence of the modern world.

CULTURE AND HUMAN VALUES

The importance and influence of creative artists changed considerably during the Renaissance. During the Early Renaissance their role was basically defined by a continuation of the medieval guild system that trained artisans, not artists. The painters' guild to which Leonardo belonged, for example, was established primarily for people who painted walls and ceilings.

All that had changed by the time of the High Renaissance. More than anything else, the newly acquired importance of the individual helped elevate the artist to a position comparable to his or her artistic achievements. The individual was not, however, the ultimate reality, as had been the case in ancient Greece. The analogy, rather, is with ancient Rome, in which the individual was free to act in accordance with the needs of the state. Reality in the Renaissance was the division of power between the monolithic Church of Rome and the secular authority of the many ducal states that dotted western and southern Europe. For the artists, reality was the protective power of such patrons as the papacy, a dukedom, or an emerging national state.

If one had to list a single virtue in the chaos and violence marking the transition from the medieval to the modern world, that ideal quality would be survival. Artists often had to work under trying, even dangerous circumstances. Yet they survived, and some of them, like Raphael, Michelangelo, and Titian, attained enduring fame and influence. Given all the rigors of the age, one can only marvel at the artists who survived and created, and wonder even more at the quality and quantity of the art and architecture that survived the Renaissance.

CHAPTER 18

Renaissance Music: Court and Church

NORTHERN ORIGINS OF THE MUSICAL RENAISSANCE

Renaissance music dates from about 1420 to 1600, music that can be characterized, in large part, as optimistic, lively, and worldly. The once-rigid distinctions between sacred and secular music no longer applied. Sacred music was not always synonymous with devotional, noble, and edifying sounds any more than secular music was necessarily shallow, common, or folksy. The subject matter rather than the style now determined whether the work was sacred or secular. Just as a painter's model could become a madonna, or nymph, or Venus, so composers used melodies where they worked best, with popular songs sometimes serving as a basis for liturgical motets or **Masses**.

As previously discussed, the Renaissance began around 1350 in Italy and eventually moved north to encompass most of Europe. For reasons still not clearly understood, the musical Renaissance began in the North—in England, the Low Countries, and northern France. The most notable of the English composers, John Dunstable (1380?–1453), was a contemporary of the early Renaissance composers on the continent and probably influenced them with what his admirers called his "sweet style." On the continent some court and church composers of northern France and the Low Countries (Flanders) formed a group known today as the Franco-Flemish school. True Renaissance artists, they were individualistic, materialistic, and boldly experimental. They had mastered the craft and art of a new style of music, and they delighted in demonstrating their compositional skills with intricate **canons** and musical puzzles for educated amateurs.

In their quest for new materials and fresh ideas they traveled to Italy, where the simple folk melodies and dance tunes provided further opportunities for **polyphonic** devices and techniques. Considering the travel hardships then, the mobility of Franco-Flemish composers in the fifteenth century was astounding. The composer Dufay, for example, was discovered at the age of nine in Cambrai in France by talent scouts seeking out precocious young musicians. Before he was twenty-six, Dufay had traveled to Italy, studied in Paris, held a post in northern France, served the court in Bologna, and sung in the papal choir in Rome.

Franco-Flemish composers such as Dufay and others dominated Italian musical life in the courts and in the churches for over a century. St. Mark's in Venice, one of the most important musical centers in Europe, employed only Flemish composers until the latter part of the sixteenth century. When Florence dedicated its magnificent cathedral in 1436, Dufay was commissioned to write special music for the occasion.

Music was an integral part of the complex fabric of Renaissance society. A retinue of musicians became a fixture of court life, with the dukes of Burgundy setting the style. Castiglione (see pp. 76 and 95–9), the chief social arbiter of the Renaissance, viewed his ideal courtier as proficient in both vocal and instrumental music:

> I regard as beautiful music, to sing well by note, with ease and beautiful style; but as even far more beautiful, to sing to the accompaniment of the viol, because nearly all the sweetness lies in the solo part, and we note and observe the fine manner and the melody with much greater attention when our ears are not occupied with more than a single voice, and moreover every little fault is more clearly discerned,—which is not the case when several sing together, because each singer helps his neighbor. But above all, singing to the viol by way of recitative seems to me most delightful, which adds to the words a charm and grace that are very admirable.
>
> All keyed instruments also are pleasing to the ear, because they produce very perfect consonances, and upon them one can play many things that fill the mind with musical delight. And not less charming is the music of the stringed quartet, which is most sweet and exquisite. The human voice lends much ornament and grace to all these instruments, with which I would have our Courtier at least to some degree acquainted, albeit the more he excels with them, the better.[1]

Opposite St Mark's, Venice, interior, arch showing the Passion of Christ and domes depicting the coming of the Holy Spirit at Pentecost and the Ascension of Christ. 12th century and ca. 1200. Mosaic. Photo: A.K.G., London.

1. Baldassare Castiglione, *The Book of the Courtier* (trans. Leonard Eckstein Opdycke) (New York: Horace Liveright, 1929).

The Courts of Burgundy

At different times a kingdom, a county, and a duchy, Burgundy became the most powerful and influential political entity in Europe in the first half of the fifteenth century. From Philip the Bold in 1336 through John the Fearless and Philip the Good to Charles the Bold (reigned 1467–77), the rulers of Burgundy made the court in the capital city of Dijon one of the most magnificent in Europe (map 18.1).

The Flemish painter Jan van Eyck served the "court of plume and panoply" of Philip the Good at the time of its greatest splendor. The court was ostentatious and even flamboyant, but nevertheless, according to contemporary accounts, it resembled a sort of fairyland. Women wore hennins, cone-shaped headdresses with long sheer veils hanging from the pointed tops. Their gowns were opulent, frequently decorated with fur and set off by gold throat bands and necklaces. Elaborate furniture and interior designs provided a tasteful setting for the elegance of the court.

The ducal court set the styles in dress, manners, dancing, music, and the other arts. The principal court dance was the *basse danse,* which was performed with gliding steps, possibly accounting for the designation *basse* (Fr. "low"). The *basse danse* belonged to a family of related dances: the *basse danse* proper and the *pas de Brabant* (It. *saltarello*). It was the custom to follow the dignified *basse danse*, referred to as the "imperial measure," by the quicker *pas de Brabant*, thus producing a contrasting pair of slow and fast dance movements, a typical procedure for Renaissance dances. Both used the same basic music; only the rhythms were changed.

Tapestries and miniatures of the period show various instrumental ensembles playing for the dancers. The standard group of instruments consisted of two shawms (early **oboes**) and a slide-trumpet, with the harp, **lute**, and **flute** forming the other group. The former group consisted of *haut* (Fr. "high, loud") instruments, the latter of *bas* (Fr. "low, soft") instruments. The *haut* instruments were used for festive occasions and were usually played from a balcony or *loggia*. The *bas* instruments were used for more intimate dancing and were placed near the dancers.

Court life at Dijon was lively and elegant. It was, in many respects, an updated version of the medieval Court of Love with music, both lively and sedate, for dancing and for songs, true French **chansons** extolling love, joy, and beauty. Secular music was in great demand for everything from the intimate rites of courtship to elaborate ceremonial music for the court. There was a remarkable development of sophisticated secular music, but not at the expense of sacred music, which incorporated the techniques and some of the melodies of secular music into a highly refined style.

Map 18.1 Lands of the Dukes of Burgundy, 1477.

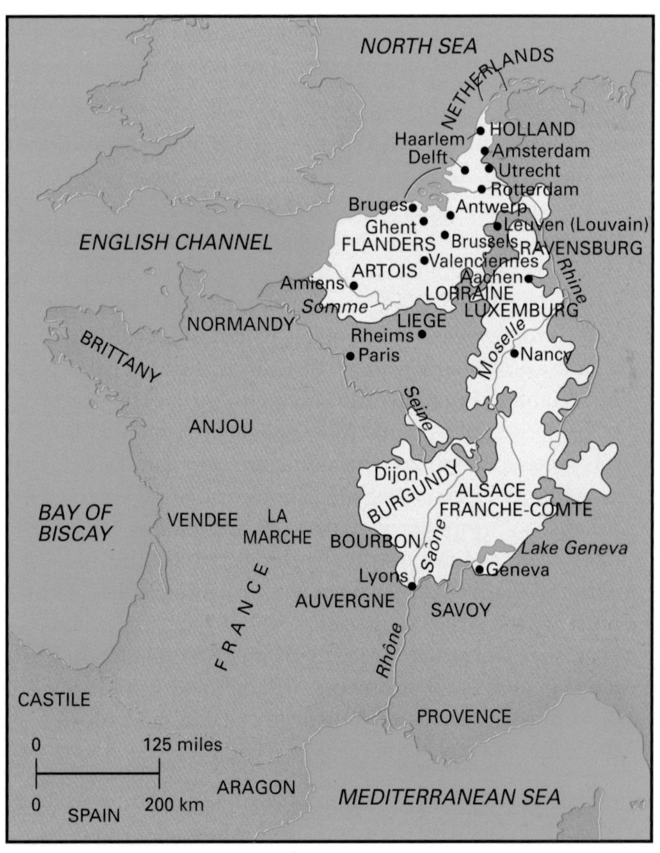

The Burgundian School

Guillaume Dufay, ca. 1400–74

Dufay (doo-FYE) was the most famous composer of the Burgundian school of the Franco-Flemish tradition and one of the greatest of French composers. Following is the beginning of a Dufay Mass movement that illustrates the smooth, rich sounds of Renaissance music. Dufay broke down the "Kyrie eleison" into three separate movements: "Kyrie eleison," "Christe eleison," and "Kyrie eleison." The texture is characteristic of early Renaissance music with mixed vocal and instrumental sounds and with instruments playing the wordless portions of the Mass.

Listening Example 13

MASS MOVEMENT

Dufay, *Missa Se la face ay pale,* "Kyrie I"[2]
15th century

Time: 1:45
Cassette 2, track 13[3]

2. Smijers, *Algemeene Muziek Geschiedenis* (Utrecht, 1938), p.101.

Missa Se la face ay pale, "Kyrie" **Dufay (ca. 1400–74)**

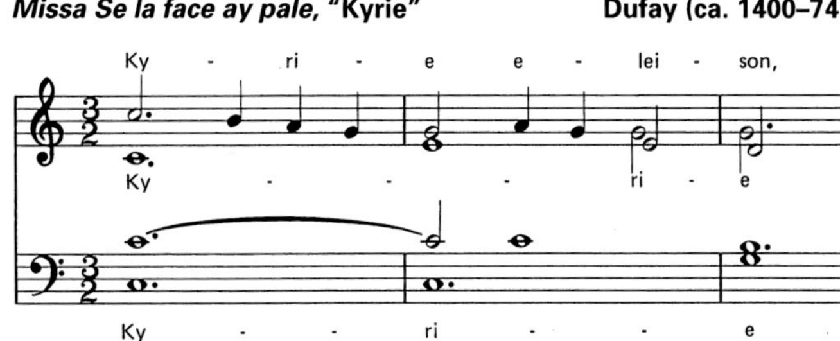

THE FRANCO-FLEMISH TRADITION

During the latter part of the fifteenth century the center of musical activity gradually shifted from Burgundy to northern France and the Low Countries of Flanders and the Netherlands. The fusion of French elegance, Flemish polyphonic techniques, and Italian vigor led to the cosmopolitan style of the Late Renaissance. Whatever followed from this—even the music of such giants as Palestrina and Lassus—was a continuation of northern genius suffused with Italian taste and supported by Italian patronage.

No one person was responsible for the development of the new music. It simply happened that many gifted northern composers were active at about the same time and that most, at varying times, were involved in Italian musical life. There were important composers from the Netherlands and northern France but Josquin of Flanders outshone them all.

Josquin des Près, ca. 1450–1521

Martin Luther reportedly said that "Others follow the notes; Josquin makes them do as he wishes." Josquin (JOSS-can) was known in his own time as the "prince of music." He and his Franco-Flemish contemporaries developed all the basic features of the Late Renaissance musical style and, in so doing, established it as an international style in western European culture. Josquin was to music what Leonardo, Michelangelo, and Raphael were to the visual arts. A master of compositional techniques, he sometimes invented and consistently refined the methods and materials of Renaissance polyphonic music.

The motet "Ave Maria" by Josquin is an example of the serene lucidity and beauty of the music of the High Renaissance. The smoothly flowing lines are woven into an elegant tapestry of luminous sound, a sound somehow comparable to the undulating arches of a Renaissance **arcade**. Motets are still sacred music, similar to polyphonic Masses, but the text is non-scriptural. Instruments are no longer combined or alternated with the voices as in Early Renaissance music; the singing is now consistently unaccompanied (**a cappella**). The vocal texture is continuous, with new phrases overlapping preceding phrases to produce an unbroken stream of simultaneous melodies. This ceaseless flow of intricately intertwined melodies is a hallmark of High and Late Renaissance vocal music.

The voices enter one at a time in imitation; that is, each of the four voices has essentially the same melodic line when it makes its entrance. Josquin used the text of the "Ave Maria" (Lat., "Hail Mary, full of grace . . .") and selected his basic theme from a portion of an "Ave Maria" chant:

Ave Maria chant theme

Listening Example 14

MOTET

Josquin des Près, "Ave Maria"
Ca. 1480; excerpt

Time: 2:06
Cassette 2, track 14[4]

"Ave Maria" **Josquin (ca. 1450–1521)**

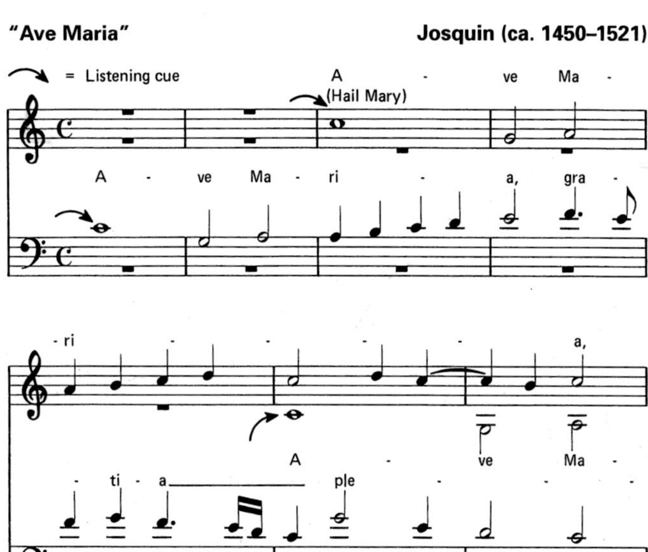

3. Musical notation is used on a modest scale throughout this book to give brief quotations from works to be studied. These are guides to listening just as literary quotations are guides to reading. Using musical quotes is a necessary, basic procedure that is in no way "technical." Performing music is technical; but reading music is a simple procedure easily learned by anyone. Please consult the Appendix: Music Listening and Notation.
4. Josquin des Près, *Werke* (Amsterdam, 1935), vol.1, p.1.

Orlando de Lassus, 1532–94

The Flemish composer Lassus was one of the finest composers of a celebrated era, the golden age of polyphony of the sixteenth century. His 1,250 compositions were literally international: Latin masses and motets; secular vocal music in French, German, and Italian; and instrumental music in different national styles. Representative of his secular music, the following Italian **madrigal** is a playful love song spiced with cheery nonsense syllables: "don don don diri diri don don don don."

Listening Example 15

ITALIAN MADRIGAL

Lassus, "Matona mia cara"
1550; excerpt

Time: 2:10
Cassette 2, track 15[5]

Matona, my beloved, be bewitched by my song. I sing beneath the window to win you for my good wife. I pray to you, listen to my pretty singing; it will make you love me more, like the obstinate Greek [Odysseus]. Command me to go hunting, to hunt with the falcon, and I will bring you a woodcock as fat as kidneys. If I were not able to speak to you with so many good reasons, Petrarch himself would not be able to, nor the Springs of Helicon [home of the Muses].

DEVELOPMENTS IN ITALY

During the latter part of the sixteenth century, Italian genius finally surfaced in the compositions of native Italians. Italian music had been invigorated by the presence of resident Flemish composers and by the dynamic Counter-Reformation response to Luther's revolt. Flemish composers had fled Spanish tyranny in the Low Countries to pursue their profession in a less hostile setting. There was, moreover, a real need to develop a new style of sacred music because things had gotten out of hand, as Erasmus of Rotterdam cogently pointed out:

> We have introduced an artificial and theatrical music into the church, a bawling and agitation of various voices, such as I believe had never been heard in the theatres of the Greeks and Romans. Horns, trumpets, pipes vie and sound along constantly with the voices. Amorous and lascivious melodies are heard such as elsewhere accompany only the dances of courtesans and clowns.[6]

The Council of Trent (1545–64) was convened to deal with the abuses pointed out by Luther and other reformers. The problem of music was only incidental to overall concerns, but musical difficulties occupied most of the attention of the Council for over a year. Final recommendations were negative rather than positive. Certain practices were forbidden and particular results were prescribed without, however, specifying the means. The canon finally adopted by the Council in 1562 banned all seductive or impure melodies, whether vocal or instrumental, all vain and worldly texts, and all outcries and uproars, so that "the House of God may in truth be called a House of prayer."

After passing the canon against decadent musical practices, the Council considered banning all polyphonic music, especially polyphonic Masses. This ultraconservative movement was countered by Lassus and Palestrina, who, among others, submitted polyphonic music to a special Commission in a successful attempt to preserve their reformed style of polyphonic music. Perhaps the Commission simply recognized its inability to appraise the quality of **liturgical** music, a judgment best made by the musicians themselves.

Giovanni Pierluigi da Palestrina, 1524/5–94

Palestrina was one of the supreme exponents of Roman Catholic polyphonic music of the Renaissance. Romanticized in the nineteenth century as a lonely and poverty-stricken artist who was wedded to the church, Palestrina was actually a successful professional musician. He briefly considered the priesthood after the death of his first wife, but chose instead to marry a wealthy widow. He was paid well for the music that he wrote for the church and even refused several more lucrative positions rather than leave Rome.

Present-day music students study Palestrina's music for classes in "strict **counterpoint**," that is, writing polyphonic music in the manner of the sixteenth century with Palestrina as the model composer. Though his compositions serve as a guide to correct contrapuntal writing, Palestrina's music is anything but dogmatic. A model it is, but one of clarity, conciseness, and consistency. Using existing **plainsong** melodies as a point of departure, he wrote in a beautifully balanced style of what can be described as simultaneous plainsong.

5. CD 1, track 9.
6. Erasmus, *Opera Omnia*, VI, 1705, col.731.

The following plainsong, "Veni sponsa Christi," forms the basis for a Palestrina Mass:

Palestrina began with this simple melody, transforming it into a serenely flowing melodic theme:

"Veni sponsa Christi" (named after the plainsong) is a short composition based on this characteristic Palestrina melody. Notice how the smoothly flowing text is fitted to graceful melodic lines.

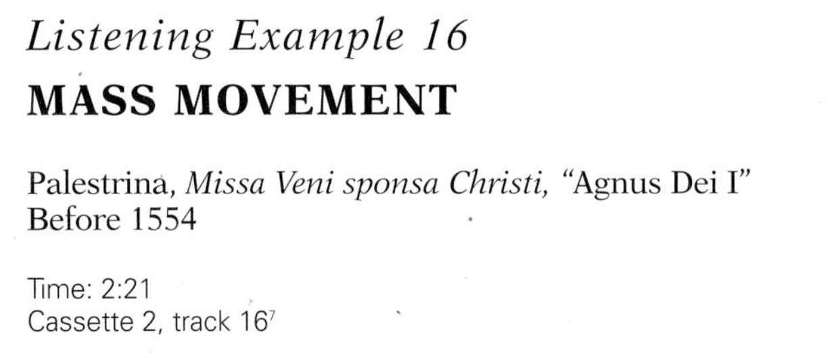

Listening Example 16

MASS MOVEMENT

Palestrina, *Missa Veni sponsa Christi,* "Agnus Dei I"
Before 1554

Time: 2:21
Cassette 2, track 16[7]

7. Ioannis Petrealoysii Praenestini, *Opera Omnia* (Leipzig, 1886), vol.18, p.35.

18.1 St. Mark's Cathedral, Venice. Begun 1063. Photo: Alinari, Florence.
With its five portals and five glittering domes, St. Mark's functioned as a sumptuous backdrop for the elaborate civic ceremonies staged in the great piazza stretched before it.

Italian Vocal-Instrumental Music

During the Late Renaissance, instrumental music began to rival the preeminence of vocal music, assisted particularly by the musical directors of the Cathedral of St. Mark's in Venice. St. Mark's Byzantine splendor was typical of the grandiose palaces, churches, ceremonies, and even paintings of that ornate city (fig. 18.1 and p. 62).

As a trading center and crossroads of the world, Venice deliberately and successfully used pomp and pageantry to impress visitors with its magnificence. Grand productions inside the cathedral were necessary for the desired effect, but the arrangement of the church did not lend itself to large musical groups.

St. Mark's floor plan formed a Greek cross (fig. 18.2). Following the conventions of the Eastern church, the main floor was reserved for men and the smaller balcony level for women. This design was exploited by creating a new polychoral style of antiphonal singing—a procedure whereby the ensemble (chorus with or without orchestra) was divided into several different groups singing and/or playing in alternation. Musical productions would include the use of the two organs in their fixed positions plus choirs and brass choirs stationed on several balconies throughout the church. The listener would be overwhelmed by vocal and instrumental music alternating between left and right, front and rear. Arrangements of choirs and brass choirs could be selected from some of the possibilities indicated in figure 18.2 (see also fig. 18.3).

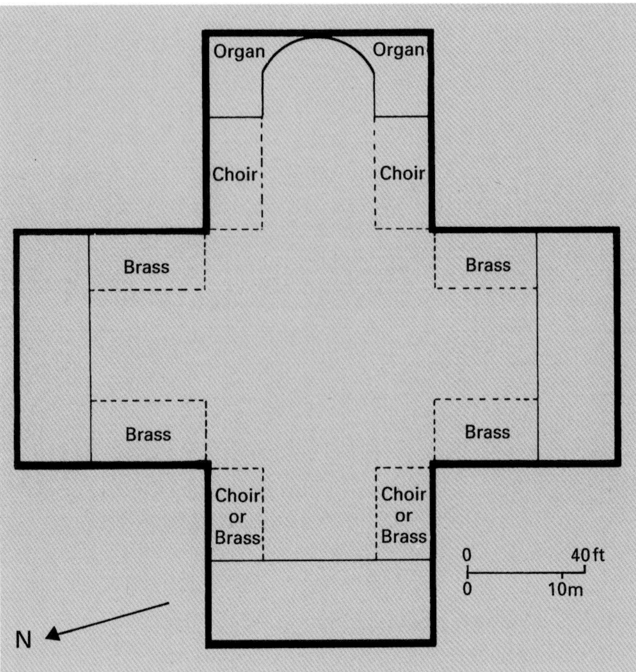

18.2 St. Mark's, Venice, simplified floor plan.

18.3 St. Mark's, Venice, interior. Photo: Marburg. This view is from the west, where one organ is located in the balcony, looking east to the small chancel with the other organ and space for a small choir. Brass choirs were placed on the balcony under massive arches at one or more of the four upper corners. The conductor stood on the high podium in front of the main-floor choir.

Listening Example 17

MOTET

Giovanni Gabrieli, "In ecclesiis"
1615; excerpt

Time: 4:20
Cassette 2, track 17

The complete motet consists of five verses and five **alleluias** and has the following overall structure of text and performing groups (which sing or play from four different locations in the church):

Verse 1	In ecclesiis benedicite Domino, (Praise the Lord in the congregation)	Sopranos (Chorus I) Organ
	Alleluia	Sopranos (Chorus I) Chorus II Organ
Verse 2	In omnia loco . . . , (In every place of worship praise him)	Tenors (Chorus I) Organ
	Alleluia	Tenors (Chorus I) Chorus II Organ
Sinfonia (orchestral interlude)		
Verse 3	In Deo, salutari meo . . . , (In God, who is my salvation and glory, is my help, and my hope is in God)	Altos (Chorus I) Tenors (Chorus I) Orchestra
	Alleluia	Altos (Chorus I) Tenors (Chorus I) Chorus II Orchestra

Music Printing

Prosperous Venice was also the setting for the development of printed music. Over 9,000,000 books had been printed by the year 1500, but no one had thought of printing music on that scale. A 1457 *Psalterium* that included music had been printed at Mainz and a Roman *Missale* was printed in 1476 in Milan using, for the first time, movable type.

Ottaviano de' Petrucci (peh-TROO-tchee; 1466–1539) used movable type in his printing shop. He was an enterprising businessman and in 1498 he petitioned the Signoria of Venice for a twenty-year license (amounting to a monopoly) to print music to meet a growing demand for domestic music. In 1501 he produced the *Harmonice*

Musices Odhecaton A (One Hundred Songs of Harmonic Music), the earliest printed collection of part-music. Rich in Franco-Flemish chansons, this anthology was followed by fifty-eight more volumes of secular and sacred music produced for music-hungry amateurs and an increasing number of professional musicians. An expanding market led, of course, to lower prices and even wider dissemination of music. By the end of the sixteenth century, music publishers were in business throughout Europe.

INSTRUMENTAL MUSIC

Renaissance instrumental music continued to be primarily functional; that is, it was associated with dances, plays, masquerades, and extravaganzas of noble courts, rather than as a performance art with its own special audience (fig. 18.4).

Dance and music have always been associated and rarely more effectively than in the sixteenth century, which has been called "the century of the dance." The church had long suppressed dancing as both heathen and lascivious, but Renaissance society ignored such medieval strictures and invented social dancing. Accompanied by wind and stringed instruments, men and women of the Italian and French courts joined hands for the first time for folklike round dances and courtly pair dances such as the *danse royale.*

18.4 *Lady playing a Dulcimer*, from the early 16th-century manuscript of the 14th-century poem, "Les Echecs amoreux," fol. 143v, Bibliothèque Nationale, Paris.
A few of the many Renaissance instruments are depicted here. The elegantly gowned lady is playing her dulcimer (an instrument still in use) with small hammers. A harp leans against the wall at the left and a portable organ rests on the floor at the right. In the background are singers and players. Reading from left to right, the instruments are: recorder (still used today: ancestor of the flute), shawm (ancestor of the oboe), and bagpipes (probably of Asian origin; introduced to Europe by the Romans during the first century AD).

Because of its portability and mellow tone the lute was the preferred instrument of the age. Its chief rival was the **harpsichord—**also called cembalo, clavecin, **virginal**, spinet—the principal keyboard instrument of the sixteenth through the eighteenth centuries. Harpsichords have various shapes, which are generally similar in external appearance to grand, upright, and spinet pianos. The tone is produced by quills plucking the strings and is bright and sharp. Unlike the piano, harpsichords cannot vary their **dynamics** (degrees of loudness or softness) except by using two keyboards, muted strings, or different types of quills. Whole sections are played at one dynamic level; variation is achieved by changing to a louder or softer tone quality in the next section.

In England, the harpsichord was called a virginal, supposedly in honor of the "maiden Queen Elizabeth." English music had flourished under Henry VIII, Edward VI, and Mary, and reached, under Elizabeth, a level rarely approached thereafter. English power and wealth, the importation of foreign talent, and increased travel all combined to assist the assimilation of the Italian style and make the sixteenth century one of the outstanding periods in English musical history. Tudor sacred music was superb, but the secular forms of English music—the madrigals, lute music, virginal music, and fancies for **viols**—had special importance in the richness of the Elizabethan age.

ENGLISH SECULAR VOCAL MUSIC

The English madrigal school was inspired by Italian models, but its growth and development have made the English madrigal virtually synonymous with Elizabethan England. A madrigal, whether English or Italian, is a secular, unaccompanied part-song, usually in four voices. English madrigals tend toward a balanced texture of polyphonic and homophonic writing, and can be either merry or melancholy. The outstanding characteristic, however, is the sheer delight in the sounds, rhythms, and meanings of the English language.

The madrigalists are fond of natural word rhythms. They also like to play with **onomatopoeia**, alliteration, **metaphor**, and **simile** and take exceptional pleasure in exploiting double meanings. Wordplay with triple meanings is even better. Word painting is another notable method by which composers manipulate the sounds of the music so that they can imitate, imply, or describe the sounds of nature and/or the meanings and sounds of words.

In the following pastoral madrigal, the composer quietly poses the question "Thyrsis? Sleepest thou?" and then continues to press the question until Thyrsis is awakened with some vigorous "hollas." The cuckoo song is imitated, the music "sighs" as the shepherd "sighed as one all undone" and requests to be "let alone alas." The repetitious text of "drive him back to London" pushes the madrigal to an animated conclusion.

Listening Example 18

MADRIGAL

Bennet, "Thyrsis? Sleepest thou?"
Before 1625

Time: 1:50
Cassette 2, track 18[8]

Opera

Opera was invented during the Renaissance in, of course, Florence. A group of humanists known as the Florentine Camerata met on a regular basis to reconstruct what ancient Greek music must have been like. They began by trying to imagine what the music of Greek drama sounded like and came up with a declamatory solo vocal line with instrumental accompaniment. This became the operatic recitative followed by the lyrical **aria**. Like the madrigal, opera migrated to England, where Henry Purcell was the greatest operatic composer. Following is a recitative and aria from Act III of Purcell's *Dido and Aeneas*.

Listening Example 19

OPERA

Purcell, *Dido and Aeneas*, Act III, "Dido's Lament"
1689

Time: 4:12[9]

Recitative
Thy hand, Belinda! darkness shades me,
On thy bosom let me rest,
More I would, but death invades me.
Death is now a welcome guest.

Aria
When I am laid in earth,
May my wrongs create no trouble in thy breast.
Remember me, but ah! forget my fate.

After the introductory recitative a descending **chromatic** bass line is heard a total of eleven times, accompanying an independent vocal melody. This is called a "ground" because it is the unvarying foundation for the vocal line.

SUMMARY

The environment of music experienced notable changes during the Renaissance, with the inevitable result that the forms of music changed accordingly. The forces of secularization, which were set in motion during the Gothic period, began to moderate the power of the church. The expansion of the universities, the development of city centers of trade and commerce, and the rise of a mercantile middle class led to a development of secular music.

Outdoor concerts using **orchestras** composed of violins, shawms, trombones, and drums, and indoor concerts of recorders, viols, and harpsichord became common. Some of the outdoor performances provided music for dancing, which had changed from improvised music for one or two instruments to composed music for groups of instruments (consorts).

The demand for musical instruments for domestic use spurred the development and production of lutes, viols, and especially the instrument that could play both homophonic and polyphonic music, the harpsichord. An even more common household instrument was the clavichord.[10]

The newly awakened interest in classical culture, in humanism, and in the creative individual was reflected in the active participation in the arts by educated amateurs. Large and small social gatherings featured performances of solo songs accompanied by lute or harpsichord (or clavichord), a variety of **chamber** music and, particularly in England, the singing of part-songs such as madrigals and catches.

8. John Bennet, *Madrigals to Four Voices* (London, 1599), no.8.
9. CD 1, track 12.
10. The tone of the clavichord is produced by depressing the keys so that metal tangents on the other end of the keys strike the strings. The instrument is portable and the tone light and flexible.

The proliferation of secular music did not provoke a decline in sacred music; rather there was a merging of techniques, instruments, and styles. Burgundian composers such as Dufay combined voices with instruments for their church music.

Josquin des Près wrote Masses and motets, Italian secular music, and French chansons. Lassus wrote 1,250 compositions in Latin, French, German, and Italian. Palestrina, serving the church in Rome, wrote much sacred music and a variety of Italian madrigals. In Venice, Gabrieli wrote antiphonal, vocal-instrumental music and considerable instrumental music. The Florentine Camerata invented opera.

The growth of music during the Renaissance was astounding. Within a single century, music changed from an esoteric, church-dominated art form to an international language heard in every court and noble residence, and in many middle-class homes throughout Europe.

CULTURE AND HUMAN VALUES

Musicians achieved the superior status accorded High Renaissance artists if they were composers or if they were amateur performers who had no need to make music for a living. Professional musicians, no matter how adept they were in the skillful manipulation of musical instruments, were ranked with cobblers, tailors, and other artisans. This situation reflected the medieval world's class division into the elite (aristocracy and clergy) and the rest of humankind.

Throughout the Renaissance the class structure gradually changed with the rise of a middle class. The new merchant class experienced its strongest growth in northern Europe, particularly in Burgundy and Flanders. And that was precisely where the musical Renaissance began and flourished. One can logically conclude that there is a connection between music and a middle class, but what is the connection?

In the first place, music is an art form that can entertain an audience of one (the performer) up to an audience of thousands. It is a social art whose appeal transcends all social barriers. Whether used in conjunction with dance, theatrical productions, or as a performing/listening art in its own right, music is generally perceived as the most universal of all art forms. Thus this most accessible and widespread art form found a new patron in the flourishing merchant class. Merchants and traders enthusiastically embraced music in all its forms, much as their seventeenth-century descendants commissioned portraits by Rembrandt, Hals, and other Dutch artists.

Did businessmen patronize music solely for its intrinsic value? Hardly. Heretofore, only the elite were patrons of the arts, literature, and theatre. What better way to announce your newly acquired wealth than to "buy in" to a higher social class by sponsoring music and, later, portraiture? This is not to say that every burgher was a calculating social climber. Some could credit sponsorship of the arts as good business, but others could truly enjoy participating in some of the "finer things of life."

For growing numbers of people the grim rounds of bleak survival in a feudal society had become a distant memory. Peasants still tilled the soil in overwhelming numbers but capitalism, trade, merchandising, and education began to change all that. For centuries people had been able only to hope for a glorious afterlife that supposedly compensated for the miseries of earthly existence. Now there was hope for a better life on this earth and, increasingly, the belief that individuals could better their lives through their own efforts took hold. Perhaps the most positive aspect of the Renaissance was the change in attitude, from mute acceptance of the old *status quo* to one of rising expectations. Envisioning something better can move mountains.

STUDY QUESTIONS

What was the long-range significance of the bourgeois aspects of fifteenth-century music? How, for example, would you categorize, in social and economic terms, today's popular music? Where does rock fit in? Jazz? Symphonic music?

ADDITIONAL LISTENING

1. Palestrina, Pope Marcellus Mass, Kyrie. This is one of the best known of the composer's liturgical compositions (CD 1, track 10).
2. Morley, "My bonny lass she smileth." This cheerful composition has five voices (CD 1, track 11).

CHAPTER 19

Shadow and Substance: Literary Insights into the Renaissance

The linguistic dualism of the Renaissance had a very positive effect on the development of literature, philosophy, and science. Church-preserved Latin was the common language of all intellectuals and, moreover, a direct link to the classical past. No wonder Petrarch and other humanists viewed Cicero and Virgil as contemporaries; all wrote in the same language. Developing during the Middle Ages as the spoken languages of the people, the vernaculars became the accepted languages of popular culture. Latin remained the proper scholarly language, but the vernaculars evolved into recognized national languages that became acceptable vehicles for literary expression. Latin provided a kind of intellectual unity, whereas English, French, Italian, and Spanish each reinforced a sense of national cohesion and purpose. Each nation developed its own modern literary tradition, but languages were not isolated by the rise of nationalism. Translations of every language, including Latin, flowed back and forth over national borders, making Renaissance literature as international, in its own way, as art and music.

RENAISSANCE AUTHORS

In a survey such as this only literary peaks can be discussed, for almost everyone of any consequence was an author of sorts, as well as an amateur painter and musician. Most of the authors possessed the quality of *virtù,* the highest ideal of a Renaissance man; they were, in some measure, universal men, active leaders in their turbulent times. Erasmus was known as the most brilliant intellect of his time, friend and adviser to popes and kings. Both Thomas More and Francis Bacon served as Lord Chancellors of England (roughly equivalent to the chief justice of the United States Supreme Court). Petrarch was among the foremost of the humanists, and both Castiglione and Machiavelli were prominent diplomats. The achievements of Michelangelo and Shakespeare were exceptional even in an age of awesome talents. Cervantes fought in the last Crusade and, a unique distinction, was captured and held prisoner by pirates. We know little about Rabelais beyond the fact that he was once a monk and priest and later a physician. He did take rakish delight in his voluntary separation from the church. The single exception among these activists was Montaigne, who retired to his study to compose his penetrating essays on Renaissance life and mores.

Miguel de Cervantes Saavedra, 1547–1616

Although he came late, in spirit it was Cervantes (sir-VAHN-teez) who tolled the knell of medievalism. Cervantes was in a better position than most of his contemporaries to utter the words that closed the Middle Ages and opened up the Renaissance; he had been a part of the final burst of chivalry, having accompanied the fleet of Don John of Austria on the last Crusade. He fought at the Battle of Lepanto (1571) and had seen, at first hand, the last knight of Christendom. Perhaps Lord Byron expressed it best in his *Don Juan*: "Cervantes smiled Spain's chivalry away."

Don Quixote is Cervantes' reaction to the medieval noble gesture. This lank, hungry, and apparently demented man rides the Spanish roads as he battles injustice. The Don's problem was his medieval point of view. His encounter with a common barber reveals a hostile knight, barmaids become noble damsels in distress, and windmills turn into giants. For Don Quixote and the medieval mind as a whole, things were never what they appeared to be. We, who are practical-minded like the people of the Renaissance, recognize that barbers are barbers and windmills are windmills, and we laugh, as did Renaissance readers, at the knight of the woeful countenance riding his flea-bitten nag. Yet the only trouble with Quixote was that he was born 100 years too late. A century earlier, he would have been the hero of a tale of chivalry, and his windmills *would* have been giants. After Cervantes, the tale of chivalry—the most popular form of medieval literature—could no longer be

Opposite Limbourg Brothers, "February," detail, from the *Très Riches Heures du Duc de Berry*. 1413–16. Illuminated manuscript. Musée Condé, Chantilly, France. Photo: Giraudon, Paris.

taken seriously. It became as outdated as the melodrama of the beautiful daughter, the mortgage coming due, the villain fingering his waxed mustache, and the hero arriving in the nick of time.

Have we lost something in giving up these fond delusions and embracing stark naturalism? Chesterton raises this question in his poem "Lepanto," in which he compares Don John, a true hero, with the paltry figures of other Renaissance rulers. Cervantes, too, must have wondered the same thing, for in the second part of his book the reader smiles at his hero, but the smile, like the author's, is sympathetic. Cervantes was apparently disillusioned with the pragmatism of the age and longed for vanished glories. This comparison of past and present, as seen in the two parts of *Don Quixote,* brings to a focus the central problem of the Renaissance, as first discussed in chapter 16. With all the new freedoms, wealth, economic order, and a science that relegated the human soul to a secondary position below sense-apparent objects—with all these, what is man? "What a piece of work is man!... And yet to me what is this quintessence of dust?" Shakespeare confronts this problem in *The Tempest* and suggests a solution.

19.1 Albrecht Dürer, *Erasmus of Rotterdam.* 1526. Engraving, 9¾ × 7½" (24.8 × 19 cm). Metropolitan Museum of Art, New York (Fletcher Fund, 1919).
The Latin inscription states that this was a drawing from life.

Petrarch (Francesco Petrarca), 1304–74

Petrarch was recognized in his own time as the preeminent poet and humanist of a new age. In 1341 the Roman Senate awarded him the laurel wreath as the first poet laureate since the ancient world. Though he cherished his elaborate Latin poems, he is best known today as the inventor of the Italian sonnet and creator of elegant Italian love poetry. As the court poet of the papal palace at Avignon, he was appalled at the decadence of the French popes of the Babylonian Captivity.

Erasmus of Rotterdam, 1466–1536

Italian humanism had a distinctly pagan flavor, but across the Alps the movement was entirely Christian, with Erasmus (fig. 19.1), the "Prince of Humanists," in the forefront. A true cosmopolitan, he made all Europe his home, from England to Italy. Although at first well-disposed toward Luther's reforms, he could not accept Luther's denial of free will. "I laid a hen's egg," wrote Erasmus; "Luther hatched a bird of quite another species."

A strong supporter of overdue reforms, Erasmus wrote that "Luther was guilty of two great crimes—he struck the Pope in his crown, and the monks in their belly." In another vein he sternly admonished the church: "By identifying the new learning with heresy you make orthodoxy synonymous with ignorance." Erasmus preferred a purified church to a divided one.

During a journey from Italy to England Erasmus conceived the idea of a satire on just about every aspect of contemporary society. Written partly during his stay with the English humanist Sir Thomas More, and dedicated to him, the book was called *Moria* (Gk. "folly") in a punning reference to his English friend's name. Appearing in thirty-six editions in his own lifetime, the *Praise of Folly* (see pp. 80–4) was, after the Bible, the most widely read book of the century. Erasmus had brilliantly reinvented the classical paradoxical encomium in which everyone and everything unworthy of praise are ironically celebrated.

Niccolò Machiavelli, 1469–1527

If man is the measure of all things, as the humanists joyously avowed, what then is man? Machiavelli (mak-ee-uh-VEL-li) attacked the problem with a clinical eye in *The Prince,* the most famous and influential of his many publications (see pp. 84–94). Having observed the confusion following the fall of Cesare Borgia's autocratic government in Urbino, Machiavelli claimed that a ruler should be pragmatic rather than virtuous. The book examines the techniques of exercising power. As such, it is rather closely allied to both the art and the science of the Renaissance. Machiavelli uses the *scientific* method of his time to dissect the successes and failures of many rulers to see what made them tick, to come to an understanding of the *art* of governing successfully. Machiavelli delineated this art with such skill and frankness that the nineteenth-century historian Jacob Burkhardt observed that a Renaissance prince manipulated the state much as an artist manipulates his art.

Machiavelli's first premise is that anything is good for a state that allows it to survive and prosper; his second premise is that any means that will work in achieving that goal is good. (Machiavelli did not write that "the end justifies the means." Rather, he used the phrase *si guarda al fine*, meaning "one considers the end.") With these two premises he sweeps aside ideals and sentiment. The state, he assumes, does not exist for the happiness or well-being of people; the people exist only for the good of the state. The resulting thinking is detached, practical, and painfully accurate, though it is based on the lowest possible estimate of the worthiness of people. Its analytic method sweeps aside all mystery and disregards previous conceptions about justice and the ruling power. A typical, but depressing example of the cold, clear vision of the age, Machiavelli gave the Renaissance its first candid picture of human nature with the idealism of medievalism and humanism stripped away. He said simply:

> For of men it may generally be affirmed that they are thankless, fickle, false, studious to avoid danger, greedy of gain, devoted to you while you are able to confer benefits upon them, and ready, as I have said before, while danger is distant, to shed their blood, and sacrifice their property, their lives and their children for you; but in the hour of need they turn against you.... Love is held by the tie of obligation, which, because men are a sorry breed, is broken on every whisper of private interest.

Machiavelli's verdict was not the opinion of a misanthrope, soured on the world, but that of a social scientist investigating human affairs with the detachment of a Kepler charting planetary orbits. After considering the fate of governments from Athens to his own time, he concluded that people were beasts, at best, and the successful ruler was one who treated them accordingly.

Disengagement: Michel de Montaigne, 1533–92

Nor was Machiavelli alone in this conclusion. Montaigne (mon-TEN-je) wrote:

> The frailest and most vulnerable of all creatures is man, and at the same time the most arrogant. He sees and feels himself lodged here in the mud and filth of the world, nailed and riveted to the worst, the deadest and most stagnant part of the universe, at the lowest story of the house and the most remote from the vault of heaven, with the animals of the worst condition of the three; and he goes and sets himself in imagination above the circle of the moon, and brings heaven under his feet.

Like Erasmus, Montaigne remained within the Catholic church, but he was far more interested in the secular world, in the classics, and in himself. Montaigne was a rationalist and a skeptic. He was convinced that all knowledge was necessarily incomplete and would always be less than total. Like More, he saw that absolutist beliefs of church or state led to religious strife and warfare. He deliberately withdrew from his troubled world to study Latin and Greek authors and to write, essentially for his own gratification, personal essays on a wide range of subjects that interested him. No other Renaissance writer speaks so openly, clearly, and unpretentiously as does Montaigne. In the foreword to his *Essays* he writes:

> This, reader, is a book without guile. Had I proposed to court the favor of the world, I had set myself out in borrowed beauties; but it was my wish to be seen in my simple, natural and ordinary garb without study or artifice, for it was myself I had to paint.

Elsewhere he wrote, "If the world finds fault with me for speaking too much of myself, I find fault with the world for not even thinking of itself."

Though not included in this text because of limited space,"On Cannibals" is one of the most candid and entertaining of the author's essays. The cannibals described by Montaigne also live in the New World, in Brazil. More used his Utopians to criticize his own society, but Montaigne is more direct. His cannibals are compared with Europeans and, cannibalism notwithstanding, judged superior:

> We may, then, well call these people barbarians in respect to the rules of reason, but not in respect to ourselves, who, in all sorts of barbarity, exceed them.

We find two disparate attitudes emerging from the new freedom of the Renaissance. The first, resulting from such opinions as those quoted above, displayed extreme pessimism and despair. Allied with that was the fear and uncertainty caused by losing the security of the old faith. But the second attitude is most commonly associated with the Renaissance. With all ties cut, with wealth abounding and frontiers stretching across the seas to unknown lands, people could be free. To secure freedom a person must obtain some kind of power, and the possibilities were apparently unlimited. Artists courted power through their own creativity and through the patronage of influential rulers; merchants achieved power by amassing money; rulers ruthlessly sought power and glory in every conceivable way. The insatiable drive for power created a dog-eat-dog situation, but the rewards were immense and they were available here and now.

A RENAISSANCE PRINCE

Soldier, politician, and ecclesiastic, Cesare Borgia (CHAYS-uh-ray BORE-ja; 1476?–1507) was, like many of his contemporaries, corrupt, treacherous, and cruel. One of the four illegitimate children of Pope Alexander VI, he was made a cardinal at the age of eighteen. His father later named him Duke of Romagna, which enabled him to extend his military conquests. When rebels attempted to reclaim the Duchy of Urbino, Cesare lured them into one of his castles, where he had all of them executed. After his father's death his many enemies deprived him of his extensive lands and had him imprisoned. He later escaped to Navarre but was killed in action in an expedition against Castile. It is generally assumed that he is the prototype of Machiavelli's prince.

François Rabelais, ca. 1490–1553

One reaction to a freewheeling society lusting after power was to withdraw from the rat race, a response that our own century has witnessed in many different forms. Symbolically this desire to retreat is revealed in the number of utopias that were written during the Renaissance. In his *Gargantua and Pantagruel* (see pp. 99–101), Rabelais (rab-uh-leh) included a brief section on "The Abbey of Theleme" as his version of utopia. Actually, the "abbey" was a country club version of a monastery that has been turned upside down. Instead of "Poverty, Chastity, and Obedience" the sole injunction is to "Do What Thou Wilt." The Abbey of Theleme was a quiet retreat where the "rougher element" (and at no time in Western history has that element been so rough as during the Renaissance) was excluded, and where everyone behaved with perfect manners.

Baldassare Castiglione, 1478–1529

An elegant aristocrat and skilled diplomat, Castiglione represented a viewpoint advocated by Rabelais but opposed to both Montaigne and Machiavelli. Little concerned with humankind's capacity for evil and very much a man in and of the world, Castiglione advocated urbane lives of mannered civility. His code for Renaissance patricians, *The Book of the Courtier* (see pp. 95–9), was a best-seller for the next two centuries.

Thomas More, 1478–1535

Sir Thomas More (fig. 19.2) quite rightly ranks as one of the heroes of the humanist movement. For his greatest work, *Utopia* (see pp. 101–6), More seized on everyone's curiosity about the New World. As a framework for his story, he relates a conversation with a sailor, Raphael Hythlodaeus, who had sailed with Amerigo Vespucci to locate a new land named Utopia. More uses this Utopia (Gk., "no place") to criticize

19.2 Hans Holbein the Younger, *Sir Thomas More*. Ca. 1530. Frick Collection, New York.
Holbein's superb portrait reveals a visionary and a man of conscience, who died at the hands of Henry VIII rather than compromise his religious conviction.

severely his own country and to describe a perfect government, which is a curious mixture of Plato's ideas and some of the most progressive concepts of More's time—or ours. Rather than the combination of private property and communism described by Plato, practically everything in Utopia is held in common. Most of the political officers are elected by the people in free elections, though More also provides for a monarch and a slave class. He believes that everybody—men and women and members of all the professions, including the clergy—should do real work, especially manual labor. With everyone working, all chores can be accomplished in a six-hour day, leaving ample time for creative leisure. His Utopians work as farmers and then move to the city to perform urban tasks. These population shifts are staggered so that the population in both country (on collective farms) and city remains constant.

More's *Utopia* has always been taken seriously, yet its conception of the state is naive. Actually, More seeks to return to medievalism while incorporating the advances of his own age. In the first place, More opposes the new capitalism, complaining of the evils that result from a society in which "money beareth all the swing." He proposes that all property should be held in common, that all houses should be the same (except for the gardens, where he allows individual initiative), and that people should trade houses at regular intervals. Gold would be used for chamber pots and jewels serve as children's toys so that citizens would not covet such things. Yet the state is to use gold and jewels to buy goods from neighboring countries.

Like Rabelais, More insists on equality and proposes representative local and federal governments similar to those of Switzerland. His equality means that every person should work at a trade except the few selected to be priests and scholars. Even with this ingenious planning, More cannot escape the dirty work done in any civilization, and he, like Plato, has slaves for labor unworthy of the Utopians. At this point, of course, his equality breaks down.

More was appalled by the ceaseless strife and warfare of his time, and he insisted that his Utopians would have none of it—or little, at least. He proposes that all wars be conducted on neighboring lands and that the Utopians hire mercenary soldiers to do the fighting. Most fortunately, a neighboring nation is inhabited by a fierce and warlike people who are eager to wage war—at a price—for the Utopians. He describes these ideal mercenaries:

> They be hideous, savage and fierce, dwelling in wild woods and high mountains, where they were bred and brought up. They be of an hard nature, able to abide and sustain heat, cold and labour, abhorring all delicate dainties, occupying no husbandry nor tillage of the ground, homely and rude both in the building of their houses and in their apparel, given unto no goodness, but only to the breeding and bringing up of cattle. The most part of their living is by hunting and stealing. They be born only to war, which they diligently and earnestly seek for. And when they have gotten it, they be wonders glad thereof. They go forth of their country in great companies together, and whosoever lacketh soldiers, there they proffer their services for small wages. This is the only craft that they have to get their living by. They maintain their life by seeking their death.

The limitation of More's thinking is paradoxical, for he can extend his ideal state only to the borders of the nation. He degrades the people of other countries so that his Utopians may live well. And how like Shakespeare's Caliban the warrior group is! The good life, it would seem, must float on a vast sea of all that we regard as evil. When we consider the Utopians and this crude race of warriors, when we consider Prospero and Caliban, we recognize that they are as unlike as day and night, yet both seem necessary for human life. More was able to place his exploitable savages just outside the borders of his nation and our consideration; yet in everyday life, they are here and now and with us always.

Particularly abhorrent for More was the religious dissension that split nations, and that would eventually cause his own death. So in *Utopia* we find complete religious freedom. Most of the people adhere to one faith, but those of other faiths or no faith are neither chastised nor penalized. Only bigots are punished, for they provoke dissension by insisting that their faith is better than any other.

More did not write a guidebook to the perfect civilization. Practically, it won't work, and he knew this as well as Plato before him. He is to be taken seriously for the ideas that lay behind the practical operation of a utopia for civilized people. Most importantly, the necessity for human equality, religious tolerance, and his conviction that life should be lived for the pleasure of each individual are grand Renaissance ideas that foreshadow the thoughts of Rousseau, Jefferson, Madison, and others of later epochs. Indeed, they are our own best ideals, and we are still at a loss for ways of making them work, even as was More.

William Shakespeare, 1564–1616

Shakespeare knew all the intricacies of the Renaissance problem, not as theory, but as one who experienced within himself the perplexities of the age. In each of his plays one finds his reactions to the nature of Renaissance people, and, as Shakespeare matured and developed, the scope of his concerns became ever more comprehensive.

In *Hamlet* the conflict is resolved by a sort of neo-Stoicism: "The readiness is all," says Hamlet at the end. In each of the plays beyond *Hamlet*, in *Othello* and in *King Lear*, we see a growing understanding of the Renaissance world. Probably more than any other tragedy, *King Lear* fills us with the emotions of pity and fear, and purges them at the end, but the experience of the audience throughout the play leaves the soul seared. The pity, of course, is for the "good" people of the drama: Lear, his fool, Gloucester, Edgar, and perhaps Kent; the fear is for ourselves and for all humankind. Lear expresses the deepest pessimism of the Renaissance but, beyond that, we see Shakespeare reaching for the conclusion that the only salvation for humankind is love and compassion.

By the time of his last complete play, *The Tempest* (see pp.106–29), Shakespeare, viewing this resolution ever more clearly, renders up his account and gives us a summation of the totality of his experience. The best of the previous plays had been tragic, but is this final play a tragedy? No, for the author has gone beyond tragedy. He places *The Tempest* in a world of imagination sufficiently removed from the workaday world to bring together all the disparate elements of the Renaissance and resolve the conflicts. Shakespeare achieves the truth-beyond-appearances on Prospero's island.

What forces are represented here? Primarily there are the dark human failings that we try to deny, but which are with us always. Among the mortals, this old evil is represented by Stephano and Trinculo, Sebastian and Antonio; among the spirits, it is symbolized by Caliban. This is the force represented by the barbaric warrior race in More's *Utopia*, the force found in the myths of every culture. It is Grendel and his mother in *Beowulf*, the mindless drives in Freudian psychology, the dark creature that the Earth-Spirit and the Walpurgis-Night Scene represent in *Faust*. Sometimes we think of this force as lust, yet that is too limited. The Caliban thrust is all the drives that make human beings distorted and destructive, the force that Dante observed in Hell.

Represented by Prospero and symbolized by Ariel, the opposing thrust is the power of the intellect, which stands at the heart of the various utopias. Prospero is the humanist who has gone stale, as humanism did in the late Renaissance, and who belatedly realizes his responsibility to humanity. He describes himself as being "for the liberal arts without a parallel: those being all my study." The Ariel force, then, represents the highest nature of humankind, the intellect, which in the Renaissance view made men and women akin to the angels.

Can we recognize any of the more earthly beings? Certainly we can, for Antonio has already usurped Prospero's dukedom, and he teaches his method to Sebastian when they plot to usurp yet another kingdom by eliminating Alonso, king of Naples. So Machiavellian are they that they form this plot even when they are marooned with apparently no chance of returning to Italy.

In such men as Adrian and Francisco we recognize opportunistic Renaissance courtiers, as they are despairingly described:

They'll take suggestion as a cat laps milk;
They'll tell the clock to any business that
We say befits the hour.

Finally, in Gonzalo, we recognize the wise old counselor, the one who has lived long enough to see and know much, but whose very age makes him if not foolish, at least ineffectual. He is a sort of redeemed Polonius.

Shakespeare's first purpose is to show these people as they are. He wants each one to find his true self. It is Gonzalo who sees through the plot to this first meaning when he says:

In one voyage
Did Claribel her husband find at Tunis,
And Ferdinand, her brother, found a wife
Where he himself was lost; Prospero his dukedom
In a poor isle; and all of us ourselves,
When no man was his own.

We explore the nature of evil with Caliban, who clearly recognizes his opposition to intellect when he speaks of his only profit from language as knowing how to curse, and when he tells Trinculo and Stephano to "burn his Book" if they want power over Prospero. Caliban's nature is confirmed when he celebrates his new "freedom" at the very moment when he is most in bondage, for he is drunk and has taken Stephano as a cruel master. Yet Caliban is more perceptive than his mortal counterparts, for when they advance with their evil purpose of overpowering Prospero, he knows the difference between the show of power (the spangled garments hung on the line) and real power, which involves pressing on about their business. His more foolish mortal masters are tricked by the flashy garb and routed by Prospero and Ariel. It is only after all these experiences that Caliban can say, "How fine my master is!... What a thrice-double ass was I, to take this drunkard for a god, And worship this dull fool!"

But the other side of the coin is that Prospero and Miranda cannot exist without Caliban. Although he is revolting in appearance and nature, so much so that Miranda says, " 'Tis a villain, sir, I do not love to look on," Prospero wisely answers,

But as 'tis
We cannot miss him: he does make our fire,
Fetch in our wood; and serves in offices
That profit us.

The Caliban nature, then, wisely used and ruled by the human will, serves a useful function in life.

But it was the state that was Shakespeare's main concern. Because the church could no longer control society, another type of order was necessary. This was the secular state, ruled by a king. Throughout the play, the political world is out of joint, for the right duke is not on the throne, and evil governs in place of good. Quite early, Shakespeare has Gonzalo propose a utopia—one not much different from that of More or of Rabelais. But the idea is ridiculous. Gonzalo starts his speech, "Had I plantation of this isle... and were the king on't," but he ends the speech, saying that there would be no sovereign. In a stroke Shakespeare dismisses the utopian dream.

But we need more than this if the state is to survive while providing a sound framework for its inhabitants. Enter Ferdinand and Miranda, who are carefully schooled throughout the play in right living. Their marriage unites the man of action with the woman of spirit. One is reminded of Plato's philosopher-king, but the philosophy here is more sprightly and lighthearted. With the consummation of this marriage, and the return to Italy, we can predict an order, neither Machiavellian (as was Alonso's) nor too idealistic (as was Prospero's). This is the proper nature of the state.

What is Shakespeare's conclusion? In the first place he recognizes the folly of most of the things people do. He realizes that ninety years hence it will make little difference what anyone has done or failed to do.

We are such stuff
As dreams are made on, and our little life
Is rounded with a sleep.

Perhaps our present activities will not affect the future but they are important here and now. Shakespeare's final choice is with humankind, men and women of good and evil mixed most wondrously. How else are we to interpret that little passage between Miranda and her father as she views all these mortals for the first time, people whom we have seen in all sorts of wicked conspiracies and evildoing? She looks on them and says:

O Wonder!
How many goodly creatures are there here!
How beauteous mankind is! O brave new world,
That has such people in 't!

And Prospero wisely answers: " 'Tis new to thee."

Is this bitter irony? Are Shakespeare and Prospero in this almost final speech venting a long-pent-up disgust with all of humanity? The brief sentence is ironic, but not bitter. Prospero knows that Miranda has much to learn about these goodly creatures, yet he has already forgiven them. In his eyes this motley crowd of good and evil that are all people is goodly, too. It is for this reason that he leaves his island, drowns the book that commanded the supernatural, leaves the spirits of Ariel and Caliban alike, and returns to Naples. With the good new rulers there, the combination of action and spirit, bound together by love, there will be a new order in human affairs. To bring the play home, we must return from the surreal to actuality and commit ourselves to proper action in the precarious balance between good and evil.

Francis Bacon and the Decline of the Renaissance

All balances must fail, which we have seen in every period that we have studied. One so delicate as that suggested in *The Tempest* cannot last for long. Sir Francis Bacon (1561–1626) proposed how the scales were to fall. He was skilled in many fields, but his greatest work lay in his scientific writing, in which he consistently revealed the clear-sighted realism that was the hallmark of the Renaissance. Among other things, he laid bare the four idols that cause errors in human vision and thinking:

1. The Idols of the Tribe. These are the fallacies that we inherit just because we are members of the human race. The greatest of these is the tendency to imagine more order in nature than actually exists there.
2. The Idols of the Cave. These are our own private prejudices that keep us from seeing things as they really are.
3. The Idols of the Marketplace. By these, Bacon was getting at the same things that modern semanticists deal with, for these are the errors into which we fall because of the imperfections of language.
4. The Idols of the Theatre. Bacon refers to the errors that people fall into because they belong to "schools" of thought. As soon as one accepts the thinking of a school or a religion, one tends to accept it all without seeing whether the individual and separate beliefs may be true or false, good or bad.

Bacon wrote a utopia called *The New Atlantis,* which, not surprisingly, is inhabited by scientists. These are men who follow the lead of Descartes in ruling by reason alone, reason divorced from the spirit. It can weigh the actions of a man such as Ferdinand, judging by the results whether they are good or bad, but reason cannot measure the loveliness of a Miranda. So Bacon and those that followed him in the next period, the Age of Reason, downplayed such qualities as imagination and sentiment. They gained greatly in sureness; their way had the hard brilliance of a diamond. But is clarity worth the price of loveliness?

This, then, was the Renaissance. Its early discoverers brought to it more new big ideas than any civilization had ever faced before. At its outset the change was overwhelming, for all the basic ideas of the Middle Ages had to be adjusted in the face of a mass of new knowledge about the world. Out of this chaos of change emerged two basic attitudes. One orientation led to the glories of the Renaissance: daring explorers, superb artists, powerful capitalists, great monarchs. Some were as fine as Leonardo or Raphael, others as corrupt as Renaissance popes or princes, or as ruthless as English sea dogs or Spanish *conquistadores*. The opposing trend of thought was one of deep pessimism. Montaigne and others who felt this assumed that somehow people were not fine enough in their basic nature properly to use their new freedom. In their dreams of the good life, these people retreated to their utopias. Near the end of his career Shakespeare saw that the balance lay in the powerful king in whose person imagination and action were joined by love. This is the pattern that enlightened despots tried to achieve, but the delicate balance was easily disturbed. In its decline it moved toward the emerging modern world in which science and technology would become ever more central to the culture.

STUDY QUESTIONS

1. Describe Machiavelli's view of human nature and explain why this might contribute to the pessimism of the time. Does Machiavelli's view apply to rulers today? Consider, for example, the various governments in the Western world, the Middle East, and selected African nations.
2. Explain Bacon's "idols" in terms of his own time, and then examine contemporary life and how his idols might still apply.

LITERARY SELECTION 42

Poetry

Petrarch (Francesco Petrarca), 1304–74

Though Petrarch intended his epic poem *Africa* to be his major work, his Italian sonnets have been far more influential. His love poetry was inspired by Laura, whom he first saw in the Church of St. Clara of Avignon on 6 April 1327. The following sonnet commemorates that momentous meeting while also alluding to the day on which Christ supposedly died: 6 April.

Sonnet III

(Era il giorno ch'al sol si scolarara)

'Twas on the morn when heaven its blessed ray
In pity to its suffering master veil'd,
First did I, lady, to your beauty yield,

Of your victorious eyes th' unguarded prey.
Ah, little reck'd I that, on such a day,
Needed against Love's arrows any shield;
And trod, securely trod, the fatal field:
Whence, with the world's, began my heart's dismay.
On every side Love found his victim bare,
And through mine eyes transfix'd my throbbing heart;
Those eyes which now with constant sorrows flow:
But poor the triumph of his boasted art,
Who thus could pierce a naked youth, nor dare
To you in armor mail'd even to display his bow!

Like Dante's Beatrice, Laura was an ideal, the object throughout Petrarch's life of an unrequited poetic passion. Unlike Beatrice, whom Dante idealized from afar, Laura accepted the poet as a friend—but no more than that. She was married and destined to be the mother of ten children. A sonnet is, by definition, a fourteen-line lyric poem that expresses a single idea or thought, in this case the poet's reaction to Laura's physical beauty.

Sonnet LXIX

(Erano i capei d'oro all' aura sparsi)

Her golden tresses were spread loose to air,
And by the wind in thousand tangles blown,
And a sweet light beyond all brightness shone
From those grand eyes, though now of brilliance bare;
And did that face a flush of feeling wear?
I now thought yes, then no, the truth unknown.
My heart was then for love like tinder grown,
What wonder if it flamed with sudden flare?
Not like the walk of mortals was her walk,
But as when angels glide; and seemed her talk
With other than mere human voice, to flow.
A spirit heavenly, a living sun
I saw, and if she be no longer so,
A wound heals not, because the bow's undone.

Petrarch was tormented by his passion, but he was also inspired as a poet because the one-way love affair appealed to his vanity. He was a Renaissance artist, a self-conscious man of letters seeking earthly fame, as the following sonnet clearly reveals.

Sonnet XLVII

(Benedetto sia l' giorno e l' mese e l' anno)

Blest be the day, and blest the month, the year,
The spring, the hour, the very moment blest,
The lovely scene, the spot, where first oppress'd
I sunk, of two bright eyes the prisoner:
And blest the first soft pang, to me most dear,
Which thrill'd my heart, when Love became its guest;
And blest the bow, the shafts which pierced my breast.
And even the wounds, which bosom'd thence I bear.
Blest too the strains which, pour'd through glade and grove,
Have made the woodlands echo with her name;
The sighs, the tears, the languishment, the love:
And blest those sonnets, sources of my fame;
And blest that thought—Oh! never to remove!—
Which turns to her alone, from her alone which came.

Laura died on 6 April 1348 of the Black Death, as did millions of Europeans during that ghastly summer. Petrarch was devastated, as well as transfixed by the date.

Sonnet CCXCII

(Gli occhi di ch' io parlai si caldamente)

Those eyes, 'neath which my passionate rapture rose,
The arms, hands, feet, the beauty that erewhile
Could my own soul from its own self beguile,
And in a separate world of dreams enclose,
The hair's bright tresses, full of golden glows,
And the soft lightning of the angelic smile
That changed this earth to some celestial isle—
Are now but dust, poor dust, that nothing knows.
And yet I live! Myself I grieve and scorn,
Left dark without the light I loved in vain,
Adrift in tempest on a bark forlorn;
Dead is the source of all my amorous strain,
Dry is the channel of my thoughts outworn,
And my sad harp can sound but notes of pain.

STUDY QUESTIONS

1. In line 11 of Sonnet III, the image of the eyes as a gateway to the heart was a poetic commonplace. Is that image still used today in poetry and songs? Give a few examples.
2. What is the meaning of the image of the "bow" in the last line of Sonnets III and LXIX?

LITERARY SELECTION 43

Praise of Folly

Desiderius Erasmus, 1466–1536

Erasmus uses a dramatic setting and a woman, Folly, who speaks wisely and foolishly, learnedly and jokingly. The underlying issue seems to be knowledge versus ignorance, with Erasmus holding to the middle ground. Don't put too much faith in knowledge and scholars, Folly implies, and try to be tolerant and gentle with fools and with ignorance.

Folly Herself Speaks
Whatever the world says of me (for I am not ignorant of
Folly's poor reputation, even among the most foolish), yet

I and I alone provide joy for gods and men. I no sooner step up to speak to this full assembly than all your faces put on a kind of new and unwonted pleasantness. So suddenly have you cleared your brows, and with so pleasant and hearty a laughter given me your applause, that in truth, as many of you as I behold on every side of me, seem to me no less than Homer's gods drunk with nectar and the drug nepenthe; whereas before, you sat as lumpish and pensive as if you had come from consulting an oracle. And as it usually happens when the sun begins to show his beams, or when after a sharp winter the spring breathes afresh on the earth, all things immediately get a new face, new color, and recover as it were a certain kind of youth again: in like manner, but by beholding me, you have in an instant gotten another kind of countenance; and so what the otherwise great orators with their tedious and long-studied speeches can hardly effect, to wit, to remove the trouble of the mind, I have done it at once, with my single look.

But if you ask me why I appear before you in this strange dress, be pleased to lend me your ears, and I will tell you; not those ears, I mean, you carry to church, but abroad with you, such as you are wont to prick up to jugglers, fools, and buffoons, and such as our friend Midas once gave to Pan. For I am disposed awhile to play the sophist with you; not of their sort who nowadays cram boys' heads with certain empty notions and curious trifles, yet teach them nothing but a more than womanish obstinacy of scolding: but I'll imitate those ancients, who, that they might the better avoid that infamous appellation of *Sophi* or *Wise,* chose rather to be called "sophists." Their business was to celebrate the praises of the gods and valiant men. And the like encomium shall you hear from me, but neither of Heracles nor Solon, but mine own dear self, that is to say, Folly.

I think it high time to look down a little on the earth; wherein you'll find nothing frolicky or fortunate, that it owes not to me. So provident has that great parent of mankind, nature, been, that there should not be anything without its mixture, as it were seasoning, of Folly. For since according to the definition of the Stoics, wisdom is nothing else than to be governed by reason; and on the contrary Folly, to be given up to the will of our passions; that the life of man might not be altogether disconsolate and hard to put up with, of how much more passion than reason has Jupiter composed us? putting in, as one would say, "scarce half an ounce to the pound." Besides, he has confined reason to a narrow corner of the brain, and left all the rest of the body to our passions; as also set up, against this one, two as it were, masterless tyrants—anger that possesses the region of the heart, and consequently the very fountain of life, the heart itself; and lust, that stretches its empire everywhere. Against which double force how powerful reason is, let common experience declare, inasmuch as she, which yet is all she can do, may call out to us until she's hoarse, and tell us the rules of honesty and virtue; while they give up the reins to their governor, and make a hideous clamor, till at last being wearied, he suffer himself to be carried wherever they please to hurry him.

Is not war the very root and matter of all famed enterprise? And yet what more foolish than to undertake it for I know not what trifles, especially when both parties are sure to lose more than they get in the bargain? For of those that are slain, not a word of them; and for the rest, when both sides are close engaged "and the trumpets make an ugly noise," what use of these wise men, I pray, that are so exhausted with study that their thin cold blood has scarcely any spirits left? No, it must be those blunt fat fellows, that by how much more they excel in courage, fall short in understanding. Unless perhaps one had rather choose Demosthenes for a soldier, who, following the example of Archilochus, threw away his arms and took to his heels e'er he had scarcely seen his enemy; as ill a soldier, as happy an orator.

But good judgment, you'll say, is not of the least concern in matters of war. In a general way I grant it; but this thing of warring is no part of philosophy, but managed by parasites, pimps, thieves, assassins, peasants, sots, spendthrifts and such other dregs of mankind, not philosophers; who how inept they are in everyday conversation, let Socrates, whom the oracle of Apollo, though not so wisely, judged "the wisest of all men living," be witness; who stepping up to speak about something, I know not what, in public, was forced to come down again well laughed at for his pains. Though yet in this he was not altogether a fool, that he refused the appellation of wise, and returning it back to the oracle, delivered his opinion that a wise man should abstain from meddling with public business; unless perhaps he should have admonished us to beware of wisdom if we intended to be reckoned among the living, there being nothing but his wisdom that first accused and afterwards sentenced him to the drinking of his poisoned cup. For while, as you find him in Aristophanes, philosophying about clouds and ideas, measuring how far a flea could leap, and admiring that so small a creature as a fly should make so great a buzz, he meddled not with anything that concerned common life.

What should I speak of Theophrastus, who being about to make a speech, became as dumb as if he had met a wolf in his way, which yet would have put courage in a man of war? Or Isocrates, who was so fainthearted that he never tried a speech? Or Tully, that great founder of the Roman eloquence, who could never begin to speak without an odd kind of trembling, like a boy that had the hiccups; which Fabius interprets as an argument of a wise orator and one that was sensible of what he was doing; and while he says it, does he not plainly confess that wisdom is a great obstacle to the true management of business? What would become of them were they to fight it out at blows, that are so dead through fear, when the contest is only with empty words?

Even among the professions those only are in high esteem that come nearest to common sense, that is to say, Folly. Theologians are half-starved, physicists out of heart, astronomers laughed at, and logicians slighted; only the physician is worth all the rest. And among them too, the more unlearned, impudent, or unadvised he is, the more he is esteemed, even among princes. For medicine, especially as it is now practised by most men, is nothing but a branch of flattery, no less so than rhetoric. Next to them, the second place is given to our lawyers, if not the first; whose profession, though I say it myself, most men laugh at as the ass of philosophy; yet there's scarcely any business, either great or small, but is managed by these asses. These purchase their great titles, while in the meantime the theologian, having run through the whole body of religious thought, sits gnawing a radish as he wars with lice and fleas.

Why should I bother discussing our professors of arts? Self-love is so natural to them all that they had rather part with their father's land than their foolish opinions; but especially actors, fiddlers, orators, and poets, of which the more ignorant each of them is, the more insolently he pleases himself, that is to say struts and spreads out his plumes. And like will to like; nay, the more foolish anything is, the more it is admired; the greater number being ever tickled at the worst things, because, as I said before, most men are so subject to Folly. And therefore if the more foolish a man is, the more he pleases himself and is admired by others, to what purpose should he beat his brains about true knowledge, which first will cost him dear, and next render him the more troublesome and less confident, and, lastly, please only a few?

And now that I consider it, nature has planted, not only in particular men but even in every nation, and scarcely any city is without it, a kind of common self-love. And thus it is that the English, besides other things, lay claim to beauty, music, and feasting. The Scots are proud of their nobility, blood-ties to the crown, and dialectical subtleties. The French think themselves the only well-bred men. The Parisians, excluding all others, arrogate to themselves the only knowledge of theological learning. The Italians affirm they are the only masters of good letters and eloquence, and flatter themselves on this account, that of all others they only are not barbarous. In which kind of happiness those of Rome claim the first place, still dreaming to themselves of somewhat, I know not what, of old Rome. The Venetians fancy themselves happy in the reputation of their nobility. The Greeks, as if they were the only authors of all learning, swell themselves with titles of ancient heroes. The Turks, and all that scum of the truly barbarous, claim for themselves the only true religion and laugh at Christians as superstitious. To this day the Jews confidently expect the coming of the Messiah and obstinately quarrel over their law of Moses. The Spaniards give place to none in the reputation of soldiery. The Germans pride themselves in their tallness of stature and skill in magic.

And not to list every instance, you see, I think, how much satisfaction this Self-love gives to mankind and, in this, her sister Flattery is nearly her equal.

Now if I seem to anyone to have spoken more boldly than truthfully, let us, if you please, look a little into the lives of men, and it will easily appear not only how much they owe to me, but how much they esteem me even from the highest to the lowest. And yet we will not run over the lives of everyone, for that would be too long; but only some few of the great ones, from whence we shall easily conjecture the rest.

For to what purpose is it to say anything of the common people, who without dispute are wholly mine? For they abound everywhere with so many several sorts of Folly, and are every day so busy in inventing new, that a thousand Demokritos's are too few for so general a laughter, though we need one more Demokritos to laugh at the thousand. It is almost incredible what sport and delight they daily provide for the Gods; for though the Gods set aside their sober morning hours to dispatch business and receive prayers, yet when they begin to be well soused with nectar, and cannot think of anything that's serious, they get themselves up into some part of heaven that's better for viewing, and then look down upon the actions of men. Nor is there anything that pleases them better. Good, good! What an excellent sight it is! How many varieties of fools! For I myself sometimes sit among the poetical Gods.

Here's one desperately in love with a young wench, and the more she slights him the more outrageously he loves her. Another marries a woman's money, not her self. Another's jealousy keeps more eyes on her than Argos. Another becomes a fulltime mourner, and how foolishly he carries it! Nay, hires others to bear him company, to make it more ridiculous. Another weeps over his mother-in-law's grave. Another spends all he can on his belly, to be the more hungry after it. Another thinks there is no happiness but in sleep and idleness. Another frets about other men's business, and neglects his own. Another thinks himself rich in refinancing and buying on credit, as we say borrowing from Peter to pay Paul, and in a short time becomes bankrupt. Another starves himself to enrich his heir. Another for a small and uncertain gain exposes his life to the dangers of seas and storms, which yet no money can restore. Another had rather get riches by war than live peaceably at home.

And some there are that think money easiest attained by courting childless old men with presents; and others again by making love to rich old women; both which afford the Gods most excellent pastime, to see them cheated by those persons they thought to have outwitted. But the most foolish and basest of all others are our merchants, to wit such as venture on everything be it never so dishonest, and manage it no better; who though they lie unceasingly, swear and perjure themselves, steal, deceive, and cheat, yet shuffle themselves into the first rank, and all because they have gold rings on their fingers. Nor are they without their flattering friars that admire them and give them openly the title of honorable, in hopes, no doubt, to get some small snip of it themselves.

There are also a kind of Pythagoreans, with whom all things are held in common, that if they get anything under their cloaks, they make no more scruple of carrying it away than if it were their own by inheritance. There are others too that are only rich in wishful thinking, and while they fancy to themselves pleasant dreams, conceive that enough to make them happy. Some desire to be accounted wealthy abroad, and are yet ready to starve at home. One makes what haste he can to fritter his money away, and another rakes it together by right or wrong. This man is ever laboring for public honors; and another lies sleeping in a chimney corner. A great many undertake endless lawsuits and outvie one another who shall most enrich the crooked judge or corrupt lawyer. One is all for innovations; and another for some great he-knows-not-what. Another leaves his wife and children at home, and goes to Jerusalem, Rome, or on a pilgrimage to St. James's, where he has no business.

In short, if a man like Menippus of old could look down from the moon, and behold those innumerable rufflings of mankind, he would think he saw a swarm of flies and gnats quarreling among themselves, fighting, laying traps for one another, snatching, playing, wantoning, growing up, growing old, and dying. Nor is it to be believed what stir, what commotions this little creature raises, and yet in how short a time it comes to nothing at all; while sometimes war, other times pestilence, sweeps many thousands away.

But let me be most foolish myself, and one whom Demokritos may not only laugh at but deride, if I go one foot further in the discovery of the follies and madnesses of the common people. I'll betake me to them that carry the reputation of wise men, and hunt after that "golden bough," as says the proverb. Among whom the school teachers hold the first place, a generation of men than whom nothing would be more miserable, nothing more wretched, nothing more hated of the Gods, did not I allay the troubles of that pitiful profession with a certain kind of pleasant madness. For they are not only subject to those five afflictions with which Homer begins his *Iliad*, but six hundred; as being ever hungry and slovenly in their schools—schools, did I say? Nay, rather prisons, sweat shops, or torture chambers—grown old among a company of boys, deaf with their noise, and wasted away in the stench and nastiness. And yet by my courtesy it is that they think themselves the most excellent of all men; so greatly do they please themselves in frightening a company of fearful boys with a thundering voice and fierce scowls; tormenting them with switches, rods, and whips; and, laying about them without fear or wit, imitate the ass in the lion's skin. In the meantime all that nastiness seems absolute spruceness, that stench a perfume, and that miserable slavery of theirs a kingdom, and such too as they would not exchange their tyranny for the empires of Phalaris or Dionysos.

Nor are they less happy in that new opinion they have taken up of being learned; for whereas most of them beat into boys' heads nothing but nonsense, yet, ye good Gods! what Palemon, what Donatus, do they not scorn in comparison with themselves? And so, I know not by what tricks, they bring it about to their boys' foolish mothers and dolt-headed fathers they pass for such as they fancy themselves.

Perhaps I had better pass over our theologians in silence and not stir this pool, or touch this fair but unsavory stinkweed; as a kind of men that are supercilious beyond comparison, and to that too, implacable; lest setting them about my ears, they attack me with proofs and force me to recant, which if I refuse, they straight away pronounce me a heretic. For this is the thunderbolt with which they frighten those whom they are resolved not to favor. And truly, though there are few others that less willingly acknowledge the kindnesses I have done for them, yet even these too are bound to me for no ordinary benefits; meanwhile being happy in their own opinion, and as if they dwelt in the third heaven, they look with haughtiness on all others as poor creeping things, and could almost find in their hearts to pity them.

And next come those that commonly call themselves "religious" and "monks"; most false in both titles, when a large part of them are farthest from religion, and no men swarm thicker in all places than themselves. Nor can I think of anything that could be more miserable, did I not support them in so many ways. For whereas all men detest them so much, that they take it for ill luck to meet one of them by chance, yet such is their happiness that they flatter themselves. For first, they reckon it one of the main points of piety if they are so illiterate that they can't so much as read. And then when they run over their Offices, which they carry about them, rather by rote than understanding, they believe the Gods more than ordinarily pleased with their braying. And some there are among them that make a great show about their pious poverty, yet roam up and down for the bread they eat; nay, there is scarcely an inn, coach, or ship into which they intrude not, to the no small damage of the common-wealth of beggars. And yet, like pleasant fellows, with all this vileness, ignorance, rudeness, and impudence, they represent to us, for so they call it, the lives of the apostles.

And as to the popes, what should I mention about them? Than most of whom though there be nothing more indebted, more servile, more witless, more contemptible, yet they would seem as they were the most excellent of all others. And yet in this only thing no men more modest, in that they are contented to wear about them gold, jewels, purple, and those other marks of virtue and wisdom, but for the study of the things themselves, they remit it to others; thinking it happiness enough for them that they can call the King Master, having learned the cringe *à la mode,* know when and where to use those titles of Your Grace, My Lord, Your Magnificence; in a word that they are past all shame and can flatter pleasantly. For these are the arts that bespeak a man truly noble and a model courtier.

But if you look into their manner of life you'll find them mere sots, as debauched as Penelope's wooers. They sleep till noon, and have their mercenary Levite come to their bedside, where he chops over his Matins before they are half up. Then to breakfast, which is scarcely done when dinner is ready for them. From thence they go to dice, tables, cards, or entertain themselves with jesters, fools, and gamblers. In the meantime they have one or two snacks and then supper, and after that a banquet, and it would be well, by Jupiter, that there be no more than one.

And in this manner do their hours, days, months, years, age slide away without the least irksomeness. Nay, I have sometimes gone away many inches fatter, to see them speak big words; while each of the ladies believes herself so much nearer the Gods, by how much the longer train she trails after her; while one cardinal edges out another, that he may get the nearer to Jupiter himself; and every one of them pleases himself the more by how much heavier is the gold chain he drapes on his shoulders, as if he meant to show his strength as well as his wealth.

But I forget myself and run beyond my bounds. Though yet, if I shall seem to have spoken anything more boldly or impertinently than I ought, be pleased to consider that not only Folly but a woman said it; remembering in the meantime that Greek proverb, "Sometimes a fool may speak a word in season," unless perhaps you'll say this concerns not women. I see you expect an Epilogue, but give me leave to tell you that you are mistaken if you think I remember anything of what I have said, having foolishly bolted out such a hodgepodge of words. It is an old proverb, "I hate one that remembers what's done over the cup." This is a new one of my own making: "I hate a man that remembers what he hears." Wherefore farewell, clap your hands, live, and drink lustily, my most excellent Disciples of Folly.

STUDY QUESTIONS

1. Try to imagine that you are a sixteenth-century college professor. What would be your reaction to Folly's description of "professors of arts." Does her account fit any of your professors?
2. Does Folly's description of "school teachers" (elementary and secondary) still have any truth today? To what extent?
3. What does the great popularity of this satire indicate about the literate public of that time? Would a twentieth-century *Praise of Folly* be equally popular? Why or why not?

LITERARY SELECTION 44

The Prince

Niccolò Machiavelli, 1469–1527

The thorough humanistic education of Niccolò Machiavelli and his own political experience helped him to reevaluate the role of the state. For medieval thinkers, the church looked after the spiritual salvation of its flock, the state attended to its physical well-being, and everything operated under Divine Law. Machiavelli observed that the Romans had encouraged civic duties and civic pride, but that Christians were supposed to detach themselves from public affairs. The obvious solution was to secularize politics, to make the state preeminent and its own justification, and to have it function in accordance with the observable facts of human nature. Machiavelli wrote *The Prince* as a guide for the man he and many other Italians longed to see: a ruler who would unite the squabbling Italian city-states under a central jurisdiction. This was a manual for action, the first objective analysis of how political power was obtained and kept. Machiavelli's brilliant analysis is detached, objective, and non-judgmental. It gave the Renaissance its first candid picture of human nature with all the idealism, both of medievalism and of humanism, stripped away. Though Italy did not achieve unification until the nineteenth century, Machiavelli's theory of absolutism became a model for the rest of Europe.

Machiavelli dedicated *The Prince* to Lorenzo de' Medici, the Magnificent, Duke of Urbino (1492–1519), who should not be confused with his illustrious grandfather, Lorenzo the Magnificent. The Duke of Urbino never measured up to Machiavelli's estimation of his potential and is remembered today by this seminal work. The translation is by Peter Bondanella and Mark Musa.

On New Principalities Acquired by One's Own Arms and Skill

No one should marvel if, in speaking of principalities that are totally new as to their prince and organization, I use the most illustrious examples; since men almost always tread the paths made by others and proceed in their affairs by imitation, although they are not completely able to stay on the path of others nor attain the skill of those they imitate, a prudent man should always enter those paths taken by great men and imitate those who have been most excellent, so that if one's own skill does not match theirs, at least it will have the smell of it; and he should proceed like those prudent archers who, aware of the strength of their bow when the target they are aiming at seems too distant, set their sights much higher than the designated target, not in order to reach to such a height with their arrow but rather to be able, with the aid of such a high aim, to strike the target.

I say, therefore, that in completely new principalities, where there is a new prince, one finds in maintaining them more or less difficulty according to the greater or lesser skill of the one who acquires them. And because this act of transition from private citizen to prince presupposes either ingenuity or fortune, it appears that either the one or the other of these two things should, in part, mitigate many of the problems; nevertheless, he who relies upon fortune less maintains his position best. Things are also facilitated when the prince, having no other dominions to govern, is constrained to come to live there in person. But to come to those who, by means of their own skill and not because of fortune, have become princes, I say that the most admirable are Moses, Cyrus, Romulus, Theseus, and the like. And although we should not discuss Moses, since he was a mere executor of things ordered by God, nevertheless he must be admired, if for nothing but that grace which made him worthy of talking with God. But let us consider Cyrus and the others who have acquired or founded kingdoms; you will find them all admirable; and if their deeds and their particular institutions are considered, they will not appear different from those of Moses, who had so great a guide. And examining their deeds and their lives, one can see that they received nothing from fortune except the opportunity, which gave them the material they could mold into whatever form they desired; and without that opportunity the strength of their spirit would have been extinguished, and without that strength the opportunity would have come in vain.

It was therefore necessary for Moses to find the people of Israel in Egypt slaves and oppressed by the Egyptians in order that they might be disposed to follow him to escape this servitude. It was necessary for Romulus not to stay in Alba and to be exposed at birth so that he might become King of Rome and founder of that nation. It was necessary for Cyrus to find the Persians discontented with the empire of the Medes, and the Medes soft and effeminate after a lengthy peace. Theseus could not have shown his skill if he had not found the Athenians scattered. These opportunities, therefore, made these men successful, and their outstanding ingenuity made that opportunity known to them, whereby their nations were ennobled and became prosperous.

Like these men, those who become princes through their skill acquire the principality with difficulty, but they hold on to it easily; and the difficulties they encounter in acquiring the principality grow, in part, out of the new institutions and methods they are obliged to introduce in order to found their state and their security. And one should bear in mind that there is nothing more difficult to execute, nor more dubious of success, nor more dangerous to administer than to introduce a new order of things; for he who introduces it has all those who profit from the old order as his enemies, and he has only lukewarm allies in all those who might profit from the new. This lukewarmness partly stems from fear of their adversaries, who have the law on their side, and partly from the skepticism of men, who do not truly believe in new things unless they have actually had personal experience of them. Therefore, it happens that whenever those who are enemies have the chance to attack, they do so enthusiastically, whereas those others defend hesitantly, so that they, together with the prince, are in danger.

It is necessary, however, if we desire to examine this subject thoroughly, to observe whether these innovators act on their own or are dependent on others: that is, if they are forced to beg or are able to use power in conducting their affairs. In the first case, they always come to a bad end and never accomplish anything; but when they depend on their own resources and can use power, then only seldom do they find themselves in peril. From this comes the fact that all armed prophets were victorious and the unarmed came to ruin. Besides what has been said, people are fickle by nature; and it is simple to convince them of something, but difficult to hold them in that conviction; and, therefore, affairs should be managed in such a way that when they no longer believe, they can be made to believe by force. Moses, Cyrus, Theseus, and Romulus could not have made their institutions long respected if they had been unarmed; as in our times happened to Brother Girolamo Savonarola, who was ruined by his new institutions when the populace began no longer to believe in them, since he had no way of holding steady those who had believed nor of making the disbelievers believe. Therefore, such men have great problems in getting ahead, and they meet all their dangers as they proceed, and they must overcome them with their skill; but once they have overcome them and have begun to be respected, having removed those who were envious of their merits, they remain powerful, secure, honoured, and happy.

On New Principalities Acquired with the Arms of Others and by Fortune

Those private citizens who become princes through fortune alone do so with little effort, but they maintain their position only with a great deal; they meet no obstacles along their way since they fly to success, but all their problems arise when they have arrived. And these are the men who are granted a state either because they have money or because they enjoy the favour of him who grants it: this occurred to many in Greece in the cities of Ionia and the Hellespont, where Darius created princes in order that he might hold these cities for his security and glory; in like manner were set up those emperors who from private citizens came to power by bribing the soldiers. Such men depend solely upon two very uncertain and unstable things: the will and the fortune of him who granted them the state; they do not know how and are not able to maintain their position. They do not know how, since if men are not of great intelligence and ingenuity, it is not reasonable that they know how to rule, having always lived as private citizens; they are not able to, since they do not have forces that are friendly and faithful. Besides, states that rise quickly, just as all the other things of nature that are born and grow rapidly, cannot have roots and ramifications; the first bad weather kills them, unless these men who have suddenly become princes, as I have noted, are of such ability that they know how to prepare themselves quickly and to preserve what fortune has put in their laps, and to construct afterwards those foundations that others have built before becoming princes.

Regarding the two methods just listed for becoming a prince, by skill or by fortune, I should like to offer two recent examples: these are Francesco Sforza and Cesare Borgia. Francesco, through the required means and with a great deal of ingenuity, became Duke of Milan from his station as a private citizen, and that which he had acquired with countless hardships he maintained with little trouble. On the other hand, Cesare Borgia (commonly called Duke Valentino) acquired the state through the favour and help of his father, and when this no longer existed, he lost it, and this despite the fact that he did everything and used every means that a prudent and skillful man ought to use in order to root himself securely in those states that the arms and fortune of others had granted him. Because, as stated above, anyone who does not lay his foundations beforehand could do so later only with great skill, although this would be done with inconvenience to the architect and danger to the building. If, therefore, we consider all the steps taken by the Duke, we shall see that he laid sturdy foundations for his future power; and I do not judge it useless to discuss them, for I would not know of any better precepts to give to a new prince than the example of his deeds; and if he did not succeed in his plans, it was not his fault, but was instead the result of an extraordinary and extreme instance of ill fortune.

On Those Who Have Become Princes Through Wickedness

But because there are yet two more ways one can from an ordinary citizen become prince, which cannot completely be attributed to either fortune or skill, I believe they should not be left unmentioned, although one of them will be discussed at greater length in a treatise on republics. These two are: when one becomes prince through some wicked and nefarious means or when a private citizen becomes prince of his native city through the favour of his fellow citizens.

In our own days, during the reign of Alexander VI, Oliverotto of Fermo, who many years before had been left as a child without a father, was brought up by his maternal uncle, Giovanni Fogliani. While still very young he was sent to serve as a soldier under Paulo Vitelli so that, once he was versed in that skill, he might attain some outstanding military position. Then, after Paulo died, he served under his brother, Vitellozzo; and in a very brief time, because of his intelligence and his vigorous body and mind, he became the commander of his troops. But since he felt it was servile to work for others, he decided to seize Fermo with the aid of some citizens of Fermo who preferred servitude to the liberty of their native city, and with the assistance of the followers of Vitellozzo; and he wrote to Giovanni Fogliani that, having been away many years from home, he wished to come to see him and his city and to inspect his own inheritance; and since he had exerted himself for no other reason than to acquire glory, he wanted to arrive in honourable fashion, accompanied by an escort of a hundred horsemen from among his friends and servants so that his fellow citizens might see that he had not spent his time in vain; and he begged his uncle to arrange for an honourable reception from the people of Fermo, one which might bring honour not only to Giovanni but also to himself, being his pupil. Giovanni, therefore, in no way failed in his duty toward his nephew: he had him received in honourable fashion by the people of Fermo, and he gave him rooms in his own house. Oliverotto, after a few days had passed and he had secretly made the preparations necessary for his forthcoming wickedness, gave a magnificent banquet to which he invited Giovanni Fogliani and all of the first citizens of Fermo. And when the meal and all the other entertainment customary at such banquets were completed, Oliverotto, according to plan, began to discuss serious matters, speaking of the greatness of Pope Alexander and his son, Cesare, and of their undertakings. After Giovanni and the others had replied to his comments, he suddenly rose up, announcing that these were matters to be discussed in a more secluded place; and he retired into another room, followed by Giovanni and all the other citizens. No sooner were they seated than from secret places in the room out came soldiers who killed Giovanni and all the others. After this murder, Oliverotto mounted his horse, paraded through the town, and besieged the chief officials in the government palace; so that out of fear they were forced to obey him and to constitute a government of which he made himself prince. And when all those were killed who, because they were discontented, might have harmed him, he strengthened himself by instituting new civil and military institutions; so that, in the space of the year that he held the principality, not only was he secure in the city of Fermo, but he had become feared by all its neighbours. His expulsion would have been difficult if he had not permitted himself to be tricked by Cesare Borgia, when at Sinigaglia, as was noted above, the Duke captured the Orsini and the Vitelli; there he, too, was captured, a year after he committed the parricide, and together with Vitellozzo, who had been his teacher in ingenuity and wickedness, he was strangled.

One might wonder how anyone, after so many betrayals and cruelties, could live for such a long time secure in their cities and defend themselves from outside enemies without being plotted against by their own citizens; many others, using cruel means, were unable even in peaceful times to hold on to their state, not to speak of the uncertain times of war. I believe that this depends on whether cruelty be well or badly used. Well used are those cruelties (if it is permitted to speak well of evil) that are carried out in a single stroke, done out of necessity to protect oneself, and are not continued but are instead converted into the greatest possible benefits for the subjects. Badly used are those cruelties which, although being few at the outset, grow with the passing of time instead of disappearing. Those who follow the first method can remedy their condition with God and with men, the others cannot possibly survive.

Wherefore it is to be noted that in taking a state its conqueror should weigh all the harmful things he must do and do them all at once so as not to have to repeat them every day, and in not repeating them to be able to make men feel secure and win them over with the benefits he bestows upon them. Anyone who does otherwise, either out of timidity or because of poor advice, is always obliged to keep his knife in his hand; nor can he ever count upon his subjects, who, because of their fresh and continual injuries, cannot feel secure with him. Injuries, therefore, should be inflicted all at the same time, for the less they are tasted, the less they offend; and benefits should be distributed a bit at a time in order that they may be savored fully. And a prince should, above all, live with his subjects in such a way that no unforeseen event, either good or bad, may make him alter his course; for when emergencies arise in adverse conditions, you are not in time to resort to cruelty, and that good you do will help you little, since it be judged a forced measure and you will earn from it no thanks whatsoever.

On the Civil Principality

But coming to the second instance, when a private citizen, not through wickedness or any other intolerable violence, but with the favour of his fellow citizens, becomes prince of his native city (this can be called a civil principality, the acquisition of which neither depends completely upon skill nor upon fortune, but instead upon a mixture of shrewdness and luck), I maintain that one reaches this princedom either with the favour of the common people or with that of the nobility. For these two different humours are found in every body politic; and they arise from the fact that the people do not wish to be commanded or oppressed by the nobles, and the nobles desire to command and to oppress the people; and from these two opposed appetites there arises one of three effects: either a principality or liberty or anarchy.

A principality is brought about either by the common people or by the nobility, depending on which of the two parties has the opportunity. For when the nobles see that they cannot resist the populace, they begin to support one among them and make him prince in order to be able, under his protection, to satisfy their appetites. The common people as well, seeing that they cannot resist the nobility, give their support to one man and make him prince in order to have the protection of his authority. He who attains the principality with the aid of the nobility maintains it with more difficulty than he who becomes prince with the assistance of the common people, for he finds himself a prince amidst many who feel themselves to be his equals, and because of this he can neither govern nor manage them as he wishes. But he who attains the principality through popular favour finds himself alone and has around him either no one or very few who are not ready to obey him. Moreover, one cannot honestly satisfy the nobles without harming others, but the common people can certainly be satisfied: their desire is more just than that of the nobles—the former want not to be oppressed and the latter want to oppress. Moreover, a prince can never make himself secure when the people are his enemy because they are so many; he can make himself secure against the nobles because they are so few. The worst that a prince can expect from a hostile people is to be abandoned by them; but with a hostile nobility not only does he have to fear being abandoned but also that they will unite against him; for, being more perceptive and shrewder, they always have time to save themselves, to seek the favours of the side they believe will win. Furthermore, a prince must always live with the same common people; but he can easily do without the same nobles, having the power to create them and to destroy them from day to day and to take away and give back their prestige as he sees fit.

A Prince's Duty Concerning Military Matters

A prince, therefore, must not have any other object nor any other thought, nor must he take anything as his profession but war, its institutions, and its disciplines; because that is the only profession which befits one who commands; and it is of such importance that not only does it maintain those who were born princes, but many times it enables men of private station to rise to that position; and, on the other hand, it is evident that when princes have given more thought to personal luxuries than to arms, they have lost their state. And the most important cause of losing it is to neglect this art; and the way to acquire it is to be well-versed in this art.

Francesco Sforza became Duke of Milan from being a private citizen because he was armed; his successors, since they avoided the inconveniences of arms, became private citizens after having been dukes. For, among the other bad effects it causes, being unarmed makes you despised; this is one of those infamies a prince should guard himself against, as will be treated below: for between an armed and an unarmed man there is no comparison whatsoever, and it is not reasonable for an armed man to obey an unarmed man willingly, nor that an unarmed man should be safe among armed servants; since, when the former is suspicious and the latter are contemptuous, it is impossible for them to work well together. And therefore, a prince who does not understand military matters, besides the other misfortunes already noted, cannot be esteemed by his own soldiers, nor can he trust them.

He should, therefore, never take his mind from this exercise of war, and in peacetime he must train himself more than in time of war; this can be done in two ways: one by action, the other by the mind. And as far as actions are concerned, besides keeping his soldiers well disciplined and trained, he must always be out hunting, and must accustom his body to hardships in this manner; and he must also learn the nature of the terrain, and know how mountains slope, how valleys open, how plains lie, and understand the nature of rivers and swamps; and he should devote much attention to such activities. Such knowledge is useful in two ways: first, one learns to know one's own country and can better understand how to defend it; second, with the knowledge and experience of the terrain, one can easily comprehend the characteristics of any other terrain that it is necessary to explore for the first time; for the hills, valleys, plains, rivers, and swamps of Tuscany, for instance, have certain similarities to those of other provinces; so that by knowing the lie of the land in one province one can easily understand it in others. And a prince who lacks this ability lacks the most important quality in a leader; because this skill teaches you to find the enemy, choose a campsite, lead troops, organize them for battle, and besiege towns to your own advantage.

On Those Things for Which Men, and Particularly Princes, Are Praised or Blamed

Now there remains to be examined what should be the methods and procedures of a prince in dealing with his subjects and friends. And because I know that many have written about this, I am afraid that by writing about it again I shall be thought of as presumptuous, since in discussing this material I depart radically from the procedures of others. But since my intention is to write something useful for anyone who understands it, it seemed more suitable to me to search after the effectual truth of the matter rather than its imagined one. And many writers have imagined for themselves republics and principalities that have never been seen nor known to exist in reality; for there is such a gap between how one lives and how one ought to live that anyone who abandons what is done for what ought to be done learns his ruin rather than his preservation: for a man who wishes to profess goodness at all times will come to ruin among so many who are not good. Hence it is necessary for a prince who wishes to maintain his position to learn how not to be good, and to use this knowledge or not to use it according to necessity.

Leaving aside, therefore, the imagined things concerning a prince, and taking into account those that are true, I say that all men, when they are spoken of, and particularly princes, since they are placed on a higher level, are judged by some of these qualities which bring them either blame or praise. And this is why one is considered generous, another miserly (to use a Tuscan word, since "avaricious" in our language is still used to mean one who wishes to acquire by means of theft; we call "miserly" one who excessively avoids using what he has); one is considered a giver, the other rapacious; one cruel, another merciful; one treacherous, another faithful; one effeminate and cowardly, another bold and courageous; one humane, another haughty; one lascivious, another chaste; one trustworthy, another frivolous; one religious, another unbelieving; and the like. And I know that everyone will admit that it would be a very praiseworthy thing to find in a prince, of the qualities mentioned above, those that are held to be good; but since it is neither possible to have them nor to observe them all completely, because the human condition does not permit it, a prince must be prudent enough to know how to escape the bad reputation of those vices that would lose the state for him, and must protect himself from those that will not lose it for him, if this is possible; but if he cannot, he need not concern himself unduly if he ignores these less serious vices. And, moreover, he need not worry about incurring the bad reputation of those vices without which it would be difficult to hold his state; since, carefully taking everything into account, he will discover that something which appears to be a virtue, if pursued, will end in his destruction; while some other thing which seems to be a vice, if pursued, will result in his safety and his well-being.

On Generosity and Miserliness

Beginning, therefore, with the first of the above-mentioned qualities, I say that it would be good to be considered generous; nevertheless, generosity used in such a manner as to give you a reputation for it will harm you; because if it is employed virtuously and as one should employ it, it will not be recognized and you will not avoid the reproach of its opposite. And so, if a prince wants to maintain his reputation for generosity among men, it is necessary for him not to neglect any possible means of lavish display; in so doing such a prince will always use up all his resources and he will be obliged, eventually, if he wishes to maintain his reputation for generosity, to burden the people with excessive taxes and to do everything possible to raise funds. This will begin to make him hateful to his subjects, and, becoming impoverished, he will not be much esteemed by anyone; so that, as a consequence of his generosity, having offended many and rewarded few, he will feel the effects of any slight unrest and will be ruined at the first sign of danger; recognizing this and wishing to alter his policies, he immediately runs the risk of being reproached as a miser.

A prince, therefore, being unable to use this virtue of generosity in a manner which will not harm himself, if he is known for it, should, if he is wise, not worry about being called a miser; for with time he will come to be considered more generous once it is evident that, as a result of his parsimony, his income is sufficient, he can defend himself from anyone who makes war against him, and he can undertake enterprises without overburdening his people, so that he comes to be generous with all those from whom he takes nothing, who are countless, and miserly with all those to whom he gives nothing, who are few. In our times we have not seen great deeds accomplished except by those who were considered miserly; the others were failures. Pope Julius II, although he made use of his reputation for generosity in order to gain the papacy, then decided not to maintain it in order to be able to wage war; the present King of France has waged many wars without imposing extra taxes on his subjects, only because his habitual parsimony has provided for the additional expenditures; the present King of Spain, if he had been considered generous, would not have engaged in or won so many campaigns.

Therefore, in order not to have to rob his subjects, to be able to defend himself, not to become poor and contemptible, and not to be forced to become rapacious, a prince must consider it of little importance if he incurs the reputation of being a miser, for this is one of those vices that permits him to rule. And if someone were to say: Caesar with his generosity achieved imperial power, and many others, because they were generous and known to be so, achieved very high positions; I would reply: you are either already a prince or you are on the way to becoming one; in the first instance such generosity is damaging; in the second it is very necessary to be thought generous. And Caesar was one of those who wanted to gain the principality of Rome; but if, after obtaining this, he had lived and had not moderated his expenditures, he would have destroyed his rule. And if someone were to reply: there have existed many princes who have accomplished great deeds with their armies who have been reputed to be generous; I would answer you: a prince either spends his own money and that of his subjects or that of others; in the first case he must be economical; in the second he must not restrain any part of his generosity. And for that prince who goes out with his soldiers and lives by looting, sacking, and ransoms, who controls the property of others, such generosity is necessary; otherwise he would not be followed by his troops. And with what does not belong to you or to your subjects you can be a more liberal giver, as were Cyrus, Caesar, and Alexander; for spending the wealth of others does not lessen your reputation but adds to it; only the spending of your own is what harms you. And there is nothing that uses itself up faster than generosity, for as you employ it you lose the means of employing it, and you become either poor and despised or else, in order to escape poverty, you become rapacious and hated. And above all other things a prince must guard himself against being despised and hated; and generosity leads you to both one and the other. So it is wiser to live with the reputation of a miser, which produces reproach without hatred, than to be forced to incur the reputation of rapacity, which produces reproach along with hatred, because you want to be considered generous.

On Cruelty and Mercy, and Whether It Is Better to Be Loved Than to Be Feared or the Contrary

Proceeding to the other qualities mentioned above, I say that every prince must desire to be considered merciful and not cruel; nevertheless, he must take care not to misuse this mercy. Cesare Borgia was considered cruel; none the less, his cruelty had brought order to Romagna, united it, restored it to peace and obedience. If we examine this carefully, we shall see that he was more merciful than the Florentine people who, in order to avoid being considered cruel, allowed the destruction of Pistoia. Therefore, a prince must not worry about the reproach of cruelty when it is a matter of keeping his subjects united and loyal; for with a very few examples of cruelty he will be more compassionate than those who, out of excessive mercy, permit disorders to continue, from which arise murders and plundering; for these usually harm the community at large, while the executions that come from the prince harm particular individuals. And the new prince, above all other princes, cannot escape the reputation of being called cruel, since new states are full of dangers. And Virgil, through Dido, states: "My difficult condition and the newness of my rule make me act in such a manner, and to set guards over my land on all sides."

Nevertheless, a prince must be cautious in believing and in acting, nor should he be afraid of his own shadow; and he should proceed in such a manner, tempered by prudence and humanity, so that too much trust may not render him imprudent nor too much distrust render him intolerable.

From this arises an argument: whether it is better to be loved than to be feared, or the contrary. I reply that one should like to be both one and the other; but since it is difficult to join them together, it is much safer to be feared than to be loved when one of the two must be lacking. For one can generally say this about men: that they are ungrateful, fickle, simulators and deceivers, avoiders of danger, greedy for gain; and while you work for their good they are completely yours, offering you their blood, their property, their lives, and their sons, as I said earlier, when danger is far away; but when it comes nearer to you they turn away. And that prince who bases his power entirely on their words, finding himself completely without other preparations, comes to ruin; for friendships that are acquired by a price and not by greatness and nobility of character are purchased but are not owned, and at the proper moment they cannot be spent. And men are less hesitant about harming someone who makes himself loved than one who makes himself feared because love is held together by a chain of obligation which, since men are wretched creatures, is broken on every occasion in which their own interests are concerned; but fear is sustained by a dread of punishment which will never abandon you.

A prince must nevertheless make himself feared in such a manner that he will avoid hatred, even if he does not acquire love; since to be feared and not to be hated can very well be combined; and this will always be so when he keeps his hands off the property and the women of his citizens and his subjects. And if he must take someone's life, he should do so when there is proper justification and manifest cause; but, above all, he should avoid seizing the property of others; for men forget more quickly the death of their father than the loss of their patrimony. Moreover, reasons for seizing their property are never lacking; and he who begins to live by stealing always finds a reason for taking what belongs to others; on the contrary, reasons for taking a life are rarer and disappear sooner.

But when the prince is with his armies and has under his command a multitude of troops, then it is absolutely necessary that he not worry about being considered cruel; for without that reputation he will never keep an army united or prepared for any combat.

I conclude, therefore, returning to the problem of being feared and loved, that since men love at their own pleasure and fear at the pleasure of the prince, a wise prince should build his foundation upon that which belongs to him, not upon that which belongs to others: he must strive only to avoid hatred, as has been said.

How a Prince Should Keep His Word

How praiseworthy it is for a prince to keep his word and to live by integrity and not by deceit everyone knows; nevertheless, one sees from the experience of our times that the princes who have accomplished great deeds are those who have cared little for keeping their promises and who have known how to manipulate the minds of men by shrewdness; and in the end they have surpassed those who laid their foundations upon loyalty.

You must, therefore, know that there are two means of fighting: one according to the laws, the other with force; the first way is proper to man, the second to beasts; but because the first, in many cases, is not sufficient, it becomes necessary to have recourse to the second. Therefore, a prince must know how to use wisely the natures of the beast and the man. This policy was taught to princes allegorically by the ancient writers, who described how Achilles and many other ancient princes were given to Chiron the Centaur to be raised and taught under his discipline. This can only mean that, having a half-beast and a half-man as a teacher, a prince must know how to employ the nature of the one and the other; and the one without the other cannot endure.

Since, then, a prince must know how to make good use of the nature of the beast, he should choose from among the beasts the fox and the lion; for the lion cannot defend himself from traps and the fox cannot protect itself from wolves. It is therefore necessary to be a fox in order to recognize the traps and a lion in order to frighten the wolves. Those who play only the part of the lion do not understand matters. A wise ruler, therefore, cannot and should not keep his word when such an observance of faith would be to his disadvantage and when the reasons which made him promise are removed. And if men were all good, this rule would not be good; but since men are a contemptible lot and will not keep their promises to you, you likewise need not keep yours to them. A prince never lacks legitimate reasons to break his promise. Of this one could cite an endless number of modern examples to show how many pacts, how many promises have been made null and void because of the infidelity of princes; and he who has known best how to use the fox has come to a better end. But it is necessary to know how to disguise this nature well and to be a great hypocrite and a liar: and men are so simple-minded and so controlled by their present needs that one who deceives will always find another who will allow himself to be deceived.

I do not wish to remain silent about one of these recent instances. Alexander VI did nothing else, he thought about nothing else, except to deceive men, and he always found the occasion to do this. And there never was a man who had more forcefulness in his oaths, who affirmed a thing with more promises, and who honoured his word less; nevertheless, his tricks always succeeded perfectly since he was well acquainted with this aspect of the world.

Therefore, it is not necessary for a prince to have all of the above-mentioned qualities, but it is very necessary for him to appear to have them. Furthermore, I shall be so bold as to assert this: that having them and practising them at all times is harmful; and appearing to have them is useful; for instance, to seem merciful, faithful, humane, trustworthy, religious, and to be so; but his mind should be disposed in such a way that should it become necessary not to be so, he will be able and know how to change to the contrary. And it is essential to understand this: that a prince, and especially a new prince, cannot observe all those things for which men are considered good, for in order to maintain the state he is often obliged to act against his promise, against charity, against humanity, and against religion. And, therefore, it is necessary that he have a mind ready to turn itself according to the way the winds of fortune and the changeability of affairs require him; and, as I said above, as long as it is possible, he should not stray from the good, but he should know how to enter into evil when necessity commands.

A prince, therefore, must be very careful never to let anything slip from his lips which is not full of the five qualities mentioned above: he should appear, upon seeing and hearing him, to be all mercy, all faithfulness, all integrity, all kindness, all religion. And there is nothing more necessary than to seem to possess this last quality. And men in general judge more by their eyes than their hands; for everyone can see but few can feel. Everyone sees what you seem to be, few touch upon what you are, and those few do not dare to contradict the opinion of the many who have the majesty of the state to defend them; and in the actions of all men, and especially of princes, where there is no impartial arbiter, one must consider the final result. Let a prince therefore act to conquer and to maintain the state; his methods will always be judged honourable and will be praised by all; for ordinary people are always deceived by appearances and by the outcome of a thing; and in the world there is nothing but ordinary people; and there is no room for the few, while the many have a place to lean on. A certain prince of the present day, whom I shall refrain from naming, preaches nothing but peace and faith, and to both one and the other he is entirely opposed; and both, if he had put them into practice, would have cost him many times over either his reputation or his state.

On Avoiding Being Despised and Hated

But now that I have talked about the most important of the qualities mentioned above, I would like to discuss the others briefly in this general manner: that the prince, as was noted above, should concentrate upon avoiding those things which make him hated and despised; and when he has avoided this, he will have carried out his duties and will find no danger whatsoever in other vices. As I have said, what makes him hated above all else is being rapacious and a usurper of the property and the women of his subjects; he must refrain from this; and in most cases, so long as you do not deprive them of either their property or their honour, the majority of men live happily; and you have only to deal with the ambition of a few, who can be restrained without difficulty and by many means. What makes him despised is being considered changeable, frivolous, effeminate, cowardly, irresolute; from these qualities a prince must guard himself as if from a reef, and he must strive to make everyone recognize in his actions greatness, spirit, dignity, and strength; and concerning the private affairs of his subjects, he must insist that his decision be irrevocable; and he should maintain himself in such a way that no man could imagine that he can deceive or cheat him.

That prince who projects such an opinion of himself is greatly esteemed; and it is difficult to conspire against a man with such a reputation and difficult to attack him, provided that he is understood to be of great merit and revered by his subjects. For a prince should have two fears: one, internal, concerning his subjects; the other, external, concerning foreign powers. From the latter he can defend himself by his good troops and friends; and he will always have good friends if he has good troops; and internal affairs will always be stable when external affairs are stable, provided that they are not already disturbed by a conspiracy; and even if external conditions change, if he is properly organized and lives as I have said and does not lose control of himself, he will always be able to withstand every attack. But concerning his subjects, when external affairs do not change, he has to fear that they may conspire secretly: the prince secures himself from this by avoiding being hated or despised and by keeping the people satisfied with him; this is a necessary accomplishment, as was treated above at length. And one of the most powerful remedies a prince has against conspiracies is not to be hated by the masses; for a man who plans a conspiracy always believes that he will satisfy the people by killing the prince; but when he thinks he might anger them, he cannot work up the courage to undertake such a deed; for the problems on the side of the conspirators are countless. And experience demonstrates that there have been many conspiracies but few have been concluded successfully; for anyone who conspires cannot be alone, nor can he find companions except from amongst those whom he believes to be dissatisfied; and as soon as you have revealed your intention to one malcontent, you give him the means to make himself content, since he can have everything he desires by uncovering the plot; so much is this so that, seeing a sure gain on the one hand and one doubtful and full of danger on the other, if he is to maintain faith with you he has to be either an unusually good friend or a completely determined enemy of the prince. And to treat the matter briefly, I say that on the part of the conspirator there is nothing but fear, jealousy, and the thought of punishment that terrifies him; but on the part of the prince there is the majesty of the principality, the laws, the defences of friends and the state to protect him; so that, with the good will of the people added to all these things, it is impossible for anyone to be so rash as to plot against him. For, where usually a conspirator has to be afraid before he executes his evil deed, in this case he must be afraid even after the crime is performed, having the people as an enemy, nor can he hope to find any refuge because of this.

How a Prince Should Act to Acquire Esteem

Nothing makes a prince more esteemed than great undertakings and examples of his unusual talents. In our own times we have Ferdinand of Aragon, the present King of Spain. This man can be called almost a new prince, since from being a weak ruler he became, through fame and glory, the first king of Christendom; and if you consider his accomplishments, you will find them all very grand and some even extraordinary. In the beginning of his reign he attacked Granada, and that enterprise was the basis of his state. First, he acted while things were peaceful and when he had no fear of opposition: he kept the minds of the barons of Castile busy with this, and they, concentrating on that war, did not consider changes at home. And he acquired, through that means, reputation and power over them without their noticing it; he was able to maintain armies with money from the Church and the people, and with that long war he laid a basis for his own army, which has since brought him honour. Besides this, in order to be able to undertake greater enterprises, always using religion for his own purposes, he turned to a pious cruelty, hunting down and clearing out the Moors from his kingdom: no example could be more pathetic or more unusual than this. He attacked Africa, under the same cloak of religion; he undertook the invasion of Italy; he finally attacked France. And in such a manner, he has always done and planned great deeds which have always kept the minds of his subjects in suspense and amazed and occupied with their outcome. And one action of his would spring from another in such a way that between one and the other he would never give men enough time to be able to work calmly against him.

A prince is also respected when he is a true friend and a true enemy; that is, when he declares himself on the side of one prince against another without any reservation. Such a policy will always be more useful than that of neutrality; for if two powerful neighbours of yours come to blows, they will be of the type that, when one has emerged victorious, you will either have cause to fear the victor or you will not. In either of these two cases, it will always be more useful for you to declare yourself and to fight an open war; for, in the first case, if you do not declare your intentions, you will always be the prey of the victor to the delight and satisfaction of the vanquished, and you will have no reason why anyone would come to your assistance; because whoever wins does not want reluctant allies who would not assist him in times of adversity; and whoever loses will not give you refuge since you were unwilling to run the risk of coming to his aid.

And it will always happen that he who is not your friend will request your neutrality and he who is your friend will ask you to declare yourself by taking up your arms. And irresolute princes, in order to avoid present dangers, follow the neutral road most of the time, and most of the time they are ruined. But when the prince declares himself vigorously in favour of one side, if the one with whom you have joined wins, although he may be powerful and you may be left to his discretion, he has an obligation to you and there does exist a bond of friendship; and men are never so dishonest that they will crush you with such a show of ingratitude; and then, victories are never so clear-cut that the victor need be completely free of caution, especially when justice is concerned. But if the one with whom you join loses, you will be taken in by him; and while he is able, he will help you, and you will become the comrade of a fortune which can rise up again.

In the second case, when those who fight together are of such a kind that you need not fear the one who wins, it is even more prudent to join his side, since you go to the downfall of a prince with the aid of another prince who should have saved him if he had been wise; and in winning he is at your discretion, and it is impossible for him not to win with your aid.

A prince also should demonstrate that he is a lover of talent by giving recognition to men of ability and by honouring those who excel in a particular field. Furthermore, he should encourage his subjects to be free to pursue their trades in tranquility, whether in commerce, agriculture, or in any other trade a man may have. And he should act in such a way that a man is not afraid to increase his goods for fear that they will be taken away from him, while another will not be afraid to engage in commerce for fear of taxes; instead, he must set up rewards for those who wish to do things, and for anyone who seeks in any way to aggrandize his city or state. He should, besides this, at the appropriate times of the year, keep the populace occupied with festivals and spectacles. And because each city is divided into guilds or clans, he should take account of these groups, meet with them on occasion, offer himself as an example of humanity and munificence, always, nevertheless, maintaining firmly the dignity of his position, for this should never be lacking in any way.

Why Italian Princes Have Lost Their States

The things written above, if followed prudently, make a new prince seem well established and render him immediately safer and more established in his state than if he had been in it for some time. For a new prince is far more closely observed in his activities than is a hereditary prince; and when his deeds are recognized to be good actions they attract men much more and bind them to him more strongly than does antiquity of lineage. For men are much more taken by present concerns than by those of the past; and when they find the present satisfactory they enjoy it and seek nothing more; in fact, they will seize every measure to defend the new prince as long as he is not lacking in his other responsibilities. And thus he will have a double glory: that of having given birth to a new principality and of having adorned it and strengthened it with good laws, good arms, and good examples; as he will have double shame who, having been born a prince, loses his principality on account of his lack of prudence.

Therefore, these princes of ours who have been in their principalities for many years, and who have then lost them, must not blame fortune, but rather their own idleness; for, never having thought in peaceful times that things might change (which is a common defect in men, not to consider in good weather the possibility of a tempest), when adverse times finally arrived they thought about running away and not about defending themselves; and they hoped that the people, angered by the insolence of the victors, would eventually recall them. This policy, when others are lacking, is good; but it is indeed bad to have disregarded all other solutions for this one; for you should never wish to fall, believing that you will find someone else to pick you up; because whether this occurs or not, it does not increase your security, that method being a cowardly defence and one not dependent upon your own resources. And those methods alone are good, are certain, are lasting, that depend on yourself and your own ingenuity.

On Fortune's Role in Human Affairs and How She Can Be Dealt With

It is not unknown to me that many have held, and still hold, the opinion that the things of this world are, in a manner, controlled by fortune and by God, that men with their wisdom cannot control them, and, on the contrary, that men can have no remedy whatsoever for them; and for this reason they might judge that they need not sweat much over such matters but let them be governed by fate. This opinion has been more strongly held in our own times because of the great variation of affairs that has been observed and that is being observed every day which is beyond human conjecture. Sometimes, as I think about these things, I am inclined to their opinion to a certain extent. Nevertheless, in order that our free will be not extinguished, I judge it to be true that fortune is the arbiter of one-half of our actions, but that she still leaves the control of the other half, or almost that, to us. And I compare her to one of those ruinous rivers that, when they become enraged, flood the plains, tear down the trees and buildings, taking up earth from one spot and placing it upon another; everyone flees from them, everyone yields to their onslaught, unable to oppose them in any way. But although they are of such a nature, it does not follow that when the weather is calm we cannot take precautions with embankments and dikes, so that when they rise up again either the waters will be channelled off or their impetus will not either be unchecked or so damaging. The same things happen where fortune is concerned: she shows her force where there is no organized strength to resist her; and she directs her impact there where she knows that dikes and embankments are not constructed to hold her. And if you consider Italy, the seat of these changes and the nation which has set them in motion, you will see a country without embankments and without a single bastion: for if she were defended by the necessary forces, like Germany, Spain, and France, either this flood would not have produced the great changes that it has or it would not have come upon us at all. And this I consider enough to say about fortune in general terms.

But, limiting myself more to particulars, I say that one sees a prince prosper today and come to ruin tomorrow without having seen him change his character or any of the reasons that have been discussed at length earlier; that is, that a prince who relies completely upon fortune will come to ruin as soon as she changes; I also believe that the man who adapts his course of action to the nature of the times will succeed and, likewise, that the man who sets his course of action out of tune with the times will come to grief. For one can observe that men, in the affairs which lead them to the end that they seek—that is, glory and wealth—proceed in different ways; one by caution, another with impetuousness; one through violence, another with guile; one with patience, another with its opposite; and each one by these various means can attain his goals. And we also see in the case of two cautious men, that one reaches his goal while the other does not; and, likewise, two men equally succeed using two different means, one being cautious and the other impetuous: this arises from nothing else than the nature of the times that either suit or do not suit their course of action. From this results that which I have said, that two men, working in opposite ways, can produce the same outcome; and of two men working in the same fashion one achieves his goal and the other does not. On this also depends the variation of what is good; for, if a man governs himself with caution and patience, and the times and conditions are turning in such a way that his policy is a good one, he will prosper; but if the times and conditions change, he will be ruined because he does not change his method of procedure. Nor is there to be found a man so prudent that he knows how to adapt himself to this, both because he cannot deviate from that to which he is by nature inclined and also because he cannot be persuaded to depart from a path, having always prospered by following it. And therefore the cautious man, when it is time to act impetuously, does not know how to do so, and he is ruined; but if he had changed his conduct with the times, fortune would not have changed.

I conclude, therefore, that since fortune changes and men remain set in their ways, men will succeed when the two are in harmony and fail when they are not in accord. I am certainly convinced of this: that it is better to be impetuous than cautious, because fortune is a woman, and it is necessary, in order to keep her down, to beat her and to struggle with her. And it is seen that she more often allows herself to be taken over by men who are impetuous than by those who make cold advances; and then, being a woman, she is always a friend of young men, for they are less cautious, more aggressive, and they command her with more audacity.

An Exhortation to Liberate Italy from the Barbarians

Considering, therefore, all of the things mentioned above, and reflecting as to whether the times are suitable, at present, to honour a new prince in Italy, and if there is the material that might give a skilful and prudent prince the opportunity to introduce a form of government that would bring him honour and good to the people of Italy, it seems to me that so many circumstances are favourable to such a new prince that I know of no other time more appropriate. And if, as I said, it was necessary that the people of Israel be slaves in Egypt in order to recognize Moses' ability, and it was necessary that the Persians be oppressed by the Medes to recognize the greatness of spirit in Cyrus, and it was necessary that the Athenians be dispersed to realize the excellence of Theseus, then, likewise, at the present time, in order to recognize the ability of an Italian spirit, it was necessary that Italy be reduced to her present condition and that she be more enslaved than the Hebrews, more servile than the Persians, more scattered than the Athenians; without a leader, without organization, beaten, despoiled, ripped apart, overrun, and prey to every sort of catastrophe.

And even though before now some glimmer of light may have shown itself in a single individual, so that it was possible to believe that God had ordained him for Italy's redemption, nevertheless it was witnessed afterwards how at the height of his career he was rejected by fortune. So now Italy remains without life and awaits the man who can heal her wounds and put an end to the plundering of Lombardy, the ransoms in the Kingdom of Naples and in Tuscany, and who can cure her of those sores which have been festering for so long. Look how she now prays to God to send someone to redeem her from these barbaric cruelties and insolence; see her still ready and willing to follow a banner, provided that there be someone to raise it up. Nor is there anyone in sight, at present, in whom she can have more hope than in your illustrious house, which, with its fortune and ability, favoured by God and by the Church, of which it is now prince, could make itself the head of this redemption. This will not be very difficult if you keep before you the deeds and the lives of those named above. And although those men were out of the ordinary and marvelous, they were nevertheless men; and each of them had less opportunity than the present one; for their enterprises were no more just, nor easier, nor was God more a friend to them than to you. Here justice is great: "Only those wars that are necessary are just, and arms are sacred when there is no hope except through arms." Here there is a great willingness; and where there is a great willingness there cannot be great difficulty, if only you will use the institutions of those men I have proposed as your target. Besides this, we now see extraordinary, unprecedented signs brought about by God: the sea has opened up; a cloud has shown you the path; the rock pours forth water; it has rained manna here; everything has converged for your greatness. The rest you must do yourself. God does not wish to do everything, in order not to take from us our free will and that part of the glory which is ours.

And it is no surprise if some of the Italians mentioned previously were not capable of doing what it is hoped may be done by your illustrious house, and if, during the many revolutions in Italy and the many campaigns of war, it always seems that her military ability is spent. This results from the fact that her ancient institutions were not good and that there was no one who knew how to discover new ones; and no other thing brings a new man on the rise such honour as the new laws and the new institutions discovered by him. These things, when they are well founded and have in themselves a certain greatness, make him revered and admirable. And in Italy there is no lack of material to be given a form: here there is great ability in her members, were it not for the lack of it in her leaders. Consider how in duels and skirmishes involving just a few men the Italians are superior in strength, dexterity, and cunning; but when it comes to armies they do not match others. And all this comes from the weakness of her leaders; for those who know are not followed; and with each one seeming to know, there has not been to the present day anyone who has known how to set himself above the others, either because of ingenuity or fortune, so that others might yield to him.

Therefore, if your illustrious house desires to follow these excellent men who redeemed their lands, it is necessary before all else, as a true basis for every undertaking, to provide yourself with your own native troops, for one cannot have either more faithful, more loyal, or better troops. And although each one separately may be brave, all of them united will become even braver when they find themselves commanded, honoured, and well treated by their own prince. It is necessary, therefore, to prepare yourself with such troops as these, so that with Italian strength you will be able to defend yourself from foreigners. And although Swiss and Spanish infantry may be reputed terrifying, nevertheless both have defects, so that a third army could not only oppose them but be confident of defeating them. For the Spanish cannot withstand cavalry and the Swiss have a fear of foot soldiers they meet in combat who are as brave as they are. Therefore, it has been witnessed and experience will demonstrate that the Spanish cannot withstand French cavalry and the Swiss are ruined by Spanish infantrymen. And although this last point has not been completely confirmed by experience, there was nevertheless a hint of it at the battle of Ravenna, when the Spanish infantry met the German battalions, who follow the same order as the Swiss; and the Spanish, with their agile bodies, aided by their spiked shields, entered between and underneath the Germans' long pikes and were safe, without the Germans having any recourse against them; and had it not been for the cavalry charge that broke them, the Spaniards would have slaughtered them all. Therefore, as the defects of both these kinds of troops are recognized, a new type can be instituted which can stand up to cavalry and will have no fear of foot soldiers: this will come about by creating new armies and changing battle formations. And these are among those matters that, when newly organized, give reputation and greatness to a new prince.

This opportunity, therefore, must not be permitted to pass by so that Italy, after so long a time, may behold its redeemer. Nor can I express with what love he will be received in all those provinces that have suffered through these foreign floods; with what thirst for revenge, with what obstinate loyalty, with what compassion, with what tears! What doors will be closed to him? Which people will deny him obedience? What jealousy could oppose him? What Italian would deny him homage? For everyone, this barbarian dominion stinks! Therefore, may your illustrious house take up this mission with that spirit and with that hope in which just undertakings are begun; so that under your banner this country may be ennobled and, under your guidance, those words of Petrarch may come true:

> Ingenuity over rage
> Will take up arms; and the battle will be short.
> For ancient valour
> In Italian hearts is not yet dead.
>
> "Italia mia" ll. 93–6

STUDY QUESTIONS

1. What does Machiavelli mean by cruelty "well used"? Give some contemporary examples of cruelty both "well used" and "badly used." Is Machiavelli correct? Have there been any twentieth-century rulers who were overthrown because of their badly used cruelties? Which ones?
2. Is it better, according to Machiavelli, to be loved or feared? How would Hitler and Stalin have responded? Does this love or fear attitude apply also to democracies? Why or why not? Is there something between love and fear that might be more apropos?
3. Machiavelli contends that a ruler does not have to keep good faith. Why not? Under what circumstances? Have any American presidents acted like "a fox and a lion"? Name one or two.

LITERARY SELECTION 45

Poetry

Michelangelo Buonarroti, 1475–1564

The musicality of sonnets by Petrarch and his followers was the accepted style of the Italian Renaissance, but Michelangelo followed his own course in his poetry just as he did in sculpting, painting, and architecture. His sonnets were, as he himself said, "unprofessional, rude, and rough." Michelangelo did not consider himself a poet in Petrarchian terms, but he was praised at the time as a poet in his own right. His sonnets, like the personality of their creator, are powerful and unique, and constitute, at their best, the finest lyric Italian poetry of the Renaissance. No knowledge of Michelangelo the sculptor and painter can be complete without knowing the artist as poet. The following poem was written for Michelangelo's close friend Tommaso de' Cavalieri.

Sonnet XXXII

(S'un casto amor)

If love be chaste, if virtue conquer ill,
  If fortune bind both lovers in one bond,
  If either at the other's grief despond,
  If both be governed by one life, one will;
If in two bodies one soul triumph still,
  Raising the twain from earth to heaven beyond,
  If Love with one blow and one golden wand
  Have power both smitten breasts to pierce and thrill;
If each the other love, himself foregoing,
  With such delight, such savor, and so well,
  That both to one sole end their wills combine;
If thousands of these thoughts, all thought outgoing,
  Fail the least part of their firm love to tell:
  Say, can mere angry spite this knot untwine?

Michelangelo met Vittoria Colonna, the Marquise of Pescara, while he was working on the *Last Judgment* (1536–1541; see fig. 17.37) in the Sistine Chapel. Probably the only woman he ever loved, Vittoria was an astute judge of his work, but valued the man even above his creations. Michelangelo viewed her as "God inside a woman." Her death in 1547 was a painful loss for a seventy-two-year-old artist who was already obsessed with the fear of death and hell. In much of the poetry written for Vittoria, Michelangelo used sculpture as a theme; God had created Adam and that made him a sculptor.

Sonnet LXI

(Se'l mie rozzo martello)

After the Death of Vittoria Colonna

When my rude hammer to the stubborn stone
Gives human shape, now that, now this, at will,
Following his hand who wields and guides it still,
It moves upon another's feet alone:
But that which dwells in heaven, the world doth fill
With beauty by pure motions of its own;
And since tools fashion tools which else were none,
Its life makes all that lives with living skill.
Now, for that every stroke excels the more
The higher at the forge it doth ascend,
Her soul that fashioned mine hath sought the skies:
Wherefore unfinished I must meet my end,
If God, the great artificer, denies
That aid which was unique on earth before.

STUDY QUESTIONS

1. Contrast these sonnets with those of Petrarch, granting that all are in English translation. Compare, for example, the use of verbs. Petrarch uses "shone," "flamed," "flow," "beguile," "smile," and "rising"; Michelangelo uses "fly," "stirreth," "strain," "bind," "conquer," "pierce," "thrill," and "spite."
2. Are there similar contrasts in their adjectives and adverbs?

LITERARY SELECTION 46

The Book of the Courtier

Baldassare Castiglione, 1478–1529

Renaissance civilization reasserted "the dignity of the human race" (Cicero) and the worth of the individual. Life and human institutions could be shaped to be more efficient and more pleasant, leading to a good life that became, at its best, an art form—the art of gracious living. True ladies and gentlemen had disciplined intellects, good manners, and impeccable taste. Those who aspired to this ideal studied the countless manuals that became available, most especially *The Book of the Courtier* (1528) by Count Baldassare Castiglione (kas-teel-YO-nay; see fig. 17.34). Using personalities from his own circle at the court of the Duke of Urbino, Castiglione designed a kind of Platonic dialogue to set up his utopian social society, a model for civilized people of every age, including our own.

As was the custom, the evening gathering of the court circle proposed various games, actually civil discourses about subjects agreeable to all. This selection begins in Book I, chapter 12, when Federico Fregoso proposes the game that will be played for four evenings.

"My Lady, I would it were permitted me, as it sometimes is, to assent to another's proposal; since for my part I would readily approve any of the games proposed by these gentlemen, for I really think that all of them would be amusing. But not to break our rule, I say that anyone who wished to praise our court,—laying aside the merit of our lady Duchess, which with her divine virtue would suffice to lift from earth to heaven the meanest souls that are in the world,—might well say without suspicion of flattery, that in all Italy it would perhaps be hard to find so many cavaliers so singularly admirable and so excellent in divers other matters besides the chief concerns of chivalry, as are now to be found here: wherefore if anywhere there be men who deserve to be called good Courtiers and who are able to judge of what pertains to the perfection of Courtiership, it is reasonable to believe that they are here. So, to repress the many fools who by impudence and folly think to win the name of good Courtier, I would that this evening's game might be, that we select some one of the company and give him the task of portraying a perfect Courtier, explaining all the conditions and special qualities requisite in one who deserves this title; and as to those things that shall not appear sound, let everyone be allowed to contradict, as in the schools of the philosophers it is allowed to contradict anyone who proposes a thesis."

Messer Federico was continuing his discourse still further, when my lady Emilia interrupted him and said:

"This, if it pleases my lady Duchess, shall for the present be our game."

My lady Duchess answered:

"It does please me."

Then nearly all those present began to say, both to my lady Duchess and among themselves, that this was the finest game that could possibly be; and without waiting for each other's answer, they entreated my lady Emilia to decide who should begin. She turned to my lady Duchess and said:

"Command, my Lady, him who it best pleases you should have this task; for I do not wish, by selecting one rather than another, to seem to decide whom I think more competent in this matter than the rest, and so do wrong to anyone."

My lady Duchess replied:

"Nay, make this choice yourself, and take heed lest by not obeying you give an example to the others, so that they too prove disobedient in their turn."

13.—At this my lady Emilia laughed and said to Count Ludovico da Canossa:

"Then not to lose more time, you, Count, shall be the one to take this enterprise after the manner that messer Federico has described; not indeed because we account you so good a Courtier that you know what befits one, but because, if you say everything wrong as we hope you will, the game will be more lively, for everyone will then have something to answer you; while if someone else had this task who knew more than you, it would be impossible to contradict him in anything, because he would tell the truth, and so the game would be tedious."

The Count answered quickly:

"Whoever told the truth, my Lady, would run no risk of lacking contradiction, so long as you were present;" and after some laughter at this retort, he continued: "But truly I would fain escape this burden, it seeming to me too heavy, and I being conscious that what you said in jest is very true; that is, that I do not know what befits a good Courtier: and I do not seek to prove this with further argument, because, as I do not practice the rules of Courtiership, one may judge that I do not know them; and I think my blame may be the less, for sure it is worse not to wish to do well than not to know how. Yet, since it so happens that you are pleased to have me bear this burden, I neither can nor will refuse it, in order not to contravene our rule and your judgment, which I rate far higher than my own."

14.—"I wish, then, that this Courtier of ours should be nobly born and of gentle race; because it is far less unseemly for one of ignoble birth to fail in worthy deeds, than for one of noble birth, who, if he strays from the path of his predecessors, stains his family name, and not only fails to achieve but loses what has been achieved already; for noble birth is like a bright lamp that manifests and makes visible good and evil deeds, and kindles and stimulates to virtue both by fear of shame and by hope of praise. And since this splendor of nobility does not illumine the deeds of the humbly born, they lack that stimulus and fear of shame, nor do they feel any obligation to advance beyond what their predecessors have done; while to the nobly born it seems a reproach not to reach at least the goal set them by their ancestors.

"It is true that, by favour of the stars or of nature, some men are endowed at birth with such graces that they seem not to have been born, but rather as if some god had formed them with his very hands and adorned them with every excellence of mind and body. So too there are many men so foolish and rude that one cannot but think that nature brought them into the world out of contempt or mockery. Just as these can usually accomplish little even with constant diligence and good training, so with slight pains those others reach the highest summit of excellence. And to give you an instance: you see my lord Don Ippolito d'Este, Cardinal of Ferrara, who has enjoyed such fortune from his birth, that his person, his aspect, his words and all his movements are so disposed and imbued with this grace, that—although he is young—he exhibits among the most aged prelates such weight of character that he seems fitter to teach than to be taught; likewise in conversation with men and women of every rank, in games, in pleasantry and in banter, he has a certain sweetness and manners so gracious, that whoso speaks with him or even sees him, must needs remain attached to him forever.

"But to return to our subject: I say that there is a middle state between perfect grace on the one hand and senseless folly on the other; and those who are not thus perfectly endowed by nature, with study and toil can in great part polish and amend their natural defects. Besides his noble birth, then, I would have the Courtier favored in this regard also, and endowed by nature not only with talent and beauty of person and feature, but with a certain grace and (as we say) air that shall make him at first sight pleasing and agreeable to all who see him; and I would have this an ornament that should dispose and unite all his actions, and in his outward aspect give promise of whatever is worthy the society and favour of every great lord."

15.—Here, without waiting longer, my lord Gaspar Pallavicino said:

"I quite agree with what you say as to the good fortune of those endowed from birth with advantages of mind and body: but this is seen as well among the humbly born as among the nobly born, since nature has no such subtle distinctions as these; and often, as I said, the highest gifts of nature are found among the most obscure. Therefore, since this nobility of birth is won neither by talent nor by strength nor by craft, and is rather the merit of our predecessors than our own, it seems to me too extravagant to maintain that if our Courtier's parents be humbly born, all his good qualities are spoiled, and that all those other qualifications that you mentioned do not avail to raise him to the summit of perfection; I mean talent, beauty of feature, comeliness of person, and that grace which makes him always charming to everyone at first sight."

16.—Then Count Ludovico replied:

"I do not deny that the same virtues may rule the low-born and the noble: but (not to repeat what we have said already or the many other arguments that could be adduced in praise of noble birth, which is honored always and by everyone, it being reasonable that good should beget good), since we have to form a Courtier without flaw and endowed with every praiseworthy quality, it seems to me necessary to make him nobly born, as well for many other reasons as for universal opinion, which is at once disposed in favor of noble birth. For if there be two Courtiers who have as yet given no impression of themselves by good or evil acts, as soon as the one is known to have been born a gentleman and the other not, he who is low-born will be far less esteemed by everyone than he who is high-born, and will need much effort and time to make upon men's minds that good impression which the other will have achieved in a moment and merely by being a gentleman. And how important these impressions are, everyone can easily understand: for in our own case we have seen men present themselves in this house, who, being silly and awkward in the extreme, yet had throughout Italy the reputation of very great Courtiers; and although they were detected and recognized at last, still they imposed upon us for many days, and maintained in our minds that opinion of them which they first found impressed there, although they conducted themselves after the slightness of their worth. We have seen others, held at first in small esteem, then admirably successful at the last.

17.—"But to come to some details, I am of opinion that the principal and true profession of the Courtier ought to be that of arms; which I would have him follow actively above all else, and be known among others as bold and strong, and loyal to whomsoever he serves. And he will win a reputation for these good qualities by exercising them at all times and in all places, since one may never fail in this without severest censure. And just as among women, their fair fame once sullied never recovers its first luster, so the reputation of a gentleman who bears arms, if once it be in the least tarnished with cowardice or other disgrace, remains forever infamous before the world and full of ignominy. Therefore the more our Courtier excels in this art, the more he will be worthy of praise; and yet I do not deem essential in him that perfect knowledge of things and those other qualities that befit a commander; since this would be too wide a sea, let us be content, as we have said, with perfect loyalty and unconquered courage, and that he be always seen to possess them. For the courageous are often recognized even more in small things than in great; and frequently in perils of importance and where there are many spectators, some men are to be found, who, although their hearts be dead within them, yet, moved by shame or by the presence of others, press forward almost with their eyes shut, and do their duty God knows how. While on occasions of little moment, when they think they can avoid putting themselves in danger without being detected, they are glad to keep safe. But those who, even when they do not expect to be observed or seen or recognized by anyone, show their ardor and neglect nothing, however paltry, that may be laid to their charge,—they have that strength of mind which we seek in our Courtier.

"Therefore let the man we are seeking be very bold, stern, and always among the first, where the enemy are to be seen; and in every other place, gentle, modest, reserved, above all things avoiding ostentation and that impudent self-praise by which men ever excite hatred and disgust in all who hear them."

18.—Then my lord Gaspar replied:

"As for me, I have known few men excellent in anything whatever, who do not praise themselves; and it seems to me that this may well be permitted them; for when anyone who feels himself to be of worth, sees that he is not known to the ignorant by his works, he is offended that his worth should lie buried, and needs must in some way hold it up to view, in order that he may not be cheated of the fame that is the true reward of worthy effort. Thus among the ancient authors, whoever carries weight seldom fails to praise himself. They indeed are insufferable who do this without desert, but such we do not presume our Courtier to be."

The Count then said:

"If you heard what I said, it was impudent and indiscriminate self-praise that I censured: and as you say, we surely ought not to form a bad opinion of a brave man who praises himself modestly, nay we ought rather to regard such praise as better evidence than if it came from the mouth of others. I say, however, that he, who in praising himself runs into no error and incurs no annoyance or envy at the hands of those that hear him, is a very discreet man indeed and merits praise from others in addition to that which he bestows upon himself; because it is a very difficult matter."

Then my lord Gaspar said:

"You must teach us that."

The Count replied:

"Among the ancient authors there is no lack of those who have taught it; but to my thinking, the whole art consists in saying things in such a way that they shall not seem to be said to that end, but let fall so naturally that it was impossible not to say them, and while seeming always to avoid self-praise, yet to achieve it; but not after the manner of those boasters, who open their mouths and let the words come forth haphazard. Like one of our friends a few days ago, who, being quite run through the thigh with a spear at Pisa, said he thought it was a fly that had stung him; and another man said he kept no mirror in his room because, when angry, he became so terrible to look at, that the sight of himself would have frightened him too much."

Everyone laughed at this, but messer Cesare Gonzaga added:

"Why do you laugh? Do you not know that Alexander the Great, on hearing the opinion of a philosopher to be that there was an infinite number of worlds, began to weep, and being asked why he wept, replied, 'Because I have not yet conquered one of them;' as if he would fain have vanquished all? Does not this seem to you a greater boast than that about the fly-sting?"

19.—The Count now paused a little, and messer Bernardo Bibbiena said, laughing:

"I remember what you said earlier, that this Courtier of ours must be endowed by nature with beauty of countenance and person, and with a grace that shall make him so agreeable. Grace and beauty of countenance I think I certainly possess, and this is the reason why so many ladies are ardently in love with me, as you know; but I am rather doubtful as to the beauty of my person, especially as regards these legs of mine, which seem to me decidedly less well proportioned than I should wish: as to my bust and other members however, I am quite content. Pray, now, describe a little more in particular the sort of body that the Courtier is to have, so that I may dismiss this doubt and set my mind at rest."

After some laughter at this, the Count continued:

"Of a certainty that grace of countenance can be truly said to be yours, nor need I cite further example than this to show what manner of thing it is, for we unquestionably perceive your aspect to be most agreeable and pleasing to everyone, albeit the lineaments of it are not very delicate. Still it is of a manly cast and at the same time full of grace; and this characteristic is to be found in many different types of countenance. And of such sort I would have our Courtier's aspect; not so soft and effeminate as is sought by many, who not only curl their hair and pluck their brows, but gloss their faces with all those arts employed by the most wanton and unchaste women in the world; and in their walk, posture and every act, they seem so limp and languid that their limbs are like to fall apart; and they pronounce their words so mournfully that they appear about to expire upon the spot: and the more they find themselves with men of rank, the more they affect such tricks. Since nature has not made them women, as they seem to wish to appear and be, they should be treated not as good women but as public harlots, and driven not merely from the courts of great lords but from the society of honest men.

20.—"Then coming to the bodily frame, I say it is enough if this be neither extremely short nor tall, for both of these conditions excite a certain contemptuous surprise, and men of either sort are gazed upon in much the same way that we gaze on monsters. Yet if we must offend in one of the two extremes, it is preferable to fall a little short of the just measure of height than to exceed it, for besides often being dull of intellect, men thus huge of body are also unfit for every exercise of agility, which thing I should much wish in the Courtier.

21.—"Moreover I deem it very important to know how to wrestle, for it is a great help in the use of all kinds of weapons on foot. Then, both for his own sake and for that of his friends, he must understand the quarrels and differences that may arise, and must be quick to seize an advantage, always showing courage and prudence in all things. Nor should he be too ready to fight except when honor demands it; for besides the great danger that the uncertainty of fate entails, he who rushes into such affairs recklessly and without urgent cause, merits the severest censure even though he be successful. But when he finds himself so far engaged that he cannot withdraw without reproach, he ought to be most deliberate, both in the preliminaries to the duel and in the duel itself, and always show readiness and daring. Nor must he act like some, who fritter the affair away in disputes and controversies, and who, having the choice of weapons, select those that neither cut nor pierce, and arm themselves as if they were expecting a cannonade; and thinking it enough not to be defeated, stand ever on the defensive and retreat,—showing therein their utter cowardice.

22.—"There are also many other exercises, which although not immediately dependent upon arms, yet are closely connected therewith, and greatly foster manly sturdiness; and one of the chief among these seems to me to be the chase, because it bears a certain likeness to war: and truly it is an amusement for great lords and befitting a man at court, and furthermore it is seen to have been much cultivated among the ancients. It is fitting also to know how to swim, to leap, to run, to throw stones, for besides the use that may be made of this in war, a man often has occasion to show what he can do in such matters; whence good esteem is to be won, especially with the multitude, who must be taken into account withal. Another admirable exercise, and one very befitting a man at court, is the game of tennis, in which are well shown the disposition of the body, the quickness and suppleness of every member, and all those qualities that are seen in nearly every other exercise. Nor less highly do I esteem vaulting on horse, which although it be fatiguing and difficult, makes a man very light and dexterous more than any other thing; and besides its utility, if this lightness is accompanied by grace, it is to my thinking a finer show than any of the others. Our Courtier having once become more than fairly expert in these exercises, I think he should leave the others on one side: such as turning summersaults, rope-walking, and the like, which savor of the mountebank and little befit a gentleman.

"But since one cannot devote himself to such fatiguing exercises continually, and since repetition becomes very tiresome and abates the admiration felt for what is rare, we must always diversify our life with various occupations. For this reason I would have our Courtier sometimes descend to quieter and more tranquil exercises, and in order to escape envy and to entertain himself agreeably with everyone, let him do whatever others do, yet never departing from praiseworthy deeds, and governing himself with that good judgment which will keep him from all folly; but let him laugh, jest, banter, frolic and dance, yet in such fashion that he shall always appear genial and discreet, and that everything he may do or say shall be stamped with grace."

Book III

Book III is devoted to the qualities of the court lady, who should be affable, modest, decorous, virtuous, courageous, educated, and intelligent. The following excerpt summarizes the qualities of the ideal court lady.

9.—"And since my lord Gaspar further asks what these many things are whereof she ought to have knowledge, and in what manner she ought to converse, and whether her virtues ought to contribute to her conversation,—I say I would have her acquainted with that which these gentlemen wished the Courtier to know. And of the exercises that we have said do not befit her, I would have her at least possess such understanding as we may have of things that we do not practice; and this in order that she may know how to praise and value cavaliers more or less, according to their deserts.

"And to repeat in a few words part of what has been already said, I wish this Lady to have knowledge of letters, music, painting, and to know how to dance and make merry; accompanying the other precepts that have been taught the Courtier with discreet modesty and with the giving of a good impression of herself. And thus, in her talk, her laughter, her play, her jesting, in short, in everything, she will be very graceful, and will entertain appropriately, and with witticisms and pleasantries befitting her, everyone who shall come before her. And although continence, magnanimity, temperance, strength of mind, prudence, and the other virtues seem to have little to do with entertainment, I would have her adorned with all of them, not so much for the sake of entertainment (albeit even there they can be of service), as in order that she may be full of virtue, and to the end that these virtues may render her worthy of being honored, and that her every act may be governed by them."

10.—My lord Gaspar then said, laughing:

"Since you have given women letters and continence and magnanimity and temperance, I only marvel that you would not also have them govern cities, make laws, and lead armies, and let the men stay at home to cook or spin."

The Magnifico replied, also laughing:

"Perhaps even this would not be amiss." Then he added: "Do you not know that Plato, who certainly was no great friend to women, gave them charge over the city, and gave all other martial duties to the men? Do you not believe that there are many to be found who would know how to govern cities and armies as well as men do? But I have not laid these duties on them, because I am fashioning a Court Lady and not a Queen."

Castiglione wrote his book as a tribute to Giubaldo di Montefeltro, Duke of Urbino (1472–1509), who was a real-life courtier. Isabella d'Este, Marchioness of Mantua (1474–1539), epitomized the court lady. Praised by Castiglione and many others for her intellect and moral qualities, she used her fine literary and artistic training to create a court at Mantua that became one of the brightest centers of Italian culture. Her reputation was so widespread that she was known as the "first woman of Europe." She was also called "Machiavelli in skirts," which was probably an acknowledgment of her ability, authority, and influence.

STUDY QUESTIONS

1. According to Castiglione, "the principal and true profession of the courtier ought to be that of arms." What is your reaction to this statement? Why?
2. List the virtues of a courtier. Which of these still apply in contemporary society? Which do not? How do you account for the changes in attitude?
3. Compare the virtues of a court lady with those of a courtier. How might modern feminists react to these statements? Would they, for example, prefer a queen to a court lady?

LITERARY SELECTION 47

Gargantua and Pantagruel

François Rabelais, 1494?–1553

An ebullient humanist and an outspoken rebel who detested all regimentation, Rabelais insisted that the good life was a natural consequence of freedom combined with a solid classical education. His masterwork, *Gargantua and Pantagruel,* is a collection of long, boisterous fables about two giant-kings, father and son. In the following excerpt Gargantua writes to his son in Paris, where he was receiving, like his father before him, the best possible education. Eloquent in the manner of Cicero, the letter summarizes the ideal education expected of the intellectual elite.

Chapter VIII

How Pantagruel, being at Paris, received letters from his father, Gargantua, and the copy of them.

Pantagruel studied very hard, as you may well conceive, and profited accordingly; for he had an excellent understanding and notable wit, together with a capacity in memory equal to the measure of twelve oil budgets or butts of olives. And, as he was there abiding one day, he received a letter from his father in manner as followeth.

Most dear Son,—Amongst the gifts, graces, and prerogatives, with which the sovereign psalmator God Almighty hath endowed and adorned human nature at the beginning, that seems to me most singular and excellent, by which we may in a moral state attain to a kind of immortality, and in the course of this transitory life perpetuate our name and seed, which is done by a progeny issued from us in the lawful bonds of matrimony. Whereby that in some measure is restored unto us which was taken from us by the sin of our first parents, to whom it was said that, because they had not obeyed the commandment of God their Creator, they should die, and by death should be brought to nought that so stately frame and psalmature wherein the man at first had been created.

But by this means of seminal propagation there continueth in the children what was lost in the parents, and in the grandchildren that which perished in their fathers, and so successively until the day of the last judgment, when Jesus Christ shall have rendered up to God the Father his kingdom in a peaceable condition, out of all danger and contamination of sin; for then shall cease all generations and corruptions, and the elements leave off their continual transmutations, seeing the so much desired peace shall be attained unto and enjoyed, and that all things shall be brought to their end and period. And, therefore, not without just and reasonable cause do I give thanks to God my Savior and Preserver, for that he hath enabled me to see my bald old age reflourish in thy youth; for when, at his good pleasure, who rules and governs all things, my soul shall leave this mortal habitation, I shall not account myself wholly to die, but to pass from one place unto another, considering that, in and by that, I continue in my visible image living in the world, visiting and conversing with people of honor, and other my good friends, as I was wont to do.

Wherefore, if those qualities of the mind but shine in thee wherewith I am endowed, as in thee remaineth the perfect image of my body, thou wilt be esteemed by all men to be the perfect guardian and treasure of the immortality of our name. But, if otherwise, I shall truly take but small pleasure to see it, considering that the lesser part of me, which is the body, would abide in thee, and the best, to wit, that which is the soul, and by which our name continues blessed amongst men, would be degenerate and bastardized. This I do not speak out of any distrust that I have of thy virtue, which I have heretofore already tried, but to encourage thee yet more earnestly to proceed from good to better. And that which I now write unto thee is not so much that thou shouldst live in this virtuous course, as that thou shouldst rejoice in so living and having lived, and cheer up thyself with the like resolution in time to come; to the prosecution and accomplishment of which enterprise and generous undertaking thou mayst easily remember how that I have spared nothing, but have so helped thee, as if I had had no other treasure in this world, but to see thee once in my life completely well-bred and accomplished as well in virtue, honesty, and valor, as in all liberal knowledge and civility, and so to leave thee after my death, as a mirror representing the person of me thy father, and if not so excellent, and such in deed as I do wish thee, yet such is my desire.

But although my deceased father of happy memory, Grangousier, had bent his endeavors to make me profit in all perfection and political knowledge, and that my labor and study was fully correspondent to, yea, went beyond his desire, nevertheless, as thou mayst well understand, the time then was not so proper and fit for learning as it is at present, neither had I plenty of such good masters as thou hast had. For that time was darksome, obscured with clouds of ignorance, and savoring a little of the infelicity and calamity of the Goths, who had, wherever they set footing, destroyed all good literature, which in my age hath by the divine goodness been restored unto its former light and dignity, and that with such amendment and increase of the knowledge, that now hardly should I be admitted unto the first form of the little grammar-schoolboys—I say, I, who in my youthful days was, and that justly, reputed the most learned of that age.

Now is it that the minds of men are qualified with all manner of discipline, and the old sciences revived which for many ages were extinct. Now is it that the learned languages are to their pristine purity restored, viz., Greek, without which a man may be ashamed to account himself a scholar, Hebrew, Arabic, Chaldean, and Latin. Printing likewise is now in use, so elegant and so correct that better cannot be imagined, although it was found out but in my time by divine inspiration, as by a diabolical suggestion on the other side was the invention of ordnance. All the world is full of knowing men, of most learned schoolmasters, and vast libraries; and it appears to me as a truth, that neither in Plato's time, nor Cicero's, nor Papinian's, there was ever such conveniency for studying as we see at this day there is. Nor must any adventure henceforward to come in public, or present himself in company, that hath not been pretty well polished in the shop of Minerva. I see robbers, hangmen, freebooters, tapsters, ostlers, and such like, of the very rubbish of the people, more learned now than the doctors and preachers were in my time.

What shall I say? The very women and children have aspired to this praise and celestial manner of good learning. Yet so it is that, in the age I am now of, I have been constrained to learn the Greek tongue—which I contemned not like Cato, but had not the leisure in my younger years to attend the study of it—and take much delight in the reading of Plutarch's Morals, the pleasant Dialogues of Plato, the Monuments of Pausanias, and the Antiquities of Athenaeus, in waiting on the hour wherein God my Creator shall call me and command me to depart from this earth and transitory pilgrimage. Wherefore, my son, I admonish thee to employ thy youth to profit as well as thou canst, both in thy studies and in virtue. Thou art at Paris, where the laudable examples of many brave men may stir up thy mind to gallant actions, and hast likewise for thy tutor and pedagogue the learned Epistemon, who by his lively and vocal documents may instruct thee in the arts and sciences.

I intend, and will have it so, that thou learn the languages perfectly; first of all, the Greek, as Quintilian will have it; secondly, the Latin; and then the Hebrew, for the Holy Scripture sake; and then the Chaldee and Arabic likewise, and that thou frame thy style in Greek in imitation of Plato, and for the Latin after Cicero. Let there be no history which thou shalt not have ready in thy memory; unto the prosecuting of which design, books of cosmography will be very conducible and help thee much. Of the liberal arts of geometry, arithmetic, and music, I gave thee some taste when thou wert yet little, and not above five or six years old. Proceed further in them, and learn the remainder if thou canst. As for astronomy, study all the rules thereof. Let pass, nevertheless, the divining and judicial astrology, and the art of Lullius, as being nothing else but plain abuses and vanities. As for the civil law, of that I would have thee to know the texts by heart, and then to confer them with philosophy.

Now, in matter of the knowledge of the works of nature, I would have thee to study that exactly, and that so there be no sea, river, nor fountain, of which thou dost not know the fishes; all the fowls of the air; all the several kinds of shrubs and trees, whether in forests or orchards; all sorts of herbs and flowers that grow upon the ground; all the various metals that are hid within the bowels of the earth; together with all the diversity of precious stones that are to be seen in the orient and south parts of the world. Let nothing of all these be hidden from thee. Then fail not most carefully to peruse the books of the Greek, Arabian, and Latin physicians, not despising the Talmudists and Cabalists; and by frequent anatomies get thee the perfect knowledge of the other world, called microcosm, which is man. And at some hours of the day apply thy mind to the study of the Holy Scriptures; first in Greek, the New Testament, with the Epistles of the Apostles; and then the old Testament in Hebrew. In brief, let me see thee an abyss and bottomless pit of knowledge; for from hence forward as thou growest great and becomest a man, thou must part from this tranquility and rest of study, thou must learn chivalry, warfare, and the exercises of the field, the better thereby to defend my house and our friends, and to succor and protect them at all their needs against the invasion and assaults of evildoers.

Furthermore, I will that very shortly thou try how much thou hast profited, which thou canst not better do than by maintaining publicly theses and conclusions in all arts against all persons whatsoever, and by haunting the company of learned men, both at Paris and otherwhere. But because, as the wise man Solomon saith, Wisdom entereth not into a malicious mind, and that knowledge without conscience is but the ruin of the soul, it behooveth thee to serve, to love, to fear God, and on him to cast all thy thoughts and all thy hope, and by faith formed in charity to cleave unto him, so that thou mayst never be separated from him by thy sins. Suspect the abuses of the world. Set not thy heart upon vanity, for this life is transitory, but the Word of the Lord endureth for ever. Be serviceable to all thy neighbors, and love them as thyself. Reverence thy preceptors: shun the conversation of those whom thou desirest not to resemble, and receive not in vain the graces which God hath bestowed upon thee. And, when thou shalt see that thou hast attained to all the knowledge that is to be acquired in that part, return unto me, that I may see thee and give thee my blessing before I die. My son, the peace and grace of our Lord be with thee. Amen.

Thy Father Gargantua.

From Utopia the 17th day of the month of March.

These letters being received and read, Pantagruel plucked up his heart, took a fresh courage to him, and was inflamed with a desire to profit in his studies more than ever, so that if you had seen him, how he took pains, and how he advanced in learning, you would have said that the vivacity of his spirit amidst the books was like a great fire amongst dry wood, so active it was, vigorous and indefatigable.

STUDY QUESTIONS

1. Gargantua writes about his son's education but not his vocation. Why not? What does this imply? Is education more important than what one does for a living? Should education be more important than a particular job?
2. Compare the education of Pantagruel with today's typical B.A. in a liberal arts discipline. What happened? Why? Would you aspire to Pantagruel's college education? Why or why not?

LITERARY SELECTION 48

Utopia

Thomas More, 1478–1535

Gargantua wrote his letter from "Utopia," a commonly used term after the appearance of Sir Thomas More's *Utopia*, a philosophical romance about an ideal state. Utopianism was in the air. Machiavelli's prince was an ideal autocrat, Castiglione's courtier functioned gracefully in an ideal society, and Pantagruel received an ideal education. Europeans were therefore entranced with the hope and promise of the New World. It was in these newly discovered lands that More (see fig. 19.2) placed his *Utopia* (1516).

The island of Utopia containeth in breadth in the middle part of it (for there it is broadest) two hundred miles. Which breadth continueth through the most part of the land, saving that by little and little it cometh in, and waxeth narrower towards both the ends. Which fetching about a circuit or compass of five hundred miles, do fashion the whole island like to the new moon. Between these two corners the sea runneth in, dividing them asunder by the distance of eleven miles or thereabouts, and there surmounteth into a large and wide sea, which by reason that the land on every side compasseth it about, and sheltereth it from the winds, is not rough, nor mounteth not with great waves, but almost floweth quietly, not much unlike a great standing pool: and maketh almost all the space within the belly of the land in manner of a haven: and to the great commodity of the inhabitants receiveth in ships towards every part of the land. The forefronts or frontiers of the two corners, what with fords and shelves, and what with rocks be very jeopardous and dangerous. In the middle distance between them both standeth up above the water a great rock, which therefore is nothing perilous because it is in sight. Upon the top of this rock is a fair and a strong tower builded, which they hold with a garrison of men. Other rocks there be that lie hid under the water, and therefore be dangerous. The channels be known only to themselves. And therefore it seldom chanceth that any stranger unless he be guided by a Utopian can come into this haven. Insomuch that they themselves could scarcely enter without jeopardy, but that their way is directed and ruled by certain landmarks standing on the shore. By turning, translating, and removing these marks into other places they may destroy their enemies' navies, be they never so many. The outside of the land is also full of havens, but the landing is so surely defenced, what by nature, and what by workmanship of man's hand, that a few defenders may drive back many armies.

There be in the island fifty-four large and fair cities, or shire towns, agreeing all together in one tongue, in like manners, institutions and laws. They be all set and situate alike, and in all points fashioned alike, as far forth as the place or plot suffereth.

Of these cities they that be nighest together be twenty-four miles asunder. Again there is none of them distant from the next above one day's journey afoot. There come yearly to Amaurote out of every city three old men wise and well experienced, there to entreat and debate, of the common matters of the land. For this city (because it standeth just in the midst of the island, and is therefore most meet for the ambassadors of all parts of the realm) is taken for the chief and head city. The precincts and bounds of the shires be so commodiously appointed out, and set forth for the cities, that never a one of them all hath of any side less than twenty miles of ground, and of some side also much more, as of that part where the cities be of farther distance asunder. None of the cities desire to enlarge the bounds and limits of their shires. For they count themselves rather the good husbands[1] than the owners of their lands. They have in

1. Husbands—caretakers or farmers.

the country in all parts of the shire houses or farms builded, well appointed and furnished with all sorts of instruments and tools belonging to husbandry. These houses be inhabited of the citizens, which come thither to dwell by course. No household or farm in the country hath fewer than forty persons, men and women, besides two bondmen, which be all under the rule and order of the good man, and the good wife of the house, being both very sage and discreet persons. And every thirty farms or families have one head ruler, which is called a philarch, being as it were a head bailiff. Out of every one of these families or farms cometh every year into the city twenty persons which have continued two years before in the country. In their place so many fresh be sent thither out of the city, which of them that have been there a year already, and be therefore expert and cunning in husbandry, shall be instructed and taught. And they the next year shall teach others. This order is used for fear that either scarceness of victuals, or some other like incommodity should chance, through lack of knowledge, if they should be altogether new, and fresh, and unexpert in husbandry. This manner and fashion of yearly changing and renewing the occupiers of husbandry, though it be solemn and customably used, to the intent that no man shall be constrained against his will to continue long in that hard and sharp kind of life, yet many of them have such a pleasure and delight in husbandry, that they obtain a longer space of years. These husbandmen plough and till the ground, and breed up cattle, and make ready wood, which they carry to the city either by land, or by water, as they may most conveniently. They bring up a great multitude of poultry, and that by a marvellous policy. For the hens do not sit upon the eggs; but by keeping them in a certain equal heat they bring life into them, and hatch them. The chickens, as soon as they come out of the shell, follow men and women instead of the hens. They bring up very few horses: nor none, but very fierce ones: and for none other use or purpose, but only to exercise their youth in riding and feats of arms. For oxen be put to all the labour of ploughing and drawing. Which they grant to be not so good as horses at a sudden brunt, and (as we say) at a dead lift, but yet they hold opinion that they will abide and suffer much more labour and pain than horses will. And they think that they be not in danger and subject unto so many diseases, and that they be kept and maintained with much less cost and charge: and finally that they be good for meat, when they be past labour. They sow corn only for bread. For their drink is either wine made of grapes, or else of apples, or pears, or else it is clean water. And many times mead made of honey or liquorice sodden in water, for thereof they have great store. And though they know certainly (for they know it perfectly indeed) how much victuals the city with the whole country or shire round about it doth spend: yet they sow much more corn, and breed up much more cattle, than serveth for their own use, and the over-plus they part among their borderers.[2] Whatsoever necessary things be lacking in the country, all such stuff they fetch out of the city: where without any exchange they easily obtain it of the magistrates of the city. For every month many of them go into the city on the holy day. When their harvest day draweth near and is at hand, then the philarchs, which be the head officers and bailiffs of husbandry, send word to the magistrates of the city what number of harvest men is needful to be sent to them out of the city. The which company of harvest men being there ready at the day appointed, almost in one fair day despatcheth all the harvest work.

Of the Cities, and Namely of Amaurote

As for their cities, he that knoweth one of them, knoweth them all: they be all like one to another, as farforth as the nature of the place permitteth. I will describe therefore to you one or other of them, for it skilleth[3] not greatly which: but which rather than Amaurote? Of them all this is the worthiest and of most dignity. For the residue acknowledge it for the head city, because there is the council house. Nor to me any of them all is better beloved, as wherein I lived five whole years together. The city of Amaurote standeth upon the side of a low hill in fashion almost four square. For the breadth of it beginneth a little beneath the top of the hill, and still continueth by the space of two miles, until it come to the river of Anyder. The length of it, which lieth by the river's side, is somewhat more. The river of Anyder riseth twenty-four miles above Amaurote out of a little spring. But being increased by other small floods and brooks that run into it, and among other two somewhat big ones, before the city it is half a mile broad, and farther broader. And sixty miles beyond the city it falleth into the Ocean sea. By all that space that lieth between the sea and the city, and a good sort of miles also above the city, the water ebbeth and floweth six hours together with a swift tide. When the sea floweth in, for the length of thirty miles it filleth all the Anyder with salt water, and driveth back the fresh water of the river. And somewhat further it changeth the sweetness of the fresh water with saltness. But a little beyond that the river waxeth sweet, and runneth forby the city fresh and pleasant. And when the sea ebbeth, and goeth back again, the fresh water followeth it almost even to the very fall into the sea. There goeth a bridge over the river made not of piles of timber, but of stonework with gorgeous and substantial arches at that part of the city that is farthest from the sea: to the intent that ships may go along forby all the side of the city without let.[4] They have also another river which indeed is not very great. But it runneth gently and pleasantly. For it riseth even out of the same hill that the city standeth upon, and runneth down a slope through the midst of the city into Anyder. And because it riseth a little without the city, the Amaurotians have inclosed the head spring of it with strong fences and bulwarks, and so have joined it to the city. This is done to the intent that the water should not be stopped nor turned away, or poisoned, if their enemies should chance to come upon them. From thence the water is derived and brought down in canals of brick divers ways into the lower parts of

2. Borderers—the surrounding countries.
3. Skilleth—matters.
4. Let—hindrance.

the city. Where that cannot be done, by reason that the place will not suffer it, there they gather the rain water in great cisterns, which doth them as good service. The city is compassed about with a high and thick wall full of turrets and bulwarks. A dry ditch, but deep, and broad, and overgrown with bushes, briers and thorns, goeth about three sides or quarters of the city. To the fourth side the river itself serveth for a ditch. The streets be appointed and set forth very commodious and handsome, both for carriage, and also against the winds. The houses be of fair and gorgeous building, and in the street side they stand joined together in a long row through the whole street without any partition or separation. The streets be twenty feet broad. On the back side of the houses through the whole length of the street, lie large gardens which be closed in round about with the back part of the streets. Every house hath two doors, one into the street, and a postern door on the back side into the garden. These doors be made with two leaves, never locked nor bolted, so easy to be opened, that they will follow the least drawing of a finger, and shut again by themselves. Every man that will, may go in, for there is nothing within the houses that is private, or any man's own. And every tenth year they change their houses by lot. They set great store by their gardens. In them they have vineyards, all manner of fruit, herbs, and flowers, so pleasant, so well furnished and so finely kept, that I never saw a thing more fruitful, nor better trimmed in any place. Their study and diligence herein cometh not only of pleasure, but also of a certain strife and contention that is between street and street, concerning the trimming, husbanding, and furnishing of their gardens: every man for his own part. And verily you shall not lightly find in all the city anything that is more commodious, either for the profit of the citizens, or for pleasure.

Of the Magistrates

Every thirty families or farms choose them yearly an officer, which is called the philarch. Every ten philarchs with all their 300 families be under an officer which is called the chief philarch. Moreover, as concerning the election of the prince, all the philarchs which be in number 200, first be sworn to choose him whom they think most meet and expedient. Then by a secret election, they name prince, one of those four whom the people before named unto them. For out of the four quarters of the city there be four chosen, out of every quarter one, to stand for the election: which be put up to the council. The prince's office continueth all his lifetime, unless he be deposed or put down for suspicion of tyranny. They choose the chief philarchs yearly, but lightly they change them not. All the other offices be but for one year. The chief philarchs every third day, and sometimes, if need be, oftener, come into the council house with the prince. Their council is concerning the commonwealth. If there be any controversies among the commoners, which be very few, they despatch and end them by-and-by. They take ever two philarchs to them in counsel, and every day a new couple. And it is provided that nothing touching the commonwealth shall be confirmed and ratified unless it have been reasoned of and debated three days in the council, before it be decreed. It is death to have any consultation for the commonwealth out of the council, or the place of the common election. This statute, they say, was made to the intent that the prince and chief philarchs might not easily conspire together to oppress the people by tyranny, and to change the state of the weal public. Therefore matters of great weight and importance be brought to the election house of the philarchs, which open the matter to their families. And afterward, when they have consulted among themselves, they show their device to the council. Sometimes the matter is brought before the council of the whole island. Furthermore this custom also the council useth, to dispute or reason of no matter the same day that it is first proposed or put forth, but to defer it to the next sitting of the council. Because that no man when he hath rashly there spoken what cometh first to his tongue's end, shall then afterwards rather study for reasons wherewith to defend and confirm his first foolish sentence, than for the commodity of the commonwealth: as one rather willing the harm or hindrance of the weal public than any loss or diminution of his own existimation. And as one that would not for shame (which is a very foolish shame) be counted anything overseen in the matter at the first. Who at the first ought to have spoken rather wisely, then hastily, or rashly.

Of Sciences, Crafts, and Occupations

Husbandry is a science common to them all in general, both men and women, wherein they be all expert and cunning. In this they be all instruct even from their youth: partly in schools with traditions and precepts, and partly in the country nigh the city, brought up as it were in playing, not only beholding the use of it, but by occasion of exercising their bodies practising it also. Besides husbandry, which (as I said) is common to them all, every one of them learneth one or other several and particular science, as his own proper craft. That is most commonly either clothworking in wool or flax, or masonry, or the smith's craft, or the carpenter's science. For there is none other occupation that any number to speak of doth use there. For their garments, which throughout all the island be of one fashion (saving that there is a difference between the man's garment and the woman's, between the married and the unmarried) and this one continueth for evermore unchanged, seemly and comely to the eye, no let to the moving and wielding of the body, also fit both for winter and summer: as for these garments (I say) every family maketh their own. But of the other foresaid crafts every man learneth one. And not only the men, but also the women. But the women, as the weaker sort, be put to the easier crafts: they work wool and flax. The other more laboursome sciences be committed to the men. For the most part every man is brought up in his father's craft. For most commonly they be naturally thereto bent and inclined. But if a man's mind stand to any other, he is by adoption put into a family of that occupation, which he doth most fantasy.[5] Whom not only

5. Fantasy—desire or choose.

his father, but also the magistrates do diligently look to, that he be put to a discreet and an honest householder. Yea, and if any person, when he hath learned one craft, be desirous to learn also another, he is likewise suffered and permitted.

When he hath learned both, he occupieth whether he will: unless the city have more need of the one, than of the other. The chief and almost the only office of the philarchs is to see and take heed that no man sit idle: but that every one apply his own craft with earnest diligence. And yet for all that, not be wearied from early in the morning, to late in the evening, with continual work, like labouring and toiling beasts.

For this is worse than the miserable and wretched condition of bondmen. Which nevertheless is almost everywhere the life of workmen and artificers, saving in Utopia. For they dividing the day and the night into twenty-four just hours, appoint and assign only six of those hours to work; three before noon, upon the which they go straight to dinner: and after dinner, when they have rested two hours, then they work three and upon that they go to supper. About eight of the clock in the evening (counting one of clock as the first hour after noon) they go to bed: eight hours they give to sleep. All the void time, that is between the hours of work, sleep, and meat, that they be suffered to bestow, every man as he liketh best himself. Not to the intent that they should misspend this time in riot or slothfulness: but being then licensed from the labour of their own occupations, to bestow the time well and thriftly upon some other good science, as shall please them. For it is a solemn custom there, to have lectures daily early in the morning, where to be present they only be constrained that be chosen and appointed to learning. Howbeit a great multitude of every sort of people, both men and women, go to hear lectures, some one and some another, as every man's nature is inclined. Yet, this notwithstanding, if any man had rather bestow this time upon his own occupation (as it chanceth in many, whose minds rise not in the contemplation of any science liberal) he is not letted, nor prohibited, but is also praised and commended, as profitable to the commonwealth. After supper they bestow one hour in play: in summer in their gardens: in winter in their common halls: where they dine and sup. There they exercise themselves in music, or else in honest and wholesome communication. But lest you be deceived, one thing you must look more narrowly upon. For seeing they bestow but six hours in work perchance you may think that the lack of some necessary things hereof may ensue. But this is nothing so. For that small time is not only enough but also too much for the store and abundance of all things that be requisite, either for the necessity, or commodity of life. The which thing you also shall perceive, if you weigh and consider with yourselves how great a part of the people in other countries liveth idle. First almost all women, which be the half of the whole number: or else if the women be anywhere occupied, there most commonly in their stead the men be idle. Beside this how great, and how idle a company is there of priests, and religious men, as they call them? Put thereto all rich men, especially all landed men, which commonly be called gentlemen, and noblemen. Take into this number also their servants: I mean all that flock of stout bragging rush-bucklers. Join to them also sturdy and valiant beggars, cloaking their idle life under the colour of some disease or sickness. And truly you shall find them much fewer than you thought, by whose labour all these things be gotten that men use and live by. Now consider with yourself, of these few that do work, how few be occupied, in necessary works. For where money beareth all the swing, there many vain and superfluous occupations must needs be used, to serve only for riotous superfluity and unhonest pleasure. For the same multitude that now is occupied in work, if they were divided into so few occupations as the necessary use of nature requireth; in so great plenty of things as then of necessity would ensue, doubtless the prices would be too little for the artificers to maintain their livings. But if all these, that be now busied about unprofitable occupations, with all the whole flock of them that live idly and slothfully, which consume and waste every one of them more of these things that come by other men's labour, then two of the workmen themselves do: if all these (I say) were set to profitable occupations, you easily perceive how little time would be enough, yea and too much to store us with all things that may be requisite either for necessity, or for commodity, yea or for pleasure, so that the same pleasure be true and natural. And this in Utopia the thing itself maketh manifest and plain. For there in all the city, with the whole country, or shire adjoining to it scarcely 500 persons of all the whole number of men and women, that be neither too old, nor too weak to work, be licensed from labour. Among them be the philarchs which (though they be by the laws exempt and privileged from labour) yet they exempt not themselves: to the intent they may the rather by their example provoke others to work. The same vacation from labour do they also enjoy, to whom the people persuaded by the commendation of the priests, and secret election of the philarchs, have given a perpetual license from labour to learning. But if any one of them prove not according to the expectation and hope of him conceived, he is forthwith plucked back to the company of artificers. And contrariwise, often it chanceth that a handicraftsman doth so earnestly bestow his vacant and spare hours in learning, and through diligence to profit therein, that he is taken from his handy occupation, and promoted to the company of the learned. Out of this order of the learned be chosen ambassadors, priests, chief philarchs, and finally the prince himself.

Of Warfare

Immediately after that war is once solemnly announced, they procure many proclamations signed with their own common seal to be set up privily at one time in their enemies' land, in places most frequented. In these proclamations they promise great rewards to him that will kill their enemies' prince, and somewhat less gifts, but them very great also, for every head of them, whose names be in the said proclamations contained. They be those whom they count their chief adversaries, next unto the prince. Whatsoever is prescribed unto him that killeth any of the proclaimed persons, that is doubled to him that bringeth any of the same to them alive; yea, and to the proclaimed persons themselves, if they will change their minds and come into them, taking their parts, they proffer the same great rewards with pardon and surety of their lives. Therefore it quickly cometh to pass that they have all other men in suspicion, and be unfaithful and mistrusting among themselves one to another, living in great fear, and in no less jeopardy. For it is well known, that divers times the most part of them (and specially the prince himself) hath been betrayed of them, in whom they put their most hope and trust. So that there is no manner of act nor deed that gifts and rewards do not enforce men unto. And in rewards they keep no measure. But remembering and considering into how great hazard and jeopardy they call them, endeavour themselves to recompense the greatness of the danger with like great benefits. And therefore they promise not only wonderful great abundance of gold, but also lands of great revenues lying in most places among their friends. And their promises they perform faithfully without any fraud or deceit. This custom of buying and selling adversaries among other people is disallowed, as a cruel act of a base and a cowardish mind. But they in this behalf think themselves much praiseworthy, as who like wise men by this means despatch great wars without any battle or skirmish. Yea they count it also a deed of pity and mercy, because that by the death of a few offenders the lives of a great number of innocents, as well of their own men as also of their enemies, be ransomed and saved, which in fighting should have been slain. For they do no less pity the base and common sort of their enemies' people, than they do their own; knowing that they be driven to war against their wills by the furious madness of their princes and heads. If by none of these means the matter go forward as they would have it, then they procure occasions of debate and dissension to be spread among their enemies. As by causing the prince's brother, or some of the noblemen, to hope to obtain the kingdom. If this way prevail not, then they raise up the people that be next neighbours and borderers to their enemies, and them they set in their necks under the colour of some old title of right, such as kings do never lack. To them they promise their help and aid in their war. And as for money they give them abundance. But of their own citizens they send to them few or none. Whom they make so much of and love so entirely, that they would not be willing to change any of them for their adversary's prince. But their gold and silver, because they keep it all for this only purpose, they lay it out frankly and freely; as who[6] should live even as wealthily, if they had bestowed it every penny. Yea, and besides their riches, which they keep at home, that have also an infinite treasure abroad, by reason that (as I said before) many nations be in their debt. Therefore they hire soldiers out of all countries and send them to battle, but chiefly of the Zapoletes. This people is five hundred miles from Utopia eastward. They be hideous, savage and fierce, dwelling in wild woods and high mountains, where they were bred and brought up. They be of an hard nature, able to abide and sustain heat, cold and labour, abhorring from all delicate dainties, occupying no husbandry nor tillage of the ground, homely and rude both in the building of their houses and in their apparel, given unto no goodness, but only to the breeding and bringing up of cattle. The most part of their living is by hunting and stealing. They be born only to war, which they diligently and earnestly seek for. And when they have gotten it, they be wonders glad thereof. They go forth of their country in great companies together, and whosoever lacketh soldiers, there they proffer their service for small wages. This is the only craft that they have to get their living by. They maintain their life by seeking their death. For them with whom they be in wages they fight hardily, fiercely, and faithfully. But they bind themselves for no certain time. But upon this condition they enter into bonds, that the next day they will take part with the other side for greater wages, and the next day after that, they will be ready to come back again for a little more money. There be few wars thereaway, wherein is not a great number of them in both parties. Therefore it daily chanceth that nigh kinsfolk, which were hired together on one part, and there very friendly and familiarly used themselves one with another, shortly after being separate into contrary parts, run one against another enviously and fiercely, and forgetting both kindred and friendship, thrust their swords one in another. And that for none other cause, but that they be hired of contrary princes for a little money. Which they do so highly regard and esteem, that they will easily be provoked to change parts for a halfpenny more wages by the day. So quickly they have taken a smack in covetousness. Which for all that is to them no profit. For that they get by fighting, immediately they spend unthriftily and wretchedly in riot. This people fight for the Utopians against all nations, because they give them greater wages than any other nation will. For the Utopians like as they seek good men to use well, so they seek these evil and vicious men to abuse. Whom, when need requireth, with promises of great rewards, they put forth into great jeopardies. From whence the most part of them never cometh again to ask their rewards. But to them that remain alive they pay that which they promised faithfully, that they may be more willing to put themselves in like dangers another time. Nor the Utopians pass not how many of them they bring to destruction. For they believe that they should do a very good deed for all mankind, if they could rid out of the world all that foul stinking den of that most wicked and cursed people.

Of the Religions in Utopia

There be divers kinds of religion not only in sundry parts of the island, but also in divers places of every city. Some worship for God, the sun; some, the moon; some other of the planets. There be that give worship to a man that was once of excellent virtue or of famous glory, not only as God, but also as the chiefest and highest God. But the

6. "As who should live," etc.: read this "as people who would live just as richly. . ."

most and the wisest part (rejecting all these) believe that there is a certain godly power unknown, everlasting, incomprehensible, inexplicable, far above the capacity and reach of man's wit, dispersed throughout all the world, not in bigness, but in virtue and power. Him they call the father of all. To him alone they attribute the beginnings, the increasings, the proceedings, the changes and the ends of all things. Neither they give divine honours to any other than to him. Yea all the other also, though they be in divers opinions, yet in this point they agree all together with the wisest sort, in believing that there is one chief and principal God, the maker and ruler of the whole world: whom they all commonly in their country language call Mithra. But after they heard us speak of the name of Christ, of his doctrine, laws, miracles, and of the no less wonderful constancy of so many martyrs, whose blood willingly shed brought a great number of nations throughout all parts of the world into their sect; you will not believe with how glad minds, they agreed unto the same: whether it were by the secret inspiration of God, or else for that they thought it next unto that opinion, which among them is counted the chiefest. Howbeit I think this was no small help and furtherance in the matter, that they heard us say, that Christ instituted among his, all things common; and that the same community doth yet remain amongst the rightest Christian companies. Verily howsoever it come to pass, many of them consented together in our religion, and were washed in the holy water of baptism. They also which do not agree to Christ's religion, fear no man from it, nor speak against any man that hath received it. Saving that one of our company in my presence was sharply punished. He as soon as he was baptised began against our wills, with more earnest affection than wisdom, to reason of Christ's religion; and began to wax so hot in his matter, that he did not only prefer our religion before all other, but also did utterly despise and condemn all other, calling them profane, and the followers of them wicked and devilish and the children of everlasting damnation. When he had thus long reasoned the matter, they laid hold on him, accused him and condemned him into exile, not as a despiser of religion, but as a seditious person and a raiser up of dissension among the people. For this is one of the ancientest laws among them; that no man shall be blamed for reasoning in the maintenance of his own religion. For King Utopus, even at the first beginning, hearing that the inhabitants of the land were, before his coming thither, at continual dissension and strife among themselves for their religions; as soon as he had gotten the victory, first of all he made a decree, that it should be lawful for every man to favour and follow what religion he would, and that he might do the best he could to bring other to this opinion, so that he did it peaceably, gently, quietly, and soberly, without haste and contentious rebuking and inveighing against other. If he could not by fair and gentle speech induce them unto his opinion yet he should use no kind of violence, and refrain from displeasant and seditious words. To him that would vehemently and fervently in this cause strive and contend was decreed banishment or bondage. This law did King Utopus make not only for the maintenance of peace, which he saw through continual contention and mortal hatred utterly extinguished; but also because he thought this decree should make for the furtherance of religion. Whereof he durst define and determine nothing unadvisedly, as doubting whether God desiring manifold and divers sorts of honour, would inspire sundry men with sundry kinds of religion. And this surely he thought a very unmeet and foolish thing, and a point of arrogant presumption, to compel all other by violence and threatenings to agree to the same that thou believest to be true. Furthermore though there be one religion which alone is true, and all other vain and superstitious, yet did he well foresee (so that the matter were handled with reason, and sober modesty) that the truth of its own power would at the last issue out and come to light. But if contention and debate in that behalf should continually be used, as the worst men be most obstinate and stubborn, and in their evil opinion most constant; he perceived that then the best and holiest religion would be trodden underfoot and destroyed by most vain superstitions, even as good corn is by thorns and weeds overgrown and choked. Therefore all this matter he left undiscussed, and gave to every man free liberty and choice to believe what he would.

STUDY QUESTIONS

1. Try making a sketch-map or diagram of Amaurote, the Utopian capital. What considerations or specifications does More give that are unnecessary in a modern American city? Are there any specifications that might improve American cities? What are they?
2. The Zapoletes, Utopia's mercenary soldiers, must have presented some problems to their employers. What might these be? Would you be willing to serve as a mercenary soldier? Why or why not?

LITERARY SELECTION 49

The Tempest

William Shakespeare, 1564–1616

Will Shakespeare was not a classical scholar, having "small Latin and less Greek," as Ben Jonson described him. His formal schooling was limited. His plots were mostly borrowed and his plays intended as box-office hits, which they were. Yet he is the supreme figure of Renaissance literature and the most quoted writer in the English language. How can this be? Critics have said that no human being could have written Mozart's music, and the same can be said for the plays of Shakespeare. There is no accounting for genius; we have the music and the plays, and the world is infinitely richer because of them. Shakespeare understood human nature in all its complexity and perversity and was able to translate his perceptions into dramatic speech and action.

The themes in the thirty-seven plays—chronicle-plays, comedies, and tragedies—are timeless, but the flavor of the Renaissance is unmistakable. Like other Renaissance writers, Shakespeare was concerned with the active role of men and women in the lusty and prosperous Elizabethan age: their passions, problems, and aspirations. Like Machiavelli, he saw people as they really were and the vision was, for Shakespeare if not for Machiavelli, profoundly disturbing. Nevertheless, his pessimistic view of people's baser instincts was tempered by his belief in their ability to achieve, usually through suffering, some measure of dignity and even nobility.

Shakespeare himself had led a turbulent life and had known all sorts of people. In the midst of the vigorous and violent life of Elizabethan England he had carved a name for himself and made a fortune, enabling him to retire to his home in Stratford-on-Avon. Here he wrote *The Tempest*, the last play to come entirely from his own hand. We may consider it as a sort of final report on all his experiences, a summary of his insights and discoveries about how people lived their lives.

The play is set in a never-never land, a Mediterranean island where anything can happen. Though removed from ordinary experience, this device enables Shakespeare to enlarge the scope of the play. He can order people and events as he wills them, create Prospero the wise magician, bestial Caliban, and spritely Ariel. The play is, of course, symbolic. Caliban represents the dark side of human nature that caused so much Renaissance pessimism; Ariel, the blithe spirit, represents the higher nature of human intellect. Prospero may be Shakespeare himself or he may simply be humankind. No matter, he is the agent who must create the balance between opposing forces. He controls the rival spirits of Ariel and Caliban and through them brings balance and order to the mortals whom he brings to his fantastic kingdom. It is he who helps all of them find themselves. And finally, it is Prospero who returns with them to the land of the living, with a new and higher order established, and with kingly power resting with the young couple, neither of whom had been a party to the long evil history behind them. The king is the young man of action; the queen is the young woman of spirit, educated by Prospero to assume her rightful place in the "brave new world."

CHARACTERS

Alonzo, King of Naples
Sebastian, his brother
Prospero, the right Duke of Milan
Antonio, his brother, the usurping Duke of Milan
Ferdinand, son to the King of Naples
Gonzalo, an honest old Counsellor
Adrian and **Francisco**, lords
Caliban, a savage and deformed slave
Trinculo, a jester
Stephano, a drunken butler
Master of a ship
Boatswain
Mariners
Miranda, daughter to Prospero
Ariel, an airy spirit

Iris, **Nymphs**, **Juno**, **Ceres**, **Reapers** — Spirits

Act I

Scene 1

[On a ship at sea. A tempestuous noise of thunder and lightning heard.]
[Enter a SHIPMASTER and a BOATSWAIN.]

Master: Boatswain!
Boatswain: Here, master. What cheer?
Master: Good,[7] speak to th' mariners. Fall to 't yarely,[8] or we run ourselves aground. Bestir, Bestir! *[Exit.]*
[Enter MARINERS.]
Boatswain: Heigh, my hearts! cheerly, cheerly, my hearts! yare, yare! Take in the topsail! Tend to th' master's whistle! Blow till thou burst thy wind, if room enough![9]
[Enter ALONZO, SEBASTIAN, ANTONIO, FERDINAND, GONZALO, and others.]
Alonzo: Good boatswain, have care. Where's the master? Play the men.
Boatswain: I pray now, keep below.
Antonio: Where is the master, boatswain?
Boatswain: Do you not hear him? You mar our labour: keep your cabins: you do assist the storm.
Gonzalo: Nay, good, be patient.
Boatswain: When the sea is. Hence! What care these roarers for the name of King? To cabin: silence! trouble us not!
Gonzalo: Good, yet remember whom thou hast aboard.
Boatswain: None that I more love than myself. You are a counsellor; if you can command these elements to silence, and work the peace of the presence, we will not hand a rope more; use your authority: if you cannot, give thanks you have lived so long, and make yourself ready in your cabin for the mischance of the hour, if it so hap. Cheerly, good hearts! Out of our way, I say. *[Exit.]*
Gonzalo: I have great comfort from this fellow: methinks he hath no drowning mark upon him; his complexion is perfect gallows. Stand fast, good Fate, to his hanging: make the rope of his destiny our cable, for our own doth little advantage. If he be not born to be hanged, our case is miserable. *[Exeunt.]*
[Re-enter BOATSWAIN.]
Boatswain: Down with the topmast! yare! lower, lower! Bring her to try with maincourse. *[A cry within.]* A plague upon this howling! they are louder than the weather or our office.
[Re-enter SEBASTIAN, ANTONIO, and GONZALO.]
Yet again! what do you here? Shall we give o'er, and drown? Have you a mind to sink?
Sebastian: A pox o' your throat, you bawling, blasphemous, incharitable dog!
Boatswain: Work you then!
Antonio: Hang, cur! hang, you whoreson, insolent noisemaker. We are less afraid to be drowned than thou art.
Gonzalo: I'll warrant him for drowning, though the ship were no stronger than a nutshell, and as leaky as an unstanched wench.

7. Good fellow.
8. Briskly.
9. If we have enough sea room.

Boatswain: Lay her a-hold, a-hold! set her two courses!
off to sea again! lay her off.
[Enter MARINERS, wet.]
Mariners: All lost, to prayers, to prayers! all lost!
Boatswain: What, must our mouths be cold?
Gonzalo: The King and Prince at prayers! Let's assist
them,
For our case is as theirs.
Sebastian: I am out of patience.
Antonio: We are merely cheated of our lives by
drunkards:
This wide-chapped rascal!—Would thou mightst lie
drowning
The washing of ten tides!
Gonzalo: He'll be hanged yet,
Though every drop of water swear against it,
And gape at wid'st to glut him.
[A confused noise within.] "Mercy on us!"—
"We split, we split!"—"Farewell, my wife and children!"—
"Farewell, brother!"—"We split, we split, we split!"
Antonio: Let's all sink wi' th' King.
Sebastian: Let's take leave of him. *[Exeunt.]*
Gonzalo: Now would I give a thousand furlongs of sea
for an acre of barren ground, long heath, broom, furze,
anything. The wills above be done! but I would fain die a
dry death. *[Exeunt.]*

Scene 2

[The Island. Before Prospero's cell.]
[Enter PROSPERO and MIRANDA.]
Miranda: If by your Art, my dearest father, you have
Put the wild waters in this roar, allay them.
The sky, it seems, would pour down stinking pitch
But that the sea, mounting to th' welkin's cheek,
Dashes the fire out. O, I have suffered
With those that I saw suffer! a brave vessel,
(Who had, no doubt, some noble creature in her,)
Dashed all to pieces! O, the cry did knock
Against my very heart! Poor souls, they perish'd!
Had I been any god of power, I would
Have sunk the sea within the earth, or ere
It should the good ship so have swallow'd, and
The fraughting[10] souls within her.
Prospero: Be collected:
No more amazement: tell your piteous heart
There's no harm done.
Miranda: O, woe the day!
Prospero: No harm.
I have done nothing but in care of thee,
Of thee, my dear one, thee, my daughter, who
Art ignorant of what thou art; nought knowing
Of whence I am, nor that I am more better
Than Prospero, master of a full poor cell,
And thy no greater father.
Miranda: More to know
Did never meddle with my thoughts.
Prospero: 'Tis time
I should inform thee farther. Lend thy hand
And pluck my magic garment from me.— So:
[Lays down his mantle.]
Lie there, my Art. Wipe thou thine eyes; have comfort.
The direful spectacle of the wrack, which touch'd
The very virtue of compassion in thee,
I have with such provision in mine Art
So safely ordered that there is no soul—
No, not so much perdition as an hair
Betid to any creature in the vessel
Which thou heard'st cry, which thou saw'st sink. Sit
down;
For thou must now know farther.
Miranda: You have often
Begun to tell me what I am, but stopp'd
And left me to a bootless inquisition,[11]
Concluding "Stay! not yet."
Prospero: The hour's now come;
The very minute bids thee ope thine ear,
Obey, and be attentive. Canst thou remember
A time before we came unto this cell?
I do not think thou canst, for then thou wast not
Out[12] three years old.
Miranda: Certainly, sir, I can.
Prospero: By what? by any other house or person?
Of any thing the image tell me, that
Hath kept with thy remembrance.
Miranda: 'Tis far off,
And rather like a dream than an assurance
That my remembrance warrants. Had I not
Four or five women once that tended me?
Prospero: Thou hadst, and more, Miranda. But how is it
That this lives in thy mind? What seest thou else
In the dark backward and abysm of time?
If thou remembʼrest aught ere thou cam'st here,
How thou cam'st here thou mayst.
Miranda: But that I do not.
Prospero: Twelve year since, Miranda, twelve year since,
Thy father was the Duke of Milan, and
A prince of power.
Miranda: Sir, are not you my father?
Prospero: Thy mother was a piece of virtue, and
She said thou wast my daughter; and thy father
Was Duke of Milan, and thou his only heir
And princess—no worse issued.
Miranda: O the heavens!
What foul play had we, that we came from thence?
Or blessed was't we did?
Prospero: Both, both, my girl:
By foul play, as thou say'st, were we heav'd thence,
But blessedly holp hither.
Miranda: O, my heart bleeds
To think o' th' teen[13] that I have turn'd you to,
Which is from my remembrance! Please you, farther.
Prospero: My brother and my uncle, call'd Antonio,—
I pray thee, mark me, that a brother should
Be so perfidious!—he whom next thyself
Of all the world I lov'd, and to him put
The manage of my state; as at that time
Through all the signories it was the first,

10. Fraughting—composing the freight.
11. Useless inquiry.
12. Fully.
13. Trouble.

And Prospero the prime duke, being so reputed
In dignity, and for the liberal Arts
Without a parallel; those being all my study,
The government I cast upon my brother,
And to my state grew stranger, being transported
And rapt in secret studies. Thy false uncle—
Dost thou attend me?
Miranda: Sir, most heedfully.
Prospero: Being once perfected how to grant suits,
How to deny them, who t' advance, and who
To trash for over-topping, new-created
The creatures that were mine, I say, or chang'd 'em,
Or else new-form'd 'em; having both the key
Of officer and office, set all hearts i' th' state
To what tune pleas'd his ear, that now he was
The ivy which had hid my princely trunk
And suck'd my verdure out on 't. Thou attend'st not?
Miranda: O, good sir, I do!
Prospero: I pray thee, mark me.
I, thus neglecting worldly ends, all dedicated
To closeness and the bettering of my mind
With that which, but by being so retir'd
O'er-prized all popular rate, in my false brother
Awak'd an evil nature; and my trust,
Like a good parent, did beget of him
A falsehood in its contrary as great
As my trust was; which had indeed no limit,
A confidence sans bound. He being thus lorded,
Not only with what my revenue yielded,
But what my power might else exact, like one
Who having into truth, by telling of it,
Made such a sinner of his memory,
To credit his own lie, he did believe
He was indeed the duke; out o' th' substitution
And executing the outward face of royalty,
With all prerogative; —hence his ambition growing,—
Dost thou hear?
Miranda: Your tale, sir, would cure deafness.
Prospero: To have no screen between this part he play'd
And him he play'd it for, he needs will be
Absolute Milan.[14] Me, poor man, my library
Was dukedom large enough: of temporal royalties
He thinks me now incapable; confederates,
So dry he was for sway, wi' th' King of Naples
To give him annual tribute, do him homage,
Subject his coronet to his crown, and bend
The dukedom yet unbow'd—alas poor Milan!—
To most ignoble stooping.
Miranda: O the heavens!
Prospero: Mark his condition, and th' event; then tell me
If this might be a brother.
Miranda: I should sin
To think but nobly of my grandmother:
Good wombs have borne bad sons.
Prospero: Now the condition.
This King of Naples, being an enemy
To me inveterate, hearkens my brother's suit;
Which was, that he, in lieu o' th' premises
Of homage and I know not how much tribute,
Should presently extirpate me and mine
Out of the dukedom, and confer fair Milan,
With all the honours, on my brother: whereon,
A treacherous army levied, one midnight
Fated to th' purpose, did Antonio open
The gates of Milan; and, i' th' dead of darkness
The ministers for th' purpose hurried thence
Me and thy crying self.
Miranda: Alack, for pity!
I, not rememb'ring how I cried out then,
Will cry it o'er again: it is a hint
That wrings mine eyes to't.
Prospero: Hear a little further,
And then I'll bring thee to the present business
Which now's upon 's; without the which, this story
Were most impertinent.
Miranda: Wherefore did they not
That hour destroy us?
Prospero: Well demanded, wench:
My tale provokes that question. Dear, they durst not,
So dear the love my people bore me; nor set
A mark so bloody on the business; but
With colours fairer painted their foul ends.
In few, they hurried us aboard a bark,
Bore us some leagues to sea; where they prepared
A rotten carcass of a boat, not rigg'd,
Nor tackle, sail, nor mast; the very rats
Instinctively have quit it: there they hoist us,
To cry to th' sea that roar'd to us; to sigh
To th' winds, whose pity, sighing back again,
Did us but loving wrong.
Miranda: Alack, what trouble
Was I then to you!
Prospero: O, a cherubin
Thou wast that did preserve me. Thou didst smile,
Infused with a fortitude from heaven
When I have deck'd the sea with drops full salt,
Under my burthen groan'd; which rais'd in me
An undergoing stomach,[15] to bear up
Against what should ensue.
Miranda: How came we ashore?
Prospero: By Providence divine.
Some food we had, and some fresh water, that
A noble Neapolitan, Gonzalo,
Out of his charity, being then appointed
Master of this design, did give us, with
Rich garments, linens, stuffs and necessaries
Which since have steaded much; so, of his gentleness,
Knowing I lov'd my books, he furnish'd me
From mine own library with volumes that
I prize above my dukedom.
Miranda: Would I might
But ever see that man!
Prospero: Now I arise:
Sit still, and hear the last of our sea-sorrow.
Here in this island we arriv'd; and here
Have I, thy schoolmaster, made thee more profit
Than other princess' can, that have more time
For vainer hours, and tutors not so careful.
Miranda: Heavens thank you for't. And now, I pray you, sir,

14. Duke of Milan.
15. Courage and strength.

For still 'tis beating in my mind, your reason
For raising this sea-storm?
Prospero: Know thus far forth.
By accident most strange, bountiful Fortune,
(Now my dear lady) hath mine enemies
Brought to this shore; and by my prescience
I find my zenith[16] doth depend upon
A most auspicious star, whose influence
If now I court not, but omit, my fortunes
Will ever after droop. Here cease more questions:
Thou art inclin'd to sleep; 'tis a good dullness,
And give it way: I know thou canst not choose.
[Miranda sleeps.]
Come away, servant, come. I am ready now.
Approach, my Ariel, come.
[Enter ARIEL.]
Ariel: All hail, great master! grave sir, hail! I come
To answer thy best pleasure; be't to fly,
To swim, to dive into the fire, to ride
On the curl'd clouds, to thy strong bidding task
Ariel and all his quality.
Prospero: Hast thou, spirit,
Perform'd to point the tempest that I bade thee?
Ariel: To every article.
I boarded the king's ship; now on the beak,
Now in the waist, the deck, in every cabin,
I flam'd amazement. sometime I'd divide,
And burn in many places; on the topmast,
The yards and bovesprit, would I flame distinctly,
Then meet and join. Jove's lightnings, the precursors
O' th' dreadful thunderclaps, more momentary
And sight-outrunning were not: the fire and cracks
Of sulphurous roaring the most mighty Neptune
Seem to besiege and make his bold waves tremble;
Yea, his dread trident shake.
Prospero: My brave spirit!
Who was so firm, so constant, that this coil[17]
Would not infect his reason?
Ariel: Not a soul
But felt a fever of the mad, and play'd
Some tricks of desperation. All but mariners
Plung'd in the foaming brine, and quit the vessel,
Then all afire with me: the King's son, Ferdinand,
With hair up-staring,—then like reeds, not hair,—
Was the first man that leap'd; cried, "Hell is empty,
And all the devils are here."
Prospero: Why, that's my spirit!
But was not this nigh shore?
Ariel: Close by, my master.
Prospero: But are they, Ariel, safe?
Ariel: Not a hair perish'd;
On their sustaining garments not a blemish,
But fresher than before: and, as thou bad'st me.
In troops I have dispers'd them 'bout the isle.
The King's son have I landed by himself,
Whom I left cooling of the air with sighs
In an odd angle[18] of the isle and sitting,
His arms in this sad knot.
Prospero: Of the King's ship,
The mariners, say how thou hast dispos'd,
And all the rest o' th' fleet.
Ariel: Safely in harbour
Is the King's ship; in the deep nook, where once
Thou call'dst me up at midnight to fetch dew
From the still-vexed Bermoothes, there she's hid:
The mariners all under hatches stow'd,
Who, with a charm join'd to their suffer'd labour,
I have left asleep: and for the rest o' th' fleet,
Which I dispers'd, they all have met again,
And are upon the Mediterranean flote,[19]
Bound sadly home for Naples;
Supposing that they saw the King's ship wrack'd
And his great person perish.
Prospero: Ariel, thy charge
Exactly is perform'd; but there's more work.
What is the time o' th' day?
Ariel: Past the mid season.
Prospero: At least two glasses.[20] The time 'twixt six and now
Must by us both be spent most preciously.
Ariel: Is there more toil? Since thou dost give me pains,
Let me remember thee what thou hast promis'd,
Which is not yet perform'd me.
Prospero: How now? moody?
What is't thou canst demand?
Ariel: My liberty.
Prospero: Before the time be out? no more!
Ariel: I prithee,
Remember I have done thee worthy service;
Told thee no lies, made no mistakings, serv'd
Without or grudge or grumblings: thou didst promise
To bate me a full year.
Prospero: Dost thou forget
From what a torment I did free thee?
Ariel: No.
Prospero: Thou dost; and think'st it much to tread the ooze
Of the salt deep,
To run upon the sharp wind of the north,
To do me business in the veins o' th' earth
When it is bak'd with frost.
Ariel: I do not, sir.
Prospero: Thou liest, malignant thing! Hast thou forgot
The foul witch Sycorax, who with age and envy
Was grown into a hoop? hast thou forgot her?
Ariel: No, sir.
Prospero: Thou hast. Where was she born? speak; tell me.
Ariel: Sir, in Argier.[21]
Prospero: O, was she so? I must
Once in a month recount what thou hast been,
Which thou forget'st. This damn'd witch Sycorax,
For mischiefs manifold, and sorceries terrible
To enter human hearing, from Argier,
Thou know'st, was banished; for one thing she did
They would not take her life. Is not this true?

16. Highest fortune.
17. Turmoil.
18. An out-of-the-way corner.
19. Sea.
20. Two hourglasses. It is two o'clock.
21. Algiers.

Ariel: Ay, sir.
Prospero: This blue-eyed hag was hither brought with child,
And here was left by th' sailors. Thou, my slave,
As thou report'st thyself, was then her servant;
And, for thou wast a spirit too delicate
To act her earthy and abhorr'd commands,
Refusing her grand hests,[22] she did confine thee,
By help of her more potent ministers,
And in her most unmitigable rage,
Into a cloven pine; within which rift
Imprison'd thou didst painfully remain
A dozen years; within which space she died,
And left thee there; where thou didst vent thy groans
As fast as millwheels strike. Then was this island—
Save for the son that she did litter here,
A freckled whelp, hag-born—not honour'd with
A human shape.
Ariel: Yes, Caliban her son.
Prospero: Dull thing, I say so; he, that Caliban,
Whom now I keep in service. Thou best know'st
What torment I did find thee in; thy groans
Did make wolves howl, and penetrate the breasts
Of ever-angry bears: it was a torment
To lay upon the damn'd, which Sycorax
Could not again undo: it was mine Art,
When I arriv'd and heard thee, that made gape
The pine, and let thee out.
Ariel: I thank thee, master.
Prospero: If thou murmur'st, I will rend an oak
And peg thee in his knotty entrails, till
Thou hast howl'd away twelve winters.
Ariel: Pardon, master.
I will be correspondent to command,
And do my spriting gently.
Prospero: Do so; and after two days
I will discharge thee.
Ariel: That's my noble master!
What shall I do? say what; what shall I do?
Prospero: Go make thyself like a nymph o' th' sea.
Be subject to
No sight but thine and mine; invisible
To every eyeball else. Go take this shape,
And hither come in't: go; hence
With diligence. *[Exit ARIEL.]*
Awake, dear heart, awake! Thou hast slept well;
Awake!
Miranda: The strangeness of your story put
Heaviness in me.
Prospero: Shake it off. Come on;
We'll visit Caliban my slave, who never
Yields us kind answer.
Miranda: 'Tis a villain, sir,
I do not love to look on.
Prospero: But, as 'tis,
We cannot miss him:[23] he does make our fire,
Fetch in our wood, and serves in offices
That profit us. What ho! slave! Caliban!
Thou earth, thou! speak!
Caliban: *[Within.]* There's wood enough within.
Prospero: Come forth, I say! there's other business for thee;
Come, thou tortoise! When!
[Re-enter ARIEL like a water nymph.]
Fine apparition! My quaint Ariel,
Hark in thine ear.
Ariel: My lord, it shall be done. *[Exit.]*
Prospero: Thou poisonous slave, got by the devil himself
Upon thy wicked dam, come forth!
[Enter CALIBAN.]
Caliban: As wicked dew as e'er my mother brush'd
With raven's feather from unwholesome fen
Drop on you both! a south-west blow on ye
And blister you all o'er!
Prospero: For this, be sure, tonight thou shalt have cramps,
Side-stitches that shall pen thy breath up; urchins
Shall, for that vast of night that they may work,
All exercise on thee; thou shalt be pinch'd
As thick as honeycomb, each pinch more stinging
Than bees that made 'em.
Caliban: I must eat my dinner.
This island's mine, by Sycorax my mother,
Which thou tak'st from me. When thou cam'st first,
Thou strok'st me and made much of me; wouldst give me
Water with berries in't; and teach me how
To name the bigger light, and how the less,
That burn by day and night; and then I lov'd thee
And showed thee all the qualities o' th' isle,
The fresh springs, brine-pits, barren place and fertile:
Curs'd be I that did so! All the charms
Of Sycorax, toads, beetles, bats, light on you!
For I am all the subjects that you have,
Which first was mine own King: and here you sty me
In this hard rock, whiles you do keep from me
The rest o' th' island.
Prospero: Thou most lying slave,
Whom stripes may move, not kindness! I have us'd thee,
Filth as thou art, with human care; and lodg'd thee
In mine own cell, till thou didst seek to violate
The honour of my child.
Caliban: O ho, O ho! Would't had been done!
Thou didst prevent me; I had peopled else
This isle with Calibans.
Prospero: Abhorred slave,
Which any print of goodness wilt not take,
Being capable of all ill! I pitied thee,
Took pains to make thee speak, taught thee each hour
One thing or other: when thou didst not, savage,
Know thine own meaning, but wouldst gabble like
A thing most brutish, I endow'd thy purposes
With words that made them known. But thy vile race,
Though thou didst learn, had that in't which good natures
Could not abide to be with; therefore wast thou
Deservedly confin'd into this rock,
Who hadst deserv'd more than a prison.
Caliban: You taught me language, and my profit on't
Is, I know how to curse. The red plague rid[24] you
For learning me your language!

22. Commands.
23. Do without.
24. Destroy.

Prospero: Hag-seed, hence!
Fetch us in fuel; and be quick, thou'rt best,
To answer other business. Shrug'st thou, malice?
If thou neglect'st, or dost unwillingly
What I command, I'll rack thee with old cramps,
Fill all thy bones with aches, make thee roar
That beasts shall tremble at thy din.
Caliban: No, pray thee.
[Aside.] I must obey: his Art is of such pow'r,
It would control my dam's god, Setebos,
And make a vassal of him.
Prospero: So, slave; hence! *[Exit CALIBAN.]*
[Re-enter ARIEL (invisible) playing and singing; FERDINAND following.]

ARIEL['s] Song

Come unto these yellow sands,
And then take hands.
Curtsied when you have and kissed,
The wild waves whist,
Foot it featly here and there;
And sweet sprites, bear.
The burthen. Hark, hark!
[Burthen[25] dispersedly.] Bow-wow.

Ariel: The watchdogs bark:
[Burthen dispersedly.] Bow-wow!
Ariel: Hark, hark! I hear
The strain of strutting chanticleer
Cry— *[Burthen dispersedly.]* Cock a diddle dow.
Ferdinand: Where should this music be? i' th' air or th' earth?
It sounds no more; and, sure, it waits upon
Some god o' th' island. Sitting on a bank,
Weeping again the King my father's wrack,
This music crept by me upon the waters,
Allaying both their fury and my passion
With its sweet air: thence I have follow'd it,
Or it hath drawn me rather; but 'tis gone.
No, it begins again.

ARIEL['s] Song

Full fathom five thy father lies;
Of his bones are coral made;
Those are pearls that were his eyes:
Nothing of him that doth fade,
But doth suffer a sea-change
Into something rich and strange.
Sea-nymphs hourly ring his knell—
[Burthen.] Ding-dong!

Ariel: Hark! now I hear them,—Ding-dong, bell.
Ferdinand: The ditty does remember my drown'd father.
This is no mortal business, nor no sound
That the earth owes:[26]—I hear it now above me.
Prospero: The fringed curtains of thine eye advance[27]
And say what thou seest yond.
Miranda: What, is't? a spirit?
Lord, how it looks about! Believe me, sir,
It carries a brave form. But 'tis a spirit.
Prospero: No, wench. It eats and sleeps and hath such senses
As we have, such. This gallant which thou seest
Was in the wrack; and, but he's somewhat stain'd
With grief (that's beauty's canker) thou mightst call him
A goodly person: he hath lost his fellows,
And strays about to find 'em.
Miranda: I might call him
A thing divine; for nothing natural
I ever saw so noble.
Prospero: *[Aside.]* It goes on, I see,
As my soul prompts it. Spirit, fine spirit! I'll free thee
Within two days for this.
Ferdinand: Most sure the goddess
On whom these airs attend! Vouchsafe my prayer
May know if you remain upon this island;
And that you will some good instruction give
How I may bear me here: my prime[28] request,
Which I do last pronounce, is, O you wonder!
If you be maid or no?
Miranda: No wonder, sir;
But certainly a maid.
Ferdinand: My language! heavens!
I am the best of them that speak this speech,
Were I but where 'tis spoken.
Prospero: How? the best?
What wert thou, if the King of Naples heard thee?
Ferdinand: A single thing, as I am now, that wonders
To hear thee speak of Naples.[29] He does hear me;
And that he does I weep: myself am Naples,
Who with mine eyes, never since at ebb, beheld
The King my father wrack'd.
Miranda: Alack, for mercy!
Ferdinand: Yes, faith, and all his lords; the Duke of Milan
And his brave son being twain.
Prospero: *[Aside.]* The Duke of Milan
And his more braver daughter could control thee,
If now 'twere fit to do't. At the first sight
They have chang'd eyes. Delicate Ariel,
I'll set thee free for this! *[To FERDINAND.]* A word, good sir;
I fear you have done yourself some wrong:[30] a word.
Miranda: Why speaks my father so ungently? This
Is the third man that e'er I saw; the first
That e'er I sighed for: pity move my father
To be inclin'd my way!
Ferdinand: O, if a virgin,
And your affection not gone forth, I'll make you
The Queen of Naples.
Prospero: Soft, sir! one word more!
[Aside.] They are both in either's pow'rs: but this swift business
I must uneasy make, lest too light winning
Make the prize light. *[To FERDINAND.]* One word more; I charge thee
That thou attend me: thou dost here usurp

25. The word *Burthen* indicates a refrain or chorus, probably sung by invisible spirits.
26. Owns.
27. Lift up.
28. First and most important.
29. The King of Naples.
30. Made a false claim about yourself.

The name thou ow'st not, and hast put thyself
Upon this island as a spy, to win it
From me, the lord on 't.
Ferdinand: No, as I am man!
Miranda: There's nothing ill can dwell in such a temple:
If the ill spirit have so fair a house,
Good things will strive to dwell with 't.
Prospero: Follow me.
Speak not you for him: he's a traitor. Come;
I'll manacle thy neck and feet together:
Sea-water shalt thou drink; thy food shall be
The fresh-brook mussels, wither'd roots, and husks
Wherein the acorn cradled. Follow!
Ferdinand: No;
I will resist such entertainment till
Mine enemy has more pow'r.
[He draws, and is charmed from moving.]
Miranda: O dear father,
Make not too rash a trial of him, for
He's gentle, and not fearful.
Prospero: What, I say,
My foot[31] my tutor?—Put thy sword up, traitor;
Who mak'st a show, but dar'st not strike, thy conscience
Is so possess'd with guilt: come from thy ward;[32]
For I can here disarm thee with this stick
And make thy weapon drop.
Miranda: Beseech you, father.
Prospero: Hence! hang not on my garments.
Miranda: Sir, have pity;
I'll be his surety.
Prospero: Silence! one word more
Shall make me chide thee, if not hate thee. What!
An advocate for an impostor! Hush!
Thou think'st there is no more such shapes as he,
Having seen but him and Caliban: foolish wench!
To th' most of men this is a Caliban,
And they to him are angels.
Miranda: My affections
Are then most humble; I have no ambition
To see a goodlier man.
Prospero: Come on; obey:
Thy nerves are in their infancy again,
And have no vigour in them.
Ferdinand: So they are:
My spirits, as in a dream, are all bound up.
My father's loss, the weakness which I feel,
The wrack of all my friends, nor this man's threats,
To whom I am subdued, are but light to me,
Might I but through my prison once a day
Behold this maid: all corners else o' th' earth
Let liberty make use of; space enough
Have I in such a prison.
Prospero: *[Aside.]* It works. *[To FERDINAND.]* Come on.
[To ARIEL.] Thou hast done well, fine Ariel! Follow me;
Hark what thou else shalt do me.
Miranda: Be of comfort.
My father's of a better nature, sir,
Than he appears by speech: this is unwonted
Which now came from him.
Prospero: Thou shalt be as free
As mountain winds: but then exactly do
All points of my command.
Ariel: To the syllable.
Prospero: Come, follow. *[To MIRANDA.]* Speak not for him. *[Exeunt.]*

Act II

Scene 1

[Another part of the island.]
[Enter ALONSO, SEBASTIAN, ANTONIO, GONZALO, ADRIAN, FRANCISCO and others.]

Gonzalo: Beseech you, sir, be merry; you have cause,
So have we all, of joy; for our escape
Is much beyond our loss. Our hint of woe
Is common; every day some sailor's wife,
The masters of some merchant,[33] and the merchant,
Have just our theme of woe; but for the miracle,
I mean our preservation, few in millions
Can speak like us: then wisely, good sir, weigh
Our sorrow with our comfort.
Alonso: Prithee, peace.
Sebastian: *[Aside to ANTONIO.]* He receives comfort like cold porridge.
Antonio: *[Aside to SEBASTIAN.]* The visitor will not give him o'er so.
Sebastian: *[Aside to ANTONIO.]* Look, he's winding up the watch of his wit; by and by it will strike.
Gonzalo: Sir,
Sebastian: One: tell.
Gonzalo: When every grief is entertained that offer'd,
Comes to the entertainer—
Sebastian: A dollar.
Gonzalo: Dolour comes to him, indeed. You have spoken truer than you purposed.
Sebastian: You have taken it wiselier than I meant you should.
Gonzalo: Therefore, my lord—
Antonio: Fie, what a spendthrift is he of his tongue!
Alonso: I prithee, spare.
Gonzalo: Well, I have done: but yet,—
Sebastian: He will be talking.
Antonio: Which, of he or Adrian, for a good wager, first begins to crow?
Sebastian: The old cock.
Antonio: The cockerel.
Sebastian: Done. The wager?
Antonio: A laughter.
Sebastian: A match!
Adrian: Though this island seem to be desert,—
Antonio: Ha, ha ha!
Sebastian: So. You're paid.
Adrian: Uninhabitable and almost inaccessible,—
Sebastian: Yet,—
Adrian: Yet,—
Antonio: He could not miss 't.
Adrian: It must needs be of subtle, tender, and delicate temperance.[34]

31. My inferior.
32. Position of defense.
33. The owners of a merchant ship.
34. Temperature.

Antonio: Temperance was a delicate wench.
Sebastian: Ay, and a subtle; as he most learnedly deliver'd.
Adrian: The air breathes upon us here most sweetly.
Sebastian: As if it had lungs, and rotten ones.
Antonio: Or as 'twere perfum'd by a fen.
Gonzalo: Here is everything advantageous to life.
Antonio: True; save means to live.
Sebastian: Of that there's none, or little.
Gonzalo: How lush and lusty the grass looks! how green!
Antonio: The ground, indeed, is tawny.
Sebastian: With an eye[35] of green in't.
Antonio: He misses not much.
Sebastian: No; he doth but mistake the truth totally.
Gonzalo: But the rarity of it is,—which is indeed almost beyond credit,—
Sebastian: As many vouch'd rarities are.
Gonzalo: That our garments, being, as they were, drenched in the sea, hold, notwithstanding, their freshness and glosses, being rather new-dyed than stained with salt water.
Antonio: If but one of his pockets would speak, would it not say he lies?
Sebastian: Ay, or very falsely pocket up his report.
Gonzalo: Methinks our garments are now as fresh as when we put them on first in Afric, at the marriage of the King's fair daughter Claribel to the King of Tunis.
Sebastian: 'Twas a sweet marriage, and we prosper well in our return.
Adrian: Tunis was never grac'd before with such a paragon to their Queen.
Gonzalo: Not since widow Dido's time.
Antonio: Widow! A pox o' that! How came that widow in? widow Dido!
Sebastian: What if he had said "widower Aeneas" too? Good Lord, how you take it!
Adrian: "Widow Dido" said you? you make me study of that: she was of Carthage, not of Tunis.
Gonzalo: This Tunis, sir, was Carthage.
Adrian: Carthage?
Gonzalo: I assure you, Carthage.
Antonio: His word is more than the miraculous harp.
Sebastian: He hath rais'd the wall, and houses too.
Antonio: What impossible matter will he make easy next?
Sebastian: I think he will carry this island home in his pocket, and give it his son for an apple.
Antonio: And sowing the kernels of it in the sea, bring forth more islands.
Gonzalo: Ay.
Antonio: Why, in good time.
Gonzalo: *[To ALONSO.]* Sir, we were talking that our garments seem now as fresh as when we were at Tunis at the marriage of your daughter, who is now Queen.
Antonio: And the rarest that e'er came there.
Sebastian: Bate, I beseech you, widow Dido.
Antonio: O, widow Dido! ay, widow Dido.
Gonzalo: Is not, sir, my doublet as fresh as the first day I wore it? I mean in a sort.
Antonio: That sort was well fish'd for.
Gonzalo: When I wore it at your daughter's marriage?
Alonso: You cram these words into mine ears against
The stomach of my sense. Would I had never
Married my daughter there! for, coming thence,
My son is lost; and, in my rate, she too,
Who is so far from Italy removed
I ne'er again shall see her. O thou mine heir
Of Naples and of Milan, what strange fish
Hath made his meal on thee?
Francisco: Sir, he may live:
I saw him beat the surges under him,
And ride upon their backs; he trod the water,
Whose enmity he flung aside, and breasted
The surge most swoln that met him; his bold head
'Bove the contentious waves he kept, and oared
Himself with his good arms in lusty stroke
To th' shore, that o'er his wave-worn basis bowed,
As stooping to relieve him: I not doubt
He came alive to land.
Alonso: No, no, he's gone.
Sebastian: Sir, you may thank yourself for this great loss,
That would not bless our Europe with your daughter,
But rather lose her to an African;
Where she, at least, is banished from your eye,
Who hath cause to wet the grief on 't.
Alonso: Prithee peace.
Sebastian: You were kneel'd to and importun'd otherwise,
By all of us; and the fair soul herself
Weigh'd, between loathness and obedience, at
Which end o' th' beam should bow. We have lost your son,
I fear, forever: Milan and Naples have
Mo' widows in them of this business' making
Than we bring men to comfort them:
The fault's your own.
Alonso: So is the dear'st o' the loss.
Gonzalo: My Lord Sebastian,
The truth you speak doth lack some gentleness,
And time to speak it in: you rub the sore,
When you should bring the plaster.
Sebastian: Very well.
Antonio: And most chirurgeonly.[36]
Gonzalo: It is foul weather in us all, good sir,
When you are cloudy.
Sebastian: *[Aside to ANTONIO.]* Fowl weather?
Antonio: *[Aside to SEBASTIAN.]* Very foul.
Gonzalo: Had I plantation[37] of this isle, my lord,—
Antonio: *[Aside to SEBASTIAN.]* He'd sow 't with nettle-seed.
Sebastian: *[Aside to ANTONIO.]* Or docks, or mallows.
Gonzalo: And were the King on't, what would I do?
Sebastian: *[Aside to ANTONIO.]* 'Scape being drunk for want of wine.
Gonzalo: I' th' commonwealth I would be contraries
Execute all things; for no kind of traffic
Would I admit; no name of magistrate;
Letters should not be known; riches, poverty,

35. Tinge.
36. Like a doctor.
37. Colonization.

And use of service, none; contract, succession,
Bourn, bound of land, tilth, vineyard, none;
No use of metal, corn, or wine, or oil;
No occupation; all men idle, all;
And women too, but innocent and pure:
No sovereignty;—
Sebastian: *[Aside to ANTONIO.]* Yet he would be King
on't.
Antonio: *[Aside to SEBASTIAN.]* The latter end of his
commonwealth forgets the beginning.
Gonzalo: All things in common Nature should produce
Without sweat or endeavor: treason, felony,
Sword, pike, knife, gun, or need of any engine,
Would I not have; but Nature should bring forth,
Of it own kind, all foison,[38] all abundance,
To feed my innocent people.
Sebastian: *[Aside to ANTONIO.]* No marrying 'mong his
subjects?
Antonio: *[Aside to SEBASTIAN.]* None, man, all idle;
whores and knaves.
Gonzalo: I would with such perfection govern, sir,
To excel the Golden Age.
Sebastian: 'Save his Majesty!
Antonio: Long live Gonzalo!
Gonzalo: And,—do you mark me, sir?
Alonso: Prithee no more: thou dost talk nothing to me.
Gonzalo: I do well believe your highness; and did it to
minister occasion to these gentlemen, who are of such
sensible[39] and nimble lungs that they always use to laugh
at nothing.
Antonio: 'Twas you we laughed at.
Gonzalo: Who in this kind of merry fooling am nothing to
you: so you may continue, and laugh at nothing still.
Antonio: What a blow was there given!
Sebastian: An it had not fall'n flat-long.
Gonzalo: You are gentlemen of brave metal; you would
lift the moon out of her sphere, if she would continue in it
five weeks without changing.
[Enter ARIEL (invisible) playing solemn music.]
Sebastian: We would so, and then go a bat-fowling.
Antonio: Nay, good my lord, be not angry.
Gonzalo: No, I warrant you, I will not adventure my discretion
so weakly. Will you laugh me asleep, for I am
very heavy?
Antonio: Go sleep, and hear us.
[All sleep except ALONSO, SEBASTIAN, and ANTONIO.]
Alonso: What, all so soon asleep! I wish mine eyes
Would, with themselves, shut up my thoughts. I find
They are inclin'd to do so.
Sebastian: Please you, sir,
Do not omit the heavy offer of it:
It seldom visits sorrow; when it doth,
It is a comforter.
Antonio: We two, my lord,
Will guard your person while you take your rest,
And watch your safety.
Alonso: Thank you.—Wondrous heavy.
[ALONSO sleeps. Exit ARIEL.]
Sebastian: What a strange drowsiness possesses them!
Antonio: It is the quality o' th' climate.
Sebastian: Why
Doth it not then our eyelids sink? I find not
Myself dispos'd to sleep.
Antonio: Nor I. My spirits are nimble.
They fell together all, as by consent;
They dropp'd, as by a thunder-stroke. What might,
Worthy Sebastian?—O, what might?— No more: —
And yet methinks I see it in thy face,
What thou shouldst be: th' occasion speaks thee; and
My strong imagination sees a crown
Dropping upon thy head.
Sebastian: What, art thou waking?
Antonio: Do you not hear me speak?
Sebastian: I do; and surely
It is a sleepy language, and thou speak'st
Out of thy sleep. What is it thou didst say?
This is a strange repose, to be asleep
With eyes wide open; standing, speaking, moving;
And yet so fast asleep.
Antonio: Noble Sebastian,
Thou let'st thy fortune sleep—die, rather; wink'st
Whiles thou art waking.
Sebastian: Thou dost snore distinctly;
There's meaning in thy snores.
Antonio: I am more serious than my custom. You
Must be so too, if heed me; which to do
Trebles thee o'er.[40]
Sebastian: Well, I am standing water.
Antonio: I'll teach you how to flow.
Sebastian: Do so: to ebb
Hereditary sloth instructs me.
Antonio: O,
If you but knew how you the purpose cherish
Whiles thus you mock it! how, in stripping it,
You more invest it! Ebbing men, indeed,
Most often do so near the bottom run
By their own fear or sloth.
Sebastian: Prithee say on:
The setting of thine eye and cheek proclaim
A matter from thee; and a birth, indeed,
Which throes thee much to yield.
Antonio: Thus, sir:
Although this lord of weak remembrance, this,
Who shall be of as little memory
When he is earth'd, hath here almost persuaded,—
For he's a spirit of persuasion, only
Professes to persuade,— the King his son's alive,
'Tis as impossible that he's undrown'd
As he that sleeps here swims.
Sebastian: I have no hope
That he's undrown'd.
Antonio: O, out of that "no hope"
What great hope have you! no hope that way is
Another way so high a hope, that even
Ambition cannot pierce a wink beyond,
But doubt discovery there. Will you grant with me
That Ferdinand is drown'd?
Sebastian: He's gone.
Antonio: Then tell me,

38. Plenteous harvest.
39. Sensitive.
40. Makes you three times as great.

Who's the next heir of Naples?
Sebastian: Claribel.
Antonio: She that is Queen of Tunis; she that dwells
Ten leagues beyond man's life; she that from Naples
Can have no note, unless the sun were post,—
The man i' th' moon's too slow,—till newborn chins
Be rough and razorable; she that from whom
We all were sea-swallow'd, though some cast again,
And that by destiny, to perform an act
Whereof what's past is prologue; what to come
In yours and my discharge.
Sebastian: What stuff is this? how say you?
'Tis true my brother's daughter's Queen of Tunis;
So is she heir of Naples; 'twixt which regions
There is some space.
Antonio: A space whose ev'ry cubit
Seems to cry out, "How shall that Claribel
Measure us back to Naples? Keep in Tunis
And let Sebastian wake." Say, this were death
That now hath seiz'd them; why, they were no worse
Than now they are. There be that can rule Naples
As well as he that sleeps; lords that can prate
As amply and unnecessarily
As this Gonzalo; I myself could make
A chough of as deep chat. O, that you bore
The mind that I do! what a sleep were this
For your advancement! Do you understand me?
Sebastian: Methinks I do.
Antonio: And how does your content
Tender your own good fortune?
Sebastian: I remember
You did supplant your brother Prospero.
Antonio: True:
And look how well my garments sit upon me;
Much feater than before: my brother's servants
Were then my fellows; now they are my men.
Sebastian: But for your conscience.
Antonio: Ay, sir, where lies that? If 'twere a kibe,[41]
'Twould put me to my slipper: but I feel not
This deity in my bosom: twenty consciences
That stand 'twixt me and Milan, candied be they
And melt, ere they molest! Here lies your brother,
No better than the earth he lies upon,
If he were that which now he's like, that's dead;
Whom I, with this obedient steel, three inches of it,
Can lay to bed forever; whiles you, doing thus,
To the perpetual wink for aye might put
This ancient morsel, this Sir Prudence, who
Should not upbraid our course. For all the rest,
They'll take suggestion as a cat laps milk;
They'll tell the clock to any business that
We say befits the hour.
Sebastian: Thy case, dear friend,
Shall be my precedent; as thou got'st Milan,
I'll come by Naples. Draw thy sword: one stroke
Shall free thee from the tribute which thou payest;
And I the King shall love thee.
Antonio: Draw together;
And when I rear my hand, do you the like,
To fall it on Gonzalo.
Sebastian: O, but one word.

[They talk apart.]
[Re-enter ARIEL (invisible).]
Ariel: My master through his Art foresees the danger
That you, his friend, are in; and sends me forth,—
For else his project dies, —to keep them living.
[Sings in GONZALO's ear.]
While you here do snoring lie,
Open-ey'd conspiracy
His time doth take.
If of life you keep a care,
Shake off slumber and beware:
Awake, Awake!
Antonio: Then let us both be sudden.
Gonzalo: *[Awakes.]* Now, good angels
Preserve the King!
[The others awake.]
Alonso: Why, how now? ho, awake?—Why are you drawn?
Wherefore this ghastly looking?
Gonzalo: What's the matter?
Sebastian: Whiles we stood here securing your repose,
Even now, we heard a hollow burst of bellowing
Like bulls, or rather lions; did 't not wake you?
It struck mine ear most terribly.
Alonso: I heard nothing.
Antonio: O, 'twas a din to fright a monster's ear,
To make an earthquake! sure, it was the roar
Of a whole herd of lions.
Alonso: Heard you this, Gonzalo?
Gonzalo: Upon mine honour, sir, I heard a humming,
And that a strange one too, which did awake me.
I shak'd you, sir, and cried: as mine eyes open'd,
I saw their weapons drawn: —there was a noise,
That's verily. 'Tis best we stand upon our guard,
Or that we quit this place: let's draw our weapons.
Alonso: Lead off this ground; and let's make further search
For my poor son.
Gonzalo: Heavens keep him from these beasts!
For he is, sure, i' the island.
Alonso: Lead away.
Ariel: Prospero my lord shall know what I have done;
So, King, go safely on to seek thy son. *[Exeunt.]*

Scene 2

[Another part of the island. Enter CALIBAN with a burden of wood. A noise of thunder heard.]
Caliban: All the infections that the sun sucks up
From bogs, fens, flats on Prosper fall, and make him
By inch-meal a disease! his spirits hear me,
And yet I needs must curse. But they'll nor pinch,
Fright me with urchin-shows, pitch me i' th' mire,
Nor lead me, like a firebrand, in the dark
Out of my way, unless he bid 'em: but
For every trifle are they set upon me;
Sometimes like apes that mow[42] and chatter at me,
And after bite me; then like hedgehogs, which
Lie tumbling in my barefoot way, and mount
Their pricks at my footfall; sometime am I
All wound with adders, who with cloven tongues

41. Sore heel.
42. Make faces.

Do hiss me into madness.
[Enter TRINCULO.]
Lo, now, lo!
Here comes a spirit of his, and to torment me
For bringing wood in slowly. I'll fall flat;
Perchance he will not mind me.
[Lies down and draws his cloak over him.]

Trinculo: Here's neither bush nor shrub to bear off any weather at all, and another storm brewing. I hear it sing i' th' wind: yond same black cloud, yond huge one, looks like a foul bombard[43] that would shed his liquor. If it should thunder as it did before, I know not where to hide my head: yond same cloud cannot choose but fall by pailfuls. What have we here? a man or a fish? dead or alive? A fish: he smells like a fish; a very ancient and fishlike smell; a kind of not of the newest Poor-John.[44] A strange fish! Were I in England now, as once I was, and had but this fish painted, not a holiday fool there but would give a piece of silver: there would this monster make a man;[45] any strange beast there makes a man: when they will not give a doit[46] to relieve a lame beggar, they will lay out ten to see a dead Indian. Legg'd like a man! and his fins like arms! Warm, o' my troth! I do now let loose my opinion, hold it no longer: this is no fish, but an islander that hath lately suffered by a thunderbolt. *[Thunder.]* Alas, the storm is come again! my best way is to creep under his gaberdine; there is no other shelter hereabout: misery acquaints a man with strange bed-fellows. I will here shroud till the dregs of the storm be past.

[Enter STEPHANO, singing, a bottle in his hand.]

Stephano: I shall no more to sea, to sea;
Here shall I die ashore.
This is a very scurvy tune to sing at a man's funeral;
Well, here's my comfort. *[Drinks.]*
[Sings.]
The master, the swabber, the boatswain, and I,
The gunner, and his mate,
Lov'd Mall, Meg, and Marian, and Margery,
But none of us car'd for Kate;
For she had a tongue with a tang,
Would cry to a sailor, "Go hang!"
She lov'd not the savour of tar nor of pitch;
Yet a tailor might scratch her where'er she did itch.
Then to sea, boys, and let her go hang!
This is a scurvy tune too: but here's my comfort. *[Drinks.]*

Caliban: Do not torment me: —O!

Stephano: What's the matter? Have we devils here? Do you put tricks upon 's with savages and men of Ind, ha? I have not 'scaped drowning to be afeard now of your four legs; for it hath been said, As proper a man as ever went on four legs cannot make him give ground; and it shall be said so again, while Stephano breathes at' nostrils.

Caliban: The spirit torments me: —O!

Stephano: This is some monster of the isle with four legs, who hath got, as I take it, an ague. Where the devil should he learn our language? I will give him some relief, if it be but for that. If I can recover him, and keep him tame, and get to Naples with him, he's a present for any emperor that ever trod on neat's leather.

Caliban: Do not torment me prithee! I'll bring my wood home faster.

Stephano: He's in his fit now, and does not talk after the wisest. He shall taste of my bottle: if he have never drunk wine afore, it will go near to remove his fit. If I can recover him and keep him tame, I will not take too much for him; he shall pay for him that hath him and that soundly.

Caliban: Thou dost me yet but little hurt; thou wilt anon. I know it by thy trembling: now Prospero works upon thee.

Stephano: Come on your ways; open your mouth; here is that which will give language to you, cat: open your mouth; this will shake your shaking, I can tell you, and that soundly. *[CALIBAN drinks.]* You cannot tell who's your friend: open your chaps again.

Trinculo: I should know that voice: it should be—but he is drowned; and these are devils: —O, defend me!

Stephano: Four legs and two voices,—a most delicate monster! His forward voice, now, is to speak well of his friend; his backward voice is to utter foul speeches and to detract. If all the wine in my bottle will recover him, I will help his ague. Come: —Amen! I will pour some in thy other mouth.

Trinculo: Stephano!

Stephano: Doth thy other mouth call me? Mercy, mercy! This is a devil, and no monster: I will leave him; I have no long spoon.

Trinculo: Stephano! If thou beest Stephano, touch me and speak to me, for I am Trinculo,—be not afeard,—thy good friend Trinculo.

Stephano: If thou beest Trinculo, come forth. I'll pull thee by the lesser legs: if any be Trinculo's legs, these are they. Thou art very Trinculo indeed! How cam'st thou to be the siege[47] of this moon-calf? can he vent Trinculos?

Trinculo: I took him to be killed with a thunderstroke. But art thou not drown'd, Stephano? I hope, now, thou art not drown'd. Is the storm overblown? I hid me under the dead moon-calf's gaberdine for fear of the storm. And art thou living, Stephano? O Stephano, two Neapolitans 'scap'd!

Stephano: Prithee do not turn me about; my stomach is not constant.

Caliban: *[Aside.]* These be fine things, an if they be not sprites.
That's a brave god, and bears celestial liquor.
I will kneel to him.

Stephano: How didst thou 'scape? How cam'st thou hither? swear by this bottle, how thou cam'st hither. I escap'd upon a butt of sack,[48] which the sailors heaved o'erboard, by this bottle! which I made of the bark of a tree with mine own hands, since I was cast ashore.

Caliban: I'll swear, upon that bottle, to be thy true subject; for the liquor is not earthly.

Stephano: Here; swear, then, how thou escap'dst.

Trinculo: Swum ashore, man, like a duck: I can swim like a duck, I'll be sworn.

43. A leather wineskin.
44. Dried and salted fish of the cheapest kind.
45. Make a man's fortune.
46. Farthing.
47. Seat.
48. A Spanish white wine.

Stephano: Here, kiss the book.[49] Though thou canst swim like a duck, thou art made like a goose.
Trinculo: O Stephano, hast any more of this?
Stephano: The whole butt, man: my cellar is in a rock by th' seaside, where my wine is hid. How now, moon-calf! how does thine ague?
Caliban: Hast thou not dropp'd from heaven?
Stephano: Out o' the moon, I do assure thee: I was the Man i' th' Moon when time was.
Caliban: I have seen thee in her, and I do adore thee:
My mistress show'd me thee, and thy dog, and thy bush.
Stephano: Come, swear to that; kiss the book: I will furnish it anon with new contents: swear.
Trinculo: By this good light, this is a very shallow monster; I afeard of him? A very weak monster! The man i' th' moon! A most poor credulous monster! Well drawn, monster, in good sooth!
Caliban: I'll show thee every fertile inch o' th' island: and I will kiss thy foot: I prithee, be my god.
Trinculo: By this light, a most perfidious and drunken monster! when 's god's asleep, he'll rob his bottle.
Caliban: I'll kiss thy foot; I'll swear myself thy subject.
Stephano: Come on, then; down, and swear.
Trinculo: I shall laugh myself to death at this puppy-headed monster. A most scurvy monster! I could find in my heart to beat him,—
Stephano: Come, kiss.
Trinculo: But that the poor monster's in drink. An abominable monster!
Caliban: I'll show thee the best springs; I'll pluck thee berries;
I'll fish for thee, and get thee wood enough.
A plague upon the tyrant that I serve!
I'll bear him no more sticks, but follow thee,
Thou wondrous man.
Trinculo: A most ridiculous monster, to make a wonder of a poor drunkard!
Caliban: I prithee, let me bring thee where crabs[50] grow;
And I with my long nails will dig thee pig-nuts;
Show thee a jay's nest, and instruct thee how
To snare the nimble marmoset; I'll bring thee
To clustering filberts, and sometimes I'll get thee
Young scamels from the rock. Wilt thou go with me?
Stephano: I prithee now, lead the way without any more talking. Trinculo, the King and all our company else being drown'd, we will inherit here: here; bear my bottle: fellow Trinculo, we'll fill him by and by again.
Caliban: *[Sings drunkenly.]*
Farewell, master, farewell, farewell!
Trinculo: A howling monster; a drunken monster!
Caliban: No more dams I'll make for fish;
Nor fetch in firing
At requiring;
Nor scrape trenchering, nor wash dish:
'Ban, 'Ban, Ca-Caliban
Has a new master: —get a new man.
Freedom, high-day! high-day, freedom! freedom, high-day, freedom!
Stephano: O brave monster! lead the way. *[Exeunt.]*

49. The book is the bottle. Imagine how they kiss the book.
50. Crab-apples.

Act III

Scene 1

[Before Prospero's cell. Enter FERDINAND, bearing a log.]
Ferdinand: There be some sports are painful, and their labour
Delight in them sets off: some kinds of baseness
Are nobly undergone; and most poor matters
Point to rich ends. This my mean task
Would be as heavy to me as odious, but
The mistress which I serve quickens what's dead
And makes my labours pleasures: O, she is
Ten times more gentle than her father's crabbed,
And he's compos'd of harshness. I must remove
Some thousands of these logs, and pile them up,
Upon a sore injunction: my sweet mistress
Weeps when she sees me work, and says, such baseness
Had never like executor. I forget:
But these sweet thoughts do even refresh my labours,
Most busilest when I do it.
[Enter MIRANDA; and PROSPERO (concealed).]
Miranda: Alas now, pray you,
Work not so hard: I would the lightning had
Burnt up those logs that you are enjoin'd to pile!
Pray, set it down, and rest you: when this burns,
'Twill weep for having wearied you. My father
Is hard at study; pray now rest yourself:
He's safe for these three hours.
Ferdinand: O most dear mistress,
The sun will set before I shall discharge
What I must strive to do.
Miranda: If you'll sit down,
I'll bear your logs the while: pray give me that;
I'll carry it to the pile.
Ferdinand: No, precious creature,
I had rather crack my sinews, break my back,
Than you should such dishonour undergo,
While I sit lazy by.
Miranda: It would become me
As well as it does you: and I should do it
With much more ease; for my good will is to it,
And yours it is against.
Prospero: *[Aside.]* Poor worm, thou art infected!
This visitation shows it.
Miranda: You look wearily.
Ferdinand: No, noble mistress: 'tis fresh morning with me
When you are by at night. I do beseech you,—
Chiefly that I might set it in my prayers,—
What is your name?
Miranda: Miranda. —O my father,
I have broke your hest to say so!
Ferdinand: Admir'd Miranda!
Indeed the top of admiration! worth
What's dearest to the world! Full many a lady
I have ey'd with best regard, and many a time
The harmony of their tongues hath into bondage
Brought my too diligent ear: for several virtues
Have I lik'd several women; never any
With so full soul, but some defect in her
Did quarrel with the noblest grace she ow'd,
And put it to the foil;[51] but you, O you,

So perfect and so peerless, are created
Of every creature's best!
Miranda: I do not know
One of my sex; no woman's face remember,
Save, from my glass, mine own; nor have I seen
More that I may call men than you, good friend,
And my dear father: how features are abroad,
I am skilless of; but, by my modesty,
The jewel in my dower, I would not wish
Any companion in the world but you;
Nor can imagination form a shape,
Besides yourself, to like of. But I prattle
Something too wildly, and my father's precepts
I therein do forget.
Ferdinand: I am in my condition
A prince, Miranda; I do think a king
I would not so!—and would no more endure
This wooden slavery than to suffer
The flesh-fly blow my mouth. Hear my soul speak:
The very instant that I saw you, did
My heart fly to your service; there resides,
To make me slave to it; and for your sake
Am I this patient log-man.
Miranda: Do you love me?
Ferdinand: O heaven, O earth, bear witness to this sound,
And crown what I profess with kind event
If I speak true! if hollowly, invert
What best is boded me to mischief! I,
Beyond all limit of what else i' th' world,
Do love, prize, honour you.
Miranda: I am a fool
To weep at what I am glad of.
Prospero: *[Aside.]* Fair encounter
Of two most rare affections! Heavens rain grace
On that which breeds between 'em!
Ferdinand: Wherefore weep you?
Miranda: At mine unworthiness, that dare not offer
What I desire to give, and much less take
What I shall die to want. But this is trifling;
And all the more it seeks to hide itself,
The bigger bulk it shows. Hence, bashful cunning!
And prompt me plain and holy innocence!
I am your wife if you will marry me,
If not, I'll die your maid: to be your fellow
You may deny me; but I'll be your servant,
Whether you will or no.
Ferdinand: My mistress, dearest;
And I thus humble ever.
Miranda: My husband, then?
Ferdinand: Ay, with a heart as willing
As bondage e'er of freedom:[52] here's my hand.
Miranda: And mine, with my heart in't; and now farewell
Till half an hour hence.
Ferdinand: A thousand thousand![53] *[Exeunt.]*
Prospero: So glad of this as they I cannot be,
Who are surpris'd with all; but my rejoicing
At nothing can be more. I'll to my book;
For yet, ere supper time, must I perform
Much business appertaining. *[Exit.]*

51. Defeat.
52. As a slave ever accepted freedom.
53. A thousand thousand farewells.
54. Idiot.

Scene 2

[Another part of the island. Enter CALIBAN, STEPHANO, and TRINCULO.]

Stephano: Tell not me;—when the butt is out, we will drink water; not a drop before: therefore bear up and board 'em! Servant-monster, drink to me.

Trinculo: Servant-monster! the folly of this island! They say there's but five upon this isle: we are three of them. If th' other two be brain'd like us, the state totters.

Stephano: Drink, servant-monster, when I bid thee: thy eyes are almost set in thy head.

Trinculo: Where should they be set else? he were a brave monster indeed if they were set in his tail.

Stephano: My man-monster hath drown'd his tongue in sack: for my part, the sea cannot drown me; I swam, ere I could recover the shore, five-and-thirty leagues off and on. By this light, thou shalt be my lieutenant, monster, or my standard.

Trinculo: Your lieutenant, if you list; he's no standard.

Stephano: We'll not run, Monsieur Monster.

Trinculo: Nor go neither, but you'll lie, like dogs, and yet say nothing neither.

Stephano: Moon-calf, speak once in thy life, if thou beest a good moon-calf.

Caliban: How does thy honour? Let me lick thy shoe: I'll not serve him; he is not valiant.

Trinculo: Thou liest, most ignorant monster: I am in case to jostle a constable. Why, thou debosh'd fish, thou, was there ever man a coward that hath drunk so much sack as I today? Wilt thou tell a monstrous lie, being but half a fish and half a monster?

Caliban: Lo, how he mocks me! wilt thou let him, my lord?

Trinculo: "Lord," quoth he? That a monster should be such a natural![54]

Caliban: Lo, lo, again! bite him to death, I prithee.

Stephano: Trinculo, keep a good tongue in your head: if you prove a mutineer,—the next tree! The poor monster's my subject, and he shall not suffer indignity.

Caliban: I thank my noble lord. Wilt thou be pleas'd to hearken once again to the suit I made to thee?

Stephano: Marry, will I: kneel and repeat it; I will stand, and so shall Trinculo.

[Enter ARIEL (invisible).]

Caliban: As I told thee before, I am subject to a tyrant, a sorcerer, that by his cunning hath cheated me of the island.

Ariel: Thou liest.

Caliban: "Thou liest," thou jesting monkey, thou!
I would my valiant master would destroy thee.
I do not lie.

Stephano: Trinculo, if you trouble him any more in 's tale, by this hand, I will supplant some of your teeth.

Trinculo: Why, I said nothing.

Stephano: Mum then, and no more. Proceed.

Caliban: I say, by sorcery he got this isle;
From me he got it. If thy greatness will

Revenge it on him,—for I know thou dar'st,
But this thing dare not,—
Stephano: That's most certain.
Caliban: Thou shalt be lord of it, and I'll serve thee.
Stephano: How now shall this be compassed? Canst thou bring me to the party?
Caliban: Yea, yea, my lord! I'll yield him thee asleep,
Where thou mayst knock a nail into his head.
Ariel: Thou liest; thou canst not.
Caliban: What a pied ninny's this! Thou scurvy patch!
I do beseech thy greatness give him blows
And take his bottle from him: when that's gone,
He shall drink nought but brine; for I'll not show him
Where the quick freshes are.
Stephano: Trinculo, run into no further danger: interrupt the monster one word further and, by this hand, I'll turn my mercy out o' doors and make a stock-fish of thee.
Trinculo: Why, what did I? I did nothing. I'll go farther off.
Stephano: Didst thou not say he lied?
Ariel: Thou liest.
Stephano: Do I so? take thou that. *[Beats TRINCULO.]*
As you like this, give me the lie another time.
Trinculo: I did not give thee the lie. Out o' your wits, and hearing too? A pox o' your bottle! this can sack and drinking do. A murrain on your monster, and the devil take your fingers!
Caliban: Ha, ha, ha!
Stephano: Now, forward with your tale.—Prithee, stand further off.
Caliban: Beat him enough. After a little time,
I'll beat him too.
Stephano: Stand farther.—Come, proceed.
Caliban: Why, as I told thee, 'tis a custom with him
I' th' afternoon to sleep: there thou mayst brain him,
Having first seiz'd his books; or with a log
Batter his skull, or paunch him with a stake,
Or cut his wezand[55] with thy knife. Remember
First to possess his books; for without them
He's but a sot, as I am, nor hath not
One spirit to command: they all do hate him
As rootedly as I. Burn but his books.
He has brave utensils,—for so he calls them,—
Which, when he has a house, he'll deck withal.
And that most deeply to consider is
The beauty of his daughter; he himself
Calls her a nonpareil; I never saw a woman
But only Sycorax my dam and she,
But she as far surpasseth Sycorax
As great'st does least.
Stephano: Is it so brave a lass?
Caliban: Ay, lord; she will become thy bed, I warrant,
And bring thee forth brave brood.
Stephano: Monster, I will kill this man: his daughter and I will be king and queen,—save our graces!—and Trinculo and thyself shall be viceroys. Dost thou like the plot, Trinculo?
Trinculo: Excellent.
Stephano: Give me thy hand. I am sorry I beat thee; but, while thou liv'st, keep a good tongue in thy head.
Caliban: Within this half hour will he be asleep:
Wilt thou destroy him then?
Stephano: Ay, on mine honour.
Ariel: This will I tell my master.
Caliban: Thou mak'st me merry; I am full of pleasure.
Let us be jocund: will you troll the catch
You taught me but while-ere?[56]
Stephano: At thy request, monster, I will do reason, any reason.—Come on, Trinculo, let us sing. *[Sings.]*
Flout 'em and scout 'em
And scout 'em and flout 'em;
Thought is free.
Caliban: That's not the tune.
[ARIEL plays the tune on a tabor[57] and pipe.]
Stephano: What is this same?
Trinculo: This is the tune of our catch, played by the picture of Nobody.
Stephano: If thou beest a man, show thyself in thy likeness: if thou beest a devil, tak't as thou list.
Trinculo: O, forgive me my sins!
Stephano: He that dies pays all debts: I defy thee. Mercy upon us!
Caliban: Art thou afeard?
Stephano: No, monster, not I.
Caliban: Be not afeard; the isle is full of noises,
Sounds and sweet airs, that give delight and hurt not.
Sometimes a thousand twangling instruments
Will hum about mine ears; and sometime voices,
That, if I then had wak'd after long sleep,
Will make me sleep again: and then, in dreaming,
The clouds methought would open, and show riches
Ready to drop upon me; that, when I wak'd,
I cried to dream again.
Stephano: This will prove a brave kingdom to me, where I shall have my music for nothing.
Caliban: When Prospero is destroy'd.
Stephano: That shall be by and by: I remember the story.
Trinculo: The sound is going away; let's follow it, and after do our work.
Stephano: Lead, monster; we'll follow. I would I could see this taborer; he lays it on. Wilt come?
Trinculo: I'll follow, Stephano. *[Exeunt.]*

Scene 3

[Another part of the island.]
[Enter ALONSO, SEBASTIAN, ANTONIO, GONZALO, ADRIAN, FRANCISCO, and others.]
Gonzalo: By'r lakin, I can go no further, sir;
My old bones ache: here's a maze trod, indeed.
Through forthrights and meanders! By your patience,
I needs must rest me.
Alonso: Old lord, I cannot blame thee,
Who am myself attach'd with weariness
To th' dulling of my spirits: sit down and rest.
Even here I will put off my hope, and keep it
No longer for my flatterer: he is drowned
Whom thus we stray to find; and the sea mocks
Our frustrate search on land. Well, let him go.
Antonio: *[Aside to SEBASTIAN.]* I am right glad that he's so out of hope.

55. Windpipe.
56. A little while ago.
57. A small drum.

Do not, for one repulse, forgo the purpose
That you resolv'd t' effect.
Sebastian: *[Aside to ANTONIO.]* The next advantage
Will we take thoroughly.
Antonio: *[Aside to SEBASTIAN.]* Let it be tonight;
For, now they are oppress'd with travel, they
Will not, nor cannot, use such vigilance
As when they are fresh.
Sebastian: *[Aside to ANTONIO.]* I say tonight, no more.
[Solemn and strange music.]
Alonso: What harmony is this? My good friends, hark!
Gonzalo: Marvellous sweet music!
[PROSPERO on the top, invisible. Enter several strange Shapes, bringing in a banquet; and dance about it with gentle actions of salutations; and inviting the King etc. to eat, they depart.]
Alonso: Give us kind keepers, heavens!—What were these?
Sebastian: A living drollery. Now I will believe
That there are unicorns; that in Arabia
There is one tree, the phoenix' throne, one phoenix
At this hour reigning there.
Antonio: I'll believe both;
And what does else want credit, come to me,
And I'll be sworn 'tis true: travellers ne'er did lie,
Though fools at home condemn 'em.
Gonzalo: If in Naples
I should report this now, would they believe me?
If I should say I saw such islanders,—
For, certes, these are people of the island,—
Who though they are of monstrous shape, yet, note,
Their manners are more gentle, kind, than of
Our human generation you shall find
Many, nay, almost any.
Prospero: *[Aside.]* Honest lord,
Thou hast said well; for some of you there present
Are worse than devils.
Alonso: I cannot too much muse
Such shapes, such gesture, and such sound, expressing—
Although they want the use of tongue—a kind
Of excellent dumb discourse.
Prospero: *[Aside.]* Praise in departing.
Francisco: They vanish'd strangely.
Sebastian: No matter, since
They have left their viands behind; for we have stomachs.—
Will 't please you taste of what is here?
Alonso: Not I.
Gonzalo: Faith, sir, you need not fear. When we were boys,
Who would believe that there were mountaineers
Dew-lapped like bulls, whose throats had hanging at 'em
Wallets of flesh? or that there were such men
Whose heads stood in their breasts? which now we find
Each putter-out of five for one will bring us
Good warrant of.
Alonso: I will stand to, and feed;
Although my last, no matter, since I feel
The best is past. Brother, my lord the Duke,
Stand to, and do as we.
[Thunder and lightning. Enter ARIEL like a Harpy; claps his wings upon the table; and with a quaint device, the banquet vanishes.]
Ariel: You are three men of sin, whom Destiny,—
That hath to instrument this lower world
And what is in't,—the never-surfeited sea
Hath caus'd to belch up you; and on this island,
Where man doth not inhabit,—you 'mongst men
Being most unfit to live, I have made you mad;
And even with such-like valor men hang and drown
Their proper selves.
[ALONSO, SEBASTIAN etc., draw their swords.]
You fools! I and my fellows
Are ministers of Fate: the elements,
Of whom your swords are temper'd, may as well
Wound the loud winds, or with bemock'd-at stabs
Kill the still-closing waters, as diminish
One dowle that's in my plume: my fellow-ministers
Are like invulnerable. If you could hurt,
Your swords are now too massy for your strengths,
And will not be uplifted. But remember,—
For that's my business to you,—that you three
From Milan did supplant good Prospero:
Expos'd unto the sea, which hath requit it,
Him and his innocent child: for which foul deed
The powers, delaying, not forgetting, have
Incens'd the seas and shores, yea all the creatures,
Against your peace. Thee of thy son, Alonso,
They have bereft; and do pronounce by me
Ling'ring perdition—worse than any death
Can be at once—shall step by step attend
You and your ways; whose wraths to guard you from,[58]
Which here, in this most desolate isle, else falls
Upon your heads,—is nothing but heart-sorrow
And a clear life ensuing.
[He vanishes in thunder; then, to soft music, enter the SHAPES again, and dance, with mocks and mows, and carrying out the table.]
Prospero: Bravely the figure of this Harpy hast thou
Perform'd, my Ariel; a grace it had, devouring:
Of my instruction hast thou nothing bated
In what thou hadst to say: so, with good life
And observation strange, my meaner ministers
Their several kinds have done. My high charms work,
And these mine enemies are all knit up
In their distractions: they now are in my power;
And in these fits I leave them, while I visit
Young Ferdinand,—whom they suppose is drown'd,—
And his and mine lov'd darling. *[Exit.]*
Gonzalo: I' the name of something holy, sir, why stand you
In this strange stare?
Alonso: O, it is monstrous, monstrous!
Methought the billows spoke and told me of it;
The winds did sing it to me; and the thunder,
That deep and dreadful organ-pipe, pronounc'd
The name of Prosper; it did bass[59] my trespass.
Therefor my son i' th' ooze is bedded; and

58. This passage means "only repentance and a reformed life will deliver you from their wrath."
59. In a bass voice.

I'll seek him deeper than e'er plummet sounded,
And with him there lie mudded. *[Exit.]*
Sebastian: But one fiend at a time,
I'll fight their legions o'er.
Antonio: I'll be thy second.
[Exeunt SEBASTIAN and ANTONIO.]
Gonzalo: All three of them are desperate: their great guilt,
Like poison given to work a great time after,
Now 'gins to bite the spirits. I do beseech you,
That are of suppler joints, follow them swiftly
And hinder them from what this ecstasy[60]
May now provoke them to.
Adrian: Follow, I pray you. *[Exeunt.]*

Act IV

Scene 1

[Before Prospero's cell.]
[Enter PROSPERO, FERDINAND, and MIRANDA.]
Prospero: If I have too austerely punish'd you,
Your compensation makes amends; for I
Have given you here a third of mine own life,
Or that for which I live; who once again
I tender to thy hand: all thy vexations
Were but my trials of thy love, and thou
Hast strangely stood the test: here, afore Heaven,
I ratify this my rich gift. O Ferdinand,
Do not smile at me that I boast her off,
For thou shalt find she will outstrip all praise,
And make it halt behind her.
Ferdinand: I do believe it.
Against an oracle.
Prospero: Then, as my gift, and thine own acquisition
Worthily purchas'd, take my daughter: but
If thou dost break her virgin-knot before
All sanctimonious ceremonies may
With full and holy rite be minister'd,
No sweet aspersion shall the heavens let fall
To make this contract grow; but barren hate,
Sour-ey'd disdain and discord shall bestrew
The union of your bed with weeds so loathly
That you shall hate it both; therefore take heed,
As Hymen's lamp shall light you.
Ferdinand: As I hope
For quiet days, fair issue and long life,
With such love as 'tis now, the murkiest den,
The most opportune place, the strong'st suggestion
Our worser genius can, shall never melt
Mine honour into lust, to take away
The edge of that day's celebration
When I shall think, or Phoebus' steeds are founder'd,
Or Night kept chain'd below.
Prospero: Fairly spoke.
Sit, then, and talk with her; she is thine own.
What Ariel! My industrious servant, Ariel!
[Enter ARIEL.]
Ariel: What would my potent master? here I am.
Prospero: Thou and thy meaner fellows your last service
Did worthily perform; and I must use you
In such another trick. Go bring the rabble,[61]
O'er whom I give thee power, here to this place:
Incite them to quick motion; for I must
Bestow upon the eyes of this young couple
Some vanity of mine Art: it is my promise,
And they expect it from me.
Ariel: Presently?
Prospero: Ay, with a twink.
Ariel: Before you can say, "come," and "go,"
And breathe twice, and cry "so, so,"
Each one, tripping on his toe,
Will be here with mop and mow.
Do you love me, master? no?
Prospero: Dearly, my delicate Ariel. Do not approach
Till thou dost hear me call.
Ariel: Well, I conceive. *[Exit.]*
Prospero: Look thou be true; do not give dalliance
Too much the rein: the strongest oaths are straw
To th' fire i' th' blood: be more abstemious,
Or else, good night your vow!
Ferdinand: I warrant you, sir;
The white cold virgin snow upon my heart
Abates the ardour of my liver.
Prospero: Well.
Now come, my Ariel! bring a corollary
Rather than want a spirit: appear, and pertly!
No tongue! all eyes! be silent.
[Soft music.]
[Enter IRIS.]
Iris: [62] Ceres, most bounteous lady, thy rich leas
Of wheat, rye, barley, vetches, oats, and pease;
Thy turfy mountains, where live nibbling sheep,
And flat meads thatch'd with stover, them to keep;
Thy banks with pioned and twilled brims,
Which spongy April at thy hest betrims
To make cold nymphs chaste crowns; and thy broom-groves,
Whose shadow the dismissed bachelor loves,
Being lasslorn; thy poll-clipt vineyard;
And thy sea-marge, sterile and rocky-hard,
Where thou thyself dost air;—the queen o' th' sky.
Whose wat'ry arch and messenger am I,
Bids thee leave these, and with her sovereign grace,
[JUNO descends.]
Here on this grass-plot, in this very place,
To come and sport: —her peacocks fly amain:
Approach, rich Ceres, her to entertain.
[Enter CERES.]
Ceres: Hail, many-colour'd messenger, that ne'er
Dost disobey the wife of Jupiter;
Who, with thy saffron wings, upon my flowers
Diffusest honey-drops, refreshing showers;
And with each end of thy blue bow dost crown
My bosky acres and my unshrubb'd down,
Rich scarf to my proud earth; why hath thy queen
Summon'd me hither to this short-grass'd green?
Iris: A contract of true love to celebrate;
And some donation freely to estate

60. Madness.
61. Simply the crowd or group.
62. We shall not attempt to render the obscure words into modern English. This whole scene is an interlude in praise of nature and fertility, all in the classical manner.

On the blest lovers.
Ceres: Tell me, heavenly bow,
If Venus or her son, as thou dost know,
Do now attend the queen? Since they did plot
The means that dusky Dis my daughter got,
Her and her blind boy's scandal'd company
I have forsworn.
Iris: Of her society
Be not afraid: I met her deity
Cutting the clouds towards Paphos, and her son
Dove-drawn with her. Here thought they to have done
Some wanton charm upon this man and maid,
Whose vows are, that no bed-right shall be paid
Till Hymen's torch be lighted: but in vain;
Mars's hot minion is return'd again.
Her waspish-headed son has broke his arrows,
Swears he will shoot no more, but play with sparrows,
And be a boy right out.
Ceres: Highest queen of state,
Great Juno comes; I know her by her gait.
[Enter JUNO.]
Juno: How does my bounteous sister? Go with me
To bless this twain, that they may prosperous be,
And honour'd in their issue.
[They sing.]
Juno: Honour, riches, marriage-blessing,
Long continuance, and increasing,
Hourly joys be still upon you!
Juno sings her blessings on you.
Ceres: Earth's increase, foison plenty,
Barns and garners never empty;
Vines with clust'ring bunches growing;
Plants with goodly burthen bowing;
Spring come to you at the farthest
In the very end of harvest!
Scarcity and want shall shun you;
Ceres' blessing so is on you.
Ferdinand: This is a most majestic vision, and
Harmonious charmingly. May I be bold
To think these spirits?
Prospero: Spirits, which by mine Art
I have from their confines call'd to enact
My present fancies.
Ferdinand: Let me live here ever;
So rare a wonder'd father and a wise
Makes this place Paradise.
[JUNO and CERES whisper, and send IRIS on employment.]
Prospero: Sweet, now, silence!
Juno and Ceres whisper seriously;
There's something else to do: hush, and be mute,
Or else our spell is marr'd.
Iris: You nymphs, call'd Naiads, of the windring brooks,
With your sedg'd crowns and ever-harmless looks,
Leave your crisp channels, and on this green land
Answer your summons; Juno does command:
Come, temperate nymphs, and help to celebrate
A contract of true love; be not too late.
[Enter certain NYMPHS.]
You sunburn'd sicklemen, of August weary,
Come hither from the furrow and be merry:
Make holiday; your rye-straw hats put on,
And these fresh nymphs encounter every one
In country footing.
[Enter certain REAPERS, properly habited: they join with the NYMPHS in a graceful dance; towards the end whereof PROSPERO starts suddenly, and speaks; after which, to a strange, hollow, and confused noise, they heavily vanish.]
Prospero: *[Aside.]* I had forgot that foul conspiracy
Of the beast Caliban and his confederates
Against my life: the minute of their plot
Is almost come. *[To the SPIRITS.]* Well done! Avoid![63] No more!
Ferdinand: This is strange: your father's in some passion
That works him strongly.
Miranda: Never till this day
Saw I him touch'd with anger, so distemper'd.
Prospero: You do look, my son, in a mov'd sort,
As if you were dismay'd: be cheerful, sir.
Our revels now are ended. These our actors,
As I foretold you, were all spirits, and
Are melted into air, into thin air:
And, like the baseless fabric of this vision,
The cloud-capp'd towers, the gorgeous palaces,
The solemn temples, the great globe itself,
Yea, all which it inherit, shall dissolve,
And, like this insubstantial pageant faded,
Leave not a rack[64] behind. We are such stuff
As dreams are made on; and our little life
Is rounded with a sleep. Sir, I am vexed;
Bear with my weakness; my old brain is troubled:
Be not disturb'd with my infirmity:
If you be pleas'd, retire into my cell
And there repose: a turn or two I'll walk,
To still my beating mind.
Ferdinand, Miranda: We wish your peace. *[Exeunt.]*
Prospero: Come with a thought! I thank thee. Ariel: come.
[Enter ARIEL.]
Ariel: Thy thoughts I cleave to. What's thy pleasure?
Prospero: Spirit,
We must prepare to meet with Caliban.
Ariel: Ay, my commander: when I presented Ceres,
I thought to have told thee of it; but I fear'd
Lest I might anger thee.
Prospero: Say again, where didst thou leave these varlets?
Ariel: I told you, sir they were redhot with drinking;
So full of valour that they smote the air
For breathing in their faces; beat the ground
For kissing of their feet; yet always bending
Towards their project. Then I beat my tabor;
At which, like unback'd colts, they prick'd their ears,
Advanc'd their eyelids, lifted up their noses
As they smelt music: so I charm'd their ears,
That, calf-like, they my lowing follow'd, through
Tooth'd briers, sharp furzes, pricking goss,[65] and thorns,
Which enter'd their frail shins: at last I left them

63. Be gone.
64. Film of cloud.
65. Gorse.

I' th' filthy-mantled pool beyond your cell,
There dancing up to th' chins, that the foul lake
O'erstunk their feet.
Prospero: This was well done, my bird.
Thy shape invisible retain thou still:
The trumpery in my house, go bring it hither,
For stale to catch these thieves.
Ariel: I go, I go. *[Exit.]*
Prospero: A devil, a born devil, on whose nature
Nurture can never stick! on whom my pains,
Humanely taken, all, all lost, quite lost;
And as with age his body uglier grows,
So his mind cankers. I will plague them all,
Even to roaring.
[Enter ARIEL, loaden with glistering apparel, etc.]
Come, hang them on this line.
[Enter CALIBAN, STEPHANO, and TRINCULO, all wet.]
[PROSPERO and ARIEL remain, invisible.]
Caliban: Pray you, tread softly, that the blind mole may not
Hear a foot fall: we now are near his cell.
Stephano: Monster, your fairy, which you say is a harmless fairy, has done little better than played the Jack with us.
Trinculo: Monster, I do smell all horse-piss; at which my nose is in great indignation.
Stephano: So is mine. Do you hear, monster? If I should take a displeasure against you, look you,—
Trinculo: Thou wert but a lost monster.
Caliban: Good my lord, give me thy favour still.
Be patient, for the prize I'll bring thee to
Shall hoodwink this mischance: therefore speak softly.
All's hush'd as midnight yet.
Trinculo: Ay, but to lose our bottles in the pool,—
Stephano: There is not only disgrace and dishonour in that, monster, but an infinite loss.
Trinculo: That's more to me than my wetting: yet this is your harmless fairy, monster.
Stephano: I will fetch off my bottle, though I be o'er ears for my labour.
Caliban: Prithee, my King, be quiet. Seest thou here,
This is the mouth o' th' cell: no noise, and enter.
Do that good mischief which may make this island
Thine own for ever, and I, thy Caliban,
For aye thy foot-licker.
Stephano: Give me thy hand. I do begin to have bloody thoughts.
Trinculo: O King Stephano! O peer! O worthy Stephano! look what a wardrobe here is for thee!
Caliban: Let it alone, thou fool! It is but trash.
Trinculo: O, ho, monster! we know what belongs to a frippery.[66] O King Stephano!
Stephano: Put off that gown, Trinculo; by this hand, I'll have that gown!
Trinculo: Thy grace shall have it.
Caliban: The dropsy drown this fool! what do you mean
To dote thus on such luggage? Let 's alone,
And do the murder first: if he awake,
From toe to crown he'll fill our skins with pinches,
Make us strange stuff.
Stephano: Be you quiet, monster. Mistress line, is not this my jerkin? Now is the jerkin under the line: now, jerkin, you are like to lose your hair, and prove a bald jerkin.
Trinculo: Do, do. We steal by line and level, an 't like your grace.
Stephano: I thank thee for that jest; here's a garment for't: wit shall not go unrewarded while I am King of this country. "Steal by line and level" is an excellent pass of pate;[67] there's another garment for't.
Trinculo: Monster, come, put some lime upon your fingers, and away with the rest.
Caliban: I will have none on't: we shall lose our time,
And all be turnid to barnacles,[68] or to apes
With foreheads villainous low.
Stephano: Monster, lay-to your fingers: help to bear this away where my hogshead of wine is, or I'll turn you out of my kingdom: go to, carry this.
Trinculo: And this.
Stephano: Ay, and this.
[A noise of hunters heard. Enter divers SPIRITS, in shape of dogs and hounds, hunting them about; PROSPERO and ARIEL setting them on.]
Prospero: Hey, Mountain, hey!
Ariel: Silver! there it goes, Silver!
Prospero: Fury, Fury! there, Tyrant, there! hark, hark!
[CALIBAN, STEPHANO, and TRINCULO are driven out.]
Go, charge my goblins that they grind their joints
With dry convulsions; shorten up their sinews
With aged cramps; and more pinch-spotted make them
Than pard[69] or cat-o'-mountain.
Ariel: Hark, they roar!
Prospero: Let them be hunted soundly. At this hour
Lies at my mercy all mine enemies.
Shortly shall all my labours end, and thou
Shalt have the air at freedom: for a little
Follow, and do me service. *[Exeunt.]*

Act V

Scene 1

[Before Prospero's cell.]
[Enter PROSPERO in his magic robes, and ARIEL.]
Prospero: Now does my project gather to a head:
My charms crack not; my spirits obey; and time
Goes upright with his carriage.[70] How's the day?
Ariel: On the sixth hour; at which time, my lord,
You said our work should cease.
Prospero: I did say so
When first I raised the tempest. Say, my spirit,
How fares the King and 's followers?
Ariel: Confin'd together
In the same fashion as you gave in charge,
Just as you left them; all prisoners, sir,
In thy lime-grove which weather-fends your cell.
They cannot budge till your release. The King,
His brother, and yours, abide all three distracted,

66. Secondhand clothing store.
67. Stroke of foolishness.
68. Geese.
69. Leopard.
70. Burden.

And the remainder mourning over them,
Brimful of sorrow and dismay; but chiefly
Him you term'd, sir, "the good old lord, Gonzalo";
His tears runs down his beard like winter's drops
From eaves of reeds. Your charm so strongly works 'em,
That if you now beheld them, your affections
Would become tender.
Prospero: Dost thou think so, spirit?
Ariel: Mine would, sir, were I human.
Prospero: And mine shall.
Hast thou, which art but air, a touch, a feeling
Of their afflictions, and shall not myself,
One of their kind, that relish all as sharply
Passion as they, be kindlier mov'd than thou art?
Though with their high wrongs I am struck to th' quick,
Yet with my nobler reason 'gainst my fury
Do I take part: the rarer action is
In virtue than in vengeance: they being penitent,
The sole drift of my purpose doth extend
Not a frown further. Go release them, Ariel:
My charms I'll break, their senses I'll restore,
And they shall be themselves.
Ariel: I'll fetch them, sir. *[Exit.]*
Prospero: Ye elves of hills, brooks, standing lakes, and groves,
And ye that on the sands with printless foot
Do chase the ebbing Neptune, and do fly him
When he comes back; you demi-puppets that
By moonshine do the green sour ringlets make,
Whereof the ewe not bites; and you whose pastime
Is to make midnight mushrooms, that rejoice
To hear the solemn curfew; by whose aid—
Weak masters though ye be—I have bedimm'd
The noontide sun, call'd forth the mutinous winds,
And 'twixt the green sea and the azured vault
Set roaring war: to the dread rattling thunder
Have I given fire and rifted Jove's stout oak
With his own bolt; the strong-bas'd promontory
Have I made shake and by the spurs[71] pluck'd up
The pine and cedar; graves at my command
Have wak'd their sleepers, op'd, and let 'em forth
By my so potent Art. But this rough magic
I here abjure; and when I have requir'd
Some heavenly music,—which even now I do,—
To work mine end upon their senses, that
This airy charm is for, I'll break my staff,
Bury it certain fadoms in the earth,
And deeper than did ever plummet sound
I'll drown my book.
[Solemn music.]
[Here enters ARIEL before; then ALONSO with a frantic gesture, attended by GONZALO; SEBASTIAN and ANTONIO in like manner, attended by ADRIAN and FRANCISCO: they all enter the circle which PROSPERO had made, and there stand charm'd; which PROSPERO observing, speaks.]
A solemn air, and the best comforter
To an unsettled fancy, cure thy brains,
Now useless, boil'd within thy skull! There stand,
For you are spell-stopped.
Holy Gonzalo, honourable man,
Mine eyes ev'n sociable[72] to show of thine
Fall fellowly drops. The charm dissolves apace.
And as the morning steals upon the night,
Melting the darkness, so their rising senses
Begin to chase the ignorant fumes that mantle
Their clearer reason. O good Gonzalo,
My true preserver, and a loyal sir
To him thou follow'st! I will pay thy graces
Home both in word and deed. Most cruelly
Didst thou, Alonso, use me and my daughter:
Thy brother was a furtherer in the act.
Thou art pinch'd for't now, Sebastian. Flesh and blood,
You, brother mine, that entertain'd ambition,
Expell'd remorse and nature; whom, with Sebastian,—
Whose inward pinches therefore are most strong,—
Would here have kill'd your King; I do forgive thee,
Unnatural though thou art. Their understanding
Begins to swell; and the approaching tide
Will shortly fill the reasonable[73] shore
That now lies foul and muddy. Not one of them
That yet looks on me, or would know me: Ariel,
Fetch me the hat and rapier in my cell:
I will discase[74] me, and myself present
As I was sometime Milan: quickly, spirit;
Thou shalt ere long be free.
[ARIEL sings and helps to attire him.]
Where the bee sucks, there suck I;
In a cowslip's bell I lie;
There I couch when owls do cry.
On the bat's back I do fly
After summer merrily.
Merrily, merrily shall I live now
Under the blossom that hangs on the bough.
Prospero: Why, that's my dainty Ariel! I shall miss thee;
But yet thou shalt have freedom: so, so, so.
To the King's ship, invisible as thou art;
There shalt thou find the mariners asleep
Under the hatches; the master and the boatswain
Being awake, enforce them to this place,
And presently, I prithee.
Ariel: I drink the air before me, and return
Or ere your pulse twice beat. *[Exit.]*
Gonzalo: All torment, trouble, wonder, and amazement
Inhabits here: some heavenly power guide us
Out of this fearful country!
Prospero: Behold, sir King,
The wronged Duke of Milan, Prospero.
For more assurance that a living prince
Does now speak to thee, I embrace thy body;
And to thee and thy company I bid
A hearty welcome.
Alonso: Whe'er thou be'st he or no,
Or some enchanted trifle to abuse me,
As late I have been, I not know: thy pulse
Beats, as of flesh and blood; and since I saw thee,
Th' affliction of my mind amends, with which,
I fear, a madness held me: this must crave—

71. Roots.
72. In sympathy.
73. Their power of reason.
74. Take off my robe.

An if this be at all—a most strange story.
Thy dukedom I resign, and do entreat
Thou pardon me my wrongs.—But how should Prospero
Be living and be here?
Prospero: First, noble friend,
Let me embrace thine age, whose honour cannot
Be measur'd or confin'd.
Gonzalo: Whether this be
Or be not, I'll not swear.
Prospero: You do yet taste
Some subtleties o' the isle, that will not let you
Believe things certain. Welcome, my friends all!
[Aside to SEBASTIAN and ANTONIO.]
But you, my brace of lords, were I so minded,
I here could pluck his highness' frown upon you
And justify you traitors: at this time
I will tell no tales.
Sebastian: *[Aside.]* The devil speaks in him.
Prospero: No.
For you, most wicked sir, whom to call brother
Would even infect my mouth, I do forgive
Thy rankest fault,—all of them; and require
My dukedom of thee, which perforce, I know,
Thou must restore.
Alonso: If thou be'st Prospero,
Give us particulars of thy preservation;
How thou hast met us here, who three hours since
Were wrack'd upon this shore; where I have lost—
How sharp the point of this remembrance is!—
My dear son Ferdinand.
Prospero: I am woe for't, sir.
Alonso: Irreparable is the loss; and patience
Says it is past her cure.
Prospero: I rather think
You have not sought her help, of whose soft grace
For the like loss I have her sovereign aid,
And rest myself content.
Alonso: You the like loss?
Prospero: As great to me, as late; and, supportable
To make the dear loss, have I means much weaker
Than you may call to comfort you, for I
Have lost my daughter.
Alonso: A daughter?
O heavens, that they were living both in Naples,
The King and Queen there! that they were, I wish
Myself were mudded in that oozy bed
Where my son lies. When did you lose your daughter?
Prospero: In this last tempest. I perceive, these lords
At this encounter do so much admire[75]
That they devour their reason, and scarce think
Their eyes do offices of truth, their words
Are natural breath: but, howsoe'er you have
Been justled from your senses, know for certain
That I am Prospero, and that very duke
Which was thrust forth of Milan; who most strangely
Upon this shore, where you were wrack'd, was landed,
To be the lord on't. No more yet of this;
For 'tis a chronicle of day by day,
Not a relation for a breakfast, nor
Befitting this first meeting. Welcome, sir;
This cell's my court: here have I few attendants,
And subjects none abroad: pray you, look in.
My dukedom since you have given me again,
I will requite you with as good a thing;
At least bring forth a wonder, to content ye
As much as me my dukedom.
[Here PROSPERO discovers FERDINAND and MIRANDA playing at chess.]
Miranda: Sweet lord, you play me false.
Ferdinand: No, my dearest love,
I would not for the world.
Miranda: Yes, for a score of kingdoms you should wrangle,
And I would call it fair play.
Alonso: If this prove
A vision of the island, one dear son
Shall I twice lose.
Sebastian: A most high miracle!
Ferdinand: Though the seas threaten, they are merciful;
I have curs'd them without cause. *[Kneels.]*
Alonso: Now all the blessings
Of a glad father compass thee about!
Arise, and say how thou cam'st here.
Miranda: O, wonder!
How many goodly creatures are there here!
How beauteous mankind is! O brave new world,
That has such people in't!
Prospero: 'Tis new to thee.
Alonso: What is this maid with whom thou wast at play?
Your eld'st acquaintance cannot be three hours:
Is she the goddess that hath sever'd us,
And brought us thus together?
Ferdinand: Sir, she is mortal;
But by immortal Providence she's mine:
I chose her when I could not ask my father
For his advice, nor thought I had one. She
Is daughter to this famous Duke of Milan,
Of whom so often I have heard renown,
But never saw before; of whom I have
Receiv'd a second life; and second father
This lady makes him to me.
Alonso: I am hers.
But, O, how oddly will it sound that I
Must ask my child forgiveness!
Prospero: There, sir, stop:
Let us not burthen our remembrance' with
A heaviness that's gone.
Gonzalo: I have inly wept,
Or should have spoke ere this. Look down, you gods,
And on this couple drop a blessed crown!
For it is you that have chalk'd forth the way
Which brought us hither.
Alonso: I say amen, Gonzalo!
Gonzalo: Was Milan thrust from Milan, that his issue
Should become Kings of Naples? O, rejoice
Beyond a common joy! and set it down
With gold on lasting pillars: in one voyage
Did Claribel her husband find at Tunis,
And Ferdinand, her brother, found a wife
Where he himself was lost, Prospero his dukedom

75. Their wonder almost overcomes their reason.

In a poor isle, and all of us ourselves
When no man was his own.
Alonso: *[To FERDINAND and MIRANDA.]* Give me your hands:
Let grief and sorrow still embrace his heart
That doth not wish you joy!
Gonzalo: Be it so! Amen!
[Re-enter ARIEL, with the MASTER and BOATSWAIN amazedly following.]
O, look, sir, look sir! here is more of us:
I prophesied, if a gallows were on land,
This fellow could not drown. Now, blasphemy,
That swear'st grace o'erboard, not an oath on shore?
Hast thou no mouth by land? What is the news?
Boatswain: The best news is, that we have safely found
Our King, and company; the next, our ship—
Which, but three glasses since, we gave out split—
Is tight and yare and bravely rigg'd as when
We first put out to sea.
Ariel: *[Aside to PROSPERO.]* Sir, all this service
Have I done since I went.
Prospero: *[Aside to ARIEL.]* My tricksy spirit!
Alonso: These are not natural events; they strengthen
From strange to stranger. Say, how came you hither?
Boatswain: If I did think, sir, I were well awake,
I'd strive to tell you. We were dead of sleep
And—how we know not—all clapp'd under hatches;
Where, but even now, with strange and several noises
Of roaring, shrieking, howling, jingling chains,
And more diversity of sounds, all horrible,
We were awak'd; straightway, at liberty;
Where we, in all her trim, freshly beheld
Our royal, good, and gallant ship, our master
Cap'ring to eye her:—on a trice, so please you,
Even in a dream, were we divided from them
And were brought moping hither.
Ariel: *[Aside to PROSPERO.]* Was't well done?
Prospero: *[Aside to ARIEL.]* Bravely, my diligence. Thou shalt be free.
Alonso: This is as strange a maze as e'er men trod,
And there is in this business more than nature
Was ever conduct of: some oracle
Must rectify our knowledge.
Prospero: Sir, my liege,
Do not infest your mind with beating on
The strangeness of this business; at pick'd leisure
Which shall be shortly, single I'll resolve you,[76]
Which to you shall seem probable, of every
These happen'd accidents; till when, be cheerful,
And think of each thing well. *[Aside to ARIEL.]* Come hither, spirit.
Set Caliban and his companions free;
Untie the spell. *[Exit ARIEL.]* How fares my gracious sir?
There are yet missing of your company
Some few odd lads that you remember not.
[Re-enter ARIEL, driving in CALIBAN, STEPHANO, and TRINCULO, in their stol'n apparel.]

Stephano: Every man shift for all the rest, and let no man take care for himself; for all is but fortune.—Coragio, bully-monster, coragio!
Trinculo: If these be true spies which I wear in my head, here's a goodly sight.
Caliban: O Setebos, these be brave spirits indeed!
How fine my master is! I am afraid
He will chastise me.
Sebastian: Ha, ha!
What things are these, my lord Antonio?
Will money buy 'em?
Antonio: Very like; one of them
Is a plain fish, and, no doubt, marketable.
Prospero: Mark but the badges[77] of these men, my lords,
Then say if they be true. This mis-shapen knave,
His mother was a witch; and one so strong
That could control the moon, make flows and ebbs,
And deal in her command, without her power.
These three have robb'd me, and this demi-devil—
For he's a bastard one—had plotted with them
To take my life. Two of these fellows you
Must know and own; this thing of darkness I
Acknowledge mine.
Caliban: I shall be pinch'd to death.
Alonso: Is not this Stephano, my drunken butler?
Sebastian: He is drunk now: where had he wine?
Alonso: And Trinculo is reeling ripe: where should they
Find this grand liquor that hath gild'd 'em?—
How cam'st thou in this pickle?
Trinculo: I have been in such a pickle, since I saw you last, that, I fear me, will never out of my bones: I shall not fear fly-blowing.
Sebastian: Why, how now, Stephano!
Stephano: O, touch me not;—I am not Stephano, but a cramp.
Prospero: You'ld be king o' the isle, sirrah?
Stephano: I should have been a sore one, then.
Alonso: This is as strange a thing as e'er I looked on.
Prospero: He is as disproportion'd in his manners
As in his shape. Go, sirrah, to my cell;
Take with you your companions. As you look
To have my pardon, trim it handsomely.
Caliban: Ay, that I will; and I'll be wise hereafter,
And seek for grace. What a thrice-double ass
Was I, to take this drunkard for a god
And worship this dull fool!
Prospero: Go to; away!
Alonso: Hence, and bestow your luggage where you found it.
Sebastian: Or stole it rather.
Prospero: Sir, I invite your Highness and your train
To my poor cell, where you shall take your rest
For this one night; which, part of it, I'll waste
With such discourse as, I not doubt, shall make it
Go quick away: the story of my life,
And the particular accidents gone by
Since I came to this isle: and in the morn
I'll bring you to your ship, and so to Naples,
Where I have hope to see the nuptial
Of these our dear-belov'd solemnized;
And thence retire me to my Milan, where

76. Alone, I'll explain to you.
77. The coats-of-arms; worn on the clothes.

Every third thought shall be my grave.
Alonso: I long
To hear the story of your life, which must
Take the ear strangely.
Prospero: I'll deliver all;
And promise you calm seas, auspicious gales,
And sail so expeditious, that shall catch
Your royal fleet far off. *[Aside to ARIEL.]* My Ariel, chick,
That is thy charge: then to the elements
Be free, and fare thou well! Please you, draw
near. *[Exeunt.]*

Epilogue

[Spoken by PROSPERO.]
Now my charms are all o'erthrown,
And what strength I have's mine own,
Which is most faint: now, 'tis true
I must be here confin'd by you,
Or sent to Naples. Let me not,
Since I have my dukedom got
And pardon'd the deceiver, dwell
In this bare island by your spell
But release me from my bands
With the help of your good hands:
Gentle breath of yours my sails
Must fill, or else my project fails,
Which was to please. Now I want
Spirits to enforce, Art to enchant,
And my ending is despair,
Unless I be reliev'd by prayer,
Which pierces so, that it assaults
Mercy itself, and frees all faults.
As you from crimes would pardon'd be,
Let your indulgence set me free. *[Exit.]*

Finis.

STUDY QUESTIONS

1. In reading any piece of literature, the first thing to do is to be sure that you understand the surface meaning and the story. As the first step into this, learn the names of the characters and be able to identify each of them in terms of what they do or have done.
   - **a.** Scene 1 presents the scene of the shipwreck. In Scene 2 what do we learn about the cause of the storm and the fate of the ship and all the people on it?
   - **b.** Also in Scene 2, what are the specific facts that we learn about Prospero's history before he came to the island?
   - **c.** And finally, in Scene 2, what happens in the meeting between Ferdinand and Miranda? As you read this, try to imagine to whom each character is speaking, and the tone of voice in which the speech should be spoken, for the tone will indicate the feelings and emotions of the speaker and add much to the meaning of the play as a whole.
   - **d.** In Act II, Scene 1, we get our first glimpse of the group of courtiers on the island. How would you sum up the character of each one? What evidence do you have for your belief?
   - **e.** What is the plot that Antonio and Sebastian make? At the end of the scene, what happens to their scheme?
   - **f.** In Act II, Scene 2, we encounter another group on the island. What did Stephano bring with him from the supposed shipwreck? And what happens when Caliban is invited to "kiss the book"? What plot does Caliban propose to Stephano and Trinculo?
   - **g.** In Act III we have three scenes, each dealing with one of the groups of shipwrecked people. How far does each of their plots progress, and to what extent is Prospero controlling each group?
   - **h.** Act IV brings the stories of two of the groups to a temporary halt. What happens to each?
   - **i.** Finally in Act V, balance is restored, and each person in the play finds his proper place in life. What is the conclusion for each person or group of persons?
2. In the introductory chapters we have spoken about various forces and influences which shaped the Renaissance. List evidences in this play of each of the following:
   - **a.** The Machiavellian idea of the nature of the ruler, and of human nature in general.
   - **b.** Humanism.
   - **c.** The utopian ideal as we saw it in More's *Utopia*.
   - **d.** The idea of the right king as the only source of health and proper discipline within a state.
   - **e.** The opposite poles of the good and evil nature of men and women. In this connection, what use should be made of each, or can the evil nature of human beings be stamped out, as was suggested in the utopian ideal?
3. Considering the ideas and forces listed above, what is Shakespeare's conclusion about each one?

19.3 *Above* Robert Dudley, "Heavens!—What were these?", illustration for Act III Scene 3 of *The Tempest* (see p.121). Colored etching from *The Library Shakespeare* (London, 1856 ff.) Photo: A.K.G., London.

19.4 John Gilbert, Title page for *The Tempest*. Wood engraving after Dalziel, from *The Library Shakespeare* (London, 1856 ff.) Photo: A.K.G., London.

SUMMARY

The dynamic Renaissance was notable for its artistic creativity, intellectual energy, widespread violence, and almost constant warfare. Almost everything was writ large because European civilization experienced drastic changes over a relatively short period of time. The Middle Ages died hard, partly because of the intransigent stance of the church. Determined to relinquish none of its vast power, the Church of Rome ultimately lost some of its authority in southern Europe and all control in northern Europe.

Critical elements of the Italian Renaissance were the rise of humanism and the retrieval of the Graeco-Roman heritage. Other factors included the expansion of capitalism and a steady increase in trade, industry, and banking. Northern Europe had no classical heritage, but its livelier economy, coupled with creative enterprise, produced considerable prosperity and a growing middle class.

Science made notable advances with the Copernican theory replacing the old Ptolemaic system and with Galileo's development of his laws of motion. Using his improved telescope, Galileo also helped confirm the Copernican thesis.

This was the age of exploration, with the magnetic compass, astrolabe, and tables of Henry the Navigator assisting the voyages of discovery of Columbus, Cabral, Cabot, and Magellan. The New World was explored by Cartier, Champlain, and Hudson; Cortés conquered the Aztec empire in Mexico, and Pizarro captured the Inca empire in Peru.

Assisted mightily by the invention of movable type, the Reformation broke the universal power of the Church of Rome. Led by Martin Luther, John Calvin, and others, the Protestant reformers established a variety of denominations throughout northern Europe. Politically, the Renaissance saw the rise of nation-states that in many ways supplanted the controlling power of the Roman church. The new nations of England, France, and Spain became the most powerful in Europe.

All of these forces contributed significantly to human freedom, but they raised the question of whether human beings were equipped to use their freedom wisely. Could selfish, greedy people rise above their animal natures to become what the Renaissance called the "noblest creatures of God" and use their God-given capacities to transform the world? That remained, for the Renaissance, an open question.

CULTURE AND HUMAN VALUES

If one were to ask what final answers were arrived at for the Renaissance problems stated here and in previous chapters, one would have to look not so much to ideas as to the lives of individuals. These were people who fulfilled the concept of "universal." This kind of person was completely free to live as he or she pleased, gaining freedom along with the ability to master knowledge and power.

Symbolic of this Renaissance person is Michelangelo's *Creation of Adam* (see fig. 17.31). One sees in the eyes of the reclining figure infinite longing, the type of yearning that will carry this man far. In the strongly muscled body one sees the strength that will help him fulfill that longing. Representing both of the sexes, this person is free, with the creative vigor to conquer new worlds, to unlock the secrets of the universe, to dare and to do in a world welcoming ambition and achievement.

UNIT 7

The Early Modern World, 1600–1789

The Early Modern World

1600–1789

	People and Events	Art and Architecture	Literature and Music	Philosophy and Science
1600	**1600** English East India Company founded **1602** Dutch East India Company founded **1609** Truce in Dutch revolt against Spain **1603–25** James I of England **1618–48** Thirty Years' War **1621–65** Philip IV of Spain **1625–49** Charles I of England **1632** Galileo condemned by Inquisition **1635** French Academy of Language and Literature established **1642–6** English Civil War **1643–1715** Louis XIV of France **1648** French Academy of Painting and Sculpture established **1649** Charles I of England executed **1649–60** Cromwell's Commonwealth **1660–85** Restoration: Charles II of England **1666** Great Fire of London **1669** Paris Opera established **1682–1725** Peter the Great of Russia **1685** Louis XIV revokes Edict of Nantes **1685–8** James II of England **1688** England's Glorious Revolution **1688–1702/1694** William and Mary of England	**Vignola** 1507–73 Il Gesù **Jones** 1573–1652 Queen's House **Caravaggio** 1573–1610 *The Conversion of St. Paul* **Rubens** 1577–1640 *The Assumption of the Virgin* **Hals** ca. 1580–1666 *The Laughing Cavalier* **Gentileschi** 1593–1652 *Judith Slaying Holofernes* **Poussin** 1594–1665 *Holy Family on the Steps* **Bernini** 1598–1680 St. Peter's Piazza and Colonnade **Borromini** 1599–1644 S. Carlo alle Quattro Fontane **Velasquez** 1599–1660 *Maids of Honor* **van Dyck** 1599–1641 *Charles I of England* **Rembrandt** 1606–69 *The Descent from the Cross* **Leyster** 1609–60 *Self-Portrait* **Ruisdael** 1628–82 *View of Haarlem from the Dunes at Overveen* **Vermeer** 1632–75 *The Girl with the Red Hat* **Wren** 1632–1723 St. Paul's **Pozzo** 1642–1709 *Apotheosis of Saint Ignatius* **Mansart** 1646–1708 Palace of Versailles	**Donne** 1573–1631 *Holy Sonnets* **Milton** 1608–74 *Paradise Lost On His Blindness* **Molière** 1622–73 *Tartuffe*	**Bacon** 1561–1626 *Novum Organum* **Galileo** 1564–1642 *Dialogues Concerning the Two Chief World Systems* **Kepler** 1571–1630 elliptical planetary orbits **Hobbes** 1588–1679 *Leviathan* **Descartes** 1596–1650 *Discourse on Method* **Spinoza** 1632–77 God in nature **Locke** 1632–1704 *Two Treatises of Government*
1700	**1701–13** Frederick I of Prussia **1702–14** Anne of England **1713–40** Frederick William I of Prussia **1714–27** George I of England **1715–74** Louis XV of France **1727–60** George II of England **1740–86** Frederick the Great of Prussia **1748** Excavations begin at Pompeii **1755** Lisbon earthquake **1760–1820** George III of England **1762–91** Catherine the Great of Russia **1774–93** Louis XVI of France **1775** Watt's improved steam engine **1775–83** American Revolution **1780–90** Joseph II Emperor of Austria	**Watteau** 1684–1721 *A Pilgrimage to Cythera* **Hogarth** 1697–1764 *Marriage à La Mode* **Chardin** 1699–1779 *The Kitchen Maid* **Boucher** 1703–70 *Venus Consoling Love* **Gainsborough** 1727–88 *Mrs. Richard Brinsley Sheridan* **Fragonard** 1732–1806 *The Swing* **Kauffmann** 1741–1807 *Pliny the Younger and His Mother at Misenum* **Houdon** 1741–1828 *Voltaire* **David** 1748–1825 *Death of Socrates*	**Swift** 1667–1745 *Gulliver's Travels; A Modest Proposal* **Couperin** 1688–1733 *Le Croc-en-jambe* **Bach** 1685–1750 French Suite No. 4 **Vivaldi** 1685–1743 *The Four Seasons* **Handel** 1685–1759 *Messiah* **Pope** 1688–1744 *Essay on Man* **Montesquieu** 1669–1755 *Spirit of the Laws* **Voltaire** 1694–1778 *Candide* **Rousseau** 1712–78 *Confessions* **Diderot** 1713–84 *Encyclopedia* **Haydn** 1732–1809 String Quartet in C Major **Mozart** 1756–91 Symphony No. 35	**Newton** 1642–1727 *Principia Mathematica* **Bayle** 1647–1706 *Historical and Critical Dictionary* **Halley** 1656–1742 Halley's comet **Hume** 1711–76 *A Treatise of Human Nature* **Smith** 1723–90 *Wealth of Nations* **Kant** 1724–1804 *Critique of Pure Reason*
1800	**1789–1815** French Revolution	**Stuart** 1755–1828 *Mrs. Richard Yates* **Canova** 1757–1822 *Pauline Borghese as Venus* **Johnson** 1765–1830 *The Westwood Children* **Charpentier** 1767–1849 *Mlle. Charlotte du Val d'Ognes*	**Jefferson** 1743–1826 *Declaration of Independence* **Beethoven** 1770–1827 Symphony No. 5	**Laplace** 1749–1827 French astronomer

The 1456 appearance of Halley's comet, from Conrad Lycosthenes, *Prodigiorum ac ostentorum chronicon.* 1557. Woodcut. Photo: Ann Ronan Picture Library, Taunton, U.K.

CHAPTER 20

Science, Reason, and Absolutism

THE SEVENTEENTH CENTURY

Europe emerged from medievalism into what is generally called the Modern World[1] during the tumultuous Renaissance, but not until 1648 did the passions unleashed by the Reformation and Counter-Reformation begin to subside. Initially a conflict between Catholics and Protestants, the Thirty Years' War (1618–48) evolved into an international conflict between modern nation-states. The Peace of Westphalia of 1648 that ended the slaughter was a landmark in European history, finally laying to rest the last vestiges of medievalism. Once viable values and institutions completely disappeared. As viewed from the early modern world, the medieval idea of a unified Christian commonwealth was a relic of the distant past as were papal claims to political power. Adopting the strategies of diplomacy and alliances initiated by Italian city-states, sovereign nations staked out boundaries and competed with each other in the struggle for a new balance of power. The strongest competing powers were France, England, the Hapsburg empires of Austria and Spain, and the Ottoman empire (map 20.1).

Rapid advances in science and technology revealed vast new horizons, and international trade opened up the whole world to European dominance and, inevitably, European exploitation. The English East Indies Company was founded in 1600; its Dutch counterpart was chartered two years later, followed by the French. The prevailing mood in northern Europe, with its growing power and wealth, was as positive as the joyful optimism voiced by Miranda in Shakespeare's *The Tempest* (see pp. 106–29).

1. Our modern world began in around 1600 but the difference between "modern" in that sense and "modern" meaning our own century can sometimes be confusing. The modern period is frequently divided into three parts: the Early Modern World: 1600–1789; the Middle Modern World: 1789–1914; the Twentieth Century. The French Revolution of 1789 marked a major change from one era to another as did the onset of World War I in 1914. The Baroque, the Age of Reason, the Enlightenment, and so forth are, of course, subheads within the modern period.

Science and Philosophy

Francis Bacon, 1561–1626

The career of Francis Bacon spanned the late Renaissance and the emerging modern world, which is why he is discussed here and in the preceding chapter. Along with Galileo and Descartes, he ranks as one of the founders of modern science and philosophy. He formulated no new scientific hypotheses nor did he make any dramatic discoveries, but he did inquire into the function and ethics of science and scientific research in relation to human life. For Bacon, knowledge was not recognition of any given reality but a search for truth, a journey rather than a destination. Bacon knew that the old culture was being replaced by a dramatically new epoch. Inventions such as gunpowder, the printing press, the compound microscope (ca. 1590), and the telescope (ca. 1608) changed the material world, spawning new beliefs, institutions, and values. Scientific knowledge and invention, Bacon believed, should be public property to be shared democratically and to be used for the benefit of all people. In his *Novum Organum* (1620) Bacon stated the logic of scientific inquiry and the principles of the inductive method. Factual information would be collected through experiment and observation, leading to general statements based solely on observable data. For Bacon the principal task of scientific investigation was to remedy the poverty of factual data, to embark on an exhilarating voyage of scientific discovery that had been delayed about 2,000 years. There was an explosion of knowledge as seventeenth-century scientists explored a world that had been virtually unknown since the groundbreaking efforts of the Hellenistic scientists of the ancient world (map 20.2).

Galileo Galilei, 1564–1642

Professor of mechanics and astronomy at the University of Padua, Galileo Galilei contributed mightily to the accumulation of factual information. His was a threefold scientific method based on a Pythagorean faith in a mathematical order of nature, the practice of abstracting and intuiting mathematical laws, and, most importantly, experimentation under rigidly controlled conditions. With his improved telescope he empirically proved the heliocentric theory, discovered sun spots, and viewed the moons of Jupiter. He

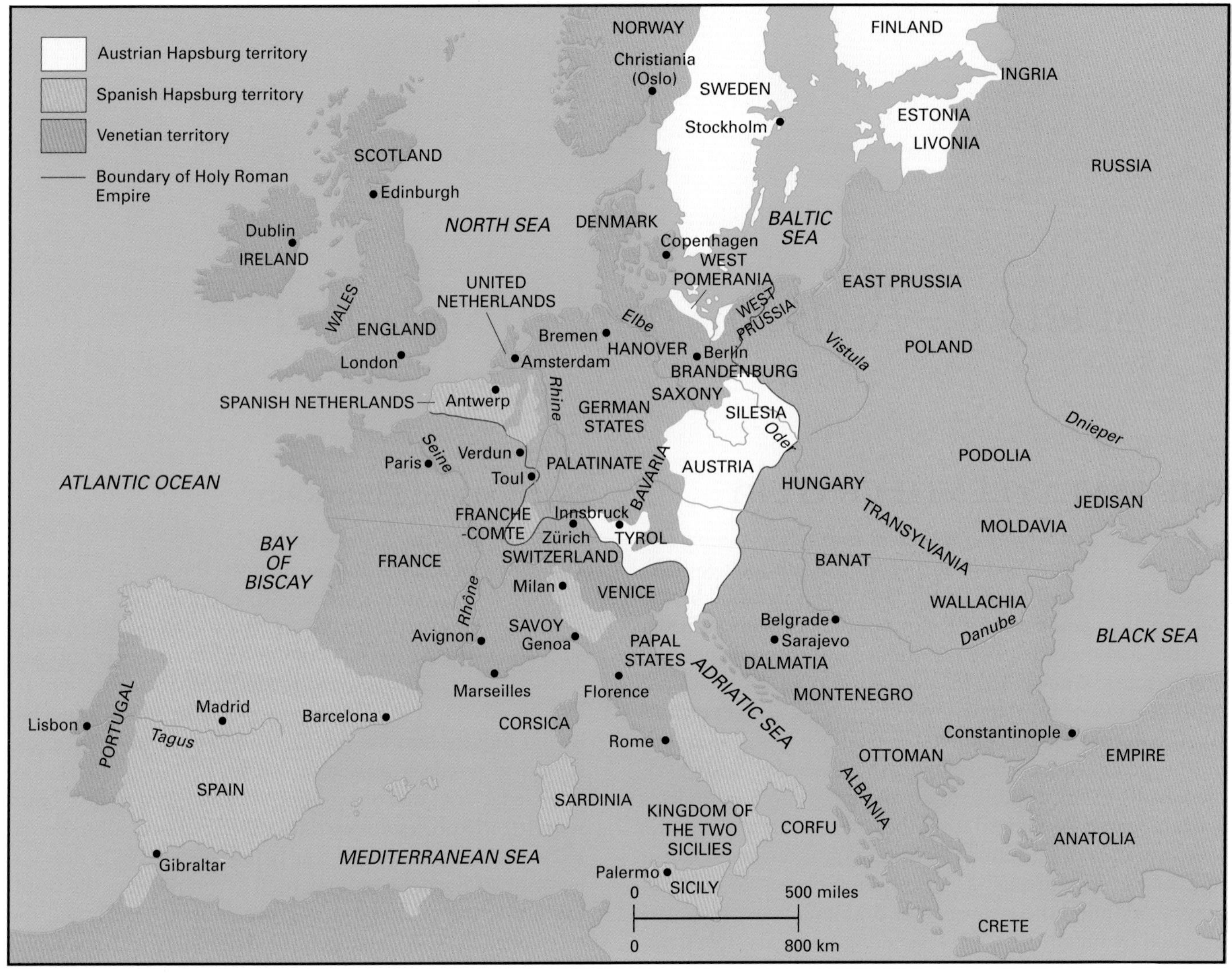

Map 20.1 Europe in the 17th century.

devised two laws of motion, invented the thermometer, improved the compound microscope, investigated the principles of the lever and the pulley, measured air pressure, and studied the properties of magnetism and sound vibrations. Even more importantly, he invented the modern method of forming a theory, testing it experimentally, and adjusting the theory to conform to observable results.

It can be said that modern science began on 24 August 1609, the date of Galileo's letter to the Doge of Venice in which he described his telescopic observations. But Galileo's was the only voice promoting examination of the heavens with his improved telescope. His fellow scientists unanimously rejected this marvelous new scientific instrument. Why was this so?

The magnifying power of a convex mirror was known to Euclid in 300 BC, but for the next 1,900 years no one was interested in concave mirrors nor were they concerned with the three-power spyglass that Dutch artisans had copied from a 1590 Italian model. Philosophers and scientists had learned not to trust the senses, especially visual phenomena. The problem was compounded because lenses and concave mirrors made one see figures that were contradicted by the sense of touch. Galileo's thirty-power telescope was therefore rejected as dispensing false information. The Catholic cardinals who refused to view moon craters through Galileo's instrument had a long tradition behind them.

The startling contents of the famous letter to the Doge became common knowledge, leading to ever-growing controversy. After Galileo published his *Dialogues Concerning the Two Chief World Systems* (1632), the Inquisition charged him with heresy. The Holy Office (Inquisition) claimed that Galileo had agreed, in a signed statement, not to promulgate his heliocentric views. The statement was a forgery, and Galileo was not allowed to appear before the court in his own defense. He was judged, nevertheless, a heretic, forced to recant, and sentenced to lifetime house arrest. First condemned to public burning, the book was later merely prohibited.

Galileo managed to get his book published in Switzerland and followed that with the publication (in Holland) of *The New Sciences* (1638), the first great work on modern physics. Galileo had successfully defied Rome but his life was a shambles and Italian science was set back for generations. (In October 1992 the Church of Rome officially declared that Galileo had been treated unfairly.)

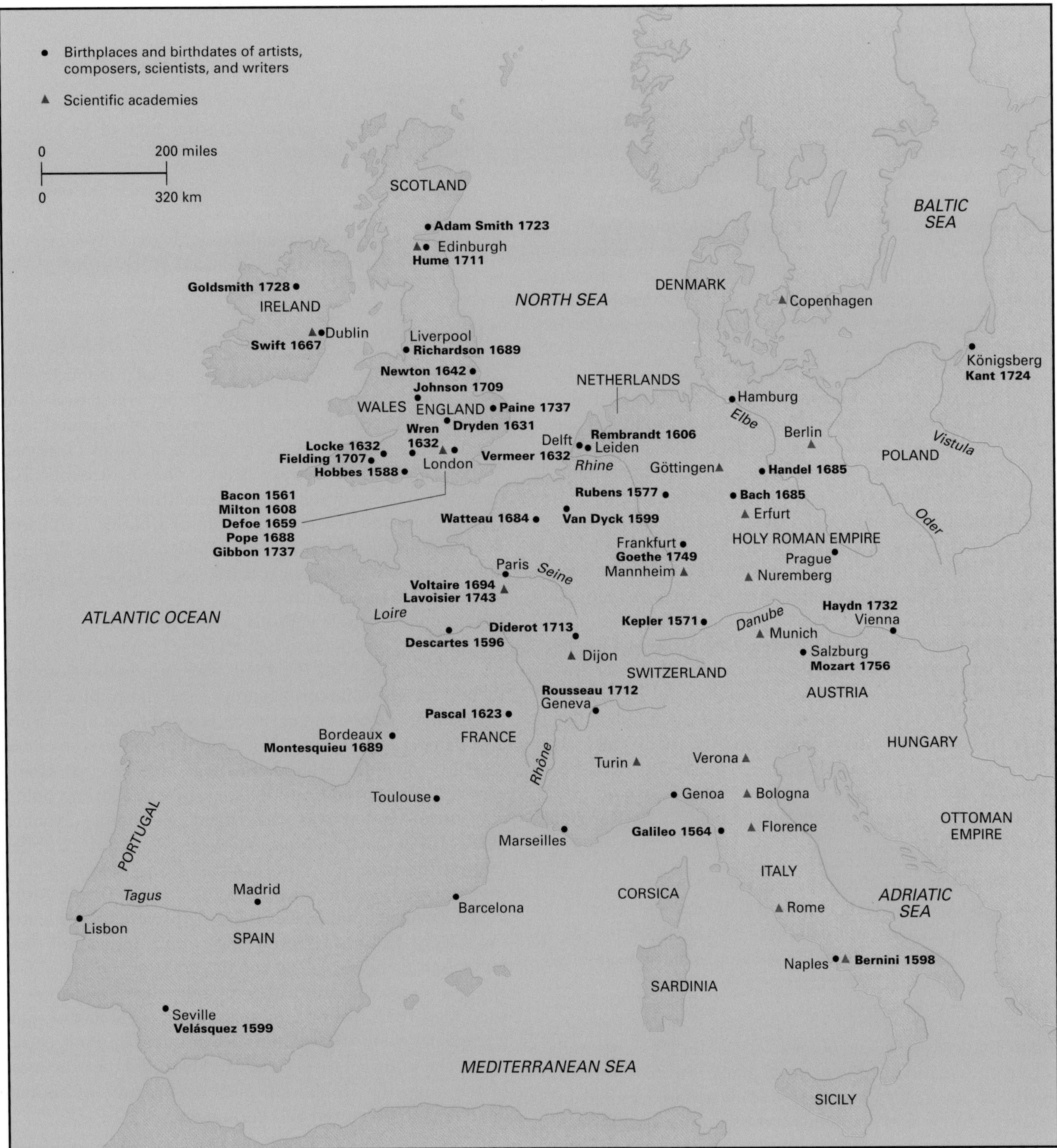

Map 20.2 The spread of the intellectual revolution in 17th- and 18th-century Europe.

René Descartes, 1596–1650

The Reformation raised the question of the reliability of religious knowledge, of whether Catholic beliefs were more or less true than Protestant or any other creeds. The rise of science extended the question to the reliability of all knowledge. Skeptics maintained that doubt was always present, with no certain knowledge possible, but Bacon argued that the inductive method, augmented by mechanical aids such as the compound microscope, provided certain knowledge about the world. Like many philosophers and scientists, René Descartes distrusted sensory evidence. Indeed, he went even further, following the arguments of skeptics such as Montaigne and Mersenne to their logical conclusion and rejecting everything as "true" or knowable except his own mental existence: *"Cogito, ergo sum"* ("I think, therefore I am"). On this foundation of "Cartesian doubt," he was able to erect a system, or method, of discovering truth.

In his *Discourse on Method* (1637) Descartes formulated his "natural method," which was to accept nothing as true except what "clearly and distinctly" presented itself to his mind. It was not until his *Meditations* (1641) that Descartes responded to attacks on all knowledge. Admitting that the senses could not be trusted, Descartes postulated an evil demon who confused people about the truth or falsity of anything, even whether a square had four sides. The Cartesian solution was to exorcise the demon by believing in the goodness of the all-powerful God. Descartes doesn't doubt that God exists, but how does he know that he himself exists? He finds his answer in the realization that he is a thinking person: *"Cogito ergo sum."*

Whatever is clearly and distinctly perceived by the mind is true. From this point Descartes constructed a rational philosophy that established the reliability of the senses and proved the existence of the physical world. He believed, further, that God had created two substances, spirit and matter. The mind was spirit and its essence was consciousness; the essence of the body, or matter, was extension and movement in space. Cartesian dualism thus established a gulf between mind and body that later philosophers removed by arguing that mind, body, and nature were all interconnected.

Descartes reaffirmed the ideas first expressed by the Greek atomist Democritos that the whole of matter was composed of items of identical substance. All reality, for Descartes, lay in the motion of this absolute substance through space and time. For him and the many who followed him, the perfect God had created a flawless (mathematical) world; God was an engineer who had built and set in motion a very complicated machine. As Randall summarizes:

> To Descartes thenceforth space or extension became the fundamental reality in the world, motion the source of all change, and mathematics the only relation between its parts. . . . He made of nature a machine and nothing but a machine; purposes and spiritual influences alike vanished.[2]

Mathematics was "queen of the sciences" for Descartes and all anyone needed to explain a mechanical universe. Applied mathematics enabled scientists to study and understand an orderly cosmos that operated according to natural laws, a position with which Galileo was in complete agreement. Copernicus had proposed the heliocentric theory; Kepler had confirmed it by observation and, with mathematics, determined the three laws of planetary motion:

1. The planets move around the sun in ellipses with the sun at one focus of the ellipse.
2. We can imagine a line joining the sun and a planet. Though the planet's speed varies in its orbit around the sun, yet this imaginary line "sweeps out" equal areas in equal times.
3. The square of the time for one complete revolution of each planet is proportional to the cube of its average distance from the sun.

Bacon, Galileo, Descartes, and the early astronomers built a firm foundation for the scientific eruption that inspired Newton and that subsequently made Western culture unrivaled among the civilizations of the world.

Absolutism

At the beginning of the century both England and France were governed by absolute monarchs who based their claims on Divine Right. The thrones of England and Scotland were united by the accession of James I (reigned 1603–25), the son of Mary Stuart, Queen of Scots. His attempt to govern absolutely brought him into conflict with Parliament, and the absolute rule of Charles I (reigned 1625–49) finally led to Civil War (1642–6) between the king and Parliament. Charles I was tried and executed for treason and the Interregnum began, the Puritan era of the Commonwealth and the Protectorate (1649–59) under what amounted to the dictatorship of Oliver Cromwell.

Beginning with the Civil War, the Social Contract theory of government became ever more prominent. Government by consent of the governed did not imply a liberal democracy, however, but only that the power of the wealthy and influential classes was able to curb kingly excesses. The Social Contract concept was a strong political current but it was challenged by Thomas Hobbes (1588–1679) in *Leviathan*, published in 1651. Hobbes revived the idea of a contract based on subjection to a monarch's sovereign power, but ruled out a Divine Right king. Convinced that peace and security were prerequisites for society, Hobbes believed that certain individual freedoms had to be sacrificed for the good of the state. For Hobbes a state of nature was anarchy; there had to be a superior force to restore and maintain the stability of society, and that would be the unlimited power of the king. Given the Social Contract theory, the Civil War, and the execution of the king, the Hobbesian position became, of course, anathema to Cromwell and Parliament.

On the death of Cromwell in 1659, power passed to his son, Richard, but within a year Charles II (reigned 1660–85), son of Charles I, was invited to restore the Stuart line. Charles managed to go his own way without openly confronting Parliament, but James II (reigned 1685–8) was not so clever and was forced to abdicate, leaving in his wake the conviction that a Catholic king was dangerous to English liberties. Mary, the daughter of James II, was Protestant and married to William of Orange, a Dutch Protestant. Providing they accepted the new Bill of Rights, William and Mary were invited to ascend the English throne. This was the bloodless Glorious Revolution of 1688 that established a constitutional monarchy. Absolutism was virtually finished in England.

2. J. H. Randall, Jr., *The Making of the Modern Mind* (New York: Columbia University Press, 1976), pp. 241–2.

Absolutism in France had a far longer and more violent history. Succeeding to the throne after the assassination of Henry IV, Louis XIII reigned from 1610 to 1643, but royal power was gradually taken over by his chief minister, Cardinal Richelieu, who operated as a virtual dictator from 1624 to 1642. It was Richelieu who established the royal absolutism to which Louis XIV succeeded in 1643 at the age of five under the regency of his mother. During the longest reign of any French monarch, Louis XIV (1643–1715; fig. 20.1) promoted the arts, built the magnificent palace at Versailles (see fig. 21.16), and made France the most powerful monarchy in Europe. The nation was crippled, however, by an archaic economic system with local customs barriers, tax farming, and a nobility that paid no taxes at all. Raising revenues simply increased the misery of the people. Further, the king's revocation of the Edict of Nantes (1685), that protected the Huguenots (French Protestants) from persecution, was a disaster. Over 250,000 mostly middle-class craftsmen and their families fled the country, marking the beginning of the end of Louis' greatness and, ultimately, of the French monarchy itself.

20.1 French school after Gianlorenzo Bernini, *Bust of Louis XIV*. Ca. 1700. Bronze, 33⅛ × 39⅜ × 17" (84.2 × 100 × 43.2cm). National Gallery of Art, Washington, D.C. (Samuel H. Kress Collection).
Versailles was decorated and furnished in the Baroque style represented by this bust, but the exterior is essentially Neoclassic, the preferred architectural style of Louis XIV.

THE EIGHTEENTH CENTURY

The Enlightenment, ca. 1687–1789

"Enlightenment" and "Age of Reason" are the two terms that describe the intellectual characteristics of the eighteenth century. The Enlightenment is usually dated from 1687, the year in which Newton's epochal *Principia Mathematica (Mathematical Principles of Natural Philosophy)* appeared, to the beginning of the French Revolution in 1789. An alternative beginning date would be 1688, the year of the Glorious Revolution in England. No matter; the *Principia* and the Glorious Revolution were major milestones marking the advance of science, rationalism, and freedom.

The Enlightenment was a self-conscious and extremely articulate movement that was to transform all Western societies. Europe had experienced some rude shocks, what some writers called the "three humiliations": the earth was not at the center of the universe; people were creatures of nature like other animals; and their reason was subject to passions and instincts. These new truths represented intellectual advances that enabled people to redefine their responsibilities: discover truth through science; achieve personal happiness in a viable society; explore the full meaning, and limitations, of liberty. Newton's discoveries provided convincing evidence that the world was orderly and knowable and that, by the same token, human societies could be made orderly and rational through the exercise of enlightened reason.

Montesquieu (1689–1755) was apparently among the first to expand Cartesian ideas about natural law, contending that both physical and political phenomena were subject to general laws. The Marquis de Condorcet (1743–94) went still further. He assumed that one could discover universally valid truths in ethics, economics, and government that were as certain as the facts of mathematics and science. The accumulation of new knowledge would guide decisions and actions and help to free men and women from prejudices, superstitions, and undesirable restraints of society and government. This was the doctrine of progress that so fascinated the intellectuals of the Enlightenment. Just as the sciences progressed ever upward by discovering new facts, so would society move to an ever fuller realization of human potential. These optimistic beliefs had the force of self-fulfilling prophecies, leading to major improvements in many areas before the realization dawned that ethics, economics, society, and government had far more variables than anyone had ever dreamed.

Science and Philosophy: Newton and Locke

Isaac Newton, 1642–1727

Newton was the scientific hero of the Enlightenment. He electrified Western culture with his discovery of the universal law of gravitation, made important investigations into optics, and invented the branch of mathematics known as calculus (also invented independently by Baron von Leibniz; 1646–1716). As important as these specific discoveries were, Newton was revered by his peers more for his methodology. Some of Newton's discoveries have been modified by later scientists, but his scientific method stands to this day as a model for every scientist. Willing to give credit where it was due, Newton supposedly remarked, "If I have seen a little farther than others, it is because I have stood on the shoulders of giants." There were many giants, including Copernicus, Brahe, Bruno, Kepler, and Galileo, but Newton effected the grand synthesis that explained the operation of the cosmos. First, he refined Galileo's laws of motion:

1. A body remains in a state of rest or of uniform motion in a straight line unless compelled by an external force to change that state. In other words, a body's inertia keeps it in a state of rest or its inertia keeps it moving in a straight line. External force has to be applied to move it from either its state of rest or its straight-line motion.
2. A change in momentum is proportional to the force causing the change and takes place in the direction in which the force is acting. In other words, the increase or decrease in velocity is proportional to the force.
3. To every action there is an equal and opposite reaction. We see this law in action every time a rocket roars into space.

Celestial Calculations

Galileo had demonstrated the principles of movement of bodies on earth, but not the motion of heavenly bodies. Why were their orbits curved? Newton hypothesized that all celestial bodies were mutually attracted to each other. He concentrated his studies on the moon's inertial movement in space, and then determined that its orbit was curved because it was continuously falling toward the earth (fig. 20.2). Its inertia causes it to fly out in a straight line, as shown by the dotted arrows, but the gravitational pull of the earth overcomes the straight-line tendency. Action and reaction are equal and the moon remains in orbit at a standard distance from the earth, just as today's manufactured satellites remain in orbit. Newton calculated the mass of the moon and its distance from the earth and determined that the gravitational pull was inversely proportional to the square of its distance from the earth. Newton also calculated the mass of the sun, the planets, and their moons and discovered that each planet would travel according to Kepler's laws by using the same formula: the gravitational pull of the sun was inversely proportional to the square of a planet's distance from the sun. The mathematical formula was the same whether the object was an apple falling from a tree or the moon, a law that worked here on earth and far out in space. This was the universal law of gravitation.

20.2 Forces acting on the moon to determine its motion.

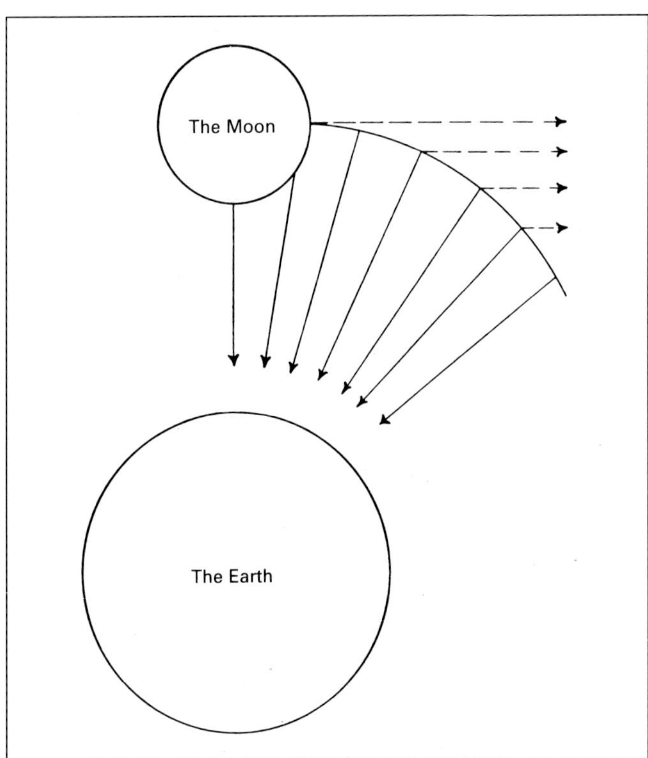

Universal Principles

Newton (and Edmund Halley; fig. 20.3) demonstrated that comets obey the same universal principle. Newton measured the flattening of the earth at its poles due to its rotation and proved that the size of a planet determined the length of its day. He showed the effect of latitude on the weight of an object and explained that the tides resulted from the combined attraction of the sun and the moon. All these examples of gravitation illustrate some of the different phenomena that can be explained with one law. No wonder Alexander Pope wrote:

> Nature and Nature's laws lay hid in night:
> God said, *Let Newton be*! and all was light.

The philosophic implications of this unification of scientific principles were astounding. Picture the universe as Newton saw it, a vast and intricate system of whirling bodies in space, a configuration both orderly and predictable. Each planet, each moon, each solar system was balanced in the cosmic plan, a balance determined by mechanical forces pulling against each other. Absolute and unvarying, these forces would keep the machine in working order. What, then, was God's place? For all practical purposes God was ruled out, but Newton assigned two functions to the Divinity. Scientists noticed slight irregularities in the motions of the heavenly bodies in terms of Newtonian physics. Therefore one function of God was to make certain periodic readjustments, with a second function the maintenance of an even flow of time and space. Thus God became a sort of celestial engineer, turning a wheel here, opening a valve there, keeping an eye on the dials. Even before the close of the eighteenth century, however, a French astronomer, the Marquis de Laplace, extended the mechanism of gravitation and proved that the irregularities were periodical and subject to a law that kept them within bounds. This led to the belief held by certain deists that God existed as the master designer of a perfect world-machine needing no further tending.

Given these developments, we see clearly and distinctly the reliance on intellect that characterized the Enlightenment. Human beings using the marvelous mechanisms of their minds could, in time, unlock the most hidden secrets of the universe. And what of human institutions? The cosmos was orderly, rational, and knowable; why couldn't people use their reason to design an orderly, rational society? It was precisely this optimism that inspired the American Founding Fathers to construct a democracy that would be a model and a beacon of hope for the entire world.

John Locke, 1632–1704

The founders of the American republic had derived some political ideas from Montesquieu's *Spirit of the Laws* (1748), but they drew mainly from John Locke. Returning from exile after the Glorious Revolution, Locke wrote his *Two Treatises of Government* (1690) to justify constitutional monarchy. In the fifteenth essay from his *Second Treatise on Civil Government* Locke takes this position:

> Now this power, which every man has in the state of Nature, and which he parts with to the society in all such cases where the society can secure him, is to use such means for the preserving of his own property as he thinks good and Nature allows him; and to punish the breach of the law of Nature in others; so as (according to the best of his reason) may most conduce to the preservation of himself and the rest of mankind. So that the end and measure of this power, when in every other man's hands, in the state of Nature, being the preservation of all his society, that is, all mankind in general; it can have no other end or measure, when in the hands of the magistrate, but to preserve the members of that society in their lives, liberties, and possessions.

Locke assumed a natural law that operated in the affairs of human beings much as Newton's world-machine functioned according to natural law, a position also reflected in the opening paragraph of the Declaration of Independence as composed by Thomas Jefferson:

> When, in the course of human events, it becomes necessary for one people to dissolve the political bands which have connected them with another, and to assume, among the powers of the earth, the separate and equal station to which the laws of nature and of nature's God entitle them, a decent respect to the opinions of mankind requires that they should declare the causes which impel them to the separation.

According to Locke, this natural law gave people certain rights that were unalienable, and these were life, liberty, and property. Jefferson substituted for "property" a much more striking and challenging phrase:

20.3 The 1456 appearance of Halley's comet, from Conrad Lycosthenes, *Prodigiorum ac ostentorum chronicon*. 1557. Woodcut. Photo: Ann Ronan Picture Library, Taunton, U.K.

> We hold these truths to be self-evident, that all men are created equal, that they are endowed by their Creator with certain unalienable Rights, that among these are Life, Liberty, and the pursuit of Happiness. That to secure these rights, Governments are instituted among Men, deriving their just powers from the consent of the governed.

Jefferson later explained how he regarded the Declaration:

> Neither aiming at originality of principles or sentiments, nor yet copied from any particular or previous writing, it was intended to be an expression of the American mind.

Locke wrote that government existed and had authority only because the people brought it into existence and gave it its authority. If the government violated its trust, the people had a natural right to set up a new government. They had a right to revolt.

The Wealth of Nations: Adam Smith, 1723–90

Exactly as Locke and Jefferson sought natural law as a guide to political affairs and Newton found such a law to be the binding force of the universe, so did Adam Smith seek a unifying principle for economic affairs. His work, interestingly enough, followed the scientific method that Bacon had established in the previous epoch; his investigations of the facts of economic life were conducted in a pin factory, leading to generalizations based on his factual findings.

Smith presented his principles of capitalism in 1776 in a book that quickly became a classic: *An Inquiry into the Nature and Causes of the Wealth of Nations.* In Smith's day capitalism had taken the form called mercantilism, a strictly regulated trade system controlled by each nation's government and based on the assumption that wealth depended on how much gold and silver that nation possessed. Increasing the supply of precious metals required a favorable balance of trade, i.e., more exports than imports. With every nation seeking a favorable trade balance the system will inevitably collapse—with one way out. A colonial nation can exploit its colonies as a source of cheap raw materials and a dumping ground for more expensive manufactured goods—so England treated its American colonies. Eventually, colonies will either develop their own manufacturing or be bled dry by the mother country. The system fails again.

Some French economists, called physiocrats, were the first to revolt against mercantilism. They claimed that a nation's wealth depended on its raw materials rather than the supply of money. They also believed that government regulation of trade and commerce was detrimental to economic well-being and progress. Adam Smith studied with this group while fleshing out his own theories.

Smith sought a reasonable balance in economic affairs that would insure an adequate supply of goods to meet the needs of human beings. He wanted these produced and sold at a fair price so that most people could buy the goods while the laborer earned a decent wage and the manufacturer reaped a reasonable profit. To solve this intricate problem he proposed a return to nature in economic affairs: the removal of all restrictions on wages and the manufacture and sale of goods. This is the unfettered competition called *laissez-faire* that can be demonstrated by the following example.

Smith's first premise is that people are acquisitive by nature with an endless craving for wealth. So an enterpriser with investment capital sees that people need shoes. He builds a shoe factory and charges whatever the traffic will bear. Other capitalists eye the large profits and rush into the shoe business. As the number of shoes increases, the price necessarily drops if, according to *laissez-faire* doctrine, everyone has equal access to raw materials and to markets with no regulation whatever. Eventually there are more shoes than buyers and prices are slashed to stimulate sales, driving the least efficient manufacturers out of business. As demand overtakes supply the price begins to regulate itself. Finally, production is adequate for people's needs, the price is stable, and the most efficient producers can make a fair profit. Labor, however, is still missing from this formula.

Labor, says Smith, is a commodity for sale just like shoes. Wages will be high in a new field and laborers will flock to this work, but wages will decline as workers become plentiful. Finally, the labor market in shoe production will become glutted, and wages will fall to less than a living wage, forcing the least competent workers into other employment. Eventually the price of labor, like that of shoes, will stabilize, with the most efficient workers employed at a fair wage. Those laid off will find other work at which they are more efficient, and, presumably, better able to make a living.

From these examples we can abstract the principles of Smith's *laissez-faire* economy. First, labor is the source of a nation's wealth. Second, all people are acquisitive. Third, there must be unregulated access to raw materials, labor, and markets. Fourth, each person has a natural endowment of skills that should determine the kind of work to be done; a free choice of employment should lead the worker into the most congenial job. Fifth, if all the conditions above exist, the law of supply and demand will solve the problem of sufficient goods, satisfactory price, adequate profit, and fair wages. Furthermore, each person will be doing what he or she can do best, and thus the most enjoyable kind of occupation. Q.E.D.

Or almost Q.E.D. One problem remained, which Smith recognized, without producing an adequate solution. He realized that monopolies might limit or eliminate competition and proposed that governments protect free competition by controlling monopolies; he could not, however, suggest any procedures that did not also regulate industry. Modern capitalist nations have solved the problem with regulations and controls that still permit the operation of Smith's laws of supply and demand in a relatively free marketplace. Constant vigilance against monopolies is, of course, essential.

Smith's economic system was similar to Locke's political philosophy and to the universal law of gravitation. The first step is a return to nature; human differences and limitations are the natural parameters. Nature will then provide a self-regulating economic mechanism. The natural forces of supply and demand, like the mutual gravitational pulls of planets and suns, like the pulls of executive and legislative branches of government, will shape the economy into a smoothly operating machine. Adam Smith contributed a principle on which an economy could be organized and operated, leading, in the fullness of time, to productive and affluent societies. Today's capitalistic economies do not function as well as everyone would like, but there is no doubt that modern capitalism, like modern democracy, functions better than anything else yet devised. The catastrophic failure of socialism's central-planning economies that had neither private property nor free enterprise vividly highlights the basic validity of Smith's theories.

Philosophy and *Les Philosophes*

Locke and Educational Theory

John Locke made yet another contribution that greatly influenced education and other human institutions. He said that the mind, at birth, was a complete blank, a *tabula rasa* (Lat., "blank slate"). This contradicted royalists, clergymen, and others, who insisted that the natural inclination, at birth, was submission to authority. Not so, said Locke. The mind was a spotless tablet on which would be written all the experiences the individual had throughout life. Shaping men and women into good citizens who were honest and responsible members of society required, therefore, positive, reinforcing experiences beginning early in life. Beyond the family, a formal education, according to Locke, was the best way of providing the good experiences that help form healthy and independent personalities.

The process is rational. One starts with the human mind as raw material and molds it, so to speak, with a solid education. The finished product is, at least theoretically, a good person. The process can, of course, work in the opposite direction, for bad experiences could produce a bad person. Most of our current ideas of universal education in a constructive environment are based on Locke's educational philosophy. Along with Socrates, men and women of the Enlightenment believed that virtue was knowledge and ignorance vice, and that an educated mind was its own reward. It still is.

David Hume, 1711–76

Locke's theories of mind and understanding revealed some inconsistencies that were later filled in by the Scottish philosopher David Hume, a lucid and urbane man who epitomized the enlightened thinker. Beginning with Locke's empiricist theory of knowledge, Hume proved that human reason has its limits. Anticipating a great public outcry, he published, in three volumes, *A Treatise of Human Nature, being an Attempt to Introduce the Experimental Method of Reasoning into Moral Subjects* (1739–40). Instead, no one noticed the book at the time; as Hume sadly noted, "it fell dead-born from the press." It could not, however, be ignored for long. In the first volume Hume granted certain knowledge only to arithmetic and algebra, and to geometry providing the axioms are true. Beyond that, he said, there was only probable knowledge, thus anticipating modern scientific thought.

Hume's principal concern was with cause and effect, or causality. If we observe that a certain event A is always followed by B, then we assume that A causes B. If, for example, we hold a match to a piece of paper and see the paper burn, we connect the two events and say that the flaming match caused the paper to burn. Not so, says Hume. That paper always burns when a match is held to it is a *belief* developed through *custom*, that is, experience. Because we have seen this happen so often we assume that it must happen every time. Therein lies the rub. Because A (the match) does not cause B (paper) to burn, we cannot assume that the paper is certain to burn; it is a probability but not a certainty. The paper, for example, could have been soaked in a chemical that no amount of flame would set afire. Further, we cannot bite into an apple with the certainty that it will taste like an apple; it could taste like roast pork. We assume that the sun will rise tomorrow, but it is impossible to establish that it must necessarily rise. Newton's law of universal gravitation is therefore probable and not necessarily universal. As space vehicles have probed ever deeper into the cosmos, scientists have watched with extreme curiosity to see if Newton's law remains valid. There have been no inconsistencies to date, but no scientist would be willing to predict what the situation might be somewhere way out there. As Hume says, human reason has its limits. He accepted a world based on probability rather than certainty. Through observation and reasoning we can determine, short of certainty, how nature operates, but not why.

Hume's skepticism also applied to religion and religious beliefs and followed a long history of serious doubts about the truths of Judaism and Christianity. In the sixteenth century Uriel da Costa, a Portuguese Jewish refugee in Holland, started out questioning the truths of orthodox Judaism and ended up maintaining that all religions were made by human beings. The French skeptic Isaac la Peyrère wrote *Man Before Adam* (1656) in which he claimed that there were people all over the world before Adam; therefore, the Bible could not be an accurate account of human history. La Peyrère's work led two biblical scholars, Baruch de Spinoza (1632–77) and Father Richard Simon (1638–1712), to reexamine religious knowledge. Spinoza concluded that the Bible was not divine revelation but merely a history of Jewish activities and superstitions. He proposed instead a religious pantheism in which all existence was embraced in one substance (God or Nature), a position that would appeal to the coming Romantic movement. Father Simon, the greatest biblical scholar of his age, declared that scholars could never find an accurate text of the Bible nor discover what it really meant. Unlike Spinoza, Simon was convinced that there was a biblical message and tried, in vain, to determine what the message was.

The most famous of the French skeptics, Pierre Bayle (1647–1706), wrote a *Historical and Critical Dictionary* (1697–1702), in which he undermined the metaphysical theories of Descartes, Spinoza, Locke, and Leibniz, attacked all existing theologies, ridiculed the heroes of the Old Testament, and challenged all rational knowledge. He advocated abandoning reason in favor of blind faith, for all things, all understandings, were doubtful—except, perhaps, historical descriptions. Voltaire called Bayle's *Dictionary* the "Arsenal of the Enlightenment."

An avid reader of Bayle, Hume saw, as apparently no other Enlightenment thinker did, the plight of human beings if Bayle's skepticism could not be countered. Hume never doubted that people could be certain about the evils of murder, stealing, and the like, nor need they be unsure about Newton's laws. Uncertainty belonged in the philosopher's study. Hume anticipated modern science by stating that there were no absolute truths and, further, that one should not, must not, believe anything absolutely. He was particularly concerned about religious conflicts. "Errors in religion," he wrote, "are dangerous; those in philosophy only ridiculous." He believed, in the final analysis, that people could lead their lives as he did his, exercising their natural passions and common sense as they cheerfully enjoyed the uncertainties of everyday life.

NATURAL DISASTER AND THE ENLIGHTENMENT

On 1 November 1755 Lisbon, in Portugal, was a wealthy trading city widely known for great piety. The three tremendous earthquakes that shook and burned and flooded the city on that day destroyed most of the wealth, 17,000 out of 20,000 homes, and the lives of over 60,000 people. Why Lisbon? Stern priests daily preached hundreds of sermons telling the stunned survivors that God was punishing them for their sins and would do so again if they did not repent. But, knowing how many children had perished on that dreadful day, people began to question God's mercy and compassion. Further, they asked the priests why God destroyed so many churches while sparing a whole street of brothels. No one had an answer. Among those writing pamphlets on the controversy were scientists who blamed the quake not on human sins but on movements of the earth. The relentless priests were eventually jailed to shut them up. The Lisbon earthquake marked a critical turning point in human attitudes toward natural disasters.

Immanuel Kant, 1724–1804

The leading thinker of the German Enlightenment, Kant responded to Hume's skepticism with the famous remark that he had been "awakened from his dogmatic slumbers." In his three *Critiques* (*Pure Reason,* 1781; *Practical Reason,* 1788; *Judgement,* 1793) Kant presented a complete philosophical system. He showed that knowledge *a priori* was possible because people could perceive the world of space, forms, and causality and, because of the intrinsic nature of the human mind, understand phenomena. As he said, we can know only such appearances as colors, shapes, and sounds, but never the thing-in-itself; true knowledge cannot transcend experience. But we can have reliable knowledge because all minds function in the same way.

In ethics Kant stated that good actions must be performed from a sense of duty and that moral law was derived from his categorical imperative: "Act only according to the maxim which you at the same time will to be a universal law." People, he said, were independent moral agents with the freedom to choose right actions. As a practical necessity Kant postulated the existence of God for those who desired (or required) a belief in divinity, so that virtue could be crowned with happiness and immortality, and the pursuit of moral perfection continue in the afterlife.

With ethical and moral theories that appealed to the heart as opposed to Hume's dispassionate rationalism, Kant was the founder of the German philosophical tendency known as Idealism. Subsequently, his philosophy had enormous appeal for the German Romantic movement. Kant was, however, an enlightened rather than a proto-Romantic thinker. His principle that every person had to be considered as an end in herself or himself is a form of the Enlightenment doctrine of the Rights of Man. Kant coined, moreover, the prevailing motto for the Enlightenment: "Dare to Know!"

Les Philosophes

Called *les philosophes* ("the philosophers") or *Encyclopédistes* because most of them wrote articles for Diderot's monumental *Encyclopedia,* the *philosophes* included writers, poets, artists, dramatists, mathematicians, and scientists. What they had in common was the French language, which had become the international language of the Enlightenment, leading to the comment that everyone had two homelands: his own and France. One of the leading *philosophes,* Denis Diderot (dee-duh-ro; 1713–84), was editor-in-chief of the *Encyclopedia* (1747–72), which he conceived of after he had translated the groundbreaking *Cyclopedia* of the Scotsman Ephraim Chambers. With characteristic wit he remarked that "there is no need to understand a language to translate it, since one translates it only for people who understand it not." For Diderot translation became creation, leading to his own *Encyclopedia.* For Diderot and the other *philosophes,* it was time for a secular, more democratic, world to replace a hierarchical, religious one. Published in twenty-eight volumes but suppressed in 1759 by the government and thereafter printed clandestinely, the work was a summary of all human knowledge, a brilliant response to Kant's "Dare to Know!" Its prevailing spirit was scorn for the past and for all organized religions, and glorification of reason, the arts, the experimental sciences, and industry. The *Encyclopedia* assumed that religious toleration and freedom of thought would win out and implied throughout that the condition of the common people should be the main concern of the government. A call to arms in twenty-eight volumes, the *Encyclopedia* was probably, for the intellectuals, the key influence that led to the French Revolution.

In his *Persian Letters* (published anonymously in 1721) Montesquieu (mon-tes-kyu; 1689–1755) satirized European, especially French, society, leaving no phase of human activity untouched by his devastating wit and irony. His most influential book, *The Spirit of the Laws* (1748), was a scientific study of comparative government whose theories of checks and balances found their way into the United States Constitution.

Diderot, Voltaire, and Rousseau were the most influential of the French *philosophes.* Voltaire and his satirical novel *Candide* are discussed on page 175. A kind of reverse image of Voltaire the rationalist, Rousseau was a powerful influence on the Romantic movement (see p. 239).

Absolutism and the Enlightenment

Louis XIV was a despot but, with some justification, he could also be called an enlightened monarch. The same cannot be said for the next two kings. Louis XV, great grandson of Louis XIV, ruled ineptly but luxuriously from 1715 to 1774, and his weak and vacillating grandson, Louis XVI (reigned 1774–93), went to the guillotine.

A rival state, the kingdom of Brandenburg-Prussia, rose to power during the decline of French authority. Frederick I was crowned the first king of Prussia in 1701, followed by Frederick William I (reigned 1713–40), who began Prussian expansion. Frederick the Great (reigned 1740–86) excelled at waging war and made Prussia the dominant military power in Europe. Known as a "benevolent despot," he promoted social and legal reforms and established a glittering court with musical performances by Johann Sebastian Bach and by Frederick himself. But the king did remark that "my people say what they please and I do as I please." Enlightenment had a way to go.

The founder of the modern Russian state, Peter the Great (reigned 1682–1725), mercilessly "westernized" his country and savagely destroyed his enemies. He was admittedly a genius and undoubtedly more than a bit mad. To this day he has been admired as an enlightened leader and viewed with horror as a sadistic monster. Catherine the Great (reigned 1762–91) was of German birth, but she became thoroughly Russianized. Influenced by the Enlightenment, she planned vast reforms, but a peasant revolt in 1773–5 and the French Revolution caused her to reverse course. She issued, among other authoritarian decrees, one to enslave the peasants. Absolutism during the Enlightenment was anything but enlightened.

Only in Great Britain was there any real political freedom. Under the Hanoverian kings George I (reigned 1714–27) and George II (reigned 1727–60), Robert Walpole became, in fact if not in name, the prime minister (in office 1721–42). William Pitt (in office 1757–61) was a strong prime minister, but resigned when the next king, George III (reigned 1760–1820), decided he wanted to direct policy. Lord North was an acquiescent prime minister and between king and prime minister they inadvertently brought a new democratic republic into being.

THE SALONS OF PARIS

Invented in Paris in the early seventeenth century, the European Salon rose to great popularity during the eighteenth century in Rome, Vienna, Berlin, London, and, especially, in Paris. Salons were usually formed by women, *salonières*, who opened their homes to the intellectual, artistic, and social elite of the time. The most fashionable salons were hosted by witty, well-informed, and intelligent *salonières* who provided a gracious atmosphere, fine foods, and a large number of very interesting guests. Attended mostly by men, including Voltaire, Hume, and many of the Encyclopedists, salons were increasingly criticized later in the century because they were controlled by women. David Hume chided France for allowing itself to be governed by women. John Locke omitted women from his idea of natural freedom and Rousseau contended that women should stick to their domestic activities and leave intellectual and artistic pursuits to men. The demise of the salon was not far behind.

LITERATURE, 1600–1789

John Donne, 1573–1631

Although the seventeenth century is often referred to as the Baroque era, the term is more appropriate for art and music (see chapters 21 and 22) than it is for literature. Donne's poetry does display some of the opulence and splendor associated with the Baroque, but Donne has, instead, been characterized as the leader of the Metaphysical school, referring, in general, to the powerful intellectual content of his work, his concentrated images, and his remarkable ability to range between the intensely personal and the cosmic. Poets such as Andrew Marvell were influenced by Donne, but they formed no organized school nor would they have endorsed the Metaphysical label that John Dryden and Samuel Johnson affixed to the poetry of Donne and Marvell.

Poet, prose stylist, and preacher, John Donne was an experienced man of the world who spoke with great intellectual vigor in his love poems and in his Holy Sonnets. Neglected for three centuries after his death, he is now recognized as one of the finest poets in the English language.

In the following song (given here in modernized spelling) Donne uses six vivid images to express the impossibility, as he saw it, of woman's constancy.

LITERARY SELECTION 50

Song

John Donne

Go and catch a falling star,
    Get with child a mandrake root,
Tell me, where all past years are,
    Or who cleft the devil's foot,
Teach me to hear mermaids singing,
Or to keep off envy's stinging,
    And find
    What wind
Serves to advance an honest mind.

If thou be'st born to strange sights,
    Things invisible to see,
Ride ten thousand days and nights,
    Till age snow white hairs on thee;
Thou, when thou return'st, wilt tell me
All strange wonders that befell thee,
    And swear
    Nowhere
Lives a woman true and fair.

If thou find'st one, let me know,
    Such a pilgrimage were sweet;

Yet do not, I would not go,
Though at next door we might meet,
Though she were true when you met her,
And last, till you write your letter,
Yet she
Will be
False, ere I come, to two, or three.

The following poem employs unique images that reflect Donne's secret marriage to his patron's niece, a happy union but one that clouded the rest of the poet's life. Only John Donne could effectively express life, love, and loving in terms of a flea.

The Flea

John Donne

Mark but this flea, and mark in this,
How little that which thou deniest me is;
It sucked me first, and now sucks thee,
And in this flea, our two bloods mingled be;
Thou know'st that this cannot be said
A sin, nor shame, nor loss of maidenhead,
Yet this enjoys before it woo,
And pampered swells with one blood made of two,
And this, alas! is more than we would do.

Oh stay, three lives in one flea spare,
Where we almost, yea more than married are.
This flea is you and I, and this
Our marriage-bed, and marriage-temple is;
Though parents grudge, and you, we're met
And cloistered in these living walls of jet.
Though use make you apt to kill me,
Let not, to that, self-murder added be,
And sacrilege, three sins in killing three.

Cruel and sudden, hast thou since
Purpled thy nail, in blood of innocence?
In what could this flea guilty be,
Except in that drop which it sucked from thee?
Yet thou triumph'st, and say'st that thou
Find'st not thyself, nor me the weaker now;
'Tis true, then learn how false, fears be;
Just so much honor, when thou yield'st to me,
Will waste, as this flea's death took life from thee.

Of Donne's large volume of religious poetry some, near the end of his career, reflected his obsession with the thought of death. In the following Holy Sonnet he uses intense language and vivid images to put death in perspective.

Holy Sonnet X

John Donne

Death, be not proud, though some have called thee
Mighty and dreadful, for thou art not so;
For those whom thou think'st thou dost overthrow
Die not, poor Death, nor yet canst thou kill me.
From rest and sleep, which but thy pictures be,
Much pleasure, then from thee much more must flow;
And soonest our best men with thee do go,
Rest of their bones, and soul's delivery.
Thou art slave to Fate, chance, kings, and desperate men,
And dost with poison, war, and sickness dwell,
And poppy or charms can make us sleep as well
And better than thy stroke; why swell'st thou then?
One short sleep past, we wake eternally
And Death shall be no more; Death, thou shalt die.

STUDY QUESTIONS

1. Donne's poetry has been aptly called "strong-lined" because of his powerful images and sharp changes in rhythm. Try reading his "Song" aloud, listening for the abrupt change in rhythm of "And find/What wind" plus similar changes in the second and third stanzas. How much do these contribute to "strong-lined" poetry?
2. In the "Holy Sonnet" Donne equates death with extended, restful sleep. Is his point of view convincing? Would it persuade an atheist?

Andrew Marvell, 1621–78

Late in his career Marvell wrote stinging political satires, but he is best known today for his classically inspired lyric poetry about love and nature. "To His Coy Mistress" is a seduction poem in the tradition of Catullus and other classical writers. The theme is the fleeting moment and the tone is urgent. We must seize the moment and make love now. Though the theme is serious, the style is both graceful and playful.

LITERARY SELECTION 51

To His Coy Mistress

Andrew Marvell

Had we but World enough, and Time,
This coyness Lady were no crime.
We would sit down, and think which way
To walk, and pass our long Loves Day.
Thou by the *Indian Ganges* side
Should'st Rubies find: I by the Tide
Of *Humber* would complain. I would
Love you ten years before the Flood:
And you should if you please refuse
Till the Conversion of the *Jews*.
My vegetable Love should grow
Vaster than Empires, and more slow.

An hundred years should go to praise
Thine Eyes, and on thy Forehead Gaze.
Two hundred to adore each Breast:
But thirty thousand to the rest.
An Age at least to every part,
And the last Age should show your Heart.
For Lady you deserve this State;
Nor would I love at lower rate.
But at my back I alwaies hear
Times winged Charriot hurrying near:
And yonder all before us lye
Deserts of vast Eternity.
Thy Beauty shall no more be found,
Nor, in thy marble Vault, shall sound
My echoing Song: then Worms shall try
That long preserv'd Virginity:
And your quaint Honour turn to dust;
And into ashes all my Lust.
The Grave's a fine and private place,
But none I think do there embrace.
Now therefore, while the youthful hew
Sits on thy skin like morning dew,
And while thy willing Soul transpires
At every pore with instant Fires,
Now let us sport us while we may;
And now, like am'rous birds of prey,
Rather at once our Time devour,
Than languish in his slow-chapt pow'r.
Let us roll all our Strength, and all
Our sweetness, up into one Ball:
And tear our Pleasures with rough strife,
Thorough the Iron gates of Life.
Thus, though we cannot make our Sun
Stand still, yet we will make him run.

STUDY QUESTION

Did the Coy Mistress acquiesce? Look again at the first and last lines, at the progression from not having enough time to the illusion of time flying by.

John Milton, 1608–74

An ardent supporter of the Puritan cause, Milton became Latin secretary in Cromwell's government and, in several important tracts, one of its principal defenders. On the restoration of the Stuart monarchy with Charles II (1660), Milton was fined and forced to retire, after which he dictated his epic poems, *Paradise Lost* (1667) and *Paradise Regained* (1671). One of the world's great epic poems, *Paradise Lost* relates the story of Satan's rebellion against God and the Fall of Man. Milton's intention was, as he said, to "justify the ways of God to man."

The epic poems were among the first to use blank verse (unrhymed iambic pentameter), but Milton also wrote some notable sonnets. Considered to be among his finest work in small form, the two sonnets given below are in the standard form of fourteen lines in rhymed iambic pentameter.

On Easter Sunday in 1655, in the Piedmont region of northwestern Italy, the Duke of Savoy slaughtered about 1,700 members of the Protestant Waldensian sect that dated back to 1170. The pope celebrated the occasion with a special Mass but Protestant Europe was horrified; Milton's response was a sonnet tense with low-keyed fury. The "martyred blood" refers to Tertullian's statement that "the blood of the martyrs is the seed of the Church." The "triple Tyrant" is the pope, whose tiara has three crowns, and "Babylonian woe" is a reference to Revelation 18 in which the obliteration of the city of luxury and vice is described. Along with many Protestants, especially Puritans, Milton saw the destruction of Babylon as an allegory of the ultimate fate of the Church of Rome.

LITERARY SELECTION 52

On the Late Massacre in Piedmont (1655)

John Milton

Avenge, O Lord, thy slaughtered Saints, whose bones
Lie scattered on the Alpine mountains cold;
Even them who kept thy truth so pure of old,
When all our fathers worshipped stocks and stones,
Forget not: in thy book record their groans
Who were thy sheep, and in their ancient fold
Slain by the bloody Piedmontese, that rolled
Mother with infant down the rocks. Their moans
The vales redoubled to the hills, and they
To heaven. Their martyred blood and ashes sow
O'er all the Italian fields, where still doth sway
The triple Tyrant; that from these may grow
A hundredfold, who, having learnt thy way,
Early may fly the Babylonian woe.

Milton's eyesight, owing to overwork, had become impaired as early as 1644, and by 1652 he was totally blind. The first of two sonnets about his blindness, the following poem signals the poet's submission to fate though he had not yet found his way to using, in darkness, "that one talent which is death to hide."

On His Blindness (1655)

John Milton

When I consider how my light is spent
Ere half my days in this dark world and wide,
And that one Talent which is death to hide
Lodged with me useless, though my soul more bent
To serve therewith my Maker, and present

My true account, lest He returning chide,
"Doth God exact day-labour, light denied?"
I fondly ask. But Patience, to prevent
That murmur, soon replies, "God doth not need
Either man's work or his own gifts. Who best
Bear his mild yoke, they serve him best. His state
Is kingly: thousands at his bidding speed,
And post o'er land and ocean without rest;
They also serve who only stand and wait."

STUDY QUESTION

Milton seethes with indignation over the fate of the slaughtered saints in Italy, but not over the loss of his sight. What are some of the words that convey this mood of resignation? Consider, for example, such words as "spent," "bent," "mild," and "murmur."

Jean-Baptiste Poquelin Molière, 1622–73

Milton's poetry has Baroque elements, but the arts in seventeenth-century France rarely ventured far from the classical ideals of Graeco-Roman civilization. The French seem always to view themselves as rational people living a civilized life in a sane and sensible society. Louis XIV was regarded as the new Caesar Augustus with Paris as the New Rome or New Athens. The painter Poussin and the playwrights Racine and Molière worked in a context that combined Renaissance ideals with the less flamboyant aspects of the Counter-Reformation. France was a Roman Catholic country with a centralized government, but with a definite secular orientation. It was perhaps the most restrained of Catholic countries, especially when compared with Spain or Ireland.

Some French intellectuals believed they lived in a Christian state of grace, but numerous others perceived themselves in a state of nature in a secular society. These contrasting views led to the famous "Quarrel of the Ancients and Moderns." (The French adore intellectual disputes.) Both sides revered classical antiquity, but the Ancients believed they were only modest heirs of classical civilization. The Moderns were convinced they could not only emulate the Greeks and Romans but actually improve on their civilization. This notion of historical progress was, at the time, relatively new, terribly enticing, and distinctly secular. The French were convinced they had invented modern European civilization, with subsequent events only tending to confirm this sweeping supposition.

Comic playwright Molière lived and worked in this Neoclassical climate. He was a rational humanist, creating characters "untouched by any thought of Christian grace," according to an early critic. People, to Molière, were products of the social order. As such, they should possess the virtues of moderation, common sense, and good taste in an urban setting that was rational and sophisticated.

Molière's comedies examine the failure of one or more individuals to measure up to these classical virtues. The title character of *Tartuffe,* for example, has none of these qualities, being a liar, cheat, rogue, and all-round scoundrel. Masquerading as a virtuous fellow of great religiosity, he is a hypocrite; his protector, Orgon, is a foolish dupe; and Orgon's mother is an arrogant snob. In his *Devil's Dictionary* Ambrose Bierce defined a hypocrite as "one who, professing virtues that he does not respect, secures the advantage of seeming to be what he despises." So it was with Tartuffe.

To stage his play Molière had to address several petitions to Louis XIV explaining that, although some religious groups accused him of attacking religious beliefs, in fact he was exposing a hypocrite who used his pretended religion to seduce women and cheat foolish people out of their money and property. Tartuffe represents all those who manipulate people's religious beliefs for personal gain. As Molière knew full well, there had undoubtedly been Tartuffes around since the beginning of civilization; they seem to be rather numerous in our own time, particularly on television. The translation is by Richard Wilbur.

LITERARY SELECTION 53

Tartuffe (1669)

Jean-Baptiste Molière

CHARACTERS[3]
Madame Pernelle, Orgon's mother
Orgon, Elmire's husband
Elmire, Orgon's wife
Damis, Orgon's son, Elmire's stepson
Mariane, Orgon's daughter, Elmire's stepdaughter, in love with Valère
Valère, in love with Mariane
Cléante, Orgon's brother-in-law
Tartuffe, a hypocrite
Dorine, Mariane's lady's-maid
M. Loyal, a bailiff
A Police Officer
Flipote, Mme. Pernelle's maid

3. The name *Tartuffe* has been traced back to an older word associated with liar or charlatan: *truffer*, "to deceive" or "to cheat." Then there was also the Italian actor, Tartufo, physically deformed and truffle-shaped. Most of the other names are typical of this genre of court-comedy and possess rather elegant connotations of the pastoral. Dorine would be a *demoiselle de compagne* and not a mere maid; that is, a female companion to Mariane of roughly the same social status. This in part accounts for the liberties she takes in conversation with Orgon, Madame Pernelle, and others. Her name is short for Théodorine.

The Scene throughout: Orgon's house in Paris.

Act I

Scene 1

MADAME PERNELLE *and* FLIPOTE, *her maid,* ELMIRE, MARIANE, DORINE, DAMIS, CLEANTE.

Madame Pernelle: Come, come, Flipote; it's time I left this place.
Elmire: I can't keep up, you walk at such a pace.
Madame Pernelle: Don't trouble, child; no need to show me out.
It's not your manners I'm concerned about.
Elmire: We merely pay you the respect we owe.
But, Mother, why this hurry? Must you go?
Madame Pernelle: I must. This house appalls me. No one in it
Will pay attention for a single minute.
I offer good advice, but you won't hear it.
Children, I take my leave much vexed in spirit.
You all break in and chatter on and on.
It's like a madhouse[4] with the keeper gone.
Dorine: If . . .
Madame Pernelle: Girl, you talk too much, and I'm afraid
You're far too saucy for a lady's-maid.
You push in everywhere and have your say.
Damis: But . . .
Madame Pernelle: You, boy, grow more foolish every day.
To think my grandson should be such a dunce!
I've said a hundred times, if I've said it once,
That if you keep the course on which you've started,
You'll leave your worthy father broken-hearted.
Mariane: I think . . .
Madame Pernelle: And you, his sister, seem so pure,
So shy, so innocent, and so demure.
But you know what they say about still waters.
I pity parents with secretive daughters.
Elmire: Now, Mother . . .
Madame Pernelle: And as for you, child, let me add
That your behavior is extremely bad,
And a poor example for these children, too.
Their dear, dead mother did far better than you.
You're much too free with money, and I'm distressed
To see you so elaborately dressed.
When it's one's husband that one aims to please,
One has no need of costly fripperies.
Cléante: Oh, Madam, really . . .
Madame Pernelle: You are her brother, Sir,
And I respect and love you; yet if I were
My son, this lady's good and pious spouse,
I wouldn't make you welcome in my house.
You're full of worldly counsels which, I fear,
Aren't suitable for decent folk to hear.
I've spoken bluntly, Sir; but it behooves us
Not to mince words when righteous fervor moves us.
Damis: Your man Tartuffe is full of holy speeches . . .
Madame Pernelle: And practices precisely what he preaches.
He's a fine man, and should be listened to.
I will not hear him mocked by fools like you.
Damis: Good God! Do you expect me to submit
To the tyranny of that carping hypocrite?
Must we forgo all joys and satisfactions
Because that bigot censures all our actions?
Dorine: To hear him talk—and he talks all the time—
There's nothing one can do that's not a crime.
He rails at everything, your dear Tartuffe.
Madame Pernelle: Whatever he reproves deserves reproof.
He's out to save your souls, and all of you
Must love him, as my son would have you do.
Damis: Ah no, Grandmother, I could never take
To such a rascal, even for my father's sake.
That's how I feel, and I shall not dissemble.
His every action makes me seethe and tremble,
With helpless anger, and I have no doubt
That he and I will shortly have it out.
Dorine: Surely it is a shame and a disgrace
To see this man usurp the master's place—
To see this beggar who, when first he came,
Had not a shoe or shoestring to his name,
So far forget himself that he behaves
As if the house were his, and we his slaves.
Madame Pernelle: Well, mark my words, your souls would fare far better
If you obeyed his precepts to the letter.
Dorine: You see him as a saint. I'm far less awed;
In fact, I see right through him. He's a fraud.
Madame Pernelle: Nonsense!
Dorine: His man Laurent's the same, or worse; —
I'd not trust either with a penny purse.
Madame Pernelle: I can't say what his servant's morals may be;
His own great goodness I can guarantee.
You all regard him with distaste and fear
Because he tells you what you're loath to hear,
Condemns your sins, points out your moral flaws,
And humbly strives to further Heaven's cause.
Dorine: If sin is all that bothers him, why is it
He's so upset when folk drop in to visit?
Is Heaven so outraged by a social call
That he must prophesy against us all?
I'll tell you what I think: if you ask me,
He's jealous of my mistress' company.
Madame Pernelle: Rubbish! *[To ELMIRE.]* He's not alone, child, in complaining
Of all of your promiscuous entertaining.
Why, the whole neighborhood's upset, I know,
By all these carriages that come and go,
With crowds of guests parading in and out
And noisy servants loitering about.
In all of this, I'm sure there's nothing vicious;
But why give people cause to be suspicious?
Cléante: They need no cause; they'll talk in any case.
Madam, this world would be a joyless place
If, fearing what malicious tongues might say,
We locked our doors and turned our friends away.

4. In the original, *la cour du roi Pétaud*, the Court of King Pétaud where all are masters; a house of misrule.

And even if one did so dreary a thing,
D'you think those tongues would cease their chattering?
One can't fight slander; it's a losing battle;
Let us instead ignore their tittle-tattle.
Let's strive to live by conscience' clear decrees,
And let the gossips gossip as they please.
Dorine: If there is talk against us, I know the source:
It's Daphne and her little husband, of course.
Those who have greatest cause for guilt and shame
Are quickest to besmirch a neighbor's name.
When there's a chance for libel, they never miss it;
When something can be made to seem illicit
They're off at once to spread the joyous news,
Adding to fact what fantasies they choose.
By talking up their neighbor's indiscretions
They seek to camouflage their own transgressions,
Hoping that others' innocent affairs
Will lend a hue of innocence to theirs,
Or that their own black guilt will come to seem
Part of a general shady color-scheme.
Madame Pernelle: All this is quite irrelevant. I doubt
That anyone's more virtuous and devout
Than dear Orante; and I'm informed that she
Condemns your mode of life most vehemently.
Dorine: Oh, yes, she's strict, devout, and has no taint
Of worldliness; in short, she seems a saint.
But it was time which taught her that disguise;
She's thus because she can't be otherwise.
So long as her attractions could enthrall,
She flounced and flirted and enjoyed it all,
But now that they're no longer what they were
She quits a world which fast is quitting her,
And wears a veil of virtue to conceal
Her bankrupt beauty and her lost appeal.
That's what becomes of old coquettes today:
Distressed when all their lovers fall away,
They see no recourse but to play the prude,
And so confer a style on solitude.
Thereafter, they're severe with everyone,
Condemning all our actions, pardoning none,
And claiming to be pure, austere, and zealous
When, if the truth were known, they're merely jealous,
And cannot bear to see another know
The pleasures time has forced them to forgo.
Madame Pernelle: *[Initially to ELMIRE.]* That sort of talk[5]
is what you like to hear;
Therefore you'd have us all keep still, my dear,
While Madam rattles on the livelong day.
Nevertheless, I mean to have my say.
I tell you that you're blest to have Tartuffe
Dwelling, as my son's guest, beneath this roof;
That Heaven has sent him to forestall its wrath
By leading you, once more, to the true path;
That all he reprehends is reprehensible,
And that you'd better heed him, and be sensible.
These visits, balls, and parties in which you revel
Are nothing but inventions of the Devil.
One never hears a word that's edifying:
Nothing but chaff and foolishness and lying,
As well as vicious gossip in which one's neighbor
Is cut to bits with épée, foil, and saber.
People of sense are driven half-insane
At such affairs, where noise and folly reign
And reputations perish thick and fast.
As a wise preacher said on Sunday last,
Parties are Towers of Babylon,[6] because
The guests all babble on with never a pause;
And then he told a story which, I think . . .
[To CLEANTE.] I heard that laugh, Sir, and I saw that wink!
Go find your silly friends and laugh some more!
Enough; I'm going; don't show me to the door.
I leave this household much dismayed and vexed;
I cannot say when I shall see you next.
[Slapping FLIPOTE.] Wake up, don't stand there gaping
into space!
I'll slap some sense into that stupid face.
Move, move, you slut.

Scene 2

CLEANTE, DORINE.
Cléante: I think I'll stay behind;
I want no further pieces of her mind.
How that old lady . . .
Dorine: Oh, what wouldn't she say
If she could hear you speak of her that way!
She'd thank you for the *lady*, but I'm sure
She'd find the *old* a little premature.
Cléante: My, what a scene she made, and what a din!
And how this man Tartuffe has taken her in!
Dorine: Yes, but her son is even worse deceived;
His folly must be seen to be believed.
In the late troubles,[7] he played an able part
And served his king with wise and loyal heart,
But he's quite lost his senses since he fell
Beneath Tartuffe's infatuating spell.
He calls him brother, and loves him as his life,
Preferring him to mother, child, or wife.
In him and him alone will he confide;
He's made him his confessor and his guide;
He pets and pampers him with love more tender
Than any pretty maiden could engender,
Gives him the place of honor when they dine,
Delights to see him gorging like a swine,
Stuffs him with dainties till his guts distend,
And when he belches, cries "God bless you, friend!"
In short, he's mad; he worships him; he dotes;
His deeds he marvels at, his words, he quotes,
Thinking each act a miracle, each word
Oracular as those that Moses heard.
Tartuffe, much pleased to find so easy a victim,
Has in a hundred ways beguiled and tricked him,

5. In the original, a reference to a collection of novels about chivalry found in *La Bibliothèque bleue* ("The Blue Library"), written for children.
6. That is, the Tower of Babel. Mme. Pernelle's malapropism is the cause of Cléante's laughter.
7. A series of political disturbances during the minority of Louis XIV. Specifically these consisted of the *Fronde* ("opposition") of the Parlement (1648–9) and the *Fronde* of the Princes (1650–3). Orgon is depicted as supporting Louis XIV in these outbreaks and their resolution.

Milked him of money, and with his permission
Established here a sort of Inquisition.
Even Laurent, his lackey, dares to give
Us arrogant advice on how to live;
He sermonizes us in thundering tones
And confiscates our ribbons and colognes.
Last week he tore a kerchief into pieces
Because he found it pressed in a *Life of Jesus*:
He said it was a sin to juxtapose
Unholy vanities and holy prose.

Scene 3

ELMIRE, MARIANE, DAMIS, CLEANTE, DORINE.
Elmire: *[To CLEANTE.]* You did well not to follow; she stood in the door
And said *verbatim* all she'd said before.
I saw my husband coming. I think I'd best
Go upstairs now, and take a little rest.
Cléante: I'll wait and greet him here; then I must go.
I've really only time to say hello.
Damis: Sound him about my sister's wedding, please.
I think Tartuffe's against it, and that he's
Been urging Father to withdraw his blessing.
As you well know, I'd find that most distressing.
Unless my sister and Valère can marry,
My hopes to wed *his* sister will miscarry.
And I'm determined . . .
Dorine: He's coming.

Scene 4

ORGON, CLEANTE, DORINE.
Orgon: Ah, Brother, good-day.
Cléante: Well, welcome back, I'm sorry I can't stay.
How was the country? Blooming, I trust, and green?
Orgon: Excuse me, Brother; just one moment. *[To DORINE.]* Dorine . . .
[To CLEANTE.] To put my mind at rest, I always learn
The household news the moment I return.
[To DORINE.] Has all been well, these two days I've been gone?
How are the family? What's been going on?
Dorine: Your wife, two days ago, had a bad fever,
And a fierce headache which refused to leave her.
Orgon: Ah. And Tartuffe?
Dorine: Tartuffe? Why, he's round and red.
Bursting with health, and excellently fed.
Orgon: Poor fellow!
Dorine: That night, the mistress was unable
To take a single bite at the dinner-table.
Her headache-pains, she said, were simply hellish.
Orgon: Ah. And Tartuffe?
Dorine: He ate his meal with relish,
And zealously devoured in her presence
A leg of mutton and a brace of pheasants.
Orgon: Poor fellow!
Dorine: Well, the pains continued strong,
And so she tossed and tossed the whole night long,
Now icy-cold, now burning like a flame.
We sat beside her bed till morning came.
Orgon: Ah. And Tartuffe?
Dorine: Why, having eaten, he rose
And sought his room, already in a doze,
Got into his warm bed, and snored away
In perfect peace until the break of day.
Orgon: Poor fellow!
Dorine: After much ado, we talked her
Into dispatching someone for the doctor.
He bled her, and the fever quickly fell.
Orgon: Ah. And Tartuffe?
Dorine: He bore it very well.
To keep his cheerfulness at any cost,
And make up for the blood Madam had lost,
He drank, at lunch, four beakers full of port.
Orgon: Poor fellow.
Dorine: Both are doing well, in short.
I'll go and tell Madam that you've expressed
Keen sympathy and anxious interest.

Scene 5

ORGON, CLEANTE.
Cléante: That girl was laughing in your face, and though
I've no wish to offend you, even so
I'm bound to say that she had some excuse.
How can you possibly be such a goose?
Are you so dazed by this man's hocus-pocus
That all the world, save him, is out of focus?
You've given him clothing, shelter, food, and care;
Why must you also . . .
Orgon: Brother, stop right there.
You do not know the man of whom you speak.
Cléante: I grant you that. But my judgment's not so weak
That I can't tell, by his effect on others . . .
Orgon: Ah, when you meet him, you two will be like brothers!
There's been no loftier soul since time began.
He is a man who . . . a man who . . . an excellent man.
To keep his precepts is to be reborn,
And view this dunghill of a world with scorn.
Yes, thanks to him I'm a changed man indeed.
Under his tutelage my soul's been freed
From earthly loves, and every human tie:
My mother, children, brother, and wife could die,
And I'd not feel a single moment's pain.
Cléante: That's a fine sentiment, Brother; most humane.
Orgon: Oh, had you seen Tartuffe as I first knew him,
Your heart, like mine, would have surrendered to him,
He used to come into our church each day
And humbly kneel nearby, and start to pray.
He'd draw the eyes of everybody there
By the deep fervor of his heartfelt prayer;
He'd sigh and weep, and sometimes with a sound
Of rapture he would bend and kiss the ground;
And when I rose to go, he'd run before
To offer me holy-water at the door.
His serving-man, no less devout than he,
Informed me of his master's poverty;
I gave him gifts, but in his humbleness
He'd beg me every time to give him less.

"Oh, that's too much," he'd cry, "too much by twice!
I don't deserve it. The half, Sir, would suffice."
And when I wouldn't take it back, he'd share
Half of it with the poor, right then and there.
At length, Heaven prompted me to take him in
To dwell with us, and free our souls from sin.
He guides our lives, and to protect my honor
Stays by my wife, and keeps an eye upon her;
He tells me whom she sees, and all she does,
And seems more jealous than I ever was!
And how austere he is! Why, he can detect
A moral sin where you would least suspect;
In smallest trifles, he's extremely strict.
Last week, his conscience was severely pricked
Because, while praying, he had caught a flea
And killed it, so he felt, too wrathfully.[8]
Cléante: Good God, man! Have you lost your common sense—
Or is this all some joke at my expense?
How can you stand there and in all sobriety . . .
Orgon: Brother, your language savors of impiety.
Too much free-thinking's made your faith unsteady,
And as I've warned you many times already,
'Twill get you into trouble before you're through.
Cléante: So I've been told before by dupes like you:
Being blind, you'd have all others blind as well;
The clear-eyed man you call an infidel,
And he who sees through humbug and pretense
Is charged, by you, with want of reverence.
Spare me your warnings, Brother; I have no fear
Of speaking out, for you and Heaven to hear,
Against affected zeal and pious knavery.
There's true and false in piety, as in bravery,
And just as those whose courage shines the most
In battle, are the least inclined to boast,
So those whose hearts are truly pure and lowly
Don't make a flashy show of being holy.
There's a vast difference, so it seems to me,
Between true piety and hypocrisy:
How do you fail to see it, may I ask?
Is not a face quite different from a mask?
Cannot sincerity and cunning art,
Reality and semblance, be told apart?
Are scarecrows just like men, and do you hold
That a false coin is just as good as gold?
Ah, Brother, man's strangely fashioned creature
Who seldom is content to follow Nature,
But recklessly pursues his inclination
Beyond the narrow bounds of moderation,
And often, by transgressing Reason's laws,
Perverts a lofty aim or noble cause.
A passing observation, but it applies.
Orgon: I see, dear Brother, that you're profoundly wise;
You harbor all the insight of the age.
You are our one clear mind, our only sage,
The era's oracle, its Cato[9] too,
And all mankind are fools compared to you.
Cléante: Brother, I don't pretend to be a sage,
Nor have I all the wisdom of the age.
There's just one insight I would dare to claim:
I know that true and false are not the same;
And just as there is nothing I more revere
Than a soul whose faith is steadfast and sincere,
Nothing that I more cherish and admire
Than honest zeal and true religious fire,
So there is nothing that I find more base
Than specious piety's dishonest face—
Than these bold mountebanks, these histrios
Whose impious mummeries and hollow shows
Exploit our love of Heaven, and make a jest
Of all that men think holiest and best;
These calculating souls who offer prayers
Not to their Maker, but as public wares,
And seek to buy respect and reputation
With lifted eyes and sighs of exaltation;
These charlatans, I say, whose pilgrim souls
Proceed, by way of Heaven, toward earthly goals,
Who weep and pray and swindle and extort,
Who preach the monkish life; but haunt the court,
Who make their zeal the partner of their vice—
Such men are vengeful, sly, and cold as ice,
And when there is an enemy to defame
They cloak their spite in fair religion's name,
Their private spleen and malice being made
To seem a high and virtuous crusade,
Until, to mankind's reverent applause,
They crucify their foe in Heaven's cause.
Such knaves are all too common; yet, for the wise,
True piety isn't hard to recognize,
And, happily, these present times provide us
With bright examples to instruct and guide us.
Consider Ariston and Périandre;
Look at Oronte, Alcidamas, Clitandre;[10]
Their virtue is acknowledged; who could doubt it?
But you won't hear them beat the drum about it.
They're never ostentatious, never vain,
And their religion's moderate and humane;
It's not their way to criticize and chide:
They think censoriousness a mark of pride,
And therefore, letting others preach and rave,
They show, by deeds, how Christians should behave.
They think no evil of their fellow man,
But judge of him as kindly as they can.
They don't intrigue and wangle and conspire;
To lead a good life is their one desire;
The sinner wakes no rancorous hate in them;
It is the sin alone which they condemn;
Nor do they try to show a fiercer zeal
For Heaven's cause than Heaven itself could feel.
These men I honor, these men I advocate
As models for us all to emulate.

8. In the *Golden Legend* (*Legenda santorum*), a popular collection of the lives of the saints written in the thirteenth century, it is said of St. Marcarius the Elder (d. 390) that he dwelt naked in the desert for six months, in penance for having killed a flea.
9. Roman statesman (95–46 BC) with an enduring reputation for honesty and incorruptibility.
10. Vaguely Greek and Roman names derived from the elegant literature of the day; not names of actual persons.

Your man is not their sort at all, I fear:
And, while your praise of him is quite sincere,
I think that you've been dreadfully deluded.
Orgon: Now then, dear Brother, is your speech
concluded?
Cléante: Why, yes.
Orgon: Your servant, Sir. *[He turns to go.]*
Cléante: No, Brother; wait.
There's one more matter. You agreed of late
That young Valère might have your daughter's hand.
Orgon: I did.
Cléante: And set the date, I understand.
Orgon: Quite so.
Cléante: You've now postponed it; is that true?
Orgon: No doubt.
Cléante: The match no longer pleases you?
Orgon: Who knows?
Cléante: D'you mean to go back on your word?
Orgon: I won't say that.
Cléante: Has anything occurred
Which might entitle you to break your pledge?
Orgon: Perhaps.
Cléante: Why must you hem, and haw, and hedge?
The boy asked me to sound you in this affair . . .
Orgon: It's been a pleasure.
Cléante: But what shall I tell Valère?
Orgon: Whatever you like.
Cléante: But what have you decided?
What are your plans?
Orgon: I plan, Sir, to be guided
By Heaven's will.
Cléante: Come, Brother, don't talk rot.
You've given Valère your word; will you keep it, or not?
Orgon: Good day.
Cléante: This looks like poor Valère's undoing;
I'll go and warn him that there's trouble brewing.

Act II

Scene 1

ORGON, MARIANE.
Orgon: Mariane.
Mariane: Yes, Father?
Orgon: A word with you; come here.
Mariane: What are you looking for?
Orgon: *[Peering into a small closet.]* Eavesdroppers, dear.
I'm making sure we shan't be overheard.
Someone in there could catch our every word.
Ah, good, we're safe. Now, Mariane, my child,
You're a sweet girl who's tractable and mild,
Whom I hold dear, and think most highly of.
Mariane: I'm deeply grateful, Father, for your love.
Orgon: That's well said, Daughter; and you can repay me
If, in all things, you'll cheerfully obey me.
Mariane: To please you, Sir, is what delights me best.
Orgon: Good, good. Now, what d'you think of Tartuffe,
our guest?
Mariane: I, Sir?
Orgon: Yes. Weigh your answer; think it through.
Mariane: Oh, dear. I'll say whatever you wish me to.
Orgon: That's wisely said, my Daughter. Say of him,
then,
That he's the very worthiest of men,
And that you're fond of him, and would rejoice
In being his wife, if that should be my choice.
Well?
Mariane: What?
Orgon: What's that?
Mariane: I . . .
Orgon: Well?
Mariane: Forgive me, pray.
Orgon: Did you not hear me?
Mariane: Of *whom*, Sir, must I say
That I am fond of him, and would rejoice
In being his wife, if that should be your choice?
Orgon: Why, of Tartuffe.
Mariane: But, Father, that's false, you know.
Why would you have me say what isn't so?
Orgon: Because I am resolved it shall be true.
That it's my wish should be enough for you.
Mariane: You can't mean, Father . . .
Orgon: Yes, Tartuffe shall be
Allied by marriage[11] to this family,
And he's to be your husband, is that clear?
It's a father's privilege . . .

Scene 2

DORINE, ORGON, MARIANE.
Orgon: *[To DORINE.]* What are you doing in here?
Is curiosity so fierce a passion
With you, that you must eavesdrop in this fashion?
Dorine: There's lately been a rumor going about—
Based on some hunch or chance remark, no doubt—
That you mean Mariane to wed Tartuffe.
I've laughed it off, of course, as just a spoof.
Orgon: You find it so incredible?
Dorine: Yes, I do.
I won't accept that story, even from you.
Orgon: Well, you'll believe it when the thing is done.
Dorine: Yes, yes, of course. Go on and have your fun.
Orgon: I've never been more serious in my life.
Dorine: Ha!
Orgon: Daughter, I mean it; you're to be his wife.
Dorine: No, don't believe your father; it's all a hoax.
Orgon: See here, young woman . . .
Dorine: Come Sir, no more jokes;
You can't fool us.
Orgon: How dare you talk that way?
Dorine: All right, then: we believe you, sad to say.
But how a man like you, who looks so wise
And wears a moustache of such splendid size,
Can be so foolish as to . . .

11. This assertion is important and more than a mere device in the plot of the play. The second *placet* or petition insists that Tartuffe be costumed as a layman, and Orgon's plan for him to marry again asserts Tartuffe's position in the laity. In the 1664 version of the play Tartuffe had been dressed in a cassock suggestive of the priesthood, and Molière was now eager to avoid any suggestion of this kind.

Orgon: Silence, please!
My girl, you take too many liberties.
I'm master here, as you must not forget.
Dorine: Do let's discuss this calmly; don't be upset.
You can't be serious, Sir, about this plan.
What should that bigot want with Mariane?
Praying and fasting ought to keep him busy.
And then, in terms of wealth and rank, what is he?
Why should a man of property like you
Pick out a beggar son-in-law?
Orgon: That will do.
Speak of his poverty with reverence.
His is a pure and saintly indigence
Which far transcends all worldly pride and pelf.
He lost his fortune, as he says himself,
Because he cared for Heaven alone, and so
Was careless of his interests here below.
I mean to get him out of his present straits
And help him to recover his estates—
Which, in his part of the world, have no small fame.
Poor though he is, he's a gentleman just the same.
Dorine: Yes, so he tells us; and, Sir, it seems to me
Such pride goes very ill with piety.
A man whose spirit spurns this dungy earth
Ought not to brag of lands and noble birth;
Such worldly arrogance will hardly square
With meek devotion and the life of prayer.
. . . But this approach, I see, has drawn a blank;
Let's speak, then, of his person, not his rank.
Doesn't it seem to you a trifle grim
To give a girl like her to a man like him?
When two are so ill-suited, can't you see
What the sad consequence is bound to be?
A young girl's virtue is imperilled, Sir,
When such a marriage is imposed on her;
For if one's bridegroom isn't to one's taste,
It's hardly an inducement to be chaste,
And many a man with horns upon his brow
Has made his wife the thing that she is now.
It's hard to be a faithful wife, in short,
To certain husbands of a certain sort,
And he who gives his daughter to a man she hates
Must answer for her sins at Heaven's gates.
Think, Sir, before you play so risky a role.
Orgon: This servant-girl presumes to save my soul!
Dorine: You would do well to ponder what I've said.
Orgon: Daughter, we'll disregard this dunderhead.
Just trust your father's judgment. Oh, I'm aware
That I once promised you to young Valère;
But now I hear he gambles, which greatly shocks me;
What's more, I've doubts about his orthodoxy.
His visits to church, I note, are very few.
Dorine: Would you have him go at the same hours as you,
And kneel nearby, to be sure of being seen?
Orgon: I can dispense with such remarks, Dorine.
[To MARIANE.] Tartuffe, however, is sure of Heaven's blessing.
And that's the only treasure worth possessing.
This match will bring you joys beyond all measure;
Your cup will overflow with every pleasure;
You two will interchange your faithful loves
Like two sweet cherubs, or two turtle-doves.
No harsh word shall be heard, no frown be seen,
And he shall make you happy as a queen.
Dorine: And she'll make him a cuckold, just wait and see.
Orgon: What language!
Dorine: Oh, he's a man of destiny;
He's *made* for horns, and what the stars demand
Your daughter's virtue surely can't withstand.
Orgon: Don't interrupt me further. Why can't you learn
That certain things are none of your concern?
Dorine: It's for your own sake that I interfere.
[She repeatedly interrupts ORGON just as he is turning to speak to his daughter.]
Orgon: Most kind of you. Now, hold your tongue, d'you hear?
Dorine: If I didn't love you . . .
Orgon: Spare me your affection.
Dorine: I'll love you, Sir, in spite of your objection.
Orgon: Blast!
Dorine: I can't bear, Sir, for your honor's sake,
To let you make this ludicrous mistake.
Orgon: You mean to go on talking?
Dorine: If I didn't protest
This sinful marriage, my conscience couldn't rest.
Orgon: If you don't hold your tongue, you little shrew . . .
Dorine: What, lost your temper? A pious man like you?
Orgon: Yes! Yes! You talk and talk. I'm maddened by it.
Once and for all, I tell you to be quiet.
Dorine: Well, I'll be quiet, but I'll be thinking hard.
Orgon: Think all you like, but you had better guard
That saucy tongue of yours, or I'll . . . *[Turning back to MARIANE.]* Now, child,
I've weighed this matter fully.
Dorine: *[Aside.]* It drives me wild
That I can't speak.
[ORGON turns his head, and she is silent.]
Orgon: Tartuffe is no young dandy,
But, still, his person . . .
Dorine: *[Aside.]* Is as sweet as candy.
Orgon: Is such that, even if you shouldn't care
For his other merits . . .
[He turns and stands facing DORINE, arms crossed.]
Dorine: *[Aside.]* They'll make a lovely pair.
If I were she, no man would marry me
Against my inclination, and go scot-free.
He'd learn, before the wedding-day was over,
How readily a wife can find a lover.
Orgon: *[To DORINE.]* It seems you treat my orders as a joke.
Dorine: Why, what's the matter? 'Twas not to you I spoke.
Orgon: What *were* you doing?
Dorine: Talking to myself, that's all.
Orgon: Ah! *[Aside.]* One more bit of impudence and gall,
And I shall give her a good slap in the face.
[He puts himself in position to slap her; DORINE, whenever he glances at her, stands immobile and silent.]
Daughter, you shall accept, and with good grace,
The husband I've selected . . . Your wedding-day . . .
[To DORINE.] Why don't you talk to yourself?
Dorine: I've nothing to say.

Orgon: Come, just one word.
Dorine: No thank you, Sir, I pass.
Orgon: Come, speak; I'm waiting.
Dorine: I'd not be such an ass.
Orgon: *[Turning to MARIANE.]* In short, dear Daughter, I mean to be obeyed,
And you must bow to the sound choice I've made.
Dorine: *[Moving away.]* I'd not wed such a monster, even in jest.
[ORGON attemps to slap her, but misses.]
Orgon: Daughter, that maid of yours is a thorough pest;
She makes me sinfully annoyed and nettled.
I can't speak further; my nerves are too unsettled.
She's so upset me by her insolent talk,
I'll calm myself by going for a walk.

Scene 3

DORINE, MARIANE.
Dorine: *[Returning.]* Well, have you lost your tongue, girl? Must I play
Your part, and say the lines you ought to say?
Faced with a fate so hideous and absurd,
Can you not utter one dissenting word?
Mariane: What good would it do? A father's power is great.
Dorine: Resist him now, or it will be too late.
Mariane: But . . .
Dorine: Tell him one cannot love at a father's whim;
That you shall marry for yourself, not him;
That since it's you who are to be the bride,
It's you, not he, who must be satisfied;
And that if his Tartuffe is so sublime,
He's free to marry him at any time.
Mariane: I've bowed so long to Father's strict control,
I couldn't oppose him now, to save my soul.
Dorine: Come, come, Mariane. Do listen to reason, won't you?
Valère has asked your hand. Do you love him, or don't you?
Mariane: Oh, how unjust of you! What can you mean
By asking such a question, dear Dorine?
You know the depth of my affection for him;
I've told you a hundred times how I adore him.
Dorine: I don't believe in everything I hear;
Who knows if your professions were sincere?
Mariane: They were, Dorine, and you do me wrong to doubt it;
Heaven knows that I've been all too frank about it.
Dorine: You love him, then?
Mariane: Oh, more than I can express.
Dorine: And he, I take it, cares for you no less?
Mariane: I think so.
Dorine: And you both, with equal fire,
Burn to be married?
Mariane: That is our one desire.
Dorine: What of Tartuffe, then? What of your father's plan?
Mariane: I'll kill myself, if I'm forced to wed that man.
Dorine: I hadn't thought of that recourse. How splendid!
Just die, and all your troubles will be ended!
A fine solution. Oh, it maddens me
To hear you talk in that self-pitying key.
Mariane: Dorine, how harsh you are! It's most unfair.
You have no sympathy for my despair.
Dorine: I've none at all for people who talk drivel
And, faced with difficulties, whine and snivel.
Mariane: No doubt I'm timid, but it would be wrong . . .
Dorine: True love requires a heart that's firm and strong.
Mariane: I'm strong in my affection for Valère,
But coping with my father is his affair.
Dorine: But if your father's brain has grown so cracked
Over his dear Tartuffe that he can retract
His blessing, though your wedding-day was named,
It's surely not Valère who's to be blamed.
Mariane: If I defied my father, as you suggest,
Would it not seem unmaidenly, at best?
Shall I defend my love at the expense
Of brazenness and disobedience?
Shall I parade my heart's desires, and flaunt . . .
Dorine: No, I ask nothing of you. Clearly you want
To be Madame Tartuffe, and I feel bound
Not to oppose a wish so very sound.
What right have I to criticize the match?
Indeed, my dear, the man's a brilliant catch.
Monsieur Tartuffe! Now, there's a man of weight!
Yes, yes, Monsieur Tartuffe, I'm bound to state,
Is quite a person; that's not to be denied;
'Twill be no little thing to be his bride.
The world already rings with his renown;
He's a great noble—in his native town;
His ears are red, he has a pink complexion,
And all in all, he'll suit you to perfection.
Mariane: Dear God!
Dorine: Oh, how triumphant you will feel
At having caught a husband so ideal!
Marine: Oh, do stop teasing, and use your cleverness
To get me out of this appalling mess.
Advise me, and I'll do whatever you say.
Dorine: Ah, no, a dutiful daughter must obey
Her father, even if he weds her to an ape.
You've a bright future; why struggle to escape?
Tartuffe will take you back where his family lives,
To a small town aswarm with relatives—
Uncles and cousins whom you'll be charmed to meet.
You'll be received at once by the elite,
Calling upon the bailiff's wife,[12] no less—
Even, perhaps, upon the mayoress,[13]
Who'll sit you down in the *best* kitchen chair.[14]
Then, once a year, you'll dance at the village fair
To the drone of bagpipes—two of them, in fact—
And see a puppet-show, or an animal act.[15]

12. A bailiff was a high-ranking official in the judiciary, not simply a sheriff's deputy as today.
13. The wife of a tax collector (*élu*), an important official controlling imports, elected by the Estates General.
14. In elegant society of Molière's day, there was a hierarchy of seats and the use of each was determined by rank. The seats descended from *fauteuils, chaises, perroquets, labourets* to *pliants*. Thus Mariane would get the lowest seat in the room.
15. In the original, *fagotin*, literally a monkey dressed up in a man's clothing.

Your husband . . .
Mariane: Oh, you turn my blood to ice!
Stop torturing me, and give me your advice.
Dorine: *[Threatening to go.]* Your servant, Madam.
Mariane: Dorine, I beg of you . . .
Dorine: No, you deserve it; this marriage must go through.
Mariane: Dorine!
Dorine: No.
Mariane: Not Tartuffe! You know I think him . . .
Dorine: Tartuffe's your cup of tea, and you shall drink him.
Mariane: I've always told you everything, and relied . . .
Dorine: No. You desire to be tartuffified.
Mariane: Well, since you mock me and refuse to care,
I'll henceforth seek my solace in despair:
Despair shall be my counsellor and friend,
And help me bring my sorrows to an end. *[She starts to leave.]*
Dorine: There now, come back; my anger has subsided.
You do deserve some pity, I've decided.
Mariane: Dorine, if Father makes me undergo
This dreadful martyrdom, I'll die, I know.
Dorine: Don't fret; it won't be difficult to discover
Some plan of action . . . But here's Valère, your lover.

Scene 4

VALERE, MARIANE, DORINE.
Valère: Madam, I've just received some wondrous news
Regarding which I'd like to hear your views.
Mariane: What news?
Valère: You're marrying Tartuffe.
Mariane: I find
That Father does have such a match in mind.
Valère: Your father, Madam . . .
Mariane: . . . has just this minute said
That it's Tartuffe he wishes me to wed.
Valère: Can he be serious?
Mariane: Oh, indeed he can;
He's clearly set his heart upon the plan.
Valère: And what position do you propose to take,
Madam?
Mariane: Why—I don't know.
Valère: For heaven's sake—
You don't know?
Mariane: No.
Valère: Well, well!
Mariane: Advise me, do.
Valère: Marry the man. That's my advice to you.
Mariane: That's your advice?
Valère: Yes.
Mariane: Truly?
Valère: Oh, absolutely.
You couldn't choose more wisely, more astutely.
Mariane: Thanks for this counsel; I'll follow it, of course.
Valère: Do, do; I'm sure 'twill cost you no remorse.
Mariane: To give it didn't cause your heart to break.
Valère: I gave it, Madam, only for your sake.
Mariane: And it's for your sake that I take it, Sir.
Dorine: *[Withdrawing to the rear of the stage.]*
Let's see which fool will prove the stubborner.
Valère: So! I am nothing to you, and it was flat
Deception when you . . .
Mariane: Please, enough of that.
You've told me plainly that I should agree
To wed the man my father's chosen for me,
And since you've deigned to counsel me so wisely,
I promise, Sir, to do as you advise me.
Valère: Ah, no, 'twas not by me that you were swayed.
No, your decision was already made;
Though now, to save appearances, you protest
That you're betraying me at my behest.
Mariane: Just as you say.
Valère: Quite so. And I now see
That you were never truly in love with me.
Mariane: Alas, you're free to think so if you choose.
Valère: I choose to think so, and here's a bit of news:
You've spurned my hand, but I know where to turn
For kinder treatment, as you shall quickly learn.
Mariane: I'm sure you do. Your noble qualities
Inspire affection . . .
Valère: Forget my qualities, please.
They don't inspire you overmuch, I find.
But there's another lady I have in mind
Whose sweet and generous nature will not scorn
To compensate me for the loss I've borne.
Mariane: I'm no great loss, and I'm sure that you'll transfer
Your heart quite painlessly from me to her.
Valère: I'll do my best to take it in my stride.
The pain I feel at being cast aside
Time and forgetfulness may put an end to.
Or if I can't forget, I shall pretend to.
No self-respecting person is expected
To go on loving once he's been rejected.
Mariane: Now, that's a fine, high-minded sentiment.
Valère: One to which any sane man would assent.
Would you prefer it if I pined away
In hopeless passion till my dying day?
Am I to yield you to a rival's arms
And not console myself with other charms?
Mariane: Go then; console yourself; don't hesitate.
I wish you to; indeed, I cannot wait.
Valère: You wish me to?
Mariane: Yes.
Valère: That's the final straw.
Madam, farewell. Your wish shall be my law.
[He starts to leave, and then returns: this repeatedly.]
Mariane: Splendid.
Valère: *[Coming back again.]* This breach, remember, is of your making;
It's you who've driven me to the step I'm taking.
Mariane: Of course.
Valère: *[Coming back again.]* Remember, too, that I am merely
Following your example.
Mariane: I see that clearly.
Valère: Enough. I'll go and do your bidding, then.
Mariane: Good.
Valère: *[Coming back again.]* You shall never see my face again.

Mariane: Excellent.
Valère: *[Walking to the door, then turning about.]* Yes?
Mariane: What?
Valère: What's that? What did you say?
Mariane: Nothing. You're dreaming.
Valère: Ah. Well, I'm on my way.
Farewell, Madam.
Mariane: Farewell.
Dorine: *[To MARIANE.]* If you ask me,
Both of you are as mad as mad can be.
Do stop this nonsense, now. I've only let you
Squabble so long to see where it would get you.
Whoa there, Monsieur Valère!
[She goes and seizes VALERE by the arm; he makes a great show of resistance.]
Valère: What's this, Dorine?
Dorine: Come here.
Valère: No, no, my heart's too full of spleen.
Don't hold me back; her wish must be obeyed.
Dorine: Stop!
Valère: It's too late now; my decision's made.
Dorine: Oh, pooh!
Mariane: *[Aside.]* He hates the sight of me, that's plain.
I'll go, and so deliver him from pain.
Dorine: *[Leaving VALERE, running after MARIANE.]*
And now *you* run away! Come back.
Mariane: No, no
Nothing you say will keep me here. Let go!
Valère: *[Aside.]* She cannot bear my presence, I perceive.
To spare her further torment, I shall leave.
Dorine: *[Leaving MARIANE, running after VALERE.]*
Again! You'll not escape, Sir; don't you try it.
Come here, you two. Stop fussing and be quiet.
[She takes VALERE by the hand, then MARIANE, and draws them together.]
Valère: *[To DORINE.]* What do you want of me?
Mariane: *[To DORINE.]* What is the point of this?
Dorine: We're going to have a little armistice.
[To VALERE.] Now, weren't you silly to get so overheated?
Valère: Didn't you see how badly I was treated?
Dorine: *[To MARIANE.]* Aren't you a simpleton, to have lost your head?
Mariane: Didn't you hear the hateful things he said?
Dorine: *[To VALERE.]* You're both great fools. Her sole desire, Valère,
Is to be yours in marriage. To that I'll swear.
[To MARIANE.] He loves you only, and he wants no wife
But you, Mariane. On that I'll stake my life.
Mariane: *[To VALERE]* Then why you advised me so, I cannot see.
Valère: *[To MARIANE.]* On such a question, why ask advice of *me*?
Dorine: Oh, you're impossible. Give me your hands, you two.
[To VALERE.] Yours first.
Valère: *[Giving DORINE his hand.]* But why?
Dorine: *[To MARIANE.]* And now a hand from you.
Mariane: *[Also giving DORINE her hand.]*
What are you doing?
Dorine: There: a perfect fit.
You suit each other better than you'll admit.
[VALERE and MARIANE hold hands for some time without looking at each other.]
Valère: *[Turning toward MARIANE.]* Ah, come, don't be so haughty. Give a man
A look of kindness, won't you, Mariane?
[MARIANE turns toward VALERE and smiles.]
Dorine: I tell you, lovers are completely mad!
Valère: *[To MARIANE.]* Now come, confess that you were very bad
To hurt my feelings as you did just now.
I have a just complaint, you must allow.
Mariane: *You* must allow that you were most unpleasant . . .
Dorine: Let's table that discussion for the present;
Your father has a plan which must be stopped.
Mariane: Advise us, then; what means must we adopt?
Dorine: We'll use all manner of means, and all at once.
[To MARIANE.] Your father's addled; he's acting like a dunce.
Therefore you'd better humor the old fossil.
Pretend to yield to him, be sweet and docile,
And then postpone, as often as necessary,
The day on which you have agreed to marry.
You'll thus gain time, and time will turn the trick.
Sometimes, for instance, you'll be taken sick,
And that will seem good reason for delay;
Or some bad omen will make you change the day—
You'll dream of muddy water, or you'll pass
A dead man's hearse, or break a looking-glass.
If all else fails, no man can marry you
Unless you take his ring and say "I do."
But now, let's separate. If they should find
Us talking here, our plot might be divined.
[To VALERE.] Go to your friends, and tell them what's occurred,
And have them urge her father to keep his word.
Meanwhile, we'll stir her brother into action,
And get Elmire,[16] as well, to join our faction.
Good-bye.
Valère: *[To MARIANE.]* Though each of us will do his best,
It's your true heart on which my hopes shall rest.
Mariane: *[To VALERE.]* Regardless of what Father may decide,
None but Valère shall claim me as his bride.
Valère: Oh, how those words content me! Come what will . . .
Dorine: Oh, lovers, lovers! Their tongues are never still.
Be off, now.
Valère: *[Turning to go, then turning back.]* One last word . . .
Dorine: No time to chat:
You leave by this door; and *you* leave by that.
[DORINE pushes them, by the shoulders, toward opposing doors.]

16. Orgon's second wife.

Act III

Scene 1

DAMIS, DORINE.
Damis: May lightning strike me even as I speak,
May all men call me cowardly and weak,
If any fear or scruple holds me back
From settling things, at once, with that great quack!
Dorine: Now, don't give way to violent emotion.
Your father's merely talked about this notion,
And words and deeds are far from being one.
Much that is talked about is never done.
Damis: No, I must stop that scoundrel's machinations;
I'll go and tell him off; I'm out of patience.
Dorine: Do calm down and be practical, I had rather
My mistress dealt with him—and with your father.
She has some influence with Tartuffe, I've noted.
He hangs upon her words, seems most devoted,
And may, indeed, be smitten by her charm.
Pray Heaven it's true! 'Twould do our cause no harm.
She sent for him, just now, to sound him out
On this affair you're so incensed about;
She'll find out where he stands, and tell him, too,
What dreadful strife and trouble will ensue
If he lends countenance to your father's plan.
I couldn't get in to see him, but his man
Says that he's almost finished with his prayers.
Go, now. I'll catch him when he comes downstairs.
Damis: I want to hear this conference, and I will.
Dorine: No, they must be alone.
Damis: Oh, I'll keep still.
Dorine: Not you. I know your temper. You'd start a brawl,
And shout and stamp your foot and spoil it all.
Go on.
Damis: I won't; I have a perfect right . . .
Dorine: Lord, you're a nuisance! He's coming; get out of sight.
[DAMIS conceals himself in a closet at the rear of the stage.]

Scene 2

TARTUFFE, DORINE.
Tartuffe: *[Observing DORINE, and calling to his manservant offstage.]*
Hang up my hair-shirt, put my scourge in place,
And pray, Laurent, for Heaven's perpetual grace.
I'm going to the prison now, to share
My last few coins with the poor wretches there.
Dorine: *[Aside.]* Dear God, what affectation! What a fake!
Tartuffe: You wished to see me?
Dorine: Yes . . .
Tartuffe: *[Taking a handkerchief from his pocket.]*
For mercy's sake,
Please take this handkerchief, before you speak.
Dorine: What?
Tartuffe: Cover that bosom,[17] girl. The flesh is weak.
And unclean thoughts are difficult to control.
Such sights as that can undermine the soul.
Dorine: Your soul, it seems, has very poor defenses,
And flesh makes quite an impact on your senses.
It's strange that you're so easily excited;
My own desires are not so soon ignited,
And if I saw you naked as a beast,
Not all your hide would tempt me in the least.
Tartuffe: Girl, speak more modestly; unless you do,
I shall be forced to take my leave of you.
Dorine: Oh, no, it's I who must be on my way;
I've just one little message to convey.
Madam is coming down, and begs you, Sir,
To wait and have a word or two with her.
Tartuffe: Gladly.
Dorine: *[Aside.] That* had a softening effect!
I think my guess about him was correct.
Tartuffe: Will she be long?
Dorine: No: that's her step I hear.
Ah, here she is, and I shall disappear.

Scene 3

ELMIRE, TARTUFFE.
Tartuffe: May Heaven, whose infinite goodness we adore,
Preserve your body and soul forevermore,
And bless your days, and answer thus the plea
Of one who is its humblest votary.
Elmire: I thank you for that pious wish. But please,
Do take a chair and let's be more at ease.
[They sit down.]
Tartuffe: I trust that you are once more well and strong?
Elmire: Oh, yes: the fever didn't last for long.
Tartuffe: My prayers are too unworthy, I am sure,
To have gained from Heaven this most gracious cure;
But lately, Madam, my every supplication
Has had for object your recuperation.
Elmire: You shouldn't have troubled so. I don't deserve it.
Tartuffe: Your health is priceless, Madam, and to preserve it
I'd gladly give my own, in all sincerity.
Elmire: Sir, you outdo us all in Christian charity.
You've been most kind. I count myself your debtor.
Tartuffe: 'Twas nothing, Madam. I long to serve you better.
Elmire: There's a private matter I'm anxious to discuss.
I'm glad there's no one here to hinder us.
Tartuffe: I too am glad; it floods my heart with bliss
To find myself alone with you like this.
For just this chance I've prayed with all my power—
But prayed in vain, until this happy hour.
Elmire: This won't take long, Sir, and I hope you'll be
Entirely frank and unconstrained with me.
Tartuffe: Indeed, there's nothing I had rather do
Than bare my inmost heart and soul to you.
First, let me say that what remarks I've made
About the constant visits you are paid

17. The Brotherhood of the Holy Sacrament practiced almsgiving to prisoners and kept a careful, censorious check on female wearing apparel if they deemed it lascivious. Thus, Molière's audience would have identified Tartuffe as sympathetic—hypocritically—to the aims of the organization.

Were prompted not by any mean emotion,
But rather by a pure and deep devotion,
A fervent zeal . . .
Elmire: No need for explanation.
Your sole concern, I'm sure, was my salvation.
Tartuffe: *[Taking ELMIRE'S hand and pressing her fingertips.]*
Quite so; and such great fervor do I feel . . .
Elmire: Ooh! Please! You're pinching!
Tartuffe: 'Twas from excess of zeal.
I never meant to cause you pain, I swear.
I'd rather . . .
Elmire: What can your hand be doing there?
Tartuffe: Feeling your gown: what soft, fine-woven stuff!
Elmire: Please, I'm extremely ticklish. That's enough.
[She draws her chair away; TARTUFFE pulls his after her.]
Tartuffe: *[Fondling the lace collar of her gown.]*
My, my, what lovely lacework on your dress!
The workmanship's miraculous, no less.
I've not seen anything to equal it.
Elmire: Yes, quite. But let's talk business for a bit.
They say my husband means to break his word
And give his daughter to you, Sir. Had you heard?
Tartuffe: He did once mention it. But I confess
I dream of quite a different happiness.
It's elsewhere, Madam, that my eyes discern
The promise of that bliss for which I yearn.
Elmire: I see: you care for nothing here below.
Tartuffe: Ah, well—my heart's not made of stone, you know.
Elmire: All your desires mount heavenward, I'm sure,
In scorn of all that's earthly and impure.
Tartuffe: A love of heavenly beauty does not preclude
A proper love for earthly pulchritude,
Our senses are quite rightly captivated
By perfect works our Maker has created.
Some glory clings to all that Heaven has made;
In you, all Heaven's marvels are displayed.
On that fair face, such beauties have been lavished,
The eyes are dazzled and the heart is ravished;
How could I look on you, O flawless creature,
And not adore the Author of all Nature,
Feeling a love both passionate and pure
For you, his triumph of self-portraiture?
At first, I trembled lest that love should be
A subtle snare that Hell had laid for me;
I vowed to flee the sight of you, eschewing
A rapture that might prove my soul's undoing;
But soon, fair being, I became aware
That my deep passion could be made to square
With rectitude, and with my bounden duty,
I thereupon surrendered to your beauty.
It is, I know, presumptuous on my part
To bring you this poor offering of my heart,
And it is not my merit, Heaven knows,
But your compassion on which my hopes repose.
You are my peace, my solace, my salvation;
On you depends my bliss—or desolation;
I bide your judgment and, as you think best,
I shall be either miserable or blest,
Elmire: Your declaration is most gallant, Sir,
But don't you think it's out of character?
You'd have done better to restrain your passion
And think before you spoke in such a fashion.
It ill becomes a pious man like you . . .
Tartuffe: I may be pious, but I'm human too:
With your celestial charms before his eyes,
A man has not the power to be wise.
I know such words sound strangely, coming from me,
But I'm no angel, nor was meant to be,
And if you blame my passion, you must needs
Reproach as well the charms on which it feeds.
Your loveliness I had no sooner seen
Than you became my soul's unrivaled queen;
Before your seraph glance, divinely sweet,
My heart's defenses crumbled in defeat,
And nothing fasting, prayer, or tears might do
Could stay my spirit from adoring you.
My eyes, my sighs have told you in the past
What now my lips make bold to say at last,
And if, in your great goodness, you will deign
To look upon your slave, and ease his pain—
If, in compassion for my soul's distress,
You'll stoop to comfort my unworthiness,
I'll raise to you, in thanks for that sweet manna,
An endless hymn, an infinite hosanna.
With me, of course, there need be no anxiety,
No fear of scandal or of notoriety.
These young court gallants, whom all the ladies fancy,
Are vain in speech, in action rash and chancy;
When they succeed in love, the world soon knows it;
No favor's granted them but they disclose it
And by the looseness of their tongues profane
The very altar where their hearts have lain.
Men of my sort, however, love discreetly,
And one may trust our reticence completely.
My keen concern for my good name insures
The absolute security of yours;
In short, I offer you, my dear Elmire,
Love without scandal, pleasure without fear.
Elmire: I've heard your well-turned speeches to the end,
And what you urge I clearly apprehend.
Aren't you afraid that I may take a notion
To tell my husband of your warm devotion,
And that, supposing he were duly told,
His feelings toward you might grow rather cold?
Tartuffe: I know, dear lady, that your exceeding charity
Will lead your heart to pardon my temerity;
That you'll excuse my violent affection
As human weakness, human imperfection;
And that—O fairest!—you will bear in mind
That I'm but flesh and blood, and am not blind.
Elmire: Some women might do otherwise, perhaps,
But I shall be discreet about your lapse;
I'll tell my husband nothing of what's occurred
If, in return, you'll give your solemn word
To advocate as forcefully as you can
The marriage of Valère and Mariane,
Renouncing all desire to dispossess
Another of his rightful happiness,
And . . .

Scene 4

DAMIS, ELMIRE, TARTUFFE.
Damis: *[Emerging from the closet where he has been hiding.]*
No! We'll not hush up this vile affair;
I heard it all inside that closet there,
Where Heaven, in order to confound the pride
Of this great rascal, prompted me to hide.
Ah, now I have my long-awaited chance
To punish his deceit and arrogance,
And give my father clear and shocking proof
Of the black character of his dear Tartuffe.
Elmire: Ah no, Damis; I'll be content if he
Will study to deserve my leniency.
I've promised silence—don't make me break my word;
To make a scandal would be too absurd.
Good wives laugh off such trifles, and forget them;
Why should they tell their husbands, and upset them?
Damis: You have your reasons for taking such a course,
And I have reasons, too, of equal force.
To spare him now would be insanely wrong.
I've swallowed my just wrath for far too long
And watched this insolent bigot bringing strife
And bitterness into our family life.
Too long he's meddled in my father's affairs,
Thwarting my marriage-hopes, and poor Valère's.
It's high time that my father was undeceived,
And now I've proof that can't be disbelieved—
Proof that was furnished me by Heaven above.
It's too good not to take advantage of.
This is my chance, and I deserve to lose it
If, for one moment, I hesitate to use it.
Elmire: Damis . . .
Damis: No, I must do what I think right.
Madam, my heart is bursting with delight,
And, say whatever you will, I'll not consent
To lose the sweet revenge on which I'm bent.
I'll settle matters without more ado;
And here, most opportunely, is my cue.[18]

Scene 5

ORGON, DAMIS, TARTUFFE, ELMIRE.
Damis: Father, I'm glad you've joined us. Let us advise you
Of some fresh news which doubtless will surprise you.
You've just now been repaid with interest
For all your loving kindness to our guest.
He's proved his warm and grateful feelings toward you;
It's with a pair of horns he would reward you.
Yes, I surprised him with your wife, and heard
His whole adulterous offer, every word.
She, with her all too gentle disposition,
Would not have told you of his proposition;
But I shall not make terms with brazen lechery,
And feel that not to tell you would be treachery.
Elmire: And I hold that one's husband's peace of mind
Should not be spoilt by tattle of this kind.
One's honor doesn't require it: to be proficient
In keeping men at bay is quite sufficient.
These are my sentiments, and I wish, Damis,
That you had heeded me and held your peace.

Scene 6

ORGON, DAMIS, TARTUFFE.
Orgon: Can it be true, this dreadful thing I hear?
Tartuffe: Yes, Brother, I'm a wicked man, I fear:
A wretched sinner, all depraved and twisted,
The greatest villain that has ever existed.
My life's one heap of crimes, which grows each minute;
There's naught but foulness and corruption in it;
And I perceive that Heaven, outraged by me,
Has chosen this occasion to mortify me.
Charge me with any deed you wish to name;
I'll not defend myself, but take the blame.
Believe what you are told, and drive Tartuffe
Like some base criminal from beneath your roof;
Yes, drive me hence, and with a parting curse:
I shan't protest, for I deserve far worse.
Orgon: *[To DAMIS.]* Ah, you deceitful boy, how dare you try
To stain his purity with so foul a lie?
Damis: What! Are you taken in by such a fluff?
Did you not hear . . . ?
Orgon: Enough, you rogue, enough!
Tartuffe: Ah, Brother, let him speak; you're being unjust.
Believe his story; the boy deserves your trust.
Why, after all, should you have faith in me?
How can you know what I might do, or be?
Is it on my good actions that you base
Your favor? Do you trust my pious face?
Ah, no, don't be deceived by hollow shows;
I'm far, alas, from being what men suppose;
Though the world takes me for a man of worth,
I'm truly the most worthless man on earth.
[To DAMIS.] Yes, my dear son, speak out now: call me the chief
Of sinners, a wretch, a murderer, a thief;
Load me with all the names men most abhor;
I'll not complain; I've earned them all, and more;
I'll kneel here while you pour them on my head
As a just punishment for the life I've led.
Orgon: *[To TARTUFFE.]* This is too much, dear Brother.
[To DAMIS.] Have you no heart?
Damis: Are you so hoodwinked by this rascal's art . . . ?
Orgon: Be still, you monster. *[To TARTUFFE.]* Brother, I pray you, rise.
[To DAMIS.] Villain!
Damis: But . . .
Orgon: Silence!
Damis: Can't you realize . . . ?
Orgon: Just one word more, and I'll tear you limb from limb.
Tartuffe: In God's name, Brother, don't be harsh with him.

18. In the original stage directions, Tartuffe now reads silently from his breviary—in the Roman Catholic Church, the book containing the Divine Office for each day, which those in holy orders are required to recite.

I'd rather far be tortured at the stake
Than see him bear one scratch for my poor sake.
Orgon: *[To DAMIS.]* Ingrate!
Tartuffe: If I must beg you, on bended knee,
To pardon him . . .
Orgon: *[Falling to his knees, addressing TARTUFFE.]*
Such goodness cannot be!
[To DAMIS.] Now, *there's* true charity!
Damis: What, you . . . ?
Orgon: Villain, be still!
I know your motives; I know you wish him ill:
Yes, all of you—wife, children, servants, all—
Conspire against him and desire his fall,
Employing every shameful trick you can
To alienate me from this saintly man.
Ah, but the more you seek to drive him away,
The more I'll do to keep him. Without delay,
I'll spite this household and confound its pride
By giving him my daughter as his bride.
Damis: You're going to force her to accept his hand?
Orgon: Yes, and this very night, d'you understand?
I shall defy you all, and make it clear
That I'm the one who gives the orders here.
Come, wretch, kneel down and clasp his blessed feet,
And ask his pardon for your black deceit.
Damis: I ask that swindler's pardon? Why, I'd rather . . .
Orgon: So! You insult him, and defy your father!
A stick! A stick! *[To TARTUFFE.]* No, no—release me, do.
[To DAMIS.] Out of my house this minute! Be off with you,
And never dare set foot in it again.
Damis: Well, I shall go, but . . .
Orgon: Well, go quickly, then.
I disinherit you; an empty purse
Is all you'll get from me—except my curse!

Scene 7

ORGON, TARTUFFE.
Orgon: How he blasphemed your goodness! What a son!
Tartuffe: Forgive him, Lord, as I've already done.
[*To ORGON.]* You can't know how it hurts when someone tries
To blacken me in my dear brother's eyes.
Orgon: Ahh!
Tartuffe: The mere thought of such ingratitude
Plunges my soul into so dark a mood . . .
Such horror grips my heart . . . I gasp for breath,
And cannot speak, and feel myself near death.
Orgon: *[He runs, in tears, to the door through which he has just driven his son.]*
You blackguard! Why did I spare you? Why did I not
Break you in little pieces on the spot?
Compose yourself, and don't be hurt, dear friend.
Tartuffe: These scenes, these dreadful quarrels, have got to end.
I've much upset your household, and I perceive
That the best thing will be for me to leave.
Orgon: What are you saying!
Tartuffe: They're all against me here;
They'd have you think me false and insincere.
Orgon: Ah, what of that? Have I ceased believing in you?
Tartuffe: Their adverse talk will certainly continue,
And charges which you now repudiate
You may find credible at a later date.
Orgon: No, Brother, never.
Tartuffe: Brother, a wife can sway
Her husband's mind in many a subtle way.
Orgon: No, no.
Tartuffe: To leave at once is the solution;
Thus only can I end their persecution.
Orgon: No, no, I'll not allow it; you shall remain.
Tartuffe: Ah, well; 'twill mean much martyrdom and pain,
But if you wish it . . .
Orgon: Ah!
Tartuffe: Enough; so be it.
But one thing must be settled, as I see it.
For your dear honor, and for our friendship's sake,
There's one precaution I feel bound to take.
I shall avoid your wife, and keep away . . .
Orgon: No, you shall not, whatever they may say.
It pleases me to vex them, and for spite
I'd have them see you with her day and night.
What's more, I'm going to drive them to despair
By making you my only son and heir;
This very day, I'll give to you alone
Clear deed and title to everything I own.
A dear, good friend and son-in-law-to-be
Is more than wife, or child, or kin to me.
Will you accept my offer, dearest son?
Tartuffe: In all things, let the will of Heaven be done.
Orgon: Poor fellow! Come, we'll go draw up the deed.
Then let them burst with disappointed greed!

Act IV

Scene 1

CLEANTE, TARTUFFE.
Cléante: Yes, all the town's discussing it, and truly,
Their comments do not flatter you unduly.
I'm glad we've met, Sir, and I'll give my view
Of this sad matter in a word or two.
As for who's guilty, that I shan't discuss;
Let's say it was Damis who caused the fuss;
Assuming, then, that you have been ill-used
By young Damis, and groundlessly accused,
Ought not a Christian to forgive, and ought
He not to stifle every vengeful thought?
Should you stand by and watch a father make
His only son an exile for your sake?
Again I tell you frankly, be advised:
The whole town, high and low, is scandalized;
This quarrel must be mended, and my advice is
Not to push matters to a further crisis.
No, sacrifice your wrath to God above,
And help Damis regain his father's love.
Tartuffe: Alas, for my part I should take great joy
In doing so. I've nothing against the boy.
I pardon all, I harbor no resentment;
To serve him would afford me much contentment.
But Heaven's interest will not have it so:

If he comes back, then I shall have to go.
After his conduct—so extreme, so vicious—
Our further intercourse would look suspicious.
God knows what people would think! Why, they'd describe
My goodness to him as a sort of bribe;
They'd say that out of guilt I made pretense
Of loving-kindness and benevolence—
That, fearing my accuser's tongue, I strove
To buy his silence with a show of love.
Cléante: Your reasoning is badly warped and stretched,
And these excuses, Sir, are most far-fetched.
Why put yourself in charge of Heaven's cause?
Does Heaven need our help to enforce its laws?
Leave vengeance to the Lord, Sir; while we live,
Our duty's not to punish, but forgive;
And what the Lord commands, we should obey
Without regard to what the world may say.
What! Shall the fear of being misunderstood
Prevent our doing what is right and good?
No, no: let's simply do what Heaven ordains,
And let no other thoughts perplex our brains.
Tartuffe: Again, Sir, let me say that I've forgiven
Damis, and thus obeyed the laws of Heaven;
But I am not commanded by the Bible
To live with one who smears my name with libel.
Cléante: Were you commanded, Sir, to indulge the whim
Of poor Orgon, and to encourage him
In suddenly transferring to your name
A large estate to which you have no claim?
Tartuffe: 'Twould never occur to those who know me best
To think I acted from self-interest,
The treasures of this world I quite despise;
Their specious glitter does not charm my eyes;
And if I have resigned myself to taking
The gift which my dear Brother insists on making,
I do so only, as he well understands,
Lest so much wealth fall into wicked hands,
Lest those to whom it might descend in time
Turn it to purposes of sin and crime,
And not, as I shall do, make use of it
For Heaven's glory and mankind's benefit.
Cléante: Forget these trumped-up fears. Your argument
Is one the rightful heir might well resent;
It *is* a moral burden to inherit
Such wealth, but give Damis a chance to bear it.
And would it not be worse to be accused
Of swindling, than to see that wealth misused?
I'm shocked that you allowed Orgon to broach
This matter, and that you feel no self-reproach;
Does true religion teach that lawful heirs
May freely be deprived of what is theirs?
And if the Lord has told you in your heart
That you and young Damis must dwell apart,
Would it not be the decent thing to beat
A generous and honorable retreat,
Rather than let the son of the house be sent,
For your convenience, into banishment?
Sir, if you wish to prove the honesty
Of your intentions . . .
Tartuffe: Sir, it is a half past three.
I've certain pious duties to attend to,
And hope my prompt departure won't offend you.
Cléante: *[Alone.]* Damn.

Scene 2

ELMIRE, MARIANE, CLEANTE, DORINE.
Dorine: Stay, Sir, and help Mariane, for Heaven's sake!
She's suffering so, I fear her heart will break.
Her father's plan to marry her off tonight
Has put the poor child in a desperate plight.
I hear him coming. Let's stand together, now,
And see if we can't change his mind, somehow,
About this match we all deplore and fear.

Scene 3

ORGON, MARIANE, CLEANTE, ELMIRE, DORINE.
Orgon: Hah! Glad to find you all assembled here.
[To MARIANE.] This contract, child, contains your happiness,
And what it says I think your heart can guess.
Mariane: *[Falling to her knees.]*
Sir, by that Heaven which sees me here distressed,
And by whatever else can move your breast,
Do not employ a father's power, I pray you,
To crush my heart and force it to obey you,
Nor by your harsh commands oppress me so
That I'll begrudge the duty which I owe—
And do not so embitter and enslave me
That I shall hate the very life you gave me.
If my sweet hopes must perish, if you refuse
To give me to the one I've dared to choose,
Spare me at least—I beg you, I implore—
The pain of wedding one whom I abhor;
And do not, by a heartless use of force,
Drive me to contemplate some desperate course.
Orgon: *[Feeling himself touched by her.]*
Be firm, my soul. No human weakness, now.
Mariane: I don't resent your love for him. Allow
Your heart free rein, Sir; give him your property,
And if that's not enough, take mine from me;
He's welcome to my money, take it, do,
But don't, I pray, include my person too.
Spare me, I beg you; and let me end the tale
Of my sad days behind a convent veil.
Orgon: A convent! Hah! When crossed in their amours,
All lovesick girls have the same thought as yours.
Get up! The more you loathe the man, and dread him,
The more ennobling it will be to wed him.
Marry Tartuffe, and mortify your flesh!
Enough; don't start that whimpering afresh.
Dorine: But why . . . ?
Orgon: Be still, there. Speak when you're spoken to.
Not one more bit of impudence out of you.
Cléante: If I may offer a word of counsel here . . .
Orgon: Brother, in counselling you have no peer;
All your advice is forceful, sound, and clever;
I don't propose to follow it, however.
Elmire: *[To ORGON.]* I am amazed, and don't know what to say;

Your blindness simply takes my breath away.
You are indeed bewitched, to take no warning
From our account of what occurred this morning.
Orgon: Madam, I know a few plain facts, and one
Is that you're partial to my rascal son;
Hence, when he sought to make Tartuffe the victim
Of a base lie, you dared not contradict him.
Ah, but you underplayed your part, my pet;
You should have looked more angry, more upset.
Elmire: When men make overtures, must we reply
With righteous anger and a battle-cry?
Must we turn back their amorous advances
With sharp reproaches and with fiery glances?
Myself, I find such offers merely amusing,
And make no scenes and fusses in refusing;
My taste is for good-natured rectitude,
And I dislike the savage sort of prude
Who guards her virtue with her teeth and claws,
And tears men's eyes out for the slightest cause:
The Lord preserve me from such honor as that,
Which bites and scratches like an alley-cat!
I've found that a polite and cool rebuff
Discourages a lover quite enough.
Orgon: I know the facts, and I shall not be shaken.
Elmire: I marvel at your power to be mistaken.
Would it, I wonder, carry weight with you
If I could *show* you that our tale was true?
Orgon: Show me?
Elmire: Yes.
Orgon: Rot.
Elmire: Come, what if I found a way
To make you see the facts as plain as day?
Orgon: Nonsense.
Elmire: Do answer me; don't be absurd.
I'm not now asking you to trust our word.
Suppose that from some hiding-place in here
You learned the whole sad truth by eye and ear—
What would you say of your good friend, after that?
Orgon: Why, I'd say . . . nothing, by Jehoshaphat!
It can't be true.
Elmire: You've been too long deceived,
I'm quite tired of being disbelieved.
Come now: let's put my statements to the test,
And you shall see the truth made manifest.
Orgon: I'll take that challenge. Now do your uttermost.
We'll see how you make good your empty boast.
Elmire: *[To DORINE.]* Send him to me.
Dorine: He's crafty; it may be hard
To catch the cunning scoundrel off his guard.
Elmire: No, amorous men are gullible. Their conceit
So blinds them that they're never hard to cheat.
Have him come down.
[To CLEANTE and MARIANE.] Please leave us, for a bit.

Scene 4

ELMIRE, ORGON.
Elmire: Pull up this table, and get under it.
Orgon: What?
Elmire: It's essential that you be well-hidden.
Orgon: Why there?
Elmire: Oh, Heavens! Just do as you are bidden.
I have my plans; we'll soon see how they fare.
Under the table, now; and once you're there,
Take care that you are neither seen nor heard.
Orgon: Well, I'll indulge you, since I gave my word
To see you through this infantile charade.
Elmire: Once it is over, you'll be glad we played.
[To her husband, who is now under the table.]
I'm going to act quite strangely, now, and you
Must not be shocked at anything I do.
Whatever I may say, you must excuse
As part of that deceit I'm forced to use.
I shall employ sweet speeches in the task
Of making that impostor drop his mask;
I'll give encouragement to his bold desires,
And furnish fuel to his amorous fires.
Since it's for your sake, and for his destruction,
That I shall seem to yield to his seduction,
I'll gladly stop whenever you decide.
That all your doubts are fully satisfied.
I'll count on you, as soon as you have seen
What sort of man he is, to intervene,
And not expose me to his odious lust
One moment longer than you feel you must.
Remember: You're to save me from my plight
Whenever . . . He's coming! Hush! Keep out of sight!

Scene 5

TARTUFFE, ELMIRE, ORGON.
Tartuffe: You wish to have a word with me, I'm told.
Elmire: Yes, I've a little secret to unfold.
Before I speak, however, it would be wise
To close that door, and look about for spies.
[TARTUFFE goes to the door, closes it, and returns.]
The very last thing that must happen now
Is a repetition of this morning's row.
I've never been so badly caught off guard.
Oh, how I feared for you! You saw how hard
I tried to make that troublesome Damis
Control his dreadful temper, and hold his peace.
In my confusion, I didn't have the sense
Simply to contradict his evidence;
But as it happened, that was for the best,
And all has worked out in our interest.
This storm has only bettered your position;
My husband doesn't have the least suspicion,
And now, in mockery of those who do,
He bids me be continually with you.
And that is why, quite fearless of reproof,
I now can be alone with my Tartuffe,
And why my heart—perhaps too quick to yield—
Feels free to let its passion be revealed.
Tartuffe: Madam, your words confuse me. Not long ago,
You spoke in quite a different style, you know.
Elmire: Ah, Sir, if that refusal made you smart,
It's little that you know of woman's heart,
Or what that heart is trying to convey
When it resists in such a feeble way!
Always, at first, our modesty prevents
The frank avowal of tender sentiments:

However high the passion which inflames us,
Still, to confess its power somehow shames us.
Thus we reluct, at first, yet in a tone
Which tells you that our heart is overthrown,
That what our lips deny, our pulse confesses,
And that, in time, all noes will turn to yesses.
I fear my words are all too frank and free,
And a poor proof of woman's modesty;
But since I'm started, tell me, if you will—
Would I have tried to make Damis be still,
Would I have listened, calm and unoffended,
Until your lengthy offer of love was ended,
And been so very mild in my reaction,
Had your sweet words not given me satisfaction?
And when I tried to force you to undo
The marriage-plans my husband has in view,
What did my urgent pleading signify
If not that I admired you, and that I
Deplored the thought that someone else might own
Part of a heart I wished for mine alone?
Tartuffe: Madam, no happiness is so complete
As when, from lips we love, come words so sweet;
Their nectar floods my every sense, and drains
In honeyed rivulets through all my veins.
To please you is my joy, my only goal;
Your love is the restorer of my soul;
And yet I must beg leave, now, to confess
Some lingering doubts as to my happiness.
Might this not be a trick? Might not the catch
Be that you wish me to break off the match
With Mariane, and so have feigned to love me?
I shan't quite trust your fond opinion of me
Until the feelings you've expressed so sweetly
Are demonstrated somewhat more concretely,
And you have shown, by certain kind concessions,
That I may put my faith in your professions
Elmire: *[She coughs, to warn her husband.]*
Why be in such a hurry? Must my heart
Exhaust its bounty at the very start?
To make that sweet admission cost me dear,
But you'll not be content, it would appear,
Unless my store of favors is disbursed
To the last farthing, and at the very first.
Tartuffe: The less we merit, the less we dare to hope,
And with our doubts, mere words can never cope.
We trust no promised bliss till we receive it;
Not till a joy is ours can we believe it.
I, who so little merit your esteem,
Can't credit this fulfillment of my dream,
And shan't believe it, Madam, until I savor
Some palpable assurance of your favor.
Elmire: My, how tyrannical your love can be,
And how it flusters and perplexes me!
How furiously you take one's heart in hand,
And make your every wish a fierce command!
Come, must you hound and harry me to death?
Will you not give me time to catch my breath?
Can it be right to press me with such force,
Give me no quarter, show me no remorse,
And take advantage, by your stern insistence,
Of the fond feelings which weaken my resistance?
Tartuffe: Well, if you look with favor upon my love,
Why, then, begrudge me some clear proof thereof?
Elmire: But how can I consent without offense
To Heaven, toward which you feel such reverence?
Tartuffe: If Heaven is all that holds you back, don't worry.
I can remove that hindrance in a hurry.
Nothing of that sort need obstruct our path.
Elmire: Must one not be afraid of Heaven's wrath?
Tartuffe: Madam, forget such fears, and be my pupil,
And I shall teach you how to conquer scruple.
Some joys, it's true, are wrong in Heaven's eyes;
Yet Heaven is not averse to compromise;
There is a science, lately formulated,
Whereby one's conscience may be liberated,[19]
And any wrongful act you care to mention
May be redeemed by purity of intention.
I'll teach you, Madam, the secrets of that science;
Meanwhile, just place on me your full reliance.
Assuage my keen desires, and feel no dread:
The sin, if any, shall be on my head.
[ELMIRE coughs, this time more loudly.]
You've a bad cough.
Elmire: Yes, yes, it's bad indeed.
Tartuffe: *[Producing a little paper bag.]*
A bit of licorice may be what you need.
Elmire: No, I've a stubborn cold, it seems. I'm sure it
Will take much more than licorice to cure it.
Tartuffe: How aggravating.
Elmire: Oh, more than I can say.
Tartuffe: If you're still troubled, think of things this way:
No one shall know our joys, save us alone,
And there's no evil till the act is known;
It's scandal, Madam, which makes it an offense,
And it's no sin to sin in confidence.
Elmire: *[Having coughed once more.]*
Well, clearly I must do as you require,
And yield to your importunate desire.
It is apparent, now, that nothing less
Will satisfy you, and so I acquiesce.
To go so far is much against my will;
I'm vexed that it should come to this; but still,
Since you are so determined on it, since you
Will not allow mere language to convince you,
And since you ask for concrete evidence, I
See nothing for it, now, but to comply.
If this is sinful, if I'm wrong to do it,
So much the worse for him who drove me to it.
The fault can surely not be charged to me.
Tartuffe: Madam, the fault is mine, if fault there be,
And . . .
Elmire: Open the door a little, and peek out;
I wouldn't want my husband poking about.
Tartuffe: Why worry about the man? Each day he grows
More gullible; one can lead him by the nose.
To find us here would fill him with delight,
And if he saw the worst, he'd doubt his sight.
Elmire: Nevertheless, do step out for a minute
Into the hall, and see that no one's in it.

19. Molière appended his own footnote to this line: "It is a scoundrel who speaks."

Scene 6

ORGON, ELMIRE.
Orgon: *[Coming out from under the table.]*
That man's a perfect monster, I must admit!
I'm simply stunned. I can't get over it.
Elmire: What, coming out so soon? How premature!
Get back in hiding, and wait until you're sure.
Stay till the end, and be convinced completely;
We mustn't stop till things are proved concretely.
Orgon: Hell never harbored anything so vicious!
Elmire: Tut, don't be hasty. Try to be judicious.
Wait, and be certain that there's no mistake.
No jumping to conclusions, for Heaven's sake!
[She places ORGON behind her, as TARTUFFE reenters.]

Scene 7

TARTUFFE, ELMIRE, ORGON.
Tartuffe: *[Not seeing ORGON.]*
Madam, all things have worked out to perfection;
I've given the neighboring rooms a full inspection;
No one's about; and now I may at last . . .
Orgon: *[Intercepting him.]* Hold on, my passionate fellow, not so fast!
I should advise a little more restraint.
Well, so you thought you'd fool me, my dear saint!
How soon you wearied of the saintly life—
Wedding my daughter, and coveting my wife!
I've long suspected you, and had a feeling
That soon I'd catch you at your double-dealing.
Just now, you've given me evidence galore;
It's quite enough; I have no wish for more.
Elmire: *[To TARTUFFE.]* I'm sorry to have treated you so slyly,
But circumstances forced me to be wily.
Tartuffe: Brother, you can't think . . .
Orgon: No more talk from you;
Just leave this household, without more ado.
Tartuffe: What I intended . . .
Orgon: That seems fairly clear.
Spare me your falsehoods and get out of here.
Tartuffe: No, I'm the master, and you're the one to go!
This house belongs to me, I'll have you know,
And I shall show you that you can't hurt *me*
By this contemptible conspiracy,
That those who cross me know not what they do,
And that I've means to expose and punish you,
Avenge offended Heaven, and make you grieve
That ever you dared order me to leave.

Scene 8

ELMIRE, ORGON.
Elmire: What was the point of all that angry chatter?
Orgon: Dear God, I'm worried. This is no laughing matter.
Elmire: How so?
Orgon: I fear I understood his drift.
I'm much disturbed about that deed of gift.
Elmire: You gave him . . . ?
Orgon: Yes, it's all been drawn and signed.
But one thing more is weighing on my mind.
Elmire: What's that?
Orgon: I'll tell you; but first let's see if there's
A certain strong-box in his room upstairs.

Act V

Scene 1

ORGON, CLEANTE.
Cléante: Where are you going so fast?
Orgon: God knows!
Cléante: Then wait;
Let's have a conference, and deliberate
On how this situation's to be met.
Orgon: That strong-box has me utterly upset;
This is the worst of many, many shocks.
Cléante: Is there some fearful mystery in that box?
Orgon: My poor friend Argas brought that box to me
With his own hands, in utmost secrecy;
'Twas on the very morning of his flight.
It's full of papers which, if they came to light,
Would ruin him—or such is my impression.
Cléante: Then why did you let it out of your possession?
Orgon: Those papers vexed my conscience, and it seemed best
To ask the counsel of my pious guest.
The cunning scoundrel got me to agree
To leave the strong-box in his custody,
So that, in case of an investigation,
I could employ a slight equivocation
And swear I didn't have it and thereby,
At no expense to conscience, tell a lie.
Cléante: It looks to me as if you're out on a limb.
Trusting him with that box, and offering him
That deed of gift, were actions of a kind
Which scarcely indicate a prudent mind.
With two such weapons, he has the upper hand,
And since you're vulnerable as matters stand,
You erred once more in bringing him to bay.
You should have acted in some subtler way.
Orgon: Just think of it: behind that fervent face,
A heart so wicked, and a soul so base!
I took him in, a hungry beggar, and then . . .
Enough, by God! I'm through with pious men:
Henceforth I'll hate the whole false brotherhood,
And persecute them worse than Satan could.
Cléante: Ah, there you go—extravagant as ever!
Why can you not be rational? You never
Manage to take the middle course, it seems,
But jump, instead, between absurd extremes.
You've recognized your recent grave mistake
In falling victim to a pious fake;
Now, to correct that error, must you embrace
An even greater error in its place,
And judge our worthy neighbors as a whole
By what you've learned of one corrupted soul?
Come, just because one rascal made you swallow
A show of zeal which turned out to be hollow,
Shall you conclude that all men are deceivers,
And that, today, there are no true believers?
Let atheists make that foolish inference;
Learn to distinguish virtue from pretense,
Be cautious in bestowing admiration,

And cultivate a sober moderation.
Don't humor fraud, but also don't asperse
True piety; the latter fault is worse,
And it is best to err, if err one must,
As you have done, upon the side of trust.

Scene 2

DAMIS, ORGON, CLEANTE.
Damis: Father, I hear that scoundrel's uttered threats
Against you; that he pridefully forgets
How, in his need, he was befriended by you,
And means to use your gifts to crucify you.
Orgon: It's true, my boy. I'm too distressed for tears.
Damis: Leave it to me, Sir; let me trim his ears.
Faced with such insolence, we must not waver.
I shall rejoice in doing you the favor
Of cutting short his life, and your distress.
Cléante: What a display of young hotheadedness!
Do learn to moderate your fits of rage.
In this just kingdom, this enlightened age,
One does not settle things by violence.

Scene 3

MADAME PERNELLE, MARIANE, ELMIRE, DORINE,
DAMIS, ORGON, CLEANTE.
Madame Pernelle: I hear strange tales of very strange events.
Orgon: Yes, strange events which these two eyes beheld.
The man's ingratitude is unparalleled.
I save a wretched pauper from starvation,
House him, and treat him like a blood relation,
Shower him every day with my largesse,
Give him my daughter, and all that I possess;
And meanwhile the unconscionable knave
Tries to induce my wife to misbehave;
And not content with such extreme rascality,
Now threatens me with my own liberality,
And aims, by taking base advantage of
The gifts I gave him out of Christian love,
To drive me from my house, a ruined man,
And make me end a pauper, as he began.
Dorine: Poor fellow!
Madame Pernelle: No, my son, I'll never bring
Myself to think him guilty of such a thing.
Orgon: How's that?
Madame Pernelle: The righteous always were maligned.
Orgon: Speak clearly, Mother. Say what's on your mind.
Madame Pernelle: I mean that I can smell a rat, my dear.
You know how everybody hates him, here.
Orgon: That has no bearing on the case at all.
Madame Pernelle: I told you a hundred times, when you were small,
That virtue in this world is hated ever;
Malicious men may die, but malice never.
Orgon: No doubt that's true, but how does it apply?
Madame Pernelle: They've turned you against him by a clever lie.
Orgon: I've told you, I was there and saw it done.
Madame Pernelle: Ah, slanderers will stop at nothing, Son.
Orgon: Mother, I'll lose my temper . . . For the last time,
I tell you I was witness to the crime.
Madame Pernelle: The tongues of spite are busy night and noon,
And to their venom no man is immune.
Orgon: You're talking nonsense. Can't you realize
I saw it; saw it; saw it with my eyes?
Saw, do you understand me? Must I shout it
Into your ears before you'll cease to doubt it?
Madame Pernelle: Appearances can deceive, my son. Dear me,
We cannot always judge by what we see.
Orgon: Drat! Drat!
Madame Pernelle: One often interprets things awry;
Good can seem evil to a suspicious eye.
Orgon: Was I to see his pawing at Elmire
As an act of charity?
Madame Pernelle: 'Till his guilt is clear,
A man deserves the benefit of the doubt.
You should have waited, to see how things turned out.
Orgon: Great God in Heaven, what more proof did I need?
Was I to sit there, watching, until he'd . . .
You drive me to the brink of impropriety.
Madame Pernelle: No, no, a man of such surpassing piety
Could not do such a thing. You cannot shake me.
I don't believe it, and you shall not make me.
Orgon: You vex me so that, if you weren't my mother,
I'd say to you . . . some dreadful thing or other.
Dorine: It's your turn now, Sir, not to be listened to;
You'd not trust us, and now she won't trust you.
Cléante: My friends, we're wasting time which should be spent
In facing up to our predicament.
I fear that scoundrel's threats weren't made in sport.
Damis: Do you think he'd have the nerve to go to court?
Elmire: I'm sure he won't; they'd find it all too crude
A case of swindling and ingratitude.
Cléante: Don't be too sure. He won't be at a loss
To give his claims a high and righteous gloss;
And clever rogues with far less valid cause
Have trapped their victims in a web of laws.
I say again that to antagonize
A man so strongly armed was most unwise.
Orgon: I know it; but the man's appalling cheek
Outraged me so, I couldn't control my pique.
Cléante: I wish to Heaven that we could devise
Some truce between you, or some compromise.
Elmire: If I had known what cards he held, I'd not
Have roused his anger by my little plot.
Orgon: *[To DORINE, as MONSIEUR LOYAL enters.]*
What is that fellow looking for? Who is he?
Go talk to him—and tell him that I'm busy.

Scene 4

MONSIEUR LOYAL, MADAME PERNELLE, ORGON,
DAMIS, MARIANE, DORINE, ELMIRE, CLEANTE.
Monsieur Loyal: Good day, dear sister. Kindly let me see
Your master.

Dorine: He's involved with company,
And cannot be disturbed just now, I fear.
Monsieur Loyal: I hate to intrude; but what has brought me here
Will not disturb your master, in any event.
Indeed, my news will make him most content.
Dorine: Your name?
Monsieur Loyal: Just say that I bring greetings from
Monsieur Tartuffe, on whose behalf I've come.
Dorine: *[To ORGON.]* Sir, he's a very gracious man, and bears
A message from Tartuffe, which, he declares,
Will make you most content.
Cléante: Upon my word,
I think this man had best be seen, and heard.
Orgon: Perhaps he has some settlement to suggest.
How shall I treat him? What manner would be best?
Cléante: Control your anger, and if he should mention
Some fair adjustment, give him your full attention.
Monsieur Loyal: Good health to you, good Sir. May Heaven confound
Your enemies, and may your joys abound.
Orgon: *[To CLEANTE.]* A gentle salutation: it confirms
My guess that he is here to offer terms.
Monsieur Loyal: I've always held your family most dear;
I served your father, Sir, for many a year.
Orgon: Sir, I must ask your pardon; to my shame,
I cannot now recall your face or name.
Monsieur Loyal: Loyal's my name; I come from Normandy,
And I'm a bailiff, in all modesty.
For forty years, praise God, it's been my boast
To serve with honor in that vital post,
And I am here, Sir, if you will permit
The liberty, to serve you with this writ . . .
Orgon: To—*what?*
Monsieur Loyal: Now, please, Sir, let us have no friction:
It's nothing but an order of eviction.
You are to move your goods and family out
And make way for new occupants, without
Deferment or delay, and give the keys . . .
Orgon: I? Leave this house?
Monsieur Loyal: Why yes, Sir, if you please.
This house, Sir, from the cellar to the roof,
Belongs now to the good Monsieur Tartuffe,
And he is lord and master of your estate
By virtue of a deed of present date,
Drawn in due form, with clearest legal phrasing . . .
Damis: Your insolence is utterly amazing!
Monsieur Loyal: Young man, my business here is not with you
But with your wise and temperate father, who,
Like every worthy citizen, stands in awe
Of justice, and would never obstruct the law.
Orgon: But . . .
Monsieur Loyal: Not for a million, Sir, would you rebel
Against authority; I know that well.
You'll not make trouble, sir, or interfere
With the execution of my duties here.
Damis: Someone may execute a smart tattoo
On that black jacket of yours, before you're through.
Monsieur Loyal: Sir, bid your son be silent. I'd much regret
Having to mention such a nasty threat
Of violence, in writing my report.
Dorine: *[Aside.]* This man Loyal's a most disloyal sort!
Monsieur Loyal: I love all men of upright character,
And when I agreed to serve these papers, Sir,
It was your feelings that I had in mind.
I couldn't bear to see the case assigned
To someone else, who might esteem you less
And so subject you to unpleasantness.
Orgon: What's more unpleasant than telling a man to leave
His house and home?
Monsieur Loyal: You'd like a short reprieve?
If you desire it, Sir, I shall not press you,
But wait until tomorrow to dispossess you.
Splendid. I'll come and spend the night here, then,
Most quietly, with half a score of men.
For form's sake, you might bring me, just before
You go to bed, the keys to the front door.
My men, I promise, will be on their best
Behavior, and will not disturb your rest.
But bright and early, Sir, you must be quick
And move out all your furniture, every stick:
The men I've chosen are both young and strong,
And with their help it shouldn't take you long.
In short, I'll make things pleasant and convenient,
And since I'm being so extremely lenient,
Please show me, Sir, a like consideration,
And give me your entire cooperation.
Orgon: *[Aside.]* I may be all but bankrupt, but I vow
I'd give a hundred louis, here and now,
Just for the pleasure of landing one good clout
Right on the end of that complacent snout.
Cléante: Careful; don't make things worse.
Damis: My bootsole itches
To give that beggar a good kick in the breeches.
Dorine: Monsieur Loyal, I'd love to hear the whack
Of a stout stick across your fine broad back.
Monsieur Loyal: Take care: a woman too may go to jail if
She uses threatening language to a bailiff.
Cléante: Enough, enough, Sir. This must not go on.
Give me that paper, please, and then begone.
Monsieur Loyal: Well, *au revoir*. God give you all good cheer!
Orgon: May God confound you, and him who sent you here!

Scene 5

ORGON, CLEANTE, MARIANE, ELMIRE, MADAME PERNELLE, DORINE, DAMIS.

Orgon: Now, Mother, was I right or not? This writ
Should change your notion of Tartuffe a bit.
Do you perceive his villainy at last?
Madame Pernelle: I'm thunderstruck. I'm utterly aghast.
Dorine: Oh, come, be fair. You mustn't take offense
At this new proof of his benevolence.
He's acting out of selfless love, I know.
Material things enslave the soul, and so

He kindly has arranged your liberation
From all that might endanger your salvation.
Orgon: Will you not ever hold your tongue, you dunce?
Cléante: Come, you must take some action, and at once.
Elmire: Go tell the world of the low trick he's tried.
The deed of gift is surely nullified
By such behavior, and public rage will not
Permit the wretch to carry out his plot.

Scene 6

VALERE, ORGON, CLEANTE, ELMIRE, MARIANE, MADAME PERNELLE, DAMIS, DORINE.

Valère: Sir, though I hate to bring you more bad news.
Such is the danger that I cannot choose.
A friend who is extremely close to me
And knows my interest in your family
Has, for my sake, presumed to violate
The secrecy that's due to things of state,
And sends me word that you are in a plight
From which your one salvation lies in flight.
That scoundrel who's imposed upon you so
Denounced you to the King an hour ago
And, as supporting evidence, displayed
The strong-box of a certain renegade
Whose secret papers, so he testified,
You had disloyally agreed to hide.
I don't know just what charges may be pressed,
But there's a warrant out for your arrest;
Tartuffe has been instructed, furthermore,
To guide the arresting officer to your door.
Cléante: He's clearly done this to facilitate
His seizure of your house and your estate.
Orgon: That man, I must say, is a vicious beast!
Valère: You can't afford to delay, Sir, in the least.
My carriage is outside, to take you hence;
This thousand louis should cover all expense.
Let's lose no time, or you shall be undone;
The sole defense, in this case, is to run.
I shall go with you all the way, and place you
In a safe refuge to which they'll never trace you.
Orgon: Alas, dear boy, I wish that I could show you
My gratitude for everything I owe you.
But now is not the time; I pray the Lord
That I may live to give you your reward.
Farewell, my dears; be careful . . .
Cléante: Brother, hurry.
We shall take care of things; you needn't worry.

Scene 7

THE OFFICER, TARTUFFE, VALERE, ORGON, ELMIRE, MARIANE, MADAME PERNELLE, DORINE, CLEANTE, DAMIS.

Tartuffe: Gently, Sir, gently; stay right where you are.
No need for haste; your lodging isn't far.
You're off to prison, by order of the Prince.
Orgon: This is the crowning blow, you wretch; and since
It means my total ruin and defeat,
Your villainy is now at last complete.
Tartuffe: You needn't try to provoke me; it's no use.
Those who serve Heaven must expect abuse.
Cléante: You are indeed most patient, sweet, and blameless.
Dorine: How he exploits the name of Heaven! It's shameless.
Tartuffe: Your taunts and mockeries are all for naught;
To do my duty is my only thought.
Mariane: Your love of duty is most meritorious,
And what you've done is little short of glorious.
Tartuffe: All deeds are glorious, Madam, which obey
The sovereign Prince who sent me here today.
Orgon: I rescued you when you were destitute;
Have you forgotten that, you thankless brute?
Tartuffe: No, no, I well remember everything;
But my first duty is to serve my King.
That obligation is so paramount
That other claims, beside it, do not count;
And for it I would sacrifice my wife,
My family, my friend, or my own life.
Elmire: Hypocrite!
Dorine: All that we most revere, he uses
To cloak his plots and camouflage his ruses.
Cléante: If it is true that you are animated
By pure and loyal zeal, as you have stated,
Why was this zeal not roused until you'd sought
To make Orgon a cuckold, and been caught?
Why weren't you moved to give your evidence
Until your outraged host had driven you hence?
I shan't say that the gift of all his treasure
Ought to have damped your zeal in any measure;
But if he is a traitor, as you declare,
How could you condescend to be his heir?
Tartuffe: *[To the OFFICER.]* Sir, spare me all this clamor; it's growing shrill.
Please carry out your orders, if you will.
Officer:[20] Yes, I've delayed too long, Sir. Thank you kindly.
You're just the proper person to remind me.
Come, you are off to join the other boarders
In the King's prison, according to his orders.
Tartuffe: Who? I, Sir?
Officer: Yes.
Tartuffe: To prison? This can't be true!
Officer: I owe an explanation, but not to you.
[To ORGON.] Sir, all is well; rest easy, and be grateful.
We serve a Prince to whom all sham is hateful,
A Prince who sees into our inmost hearts,
And can't be fooled by any trickster's arts.
His royal soul, though generous and human,
Views all things with discernment and acumen;
His sovereign reason is not lightly swayed,
And all his judgments are discreetly weighed.
He honors righteous men of every kind,
And yet his zeal for virtue is not blind,
Nor does his love of piety numb his wits
And make him tolerant of hypocrites.
'Twas hardly likely that this man could cozen

20. In the original, *un exempt*. He would actually have been a gentleman from the king's personal bodyguard with the rank of lieutenant-colonel or "master of the camp."

A King who's foiled such liars by the dozen.
With one keen glance, the King perceived the whole
Perverseness and corruption of his soul,
And thus high Heaven's justice was displayed:
Betraying you, the rogue stood self-betrayed.
The King soon recognized Tartuffe as one
Notorious by another name, who'd done
So many vicious crimes that one could fill
Ten volumes with them, and be writing still.
But to be brief: our sovereign was appalled
By this man's treachery toward you, which he called
The last, worst villainy of a vile career,
And bade me follow the impostor here
To see how gross his impudence could be,
And force him to restore your property.
Your private papers, by the King's command,
I hereby seize and give into your hand.
The King, by royal order, invalidates
The deed which gave this rascal your estates,
And pardons, furthermore, your grave offense
In harboring an exile's documents.
By these decrees, our Prince rewards you for
Your loyal deeds in the late civil war,
And shows how heartfelt is his satisfaction
In recompensing any worthy action,
How much he prizes merit, and how he makes
More of men's virtues than of their mistakes.
Dorine: Heaven be praised!
Madame Pernelle: I breathe again, at last.
Elmire: We're safe.
Mariane: I can't believe the danger's past.
Orgon: *[To TARTUFFE.]* Well, traitor, now you see . . .
Cléante: Ah, brother, please,
Let's not descend to such indignities.
Leave the poor wretch to his unhappy fate,
And don't say anything to aggravate
His present woes; but rather hope that he
Will soon embrace an honest piety,
And mend his ways, and by a true repentance
Move our just King to moderate his sentence.
Meanwhile, go kneel before your sovereign's throne
And thank him for the mercies he has shown.
Orgon: Well said: let's go at once and, gladly kneeling,
Express the gratitude which all are feeling.
Then, when that first great duty has been done,
We'll turn with pleasure to a second one,
And give Valère, whose love has proven so true,
The wedded happiness which is his due.

STUDY QUESTIONS

1. Imagine that you are casting *Tartuffe* for a movie production. Select the actor whose appearance, personality, and acting skills make her/him the best person for each major role.
2. Why does Molière delay Tartuffe's entrance until Act III? Why does he have Tartuffe encounter Dorine first? Why not Orgon?
3. Describe the character traits of Orgon that make him so vulnerable to a villain like Tartuffe. Why aren't the others duped?
4. Name some people whom you suspect of being Tartuffes. Describe them, how they operate, and why you are suspicious of their motives.

Alexander Pope, 1688–1744

Neoclassicism became the dominant style in eighteenth-century Europe, especially in France and England. The most influential Neoclassic poet in England, Alexander Pope, formulated the aesthetics of poetry in *Essay on Criticism*, emphasizing the necessity for precise language, logical order, and clear form. Pope's own poetry was didactic, witty, satiric, technically superb; it epitomized the Neoclassic style of eighteenth-century England. Pope, in fact, expressed his goal in his own verse:

> True wit is nature to advantage dressed,
> What oft was thought, but ne'er so well expressed.

His *Essay on Man* (1733–4) optimistically summarizes eighteenth-century views on the rational universe, reasonable behavior, and deism. Though not philosophically profound, the poem is esteemed for its skillful craftsmanship and sparkling wit. Pope's optimism was rejected by the skeptical Voltaire in *Candide*, as discussed later.

LITERARY SELECTION 54

Essay on Man

Alexander Pope

Epistle I

Awake, my St. John! leave all meaner things
To low ambition and the pride of kings.
Let us (since life can little more supply
Than just to look about us and to die)
Expatiate free o'er all this scene of man;
A mighty maze! but not without a plan;
A wild, where weeds and flowers promiscuous shoot;
Or garden, tempting with forbidden fruit.
Together let us beat this ample field,
Try what the open, what the covert yield;
The latent tracts, the giddy heights, explore,
Of all who blindly creep, or sightless soar;
Eye Nature's walks, shoot Folly as it flies,
And catch the manners living as they rise;
Laugh where we must, be candid where we can;
But vindicate the ways of God to man.

I

Say first, of God above or man below,
What can we reason but from what we know?
Of man, what see we but his station here,
From which to reason, or to which refer?
Through worlds unnumber'd though the God be known,
'Tis ours to trace him only in our own.
He, who through vast immensity can pierce,
See worlds on worlds compose one universe,
Observe how system into system runs,
What other planets circle other suns,
What varied being peoples every star,
May tell why Heav'n has made us as we are.
But of this frame, the bearings and the ties,
The strong connections, nice dependencies,
Gradations just, has thy pervading soul
Looked through, or can a part contain the whole?
Is the great chain that draws all to agree,
And drawn supports, upheld by God or thee?

II

Presumptuous man! the reason wouldst thou find,
Why form'd so weak, so little, and so blind?
First, if thou canst, the harder reason guess,
Why form'd no weaker, blinder, and no less?
Ask of thy mother earth, why oaks are made
Taller or stronger than the weeds they shade!
Or ask of yonder argent fields above
Why Jove's satellites are less than Jove!
   Of systems possible, if 'tis confest
That wisdom infinite must form the best,
Where all must full or not coherent be,
And all that rises rise in due degree,
Then, in the scale of reas'ning life, 'tis plain
There must be somewhere such a rank as Man:
And all the question (wrangle e'er so long)
Is only this, if God has placed him wrong?
   Respecting Man, whatever wrong we call,
May, must be right, as relative to all,
In human works, though labour'd on with pain,
A thousand movements scarce one purpose gain;
In God's, one single can its end produce;
Yet serves to second too some other use.
So Man, who here seems principal alone,
Perhaps acts second to some sphere unknown,
Touches some wheel, or verges to some goal;
'Tis but a part we see, and not a whole.
   When the proud steed shall know why man restrains
His fiery course, or drives him o'er the plains;
When the dull ox, why now he breaks the clod,
Is now a victim, and now Egypt's god;
Then shall man's pride and dullness comprehend
His actions', passions', being's, use and end;
Why doing, suff'ring, check'd, impell'd; and why
This hour a slave, the next a deity.
   Then say not man's imperfect, Heav'n in fault;
Say rather man's as perfect as he ought:
His knowledge measur'd to his state and place,
His time a moment, and a point his space.
If to be perfect in a certain sphere,
What matter soon or late, or here or there?
The blest today is as completely so,
As who began a thousand years ago.

III

Heav'n from all creatures hides the book of Fate,
All but the page prescrib'd, their present state:
From brutes what men, from men what spirits know:
Or who could suffer Being here below?
The lamb thy riot dooms to bleed today,
Had he thy reason, would he skip and play?
Pleas'd to the last, he crops the flow'ry food,
And licks the hand just rais'd to shed his blood.
Oh blindness to the future! kindly giv'n,
That each may fill the circle mark'd by Heav'n:
Who sees with equal eye, as God of all,
A hero perish, or a sparrow fall,
Atoms or systems into ruin hurl'd,
And now a bubble burst, and now a world.
   Hope humbly then; with trembling pinions soar;
Wait the great teacher Death, and God adore!
What future bliss he gives not thee to know,
But gives that hope to be thy blessing now.
Hope springs eternal in the human breast;
Man never is, but always to be blest.
The soul, uneasy, and confin'd from home,
Rests and expatiates in a life to come.
   Lo! the poor Indian, whose untutor'd mind
Sees God in clouds, or hears him in the wind;
His soul proud Science never taught to stray
Far as the solar walk or milky way;
Yet simple Nature to his hope has giv'n,
Behind the cloud-topt hill, an humbler heav'n;
Some safer world in depth of woods embrac'd,
Some happier island in the watery waste,
Where slaves once more their native land behold,
No fiends torment, no Christians thirst for gold!
To be, contents his natural desire;
He asks no angel's wing, no seraph's fire;
But thinks, admitted to that equal sky,
His faithful dog shall bear him company.

IV

Go, wiser thou! and in thy scale of sense,
Weigh thy opinion against Providence;
Call imperfection what thou fancy'st such,
Say, Here he gives too little, there too much!
Destroy all creatures for thy sport or gust,
Yet cry, If man's unhappy, God's unjust;
If man alone engross not Heav'n's high care,
Alone made perfect here, immortal there:
Snatch from his hand the balance and the rod,
Rejudge his justice, be the God of God!
In pride, in reas'ning pride, our error lies;
All quit their sphere and rush into the skies.
Pride still is aiming at the blest abodes,
Men would be angels, angels would be gods.
Aspiring to be gods if angels fell,
Aspiring to be angels, men rebel:
And who but wishes to invert the laws
Of order, sins against the Eternal Cause.

V

Ask for what end the heav'nly bodies shine,
Earth for whose use? Pride answers, " 'Tis for mine!
For me kind Nature wakes her genial pow'r,
Suckles each herb, and spreads out ev'ry flow'r;
Annual for me, the grape, the rose renew
The juice nectarous and the balmy dew;
For me the mine a thousand treasures brings;
For me health gushes from a thousand springs;
Seas roll to waft me, suns to light me rise;
My footstool earth, my canopy the skies."
But errs not Nature from this gracious end,
From burning suns when livid deaths descend,
When earthquakes swallow, or when tempests sweep
Towns to one grave, whole nations to the deep?
"No," 'tis reply'd, "the first Almighty Cause
Acts not by partial but by gen'ral laws:
Th' exceptions few; some change since all began;
And what created perfect?"—Why then man?
If the great end be human happiness,
Then Nature deviates; and can man do less?
As much that end a constant course requires
Of show'rs and sunshine, as of man's desires:
As much eternal springs and cloudless skies,
As men forever temp'rate, calm, and wise.
If plagues or earthquakes break not Heav'n's design,
Why then a Borgia or a Catiline?
Who knows but he, whose hand the lightning forms,
Who heaves old ocean, and who wings the storms,
Pours fierce ambition in a Caesar's mind,
Or turns young Ammon loose to scourge mankind?
From pride, from pride our very reas'ning springs;
Account for moral, as for natural things:
Why charge we Heav'n in those, in these acquit?
In both, to reason right is to submit.
Better for us, perhaps, it might appear,
Were there all harmony, all virtue here;
That never air or ocean felt the wind;
That never passion discompos'd the mind.
But all subsists by elemental strife;
And passions are the elements of life.
The gen'ral order, since the whole began,
Is kept in Nature, and is kept in man.

VI

What would this man? Now upward will he soar,
And little less than angel, would be more!
Now looking downwards, just as griev'd appears
To want the strength of bulls, the fur of bears.
Made for his use all creatures if he call,
Say what their use, had he the pow'rs of all?
Nature to these, without profusion, kind,
The proper organs, proper pow'rs assign'd;
Each seeming want compensated of course,
Here with degrees of swiftness, there of force:
All in exact proportion to the state;
Nothing to add, and nothing to abate;
Each beast, each insect happy in its own:
Is Heav'n unkind to man, and man alone?
Shall he alone, whom rational we call,
Be pleas'd with nothing, if not bless'd with all?
The bliss of man (could pride that blessing find),
Is not to act or think beyond mankind;
No powers of body or of soul to share,
But what his nature and his state can bear.
Why has not man a microscopic eye?
For this plain reason, man is not a fly.
Say what the use, were finer optics giv'n,
To inspect a mite, not comprehend the heav'n?
Or touch, if tremblingly alive all o'er,
To smart and agonize at every pore?
Or quick effluvia darting through the brain,
Die of a rose in aromatic pain?
If Nature thunder'd in his opening ears,
And stunn'd him with the music of the spheres,
How would he wish that Heav'n had left him still
The whisp'ring zephyr and the purling rill?
Who finds not Providence all good and wise,
Alike in what it gives, and what denies?

VII

Far as creation's ample range extends,
The scale of sensual, mental powers ascends.
Mark how it mounts to man's imperial race,
From the green myriads in the peopled grass;
What modes of sight betwixt each wide extreme,
The mole's dim curtain, and the lynx's beam:
Of smell, the headlong lioness between,
And hound sagacious on the tainted green:
Of hearing, from the life that fills the flood,
To that which warbles through the vernal wood:
The spider's touch how exquisitely fine!
Feels at each thread, and lives along the line:
In the nice bee, what sense so subtly true
From pois'nous herbs extracts the healing dew?
How instinct varies in the grov'ling swine,
Compar'd, half-reas'ning elephant, with thine!
'Twixt that and reason, what a nice barrier;
Forever sep'rate, yet forever near!
Remembrance and reflection, how ally'd;
What thin partitions sense from thought divide;
And middle natures, how they long to join,
Yet never pass th' insuperable line!
Without this just gradation, could they be
Subjected, these to those, or all to thee?
The pow'rs of all subdu'd by thee alone,
Is not thy reason all these pow'rs in one?

VIII

See, through this air, this ocean, and this earth,
All matter quick, and bursting into birth.
Above, how high progressive life may go!
Around, how wide! how deep extend below!
Vast Chain of Being! which from God began,
Natures ethereal, human, angel, man,
Beast, bird, fish, insect, what no eye can see,
No glass can reach; from infinite to thee,
From thee to nothing. On superior pow'rs
Were we to press, inferior might on ours:
Or in the full creation leave a void,
Where, one step broken, the great scale's destroy'd:
From Nature's chain whatever link you strike,

Tenth or ten thousandth, breaks the chain alike.
And if each system in gradation roll
Alike essential to the amazing Whole,
The least confusion but in one, not all
That system only, but the Whole must fall.
Let earth unbalanc'd from her orbit fly,
Planets and suns run lawless through the sky;
Let ruling angels from their spheres be hurl'd,
Being on being wreck'd, and world on world;
Heav'n's whole foundations to their centre nod,
And Nature tremble to the throne of God!
All this dread Order break—for whom? for thee?
Vile worm!—Oh! madness! pride! impiety!

IX

What if the foot, ordain'd the dust to tread,
Or hand, to toil, aspir'd to be the head?
What if the head, the eye, or ear repin'd
To serve mere engines to the ruling Mind?
Just as absurd for any part to claim
To be another in this gen'ral frame;
Just as absurd to mourn the tasks or pains
The great directing Mind of All ordains.
All are but parts of one stupendous whole,
Whose body Nature is, and God the soul;
That, chang'd through all, and yet in all the same,
Great in the earth, as in th' ethereal frame,
Warms in the sun, refreshes in the breeze,
Glows in the stars, and blossoms in the trees,
Lives through all life, extends through all extent,
Spreads undivided, operates unspent;
Breathes in our soul, informs our mortal part,
As full, as perfect in a hair as heart;
As full, as perfect in vile man that mourns,
As the rapt seraph that adores and burns:
To him no high, no low, no great, no small;
He fills, he bounds, connects, and equals all.

X

Cease then, nor Order imperfection name:
Our proper bliss depends on what we blame.
Know thy own point: this kind, this due degree
Of blindness, weakness, Heav'n bestows on thee.
Submit: in this or any other sphere,
Secure to be as blest as thou canst bear;
Safe in the hand of one disposing Pow'r
Or in the natal, or the mortal hour.
All Nature is but art unknown to thee;
All chance, direction which thou canst not see;
All discord, harmony not understood;
All partial evil, universal good;
And, spite of pride, in erring reason's spite,
One truth is clear, *whatever is, is right.*

Epistle II

I

Know then thyself, presume not God to scan:
The proper study of mankind is Man.
Plac'd on this isthmus of a middle state,
A being darkly wise and rudely great:
With too much knowledge for the sceptic side,
With too much weakness for the Stoic's pride,
He hangs between; in doubt to act, or rest;
In doubt to deem himself a god or beast;
In doubt his mind or body to prefer;
Born but to die, and reas'ning but to err;
Alike in ignorance, his reason such,
Whether he thinks too little or too much:
Chaos of thought and passion, all confus'd;
Still by himself abus'd, or disabus'd;
Created half to rise, and half to fall;
Great lord of all things, yet a prey to all;
Sole judge of truth, in endless error hurl'd;
The glory, jest, and riddle of the world! . . .

II

Two principles in human nature reign;
Self-love to urge, and reason to restrain;
Nor this a good, nor that a bad we call,
Each works its end to move or govern all:
And to their proper operation still
Ascribe all good; to their improper, ill.
Self-love, the spring of motion, acts the soul;
Reason's comparing balance rules the whole.
Man, but for that, no action could attend,
And, but for this, were active to no end:
Fix'd like a plant on his peculiar spot,
To draw nutrition, propagate, and rot;
Or, meteor-like, flame lawless thro' the void,
Destroying others, by himself destroyed.
Most strength the moving principle requires;
Active its task, it prompts, impels, inspires.
Sedate and quiet, the comparing lies,
Form'd but to check, deliberate, and advise.
Self-love still stronger, as its objects nigh;
Reason's at distance and in prospect lie:
That sees immediate good by present sense;
Reason, the future and the consequence.
Thicker than arguments, temptations throng,
At best more watchful this, but that more strong.
The action of the stronger to suspend,
Reason still use, to reason still attend.
Attention, habit and experience gains;
Each strengthens reason, and self-love restrains . . .

V

Vice is a monster of so frightful mien,
As to be hated needs but to be seen;
Yet seen too oft, familiar with her face,
We first endure, then pity, then embrace:
But where the extreme of vice was ne'er agreed:
Ask where's the north? at York, 'tis on the Tweed;
In Scotland, at the Orcades; and there,
At Greenland, Zembla, or the Lord knows where.
No creature owns it in the first degree,
But thinks his neighbor farther gone than he;
Even those who dwell beneath its very zone;
Or never feel the rage, or never own;
What happier natures shrink at with affright
The hard inhabitant contends is right.

VI

Virtuous and vicious every man must be;
Few in the extreme, but all in the degree:
The rogue and fool by fits is fair and wise;
And ev'n the best, by fits, what they despise.
'Tis but by parts we follow good or ill;
For, vice or virtue, self directs it still;
Each individual seeks a sev'ral goal;
But Heav'n's great view is one, and that the whole . . .

Epistle III

Here then we rest: "The Universal Cause
Acts to one end, but acts by various laws."
In all the madness of superfluous health,
The trim of pride, the impudence of wealth,
Let this great truth be present night and day:
But most be present, if we preach or pray.

I

Look round our world, behold the chain of love
Combining all below and all above.
See plastic Nature working to this end:
The single atoms each to other tend;
Attract, attracted to, the next in place
Form'd and impell'd its neighbour to embrace.
See matter next with various life endu'd,
Press to one centre still, the gen'ral good.
See dying vegetables life sustain,
See life dissolving vegetate again:
All forms that perish other forms supply,
(By turns we catch the vital breath, and die.)
Like bubbles on the sea of matter borne,
They rise, they break, and to that sea return.
Nothing is foreign; parts relate to whole;
One all-extending, all-preserving soul
Connects each being, greatest with the least;
Made beast in aid of man, and man of beast;
All serv'd, all serving: nothing stands alone;
The chain holds on, and where it ends, unknown . . .

STUDY QUESTIONS

1. Pope speaks of man as the glory, the jest, and the riddle of the world. In what sense does he use each term? Name three men or women, or one person in three different situations, that would explain Pope's meaning.
2. Who would have given the more favorable review of the *Essay on Man* (if he could have read it!): Newton or the pope? Dante or Machiavelli? Shakespeare or Donne? Why do you think so?

Jonathan Swift, 1667–1745

Born in Ireland of English parents, Jonathan Swift (fig. 20.4) is identified with Ireland and its political troubles and yet, for most of his life, he tried to break away from Ireland. His dream of becoming an English bishop failed; instead he was awarded the deanship of St. Patrick's Cathedral in Dublin. At first feeling exiled in Ireland, he later became closely identified with its pervasive poverty and political privation.

A master of language employed in a lucid and forceful style, Swift was the greatest English satirist in an age of satire, perhaps because he was more detached, critically viewing English life and customs from his vantage point in Ireland. His masterpiece, *Gulliver's Travels* (1726), savagely exposed and attacked every human weakness and vice over there in England. His brilliant pamphlet, "A Modest Proposal," was written in the white heat of indignation. Ireland's poverty and misery, in his own words, did "tear his heart." His proposal is all the more horrendous in its reasoned logic as he ironically suggests a practical solution to the destitution of the downtrodden Irish.

LITERARY SELECTION 55

A Modest Proposal

for Preventing the Children of Poor People in Ireland from Being a Burden to Their Parents or Country, and for Making Them Beneficial to the Public

Jonathan Swift

It is a melancholy object to those who walk through this great town, or travel in the country, when they see the streets, the roads, and cabin-doors, crowded with beggars of the female sex, followed by three, four, or six children, all in rags, and importuning every passenger for an alms. These mothers, instead of being able to work for their honest livelihood, are forced to employ all their time in strolling to beg sustenance for their helpless infants: who, as they grow up, either turn thieves for want of work, or leave their dear native country to fight for the Pretender in Spain, or sell themselves to the Barbadoes.

I think it is agreed by all parties, that this prodigious number of children in the arms, or on the backs, or at the heels of their mothers, and frequently of their fathers, is, in the present deplorable state of the kingdom, a very great additional grievance; and, therefore, whoever could find out a fair, cheap, and easy method of making these children sound, useful members of the commonwealth, would deserve so well of the public, as to have his statue set up for a preserver of the nation.

But my intention is very far from being confined to provide only for the children of professed beggars; it is of a much greater extent, and shall take in the whole

20.4 Dean Jonathan Swift. Copperplate engraving. Photo: North Wind Picture Archives, Alfred, Maine.

number of infants at a certain age, who are born of parents in effect as little able to support them, as those who demand our charity in the streets.

As to my own part, having turned my thoughts for many years upon this important subject, and maturely weighed the several schemes of our projectors, I have always found them grossly mistaken in their computation. It is true, a child, just born, may be supported by its mother's milk for a solar year, with little other nourishment; at most, not above the value of two shillings, which the mother may certainly get, or the value in scraps, by her lawful occupation of begging; and it is exactly at one year old that I propose to provide for them in such a manner, as, instead of being a charge upon their parents, or the parish, or wanting food and raiment for the rest of their lives, they shall, on the contrary, contribute to the feeding, and partly to the clothing, of many thousands.

There is likewise another great advantage in my scheme, that it will prevent those voluntary abortions, and that horrid practice of women murdering their bastard children, alas, too frequent among us! sacrificing the poor innocent babes, I doubt more to avoid the expense than the shame, which would move tears and pity in the most savage and inhuman breast.

The number of souls in this kingdom being usually reckoned one million and a half, of these I calculate there may be about two hundred thousand couple whose wives are breeders; from which number I subtract thirty thousand couple, who are able to maintain their own children, (although I apprehend there cannot be so many, under the present distresses of the kingdom;) but this being granted, there will remain a hundred and seventy thousand breeders. I again subtract fifty thousand, for those women who miscarry, or whose children die by accident or disease within the year. There only remain a hundred and twenty thousand children of poor parents annually born. The question therefore is, How this number shall be reared and provided for? which, as I have already said, under the present situation of affairs, is utterly impossible by all the methods hitherto proposed. For we can neither employ them in handicraft or agriculture; we neither build houses (I mean in the country,) nor cultivate land: they can very seldom pick up a livelihood by stealing, till they arrive at six years old, except where they are of towardly parts; although I confess they learn the rudiments much earlier; during which time they can, however, be properly looked upon only as probationers; as I have been informed by a principal gentleman in the county of Cavan, who protested to me, that he never knew above one or two instances under the age of six, even in a part of the kingdom so renowned for the quickest proficiency in that art.

I am assured by our merchants, that a boy or a girl before twelve years old is no saleable commodity; and even when they come to this age they will not yield above three pounds or three pounds and half-a-crown at most, on the exchange; which cannot turn to account either to the parents or kingdom, the charge of nutriment and rags having been at least four times that value.

I shall now, therefore, humbly propose my own thoughts, which I hope will not be liable to the least objection.

I have been assured by a very knowing American of my acquaintance in London, that a young healthy child, well nursed, is, at a year old, a most delicious, nourishing, and wholesome food, whether stewed, roasted, baked, or boiled; and I make no doubt that it will equally serve in a fricassee or a ragout.

I do therefore humbly offer it to public consideration, that of the hundred and twenty thousand children already computed, twenty thousand may be reserved for breed, whereof only one-fourth part to be males; which is more than we allow to sheep, black-cattle, or swine; and my reason is, that these children are seldom the fruits of marriage, a circumstance not much regarded by our savages, therefore one male will be sufficient for four females. That the remaining hundred thousand may, at a year old, be offered in sale to the persons of quality and fortune through the kingdom; always advising the mother to let them suck plentifully in the last month, so as to render them plump and fat for a good table. A child will make two dishes at an entertainment for friends; and when the family dines alone, the fore or hind quarter will make a reasonable dish, and, seasoned with a little pepper or salt, will be very good boiled on the fourth day, especially in winter.

I have reckoned, upon a medium, that a child just born will weigh twelve pounds, and in a solar year, if tolerably nursed, will increase to twenty-eight pounds.

I grant this food will be somewhat dear, and therefore very proper for landlords, who, as they have already devoured most of the parents, seem to have the best title to the children.

Infants' flesh will be in season throughout the year, but more plentifully in March, and a little before and after: for we are told by a grave author, an eminent French physician, that fish being a prolific diet, there are more children born in Roman Catholic countries about nine months after Lent, than at any other season; therefore, reckoning a year after Lent, the markets will be more glutted than usual, because the number of Popish infants is at least three to one in this kingdom; and therefore it will have one other collateral advantage, by lessening the number of Papists among us.

I have already computed the charge of nursing a beggar's child (in which list I reckon all cottagers, labourers, and four-fifths of the farmers) to be about two shillings per annum, rags included; and I believe no gentleman would repine to give ten shillings for the carcass of a good fat child, which, as I have said, will make four dishes of excellent nutritive meat, when he has only some particular friend, or his own family, to dine with him. Thus the squire will learn to be a good landlord, and grow popular among his tenants; the mother will have eight shillings net profit, and be fit for work till she produces another child.

Those who are more thrifty (as I must confess the times require) may flay the carcass; the skin of which, artificially dressed, will make admirable gloves for ladies, and summer-boots for fine gentlemen. As to our city of Dublin, shambles may be appointed for this purpose in the most convenient parts of it, and butchers we may be assured will not be wanting; although I rather recommend buying the children alive, then dressing them hot from the knife, as we do roasting pigs.

A very worthy person, a true lover of his country, and whose virtues I highly esteem, was lately pleased, in discoursing on this matter, to offer a refinement upon my scheme. He said, that many gentlemen of this kingdom, having of late destroyed their deer, he conceived that the want of venison might be well supplied by the bodies of young lads and maidens, not exceeding fourteen years of age, nor under twelve; so great a number of both sexes in every country being now ready to starve for want of work and service; and these to be disposed of by their parents, if alive, or otherwise by their nearest relations. But, with due deference to so excellent a friend, and so deserving a patriot, I cannot be altogether in his sentiments; for as to the males, my American acquaintance assured me, from frequent experience, that their flesh was generally tough and lean, like that of our schoolboys, by continual exercise, and their taste disagreeable; and to fatten them would not answer the charge. Then as to the females, it would, I think, with humble submission, be a loss to the public, because they soon would become breeders themselves: and besides, it is not improbable that some scrupulous people might be apt to censure such a practice, (although indeed very unjustly,) as a little bordering upon cruelty; which, I confess, has always been with me the strongest objection against any project, how well soever intended.

But in order to justify my friend, he confessed that this expedient was put into his head by the famous Psalmanazar, a native of the island Formosa, who came from thence to London above twenty years ago; and in conversation told my friend, that in his country, when any young person happened to be put to death, the executioner sold the carcass to persons of quality as a prime dainty; and that in his time the body of a plump girl of fifteen, who was crucified for an attempt to poison the emperor, was sold to his imperial majesty's prime minister of state, and other great mandarins of the court, in joints from the gibbet, at four hundred crowns. Neither indeed can I deny, that if the same use were made of several plump young girls in this town, who, without one single groat to their fortunes, cannot stir abroad without a chair, and appear at playhouse and assemblies in foreign fineries which they never will pay for, the kingdom would not be the worse.

Some persons of a desponding spirit are in great concern about that vast number of poor people, who are aged, diseased, or maimed; and I have been desired to employ my thoughts, what course may be taken to ease the nation of so grievous an encumbrance. But I am not in the least pain upon that matter, because it is very well known, that they are every day dying, and rotting, by cold and famine, and filth and vermin, as fast as can be reasonably expected. And as to the young labourers, they are now in almost as hopeful a condition: they cannot get work, and consequently pine away for want of nourishment, to a degree, that if at any time they are accidentally hired to common labour, they have not strength to perform it; and thus the country and themselves are happily delivered from the evils to come.

I have too long digressed, and therefore shall return to my subject. I think the advantages by the proposal which I have made, are obvious and many, as well as of the highest importance.

For first, as I have already observed, it would greatly lessen the number of Papists, with whom we are yearly over-run, being the principal breeders of the nation, as well as our most dangerous enemies; and who stay at home on purpose to deliver the kingdom to the Pretender, hoping to take their advantage by the absence of so many good Protestants, who have chosen rather to leave their country, than stay at home and pay tithes against their conscience to an Episcopal curate.

Secondly, The poorer tenants will have something valuable of their own, which by law may be made liable to distress, and help to pay their landlord's rent; their corn and cattle being already seized, and money a thing unknown.

Thirdly, Whereas the maintenance of a hundred thousand children, from two years old and upward, cannot be computed at less than ten shillings a piece per annum, the nation's stock will be thereby increased fifty thousand pounds per annum, beside the profit of a new dish introduced to the tables of all gentlemen of fortune in the kingdom, who have any refinement in taste. And the money will circulate among ourselves, the goods being entirely of our own growth and manufacture.

Fourthly, The constant breeders, beside the gain of eight shillings sterling per annum by the sale of their children, will be rid of the charge of maintaining them after the first year.

Fifthly, This food would likewise bring great custom to taverns; where the vintners will certainly be so prudent as to procure the best receipts for dressing it to perfection, and, consequently, have their houses frequented by all the fine gentlemen, who justly value themselves upon their knowledge in good eating: and a skilful cook, who understands how to oblige his guests, will contrive to make it as expensive as they please.

Sixthly, This would be a great inducement to marriage,

which all wise nations have either encouraged by rewards, or enforced by laws and penalties. It would increase the care and tenderness of mothers toward their children, when they were sure of a settlement for life to the poor babes, provided in some sort by the public, to their annual profit or expense. We should see an honest emulation among the married women, which of them could bring the fattest child to the market. Men would become as fond of their wives during the time of their pregnancy, as they are now of their mares in foal, their cows in calf, their sows when they are ready to farrow; nor offer to beat or kick them (as is too frequent a practice) for fear of a miscarriage.

Many other advantages might be enumerated. For instance, the addition of some thousand carcasses in our exportation of barrelled beef; the propagation of swine's flesh, and improvement in the art of making good bacon, so much wanted among us by the great destruction of pigs, too frequent at our table; which are no way comparable in taste or magnificence to a well-grown, fat, yearling child, which, roasted whole, will make a considerable figure at a lord mayor's feast, or any other public entertainment. But this, and many others, I omit, being studious of brevity.

Supposing that one thousand families in this city would be constant customers for infants' flesh, beside others who might have it at merry-meetings, particularly at weddings and christenings, I compute that Dublin would take off annually about twenty thousand carcasses; and the rest of the kingdom (where probably they will be sold somewhat cheaper) the remaining eighty thousand.

I can think of no one objection, that will possibly be raised against this proposal, unless it should be urged, that the number of people will be thereby much lessened in the kingdom. This I freely own, and it was indeed one principal design in offering it to the world. I desire the reader will observe, that I calculate my remedy for this one individual kingdom of Ireland, and for no other that ever was, is, or I think ever can be, upon earth. Therefore let no man talk to me of other expedients: of taxing our absentees at five shillings a pound: of using neither clothes, nor household-furniture, except what is our own growth and manufacture: of utterly rejecting the materials and instruments that promote foreign luxury: of curing the expensiveness of pride, vanity, idleness, and gaming in our women; of introducing a vein of parsimony, prudence, and temperance: of learning to love our country, in the want of which we differ even from LAPLANDERS, and the inhabitants of TOPINAMBOO: of quitting our animosities and factions, nor acting any longer like the Jews, who were murdering one another at the very moment their city was taken: of being a little cautious not to sell our country and conscience for nothing: of teaching landlords to have at least one degree of mercy toward their tenants: lastly, of putting a spirit of honesty, industry, and skill into our shopkeepers; who, if a resolution could now be taken to buy only our native goods, would immediately unite to cheat and exact upon us in the price, the measure, and the goodness, nor could ever yet be brought to make one fair proposal of just dealing, though often and earnestly invited to it.

Therefore I repeat, let no man talk to me of these and the like expedients, till he has at least some glimpse of hope, that there will be ever some hearty and sincere attempt to put them in practice. But, as to myself, having been wearied out for many years with offering vain, idle, visionary thoughts, and at length utterly despairing of success, I fortunately fell upon this proposal; which, as it is wholly new, so it has something solid and real, of no expense and little trouble, full in our own power, and whereby we can incur no danger in disobliging ENGLAND. For this kind of commodity will not bear exportation, the flesh being of too tender a consistence to admit a long continuance in salt, although perhaps I could name a country, which would be glad to eat up our whole nation without it.

After all, I am not so violently bent upon my own opinion as to reject any offer proposed by wise men, which shall be found equally innocent, cheap, easy, and effectual. But before something of that kind shall be advanced in contradiction to my scheme, and offering a better, I desire the author, or authors, will be pleased maturely to consider two points. First, as things now stand, how they will be able to find food and raiment for a hundred thousand useless mouths and backs. And, secondly, there being a round million of creatures in human figure throughout this kingdom, whose whole subsistence put into a common stock would leave them in debt two millions of pounds sterling, adding those who are beggars by profession, to the bulk of farmers, cottagers, and labourers, with the wives and children who are beggars in effect; I desire those politicians who dislike my overture, and may perhaps be so bold as to attempt an answer, that they will first ask the parents of these mortals, whether they would not at this day think it a great happiness to have been sold for food at a year old, in the manner I prescribe, and thereby have avoided such a perpetual scene of misfortunes, as they have since gone through, by the oppression of landlords, the impossibility of paying rent without money or trade, the want of common sustenance, with neither house nor clothes to cover them from the inclemencies of the weather, and the most inevitable prospect of entailing the like, or greater miseries, upon their breed for ever.

I profess, in the sincerity of my heart, that I have not the least personal interest in endeavouring to promote this necessary work, having no other motive than the public good of my country, by advancing our trade, providing for infants, relieving the poor, and giving some pleasure to the rich. I have no children by which I can propose to get a single penny; the youngest being nine years old, and my wife past child-bearing.

---

21. Westphalia—one of the small Prussian states of Germany.
22. Almoner—official whose duty is to distribute alms.
23. This is not far from Pope's statement, "Whatever is, is right." Actually it comes from the German philosopher, Leibniz.

STUDY QUESTIONS

The Irish complained that "the English are devouring the Irish." Swift turned the metaphor into "A Modest Proposal." Disregarding the actual subject matter for the moment, is this proposal rational and practical? Will it help relieve poverty by reducing the population while increasing family incomes? If you answered these questions in the affirmative, you are beginning to appreciate the intellectual nature of satire, for satire must be logical and persuasive if it is to accomplish its purpose. The proposal is made all the more horrible by Swift's dispassionate tone and flawless logic.

Voltaire (François Marie de Arouet), 1694–1778

As philosopher, critic, and writer, Voltaire was the preeminent intellectual of the Enlightenment. A tireless opponent of the *ancien régime* of the Bourbon kings and of the Church of Rome, he was twice imprisoned in the Bastille (1717, 1726) and exiled in 1726. In England his studies of Newton and Locke reinforced his hatred of absolutism and heightened his admiration of English liberalism. On his return to France he published a veritable torrent of works that criticized all the existing conditions. Pope had written, "Whatever is, is right," but Voltaire's motto might well have been, "Whatever is, is wrong," especially in France.

Voltaire first sought his freedom at the court of Frederick the Great, where he lived for three years, but found the German king as arrogant a despot as the French monarch. So he established himself near Geneva, where he spent most of the last quarter century of his life. Some of his critics questioned Voltaire's sincerity, for he was always concerned with his personal comfort and wealth; he certainly displayed no concern for the cause of freedom when he sought Frederick's protection.

Whatever one may say of Voltaire's personal life, his doubting and skeptical works found a wide and receptive audience. Of his incredible output *Candide* was as important as anything he ever wrote, for it ridiculed everything that Europe held dear. The champion debunker of the age, Voltaire faced the dilemma that confronts all debunkers: he had little better to offer. Everything in his world seemed futile and silly: the "glories" of war; the church, both Catholic and Protestant; even nature itself. All was senseless and unreasonable. He has Candide suggest retirement to a farm, where one can at least cultivate one's garden. Whether or not he speaks for Voltaire is an open question.

Voltaire's critical contribution was an unerring pen that targeted the faults of his age, a mighty weapon helping spark the revolutions that doomed absolutism. Perhaps the painter Jacques Louis David best summarized Voltaire's legacy. During the ceremony of 10 July 1791, when Voltaire's body was transferred to an honored site in the Pantheon, David said, simply: "He taught us to be free."

LITERARY SELECTION 56

Candide

Voltaire

In a castle of Westphalia,[21] belonging to the Baron of Thunder-ten-Tronckh, lived a youth whom nature had endowed with the most gentle manners. His countenance was a true picture of his soul. He combined a true judgment with simplicity of spirit, which was the reason, I apprehend, of his being called Candide. The old servants of the family suspected him to have been the son of the Baron's sister, by a good, honest gentleman of the neighborhood, whom that young lady would never marry because he had been able to prove only seventy-one quarterings, the rest of his genealogical tree having been lost through the injuries of time.

The Baron was one of the most powerful lords in Westphalia, for his castle had not only a gate, but windows. His great hall, even, was hung with tapestry. All the dogs of his farmyards formed a pack of hounds at need; his grooms were his huntsmen; and the curate of the village was his grand almoner.[22] They called him "My Lord," and laughed at all his stories.

The Baron's lady weighed about three hundred and fifty pounds, and was therefore a person of great consideration, and she did the honors of the house with a dignity that commanded still greater respect. Her daughter Cunegonde was seventeen years of age, fresh-colored, comely, plump, and desirable. The Baron's son seemed to be in every respect worthy of his father. The Preceptor Pangloss was the oracle of the family, and little Candide heard his lessons with all the good faith of his age and character.

Pangloss was professor of metaphysicotheologico-cosmolo-nigology. He proved admirably that there is no effect without a cause, and that in this best of all possible worlds, the Baron's castle was the most magnificent of castles, and his lady the best of all possible Baronesses.

"It is demonstrable," said he, "that things cannot be otherwise than as they are; for all being created for an end, all is necessarily for the best end. Observe, that the nose has been formed to bear spectacles—thus we have spectacles. Legs are visibly designed for stockings—and we have stockings. Stones were made to be hewn, and to construct castles—therefore my lord has a magnificent castle; for the greatest baron in the province ought to be the best lodged. Pigs were made to be eaten—therefore we eat pork all the year round. Consequently they who assert that all is well have said a foolish thing; they should have said all is for the best."[23]

Candide listened attentively and believed innocently;

for he thought Miss Cunegonde extremely beautiful, though he never had the courage to tell her so. He concluded that after the happiness of being born of the Baron of Thunder-ten-Tronckh, the second degree of happiness was to be Miss Cunegonde, the third that of seeing her every day, and the fourth that of hearing Master Pangloss, the greatest philosopher of the whole world.

One day when Miss Cunegonde went to take a walk in a little neighboring wood which was called a park, she saw, through the bushes, the sage Doctor Pangloss giving a lecture in experimental philosophy to her mother's chambermaid, a little brown wench, very pretty, and very tractable. As Miss Cunegonde had a great disposition for the sciences, she observed with the utmost attention the experiments which were repeated before her eyes; she perfectly well understood the force of the doctor's reasoning upon causes and effects. She retired greatly flurried, quite pensive and filled with the desire of knowledge, imagining that she might well be a *sufficient reason* for young Candide, her cousin, and he for her.

She met Candide on reaching the castle and blushed; Candide blushed also; she wished him good morrow in a faltering tone, and Candide spoke to her without knowing what he said. The next day after dinner, as they went from table, Cunegonde and Candide found themselves behind a screen; Cunegonde let fall her handkerchief, Candide picked it up, she took him innocently by the hand, the youth as innocently kissed the young lady's hand with particular vivacity, sensibility, and grace; their lips met, their eyes sparkled, their knees trembled. Baron Thunder-ten-Tronckh passed near the screen and beholding this cause and effect chased Candide from the castle with great kicks; Cunegonde fainted away; she was boxed on the ears by the Baroness, as soon as she came to herself; and all was consternation in this most magnificent and most agreeable of all possible castles.

Candide, driven from this terrestrial paradise, walked a long while without knowing where, weeping, raising his eyes to heaven, turning them often toward the most magnificent of castles which imprisoned the purest of noble young ladies. He lay down to sleep without supper, in the middle of a field between two furrows. The snow fell in large flakes. Next day Candide, all benumbed, dragged himself towards the neighboring town which was called Waldberghofftrarbkdikdorff. Having no money, dying of hunger and fatigue, he stopped sorrowfully at the door of an inn. Two men dressed in blue observed him.

"Comrade," said one, "here is a well-built young fellow, and of proper height."

They went up to Candide and very civilly invited him to dinner.

"Gentlemen," replied Candide, with a most engaging modesty, "you do me great honor, but I have not wherewithal to pay my share."

"Oh, sir," said one of the blues to him, "people of your appearance and of your merit never pay anything: are you not five feet five inches high?"

"Yes, sir, that is my height," answered he, making a low bow.

"Come, sir, seat yourself; not only will we pay your reckoning, but we will never suffer such a man as you to want money; men are only born to assist one another."

"You are right," said Candide; "this is what I was always taught by Mr. Pangloss, and I see plainly that all is for the best."

They begged of him to accept a few crowns. He took them, and wished to give them his note; they refused; they seated themselves at table.

"Love you not deeply?"

"Oh, yes," answered he; "I deeply love Miss Cunegonde."

"No," said one of the gentlemen, "we ask you if you do not deeply love the King of the Bulgarians?"

"Not at all," said he; "for I have never seen him."

"What! he is the best of kings, and we must drink his health."

"Oh! very willingly, gentlemen," and he drank.

"That is enough," they told him. "Now you are the help, the support, the defender, the hero of the Bulgarians. Your fortune is made, and your glory is assured."

Instantly they fettered him, and carried him away to the regiment. There he was made to wheel about to the right, and to the left, to draw his rammer,[24] to return his rammer, to present, to fire, to march, and they gave him thirty blows with a cudgel. The next day he did his exercise a little less badly, and he received but twenty blows. The following they gave him only ten, and he was regarded by his comrades as a prodigy.

Candide, all stupefied, could not yet very well realize how he was a hero. He resolved one fine day in spring to go for a walk, marching straight before him, believing that it was a privilege of the human as well as of the animal species to make use of their legs as they pleased. He had advanced two leagues when he was overtaken by four others, heroes of six feet, who bound him and carried him to a dungeon. He was asked which he would like the best, to be whipped six-and-thirty times through all the regiment, or to receive at once twelve balls of lead in his brain. He vainly said that human will is free, and that he chose neither the one nor the other. He was forced to make a choice; he determined, in virtue of that gift of God called liberty, to run the gauntlet six-and-thirty times. He bore this twice. The regiment was composed of two thousand men; that composed for him four thousand strokes, which laid bare all his muscles and nerves, from the nape of his neck quite down to his rump. As they were going to proceed to a third whipping, Candide, able to bear no more, begged as a favor that they would be so good as to shoot him. He obtained this favor; they bandaged his eyes and bade him kneel down. The King of the Bulgarians passed at this moment and ascertained the nature of the crime. As he had great talent, he understood from all that he learned of Candide that he was a young metaphysician, extremely ignorant of the things of this world, and he accorded him his pardon with a clemency which will bring him praise in all the journals, and throughout all ages.

An able surgeon cured Candide in three weeks by means of emollients taught by Dioscorides.[25] He had already a little skin, and was able to march when the King of the Bulgarians gave battle to the King of the Abares.

There was never anything so gallant, so spruce, so brilliant, and so well disposed as the two armies. Trumpets, fifes, hautboys,[26] drums, and cannon made music such as Hell itself had never heard. The cannons first of all laid flat about six thousand men on each side; the muskets swept away from this best of worlds nine or ten thousand ruffians who infested its surface. The bayonet was also a *sufficient reason* for the death of several thousands. The whole might amount to thirty thousand souls. Candide, who trembled like a philosopher, hid himself as well as he could during this heroic butchery.

At length, while the two kings were causing *Te Deum*[27] to be sung each in his own camp, Candide resolved to go and reason elsewhere on effects and causes. He passed over heaps of dead and dying, and first reached a neighboring village; it was in cinders; it was an Abare village which the Bulgarians had burnt according to the laws of war. Here, old men covered with wounds beheld their wives, hugging their children to their bloody breasts, massacred before their faces; there, their daughters, disemboweled and breathing their last after having satisfied the natural wants of Bulgarian heroes, while others, half burnt in the flames, begged to be dispatched. The earth was strewn with brains, arms, and legs.

Candide fled quickly to another village; it belonged to the Bulgarians; and the Abarian heroes had treated it in the same way. Candide, walking always over palpitating limbs or across ruins, arrived at last beyond the seat of war, with a few provisions in his knapsack, and Miss Cunegonde always in his heart. His provisions failed him when he arrived in Holland; but having heard that everyone was rich in that country, and that they were Christians, he did not doubt but he should meet with the same treatment from them as he had met with in the Baron's castle, before Miss Cunegonde's bright eyes were the cause of his expulsion thence.

He asked alms of several grave-looking people, who all answered him that if he continued to follow this trade they would confine him to the house of correction, where he should be taught to get a living.

The next he addressed was a man who had been haranguing a large assembly for a whole hour on the subject of charity. But the orator, looking askew, said:

"What are you doing here? Are you for the good cause?"

"There can be no effect without a cause," modestly answered Candide; "the whole is necessarily concatenated and arranged for the best. It was necessary for me to have been banished from the presence of Miss Cunegonde, to have afterwards run the gauntlet, and now it is necessary I should beg my bread until I learn to earn it; all this cannot be otherwise."

"My friend," said the orator to him, "do you believe the Pope to be Anti-Christ?"

"I have not heard it," answered Candide; "but whether he be, or whether he be not, I want bread."

"Thou dost not deserve to eat," said the other. "Begone, rogue; begone, wretch; do not come near me again."

The orator's wife, putting her head out of the window, and spying a man that doubted whether the Pope was Anti-Christ, poured over him a full bucket of slops. Oh, heavens! to what excess does religious zeal carry the ladies.

A man who had never been christened, a good Anabaptist, named James, beholding the cruel and ignominious treatment shown to one of his brethren, an unfeathered biped with a rational soul, he took him home, cleaned him, gave him bread and beer, presented him with two florins, and even wished to teach him the manufacture of Persian stuffs, which they make in Holland. Candide, almost prostrating himself before him, cried:

"Master Pangloss has well said that all is for the best in this world, for I am infinitely more touched by your extreme generosity than with the inhumanity of that gentleman in the black coat and his lady."

The next day, as he took a walk, he met a beggar all covered with scabs, his eyes diseased, the end of his nose eaten away, his mouth distorted, his teeth black, choking in his throat, tormented with a violent cough, and spitting out a tooth at each effort.

Candide, yet more moved with compassion than with horror, gave to this shocking beggar the two florins which he had received from the honest Anabaptist James. The specter looked at him very earnestly, dropped a few tears, and fell upon his neck. Candide recoiled in disgust.

"Alas!" said one wretch to the other, "do you no longer know your dear Pangloss?"

"What do I hear? You, my dear master! You in this terrible plight! What misfortune has happened to you? Why are you no longer in the most magnificent of castles? What has become of Miss Cunegonde, the pearl of girls, and nature's masterpiece?"

"I am so weak that I cannot stand," said Pangloss.

Upon which Candide carried him to the Anabaptist's stable, and gave him a crust of bread. As soon as Pangloss had refreshed himself a little:

"Well," said Candide, "Cunegonde?"

"She is dead," replied the other.

Candide fainted at this word; his friend recalled his senses with a little bad vinegar which he found by chance in the stable. Candide reopened his eyes.

"Cunegonde is dead! Ah, best of worlds, where art thou? But of what illness did she die? Was it not for grief, upon seeing her father kick me out of his magnificent castle?"

"No," said Pangloss, "she was stabbed by the Bulgarian soldiers, they broke the Baron's head for attempting to defend her; my lady, her mother, was cut in pieces; my poor pupil was served just in the same manner as his sister; and as for the castle, they have not

24. Rammer—rod with which to load a muzzle-loading rifle.
25. Dioscorides—ancient Greek medical writer.
26. Hautboys—old form of the modern oboe.
27. Te Deum—canticle of the church in praise of God, used by France to celebrate military victory.

left one stone upon another, not a bar, nor a sheep, nor a duck, nor a tree; but we have had our revenge, for the Abares have done the very same thing to a neighboring barony, which belonged to a Bulgarian lord. . . "

"Well, this is wonderful!" said Candide, "but you must be cured."

"Alas! how can I?" said Pangloss. "I have not a farthing, my friend, and all over the globe there is no letting of blood or taking a glister[28] without paying, or somebody paying for you."

These last words determined Candide; he went and flung himself at the feet of the charitable Anabaptist James, and gave him so touching a picture of the state to which his friend was reduced that the good man did not scruple to take Dr. Pangloss into his house, and had him cured at his expense. In the cure Pangloss lost only an eye and an ear. He wrote well, and knew arithmetic perfectly. The Anabaptist James made him his bookkeeper. At the end of two months, being obliged to go by sea to Lisbon about some mercantile affairs, he took the two philosophers with him in his ship. Pangloss explained to him how everything was so constituted that it could not be better. James was not of this opinion.

"It is more likely," said he, "mankind have a little corrupted nature, for men were not born wolves, and they have become wolves; God has given them neither cannon or four-and-twenty pounders nor bayonets; and yet they have made cannon and bayonets to destroy one another. Into this account I might throw not only bankrupts, but Justice which seizes on the effects of bankrupts to cheat the creditors."

"All this was indispensable," replied the one-eyed doctor, "for private misfortunes make the general good, so that the more private misfortunes there are the greater is the general good."

While he reasoned, the sky darkened, the winds blew from the four quarters, and the ship was assailed by a most terrible tempest within sight of the port of Lisbon.

Half dead of that inconceivable anguish which the rolling of a ship produces, one half of the passengers were not even sensible of the danger. The other half shrieked and prayed. The sheets were rent, the masts broken, the vessel gaped. Work who would, no one heard, no one commanded. The Anabaptist, being upon deck, bore a hand; then a brutish sailor struck him roughly and laid him sprawling; but with the violence of the blow he himself tumbled head foremost overboard, and struck upon a piece of the broken mast. Honest James ran to his assistance, hauled him up, and from the effort he made was precipitated into the sea in sight of the sailor, who left him to perish, without deigning to look at him. Candide drew near and saw his benefactor, who rose above the water one moment and was then swallowed up forever. He was just going to jump after him, but was prevented by the philosopher Pangloss, who demonstrated to him that the Bay of Lisbon had been made on purpose for the Anabaptist to be drowned. While he was proving this *a priori*, the ship foundered; all perished except Pangloss, Candide, and the brutal sailor who had drowned the good Anabaptist. The villain swam safely to the shore, while Pangloss and Candide were borne thither upon a plank.

As soon as they recovered themselves a little, they walked toward Lisbon. They had some money left, with which they hoped to save themselves from starving, after they had escaped drowning. Scarcely had they reached the city, lamenting the death of their benefactor, when they felt the earth tremble under their feet. The sea swelled and foamed in the harbor and beat to pieces the vessels riding at anchor. Whirlwinds of fire and ashes covered the streets and public places, houses fell, roofs were flung upon the pavements, and the pavements were scattered. Thirty thousand inhabitants of all ages and sexes were crushed under the ruins. The sailor, whistling and swearing, said booty was to be gained here.

"What can be the *sufficient reason* of this phenomenon?" said Pangloss.

"This is the Last Day!" cried Candide.

The sailor ran among the ruins, facing death to find money; finding it, he took it, and got drunk . . . .

Some falling stones had wounded Candide. He lay stretched in the street covered with rubbish.

"Alas!" said he to Pangloss, "get me a little wine and oil; I am dying."

"This concussion of the earth is no new thing," answered Pangloss. "The city of Lima, in America, experienced the same convulsions last year; the same cause, the same effects; there is certainly a train of sulphur underground from Lima to Lisbon."

"Nothing more probable," said Candide; "but for the love of God get me a little oil and wine."

"How, probable?" replied the philosopher. "I maintain that the point is capable of being demonstrated."

Candide fainted away, and Pangloss fetched him some water from a neighboring fountain. The following day they rummaged among the ruins and found provisions, with which they repaired their exhausted strength. After this they joined with others in relieving those inhabitants who had escaped death. Some, whom they had succored, gave them as good a dinner as they could in such disastrous circumstances; true, the repast was mournful, and the company moistened their bread with tears; but Pangloss consoled them, assuring them that things could not be otherwise.

"For," said he, "all that is is for the best. If there is a volcano at Lisbon it cannot be elsewhere. It is impossible that things should be other than they are; for everything is right."

[In the passage which follows, Candide is whipped and Pangloss is hanged. Candide then meets Cunegonde, who had not been killed in Westphalia. Candide kills two men and flees with Cunegonde and her maid, an old woman, to Cadiz.]

Candide, Cunegonde, and the old woman, having passed through Lucena, Chillas, and Lebrixa, arrived at length at Cadiz. A fleet was there getting ready, and troops assembling to bring to reason the reverend Jesuit Fathers of Paraguay, accused of having made one of the native tribes in the neighborhood of San Sacrament revolt against the kings of Spain and Portugal. Candide, having

28. Glister—a medical treatment.

been in the Bulgarian service, performed the military exercise before the general of this little army with so graceful an address, with so intrepid an air, and with such agility and expedition, that he was given the command of a company of foot. Now, he was a captain! He set sail with Miss Cunegonde, the old woman, two valets, and two Andalusian horses, which had belonged to the Grand Inquisitor of Portugal.

During their voyage they reasoned a good deal on the philosophy of poor Pangloss.

"We are going into another world," said Candide; "and surely it must be there that all is for the best. For I must confess there is reason to complain a little of what passeth in our world in regard to both natural and moral philosophy."

"I love you with all my heart," said Cunegonde; "but my soul is still full of fright at that which I have seen and experienced."

"All will be well," replied Candide; "the sea of this new world is already better than our European sea; it is calmer, the winds more regular. It is certainly the New World which is the best of all possible worlds."

[After landing in Buenos Aires, Candide and his valet, Cacambo, are separated from Cunegonde. Then, Candide, in self-defense, kills an inquisitor, and the two men are forced to flee over much of South America.]

"You see," said Cacambo to Candide, as soon as they had reached the frontiers of the Oreillons, "that this hemisphere is not better than the other, take my word for it; let us go back to Europe by the shortest way."

"How go back?" said Candide, "and where shall we go? to my own country? The Bulgarians and the Abares are slaying all; to Portugal? there I shall be burnt; and if we abide here, we are every moment in danger of being spitted. But how can I resolve to quit a part of the world where my dear Cunegonde resides?"

"Let us turn toward Cayenne," said Cacambo; "there we shall find Frenchmen, who wander all over the world; they may assist us; God will perhaps have pity on us."

It was not easy to get to Cayenne; they knew vaguely in which direction to go, but rivers, precipices, robbers, savages obstructed them all the way. Their horses died of fatigue. Their provisions were consumed; they fed a whole month upon wild fruits, and found themselves at last near a little river bordered with cocoa trees, which sustained their lives and their hopes.

Cacambo, who was a good counselor, said to Candide:

"We are able to hold out no longer; we have walked enough. I see an empty canoe near the riverside; let us fill it with cocoa-nuts, throw ourselves into it, and go with the current; a river always leads to some inhabited spot. If we do not find pleasant things, we shall at least find new things."

"With all my heart," said Candide; "let us recommend ourselves to Providence."

They rowed a few leagues, between banks, in some places flowery, in others barren; in some parts smooth, in others rugged. The stream widened, and at length lost itself under an arch of frightful rocks which reached to the sky. The two travelers had the courage to commit themselves to the current. The river, suddenly contracting at this place, whirled them along with a dreadful noise and rapidity. At the end of four-and-twenty hours they saw daylight again, but their canoe was dashed to pieces against the rocks. For a league they had to creep from rock to rock, until at length they discovered an extensive plain, bounded by inaccessible mountains. The country was cultivated as much for pleasure as for necessity. On all sides the useful was also the beautiful. The roads were covered, or rather adorned, with carriages of a glittering form and substance, in which were men and women of surprising beauty, drawn by large red sheep which surpassed in fleetness the finest coursers of Andalusia, Tetuan, and Mequinez.

"Here, however, is a country," said Candide, "which is better than Westphalia."

He stepped out with Cacambo toward the first village which he saw. Some children dressed in tattered brocades played at quoits on the outskirts. Our travelers from the other world amused themselves by looking on. The quoits were large round pieces, yellow, red, and green, which cast a singular luster! The travelers picked a few of them off the ground; this was of gold, that of emeralds, the other of rubies—the least of them would have been the greatest ornament on the Mogul's throne.

"Without doubt," said Cacambo, "these children must be the king's sons that are playing at quoits!"

The village schoolmaster appeared at this moment and called them to school.

"There," said Candide, "is the preceptor of the royal family."

The little truants immediately quitted their game, leaving the quoits on the ground with all their other playthings. Candide gathered them up, ran to the master, and presented them to him in a most humble manner, giving him to understand by signs that their royal highnesses had forgotten their gold and jewels. The schoolmaster, smiling, flung them upon the ground; then, looking at Candide with a good deal of surprise, went about his business.

The travelers, however, took care to gather up the gold, the rubies, and the emeralds.

"Where are we?" cried Candide. "The king's children in this country must be well brought up, since they are taught to despise gold and precious stones."

Cacambo was as much surprised as Candide. At length they drew near the first house in the village. It was built like an European palace. A crowd of people pressed about the door, and there were still more in the house. They heard most agreeable music, and were aware of a delicious odor of cooking. Cacambo went up to the door and heard they were talking Peruvian; it was his mother's tongue, for it is well known that Cacambo was born in Tucuman, in a village where no other language was spoken.

"I will be your interpreter here," said he to Candide; "let us go in; it is a public house."

Immediately two waiters and two girls, dressed in cloth of gold, and their hair tied up with ribbons, invited them to sit down to table with the landlord. They served four dishes of soup, each garnished with two young parrots; a boiled condor which weighed two hundred pounds; two roasted monkeys, of excellent flavor; three hundred hummingbirds in one dish, and six hundred fly-birds in another; exquisite ragouts,[29] delicious pastries; the whole served up in dishes of a kind of rock crystal. The waiters and girls poured out several liqueurs drawn from the sugar cane.

Most of the company were chapmen[30] and wagoners, all extremely polite; they asked Cacambo a few questions with the greatest circumspection, and answered his in the most obliging manner.

As soon as dinner was over, Cacambo believed as well as Candide that they might well pay their reckoning by laying down two of those large gold pieces which they had picked up. The landlord and landlady shouted with laughter and held their sides. When the fit was over:

"Gentlemen," said the landlord, "it is plain you are strangers, and such guests we are not accustomed to see; pardon us therefore for laughing when you offered us the pebbles from our highroads in payment of your reckoning. You doubtless have not the money of the country; but it is not necessary to have any money at all to dine in this house. All hostelries established for the convenience of commerce are paid by the government. You have fared but very indifferently because this is a poor village; but everywhere else, you will be received as you deserve."

Cacambo explained this whole discourse with great astonishment to Candide, who was as greatly astonished to hear it.

"What sort of a country then is this," said they to one another; "a country unknown to all the rest of the world, and where nature is of a kind so different from ours? It is probably the country where all is well; for there absolutely must be one such place. And, whatever Master Pangloss might say, I often found that things went very ill in Westphalia."

Cacambo expressed his curiosity to the landlord, who made answer:

"I am very ignorant, but not the worse on that account. However, we have in this neighborhood an old man retired from Court who is the most learned and most communicative person in the kingdom."

At once he took Cacambo to the old man. Candide acted now only a second character, and accompanied his valet. They entered a very plain house, for the door was only of silver, and the ceilings were only of gold, but wrought in so elegant a taste as to vie with the richest. The antechamber, indeed, was only encrusted with rubies and emeralds, but the order in which everything was arranged made amends for this great simplicity.

The old man received the strangers on his sofa, which was stuffed with hummingbirds' feathers, and ordered his servants to present them with liqueurs in diamond goblets; after which he satisfied their curiosity in the following terms:

"I am now one hundred and seventy-two years old, and I learned of my late father, Master of the Horse to the King, the amazing revolutions of Peru, of which he had been an eyewitness. The kingdom we now inhabit is the ancient country of the Incas, who quitted it very imprudently to conquer another part of the world, and were at length destroyed by the Spaniards.

"More wise by far were the princes of their family, who remained in their native country; and they ordained, with the consent of the whole nation, that none of the inhabitants should ever be permitted to quit this little kingdom; and this has preserved our innocence and happiness. The Spaniards have had a confused notion of this country, and have called it *El Dorado*; and an Englishman, whose name was Sir Walter Raleigh, came very near it about a hundred years ago; but being surrounded by inaccessible rocks and precipices, we have hitherto been sheltered from the rapaciousness of European nations, who have an inconceivable passion for the pebbles and dirt of our land, for the sake of which they would murder us to the last man."

The conversation was long: it turned chiefly on their form of government, their manners, their women, their public entertainments, and the arts. At length Candide, having always had a taste for metaphysics, made Cacambo ask whether there was any religion in that country.

The old man reddened a little.

"How then," said he, "can you doubt it? Do you take us for ungrateful wretches?"

Cacambo humbly asked, "What is the religion in El Dorado?"

The old man reddened again, but continued.

"Can there be two religions?" said he. "We have, I believe, the religion of all the world: we worship God night and morning."

"Do you worship but one God?" said Cacambo, who still acted as interpreter in representing Candide's doubts.

"Surely," said the old man, "there are not two, nor three, nor four. I must confess the people from your side of the world ask very extraordinary questions."

Candide was not yet tired of interrogating the good old man; he wanted to know in what manner they prayed to God in El Dorado.

"We do not pray to Him," said the worthy sage; "we have nothing to ask of Him; He has given us all we need, and we return Him thanks without ceasing."

Candide, having a curiosity to see the priests, asked where they were. The good old man smiled.

"My friend," said he, "we are all priests. The King and all the heads of families sing solemn canticles of thanksgiving every morning, accompanied by five or six thousand musicians . . ."

During this whole discourse Candide was in raptures, and he said to himself:

"This is vastly different from Westphalia and the Baron's castle. Had our friend Pangloss seen El Dorado he would no longer have said that the castle of Thunder-ten-Tronckh was the finest upon earth. It is evident that one must travel."

After this long conversation the old man ordered a coach and six sheep to be got ready, and twelve of his domestics to conduct the travelers to Court.

"Excuse me," said he, "if my age deprives me of the

29. Ragout—highly seasoned stew.
30. Chapmen—peddlers; traders.

honor of accompanying you. The King will receive you in a manner that cannot displease you; and no doubt you will make there a better entertainment."

Never was more wit shown at a table than that which fell from His Majesty. Cacambo explained the King's *bons mots* to Candide, and notwithstanding they were translated they still appeared to be *bons mots.* Of all the things that surprised Candide this was not the least.

They spent a month in this hospitable place. Candide frequently said to Cacambo:

"I own, my friend, once more that the castle where I was born is nothing in comparison with this; but, after all, Miss Cunegonde is not here, and you have, without doubt, some mistress in Europe. If we abide here we shall only be upon a footing with the rest, whereas, if we return to our old world, only with twelve sheep laden with the pebbles of El Dorado, we shall be richer than all the kings in Europe. We shall have no more Inquisitors to fear, and we may easily recover Miss Cunegonde."

This speech was agreeable to Cacambo; mankind are so fond of roving, of making a figure in their own country, and of boasting of what they have seen in their travels that the two happy ones resolved to be no longer so, but to ask His Majesty's leave to quit the country.

"You are foolish," said the King. "I am sensible that my kingdom is but a small place, but when a person is comfortably settled in any part he should abide there. I have not the right to detain strangers. It is a tyranny which neither our manners nor our laws permit. All men are free. Go when you wish, but the going will be very difficult. It is impossible to ascend that rapid river on which you came as by a miracle, and which runs under vaulted rocks. The mountains which surround my kingdom are ten thousand feet high, and as steep as walls; they are each over ten leagues in breadth, and there is no other way to descend them than by precipices. However, since you absolutely wish to depart, I shall give orders to my engineers to construct a machine that will convey you very safely. When we have conducted you over the mountains no one can accompany you further, for my subjects have made a vow never to quit the kingdom, and they are too wise to break it. Ask me besides anything that you please."

"We desire nothing of Your Majesty," said Candide, "but a few sheep laden with provisions, pebbles, and the earth of this country."

The King laughed.

"I cannot conceive," said he, "what pleasure you Europeans find in our yellow clay, but take as much as you like, and great good may it do you!"

At once he gave directions that his engineers should construct a machine to hoist up these two extraordinary men out of the kingdom. Three thousand good mathematicians went to work; it was ready in fifteen days, and did not cost more than twenty million sterling in the specie of that country. They placed Candide and Cacambo on the machine. There were two great red sheep saddled and bridled to ride upon as soon as they were beyond the mountains, twenty pack-sheep laden with provisions, thirty with presents of the curiosities of the country, and fifty with gold, diamonds, and precious stones. The King embraced the two wanderers very tenderly.

Their departure, with the ingenious manner in which they and their sheep were hoisted over the mountains, was a splendid spectacle. The mathematicians took their leave after conveying them to a place of safety, and Candide had no other desire, no other aim, than to present his sheep to Miss Cunegonde.

"Now," said he, "we are able to pay the Governor of Buenos Aires if Miss Cunegonde can be ransomed. Let us journey towards Cayenne. Let us embark, and we will afterwards see what kingdom we shall be able to purchase."

Our travelers spent the first day very agreeably. They were delighted with possessing more treasure than all Asia, Europe, and Africa could scrape together. Candide, in his raptures, cut Cunegonde's name on the trees. The second day two of their sheep plunged into a morass, where they and their burdens were lost; two more died of fatigue a few days after; seven or eight perished with hunger in a desert; and others subsequently fell down precipices. At length, after traveling a hundred days, only two sheep remained. Said Candide to Cacambo:

"My friend, you see how perishable are the riches of this world; there is nothing solid but virtue, and the happiness of seeing Cunegonde once more."

"I grant all you say," said Cacambo, "but we have still two sheep remaining, with more treasure than the King of Spain will ever have; and I see a town which I take to be Surinam, belonging to the Dutch. We are at the end of all our troubles, and at the beginning of happiness."

As they drew near the town, they saw a Negro stretched upon the ground, with only one moiety of his clothes, that is, of his blue linen drawers; the poor man had lost his left leg and his right hand.

"Good God!" said Candide in Dutch, "what art thou doing there, friend, in that shocking condition?"

"I am waiting for my master, Mynheer Vanderdendur, the famous merchant," answered the Negro.

"Was it Mynheer Vanderdendur," said Candide, "that treated thee thus?"

"Yes, sir," said the Negro, "it is the custom. They give us a pair of linen drawers for our whole garment twice a year. When we work at the sugar canes, and the mill snatches hold of a finger, they cut off the hand; and when we attempt to run away, they cut off the leg; both cases have happened to me. This is the price at which you eat sugar in Europe. Yet when my mother sold me for ten patagons on the coast of Guinea, she said to me: 'My child, bless our fetishes, adore them forever; they will make thee live happily, thou hast the honor of being the slave of our lord the whites, which is making the fortune of thy father and mother.' Alas! I know not whether I have made their fortunes; this I know, that they have not made mine. Dogs, monkeys, and parrots are a thousand times less wretched than I. The Dutch fetishes, who have converted me, declare every Sunday that we are all of us children of Adam—blacks as well as whites. I am not a genealogist, but if these preachers tell truth, we are all second cousins. Now, you must agree with me it is impossible to treat one's relations in a more barbarous manner."

"Oh, Pangloss!" cried Candide, "thou hadst not guessed at this abomination; it is the end. I must at last renounce thy optimism."

"What is this optimism?" said Cacambo.

"Alas!" said Candide, "it is the madness of maintaining that everything is right when it is wrong."

Looking at the Negro, he shed tears, and weeping, he entered Surinam.

The first thing they inquired after was whether there was a vessel in the harbor which could be sent to Buenos Aires. The person to whom they applied was a Spanish sea-captain, who offered to take them there upon reasonable terms. He appointed to meet them at a public house, whither Candide and the faithful Cacambo went with their two sheep, and awaited his coming.

Candide, who had his heart upon his lips, told the Spaniard all his adventures, and avowed that he intended to elope with Miss Cunegonde.

"Then I will take good care not to carry you to Buenos Aires," said the seaman. "I should be hanged, and so would you. The fair Cunegonde is my lord's favorite mistress!"

This was a thunderclap for Candide: he wept for a long while. At last he drew Cacambo aside.

"Here, my dear friend," said he to him, "this thou must do. We have, each of us in his pocket, five or six millions in diamonds; you are more clever than I; you must go and bring Miss Cunegonde from Buenos Aires. If the Governor makes any difficulty, give him a million; if he will not relinquish her, give him two; as you have not killed an Inquisitor, they will have no suspicion of you; I'll get another ship, and go and wait for you at Venice; that's a free country, where there is no danger either from Bulgarians, Abares . . . or Inquisitors."

Cacambo applauded this wise resolution. He despaired at parting from so good a master, who had become his intimate friend; but the pleasure of serving him prevailed over the pain of leaving him. They embraced with tears; Candide charged him not to forget the good old woman who had aided them to escape to South America. Cacambo set out that very same day. This Cacambo was a very honest fellow.

Candide stayed some time longer in Surinam, waiting for another captain to carry him and the two remaining sheep to Italy. After he had hired domestics, and purchased everything necessary for a long voyage, Mynheer Vanderdendur, captain of a large vessel, came and offered his services.

"How much will you charge," said he to this man, "to carry me straight to Venice—me, my servants, my baggage, and these two sheep?"

The skipper asked ten thousand piastres. Candide did not hesitate.

"Oh! oh!" said the prudent Vanderdendur to himself, "this stranger gives ten thousand piastres unhesitatingly! He must be very rich."

Returning a little while after, he let him know that, upon second consideration, he could not undertake the voyage for less than twenty thousand piastres.

"Well, you shall have them," said Candide.

"Ay!" said the skipper to himself, "this man agrees to pay twenty thousand piastres with as much ease as ten."

He went back to him again, and declared that he could not carry him to Venice for less than thirty thousand piastres.

"Then you shall have thirty thousand," replied Candide.

"Oh! oh!" said the Dutch skipper once more to himself, "thirty thousand piastres are a trifle to this man; surely these sheep must be laden with an immense treasure; let us say no more about it. First of all, let him pay down the thirty thousand piastres; then we shall see."

Candide sold two small diamonds, the least of which was worth more than what the skipper asked for his freight. He paid him the money in advance.

The two sheep were put on board. Candide followed in a little boat to join the vessel in the roads. The skipper seized his opportunity, set sail, and put out to sea, the wind favoring him. Candide, dismayed and stupefied, soon lost sight of the vessel.

"Alas!" said he, "this is a trick worthy of the old world!"

[Many adventures follow this one in this best of all possible worlds. Finally Candide, Cunegonde, Pangloss (who did not die of hanging), and all the other characters of the story are reunited in Turkey, where they bought a little farm.]

In the neighborhood there lived a very famous Dervish who was esteemed the best philosopher in all Turkey, and so they went to consult him. Pangloss was the speaker.

"Master," said he, "we come to beg you to tell why so strange an animal as man was made."

"With what meddlest thou?" said the Dervish. "Is it thy business?"

"But, reverend father," said Candide, "there is horrible evil in this world."

"What signifies it," said the Dervish, "whether there be evil or good? When His Highness sends a ship to Egypt, does he trouble his head whether the mice on board are at their ease or not?"

"What, then, must we do?" said Pangloss.

"Hold your tongue," answered the Dervish.

"I was in hopes," said Pangloss, "that I should reason with you a little about causes and effects, about the best of possible worlds, the origin of evil, the nature of the soul, and the preestablished harmony."

At these words, the Dervish shut the door in their faces.

During this conversation, the news was spread that two Viziers and the Mufti had been strangled at Constantinople, and that several of their friends had been impaled. This catastrophe made a great noise for some hours. Pangloss, Candide, and Martin, returning to the little farm, saw a good old man taking the fresh air at his door under an orange bower. Pangloss, who was as inquisitive as he was argumentative, asked the old man what was the name of the strangled Mufti.

"I do not know," answered the worthy man, "and I have not known the name of any Mufti, nor of any Vizier. I am entirely ignorant of the event you mention; I presume in general that they who meddle with the administration of public affairs die sometimes miserably, and that they deserve it; but I never trouble my head about what is transacting at Constantinople; I content myself with sending there for sale the fruits of the garden which I cultivate."

Having said these words, he invited the strangers into his house; his two sons and two daughters presented them with several sorts of sherbet, which they made themselves, with Kaimak enriched with the candied peel of citrons, with oranges, lemons, pineapples, pistachio nuts, and Mocha coffee unadulterated with the bad coffee of Batavia or the American islands; after which the two daughters of the honest Mussulman perfumed the strangers' beards.

"You must have a vast and magnificent estate," said Candide to the Turk.

"I have only twenty acres," replied the old man, "I and my children cultivate them; our labor preserves us from three great evils—weariness, vice, and want."

Candide, on his way home, made profound reflections on the old man's conversation.

"This honest Turk," said he to Pangloss and Martin, "seems to be in a situation far preferable to that of the six kings with whom we had the honor of supping."

"Grandeur," said Pangloss, "is extremely dangerous, according to the testimony of philosophers . . ."

"I know also," said Candide, "that we must cultivate our garden."

"You are right," said Pangloss, "for when man was first placed in the Garden of Eden, he was put there *ut operaretur eum*, that he might cultivate it; which shows that man was not born to be idle."

"Let us work," said Martin, "without disputing; it is the only way to render life tolerable."

The whole little society entered into this laudable design, according to their different abilities. Their little plot of land produced plentiful crops . . . They were all of some service or other . . .

Pangloss sometimes said to Candide:

"There is a concatenation of events in this best of all possible worlds; for if you had not been kicked out of a magnificent castle for love of Miss Cunegonde; if you had not suffered misfortune in Portugal; if you had not walked over America; if you had not stabbed the Baron; if you had not lost all your sheep from the fine country of El Dorado, you would not be here eating preserved citrons and pistachio nuts."

"All that is very well," answered Candide, "but let us cultivate our garden."

STUDY QUESTIONS

1. "El Dorado" sounds suspiciously like "Utopia," at first acquaintance; what different aspects are emphasized from those in More's account?
2. The only "answer" that Candide comes up with is "Let us cultivate our garden." What would Pericles say about such an answer? How good an answer is it? What are some of its defects—and virtues?
3. How important a figure is Cunegonde? Why have we not encountered such a figure earlier? In what way is she part of the "New Look" of the eighteenth century?

Thomas Jefferson, 1743–1826

The American Revolution (1775–1783) was hailed as the first significant triumph of rationalism. The causes of the uprising were certainly as much economic as ideological, yet liberal rational beliefs prevailed over the imposition of absolute authority. One of the clearest voices of the new nation was that of Thomas Jefferson, author of the Declaration of Independence, third president of the United States, and founder of the University of Virginia, the last being, for Jefferson, his most significant achievement. Jefferson's address on first assuming the presidency is a masterful speech that summarizes the ideals of the Enlightenment.

LITERARY SELECTION 57

First Inaugural Address (1801)

Thomas Jefferson

During the contest of opinion through which we have passed, the animation of discussions and of exertions has sometimes worn an aspect which might impose on strangers unused to think freely and to speak and to write what they think; but this being now decided by the voice of the nation, announced according to the rules of the constitution, all will, of course, arrange themselves under the will of the law, and unite in common efforts for the common good. All, too, will bear in mind this sacred principle, that though the will of the majority is in all cases to prevail, that will, to be rightful, must be reasonable; that the minority possess their equal rights, which equal laws must protect, and to violate which would be oppression. Let us then, fellow citizens, unite with one heart and one mind. Let us restore to social intercourse that harmony and affection without which liberty and even life itself are but dreary things. And let us reflect that having banished from our land that religious intolerance under which mankind so long bled and suffered, we have yet gained little if we countenance a political intolerance as despotic, as wicked, and capable of as bitter and bloody persecutions. During the throes and convulsions of the ancient world, during the agonizing spasms of infuriated man, seeking through blood and slaughter his long-lost liberty, it was not wonderful that the agitation of the billows should reach even this distant and peaceful shore; that this should be more felt and feared by some and less by others; that this should divide opinions as to measures of safety. But every difference of opinion is not a difference of principle. We have called by different names brethren of the same principle. We are all republicans—we are all federalists. If there be any among us who would wish to dissolve this Union or to change its republican form, let them stand undisturbed as monuments of the safety with which error of opinion may be tolerated where reason is left free to combat it. I know, indeed, that some honest men fear that a republican government cannot be strong; that this government is not strong enough. But would the honest patriot, in the full tide of successful experiment, abandon a government which has so far kept us free and firm, on the theoretic and visionary fear that this government, the world's best hope, may by possibility want energy to preserve itself? I trust not. I believe this, on the contrary, the strongest government on earth. I believe it is the only one where every man, at the call of the law, would fly to the standard of the law, and would meet invasions of the public order as his own personal concern. Sometimes it is said that man cannot be trusted with the government of himself. Can he, then, be trusted with the government of others? Or have we found angels in the form of kings to govern him? Let history answer this question.

Let us, then, with courage and confidence pursue our own federal and republican principles, our attachment to our union and representative government. Kindly separated by nature and a wide ocean from the exterminating havoc of one quarter of the globe; too high-minded to endure the degradations of the others; possessing a chosen country, with room enough for our descendants to the hundredth and thousandth generation; entertaining a due sense of our equal right to the use of our own faculties, to the acquisitions of our own industry, to honor and confidence from our fellow citizens, resulting not from birth but from our actions and their sense of them; enlightened by a benign religion, professed, indeed, and practiced in various forms, yet all of them inculcating honesty, truth, temperance, gratitude, and the love of man; acknowledging and adoring an overruling Providence, which by all its dispensations proves that it delights in the happiness of man here and his greater happiness hereafter; with all these blessings, what more is necessary to make us a happy and a prosperous people? Still one thing more, fellow citizens—a wise and frugal government, which shall restrain men from injuring one another, shall leave them otherwise free to regulate their own pursuits of industry and improvement, and shall not take from the mouth of labor the bread it has earned. This is the sum of good government, and this is necessary to close the circle of our felicities.

About to enter, fellow citizens, on the exercise of duties which comprehend everything dear and valuable to you, it is proper that you should understand what I deem the essential principles of our government, and consequently which ought to shape its administration. I will compress them within the narrowest compass they will bear, stating the general principle, but not all its limitations. Equal and exact justice to all men, of whatever state or persuasion, religious or political; peace, commerce, and honest friendship, with all nations—entangling alliances with none; the support of the state governments in all their rights, as the most competent administrations for our domestic concerns and the surest bulwarks against anti-republican tendencies; the preservation of the general government in its whole constitutional vigor, as the sheet anchor of our peace at home and safety abroad; a jealous care of the right of election by the people—a mild and safe corrective of abuses which are lopped by the sword of revolution where peaceable remedies are unprovided; absolute acquiescence in the decisions of the majority—the vital principle of republics, from which is no appeal but to force, the vital principle and immediate parent of despotism; a well-disciplined militia—our best reliance in peace and for the first moments of war, till regulars may relieve them; the supremacy of the civil over the military authority; economy in the public expense, that labor may be lightly burdened; the honest payment of our debts and sacred preservation of the public faith; encouragement of agriculture, and of commerce as its handmaid: the diffusion of information and arraignment of all abuses at the bar of public reason; freedom of religion; freedom of the press; and freedom of person under the protection of the *habeas corpus*; and trial by juries impartially selected—these principles form the bright constellation which has gone before us, and guided our steps through an age of revolution and reformation. The wisdom of our sages and the blood of our heroes have been devoted to their attainment. They should be the creed of our political faith—the text of civil instruction—the touchstone by which to try the services of these we trust; and should we wander from them in moments of error or alarm, let us hasten to retrace our steps and to regain the road which alone leads to peace, liberty, and safety.

I repair, then, fellow citizens, to the post you have assigned me. With experience enough in subordinate offices to have seen the difficulties of this, the greatest of all, I have learned to expect that it will rarely fall to the lot of imperfect man to retire from this station with the reputation and the favor which bring him to it. Without pretensions to that high confidence you reposed in our first and great revolutionary character, whose preeminent services had entitled him to the first place in his country's love, and destined for him the fairest page in the volume of faithful history, I ask so much confidence only as may give firmness and effect to the legal administration of your affairs. I shall often go wrong through defect of judgment. When right, I shall often be thought wrong by those whose positions will not command a view of the whole ground. I ask your indulgence for my errors, which will never be intentional; and your support against the errors of others, who may condemn what they would not if seen in all its parts. The approbation implied by your suffrage is a consolation to me for the past; and my future solicitude will be to retain the good opinion of those who have bestowed it in advance, to conciliate that of others by doing them all the good in my power and to be instrumental in the happiness and freedom of all.

Relying, then, on the patronage of your good will, I advance with obedience to the work, ready to retire from it whenever you become sensible how much better choice it is in your power to make. And may that Infinite Power which rules the destinies of the universe, lead our councils to what is best, and give them a favorable issue for your peace and prosperity.

STUDY QUESTIONS

1. What does Jefferson mean by "we are all republicans—we are all federalists"?
2. Why is he so opposed to political and/or religious intolerance? What is the fundamental problem in encountering intolerance?

SUMMARY

It was not until the 1648 Peace of Westphalia that Europe was fully launched on a new age freed from medievalism. The physical world had been transformed by inventions such as gunpowder and the printing press, and the work of Bacon, Descartes, and Galileo began to change ways of thinking about the world.

At the beginning of the seventeenth century England and France had absolute monarchs, but the Glorious Revolution of 1688 saw William and Mary on the English throne as rulers of a constitutional monarchy. In France, however, Louis XIV was a divine-right king throughout the longest reign (1643–1715) of any monarch.

The publication of Newton's *Principia* in 1687 marked the dawn of the Enlightenment, an optimistic new age that relied on the intellect to design a rational society in a knowable universe. Newton had discovered the law of universal gravitation, John Locke relied on natural law as a guide to political affairs, and Adam Smith developed a similar unifying principle for economic affairs. Locke's theories of knowledge were later refined by David Hume, who granted certain knowledge only to mathematics, with all other knowledge as only probable. Immanuel Kant reacted to Hume's skepticism with an idealistic philosophy that highlighted the German Enlightenment. In France, the *philosophes* Diderot, Montesquieu, Voltaire, and others wrote articles for the *Encyclopedia*, a monumental summary of all human knowledge.

Paradoxically, the Enlightenment had little influence on the absolute rulers in France, Prussia, and Russia. Only in England was there any political freedom; the most democratic nation in Europe set the forces in motion that led to the triumph of the Enlightenment in the New World.

CULTURE AND HUMAN VALUES

The Enlightenment was victorious in the United States from 1776 but failed in France only thirteen years later. How could the Enlightenment fail in its country of origin—the land of Voltaire, Diderot, and Montesquieu?

Both revolutions intended to replace an autocratic regime with a republican form of government, but there the similarity ends. A prime ingredient in the American success story was the extended and invaluable experience in the art of self-government. The British crown had long pursued a policy of benign neglect; acts of the colonial assemblies were rarely questioned, let alone vetoed by a royally appointed governor or the king himself. There was no titled nobility and, most importantly, no state church. Colonial society had a backbone of a solid middle class of farmers and merchants, particularly in the northern colonies. Further, the Founding Fathers, firmly grounded in Enlightenment ideals, were convinced that human beings had the ability to govern themselves in a sane and rational manner. They not only assumed that people could realize their potential, but designed a government and a constitution that enabled its citizens to do so.

The French revolted against a royal power unchallenged for centuries, a creaking monarchy that had piled up a mountain of abuses. It was not the only problem, however. France was more advanced than other continental nations, but its social organization was inherited from the Middle Ages. By the eighteenth century the class structure had evolved into a First Estate (clergy), a Second Estate (nobility), with 97 percent of the population lumped into a Third Estate (commoners). The Third Estate and some of the clergy and nobility favored reforms, but the commoners had been abused by everyone and longed for an end to the throne, the nobility, and the church. But, with no experience in government, there was no workable alternative to the Old Regime.

Hatred of the Old Regime and its abuses was such a dominant factor there was no room left for restraint and reason. Liberty was quickly achieved, but equality was an impossible dream. Within just a few years any feelings of fraternity had vanished during the unleashed passions that led to the Reign of Terror and, finally, to the dictatorship of Napoleon and the Napoleonic Wars. The French Revolution had, at the time, failed just as completely as the American Revolution had succeeded. But it was the establishment of a New World democracy that provided hope and inspiration for a weary Old World.

In terms of the culture-epoch theory the period from 1600 to 1789, the Early Modern World, can be seen, in retrospect, as one of relative balance, preceded by the tumultuous Renaissance and followed by the French Revolution and the Napoleonic Wars. Certainly both the seventeenth and eighteenth centuries were glorious years of superb artistic achievement.

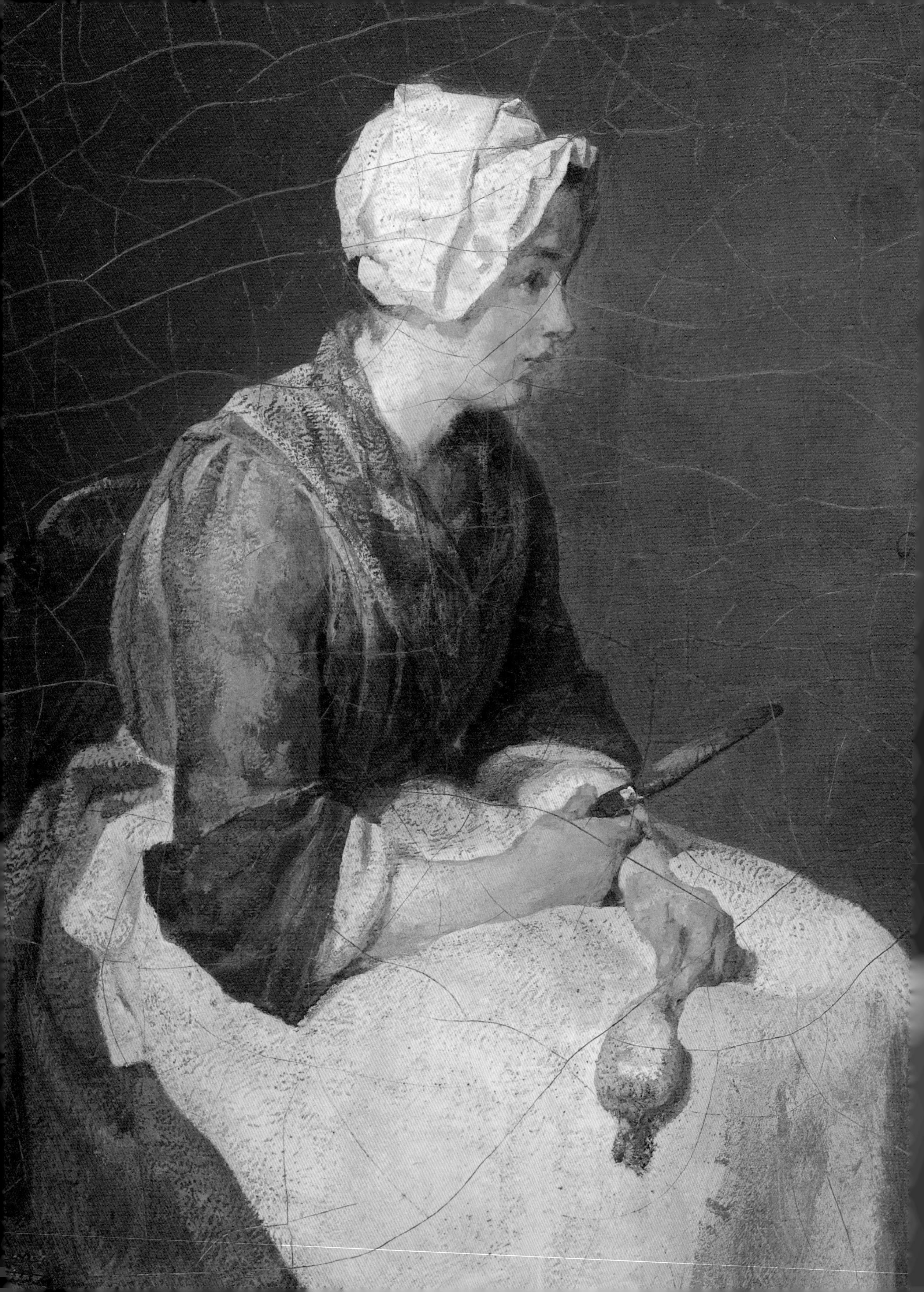

CHAPTER 21

Art: Baroque, Rococo, and Neoclassic

THE BAROQUE AGE, CA. 1580–1700

An age of expansion following the Renaissance era of discovery, the Baroque was a period of conflicts and contradictions that encompassed extremes: Louis XIV and Rembrandt; Bernini and Descartes; Milton and Bach. In architecture and the visual arts the Baroque began in the last quarter of the sixteenth century; and it extended into the eighteenth, culminating in the music of Bach and Handel (see pp. 216–19).

The characteristics of Baroque art are movement, intensity, tension, and energy, traits that are more often associated with music than with the more static arts of painting, sculpture, and architecture. Nevertheless, revolutionary innovations in all the arts generated a Baroque style that could be extravagant, excessive, or even grotesque. At its best, Baroque art is vigorous, dazzling, opulent, colorful, and frequently theatrical, all in marked contrast to the High Renaissance canon of balance, restraint, and control. Most especially, the new style proclaimed the vigorous beginning of the contentious Early Modern World.

The sometimes contradictory variations of the Baroque style can be examined under three broad categories of patrons: the Counter-Reformation Church of Rome; the aristocratic courts of Louis XIV of France and the Stuarts of England; and the bourgeois merchants of Holland. Though drive, intensity, and contrast are common characteristics of all Baroque art, the style will be considered here as a set of reactions to the needs of these patrons and labeled Counter-Reformation, aristocratic, and bourgeois Baroque art.

Counter-Reformation Baroque

Founded in 1534 by Ignatius of Loyola, the Society of Jesus (Jesuits) formed the spearhead of the Counter-Reformation. The mother church of the order, Il Gesù ("Church of Jesus"), was the first building in the new style. It became a model for church design throughout the Roman Catholic world, especially in Latin America (fig. 21.1). The four pairs of pilasters on each level visually stabilize the facade and add a rhythmic punctuation that the evenly spaced **columns** of the classical style do not have (see fig. 17.4). Baroque architecture, from its very beginning, is characterized by the strong accents of paired columns or pilasters. The dramatic effect of paired pilaster and column framing a central portal under a double **cornice** exemplifies the theatricality of the Baroque style, making the entrance seem like an invitation to hurry into the church. The proportions of the two stories and the framing volutes are derived from Alberti's Santa Maria Novella (see fig. 17.13), whereas the classical **pediment** is reminiscent of Palladio (see fig. 17.45). Il Gesù

21.1 *Right* G. B. Vignola (plan) and G. C. della Porta (facade), Il Gesù, Rome, 1568–84. Photo: Scala, Florence.

Opposite Jean-Baptiste-Siméon Chardin, *The Kitchen Maid*, detail of fig. 21.27, 1738. Oil on canvas, full painting 18⅛ × 14¾" (46.2 × 37.5 cm). National Gallery of Art, Washington, D.C. (Samuel H. Kress Collection).

21.2 Il Gesù, interior. Photo: Scala, Florence.

21.3 Caravaggio, *The Conversion of St. Paul*. Ca. 1601. Oil on canvas, 7' 6" × 5' 9" (2.29 × 1.75 m). Sta. Maria del Popolo, Rome.

is not a wholly new design but rather a skillful synthesis of existing elements in a new and dramatic style.

In the interior (fig. 21.2), chapels recessed in the walls replace side aisles, making the richly decorated central space a theatre for the enactment of the Lord's Supper. Light pours through the dome windows and on the high altar in this architectural embodiment of the militant and mystical Society of Jesus.

Michelangelo Merisi da Caravaggio, 1573–1610

The Baroque style of painting appeared abruptly in the person of the northern Italian artist called Caravaggio (ca-ra-VOD-jo), perhaps the first artist to deliberately shock not only the public but also his fellow artists. The most important Italian painter of the seventeenth century, Caravaggio was militantly opposed to such classical concepts as balance and restraint, claiming that nature would be his only teacher. Using chiaroscuro and nonrealistic dramatic lighting, his paintings had an intense psychological impact that profoundly influenced most Baroque artists, including Rembrandt and Velasquez. *The Conversion of St. Paul* (fig. 21.3) must have shocked everyone who saw it, for this is no reverent depiction of a biblical scene. This is the moment after Saul of Tarsus, while riding on the road to Damascus, experiences his vision of Christ, who asks why Saul persecutes him. In that instant Paul becomes a missionary for the new religion. The lighting is harsh and dramatic and the effect highly theatrical. The vivid contrast between light and dark (chiaroscuro) was a major innovation, one that first shocked and then enthralled contemporary artists. In a composition further dramatized by slashing diagonals, the realistically depicted horse towers over the recumbent Paul. Caravaggio was vividly explicit about his rejection of tradition, especially Renaissance idealism, which would hardly surprise anyone viewing this painting.

Caravaggio's life was as dramatic as his art. A man of violent passions, he killed another man in a fight and, badly wounded, fled Rome for Naples. Later thrown into prison, he violated his oath of obedience and escaped to Sicily, but subsequently returned to Naples where he was nearly fatally wounded in another fight. Destitute and ill with malaria, he died during a violent rage over a misunderstanding on the very day that his papal pardon was announced.

Artemisia Gentileschi, 1593–1652/3

A student of her father, who was a follower of Caravaggio, Gentileschi (jen-ti-LES-ki) was also strongly influenced by that artist's use of chiaroscuro and his frequently violent subject matter. Her preferred subjects were heroic women, particularly Judith, whom she portrayed many times. In *Judith Slaying Holofernes* (fig. 21.4) she selected the exact moment in which Judith beheaded the enemy general, having tricked him to gain access to his tent. The Hebrew heroine works with the cold efficiency of an executioner as she also avoids the rush of blood. The extreme chiaroscuro emphasizes the drama and horror of the scene. Criticism from some of her contemporaries that her violent images were not "feminine" deterred her not at all. Unlike most women of her day, she had received a good education in painting solely because her father was a highly skilled artist, and she took full advantage of that training.

21.4 Artemisia Gentileschi, *Judith Slaying Holofernes*. 1620. Oil on canvas, 6' 6" × 5' 4" (1.98 × 1.63 m). Galleria degli Uffizi, Florence. Photo: Scala, Florence.

21.5 Gianlorenzo Bernini, *David*. 1623. Marble, life-size. Galleria Borghese, Rome. Photo: Alinari, Florence.

Gianlorenzo Bernini, 1598–1680

In his life and in his art Caravaggio was at odds with his time, but Bernini (bear-NEE-nee) was the Counter-Reformation personified. A superbly gifted sculptor and architect, with a virtuosity comparable to that of Michelangelo, Bernini was regarded in his own century as not only its best artist but also its greatest man. He himself saw that his renown would decline with the waning of Counter-Reformation energy, but his emotional art has now regained some of its luster. His *David* (fig. 21.5) is a young warrior tensely poised over his discarded armor and harp; every muscle strains to hurl the fatal stone at an unseen Goliath, who seems to be approaching from behind and above the level of the viewer. Compared with Michelangelo's *David* (see fig. 17.30), Bernini's sculpture has the intense energy of the Baroque, so much so that there is an impulse to leap out of the way of the stone missile. The bit lip is Bernini's own expression as copied from a mirror, and realism is further heightened by the grip of David's foot on the actual base of the statue. Completed just nine years before the Inquisition condemned Galileo (in 1632), *David* epitomizes Counter-Reformation fervor.

Rome was Bernini's city and he left his stamp on it literally everywhere, but nowhere else so effectively as in his enhancement of St. Peter's (fig. 21.6). The oval piazza, together with the embracing arms of the colossal **colonnade**, form a spectacular entrance to the largest church in Christendom. The 284 massive Doric columns are 39 feet (11.7 m) in height and are topped with 15-foot (4.5-m) statues of 96 saints, demarcating a piazza that can accommodate about 250,000 people. Bernini used the pavement design, the Egyptian obelisk, and the two fountains to unify the piazza and give it human scale. This fifty-year project was the crowning architectural achievement of the Counter-Reformation. Ironically, it was completed one year after the Great Fire of London had reduced much of that Protestant stronghold to rubble.

21.6 St. Peter's, Rome. Apse and dome by Michelangelo (1547–64); nave and facade by Carlo Maderno (1607–26); colonnade and piazza by Gianlorenzo Bernini (1617–67). Photo: Spectrum, London.

Once in the awesome nave of the church, the visitor is surrounded by other manifestations of Bernini's genius: monumental sculptures, the Throne of St. Peter, elegant relief carvings, even the patterned marble floor. Under Michelangelo's soaring dome stands the Baldacchino (ball-da-KEY-no; fig. 21.7), a canopy 85 feet (25.5 m) in height over the tomb of St. Peter. The title is derived from the Italian: *baldacco* is a silk cloth draped as a canopy over important people or places. In this case, the drapery is bronze as is the entire canopy, including the intricate designs covering the four columns. The Baldacchino was commissioned by the Barberini Pope Urban VIII, who ordered the bronze plates to be removed from the dome of the Pantheon and melted down, prompting the pope's physician to remark that "what the barbarians didn't do the Barberini did." Bernini patterned the serpentine column design after the twisted marble columns saved from Old St. Peter's, which were thought by Constantine to have survived from Solomon's Temple. Some critics refer to the Baldacchino as architecture and others as sculpture; in either case, it is an artistic triumph under difficult circumstances. It had to be large enough to be significant under Michelangelo's enormous dome, but not disproportionate to the size of the nave. Bernini himself called the solution one that "came out well by luck."

21.7 Gianlorenzo Bernini, Baldacchino. 1624–33. St Peter's, Rome. Photo: Scala, Florence.

21.8 Gianlorenzo Bernini, *Ecstasy of St. Theresa*. 1645–52. Marble and gilt, life-size. Cornaro Chapel, Sta. Maria della Vittoria, Rome. Photo: Scala, Florence.

The appeal of Bernini's *Ecstasy of St. Theresa* (fig. 21.8) is emotional, mystical, spiritual, and, withal, palpably sensual. It is based on the writings of St. Theresa, the Spanish mystic, who is depicted in the throes of rapture as the angel is about to pierce her with the golden arrow of Divine Love. Epitomizing the Roman High Baroque, the altarpiece has become a stage for a theatrical work of intense religiosity, a visual counterpart of the *Spiritual Exercises* of Ignatius of Loyola that Bernini himself practiced every day.

Francesco Borromini, 1599–1644

Bernini was Pope Urban VIII's favorite, but by no means the only artist supported by the lavish building program that drained the Vatican treasury. One of Bernini's severest critics was rival architect Borromini (bor-o-ME-nee), a brooding and introspective genius who resented Bernini's favored status and grand reputation. Rejecting Bernini's predilection for rich marbles and lavishly painted stucco, Borromini concentrated on the interplay of elaborate curves and lines. In the small monastic Church of S. Carlo alle Quattro Fontane (fig. 21.9), Borromini used a series of intersecting ellipses in an undulating facade richly embellished with columns, sculpture, plaques, and scrolls, all in stone and

21.9 Francesco Borromini, S. Carlo alle Quattro Fontane, Rome. Begun 1638. Photo: Alinari, Florence.

relying for their effect on design rather than on opulent materials. The impression of restless, mystical passion must have had great appeal, for this small church was emulated throughout southern Europe.

Diego Velasquez, 1599–1660

Unlike his Spanish contemporaries, Velasquez (ve-LASS-kis) was not interested in religious subjects. Allegorical figures, swirling clouds, and rhapsodic faces were never part of a unique style that was concerned with nature and the optical effects of light. During his studies in Italy he became fascinated with the paintings of Titian and Tintoretto, but he cared not at all for the style of Raphael, nor was he influenced by Rubens even though they were friends. A court painter to King Philip IV for thirty years, Velasquez worked with the effects of light on objects and colors, producing candid portraits that never descended to the level of common courtly pictures. His *Maids of Honor* (fig. 21.10) is his acknowledged triumph and one of the most celebrated works of the century. The painting is a symphony of deep pictorial space, light, and images of reality, including what we actually see in the room and also the implied presence of the king and queen, whose images are reflected in the mirror. The artist apparently adapted the mirror idea from van Eyck's *Arnolfini Wedding Portrait* (see fig. 17.23), which was then in the Spanish Royal Collection.

21.10 Diego Velasquez, *Maids of Honor* (*Las Meninas*). 1656. Oil on canvas, 10' 5" × 9' (3.18 × 2.74 m). Museo del Prado, Madrid. Photo: Oronoz, Madrid.

The painter himself looks back at us as he works on a painting that is probably the one at which we are looking. At the front of the picture plane light falls on the dog with the child's foot placed on its back, on the court dwarf, and, in the near foreground, on the Infanta Margarita and her two attendants. Standing behind a lady-in-waiting and wearing the cross of the Order of Santiago, the artist pauses with paintbrush poised; slightly deeper in the middle ground we see a couple engaged in conversation. The mirror on the back wall marks the next step in receding space and, behind the courtier in the open doorway, space recedes to infinity. What at first looks like a genre scene in the artist's studio is actually a stunning spatial composition of five or six receding planes. As it is usually displayed in the Prado Museum, the painting faces a mirror on the opposite wall in which the spectator sees an electrifying image of receding space, an illusion that further confuses reality because the mirror includes the viewer as part of the painting. Space was a major preoccupation of the Baroque, from the large interiors of Baroque churches to the great piazza fronting St. Peter's, and the fascinating illusion of deep space in the *Maids of Honor*. Like most of the paintings of the period, the title was added in the nineteenth century when it was viewed by people other than the royal couple for whom it was originally painted. *Maids of Honor* so fascinated Pablo Picasso that he painted, in 1957, no less than forty-five different studies of all or part of this monumental creation.

Andrea Pozzo, 1642–1709

Among the most extravagant examples of Counter-Reformation power and religious rapture are the ceiling paintings found in many Baroque churches. Late in the period, Pozzo (POET-zo) painted a phenomenal work on the barrel-vaulted ceiling of Sant' Ignazio, a sister church of Il Gesù (fig. 21.11). Depicting the ascent of Ignatius Loyola into heaven, the illusion is dazzling, as if the ceiling has opened up to admit the saint and accompanying saints, angels, and cherubs into the heavenly kingdom. The exuberant design expresses far better than mere words the fervor and dedication of the Society of Jesus in its mission to reform and inspire the church.

Aristocratic Baroque

Peter Paul Rubens, 1577–1640

Rubens lived during an age marked by extremes. Galileo, Kepler, and Descartes were helping shape a new vision of the world, but there was also the dark and bloody side of misogynistic witchcraft trials, the Inquisition, and the savage Thirty Years' War. Throughout his entire lifetime Rubens' own country, the Netherlands, was struggling to free itself from ruthless Spanish power with its pitiless Spanish Inquisition, and yet Rubens painted works that jubilantly praised the human spirit and celebrated the beauty of the natural world. He was not indifferent to human suffering—far from it—but his temperament was wholly

21.11 Andrea Pozzo, *Apotheosis of Saint Ignatius*. Nave ceiling, Sant' Ignazio, Rome. 1691. Photo: Scala, Florence.

21.12 Peter Paul Rubens, *The Assumption of the Virgin*. Ca. 1626. Oil on panel, 49⅜ × 37⅛" (125.4 × 94.2 cm). National Gallery of Art, Washington, D.C. (Samuel H. Kress Collection).

sunny and positive. He possessed a rare combination of robust health, good looks, common sense, a talent for business, phenomenal artistic ability, and a remarkable intellect. He was fluent in six modern languages and classical Latin and was reputed to be capable of listening to a learned lecture while painting, conversing, and dictating letters. One of the most gifted and accomplished painters who ever lived, Rubens amassed a fortune and enjoyed it all.

In only eight years of study in Italy Rubens mastered the classical style of ancient Rome plus the styles of the High and Late Renaissance. On completing a series of paintings for Marie de' Medici, the Dowager Queen of France, he established his reputation as the preeminent painter for kings, nobles, and princes of the church. *The Assumption of the Virgin* (fig. 21.12), though considerably smaller than his many giant paintings, is charged with the boundless energy that characterizes all his work. In diametric opposition to Caravaggio's stark realism, his figures are richly and colorfully garbed, with pink and chubby cherubs and solicitous angels effortlessly wafting the Virgin into heaven. The rich sensual quality of Rubens' work was prized by aristocratic patrons and by the church; glamor, grandeur, and glory provided favorable answers to any doubts of the faithful, assuring them that heaven and earth alike were equally splendid.

Anthony van Dyck, 1599–1641

No one knows how many assistants Rubens employed in his huge studio in Antwerp. As a court painter he paid no guild tax and therefore kept no records of the people who copied popular works or roughed out canvases that the master would complete and sell at a price based on the square footage and the extent of his involvement. Of the few assistants who were successful in their own right, van Dyke is by far the most notable. Unable to develop his talents in the overpowering presence of his teacher, van Dyck left to seek his fortune, which he found in abundance at the court of Charles I of England. With his aristocratic and refined style, van Dyck became the century's foremost portrait painter for court and church, producing elegant portrayals that always improved on the appearance of the model. Van Dyck portrays Charles I in a quiet moment in a beautiful English landscape (fig. 21.13). He conveys a feeling of both dignity and certitude, for this is no tentative monarch. This is a model of the art of portraiture in the grand manner.

Nicolas Poussin, 1594–1665

Throughout his mature career Poussin (poo-sã) painted in the grand manner, but in a style entirely different from that of van Dyck and especially Rubens. Emphasizing line, lucidity, and control, Poussin chose only lofty subject matter drawn from ancient history, mythology, and biblical stories. He was an elitist, an aristocrat of paint and canvas, a French classicist in an age of Baroque exuberance. Religious subjects were treated, he thought, in a base and vulgar manner in most of the works by Caravaggio and his followers. Poussin's Baroque classical style attracted followers just as did the quite different Baroque style of Rubens, touching off a controversy between "Rubenists" and "Poussinists" that may never be resolved. The basic disagreement was between color and line. Line and drawing were absolute values in representing things according to the Poussinists, and color was merely accidental because it depended on light. Color was, of course, what fascinated Rubens and his followers. Rubenists painted the multicolored world as they perceived it, whereas the Poussinists constructed idealized forms of the world as it should be. Actually, the conflict was not just Rubenists versus Poussinists but the eternally opposing views of artists who were, in general, inclined toward romanticism as opposed to artists who were classically oriented. Romanticism in the nineteenth century is a stylistic period and is not to be confused with romantic or classical tendencies of artists in any period. When considered in very broad terms, the Renaissance was classically oriented, whereas the Baroque was inclined toward romanticism except, of course, for Poussin. Classicists emphasize objectivity, rationality, balance, and control; romanticists stress subjectivity, nonrationality, and the restless expression of emotion. Leonardo, Raphael, Poussin, Haydn, and Mozart are classicists; Tintoretto, the later Michelangelo, El Greco, Rubens, Verdi, Tchaikovsky, and Delacroix are romanticists.

21.13 Anthony van Dyck, *Charles I of England*. 1635. Oil on canvas, 8' 8¾" × 6' 9½" (2.66 × 2.07 m). Louvre, Paris. Photo: R.M.N., Paris.

In *Holy Family on the Steps* (fig. 21.14) Poussin has designed an upward-angled perspective that is enforced by the steps across the bottom of the painting. Reminiscent of Raphael's style that Poussin studied assiduously, the triangular composition is slightly off-center, putting the head of Christ almost precisely in the mathematical center of the painting. From vases to temples the setting is Roman and the mode is derived, according to Poussin, from the ethos of the Greek musical scales which, in this case, may be the sweetly lyrical quality of the Ionic scale. Appearing at first to be starkly geometric, the composition has a drama and a classical beauty that are apparent in the balance of solids and voids, cylinders and cubes, and in the balanced

21.14 Nicolas Poussin, *Holy Family on the Steps*. 1648. Oil on canvas 27 × 38½" (68.6 × 97.8 cm). National Gallery of Art, Washington, D.C. (Samuel H. Kress Collection).

21.15 Hyacinthe Rigaud, *Portrait of Louis XIV*. 1701. Oil on canvas, 9' 1½ " × 6' 2⅝" (2.78 × 1.9 m). Louvre, Paris. Photo: R.M.N., Paris.

21.16 Louis le Vau and Jules Hardouin Mansart, Palace of Versailles, central section of garden facade. 1669–85. Photo: Robert Harding, London.

contrast of hard stone and soft foliage, drapery and coolly supple flesh. To compare this work with the Rubens painting (fig. 21.12) is to understand the difference between classicism and romanticism in the broad sense in which these terms are used here.

Louis XIV and Versailles

French tastes were attuned to a rationalized version of the Baroque as represented in the work of Poussin and, on a grand scale, in the enormous royal palace at Versailles. Soon after Louis XIV assumed full control of the government in 1661, French classicism was deliberately used to create a "royal style" that reinforced and enhanced the absolute rule of the king of the most powerful nation in Europe. Classical architecture has, since that time, been used by banks to indicate their financial stability and by rulers and dictators from Napoleon to Hitler and Stalin to symbolize authority and power.

Originally a hunting lodge for Louis XIII, the Palace of Versailles was rebuilt and vastly enlarged for Louis XIV, the self-styled "Sun King" whose power was so immense that he supposedly declared that *"L'état, c'est moi"* ("I am the state"). He certainly said, "It is legal because I wish it." The royal portrait (fig. 21.15) illustrates the judgment of the English statesman Viscount Bolingbroke: "If he was not the greatest king, he was the best actor of majesty that ever filled a throne." Designed initially by Louis le Vau (VO; 1612–70) and completed by Jules Hardouin Mansart (mã-sar; 1646–1708), the Palace was oriented along an east-west axis with the western front facing the extensive gardens (fig. 21.16 and p. 131). Far too large to photograph at ground level in its entirety, the view shown is part of the garden facade. The three-floor design is basically classical, with windows equally spaced and lined up above each other from ground-level French doors to the square top windows. The paired Ionic columns on the projecting fronts are Baroque and intended to enliven an exterior that would otherwise be bland and boring.

The vastness of the palace can be overpowering except when viewed as intended, as the principal structure set within the spacious formal gardens designed by André le Nôtre (nah-truh; 1613–1700), which are classical in every respect except for the Baroque scale and the vast extension of space. Every flower, shrub, hedge, and tree is set precisely in place and enlivened by reflecting pools and 1,200 fountains, a superb setting for a king who imposed his will even on nature. Because the king's minister of finance concealed expenditures, there are no reliable figures on what it cost to build and maintain Versailles, but today the French government can afford to operate the fountains only on Sunday evenings during the summer tourist season.

21.17 *Opposite* Frans Hals, *The Laughing Cavalier*. 1624. Oil on canvas, 33¼ × 27" (85.7 × 68.6 cm). Wallace Collection, London.

Bourgeois Baroque

Dutch art flourished in an environment utterly unlike the regal splendor of France or the flamboyant Baroque of the southern Catholic countries. Freed at last from the Spanish yoke, Holland became a prosperous trading nation: Protestant, hard-working, and predominantly middle class. Calvinism opposed images in churches, and there was no royal court or hereditary nobility, meaning that there were no traditional patrons of the arts. The new patrons were private collectors and there were many. Just about everyone in the nation of nearly 2,000,000 inhabitants wanted paintings for their living rooms, and schools of painting at Amsterdam, Haarlem, Delft, and Utrecht labored to supply a demand somewhat comparable to the Golden Age of Greece or fifteenth-century Florence.

Frans Hals, ca. 1580–1666

The first of the great Dutch masters, Hals was one of history's most brilliant portraitists. There is no precedent for the liveliness of his canvases or the spontaneous brilliance of his brushwork. In *The Laughing Cavalier* (fig. 21.17), a

21.18 Judith Leyster, *Self-Portrait*. Ca. 1630. Oil on canvas, 29⅜ × 25⅞" (74.6 × 65.7 cm). National Gallery of Art, Washington, D.C. (Gift of Mr. and Mrs. Robert Woods Bliss). Photo: Lorene Emerson.

21.19 Rembrandt van Rijn, *The Descent from the Cross*. 1650–5. Oil on canvas, 4' 8¼" × 3' 7¾" (1.43 × 1.11 m). National Gallery of Art, Washington, D.C. (Widener Collection). Photo: Richard Carafelli.

portly gentleman with hand on hip, his head jauntily tilted, stares at the viewer. Large surfaces are treated casually but the lacework and brocade are incredibly precise. Not a deep character study, this is a portrait of a passing acquaintance captured in a brief moment, but rendered as a momentary but uncompromising truth.

Judith Leyster, 1609–60

Leyster (LIE-ster) specialized in genre paintings, especially of musicians, and was one of the few artists prior to this century who could suggest musical performance through form, line, and color. In *Self-Portrait* (fig. 21.18) Leyster portrays herself in formal dress but in a relaxed and casual pose that echoes, in a lower key, the laughing violinist on her canvas, who is actually playing the instrument rather than just holding it. Although influenced by the Utrecht school of Caravaggio disciples and her teacher, Frans Hals, her style is clearly her own. However, it was not until this century that "Leyster" replaced "Hals" on several paintings that she had com-pleted during her late teens or early twenties. She was, in fact, a well-known artist at the age of eighteen and the only woman among the thirty or more master painters in the Haarlem guild in the 1630s. However, she did not receive her first retrospective until 1993 when "A Dutch Master and Her World" opened at the Worcester Art Museum in Massachusetts.

Dutch artists were proud of their craft, and this attitude is reflected in the jaunty ease and confident self-assertion of the artist. Italian artists of the High Renaissance promoted the idea of the artist as a noble creator, but in bourgeois Holland, superlative skills in the crafts were valued on their own merits.

At this point let us compare the four basic Baroque styles: Bourgeois, French Classical, Aristocratic, and Counter-Reformation. The pertinent illustrations, in the same order, are figures 21.18, 21.14, 21.15, and 21.3. The radical differences in subject matter, line, color, design, and technique illustrate the extremes coexisting in this dynamic first century of the modern era.

Rembrandt van Rijn, 1606–69

Some Dutch artists such as Hals specialized in portraits, Leyster painted genre scenes, and others concentrated on history or landscapes. Rembrandt, however, worked with consummate ease in all areas. Sometimes called the Shakespeare of seventeenth-century painters, he is one of a handful of supreme masters of the entire European tradition. Calvinism frowned on religious images, which may explain why sculpture was not popular, but, on the other hand, the Reformed Church rejected all authority except individual conscience. This meant, in effect, that artists could study the Bible and create sacred images as they personally envisioned them, which is precisely what Rembrandt did. He could not accept the stern God of the Calvinists and he never painted a Last Judgment. He was concerned instead with the human drama of the Old

Testament, the loving and forgiving God of the New Testament, and the life and passion of Christ. In *The Descent from the Cross* (fig. 21.19) the two main focal points of the drama are the body of Christ and the face of his fainting mother. Eliminating all superfluous details with his characteristic dark background, the artist conveys the tenderness with which the broken body is being lowered from the cross. The composition is extremely tight, concentrating our attention on the key figures and, through the skillful use of chiaroscuro, flooding the canvas with the most profound grief. Rembrandt never surpassed the expressive combination of space and light that he achieved in this painting.

21.20 Jan Vermeer, *Woman Holding a Balance*. Ca. 1664. Oil on canvas, 16¾ × 15" (42.5 × 38.1 cm). National Gallery of Art, Washington, D.C. (Widener Collection).

Jan Vermeer, 1632–75

Vermeer (ver-MEER) did not paint monumental subjects with the passion of Rembrandt, but he did possess a special magic that transmuted everyday reality into eternal symbols. Fewer than forty of his paintings survive, and all but three are of sparsely furnished interiors of modest size. Vermeer, in fact, did for ordinary rooms what High Renaissance artists did for ordinary human bodies: elevated them to the level of universals. With an eye for detail comparable to van Dyck's, Vermeer specialized in light—natural light streaming into the interior, usually from the left, and filling a space punctuated by objects. His figures are seemingly suspended in light. In *Woman Holding a Balance* (fig. 21.20) Vermeer has created an apparently simple scene of a woman, probably his wife, Catharina, in one of her eleven pregnancies, holding an empty balance. With jewelry on the table and a painting of the Last Judgment on the wall, one might assume that this is a moral analogy, a weighing of worldly possessions against a background of divine judgment. Dutch Calvinists would not have had a Last Judgment anywhere in the house, but this may be Catharina's room and she, unlike her husband, was Catholic. Nevertheless, the mood is introspective and her expression serene. Catharina was married to a painter who never sold a painting, a man of extravagant tastes with a host of creditors, and in this painting she may simply be contentedly contemplating jewelry received from her loving husband. The highest level of art may not be to encourage laughter, passion, or tears but to invoke dreams, and dreams are perhaps best left unexplained.

After Vermeer's premature death, his paintings were used to satisfy creditors who undoubtedly had no more appreciation of his worth than the rest of a society that had ignored him. Not rediscovered until the 1860s, his paintings, with their use of color and light, were a revelation to the Impressionists, who thought themselves the first to discover that shadows were not black but also had color. In *The Girl with the Red Hat* (fig. 21.21), there is a technical mastery that, in combination with Vermeer's scientific study of light, makes this one of the finest works of the artist's brief mature period. Remarkable in its own right, the painting is also a tribute to the rapidly developing science of optics, for it is virtually certain that Jan Vermeer actually sought to

21.21 Jan Vermeer, *The Girl with the Red Hat*, after restoration. Ca. 1665. Oil on panel, 9⅛ × 7⅛" (23.2 × 18.1 cm). National Gallery of Art, Washington, D.C. (Andrew W. Mellon Collection). Photo: Richard Carafelli.

21.22 Jacob van Ruisdael, *View of Haarlem from the Dunes at Overveen*. Ca. 1670. Oil on canvas, 25 × 22" (63.5 × 55.9 cm). Mauritshuis, The Hague.

simulate the camera obscura's effects. The principle of the camera obscura was described by Leonardo da Vinci and developed by Johannes Kepler: light passing through a small hole in the side wall of a dark room projects an image of outside objects onto an interior wall. Filling the hole with one of the new improved lenses would make the inside image as vivid as a color photograph. The artist did not copy the camera image; rather, he suggested the luminosity of such an image. Here, as if they were visualized molecules, we see floating globules of colored light. Light glints from an eye, an earring, and the lips of a young woman unexpectedly caught in a soft-focus candid "photograph." Under the spectacular hat, light and shadow are painted in subtle gradations of color emphasized by the gleaming white ruff. Never receiving a commission, Vermeer created whatever he wished, applying paint to canvas with a remarkable dexterity and charm.

Jacob van Ruisdael, 1628–82

Vermeer exploited color and light, but Ruisdael (ROIS-dale) specialized in space. The finest Dutch landscape painter and one of the greatest in Western art, Ruisdael painted the immensity of space from memory and imagination. In his *View of Haarlem* (fig. 21.22) a spacious sky dominates the composition, taking up over two-thirds of the canvas. Ruisdael's landscapes are frequently devoid of people and when they are present, as here, they are inconsequential figures compared with the magnificence of nature. The atmospheric perspective encourages the illusion that we are looking into space so deep it verges on infinity.

Rachel Ruysch, 1664–1750

Emerging late in the Dutch Baroque style, Ruysch (roys) became one of the leading still-life painters of the era. Court painter to the Elector Palatine at Düsseldorf, she

21.23 Rachel Ruysch, *Flowers in a Vase*. 1698. Oil on canvas, 23 × 17½" (58.5 × 44.5 cm). Städelsches Institut, Frankfurt am Main.

successfully combined her profession with marriage and children. Though she has the characteristic Dutch dark background for her flower arrangement (fig. 21.23), she uses vivid colour to enliven and dramatize her composition.

The subject matter of the paintings illustrated reveals the generally secular orientation of Dutch artists, indeed of the entire nation. From the last quarter of the sixteenth century through three-quarters of the seventeenth, the tiny Dutch nation (United Provinces of the Northern Netherlands) was a great power throughout the world, with colonies in Asia, Africa, and the Americas. With virtually no aristocracy, this was the first notable middle-class nation in Europe; its wealth and authority derived from vigorous international trade protected by the world's most powerful navy.

ROCOCO ART, CA. 1715–89

With the death of Louis XIV in 1715 the academic classical art of the Baroque lost its chief patron. It was with immense relief that the French court abandoned the palace of Versailles and the Baroque, moving back to Paris and to a new way of life in elegant townhouses, where manners and charm were far more interesting than grandeur and geometric order. This was the Age of Enlightenment and of the Rococo style of art, contradictory but not mutually exclusive. In fact, the Enlightenment and the American and French revolutions cannot be fully understood without knowing what the Rococo was all about. That Rococo is merely Baroque made small or Baroque made light are bromides that do have a certain element of truth, but Rococo is also a style in its own right. Rococo art illustrates with astonishing accuracy the superficial values of an aristocracy whose languid days were numbered. Imposing Baroque forms were reduced to depictions of the pursuit of pleasure and escape from boredom. Rococo art was not decadent but the society it portrayed most certainly was.

France

Jean Antoine Watteau, 1684–1721

Watteau (vah-toe), the first and greatest French Rococo artist, was born of Flemish parents in Valenciennes, a city that had been French for only six years. Yet he transformed French art from the classicism of Poussin into a new style of gaiety and tenderness, casual but elegant, that even today is recognized as Parisian in the sophisticated tradition later reinforced by artists such as Renoir and Degas. Watteau's *Embarkation for Cythera* (fig. 21.24), an early Rococo work completed only two years after the death of Louis XIV, is also the most important. Cythera was the legendary island of Venus, whose statue at the right presides over the amorous festivities. Grouped couple by couple, the elegantly garbed party is preparing to board a fanciful boat attended by cherubs, anticipating the pleasures to be enjoyed on the isle of love. Characteristic of Rococo design is the reverse *C* that can be traced from the heads at the lower left, curving past the couple on the hillock, and then turning back to the left along the delicate tips of the tree branches. Though it is a large painting, the scene is remarkably intimate. Each couple is totally preoccupied with itself and forms a distinct unit as they talk, smile, whisper, or touch. Beneath the frivolity and charm is a warm feeling of agreeable people and pleasant times. Watteau has transformed the amorous dalliances of an idle and privileged class into lyric poetry.

François Boucher, 1703–70

Venus was queen of the Rococo at its height in the 1750s, and Boucher (boo-shay) was her most talented interpreter. The protégé of Madame de Pompadour, mistress of Louis XV and arbiter of Rococo style, Boucher was a master of the sensual and frequently erotic art of the period. With astounding energy and prodigious virtuosity he produced paintings, designed tapestries, decorated porcelain, and created opera and ballet settings. With his many students and widely circulated engravings, he became the most influential artist in Europe. His *Venus Consoling Love* (fig. 21.25) depicts a slim and delicate beauty who would be more comfortable at the French court than on Mount Olympos. She was, in fact, at the French court, for this is one of

21.24 *Above* Jean Antoine Watteau, *Embarkation for Cythera*. 1717. Oil on canvas 4' 3" × 6' 2½" (1.3 × 1.89 m). Louvre, Paris. Photo: R.M.N., Paris.

ROYAL MISTRESSES

Louis XV's failure to provide strong leadership and badly needed reforms contributed mightily to the coming revolution. He was more interested in his sensual pleasures and many mistresses than affairs of state. Well-educated, artistic, and musical, the Marquise de Pompadour arranged the king's entertainments and helped design many public buildings and mansions. Her greatest service to the state was her defense of Diderot's *Encyclopedia*.

Another mistress, the Comtesse du Barry, was not so politically powerful as Pompadour, but she was a generous patron of the arts and letters who was known for her wit and beauty. She commissioned a set of erotic paintings by Fragonard that now reside in the Frick Collection in New York. During the French Revolution she tried to aid some royalist émigrés in England and then made the mistake of returning to France, where she was arrested and guillotined.

21.25 François Boucher, *Venus Consoling Love*. 1751. Oil on canvas, 42⅛ × 33⅜" (107 × 84.8 cm). National Gallery of Art, Washington, D.C. (Chester Dale Collection).

21.26 Jean-Honoré Fragonard, *The Swing*. 1766. Oil on canvas, 32 × 25½" (81.3 × 64.8 cm). Wallace Collection, London.

Boucher's many portraits of Mme. de Pompadour, to whom the painting belonged. Here are the characteristic ivory, pink, blue, silver, and gold colors of the Rococo, all elegantly detailed by one of the virtuosos of the painter's brush. The painting is frankly pretty, and meant to be, but its subtle design is a carefully controlled interplay of sinuous curves; nowhere is there a straight line. A study of the apparent diagonals of the goddess' body discloses a series of curves, flattering curls of supple and creamy flesh. This is an idealized version of Pompadour, totally different from other Boucher paintings that reveal her intellectual brilliance. Her physician, Dr. Quesway, quoted her foreboding remark, *"Après moi le déluge!"* ("After me the flood!", that is, disaster), and Voltaire wrote, on the occasion of her death in 1764, that he would miss her because "she was one of us; she protected Letters to the best of her power."

Jean-Honoré Fragonard, 1732–1806

The most eminent pupil of Boucher and Chardin and the last of the exceptional Rococo artists, Fragonard (frah-go-nar) lived to see the revolution destroy the Rococo age and all it represented. A master of the elegantly erotic paintings that delighted his patrons, Fragonard also had a technical skill and an eye for composition that enabled him to make powerful artistic statements. *The Swing* (fig. 21.26) is an apparently lightweight erotic diversion with a statue of Cupid at the left and the lolling figure of a young man below,

21.27 Jean-Baptiste-Siméon Chardin, *The Kitchen Maid.* 1738. Oil on canvas, 18⅛ × 14¾" (46.2 × 37.5 cm). National Gallery of Art, Washington, D.C. (Samuel H. Kress Collection).

21.28 Thomas Gainsborough, *Mrs. Richard Brinsley Sheridan.* Ca. 1783. Oil on canvas, 7' 2½" × 5' ½" (2.2 × 1.5 m). National Gallery of Art, Washington, D.C. (Andrew W. Mellon Collection).

actually Baron de Saint-Julien, who commissioned the work. As directed by the baron, Fragonard has shown his lady friend whimsically kicking her pump off to give him a better view up her skirt. Almost unnoticed is the key to the composition, the swing-pulling servant in the right background. Fragonard has portrayed a decadent class that neither works nor pays taxes, a frivolous aristocracy totally supported by the labors (and taxes) of 97 percent of a population symbolized by the shadowy figure of the servant. This was painted when the publication of Diderot's *Encyclopedia* was nearing completion and the revolution itself was waiting impatiently in the wings.

Jean-Baptiste-Siméon Chardin, 1699–1779

But there was another current, one that celebrated the sober virtues of the middle class. Chardin (shar-dã) sought the underlying nobility that could be found in scenes of daily life. Nothing was so humble that his brush could not reveal its charm. *The Kitchen Maid* (fig. 21.27 and p. 186) has a natural dignity in sharp contrast to the artificiality of the courtly Rococo style. Chardin painted what he saw, which was, essentially, light falling on pleasing shapes: face, apron, basin, turnips. The result is a quietly beautiful composition by the finest **still-life** painter of the eighteenth century.

England

Thomas Gainsborough, 1727–88

The artificial elegance of the French Rococo had no place in an English society that was less frivolous than the French and certainly less decadent. In both subject matter and style Gainsborough's portrait of *Mrs. Richard Brinsley Sheridan* (fig. 21.28) symbolizes the dashing, worldly taste of English high society. This is the beautiful singer who married Sheridan, the wit, brilliant member of Parliament, and writer of such plays as *School for Scandal* and *The Rivals.* Here nature is synthetic, arranged as a proper background to highlight the natural beauty and unpretentious air of the sitter. In contrast to the sprightly sophistication of Boucher's women, Mrs. Sheridan is the very picture of the tasteful elegance so admired by British society.

William Hogarth, 1697–1764

Painter, engraver, and above all a master satirist, Hogarth delighted in attacking foolishness, frivolity, hypocrisy, and other vulnerable aspects of English society. He can, in fact, be considered a visual Jonathan Swift. Perhaps his finest work is the series of six paintings entitled *Marriage à la Mode* in which he satirized everything that could go wrong in marriage for money. When the engravings were published in 1745 there were very many indignant people all over London. In the second engraving (fig. 21.29) the husband is sprawled on a chair, obviously exhausted from a night out with a woman friend, whose hat the dog is drawing from his pocket. The black mark on the husband's neck indicates the presence of syphilis. The wife leans back in a suggestive

21.29 *Above* William Hogarth, *Marriage à la Mode II*. 1745. Engraving by B. Baron after an oil painting of 1743. British Museum, London.

21.30 Dominikus Zimmermann, Wieskirche, Upper Bavaria, Germany. 1745–54. Photo: Angelo Hornak, London.

pose, probably indicating some interrupted activity on her part, perhaps with a hastily departed music teacher. Her father protests to heaven about the accumulating bills but he must know there is no end in sight. The design of the two rooms is clearly Palladian and made even more classical by the huge number of Rococo decorations and furnishings.

Rococo Architecture

Rococo architecture is charming and beguiling in small structures and, when tastefully done, even in larger buildings. The pilgrimage church of Wieskirche (VEEZ-keer-ka; Church in the Meadow) was built in a remote rural area where the faithful believed a miracle had transpired. Pilgrims from near and far would travel to a pilgrimage church in the expectation of a miraculous cure or deliverance from some sort of evil. The interior of the church (fig. 21.30) is a celestial arrangement of white **stucco**, gold gilt, and profuse decoration set off to best advantage by the north-south orientation of the building and the large clear-glass windows. Most of the elegantly textured decorations are carved wood, and the "marble" columns are wood painted to look like marble. The spritely terra-cotta angels pose gracefully on stucco clouds, above which the painted vaulting soars effortlessly. Despite the multiplicity of details the rich ensemble is completely harmonious; the overwhelming impression is a mystical, deeply emotional experience.

NEOCLASSIC ART

English Architecture

The visual arts of the Renaissance and the Baroque made little impact on English culture. Apparently preoccupied with their justly celebrated achievements in dramatic literature, poetry, and music, the English continued to build in the Gothic and Tudor styles and to import painters such as Holbein, Rubens, and van Dyck. After a visit to Italy, Inigo Jones (1573–1652), the king's surveyor (architect), inaugurated a revolution in English architecture. Jones' middle-class sensibilities were offended by the extravagance of Michelangelo's style, but he was profoundly impressed with Palladio's architectural designs. Jones did not copy Palladian buildings, but instead selected classical characteristics as a basis for his own architectural style. His Queen's House (fig. 21.31) is the first English building designed in the Neoclassic style that was to become so prominent in England and North America. Chaste and clean with the poise of pure Roman classicism, the house has slight rustication on the ground floor derived from an early Renaissance style long since abandoned by the Italians (see fig. 17.12). With simple window openings and matching lower and upper balustrades, the curving double stairway adds a discreet touch of dignity and grace.

21.31 *Above* Inigo Jones, Queen's House, Greenwich, England, north facade, 1610–18. Photo: Topham, Edenbridge, U.K. (William Gordon Davis).

English architecture was influenced by Palladian and Baroque characteristics more rapidly than anyone might have anticipated. In 1666 King Charles II commissioned Christopher Wren (1632–1723) to design a new dome for the Gothic Cathedral of St. Paul's, a design that Wren planned in the "Roman manner." A professor of astronomy at Oxford and an amateur architect, Wren soon had more than he bargained for; the Great Fire of 1666 destroyed most of London, necessitating a major rebuilding program with Wren as the chief architect. Of the more than fifty churches that Wren designed, the most important was the new St. Paul's, an eclectic design influenced by Jones, Palladio, and

21.32 Christopher Wren, St. Paul's Cathedral, London, west facade. 1675–1710. Photo: Angelo Hornak, London.

the French and Italian Baroque, and masterfully synthesized by Wren (fig. 21.32). St. Paul's is one of a limited number of English buildings with Baroque characteristics, but overall the design is dominated by the classical dome that is reminiscent, on a massive scale, of Bramante's Tempietto (see fig. 17.32). Punctuated by paired Corinthian columns in the Baroque manner, the facade is basically classical, but the ornate twin towers are similar to Borromini's curvilinear style (see fig. 21.9). None of Wren's London churches is quite like any other, though most are classical; some have towers, others steeples, and a few are crowned with domes.

Variations on the Palladian style spread throughout England in the designs of stately homes and their interiors, including furniture. The drawing room of Townhouse No. 1, Royal Crescent, Bath, (fig. 21.33) contains an Axminster carpet, a fireplace of Italian Carrara marble, Sheraton cabinets, a Chippendale card table, and a Hepplewhite sofa and wooden chairs, all in the Neoclassic style. The 1798 piano is Neoclassic as are the spacious windows. The two mirrors add a Rococo touch to an interior design that, with many variations, became fashionable in comparable American homes of the late eighteenth and early nineteenth centuries.

THE GREAT FIRE

The fire began in a baker's shop on Pudding Lane between London Bridge and the Tower of London. Awakened in the middle of the night, the Lord Mayor saw a poor section of his city burning and went back to bed. But these were wooden houses—weatherboarding covered with pitch—on streets so narrow that the projecting upper stories of the houses nearly touched one another. Within hours the fire was out of control and burning better-class districts. Diarist Samuel Pepys wrote that "it made me weep to see it" when he saw St. Paul's in flames, whose six acres of leaden roofs poured down into the churchyard "like snow before the sun." On the fourth day the firefighters began blowing up houses to set up fire lanes, but five-sixths of the largely medieval city was gone. Over 100,000 people were homeless and 85 churches and 13,000 houses were destroyed. Christopher Wren's rebuilding plan would have made London the finest city in Europe but the conservative English stubbornly rebuilt their city just as it was, except for the significant ban on wooden houses. Wren was left to rebuild churches.

French Neoclassicism

In France the Rococo style was deemed too frivolous for public buildings and the Baroque too elaborate, leaving the way open for a French version of Neoclassicism. Ange-Jacques Gabriel (1698–1782), court architect for Louis XV, made his reputation with his design for the Petit Trianon on the royal grounds at Versailles (fig. 21.34). Restrained, symmetrical, and exquisitely proportioned, the diminutive palace was constructed for Mme. de Pompadour who was, in effect, the ruler of France in place of the inept Louis XV. Clearly reflecting her classical architectural tastes, the Petit Trianon is in the austere Augustan style of republican Rome, a style that became dominant in Paris and other French cities during the second half of the eighteenth century.

The gap between the aristocracy and the middle class was probably no greater than it had been for generations, but by the last quarter of the century it had become far more noticeable. The *philosophes* expounded on the gap along with revolutionary political and economic ideas that had become active principles in England's rebellious American colonies. Seeking an art to reflect their revolutionary fervor,

21.33 No. 1, Royal Crescent, Bath, England, drawing room.

21.34 Ange-Jacques Gabriel, Petit Trianon, Versailles, south facade. 1762–8. Photo: Giraudon, Paris.

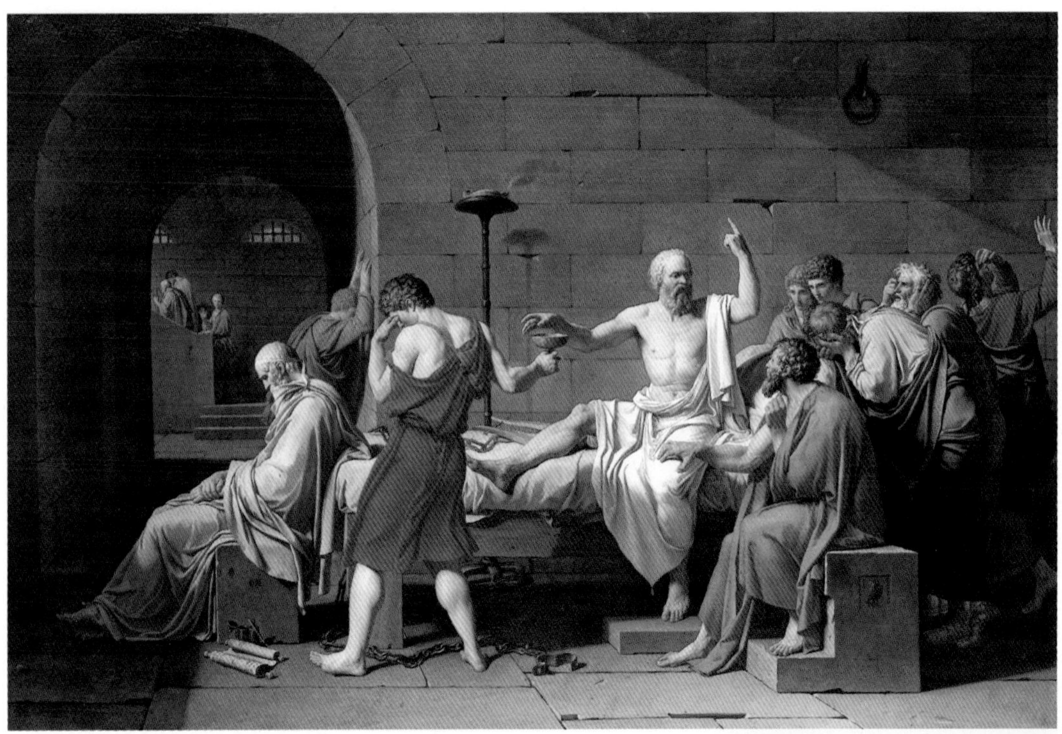

21.35 *Above* Jacques-Louis David, *The Death of Socrates*. 1787. Oil on canvas, 4' 3" × 6' 5¼" (1.3 × 1.96 m). Metropolitan Museum of Art, New York (Wolfe Fund, 1931. Catharine Lorillard Wolfe Collection 31.45).

21.36 Circle of David, *Portrait of a Lady*. Ca. 1800. Oil on canvas, 39½ × 32⅛" (100.3 × 81.6 cm). San Diego Museum of Art, California (Gift of Anne R. and Amy Putnam).

21.37 Constance Marie Charpentier, *Mlle. Charlotte du Val d'Ognes*. 1785. Oil on canvas, 5' 3½" × 4' 2⅝" (1.61 × 1.29 m). Formerly attributed to David. Metropolitan Museum of Art, New York (Mr. and Mrs. Isaac D. Fletcher Collection; bequest of Isaac D. Fletcher, 1917.17.120.204).

the *philosophes* turned to Neoclassicism. Excavations at Pompeii and Herculaneum, begun in 1748 under the aegis of King Charles of Bourbon, were bringing to light a new chapter from the history of ancient Rome, sparking a renewed interest in antiquity that was not confined to the arts. Political theorists who were advocating democratic equality, fervent patriotism, and the rule of reason thought they had found all this in republican Rome.

Jacques-Louis David, 1748–1825

Both a gifted and a visionary artist, David (da-veed) developed his Neoclassic style during his studies in Rome (1775–81). Refusing to merely copy Roman statues and paintings, to become an antiquarian, he chose instead to be a propagandist, to place his talent at the service of revolutionary ideals. David used the forms of ancient art to extol the virtues of patriotism and democracy. Painted shortly before the French Revolution, *The Death of Socrates* (fig. 21.35) became one of the most popular paintings of the century and set the tone for didactic art of the highest quality. The Greek philosopher is depicted here as the apostle of reason, the patron saint of such Roman Stoics as Epictetus and Marcus Aurelius. With the body of a young athlete and the face of a benign sage, Socrates dominates a sharply focused composition that recalls Caravaggio's dramatic use of chiaroscuro. The figures of the twelve disciples—no coincidence—are rendered as precisely as marble statues, meticulous detail being a David trademark. David's message is unmistakable: men of principle should be willing to die in defense of their ideals. Nobles and tradesmen, philosophers and priests, seemingly everyone bought an **engraving** of the painting, including the doomed Louis XVI, who admired its noble sentiments.

David's works, with their detailed, painstaking realism and appeal to reason, were conceived and executed as cries for revolution. During the revolution itself David was a member of the Convention that sentenced Louis XVI and Marie Antoinette to death. For twenty-five years he was a virtual dictator of the arts in France. Following his dicta, Rococo salons were stripped of their sensuous paintings and curvaceous furnishings, remodeled in Neoclassic style, and equipped with furniture patterned after Greek vase paintings and Pompeiian murals. Fashionable men and women adopted Roman names such as Portia and Brutus, styled their hair in the antique manner, and even costumed themselves in classical togas (fig. 21.36). This was the approved new look of the revolution as painted in the style of David by an unknown artist.

Constance Marie Charpentier, 1767–1849

David was a highly successful artist with many students and, of course, numerous imitators. As with any well-known artist, paintings were sometimes attributed to him so they could command a higher price, which is what happened with the portrait of *Mlle. Charlotte du Val d'Ognes* (fig. 21.37). Purchased in 1917 as a David for $200,000, the painting has since been attributed to Charpentier (shar-pã-ty-ay), a Parisian artist who studied with David and several other noted painters. Winner of a gold medal and an exhibitor in ten salons, her work appears to be hidden away—either in private collections or behind the names of more famous artists. That the painting could ever have been attributed to David is very odd. Though the style is Neoclassic, the brushwork firm and lucid, and the garb elegantly classical, the mood is totally alien to David's style. Strangely haunting, the work has a brooding and unreal quality that prompted critics to call it a "mysterious masterpiece." André Malraux described it as "a merciless portrait of an intelligent, homely woman against the light and bathed in shadow and mystery. The colors have the subtlety and singularity of those of Vermeer. A perfect picture, unforgettable." Made while the painting bore David's name, these comments are just as appropriate for a masterpiece by Charpentier.

Angelica Kauffmann, 1741–1807

Daughter and pupil of the artist J. J. Kauffmann, the Swiss painter became, at age twenty-four, a member of the Accademia di San Luca in Italy but was not allowed in the nude drawing classes because she was a woman. She nevertheless had a successful career as a history painter. One of the founding members of the British Royal Academy of Art, she produced hundreds of portraits and also designed the interiors of houses—mainly homes conceived by classicist Robert Adam. Upon marrying Antonio Zucchi and returning to Rome, she became the unofficial head of the Roman school of painting. Bristling with contained emotion, her painting shows Pliny the Younger and his mother, sister to Pliny the Elder, fearfully awaiting the news that the ever-so-curious Elder had lost his life as he investigated the eruption of Vesuvius at Pompeii (fig. 21.38).

Elisabeth Vigée-Le Brun, 1755–1842

A student of her father, a portrait artist, Le Brun was already supporting her family at the age of fifteen. She married Le Brun, an art dealer and inveterate gambler, but chose to pursue a career as an internationally recognized portrait painter with over 900 paintings to her credit, a virtual *Who's Who* of late-eighteenth- and early-nineteenth-century European aristocrats. She served as painter to Queen Marie Antoinette but escaped, after the French Revolution, with her daughter to Italy, and continued to receive commissions throughout Europe. Her *Self-Portrait* (fig. 21.39) shows the artist painting a portrait of her daughter, whose face is captured in almost ghostlike fashion. Meticulously detailed from sash to lacework to hat, this is classical portraiture at its best. Particularly notable is the strong light on the hat and collar that creates a virtual miniature portrait of the head and shoulders.

Jean Antoine Houdon, 1741–1828

Portrait sculpture, as might be expected, was a natural for the Neoclassic style, but there were no sculptors comparable to David. Houdon (ooh-dõ), the finest French sculptor

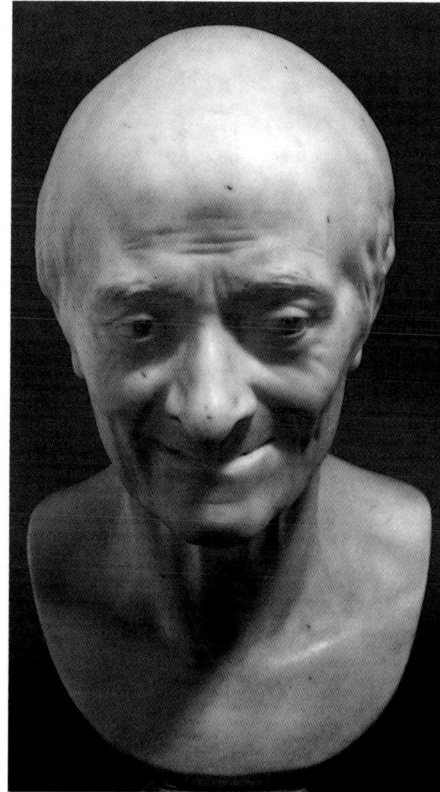

21.38 *Above* Angelica Kauffmann, *Pliny the Younger and his Mother at Misenum, AD 79.* 1785. Oil on canvas, 3' 4½" × 4' 2½" (1.03 × 1.28 m). Art Museum, Princeton University (Museum Purchase, Gift of Franklin H. Kissner).

21.40 Jean-Antoine Houdon, *Voltaire*. 1778. Marble, 20¾ × 17⅞ × 13⅛" (52.7 × 45.5 × 33.3 cm). National Gallery of Art, Washington, D.C. (Widener Collection).

of the age, was admired by the *philosophes*, many of whom he portrayed with great accuracy. His reputation led to a commission in the United States for a statue of George Washington. His portrait bust of Voltaire (fig. 21.40) is a realistic depiction of the aging writer, clearly communicating his personality with twinkling eyes and wry and cynical smile.

Antonio Canova, 1757–1822

Houdon was acquainted with other revolutionaries, including George Washington and Benjamin Franklin, and created a portrait of Franklin and two statues of Washington. Despite his revolutionary background and realistic portraits, Houdon won only reluctant acceptance from Napoleon, who much preferred the Neoclassic style of Italian sculptor Canova (ka-NO-va), whose art, like that of David, became a propaganda tool for the Empire. Canova's lovely study of *Pauline Borghese as Venus* (fig. 21.41) is an idealized version of feminine charm, a very sensual portrait of Napoleon's sister and, though classical, an evocation of imperial luxury rather than the noble dignity of Republican Rome.

21.39 Elisabeth Vigée-Le Brun, *Self-Portrait*. 1791. Oil on canvas, 39 × 31¾" (99.1 × 80.6 cm). Ickworth, Suffolk, U.K. Photo: National Trust Photographic Library, London (Angelo Hornak).

21.41 Antonio Canova, *Pauline Borghese as Venus*. 1805. Marble, life-size. Galleria Borghese, Rome. Photo: Scala, Florence.

21.42 Gilbert Stuart, *Mrs. Richard Yates*, 1793. Oil on canvas, 30¼ × 25" (76.8 × 63.5 cm). National Gallery of Art, Washington, D.C. (Andrew W. Mellon Collection).

Neoclassicism in the United States

Gilbert Stuart, 1755–1828

The Neoclassic style found a congenial home in the young republic of the New World. The leading American painter was Stuart, who painted many Founding Fathers, particularly George Washington, whose portrait on the dollar bill is from a Stuart work. In his portraits Stuart displayed a mastery of flesh tones, having determined, like the much later Impressionists, that flesh coloration was a combination of colors. His portrait of *Mrs. Richard Yates* (fig. 21.42) is typical of the Neoclassic style in a new democracy in which neither dress nor background gives a clue to the social status of the sitter. European portraiture customarily added a proper setting and adornment indicating a regal or noble subject. In this portrait of the wife of a New York importer we see a coolly poised and confident woman. Her strongly featured face with the raised eyebrows and slightly drooping eyelids is faintly skeptical, the face of a shrewd and capable Yankee.

Joshua Johnson, 1765–1830

Johnson was one of the most celebrated of a long line of limners who traveled through New England and New York painting family portraits. The name was derived from "illuminator," a decorator of illuminated manuscripts. Though

21.43 Joshua Johnson, *The Westwood Children*. Ca. 1807. Oil on canvas, 3' 5⅛" × 3' 10" (1.04 × 1.17 m). National Gallery of Art, Washington, D.C. (Gift of Edgar William and Bernice Chrysler Garbisch).

the National Gallery has a number of Johnson's portraits, many are still retained by descendants of the original families. *The Westwood Children* (fig. 21.43) has a charming modern appeal with its artful asymmetrical arrangement of the children, the dog, and the tree outside. The children are dressed in identical outfits but each is distinguished by hair style, placement of the feet, and the held objects. It was customary for limners to have the clothing already painted with faces and other personal factors added later.

Thomas Jefferson, 1743–1826

As United States Minister to France, Jefferson had an opportunity to study French Neoclassic architecture and especially Roman architecture in France and Italy. In particular, he was fascinated by the Maison Carrée in southern France. The first time he visited the building he studied it for seven hours, remarking afterward that he was as transfixed as a man admiring his beautiful mistress. His love affair with this temple compelled him to introduce Roman architecture into the United States. Jefferson's design of the State Capitol of Virginia (fig. 21.44) was patterned after the Maison Carrée, but with Ionic capitals, and constructed of wood painted gleaming white. Larger than the Roman temple, the Virginia Capitol has an aura of noble dignity precisely as intended by its designer.

Neoclassicism is popular because it is easily comprehended. Political themes and purposes aside, the classical impulse is toward physical and intellectual perfection as embodied in buildings that express the essence of poised, serene beauty. The Greeks not only invented the style but perfected it, and for twenty-five centuries the Western world has copied it.

21.44 Thomas Jefferson, State Capitol, Richmond, Virginia, from roof of Sovran Bank. 1785–9. Photo: Library of Virginia (Mark Ranier).

STUDY QUESTIONS

1. Compare and contrast the Davids by Donatello, Verrocchio, Michelangelo, and Bernini. Which, in your opinion, best exemplifies the shepherd boy of the Old Testament? How does the Bernini statue symbolize the Baroque, particularly when compared with Michelangelo's *David*?
2. Explain the similarities and differences between Baroque and Rococo art. Identify current manifestations of the Rococo style in modern furniture and interior design.
3. Identify buildings in your area that are basically Neoclassic.

SUMMARY

The seventeenth and eighteenth centuries witnessed diversity and conflict in virtually every field of human endeavor. In the arts, the term Baroque embraced contradictory styles and trends, all of which had a common denominator of restless and powerful energy. The emergence of the Modern World in the seventeenth century was reflected in the development of four predominant styles in response to three categories of patronage:

1. The Counter-Reformation Baroque, a dynamic, colorful, and frequently flamboyant style favored by the Counter-Reformation Church of Rome. Leading artists included Caravaggio, Bernini, and Borromini.
2. The aristocratic Baroque, a splendidly regal style as embodied in the work of Rubens and van Dyck, and largely supported by the court nobles of France and England.
3. The Baroque classical style of Nicolas Poussin, a typically rationalistic French counterpart of the aristocratic style. Poussin emphasized line as opposed to the use of color by Rubens, setting up a confrontation between Poussinists and Rubenists, between painters who objectively controlled the lines and those who expressed themselves through color.
4. The bourgeois Baroque as exemplified in the painting of Hals, Rembrandt, Leyster, Ruisdael, and Vermeer, and patronized by the bourgeois merchants of Holland. As an artistic style by and for the Protestant middle class, this contradicted the aristocratic style and, most emphatically, the Counter-Reformation Baroque of the Church of Rome.

In retrospect, we can see the first two styles as the beginning of the end of the old world, whereas the bourgeois Baroque signified the coming age of world trade, free enterprise, industrial development, and democratic societies.

These multiple aspects of the Baroque had in common a presentation of monumental form; an exuberance of action, expression, and idealism; and an audience that was international. To this audience Baroque artists, with their outstanding accomplishments, brought Western men and women to a realization of their potential as enterprising and creative human beings. This was probably the greatest achievement of the Baroque.

With the death of the "Sun King", Louis XIV, in 1715, the academic classical art of the Baroque lost its chief secular patron. The French court and the aristocracy moved from Versailles, that most monumental of Baroque palaces, and began a new way of life in the elegant, intimate salons of their Parisian townhouses, where manners and charm were emphasized over splendor in the grand manner. Although the eighteenth century was the Age of the Enlightenment, and science was thought to be the key to most aspects of life, in art the refinement of men, women, and nature was the overriding concept. The artists of the Rococo celebrated the cult of pleasure and sentimentality, of genteel seduction and love in an enchanted land. Watteau was elegant and refined; Boucher was the flashy style-setter; Fragonard was unabashedly sensual.

By mid-century the antagonism between the aristocracy and the bourgeoisie had become blatantly apparent. The *philosophes* celebrated middle-class morality and the simple life as embodied in the art of Chardin but found their ultimate artistic exemplar in Jacques-Louis David, who turned to classical antiquity for literary and stylistic inspiration. David placed his talent at the service of revolutionary ideals and painted to inspire honor, duty, and patriotism.

By the end of the eighteenth century all Europe was ablaze with revolutionary fervor and Neoclassicism reigned supreme. The Neoclassic style gave historical sanction to both liberalism and conservatism because it was so readily comprehensible. Any power structure could manipulate the style to defend and justify its existence.

CULTURE AND HUMAN VALUES

There was a critical change in art patronage during the Early Modern Age that foretold the growth of capitalism and the rise of a middle class. Churches and courts were still the main supporters of working artists, but the bourgeois Baroque style was a clear sign of something new and different; nor was the middle-class sponsorship of art the only indication of a significant change in European society. The founding of the Dutch and English East India societies formed the leading edge of the coming European domination of international trade that gradually evolved into imperialism. Increased trade meant greater prosperity for a growing number of capitalists. No longer was a title or a bishop's mitre the only way to power and recognition in this world; money and power were there for the taking by a growing class of bourgeois capitalists.

The view of reality had changed again, from the Renaissance idea of individuals as the most beloved of God's creations to a materialistic view as described by Newton: a world that operated like a machine. Further, the world machine was inhabited by societies that, according to the Enlightenment, functioned rationally—a view confirmed by the American Revolution, but denied by the French Revolution that ended the Enlightenment in Europe.

CHAPTER 22

Music: Baroque, Rococo, and Classical

BAROQUE MUSIC, 1600–1750

Modern music, music as we know it, began sometime around the year 1600 as the Renaissance waned and the new Age of Reason began to take shape. The unbroken line of development leading from early **organum** to the smoothly flowing symmetry of the *a cappella* vocal music of the golden age of polyphony came to an end. The old world of private music for the church, the courts, and a cultural elite steadily declined in influence and importance. The modern world in which music became a public art was taking shape amid the intellectual, political, and social ferment of the seventeenth century.

Given the continuing rivalry between the Reformation and Counter-Reformation, churches could no longer take the faith of their congregations for granted. They built edifices with a maximum of floor space that resembled theatres more than they did Gothic or Renaissance churches. In a setting bursting with agitated forms and twisting, curving shapes with elaborate decorative details, these audiences were preached to, firmly and fervently.

This new Baroque style was applied to all public buildings whether they were churches, concert halls, or opera houses. Even the Baroque palaces (such as Versailles) of ruling heads of state assumed a quasi-public character in their dual roles as royal residences and showcases of national prestige and power.

There was a consistent dualism in the Baroque era, a sometimes precarious balance of opposing forces: church and state, aristocracy and affluent middle class. Baroque architecture reflected this dualism, achieving a sculptured effect by balancing the massiveness of its basic structure with elaborate decoration and exploitation of three-dimensional effects. Even the cylindrical columns of the facades were grouped in pairs. Baroque music displayed its dualism with balanced vocal-instrumental groups, consistent use of two-part (binary) forms, and the reduction of the eight church modes to the two modes of either major or minor.

The emergence of instrumental music to a position of equal importance with vocal music virtually eliminated the *a cappella* style. All Baroque vocal music had an instrumental accompaniment, whether it was a mass, motet, **oratorio**, passion, **cantata**, or opera. Purely instrumental music established new forms such as the balanced participation of small and large groups in the **concerto grosso** and the pieces for two solo instruments with keyboard accompaniment called trio sonatas. Even the dynamics were dualistic, with consistent use of alternating loud and soft passages.

KEYBOARD MUSIC

Harpsichord

Dance Suite

Dancing has been a fundamental activity since the dim dawn of the human race—dances to appease the gods, to exorcise evil spirits, to invoke fertility, and for the sheer exhilaration of physical and emotional release. Dancing attained a new prestige during the seventeenth century, with magnificent balls in the great royal courts. Lords and ladies refined lusty and sometimes crude peasant dances into a social art of grace and charm (fig. 22.1 and chapter opener opposite).

22.1 Anonymous, *Queen Elizabeth I Dancing the Volta with Robert Dudley, Earl of Leicester*; detail opposite. Late 16th century. Oil on canvas. Private collection, England. Photo: A.K.G., London.

During the early Baroque period, short instrumental pieces were composed in the manner and style of various popular dances. The exotic and erotic sarabande, for example, was transformed into a stylized and sophisticated art form that sometimes subtly implied what the original boldly proclaimed. Later on, in the nineteenth century, a similar process changed the waltz from an "indecent" dance into a popular social dance, leading finally to an art form, for example, "The Blue Danube" by Johann Strauss, Jr. Late twentieth-century composers are likely to accord similar treatment to dances of the 1980s and 1990s. During the seventeenth century these stylized dances were combined in collections of chamber music called suites, which were played by harpsichords, other solo instruments, and various instrumental ensembles. There are usually five or six dances (or movements) in a suite, each a different type of dance with a standard sequence: allemande, courante, sarabande, gigue. The suite was truly international in character; the original folk dances were, respectively, German, French, Spanish, and English (jig). Each dance suite had, however, a basic unity: each dance was in the same key.

For the first time in history, music acquired a firm and rational foundation: a key. Centuries before, the many modes of the Greeks had been reduced to the eight church modes that formed the musical material of everything from plainsong to Renaissance polyphonic music. The Baroque saw the emergence of two new concepts:

1. all music came to be written in a consistent pitch relationship called a key, with a choice of either major or minor mode, and
2. a temporary disenchantment with the complexities of polyphonic music led to compositions based on blocks of sound called **chords** or harmony.

By exploiting homophonic (one-sound) music (that is, one block of harmony following another) and a fixed pitch relationship, composers were merely reflecting the new view of reality. The "old music" was gradually replaced by less complicated music that was considered to be lucid and rational, though of course always expressive. This is not to say that this was a conscious decision by anyone or that there was instant recognition of the drastic changes that had taken place. Rather, musicians, like all artists, reacted to the new view of reality with a combination of old and new techniques that gave a fresh sound to a new age.

This new sound, as in the music of Johann Sebastian Bach, can be considered the beginning of modern music. Compositions by twentieth-century composers such as Stravinsky, Prokofiev, and Bartók are more closely related to the music of Bach than Bach's is, in turn, to the Renaissance. Palestrina, Lassus, and other Renaissance musicians were writing for the Church of Rome and for an educated aristocracy. Bach, though sometimes serving as a court composer, wrote, played, and conducted music for the largely middle-class Lutheran church.

The music of Bach is admired for its artistry and its superb craftsmanship. In his own day, however, Bach composed much of his music in response to specific demands. Many of his organ works were written and performed for church services and special programs. His sacred cantatas, written for particular Sundays of the liturgical year, were normally performed only once. Having served their purpose, they were consigned to storage where, many years later, a young Mozart could discover them and exclaim, "Now here is a man from whom I can learn," or words to that effect.

Much of Bach's output was intended for performance by amateur musicians and, more importantly, to be listened to by audiences composed essentially of middle-class German burghers. This middle class, of increasing affluence and influence, was becoming the primary audience not only of that period, but of all subsequent periods. Today's mass audience is a logical development of the processes that began during the eighteenth century.

The following dance suite for harpsichord is typical of solo keyboard music of the Baroque. The performance could be as simple as an amateur playing in the parlor of a middle-class home or as elaborate as a professional playing at a royal court on a highly decorated harpsichord like that in figure 22.2. The suite is in six movements.

Listening Example 20

DANCE SUITE

J. S. Bach, French Suite No. 4 in E-Flat Major, 6th movement, Gigue
1720–4

Time: 2:34
Cassette 2, track 19[1]

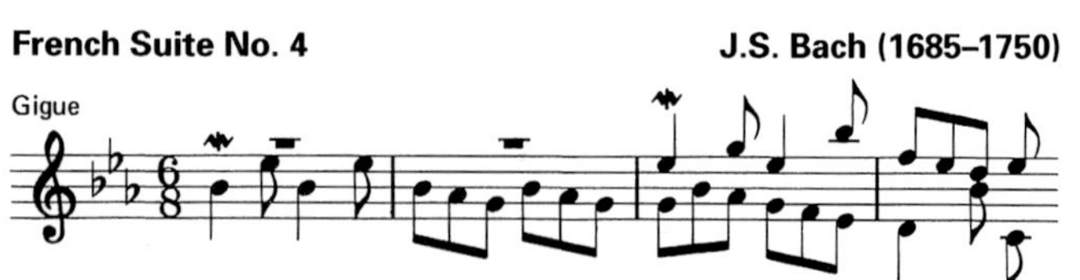

Organ

The prime keyboard instrument for the performance of preludes, **fugues** and chorale preludes was the pipe **organ**. Baroque organs were solo instruments capable of filling Baroque churches and concert halls with a variety and volume of sound unequaled by any other instrument. The clarity and grandeur of these magnificent instruments have never been surpassed. The proof of this statement can still be heard throughout Europe; many of the original instruments have never ceased pouring forth the unique color and brilliance of the Baroque (fig. 22.3).

Chorale Prelude

An organ composition consisting of variations on a **chorale** melody is called a chorale prelude. The variations are to be played before the congregation sings the chorale (what Lutherans call a hymn)—hence the term "prelude." The intention of the organist is to set the general mood of the chorale so that the congregation can sing it with more understanding.

The following chorale prelude is based on the Lutheran chorale "Wachet auf" ("Sleepers, Awake"). The opening section has a sprightly melody over a smoothly striding bass. The first part of the chorale melody becomes a third voice about halfway through the opening section, after which the entire section is repeated. In the second (concluding) section the chorale melody is interspersed throughout.

Listening Example 21

CHORALE PRELUDE

J. S. Bach, Schubler Chorale Prelude No. 1, BWV 645, "Wachet auf"
1746

Time: 4:40
Cassette 2, track 21[2]

INSTRUMENTAL MUSIC

Trio Sonata

Baroque music was particularly notable for the widespread development of private music-making by performers who played or sang for the sheer joy of making their own music. Not all of them were as skilled as professionals, but self-expression was more important than technical proficiency. These multitudes of musicians, whose personal pleasure was more than sufficient payment for performance, were amateurs: truc lovers of music in the best sense of the term.

Musical instruments became necessary functional furniture for a burgeoning middle class growing ever more

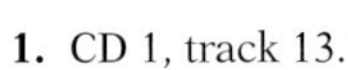
1. CD 1, track 13.

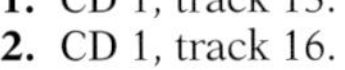
2. CD 1, track 16.

22.2 Pascal Taskin, Harpsichord, 1786. Victoria & Albert Museum, London.

22.3 Christian Müller, Baroque pipe organ, Grote Kerk, Haarlem, Holland. 1735–8, with casework probably by J. van Logteren.
Organ designers were as concerned with the exterior design of the case as with the tonal quality of the pipes.

affluent. Baroque music was, however, in many respects difficult for amateur performances. Composers did not indicate the exact speed or tempo of their compositions, nor did they do more than provide occasional directions regarding dynamics (relative loudness or softness). These procedures gave amateurs considerable margin for error. Moreover, specific directions as to which instruments were to be used were frequently omitted, leaving it to the discretion, and resources, of the performers.

The ubiquitous trio sonata provided ideal material for amateurs because it was written in the conventional form of two melodic lines plus generalized directions for keyboard accompaniment. The two melodies could be performed by any two available instruments and the accompaniment by any keyboard instrument (clavichord, harpsichord, or pipe organ). The pivotal figures in trio sonatas (and large compositions) were the keyboard performers; it was assumed that they were the most competent musicians, which was usually the case. They provided the foundation for the continuation of the piece, which led to the adoption of the Italian word *continuo* to describe the function of the keyboard musicians. It was up to them to fill in the harmony and to cover up the blank spots whenever the less expert performers played wrong notes, lost their place, or otherwise strayed from grace.

Baroque chamber music was highly improvisational (as were arias in operas and oratorios) because performers were expected to add their personal touches to a given melodic line. Compositions were "personalized" through available instruments, the expertise and imagination of performers and, most importantly, the musical challenge presented by the composer. Not until jazz appeared on the scene during the latter part of the nineteenth century did performers again have so much individual freedom as that accorded amateur and professional musicians of the Baroque period.

Concerto

The classic Baroque **concerto** was the *concerto grosso* in which a small group of soloists (*concertino*) performed in conjunction with a full orchestra (*tutti* or *concerto grosso*). Bach, Handel, and Vivaldi did write solo concertos for single instruments, but Baroque composers generally preferred the sonority of the concertino as it blended and contrasted with the full orchestra.

The Italian composer Antonio Vivaldi wrote more than 450 concertos, the most famous of which are *The Four Seasons* for solo violin and orchestra. Each season—spring, summer, autumn, winter—has three movements that together evoke different aspects of the season. The four concertos are remarkable early examples of **program music**, that is, music describing or communicating extra-musical ideas. As might be expected, the first concerto is bright and cheerful, full of allusions to nature's annual rebirth.

Listening Example 22

VIOLIN CONCERTO

Vivaldi, *The Four Seasons,* "Spring," 1st movement
Before 1725; excerpt

Time: 2:25
Cassette 2, track 20

The Four Seasons, "Spring" **Vivaldi (ca. 1675–1741)**

VOCAL-INSTRUMENTAL MUSIC

Chorale

Martin Luther translated the Bible into German because he believed that every Christian should have direct access to the text. He was also concerned about congregational participation in the service of worship because it tended to bind the congregation and the clergy together in a common endeavor. Moreover, music had, in Luther's opinion, a spiritual, transcendental quality that enriched and elevated worship. Unlike John Calvin, Luther, once a priest of the Church of Rome, culled the rich musical heritage of the church, selecting and adapting plainsong to the needs and capabilities of Protestant congregations. For the first time in many centuries, common people once again took an active part in worship as they raised their voices in song. They sang what we would call hymns, though hymn tunes of the Lutheran church are called "chorales."

The typical Lutheran service of the eighteenth century began at 7:00 A.M. and concluded at noon. In the larger churches professional musicians (such as Bach) were expected to teach school during the week, maintain the organ, train a volunteer choir, compose special instrumental and vocal music for each Sunday of the year, and play the organ and direct the choir during the Sunday service. Each Sunday occupied a specific place in the liturgical year, with special emphasis on Advent, Epiphany, Easter, and Pentecost. The music for each Sunday had to correspond with the special meaning of that Sunday—from the opening chorale prelude through the hymns, the cantata, and the concluding postlude.

Oratorio

An oratorio is a sacred or epic text set to music and performed in a church or concert hall by soloists, chorus, and orchestra; it can also be described, somewhat loosely, as a concert version of a sacred opera. In the latter part of his career George Frederick Handel, the foremost composer in eighteenth-century London, turned from composing operas for an indifferent nobility to writing oratorios for the middle class. Of his twenty-one oratorios, the most celebrated is *Messiah.* This extended composition was written in feverish haste—completed in only three weeks—leading Handel to believe it was divinely inspired. Based mainly on the New Testament, it is divided into three sections. Concluding the second section, the brilliant Hallelujah Chorus so impressed George II that he spontaneously rose to his feet, thus setting the tradition of a standing audience for this stirring chorus. The text consists primarily of "hallelujah," a Hebrew word of jubilation that has been called the college cheer of Christendom.

> *Listening Example 23*
>
> **ORATORIO**
>
> Handel, *Messiah,* 44th movement, Hallelujah Chorus 1742
>
> Time: 3:59
> Cassette 2, track 22

***Messiah,* Hallelujah Chorus** **Handel (1685–1759)**

Opera

Opera (It., from Lat. *opera,* "works") is generally considered to be the most "Baroque" of all the artistic media of the age. As discussed earlier, opera began as a "reform" movement, an attempt to return to the proper combination of words and music in ancient Greek tragedies. Text was all-important, vocal lines were sparse, and accompaniment minimal. However, within a remarkably short period opera developed into full-blown music drama with elaborate sets, costumes, and choruses. Despite various regional differences in style between Florence, Rome, Venice, Vienna, Paris, and London, opera became the most popular and spectacular art form of the period. Elaborate opera houses were built all over Europe for an art form which, in a manner of speaking, put the vitality of an era on stage for all to see and hear.

Italian operas became the favorite artistic import for most of the nations of western Europe. French nationalism, however, strongly resisted the dominance of Italian music. Critics lambasted Italian operas as being too long, monotonous, too arty, archaic in language, and with flamboyant singing that obscured the sound and the sense of the words, thus leaving no appeal to the logical French mind. Additionally, the male sopranos and altos—the *castrati*—were said to horrify the women and to cause the men to snicker. But the French resisted Italian opera because they valued dance over drama. Dance—French ballet—was central to the French musical stage but only minimal in Italian opera.

The struggle between French and Italian music became an actual confrontation when the Italian opera composer, Pietro Francesco Cavalli (1602–76), was commissioned to write a festive opera for the wedding of Louis XIV. The director of the king's music, Jean-Baptiste Lully (1632–87)—born Gianbattista Lulli in Florence—turned the occasion to his advantage. The opera was indeed performed in 1662 for the king's wedding and it was monumental, lasting some six hours. However, each act concluded with one of Lully's large-scale ballets. The French reaction to this spectacle was interesting: the production was seen, not as a music drama with interpolated dances, but as a gigantic ballet with operatic interludes. Cavalli returned to Italy, vowing never to write another opera while Lully continued his intrigues becoming, in time, as absolute a sovereign in music as Louis XIV was in affairs of state. Cavalli's career was finished but Lully went on to accumulate one of the greatest fortunes ever amassed by a musician.

ROCOCO, 1725–75

In art and architecture the last stage of the Baroque period is characterized by an even more elaborate style called Rococo (from the Fr., *rocaille,* "rock," and *coquilles,* "shells"). The grandeur of the Baroque was scaled down to an emphasis on interior design and decorative scroll and shell work, resulting in a sort of domesticated, sometimes decadent, Baroque.

In music, Rococo is the "gallant style," a highly refined art of elegant pleasantness suitable for intimate social gatherings in fashionable salons. Among the chief exponents were François Couperin and Domenico Scarlatti with styles comparable to the paintings of Watteau, Boucher, and Fragonard.

François Couperin (1668–1733)

The foremost Rococo composer was Couperin, usually referred to as "le Grand." His music crystallizes the miniature world of the Rococo. French to the core, it is scintillating, elegant, refined, and witty. He wrote twenty-seven *ordres* or sets of dances for harpsichord, all with evocative titles. The name of the following composition is typically whimsical. It translates literally as "hook in leg" and means tripping someone. In this case it is the music that goes tripping along, lighthearted and saucy.

Listening Example 24

DANCE MOVEMENT FOR HARPSICHORD

Couperin, Ordre No. 22, *Le Croc-en-jambe*
1730

Time: 2:14
Cassette 2, track 23

Ordre No. 22, *Le Croc-en-jambe* **Couperin (1668–1733)**

CLASSICISM IN MUSIC, 1760–1827

The Classical period in music dates from about 1760, the beginning of Haydn's mature style, to about 1827, the year of Beethoven's death. Haydn, Mozart, and Beethoven were musical giants in what has been called the golden age of music, an era of extraordinary musical achievements. Other eras have perhaps been as musically productive, but none has become so mutually identifiable as the Classical period, the golden age, and the musical output of Haydn, Mozart, and Beethoven. The basic homophonic style of Classicism has many antecedents in several earlier periods of music. It is therefore appropriate to briefly review these earlier periods.

Renaissance music was primarily polyphonic and written in the old liturgical modes. On the other hand, some Renaissance music, English madrigals in particular, was quite homophonic and was, moreover, tonal; that is, it was written in either a major or a minor key rather than in a liturgical mode. The music of Gabrieli in Venice was also strongly homophonic with a preference for sonorous harmonies rather than the multiple melody lines used by Renaissance composers such as Josquin, Lassus, and Palestrina.

At the beginning of the seventeenth century there was a relatively brief period of strongly homophonic music as composers attempted to re-create what they thought was the text-oriented musical style of the ancient Greeks. These experiments in words and music led to the development of the new style of music called opera. Opera, the epitome of the new Baroque style, quickly became elaborate and ornate and combined homophonic and polyphonic music. The vocal-instrumental music of the age developed a new and complex style of polyphony, culminating in the music of Handel and Bach.

Rococo music used Baroque **ornamentation**, but the style was much more homophonic, less profound, and more stylishly elegant. Some characteristics of the Rococo, notably the less complex homophonic techniques, were incorporated into a new style called Classicism, Neoclassicism, or Viennese Classicism. Classicism is the preferred term for music of the period, whereas Neoclassicism is generally applied to the sister arts.

At no time are the stylistic periods of the arts precisely synchronized. Careful study of the comparative outline given (table 22.1, p. 222) will indicate that the prevailing world-views of the periods since the Renaissance are reflected in the arts at different times. Any number of inferences can be drawn regarding the influence of an era on the arts and the arts on each other. However, the artistic production of specific individuals is of paramount concern. The uniqueness of a work of art reflects the uniqueness of the individual artist who created it.

The Classical period of music might also be called the "Advanced Age of the Amateur Musician." Baroque music, with its figured bass accompaniments and demands for improvisation, was partially the province of the professional but with real possibilities for gifted amateurs. On the other hand, the latter part of the eighteenth century featured modern notation, with every note written down plus indications for interpretation (tempo, dynamics, etc.), thus providing an even better opportunity for music-making by amateurs. Baroque musicians could improvise and stray from the musical score but, in the Age of Reason, you acceded to the composer's intentions by playing the music exactly as written.

The vastly increased demand for music for all occasions resulted in a flood of mostly instrumental compositions. There were serenades for outdoor parties, chamber music for indoor gatherings, **symphonies** for the newly established symphony orchestras, and operas for the increasing number of private and public opera houses. The newly invented piano (ca. 1710 by Cristofori), with its ability to play soft and loud (It. *pianoforte*) on a single keyboard, rapidly replaced the harpsichord and the clavichord as the standard home instrument for amateur performance. Amateur chamber music societies were organized for the presentation of programs ranging from **sonatas** to duets and trios for the various instruments, including the quartets for a homogeneous group of string instruments called, naturally enough, string quartets.

All of this musical activity was of little benefit to those who tried to earn a living from their music. Eighteenth-century musicians were, on the whole, accorded a lowly position on the social scale. Typically, composers such as Franz Joseph Haydn worked for a noble family like the Esterhazy, wore servant's livery, and sat at the dinner table "below the salt." Not until the latter part of his life did Haydn achieve any financial independence, and he had to go to the London concert scene to do it. Ironically, the descendants of the once powerful Esterhazy family are notable today only to the extent that some of Haydn's unpublished music may still be in their possession.

Franz Joseph Haydn, 1732–1809

Haydn's professional life was typical of the vicissitudes of a musical career, yet he fared better than many of his contemporaries. In a short sketch that he contributed to a 1776 yearbook, Haydn wrote that he sang at court in Vienna and in St. Stephen's Cathedral until his voice changed and he was summarily dismissed.

> When my voice finally changed I barely managed to stay alive by giving music lessons to children for about eight years. In this way many talented people are ruined: they have to earn a miserable living and have no time to study.

There were numerous musical opportunities for a musician in Vienna, but most of them paid very little. Musicians were forced to hold down a number of positions in order to survive. Haydn had as many as three jobs on a Sunday morning: playing the violin at one church, the organ at another, and singing in the choir at a third. When he finally achieved full employment with the Esterhazy family, he was quite willing, at that time, to relinquish a certain amount of personal freedom.

Classical composers had tired of the late Baroque proclivity for ever more elaborate and sometimes ponderous polyphony. A simpler homophonic style emerged and began gradually to replace the polyphonic manipulation of a single musical theme. By abandoning the polyphonic vocal-instrumental style, composers were faced with a dilemma: how to develop a coherent style of purely instrumental music. A certain unity was inherent in vocal music because of the text. Without a text, composers were faced with the possibility of a chaotic mass of instrumental sounds. One of the solutions was to give shape to instrumental music by using the form of theme and variations: a long subject or theme was followed by a series of variations that, usually, grew gradually more distant from the theme, before concluding with the original theme.

Haydn, as the first of the composers in the Classical style, led the way in establishing such basic instrumental ensembles as the symphony orchestra and the string quartet. Large enough to produce a rich, full tone but small enough to be intimate and to leave room for personal expression, the string quartet was the preferred Classical musical group. Consisting of first and second violin, viola, and cello, corresponding to the SATB division of voices in choral music, the three members of the violin family can achieve a fine balance of unified tone. The second movement of his String Quartet in C has the Theme and Variations form. Further, the theme was Haydn's gift to the Austrian people, the Austrian national anthem, best known as the Austrian National Hymn.

Listening Example 25

SLOW MOVEMENT OF STRING QUARTET

Haydn, String Quartet in C, Op. 76 No. 3, "Emperor," 2nd movement
1798

Time: 7:33[3]

Wolfgang Amadeus Mozart, 1756–91

Musical genius has been a subject of considerable interest to twentieth-century psychologists, but the exact nature of the qualities that can be labeled "genius" remains tantalizingly elusive. Thus the accomplishments of Mozart, possibly the greatest musical genius who ever lived, are both awesome and inexplicable.

Mozart devoted virtually his entire life to the composition and performance of music. Like Haydn, he endured the slights of a society as yet unready and unwilling to recognize, let alone support, his incredible gifts. Unlike Haydn, he never found a noble patron. His brief, poverty-stricken life and eventual burial in an unmarked grave testify eloquently to the status of a musician in Vienna during the golden age of music.

There are many accounts of Mozart's precocity but none more typical of his manner of composition—and lifestyle—than the premiere of his opera *Don Giovanni*. The opera was complete except for the overture that was, according to the composer, "finished." On the day of the premiere, Mozart was busily engaged in shooting billiards, one of his favorite occupations. In reply to urgent questioning, he reiterated that he had completed the overture. When pressed to produce a musical score, he finally admitted that the piece was indeed completed—in his head—but not yet written down. Many cups of coffee later, the complete parts, still dripping with wet ink, were rushed to the opera house where the orchestra had to sightread the music. Characteristically, the thousands of musical notes that Mozart had mentally arranged added up to a gem in operatic literature. Some critics feel, in fact, that *Don Giovanni* is the greatest opera ever written but others single out *The Marriage of Figaro* or *The Magic Flute*, also by Mozart.

Mozart wrote over fifty symphonies, with most of the movements using sonata form,[4] which neither he nor Haydn is credited with inventing. The inventor is, in fact, unknown. Sonata form was the prime eighteenth-

3. CD 2, track 1.
4. Sonata form was not limited to sonatas, which are compositions for piano or a solo instrument with accompaniment. The form was also used for trios, quartets, concertos, and symphonies.

century solution to the problem of finding a rational design for instrumental music. In a very real sense, sonata form reflected Enlightenment ideals: it was lucid, logical, and symmetrical.

The technical term "sonata form" is a label for a procedure that uses a dual subject rather than the single subject of the Baroque style. The first of these two subjects is usually vigorous and dynamic, while the second is generally quieter and more lyrical. The two subjects should be, musically speaking, logical parts of the whole; the second subject should somehow complement and balance the first.

The dual subjects of sonata form are theme A and theme B. These two contrasting subjects (or themes) are connected by a bridge, a transitional passage, which leads smoothly from theme A to theme B. Following theme B there is a closing section called a codetta ("little ending"). The complete unit of two themes with connecting transition and closing section contains all the thematic material which has been presented or to which the ear has been exposed. This unit is therefore called an exposition and can be outlined as indicated below. During the Classical period expositions were normally repeated, as indicated by the sets of double dots.

Exposition
‖: theme A bridge theme B codetta :‖

After the basic material has been presented in the exposition, the composer proceeds to manipulate and exploit selected thematic material in the development section. Any and all material may be subjected to a variety of treatment.

Near the end of the development section, the composer usually introduces the return, a transitional section that prepares the way for a recapitulation of the material from the exposition. The recapitulation repeats, more or less, the material from the exposition, but there are subtle variations that help avoid monotony.

After the codetta of the recapitulation, the composer may add a final coda if he or she believes that something more is needed to bring the movement to a satisfactory conclusion. A complete sonata form can be outlined as follows:

Exposition	Development	Recapitulation
‖: A bridge B codetta :‖:		return A bridge B codetta (coda) :‖

Mozart's Symphony No. 35 was written for a festive occasion in the house of Siegmund Haffner, the mayor of Salzburg. Originally a six-movement serenade, it was completed in the amazing time of only two weeks. Six months after finishing it he wrote to his father that "the new Haffner symphony has quite astonished me, for I do not remember a note of it. It must be very effective." Mozart's evaluation of his new symphony is modest, for this is a joyful work of great brilliance. The first, second, and fourth movements use sonata form while the third movement follows the ternary form of ABA.

TABLE 22.1 COMPARISON OF STYLISTIC PERIODS OF THE ARTS

	Approx. Dates	Important Individuals
Period: The Age of Reason	1600–1700	Descartes, Galileo, Kepler, Bacon, Spinoza
Artistic Style: Baroque		
Architecture	1575–1740	Bernini, Wren, Mansart, Perrault, Le Vau
Music	1600–1750	Corelli, Lully, Vivaldi, Handel, Bach, Purcell
Painting	1600–1720	Rubens, Rembrandt, Steen, Hals, Vermeer, van Dyck, Velasquez
Sculpture	1600–1720	Bernini
Period: The Enlightenment	1687–1789	Newton, Voltaire, Diderot, Locke, Hume, Kant, Rousseau, Frederick II, Jefferson, Franklin
Artistic Style: Rococo		
Architecture	1715–60	Erlach, Hildebrandt, Asam, Cuvilliés, Fischer
Music	1725–75	Couperin, some of Haydn and Mozart
Painting	1720–89	Watteau, Chardin, Boucher, Fragonard
Sculpture	1770–1825	Clodion, Falconet
Artistic Style: Neoclassic		
Architecture	1750–1830	Chalgrin, Vignon, Fontaine
Music (Classicism)	1760–1827	Haydn, Mozart, Beethoven, Gluck
Painting	1780–1850	David, Ingres
Sculpture	1800–40	Canova, Thorwalden, Houdon

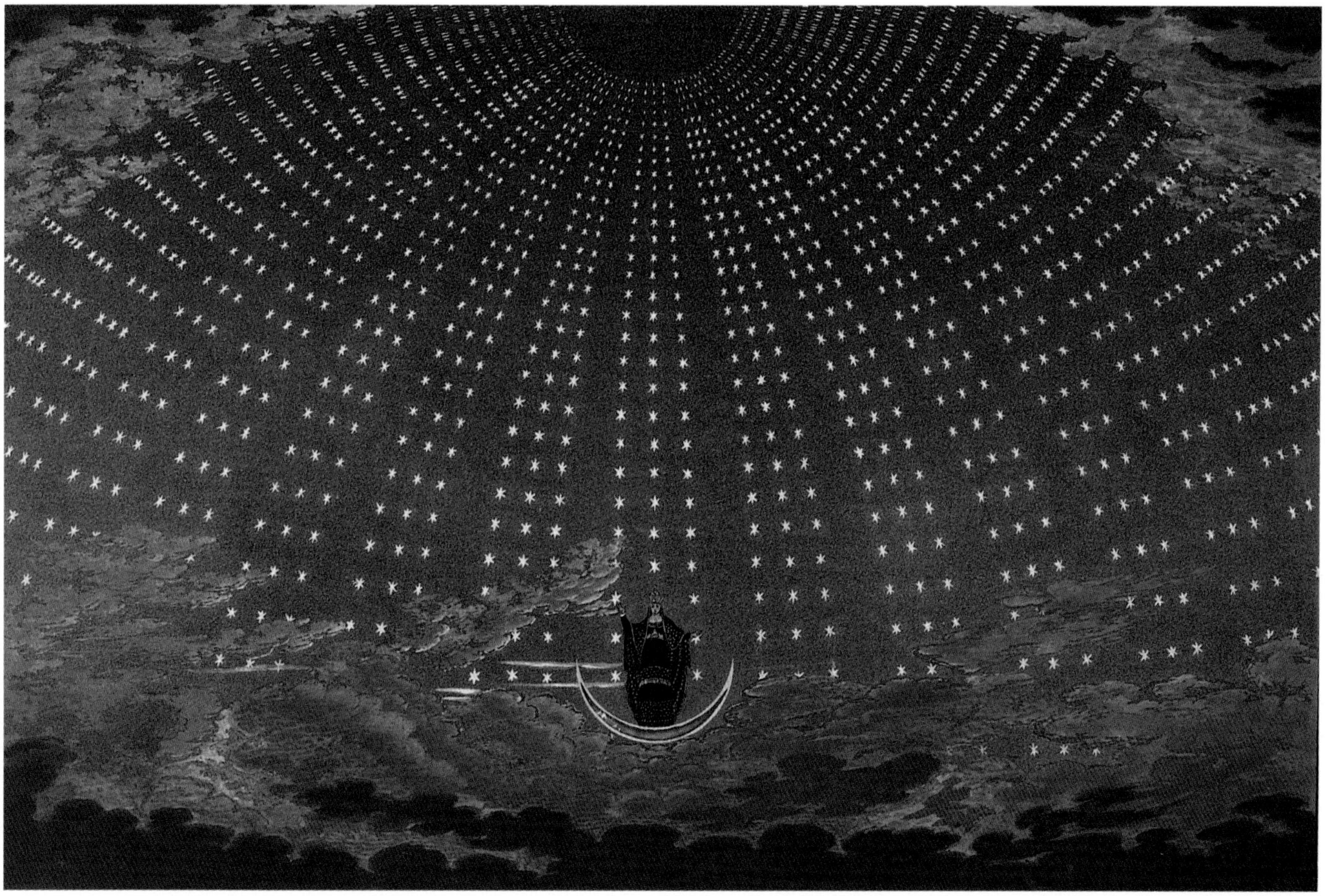

22.4 K. F. Schinkel, Design for Mozart's opera *The Magic Flute*, Act 1 Scene 6, The Queen of Night, from *Decorationen auf den Beiden*. 1823.

> *Listening Example 26*
>
> **SYMPHONY**
>
> Mozart, Symphony No. 35 in D, K.385, "Haffner"
> 1782
>
> Time: 7:59, 4:25, 3:05. 3:34
> Cassette 2, track 24 (4th movement)[5]

Symphony No. 35, "Haffner," Fourth movement **Mozart (1756–91)**

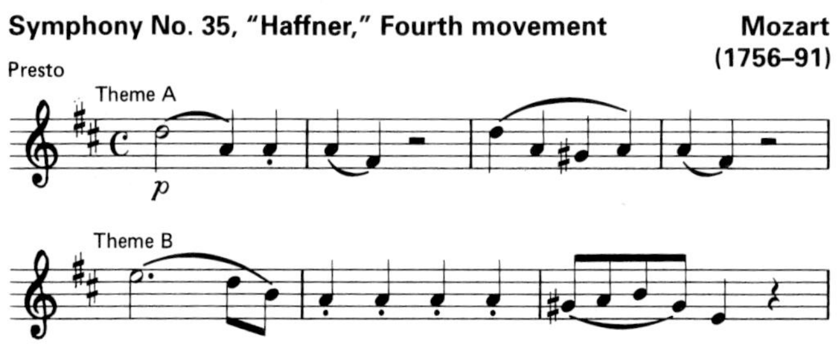

The Magic Flute is a comic opera commissioned by a theatrical impresario who wanted a popular and profitable opera, which it was. Its combination of fantasy (fig. 22.4), frolic, and solemn rites has made it popular on the operatic stage, as a movie, as several different television productions, and even as a production of the Salzburg Marionettes for the annual Mozart Festival in Salzburg. In the following solemn aria Sarastro, the high priest, comforts a despairing Pamina by assuring her that Prince Tamino will soon be free to marry her.

> *Listening Example 27*
>
> **OPERATIC ARIA**
>
> Mozart, *The Magic Flute,* Act II,"Within these hallowed portals"
> 1791
>
> Time. 4:15[6]

5. CD 1, track 19 (1st movement); CD 1 track 20 (2nd movement); CD 1, track 21 (3rd movement).
6. CD 1, track 18.

Within these hallowed portals,
Revenge and discord die;
Here when a brother falleth,
A brother's help is nigh.

Led by a kind and friendly hand,
He seeks, rejoiced, the better land. } 3 times

Here on our peaceful mountain,
In holy love we live;
And here no hatred lurketh,
But all their wrongs forgive.

He who by love is not made free,
Doth not deserve a man to be. } 3 times

English translation by Samuel Langford

Ludwig van Beethoven, 1770–1827

Unlike Haydn and Mozart, Beethoven forged a place for himself as an economically independent musician. He was not above selling the same composition to different publishers and did so quite often. He reasoned that the publishers had cheated composers long enough; he was merely collecting retribution for a long chain of abuses.

Beethoven's finances were generally sound though somewhat chaotic. His health was another matter. He noticed a hearing loss at an early age that gradually evolved into total deafness. This silence became, at times, almost more than a musician could bear. That some of Beethoven's greatest music was composed while he was completely deaf is a testament to his genius and to his unconquerable spirit. He himself conducted the premiere of his Ninth Symphony, that powerful and imposing work dedicated to the exalted ideal of world brotherhood. At the conclusion of the symphony he remained facing the orchestra, solitary in his silence, and thinking that the work had failed. Finally, someone turned him about to face the thunderous applause of an audience that was both inspired and deeply moved.

Beethoven's Third Symphony, the "Eroica," was originally dedicated to Napoleon, whom Beethoven regarded as a true Faustian man who labored to improve the lives of all the people. There were many victims of Napoleon's march to power—"while man's desires and aspirations stir, he cannot choose but err"—but it appeared that he was using his energy to make the world a better place in which people could work out their freedom. However, Napoleon declared himself emperor, and Beethoven furiously erased his name from the dedicatory page of the "Eroica," leaving the work implicitly dedicated to the heroic impulses of a Faustian man or, simply, to an unknown hero.

Beethoven poured the very essence of Classical symphonic music into his Fifth Symphony, a work that has often been cited as the perfect symphony. Though sometimes threatening to break the bounds of Classical form, Beethoven channeled all his titanic energy into the driving rhythms of this mighty work. The Fifth Symphony is a summary of many aspects of Beethoven's genius: the terse, surging energy of the first movement, the moving and mellow lyricism of the second movement, the exuberant vitality of the **scherzo**, and the sheer drive of the finale.

The orchestra as Beethoven knew it was simply not large and expressive enough for this symphony. He enlarged his tonal palette by adding instruments at both ends of the spectrum and trombones in the middle to obtain the full and rich sound that he had to have. The instrumentation for the enlarged orchestra needed to perform his Fifth Symphony is: piccolo, two flutes, two oboes, two clarinets, two bassoons, contra-bassoon, two French horns, two trumpets, three trombones, two timpani, sixteen violin I, fourteen violin II, ten violas, eight cellos, six basses. (The number of strings can vary; these are approximations.)

The Fifth Symphony achieves a maximum effect with the utmost economy of musical materials. Essentially, the entire symphony is built out of one musical interval and one rhythmic pattern:

Interval of 3rd plus pattern of ♪♪♪ | 𝅗𝅥

This motive is so brief that it is referred to as a germ motive from which the entire symphony is germinated. This first movement is in sonata form.

> *Listening Example 28*
> **SYMPHONIC MOVEMENT**
>
> Beethoven, Symphony No. 5 in C Minor, Op. 67,
> 1st movement
> 1808
>
> Time: 8:41
> Cassette 2, track 25[7]

7. CD 2, track 5.

The Fifth Symphony is a prime example of the Classical style: logical, direct and to the point, objective, controlled, achieving maximum effect with a minimum of means.

Beethoven is considered by some to be a pivotal figure in musical styles, standing midway between Classicism and the dawning age of Romanticism. However, his heroic style and even his introspective later works all testify to his fundamental Classical outlook, namely, his rational control of his material. Beethoven's music served *him;* he was the master who, with disciplined creativity, molded (and sometimes hammered) his musical materials into the structured sounds of the Classical style.

SUMMARY

From about 1600 to 1750 the Baroque style built a new kind of music on the Classical foundations of the Renaissance. The flexible modal system of the past was narrowed down to a single tonal center, or key, with the modal possibilities reduced to two: major or minor. Compensating for the limiting of tonal materials to a single major or minor key were the new possibilities for composing by contrasting keys and modulating from one key to another.

The ubiquitous trio sonata was perhaps most representative of Baroque music-making because of the emphasis on instrumental music with improvised accompaniment in the *continuo* part. Concertos were more formal because of the larger number of instrumentalists involved, but the continuo still played an important accompanying part for orchestra and soloist(s).

Following the Reformation, the German sacred songs called chorales assumed an important place in congregational singing and in organ literature in the form of chorale preludes. Cantatas, oratorios, and operas were the most important vocal forms of the Baroque, although there was still a tradition of composing Masses and motets.

The surface elements of the ornate Baroque style assumed a primary emphasis in the style called Rococo. The Rococo, or "gallant style" of music (1725–75), with its light, airy texture and elegant ornamentation, served as a bridge between the sumptuous Baroque and the gracefully refined style of the Classical period.

During the Classical period (1760–1827), instrumental musicians, whether professional or amateur, came into their own. The improvement in musical instruments and the great interest in amateur performance encouraged the composition of chamber music (sonatas, string quartets, etc.) and orchestral music ranging from serenades for soirées to symphonies for the growing number of concert halls. Monothematic polyphony was replaced by a dual-subject structure called sonata form in which composers could combine two contrasting themes into an expressive and balanced whole.

The Classical period, coinciding with the height of the Enlightenment, created chamber music and the symphony orchestra virtually as they are known today. Even more important, music progressed from a more or less private concern of the aristocracy or the church to a public art available to all.

CULTURE AND HUMAN VALUES

All of us are so accustomed to the ready availability of all kinds of music that we tend to forget that mass audiences for music are a relatively recent phenomenon. As late as the seventeenth century, the musical patrons were still the courts and, to a lesser extent, the Church of Rome. After the Reformation, Protestant churches, particularly Lutheran, became active in commissioning music and hiring organists and choirmasters. The common element in the Lutheran churches and in Holland was the growing middle class.

By the eighteenth century music had become much more of a public art. Virtually anyone with money could rent a hall and hire musicians, but few could make a living as a composer. Handel did fairly well in London, particularly with his oratorios, but Bach's reputation was largely based on his remarkable skills as a performer. Mozart attempted to survive in Vienna as a composer without a patron but only eked out a bare living. At the end of the century, however, Beethoven proved that music had finally become a profession in which one could make a living composing and performing. It was at this point that one can say musical art had gone public.

STUDY QUESTIONS

1. Explain the forces that helped convert music from a private to a public art.
2. What are the pressures when music depends on an admission-paying public?

ADDITIONAL LISTENING

1. Bach, *The Well-Tempered Clavier,* vol. I, Fugue in G minor. This is a good example of the monothematic (one-subject) Baroque style (CD 1, track 14).
2. J. S. Bach, Partita No. 3 in E for violin, Gavotte en Rondeau. This is in the rondo form of ABACAD (CD 1, track 15).
3. Beethoven, Piano Sonata No. 2 in A, Op. 2, No. 2. The fourth movement is also in rondo form (CD 2, track 2).
4. Beethoven, Piano Sonata No. 8 in C minor, Op. 13. The first movement, after the dramatic introduction, is in sonata form (CD 2, track 3).
5. Beethoven, Violin Sonata No. 5 in F, Op. 24, "Spring." The scherzo is in three-part form (ABA) (CD 2, track 4).

UNIT 8

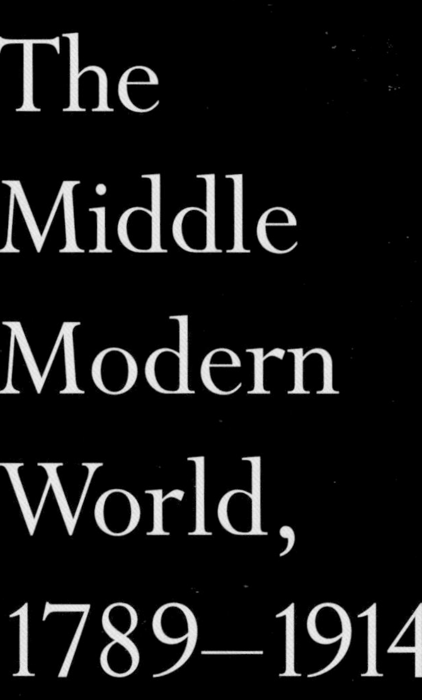

The Middle Modern World, 1789–1914

The Middle Modern World

1789–1914

	People and Events	Art and Architecture	Literature and Music	Philosophy, Science, Invention
1800	**1760–1820** George III of England **1774–93** Louis XVI of France **1789–1815** French Revolution **1801–25** Alexander I of Russia **1804–12** Napoleon Emperor of France **1814–24** Louis XVIII of France **1815** Napoleon defeated at Waterloo **1820–30** George IV of England **1821–30** Greek revolt from Turks **1824–30** Charles X of France **1825–55** Nicholas I of Russia **1830** July Revolution in France **1830–48** Louis Philippe of France, constitutional monarch **1830–7** William IV of England **1837–1901** Victoria of England **1848** *Communist Manifesto* by Marx and Engels **1851** Crystal Palace, "Great Exhibition of the Works of All Nations" **1852–70** Napoleon III of France **1853–6** Crimean War **1855–81** Alexander II of Russia **1859** *Origin of Species* by Darwin **1861–78** Victor Emmanuel II of Italy **1870–1** Franco-Prussian War **1871–1940** Third Republic in France **1871** *Descent of Man* by Darwin **1871–88** Wilhelm I, Emperor of Germany **1878–1900** Humbert I of Italy **1881–94** Alexander III of Russia **1888–1918** Wilhelm II, Emperor of Germany **1889** Paris Exhibition; Eiffel Tower **1894–1918** Nicholas II of Russia **1899–1902** Boer War	**Goya** 1746–1828 *Gran hazaña! Con muertos!* **Turner** 1775–1851 *Keelman Heaving Coals by Moonlight* **Constable** 1776–1837 *Wivenhoe Park, Essex* **Ingres** 1780–1867 *Grande Odalisque* **Géricault** 1791–1824 *The Raft of the Medusa* **Corot** 1796–1875 *Forest of Fontainebleau* **Delacroix** 1799–1863 *Arabs Skirmishing in the Mountains* **Cole** 1801–48 *Oxbow* **Paxton** 1801–65 The Crystal Palace **Daumier** 1808–79 *Third-Class Carriage* **Bingham** 1811–79 *Fur Traders Descending the Missouri* **Millet** 1814–75 *The Gleaners* **Courbet** 1819–77 *Burial at Ornans* **Manet** 1832–83 *Olympia* **Degas** 1834–1917 *Four Dancers* **Whistler** 1834–1903 *The White Girl: Symphony in White, No. 1* **Homer** 1836–1910 *Breezing Up* **Cézanne** 1839–1906 *Mont Sainte-Victoire* **Rodin** 1840–1917 *The Thinker* **Monet** 1840–1926 *Rouen Cathedral* **Renoir** 1841–1919 *Le Moulin de la Galette* **Morisot** 1841–95 *In the Dining Room* **Eakins** 1844–1916 *The Gross Clinic* **Cassatt** 1844–1926 *The Bath* **Rousseau** 1844–1910 *The Dream* **Gauguin** 1848–1903 *Where Do We Come From?* **van Gogh** 1853–90 *The Starry Night* **Seurat** 1859–91 *Sunday Afternoon on the Island of La Grande Jatte* **Toulouse-Lautrec** 1864–1901 *Quadrille at the Moulin Rouge*	**Rousseau** 1712–78 *Emile* **Goethe** 1749–1832 *Faust* **Schiller** 1759–1805 "Ode to Joy" **Blake** 1757–1827 "The Tyger" **Wordsworth** 1770–1850 "The World Is Too Much With Us" **Coleridge** 1772–1834 "Kubla Khan" **Byron** 1788–1824 "Prometheus" **Shelley** 1792–1822 "To a Skylark" **Mary Shelley** 1797–1851 *Frankenstein* **Keats** 1795–1821 "La Belle Dame Sans Merci" **Schubert** 1797–1828 *Gretchen am Spinnrade* **Berlioz** 1803–69 *Symphonie fantastique* **Emerson** 1803–82 "The Rhodora" **de Tocqueville** 1805–59 *Democracy in America* **Mendelssohn** 1809–47 Italian Symphony **Poe** 1809–49 "Annabel Lee" **Tennyson** 1809–92 "Ulysses" **Chopin** 1810–49 *Ballade in G minor* **Liszt** 1811–86 *Les Preludes* **Whitman** 1819–92 "I Hear America Singing" **Melville** 1819–91 *Moby Dick* **Dostoevsky** 1821–81 "The Grand Inquisitor" **Arnold** 1822–88 "Dover Beach" **Dickinson** 1830–86 "A Service of Song" **Brahms** 1833–97 Symphony No. 3 **Twain** 1835–1910 "The Notorious Jumping Frog of Calaveras County" **Hardy** 1840–1928 "Neutral Tones" **Tchaikovsky** 1840–93 "The Nutcracker" **Crane** 1871–1900 "War Is Kind"	**Bentham** 1748–1832 *Utilitarianism* **Hegel** 1770–1831 *Philosophy of History* **Schopenhauer** 1788–1860 *The World as Will and Idea* **Daguerre** 1799–1851 photography **Faraday** 1791–1867 electromagnetic induction **Morse** 1791–1872 painting, telegraph, and Morse Code **Mill** 1806–73 *On Liberty* **Kierkegaard** 1813–55 *Fear and Trembling* **Marx** 1818–83 *Das Kapital* **Pasteur** 1822–95 begins bacteriology **Mendel** 1822–84 genetics **Thomson** 1824–1907 transatlantic cable (1858) **Lister** 1827–1912 antiseptic surgery (1860) **James** 1842–1910 pragmatism **Nietzsche** 1844–1900 *Thus Spake Zarathustra* **Röntgen** 1845–1913 X-rays (1895) **Edison** 1847–1931 inventor **Bell** 1849–1922 telephone (1870s) **Friese-Greene** 1855–1921 movies (1880s) **Freud** 1856–1939 psychoanalysis **Hertz** 1857–1894 wireless that led to Marconi's radio in 1895 **Diesel** 1858–1913 diesel engine (1897)
1900	**1900–46** Victor Emmanuel III of Italy **1901–10** Edward VII of England	**Munch** 1864–1944 *The Scream*	**Puccini** 1858–1924 *La Bohème* **Debussy** 1862–1918 *La Mer* **Strauss** 1864–1949 *Till Eulenspiegel's Merry Pranks* **Dunbar** 1872–1906 "Sympathy"	**Planck** 1858–1947 quantum theory (1900) **Wright brothers** 1867–1912; 1871–1948 heavier-than-air flight (1903) **Curie** 1867–1934; radium (1910) **Einstein** 1879–1955 relativity (1905)

CHAPTER 23

Revolution, Romanticism, Realism

REVOLUTION TO WATERLOO

On 14 July 1789 a Parisian mob stormed the hated prison called the Bastille only to find a handful of bewildered prisoners. When Louis XVI asked the next day if this were a riot, the response was: "No sire, a revolution." The revolt erupted only eight years after French money and troops had materially helped the American colonies win their independence from Great Britain. Due partly to the American effort, the national debt was enormous and getting worse because of huge defense expenditures. Failed harvests and mismanaged financial crises led to widespread shortages and skyrocketing food prices. Whatever was wrong was blamed on the government. Hunger and anger finally touched off a revolution long in the making. The American example had inspired, of course, much revolutionary fervor, but the enemy was not a distant colonial power but the French establishment itself. Nothing less than the total destruction of the *ancien régime* would suffice. In a nation at war with its own institutions, fury and brutality energized the revolution from the storming of the Bastille to the busy guillotine and the Reign of Terror. St. Just stated the ultimate goal quite simply: "The Republic consists in the extermination of everything that opposes it." Like many revolutions (with the notable exception of the American), the political outcome was a tyranny and the economic consequences catastrophic. As Barzini observed in *The Europeans*, "the French Revolution did not correct the fundamental defects of French life. It magnified and perfected them." In retrospect we can see that this ferocious bloodbath marked the beginning of what we have called the Middle Modern World of 1789 to 1914, the period between the beginning of our modern world in about 1600 and the twentieth century.

Royalty, aristocracy, and all their properties were targeted for destruction and indeed many nobles were summarily executed while howling mobs ravaged rich estates. The revolution feasted on ferocity so pervasive that 250,000 people (one-third of the population) died in just one area of the country (the Vendée). Any who opposed, hindered, or even failed to strongly support the revolution could be consumed in the firestorm of savagery and death, and many thousands were.

The revolutionary battle cry of "Liberty, Equality, Fraternity" was a thrilling slogan that had nothing to do with reality. How can you have both total individual liberty and a strong, efficient government? How can you abolish privilege and place everyone on the same social, brotherly level in a country with few teachers, lawyers, and doctors and millions of illiterate peasants? It certainly wasn't the first time that ideals clashed with the real world.

The revolution had been incredibly destructive but there were some positive results, particularly the noble "Declaration of the Rights of Man and the Citizen" (fig. 23.1). Feudalism, titles, and privileges had been abolished, the monastic orders suppressed, and church properties confiscated, but the enemies of France were assaulting the borders and internal disorder was increasing. The execution of Robespierre in 1794 ended the Terror, but it took the establishment of the Directory in 1795 to temporarily stabilize the state. Composed of men of conspicuous wealth, the Directory ruled from 1795 to 1799 with the assistance of the military, most notably the Corsican general Napoleon Buonaparte (1769–1821). Under the guise of saving the revolution Napoleon seized power in a coup d'état in 1799 and declared himself First Consul. Proclaiming himself emperor in 1804, he launched a course of conquest that engulfed much of Europe and part of Africa. Waterloo (18 June 1815) was an anticlimax to the fall of a conqueror who lost his entire Grand Army of 500,000 men on the scorched steppes of Russia.

Napoleon saw himself as the enlightened, benevolent despot who had rescued the revolution (fig. 23.2), but he maintained order and control only with the army and, especially, his secret police. He did establish the Code Napoleon, a model of modern civil laws that buried the inequities of the *ancien régime* and set the stage for the rise of the middle class. The Napoleonic legend of the military and political genius who fostered liberalism and nationalism contains, therefore, minor elements of truth. The ideals of the French Revolution did, in time, inspire the spread of democracy throughout the Western world. The other side of the coin was dark and bloody; two decades of Napoleonic wars destroyed lives and property on a staggering scale (map 23.1).

Napoleon's conquerors were deep in deliberations at

23.1 Jacques-Louis David, *The Tennis Court Oath*. 1791. Pen and ink drawing with bistre wash, 25½ × 41⅜" (65 × 105 cm). Louvre, Paris (on loan to the museum at Versailles). Photo: A.K.G., London.

In the Tennis Court Oath of 20 June 1789 deputies of the Third Estate, locked out of their meeting place, met informally at a tennis court in Versailles to swear not to disband until the basis of a new constitution had been established.

23.2 *Opposite* Jacques-Louis David, *Napoleon in His Study*. 1812. Oil on canvas, 6' 8¼" × 4' 1¼" (2.04 × 1.25 m). National Gallery of Art, Washington, D.C. (Samuel H. Kress Collection).

Wearing the Legion of Honor, Napoleon is pictured by his court painter as a conscientious ruler who has stayed up until 4:12 A.M. working for his subjects.

Map 23.1 Napoleon's empire at its greatest extent, 1812.

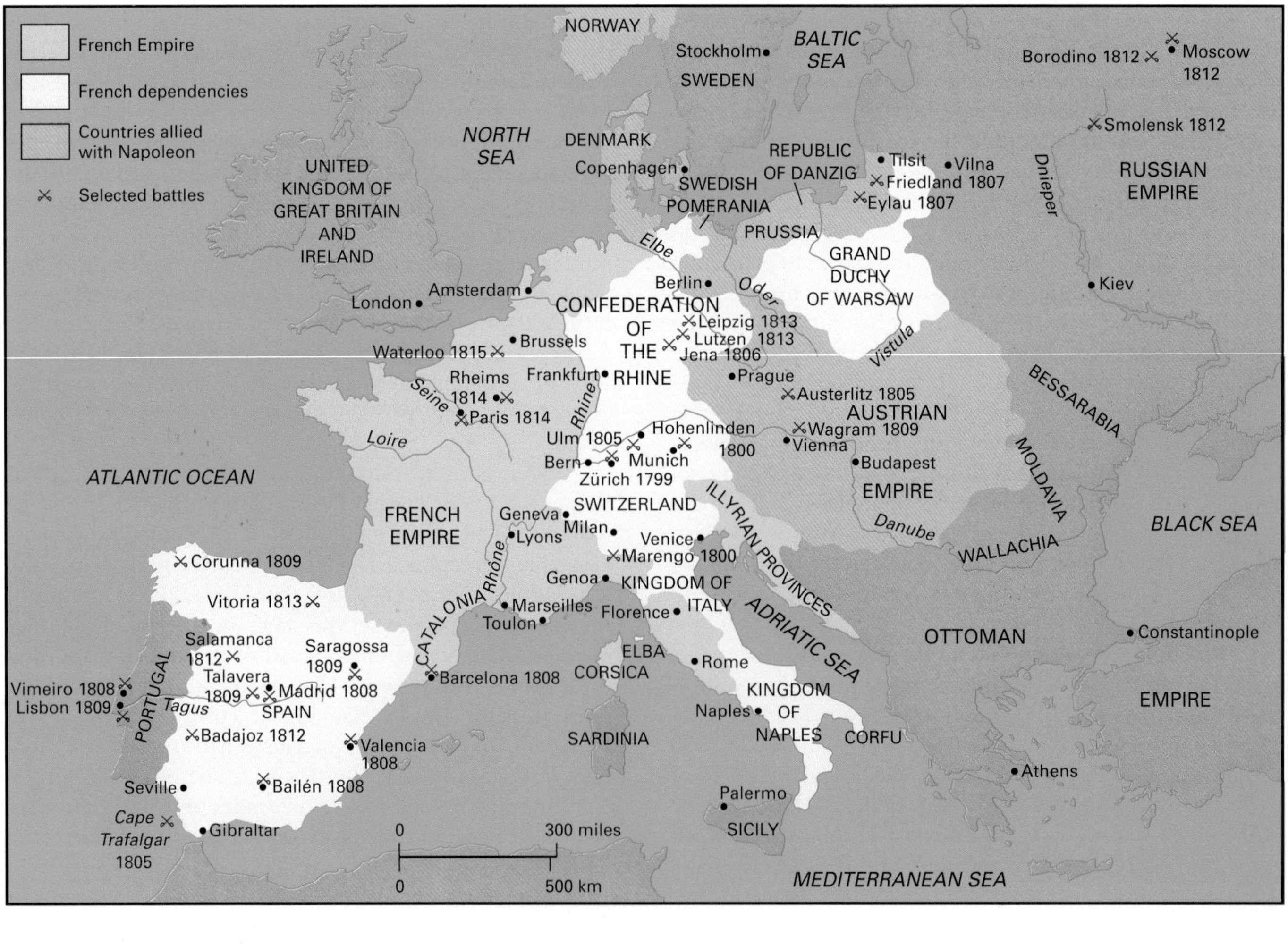

French Empire
French dependencies
Countries allied with Napoleon
Selected battles
NORWAY
Stockholm
SWEDEN
BALTIC SEA
Borodino 1812
Moscow 1812
Smolensk 1812
NORTH SEA
DENMARK
Copenhagen
SWEDISH POMERANIA
REPUBLIC OF DANZIG
Tilsit
Vilna
Friedland 1807
Eylau 1807
Dnieper
RUSSIAN EMPIRE
UNITED KINGDOM OF GREAT BRITAIN AND IRELAND
PRUSSIA
Elbe
Berlin
Oder
GRAND DUCHY OF WARSAW
Kiev
London
Amsterdam
CONFEDERATION OF THE RHINE
Leipzig 1813
Lutzen 1813
Jena 1806
Waterloo 1815
Brussels
Vistula
Rheims 1814
Frankfurt
Prague
BESSARABIA
Seine
Paris 1814
Rhine
Austerlitz 1805
AUSTRIAN EMPIRE
Loire
Ulm 1805
Hohenlinden 1800
Wagram 1809
Vienna
Bern
Munich
Zürich 1799
Budapest
MOLDAVIA
ATLANTIC OCEAN
SWITZERLAND
ILLYRIAN PROVINCES
FRENCH EMPIRE
Geneva
Lyons
Milan
Venice
Danube
WALLACHIA
BLACK SEA
Corunna 1809
Rhône
Marengo 1800
Genoa
KINGDOM OF ITALY
Vitoria 1813
CATALONIA
Marseilles
Toulon
Florence
ADRIATIC SEA
OTTOMAN EMPIRE
Constantinople
Salamanca 1812
Saragossa 1809
ELBA
CORSICA
Rome
Vimeiro 1808
Lisbon 1809
Talavera 1809
Madrid 1808
Barcelona 1808
PORTUGAL
Tagus
SPAIN
KINGDOM OF NAPLES
Naples
Badajoz 1812
Valencia 1808
SARDINIA
CORFU
Seville
Bailén 1808
Athens
Cape Trafalgar 1805
Gibraltar
Palermo
SICILY
0 300 miles
0 500 km
MEDITERRANEAN SEA

the Congress of Vienna when he escaped from Elba and rallied his still loyal armies for a Hundred Days' campaign that ended, once and for all, on the field of Waterloo. Final banishment to the remote island of St. Helena and a heavy guard assured the allies of a peace on their terms.

Called the "peace concert of Europe," the Congress of Vienna (1814–15) involved Austria, Prussia, Russia, and England, but its guiding spirit was Prince Clemens von Metternich (MEH-ter-nikh; 1773–1859), the chief minister of Austria. A reactionary and arch defender of the old order, Metternich secured a balance of power that favored Austria and reinforced established monarchies at the expense of all liberal movements, marking the period of 1815–48 as the Age of Metternich (map 23.2).

Napoleon's foreign minister, Prince Charles Maurice de Talleyrand (1754–1838), betrayed Napoleon, won easier peace terms for his country, and effected the restoration of the Bourbon kings with Louis XVIII (reigned 1814–24), the brother of Louis XVI.

Map 23.2 Europe, 1815.

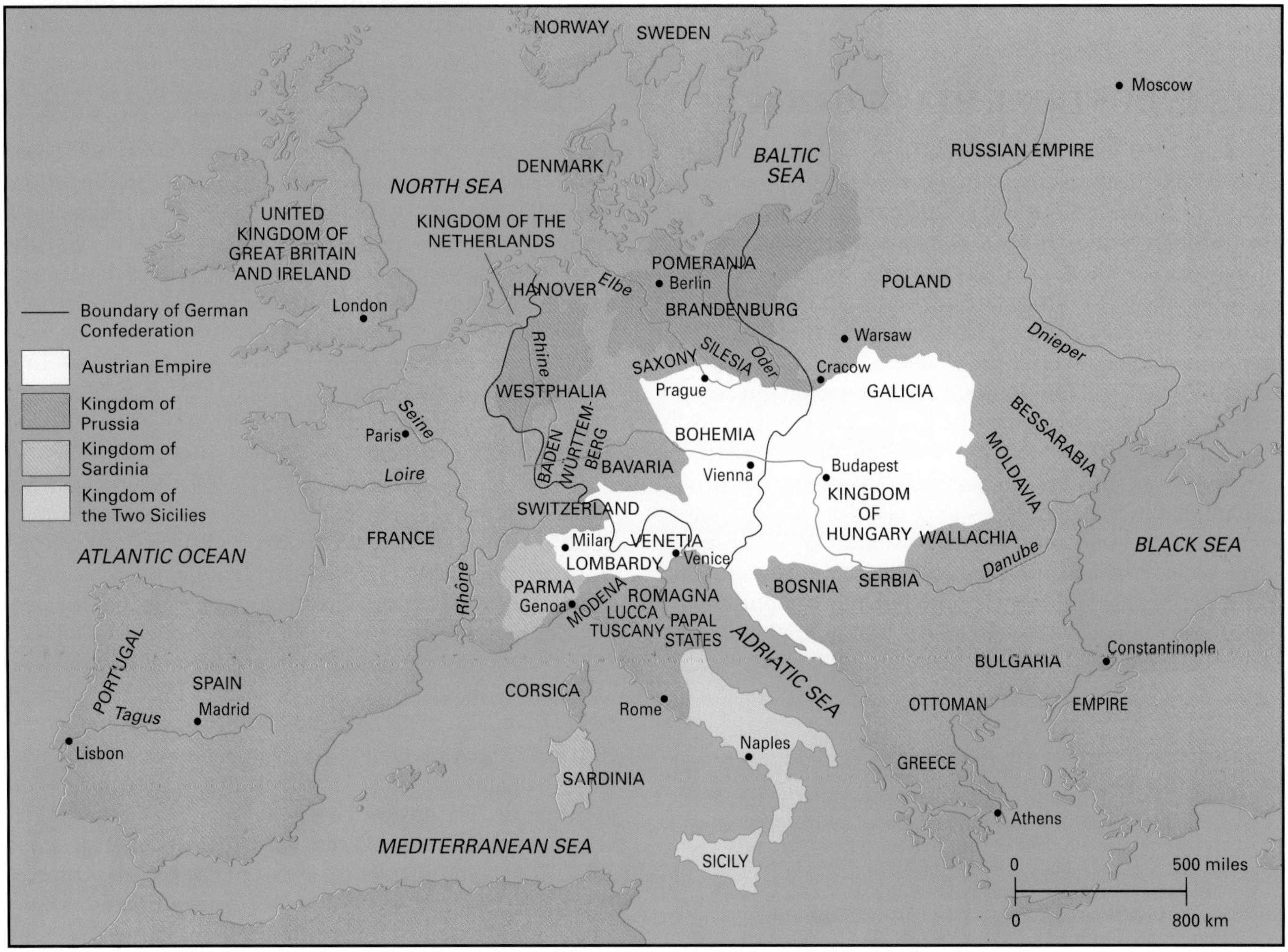

THE REVOLUTIONS OF 1830 AND 1848

The heavy-handed, reactionary rule of Charles X (1824–30), who succeeded Louis XVIII, led to the July Revolution of 1830 in which the workers of Paris challenged the government. When the troops and police refused to fire on the rioters, the king quickly abdicated, delighting the liberals, who saw a possibility of relieving the misery of workers oppressed by the monarchy and the factory-owners. On the invitation of the Chamber of Deputies, Louis Philippe (reigned 1830–48) assumed rule of a "bourgeois monarchy," which catered to the wealthy middle class and ignored the industrial workers. The brief July Revolution sparked violence in Germany, Italy, Spain, Portugal, Poland, and Belgium, all of which was overcome by force except in Belgium which, in 1831, won its independence from Holland.

A wave of revolutions swept Europe in 1848, the year in which Marx and Engels published *The Communist Manifesto.* The suppressed forces of liberalism erupted in France, Prussia, Austria, Hungary, Bohemia, Croatia, and the Italian possessions of the Hapsburgs. Repression was even more severe than in 1830 but, as Marx and Engels wrote, "The specter of Communism" was haunting Europe.

THE INDUSTRIAL REVOLUTION

Between 1750 and 1850 England's economic structure changed drastically as the nation shifted from an agrarian society to modern industrialism. The transformation was astonishingly rapid because so many important factors already existed: capitalism, international trade, mercantilism, colonialism, the Protestant work ethic. England already had hand-operated domestic (cottage) industries; what was needed was power to drive the machinery, and this became available when, in 1769, James Watt patented an improved version of the steam engine that Thomas Newcomen had invented in about 1700 to pump water out of mine shafts.[1]

Why was England the original home of the industrial revolution rather than prosperous Holland or rich and powerful France? American economic historian W. W. Rostow suggests that national pride and confidence were buoyed by a series of English military victories but, more importantly, that the mix of needed resources was best in England:

> Britain, with more basic industrial resources than the Netherlands; more nonconformists, and more ships than France; with its political, social, and religious revolution fought out by 1688—Britain alone was in a position to weave together cotton manufacture, coal and iron technology, the steam engine and ample foreign trade to pull it off.[2]

With its head start England became the textile center of the world but, after 1850, Belgium, France, Germany, the United States, and Canada were also involved not only in industrialization but in dramatic changes in communications, agricultural chemistry, machinery, and transportation. Railroads and steamships helped turn northern Europe and North America into an energetic and highly competitive complex that, in effect, functioned like an economic community.

DEVELOPMENT OF THE WESTERN NATIONS

Only in France did the 1848 revolution succeed and then just briefly. The Second Republic lasted from 1848 to 1852, followed by the Second Empire of Napoleon III (1852–70). Deliberately provoked by Bismarck, the Franco-Prussian War (1870–1) toppled the inept emperor and humiliated the nation. The Third Republic of 1871 finally exorcised the monarchy in France, but the Dreyfus Affair (1894–1906) nearly ripped the nation asunder. Falsely accused of treason, Captain Alfred Dreyfus (dray-fus; 1859–1935) was cashiered from the army and sentenced to life imprisonment on notorious Devil's Island. Generally speaking, anti-Semites, royalists, militarists, and Catholics backed the army whereas republicans, socialists, intellectuals, and anticlericals supported Dreyfus. Emile Zola, for example, was jailed for his inflammatory newspaper article, *"J'accuse"* (1898). It took a civil court to exonerate Dreyfus and reinstate him in the army as a major. Monarchists and Catholics were discredited, paving the way for the separation of church and state.

Otto Fürst von Bismarck (1815–98), the first minister of Prussia (1862–71), personally created the German Empire in 1871, when he had Wilhelm I of Prussia proclaimed emperor (reigned 1871–88). Consolidating his gains after a series of aggressive wars, the "iron chancellor" made a unified Germany the new power in Europe. Wilhelm II (reigned 1888–1918), the grandson of Queen Victoria, had his own ideas about royal power and dismissed his chancellor in 1890. Bismarck criticized the Kaiser unceasingly as the emperor armed his nation for the conflict that erupted in 1914. Wilhelm II abdicated in 1918 after leading his nation to defeat in the catastrophic Great War.

During the reign of Francis II (1792–1835) Austria was defeated on four different occasions by the French. Emperor Ferdinand (reigned 1835–48) had frequent fits of insanity, which left Metternich free to govern in his name. The 1848

1. Reinvented would be a more appropriate word. The ancient Greeks were apparently the first to invent the steam engine. Judging by the drawings of Heron (or Hero) of Alexandria (ca. second century AD), steam power was used in toy gadgets that caused birds to sing and Tritons to blow their horns. See Robert S. Brumbaugh, *Ancient Greek Gadgets and Machines* (Westport, Conn.: Greenwood Press, 1975).
2. W. W. Rostow, *The Stages of Economic Growth* (New York: Cambridge University Press, 1960), p. 33.

23.3 Eugène Delacroix, *The Massacre at Chios*. 1822–4. Oil on canvas, 13' 10"× 11' 7" (4.22 × 3.53 m). Louvre, Paris. Photo: R.M.N., Paris.

revolution drove Ferdinand from the throne and Metternich from power, but the monarchy continued under the ill-fated Franz Joseph (reigned 1848–1916), Emperor of Austria and King of Hungary. The emperor's brother, Maximilian I, was installed by Napoleon III as Emperor of Mexico (1864–7), but he was executed by the revolutionary forces of Juarez after the French emperor withdrew his troops. Franz Joseph's wife was assassinated in 1898 by an Italian anarchist, and his only son, Archduke Rudolf, was found dead (along with his mistress Baroness Maria Vetsera) at Mayerling. Thought possibly to be a double suicide, the tragedy remains a mystery. The heir-apparent to Franz Joseph, his grand-nephew Archduke Franz Ferdinand (1863–1914) was assassinated (with his wife) on 28 June 1914 by Serbian nationalists at Sarajevo, leading to the ultimate tragedy of the Great War.

Ruled by the Turks since 1456, Greece finally began, in 1821, a rebellion that engaged the romantic imagination of the Western world. Extolling ancient Greece as the birthplace of democracy and of Western culture, Philhellenic (pro-Greek) committees in Europe and North America sent supplies and money while demanding that civilized nations intervene directly. Eventually, England, France, and Russia did. The war was ferocious, with Greek peasants slaughtering every Turk in sight and the Turks retaliating, for example, by killing or selling into slavery all 30,000 residents of the island of Chios, which inspired Delacroix's painting, *The Massacre at Chios* (fig. 23.3). Lord Byron could not resist the siren call of Greek independence and died there of fever in 1824. By 1832 independence had been achieved, but Greek nationalism was not fully victorious until after World War II.

Early in the nineteenth century Italy was temporarily unified under Napoleon, but the Congress of Vienna again reduced it to petty states. Following several abortive revolts, Giuseppe Garibaldi (1807–82) spearheaded the *Risorgimento* (rie-sor-jie-MEN-toe; "resurgence") which, by 1861, established Italy, under King Victor Emmanuel II (reigned 1861–78), as a unified political entity for the first time since the demise of the Roman Empire. By 1870 the Papal States had been incorporated into the kingdom, but not until 1929 was Vatican City established by Benito Mussolini as a separate sovereign state of 108 acres.

Plagued by Czarist repression and widespread corruption, poverty, and ignorance, Russia was the most backward country in Europe. Czar Alexander I (reigned 1801–25) attempted some reforms but, under the influence of Metternich, he became a reactionary; his successor, Nicholas I (reigned 1825–55), was even more rigid. The campaign of Nicholas to dominate southeast Europe led to the Crimean War (1853–6) in which the allied powers of Turkey, England, France, and Sardinia stopped, for a time, Russian expansionism. The main battle was the successful siege of the Russian naval base at Sevastopol, but the war itself was notorious for the outrageous neglect of wounded soldiers and general incompetence of command. Nothing could save the troops from tragic blunders—epitomized by the futile gallantry of the Light Brigade. Tennyson's poem, "The Charge of the Light Brigade," typifies the romantic fantasies about national honor and glory that helped plunge Europe into the Great War of 1914–18.

ANGEL OF MERCY

Trained as a nurse in France and Germany at a time when most nurses were untrained menials, Florence Nightingale (1820–1910) offered to leave her job as a hospital superintendent in London to nurse soldiers in the Crimea. The minister of war immediately (surprisingly) accepted her proposal and helped her lead thirty-eight nurses to the pitifully inadequate hospitals behind the battlefields. Having saved untold lives, she returned to London after the war to open the Nightingale School, the first to train nurses as medical professionals. She was the very first woman to be awarded, belatedly in 1907, the British Order of Merit.

European Monarchs

The reign of Alexander II (1855–81) was about as authoritarian as that of Nicholas I, but he did belatedly liberate about 40,000,000 serfs with his 1861 Emancipation Act. The assassination of Alexander II led to the brutally oppressive regime of Alexander III (reigned 1881–94) and the inept but equally oppressive reign of Nicholas II (reigned 1894–1918), the last of the czars.

The long reign of England's George III (1760–1820) actually ended in 1811 when the king became totally insane. Functioning as Prince Regent (1811–20) and then king, George IV (reigned 1820–30) led a wildly profligate life that earned him the contempt of his subjects. William IV (reigned 1830–7) agreed to the Reform Bill of 1832 that extended suffrage to people who owned property but not to the large majority who did not. His niece, Victoria (reigned 1837–1901), reestablished the prestige of the crown while presiding over the enormous expansion of the British Empire, symbolized by her crowning as Empress of India in 1876. Though the English monarchy was largely decorative, Victoria determinedly took her role seriously (fig. 23.4), presiding over the conversion of the country into a political democracy with humanitarian reforms and a measure of social and economic democracy. Paradoxically, the British developed a liberal democracy at home while pursuing aggressive imperialism abroad.

Several decades before Victoria's death Victorian earnestness and sobriety had become, for many writers and artists, increasingly boring. They were as ready for a new era as Edward VII (reigned 1901–10) was eager to rule, having been Prince of Wales for sixty years. The Edwardian Age, as flashy and flamboyant as the king himself, was a great age for those who could afford to frolic in the grand manner. The accession of George V (reigned 1910–36) restored some measure of decorum but all that ended in 1914 with the guns of August.

America's Civil War

Inspired in part by the doctrine of **Manifest Destiny**, the United States tripled its size during the nineteenth century and increased its population twentyfold. Even more remarkable was the fact that the nation could expand so enormously and still maintain its union. The Civil War (1861–5) was a cruel test sufficient to destroy perhaps any other nation. Slavery was the basic issue but the conflict also stemmed from widely divergent ways of life and different economic structures. The mainly industrial North was vigorous and aggressive in the spirit of Calvinism, whereas the South was primarily agricultural, with a relaxed and cavalier life-style. Lee surrendered to Grant at Appomattox, the war was over, and that fact was accepted, despite the four years of ferocious combat, by most Southerners as the final end of a rebellion that would never again be seriously considered. Reconstruction would surely have proceeded less radically had Lincoln not been assassinated but, nevertheless, his views seemed to eventually temper vengeful northern radicals and encourage the moderates. In his memorable Second Inaugural Address, given just five weeks before the end of the war, Lincoln (fig. 23.5) set the tone of what would ultimately prove to be the sanest and wisest

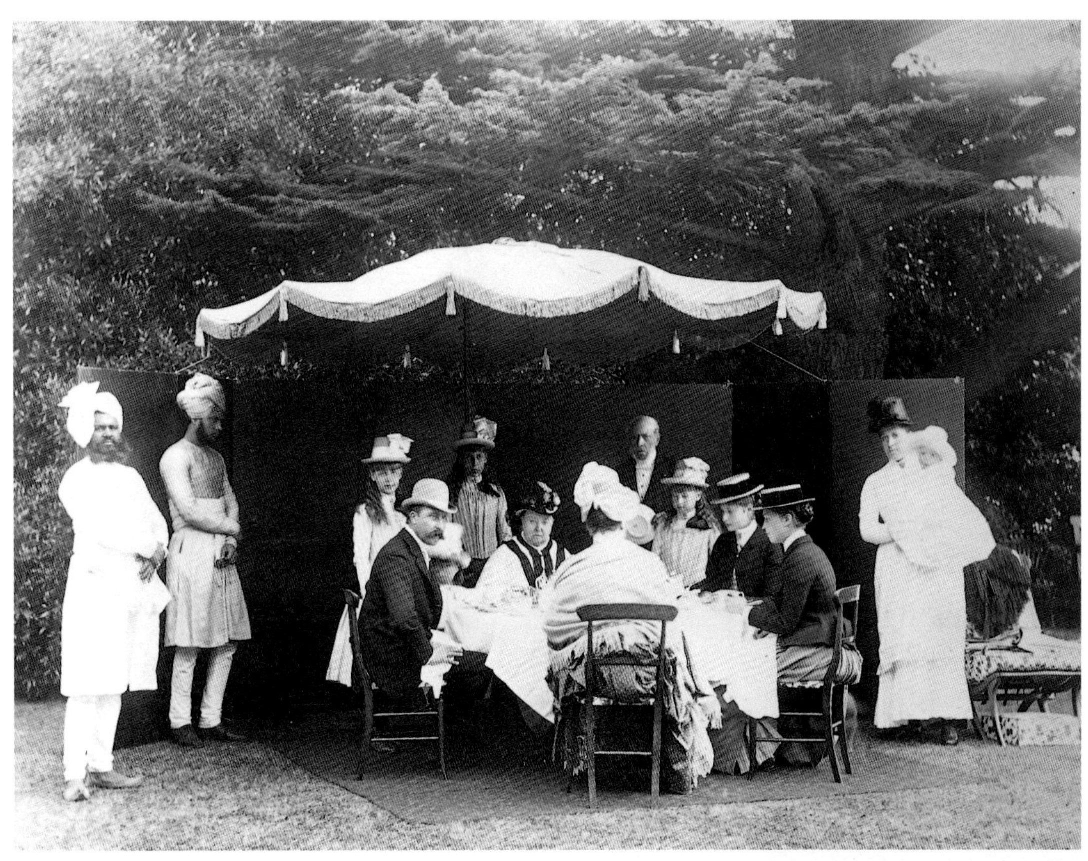

23.4 *Above* Queen Victoria in India. Photograph. Photo: By gracious permission of H.M. the Queen.

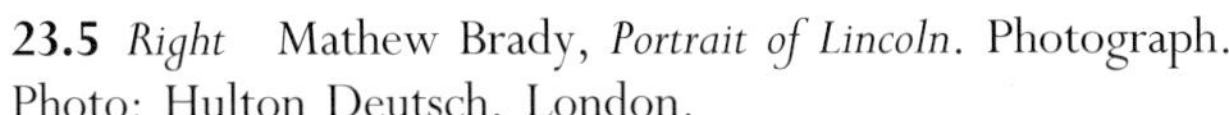

23.5 *Right* Mathew Brady, *Portrait of Lincoln*. Photograph. Photo: Hulton Deutsch, London.

attitude in the aftermath of the nation's internal agony, as summarized in the final paragraph:

> With malice toward none; with charity for all; with firmness in the right, as God gives us to see the right, let us strive on to finish the work we are in; to bind up the nation's wounds; to care for him who shall have borne the battle, and for his widow, and his orphan—to do all which may achieve and cherish a just and lasting peace among ourselves, and with all nations.

UNCLE TOM'S CABIN

The scenes of this story, as its title indicates, lie among a race hitherto ignored by the associations of polite and refined society; an exotic race, whose ancestors, born beneath a tropic sun, brought with them, and perpetuated to their descendants, a character so essentially unlike the hard and dominant Anglo-Saxon race, as for many years to have won from it only misunderstanding and contempt . . . .

But another and better day is dawning . . . . Unhappy Africa at last is remembered; Africa, who began the race of civilization and human progress in the dim, gray dawn of early time, but who, for centuries, has lain bound and bleeding at the foot of civilized and Christianized humanity, imploring compassion in vain . . . .

The object of these sketches is to awaken sympathy and feeling for the African race, as they exist among us; to show their wrongs and sorrows, under a system so necessarily cruel and unjust as to defeat and do away the good effects of all that can be attempted for them, by their best friends, under it.

From Harriet Beecher Stowe (1811–96),
Preface, *Uncle Tom's Cabin*, 1852

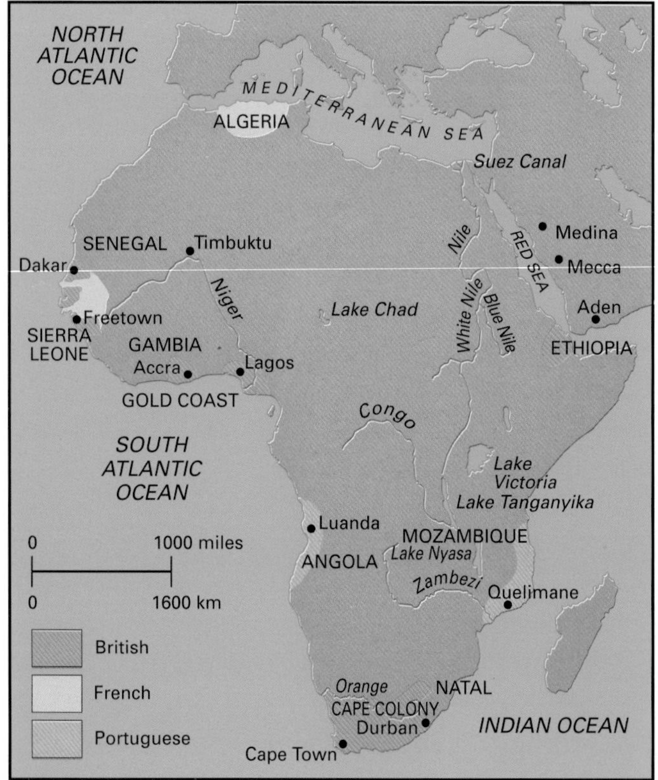

Map 23.3 European colonies in Africa, 1878.

THE END OF AN ERA

The industrial revolution was a major factor in the complex chain of events leading to the Great War. Germany, England, France, and Russia were competing in the quality and price of industrial products while also searching for new colonial markets that would absorb some of their booming production. In Europe, after the unification of Germany and Italy, there was very little territory "available" for annexation. There were, in other words, more predatory nations than suitable victims, with the latter located mainly in Africa (maps 23.3 and 23.4). To protect what they had and hoped to acquire, nations enlarged their armies and navies and equipped them with the latest weaponry.

National identity was another crucial factor. As late as the 1860s citizens of Florence, for example, saw themselves as Florentines or Tuscans; residents of Normandy were Norman rather than French; the population of Munich was Bavarian first and German second, and so on. The physical unification of Germany and Italy stimulated a sense of national identity symbolized by the powerful image of Britain as a sovereign nation, with national pride fueled by feelings of national superiority. When James Thomson wrote

The nations not so blest as thee,
Must in their turn, to tyrants fall;
Whilst thou shalt flourish great and free,
The dread and envy of them all.
"Rule, Britannia, rule the waves;
Britons never will be slaves."

he had no idea of sharing the waves or anything else with other nations.

The Romantic idea of the sovereign individual was enlarged to include each citizen as a critical component in the noble and heroic image of the sovereign state. There was for the Romantic no true identity separate from the homeland, as Sir Walter Scott emphasized, when he wrote: "Breathes there the man, with soul so dead,/Who never to himself hath said,/This is my own, my native land!"

The Balkan Tinderbox

Nations forged alliances that were supposed to maintain a balance of power and thus avoid open warfare. Bismarck effected a Triple Alliance in 1882 of Germany, Austria-Hungary, and Italy to offset French power. France and Russia countered in 1894 with a Dual Alliance that made Germany uneasy about a two-front war and, in 1907, Great Britain joined the two nations in what was called a "close understanding" (Triple Entente). The tinderbox was the Balkans, where nationalist ambitions were continually clashing. Russia wanted to make the Black Sea a Slavic lake, but Great Britain saw a Russian thrust as a threat to the empire. By this time Turkey, the "sick man of Europe," was virtually powerless, newly independent Serbia was a threat to the Austro-Hungarian Empire, and Germany had her eye on Balkan conquests. The high level of international tension

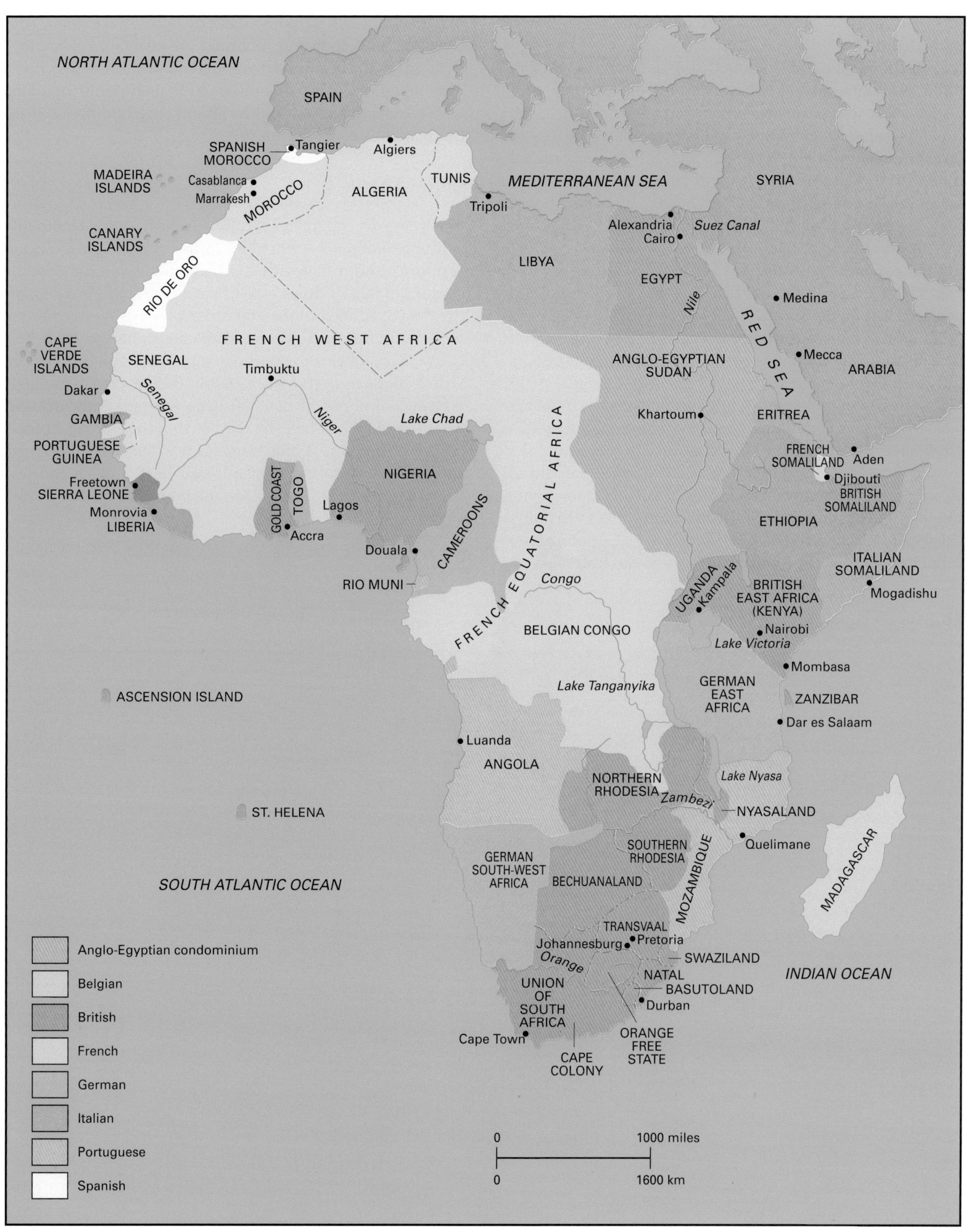

Map 23.4 European rule in Africa, 1914.

was extremely dangerous because all nations were armed to the teeth.

Nationalist activities touched a spark to the Balkan tinder and nationalist stubbornness, duty, and honor provoked a war that many diplomats and statesmen believed was preferable to seeing their nation humiliated by loss of face. On 28 June 1914, a Serbian nationalist assassinated the Austrian Archduke Franz Ferdinand and his wife. After obtaining Germany's backing for whatever it should choose to do in response—a true "blank check"—Austria delivered an ultimatum to Serbia that was promptly rejected. Claiming that compromise was inconsistent with "national honor," Austria rebuffed a British offer to mediate and declared war on Serbia on 28 July 1914. Fearful of German might, the panic-stricken Russian government ordered full mobilization, prompting a German ultimatum, ignored by the Kremlin, to cease or face a fight. On 1 August 1914 Germany began mobilizing while simultaneously declaring war, which says something about German readiness. Two days later the confident Germans declared war on the frantically mobilizing French. Great Britain dithered and delayed until Germany announced her intention to violate Belgium's neutrality as established in 1839. Great Britain's subsequent declaration of war prompted the German chancellor to sneer that the English had gone to war over a "scrap of paper." Actually, as pointed out by Barbara Tuchman,[3] the German Staff had long planned an invasion of helpless Belgium as the best route to an undefended French frontier. The "scrap of paper" slur inflamed British public opinion, which eagerly backed a government that had honored its treaty and thus the nation (map 23.5).

World War I

The war was fought, generally speaking, with twentieth-century weapons (machine guns, tanks, poison gas, artillery) and nineteenth-century tactics (mass frontal assaults, artillery duels, use of cavalry). There were many theatres of action but the 300-mile (483-km) Western Front was the main meat-grinder with mass charges launched between trenches into pointblank machine-gun fire. In four years sixteen nations had casualties (killed, died, wounded, missing) of about 50,000,000. One example indicates the extent of the slaughter. In the center of the small French village of Sully-sur-Loire stands a war memorial designed as a tall obelisk. On one side are listed, in categories, the villagers who died in World War II. The categories

3. Barbara Tuchman, *The Guns of August* (New York: Macmillan, 1962).

Map 23.5 Europe, 1914.

themselves communicate much about the conflict with Nazi Germany: "Killed in Action," "Murdered by the Gestapo," "Died in Concentration Camp," and "Missing." Eight names are engraved on the World War II side. On the opposite World War I side, the single category is "Killed in Action." There are ninety-six names.

As some historians have noted, World War I began as the most popular war in history. Just about everyone was spoiling for a fight, a chance to demonstrate the combative spirit of their country, to prove their valor and nobility, to honor their country. Those romantic notions died in the trenches and lie buried from Flanders Fields to Verdun. Throughout Western history no event has ended an era with such finality as did the Great War.

ROMANTICISM

More an attitude to be explored than a term to be defined, Romanticism began around 1780 as a reaction against the Enlightenment. The Romantic movement itself lasted from about 1780 to about 1830, but Romantic ideas and issues were present in a variety of forms right up to 1914.

In its initial stages Romanticism was mainly a German movement but it drew its inspiration from Jean-Jacques Rousseau (1712–78). Rousseau began his *Social Contract* (1762) with a ringing proclamation: "Man is born free and everywhere he is in chains." The source of the trouble, according to Rousseau, was too much education, and of the wrong kind at that. Self-forged chains could not be thrown off with more "progress"; instead, people must emulate the Noble Savage by returning to a state of innocence in nature. Civilization had corrupted us, claimed Rousseau, and a return to nature was the proper antidote. More a call to action than a coherent program, just what Rousseau meant by "back to nature" has been debated for centuries. Some idea of his attitude can be obtained from his analysis of the "wrong kind of education" in the *Discourse on the Arts and Sciences* (1749):

> Astronomy was born of superstition, eloquence of ambition, hatred, falsehood, and flattery; geometry of avarice; physics of an idle curiosity; and even moral philosophy of human pride. Thus the arts and sciences owe their birth to our vices; and we should be less doubtful of their advantages, if they had sprung from our virtues.
>
> Their evil origin is, indeed, but too plainly reproduced in their objects. What would become of the arts were they not cherished by luxury? If men were not unjust, of what use were jurisprudence? What would become of history if there were no tyrants, wars, or conspiracies? In a word, who would pass his life in barren speculations if everybody, attentive only to the obligations of humanity and the necessities of nature, spent his whole life in serving his country, obliging his friends, and relieving the unhappy?

LITERARY SELECTION 58

Emile (1762)

Jean-Jacques Rousseau

Rousseau presented his ideas about the proper education of children in the form of a novel. In the two selections given here we see first an opening essay on the nature of education, and, second, an example of the proper education of the pupil Emile.

Book I

Everything is good as it comes from the hand of the Author of things; everything degenerates in the hand of man. He forces a piece of ground to nourish harvests alien to it, a tree to bear fruit not its own; he mingles and confounds climates, elements, seasons; he mutilates his dog, his horse, his slave; he turns everything upside down, he disfigures everything; he loves deformity and monsters. He does not want anything to be as nature made it, not even man; it must be groomed for him, like a riding-school horse; it must conform to his whim like a tree in his garden . . . .

It is you I address, gentle and far-seeing mother, who know that you must withdraw yourself from the established highway and protect the tender sapling from the shock of human opinion! Cultivate, water the young plant before it dies; its fruits will one day be your greatest joy. Build early a protecting wall about the soul of your child; another may mark out the boundary, but you alone must erect the barrier.

Plants are formed by cultivation and men by education. If a man were born tall and strong, his height and strength would be worthless to him until he had learned to make use of them; both could be harmful to him, in keeping others from thinking he needed help; left to himself, he could die of misery before he understood his own needs. We pity the childish state; we do not see that the human race would have perished if man had not started out as a child.

We are born feeble, we need strength; we are born deprived of everything, we need help; we are born stupid, we need judgment. Everything we lack at our birth, but need when we are grown, is given by our education.

This education comes to us from nature, from men, or from things. The internal development of our faculties and organs is the education of nature; the use we learn to make of this development is the education of men; and the acquisition of our own experience from the objects which affect us is the education of things.

Each one of us, then, is fashioned by three sorts of teachers. The pupil in whom their various teachings clash is badly educated, and will never be at peace with himself; the one in whom they all emphasize the same purpose and tend towards the same ends, goes straight to his goal and lives harmoniously. Such an one is well educated.

Now, of these three different educations, that of nature is the only one that does not depend on us at all; that of things depends on man only in certain respects. That of man is the only one of which we are truly the masters: even here we are in control only theoretically; for who can hope to direct completely the discourse and actions of all those surrounding a child?

Since, then, education is an art, it is almost impossible that it should be successful, for the circumstances necessary to its success are determined by no one person. All that one can do with the greatest care is, more or less, to approach the goal, but one needs good luck to reach it.

What is this goal? It is the very same as nature's; that has just been proved. Since the combination of these educations is necessary for their perfecting, it is toward the one over which we have no control that we must direct the other two. But perhaps this word nature is too vague a term; we must try here to define it.

Nature, we are told, is only habit. What does that mean? Are there not habits which are developed only with effort, and which never stifle nature? Such is, for example, the habit of plants, the vertical direction of which is interfered with. Once the restraints are removed, the plant retains the inclination which it has been forced to take; but even so the sap has not changed its primitive direction, and, if the plant continues to thrive, its growth will return to the vertical. It is the same with the tendencies of man. As long as we stay in one situation, we keep those which are the result of custom and which are the least natural to us; but as soon as the situation changes the learned habit stops and the natural returns. Education is certainly a habit. Now are there not people who forget and lose their education and others who retain it? From whence comes this difference? If we limit the meaning of nature to the habits which conform to the natural, we may spare ourselves this nonsense.

We are born sensitive, and from our birth we are affected in diverse ways by the objects which surround us. As soon as we have, so to speak, the consciousness of our sensations, we are disposed to seek out or to flee from the objects which produce them, first according as to whether they are agreeable or displeasing to us, then according to the harmony or discord which we find between ourselves and these objects, and finally according to the judgments which we form concerning the idea of happiness and perfection which our reason gives us. These judgments are extended and strengthened in accordance with our becoming more sensitive and more enlightened; but limited by our habits, they are changed more or less by our opinions. Before this change, they are what I call nature in us.

It is to these primitive urges, then, that we must relate everything; and this could be done if our three educations were merely different; but what is to be done when they are opposed?—when, instead of educating a man for himself, we wish to educate him for others, then harmony is impossible. Forced to combat nature or social institutions, we must choose between making a man or a citizen; for one cannot do both at the same time.

All small societies, when confined and close-knit, draw away from the world at large. Every patriot is intolerant of foreigners; they are mere men, they have no worth to him. This difficulty is inevitable but it is a slight one. It is essential to be kind to the people with whom one lives. Outside, the Spartan was ambitious, miserly, unrighteous; but disinterestedness, justice, and concord reigned within his walls. Beware of those citizens of the world who study their books for dutiful acts which they disdain to carry out at home. This kind of philosopher loves the barbarian in order to be free from loving his neighbor.

The natural man is all for himself; he is a numerical unity, the absolute entity, in harmony only with himself or his equals. The civil man (the man in society) is but a fractional unit belonging to the denominator whose sole value is in relation to the whole, which is the social body. Good social institutions are those that know best how to strip man of his nature, to take from him his real existence and give him one which is only relative, and to add his personality to the common unity; to the end that each individual will no longer think of himself as one, but as a part of the whole, no longer a thinking being except in the group. A Roman citizen was neither a Caius nor a Lucius: he was a Roman . . . .

A woman of Sparta had five sons in the army and awaited news of the battle. A helot arrived and she asked for news, trembling. "Your five sons have been killed." "Ignoble slave, did I ask you that?" "We are victorious!" The mother ran to the temple and gave thank-offerings to the gods. There is your citizen.

One who, in civilized society, hopes to maintain the preeminence of the natural does not know what he asks. Always at odds with himself, forever vacillating between his inclinations and his duty, he will never be either man or citizen; he will be no good to himself or others. He will be one of those contemporary men, a Frenchman, an Englishman, a citizen. He will be a nonentity.

To be something, to be himself and always whole, a man must act as he speaks, he must be sure always of the road he must take, take it resolutely and follow it always. I am waiting for someone to show me such a prodigy to know if he is man or citizen, or how he undertakes to be both at the same time.

From these necessarily opposed aims come two forms of contrary institutions: the one held in common and public, the other individual and private.

If you want to get an idea of public education, read Plato's *Republic*. It is not at all a political work, as those who judge a book only by its title believe it to be: it is the finest treatise on education that anyone ever wrote.

When people want to return to a never-never land, they think of Plato's institution: if Lycurgus[4] had done no more than put his in writing, I should find it much more fanciful. Plato simply purified the heart of man: Lycurgus denaturalized it.

That public system exists no longer, and can exist no

4. Lycurgus, the Spartan king, did not write about education; he established the actual system of training in Sparta to which Rousseau refers.

longer, because where there is no nation there can be no citizen. These two words *Nation* and *Citizen* should be removed from modern languages. I know quite well the reason for this, but I do not want to discuss it: it has nothing to do with my subject.

Those laughable institutions they call "colleges" I do not think of in connection with public education. Neither do I count the education of the world, because this education leads toward two contrary goals, and misses both of them; it is useful only to produce two-faced men, who seem always to defer to others but who are really interested only in pleasing themselves. Now this behavior, being common to all, deceives no one in particular. It is so much wasted effort.

From these contradictions arises the one which we feel constantly within ourselves. Pulled by nature and by man in opposite directions; forced to divide ourselves among these different compulsions, we make compromises which lead neither to one goal nor the other. Thus besieged and vacillating during the whole course of our life, we end it without having found peace within ourselves and without having been any good to ourselves or others.

There remains finally private education, or that of nature, but what can a man mean to others if he is educated only for himself. If perhaps the proposed double object could be resolved into one, by removing the contradictions of man we could remove a great obstacle to his happiness. To make a judgment, we must see the finished man; we must have observed his tendencies, seen his progress, followed his advance; in a word, we must know the natural man. I believe you will have taken some steps (made some progress) in our research after having read this discussion.

What must we do to fashion this rare being?—much, without doubt: that is, prevent anything from being done. When it is only a question of sailing against the wind, we tack; but if the sea is high and we want to stay in one place, we must drop anchor. Take care, young pilot, that your cable does not slip or your anchor drag, and that your vessel does not drift without your noticing it.

In the social order where every place is allocated, each one must be educated for his niche. If a man leaves the place for which he was prepared, he no longer fits anywhere. Education is useful to the extent that destiny harmonizes it with the vocation of the parents; in all other instances, it is harmful to the student, if only for the prejudices it gives him. In Egypt, where the son was obliged to step into his father's place, education at least had an assured purpose: but among us where only classes remain, and where men change from one to the other constantly, no one knows whether, in educating his son to take his place, a father may be working against the son's best interests.

In the natural order, since men are equal, their common calling is man's estate, and whoever is well educated for this, cannot fill unworthily any position which relates to it. Whether I destine my pupil for the army, the church, the bar, is of little importance. No matter what the calling of his parents, nature calls him to human life. Living is the trade I should like to teach him. Leaving my hands, he will not be, I admit, magistrate, soldier, or priest; he will be first of all a man: everything that a man should be, he will know how to be, when called on, as well as any man; and in vain will fortune change his place, for he will always be at home.

. . . . . .

For a time we had noticed, my pupil and I, that amber, glass, wax, different substances when they were rubbed would attract straws, and that others did not attract them. By chance we discovered one which had a still stranger attribute, which was to attract from quite a distance and without being rubbed, filings and other bits of iron. How long this quality amused us without our being able to perceive anything beyond it! Finally we found that this characteristic was communicated to the iron, even magnetized in a certain sense. One day we went to the fair; a juggler attracted with a piece of bread a wax duck floating on a basin of water. Very much astonished, we did not call him a sorcerer, however, for we did not know what a sorcerer was. Continually struck with effects of which we did not know the causes, we were in no hurry to make judgments, and remained quietly ignorant until we found the answer.

On returning to our lodging, as a result of talking about the duck at the fair we began to try to imitate it. We took a well-magnetized needle, covered it with white wax which we shaped like a duck as best we could, in such a way that the needle traversed the body and the eye formed the beak. We placed the duck on the water and brought near the beak a key, and we saw, with what joy you may imagine, that our duck followed the piece of bread. To observe in what direction the duck faced when left quiet on the water was something for us to do another time. As for the present, full of our plans, we asked for nothing more.

The same evening we returned to the fair with some prepared bread in our pockets and as soon as the magician performed his trick, our little savant, who could hardly contain himself, said that this trick was not difficult and that he could do as well himself. He was taken at his word and at once took from his pocket the bread containing the bit of iron. As he approached the table his heart was pounding, and, almost trembling, he held out the bread. The duck came and followed it; the child cried out and quivered with joy. As people clapped and the assembly acclaimed him, his head was completely turned and he was beside himself. The juggler, overwhelmed, came, nevertheless to embrace and congratulate him and to request the honor of his presence the next day, adding that we would take pains to assemble a still larger crowd to applaud his cleverness. My proud little naturalist wanted to make a speech, but I shut him up at once and took him away, overwhelmed with praise.

The child with evident excitement counted the minutes the next day. He invited everyone he met; he wanted the whole human race to witness his glory. He could hardly wait for the time to come, he was ready ahead of time, we flew to the meeting place; the room was already full. As he entered, his young heart swelled.

Other tricks had to come first; the juggler surpassed himself and did astonishing things. The child saw nothing of all this; he was agitated, he perspired, his breathing was labored. He spent the time fingering the bread in his pocket with a hand trembling with impatience. At last it was his turn; the master announced him ceremoniously. He approached a little ashamedly, he brought out the bread. New vicissitude of human things!—the duck, so tame the day before, had become wild today. Instead of presenting its beak, it turned tail and fled; it avoided the bread and the hand which held it with the same care with which it had formerly followed them. After a thousand useless attempts, each one jeered at, the child whined, said that he was being duped, that this was another duck substituted for the first one, and defied the juggler to attract it.

The juggler, without replying, took a piece of bread and held it out to the duck; which at once followed the bread and came to the hand which held it. The child took the same piece of bread, but far from succeeding better than before, he saw the duck make fun of him and do pirouettes all around the basin; he went off at last, quite upset, and did not dare expose himself to catcalls.Then the juggler took the bread that the child had brought and made use of it as successfully as with his own: he drew out the iron (magnet) before the people, more laughter at our expense: then with the bread thus emptied he attracted the duck as before. He did the same thing with another piece, cut by a third person, he did the same with his glove, with the end of his finger; finally he went off to the center of the room and in an emphatic tone such as show people use, declaring that the duck would obey his voice no less than his gesture, he spoke and the duck obeyed: he told it to go to the right and it turned right; to come back, and it came; to turn and it turned; the movement followed close upon the order. The redoubled applause was a still greater insult to us. We slipped out without being noticed, and shut ourselves up in our room, without going about to tell everyone of our prowess, as we had planned to do.

The next morning there was a knock at the door, I opened it; there stood the juggler. He mildly objected to our behavior. What had he done to us that we would undertake to discredit his tricks and deprive him of a livelihood? What is so marvelous after all about drawing along a wax duck to cause us to purchase that ability at the expense of the living of an honest man? "By my faith, gentlemen, if I had some other talent by which to earn my living, I should hardly take pride in this one. You ought to know that a man who has spent his life continually practicing this miserable trade would know more about it than you who have spent only a few minutes on it. If I did not show you my finest tricks at once, it was because a man must not be in a hurry to display foolishly all he knows. I always take care to keep my best tricks for a great occasion, and beyond that I have still greater ones to halt young upstarts. Also, gentlemen, I come in goodwill to disclose the secret which embarrassed you so much, requesting that you will not make use of it to harm me, and that you will be more restrained another time."

Then he showed us his apparatus, and we saw with the utmost surprise that it was nothing but a strong, well mounted magnet which a child hidden under the table moved about without our realizing it.

The man put away his apparatus and after we had expressed our thanks and our apologies, we wanted to give him a present; he refused it. "No, gentlemen, I am not pleased enough with you to accept your gift; I leave you in my debt in spite of yourselves; this is my only revenge. Learn that there is generosity in all classes; I get paid for my tricks but not for my lessons."

STUDY QUESTIONS

1. What are the three aspects of education according to Rousseau? What should be the aim of the two aspects that people can do anything about?
2. What distinction does Rousseau make between the person and the citizen? What is his opinion of the citizen?
3. Some of today's educators claim that vocational training is of little value because job requirements are changing so rapidly. What would Rousseau say about this problem?

THE ROMANTIC MOVEMENT

Germany

Johann Gottfried von Herder (1744–1803) was the leader of the precursor of Romanticism, the *Sturm und Drang* (SHTOORM oont DRAHNG) movement in German literature, a term derived from Klinger's novel, *Der Wirrwarr; oder Sturm und Drang* ("Chaos; or Storm and Stress"). A passionate opponent of French rationalism and the Enlightenment, Herder emphasized the *Volksgeist* ("spirit of the people") in Germany, claiming that each *Volk* found its *Geist* in its language, literature, and religion. This was, in effect, a cultural particularism that became the basis of later German nationalism.

In his early writings Johann Wolfgang von Goethe (GUHR-tuh; 1749–1832) was one of the leading exponents of the movement. Written after an unhappy love affair, *The Sorrows of Young Werther* (1774) was a morbidly sensitive tale full of sentiment and gloomy feelings that culminated in the suicide of the tragic Werther. Though Goethe was later to regret the storm and stress of his little book, it made him an instant celebrity.

The philosopher Friedrich Wilhelm Joseph von Schelling (1775–1854) contributed the theory that nature and mind were inseparable and differed only in degree rather than in kind. For Schelling the creative artist was the "ideal Romantic man," a genius who presented his work as instinctively created apart from any conscious effort. From this idea Nietzsche developed his notion of the creative genius as a "superman" who was "beyond good and evil."

Second only to Goethe in German literature, Friedrich von Schiller (1759–1805) was influenced by Kant and, in turn, became a major inspiration for modern German literature. An idealist who hated tyranny, Schiller envisioned the universal fellowship of all humankind. It was his poem "*An die Freude*" ("To Joy") that Beethoven used in the final movement of his mighty Ninth Symphony.

Contributing his pessimistic theories to the movement, Arthur Schopenhauer (1788–1860) claimed that reality was a blind driving force manifested in individuals as Will. Individual wills inevitably clashed, causing strife and pain, from which there was no escape except by a negation of the will. Temporary escape was possible, however, through creative acts in art and science. According to Schopenhauer and other Romantics, creativity emerges from the unconscious, but there are also instinctual drives that conflict with the creative impulses. The unconscious cuts both ways and the Romantics were vividly aware of the "night-side" that could release demonic destruction, as Schopenhauer noted in *The World of Will and Idea* (1818). Blind human will achieves only unhappiness or, as Goya said, "The sleep of reason produces monsters." Schopenhauer concluded that reason must permit the release of creativity while simultaneously controlling the passions, but he was not optimistic about the outcome.

England

Romanticism was effectively expressed in nineteenth-century art and music, in historical novels, Gothic tales, and romantic stories of love and adventure. For an English-speaking audience the Romantic mood is never better expressed than in the work of the English poets.

William Blake, 1757–1827

A self-proclaimed mystic with minimal formal schooling, Blake was a fundamentalist Protestant who believed that the Bible was the sole source of religious knowledge. Very much an individualist, he detested institutionalized religion, claiming that the human imagination was the sole means of expressing the Eternal. Blake referred to people as the Divine Image, the possessors of the humane virtues of mercy, pity, peace, and love. Equally gifted as an artist, Blake illustrated all but one of his volumes of poetry plus the Book of Job, Dante, and the poems of Thomas Gray.

The collection of poems called the *Songs of Innocence* (1789) coincides with the beginning of the French Revolution that, for Blake, held so much promise of a better life for all people. The following poem from that collection celebrates the joys of a Christian life and a simple pastoral existence.

LITERARY SELECTION 59

The Lamb (1789)

William Blake

Little Lamb, who made thee?
Dost thou know who made thee?
Gave thee life, and bid thee feed,
By the stream and o'er the mead;
Gave thee clothing of delight,
Softest clothing, woolly, bright;
Gave thee such a tender voice,
Making all the vales rejoice?
Little Lamb, who made thee?
Dost thou know who made thee?

Little Lamb, I'll tell thee,
Little Lamb, I'll tell thee:
He is callèd by thy name,
For He calls Himself a Lamb.
He is meek, and He is mild;
He became a little child.
I a child, and thou a lamb,
We are callèd by His name.
Little Lamb, God bless thee!
Little Lamb, God bless thee!

The *Songs of Experience* address a sick and corrupt world in which good and evil coexist. In "The Tyger" Blake asks the age-old question: did the good God create evil?

The Tyger (1794)

William Blake

Tyger! Tyger! burning bright
In the forests of the night,
What immortal hand or eye
Could frame thy fearful symmetry?

In what distant deeps or skies
Burnt the fire of thine eyes?
On what wings dare he aspire?
What the hand dare seize the fire?

And what shoulder, and what art,
Could twist the sinews of thy heart?
And when thy heart began to beat,
What dread hand? and what dread feet?

What the hammer? what the chain?
In what furnace was thy brain?
What the anvil? what dread grasp
Dare its deadly terrors clasp?

When the stars threw down their spears,
And water'd heaven with their tears,

Did he smile his work to see?
Did he who made the Lamb make thee?

Tyger! Tyger! burning bright
In the forests of the night,
What immortal hand or eye,
Dare frame thy fearful symmetry?

STUDY QUESTIONS

In *The Marriage of Heaven and Hell* Blake wrote that "Attraction and Repulsion, Reason and Energy, Love and Hate are necessary to Human Existence." Is this attitude reflected in the poems about the lamb and the tiger? Is the tiger, in other words, evil or a symbol of necessary vigor and energy?

William Wordsworth, 1770–1850

The greatest of the English nature poets, Wordsworth was influenced by Rousseau and the spirit of the French Revolution. Strongly opposed to the flowery artificiality of Neoclassic poetry, Wordsworth and Samuel Taylor Coleridge published *Lyrical Ballads* (2nd edition, 1800), which contained a new poetic manifesto. Wordsworth referred to his poetry as "emotion recollected in tranquillity" but, as he stated in the manifesto, he deliberately chose to write in "the language of conversation in the middle and lower classes of society."

The following sonnet mourns a world so overwhelmed with materialism that it may lose its spiritual qualities. Proteus and Triton are from Greek mythology and symbolize the poet's conviction that the wonders of nature that delighted the ancients cannot, in the long run, be destroyed by the Industrial Age. Wordsworth was a Romantic optimist.

LITERARY SELECTION 60

The World is Too Much With Us (1802)

William Wordsworth

The world is too much with us; late and soon,
Getting and spending, we lay waste our powers:
Little we see in Nature that is ours;
We have given our hearts away, a sordid boon!
This Sea that bares her bosom to the moon;
The winds that will be howling at all hours,
And are up-gathered now like sleeping flowers;
For this, for everything, we are out of tune;
It moves us not.—Great God! I'd rather be
A Pagan suckled in a creed outworn;
So might I, standing on this pleasant lea,
Have glimpses that would make me less forlorn;
Have sight of Proteus rising from the sea;
Or hear old Triton blow his wreathèd horn.

STUDY QUESTIONS

If Wordsworth were to write "The World is Too Much With Us" today, would he be as optimistic about the survival of nature's wonders? Why or why not?

Samuel Taylor Coleridge, 1772–1834

Though he did not consider himself a Romantic poet, Coleridge did make a classic Romantic statement: "Each man is meant to represent humanity in his own way, combining its elements uniquely." Coleridge set great store on imagination over fancy, claiming that fancy was only the ability to copy or elaborate on previous examples; imagination was the ability to create new worlds. "Kubla Khan" is a notable example of an inspired vision whether or not, as Coleridge claimed, the poem was composed during an opium reverie and later written down. Coleridge and many other Romantics were fascinated with the exotic Orient. The grandson of Mongol conqueror Genghis Khan, Kubla Khan (1215?–94) founded the Yuan dynasty of China and sponsored Marco Polo as his agent to the West.

LITERARY SELECTION 61

Kubla Khan (1797)

Samuel Taylor Coleridge

In Xanadu did Kubla Khan
A stately pleasure-dome decree:
Where Alph, the sacred river, ran
Through caverns measureless to man
Down to a sunless sea.
So twice five miles of fertile ground
With walls and towers were girdled round:
And, there were gardens bright with sinuous rills,
Where blossomed many an incense-bearing tree
And here were forests ancient as the hills,
Enfolding sunny spots of greenery.
But oh! that deep romantic chasm which slanted
Down the green hill athwart a cedarn cover!
A savage place! as holy and enchanted
As e'er beneath a waning moon was haunted
By woman wailing for her demon-lover!
And from this chasm, with ceaseless turmoil seething,
As if this earth in fast thick pants were breathing,

A mighty fountain momently was forced,
Amid whose swift half-intermitted burst
Huge fragments vaulted like rebounding hail,
Or chaffy grain beneath the thresher's flail:
And 'mid these dancing rocks at once and ever
It flung up momently the sacred river.
Five miles meandering with a mazy motion
Through wood and dale the sacred river ran,
Then reached the caverns measureless to man,
And sank in tumult to a lifeless ocean:
And 'mid this tumult Kubla heard from far
Ancestral voices prophesying war!
The shadow of the dome of pleasure
Floated midway on the waves;
Where was heard the mingled measure
From the fountain and the caves.
It was a miracle of rare device,
A sunny pleasure-dome with caves of ice!
A damsel with a dulcimer
In a vision once I saw:
It was an Abyssinian maid,
And on her dulcimer she played,
Singing of Mount Abora.
Could I revive within me
Her symphony and song,
To such a deep delight 'twould win me,
That with music loud and long,
I would build that dome in air,
That sunny dome! those caves of ice!
And all who heard should see them there,
And all should cry, Beware! Beware!
His flashing eyes, his floating hair!
Weave a circle round him thrice,
And close your eyes with holy dread,
For he on honey-dew hath fed,
And drunk the milk of Paradise.

STUDY QUESTIONS

Coleridge claimed that "Kubla Khan" appeared to him in a dream and that what he later wrote down was "a fragment." Is the poem incomplete? Could the first thirty-six lines be an exercise in creative imagination and the remainder a lament over the loss of poetic power? In these terms is the poem complete or incomplete?

George Noel Gordon, Lord Byron, 1788–1824

The most flamboyant and controversial personality of the age, Lord Byron epitomizes the Romantic hero. With his egotism and superhuman vigor he gloried in physical and mental license, learning relatively late, and only in part, the virtue of moderation. He wrote his words, he said, "as a tiger leaps" and aimed many of them at conventional social behavior, cant, and hypocrisy. Much of his poetry was prosaic when compared with the iridescent style of Shelley and Keats but, as he said, his genius was eloquent rather than poetical. His reputation was early and firmly established with *Childe Harold's Pilgrimage,* a poetic travelogue, but his greatest work is *Don Juan,* a long poem full of irony and pathos. Byron wrote in the Dedication:

> I want a hero: an uncommon want, . . .
> But can't find any in the present age
> Fit for my poem (that is, for my new one):
> So, as I said, I'll take my friend Don Juan.

Almost to the day of his premature death Byron was torn between the heroic defiance of Prometheus and the worldly, cynical insolence of Don Juan. In the end, he tried to choose the Promethean way but died of fever during the Greek struggle for independence.

LITERARY SELECTION 62

Prometheus (1816)

Lord Byron

Titan! to whose immortal eyes
The sufferings of mortality,
Seen in their sad reality,
Were not as things that gods despise;
What was thy pity's recompense?
A silent suffering, and intense;
The rock, the vulture, and the chain,
All that the proud can feel of pain,
The agony they do not show,
The suffocating sense of woe,
Which speaks but in its loneliness,
And then is jealous lest the sky
Should have a listener, nor will sigh
Until its voice is echoless.
Titan! to thee the strife was given
Between the suffering and the will,
Which torture where they cannot kill;
And the inexorable Heaven,
And the deaf tyranny of Fate,
The ruling principle of Hate,
Which for its pleasure doth create
The things it may annihilate,
Refused thee even the boon to die:
The wretched gift eternity
Was thine—and thou hast borne it well.
All that the Thunderer wrung from thee
Was but the menace which flung back
On him the torments of thy rack;
The fate thou didst so well foresee,
But would not to appease him tell;
And in thy Silence was his Sentence,
And in his Soul a vain repentance,
And evil dread so ill dissembled,
That in his hand the lightnings trembled.

Thy Godlike crime was to be kind,
To render with thy precepts less
The sum of human wretchedness,
And strengthen Man with his own mind;
But baffled as thou wert from high,
Still in thy patient energy,
In the endurance, and repulse
Of thine impenetrable Spirit,
Which Earth and Heaven could not convulse,
A mighty lesson we inherit:
Thou art a symbol and a sign
To Mortals of their fate and force;
Like thee, Man is in part divine,
A troubled stream from a pure source;
And Man in portions can foresee
His own funereal destiny,
His wretchedness, and his resistance,
And his sad unallied existence:
To which his Spirit may oppose
Itself—and equal to all woes,
And a firm will, and a deep sense,
Which even in torture can descry
Its own concentre'd recompense,
Triumphant where it dares defy,
And making Death a Victory.

Diodati, July, 1816

Though unable to moderate his course, Byron was fully aware of the causes of his self-destruction, as revealed in several lines from his poignant "Epistle to Augusta":

I have been cunning in mine overthrow,
The careful pilot of my proper woe.
Mine were my faults, and mine be their reward.
My whole life was a contest, since the day
That gave me being, gave me that which marr'd
The gift,—a fate, or will, that walk'd astray.

STUDY QUESTIONS

Prometheus was the Titan who stole fire from Mount Olympos and gave it to humankind. Zeus, the Thunderer in the poem, had him chained to a rock where a vulture perpetually tore out his liver. What does Prometheus symbolize for Byron? Greece under Turkish tyranny? Himself? Both?

Percy Bysshe Shelley, 1792–1822

Shelley and Keats established Romantic verse as the prime poetic tradition of the period; to this day "Shelley and Keats" and "Romantic poetry" are virtually synonymous. A lifelong heretic who was expelled from Oxford because of his pamphlet, *The Necessity of Atheism,* Shelley saw all humankind as the Divine Image to whom poets spoke as the "unacknowledged legislators of the world" (*A Defence of Poetry*). His finest achievement is *Prometheus Unbound,* a lyrical drama in four acts in which he gave full expression to his "passion for reforming the world." Also written at Leghorn, Italy, and published with *Prometheus Unbound* was "To a Skylark," the composition of which was described by Mary Wollstonecraft Shelley:

> It was on a beautiful summer evening while wandering among the lanes, whose myrtle hedges were the bowers of the fireflies, that we heard the caroling of the skylark, which inspired one of the most beautiful of his poems.

LITERARY SELECTION 63

To a Skylark (1820)

Percy Bysshe Shelley

Hail to thee, blithe spirit!
Bird thou never wert,
That from heaven, or near it,
Pourest thy full heart
In profuse strains of unpremeditated art.
Higher still and higher
From the earth thou springest
Like a cloud of fire;
The blue deep thou wingest,
And singing still dost soar, and soaring ever singest.
In the golden lightning
Of the sunken sun,
O'er which clouds are brightning,
Thou dost float and run;
Like an unbodied joy whose race is just begun.
The pale purple even
Melts around thy flight;
Like a star of heaven,
In the broad day-light
Thou art unseen, but yet I hear thy shrill delight,
Keen as are the arrows
Of that silver sphere,
Whose intense lamp narrows
In the white dawn clear,
Until we hardly see, we feel that it is there.
All the earth and air
With thy voice is loud,
As, when night is bare,
From one lonely cloud
The moon rains out her beams, and heaven is overflowed.
What thou art we know not;
What is most like thee?
From rainbow clouds there flow not
Drops so bright to see,
As from thy presence showers a rain of melody.
Like a poet hidden
In the light of thought,

Singing hymns unbidden,
Till the world is wrought
To sympathy with hopes and fears it heeded not:
Like a high-born maiden
In a palace tower,
Soothing her love-laden
Soul in secret hour
With music sweet as love, which overflows her bower:
Like a glow-worm golden
In a dell of dew,
Scattering unbeholden
Its aërial hue
Among the flowers and grass, which screen it from the view:
Like a rose embowered
In its own green leaves,
By warm winds deflowered,
Till the scent it gives
Makes faint with too much sweet these heavy-winged thieves:
Sound of vernal showers
On the twinkling grass,
Rain-awakened flowers,
All that ever was
Joyous, and clear, and fresh, thy music doth surpass:
Teach us, sprite or bird,
What sweet thoughts are thine:
I have never heard
Praise of love or wine
That panted forth a flood of rapture so divine.
Chorus Hymenaeal,
Or triumphal chaunt,
Matched with thine would be all
But an empty vaunt,
A thing wherein we feel there is some hidden want.
What objects are the fountains
Of thy happy strain?
What fields, or waves, or mountains?
What shapes of sky or plain?
What love of thine own kind? what ignorance of pain?
With thy clear keen joyance
Languor cannot be:
Shadow of annoyance
Never came near thee:
Thou lovest; but ne'er knew love's sad satiety.
Waking or asleep,
Thou of death must deem
Things more true and deep
Than we mortals dream,
Or how could thy notes flow in such a crystal stream?
We look before and after,
And pine for what is not:
Our sincerest laughter
With some pain is fraught;
Our sweetest songs are those that tell of saddest thought.
Yet if we could scorn
Hate, and pride, and fear;
If we were things born
Not to shed a tear,
I know not how thy joy we ever should come near.
Better than all measures
Of delightful sound,
Better than all treasures
That in books are found,
Thy skill to poet were, thou scorner of the ground!
Teach me half the gladness
That thy brain must know,
Such harmonious madness
From my lips would flow,
The world should listen then, as I am listening now.

STUDY QUESTION

How does Shelley achieve the seemingly effortless buoyancy of "To a Skylark"? Consider the rhythm and the use of words such as "blithe," "springest," "soar," "float," and many others.

Mary Wollstonecraft Godwin Shelley, 1797–1851

Mary Shelley deserves special mention here. She was the daughter of noted feminist Mary Wollstonecraft (1759–97), author of *Vindication of the Rights of Woman* (1792; see p. 353), and the equally notable social reformer William Godwin (1756–1836), a disciple of Jeremy Bentham and a man who strongly influenced Shelley's reforming zeal. Shelley had left Harriet, his wife, for Mary and moved to the continent where he later married her. While reading ghost stories one evening, Lord Byron suggested that each should write a tale of the supernatural. Mary Shelley's contribution was *Frankenstein; or, The Modern Prometheus* (1818). Using the central themes of Faustian ambition and Promethean creativity, Mary told the story of the scientist Frankenstein who dared to create life itself. Frankenstein's creation needed love and sympathy, but was greeted instead, even by his creator, with disgust and revulsion. Symbolizing Romantic ideas of isolation and alienation, Frankenstein's creation turned from a search for love to hatred of all humankind and murderous destruction. Mary Shelley's story is even more influential today as a modern myth about the horrifying potential of human creativity such as, for example, nuclear weapons.

John Keats, 1795–1821

The poems of both Keats and Shelley have a musicality that sets them apart from all other Romantic poetry. Trained as an apothecary with no thought of becoming a poet, Keats began writing when he was eighteen with a sense of urgency, having noted the symptoms of the tuberculosis that had already carried off his mother and his brother. Keats was the first to admit that his initial volume of poetry had many flaws, but not that it was "alternately florid and arid," as one critic bitingly observed. Keats' own reaction to a barrage of criticism was quite relaxed: "About a twelvemonth since, I published a little book of verses; it was read by some dozen of my friends, who lik'd it; and some dozen whom I was unacquainted with, who did not."

Most Romantics adored what they imagined the Middle Ages to have been; none would have tolerated for a moment the reality of the medieval world. "La Belle Dame sans Merci" ("The Lovely Lady without Pity") is perhaps the finest example of Romantic medievalism. Though the title is taken from a medieval poem by Alain Chartier, the ballad is the poet's own magical version of the ageless myth of the hapless mortal who succumbs to the irresistible charms of a supernatural and pitiless seductress. The first three stanzas are addressed to the distraught knight by an unknown questioner; the balance forms his anguished reply.

LITERARY SELECTION 64

La Belle Dame Sans Merci (1819)

John Keats

O what can ail thee, knight-at-arms,
Alone and palely loitering?
The sedge has withered from the lake,
And no birds sing.

O what can ail thee, knight-at-arms,
So haggard and so woe-begone?
The squirrel's granary is full,
And the harvest's done.

I see a lily on thy brow,
With anguish moist and fever dew;
And on thy cheek a fading rose
Fast withereth too.

I met a lady in the meads,
Full beautiful—a faery's child;
Her hair was long, her foot was light,
And her eyes were wild.

I set her on my pacing steed,
And nothing else saw all day long;
For sidelong would she bend, and sing
A faery's song.

I made a garland for her head,
And bracelets too, and fragrant zone;
She looked at me as she did love,
And made sweet moan.

She found me roots of relish sweet,
And honey wild, and manna-dew;
And sure in language strange she said,
"I love thee true."

She took me to her elfin grot,
And there she wept and sighed full sore:
And there I shut her wild, wild eyes
With kisses four.

And there she lullèd me asleep,
And there I dreamed—Ah! woe betide!
The latest dream I ever dreamed,
On the cold hill-side.

I saw pale kings and princes too,
Pale warriors—death-pale were they all;
Who cried, "La Belle Dame Sans Merci
Hath thee in thrall!"

I saw their starved lips in the gloam,
With horrid warning gapèd wide;
And I awoke, and found me here
On the cold hill's side.

And this is why I sojourn here,
Alone and palely loitering;
Though the sedge is withered from the lake,
And no birds sing.

STUDY QUESTION

How does Keats maintain the medieval mood in "La Belle Dame Sans Merci"? Look, for example, at obvious words such as "thee," "knight-at-arms," and "dancing steed" and subtle words such as "meads," "garland," and "elfin."

Johann Wolfgang von Goethe, 1749–1832

Germany's greatest writer, Goethe, achieved instant fame with the publication of a Romantic novel, *The Sorrows of Young Werther* (1774), but later denounced Romanticism as "a sickness" and wrote novels and plays in the Neoclassic style. A "Renaissance man" rather than a "Romantic hero," Goethe made important contributions to botany, the theory of evolution, and physics. He devoted much of his life to retelling the legend of Dr. Johannes Faustus (ca. 1480–1540), who supposedly sold his soul to the Devil (Mephistopheles) in exchange for youth, knowledge, and power. Goethe's *Faust* (1808–32) became the mythic symbol for the restless search for the meaning of life, and the will to wrest the fullest possibilities from a lifetime of titanic deeds. In his relentless drive to enlarge the meaning of life "Faustian man" is Romantic, but his will to power and knowledge was always and inevitably doomed to failure. Ultimately, Faust's salvation lay in his heroic self-regeneration and his acceptance of his own mortality.

Late in his long career Goethe again became a Romantic poet but, as usual, in his own original fashion. Long attracted to poetry of the Middle East, Goethe published *West-Eastern Divan* (1819), his last important body of lyric poetry, in which he sought wisdom, piety, and peace through the central motif of love. Inspired by a translation of the *Divan* of Hafiz, a fourteenth-century Persian poet,

Goethe wrote twelve books of mostly love poetry. This unique collection was described by noted German poet, Heinrich Heine (1797–1856):

> The charm of the book is inexplicable; it is a votive nosegay sent from the West to the East, composed of the most precious and curious plants. This nosegay signifies that the West is tired of thin and icy-cold spirituality, and seeks warmth in the strong and healthy bosom of the East.

The selections given are the last two poems in the book in which the lovers are reunited after an extended separation (related by Hatem). The volume closes with Suleika's rhapsodic declaration of love. The idealized lovers are Goethe himself (Hatem) and Marianne von Willemer (Suleika).

LITERARY SELECTION 65

VIII Book of Suleika (1819)

Johann Wolfgang von Goethe

The Reunion

Can it be! of stars the star,
  Do I press thee to my heart?
In the night of distance far,
  What deep gulf, what bitter smart!
Yes, 'tis thou, indeed at last,
  Of my joys the partner dear!
Mindful, though, of sorrows past,
  I the present needs must fear.

When the still unfashioned earth
  Lay on God's eternal breast,
He ordained its hour of birth
  With creative joy possessed.
Then a heavy sigh arose,
  When He spake the sentence:—"Be!"
And the All, with mighty throes,
  Burst into reality.

And when thus was born the light,
  Darkness near it feared to stay,
And the elements with might
  Fled on every side away;
Each on some far-distant trace,
  Each with visions wild employed,
Numb, in boundless realms of space,
  Harmony and feeling—void.

Dumb was all, all still and dead,
  For the first time, God alone!
Then He formed the morning-red,
  Which soon made its kindness known:
It unraveled from the waste
  Bright and glowing harmony,
And once more with love was graced
  What contended formerly.

And with earnest, noble strife,
  Each its own peculiar sought;
Back to full, unbounded life,
  Sight and feeling soon were brought.
Wherefore, if 'tis done, explore
  How? why give the manner, name?
Allah need create no more,
  We his world ourselves can frame.

So, with morning pinions bright,
  To thy mouth was I impelled;
Stamped with thousand seals by night,
  Star-clear is the bond fast held.
Paragons on earth are we
  Both of grief and joy sublime,
And a second sentence:—"Be!"
  Parts us not a second time.

Suleika

With what inward joy, sweet lay,
  I thy meaning have descried!
Lovingly thou seemest to say
  That I'm ever by his side;

That he ever thinks of me,
  That he to the absent gives
All his love's sweet ecstasy,
  While for him alone she lives.

Yes, the mirror which reveals
  Thee, my loved one, is my breast;
This is the bosom, where thy seals
  Endless kisses have impressed.

Numbers sweet, unsullied truth,
  Chain me down in sympathy!
Love's embodied radiant youth,
  In the garb of Poesy!

In thousand forms mayst thou attempt surprise,
  Yet, all-belovèd one, straight know I thee;
Thou mayst with magic veils thy face disguise,
  And yet, all-present one, well I know thee!

Upon the cypress' purest, youthful bud,
  All-beauteous-growing one, straight know I thee;
In the canal's unsullied, living flood,
  All-captivating one, well know I thee!

When spreads the water-column, rising proud,
  All-sportive one, how gladly know I thee;
When, e'en in forming, is transformed the cloud,
  All-figure-changing one, there know I thee.

Veiled in the meadow-carpet's flowery charms,
  All-chequered starry fair one, know I thee;
And if a plant extend its thousand arms,
  Oh, all-embracing one, there know I thee.

When on the mount is kindled morn's sweet light,
  Straightway, all-gladdening one, salute I thee;
The arch of heaven o'er head grows pure and bright,—
  All-heart-expanding one, then breathe I thee.

That which my inward, outward sense proclaims,
Thou all-instructing one, I know through thee;
And if I utter Allah's hundred names,
A name with each one echoes, meant for thee.

STUDY QUESTIONS

1. How did the previous relationship end? Why does the poet compare the reunion with the Creation? What are the parallels?
2. What is the cumulative effect of Suleika's repeated, similar phrases ending with "thee"?

SUMMARY

The Romantic movement is perplexing if we consider only what these individual writers and philosophers advocated. What most Romantics were opposed to provides a clearer picture, and the Enlightenment was their main target. Empiricism, geometric thinking, Neoclassicism, all were areas subject to reason and, said the Romantics, all were mechanized and dehumanized. Even the great Newton had become only a materialist and a narrow materialist at that.

Romantics emphasized individuality, the non-rational component of the personality, a sense of the infinite, and a quest for religious reality beyond sensible experience to find God in nature and within the human heart. Far from a return to orthodoxy, the impulse to re-create wonder in the world by finding God in nature was common to many Romantics, except for those such as Byron and Shelley, who sought no God at all. The closest approach to a Romantic consensus was the emphasis on the primacy of human concerns, the celebration of the emotional nature of human beings, and the necessity for creative activity through the exercise of an unfettered imagination.

Perhaps more than any other period, the Romantic era was expressed as well in literature as in music and the visual arts. "Art," wrote Oscar Wilde, "is the most intense mode of individualism that the world has known." In no era was the creative role of the individual more consciously and effectively fulfilled than in the Romantic age. Art was, moreover, highly social, because it was the "result of a relationship between the artist and his time" (James Adams). This was an era of extreme sensitivity to social issues. The Romantics, whether writers, artists, or composers, were generally attuned to certain themes that were endlessly fascinating. Figure 23.6 depicts in a single work five of the most powerful of these themes: nature, the Middle Ages, mysticism, religion, and death. The fate of this painting represents a final Romantic irony.

23.6 Kaspar David Friedrich, *Cloister Graveyard Under Snow*. 1819. Oil on canvas, 3' 11" × 5' 10" (1.19 × 1.77 m). Formerly Nationalgalerie, Staatliche Museen, Berlin (destroyed in 1945 during the Battle of Berlin). Photo: B.P.K., Berlin.

PHILOSOPHY, SCIENCE, AND SOCIAL THOUGHT

Hegel and Marx

The most important German philosopher after Kant, Georg Wilhelm Hegel (HAY-gul; 1770–1831) influenced European and American philosophers, historians, theologians, and political theorists. Described by Bertrand Russell as "the hardest to understand of all the great philosophers," Hegel and those doctrines of his that influenced Karl Marx will be our focus here. Hegel believed in an all-encompassing Absolute, a world Spirit that expressed itself in the historical process. Basing his logic on the "triadic dialectic," Hegel stated that for every concept or force (thesis) there was its opposite idea (antithesis). Out of the dynamic interaction between the two extremes would emerge a synthesis that, in turn, would become a new and presumably higher thesis. Absolute Being, for example, is a thesis whereas Absolute Unbeing is its antithesis. The synthesis is Absolute Becoming, meaning that the universe is eternally re-creating itself.

The notable cultures of the past were, according to Hegel, stages in the evolutionary development of the world Spirit toward perfection and freedom. Human beings and their institutions must inevitably clash because all are subject to error; nevertheless, they must act and, through striving, find the "path of righteousness." Essentially Faustian in the conviction that perfectibility was attainable only through continuous activity and unavoidable conflict, Hegel's philosophy of history was evolutionary. Not only all humankind but the world itself was progressing ever upward, away from imperfection and toward the Absolute.

By mid-century, few could see progress of any kind, particularly for the oppressed lower class. The horrible working conditions and dismal lives of factory workers concerned social reformers throughout Europe. Many spoke out against the exploitation of the working class, but none so dramatically as the Communists in the following extracts from their *Manifesto*.

LITERARY SELECTION 66

Manifesto of the Communist Party (1848)

Karl Marx and Friedrich Engels

A spectre is haunting Europe—the spectre of Communism. All the Powers of old Europe have entered into a holy alliance to exorcize this spectre: Pope and Czar, Metternich and Guizot, French Radicals and German police spies.

Where is the party in opposition that has not been decriėd as Communistic by its opponents in power? Where the Opposition that has not hurled back the branding reproach of Communism against the more advanced opposition parties, as well as against its reactionary adversaries?

Two things result from this fact:

I. Communism is already acknowledged by all European powers to be itself a power.

II. It is high time that Communists should openly, in the face of the whole world, publish their views, their aims, their tendencies, and meet this nursery tale of the Spectre of Communism with a Manifesto of the party itself.

To this end, Communists of various nationalities have assembled in London, and sketched the following Manifesto, to be published in the English, French, German, Italian, Flemish, and Danish languages.

I Bourgeois and Proletarians

The history of all hitherto existing society is the history of class struggles.

Freeman and slave, patrician and plebeian, lord and serf, guild-master and journeyman, in a word, oppressor and oppressed, stood in constant opposition to one another, carried on an uninterrupted, now hidden, now open fight, a fight that each time ended, either in a revolutionary reconstitution of society at large, or in the common ruin of the contending classes.

In the earlier epochs of history, we find almost everywhere a complicated arrangement of society into various orders, a manifold gradation of social rank. In ancient Rome we have patricians, knights, plebeians, slaves; in the Middle Ages, feudal lords, vassals, guild-masters, journeymen, apprentices, serfs; in almost all of these classes, again, subordinate gradations.

The modern bourgeois society that has sprouted from the ruins of feudal society, has not done away with class antagonisms. It has but established new classes, new conditions of oppression, new forms of struggle in place of the old ones.

Our epoch, the epoch of the bourgeoisie, possesses, however, this distinctive feature: it has simplified the class antagonisms. Society as a whole is more and more splitting up into two great classes directly facing each other: Bourgeoisie and Proletariat . . . .

Each step in the development of the bourgeoisie was accompanied by a corresponding political advance of that class. An oppressed class under the sway of the feudal nobility, it became an armed and self-governing association in the medieval commune: here independent urban republic (as in Italy and Germany); there, taxable "third estate" of the monarchy (as in France); afterwards, in the period of manufacture, serving either the semi-feudal or the absolute monarchy as a counterpoise against the nobility, and, in fact, cornerstone of the great monarchies in general. The bourgeoisie has, at last, since the establishment of Modern Industry and of the world market, conquered for itself, in the modern representative State, exclusive political sway. The executive of the modern State is but a committee for managing the common affairs of the whole bourgeoisie . . . .

IV Position of the Communists in Relation to the Various Existing Opposition Parties

. . . The Communists turn their attention chiefly to Germany because that country is on the eve of a bourgeois revolution that is bound to be carried out under more advanced conditions of European civilization and with a much more developed proletariat than that of England in the seventeenth and of France in the eighteenth century, and because the bourgeois revolution in Germany will be but the prelude to an immediately following proletarian revolution.

In short, the Communists everywhere support every revolutionary movement against the existing social and political order of things . . . .

Finally, they labour everywhere for the union and agreement of the democratic parties of all countries.

The Communists disdain to conceal their views and aims. They openly declare that their ends can be attained only by the forcible overthrow of all existing social conditions. Let the ruling classes tremble at a Communist revolution. The proletarians have nothing to lose but their chains. They have a world to win.

WORKINGMEN OF ALL COUNTRIES, UNITE!

Translation by Samuel Moore, 1888

Because he believed in the basic goodness of human beings, Karl Marx (1818–83), along with his collaborator Friedrich Engels (1820–95), formulated a doctrine of inevitable progress that would lead to the perfect classless society in which private property and the profit motive would be relics of the imperfect past. From Hegel he took the dialectic, not as world Spirit, but as material forces, a concept espoused by the German philosopher Ludwig Feuerbach (1804–72). In effect, Marx turned Hegel's dialectic upside down, contending that it was not consciousness that determined human existence but the social existence of people that defined their consciousness.

For Marx, the way people made a living, their "means of production," determined their beliefs and institutions. To demonstrate the working of dialectical materialism Marx concentrated on medieval feudal society. The *thesis* was the ruling class of the nobility and clergy. With the development of trade an increasingly affluent middle class, the bourgeoisie, rose as the *antithesis* in the class struggle. Following the American and French revolutions the bourgeois class merged with the vanquished nobility as the *synthesis*. Traders, bankers, and factory-owners made up the ruling class of capitalists, the new thesis, whereas the oppressed workers, the proletariat, were the antithesis. The final class struggle between capitalists and workers would, according to Marx, inevitably result in victory for the proletariat, who would take over the means of production. Under the "dictatorship of the proletariat" the entire capitalist apparatus would be collectivized. With only one class remaining, the class struggle would cease. According to Marx, the state, with its laws, courts, and police served only to oppress the proletariat and would no longer be necessary; it would therefore "wither away."

It was not until late in the twentieth century that Marx was finally and decisively proven wrong, along with those who used their versions of his theories. The failure of Communism is discussed in the concluding unit of this text.

STUDY QUESTIONS

1. Marx claimed that Communism would first overcome the most advanced socities. Why didn't this happen?
2. Communism succeeded in Russia, the most backward nation in Europe. How did this happen? Why?

Charles Darwin, 1809–82

Anaximander of Miletus (610–ca. 547 BC) postulated an elementary theory of evolution, but it was not until the nineteenth century that the theories of Erasmus Darwin, Jean-Baptiste de Lamarck, Thomas Malthus, and the detailed naturalistic observations of Charles Darwin finally led to Darwin's publication of *On the Origin of Species by Means of Natural Selection* (1859). After serving as naturalist on the surveying ship *Beagle* (1831–6) Darwin read, in Thomas Malthus' *Essay on the Principle of Population* (1798), the thesis that population increased by a geometric ratio (1:2:4:16 etc.), whereas the food supply increased arithmetically (1:3:5:7:9 etc.). The limited food supply, Malthus observed, placed a natural check on population increase. Darwin wrote:

> It at once struck me that under the circumstances favourable variations would tend to be preserved and unfavourable ones destroyed. The result of this would be the formation of a new species. Here then I had a theory by which to work. This is the doctrine of natural selection, the result of chance enabling, in Herbert Spencer's phrase, the survival of the fittest.

Darwin proceeded from three facts to his deductions:

Fact 1. All organisms tend to increase geometrically.
Fact 2. The population of a given species remains more or less constant.
Fact 3. Within any species there is considerable variation.
Deduction 1. With more young produced than can survive there must be competition for survival.
Deduction 2. The variations within a species mean that a higher percentage of those with favourable variations will survive and, conversely, a higher percentage of those with unfavourable variations will die or fail to reproduce. This is natural selection. Furthermore, favourable variations are generally transmitted by heredity, meaning that natural selection will tend to maintain and act to improve the ability of the species to survive.

Modern evolution theory confirms Darwin's facts and deductions as outlined above, but adds some significant variations in terms of modifications, mutations, and recombinations. Modification is a variation due to external or internal factors and is not the result of inheritance. Take, for example, identical twins, one leading an active and healthy life and the other immersed in alcoholism. Barring an accident one twin will almost certainly survive the other.

The copying of genes in the process of reproduction is not always precise. A copy that differs slightly from the original is a mutation, and the mutated gene will continue to reproduce itself unless the mutation results in an unfavorable variation that increases the chances against survival. Mutations tend, on the whole, to result in unfavorable variations.

Darwin was not aware of the full implications of Gregor Mendel's (1822–84) experiments in genetics, specifically the fact that sexual reproduction results in a recombination of existing genetic units that may produce or modify inheritable combinations. Take, for example, twelve children born of the same parents. Though there is generally a familial resemblance, each child will be distinctly different because of the different recombination of genes.

Darwin was reluctant to publish his theories until he learned that Alfred Russel Wallace (1823–1913) had independently developed a theory of evolution. Both men submitted a paper to the Linnaean Society on the theory of natural selection; both papers were read on 1 July 1858, and later published. Even when Darwin published his *Origin of Species* the following year he considered his work a brief abstract of twenty-five years of detailed studies.

Darwin's work provoked a great controversy, of course, because it denied supernatural intervention in the functioning of the universe. He rode out the theological storm, but not the attacks of naturalists who claimed a special place for *Homo sapiens* separate from other species. In the introduction to *The Descent of Man* (1871) Darwin noted that he had many notes on the origin or descent of man, but that he had been determined "not to publish, as I thought that I should thus only add to the prejudices against my views." Indeed, *Origin of Species* implied "that man must be included with other organic beings in any general conclusion respecting his manner of appearance on this earth." *The Descent of Man* is therefore a response to hostile naturalists and a sequel to the *Origin of Species* in which Darwin discussed the evolution of *Homo sapiens* from lower forms of life. The conclusion of this work reveals Darwin as a realist and as an optimist.

LITERARY SELECTION 67

The Descent of Man (1871)

Charles Darwin

The main conclusion arrived at in this work, namely, that man is descended from some lowly organised form, will, I regret to think, be highly distasteful to many. But there can hardly be a doubt that we are descended from barbarians. The astonishment which I felt on first seeing a party of Fuegians on a wild and broken shore will never be forgotten by me, for the reflection at once rushed into my mind—such were our ancestors. These men were absolutely naked and bedaubed with paint, their long hair was tangled, their mouths, frothed with excitement, and their expression was wild, startled, and distrustful. They possessed hardly any arts, and like wild animals lived on what they could catch; they had no government, and were merciless to every one not of their own small tribe. He who has seen a savage in his native land will not feel much shame, if forced to acknowledge that the blood of some more humble creature flows in his veins. For my own part I would as soon be descended from that heroic little monkey, who braved his dreaded enemy in order to save the life of his keeper, or from that old baboon, who descending from the mountains, carried away in triumph his young comrade from a crowd of astonished dogs—as from a savage who delights to torture his enemies, offers up bloody sacrifices, practises infanticide without remorse, treats his wives like slaves, knows no decency, and is haunted by the grossest superstitions.

Man may be excused for feeling some pride at having risen, though not through his own exertions, to the very summit of the organic scale; and the fact of his having thus risen, instead of having been aboriginally placed there, may give him hope for a still higher destiny in the distant future. But we are not here concerned with hopes or fears, only with the truth as far as our reason permits us to discover it; and I have given the evidence to the best of my ability. We must, however, acknowledge, as it seems to me, that man with all his noble qualities, with sympathy which feels for the most debased, with benevolence which extends not only to other men but to the humblest living creature, with his god-like intellect which has penetrated into the movements and constitution of the solar system—with all these exalted powers—man still bears in his bodily frame the indelible stamp of his lowly origin.

What is the status of Darwinism today? As Dennis Flanagan states it, evolution by natural selection is simply "the testing of variations in the laboratory of the environment." With the theory of evolution

> the trouble lies with the word "theory." The everyday meaning of "theory" is speculation but the scientific meaning of the word is a substantial body of reasoning. It is like that with the Darwinian theory of evolution. *Evolution itself is not a theory; it is an inescapable fact.* Charles Darwin did much to call attention to that fact. Modern Darwinian theory, however, is an effort to explain how life evolves.[5]

The difference, in science, between "law" and "theory" can be further illustrated by citing the *law* of gravity, which states that objects in space are attracted to each other. The *theory* of gravity, on the other hand, is the inquiry into how and why objects attract each other. As with evolution, that inquiry continues to challenge scientists.

Social Darwinism

English philosopher Herbert Spencer (1820–1903) argued that evolution occurred not only in nature but in human institutions as well. Spencer's phrase, "survival of the fittest," meant, according to the Social Darwinists, that the rich were better adapted to the rigors of competitive life because they

5. Dennis Flanagan, *Flanagan's Version: A Spectator's Guide to Science on the Eve of the 21st Century* (New York: Alfred A. Knopf, 1988), p. 26.

were better able to survive than the poor. Opposed to government interference in economic affairs, to trade unions, and to socialist ideas such as welfare, powerful capitalists (John D. Rockefeller, Andrew Carnegie, and others) claimed that unrestrained competition had a scientific basis comparable to evolution in nature. This position was, of course, an attempt to justify *laissez-faire* capitalism.

On a larger scale, Social Darwinism reinforced the idea that some nations were more competent than others; defeating an adversary in warfare would thus demonstrate that superiority. Indeed, it became almost a moral duty, in Social Darwinian terms, to conquer "inferior" people and populate their lands with fitter human beings. Late nineteenth-century imperialism thus had an ideal social philosophy to justify the ruthless growth of empire. British imperialist Cecil Rhodes went even further by claiming that a world of Anglo-Saxons was the best of all possible worlds, thus adding racism to the social evolution theory. In 1845 a journalist and diplomat named John Louis O'Sullivan coined the term "manifest destiny"—a phrase that, when reinforced by Social Darwinism, provided the justification of American imperialism.

Darwinian views spread into every corner of the intellectual domain: anthropology, sociology, history, literature, art, music, legal and political institutions. Just about everything was investigated in terms of origin, development, and survival or disappearance.

There is no denying the enormous influence of evolutionary theory in all these areas, but great care has to be taken when applying a scientific theory to non-scientific areas. "Natural selection," for scientists, means the way things work in nature and no more than that. Social Darwinists manipulated evolutionary theory to justify individuality and unfettered competition as if the marketplace were a scientific laboratory. Scientific terminology was selected to undergird the way things were supposed to be. "Survival of the fittest" supposedly proved that the wealthy and powerful were fit and no one else. In fact, the most competent creatures in Darwin's natural world were those who, over a period of time, left the most dependents who could survive natural selection. Not necessarily the smartest, largest, or strongest; just survivors.

Furthermore, many of those who claimed that a capitalist economy was a struggle for existence with only the fittest surviving refused to compete in a free market. They wanted high tariffs to protect them from foreign competition and would tolerate no competition for improved wages and working conditions on the part of organized labor. Rockefeller and Carnegie, for example, argued for competition, but they effectively eliminated it and made billions from their virtual monopolies in oil and steel. Social Darwinism is a twisted play on the good name of Charles Darwin. The true social philosophy of America's "robber barons" at the height of *laissez-faire* capitalism can best be summed up in the callous statement attributed to William Vanderbilt: "The public be damned!"

Liberalism

Jeremy Bentham (1748–1832) was the founder of the rationalist philosophy of utilitarianism, a doctrine whose central idea is that, in themselves, actions are not right or wrong; they can be judged only by their consequences. Utilitarianism is based on the assumption that all human beings pursue happiness by seeking pleasure and avoiding pain. The criterion of the value of deeds is their utility, that is, whether they lead to the greatest happiness of the greatest number. Bentham's ethics are, in effect, an inversion of those of Kant. Kant calls for action as a duty and on principle; Bentham's values are based on the consequences of actions.

Bentham believed, along with classical (*laissez-faire*) economists, that government governs best when it governs least and that it should be relatively passive in social affairs. He was, however, an ardent reformer and his detailed studies of English institutions convinced him that the pleasure derived by some in the pursuit of self-interest caused pain for others, sometimes many, many others. He and his followers, the Philosophic Radicals, finally concluded that the state should intervene to help provide the greatest happiness for the greatest number. Their influence led to considerable administrative, legal, and economic reforms that broadened, in the twentieth century, into the concept of the welfare state that aimed to care for all its citizens "from the cradle to the grave."

John Stuart Mill, 1806–73

James Mill was a disciple of Bentham and the director of a rigorous "educational experiment" for his son, John Stuart Mill. By the age of three, young Mill had learned Greek and, at seven, he was reading Plato's dialogues. During the following year he taught Latin to his sister. By the time John Stuart Mill started college, he had what he called a twenty-five-year head start on his classmates. There were drawbacks, however. "I grew up," Mill wrote in his celebrated *Autobiography* (1873), "in the absence of love and in the presence of fear." Referring to himself as a "reasoning machine," Mill had a breakdown at twenty from which he recovered by turning to music and the Romantic poets, especially Coleridge and Wordsworth. It was also during this period of crisis that Mill met Harriet Taylor, the wife of a London merchant. A woman of remarkable intellect comparable to that of Mill, Harriet was his intense Platonic love and intellectual companion until 1851, when her husband died and they were married. The belated education in music and art plus the association with Harriet, whom Mill credited with much assistance in his writing, helped make Mill the foremost humanitarian liberal of the century.

Mill adopted utilitarianism at an early age, but he distinguished pleasures by qualities rather than by mere quantities as Bentham had done. For Mill the greatest pleasures were intellectual, ranking far above sensual pleasures. As he said, he would "rather be Socrates dissatisfied than a fool satisfied." Mill's position was comparable to that of the

23.7 "The houses of the poor are not the palaces of the rich," from Gustave Dore and Blanchard Jerrold, *London, a Pilgrimage* (London: Grant & Co.). 1872. Woodcut after Gustave Dore, 7⅞ × 9⅝" (19.9 × 24.6 cm). Photo: A.K.G., London.

Epicureans: he said that "human beings have faculties more elevated than the animal appetites, and when once conscious of them, do not regard anything as happiness which does not include their gratification." Among the greatest pleasures for Mill were freedom of thought, speech, and action, but only up to the point where this freedom might impinge on that of another. His famous political essay, *On Liberty* (1859), explores the "nature and limits of power which can be legitimately exercised over the individual." His arguments defending free speech in a democratic society are just as convincing today, and his repeated warning against the "tyranny of the majority" is equally apropos.

To help secure the greatest good for the greatest number, Mill was an extremely active reformer, pressing for extended suffrage, measures to protect children, and actions to improve the lot of the poor. Virtually alone among thinkers of his time, Mill was convinced that women were the intellectual equals of men. Vigorously opposed to the inferior status of women, he wrote the *Subjection of Women* (1869), a strongly worded book that was responsible for some altered laws and a number of modifications in opinions. Though he did not reject classical economics, Mill did see that adjustments were necessary and long overdue. In the midst of self-righteous materialistic Victorians, Mill's sane and sophisticated voice was hailed, by his supporters, as a generous breath of fresh air.

Victorian Poets

By the later Victorian period England was a bustling and prosperous country. Mechanized, industrialized, and urbanized, it was also a tiny island on whose flag the sun never set, the most powerful and far-flung empire the world had ever known. Early Romantics had envisioned a new society flourishing in a golden age, but later Victorians witnessed endless colonial wars, smoke blanketing the countryside from hundreds of belching smokestacks, and miles of dreary row houses inhabited by overworked and underpaid factory workers (fig. 23.7). The industrial revolution had defiled nature but, after Darwin, there was no solace in nature, which Tennyson described as "red in tooth and claw." What, then, was the role of the poet?

Alfred, Lord Tennyson, 1809–92

The most representative poet of the mid-Victorian era, Tennyson reflected the mood of the period in poetry that was sad, quiet, contemplative, melancholy, sometimes wistful, and often pessimistic. The old optimism of the early Romantics had vanished.

Tennyson wrote often about contemporary events such as "The Charge of the Light Brigade," but his best poetry is about the past, particularly the classical past. In "Ulysses" the Greek hero has returned, after twenty years, to Penelope, his "aged wife," and Telemachus, a dutiful son who is content to stay at home and "make mild a rugged people." Ulysses is always the man of action, the embodiment of the Faustian man, whose mission in life is succinctly stated in the last line of the poem.

LITERARY SELECTION 68

Ulysses (1842)

Alfred, Lord Tennyson

It little profits that an idle king,
By this still hearth, among these barren crags,
Matched with an aged wife, I mete and dole
Unequal laws unto a savage race,
That hoard, and sleep, and feed, and know not me.
I cannot rest from travel: I will drink
Life to the lees: all times I have enjoyed
Greatly, have suffered greatly, both with those
That loved me, and alone; on shore, and when
Through scudding drifts the rainy Hyades
Vext the dim sea. I am become a name;
For always roaming with a hungry heart
Much have I seen and known: cities of men
And manners, climates, councils, governments,
Myself not least, but honoured of them all,—
And drunk delight of battle with my peers,
Far on the ringing plains of windy Troy.
I am a part of all that I have met;
Yet all experience is an arch wherethrough
Gleams that untravelled world, whose margin fades
For ever and for ever when I move.
How dull it is to pause, to make an end,
To rust unburnished, not to shine in use!
As though to breathe were life! Life piled on life
Were all too little, and of one to me
Little remains: but every hour is saved
From that eternal silence, something more,
A bringer of new things; and vile it were
For some three suns to store and hoard myself,
And this gray spirit yearning in desire
To follow knowledge, like a sinking star,

Beyond the utmost bound of human thought.
This is my son, mine own Telemachus,
To whom I leave the sceptre and the isle—
Well-loved of me, discerning to fulfil
This labour, by slow prudence to make mild
A rugged people, and through soft degrees
Subdue them to the useful and the good.
Most blameless is he, centred in the sphere
Of common duties, decent not to fail
In offices of tenderness, and pay
Meet adoration to my household gods,
When I am gone. He works his work, I mine.

There lies the port: the vessel puffs her sail:
There gloom the dark broad seas. My mariners,
Souls that have toiled, and wrought, and thought with me—
That ever with a frolic welcome took
The thunder and the sunshine, and opposed
Free hearts, free foreheads—you and I are old;
Old age hath yet his honour and his toil;
Death closes all: but something ere the end,
Some work of noble note, may yet be done,
Not unbecoming men that strove with Gods.
The lights begin to twinkle from the rocks:
The long day wanes: the slow moon climbs: the deep
Moans round with many voices. Come, my friends,
'Tis not too late to seek a newer world.
Push off, and sitting well in order smite
The sounding furrows; for my purpose holds
To sail beyond the sunset, and the baths
Of all the western stars, until I die.
It may be that the gulfs will wash us down:
It may be we shall touch the Happy Isles,
And see the great Achilles, whom we knew.
Though much is taken, much abides; and though
We are not now that strength which in old days
Moved earth and heaven, that which we are, we are,—
One equal temper of heroic hearts,
Made weak by time and fate, but strong in will
To strive, to seek, to find, and not to yield.

STUDY QUESTIONS

In Tennyson's version is Ulysses a noble hero who refuses to submit meekly to old age and death or is he an arrogant, self-centered old man with little concern for his family? Why shouldn't he be "matched with an aged wife"? Penelope is younger than Ulysses and she did wait twenty faithful years for her husband to return from his Odyssey. Whatever your opinion, is he believable as a human being?

Matthew Arnold, 1822–88

As a poet and literary critic Arnold was as pessimistic as his colleagues about human beings and their institutions, but through sheer force of will he created a cheerful demeanor and purposeful character for himself. Possibly the most anti-Victorian figure in Victorian England, Arnold was an apostle of high culture and a lifelong enemy of Puritanism, the "Barbarians" (aristocracy), and the "Philistines" (middle class). His despairing view of human alienation in a hostile universe is memorably expressed in "Dover Beach." When the poet says to his female companion, "Ah love, let us be true to one another!" the objective is not love but survival. Arnold was a realist, not a romantic.

LITERARY SELECTION 69

Dover Beach (1867)

Matthew Arnold

The sea is calm to-night.
The tide is full, the moon lies fair
Upon the straits; on the French coast the light
Gleams and is gone; the cliffs of England stand,
Glimmering and vast, out in the tranquil bay.
Come to the window, sweet is the night air!
Only, from the long line of spray
Where the sea meets the moon-blanch'd land,
Listen! you hear the grating roar
Of pebbles which the waves draw back, and fling,
At their return, up the high strand,
Begin, and cease, and then again begin,
With tremulous cadence slow, and bring
The eternal note of sadness in.

Sophocles long ago
Heard it on the Aegaean, and it brought
Into his mind the turbid ebb and flow
Of human misery; we
Find also in the sound a thought,
Hearing it by this distant northern sea.

The Sea of Faith
Was once, too, at the full, and round earth's shore
Lay like the folds of a bright girdle furled.
But now I only hear
Its melancholy, long, withdrawing roar,
Retreating, to the breath
Of the night-wind, down the vast edges drear
And naked shingles of the world.

Ah, love, let us be true
To one another! for the world, which seems
To lie before us like a land of dreams,
So various, so beautiful, so new,
Hath really neither joy, nor love, nor light,
Nor certitude, nor peace, nor help for pain;
And we are here as on a darkling plain
Swept with confused alarms of struggles and flight,
Where ignorant armies clash by night.

STUDY QUESTIONS

1. Compare the liquid and nasal sounds of lines 1–8 with the much harsher sounds of lines 9–14. Notice, also, that the opening lines describe a lovely seascape, with a discordant tone entering at line 9 in both sounds and sense.
2. What happened to the "sea of faith"? Why?
3. What are the many implications inherent in the last line? Consider the levels of meaning in each of the key words—"ignorant," "armies," "clash," "night"—and then reflect on the entire line. How far have we come from the opening lines?

Thomas Hardy, 1840–1928

Though he denied being a pessimist, the novels, short stories, and poems of Thomas Hardy reveal a pessimism every bit as profound as that of Matthew Arnold and Feodor Dostoevsky. Hardy claimed that human effort could make the world a better place, but his prose and poetry overflow with sadness over the waste and frustration of life. Though he outlived the Victorian era, Hardy's output typifies the late Victorian mood of ironic melancholy as, for example, in "Neutral Tones" in which the imagery is consistent and convincing.

LITERARY SELECTION 70

Neutral Tones (1898)

Thomas Hardy

We stood by a pond that winter day,
And the sun was white, as though chidden of God,
And a few leaves lay on the starving sod;
—They had fallen from an ash, and were grey.
Your eyes on me were as eyes that rove
Over tedious riddles of years ago;
And some words played between us to and fro
On which lost the more by our love.
The smile on your mouth was the deadest thing
Alive enough to have strength to die;
And a grin of bitterness swept thereby
Like an ominous bird a-wing . . .
Since then, keen lessons that love deceives,
And wrings with wrong, have shaped to me
Your face, and the God-cursed sun, and a tree,
And a pond edged with greyish leaves.

Written on the last day of the nineteenth century, "The Darkling Thrush" morosely defines a century that ends, for Hardy, with a whimper, and anticipates a new hundred years that seem to offer little hope of anything better.

The Darkling Thrush (1900)

Thomas Hardy

I leant upon a coppice gate
  When Frost was spectre-grey,
And Winter's dregs made desolate
  The weakening eye of day.
The tangled bine-stems scored the sky
  Like strings of broken lyres,
And all mankind that haunted nigh
  Had sought their household fires.
The land's sharp features seemed to be
  The Century's corpse outleant,
His crypt the cloudy canopy,
  The wind his death-lament.
The ancient pulse of germ and birth
  Was shrunken hard and dry,
And every spirit upon earth
  Seemed fervourless as I.
At once a voice arose among
  The bleak twigs overhead
In a full-hearted evensong
  Of joy illimited;
An aged thrush, frail, gaunt, and small,
  In blast-beruffled plume,
Had chosen thus to fling his soul
  Upon the growing gloom.
So little cause for carolings
  Of such ecstatic sound
Was written on terrestrial things
  Afar or nigh around,
That I could think there trembled through
  His happy good-night air
Some blessed Hope, whereof he knew
  And I was unaware.

MATERIALISM AND PESSIMISM

Feodor Mikhailovich Dostoevsky, 1821–81

One of the giants of modern literature, Dostoevsky (doss-toe-EFF-ski) was deeply scarred by his sentence to hard labor in Siberia as an enemy of the Czarist government. Darkly pessimistic about the future of European civilization, the author turned to religion as a means of redemption. This was not the organized religion of Rome or of the Russian Orthodox Church, but an individual commitment to faith, action, and demonstrated compassion for all people, even the worst among them, with the expectation that all could be saved through their own individual efforts. Thus Dostoevsky can be classed with Kierkegaard and Nietzsche (see pp. 345–6) as an early exponent of existentialism.

In his monumental novel *The Brothers Karamazov* the author presents Ivan Karamazov as an atheist, whereas his brother, Aloysha, is spiritually whole and actively seeking Christianity in a secular society. Dostoevsky viewed his age as spiritually bankrupt, and vulnerable to the dictates of church and state, present or future. In this selection, extracted from the novel (Part II, Book V, Chapter 5) and translated by Ralph E. Matlaw, the author portrays the Grand Inquisitor as a symbol of everyone who embraces power and rejects freedom and self-reliance. Dostoevsky proposes the utilization of an active Christian faith to counter the totalitarian hell of a party, government, or church. His prescience immediately calls to mind the horrifying realities of Hitler, Stalin, Chairman Mao, and the attendant miseries of the twentieth century.

LITERARY SELECTION 71

The Grand Inquisitor

Feodor Dostoevsky

". . . My story [said Ivan Karamazov to Aloysha] is laid in Spain, in Seville, in the most terrible time of the Inquisition, when fires were lighted every day to the glory of God, and

In the splendid autos-da-fé
The wicked heretics were burnt.[6]

"Oh, of course, this was not the coming in which He will appear according to His promise at the end of time in all His heavenly glory, and which will be sudden 'as lightning flashing from east to west.' No, He visited His children only for a moment, and there were the flames crackling round the heretics. In His infinite mercy He came once more among men in that human shape in which He walked among men for three years fifteen centuries ago. He came down to the 'hot pavement' of the southern town in which on the day before almost a hundred heretics had, *ad majorem gloriam Dei*,[7] been burned by the cardinal, the Grand Inquisitor, in a magnificent *auto-da-fé*, in the presence of the king, the court, the knights, the cardinals, the most charming ladies of the court, and the whole population of Seville.

"He came softly, unobserved, and yet, strange to say, everyone recognized Him. The people are irresistibly drawn to Him, they flock about Him, follow Him. He moves silently in their midst with a gentle smile of infinite compassion. The sun of love burns in His heart. Light, enlightenment, and power shine from His eyes, and their radiance, shed on the people, stirs their hearts with responsive love. He holds out His hands to them, blesses them, and a healing virtue comes from contact with Him, even with His garments. An old man in the crowd, blind from childhood, cries out, 'Oh Lord, heal me and I shall see Thee!' and, as it were, scales fall from his eyes and the blind man sees Him. The crowd weeps and kisses the earth under His feet. Children throw flowers before Him, sing and cry 'Hosannah.' 'It is He—it is He!' all repeat. 'It must be He, it can be no one but Him!' He stops at the steps of the Seville cathedral at the moment when the weeping mourners are bringing in a little open

6. From a poem, "Corialanus," (1834) by A. I. Polezhaev.
7. "For the greater glory of God"—motto of the Society of Jesus.

white coffin. In it lies a child of seven, the only daughter of a prominent citizen. The dead child lies hidden in flowers. 'He will raise your child,' the crowd shouts to the weeping mother. The priest, coming to meet the coffin, looks perplexed, and frowns, but the mother of the dead child throws herself at His feet with a wail, 'If it is Thou, raise my child!' she cries, holding out her hands to Him. The procession halts, the coffin is laid on the steps at His feet. He looks with compassion, and His lips once more softly pronounce, 'Maiden arise!' and the maiden arises. The little girl sits up in the coffin and looks round, smiling with wide-open wondering eyes, holding a bunch of white roses they put in her hand.

"There are cries, sobs, confusion among the people, and at that moment the cardinal himself, the Grand Inquisitor, passes by the cathedral. He is an old man, almost ninety, tall and erect, with a withered face and sunken eyes, in which there is still a gleam of light, like a fiery spark. He is not dressed in his gorgeous cardinal's robes, as he was the day before, when he was burning the enemies of the Roman Church—at that moment he was wearing his coarse, old, monk's cassock. At a distance behind him come his gloomy assistants and slaves and the 'holy guard.' He stops at the sight of the crowd and watches it from a distance. He sees everything; he sees them set the coffin down at His feet, sees the child rise up, and his face darkens. He knits his thick grey brows and his eyes gleam with a sinister fire. He holds out his finger and bids the guards take Him. And such is his power, so completely are the people cowed into submission and trembling obedience to him, that the crowd immediately make way for the guards and in the midst of deathlike silence they lay hands on Him and lead Him away. The crowd instantly bows down to earth, like one man, before the old inquisitor. He blesses the people in silence and passes on. The guards lead their prisoner to the close, gloomy vaulted prison in the ancient palace of the Holy Inquisition and shut Him in it. The day passes and is followed by the dark, burning 'breathless' night of Seville. The air is fragrant with laurel and lemon.[8] In the pitch darkness the iron door of the prison is suddenly opened and the Grand Inquisitor himself comes in with a light in his hand. He is alone; the door is closed at once behind him. He stands in the doorway and for a long time, for a minute or two, gazes into His face. At last he goes up slowly, sets the light on the table and speaks.

" 'Is it Thou?' but receiving no answer, he adds at once, 'Don't answer, be silent. What canst Thou say, indeed? I know too well what Thou wouldst say. And Thou hast no right to add anything to what Thou hadst said of old. Why, then, art Thou come to hinder us? For Thou hadst come to hinder us, and Thou knowest that. But dost Thou know what will be tomorrow? I know not who Thou art and care not to know whether it is Thou or only a semblance of Him, but tomorrow I shall condemn Thee and burn Thee at the stake as the worst of heretics. And the very people who have today kissed Thy feet, tomorrow at the faintest sign from me will rush to heap up the timbers of Thy fire. Knowest Thou that? Yes, maybe, Thou knowest it,' he added with thoughtful penetration, never for a moment taking his eyes off the Prisoner."

"I don't quite understand, Ivan. What does it mean?" Aloysha, who had been listening in silence, said with a smile. "Is it simply a wild fantasy, or a mistake on the part of the old man—some impossible *quid pro quo?*"[9]

"Take it as the last," said Ivan, laughing, "if you are so corrupted by modern realism and can't stand anything fantastic. If you like it to be a case of *quid pro quo*, let it be so. It is true," he went on, laughing, "the old man was ninety, and he might well be crazy over his set idea. He might have been struck by the appearance of the Prisoner. It might, in fact, be simply his ravings, the delusion of an old man of ninety, approaching his death, over-excited by the *auto da fé* of a hundred heretics the day before. But does it matter to us after all whether it was a *quid pro quo* or a wild fantasy? All that matters is that the old man should speak out, should speak openly of what he has thought in silence for ninety years."

"And the Prisoner too is silent? Does He look at him and not say a word?"

"That's inevitable in any case," Ivan laughed again. "The old man has told Him He hasn't the right to add anything to what He has said of old. One may say it is the most fundamental feature of Roman Catholicism, in my opinion, at least. 'All has been given by Thee to the Pope,' they say, 'and all, therefore, is still at the Pope's hands, and there is no need for Thee to come now at all. Thou must not meddle for the time, at least.' That's how they speak and write too—the Jesuits at any rate. I have read it myself in the works of their theologians. 'Hast Thou the right to reveal to us one of the mysteries of that world from which Thou hast come?' my old man asks Him, and answers the question for Him. 'No, Thou hast not; Thou mayest not add to what has been said of old, and mayest not take from men the freedom which Thou didst exalt when Thou wast on earth. Whatsoever Thou revealest anew will encroach on men's freedom of faith; for it will be manifest as a miracle, and the freedom of their faith was dearer to Thee than anything in those days fifteen hundred years ago. Didst Thou not often say then, "I will make you free?" But now Thou hast seen these "free" men,' the old man adds suddenly, with a pensive smile. 'Yes, we've paid dearly for it,' he goes on, looking sternly at Him, 'but at last we have completed that work in Thy name. For fifteen centuries we have been wrestling with Thy freedom, but now it is ended and over for good. Dost Thou not believe that it's over for good? Thou lookest meekly at me and deignest not even to be wroth with me. But let me tell Thee that now, today, people are more persuaded than ever that they have perfect freedom, yet they have brought their freedom to us and laid it humbly at our feet. But that has been our doing. Was this what Thou didst? Was this Thy freedom?' "

"I don't understand again," Aloysha broke in. "Is he ironical, is he jesting?"

"Not a bit of it! He claims it as a merit for himself and his Church that at last they have vanquished freedom and have done so to make men happy. 'For now' (he is

8. From Pushkin's play *The Stone Guest* (Don Juan).
9. "One for the other," a mix-up, mistaken identity.

speaking of the Inquisition, of course) 'for the first time it has become possible to think of the happiness of men. Man was created a rebel; and how can rebels be happy? Thou wast warned,' he says to Him. 'Thou has had no lack of admonitions and warnings, but Thou didst not listen to those warnings; Thou didst reject the only way by which men might be made happy. But, fortunately, departing Thou didst hand on the work to us. Thou hast promised, Thou hast established by Thy word, Thou hast given to us the right to bind and unbind, and now, of course, Thou canst not think of taking it away. Why, then, hast Thou come to hinder us?' "

"And what's the meaning of 'no lack of admonitions and warnings'?" asked Aloysha.

"Why, that's the chief part of what the old man must say.

" 'The wise and dread spirit, the spirit of self-destruction and nonexistence,' the old man goes on, 'the great spirit talked with Thee in the wilderness, and we are told in the books that he "tempted" Thee. Is that so? And could anything truer be said than what he revealed to Thee in three questions and what Thou didst reject, and what in the books is called "the temptation?" And yet if there has ever been on earth a real stupendous miracle, it took place on that day, on the day of the three temptations. The statement of those three questions was itself the miracle. If it were possible to imagine simply for the sake of argument that those three questions of the dread spirit had perished utterly from the books, and that we had to restore them and to invent them anew, and to do so had gathered together all the wise men of the earth—rulers, chief priests, learned men, philosophers, poets—and had set them the task to invent three questions, such as would not only fit the occasion, but express in three words, three human phrases, the whole future history of the world and of humanity—dost Thou believe that all the wisdom of the world united could have invented anything in depth and force equal to the three questions which were actually put to Thee then by the wise and mighty spirit in the wilderness? From these questions alone, from the miracle of their statement, we can see that we have here to do not with the fleeting human intelligence, but with the absolute and eternal. For in those three questions the whole subsequent history of mankind is, as it were, brought together into one whole, and foretold, and in them are united all the unsolved historical contradictions of human nature. At the time it could not be so clear, since the future was unknown; but now that fifteen hundred years have passed, we see that everything in those three questions was so justly grasped and foretold, and has been truly fulfilled, that nothing can be added to them or taken from them.

" 'Judge Thyself who was right—Thou or he who questioned Thee then? Remember the first question; its meaning, though not the exact words, was this: "Thou wouldst go into the world, and art going with empty hands, with promise of freedom which men in their simplicity and their natural unruliness cannot even understand, which they fear and dread—for nothing has ever been more insupportable for a man and a human society than freedom. But seest Thou these stones in this parched and barren wilderness? Turn them into bread, and mankind will run after Thee like a flock, grateful and obedient, though forever trembling, lest Thou withdraw Thy hand and deny them Thy bread." But Thou wouldst not deprive man of freedom and didst reject the offer, thinking, what is that freedom worth, if obedience is bought with bread? Thou didst reply that man lives not by bread alone. But dost Thou know that for the sake of that earthly bread the spirit of the earth will rise up against Thee and will strive with Thee and overcome Thee, and all will follow him, crying, "Who can compare with this beast? He has given us fire from heaven!" Dost Thou know that the ages will pass, and humanity will proclaim by the lips of their sages that there is no crime, and therefore no sin; there is only hunger? "Feed men, and then ask of them virtue!" that's what they'll write on the banner, which they will raise against Thee, and with which they will destroy Thy temple. Where Thy temple stood will rise a new building; the terrible tower of Babel will be built again, and though, like the one of old, it will not be finished, yet Thou mightest have prevented that new tower and have cut short the sufferings of men for a thousand years; for they will come back to us after a thousand years of agony with their tower. They will seek us again, hidden underground in the catacombs, for we shall again be persecuted and tortured. They will find us and cry to us, "Feed us, for those who have promised us fire from heaven haven't given it!" And then we shall finish building their tower, for he finished the building who feeds them. And we alone shall feed them in Thy name, declaring falsely that it is in Thy name. Oh, never, never can they feed themselves without us! No science will give them bread so long as they remain free. In the end they will lay their freedom at our feet and say to us, "Make us your slaves, but feed us." They will understand themselves at last, that freedom and bread enough for all are inconceivable together, for never, never will they be able to share between them! They will be convinced, too, that they can never be free, for they are weak, vicious, worthless and rebellious. Thou didst promise the bread of Heaven, but, I repeat again, can it compare with earthly bread in the eyes of the weak, ever sinful and ignoble race of man? And if for the sake of the bread of Heaven thousands and tens of thousands shall follow Thee, what is to become of the millions and tens of thousands of millions of creatures who will not have the strength to forego the earthly bread for the sake of the heavenly? Or dost Thou care only for the tens of thousands of the great and the strong, while the millions, numerous as the sands of the sea, who are weak but love Thee, must exist only for the sake of the great and strong? No, we care for the weak too. They are sinful and rebellious, but in the end they too will become obedient. They will marvel at us and look on us as gods, because we are ready to endure the freedom which they have found so dreadful and to rule over them—so awful it will seem to be free. But we shall tell them that we are Thy servants and rule them in Thy name. We shall deceive them again, for we will not let Thee come to us again. The deception will be our suffering, for we shall be forced to lie. This is the significance of the first question in the wilderness, and this is what Thou hast rejected for the sake of that freedom which Thou hast exalted above everything. Yet in this question lies hid the great secret of this world. Choosing "bread," Thou wouldst have satisfied the universal and everlasting craving of humanity individually and together as one—to find someone to worship. So long as man remains free he strives for nothing so incessantly and so painfully as to find someone to worship. But man seeks to worship what is established beyond dispute, so that all men would agree at once to worship it. For these pitiful creatures are concerned not only to find what one or the other can worship, but to find something that all would believe in and worship; what is essential is that all may be *together* in it. This craving for *community* of worship is the chief misery of every man individually and of all humanity from the beginning of time. For the sake of common worship they've slain each other with the sword. They have set up gods and challenged one another, "Put away your gods and come and worship ours, or we will kill you and your gods!" And so it will be to the end of the world, when even gods disappear from the earth; they will fall down before idols just the same. Thou didst know, Thou couldst not but have known, this fundamental secret of human nature, but Thou didst reject the one infallible banner which was offered Thee to make all men bow down to Thee alone—the banner of earthly bread; and Thou hast rejected it for the sake of freedom and the bread of Heaven. Behold what Thou didst further. And all again in the name of freedom! I tell Thee that man is tormented by no greater anxiety than to find someone quickly to whom he can hand over that gift of freedom with which the ill-fated creature is born. But only one who can appease their conscience can take over their freedom. In bread there was offered Thee an invincible banner; give bread, and man will worship Thee, for nothing is more certain than bread. But if someone else gains possession of his conscience—oh! then he will cast away Thy bread and follow after him who has ensnared his conscience. In that Thou wast right. For the secret of man's being is not only to live but to have something to live for. Without a stable conception of the object of life, man would not consent to go on living, and would rather destroy himself than remain on earth, though he had bread in abundance. That is true. But what happened? Instead of taking men's freedom from them, Thou didst make it greater than ever! Didst Thou forget that man prefers peace, and even death, to freedom of choice in the knowledge of good and evil? Nothing is more seductive for man than his freedom of conscience, but nothing is a greater cause of suffering. And behold, instead of giving a firm foundation for setting the conscience of man at rest forever, Thou didst choose all that is exceptional, vague and enigmatic; Thou didst choose what was utterly beyond the strength of men, acting as though Thou didst not love them at all—Thou who didst come to give Thy life for them! Instead of taking possession of men's freedom, Thou didst increase it, and burdened the spiritual kingdom of mankind with its sufferings forever. Thou didst desire man's free love, that he should follow Thee freely, enticed and taken captive by Thee. In place of the rigid ancient law, man must hereafter with free heart decide for himself what is good and what is evil, having only Thy image before him as his guide. But didst Thou not know he would at last reject even Thy image and Thy truth, if he is weighed down with the fearful burden of free choice? They will cry aloud at last that the truth is not in Thee, for they could not have been left in greater confusion and suffering than Thou hast caused, laying upon them so many cares and unanswerable problems.

" 'So that, in truth, Thou didst Thyself lay the foundation for the destruction of Thy kingdom, and no one is more to blame for it. Yet what was offered Thee? There are three powers, three powers alone, able to conquer and to hold captive forever the conscience of these impotent rebels for their happiness—those forces are miracle, mystery and authority. Thou hast rejected all three and hast set the example for doing so. When the wise and dread spirit set Thee on the pinnacle of the temple and said to Thee, "If Thou wouldst know whether Thou art the Son of God then cast Thyself down, for it is written: the angels shall hold him up lest he fall and bruise himself, and Thou shalt know then whether Thou art the Son of God and shalt prove then how great is Thy faith in Thy Father." But Thou didst refuse and wouldst not cast Thyself down. Oh! of course, Thou didst proudly and well, like God; but the weak, rebellious race of men, are they gods? Oh, Thou didst know then that in taking one step, in making one movement to cast Thyself down, Thou wouldst be tempting God and have lost all Thy faith in Him, and wouldst have been dashed to pieces against that earth which Thou didst come to save. And the wise spirit that tempted Thee would have rejoiced. But I ask again, are there many like Thee? And couldst Thou believe for one moment that men, too, could face such a temptation? Is the nature of men such, that they can reject miracle, and at the great moments of their life, the moments of their deep, most agonizing spiritual difficulties, cling only to the free verdict of the heart? Oh, Thou didst know that Thy deed would be recorded in books, would be handed down to remote times and the utmost ends of the earth, and Thou didst hope that man, following Thee, would cling to God and not ask for a miracle. But Thou didst not know that when man rejects miracle he rejects God too; for man seeks not so much God as the miraculous. And as man cannot bear to be without the miraculous, he will create new miracles of his own for himself, and worship deeds of sorcery and witchcraft, though he might be a hundred times over a rebel, heretic and infidel. Thou didst not come down from the Cross when they shouted to Thee, mocking and reviling Thee, "Come down from the cross and we will believe that Thou art He." Thou didst not come down, for again Thou wouldst not enslave man by a miracle, and didst crave faith given freely, not based on miracle. Thou didst crave for free love and not the base raptures of the slave before the might that has overawed him forever. But Thou didst think too highly of men therein, for they are slaves, of course, though rebellious by nature. Look around and judge; fifteen centuries have passed, look upon them. Whom hast Thou raised up to Thyself? I swear, man is weaker and baser by nature than Thou hast believed him! Can he, can he do what Thou didst? By showing him so much respect, Thou didst, as it were, cease to feel for him, for Thou didst ask far too much from him—Thou who hast loved him more than Thyself! Respecting him less, Thou wouldst have asked less of him. That would have been more like love, for his burden would have been lighter. He is weak and vile. What though he is everywhere now rebelling against our power, and proud of his rebellion? It is the pride of a child and a schoolboy. They are little children rioting and barring out the teacher at school. But their childish delight will end; it will cost them dear. They will cast down temples and drench the earth with blood. But they will see at last, the foolish children, that, though they are rebels, they are impotent rebels, unable to keep up their own rebellion. Bathed in their foolish tears, they will recognize at last that He who created them rebels must have meant to mock at them. They will say this in despair, and their utterance will be a blasphemy which will make them more unhappy still, for man's nature cannot bear blasphemy, and in the end always avenges it on itself. And so unrest, confusion and unhappiness—that is the present lot of man after Thou didst bear so much for their freedom! Thy great prophet tells in vision and in image, that he saw all those who took part in the first resurrection and that there were of each tribe twelve thousand.[10] But if there were so many of them, they must have been not men but gods. They had borne Thy cross, they had endured scores of years in the barren, hungry wilderness, living upon locusts and roots—and Thou mayest indeed point with pride at those children of freedom, of free love, of free and splendid sacrifice for Thy name. But remember that they were only some thousands, and gods at that; and what of the rest? And how are the other weak ones to blame, because they could not endure what the strong have endured? How is the weak soul to blame that it is unable to receive such terrible gifts? Canst Thou really have come only to the elect and for the elect? But if so, it is a mystery and we cannot understand it. And if it is a mystery, we too have a right to preach a mystery, and to teach them that it's not the free judgment of their hearts, not love that matters, but a mystery which they must follow blindly, even against their conscience. So we have done. We have corrected Thy work and have founded it upon *miracle, mystery,* and *authority*. And men have rejoiced that they were again led like sheep, and that the terrible gift that had brought them such suffering was, at last, lifted from their hearts. Were we right teaching them this? Speak! Did we not love mankind, so meekly acknowledging their feebleness, lovingly lightening their burden, and permitting their weak nature even sin with our sanction? Why hast Thou come now to hinder us? And why dost Thou look silently and searchingly at me with Thy mild eyes? Be angry. I don't want Thy love, for I love Thee not. And what use is it to hide anything from Thee? Don't I know to whom I am speaking? All that I can say is known to Thee already. I can see it in Thine eyes. And is it for me to conceal from Thee our mystery? Perhaps it is Thy will to hear it from my lips. Listen, then. We are not working with Thee, but with *him*—that is our mystery. It's long—eight centuries—since we have been on *his* side and not on Thine. Just eight centuries ago we took from him what Thou didst reject with scorn, that last gift he offered Thee, showing Thee all the kingdoms of the earth. We took from him Rome and the sword of Caesar, and proclaimed ourselves sole rulers of the earth, though hitherto we have not been able to complete our work.[11] But whose fault is that? Oh, the work is only beginning, but it has begun. It has long to await completion and the earth has yet much to suffer but we shall triumph and shall be Caesars, and then we shall plan the universal happiness of man. But Thou mightest have taken even then the sword of Caesar. Why didst Thou reject that last gift? Hadst Thou accepted that last counsel of the mighty spirit, Thou wouldst have accomplished all that man seeks on earth—that is, someone to worship, someone to keep his conscience, and some means of uniting all in one unanimous and harmonious anthill, for the craving of universal unity is the third and last anguish of men. Mankind as a whole has always strived to organize a universal state. There have been many great nations with great histories, but the more highly they were developed the more unhappy they were, for they felt more acutely than other people the craving for worldwide union. The great conquerors, Tamerlane[12] and Genghis Khan,[13] whirled like hurricanes over the face of the earth striving to subdue its people, and they too were but the unconscious expression of the same craving for universal unity. Hadst Thou taken the world and Caesar's purple, Thou wouldst have founded the universal and have given universal peace. For who can rule men if not he who holds their conscience and their bread in his hands? We have taken the sword of Caesar, and in taking it, of course, have rejected Thee and followed *him.* Oh, ages are yet to come of the confusion of free thought, of their science and cannibalism. For having begun to build their tower of Babel without us, they will end, of course, with cannibalism. But then the beast will crawl to us and lick our feet and spatter them with tears of blood. And we shall sit upon the beast and raise the cup, and on it will be written, "Mystery." But then, and only then, the reign of peace and happiness will come for men. Thou art proud of Thine elect, but Thou hast only the elect, those mighty ones who could become elect, have grown weary waiting for Thee, and have transferred and will transfer the powers of their spirit and the warmth of their heart to the other camp, and end by raising their *free* banner against Thee. Thou didst Thyself lift up that banner. But with us all will be happy and will no more rebel nor destroy one another as under Thy freedom. Oh, we shall persuade them that they will only become free when they renounce their freedom to us and submit to us. And shall we be right or shall we be lying? They will be convinced

10. Revelation 8.

11. Pepin the Short, king of the Franks, granted Ravenna to Pope Stephen III in 756. This was the origin of the pope's temporal power (the sword of Caesar), which was strengthened when a later pope crowned Charlemagne Emperor on Christmas Day, AD 800 .

12. Tamerlane (1336–1406), Tartar conqueror.

13. Genghis Khan (1155–1227), Mongolian conqueror.

that we are right, for they will remember the horrors of slavery and confusion to which Thy freedom brought them. Freedom, free thought and science, will lead them into such straits and will bring them face to face with such marvels and insoluble mysteries, that some of them, the fierce and rebellious, will destroy themselves, others, rebellious but weak, will destroy one another, while the rest, weak and unhappy, will crawl fawning to our feet, and whine to us: "Yes, you were right, you alone possess His mystery, and we come back to you, save us from ourselves!" Receiving bread from us, they will of course see clearly that we take the bread made by their hands from them, to give it to them, without any miracle. They will see that we do not change the stones to bread, but in truth they will be more thankful for taking it from our hands than for the bread itself! For they will remember only too well that in the old days, without our help, even the bread they made turned to stones in their hands, while since they have come back to us, the very stones have turned to bread in their hands. Too, too well they know the value of complete submission! And until men know that, they will be unhappy. Who is most to blame for their not knowing it, speak? Who scattered the flock and sent it astray on unknown paths? But the flock will come together again and will submit once more, and then it will be once for all. Then we shall give them the quiet humble happiness of weak creatures such as they are by nature. Oh, we shall persuade them at last not to be proud, for Thou didst lift them up and thereby taught them to be proud. We shall show them that they are weak, that they are only pitiful children, but that childlike happiness is the sweetest of all. They will become timid and will look to us and huddle close to us in fear, as chicks to the hen. They will marvel at us and will be awestricken before us, and will be proud at our being so powerful and clever, that we have been able to subdue such a turbulent flock of thousands of millions. They will tremble impotently before our wrath, their minds will grow fearful, they will be quick to shed tears like women and children, but they will be just as ready at a sign from us to pass to laughter and rejoicing, to happy mirth and childlike song. Yes, we shall set them to work, but in their leisure hours we shall make their life like a child's game, with children's songs and innocent dance. Oh, we shall allow them even sin, they are weak and helpless, and they will love us like children because we allow them to sin. We shall tell them that every sin will be expiated, if it is done with our permission, that we allow them to sin because we love them, and the punishment for these sins we take upon ourselves. And we shall take it upon ourselves, and they will adore us as their saviors who have taken on themselves their sins before God. And they will have no secrets from us. We shall allow or forbid them to live with their wives and mistresses, to have or not have children—according to whether they have been obedient or disobedient—and they will submit to us gladly and cheerfully. The most painful secrets of their conscience, all, all they will bring to us, and we shall have an answer for all. And they will be glad to believe our answer, for it will save them from the great anxiety and terrible agony they endure at present in making a free decision for themselves. And all will be happy, all the millions of creatures except the hundred thousand who rule over them. For only we, we who guard the mystery, shall be unhappy. There will be thousands of millions of happy babes, and a hundred thousand sufferers who have taken upon themselves the curse of the knowledge of good and evil. Peacefully they will die, peacefully they will expire in Thy name, and beyond the grave they will find nothing but death. But we shall keep the secret, for their happiness we shall entice them with the reward of heaven and eternity. Though if there were anything in the other world, it certainly would not be for such as they. It is prophesied that Thou will come again in victory, Thou wilt come with Thy chosen, the proud and strong, but we will say that they have only saved themselves, but we have saved all. We are told that the harlot who sits upon the beast, and holds in her hands the mystery, shall be put to shame, that the weak will rise up again, and will rend her royal purple and will strip naked her "loathsome" body.[14] But then I will stand up and point out to Thee the thousand millions of happy children who have known no sin. And we who have taken their sins upon us for their happiness will stand up before Thee and say: "Judge us if Thou canst and darest." Know that I fear Thee not. Know that I too have been in the wilderness, I too have lived on roots and locusts, I too prized the freedom with which Thou hast blessed men, and I too was striving to stand among the elect, among the strong and powerful, thirsting "to make up the number." But I awakened and would not serve madness. I turned back and joined the ranks of those *who have corrected Thy work.* I left the proud and went back to the humble, for the happiness of the humble. What I say to Thee will come to pass, and our dominion will be built up. I repeat, tomorrow Thou shalt see that obedient flock who at a sign from me will hasten to heap up the hot cinders about the pile on which I shall burn Thee for coming to hinder us. For, if anyone ever deserved our fires, it is Thou. Tomorrow, I shall burn Thee. *Dixi.*' "[15]. . .

14. Revelation 17.
15. "I have spoken (finished)."

STUDY QUESTIONS

1. Defense lawyer Clarence Darrow claimed that he prepared his defense by studying the prosecutor's case. Consider the Grand Inquisitor as the prosecutor (as indeed he was) and list all the characteristics of people he considered good members of his church. Now list the human values that Dostoevsky prized. These will include those qualities specifically condemned plus the opposite of the human "virtues" praised by the cardinal.
2. The cardinal says that the church has followed the Devil for eight centuries but he names him not. Why not?

3. What does the church value that is not derived from the teachings of Christ? You should consider the whole question of an institution that burns people at the stake because the victims supposedly disagree with its teachings. Did these so-called heretics receive a fair trial in a regular court of law before an impartial judge?
4. How does the church try to maintain control over the private lives of its members?
5. What is the problem with free will? Why do so many people consider freedom of choice a kind of curse that must be countered by seeking an outside authority that will tell them what is right or wrong, good or bad? What does the church substitute for the terror of choosing between right and wrong?

ROMANTICISM AND REALISM IN AMERICA

For the United States the nineteenth century was the great age of expansion, from thirteen states to forty-five, plus three territories, Alaska, Hawaii, the Philippines, Puerto Rico, Guam, and American Samoa (see map 23.6, p. 273). Part of this growth was at the expense of the many American Indian tribes whose lands were dotted all across the country. The Indian Wars had begun in 1540 when Coronado's conquistadores first clashed with the Zuni in what is now New Mexico. Three and a half centuries later the wars ended with the 7th U.S. Cavalry massacre of Big Foot's band of Oglala Sioux at Wounded Knee, South Dakota, in 1890.

I am tired of fighting.
Our chiefs are killed.
Looking Glass is dead.
Toohulhulsote is dead.
The old men are all dead.
It is the young men who say no and yes.
He who led the young men is dead.
It is cold and we have no blankets.
The little children are freezing to death.
My people, some of them,
Have run away to the hills
And have no blankets, no food.
No one knows where they are—
Perhaps they are freezing to death.
I want to have time to look for my children
And see how many of them I can find.
Maybe I shall find them among the dead.
Hear me, my chiefs, I am tired.
My heart is sad and sick.
From where the sun now stands
I will fight no more forever.

Surrender speech of Nez Percé[16] Chief Joseph (ca. 1840–1904)

America's vast physical growth and economic development were not paralleled, however, by significant developments in the fine and literary arts—not for some time. Early in the century writers were still intimidated by British letters though seeking ways to declare their literary independence. The emergence of Romanticism in England struck a responsive spark in America, and writers such as Washington Irving (1783–1859), William Cullen Bryant (1794–1878), and James Fenimore Cooper (1789–1851) produced Romantic works in a new American style. Because of limited space we will begin with the next generation of writers and trace the development of American literature from Romanticism to Realism.

Edgar Allan Poe, 1809–49

One of the few literary figures with an international reputation that the United States has produced, Poe was a brilliant literary critic, poet, and writer of highly imaginative short stories. Among the first to condemn crass American materialism, Poe devoted himself wholly to his art, becoming the first American to live his life entirely as an artist. Poe defined poetry as "the creation of beauty" and contended that all poetry should appeal equally to reason and emotion. Poe felt that all poetry should be composed in terms of beauty, restraint, and unity of effect and, indeed, his poetry is the embodiment of his theory of art. Inspired by the loss of a beautiful woman, "Annabel Lee" is a lyric masterpiece in a lilting musical style.

LITERARY SELECTION 72

Annabel Lee

Edgar Allan Poe

It was many and many a year ago,
  In a kingdom by the sea,
That a maiden there lived whom you may know
  By the name of Annabel Lee;
And this maiden she lived with no other thought
  Than to love and be loved by me.

I was a child and she was a child,
  In this kingdom by the sea,
But we loved with a love that was more than love,
  I and my Annabel Lee;
With a love that the wingèd seraphs of heaven
  Coveted, her and me.

16. Chief Joseph was one of the Nez Percé chiefs responsible for the skillful eluding of the enemy during a 1,000-mile (1610-km) flight from Oregon to Montana, where the tribe finally surrendered to the U.S. Army.

And this was the reason that, long ago,
In this kingdom by the sea,
A wind blew out of a cloud, chilling
My beautiful Annabel Lee;

So that her highborn kinsmen came
And bore her away from me,
To shut her up in a sepulchre
In this kingdom by the sea.

The angels, not half so happy in heaven,
Went envying her and me;
Yes! that was the reason (as all men know,
In this kingdom by the sea)
That the wind came out of the cloud by night,
Chilling and killing my Annabel Lee.

But our love it was stronger by far than the love
Of those who were older than we,
Of many far wiser than we;
And neither the angels in heaven above,
Nor the demons down under the sea,
Can ever dissever my soul from the soul
Of the beautiful Annabel Lee:

For the moon never beams, without bringing me dreams
Of the beautiful Annabel Lee;
And the stars never rise, but I feel the bright eyes
Of the beautiful Annabel Lee;

And so, all the night-tide, I lie down by the side
Of my darling—my darling—my life and my bride,
In her sepulchre there by the sea,
In her tomb by the sounding sea.

Ralph Waldo Emerson, 1803–82

Poe was a conscious representative of a Southern tradition in literature, that of a Virginia Cavalier. Just as consciously, Emerson and his colleagues were New England Romantics who reconciled romantic abstractions with the hardheaded realities of Yankee individualism. The creed of Emerson, Thoreau, Margaret Fuller, and others was transcendentalism, a belief that human beings and the universe were in perfect harmony and moving in a Hegelian manner toward perfection. High-minded and highly individualistic, transcendentalists stressed the individual's conscience as the sole judge in spiritual matters, total self-reliance in all matters, and the necessity for social reforms.

Beauty and truth were critical issues for the transcendentalists. For Poe poetry was beauty. Emerson viewed it as a necessary function for the individual who was seeking truth. Emerson wrote his essays but, in a sense, he thought that his poems wrote him. Many of Emerson's poems are the result of the poet's attempts to perceive the deeper meaning of nature. One such was "The Rhodora," which was emblematic of the beauty bestowed by spirit on the world and implanted in human beings.

LITERARY SELECTION 73

The Rhodora

On Being Asked, Whence is the Flower?

Ralph Waldo Emerson

In May, when sea-winds pierce our solitudes,
I found the fresh Rhodora in the woods,
Spreading its leafless blooms in a damp nook,
To please the desert and the sluggish brook.
The purple petals, fallen in the pool,
Made the black water with their beauty gay;
Here might the red-bird come his plumes to cool,
And court the flower that cheapens his array.
Rhodora! if the sages ask thee why
This charm is wasted on the earth and sky,
Tell them, dear, that if eyes were made for seeing,
Then Beauty is its own excuse for being:
Why thou wert there, O rival of the rose!
I never thought to ask, I never knew:
But, in my simple ignorance, suppose
The self-same Power that brought me there brought you.

Henry David Thoreau, 1817–62

Emerson and Thoreau were close friends all their lives, but no two people were less alike personally or more alike in their transcendentalist conviction that individuals should lead active and responsible lives. Thoreau felt that most people lived lives of "quiet desperation" and made his point at Walden Pond by coexisting for two years in harmony with nature. His account of his experiences in *Walden* (1854) was his best work, but his thoughtful essay on "Civil Disobedience" was largely unread in his own day. Inspired probably by a night in jail because of his refusal, on principle, to pay a poll tax, "Civil Disobedience" was a major influence on Mahatma Gandhi and, later, on Martin Luther King, Jr.

LITERARY SELECTION 74

Civil Disobedience

Henry David Thoreau

I heartily accept the motto, "That government is best which governs least;" and I should like to see it acted up to more rapidly and systematically. Carried out, it finally amounts to this, which also I believe,—"That government is best which governs not at all;" and when men are prepared for it, that will be the kind of government which they will have. Government is at best but an expedient; but most governments are usually, and all governments are sometimes, inexpedient. The objections which have been brought against a standing army, and they are many and weighty, and deserve to prevail, may also at last be brought against a standing government. The standing army is only an arm of the standing government. The government itself, which is only the mode which the people have chosen to execute their will, is equally liable to be abused and perverted before the people can act through it. Witness the present Mexican war, the work of comparatively a few individuals using the standing government as their tool; for, in the outset, the people would not have consented to this measure.

This American government,—what is it but a tradition, though a recent one, endeavoring to transmit itself unimpaired to posterity, but each instant losing some of its integrity? It has not the vitality and force of a single living man; for a single man can bend it to his will. It is a sort of wooden gun to the people themselves. But it is not the less necessary for this, for the people must have some complicated machinery or other, and hear its din, to satisfy that idea of government which they have. Governments show thus how successfully men can be imposed on, even impose on themselves, for their own advantage. It is excellent, we must all allow. Yet this government never of itself furthered any enterprise, but by the alacrity with which it got out of its way. *It* does not keep the country free. *It* does not settle the West. *It* does not educate. The character inherent in the American people has done all that has been accomplished; and it would have done somewhat more, if the government had not sometimes got in its way. For government is an expedient by which men would fain succeed in letting one another alone; and, as has been said, when it is most expedient, the governed are most let alone by it. Trade and commerce, if they were not made of india-rubber, would never manage to bounce over the obstacles which legislators are continually putting in their way; and, if one were to judge these men wholly by the effects of their actions and not partly by their intentions, they would deserve to be classed and punished with those mischievous persons who put obstructions on the railroads

But, to speak practically and as a citizen, unlike those . who call themselves no-government men, I ask for, not at once no government, but *at once* a better government. Let every man make known what kind of government would command his respect, and that will be one step toward obtaining it.

After all, the practical reason why, when the power is once in the hands of the people, a majority are permitted, and for a long period continue, to rule is not because they are most likely to be in the right, nor because this seems fairest to the minority, but because they are physically the strongest. But a government in which the majority rule in all cases cannot be based on justice, even as far as men understand it. Can there not be a government in which majorities do not virtually decide right and wrong, but conscience?—in which majorities decide only those questions to which the rule of expediency is applicable? Must the citizen ever for a moment, or in the least degree, resign his conscience to the legislator? Why has every man a conscience, then? I think that we should be men first, and subjects afterward. It is not desirable to cultivate a respect for the law, so much as for the right. The only obligation which I have a right to assume is to do at any time what I think right. It is truly enough said that a corporation has no conscience; but a corporation of conscientious men is a corporation *with* a conscience. Law never made men a whit more just; and, by means of their respect for it, even the well-disposed are daily made the agents of injustice. A common and natural result of an undue respect for law is, that you may see a file of soldiers, colonel, captain, corporal, privates, powder-monkeys, and all, marching in admirable order over hill and dale to the wars, against their wills, ay, against their common sense and consciences, which makes it very steep marching indeed, and produces a palpitation of the heart. They have no doubt that it is a damnable business in which they are concerned; they are all peaceably inclined. Now, what are they? Men at all? or small movable forts and magazines, at the service of some unscrupulous man in power? Visit the Navy-Yard, and behold a marine, such a man as an American government can make, or such as it can make a man with its black arts,—a mere shadow and reminiscence of humanity, a man laid out alive and standing, and already, as one may say, buried under arms with funeral accompaniments, though it may be,—

"Not a drum was heard, not a funeral note,
As his corse to the rampart we hurried;
Not a soldier discharged his farewell shot
O'er the grave where our hero we buried."

The mass of men serve the state thus, not as men mainly, but as machines, with their bodies. They are the standing army, and the militia, jailers, constables, *posse comitatus*, etc. In most cases there is no free exercise whatever of the judgment or of the moral sense; but they put themselves on a level with wood and earth and stones; and wooden men can perhaps be manufactured that will serve the purpose as well. Such command no more respect than men of straw or a lump of dirt. They have the same sort of worth only as horses and dogs. Yet such as these even are commonly esteemed good citizens. Others—as most legislators, politicians, lawyers, ministers, and office-holders—serve the state chiefly with their heads; and, as they rarely make any moral distinctions, they are as likely to serve the devil, without *intending* it, as God. A very few—as heroes, patriots, martyrs, reformers in the great sense, and *men*—serve the state with their consciences also, and so necessarily resist it for the most part; and they are commonly treated as enemies by it.

How does it become a man to behave toward this American government to-day? I answer, that he cannot without disgrace be associated with it. I cannot for an instant recognize that political organization as *my* government which is the *slave's* government also.

All men recognize the right of revolution; that is, the right to refuse allegiance to, and to resist, the government, when its tyranny or its inefficiency are great and unendurable. But almost all say that such is not the case now. But such was the case, they think, in the Revolution of '75. If one were to tell me that this was a bad government because it taxed certain foreign commodities brought to its ports, it is most probable that I should not make an ado about it, for I can do without them. All machines have their friction; and possibly this does enough good to counterbalance the evil. At any rate, it is a great evil to make a stir about it. But when the friction comes to have its machine, and oppression and robbery are organized, I say, let us not have such a machine any longer. In other words, when a sixth of the population of a nation which has undertaken to be the refuge of liberty are slaves, and a whole country is unjustly overrun and conquered by a foreign army, and subjected to military law, I think that it is not too soon for honest men to rebel and revolutionize. What makes this duty the more urgent is the fact that the country so overrun is not our own, but ours is the invading army.

Paley, a common authority with many on moral questions, in his chapter on the "Duty of Submission to Civil Government," resolves all civil obligation into expediency; and he proceeds to say that "so long as the interest of the whole society requires it, that is, so long as the established government cannot be resisted or changed without public inconveniency, it is the will of God . . . that the established government be obeyed,—and no longer. This principle being admitted, the justice of every particular case of resistance is reduced to a computation of the quantity of the danger and grievance on the one side, and of the probability and expense of redressing it on the other." Of this, he says, every man shall judge for himself. But Paley appears never to have contemplated those cases to which the rule of expediency does not apply, in which a people, as well as an individual, must do justice, cost what it may. If I have unjustly wrested a plank from a drowning man, I must restore it to him though I drown myself. This, according to Paley, would be inconvenient. But he that would save his life, in such a case, shall lose it. This people must cease to hold slaves, and to make war on Mexico, though it cost them their existence as a people.

In their practice, nations agree with Paley; but does any one think that Massachusetts does exactly what is right at the present crisis?

"A drab of state, a cloth-o'-silver slut,
To have her train borne up, and her soul trail in the dirt."

Practically speaking, the opponents to reform in Massachusetts are not a hundred thousand politicians at the South, but a hundred thousand merchants and farmers here, who are more interested in commerce and agriculture than they are in humanity, and are not prepared to do justice to the slave and to Mexico, *cost what it may*. I quarrel not with far-off foes, but with those who, near at home, coöperate with, and do the bidding of, those far away, and without whom the latter would be harmless. We are accustomed to say, that the mass of men are unprepared; but improvement is slow, because the few are not materially wiser or better than the many. It is not so important that many should be as good as you, as that there be some absolute goodness somewhere; for that will leaven the whole lump. There are thousands who are *in opinion* opposed to slavery and to the war, who yet in effect do nothing to put an end to them; who, esteeming themselves children of Washington and Franklin, sit down with their hands in their pockets, and say that they know not what to do, and do nothing; who even postpone the question of freedom to the question of free trade, and quietly read the prices-current along with the latest advices from Mexico, after dinner, and, it may be, fall asleep over them both. What is the price-current of an honest man and patriot to-day? They hesitate, and they regret, and sometimes they petition; but they do nothing in earnest and with effect. They will wait, well disposed, for others to remedy the evil, that they may no longer have it to regret. At most, they give only a cheap vote, and a feeble countenance and God-speed, to the right, as it goes by them. There are nine hundred and ninety-nine patrons of virtue to one virtuous man. But it is easier to deal with the real possessor of a thing than with the temporary guardian of it.

All voting is a sort of gaming, like checkers or backgammon, with a slight moral tinge to it, a playing with right and wrong, with moral questions; and betting naturally accompanies it. The character of the voters is not staked. I cast my vote, perchance, as I think right; but I am not vitally concerned that that right should prevail. I am willing to leave it to the majority. Its obligation, therefore, never exceeds that of expediency. Even voting *for the right* is *doing* nothing for it. It is only expressing to men feebly your desire that it should prevail. A wise man will not leave the right to the mercy of chance, nor wish it to prevail through the power of the majority. There is but little virtue in the action of masses of men. When the majority shall at length vote for the abolition of slavery, it will be because they are indifferent to slavery, or because there is but little slavery left to be abolished by their vote. *They* will then be the only slaves. Only *his* vote can hasten the abolition of slavery who asserts his own freedom by his vote.

It is not a man's duty, as a matter of course, to devote himself to the eradication of any, even the most enormous, wrong; he may still properly have other concerns to engage him; but it is his duty, at least, to wash his hands of it, and, if he gives it no thought longer, not to give it practically his support. If I devote myself to other pursuits and contemplations, I must first see, at least, that I do not pursue them sitting upon another man's shoulders. I must get off him first, that he may pursue his contemplations too. See what gross inconsistency is tolerated. I have heard some of my townsmen say, "I should like to have them order me out to help put down an insurrection of the slaves, or to march to Mexico;—see if I would go;" and yet these very men have each, directly by their allegiance, and so indirectly, at least, by their money, furnished a substitute. The soldier is applauded who refuses to serve in an unjust war by those who do not refuse to sustain the unjust government which makes the war; is applauded by those whose own act and authority he disregards and sets at naught; as if the state were penitent to that degree that it hired one to scourge it while it sinned, but not to that degree that it left off sinning for a moment.

Thus, under the name of Order and Civil Government, we are all made at last to pay homage to and support our own meanness. After the first blush of sin comes its indifference; and from immoral it becomes, as it were, *un*moral, and not quite unnecessary to that life which we have made.

Unjust laws exist: shall we be content to obey them, or shall we endeavor to amend them, and obey them until we have succeeded, or shall we transgress them at once? Men generally, under such a government as this, think that they ought to wait until they have persuaded the majority to alter them. They think that, if they should resist, the remedy would be worse than the evil. But it is the fault of the government itself that the remedy *is* worse than the evil. *It* makes it worse. Why is it not more apt to anticipate and provide for reform? Why does it not cherish its wise minority? Why does it cry and resist before it is hurt? Why does it not encourage its citizens to be on the alert to point out its faults, and *do* better than it would have them? Why does it always crucify Christ, and excommunicate Copernicus and Luther, and pronounce Washington and Franklin rebels?

One would think, that a deliberate and practical denial of its authority was the only offence never contemplated by government; else, why has it not assigned its definite, its suitable and proportionate, penalty? If a man who has no property refuses but once to earn nine shillings for the State, he is put in prison for a period unlimited by any law that I know, and determined only by the discretion of those who placed him there; but if he should steal ninety times nine shillings from the State, he is soon permitted to go at large again.

If the injustice is part of the necessary friction of the machine of government, let it go, let it go: perchance it will wear smooth,—certainly the machine will wear out. If the injustice has a spring, or a pulley, or a rope, or a crank, exclusively for itself, then perhaps you may consider whether the remedy will not be worse than the evil; but if it is of such a nature that it requires you to be the agent of injustice to another, then, I say, break the law. Let your life be a counter-friction to stop the machine. What I have to do is to see, at any rate, that I do not lend myself to the wrong which I condemn.

As for adopting the ways which the State has provided for remedying the evil, I know not of such ways. They take too much time, and a man's life will be gone. I have other affairs to attend to. I came into this world, not chiefly to make this a good place to live in, but to live in it, be it good or bad. A man has not everything to do, but something; and because he cannot do *everything*, it is not necessary that he should do *something* wrong. It is not my business to be petitioning the Governor or the Legislature any more than it is theirs to petition me; and if they should not hear my petition, what should I do then? But in this case the State has provided no way: its very Constitution is the evil. This may seem to be harsh and stubborn and unconciliatory; but it is to treat with the utmost kindness and consideration the only spirit that can appreciate or deserves it. So is all change for the better, like birth and death, which convulse the body.

I do not hesitate to say, that those who call themselves Abolitionists should at once effectually withdraw their support, both in person and property, from the government of Massachusetts, and not wait till they constitute a majority of one, before they suffer the right to prevail through them. I think that it is enough if they have God on their side, without waiting for that other one. Moreover, any man more right than his neighbors constitutes a majority of one already.

I meet this American government, or its representative, the State government, directly, and face to face, once a year—no more—in the person of its tax-gatherer; this is the only mode in which a man situated as I am necessarily meets it; and it then says distinctly, Recognize me; and the simplest, most effectual, and, in the present posture of affairs, the indispensablest mode of treating with it on this head, of expressing your little satisfaction with and love for it, is to deny it then. My civil neighbor, the tax-gatherer, is the very man I have to deal with,—for it is, after all, with men and not with parchment that I quarrel,—and he has voluntarily chosen to be an agent of the government. How shall he ever know well what he is and does as an officer of the government, or as a man, until he is obliged to consider whether he shall treat me, his neighbor, for whom he has respect, as a neighbor and well-disposed man, or as a maniac and disturber of the peace, and see if he can get over this obstruction to his neighborliness without a ruder and more impetuous thought or speech corresponding with his action. I know this well, that if one thousand, if one hundred, if ten men whom I could name,—if ten *honest* men only—ay, if *one* HONEST man, in this State of Massachusetts, *ceasing to hold slaves*, were actually to withdraw from this copartnership, and be locked up in the county jail therefor, it would be the abolition of slavery in America. For it matters not how small the beginning may seem to be: what is once well done is done forever. But we love better to talk about it: that we say is our mission. Reform keeps many scores of newspapers in its service, but not one man.

Under a government which imprisons any unjustly, the true place for a just man is also a prison. The property place to-day, the only place which Massachusetts has provided for her freer and less desponding spirits, is in her prisons, to be put out and locked out of the State by her own act, as they have already put themselves out by their principles. It is there that the fugitive slave, and the Mexican prisoner on parole, and the Indian come to plead the wrongs of his race should find them; on that separate, but more free and honorable, ground, where the State places those who are not *with* her, but *against* her,—the only house in a slave State in which a free man can abide with honor. If any think that their influence would be lost there, and their voices no longer afflict the ear of the State, that they would not be as an enemy within its walls, they do not know by how much truth is stronger than error, nor how much more eloquently and effectively he can combat injustice who has experienced a little in his own person. Cast your whole vote, not a strip of paper merely, but your whole influence. A minority is powerless while it conforms to the majority; it is not even a minority then; but it is irresistible when it clogs by its whole weight. If the alternative is to keep all just men in prison, or give up war and slavery, the State will not hesitate which to choose. If a thousand men were not to pay their tax-bills this year, that would not be a violent and bloody measure, as it would be to pay them, and enable the State to commit violence and shed innocent blood. This is, in fact, the definition of a peaceable revolution, if any such is possible. If the tax gatherer, or any other public officer, asks me, as one has done, "But what shall I do?" my answer is "If you really wish to do anything, resign your office." When the subject has refused allegiance, and the officer has resigned his office, then the revolution is accomplished. But even suppose blood should flow. Is there not a sort of blood shed when the conscience is wounded? Through this wound a man's real manhood and immortality flow out, and he bleeds to an everlasting death. I see this blood flowing now.

I have contemplated the imprisonment of the offender, rather than the seizure of his goods,—though both will serve the same purpose,—because they who assert the purest right, and consequently are most dangerous to a corrupt State, commonly have not spent much time in accumulating property. To such the State renders comparatively small service, and a slight tax is wont to appear exorbitant, particularly if they are obliged to earn it by special labor with their hands. If there were one who lived wholly without the use of money, the State itself would hesitate to demand it of him. But the rich man—not to make any invidious comparison—is always sold to the institution which makes him rich. Absolutely speaking, the more money, the less virtue; for money comes between a man and his objects, and obtains them for him; and it was certainly no great virtue to obtain it. It puts to rest many questions which he would otherwise be taxed to answer; while the only new question which it puts is the hard but superfluous one, how to spend it. Thus his moral ground is taken from under his feet. The opportunities of living are diminished in proportion as what are called the "means" are increased. The best thing a man can do for his culture when he is rich is to endeavor to carry out those schemes which he entertained when he was poor. Christ answered the Herodians according to their condition. "Show me the tribute-money," said he;—and one took a penny out of his pocket;—if you use money which has the image of Caesar on it, and which he has made current and valuable, that is, *if you are men of the State*, and gladly enjoy the advantages of Caesar's government, then pay him back some of his own when he demands it. "Render therefore to Caesar that which is Caesar's, and to God those things which are God's,"—leaving them no wiser than before as to which was which; for they did not wish to know.

When I converse with the freest of my neighbors, I perceive that, whatever they may say about the magnitude and seriousness of the question, and their regard for the public tranquility, the long and the short of the matter is, that they cannot spare the protection of the existing government, and they dread the consequences to their property and families of disobedience to it. For my own part, I should not like to think that I ever rely on the protection of the State. But, if I deny the authority of the State when it presents its tax-bill, it will soon take and waste all my property, and so harass me and my children without end. This is hard. This makes it impossible for a man to live honestly, and at the same time comfortably, in outward respects. It will not be worth the while to accumulate property; that would be sure to go again. You must hire or squat somewhere, and raise but a small crop, and eat that soon. You must live within yourself, and depend upon yourself always tucked up and ready for a start, and not have many affairs. A man may grow rich in Turkey even, if he will be in all respects a good subject of the Turkish government. Confucius said: "If a state is governed by the principles of reason, poverty and misery are subjects of shame; if a state is not governed by the principles of reason, riches and honors are the subjects of shame." No: until I want the protection of Massachusetts to be extended to me in some distant Southern port, where my liberty is endangered, or until I am bent solely on building up an estate at home by peaceful enterprise, I can afford to refuse allegiance to Massachusetts, and her right to my property and life. It costs me less in every sense to incur the penalty of disobedience to the State than it would to obey. I should feel as if I were worth less in that case.

Some years ago, the State met me in behalf of the Church, and commanded me to pay a certain sum toward the support of a clergyman whose preaching my father attended, but never I myself. "Pay," it said, "or be locked up in the jail." I declined to pay. But, unfortunately, another man saw fit to pay it. I did not see why the schoolmaster should be taxed to support the priest, and not the priest the schoolmaster; for I was not the State's schoolmaster, but I supported myself by voluntary subscription. I did not see why the lyceum should not present its tax-bill, and have the State to back its demand, as well as the Church. However, at the request of the selectmen, I condescended to make some such statement as this in writing:—"Know all men by these presents, that I, Henry Thoreau, do not wish to be regarded as a member of any incorporated society which I have not joined." This I gave to the town clerk; and he has it. The State, having thus learned that I did not wish to be regarded as a member of that church, has never made a like demand on me since; though it said that it must adhere to its original presumption that time. If I had known how to name them, I should then have signed off in detail from all the societies which I never signed on to; but I did not know where to find a complete list.

I have paid no poll-tax for six years. I was put into a jail once on this account, for one night; and, as I stood considering the walls of solid stone, two or three feet thick, the door of wood and iron, a foot thick, and the iron grating which strained the light, I could not help being struck with the foolishness of that institution which treated me as if I were mere flesh and blood and bones, to be locked up. I wondered that it should have concluded at length that this was the best use it could put me to, and had never thought to avail itself of my services in some way. I saw that, if there was a wall of stone between me and my townsmen, there was a still more difficult one to climb or break through before they could get to be as free as I was. I did not for a moment feel confined, and the walls seemed a great waste of stone and mortar. I felt as if I alone of all my townsmen had paid my tax. They plainly did not know how to treat me, but behaved like persons who are underbred. In every threat and in every compliment there was a blunder; for they thought that my chief desire was to stand the other side of that stone wall. I could not but smile to see how industriously they locked the door on my meditations, which followed them out again without let or hindrance, and *they* were really all that was dangerous. As they could not reach me, they had resolved to punish my body; just as boys, if they cannot come at some person against whom they have a spite, will abuse his dog. I saw that the State was half-witted, that it was timid as a lone woman with her silver spoons, and that it did not know its friends from its foes, and I lost all my remaining respect for it, and pitied it.

Thus the State never intentionally confronts a man's sense, intellectual or moral, but only his body, his senses. It is not armed with superior wit or honesty, but with superior physical strength. I was not born to be forced. I will breathe after my own fashion. Let us see who is the strongest. What force has a multitude? They only can force me to obey a higher law than I. They force me to become like themselves. I do not hear of *men* being *forced* to live this way or that by masses of men. What sort of life were that to live? When I meet a government which says to me, "Your money or your life," why should I be in haste to give it my money? It may be in a great strait, and not know what to do: I cannot help that. It must help itself; do as I do. It is not worth the while to snivel about it. I am not responsible for the successful working of the machinery of society. I am not the son of the engineer. I perceive that, when an acorn and a chestnut fall side by side, the one does not remain inert to make way for the other, but both obey their own laws, and spring and grow and flourish as best they can, till one, perchance, overshadows and destroys the other. If a plant cannot live according to its nature, it dies; and so a man.

The night in prison was novel and interesting enough. The prisoners in their shirt-sleeves were enjoying a chat and the evening air in the doorway, when I entered. But the jailer said, "Come, boys, it is time to lock up;" and so they dispersed, and I heard the sound of their steps returning into the hollow apartments. My roommate was introduced to me by the jailer as "a first-rate fellow and a clever man." When the door was locked, he showed me where to hang my hat, and how he managed matters there. The rooms were whitewashed once a month; and this one, at least, was the whitest, most simply furnished, and probably the neatest apartment in the town. He naturally wanted to know where I came from, and what brought me there; and, when I had told him, I asked him in my turn how he came there, presuming him to be an honest man, of course; and, as the world goes, I believe he was. "Why," said he, "they accuse me of burning a barn; but I never did it." As near as I could discover, he had probably gone to bed in a barn when drunk, and smoked his pipe there; and so a barn was burnt.

It was like traveling into a far country, such as I had never expected to behold, to lie there for one night. It seemed to me that I never had heard the town clock strike before, nor the evening sounds of the village; for we slept with the windows open, which were inside the grating. It was to see my native village in the light of the Middle Ages, and our Concord was turned into a Rhine stream, and visions of knights and castles passed before me. They were the voices of old burghers that I heard in the streets. I was an involuntary spectator and auditor of whatever was done and said in the kitchen of the adjacent village inn,—a wholly new and rare experience to me. It was a closer view of my native town. I was fairly inside of it. I never had seen its institutions before. This is one of its peculiar institutions; for it is a shire town. I began to comprehend what its inhabitants were about.

In the morning, our breakfasts were put through the hole in the door, in small oblong-square tin pans, made to fit, and holding a pint of chocolate, with brown bread, and an iron spoon. When they called for the vessels again, I was green enough to return what bread I had left; but my comrade seized it, and said that I should lay that up for lunch or dinner. Soon after he was let out to work at haying in a neighboring field, whither he went every day, and would not be back till noon; so he bade me good-day, saying that he doubted if he should see me again.

When I came out of prison,—for some one interfered, and paid that tax,—I did not perceive that great changes had taken place on the common, such as he observed who went in a youth and emerged a tottering and gray-headed man; and yet a change had to my eyes come over the scene,—the town, and State, and country,—greater than any that mere time could effect. I saw yet more distinctly the State in which I lived. I saw to what extent the people among whom I lived could be trusted as good neighbors and friends; that their friendship was for summer weather only; that they did not greatly propose to do right; that they were a distinct race from me by their prejudices and superstitions, as the Chinamen and Malays are; that in their sacrifices to humanity they ran no risks, not even to their property; that after all they were not so noble but they treated the thief as he had treated them, and hoped, by a certain outward observance and a few prayers, and by walking in a particular straight though useless path from time to time, to save their souls. This may be to judge my neighbors harshly; for I believe that many of them are not aware that they have such an institution as the jail in their village.

It was formerly the custom in our village, when a poor debtor came out of jail, for his acquaintances to salute him, looking through their fingers, which were crossed to represent the grating of a jail window, "How do ye do?" My neighbors did not thus salute me, but first looked at me, and then at one another, as if I had returned from a long journey. I was put into jail as I was going to the shoemaker's to get a shoe which was mended. When I was let out the next morning, I proceeded to finish my errand, and, having put on my mended shoe, joined a huckleberry party, who were impatient to put themselves under my conduct; and in half an hour,—for the horse was soon tackled,—was in the midst of a huckleberry field, on one of our highest hills, two miles off, and then the State was nowhere to be seen.

This is the whole history of "My Prisons."

I have never declined paying the highway tax, because I am as desirous of being a good neighbor as I am of being a bad subject; and as for supporting schools, I am doing my part to educate my fellow-countrymen now. It is for no particular item in the tax-bill that I refuse to pay it. I simply wish to refuse allegiance to the State, to withdraw and stand aloof from it effectually. I do not care to trace the course of my dollar, if I could, till it buys a man or a musket to shoot one with,—the dollar is innocent,—but I am concerned to trace the effects of my allegiance. In fact, I quietly declare war with the State, after my fashion, though I will still make what use and get what advantage of her I can, as is usual in such cases.

If others pay the tax which is demanded of me, from a sympathy with the State, they do but what they have already done in their own case, or rather they abet injustice to a greater extent than the State requires. If they pay the tax from a mistaken interest in the individual taxed, to save his property, or prevent his going to jail, it is because they have not considered wisely how far they let their private feelings interfere with the public good.

This, then, is my position at present. But one cannot be too much on his guard in such a case, lest his action be biased by obstinacy or an undue regard for the opinions of men. Let him see that he does only what belongs to himself and to the hour.

I do not wish to quarrel with any man or nation. I do not wish to split hairs, to make fine distinctions, or set myself up as better than my neighbors. I seek rather, I may say, even an excuse for conforming to the laws of the land. I am but too ready to conform to them. Indeed, I have reason to suspect myself on this head; and each year, as the tax-gatherer comes round, I find myself disposed to review the acts and position of the general and State governments, and the spirit of the people, to discover a pretext for conformity.

"We must affect our country as our parents,
And if at any time we alienate
Our love or industry from doing it honor,
We must respect effects and teach the soul
Matter of conscience and religion,
And not desire of rule or benefit."

I believe that the State will soon be able to take all my work of this sort out of my hands, and then I shall be no better a patriot than my fellow-countrymen. Seen from a lower point of view, the Constitution, with all its faults, is very good; the law and the courts are very respectable; even this State and this American government are, in many respects, very admirable, and rare things, to be thankful for, such as a great many have described them; but seen from a point of view a little higher, they are what I have described them; seen from a higher still, and the highest, who shall say what they are, or that they are worth looking at or thinking of at all?

However, the government does not concern me much, and I shall bestow the fewest possible thoughts on it. It is not many moments that I live under a government, even in this world. If a man is thought-free, fancy-free, imagination-free, that which *is not* never for a long time appearing *to be* to him, unwise rulers or reformers cannot fatally interrupt him.

I know that most men think differently from myself; but those whose lives are by profession devoted to the study of these or kindred subjects content me as little as any. Statesmen and legislators, standing so completely within the institution, never distinctly and nakedly behold it. They speak of moving society, but have no resting-place without it. They may be men of a certain experience and discrimination, and have no doubt invented ingenious and even useful systems, for which we sincerely thank them; but all their wit and usefulness lie within certain not very wide limits. They are wont to forget that the world is not governed by policy and expediency. Webster never goes behind government, and so cannot speak with authority about it. His words are wisdom to those legislators who contemplate no essential reform in the existing government; but for thinkers, and those who legislate for all time, he never once glances at the subject. I know of those whose serene and wise speculations on this theme would soon reveal the limits of his mind's range and hospitality. Yet, compared with the cheap professions of most reformers, and the still cheaper wisdom and eloquence of politicians in general, his are almost the only sensible and valuable words, and we thank Heaven for him. Comparatively, he is always strong, original, and, above all, practical. Still, his quality is not wisdom, but prudence. The lawyer's truth is not Truth, but consistency or a consistent expediency. Truth is always in harmony with herself, and is not concerned chiefly to reveal the justice that may consist with wrong-doing. He well deserves to be called, as he has been called, the Defender of the Constitution. There are really no blows to be given by him but defensive ones. He is not a leader, but a follower. His leaders are the men of '87. "I have never made an effort," he says, "and never propose to make an effort; I have never countenanced an effort, and never mean to countenance an effort, to disturb the arrangement as originally made, by which the various States came into the Union." Still thinking of the sanction which the Constitution gives to slavery, he says, "Because it was a part of the original compact,—let it stand."

No man with a genius for legislation has appeared in America. They are rare in the history of the world. There are orators, politicians, and eloquent men, by the thousand; but the speaker has not yet opened his mouth to speak who is capable of settling the much-vexed questions of the day. We love eloquence for its own sake, and not for any truth which it may utter, or any heroism it may inspire. Our legislators have not yet learned the comparative value of free trade and of freedom, of union, and of rectitude, to a nation. They have no genius or talent for comparatively humble questions of taxation and finance, commerce and manufactures and agriculture. If we were left solely to the wordy wit of legislators in Congress for our guidance, uncorrected by the seasonable experience and the effectual complaints of the people, America would not long retain her rank among the nations. For eighteen hundred years, though perchance I have no right to say it, the New Testament has been written; yet where is the legislator who has wisdom and practical talent enough to avail himself of the light which it sheds on the science of legislation?

The authority of government, even such as I am willing to submit to,—for I will cheerfully obey those who know and can do better than I, and in many things even those who neither know nor can do so well,—is still an impure one: to be strictly just, it must have the sanction and consent of the governed. It can have no pure right over my person and the property but what I concede to it. The progress from an absolute to a limited monarchy, from a limited monarchy to a democracy, is a progress toward a true respect for the individual. Even the Chinese philosopher was wise enough to regard the individual as the basis of the empire. Is a democracy, such as we know it, the last improvement possible in government? Is it not possible to take a step further toward recognizing and organizing the rights of man? There will never be a really free and enlightened State until the State comes to recognize the individual as a higher and independent power, from which all its own power and authority are derived, and treats him accordingly. I please myself with imagining a State at last which can afford to be just to all men, and to treat the individual with respect as a neighbor; which even would not think it inconsistent with its own repose if a few were to live aloof from it, not meddling with it, nor embraced by it, who fulfilled all the duties of neighbors and fellow-men. A state which bore this kind of fruit, and suffered it to drop off as fast as it ripened, would prepare the way for a still more perfect and glorious State, which also I have imagined, but not yet anywhere seen.

Walt Whitman, 1819–92

In his essay, "The Poet," Emerson wrote that the poet has a special mission because "the experience of each new age requires a new confession, and the world seems always waiting for its poet." It was the age of affirmation of American aspirations (map 23.6), and the exuberant voice of American democracy was that of Walt Whitman, which Emerson himself immediately recognized. On receiving the first edition of *Leaves of Grass* (1855), Emerson wrote Whitman that this was "the most extraordinary piece of wit and wisdom that America has yet contributed" and greeted the poet "at the beginning of a great career." Few writers, not to mention an indifferent general public, were as perceptive as Emerson, and even he later advised Whitman to go easy on the erotic poetry, advice which Whitman consistently ignored. *Leaves of Grass* was to be the poet's only book. Through nine editions (1855–92) it grew with his life and, in effect, became his life. "This is no book," wrote Whitman; "who touches this touches a man."

A poet of many voices, Whitman rejected the genteel tradition and what he called "book-words," selecting instead the language of the common people, a unique blend of journalistic jargon, everyday speech, and a great variety of foreign words and phrases. A pantheist, mystic, and ardent patriot, Whitman advocated humanity, brotherhood, and freedom, not only in the United States, but throughout the world.

The following chantlike poem is in Whitman's "catalog style" and illustrates his lusty mode as the "bard of democracy."

LITERARY SELECTION 75

I Hear America Singing

Walt Whitman

I hear America singing, the varied carols I hear,
Those of mechanics, each one singing his as it should be blithe and strong,
The carpenter singing his as he measures his plank or beam,
The mason singing his as he makes ready for work, or leaves off work,
The boatman singing what belongs to him in his boat, the deck-hand singing on the steamboat deck,
The shoemaker singing as he sits on his bench, the hatter singing as he stands,
The wood-cutter's song, the ploughboy's on his way in the morning, or at noon intermission or at sundown,
The delicious singing of the mother, or of the young wife at work, or of the girl sewing or washing,
Each singing what belongs to him or her and to none else,
The day what belongs to the day—at night the party of young fellows, robust, friendly,
Singing with open mouths their strong melodious songs.

Always an ardent supporter of the Union, Whitman was tormented by the "peculiar institution" of slavery and became an active Abolitionist. His involvement in the Civil War turned personal when he began caring for his wounded brother, George, in an Army hospital and stayed on to nurse others stricken by the war. The following poem is from *Drum-Taps*, which was added to *Leaves of Grass* in 1865.

By the Bivouac's Fitful Flame

Walt Whitman

By the bivouac's fitful flame,
A procession winding around me, solemn and sweet and slow—but first I note,
The tents of the sleeping army, the fields' and woods' dim outline,

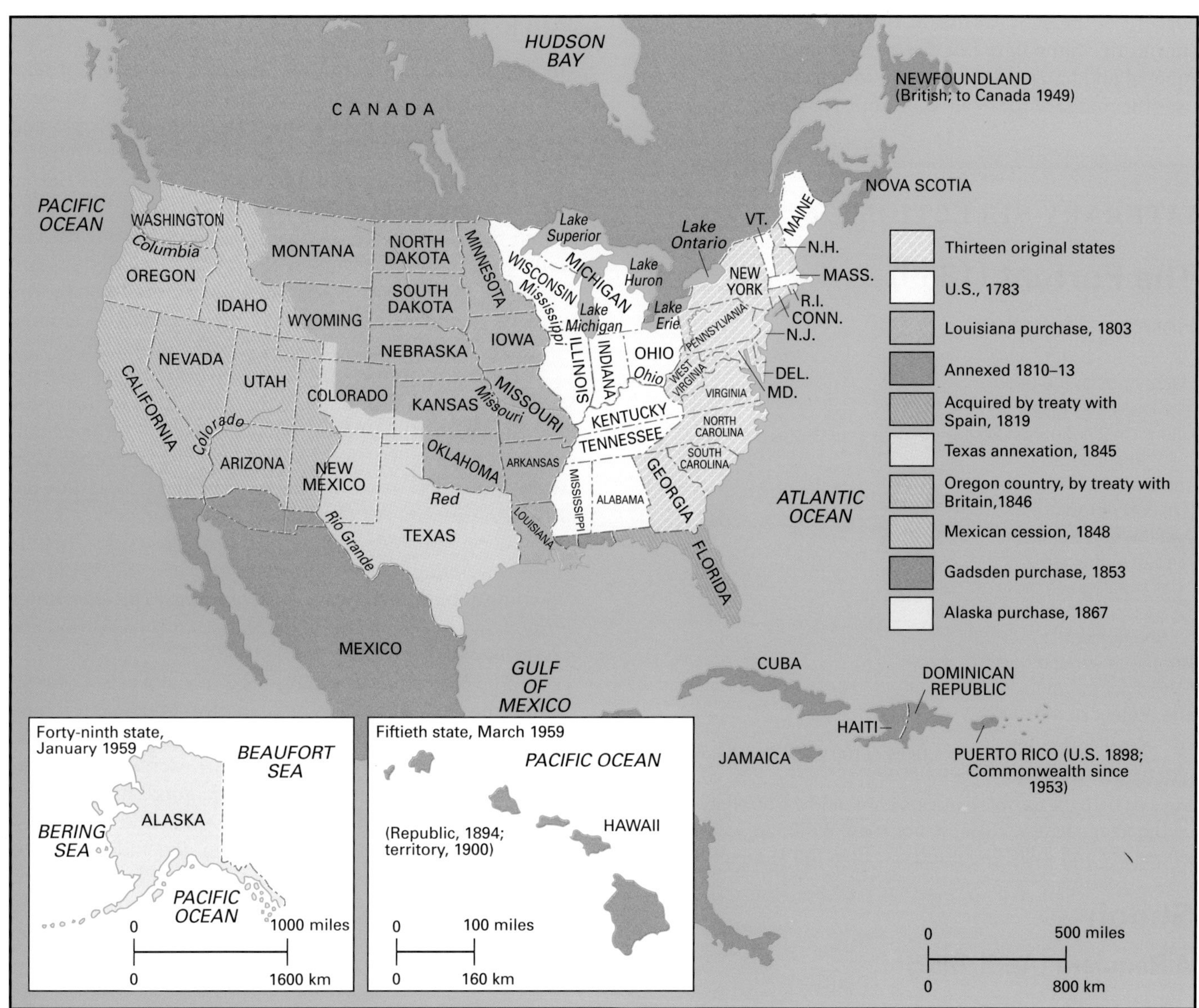

Map 23.6 Growth of the United States.

The darkness lit by spots of kindled fire, the silence,
Like a phantom far or near an occasional figure moving,
The shrubs and trees, (as I lift my eyes they seem to be
  stealthily watching me,)
While wind in procession thoughts, O tender and
  wondrous thoughts,
Of life and death, of home and the past and loved, and of
  those that are far away;
A solemn and slow procession there as I sit on the
  ground,
By the bivouac's fitful flame.

Herman Melville, 1819–91

Born in the same year as Whitman and also influenced by Emerson, Melville had not one but two literary careers. Like Whitman, Melville was fascinated by the sea and images of the sea, but Whitman's vision was essentially positive whereas Melville's was ironic and tragic, the viewpoint of a realist as opposed to Whitman the romantic. Several years after publishing his greatest novel, *Moby Dick* (1851), Melville turned, for reasons still unknown, to an exclusive preoccupation with poetry. (He did leave at his death the manuscript of *Billy Budd,* but with no clues as to when it was written.) Melville's ten-year career as a prose writer and thirty-year sequel as a poet were as unnoticed by the general public of the time as was the poetry of Whitman.

Deeply disturbed by the prospect of civil war, Melville followed the self-appointed mission of the Abolitionist John Brown who, in his zeal to free the slaves, had secured support from Emerson, Thoreau, and many others. Brown's capture of the U.S. Arsenal at Harper's Ferry was a major step in his campaign, but the government recaptured the Arsenal and hanged John Brown. Melville's brooding poem uses the image of the dead Abolitionist as a prologue to war.

LITERARY SELECTION 76

The Portent (1859)

Herman Melville

Hanging from the beam,
Slowly swaying (such the law),
Gaunt the shadow on your green,
Shenandoah!
The cut is on the crown
(Lo, John Brown),
And the stabs shall heal no more.
Hidden in the cap
Is the anguish none can draw;
So your future veils its face,
Shenandoah!
But the streaming beard is shown
(Weird John Brown),
The meteor of the war.

One of the bloodiest conflicts of the Civil War, the Battle of Shiloh (6–7 April 1862) cost the lives of thousands of soldiers and forecast both the terrible battles to come and the inevitable defeat of the Confederacy. No one, not even Whitman, wrote more eloquently and sadly about the war than did Herman Melville.

Shiloh

A Requiem (April 1862)

Herman Melville

Skimming lightly, wheeling still,
The swallows fly low
Over the field in clouded days,
The forest-field of Shiloh—
Over the field where April rain
Solaced the parched ones stretched in pain
Through the pause of night
That followed the Sunday fight
Around the church of Shiloh—
The church so lone, the log-built one,
That echoed to many a parting groan
And.natural prayer
Of dying foemen mingled there—
Foemen at morn, but friends at eve—
Fame or country least their care:
(What like a bullet can undeceive!)
But now they lie low,
While over them the swallows skim,
And all is hushed at Shiloh.

Mark Twain, 1835–1910

The second half of the century saw the emergence of realism in American literature and throughout the Western world. There was a new interest in common people and everyday facts of life. Among the new realists were Dickens, Thackeray, and George Eliot in England, Zola and Balzac in France, and William Dean Howells (1837–1921) in the United States. As editor-in-chief of the influential *Atlantic Monthly,* Howells advocated realism and supported regional writers. Mark Twain (pseudonym of Samuel Langhorne Clemens) was, however, the only major writer to emerge from what can be called the grass-roots movement.

The first important author born west of the Mississippi, Mark Twain, more than any other writer of his time, symbolized the power and exuberance of the expansive American spirit that blossomed after the Civil War. Twain spoke and wrote in the voice of the people in celebration of the winning of the West. (The later, darker Twain will not be considered here.) His major works include *Innocents Abroad* (1869) and *Roughing It* (1872), but his crowning achievement was a kind of trilogy: *The Adventures of Tom Sawyer* (1876); *Life on the Mississippi* (1883); and *The Adventures of Huckleberry Finn* (1885).

"The Notorious Jumping Frog of Calaveras County," perhaps his best short story, was an oft-told tale, but it took a Mark Twain to give it form and style. The story reprinted here is actually the first of a three-part exercise. On learning that a French critic had called it a good, but unfunny, story, Twain translated the tale into French and then translated that version into English. Twain concluded that the French-into-English version was awkward and indeed unfunny. The point is, of course, that Twain's American English was so idiomatic that it was untranslatable.

LITERARY SELECTION 77

The Notorious Jumping Frog of Calaveras County

Mark Twain

In compliance with the request of a friend of mine, who wrote me from the East, I called on good-natured, garrulous old Simon Wheeler, and inquired after my friend's friend, Leonidas W. Smiley, as requested to do, and I hereunto append the result. I have a lurking suspicion that *Leonidas W.* Smiley is a myth; that my friend never knew such a personage; and that he only conjectured that if I asked old Wheeler about him, it would remind him of his infamous *Jim* Smiley, and he would go to work and bore me to death with some exasperating reminiscence of him as long and tedious as it should be useless to me. If that was the design, it succeeded.

I found Simon Wheeler dozing comfortably by the bar-room stove of the dilapidated tavern in the decayed mining camp of Angel's, and I noticed that he was fat and bald-headed, and had an expression of winning gentleness and simplicity upon his tranquil countenance. He roused up and gave me good day. I told him that a friend of mine had commissioned me to make some inquiries about a cherished companion of his boyhood named Leonidas W. Smiley—*Rev. Leonidas W.* Smiley, a young minister of the Gospel, who he had heard was at one time a resident of Angel's Camp. I added that if Mr. Wheeler could tell me anything about this Rev. Leonidas W. Smiley, I would feel under many obligations to him.

Simon Wheeler backed me into a corner and blockaded me there with his chair, and then sat down and reeled off the monotonous narrative which follows this paragraph. He never smiled, he never frowned, he never changed his voice from the gentle-flowing key to which he tuned his initial sentence, he never betrayed the slightest suspicion of enthusiasm; but all through the interminable narrative there ran a vein of impressive earnestness and sincerity, which showed me plainly that, so far from his imagining that there was anything ridiculous or funny about his story, he regarded it as a really important matter, and admired its two heroes as men of transcendent genius in finesse. I let him go on in his own way, and never interrupted him once.

"Rev. Leonidas W. H'm, Reverend Le—well, there was a feller here once by the name of *Jim* Smiley, in the winter of '49—or maybe it was the spring of '50—I don't recollect exactly, somehow, though what makes me think it was one or the other is because I remember the big flume warn't finished when he first come to the camp; but, anyway, he was the curiousest man about always betting on anything that turned up you ever see, if he could get anybody to bet on the other side; and if he couldn't he'd change sides. Any way that suited the other man would suit *him*—any way just so's he got a bet, *he* was satisfied. But still he was lucky, uncommon lucky; he most always come out winner. He was always ready and laying for a chance, there couldn't be no solit'ry thing mentioned but that feller'd offer to bet on it, and take ary side you please, as I was just telling you. If there was a horse-race, you'd find him flush or you'd find him busted at the end of it; if there was a dog-fight, he'd bet on it; if there was a cat-fight, he'd bet on it; if there was a chicken-fight, he'd bet on it; why, if there was two birds setting on a fence, he would bet you which one would fly first; or if there was a camp-meeting, he would be there reg'lar to bet on Parson Walker, which he judged to be the best exhorter about here, and so he was too, and a good man. If he even see a straddle-bug start to go anywheres, he would bet you how long it would take him to get to—to wherever he was going to, and if you took him up, he would foller that straddle-bug to Mexico but what he would find out was where he was bound for and how long he was on the road. Lots of the boys here has seen that Smiley, and can tell you about him. Why, it never made no difference to *him*—he'd bet on *any*thing—the dangdest feller. Parson Walker's wife laid very sick once, for a good while, and it seemed as they warn't going to save her; but one morning he come in, and Smiley up and asked him how she was, and he said she was considerable better—thank the Lord for his inf'nite mercy—and coming on so smart that with the blessing of Prov'dence she'd get well yet; and Smiley, before he thought, says, 'Well, I'll risk two-and-a-half she don't anyway.'

"Thish-yer Smiley had a mare—the boys called her the fifteen-minute nag, but that was only in fun, you know, because of course she was faster than that—and he used to win money on that horse, for all she was so slow and always had the asthma, or the distemper, or the consumption, or something of that kind. They used to give her two or three hundred yards' start, and then pass her underway; but always at the fag end of the race she'd get excited and desperate like, and come cavorting and straddling up, and scattering her legs around limber, sometimes in the air, and sometimes out to one side among the fences, and kicking up m-o-r-e dust and raising m-o-r-e racket with her coughing and sneezing and blowing her nose—and *always* fetch up at the stand just about a neck ahead, as near as you could cipher it down.

"And he had a small bull-pup, that to look at him you'd think he warn't worth a cent but to set around and look ornery and lay for a chance to steal something. But as soon as money was up on him he was a different dog; his under-jaw'd begin to stick out like the fo'castle of a steamboat, and his teeth would uncover and shine like the furnaces. And a dog might tackle him and bully-rag him, and bite him, and throw him over his shoulder two or three times, and Andrew Jackson—which was the name of the pup—Andrew Jackson would never let on but what *he* was satisfied, and hadn't expected nothing else—and the bets being doubled and doubled on the other side all the time, till the money was all up; and then all of a sudden he would grab that other dog jest by the j'int of his hind leg and freeze to it—not chaw, you understand, but only just grip and hang on till they throwed up the sponge, if it was a year. Smiley always come out winner on that pup, till he harnessed a dog once that didn't have no hind legs, because they'd been sawed off in a circular saw, and when the thing had gone along far enough, and the money was all up, and he come to make a snatch for his pet holt, he see in a minute how he'd been imposed on, and how the other dog had him in the door, so to speak, and he 'peared surprised, and then he looked sorter discouraged-like, and didn't try no more to win the fight, and so he got shucked out bad. He give Smiley a look, as much as to say his heart was broke, and it was *his* fault, for putting up a dog that hadn't no hind legs for him to take holt of, which was his main dependence in a fight, and then he limped off a piece and laid down and died. It was a good pup, was that Andrew Jackson, and would have made a name for hisself if he'd lived, for the stuff was in him and he had genius—I know it, because he hadn't no opportunities to speak of, and it don't stand to reason that a dog could make such a fight as he could under them circumstances if he hadn't no talent. It always makes me feel sorry when I think of that last fight of his'n, and the way it turned out.

"Well, thish-yer Smiley had rat-terriers, and chicken

cocks, and tomcats, and all them kind of things, till you couldn't rest, and you couldn't fetch nothing for him to bet on but he'd match you. He ketched a frog one day, and took him home, and said he cal'lated to educate him; and so he never done nothing for three months but set in his back yard and learn that frog to jump. And you bet you he *did* learn him, too. He'd give him a little punch behind, and the next minute you'd see that frog whirling in the air like a doughnut—see him turn one summerset, or maybe a couple, if he got a good start, and come down flat-footed and all right, like a cat. He got him up so in the matter of catching flies, and kep' him in practice so constant, that he'd nail a fly every time as fur as he could see him. Smiley said all a frog wanted was education, and he could do 'most anything—and I believe him. Why, I've seen him set Dan'l Webster down here on this floor—Dan'l Webster was the name of the frog—and sing out, 'Flies, Dan'l, flies!' and quicker'n you could wink he'd spring straight up and snake a fly off'n the counter there, and flop down on the floor ag'in as solid as a gob of mud, and fall to scratching the side of his head with his hind foot as indifferent as if he hadn't no idea he'd been doin' any more'n any frog might do. You never see a frog so modest and straight-for'ard as he was, for all he was so gifted. And when it come to fair and square jumping on a dead level, he could get over more ground at one straddle than any animal of his breed you ever see. Jumping on a dead level was his strong suit, you understand; and when it come to that, Smiley would ante up money on him as long as he had a red. Smiley was monstrous proud of his frog, and well he might be, for fellers that had traveled and been everywheres all said he laid over any frog that ever *they* see.

"Well, Smiley kep' the beast in a little lattice box, and he used to fetch him down-town sometimes and lay for a bet. One day a feller—a stranger in the camp, he was—come acrost him with his box and says:

" 'What might it be that you've got in the box?'

"And Smiley says, sorter indifferent-like, 'It might be a parrot, or it might be a canary, maybe, but it ain't—it's only just a frog.'

"And the feller took it, and looked at it careful, and turned it round this way and that, and says, 'H'm—so 'tis. Well, what's *he* good for?'

" 'Well,' Smiley says, easy and careless, 'he's good enough for *one* thing, I should judge—he can outjump any frog in Calaveras County.'

"The feller took the box again, and took another long, particular look, and give it back to Smiley, and says, very deliberate, 'Well,' he says, 'I don't see no p'ints about that frog that's any better'n any other frog.'

" 'Maybe you don't,' Smiley says. 'Maybe you understand frogs and maybe you don't understand 'em; maybe you've had experience, and maybe you ain't only a amature, as it were. Anyways, I've got *my* opinion, and I'll resk forty dollars that he can outjump any frog in Calaveras County.'

"And the feller studied a minute, and then says, kinder sadlike, 'Well, I'm only a stranger here, and I ain't got no frog; but if I had a frog, I'd bet you.'

"And then Smiley says, 'That's all right—that's all right—if you'll hold my box a minute, I'll go and get you a frog.' And so the feller took the box, and put up his forty dollars along with Smiley's, and set down to wait.

"So he set there a good while thinking and thinking to himself, and then he got the frog out and prized his mouth open and took a teaspoon and filled him full of quail-shot—filled him pretty near up to his chin—and set him on the floor. Smiley he went to the swamp and slopped around in the mud for a long time, and finally he ketched a frog, and fetched him in, and give him to this feller and says:

" 'Now, if you're ready, set him alongside of Dan'l, with his fore paws just even with Dan'l's, and I'll give the word.' Then he says, 'One—two—three—*git!*' and him and the feller touched up the frogs from behind, and the new frog hopped off lively, but Dan'l give a heave, and hysted up his shoulders—so—like a Frenchman, but it warn't no use—he couldn't budge; he was planted as solid as a church, and he couldn't no more stir than if he was anchored out. Smiley was a good deal surprised, and he was disgusted too, but he didn't have no idea what the matter was, of course.

"The feller took the money and started away; and when he was going out the door, he sorter jerked his thumb over his shoulder—so—at Dan'l, and says again, very deliberate, 'Well,' he says, 'I don't see no p'ints about that frog that's any better'n any other frog.'

"Smiley he stood scratching his head and looking down at Dan'l a long time, and at last he says, 'I do wonder if there ain't something the matter with him—he 'pears to look mighty baggy, somehow.' And he ketched Dan'l by the nap of the neck, and hefted him, and says, 'Why blame my cats if he don't weigh five pound!' and turned him upside down and he belched out a double handful of shot. And then he sees how it was, and he was the maddest man—he set the frog down and took out after that feller, but he never ketched him. And—"

[Here Simon Wheeler heard his name called from the front yard, and got up to see what was wanted.] And turning to me as he moved away, he said: "Just set where you are, stranger, and rest easy—I ain't going to be gone a second."

But, by your leave, I did not think that a continuation of the history of the enterprising vagabond *Jim* Smiley would be likely to afford me much information concerning the Rev. *Leonidas W.* Smiley, and so I started away.

At the door I met the sociable Wheeler returning, and he buttonholed me and recommenced:

"Well, thish-yer Smiley had a yaller one-eyed cow that didn't have no tail, only just a short stump like a bannanner, and—' ''

However, lacking both time and inclination, I did not wait to hear about the afflicted cow, but took my leave.

STUDY QUESTION

This humorous classic is a virtual compendium of comic elements and devices. Considering the bet on the parson's wife, the "fifteen-minute nag," Andrew Jackson and Dan'l Webster, just how complex is this story?

Emily Dickinson, 1830–86

The poetry of the "recluse of Amherst" is also realistic. Twain's universe was the exterior world; Dickinson's was the inner world of her own psyche. Published years after her death, her 1,775 poems were written as if they were entries in a diary, the private thoughts of a solitary person who took just a little from society and shut out all the rest. Her gem-like, frequently cryptic, verses are unique, unlike poetry of any writer of any age.

LITERARY SELECTION 78

Poetry

Emily Dickinson

VI

Some keep the Sabbath going to church;
I keep it staying at home,
With a bobolink for a chorister,
And an orchard for a dome.

Some keep the Sabbath in surplice;
I just wear my wings,
And instead of tolling the bell for church,
Our little sexton sings.

God preaches,—a noted clergyman,—
And the sermon is never long;
So instead of getting to heaven at last,
I'm going all along!

XI

Much madness is divinest sense
To a discerning eye;
Much sense the starkest madness.
'Tis the majority
In this, as all, prevails.
Assent, and you are sane;
Demur,—you're straightway dangerous,
And handled with a chain.

XVII

I never saw a moor,
I never saw the sea;
Yet know I how the heather looks.
And what a wave must be.

I never spoke with God,
Nor visited in heaven;
Yet certain am I of the spot
As if the chart were given.

XXVII

Because I could not stop for Death,
He kindly stopped for me;
The carriage held but just ourselves
And Immortality.

We slowly drove, he knew no haste,
And I had put away
My labor, and my leisure too,
For his civility.

We passed the school where children played,
Their lessons scarcely done;
We passed the fields of gazing grain,
We passed the setting sun.

We paused before a house that seemed
A swelling of the ground;
The roof was scarcely visible,
The cornice but a mound.

Since then 'tis centuries; but each
Feels shorter than the day
I first surmised the horses' heads
Were toward eternity.

STUDY QUESTIONS

1. Would you call Poem VI pantheistic? Is it opposed to conventional religion or merely indifferent?
2. Poem XXVII contains many of the unusual metaphors for which Dickinson is famous. What are some of them? How effective are they?

Paul Laurence Dunbar, 1872–1906

Emancipation released the slaves from bondage only to suspend African Americans somewhere between African cultures to which they could not return and an American culture that refused to admit them. The first black poet to reach a national audience, Dunbar wrote a poignant poem still quoted today.

LITERARY SELECTION 79

Sympathy

Paul Laurence Dunbar

I know what the caged bird feels, alas!
When the sun is bright on the upland slopes;
When the wind stirs soft through the springing grass,
And the river flows like a stream of glass;
When the first bird sings and the first bud opes,
And the faint perfume from its chalice steals—
I know what the caged bird feels!

I know why the caged bird beats his wing
Till its blood is red on the cruel bars;
For he must fly back to his perch and cling
When he fain would be on the bough a-swing;
And a pain still throbs in the old, old scars
And they pulse again with a keener sting—
I know why he beats his wing!

I know why the caged bird sings, ah me,
When his wing is bruised and his bosom sore,—
When he beats his bars and he would be free;
It is not a carol of joy or glee,
But a prayer that he sends from his heart's deep core,
But a plea, that upward to Heaven he flings—
I know why the caged bird sings!

STUDY QUESTIONS

1. The caged bird is a metaphor for what? Is it a multiple metaphor?
2. What is implied by the peaceful images in stanza 1? The violent images in stanza 2?
3. Who or what will free the caged bird?

Stephen Crane, 1871–1900

Though sometimes identified as a writer in the realistic style called naturalism, Crane was actually influenced by Monet, Renoir, and other Impressionists. A journalist by profession and a war correspondent, Crane used word-painting in a manner comparable to the Impressionists' use of color. *The Red Badge of Courage* (1895) is perhaps the finest short novel in the English language, and "The Open Boat" and "The Blue Hotel" rank at the top of American short stories. Of Crane's poems, the following two seem most appropriate to conclude this survey of nineteenth-century life and literature.

LITERARY SELECTION 80

Two Poems (Untitled)

Stephen Crane

Do not weep, maiden, for war is kind.
Because your lover threw wild hands toward the sky
And the affrighted steed ran on alone,
Do not weep.
War is kind.
Hoarse, booming drums of the regiment,
Little souls who thirst for fight
These men were born to drill and die.
The unexplained glory flies above them,
Great is the battle-god, great, and his kingdom—
A field where a thousand corpses lie.
Do not weep, babe, for war is kind.
Because your father tumbled in the yellow trenches,
Raged at his breast, gulped and died,
Do not weep.
War is kind.
Swift blazing flag of the regiment,
Eagle with crest of red and gold,
These men were born to drill and die.
Point for them the virtue of slaughter,
Make plain to them the excellence of killing
And a field where a thousand corpses lie.
Mother whose heart hung humble as a button
On the bright splendid shroud of your son,
Do not weep.
War is kind.

. . . . .

A man said to the universe:
"Sir, I exist!"
"However," replied the universe,
"The fact has not created in me
A sense of obligation."

SUMMARY

The revolutionary surge that began in France in 1789 was sidetracked by the imperial conquests of Napoleon and, even more effectively, by the 1815 Congress of Vienna. From 1815 to 1848, the arch-conservatism of the age of Metternich helped to maintain the *status quo* of absolutism, disturbed only by the waves of revolution that rolled over Europe in 1830 and 1848. By mid-century the industrial revolution had helped turn western Europe and North America into a powerful economic community, but political divisions became ever sharper with the rise of militant nationalism.

Revolution, civil war, and aggressive imperial wars became the hallmark of the last half of the so-called Romantic century. The Greek struggle for independence did spark the Romantic imagination, but the Crimean and Franco-Prussian wars were bloody preludes to the Great War of 1914–18.

Italy finally became an independent nation in 1861 and, after the Civil War ended in 1865, the United States began to assume its place as a world power. In 1871 France became, once again, a republic; Bismarck proclaimed the German Empire; and the rival British Empire girdled the globe. Nationalism, imperialism, and militarism led, perhaps inevitably, to the conflict that ended what has been called the Age of Progress.

CULTURE AND HUMAN VALUES

The nineteenth century was noted for the prosperity stimulated by the industrial revolution, the growing middle class, and the enormous increase in manufactured products. The prevailing view of reality was more materialistic than ever; the world was a well-oiled machine bursting with machines turning out a flood of products. When these factors are combined with steady advances in science, transportation, communications, and other technologies, one can see why this has been grandly labeled as the Age of Progress.

This designation was, however, self-anointed and self-serving for the industrially advanced nations of western Europe and North America. And not even in these industrialized countries was "progress" even remotely uniform. A large (growing ever larger) class of underpaid industrial workers, child labor, inadequate health and safety standards, and woefully substandard sanitation and housing were just some of the basic problems plaguing the working class. The poor were without power or influence in the factory, at home, and at the voting booth, whereas the rich got richer and more powerful.

What of the rest of the world—those non-industrial nations of Central and South America, Africa, and Asia? Many of them became involuntary outposts of Western civilization. The monumental problem of the nineteenth century—that spilled over into the twentieth—was colonialism, and its negative after-effects haunt us still. In the colonies of England, Germany, France, Belgium, Italy, Spain, and Portugal, the locals (natives) had to accept whatever culture and values the foreign overlords brought with them. As arbitrary extensions or pawns of the mother country, colonies were fair game for commerce, the military, politicians, and as many industrial products as the market would bear.

In today's world the new nations that have risen from the ashes of colonialism often exhibit no imprint of the culture of the vanished colonial powers. In Indonesia, for example, there is virtually no indication that these islands were ever ruled by the Dutch for four centuries. The same generally holds true for the colonies of Portugal, Spain, Italy, Germany, and Belgium, which were exploited and plundered—as was Indonesia—solely for the benefit of the mother country with little or no regard for the welfare of the subject population.

The British did attempt to create the infrastructures of modern states, but these were designed to serve the interests of the colonial masters. Their subjects did derive some indirect benefits, while also acquiring other aspects of English civilization, particularly the language. In the Third World the residual effects of English hegemony can be seen today in such former possessions as India, Kenya, Malaysia, Zimbabwe, and Fiji.

Unique among the Western powers, the French imported and educated selected colonials in the French language and culture and installed them in key positions in their colonies. The French heritage is quite apparent, for example, in Morocco, Algeria, and Indochina. Much like the Greeks under Alexander the Great, the French were eager to share their civilization with other nationalities.

When considering the culture-epoch theory the period is full of paradoxes. On the one hand, there was the notable increase in prosperity in the industrial nations but a *status quo* at best in the colonized nations. The industrial, imperialist powers enforced a certain stability as they competed to maintain a balance of power, and certainly Europe imposed its values on much of the world. But the Age of Progress was headed for a fall signaled by the onset of the Great War, the so-called "war to end all wars."

CHAPTER 24

Romanticism in Music

The ever-changing sequence of artistic styles can be seen in broad perspective as a constant back-and-forth movement between two extremes. In painting, these outer boundaries were represented by the Rubenists, who emphasized color, and the Poussinists, who advocated line and drawing. Delacroix was a Rubenist; Ingres and David were Poussinists. These extremes are referred to, in music, as romanticism and classicism. As in painting, romantic music emphasizes color whereas the classical style stresses line and design. The two extremes can be outlined as follows:

Classicism	**Romanticism**
intellectual	emotional
objective	subjective
rational	non-rational
tranquil	restless
simple	ornate
Apollonian	Dionysian

No artistic style can be classified as wholly classic or wholly romantic. An inclination in favor of either extreme results in a classification of the style *as* that extreme, a process that can be compared to a seesaw touching ground at one end because of a slight shift of balance. Though it is absurd to consider all of Mozart's music, for example, as intellectual but not emotional, tranquil and simple rather than ornate and restless, the fact remains that Mozart's music is essentially classic in its meticulous detail, restraint, and clarity of design.

The Romantic style in music is either miniaturized or grandiose with comparatively little in between. There are intimate art songs for solo voice and piano and single-movement piano pieces at one extreme, and grandiose symphonic works at the other. The emphasis is on tone color (or sound), that fourth element of music (melody, harmony, rhythm, tone color). Symphonies have a wider range of instrumental tone color and a greater volume of sound than at any time since the invention of the symphony orchestra.

Opposite Eugène Delacroix, *Arabs Skirmishing in the Mountains*, detail of fig. 25.8. 1863. Oil on linen, 36⅜" × 29⅜" (92.5 × 74.6 cm). National Gallery of Art, Washington, D.C. (Chester Dale Fund).

The international aspects of seventeenth- and eighteenth-century music are superseded by highly individualistic styles of writing and strong nationalistic expression. The "Austrian" quality of the classical music of Haydn and Mozart is not relevant to their work. During the Romantic period, however, the "German" characteristics of Wagner, Schubert, and Schumann and the "Italian" qualities of Verdi, Rossini, and Donizetti are essential components of the stylistic picture. Along with literature and art, Romantic music mirrors the rise of nationalism.

Typical of the Romantic mode is the brooding, melancholy painting by Arnold Böcklin (BOEK-lin; 1827–1901), which the artist called "a picture for dreaming about" (fig. 24.1). The strange and mysterious scene was enormously popular; it simply exists in its own bizarre world with no explanation necessary or even desirable.

GERMAN *LIEDER*

The Romantic movement generated a new style, the setting of preexisting poetry—almost always Romantic—to music in an adroit matching of mood and meaning. Nationalism was again a salient characteristic, for the new style was a synthesis of words and music, and the language was German.

24.1 Arnold Böcklin, *Island of the Dead*. 1880. Oil on wood, 29 × 48" (73.7 × 121.9 cm). Metropolitan Museum of Art, New York (Reisinger Fund, 1926).

Viennese composer Franz Schubert (1797–1828) created the new artistic medium when, in 1814, he wrote music for "Gretchen am Spinnrade" from Goethe's *Faust*. Schubert invented the art song movement; the generic term *Lieder* applies to the German Romantic songs of Schubert, Schumann, Brahms, and others, though *Lied* is the German word for any song.

Composers have always set poetry to music, from Sappho to the troubadours to Bach and beyond. *Lieder* are not just songs, however, for German composers displayed a remarkable unity of purpose—the re-creation of a poem in musical terms. Art songs (*Lieder*) were significant miniatures in an era that indulged itself with the grandiose or doted on the diminutive. There was little middle ground, for the Romantics sought the heights and plumbed the depths with scant patience for the ordinary. Complexity was preferred and simplicity abhorred. If one art form was good then two art forms were even better. Art songs embodied the essence of Romanticism for they synthesized poetry and music in a new and rarefied style.

From the poem comes the song, which attempts to capture the feelings, the mood, indeed the essence of what the poet is saying. The rhythm, inflection, sound, and meaning of the language are corroborated and heightened by the composer's own personal language of melody, harmony, rhythm, and tone color.

Following is the Schubert *Lied* that inaugurated the German *Lieder* movement. German art songs are always sung in German because a translation spoils the unity of words and music. The German text with English translation is provided so that the listener can follow one and understand the other. There are ten verses, as indicated by the numbers in the text.

Listening Example 29

GERMAN ART SONG (*LIED*)

Schubert, "Gretchen am Spinnrade" ("Gretchen at the Spinning Wheel")
1814

Time: 3:48
Cassette 2, track 26

Synopsis: Margaret sits in her room at the spinning wheel and sings of her love for Faust, knowing that this love will prove fatal. The scene occurs near the end of Part I of *Faust*.

1. Mei-ne Ruh' ist hin, mein Herz ist schwer;
ich finde, ich finde sie nimmer und nimmer mehr.
(My peace is gone, my heart is sore:
I shall find it never and never more.)

2. Wo ich ihn nicht hab', ist mir das Grab,
die ganze Welt ist mir vergällt.
(He has left my room an empty tomb
He has gone and all my world is gall.)

3. Mein armer Kopf ist mir verrückt,
mein armer Sinn ist mir zerstückt.
(My poor head is all astray,
My poor mind fallen away.)

4. Meine Ruh' ist hin, mein Herz ist schwer;
ich finde, ich finde sie nimmer und nimmer mehr.
(My peace is gone, my heart is sore;
I shall find it never and never more.)

5. Nach ihm nur schau' ich zum Fenster hinaus,
nach ihm nur geh' ich aus dem Haus.
('Tis he that I look through the window to see
He that I open the door for—he!)

6. Sein hoher Gang, sein' edle Gestalt,
seines Mundes Lächeln, seiner Augen Gewalt,
(His gait, his figure, so grand, so high,
The smile of his mouth, the power of his eye,)

7. Und seiner Rede Zauberfluss,
sein Händedruck und ach, sein Kuss! (Piano)
(And the magic stream of his words—what bliss
The clasp of his hand and, ah, his kiss!)

8. Meine Ruh' ist hin, mein Herz ist schwer;
ich finde, ich finde sie nimmer und nimmer mehr.
(My peace is gone, my heart is sore:
I shall find it never and never more.)

9. Mein Busen drängt sich nach ihm hin.
Ach, dürft' ich fassen und halten ihn!
(My heart's desire is so strong, so vast;
Ah, could I seize him and hold him fast.)

10. Und küssen ihn, so wie ich wollt'
an seinen Küssen vergehen sollt',
O könnt' ich ihn küssen, so wie ich wollt',
an seinen Küssen vergehen sollt',
an seinen Küssen vergehen sollt'!
(And kiss him forever night and day,
And on his kisses pass away!)
Meine Ruh' ist hin, mein Herz ist schwer. (Piano)
(My peace is gone, my heart is sore.)

PIANO MUSIC

The Romantic emphasis on the uniqueness of the individual was symbolized by the dominance of the piano as the most popular musical instrument—as typical of the Romantic era as the guitar is of contemporary life. The piano was ubiquitous because it could accompany *Lieder*, blend into a chamber music ensemble or, in a piano concerto, dominate a symphony orchestra. Its prime attraction, however, was its independence, for it is a superb solo instrument.

Eighteenth-century pianos were relatively small with a clear and delicate tone. Nineteenth-century pianos were larger, more sonorous than clear, and loud enough to fill the largest concert hall. The range of tone was representative of the Romantic propensity for extremes. Whether playing the tender "Lullaby" by Brahms or the thunderous "Revolutionary Etude" by Chopin, the pianist was a commanding figure throughout the Romantic period. Pianists also dominate today's concert world because of the enduring popularity of the Romantic repertoire.

Frédéric Chopin, 1810–49

Frédéric Chopin (shaw-pã) was a superb concert pianist, but he did not confuse virtuoso performance with the circus showmanship of Paganini and Liszt. Though he was successful in the concert hall he gave fewer than seventy-five public concerts in his entire career. In temperament and style he was much more at home in the fashionable salons of Paris. He was the "poet of the keyboard," whose personal style epitomizes the Romantic spirit (fig. 24.2).

His musical poetry is not unlike the blending of words and music in German art songs. The formal designs of his music—sonata form, binary, and ternary forms—are traditional, but the content is unique. Some of the range of Chopin's piano style can be appreciated by considering just three compositions: two preludes and an étude.

Chopin wrote twenty-four preludes in Opus 28, each in a different key. As befits a prelude, which for Chopin is a short piano piece in one movement, there is only one subject. Prelude No. 4 is a short and melancholy meditation in the minor mode. Prelude No. 7 is a very brief and beautiful composition in the major mode.

24.2 Eugène Delacroix, *Frédéric Chopin*. 1838. Oil on canvas, 18 × 15" (45.7 × 38.1 cm). Louvre, Paris, Photo: R.M.N., Paris.
Delacroix seldom painted portraits on commission; instead, he depicted some of his personal friends, the victims, like himself, of what he and other artists called the "Romantic agony."

Listening Example 30

PIANO PRELUDES

Chopin, Preludes, Op. 28 No. 4 in E Minor and No. 7 in A Major
1839

Times: 1:53, 0:43[1]

Chopin wrote a number of studies (études) that concentrated on various technical problems in playing the piano. Brief and brilliant, the G-Flat Major ("Black Key") Etude is a delightful exercise for playing on the black keys of the piano. The problem is performing at breakneck speed on narrow keys less than half the width of the white keys—3/8" to 7/8" (0.95–2.2cm).

Listening Example 31

PIANO ETUDE

Chopin, Etude in G-Flat Major, Op. 10 No. 5
1830

Time: 1:46
Cassette 2, track 27

Etude in G-Flat Major, Op. 10, No. 5 **Chopin (1810–49)**

1. CD 2, track 9 (Prelude No. 4); CD 2, track 10 (Prelude No. 7).

SHOWMANSHIP

The nineteenth century was a fabulous age of virtuosos, which is what spectacular performers were called. Virtuosity and showmanship were so widely admired that some performers added extramusical tricks. Violin virtuoso Niccolò Paganini, for example, would conclude a concert with a razor blade hidden in his right hand. Near the end of an already sensational performance he would deftly cut the violin strings, one by one, until he could triumphantly conclude on the last remaining string.

Virtuoso pianist Franz Liszt was fond of planting a female admirer in the front row of the concert hall. At the most dramatic moment the young lady, obviously enthralled by Liszt's performance, would be drawn to her feet and then ecstatically faint away (fig. 24.3). The maestro would carry her onstage and, holding her artistically draped body over one arm, triumphantly conclude his performance with one hand.

24.3 Liszt in the concert hall, from Adolf Glasbrenner, *Berlin wie es isst und trinkt,* book 14. Book illustration. Märkisches Museum, Berlin.

THE SYMPHONY

The greatly augmented symphony orchestra with its strong brass and percussion sections and enlarged body of woodwinds provided a particularly effective medium for Romantic music. The classical orchestra had a nucleus of strings plus a small woodwind section and just a few brass and percussion instruments. Romantic composers added full sections of woodwinds and brass that could play as independent sections as well as filling in the ensemble. The comparative size of the orchestra over a single century is illustrated in table 24.1.

TABLE 24.1 COMPARATIVE SIZES OF ORCHESTRAS

	Mozart (1788)	Beethoven (1808)	Strauss (1895)
Woodwinds	flute 2 oboes 2 clarinets 2 bassoons	piccolo 2 flutes 2 oboes 2 clarinets 2 bassoons	piccolo 3 flutes 3 oboes English horn 3 clarinets bass clarinet 3 bassoons contrabassoon
Brass	2 French horns	2 French horns 2 trumpets 3 trombones	8 French horns 6 trumpets 3 trombones tuba
Percussion		timpani	timpani, snare drum, bass drum, cymbals, triangle
Strings	violin I violin II viola cello bass	violin I violin II viola cello bass	violin I violin II viola cello bass

Figure 24.5 is a seating plan observed in principle by most modern orchestras. Because of their limited volume the strings are seated in front and the woodwinds in the center; brass, bass instruments, and percussion bring up the rear (fig. 24.4).

As might be expected, composers were highly individualistic in their approach to the symphonic tradition. The remarkable variety of orchestral music will be surveyed by considering one work by three different composers: Hector Berlioz, Johannes Brahms, and Peter Tchaikovsky.

Hector Berlioz, 1803–69

Hector Berlioz (bear-lee-os; fig. 24.6) was a red-headed Romantic from the south of France, a revolutionary artist whose only personal instrument was the guitar, but whose preferred instrument was the entire symphony orchestra. Despite his flamboyance—his lifetime dream was to hear 10,000 trumpets from a mountain top—he was a solid musician and an orchestral innovator who strongly influenced Liszt, Wagner, Tchaikovsky, and Strauss.

24.4 A modern symphony orchestra in the Royal Festival Hall, London. Photo: Langham Arts, London.

24.5 Typical seating plan of a modern symphony orchestra.

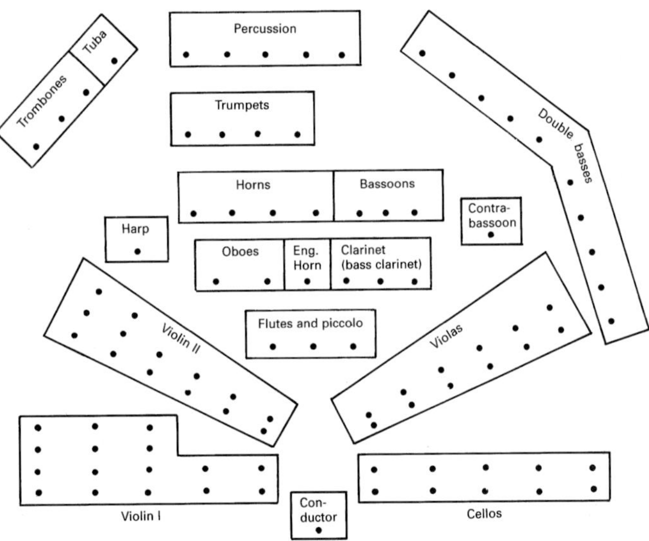

P(HINEAS) T(AYLOR) BARNUM

Though he claimed the title of "Prince of Humbugs" and frequently declared that "there's a sucker born every minute," P. T. Barnum (1810–91) was America's greatest showman. In direct contrast to William Vanderbilt, Barnum truly loved the public—and only partly because people "love to be fooled." In an age with no radios, movies, and very few theatres, Barnum gave the public what it wanted: exotic shows and curious and strange attractions—from the supposed nurse of George Washington (a former slave woman "164 years old") to a fake mermaid, a midget he named General Tom Thumb, and an African elephant named Jumbo that he called the "only mastodon on earth." These were some of the attractions in Barnum's American Museum in New York, where he sold over 41,000,000 tickets in seventeen years. Truly a gifted showman who knew the value of advertising, Barnum successfully staged the American tour of Jenny Lind, the very first concert tour by a European artist. He exceeded even himself, however, when he created the traveling Barnum Circus, museum, and menagerie and called it "The Greatest Show on Earth." When Barnum merged his show with that of his rival, James Bailey, the resulting Barnum and Bailey Circus was indeed the greatest show on earth.

One of his most successful and controversial works, the *Symphonie fantastique,* was completed in 1830, only three years after Beethoven's death. Berlioz had been influenced by the popular *Confessions of an English Opium Eater* (1821) by Thomas de Quincey and he thought of combining an opium dream with music. He also fell madly in love with a Shakespearean actress named Harriet Smithson. It is now impossible to tell what the components were of this frenzied, desperate love affair that led to a short-lived and disastrous marriage.

Entranced by what he saw as the Romantic elements in Shakespeare's plays, Berlioz was as stage-struck by the Shakespearean women played by Miss Smithson as he was infatuated with the actress herself. In the midst of their stormy marriage Berlioz blended his conception of Shakespeare's women, his passion for Harriet, and his interest in opium into the fanciful story-line (program) that created the *Symphonie fantastique.*

Berlioz viewed classical forms as empty shells. He created, instead, an *idée fixe* (Fr. "fixed idea"), a single theme that was the common thread for each of the five movements of his daring new symphony. The *idée fixe* was a kind of *Leitmotif*—a procedure that Wagner was to exploit—that represented both the ideal of perfect love and the artist's idealized version of Harriet Smithson.

Following are the titles of the five movements of the *Symphonic fantastique* plus a brief explanation of what the composer apparently had in mind when he wrote the music.

I. *Reveries—Passions* ("Daydreams—Passions"). The artist, despairing of ever possessing his beloved, attempts to poison himself with opium. What follows in this and in the other movements is a series of opium-induced dreams, fantasies, and nightmares. This first movement is a frequently euphoric reverie about the artist's passion for his beloved.

II. *Un bal* ("A ball"). There is a fancy ball at which the beloved appears, slipping in and out of the dancers. The *idée fixe,* representing the beloved, is heard as she appears among the dancers.

III. *Scène aux champs* ("Scene in the country"). An idyllic scene of calm serenity in the bucolic countryside.

IV. *Marche au supplice* ("March to the scaffold"). In his delirium, the artist imagines that he has killed his beloved and that he is being taken on a tumbrel to the guillotine.

V. *Songe d'une nuit de Sabbat* ("Dream of a Witches' Sabbath"). Following his execution the artist dreams that he is present at a gruesome Witches' Sabbath, complete with a parody of the Dies irae (Lat., "Day of Judgment") as a part of a Black Mass. The *idée fixe* is also parodied as his beloved appears as a debased prostitute.

24.6 Hector Berlioz.

Listening Example 32

PROGRAM SYMPHONY

Berlioz, *Symphonie fantastique,* 4th movement, March to the Scaffold
1830

Time: 4:56
Cassette 2, track 28

24.7 *Opposite* Peter Ilich Tchaikovsky. 1888. Photo: Free Library of Philadelphia.

Johannes Brahms, 1833–97

More than any other composer of the last half of the nineteenth century, Brahms was responsible for the reviving of "absolute music," that is, compositions that were strictly interplays of sound and totally independent of any kind of extramusical program. In this respect he was seen as a successor to Beethoven—so much so that his First Symphony was also nicknamed "Beethoven's Tenth." Brahms followed the Viennese classical tradition that emphasized form over novelties and innovations. While all of Europe was mesmerized by the special effects and innovations of Richard Wagner's operas, Brahms stubbornly stuck to the traditions of Mozart and Beethoven and thereby forged a unique place for himself as the foremost composer of the German Romantic movement. The third movement of his Second Symphony is a charming and lighthearted example of his symphonic style. The form is a five-part rondo: ABACA.

Listening Example 33

SYMPHONY

Brahms, Symphony No. 2 in D Major, Op. 73, 3rd movement
1877

Time: 5:33[2]

Peter Ilich Tchaikovsky, 1840–93

Tchaikovsky (chy-KOF-skee; fig. 24.7) seldom succeeded in mastering musical forms, but he was remarkably skillful in his handling of the symphony orchestra. The lush sounds of Tchaikovsky's orchestra have become a kind of hallmark for the dramatic intensity and emotional extremes of the Romantic movement.

Tchaikovsky's orchestral music ranges from ponderous melodrama to vapid sentimentality and yet, at his best, he has created enormously popular works for ballet—"Swan Lake," "The Nutcracker," "Sleeping Beauty"—and three successful symphonies, the Fourth, Fifth, and Sixth.

"The Nutcracker"

The subject for his ballet "The Nutcracker" was drawn from stories by Alexandre Dumas and E. T. A. Hoffmann. It begins with a Christmas tree party hosted by Marie for children and mechanical dolls. She is fascinated by a German nutcracker fashioned in the figure of an old man with massive jaws. Some rough boys break the nutcracker, and that night Marie lies sleepless in pity for it. Getting out of bed to look after her broken darling, she watches the Christmas tree grow and the toys come to life, including the cakes, tidbits, and nutcracker. Mice attack the toys and the nutcracker challenges the king of mice to single combat, a battle being won by the mouse until Marie kills it with a well-aimed shoe. The nutcracker is immediately transformed into a handsome young prince who thanks Marie for his life as he escorts her to his enchanted kingdom.

The scene in the second act is a jam mountain in the realm of the Sugarplum Fairy. There follows a series of eight dances which comprise the suite that Tchaikovsky made from the ballet score. The Russian Dance (*Trepak*) is extremely lively and is based almost entirely on the rhythmical figure in the opening measure.

Listening Example 34

BALLET MUSIC

Tchaikovsky, Suite from the ballet "The Nutcracker," Op. 71a, 4th movement, Russian Dance (*Trepak)*
1892

Time: 1:09
Cassette 2, track 29[3]

***Nutcracker Suite*, Fourth movement, "Russian Dance (Trepak)"**

Tchaikovsky (1840–93)

2. CD 2, track 19.
3. CD 3, track 2.

OPERA

Opera underwent drastic changes in style and intent during the nineteenth century. Early in the century, Beethoven's *Fidelio* (1805) represented what might be called international opera. With the emergence of Romanticism there was a corresponding rise in national schools of opera with Italy dominating the European (and American) scene.

Italian opera, as typified by Verdi's *Rigoletto* (1851), was a mélange of melodramatic plots, popular-type melodies, and "effective" solos and ensembles. There was more emphasis on *bel canto* (It., "beautiful singing") than on the development of plot and character. Later operas, Verdi's *Aïda* (1871) for example, evidenced an ever-increasing concern with dramatic values, culminating in the complex "music dramas" of Richard Wagner. Wagner conceived of opera, his *Tristan und Isolde* (1859) for example, as a super art form, a viewpoint roughly comparable to Byron's conception of himself as a superhero and Nietzsche's theory of a superman.

Wagner's insistence on the musical-literary totality of his myth-based music dramas provoked strong reactions in favor of so-called realism in subject matter and a new simplicity in musical treatment. A similar reaction against academic painting led to the emergence of such Romantic realists as Millet and Corot of the Barbizon School and, especially, the realists Daumier and Courbet. A comparable movement in literature, called naturalism, was led by Emile Zola.

Giuseppe Verdi, 1813–1901

Probably the greatest of all Italian opera composers, Verdi (VAIR-dee) had an exceptionally long and productive career. His last two operas, *Otello* (1887) and *Falstaff* (1893), based on Shakespeare and undoubtedly his best works, were composed long after most composers would have considered their careers over and done with. His operas are noted for their emotional intensity, tuneful, singable melodies, and highly dramatic characterizations. The following example is a tenor aria that deals playfully with women's frivolity: "How fickle women are, Fleeting as falling star, Changing forever; Constant, ah! never."

Listening Example 35

ITALIAN OPERA

Verdi, *Rigoletto*, Act IV, "La donna è mobile"
1851

Time: 2:11[4]

Giacomo Puccini, 1858–1924

Giacomo Puccini (poo-CHEE-nee; fig. 24.8) was the leading Romantic Realist in operatic literature. His tragic operas *La Bohème, Madame Butterfly*, and *Tosca* are among the most popular works in the standard repertoire of leading opera companies. Though not the musical or dramatic innovator that Verdi was, Puccini had an inherent feeling for the stage which, together with the instrumental colors of his orchestral writing, assured him of international success. Along with Verdi's, his work continues to define Italian opera around the world. In the following example Tosca, an opera star, sings of her lover's imminent execution: "Love and music, these I have lived for, nor ever have harmed a human being . . . why, Heavenly Father, why hast Thou forsaken me?"

Listening Example 36

ITALIAN OPERA

Puccini, *Tosca*, Act II, "Vissi d'arte"
1900

Time: 3:08[5]

24.8 Giacomo Puccini. Photo: Viollet, Paris.

Georges Bizet, 1838–75

Bizet (Bee-zay) wrote only one successful opera, but that was quite enough to make him one of the century's great operatic composers. Oddly enough, *Carmen* was poorly received when first performed, a great disappointment for the composer, who died shortly after the thirty-first performance. Bizet based his opera on the novella *Carmen* by the French author Prosper Mérimée. Numerous French Romantic writers and composers had great success in using Spanish themes and placing their work in Spain. In the following selection Carmen compares love with a bird that cannot be tamed and with a wild and lawless gypsy child, warning anyone who loves her to be forever on guard. The arrogance of the beautiful Spanish gypsy is unmistakable.

> *Listening Example 37*
>
> **OPERA**
>
> Bizet, *Carmen,* Act I, Habanera
> 1875
>
> Time: 5:38[6]

IMPRESSIONISM IN MUSIC

By the end of the nineteenth century the main stream of Romanticism had about run its course. The decline was marked by the appearance of what was thought to be the new style of Impressionism. Just as the Renaissance had faded into Mannerism and the Baroque into Rococo, the refined essence of Romanticism was distilled into a final stage named after the painting style of Monet, Degas, Renoir, and others.

The so-called "impressionistic" music of Debussy and Ravel—Debussy detested the term "impressionism"—spearheaded a French revolt against the domination of German Romanticism and particularly the overwhelming exuberance of Wagner. The competition of German and French nationalism was a major factor in the Impressionist movement. Debussy cultivated an art that was subtle, delicate, and discreet, an art that was a sensuous rather than an emotional experience. For Debussy, German Romanticism was ponderous and tedious whereas French music possessed the Gallic spirit of elegance and refinement.

Many similarities exist between the painting of the Impressionists and the sophisticated music of Debussy and Ravel. The Impressionists tried to capture the play of color and light; favorite images included dappled sunlight through leaves and the play of light on water, fields, flowers, and buildings. The musicians dealt with an art of movement that attempted to translate this interplay of color and light into shimmering sounds.

Closely related to Impressionism in painting and music was the symbolism of the French poets, Mallarmé, Verlaine, and Baudelaire. They achieved an indefiniteness with words that had been the privilege of music alone. They likened their poetry to music and sought tone color in word sounds and symbolic meanings of words rather than any definite meaning. Wordplay, as with the tonal play of impressionistic music, was, according to Verlaine, "the gray song where the indefinite meets the precise."

The effects that musical impressionism achieved were the result of a number of innovations and extensions of musical resources.

Stylistic Characteristics

Modes

The old church modes came into favor again during late Romanticism and were exploited further by the impressionists. The effects they sought were counter to the clear tonality of the major-minor system. The modes, among other scales, provided a wider range of colors and a vagueness of tonality.

Other Scales

A strong Asian influence was reflected in the use of the pentatonic scale (five-tone scale) that is the basis for the folk music of Bali, China, and other Asian cultures.

Pentatonic scale

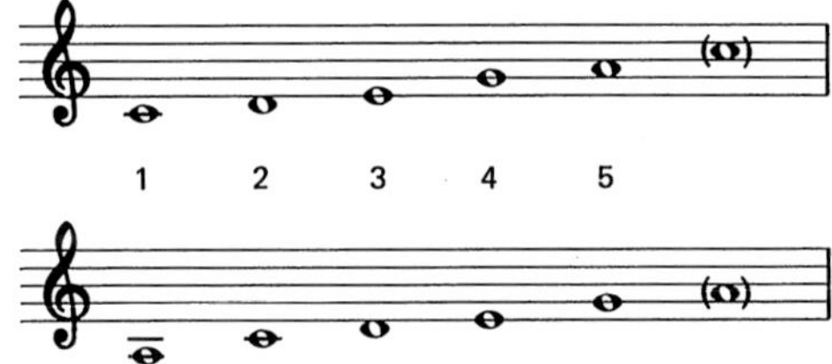

Particularly appropriate for the vague tonalities and drifting harmonies of impressionism was the whole-tone scale. This was a six-tone scale with a whole step between each pitch. With all tones equidistant, there was no clear tonal center. In fact, there were only two whole-tone scales possible: one starting on a white note and ending on a black note, and the other starting on a black note and ending on a white note.

Whole-tone scale

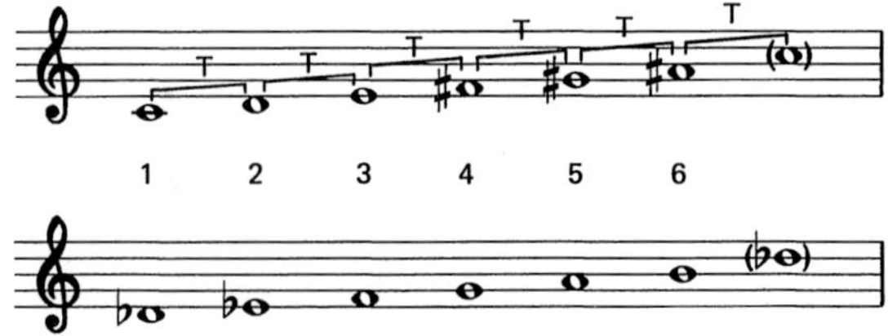

4. CD 2, track 17.
5. CD 3, track 4.
6. CD 2, track 18.

Form

Classical forms were generally abandoned in favor of the vague outlines, drifting quality, and dreamlike effects so basic to the style. This is not to say that the music is formless—there is a beginning, middle, and end—but rather that the forms are subtle and dictated by the impressions sought by the composer.

Orchestration

The massed woodwind and/or brass sounds of the orchestras of Brahms and Wagner were anathema to the impressionists. They replaced the dark and ponderous sound of the Germanic orchestras with a much lighter, shimmering effect and much more individualistic use of instruments. They delighted in the exotic sounds of the English horn and the flutes and clarinets in the low register. Violins frequently played in extremely high registers and were often muted. Trumpets and horns, too, were frequently muted. The characteristic sounds of the orchestra were supplemented by the harp, triangle, lightly brushed cymbals, and the bell tones of the small keyboard instrument called the celeste. The treatment of the pure sounds of the individual instruments was very much like the use of tiny brushstrokes of pure colors by the painters.

The piano remained a favorite instrument for the impressionists, but the sounds had little in common with the style, for example, of Chopin. The emphasis was on coloration, sensation, subtle harmonic effects, delicacy of tone. Everything was programmatic, whether a tonal description of a specific event or the evocation of a general idea, image, or sensation.

Claude Debussy, 1862–1918

Claude Debussy (deh-buh-see; fig. 24.9) used shifting harmonies and tone colors to suggest the shimmering effects of light and shade in the paintings of the Impressionists. His music has a luminous quality that compares with, for example, Renoir's sun-dappled nudes. Below is a piano composition that is titled "Voiles" (Fr., "Sails"). Using the whole-tone scale and a bit of pentatonic, Debussy weaves drifting patterns of melody and harmony that encourage the listener to make any association appropriate to the music and the ambiguous one-word title.

Listening Example 38

PIANO SOLO

Debussy, Preludes for Piano, Book I, 2nd movement, "Voiles"
1913

Time: 2:42
Cassette 2, track 30

Preludes for Piano, Book 1, Second movement, "Voiles (Sails)"

Debussy (1862–1918)

24.9 Claude Debussy. Photo: Free Library of Philadelphia.

SUMMARY

Some of the elements of nineteenth-century Romanticism were present in the later works of Beethoven, but the lyric strains of full-blown Romanticism were paramount in the vocal and instrumental works of Franz Schubert. The characteristic style of German art songs (*Lieder*) which he created was developed by the German composers Schumann, Brahms, and Wolf. Frédéric Chopin made the piano his personal instrument with his unique style, and the very nature of Romanticism reinforced this individuality of personal expression. The music of Tchaikovsky, Brahms, Verdi, Bizet, and Puccini reflected this intensely subjective approach to artistic experience. They, like Rousseau, if not better than other men, were "at least different."

The decline of absolute music in favor of a full range of miniature to grandiose program music was probably the most significant musical characteristic of the century. The abstract titles of the eighteenth century (sonata, serenade, symphony) were, to a considerable extent, abandoned for descriptive or poetic titles. Dreamy nocturnes, cute capriccios, and dashing rhapsodies were distinguished more by sound and fury than by strong intrinsic design. Filled with emotion for its own sake and thus unabashedly sentimental, and lacking also the disciplined energy of the pre-Napoleonic era, Romantic music provided the sounding-board of the age.

The latter part of the century saw a gradual leveling off in the growth of the symphony orchestra. The tone poems of Strauss and the huge vocal-instrumental works of Mahler and Bruckner represented a point of no return, a stage reached after a reaction against the grandiloquence had already set in. Brahms responded to the extravagant use of musical materials and orchestral sounds by deliberately returning to the more disciplined practices of an earlier age. Debussy, Ravel, and other impressionists sharply reduced the orchestra in order to concentrate on the pure tone colors of individual instruments. However, they did continue in the Romantic tradition of program music, carrying it to its ultimate conclusion with techniques similar to those used in the Symbolist poetry of Mallarmé and Verlaine. The transition from nineteenth-century Romanticism to the so-called "new music" of the twentieth century was accomplished in large part by the impressionists, who inaugurated many of the materials of modern music while writing the final chapter of Romantic music.

CULTURE AND HUMAN VALUES

Though we live in an era not particularly notable for romantic sentiment, nineteenth-century music still forms a large part of today's musical repertoire. Why is the Romantic style still so popular?

Some of this appeal would have to be attributed to its familiarity: American audiences are notorious for their attachment to the tried and true compositions of the past. There is, however, an additional appeal that seems to have an enduring value—the fervent individualism of Romantic composers. The music of Chopin, for example, is totally unique, as is the music of Brahms, Verdi, and others. Each Romantic composer was fiercely independent and self-consciously "different."

Many of us are painfully aware of the anonymity of modern life in which people feel that they are little more than facts and figures imprisoned in the memory bank of a computer. Romantic composers, by contrast, loom large as heroic individuals from a recent past.

Romantic music is also unabashedly emotional, dramatically revealing the strains and stresses of life in all its complexity. Restraint is not a characteristic of the Romantic style. Nor can we say that our own era is particularly noted for restraint; in fact, energy, emotion, and dramatic intensity are notable components of much of modern music, with particular reference to several styles of rock.

There is, perhaps, more than a trace of nostalgia in our fondness for the Romantic style. Here is daring and derring-do. Laced with sentiment and surging emotions, Romanticism appeals to a large and faithful cross-section of today's audiences.

STUDY QUESTIONS

What, exactly, is a virtuoso? Can you identify some of today's virtuosos?

ADDITIONAL LISTENING

1. Chopin, Mazurka No. 24 in C, Op. 33 No. 3 (1838). The form of this piano solo is ABA (CD 2, track 11).
2. Wagner, *Lohengrin*, Prelude to Act III. This is a good illustration of the dynamic Wagnerian style at its best (CD 2, track 16).
3. Franck, Violin Sonata in A, last movement. This features a canon between the violin and piano (CD 3/1).
4. Sousa, *Hands Across the Sea*. The "March King" was an outstanding Romantic composer. The form is standard march form: an introduction followed by AABBCDC (CD 3, track 3).

CHAPTER 25

Nineteenth-Century Art: Conflict and Diversity

THE ROMANTIC MOVEMENT AND THE NEOCLASSIC STYLE

The Romantic movement first manifested itself in literature and music in the poetry of Wordsworth and Coleridge and the *Lieder* of Schubert. The visual arts were, however, in thrall to David, Napoleon's court painter, and to Napoleon's determination to confirm the legitimacy of his empire with the classical architecture of Imperial Rome. In 1806 Napoleon commissioned Jean François Chalgrin (shal-gre; 1739–1811) to construct a mighty arch to honor the victories of the French fighting forces (fig. 25.1). Placed in the center of twelve radiating avenues, the arch is 164 feet (49 m) in height and 148 feet (44.5 m) wide, larger than the triumphal arch of any Caesar. It stands today at the climax of the Avenue des Champs Elysées over the tomb of the Unknown Soldier, commemorating French imperial glory and the military triumphs of an emperor who did not live to see its completion.

The Church of St. Mary Magdalen, known as The Madeleine (fig. 25.2), was originally begun in 1764 and later razed to be replaced by a building modeled after the Pantheon in Rome. Napoleon required a new temple, a massive building dedicated to the glory of his Grand Army. The Madeleine has fifty-two majestic Corinthian columns running completely round the building, each 66 feet (20 m) tall. The eight-column front and complete **peristyle** are reminiscent of the Parthenon, but the podium, 23 feet (7 m) in height, is of Roman origin and similar to the Maison Carrée. Napoleon's Temple of Glory (also completed after his death) is a skillful synthesis of Graeco-Roman elements in a unified and imposing design.

Opposite Claude, Monet, *Rouen Cathedral, West Facade Sunlight*, detail of fig. 25.28. 1894. Oil on canvas, full painting 39½ × 26" (100.3 × 66 cm). National Gallery of Art, Washington, D.C. (Chester Dale Collection).

25.1 *Above* Jean François Chalgrin (and others), Arch of Triumph, Place Charles de Gaulle, Paris, eastern facade. 1806–36. Photo: Giraudon, Paris.

25.2 *Right* Pierre Vignon, The Madeleine, Paris. 1806–42. Photo: Viollet, Paris.

Jean-Auguste-Dominique Ingres, 1780–1867

Only nine years old when the revolution began, Ingres (ãgre) was never an enthusiastic supporter of Napoleon's self-proclaimed revolutionary ideals. He was, however, David's most talented pupil and an advocate of a Neoclassic style that had evolved from revolutionary art into state-endorsed dogma. Contending that David's style was too heavily incised, Ingres developed a fluid drawing technique influenced by Pompeiian frescoes and patterned after the elegant linear figures of Greek vase paintings. His *Grande Odalisque* (fig. 25.3) is not a classical version of feminine beauty; it is, however, a superb example of the artist's unique mix of Neoclassic and Romantic ideas. The reclining-nude pose can be traced to Titian and the smoothly flowing contours of the sculpturesque body are coolly classical; but the subject is an odalisque, a harem slave girl who represents an exotic concept dear to the Romantics. The small head, elongated limbs, and languid pose are very mannered in the decorative style of Parmigianino (see fig. 17.40).

25.4 *Right* Francisco de Goya, *Majas on a Balcony*. 1810–15. Oil on canvas, 6' 4¾" × 4' 1½" (1.95 × 1.26 m). Metropolitan Museum of Art, New York (Bequest of Mrs. H. O. Havemayer, 1929; H. O. Havemeyer Collection). Photo: Bridgeman, London.

25.3 *Below* Jean-Auguste-Dominique Ingres, *Grande Odalisque*. 1814. Oil on canvas, 35¼ × 63¾" (89.5 × 161.9 cm). Louvre, Paris.

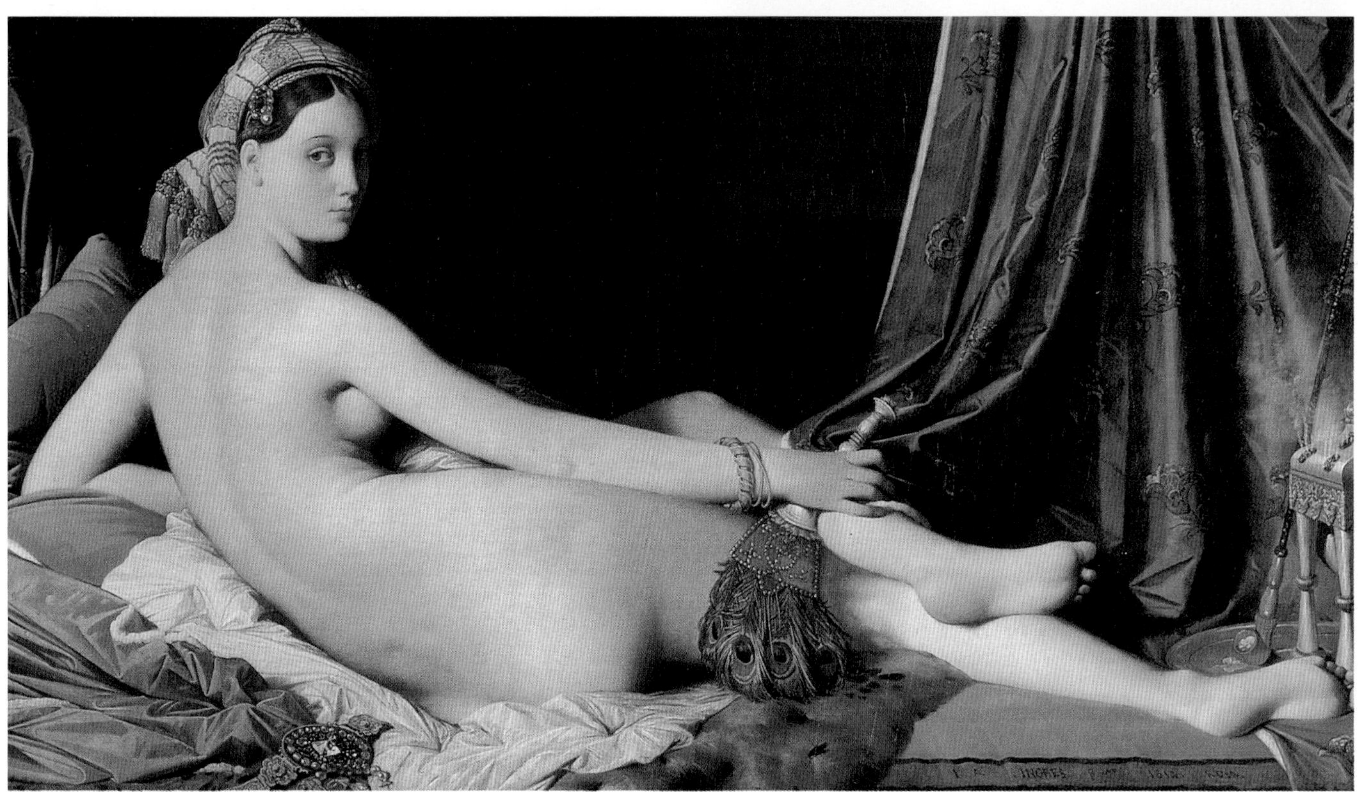

Francisco de Goya, 1746–1828

The first of the illustrious painters of the Romantic era, Goya (GO-ya) was unique even in a time of remarkably individualistic artists. A contemporary of David, with whom he had nothing in common, Goya was influenced by Velasquez and Rembrandt, but not at all by antiquity or the Renaissance. Excelling in both portraiture and vigorous action canvases, Goya was appointed painter to the court of Spain in 1799. In his many acutely candid studies of the incompetent royal family of Charles IV that presided over a corrupt and decadent administration he was both a Romantic and a realist. Representing his Romantic bent is the portraiture in *Majas on a Balcony* (fig. 25.4) which, at first glance, appears to be a lovely portrayal of two pretty, elegantly dressed women. But who are the shadowy figures in the background? The painting is a study in strong contrasts: light and dark; colorful foreground and drab background; beauty and menace. Goya may be making a statement but we cannot be certain of his intention. What is irrefutable, of course, is the ambiguity of Romantic art, of which this is a superb example.

Goya extended his critical appraisal of the royal family to a general view of human folly, vice, and stupidity as depicted in a series of eighty etchings called "The Caprices." He had sold only twenty-seven copies when the Inquisition shut down the enterprise. Then, in 1808, Napoleon's invasion and conquest of Spain provided the artist with a powerful new subject: the bestiality and utter futility of war. Goya and many of his countrymen had hoped for French reforms of the debased Spanish court; instead, the merciless brutality of French soldiers provoked an equally savage resistance. Among the tragic results were a series of executions of Spanish patriots. Commissioned in 1814 by a liberal government after the expulsion of the French, Goya selected the executions of the Third of May (fig. 25.5) to vividly portray the underside of Napoleonic conquest. The firing squad is a faceless monster with many legs. Firing at point-blank range—the usual procedure for these executions—the soldiers operate in a symbolic blackness of night illuminated only by a single lamp. This is probably the first of its kind, a work of art that protests against the barbarism of military conquest. Later in the century, so-called social-protest works of art became ever more common as artists attacked a variety of social evils. Careful study of Goya's painting, of the dead and those about to die, reveals a powerful universal statement about the lot of common people at the mercy of invading armies.

In a series of unforgettable etchings called "The Disasters of War," Goya brilliantly depicted the sordid consequences of warfare. His *Grande hazaña! Con muertos!* ("Great exploit! In corpses!"; fig. 25.6) imparts the horror of

25.5 Francisco de Goya, *The Third of May, 1808, at Madrid: The Shootings on Príncipe Pío Mountain*. 1814. Oil on canvas, 8' 8¾ × 11' 3⅞" (2.66 × 3.45 m). Museo del Prado, Madrid. Photo: Bridgeman, London.

25.6 Francisco de Goya, *Grand hazaña! Con muertos!*, from "The Disasters of War." Ca. 1814. Etching, edition of 1863. Private collection. Photo: Violllet, Paris.

25.7 Théodore Géricault, *The Raft of the "Medusa."* 1818–19. Oil on canvas, 16' × 23' 6" (4.8 × 7.05 m). Louvre, Paris.

mutilation and violent death with a startling economy of means. Goya stands with Euripides of *The Trojan Women* in his convincing portrayal of the senselessness of warfare.

Goya's art was intensely personal and impossible to classify. He was a true Romantic, however, in his refusal to place much faith in reason, that goddess of the Enlightenment—the era that ended in bloody revolution, the Reign of Terror, and Napoleon. Goya left Spain in 1824 during a period of repression and died in self-imposed exile in France. His art was not known outside Spain until late in the Romantic era.

Théodore Géricault, 1791–1824

The most talented French painter of early Romanticism, Géricault (zhay-ree-ko) won artistic immortality with his painting of *The Raft of the "Medusa"* (fig. 25.7). Like other Romantic artists, Géricault seized on a contemporary event, a tragedy that caused a national scandal, as his subject matter. Jammed with colonists bound for French West Africa in 1816, the *Medusa* ran aground off the African coast because of the incompetence of the ship's captain, who then filled the *Medusa*'s six life-boats with his own party and sailed safely to shore, leaving about 150 men and one woman to shift for themselves.[1] In the painting, the few remaining survivors on their makeshift raft have just sighted a rescue

ship on the horizon and are frantically signaling for help. This was the *Argus*, which did not sight the raft until the following day. Géricault researched the tragedy like an investigative reporter, interviewing survivors, studying corpses in the morgue, even building a raft to scale in his studio. The result is not just a realistic reporting of the event but a drama of heroic proportions of men against the sea. The slashing diagonals and vivid chiaroscuro lead our eye to the triangle formed by the extended arms, with the waving figure at the apex; all movement is projected forward toward the distant sail. There is no movement in the left foreground, however, where an older man broods over the youthful corpse sprawled across his lap. The dejected man seems to be mourning the inhuman price all of them had to pay, for this composition is taken from an earlier sketch depicting the cannibalism that kept the survivors alive. But, if these men had been adrift for fourteen days with almost no provisions, why do the figures look so muscular, so healthy? Simply stated, emaciated figures with shriveled flesh and horrible wounds would be pitiful, tugging too directly on our emotions. But these sturdy figures transmit such power that we are lifted past the particular to the universal. This is how you turn a catastrophe into art.

Géricault's graphic realism was characteristic of the Romantic intent to shock the sensibilities of the viewer and evoke an emotional response. Government attempts to cover up the errors of a French naval officer stirred the public to a frenzy and focused attention on the painting as a political statement, much to the artist's dismay. (Géricault had at first hoped to avoid this reaction by calling the painting *Scene of Shipwreck*.) However, the *Medusa* affair has receded into history, leaving behind this vivid example of social-protest art whose timeless appeal transcends the tragedy that inspired it.

Eugène Delacroix, 1799–1863

Following Géricault's early death as a result of a riding accident, Delacroix (de-la-krwah), a peerless colorist, became the leading Romantic artist. The expansion of the French colonial empire into north Africa (beginning with Algeria in 1830) opened new vistas to French writers and artists. The first major French artist to visit Islamic countries, Delacroix was fascinated with the colorful vitality of Muslim cultures. In *Arabs Skirmishing in the Mountains* (fig. 25.8 and p. 280) he demonstrates a vibrant range of intense hues and strong contrasts of light and dark. As the artist wrote in one of his journals, "the more the contrast the greater the force." His ability to capture the illusion of movement makes the dramatic impact of the pitched battle all the more convincing. Continuing the squabble between color and line (one aspect of Romanticism versus Classicism), Delacroix was the Rubenist and his rival, Ingres, the Poussinist of the early nineteenth century. For a colorist such as Delacroix the perfect style, as he said, was a combination of Michelangelo and the recently discovered Goya.

25.8 Eugène Delacroix, *Arabs Skirmishing in the Mountains*. 1863. Oil on linen, 36⅜ × 29⅜" (92.5 × 74.6 cm). National Gallery of Art, Washington, D.C. (Chester Dale Fund).

Romantic painters were enamored of the sister arts: the plays of Shakespeare, medieval romances, English romantic poetry, and especially music. Delacroix preferred, surprisingly, the classical style of Mozart to the flamboyant romanticism of his French contemporary Hector Berlioz but he was a friend of Chopin, whose poetic piano music had a special appeal, not only for Delacroix, but also for many writers and artists of the time. His portrait of Chopin (see fig. 24.2) epitomizes the melancholy suffering of the Romantic genius.

John Constable, 1776–1837

English artists responded more readily to Rousseau's back-to-nature movement than to the ideological drive of the French Revolution and subsequent Napoleonic wars. English Romantic poets—Wordsworth, Coleridge, Shelley, Keats—described the beauties of nature in highly personal

1. For details of the century's worst French scandal prior to the Dreyfus Case, see Alexander McKee's *Death Raft: The Human Drama of the Medusa Shipwreck* (New York: Warner Books, Inc., 1977).

25.9 John Constable, *Wivenhoe Park, Essex.* 1816. Oil on canvas, 22⅛ × 39⅞" (56.2 × 101.3 cm). National Gallery of Art, Washington, D.C. (Widener Collection).

terms. Landscape was prominent in their poetry but not as description for its own sake; rather, poets responded to aspects of the natural scene that stimulated their thinking, leading to meditations on nature that, as Wordsworth observed, involved the "Mind of Man." On the other hand, nature was frequently the subject matter for Romantic painters. Constable, one of the finest of all English painters, studied landscapes with a scientific objectivity. Rather than simply recording actual objects he sought the intangible qualities of atmosphere, light, and sky. The justly famed "Constable sky" is the dominating element in his poetic response to the peaceful scene at Wivenhoe Park, Essex (fig. 25.9). Sunlight shining on the wind-driven clouds and the effect of sunshine on fields and water have a luminosity rivaling even the Dutch masters, and the entire canvas has a freshness never before achieved in painting. The lustrous sky is the crowning glory of the picture, triumphantly confirming the artist's claim that this area was the "principal instrument for expressing sentiment." After his first exposure to Constable's work, Delacroix repainted the sky of an already completed work; the Impressionists were no less dazzled by the skies of Constable.

Joseph M. W. Turner, 1775–1851

The Impressionists, especially Monet, were just as enthralled by the heightened, liberated colors of Turner, Constable's eminent contemporary. A Londoner by birth and preference, Turner had none of Constable's attachment to peaceful nature. He was fascinated by light, the bright southern light of Italian cities, especially Venice. His sensitivity to light enabled him to develop a subtle, colorful art of freedom and refinement. His concentration on light and extreme effects of storms, sunsets, and fires put him ahead of his time and his indifference to finished details made his art unique. His *Keelmen Heaving Coals by Moonlight* (fig. 25.10) includes many of Turner's prized effects: moonlight, fires, and the use of color for atmospheric effects. The details are typically unclear with an overall effect that reveals Turner at his Romantic best.

25.10 Joseph M. W. Turner, *Keelmen Heaving Coals by Moonlight*. Probably 1835. Oil on canvas, 36¼ × 48¼" (92.1 × 122.5 cm). National Gallery of Art, Washington, D.C. (Widener Collection).

Thomas Cole, 1801–48

American Romanticism had all the characteristics of the European variety but with some distinct variations that reflected a youthful nation in the New World. George Catlin, for example, spent many years studying and painting various Indian tribes, and John James Audubon devoted twelve years to the publication of his monumental *Birds of America*. But it was the American landscape that enthralled Thomas Cole and many other artists.

Cole emigrated from England to Philadelphia at the age of seventeen and later became an influential member of a group of artists now known as the Hudson River School. Cole and his colleagues viewed their landscape paintings as a high moral imperative in which they celebrated the beauty and purity of the American wilderness. In his *Essay on American Scenery* Cole pointed out that "the most distinctive, and perhaps the most impressive characteristic of American scenery is its wildness." He contrasted this with civilized Europe in which "the primitive features of scenery have long since been destroyed or modified." With its relatively untouched forests and mountains and newly established republic, the United States was viewed as the new Eden, the light and hope of an exhausted Old World. Cole's view of *The Oxbow* (fig. 25.11) is an elaborate celebration of nature, a realistic depiction of an actual location with Romantic overtones of an idealized storm that, along with the twisted tree, helps frame the river. As with most of Cole's paintings, the human figure (right foreground) is dwarfed by the majesty of nature. Currently there is a considerable revival of interest in the work of the Hudson River School occasioned, in part, by environmental concerns. Depictions of the new Eden are, after all, only about a century and a half in a past that can never be recaptured.

George Caleb Bingham, 1811–79

Bingham pursued still another aspect of American Romanticism. Though he was born in Virginia he moved to Missouri when he was eight, there to paint the fur traders, boatmen, and politicians in what was then raw frontier country. This was also Mark Twain country, and one can find many images in the artist's work that illustrate life on the

25.11 Thomas Cole, *The Oxbow: View from Mount Holyoke, Northampton, Massachusetts, After a Thunderstorm*. 1836. Oil on canvas, 4' 3½" × 6' 4" (1.31 × 1.93 m). Metropolitan Museum of Art, New York (Gift of Mrs. Russel Sage, 1908. 08.228).

25.12 George Caleb Bingham, *Fur Traders Descending the Missouri*. Ca. 1845. Oil on canvas, 29 × 36½" (73.7 × 92.7 cm). Metropolitan Museum of Art, New York (Morris K. Jesup Fund, 1933.33.61).

Missouri and Mississippi rivers as described in Twain's novels. *Fur Traders Descending the Missouri* (fig. 25.12) communicates some of the mystery and mystique of life on the leading edge of a developing nation. Bingham saw these figures as exotic explorers of the American wilderness—the first title for the painting was "French Trader and Half-Breed Son." His use of primary colors (red, yellow, blue) for the figures is echoed in the landscape by paler hues throughout the composition. The two figures stare out at us as though they are momentarily frozen in time. Though the water is like a mirror we still have the impression of watery motion from right to left. This is clearly a Romantic work but there are classical overtones in the balanced design, luminous light, and meticulous purity of details.

25.13 Robert Scott Duncanson, *Blue Hole, Flood Waters, Little Miami River*. 1851. Oil on canvas, 42¼ × 29¼" (107.3 × 74.3 cm). Cincinnati Art Museum (Gift of Norbert Heerman and Arthur Helbig).

Robert Scott Duncanson, 1817–72

Influenced by the Hudson River School, Duncanson was recognized in his own time as an exceptional landscape painter. His *Blue Hole* (fig. 25.13), like much of Thomas Cole's work, has a double scale: the fishermen have been made very small so that the enlarged landscape can dominate the composition. Like other artists in the Hudson River tradition, Duncanson regarded America, with its magnificent landscapes towering over insignificant human beings, as the new Garden of Eden.

Architectural Inspiration from the Past

The largest and most successful architectural recollection of the past was the Houses of Parliament in London, designed by Sir Charles Barry (1795–1860) with the assistance of Gothic scholar Augustus Welby Pugin (1812–52; fig. 25.14). More than the French or Germans, the English felt that the Gothic style was an exemplary expression of the national past, a heritage both noble and Christian. Consequently, a parliamentary commission decreed that the

25.14 Barry and Pugin, The Houses of Parliament, London. 1836–60. Photo: John Bethell, St. Albans, U.K.

design for the new seat of government be either Gothic or Elizabethan and nothing else. Barry favored the Neoclassic style, but Pugin convinced him that the English Late Gothic style was the proper glorification of the British spirit and a celebration of medieval craftsmanship in the face of mass-produced items of the industrial age. Actually, the body of the building is symmetrical in the Palladian manner surmounted by a Gothic fantasy of turrets, towers, and battlements.

Inspired by the design of Parliament, the Gothic Revival style was enthusiastically adopted by English and American architects. Constructed at the very end of the revival by a timber contractor, the Victorian Gothic mansion in California (fig. 25.15) is a wooden frame structure with an incredible variety of surface decoration and detail. "More is better" was a Victorian preference that is exuberantly realized in this prize example of American Gothic.

REALISM

Millet, Corot, and the Barbizon School

Countering the Romantic fantasies of their literary and artistic contemporaries, the realists concentrated on the real world as they perceived it, with an objective matter-of-factness that alienated the followers of Géricault and Delacroix. Settling near the village of Barbizon in the Forest of Fontainebleau south of Paris, painters of the Barbizon School imitated Rousseau's back-to-nature movement while simultaneously escaping the disorder and confusion of the 1848 Revolution. Rousseau's "noble savage" was interpreted by Barbizon painter, François Millet (me-yay; 1814–75), as a heroic peasant who exemplified the dignity of working the land. In *The Gleaners* (fig. 25.16) Millet's peasants have the monumentality of Michelangelo and an earthy quality comparable to the bourgeois Dutch tradition. Himself the son of peasants, Millet chose to live the life of a peasant and he sympathetically depicted his figures as actors in a kind of divine drama in a style antithetical to the French academic tradition.[2]

25.15 Carson Mansion, Eureka, California. Ca. 1885. Photo: Esto (Wayne Andrews).

2. Disdained since about 1860 as artistically inferior, French academic art has, since about 1965, experienced a rebirth. See, for example, *The Encyclopedia of World Art,* vol. XVI (New York: McGraw-Hill, 1983), pp. 230–1.

Though he did not consider himself a member of the Barbizon School, Jean-Baptiste-Camille Corot (ko-row; 1796–1875) lived in the area and shared their strong commitment to direct visual experience. In the *Ville d'Avray* (fig. 25.17) Corot painted the full range of light and dark values, depicting visual reality at a single moment in time, as in a photograph. Working very quickly, Corot sought the underlying rhythm of nature, composing his landscapes so that the magic moment of truth would be revealed to all. One of the finest Western landscape painters, Corot became, according to the poet Baudelaire, "the master of an entire younger generation."

25.18 Honoré Daumier, *Le Ventre Legislatif*. 1834. Lithograph. Arizona State University Art Collections, Arizona State University, Tempe, Arizona (Gift of Oliver B. James).

Honoré Daumier, 1808–79

Corot, Millet, and the Barbizon School can be described as Romantic realists for there is an element of escapism in their work. In Paris, however, the realities of political and social unrest before and after the 1848 Revolution were of far greater concern to a hard-bitten realist such as Daumier (doe-me-ay). Known to his contemporaries as a caricaturist, Daumier created over 4,000 **lithographs**[3] satirizing the major and minor foibles of the day. In his caricature of *Le Ventre Legislatif* ("The Legislative Belly"; fig. 25.18) Daumier depicted the venality, pomposity, and stupidity of the collective "Legislative Belly," that is, "Body." With devastating candor Daumier gives us a cast of characters all too well known in the body politic of democratic societies.

Daumier was just as forceful a contemporary social critic in oils as he was in his lithographs, claiming that scenes of contemporary everyday life had to be painted because "one must be of one's own time." In *Third-Class Carriage* (fig. 25.19) he used a strong chiaroscuro in the manner of Rembrandt, whom he greatly admired, to depict the isolation of each figure in the railway car; each person is utterly alone with his or her own thoughts. This painting is both Romantic and realistic. Daumier accurately caught a stark moment in the anonymity of urban life but the painting is suffused with the emotion of an artist who has sympathetically identified with a car full of lonely strangers.

25.16 *Opposite, top* Jean-François Millet, *The Gleaners*. 1857. Oil on canvas, 33 × 44" (83.8 × 111.8 cm). Louvre, Paris. Photo: R.M.N., Paris.

25.17 *Opposite, bottom* Jean-Baptiste-Camille Corot, *Ville d'Avray*. 1870. Oil on canvas, 21⅝ × 31½" (54.9 × 80 cm). The Metropolitan Museum of Art, New York (Bequest of Catherine Lorillard Wolfe, 1887). Photo: Tintometer Ltd., Salisbury, U.K.

25.19 Honoré Daumier, *Third-Class Carriage*. Ca. 1862. Oil on canvas, 25¼ × 35½" (65.4 × 90.2 cm). Metropolitan Museum of Art, New York (Bequest of Mrs. H. O. Havemeyer, 1929; H. O. Havemeyer Collection. 29.100.129). Photo: Schecter Lee.

Gustave Courbet, 1819–77

Realism in art was given a name and a leader in the person of Courbet (koor-bay), who issued a "Manifesto of Realism." At the Andler Keller, one of the first Parisian beer halls, the swaggering, flamboyant Courbet held forth as the champion of the physical world of visible objects. "Show me an angel," he once remarked, "and I will paint you an angel."

3. One of the graphic arts, lithography is a printmaking process that was widely used in the nineteenth century for newspaper and magazine illustrations. In lithography (Gk., "writing on stone") the design is drawn on stone or a metal plate with a greasy printing ink and then reproduced by the standard printing process.

Courbet found his natural subjects in the common people of his home village of Ornans in eastern France. As he said, "to paint a bit of country, one must know it. I know my country." *Burial at Ornans* (fig. 25.20) depicts a rural scene on a monumental scale normally reserved for epic historical events. Much to the consternation of the critics, Courbet turned the somber reality of this simple country funeral into a noble occasion that he called "true history." Combining religious symbolism with realism, Courbet included the dog as it was depicted in the Office of the Dead in medieval manuscripts; the people were all painted from life in innumerable sittings demanded by the artist. Composed on a horizontal S-curve, the figures of clergy, pall-bearers, friends, and relatives stand in poses ranging from indifference to composed grief. The staff with the crucifix is positioned to give the illusion of Christ's death on Golgotha. This and other paintings were rejected by the Universal Exposition, leading to the construction of a shed, called by Courbet "The Pavilion of Realism," for the exhibition of his uncompromising works.

Winslow Homer, 1836–1910

Realism spread throughout Europe as artists were attracted to the style, but it was especially popular in the United States, where pragmatism and realism were characteristics of the American way of life. Beginning his career as an illustrator for *Harper's Weekly,* Winslow Homer was influenced by Corot and Courbet, but not at the expense of his American point of view. Homer lived during the post-Civil War era that Mark Twain called the Gilded Age, a grossly materialistic era of pretentious opulence, but his style was firmly fixed in genre paintings in the mode of American realism. In *Breezing Up* (fig. 25.21) Homer celebrated his lifelong love-affair with the sea in a joyous composition of wind, salt air, and sparkling sea. Fatigued but happy with the day's catch, the fisherman and boys are returning home. With the catboat placed at eye-level and slanting away from the viewer, we are drawn into an illusion of movement and the feeling of a job well done. Exemplifying Homer's statement, "When I have selected a thing carefully, I paint it exactly as it appears," the details are finely drawn: wrinkled clothes, light sparkling from metal fittings, a lighthouse at the lower left, a wheeling gull at the upper right. Homer's ability to give the illusion of light emanating from his canvases paralleled the development of French Impressionism across the ocean.

Homer's career was remarkably divergent from that of his older contemporary, author Herman Melville. Both were New Englanders, fascinated by the sea, but Homer's vision was generally positive whereas Melville's was darkly ambiguous. Homer covered the Civil War as an illustrator for *Harper's Weekly*; Melville wrote two volumes of war poems that were totally unknown at the time. Homer was a highly successful and popular painter; Melville was not recognized as one of America's greatest writers until many years after his unremarked death. Both were realists.

Thomas Eakins, 1844–1916

Eakins (ay-kins) called Homer the best living American artist, but Eakins himself ranks, with Homer, as one of the very best of American artists. His *The Gross Clinic* (fig. 25.22) is a monumental work. The scene is Philadelphia's Jefferson Medical Clinic, in which Dr. Gross and his surgical team are operating. Much in the manner of Rembrandt (see fig. 21.19) the focus is precisely on the chief surgeon and the incision in the leg of the anesthetized patient, whose mother on the left (present as a legal requirement) cannot bear to watch. As was customary at the time, the doctors

25.20 Gustave Courbet, *Burial at Ornans*. 1849–50. Oil on canvas, ca. 10' 6" × 13' (3.2 × 3.9 m). Musée d'Orsay, Paris. Photo: R.M.N., Paris.

25.21 *Above* Winslow Homer, *Breezing Up (A Fair Wind).* 1876. Oil on canvas, 24⅛ × 38⅛" (61.3 × 96.8 cm). National Gallery of Art, Washington, D.C. (Gift of the W. I. and May T. Mellon Foundation, 1943).

wear street clothing (as did Eakins himself, on the far right). Not surprisingly, considering the era, the uncompromising realism of the painting raised a storm of objections. Though submitted for the Philadelphia Centennial of 1876, it was shunted aside and ended up in the obscurity of the U.S. Army Post Hospital exhibit. Eakins was never popular with the general public or with most critics of the time.

Architecture

Realism in painting can be compared, to some extent, with the development of late-nineteenth-century architecture. Abandoning copies of older styles, architects turned to modern building materials to design functional structures serving specific purposes. Epitomizing the new attitude toward utilitarian design, the Crystal Palace (fig. 25.23) was constructed of 5,000 prefabricated iron columns and girders and nearly 300,000 panes of glass. A gardener and greenhouse designer by profession, Sir Joseph Paxton (1801–65) oversaw the construction of an immense structure that covered eighteen acres in Hyde Park and contained almost a million square feet of floor space. Ironically, this first truly modern building was a response to an emergency brought about by the dithering of the Building Commission, which was unable to select a winning design from the more than

25.22 Thomas Eakins, *The Gross Clinic*. 1875. Oil on canvas, 8' × 6' 6" (2.4 × 1.95 m). Jefferson Medical College of Thomas Jefferson University, Philadelphia.

25.23 Joseph Paxton, Crystal Palace, London. 1850–1. Cast iron, wrought iron, and glass. Engraving (R. P. Cuff after W. B. Brounger). Royal Institute of British Architects, London (Drawings Collection).

200 submitted. The Crystal Palace won by default because only Paxton's advanced technology could create a building in the little time remaining.

Assembled in only thirty-nine weeks, the Crystal Palace housed London's "Great Exhibition of the Works of All Nations of 1851," a triumphant display of the miracles wrought by the industrial revolution. The theme of the exhibition was "Progress," represented by the mechanized marvels within the glittering structure, itself a symbol of the "Age of Progress." The first of many similar buildings, the Crystal Palace was dismantled after the exhibition and reassembled south of London where, in 1936, it was destroyed by fire. Though cast-iron structures were vulnerable to fire, the Crystal Palace did establish the practicality of metal as a building material. With the invention of the Bessemer process of making steel in 1856, the technology became available for the construction of bridges and twentieth-century high-rise buildings.

Using iron chains, suspension bridges had been built since the early 1800s. With the use of flexible steel cables suspension bridges became the dominant form of what was known then as engineering and today as another form of architecture. The first of these structures was also one of the best, both functionally and architecturally. Designed and built by J. A. Roebling (1806–69) and his son W. A. Roebling (1837–1926), the Brooklyn Bridge (fig. 25.24) connected Manhattan with Brooklyn. Featuring Gothic pointed arches, the two massive towers are built of granite and connected by four huge parallel cables, each containing over 5,000 strands of wire spun on the site.

25.25 *Opposite* Gustave Eiffel, Eiffel Tower, Paris. 1889. Original poster produced by Ch. Parvillers. Photo: Mansell Collection, London.

25.24 John A. and W. A. Roebling, Brooklyn Bridge, New York. 1869–83. Span 1,595' (480 m). Photo: Hulton Deutsch, London.

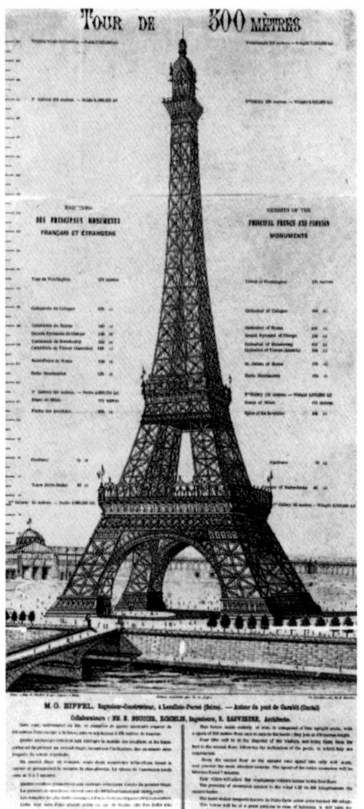

The first high-rise structure in the world was designed by an engineer who had previously devised bridges and the metal framework for the Statue of Liberty. Gustave Eiffel (I-fel; 1832–1923) designed the theme tower for the Paris Exhibition of 1889, another celebration of technological advances. Rising to an imposing height of 984 feet (295 m), the Eiffel Tower (fig. 25.25) symbolized the "Age of Progress" in France. Like a giant erector set, it was assembled on the site; 15,000 prefabricated and prepunched girders were bolted together in a masterful demonstration of precision design and production that was completed in two years, two months, and two days. The tower weighs almost 10,000 tons (10 million kg), but it is proportionately so light that a steel scale model 1 foot (30 cm) in height would weigh less than 1/4 ounce (7g). Though denounced from the outset by purists who objected to the violation of the Parisian skyline, the tower stands today as the enduring symbol of the City of Light.

IMPRESSIONISM

In one respect Impressionism was an outgrowth of realism, but in another it was a revolutionary artistic movement almost as profound in its effect as the Early Renaissance in Italy. Impressionists saw themselves as the ultimate realists whose main concern was the perception of optical sensations of light and color. Whether the Impressionists were consciously aware of photographic techniques, scientific research in optics, or the physiology of the eye is not important; they painted as if the world were not matter in space but a source of sensations of light and color. Objects were perceived as agents for the absorption and reflection of light; there were no sharp edges, indeed no lines, in nature. In nature, form and space were implied by infinitely varied intensities of color and light, and shadows were not black but colored in relation to the objects casting the shadows. This is Impressionist theory in essence, but the individual artists developed styles, of course, that sometimes contradicted the theories.

There was one characteristic of Impressionism that differentiated the movement from all other styles; it was not limited to artists. There was a generally appealing quality that drew together not only painters and their models, but a number of writers, critics, and collectors. The general public was not part of the movement, of course, for this was a consciously **avant-garde** enterprise, a confident step into the modern world.

Edouard Manet, 1832–83

"From now on I will be of our times and work with what I see," Manet (ma-nay) said to friends after destroying most of his early paintings. A major innovator in Western painting, Manet was not a member of the Impressionist group, but his influence on the movement was critical. Realizing that modeled transitions did not exist in nature, he worked instead in planes. He was also one of the first artists to paint with pure colors, eliminating dark shadows that had been used for centuries. Manet was a pioneer in the use of light as his subject; light was the actual subject matter of the painting that he submitted in 1863 to the jury of the Paris **Salon**. An unconventional painting with a conventional title, *Déjeuner sur l'herbe* ("Luncheon on the Grass"; fig. 25.26) was refused by the jury but exhibited in a special Salon des Refusés, where it caused a storm of controversy. Though the ostensible subject matter was possibly derived from Titian's *Fête Champêtre* (fig. 17.41), the contemporary dress of the men in combination with the unconcerned nakedness of the woman deeply shocked the public. Even Courbet criticized the work as flat and formless. Indeed, Manet had almost totally abandoned Renaissance

25.26 Edouard Manet, *Déjeuner sur l'herbe*. 1863. Oil on canvas, 6' 9⅛" × 8' 10¼" (2.06 × 2.7 m). Musée d'Orsay, Paris. Photo: R.M.N., Paris.

perspective, accepting the canvas for what it really was: a two-dimensional surface. For example, the background figure is much too large: if corrected for perspective she would be 9 feet (2.7 m) tall. Also, the painting is lit from two different directions. The hue and cry over the work bewildered the artist; the subject, after all was light itself—as clustered around the nude, the background figure, and the still life in the left foreground. The grouping of the dark areas further emphasized the harsh light of day, giving the painting a powerful visual impact. For Manet and the Impressionists the objects and figures in their paintings were sometimes treated impersonally, as opportunities to depict light sensations. Frequently detached and non-judgmental, Manet and the Impressionists, except for Renoir, were often more entranced with optical sensations than with humanity.

The public, however, was not detached and it was very judgmental. The reaction to Manet's *Olympia* (fig. 25.27), which he exhibited at the 1865 Salon, caused one of the greatest scandals in art history. Critics called Manet "a buffoon" and the nude a "female gorilla" and "yellow-bellied odalisque." Boisterous crowds flocked to see a work that another critic advised pregnant women and proper young ladies to avoid at all costs. Manet had painted his model, Victorine Meurend (who also posed for the *Déjeuner*), as an elegant and world-weary lady of the evening. With an orchid in her hair and wearing only a black ribbon and a bracelet, she stares disdainfully at the viewer while ignoring the bouquet proffered by her maid. Critics were no more incensed by the flagrant nakedness than by the black-on-black coloration of the maid's face against the background, not to mention the black cat at the foot of the suggestively rumpled bed, also painted against a black background. The picture became a *cause célèbre,* pitting modernists against traditionalists. In his novel *Of Human Bondage* Somerset Maugham gleefully described the Latin Quarter in which reproductions of *Olympia* were prominent in virtually every student room, bistro, and café. Even today the picture is distinctly modern. Manet forces his viewers to look *at* his flat picture rather than *into* it. The traditional boxlike space behind the frontal picture plane has been eliminated, presenting a situation that leaves much to the imagination. Further, a comparison of *Olympia* and the *Odalisque* of Ingres (see fig. 25.3) reveals the difference, at that time, between acceptable nudity and the disagreeable reality of a naked prostitute.

Following the innovations of Manet, who went on to experiment in other directions, the Impressionists developed a definite system with its own aesthetic principles. For centuries artists had been painting what they knew. The Impressionists were interested in painting what they saw.

25.27 Edouard Manet, *Olympia*. 1863. Oil on canvas, 4' 3¼" × 6' 2¾" (1.3 × 1.9 m). Musée d'Orsay, Paris. Photo: A.K.G., Berlin.

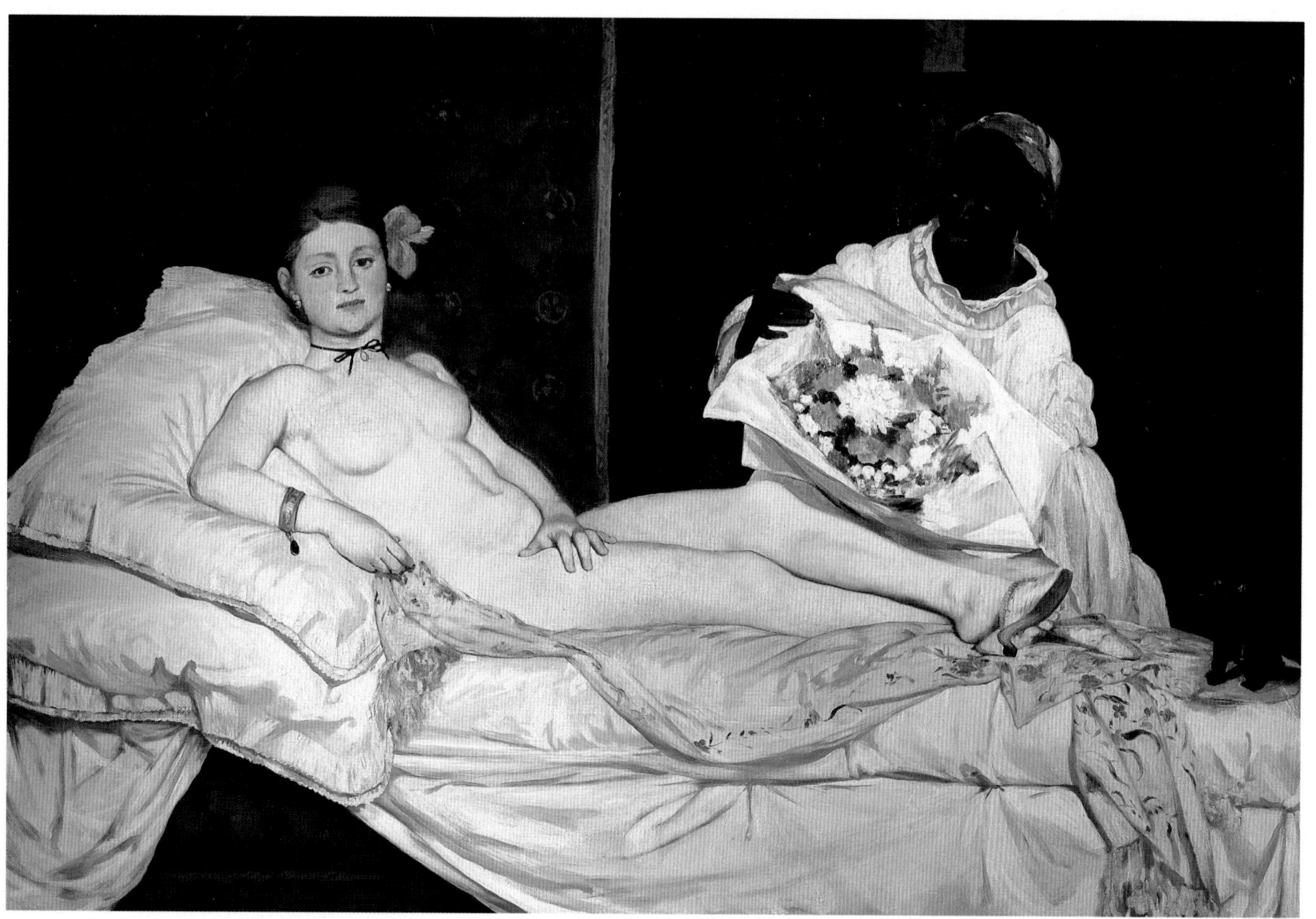

WELL-TIMED TECHNOLOGY

Until the late nineteenth century artists had to undergo the messy and time-consuming process of mixing their own paints and storing the results in jars or bladders. Advances in chemistry now produced new and brilliant pigments and the invention of collapsible tin tubes came at just the right time. With their bright colors in portable tubes artists were able to roam the countryside and paint *en plein air* ("in open air"). They were freed to paint what they saw and that was largely the glories of nature and the evanescent effects of sunlight and shade, clouds and water.

25.28 Claude Monet, *Rouen Cathedral, West Facade Sunlight.* 1894. Oil on canvas, 39½ × 26" (100.3 × 66 cm). National Gallery of Art, Washington, D.C. (Chester Dale Collection).

Claude Monet, 1840–1926

The spokesman and chief painter of the Impressionist style was Monet (mah-nay), who throughout his long and productive career relied wholly on his visual perceptions. For him, especially, there were no objects such as trees, houses, or figures. Rather, there was some green here, a patch of blue there, a bit of yellow over here, and so on. Monet was "only an eye," said Paul Cézanne, "but what an eye!"

The mechanics of vision were a major concern of Monet and the other Impressionists. To achieve intensity of color, pigments were not combined on the palette but laid on the canvas in primary hues so that the eye could do the mixing. A dab of yellow, for example, placed next to one of blue is perceived, from a distance, as green, a brilliant green because the eye accomplishes the optical recomposition. Further, each color leaves behind a visual sensation that is its after-image or complementary color. The after-image of red is blue-green and that of green is the color red. The adjacent placement of red and green reinforces each color through its after-image, making both red and green more brilliant. Impressionists generally painted with pure pigments in the colors of the spectrum; conspicuously absent from the spectrum and thus from Impressionist canvases was black, a favorite of academic painters. Monet contended that black was not a color and he was scientifically correct; black is the absence of color. This, of course, did not keep Degas and Manet from using black with dramatic effect.

Portable paints in the open sunlight and color perception were two components of Impressionist technique. The third component was speed. Making natural light explode on canvas necessitated quick brushstrokes that captured a momentary impression of reflected light, a reflection that changed from minute to minute. Monet's procedure was to paint furiously for seven or eight minutes and then move quickly to another canvas to capture a different light. Should a painting require additional effort he would return to the same spot the following day at the same time, a procedure he followed in his forty paintings of Rouen Cathedral done at different times of day. Early in the morning the elaborate Gothic facade would appear to be quite solid, but later in the day, as in *Rouen Cathedral, West Facade Sunlight* (fig. 25.28 and p. 292), the stonework has dissolved into a luminous haze of warm colors. Monet was the first artist since the Renaissance to investigate the dimension of time.

"Impressionism" is a term used derisively by a critic who, on seeing Monet's 1872 painting entitled *Impression, Sunrise,* remarked that it was "only an impression." That the term is generally apropos is apparent in Monet's impression of sunlight on medieval stonework. An interesting and telling sidelight is the 1872 date of this important painting. This was only a year after France had been humiliated by Germany in the Franco-Prussian War of 1870–1. A study of French artistic output of the period points up the artists' total unconcern with politics and so-called national honor.

Auguste Renoir, 1841–1919

Monet was a magnificent "eye" whose achievements are far more appreciated today than in his own time. On the other hand, the work of his celebrated contemporary, Auguste Renoir (re-nwar), has always had great appeal, possibly because Renoir portrayed people rather than buildings, landscapes, or lily ponds. The finest painter of luscious nudes since Rubens, Renoir had a unique ability to create the illusion of soft and glowing human flesh. He painted females of all ages, once exclaiming that if "God had not created woman I don't know whether I would have become a painter!"

Much of the art of Millet and the realists depicts laborers at various tasks, but the Impressionists viewed a world without work. An astonishing number of Impressionist works portrayed people enjoying leisure activities: boating, bathing, picnicking, promenading, dancing, attending the theatre, opera, ballet, or music hall, going to the races. There is no finer representation of exuberant pleasure than Renoir's *Le Moulin de la Galette* (fig. 25.29 and p. 227), a dazzling display of painterly virtuosity. The scene is an outdoor café with a large and crowded dance floor. The radiant color and shimmering light emphasize the fresh and youthful vigor of the participants, especially the women; nowhere is there a trace of black for all shadows have some degree of color. Light, air, color, and the captured moment, this is what Impressionism is all about. Further, Impressionism also functioned as a social history of France in the latter part of the nineteenth century. People were shown enjoying leisure activities because so many more of them had the time and money to do so. The growth and rise of the middle class is right there in Renoir's painting for all to see.

25.29 Pierre Auguste Renoir, *Le Moulin de la Galette*. 1876. Oil on canvas, 4' 3½" × 5' 9" (1.31 × 1.75 m). Musée d'Orsay, Paris. Photo: R.M.N., Paris.

Edgar Degas, 1834–1917

Degas (day-gah) also specialized in women, but women in their casual and graceful roles as ballet dancers. Delighting in studying forms in motion, he drew dancers and race horses with a remarkable vitality. *Four Dancers* (fig. 25.30) was one of his last large oil paintings, and it shows the influence

25.30 Edgar Degas, *Four Dancers*. Ca. 1899. Oil on canvas, 4' 11½" × 5' 11" (1.51 × 1.8 m). National Gallery of Art, Washington, D.C. (Chester Dale Collection).

of the pastel medium that he used in most of his later works. Of all the Impressionists, Degas was most interested in photography, both in taking pictures and in basing some of his works on photographs. This off-stage ballet scene has the appearance of a candid snapshot of dancers limbering up and checking their costumes before going on-stage. Actually, Degas posed dancers in his studio to create the illusion of spontaneity. Degas' concern with composition—and his use of black—make his style less Impressionist than that of Monet or Renoir.

Berthe Morisot, 1841–95

The Impressionists were a cohesive group of *avant-garde* artists who revolved around the central personality of Manet. The regular meeting place of Manet's "school" was the Café Guerbois, where Manet, Monet, Renoir, Degas, Whistler, the photographer Nadar, Emile Zola, Baudelaire, and others congregated to argue passionately about the role of the modern artist. Morisot (more-ee-so) was a member of the group but, as a proper young woman, she was denied the opportunity to socialize at the café with her colleagues. A student of both Corot and Manet, she earned the unusual distinction of having her work accepted by both the Impressionists and the Salon. She was, in fact, one of the organizers of the first Impressionist exhibition at Nadar's Gallery in 1874. *In the Dining Room* (fig. 25.31) depicts her maid and a little white dog in a setting in which the forms are silhouetted as elements in a design literally flooded with shimmering color and light. Mallarmé, an enthusiastic admirer of her art, wrote in his catalog for an exhibition of her work: "To make poetry in the plastic arts demands that the artist portray on the surface the luminous secret of things, simply, directly, without extraneous detail."

Mary Cassatt, 1844–1926

Both of the American painters who exhibited with the Impressionists, Mary Cassatt and James Whistler, drew inspiration from Impressionist techniques, but each developed a different and very personal style. Cassatt was American by birth and training and, though she lived in

25.31 Berthe Morisot, *In the Dining Room*. 1886. Oil on canvas, 24⅛ × 19¾" (61.3 × 50 cm). National Gallery of Art, Washington, D.C. (Chester Dale Collection).

25.32 Mary Cassatt, *The Bath*. Ca. 1891–2. Oil on canvas, 39¼ × 26" (99.7 × 66 cm). Art Institute of Chicago (Robert A. Waller Fund). Photo: Arlette Mellaart.

France for much of her life, is considered by the French to be the best artist America has yet produced. The influence of two-dimensional Japanese woodcuts (see fig. 25.37) is apparent in *The Bath* (fig. 25.32), but the extraordinary fluidity of the lines is uniquely her own. Both decorative and functional, they enclose what seems at first to be a simple domestic scene. But this is a highly stylized composition that we look down on, an intimate and tender moment presented in a closed form that shuts out the viewer and the world. We experience the rich warmth of the scene but we are not a part of it. The frequently caustic and always chauvinistic Degas remarked, after examining her work in her studio, "These are real. Most women paint pictures as though they were trimming hats, not you." For Degas, this was high praise for a great artist.

James McNeill Whistler, 1834–1903

Whistler and Henry James considered American civilization an embarrassment. Like James, Whistler became an expatriate, even denying that he was born in Lowell, Massachusetts: "I shall be born when and where I want, and I do not choose to be born in Lowell." Whistler was highly critical, naturally, of American realists such as Winslow Homer (see fig. 25.21), advocating instead "art for art's sake." The Impressionists were sufficiently artistic for his tastes, and he adapted some of their modern techniques to his uniquely personal style. Subject matter, he felt, was of no importance. Of his *The White Girl (Symphony in White, No. 1)* (fig. 25.33) Whistler remarked that no one could possibly be interested in the model, who happened to be the artist's mistress, Joanna Heffernan. Whistler added the subtitle several years after exhibiting the painting to emphasize the aesthetic appeal of his use of rhythm and harmony in the manner of music. Some of his *avant-garde* colleagues recognized that art was its own subject matter, but not the art establishment. Rejected by both the Royal Academy in London and the Paris Salon, the painting became as notorious as Manet's *Déjeuner* (see fig. 25.26). Light was the subject of one painting and white the subject of the other.

25.33 James McNeill Whistler, *The White Girl (Symphony in White No. 1)*, after restoration. 1862. Oil on canvas, 7' ½" × 3' 6½" (2.15 × 1.08 m). National Gallery of Art, Washington, D.C. (Harris Whittemore Collection). Photo: Richard Carafelli.

Auguste Rodin, 1840–1917

During the eighteenth and nineteenth centuries sculpture failed to keep pace with painting and architecture. The work of Houdon (see fig. 21.40) was significant, but the sculptures of Daumier and Degas were scarcely known at the time. And then there was Rodin (ro-dã), the greatest sculptor since Bernini, a dynamo of a man who captured the spontaneity and immediacy of Impressionism in three-dimensional form. Like Renoir and Degas, Rodin was concerned with the human figure but, totally unlike any Impressionist, he depicted his figures in moments of stress or tension. *The Walking Man* (fig. 25.34), intended originally as a study for *St. John the Baptist Preaching,* is a study in

25.34 Auguste Rodin, *The Walking Man*. Probably ca. 1900. Bronze, 33¼ × 16¾ × 21⅞" (84.5 × 42.6 × 55.5 cm). National Gallery of Art, Washington, D.C. (Gift of Mrs. John W. Simpson).

25.35 Auguste Rodin, *The Thinker*. 1880. Bronze, 28⅛ × 14⅜ × 23½" (71.5 × 36.4 × 59.5 cm). National Gallery of Art, Washington, D.C. (Gift of Mrs. John W. Simpson).

motion—and motion is all that we sense. Headless and armless, the figure has neither expression nor gesture to distract our attention from the strongly striding torso moving its muscular legs in long steps. The surface shimmers with light, shaped by the artist to heighten the illusion of motion.

Rodin's commission for *The Gates of Hell* produced a number of figures extracted from a monumental work that was never finished. *The Thinker* (fig. 25.35), sitting atop the gates and brooding over Rodin's conception of Dante's *Inferno,* is a prodigious representation of tension in repose. Similar to Michelangelo's superhuman forms (which Rodin studied in detail), the figure is sunk deep in thought. What is he thinking of? Rodin said at one time that it was Dante contemplating his poem and at other times that it was a dreamer or a creator. Whether writer, dreamer, or creator, *The Thinker* remains a fascinating enigma.

POSTIMPRESSIONISM

Paul Cézanne, 1839–1906

Postimpressionism is a catch-all term for some highly individual artists who reacted against the purely visual emphasis of Impressionism. The first and foremost of the Postimpressionists, Cézanne (say-zan) was, in fact, one of the giants of European painting. His art lay somewhere between representation and abstraction, an intellectualized approach to applying paint to canvas. For Cézanne the whole purpose of painting was to express the emotion that the forms and colors of the natural world evoked in the artist. His landscapes look like his native Provence but not literally; everything has been clarified and concentrated. Cézanne took liberties with ordinary visual experience that challenge our perceptions and force us to view the world in a new way, in Cézanne's way. In *Mont Sainte-Victoire seen from Les Lauves* (fig. 25.36) Cézanne gives us one of many versions of his favorite mountain. In common with his other landscapes, it contains no living creatures and the forms of the trees and houses are synthesized with the artist's characteristically muted blue-green and orange hues. The Impressionists used color to dissolve form and space; Cézanne did precisely the opposite, using color to define form in a tangible space. Cézanne constructed his paintings slowly, methodically, with an intellectual control comparable to that of Poussin. *Mont Sainte-Victoire* has what he called a "durable museum quality" because Cézanne painted not just what he saw but what he knew.

25.36 *Opposite* Paul Cézanne, *Mont Sainte-Victoire seen from Les Lauves*. 1902–4. Oil on canvas, 27⅞ × 36⅛" (70.8 × 91.8 cm). Philadelphia Museum of Art (George W. Elkins Collection).

Vincent van Gogh, 1853–90

Cézanne sold some of his paintings for as little as nine dollars but the Dutch artist van Gogh (van-go) sold only one painting during his ten-year career, depending entirely on his brother for support. Van Gogh began as an Impressionist but changed his style drastically after studying Japanese prints, which he found "extremely clear, never tedious, as simple as breathing" (fig. 25.37). Though van Gogh never attained this degree of facility, he did learn to treat the picture surface as an area to be decorated in masses of flat or slightly broken color. In *La Mousmé* (fig. 25.38) he painted a young girl from Provence, to which he had moved in 1888 to capture in the brilliant sunlight some of the beauty that he imagined existed in Japan. The word *mousmé* was used

25.37 *Right* Kitagawa Utamaro, *Uwaki, Half-Length Portrait,* from the series *Fujin Sogaku Jittai: Studies in Physiognomy; Ten Kinds of Women*. Ca. 1794. Print; color and mica on paper, 14½ × 10" (36.8 × 25.4 cm). Cleveland Museum of Art (Bequest of Edward L. Whittemore).

JAPANESE PRINTS

The Japanese *ukiyo-e* prints that inspired Mary Cassatt and Vincent van Gogh were popular during the eighteenth and nineteenth centuries (Edo period) in Japan. *Ukiyo-e* ("pictures of the floating world") was a tradition in Japanese painting and printmaking that tried to capture pleasurable scenes from everyday life: love or sexual scenes, festivals, theatrical performances, portraits of actors and dancers, and so forth.

Ukiyo-e prints were widely popular as independent, affordable works of art and book illustrations. Their commercial nature seems to have made the workshops less conservative than other art areas and open to large numbers of aspiring artists who signed on as apprentices in workshops run by master artists. A number of women artists also became apprentices in these workshops, leading some to credit the more liberal mercantile atmosphere for the unusual opportunity afforded women. Even more than European women, Japanese women were traditionally limited in their education and tied to domestic responsibilities. But further research identifies many of these women artists as producing art in a workshop run by a famous artist who was also their father. Not until well after World War II were Japanese women able to pursue careers in art or the professions.

25.38 Vincent van Gogh, *La Mousmé*. 1888. Oil on canvas, 28⅞ × 23¾" (73.3 × 60.3 cm). National Gallery of Art, Washington, D.C. (Chester Dale Collection). Photo: Bob Grove.

in a contemporary romantic novel to characterize the innocent charm of youthful Japanese teahouse attendants. Poised motionless against a neutral background and holding some oleander flowers, the thirteen-year-old peasant girl seems totally removed from everyday experience. She represents the artist's aim "to paint men and women with that quality of the eternal which used to be suggested by the halo."

Twice confined to a hospital in Arles after an apparent mental breakdown in 1889, van Gogh resumed painting and continued to produce during his subsequent year-long confinement in an asylum at St.-Rémy. Painted in a field near the hospital, *The Starry Night* (fig. 25.39) is an ecstatic vision of the power and glory of the universe. A tall cypress flames toward the whirling and exploding stars of a cosmic drama unknown to the inhabitants of the peaceful village below. This expressive work represents the artist's reverent celebration of the wonders of nature and is not, as some have contended, symptomatic of mental problems, although recent research has determined that the artist probably suffered from a debilitating illness called Ménière's disease. Symptoms include hallucinations and a ringing in the ears.

Moving northwest of Paris to the village of Auvers-sur-Oise after his release from the asylum, van Gogh completed about sixty paintings during the last two months of his tragic life. Why he chose to commit suicide at age thirty-seven with a bullet to the abdomen (that killed him several agonizing days later) has never been satisfactorily explained.

At his funeral his friend and physician, Dr. Paul Gachet, said: "He was an honest man and a great artist. He had only two aims: humanity and art. It was the art that . . . will insure his survival."

25.39 Vincent van Gogh, *The Starry Night*. 1889. Oil on canvas 29 × 36¼" (73.7 × 92.1 cm). The Museum of Modern Art, New York (Acquired through the Lillie P. Bliss Bequest). Photo: © 1996 The Museum of Modern Art, New York.

Paul Gauguin, 1848–1903

Van Gogh's onetime friend, Gauguin (go-gã), has been a kind of folk hero for desk-bound romantics who dream of dropping out of the rat race to pursue their artistic muse. The reality of Gauguin's life and career is, however, not the stuff of dreams. An amateur painter for many years, Gauguin naively assumed that he would be as successful as a full-time painter as he had been as a stockbroker. Within three years of giving up his financial career in 1883 (because of a stock market crash), everything was gone: wife, family, money. He found himself living on borrowed funds at a run-down country inn in Brittany.

A rebel at odds with conventional behavior and society in general, Gauguin was seldom plagued with self-doubt. Writing to his absent wife (whom he had abandoned), he proclaimed that "I am a great artist and I know it." Much of his work was inspired by Japanese prints, and his *Self-Portrait* (fig. 25.40), a strikingly off-centered composition, has a slightly oriental cast to the eyes. He has given himself an ironic halo, and his temptations are symbolized by the sharply outlined apples and the snake that he holds like a cigarette. The portrait is painted in the manner of a **cloisonné enamel**, the vivid colors being divided by incised lines, with everything flattened except the arrogant but sadly reflective face of a man who once wrote that he felt "like a brigand, which, for that matter, I am to many people."

Forever restless, Gauguin was drawn to the warm weather of Provence where he roomed briefly, and

25.40 Paul Gauguin, *Self-Portrait*, after restoration. 1889. Oil on wood, 31¼ × 20¼" (79.2 × 51.3 cm). National Gallery of Art, Washington, D.C. (Chester Dale Collection).

quarreled, with van Gogh. He then drifted to tropical climates: Panama, Martinique, Tahiti, and the Marquesas, where he died. In Tahiti Gauguin found, he thought, an antidote to the sickness of European civilization, a "primitive life" that would nurture his style. Actually, the Society Islands were governed by the French and Gauguin had evolved his tropical style before settling down in Polynesia. Gauguin's dream of "solitude under the tropical sun" was compromised by illness, poverty, and harassment by French authorities, but his work did acquire a new vigor.

While critics of the time found Gauguin's colors bizarre and his drawing crude, the public accepted the content of his paintings as actual illustrations of Tahitian life and customs. Tahiti was, however, Westernized and middle-class, with a snobbish colonial bureaucracy and a pervasive overlay of Western missionary zeal. One looks in vain in a Gauguin painting for anything resembling the everyday details of colonial life: no officials, traders, sailors, ships, or any possessions of the Europeans who had been running this colonial outpost for sixty years. The Polynesia that we see in Gauguin's art was the creation of the artist.

Though Gauguin admitted that his Tahiti was a subjective interpretation of what was "vaguest and most universal in nature," we still have a romantic image of Tahiti in Gauguin's mode. In *Where Do We Come From? What Are We? Where Are We Going?* (fig. 25.41) Gauguin executed what he called his "spiritual testament," completed shortly before his abortive suicide attempt. Stating that "I will never do anything better or even like it," Gauguin painted this as a voyage of discovery, not as a statement of his rather confused ideas about birth, life, and death. The painting is a fusion of antitheses: sunlight and moonlight; night and day; the warmness of life and the coldness of death. The cycle of life can be read from childhood on the right to the old woman waiting for death at the left. Ultimately, this work attests, as Gauguin said, to "the futility of words" in any attempt to express the wonder and mystery of life. It may have been this painting that the Symbolist poet Mallarmé called a "musical poem that needs no libretto."

Georges Seurat, 1859–91

Causing nearly as much controversy as Manet and Whistler, Seurat (sue-rah) exhibited *Sunday Afternoon on the Island of La Grande Jatte* (fig. 25.42) at the eighth and final Impressionist show of 1886. Critics had a field day lambasting the dots of color, the "procession of pharaohs," and a "clearance sale of Nuremberg toys." Favorable critics, and there were some, labeled the new style "Neoimpressionism" or "Divisionism," though Paris wits chose the word "confettism." Seurat himself used the term "chromo-luminarium" to describe his method of painting with tiny dots using the colors of the spectrum. Aspiring to paint in a scientific manner based on the optical theories of Helmholtz and others, Seurat used his *petits points,* his dots, to construct

25.41 Paul Gauguin, *Where Do We Come From? What Are We? Where Are We Going?* 1897. Oil on canvas, 4' 6¾" × 12' 3½" (1.39 × 3.75 m). Museum of Fine Arts, Boston (Tompkins Collection).

25.42 Georges Seurat, *Sunday Afternoon on the Island of La Grande Jatte*. 1884–6. Oil on canvas, 10' 6" × 6' 9" (3.2 × 2.06 m). Art Institute of Chicago (Helen Birch Bartlett Memorial Collection).

a monumental composition of "museum quality," as advocated by Cézanne. The scene is a popular summer resort near Paris where middle-class city dwellers could bathe, picnic, and promenade. Though the dots of pure color were supposed to fuse in the eye this does not happen, save in the luminosity of the river. Instead, the spectator is conscious of the myriads of dots that, in a non-chromatic way, contribute as units of scale to the grandeur that Seurat achieved; his optical theories were, in practice, more artistic than scientific. In addition, he developed a control of line, proportions, and masses of light and shade that make this a classical composition in the manner of Poussin and David. In its psychological impact the work is curiously modern. People, animals, hats, and parasols are structural and decorative elements, as isolated from each other as the passengers in *Third-Class Carriage* (see fig. 25.19). A typical Impressionist genre scene has become a melancholic comment on alienation and isolation in late Victorian society, symbolizing the underlying pessimism of the age.

25.43 Henri Rousseau, *The Dream*. 1910. Oil on canvas, 6' 8½" × 9' 9½" (2.40 × 2.98 m). The Museum of Modern Art, New York (Gift of Nelson A. Rockefeller). Photo: © 1996 The Museum of Modern Art, New York.

Henri Rousseau, 1844–1910

The most influential of the Postimpressionists were Cézanne and an obscure toll collector named Rousseau. An isolated and enigmatic genius who began painting late in life, Rousseau taught himself to paint "alone," as he said, "and without any master but nature." His naive ideal was what he called the "truth" of the camera; he was actually convinced that his paintings were as "realistic" as photographs. His jungle landscapes were painted with a startling directness of vision that influenced Picasso and others, but these were tropics of the mind produced by the magical vision of a simple man who, apparently, never left France. Nothing in *The Dream* (fig. 25.43) is identifiable in botanical terms. What we see is a brooding and sinister jungle inhabited by a nude on a Victorian couch, some apparently tame animals, and a creature both animal and human who plays a musical instrument. Rousseau has combined the subjectivity of Romanticism with the so-called objectivity that was aspired to by the realists and Impressionists, giving us a vivid illustration of the never-never land between the two extremes.

Edvard Munch, 1864–1944

Van Gogh, Gauguin, Seurat, and Rousseau were critical of the disease of civilization, but their pervasive pessimism was not limited to French urban culture. The Norwegian painter Munch (moonk) manipulated themes of evil, terror, and death to depict the plight, as he saw it, of *fin de siècle* European civilization, themes similar to those of the poets Matthew Arnold and Thomas Hardy (see pp. 256–8). In *The Scream* (fig. 25.44) Munch portrayed a terror-stricken person whose sexual and facial identity has been obliterated by a piercing scream that is echoed in undulating lines of the landscape. Like his friend and associate, Henrik Ibsen, Munch dealt with the unbearable tensions of the modern world that led to anxiety, alienation, and, as here, terror. Though his **iconography** was intensely personal, Munch's pessimistic vision strongly influenced the later German Expressionist movement (see p. 369).

A rather impromptu special event, the *banquet Rousseau,* symbolically marked the end of an era and the advent of the twentieth-century *avant-garde*. Held in the studio of Picasso in 1908, three years after the revolutionary show of the Fauves (see p. 365), the guest of honor was Henri Rousseau, nearing the end of his career and still unrecognized by the public. Guests included artists Georges Braque and Marie Laurencin, writers Apollinaire, Max Jacob, and Gertrude Stein, and other luminaries of the new epoch. Picasso had ordered the food for the wrong day but there was ample wine and abundant good spirits, with violin entertainment provided by the guest of honor. The only real tribute the unassuming toll-collector-cum-painter ever received prompted him to whisper confidentially to Picasso that "after all, you and I are both great painters: I in the Modern style and you in the Egyptian." Though Picasso's "Egyptian" style was actually his African mask period, Henri Rousseau's remark was correct on both counts.

25.44 Edvard Munch, *The Scream*. 1893. Tempera and casein on cardboard, 36 × 29" (91.4 × 73.7 cm). National Museum, Oslo, Norway.

SUMMARY

Romanticism was a reaction in all the arts against the Enlightenment. For a time, however, the visual arts in France were in the service of Napoleon and David, his court painter. The Arch of Triumph and Church of the Madeleine made significant contributions to the neoclassic face of Paris, and the paintings of Ingres established an academic style against which later artists were to rebel.

Painting in a style uniquely his own, Goya was one of the most important painters of the century. The French Romantic style was established by the dramatic work of Géricault and continued by the peerless colorist Delacroix. John Constable was the leading Romantic landscape painter in England whereas Romantic architecture was revivalist, as manifested in the Gothic Revival Houses of Parliament. The art of Turner was a Romantic style in and of itself. The Romanticism of Cole, Duncanson, and Bingham had a distinctly American flavor.

By the second half of the century realists such as Millet, Corot, Daumier, and Courbet were dominating the Parisian art scene while, in America, Winslow Homer and Thomas Eakins were leading artists in the ongoing tradition of American realism. Imaginative uses of industrial technology saw the construction of prefabricated structures such as the Crystal Palace and the Eiffel Tower.

Led by the innovations of Manet, the Impressionist movement became the *avant-garde* of European art. Considering themselves the ultimate realists, Monet, Renoir, Degas, Morisot, Cassatt, and others helped to establish Impressionism as one of the most influential of all artistic styles. Whistler did his own personal version of modern art and, in Paris, Rodin produced the most dramatic and expressive sculpture since the High Renaissance.

Reacting against the visual emphasis of Impressionism in very personal terms, the Postimpressionists included Cézanne, who distilled on canvas the forms and colors of the natural world, and Seurat, who used a similar approach but with dots of color. Van Gogh and Gauguin employed vivid colors to create very expressive works in very different styles. Rousseau created works from his private dream world that were a revelation to Picasso and others of the new *avant-garde*. Like many artists and writers of the late Victorian era, Munch reacted against modern urban society with themes of alienation and terror. A century that began with the Arch of Triumph ended with *The Scream*.

CULTURE AND HUMAN VALUES

The facts of science, a secular worldview, and materialism were the realities of the nineteenth century. Other factors included imperialism, the rising tide of nationalism, and the sporadic violence of an almost endless procession of revolutions and wars. The optimism of the Enlightenment seemed as remote as the Middle Ages. Though pessimism was not yet endemic, there were many, especially among writers and artists, who had strong feelings of foreboding. There is no more poignant expression of the doleful end of the century than Thomas Hardy's poem "The Darkling Thrush" (see p. 258). The entire age is brilliantly summed up by Stephen Crane's two untitled poems that end chapter 23.

STUDY QUESTIONS

1. Explain the basic differences between nineteenth-century Neoclassic and Romantic art by using two works from this chapter. Then repeat this exercise using two works not in this book.
2. One of the purposes of art is pleasure. Explain in detail why and how you enjoy a particular work presented in this chapter. There is no need to try for a balance between subjective and objective reactions.
3. Like most reproductions, the ones in this chapter are inadequate; art works are best appreciated when you view the real thing. You very likely have access to art in your school or community, including some by the artists discussed in this chapter. Seek these out and compare them with the works shown in this chapter. Compare the works stylistically and, especially, compare the quality of the original works as opposed to book illustrations.
4. Find some paintings by the Impressionists (originals or reproductions) and match them as closely as possible with the composition by Debussy on page 290.
5. What relationships can you find between the pessimistic Victorian poets in chapter 23 and some of the works discussed in this chapter? Relate all of these to some of the events of the period as outlined in the Time Chart for the Middle Modern World (see p. 228).

UNIT 9

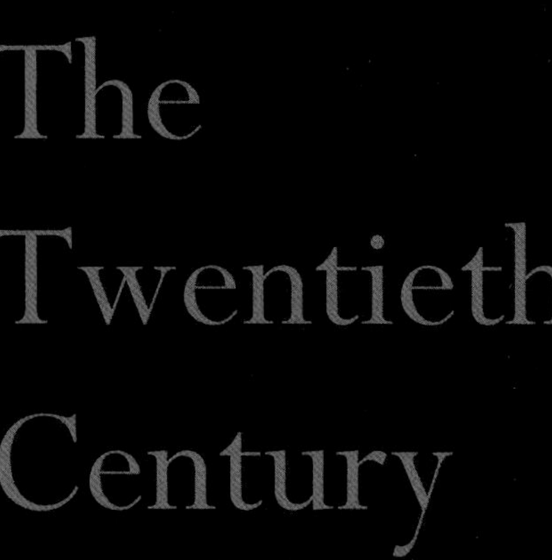

The Twentieth Century

The Twentieth Century

People and Events

1905 Unsuccessful revolution in Russia; Fauves in Paris
1906 San Francisco earthquake
1907 Cubism in Paris
1909 Founding of NAACP
1910–36 George V of England
1913 Armory Show in New York; Stravinsky *Rite of Spring; Ballet Russe* in Paris
1914–18 World War I
1916 Beginning of Dada movement
1917 Lenin triumphs in Russia; U.S. enters WWI; beginning of International Style
1918 Worldwide flu epidemic kills 20 million
1919 Treaty of Versailles
1919–33 Weimar Republic
1919–39 League of Nations
1920 U.S. women win right to vote
1920–33 Volstead Act (prohibition)
1922 Mussolini triumphs in Italy
1924 Surrealist Manifesto in Paris
1927 Stalin dictator in Russia
1929 Great Depression begins
1931–45 Sino-Japanese War
1932–4 Geneva Disarmament Conference
1933–45 Hitler dictator of Germany
1933–45 Roosevelt U.S. president
1934–8 The Great Terror: Stalin's purges
1935 Congress passes Social Security Act
1935–6 Italy conquers Ethiopia
1935–40 WPA Art Project
1936 Edward VIII of England
1936–9 Spanish Civil War
1936–52 George VI of England
1938 Germany annexes Austria; Czechoslovakia dismembered
1939–45 World War II
1941 Pearl Harbor: U.S. enters war
1944 Beginning of modern jazz
1945 United Nations organized; atomic bombs on Japan
1945–90 The Cold War
1947 Beginning of Marshall Plan
1948 Israel becomes independent state
1950 U.S. advisors sent to Vietnam
1950–3 Korean War
1952 Elizabeth II of England
1954 School segregation disallowed
1955 Civil Rights movement begins
1961–89 Berlin Wall
1963 President Kennedy assassinated
1964–75 Vietnam War
1965 M. L. King leads Selma march; beginning of protests, hippies, flower children
1968 Assassination of M. L. King, R. F. Kennedy
1969 U.S. lunar landing; race riots in Watts, Detroit, New York
1970 National Guard kills 4 students at Kent State University
1974 Nixon resigns presidency
1979 American hostages seized in Iran
1980–8 The Reagan era
1989 Beginning worldwide collapse of Communism
1990 End of Cold War

Literature

Olive Schreiner 1855–1920 "Somewhere, Some Time, Some Place"
William Butler Yeats 1865–1939 "The Second Coming"
Sidonie Gabrielle Colette 1873–1954 "The Other Wife"
Virginia Woolf 1882–1941 "If Shakespeare Had a Sister"
Countee Cullen 1887–1946 "Yet Do I Marvel"
Robinson Jeffers 1887–1962 "Shine, Perishing Republic"
T. S. Eliot 1888–1965 "The Love Song of J. Alfred Prufrock"
Wilfred Owen 1893–1918 "Dulce et Decorum Est"
e e cummings 1894–1962 "anyone lived in a pretty how town"
Jorge Luis Borges 1899–1986 "The Disinterested Killer Bill Harrigan"
George Seferis 1900–71 "Helen"
Langston Hughes 1902–67 "Harlem"
Richard Eberhart 1904– "The Fury of Aerial Bombardment"
Jean-Paul Sartre 1905–80 "Existentialism"
Samuel Beckett 1906–89 *Waiting for Godot*
Naguib Mahfouz 1911– "The Happy Man"
Albert Camus 1913–66 "The Myth of Sisyphus"
Dylan Thomas 1914–53 "When All My Five and Country Senses See"
Ralph Ellison 1914–94 *Invisible Man*
Gwendolyn Brooks 1917– "We Real Cool"
James Dickey 1923– "Adultery"
Joseph Heller 1923– *Catch 22*
Yehuda Amichai 1924– "Jews in the Land of Israel"
Adrienne Rich 1929– "Two Songs"
Martin Luther King, Jr. 1929–68 "Letter from Birmingham Jail"
N. Scott Momaday 1934– *House Made of Dawn*
Kofi Awoonor 1935– "Night of My Blood"
Gail Godwin 1937– "A Sorrowful Woman"
Susan Griffin 1943– "I Like to Think of Harriet Tubman"

Art

Wassily Kandinsky 1866–1944 *Panel 3*
Käthe Kollwitz 1867–1945 *The Only Good Thing*
Henri Matisse 1869–1954 *The Blue Window*
Georges Rouault 1871–1958 *Christ Mocked by Soldiers*
John Sloan 1871–1952 *Roof Gossips*
Piet Mondrian 1872–1944 *Broadway Boogie Woogie*
Constantin Brancusi 1876–1956 *Bird in Space*
Paul Klee 1879–1940 *Twittering Machine*
Pablo Picasso 1881–1973 *Guernica*
Edward Hopper 1882–1967 *Nighthawks*
José Orozco 1883–1949 *Zapatistas*
Diego Rivera 1886–1957 *Liberation of the Peon*
Kurt Schwitters 1887–1948 *Sichtbar*
Marcel Duchamp 1887–1968 *The Bride Stripped Bare by Her Bachelors, Even*
Marc Chagall 1887–1985 *I and the Village*
Georgia O'Keeffe 1887–1986 *Jack-in-the-Pulpit*
Giorgio de Chirico 1888–1978 *The Nostalgia of the Infinite*
Josef Albers 1888–1976 *Homage to the Square*
Horace Pippin 1888–1946 *Victorian Interior*
George Grosz 1893–1959 *I Am Glad I Came Back*
Joan Miró 1893–1983 *Person Throwing a Stone at a Bird*
Stuart Davis 1894–1964 *Radio Tubes*
David Siqueiros 1896–1974 *Echo of a Scream*
Alexander Calder 1898–1976 *Many Pierced Discs*
Henry Moore 1898–1986 *Family Group*
René Magritte 1896–1967 *The False Mirror*
Jean Dubuffet 1901–85 *Portrait of Henri Michaux*
Mark Rothko 1903–70 *Number 10*
Willem de Kooning 1904– *Woman I*
Salvador Dali 1904–89 *The Persistence of Memory*
David Smith 1906–65 *Cubi XV*
Francis Bacon 1910– *Number VII from Eight Studies for a Portrait*
Jackson Pollock 1912–56 *Autumn Rhythm, No. 30, 1950*
Meret Oppenheim 1913– *Object*
Jacob Lawrence 1917– *Daybreak—A Time to Rest*
Roy Lichtenstein 1923– *Drowning Girl*
Robert Colescott 1925– *Les Demoiselles d'Alabama: Vestidas*
Robert Rauschenberg 1925– *Monogram*
Edward Kienholz 1927– *State Hospital*
Tony DeLap 1927– *Sentaro*
Helen Frankenthaler 1928– *Interior Landscape*
Marisol 1930– *Women and Dog*
Audrey Flack 1931– *World War II, April 1945*
Bridget Riley 1921– *Crest*
Christo and **Jeanne-Claude** 1935– *Running Fence*
Fritz Scholder 1937– *Waiting Indian No. 4*
Robert Smithson 1938–73 *Spiral Jetty*
Otto Duecker 1948– *Russell, Terry, J. T.*
Gerhard Richter 1932– *Vase*

Architecture, Music, Photography

Mathew Brady 1823–96 *Abraham Lincoln*
Antonio Gaudi 1852–1926 Church of the Holy Family
Alfred Stieglitz 1863–1946 *The Terminal*
Frank Lloyd Wright 1869–1959 "Falling Water"
W. C. Handy 1873–1958 "St. Louis Blues"
Charles Ives 1874–1954 *Three Places in New England*
Béla Bartók 1881–1945 *Concerto for Orchestra*
Igor Stravinsky 1882–1971 *The Rite of Spring*
Anton Webern 1883–1945 *Three Songs*
Walter Gropius 1883–1969 Bauhaus
Alban Berg 1885–1935 Violin Concerto
Ludwig Mies van der Rohe 1886–1969 Seagram Building
Le Corbusier 1887–1965 Notre Dame-du-Haut
Wallace Harrison 1895–1981 Secretariat Building of the United Nations
Paul Hindemith 1895–1963 *Mathis der Maler*
Dorothea Lange 1895–1965 *Migrant Mother*
Duke Ellington 1899–1974 "Old King Dooji"
Benny Goodman 1900–80 "Dizzy Spells"
Ansel Adams 1902–84 *Moonrise*
Margaret Bourke-White 1904–71 *Two Women, Lansdale, Arkansas*
Philip Johnson 1906– Chippendale Skyscraper
Eero Saarinen 1910–61 TWA Terminal
John Cage 1912–92 Aleatory music
Joern Utzon 1918– Sydney Opera House
W. Eugene Smith 1918–78 *Spanish Wake*
Michael Graves 1937– The Portland
Barton McLean 1938– *Etunytude*

Invention, Science, Philosophy

1900 Freud *The Interpretation of Dreams:* Planck's constant; quantum theory
1901 first transatlantic radio telegraphic transmission
1902 first phonograph recordings
1903 Wright brothers' first flight
1905 Einstein Special Theory of Relativity; first U.S. motion pictures
1908 Ford introduces Model T
1909 wireless radio
1912 discovery of insulin
1914 discovery of vitamins
1916 Einstein General Theory of Relativity
1922 radar invented
1926 first TV transmission; first liquid-fuel rocket
1927 Heisenberg Principle of Uncertainty
1928 first sound movie
1930 discovery of penicillin
1934 first use of antibiotics
1939 first commercial TV; first jet engine; automatic sequence computer
1940 first successful plutonium fission
1942 uranium fission, atomic reactor
1948 LP recordings marketed
1951 inauguration of transcontinental TV
1951 U.S. explodes hydrogen bomb
1956 first transatlantic telephone; inauguration of interstate highway system
1957 first earth satellite (U.S.S.R.)
1958 beginning of jet airline passenger service; laser beam invented
1961 first manned orbital flight (U.S.S.R.)
1962 Rachel Carson's *Silent Spring* launches environmentalist movement
1963 quasars discovered
1964 China detonates atom bomb
1965 foundation of National Organization for Women (NOW)
1967 first heart transplant
1972 UN Conference on the Human Environment
1973 first orbital laboratory (Skylab)
1974 first energy crisis
1976 genetic engineering developed
1978 first test-tube baby
1981 beginning of space shuttle flights
1990s expansion of high tech: computers, robotics, global communications

CHAPTER 26

Things Fall Apart: The Center Cannot Hold

HISTORICAL OVERVIEW, 1914–39

World War I can be viewed as Act 1 in a drama that began in 1871 with Bismarck's formation of the German Empire (the Prologue) and continued with World War II as Act 2 in a tragedy that engulfed most of the world. The period of 1918–39 can be seen, in retrospect, as an entr'acte that set the stage for what may or may not be the last act. When the Allies and Germany agreed to an Armistice on 11 November 1918 the stated intent was to stop the fighting and arrange for a just peace. However, the Treaty of Versailles, signed on 28 June 1919, was harshly punitive. Germany and its allies were forced to sign the "war guilt" clause and to accept all responsibility for causing the war. War reparations were to be paid to all thirty-two allies; Germany lost virtually its entire armed services and overseas colonies plus large portions of its land area. Woodrow Wilson's attempts to curb the nationalistic zeal of Britain's Lloyd George and France's Clemenceau were essentially futile. Even Wilson's prize project, the League of Nations that was part of the Peace of Versailles, ended, finally, in failure—caused, in part, by the refusal of the United States to join this valiant, doomed attempt to civilize the conduct of nations. The League of Nations did settle a few disputes but it was powerless to prevent Japan's invasion of Manchuria in 1931, Germany's withdrawal from the League in 1933 in order to rearm, and Mussolini's invasion of Ethiopia in 1935.

The Allies had convinced the Germans that Kaiser Wilhelm II and his imperial government were primarily responsible for the war. But it was the new Weimar Republic that signed the dictated peace and it was the Republic that bore the onus of German humiliation at the conference table. Moreover, the Treaty of Versailles made no provision for the economic rehabilitation of Europe. Nor were there any assurances for the futures of new nations—Czechoslovakia and Yugoslavia—that had been carved out of the dismembered Austro-Hungarian empire. The Treaty of Versailles caused more discontent and unrest than even the 1815 Vienna Settlement after the Napoleonic wars.

The March 1917 revolution in Russia had disposed of the czar, but the new Provisional government, despite rising unrest, continued to pursue the war. V. I. Lenin (1870–1924) capitalized on new defeats at the front to seize the government and establish the All-Russian Congress of the Soviets. Concluding a separate disastrous peace with Germany, Lenin established a dictatorship of the Communist party that barely survived the ferocious Civil War of 1918–21. Under Leon Trotsky (1877–1940) a new Red Army destroyed the rebel White armies and then helped Lenin solidify his hold on the government. Lenin established himself as the unchallenged leader by having his secret police (Cheka) murder all his political opponents and potential opponents (some 60,000 or more), conforming to the dictator's rationale: "We are exterminating the bourgeosie as a class. This is the essence of the Red Terror."[1] The Russian aristocracy had already been eliminated and the vast body of peasants posed no threat. Following Lenin's death in 1924, a power struggle between Trotsky and Joseph Stalin (1879–1953) saw Stalin emerge, in 1927, as the absolute dictator of the Soviet Union (fig. 26.1).

26.1 Gustav Kluzi, "Lenin's Banner." 1933. Poster: photomontage with portrait of Stalin. Galerie Avantgarde N. Fedorowskij, Berlin. Photo: A.K.G., London.

1. Paul Johnson, *Modern Times: The World from the Twenties to the Eighties* (New York: Harper & Row, 1983), p. 71.

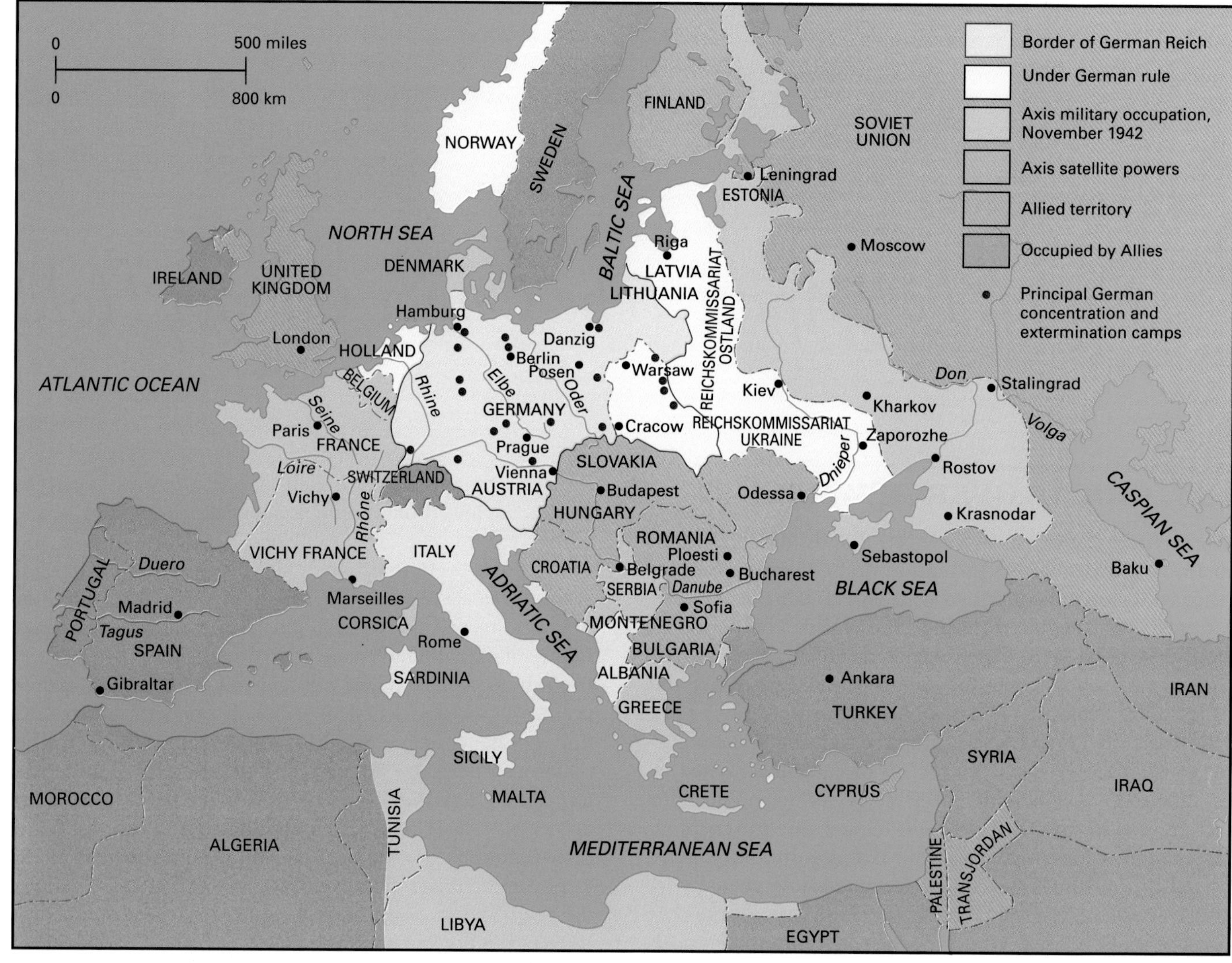

Map 26.1 World War II in Europe.

The democracies were beset by economic difficulties in the 1920s and assaulted by Communists on the left and hard-core nationalists on the right. Benito Mussolini (1883–1945) marched on Rome in 1922 and assumed full dictatorial powers by 1926. Designed to produce a corporate totalitarian state, the doctrines of Italian fascism stressed the dominance of the state and the subordination of the individual, the desirability of war, and the Social Darwinian "right" of Italy to expand at the expense of "inferior" nations.

The initial successes of Italian fascism impressed not only the older Western democracies but also many malcontents in Germany, who bitterly resented the war-guilt clause of the Treaty of Versailles. Compounding the discontent, the German military clique fostered the false belief that Germany had never been defeated on the field of battle; it had been betrayed at home, said the military, by pacifist liberals. Following the disastrous inflation of 1923 the National Socialist German Workers Party (Nazis) launched a propaganda campaign that capitalized on the supposed sellout at Versailles. Coupled with the barrage was a virulent anti-Semitism that blamed the Jews for many of Germany's postwar problems while proclaiming the absolute supremacy of the Aryan master race. A spellbinding political orator, Nazi leader Adolf Hitler (1889–1945) mesmerized his audiences with what he called the Big Lie: "If you keep it simple, say it often, and make it burn the public will believe anything." The Nazis gained power when, in 1933, President von Hindenburg appointed Hitler as Chancellor of the Republic. Using the emergency powers of Article 48 of the constitution, Hitler eradicated all opposition with his bloody purge of 1934. He was now absolute ruler of a Third Reich that was to "last for a thousand years."

The direct road to World War II began, probably, with Japan's seizure of Manchuria in 1931; it was followed by her withdrawal from the League of Nations in 1933 and her invasion of China four years later. In order to arm secretly for war, Germany withdrew from the League in 1933, the year in which Hitler opened the first concentration camp at Dachau (DAH-kow; see p. 344). Defying the Treaty of Versailles, Hitler occupied the Rhineland in 1936, a fateful step that is now seen as the last opportunity for England and France to avert war in Europe. From then on Hitler had the might to back up his threats.

The Spanish Civil War of 1936–9 had the effect of polarizing world opinion between the fascists and monarchists of "loyalist" Francisco Franco (1892–1975) and rebel

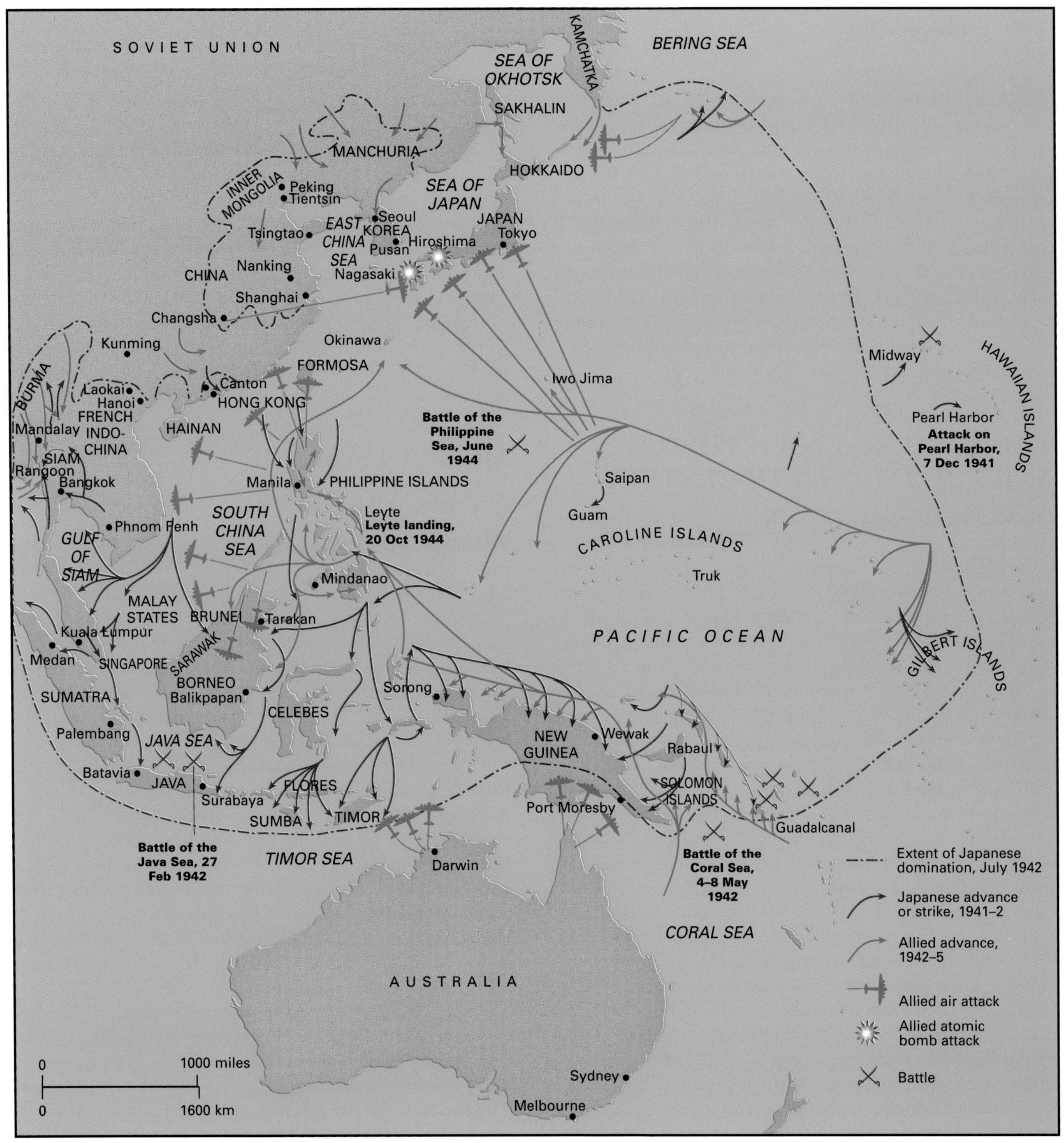

Map 26.2 World War II in the Pacific.

factions led by anarchists, socialists, communists, and an assortment of liberals. Hitler backed Franco, using the opportunity to field-test his new war machines. It was German bombers that attacked the undefended Basque town of Guernica, an atrocity immortalized on canvas by Picasso (see fig. 28.13).

After signing the Rome-Berlin treaty with Mussolini in 1936, Hitler launched his campaign for a union (*Anschluss*) with German-speaking Austria, which he occupied in early 1938. The next target was the German-speaking Sudeten area of Czechoslovakia. After working up a full-scale crisis with his oratory, Hitler agreed to a four-power conference at Munich on 29 September 1938. Hitler, Mussolini, British Prime Minister Neville Chamberlain, and Premier Edouard Daladier of France conferred in an atmosphere of conciliation artfully orchestrated by Hitler. Chamberlain returned to England proclaiming "peace in our time" even though England and France had helped to dismember hapless Czechoslovakia. Hitler acquired the Sudetenland at Munich and all of Czechoslovakia by the following spring.

The final step was Poland. Germany and Russia signed a non-aggression pact on 23 August 1939 that relieved Hitler of his concerns about waging a two-front war. The secret portion of the pact carved up Poland and eastern Europe between Germany and Russia and "awarded" the Baltic republics of Lithuania, Estonia, and Latvia to Stalin. On 1 September 1939 the German armies rolled into Poland and, two days later, England and France honored their commitment to Poland by declaring war on Germany. The Treaty of Versailles that was supposed to confirm the Great War as the "war to end all wars" had lasted a scant twenty years (maps 26.1 and 26.2).

THE CULTURE-EPOCH THEORY AND THE TWENTIETH CENTURY

Our distance from past ages enables us to perceive the periods when a culture was balanced, when the balance tipped into chaos, when the adjustment began that led to a new period of balance, and so on (see pp. 3–5). Analyzing our own age is far more difficult, perhaps impossible, yet we try to understand where we are and where we might be going.

During the past several decades new attitudes have become increasingly important. We know through evolutionary studies, for example, that all living things are evolving—everything in the cosmos, in fact. Led by molecular biologists, the overwhelming consensus among today's scientists is that human beings, chimpanzees, and gorillas evolved from a common ancestor between 3,000,000 and 8,000,000 years ago. Human beings, chimps, and gorillas are more closely related to each other than any of them is to other primates. The DNA sequences of hemoglobin from human beings and chimps are 98.4 percent identical and the sequences from human beings and gorillas are 98.3 percent identical. Right down to the bottom of the great chain of being, all living creatures are interrelated. *Homo sapiens* has no proper claim to dominion over the globe or over so-called lower forms of life. Moreover, the balance of life in our world is precarious; we know, or should know, that we cannot alter our environment without worldwide repercussions and we cannot damage our environment without ultimately harming ourselves. It is a scientific fact that the flight of a butterfly over Tokyo can in some still unexplained way—the famous "butterfly effect"—influence the weather of New York City.

This holistic view of living things expands to include our concept of the cosmos as expressed by modern science and applies to the inner world of the human personality as probed by Freud and other psychologists. Contemporary holistic views of evolving personality, society, the environment, and the cosmos suggest a new age that may be called a planet in process, a world in which everything is in a continual stage of becoming. Goal-oriented cultures of the past may be replaced by change-oriented cultures of the future. Once people begin viewing their cultural identities as journeys rather than as destinations, the new age may have begun.

In this and the following chapters we will consider the status of modern science, the Information Age, the Global Village, the failure of Marxist-Leninism and the resurgence of free enterprise in democratic societies, massive damage to the environment, racism, nascent nationalism, gender issues, and the reactions of artists to the chaos, adjustment, and new directions of the twentieth century.

MODERN SCIENCE

Quantum Theory

The old social order was in disarray by about 1914, but the predictable world-machine described by Newtonian science was overthrown even earlier. In 1900 Max Planck (1858–1947) took a giant stride away from visible perceptions of the physical world to a theory that described the microcosmos by using mathematical abstractions. While studying the radiant energy given off by heated bodies, Planck discovered that energy was radiated, not in unbroken streams, but in discontinuous bits or portions that he called *quanta*. In terms of both the emission and the absorption of atomic and subatomic particles, Planck hypothesized that the energy transfer was discontinuous and involved a unit of energy (quantum) that could be calculated: "The uncertainty in the position of a particle times the uncertainty in its velocity times its mass can never be smaller than a certain quantity," which is known as Planck's constant.[2] Roughly a decimal point followed by 26 zeroes and ending in 6624, this minuscule number remains one of nature's most fundamental constants.

In conjunction with quantum theory, Werner Heisenberg (1901–76) developed, in 1927, his "Principle of Uncertainty," which states that, in effect, theory can accurately predict the behavior of statistically large numbers of particles, but not the behavior of individual particles. It is impossible simultaneously to determine the position and the velocity of, for example, an electron. If the position is observed, that act of observing will alter its velocity; conversely, the more accurate the determination of its velocity the more indefinite is the position of the electron. The fundamental equation of quantum mechanics is this: there is no such thing as an electron that possesses both a precise momentum and a precise position. The old science relied on a study of cause and effect (or causality and determinism), but the Principle of Uncertainty toppled these formerly sturdy pillars. Heisenberg won the Nobel Prize in 1932 for his work in quantum mechanics. His leadership of the German scientists who kept Hitler from developing the atomic bomb is also worthy of mention.[3] Even now the

2. Stephen Hawking, *A Brief History of Time: From the Big Bang to Black Holes* (New York: Bantam Books, 1988), p. 55.
3. See Mark Walker, *German National Socialism and the Quest for Nuclear Power: 1939–1949* (Cambridge: Cambridge University Press, 1990).

vision of Hitler with the bomb is just too dreadful to contemplate.

Quantum theory is strange and fascinating. Niels Bohr, Heisenberg's mentor and a leading physicist on the Manhattan Project that developed the bomb, cogently proclaimed that "anyone who is not shocked by quantum theory has not understood it." What is so astonishing?

In the first place, no one knows how the quantum world behaves the way it does; scientists simply do know that it behaves the way it does. "In the quantum world what you see is what you get, and nothing is real; the best you can hope for is a set of delusions that agree with one another."[4]

The double-hole experiment is perhaps the best way to view the eerie quantum world. Picture two walls separated by several feet with a small hole in each wall, either of which can be covered up. A single electron, or a single photon, on its way through one hole in the wall, obeys statistical laws which are appropriate only when it "knows" if the other hole is open.

> *This is the central mystery of the quantum world.* The electrons not only know whether or not both holes are open, they know whether or not we are watching them, and they adjust their behavior accordingly.[5]

Scientists had shown in theory, in 1970, that an atom in one energy state cannot change its energy so long as it is being observed. By 1990 scientists at the National Institute of Standards and Technology had demonstrated that the act of looking at an atom prevented it from decaying. What still remains to be proved is that continuous observation of unstable radioactive isotopes can prevent them from disintegrating radioactively. Theoretically, if a nuclear bomb were watched intently enough, it could not explode!

All of this bizarre behavior leads one to ask if there are any practical ways to convert quantum theory into quantum mechanics.

> The physics is impossible, but the math is clean and simple, familiar equations to any physicist. As long as you avoid asking what it means there are no problems. Ask why the world should be like this, however, and the reply is: "we have no idea."[6]

Mathematical formulas based on quantum theory are basic to the development of television, VCRs, computers, and other high-tech marvels. Further, quantum theory has opened up a whole new area of philosophic speculation. Given a fantastic world that can be used but not explained, what, then, is reality?

4. John Gribbin, *In Search of Schrödinger's Cat: Quantum Physics and Reality* (New York: Bantam Books, 1984), p. 162.
5. *Ibid.*, p. 171.
6. *Ibid.*, p. 174.

Einstein and Relativity

Five years after Planck discovered quanta Albert Einstein (1879–1955; fig. 26.2) hammered another nail into the coffin of the Newtonian world-machine. He postulated that light photons were also quanta and developed his Special Theory of Relativity (1905). In essence, his Special Theory rests on the hypothesis that neither space nor time has an objective reality. Space is an arrangement of perceived objects and time has no independent existence apart from our measurements of a sequence of events. Our clocks are geared to our solar system. What we call an hour is actually a measurement of an arc of 15 degrees in space based on the apparent movement of the sun. A year is, therefore, the time it takes the earth to orbit the sun, which is 365¼ days. Mercury has an eighty-eight-day year and other planets have their own time-frame. As Einstein said, time is subjective and based on how people remember events as a sequence of "earlier" and "later" episodes.

Einstein's Special Theory stipulates, in particular, that the velocity of light is constant for all uniformly moving systems anywhere in the universe. There is neither absolute space nor absolute time, but the velocity of light is the absolute speed limit of the universe. There can be no fixed interval of time independent of the system to which it is referred nor can there be simultaneity independent of an established reference. Einsteinian physics assumes, for example, that there is an observer seated beside a railroad track who sees a bolt of lightning at the far left (bolt A) and another at the far right (bolt B). Assuming that the observer is positioned precisely between A and B, the bolts will be

26.2 Albert Einstein playing a violin at a chamber music rehearsal in Princeton, N.J. Photo: Bettmann Archive, New York.

perceived as simultaneous because all events have the same frame of reference. Now, assume that a train is moving along the track from right to left at the brisk speed of light (186,284 miles or 300,000 km per second) and that another observer is riding on the top of the train. Assume, further, that observer 2 is exactly opposite observer 1 at the precise moment that bolts A and B strike. Observer 2 will perceive bolt A but not bolt B. The train is moving away from bolt B at the speed of light, meaning that the light waves of bolt B will never catch up with the train. Observer 2 is in a different frame of reference from the one occupied by observer 1.

Based on his Special Theory, Einstein determined that with an increase in velocity the mass of an object will also increase relative to an observer. Because motion is a form of kinetic energy, the increase in motion that leads to an increase in mass means that the mass has increased in energy. Einstein computed the value of the equivalent mass (m) in any unit of energy (e), leading to the equation that mass is equal to its energy over the square of the speed of light (c^2). The remaining algebraic step results in the equation $e = mc^2$, the most famous equation of our age. As Einstein demonstrated mathematically, mass and energy were equivalent. What we normally call mass is concentrated energy that, with the proper trigger, can be released. The detonation of the first atomic device at Alamogordo, New Mexico, on 16 July 1945 demonstrated the transmutation of matter into energy in the forms of light, heat, sound, and motion.

Newton's laws still satisfactorily explain phenomena based on human experiences, but they cannot cope with modern physics. Einstein's laws of motion are based on the relativity of distance, time, and mass, what he called the "four-dimensional space-time continuum," that is, three dimensions of space and one of time. Relativity thus gives scientists the means to provide better descriptions of the workings of nature.

Einstein later expanded his system into the General Theory of Relativity, in which he examined what it is that guides all moving systems. His Special Theory had stated that the velocity of light was constant for all uniformly moving systems. His General Theory is broader and states that the laws of nature are the same for all systems regardless of their states of motion. The basic premise of his Special Theory—that all motion, uniform or non-uniform, had to be judged within some system of reference because absolute motion did not exist—held true. He could not, however, distinguish between the motion caused by inertial forces (acceleration, centrifugal forces, etc.) and motion caused by gravitation. This led to his Principle of the Equivalence of Gravitation and Inertia, a new theory of gravitation more accurate and complete than Newton's Law of Universal Gravitation. Newton had postulated gravitation as a force or attraction, but Einstein's Law of Gravitation simply describes the behavior of objects in a gravitational field by depicting the paths they follow.

Gravitation, for Einstein, was a form of inertia, leading him to conclude that light, like any material body, was subject to gravitation when passing through a very strong gravitational field. He then proved that light travels in a predictable curve given sufficient gravitational pull. Einstein's universe has no straight lines. Euclidean geometry defines a straight line as the shortest distance between two points but there are only vast circles delineating all of space that, though finite, is unbounded.

It took only a few years to verify Einstein's General Theory of Relativity:

> The modern world began on 29 May 1919 when photographs of a solar eclipse, taken on the island of Principe off the coast of West Africa and at Sobral in Brazil, confirmed the truth of a new theory of the universe.[7]

As Einstein observed, relativity defined the outer limits of our knowledge and quantum theory delineated the inner limits. What bothered him was that the two systems were unrelated to each other: "The idea that there are two structures of space independent of each other, the metric-gravitational and the electromagnetic is intolerable to the theoretical spirit." He went on to declare that "God does not play dice with the universe." A persistent believer in the fundamental uniformity and harmony of nature, Einstein devoted the latter part of his career to a futile search for a Unified Field Theory that would construct a bridge between relativity and quantum theory.

But Einstein was mistaken about the dice. In terms of quantum theory, physicist Stephen W. Hawking has declared that "God not only plays dice, he sometimes throws the dice where they cannot be seen." Physicist Joseph Ford approached the problem from another perspective, stating that "God plays dice with the universe, but they're loaded dice. And the main objective of physics now is to find out by what rules they were loaded and how we can use them for our own ends."[8]

The New Science of Chaos

Relativity eliminated the Newtonian illusion of absolute space and time; quantum theory abolished the Newtonian dream of a precise and controllable measurement process; chaos dispensed with the long-held belief that random events could not be subjected to scientific analysis.

That the remarkable scientific advances of this century have led to a brand new science should not be surprising. Since about 1976 physicists, biologists, astronomers, and economists have created a new way of understanding the evolution of complexity in nature. This new science of chaos is a way of seeing order and pattern where formerly only the erratic, the random, the unpredictable—the chaotic—had been observed. According to mathematician

7. Johnson, *op. cit.*, p. 1.
8. Joseph Ford, as quoted in James Gleich, *Chaos: Making a New Science* (New York: Viking, 1987), p. 314.

Douglas Hofstadter, "it turns out that an eerie type of chaos can lurk just behind a facade of order—and yet, deep inside the chaos lurks an eerier kind of order."

> Where chaos begins, classical science stops. For as long as the world has physicists inquiring into the laws of nature, it has suffered a special ignorance about disorder in the atmosphere, in the turbulent sea, in the fluctuations of wildlife populations, in the oscillations of the heart and the brain.[9]

Chaos has been used to study, among other things, weather patterns to determine how to make long-range predictions. Consider, for example, the "butterfly effect." Could the flight of a butterfly over Tokyo somehow affect the weather of New York City? The surprising answer is Yes!, though no one knows how this happens, there being so many variables (known and unknown). The variables are, in fact, so numerous that long-range predictions (more than five days) are impossible. Chaos mathematics has identified patterns that permit short-range weather forecasts, which become increasingly inaccurate after one, two, three, and four days. Chaos has also been used to study wave motion, water turbulence, economic activity, wildlife populations, and other phenomena that were heretofore totally unpredictable, leading to the discovery that there are indeed underlying patterns that reveal "an eerier kind of order."

Chaos is a science in its infancy with no idea where its analyses of previously hidden patterns will lead. As with all science, the search is endlessly exciting because the explorers are moving ahead into what was not only unknown but, in this case, totally unexpected.

Another relatively new scientific area is complexity theory, which has been described as a first cousin to chaos theory. Complexity theory may, eventually, explain life on this planet. Scientists ask how it is that a chaotic universe organized itself into stars, galaxies, and planets and, against all known odds, produced a wild diversity of life on planet Earth. There may never be satisfactory answers but, this being what science is basically all about, the search is on.

How do relativity, quantum mechanics, complexity, and chaos affect us as human beings? In the first place, human mental processes cannot be explained by existing laws of physics. The answer may come, scientists believe, with the merger of general relativity, which concerns itself with gravity, and quantum theory, which governs the submicroscopic world, a bridge that Einstein called the Unified Field Theory. The two theories are mathematically incompatible but scientists, led by Stephen Hawking, are laboring to create a quantum version of gravity. One consequence would be to establish the boundaries of quantum mechanics, which says that particles can suddenly leap from one space to another without traversing the space between. What if these properties also apply to something as large as human brain cells in the process of creative thinking?

Indeed, quantum gravity could be behind consciousness itself. Consciousness has a peculiar quality that baffles physics: all humans perceive time as moving forward rather than backward. But virtually all the laws of physics are time-symmetric, working equally well either forward or backward. The speculative answer is that when quantum gravity is finally constructed it will begin with the Big Bang theory of creation and thus move only forward. Some scientists believe that human creativity and consciousness are the perceptible workings of the most basic laws of the universe, laws that are being explored using quantum, complexity, and chaos theories.

The uncertainty principle applies to virtually everything in our universe with only three fundamental constants remaining: gravity, Planck's constant, and the speed of light. Given so much uncertainty, philosophers have renewed their arguments for the existence of free will. Moreover, contemporary thinkers in many fields are exploring the nature of reality given the unexplained mysteries of quantum theory and the incompatibility of the mathematics of general relativity and quantum mechanics. If physical events can be neither plotted nor explained, nor predicted with any certainty, then perhaps the still relatively unknown capabilities of the human intellect will be a decisive factor in the destiny of humankind.[10]

FREUD AND THE INNER WORLD

Though he wrote his celebrated *The Interpretation of Dreams* in 1900 and *The Psychopathology of Everyday Life* in 1904, the psychological theories of Sigmund Freud (1856–1939; fig. 26.3) did not become influential until after World War I. Freud evolved a theory of the tripartite personality consisting of the *id, ego,* and *superego*. There are no clear boundaries between these concepts but each can be described in isolation. Representing our biological endowment, the *id* (Lat., "it") resides in our unconscious as an amalgam of our drives and instincts. Hunger, thirst, elimination, and sex are some of the drives that compel us to avoid pain and to seek pleasure through gratification. Either through action or wish-fulfillment, pent-up energy is discharged and tension relieved. Freud considered life and love as positive life forces (*libido* or *Eros*) and aggressiveness, destruction, and the death-wish as negative forces.

The *ego*, according to Freud, is the reality-principle, the thinking, conscious self that interacts with objective reality. The well-developed *ego* controls the *id*, determining when and how instinctive drives are satisfied.

9. *Ibid.*, p. 3.

10. Though this chapter is primarily concerned with the 1914–39 period, the discussion of twentieth-century science includes contemporary science because scientific knowledge and theory are continually evolving into ever more complex mosaics that encompass new discoveries and/or affirmations or denials of all past knowledge. A similar rationale also applies to the discussion of Freud and his contemporary critics.

26.3 Sigmund Freud. Ca. 1921. Photo: Mary Evans, London (Max Halberstadt, courtesy of W. E. Freud).

Freud's *superego* is a combination of the moral code of the parents and the person, a kind of conscience that is a product of socialization and cultural traditions. Motivated by fear of punishment and desire for approval, the *superego* can perhaps be best described as a synthesis of the *ego*-ideal and conscience. The psychological rewards for the *superego* are feelings of pride and accomplishment; psychological punishment causes feelings of inferiority and guilt.

The well-balanced personality has a strong *ego* generally in control of the *id* and *superego*, restraining the *id* while recognizing the censorship of the *superego*. A neurotic person has lost some control, for whatever reason, over conscious actions, giving in to aggressive instincts from the *id*, or succumbing to feelings of guilt and inferiority exacted by the *superego*. Psychosis is a serious mental illness in which the patient has lost all touch with reality.

Freud invented what he called psychoanalysis, a systematic therapy for the treatment of neurosis. The task of the analyst was to help the patient uncover repressed matter, mainly through free association and the interpretation of dreams. Essentially, the analyst assisted the patient in understanding the reasons for abnormal behavior; once the patient uncovered the repressions that caused undesirable actions, the *ego* could consciously deal with the problem. Recognition of the basic problem(s) would theoretically help restore emotional balance.

Partly because he treated mostly neurotic patients, and partly because any new idea is likely to carry its originator to extremes, Freud rode his interpretations very hard in one direction. He believed that virtually all the mental disorders he treated were ultimately traceable to one basic frustration: the denial of the life-force, the *libido* or sex-drive. Freud's discovery that sexuality goes far back into childhood, even infancy, was a radical departure from the views of his day. It is, therefore, quite understandable that the sexual factor should loom so large in his investigations, for this human drive is hedged about with all sorts of taboos. Even in our own time, supposedly sexually liberated, there are a variety of sexual mores about how one should and should not act.

A number of scientists, including Adolf Grünbaum, Marshall Edelson, Frank J. Sulloway, and Peter Medawar now claim that none of Freud's concepts or hypotheses stand up to scientific scrutiny.[11] Most of his theories were not based on observation but derived from his premise that repression was the driving force of a neurosis. No one has been able to prove scientifically that this is indeed the case. Much of his work has, for this reason, been invalidated. As demonstrated by Marx's mistaken view of history, a correct doctrine cannot be erected on a false premise.

Why, then, was Freudian psychology so influential? Primarily, the time was ripe for his theories because they contributed to a new spirit of liberation. Freud's unchallenged achievement was to show that men and women were not always guided by their reason but driven to action by their impulses and passions. They did not, in other words, deliberately choose to act destructively. The liberating factor was that blame or censure need not focus on bad decisions; instead, one could consider the reasons why a person failed to control unconscious passions that produced negative results. The notion of "inner drives" was an idea whose time had come. Sigmund Freud was the first person to attempt a "scientific" exploration of the mysterious inner world of the human personality and for that alone he deserves a special place in the history of science. Moreover, as one critic (Michael Molnar, an editor of Freud's diaries) remarked, "Freud is in better shape than Marx."

Whatever illusions the nineteenth century may have preserved about the perfectibility of human behavior and human institutions perished during the four dreadful years of World War I. Much of the art and literature of the postwar period reflected a profound pessimism, a feeling that Western civilization carried the seeds of its own destruction. The following poems and essay express some of the prevailing sentiments, some of the loneliness, alienation, and despair experienced by the postwar generation. And little did anyone know that within less than a generation the Great War was to receive a number.

11. According to Medawar, "psychoanalysis is akin to mesmerism and phrenology: it contains isolated nuggets of truth, but the general theory is false." Johnson, *op. cit.*, p. 6.

LITERARY SELECTION 81

The Love Song of J. Alfred Prufrock

Thomas Stearns Eliot, 1888–1965

Written in England around the beginning of World War I, *Prufrock* is a dramatic monologue of a middle-aged and frustrated social misfit who is vainly trying to adjust to a petty and superficial society. The larger perspective is that of bankrupt idealism, a decaying of nations, societies, and religious institutions. With juxtaposed images enlarged by dramatic echoes of Hesiod, Dante, and Shakespeare, Eliot builds a mood of futility and despair.

S'io credesse che mia risposta fosse
a persona che mai tornasse al mondo,
questa fiamma staria senza più scosse.
Ma per ciò che giammai di questo fondo
non torno vivo alcun, s'i'odo il vero,
senza tema d'infamia ti rispondo.[12]

Let us go then, you and I,
When the evening is spread out against the sky
Like a patient etherised upon a table;
Let us go, through certain half-deserted streets,
The muttering retreats
Of restless nights in one-night cheap hotels
And sawdust restaurants with oyster-shells:
Streets that follow like a tedious argument
Of insidious intent
To lead you to an overwhelming question . . .
Oh, do not ask, "What is it?"
Let us go and make our visit.

In the room the women come and go
Talking of Michelangelo.

The yellow fog that rubs its back upon the window-panes,
The yellow smoke that rubs its muzzle on the window-panes
Licked its tongue into the corners of the evening,
Lingered upon the pools that stand in drains,
Let fall upon its back the soot that falls from chimneys,
Slipped by the terrace, made a sudden leap,
And seeing that it was a soft October night,
Curled once about the house, and fell asleep.

12. "If I thought I were making answer to one that might return to view the world, this flame should evermore cease shaking. But since from the abyss, if I hear true, none ever came alive, I have no fear of infamy, but give thee answer due." The speaker is Guido da Montefeltro, who was condemned to Hell as a Counsellor of Fraud (Dante, *Inferno*, XXVII, 61–6). Dante has asked him why he is being punished and Guido, still fearful of what might be said about him, answers truthfully because he thinks Dante is also dead. Prufrock, like Guido, is fearful of society's judgment.

And indeed there will be time
For the yellow smoke that slides along the street
Rubbing its back upon the window-panes;
There will be time, there will be time
To prepare a face to meet the faces that you meet;
There will be time to murder and create,
And time for all the works and days of hands[13]
That lift and drop a question on your plate;
Time for you and time for me,
And time yet for a hundred indecisions,
And for a hundred visions and revisions,
Before the taking of a toast and tea.

In the room the women come and go
Talking of Michelangelo.

And indeed there will be time
To wonder, "Do I dare?" and, "Do I dare?"
Time to turn back and descend the stair,
With a bald spot in the middle of my hair—
(They will say: "How his hair is growing thin!")
My morning coat, my collar mounting firmly to the chin,
My necktie rich and modest, but asserted by a simple pin—
(They will say: "But how his arms and legs are thin!")
Do I dare
Disturb the universe?
In a minute there is time
For decisions and revisions which a minute will reverse.

For I have known them all already, known them all—
Have known the evenings, mornings, afternoons,
I have measured out my life with coffee spoons;
I know the voices dying with a dying fall
Beneath the music from a farther room.
So how should I presume?

And I have known the eyes already, known them all—
The eyes that fix you in a formulated phrase,
And when I am formulated, sprawling on a pin,
When I am pinned and wriggling on the wall,
Then how should I begin
To spit out all the butt-ends of my days and ways?
So how should I presume?

And I have known the eyes already, known them all—
Arms that are braceleted and white and bare
(But in the lamplight, downed with light brown hair!)
Is it perfume from a dress
That makes me so digress?
Arms that lie along a table, or wrap about a shawl.
And should I then presume?
And how should I begin?

. . . . .

Shall I say, I have gone at dusk through narrow streets
And watched the smoke that rises from the pipes
Of lonely men in shirt-sleeves, leaning out of windows? . . .

I should have been a pair of ragged claws
Scuttling across the floors of silent seas.

. . . . .

And the afternoon, the evening, sleeps so peacefully!
Smoothed by long fingers,
Asleep . . . tired . . . or it malingers,
Stretched on the floor, here beside you and me.
Should I, after tea and cakes and ices,
Have the strength to force the moment to its crisis?
But though I have wept and fasted, wept and prayed,
Though I have seen my head (grown slightly bald) brought in upon a platter,
I am no prophet—and here's no great matter;[14]
I have seen the moment of my greatness flicker,
And I have seen the eternal Footman hold my coat, and snicker,
And in short, I was afraid.

And would it have been worth it, after all,
After the cups, the marmalade, the tea,
Among the porcelain, among some talk of you and me,
Would it have been worth while,
To have bitten off the matter with a smile,
To have squeezed the universe into a ball[15]
To roll it toward some overwhelming question,
To say: "I am Lazarus, come from the dead,[16]
Come back to tell you all, I shall tell you all"—
If one, settling a pillow by her head,
Should say: "That is not what I meant at all,
That is not it, at all."

And would it have been worth it, after all,
Would it have been worth while,
After the sunsets and the dooryards and the sprinkled streets,
After the novels, after the teacups, after the skirts that trail along the floor—
And this, and so much more?—
It is impossible to say just what I mean!
But as if a magic lantern threw the nerves in patterns on a screen:
Would it have been worth while
If one, settling a pillow or throwing off a shawl,
And turning toward the window, should say:
"That is not it at all,
That is not what I meant, at all."

. . . . .

No! I am not Prince Hamlet, nor was meant to be;
Am an attendant lord, one that will do

13. *Works and days* recalls Hesiod's poem entitled "Works and Days" (ca. 750 BC). Ironically contrasting with Prufrock's frivolous world, Hesiod's poem extols the virtues of hard labor on the land.

14. *I am no prophet,* that is, no John the Baptist, who was beheaded by Herod and his head brought in on a tray to please Salome, Herod's stepdaughter (Matthew 14:3–11). Prufrock views himself as a sacrificial victim, but he is neither saint nor martyr.

15. *Universe into a ball* recalls "Let us roll all our Strength, and all our sweetness, up into one Ball" from the poem "To His Coy Mistress" by Andrew Marvell (see pp. 144–5). Prufrock's attempt to raise the conversation to a cosmic level with an allusion to a love poem is doubly ironic; the imaginary lady casually brings the discussion back to trivialities (ll. 103–4).

16. *Lazarus* was raised from the grave by Christ (John 11:1–44). Can this society be brought back from the dead?

To swell a progress, start a scene or two,
Advise the prince; no doubt, an easy tool,[17]
Deferential, glad to be of use,
Politic, cautious, and meticulous;
Full of high sentence, but a bit obtuse;
At times, indeed, almost ridiculous—
Almost, at times, the Fool.

I grow old . . . I grow old . . .
I shall wear the bottoms of my trousers rolled.[18]

Shall I part my hair behind? Do I dare to eat a peach?
I shall wear white flannel trousers, and walk upon the beach.
I have heard the mermaids singing, each to each.

I do not think that they will sing to me.

I have seen them riding seaward on the waves
Combing the white hair of the waves blown back
When the wind blows the water white and black.

We have lingered in the chambers of the sea
By sea-girls wreathed with seaweed red and brown
Till human voices wake us, and we drown.

STUDY QUESTIONS

1. What kind of a society is implied in which "the women come and go/Talking of Michelangelo" (ll. 19–20)?
2. Describe, in your own words, Prufrock's physical appearance, personality, and social conduct.

LITERARY SELECTION 82

Dulce et Decorum Est

Wilfred Owen, 1893–1918

Perhaps the most promising English poet to die in the war, Wilfred Owen, unlike most of his contemporaries, saw no honor nor glory in a conflict that he referred to as "this deflowering of Europe." The closing quotation of this somber poem is from the poet Horace: "It is sweet and fitting to die for one's country." Owen apparently hoped that this "old Lie" would never again lead nations to war. He was killed in action on 4 November 1918, one week before the armistice that ended the fighting.

Bent double, like old beggars under sacks,
Knock-kneed, coughing like hags, we cursed through sludge,
Till on the haunting flares we turned our backs
And towards our distant rest began to trudge.

Men marched asleep. Many had lost their boots
But limped on, blood-shod. All went lame; all blind;
Drunk with fatigue; deaf even to the hoots
Of tired, outstripped Five-Nines that dropped behind.
Gas! Gas! Quick, boys!—An ecstasy of fumbling,
Fitting the clumsy helmets just in time,
But someone still was yelling out and stumbling
And flound'ring like a man in fire or lime . . .
Dim, through the misty panes and thick green light,
As under a green sea, I saw him drowning.

In all my dreams, before my helpless sight,
He plunges at me, guttering, choking, drowning.

If in some smothering dreams you too could pace
Behind the wagon that we flung him in,
And watch the white eyes writhing in his face,
His hanging face, like a devil's sick of sin;
If you could hear, at every jolt, the blood
Come gargling from the froth-corrupted lungs,
Obscene as cancer, bitter as the cud
Of vile, incurable sores on innocent tongues,—
My friend, you would not tell with such high zest
To children ardent for some desperate glory,
The old Lie: *Dulce et decorum est*
Pro patria mori.

STUDY QUESTIONS

1. Notice the many participles in lines 2 and 3. Is their effect active or passive?
2. Read line 6 aloud while listening to the sounds. How many weak syllables are there? Strong syllables? What is the effect?

LITERARY SELECTION 83

The Second Coming

William Butler Yeats, 1865–1939

Written by Yeats in 1920, the poem conveys a sense of the dissolution of civilization. His image of the cycle of history is a "gyre" (a rotating spiral). Imagine a falconer losing control of his falcon as the bird soars in widening circles and eventually breaks away. Lines 4–8 refer to the Russian Revolution of 1917, but they can also be taken as a portent of the rise of fascism in the twenties and thirties. *Spiritus Mundi* is the soul of the universe that connects all human souls in what Yeats calls the "Great Memory," or universal subconscious.

17. *Advise the prince* apparently refers to Polonius, the king's adviser in *Hamlet*. The cross-reference is to Guido da Montefeltro, also a false counsellor.
18. Cuffed (rolled) trousers were stylish at the time. Middle-aged and socially inept, Prufrock tries to appear young and fashionable.

Turning and turning in the widening gyre
The falcon cannot hear the falconer;
Things fall apart: the centre cannot hold;
Mere anarchy is loosed upon the world,
The blood-dimmed tide is loosed, and everywhere
The ceremony of innocence is drowned;
The best lack all conviction, while the worst
Are full of passionate intensity.

Surely some revelation is at hand:
Surely the Second Coming is at hand.
The Second Coming! Hardly are those words out
When a vast image out of *Spiritus Mundi*
Troubles my sight: somewhere in the sands of the desert
A shape with lion body and the head of a man,
A gaze blank and pitiless as the sun,
Is moving its slow thighs, while all about it
Reel shadows of the indignant desert birds.
The darkness drops again; but now I know
That twenty centuries of stony sleep
Were vexed to nightmare by a rocking cradle,
And what rough beast, its hour come round at last,
Slouches towards Bethlehem to be born?

STUDY QUESTIONS

1. What does the poet mean, in lines 7 and 8, by the "best" and the "worst"?
2. There is a name for a shape with the head of a man and the body of a lion. What is it and why does Yeats evoke this image?
3. What is the implication of the "rocking cradle"?
4. Describe the feeling aroused by the last two lines of the poem.

LITERARY SELECTION 84

Shine, Perishing Republic

Robinson Jeffers, 1887–1962

Postwar America was a world power but Jeffers saw the darker side, a crass and materialistic nation mired "in the mold of its vulgarity." The reader can determine whether the poem, written in 1924, is still apropos.

While this America settles in the mold of its vulgarity, heavily thickening to empire,
And protest, only a bubble in the molten mass, pops and sighs out, and the mass hardens,
I sadly smiling remember that the flower fades to make fruit, the fruit rots to make earth.
Out of the mother; and through the spring exultances, ripeness and decadence; and home to the mother.

You making haste haste on decay: not blameworthy; life is good, be it stubbornly long or suddenly
A mortal splendor: meteors are not needed less than mountains: shine perishing republic.
But for my children, I would have them keep their distance from the thickening center: corruption
Never has been compulsory, when the cities lie at the monster's feet there are left the mountains.
And boys, be in nothing so moderate as in love of man, a clever servant, insufferable master.
There is the trap that catches noblest spirits, that caught—they say—God, when he walked on earth.

STUDY QUESTIONS

1. Identify the images that refer to the cycle of life and death.
2. What is implied by "meteors are not needed less than mountains"?

LITERARY SELECTION 85

Yet Do I Marvel (1924, 1925)

Countee Cullen, 1887–1946

One of the leaders of a 1920s literary movement called the Harlem Renaissance, Cullen can be seen, at first glance, as a voice of moderation compared with black protests since World War II. Cullen's references are from the Western literary tradition (Greek mythology, Dante) and the form is that of a sonnet. Line 12 is derived from the last two lines of "The Tyger" by William Blake (see pp. 243–4). Blake asks how a good God can put evil in the world; Cullen ponders a similar question about the evil of racism. The tone is moderate but the sentiment is not.

I doubt not God is good, well-meaning, kind,
And did He stoop to quibble could tell why
The little buried mole continues blind,
Why flesh that mirrors Him must some day die,
Make plain the reason tortured Tantalus
Is baited by the fickle fruit, declare
If merely brute caprice dooms Sisyphus
To struggle up a never-ending stair.
Inscrutable His ways are, and immune
To catechism by a mind too strewn
With petty cares to slightly understand
What awful brain compels His awful hand.
Yet do I marvel at this curious thing:
To make a poet black, and bid him sing!

STUDY QUESTIONS

1. How many images are there of the way things are? Consider, for example, blind moles, Tantalus, and Sisyphus. (Tantalus was condemned by Zeus to stand up to his chin in water that receded everytime he tried to drink. Above his head hung fruit that the wind kept perpetually out of his reach. His name has given us the verb "tantalize." "The Myth of Sisyphus" is on pp. 347–8.)
2. The last line implies that people who can write poetry must write poetry. Why is this so?

LITERARY SELECTION 86

Somewhere, Some Time, Some Place (1920)

Olive Schreiner, 1855–1920

The originator of English-language literature in South Africa, Schreiner was also an early feminist and social reformer. Despite the efforts of Schreiner and many other activists, South Africa, with the Native Lands Act of 1913, officially launched the separation of the races called "apartheid." The following memoir may have had something to do with the thinking of those who began dismantling apartheid some seventy years after it was written.[19]

When a child, not yet nine years old I walked out one morning along the mountain tops on which my home stood. The sun had not yet risen, and the mountain grass was heavy with dew; as I looked back I could see the marks my feet had made on the long, grassy slope behind me. I walked till I came to a place where a little stream ran, which farther on passed over the precipices into the deep valley below. Here it passed between soft, earthy banks; at one place a large slice of earth had fallen away from the bank on the other side, and it had made a little island a few feet wide with water flowing all round it. It was covered with wild mint and a weed with yellow flowers and long waving grasses. I sat down on the bank at the foot of a dwarfed olive tree, the only tree near. All the plants on the island were dark with the heavy night's dew, and the sun had not yet risen.

I had got up so early because I had been awake much in the night and could not sleep longer. My heart was heavy; my physical heart seemed to have a pain in it, as if small, sharp crystals were cutting into it. All the world seemed wrong to me. It was not only that sense of the small misunderstandings and tiny injustices of daily life, which perhaps all sensitive children feel at some time pressing down on them; but the whole Universe seemed to be weighing on me.

I had grown up in a land where wars were common. From my earliest years I had heard of bloodshed and battles and hairbreadth escapes; I had heard them told of by those who had seen and taken part in them. In my native country dark men were killed and their lands taken from them by white men armed with superior weapons; even near to me such things had happened. I knew also how white men fought white men[20]; the stronger even hanging the weaker on gallows when they did not submit; and I had seen how white men used the dark as beasts of labour, often without any thought for their good or happiness. Three times I had seen an ox striving to pull a heavily loaded wagon up a hill, the blood and foam streaming from its mouth and nostrils as it struggled, and I had seen it fall dead, under the lash. In the bush in the kloof[21] below I had seen bush-bucks and little long-tailed monkeys that I loved so shot dead, not from any necessity but for the pleasure of killing, and the cock-o-veets and the honey suckers and the wood-doves that made the bush so beautiful to me. And sometimes I had seen bands of convicts going past to work on the roads, and had heard the chains clanking which went round their waists and passed between their legs to the irons on their feet; I had seen the terrible look in their eyes of a wild creature, when every man's hand is against it, and no one loves it, and it only hates and fears. I had got up early in the morning to drop small bits of tobacco at the roadside, hoping they would find them and pick them up. I had wanted to say to them, "Someone loves you"; but the man with the gun was always there. Once I had seen a pack of dogs set on by men to attack a strange dog, which had come among them and had done no harm to anyone. I had watched it torn to pieces, though I had done all I could to save it. Why did everyone press on everyone and try to make them do what they wanted? Why did the strong always crush the weak? Why did we hate and kill and torture? Why was it all as it was? Why had the world ever been made? Why, oh why, had I ever been born?

The little sharp crystals seemed to cut deeper into my heart.

And then, as I sat looking at that little, damp, dark island, the sun began to rise. It shot its lights across the long, grassy slopes of the mountains and struck the little mound of earth in the water. All the leaves and flowers and grasses on it turned bright gold, and the dewdrops hanging from them were like diamonds; and the water in the stream glinted as it ran. And, as I looked at that almost intolerable beauty, a curious feeling came over me. It was not what I *thought* put into exact words, but I seemed to *see* a world in which creatures no more hated and crushed, in which the strong helped the weak, and men understood each other, and forgave each other, and did not try to crush others, but to help. I did not think of it as something to be in a distant picture; it was there about

19. Not until 1991 was the legal framework of apartheid revoked, followed by a 1992 referendum that mandated the sharing of power between the white minority and the black majority.
20. The British versus the Dutch-descended population (Afrikaners or Boers).
21. Afrikaans, "deep ravine."

me, and I was in it, and a part of it. And there came to me, as I sat there, a joy such as never have I experienced, except perhaps once, a joy without limit.

And then, as I sat on there, the sun rose higher and higher, and shone hot on my back, and the morning light was everywhere. And slowly and slowly the vision vanished, and I began to think and question myself.

How could that glory ever really be? In a world where creature preys on creature, and man, the strongest of all, preys more than all, how could this be? And my mind went back to the dark thoughts I had in the night. In a world where the little ant-lion digs his hole in the sand and lies hidden at the bottom for the small ant to fall in and be eaten, and the leopard's eyes gleam yellow through bushes as it watches the little bush-buck coming down to the fountain to drink, and millions and millions of human beings use all they know, and their wonderful hands, to kill and press down others, what hope could there ever be? The world was as it was! And what was I? A tiny, miserable worm, a speck within a speck, an imperceptible atom, a less than a nothing! What did it matter what *I* did, how *I* lifted my hands, and how *I* cried out? The great world would roll on, and on, just as it had! What if nowhere, at no time, in no place, was there anything else?

The band about my heart seemed to grow tighter and tighter. A helpless, tiny miserable worm! Could I prevent one man from torturing an animal that was in his power; stop one armed man from going out to kill? In my own heart was there not bitterness, the anger against those who injured me or others, till my heart was like a burning coal? If the world had been made so, so it was! But, why, oh why, had I ever been born? Why did the Universe exist?

And then, as I sat on there, another thought came to me; and in some form or other it has remained with me ever since, all my life. It was like this: you cannot by willing it alter the vast world outside of you; you cannot, perhaps, cut the lash from one whip; you cannot stop the march of even one armed man going out to kill; you cannot, perhaps, strike the handcuffs from one chained hand; you cannot even remake your own soul so that there shall be no tendency to evil in it; the great world rolls on, and *you* cannot reshape it; but this one thing only you can do—in that one, small, minute, almost infinitesimal spot in the Universe, where your will rules, there where alone you are as God, *strive* to make that you hunger for real! No man can prevent you there. In your own heart strive to kill out all hate, all desire to see evil come even to those who have injured you or another; what is weaker than yourself try to help; whatever is in pain or unjustly treated and cries out, say, "I am here! I, little, weak, feeble, but I will do what I can for you." This is all you can do; but do it; it is not nothing! And then this feeling came to me, a feeling it is not easy to put into words, but it was like this: you also are a part of the great Universe; what you strive for something strives for; *and nothing in the Universe is quite alone*; you are moving on towards something.

And as I walked back that morning over the grass slopes, I was not sorry I was going back to the old life. I did not wish I was dead and that the Universe had never existed. I, also, had something to live for—and even if I failed to reach it utterly—somewhere, some time, some place, it was! I was not alone.

More than a generation has passed since that day, but it remains to me the most important and unforgettable of my life. In the darkest hour its light has never quite died out.

In the long years which have passed, the adult has seen much of which the young child knew nothing.

In my native land I have seen the horror of a great war.[22] Smoke has risen from burning homesteads; women and children by thousands have been thrown into great camps to perish there; men whom I have known have been tied in chairs and executed for fighting against strangers in the land of their own birth. In the world's great cities I have seen how everywhere the upper stone grinds hard on the nether, and men and women feed upon the toil of their fellow men without any increase of spiritual beauty or joy for themselves, only a heavy congestion; while those who are fed upon grow bitter and narrow from the loss of the life that is sucked from them. Within my own soul I have perceived elements militating against all I hungered for, of which the young child knew nothing; I have watched closely the great, terrible world of public life, of politics, diplomacy, and international relations, where, as under a terrible magnifying glass, the greed, the ambition, the cruelty and falsehood of the individual soul are seen, in so hideously enlarged and wholly unrestrained a form that it might be forgiven to one who cried out to the powers that lie behind life: "Is it not possible to put out a sponge and wipe up humanity from the earth? It is stain!" I have realized that the struggle against the primitive, self-seeking instincts in human nature, whether in the individual or in the larger social organism, is a life-and-death struggle, to be renewed by the individual till death, by the race through the ages. I have tried to wear no blinkers. I have not held a veil before my eyes, that I might profess that cruelty, injustice, and mental and physical anguish were not. I have tried to look nakedly in the face those facts which make most against all hope—and yet, in the darkest hour, the consciousness which I carried back with me that morning has never wholly deserted me; even as a man who clings with one hand to a rock, though the waves pass over his head, yet knows what his hand touches.

But, in the course of the long years which have passed, something else has happened. That which was for the young child only a vision, a flash of almost blinding light, which it could hardly even to itself translate, has, in the course of a long life's experience, become a hope, which I think the cool reason can find grounds to justify, and which a growing knowledge of human nature and human life does endorse.

Somewhere, some time, some place—even on earth!

22. The Boer war of 1899–1902 in which the invading British defeated the Afrikaners but granted the South African provinces self-government as colonies in the British empire. Complicating the resolution of the war was that over 26,000 women and children died in British concentration camps.

SUMMARY

The nineteenth-century Age of Progress had established a core of belief that held people together or provided a target against which they might revolt. World War I marked the point at which the balance was finally destroyed; after that time no such center existed and people found themselves cut loose from the comforting bonds of community and shared values, alone and alienated in a frightening new world. The Culture-Epoch theory highlights the chaotic nature of the period between the two World Wars. This, in turn, provides the framework for cultural changes later in the century.

Replacing the determinism of Newton's world-machine, the work of Planck, Heisenberg, and Einstein revolutionized scientific knowledge of the universe and how it operates. Also revolutionary, the theories of Sigmund Freud, though fatally flawed, helped prepare the way to new insights into the human personality.

In "The Love Song of J. Alfred Prufrock" and "The Second Coming" Eliot and Yeats set the theme for the postwar reaction against the spiritual bankruptcy of the age. Wilfred Owen's poem "Dulce et Decorum Est" speaks for the generation of young men wasted in the trenches and, in "Shine, Perishing Republic," Jeffers depicts bankrupt idealism in a crass and vulgar nation. Harbinger of bad times to come, Cullen's "Yet Do I Marvel" highlights the destructive effects of racism in interwar America. Schreiner's hopes for improvements in human life in her native land were finally realized many years later.

CULTURE AND HUMAN VALUES

Looking back from the distance of some three-quarters of a century, it is difficult to fully appreciate the devastating impact the Great War had on Western culture. Bad enough were the dreadful numbers killed, wounded, and maimed for life. But there was much more. Europeans considered their civilization as the world's most advanced, with the foremost science and technology, a superb educational system, and the world's highest standard of living. Science and technology, however, served the war-machines and contributed mightily to the general death and destruction. The best-educated nation in Europe—Germany—launched a long-planned war of conquest, with victims such as neutral Belgium sacrificed to imperial goals. Germany was by no means the sole transgressor; by the end of the war most nations had contributed their own barbarous acts. In the name of duty, honor, and love of country, politicians and generals violated virtually every precept of those vaunted ideals, not to mention justice and mercy.

Ideals and empires turned out to be equally vulnerable. By the end of the war the empires of Russia, Germany, and Austria-Hungary were finished and the British empire was on its last legs.

Actually, the old values had been disintegrating since the latter decades of the nineteenth century. The pressures of workers, unions, liberals, revolutionaries, socialists, and communists had forced changes on society, but not yet on the outmoded colonial empires. It remained for World War I to bring down the empires and start phasing out colonialism. We now see the war as the cataclysmic event that ended an era and set the stage for the search for new values: chaos followed by a period of adjustment.

CHAPTER 27

Ideas and Conflicts That Motivate the Twentieth Century

HISTORICAL OVERVIEW, 1939–90s

The Great Depression following the breakdown of economic systems was "cured" by the escalating production of weapons for war. England and France frantically, and belatedly, prepared for the resumption of hostilities with Germany in a war notably different from any other in humankind's interminable history of violence.

Soldiers fought in fields and pastures in the nineteenth century, in the trenches in 1914–18, but in 1939–45 the furious new battlefield described by American poet and playwright Richard Eberhart was the air itself. The bomber was the cost-efficient delivery system of World War II; targets included not only opposing armies but myriads of cities and their millions of inhabitants. Whether blasting Berlin and London, fire-bombing Dresden and Tokyo, or obliterating Hiroshima and Nagasaki, civilian casualties vastly outnumbered those of the military, and warfare was total.

DEATH OF A CITY

On 13 February 1945 Dresden, Germany, held about 1,200,000 people, about twice its normal population. Refugees had gathered there because, with no important military targets, it was the safest city in Germany. The first wave of 244 English Lancaster bombers, dropping mostly incendiaries, set fires that the next wave of 529 Lancasters fed with about 650,000 fire-bombs. The third wave of 450 American Flying Fortresses finished the city off. Over 130,000 people (including Allied prisoners of war) were dead, mostly by fire, and the entire center of the city was gone. Why was a non-industrial city full of civilians destroyed? Allied air commanders justified the fire-bombing of German cities such as Berlin, Hamburg, Cologne, and others as part of the "progressive destruction and dislocation of the German economic and industrial system." Famous for its superb old buildings and splendid art collections, Dresden was known as the "Florence of the Elbe" (fig. 27.1). The art had been stored elsewhere but the homes, churches, and palaces were gone forever.

27.1 Dresden old town before its destruction, aerial view. 1929. Photograph. Photo: A.K.G., London.

LITERARY SELECTION 87

The Fury of Aerial Bombardment[1]

Richard Eberhart, b.1904

You would think the fury of aerial bombardment
Would rouse God to relent; the infinite spaces
Are still silent. He then looks on shock-pried faces.
History, even, does not know what is meant.
You would feel that after so many centuries
God would give man to repent; yet he can kill
As Cain could, but with multitudinous will,
No farther advanced than in his ancient furies.
Was man made stupid to see his own stupidity?
Is God by definition indifferent, beyond us all?

1. The Literary Selections in this chapter were picked for two reasons: literary merit and pertinent themes that could point up or flesh out a particular idea or conflict.

Is the eternal truth man's fighting soul
Wherein the Beast ravens in its own avidity?
Of Van Wettering I speak, and Averill,
Names on a list, whose faces I do not recall
But they are gone to early death, who late in school
Distinguished the belt feed lever from the belt holding pawl.

LITERARY SELECTION 88

Chorus of the Rescued

Nelly Sachs, 1891–1970

Sachs developed her poetry as a means of expression that would "make the unspeakable bearable." She escaped to Sweden in 1940 but returned to her native Germany after the war to confront the Holocaust, the basic theme of her poetry. She shared the 1966 Nobel Prize for literature with S. Y. Agnon.

We, the rescued
From whose hollow bones death had begun to whittle his flutes,
And on whose sinews he had already stroked his bow—
Our bodies continue to lament
With their mutilated music.
We, the rescued,
The nooses wound for our necks still dangle before us in the blue air—
Hourglasses still fill with our dripping blood.
We, the rescued,
The worms of fear still feed on us.
Our constellation is buried in dust.
We, the rescued.
Beg you:
Show us your sun, but gradually.
Lead us from star to star, step by step.
Be gentle when you teach us to live again.
Lest the song of a bird,
Or a pail being filled at the well,
Let our badly sealed pain burst forth again and carry us away—
We beg you:
Do not show us an angry dog, not yet—
It could be, it could be
That we will dissolve into dust—
Dissolve into dust before your eyes.
For what binds our fabric together?
We whose breath vacated us,
Whose soul fled to Him out of that midnight
Long before our bodies were rescued
Into the ark of the moment,
We, the rescued,
We press your hand
We look into your eye—
But all that binds us together now is leave-taking,
The leave-taking in the dust
Binds us together with you.

STUDY QUESTIONS

1. Which images best indicate what these survivors have endured?
2. Will these people ever fully recover?

THE COLD WAR, CA. 1945–90

World War II ended on 14 August 1945 with the Japanese surrender, and the whole world expected a new era of peace and stability. The United States, with its nuclear monopoly and enormous industrial capacity, emerged as an unrivaled superpower. Having learned some bitter lessons from the League of Nations, the United Nations began to function as the first real consortium of nations; with the assistance of the Marshall Plan, war-ravaged nations launched recovery programs that frequently verged on the miraculous. However, the anticipated era of peace and stability was delayed indefinitely with the Soviet Union's postwar expansionism and the detonation of its own atomic bomb in 1949. The sharply reduced power of the western European nations and the shambles of the old colonial order left a vacuum that was filled by the United States and the Soviet Union. Basically the confrontation was between the Western democracies led by the United States and the Eastern Bloc led by the Soviet Union under dictator Joseph Stalin (map 27.1).[2] Stalin moved quickly in 1945, creating "people's republics" in Poland, Romania, Hungary, Bulgaria, and later in Czechoslovakia and East Germany. Soviet attempts to take over Greece and Turkey were rebuffed by the Allies but, as it had for centuries before Lenin and Stalin, Russian imperialism continued to select targets of opportunity.

Communists tried and failed to win power in the Philippines, Indonesia, and Malaysia, but they did succeed in North Korea. Russian weapons (and the connivance of Stalin and Mao Zedong) encouraged the North Koreans to invade South Korea, thus launching the Korean War (1950–53) that eventually saw the People's Republic of China enter the war against United Nations troops comprised mainly of U.S. forces. The invasion ended in a stalemate near the original boundary between the two nations. Prolonged negotiations resulted in an armistice—not a peace treaty—in July 1953 that remains in effect.

The Viet Minh revolt that erupted in French Indochina after World War II ended in 1954 when the French stronghold at Dien Bien Phu surrendered to the insurgency

2. "If we assume the viewpoint of humanity and freedom, history does not know a despot as cynical as Stalin was. He was methodical, all-embracing, and total as a criminal. He was one of those rare terrible dogmatists capable of destroying nine-tenths of the human race to 'make happy' the one tenth." Milojan Djilas, *Conversations with Stalin* (New York: Harcourt, Brace & World, 1962), p. 190.

led by Ho Chi Minh (1890–1969). A major power conference in Geneva subsequently recognized the independence of the former provinces of Cambodia and Laos. A Korean-style compromise divided the third province into Communist North Vietnam with its capital at Hanoi, and capitalist South Vietnam with Saigon as its capital.

By 1958 Communist-led guerillas, supported by Ho Chi Minh and known as the Viet Cong, had disrupted and terrorized much of South Vietnam. When the North Vietnamese army joined the Viet Cong in 1966, the American response was a rapid increase in troops, from several thousand in 1965 to 500,000 in 1967. The impact of the war on the United States was enormous, this being the first war to appear every evening on American television. The mounting casualties, the known atrocities, the corrupt South Vietnamese governments, the lack of a clear-cut rationale for an Asian war, and the inability of American arms to inflict a decisive defeat on a dedicated and relentless enemy led to massive anti-war protests in the United States.

Even now it is difficult to determine which came first: the anti-establishment free-speech revolt of the 1960s or the violent reaction to the slaughter in Vietnam that spun off a whole decade of activism, hippies, flower children, communes, campus sit-ins and riots, and the development of a drug culture. All were manifestations of a sea-change that affected every cranny of American society.

The war effectively ended the political career of President Lyndon B. Johnson and adversely affected the Nixon administration. A long-delayed cease-fire was finally arranged in January 1973, a pact that North Vietnam violated after most of the remaining American troops had left the country. Saigon fell to the North Vietnamese on 30 April 1975 as the remaining Americans frantically evacuated the American embassy on relays of helicopters. Though the war was widely believed to be an internal war of liberation, North Vietnamese leaders later admitted that they had used the Viet Cong as pawns in a well-planned war of conquest.

The war in Vietnam prompted violent reactions, but a large segment of the population tried to ignore American entanglement in an unpopular war. There was a desire not to become involved, not to think about distant, murderous jungles, especially when—as was often the case—no friends nor relatives were fighting in Asia. However, nearly 60,000 combatants died in Vietnam in the only war the United States ever lost.

Throughout the Cold War, mutual assured destruction (MAD), a balance of terror, kept nuclear weapons in their silos. So-called conventional (hot) wars, however, abounded. If a major war is defined as one in which there are more than 1,000 combatants, there have been over 100 wars since 1945. African and Asian nationalism, class conflicts in Central and South America, endless Middle East crises, including large-scale warfare—the trials and tribulations of our era never cease and yet the world looks hopefully toward better days with the freeing of captive nations and the widespread revival of democracies.

The major event—actually series of events—of the late 1980s was the widespread failure of Marxist-Leninism. The Soviet Union and its satellites had, by that time, demonstrated that Communism could not work, indeed had never achieved its goals. In *The Unperfect Society* (1969) Yugoslav author Milovan Djilas predicted the inevitable failure of Communism; he identified the source of the problem by tracing the ugly roots of Stalinism back through Lenin to Marx's utopianism, ideological rigidity, and scientific pretensions. He pointed out that Communist dictators assumed they had been named by a higher power—History—that awarded them the right to establish the Kingdom of Heaven (dictatorship of the proletariat) in this sinful capitalistic world. Why was History this higher power? Because Marx said so.

The flaw in Marxism was fundamental. Marx based his entire doctrine on the proclamation that began Section I of the *Communist Manifesto*: "The history of all hitherto existing society is the history of class struggles." If this statement were true then History was on the side of those who would eliminate class struggles by establishing a classless society. Hegel had claimed that past cultures were stages in the evolutionary development of the world Spirit toward perfection and freedom. Marx and Engels formulated a doctrine of inevitable progress leading to the perfect classless society by twisting Hegel's philosophy from the consciousness of his world Spirit to the consciousness of societies engaged in class struggle. In fact, however, some of the most important values and issues transcend class. Family, trust, loyalty, faith, fidelity, and the many varieties of love are just a few of the values that are cherished by peasants and poets, commoners and kings. The Marxian interpretation of history was, in plain words, wrong, thus making all subsequent Communist theory fatally flawed. This should not imply, however, that Marx's influence was wholly negative. He was genuinely interested in the welfare of the working class and his theories are, in part, responsible for the greatly improved status of the underprivileged of advanced societies.

In pragmatic terms, Communism failed because not one aspect of the system worked.[3] The classless society was never tried nor did the proletariat ever have any voice in the "dictatorship of the proletariat." Every Communist country suffered under a dictatorial party whose elite class controlled the masses by coercion, fear, censorship, rewriting history (of all subjects!), and the omnipresent secret police. One of the worst—and abiding—bequests of Communist inefficiency and mismanagement is the destruction of the environment. Throughout central Europe, forests, fields, streams, lakes, and the atmosphere were destroyed or

3. In 1983 Luigi Barzini wrote in *The Europeans*: "The Russian Revolution exaggerated the worst traits of Czarist authority: secret police, mass exiles to Siberia, forced labor camps, the concentration of all of the economy in the hands of the state. The Soviets dedicated the largest percentage of the national income to armaments and starved the peasantry, as has been done in Russia for centuries. In the end, the Communist regime turned out to be a caricature of what had existed before."

GENOCIDE

Not until Nazi Germany was finally defeated in 1945 did the world learn of the incredible extent of Nazi atrocities. As Allied troops liberated starving prisoners from Dachau (fig. 27.2 and p. 404), Auschwitz, Buchenwald (see fig. 28.56) and dozens more death camps, the horror grew ever greater. Of the estimated 12,000,000 victims who were gassed and cremated in the ovens, about 6,000,000 were Jews, whom Hitler's Holocaust had tried to erase from the face of the earth. The other 6,000,000 were Slavs, Gypsies, Masons, Communists, Socialists, homosexuals, prostitutes, and an unending supply of enemies of the state. Ironically, some of the troops whose relatives had been imprisoned in the United States, namely the Japanese-American 522nd Field Artillery Battalion, were among the Allied liberators.

27.2 Memorial Sculpture, Dachau, Germany. Photo: Ullstein, Berlin.

severely contaminated in futile attempts to fulfill production quotas regardless of the consequences. The won der of it all, as many have remarked, is not that Marxism-Leninism failed but that it took so long.

The most startling aspect of the demise of Communism was how abruptly it collapsed in so many countries. The sickly Soviet economy was a critical factor, of course, but one should also consider the pivotal role of the electronic devices of the Information Age. Television, camcorders, video tapes, and VCRs played a significant role in the public's knowledge of demonstrations, repression, and rebellion. It is no longer possible to keep a subject people in the dark about what transpires in the rest of the world, and this may be the most hopeful sign of what it means to live in a "Global Village."

The decisive conclusion of the Cold War followed closely on the jubilant destruction of the Berlin Wall in 1989. Stalin had reasoned that, American power notwithstanding, a divided Germany was the key to the USSR's unrivaled dominance in Europe. Germany was unified on 2 October 1990 and the Paris Charter was signed on 21 November 1990 by the United States, Canada, and every European nation except Albania. The Paris agreement guaranteed commitment to democracy and economic well-being for all signatories, thus ending the Cold War that had begun after World War II. 1990 is already viewed as one of the most important dates in the modern history of Western civilization, probably on a par with the end of the Thirty Years' War in 1648 and the termination of the Napoleonic wars in 1815.

We can now complete the dramatic allegory described on page 325 in which World War I was characterized as Act I. The entr'acte of 1918–39 connected the Great War to World War II (Act II), for the former did indeed lead to the latter. The third act was the Cold War that ended with the triumph of the Western democracies. The Western world and the European Community in particular now have a historic opportunity to secure a lasting peace. Serious problems in the Balkans, Middle East, the Far East, and Africa remain unresolved but the United Nations, with the strong backing of the United States and the EC, is in the best position in its history to bring some sort of stability to the entire world.

PHILOSOPHY

Probably every philosophical system ever invented has surfaced at one time or another during this troubled century. One of the most influential of these philosophies, existentialism, is more a mood or an attitude than a complete philosophical system. Formulated during World War II by French writer Jean-Paul Sartre during his years with the French Resistance, existentialism had an immediate appeal for a desperate world. Actually, the roots of the movement go back to several disparate personalities of the nineteenth century, particularly Kierkegaard, a Danish anticlerical theologian, and Nietzsche, a German atheist.

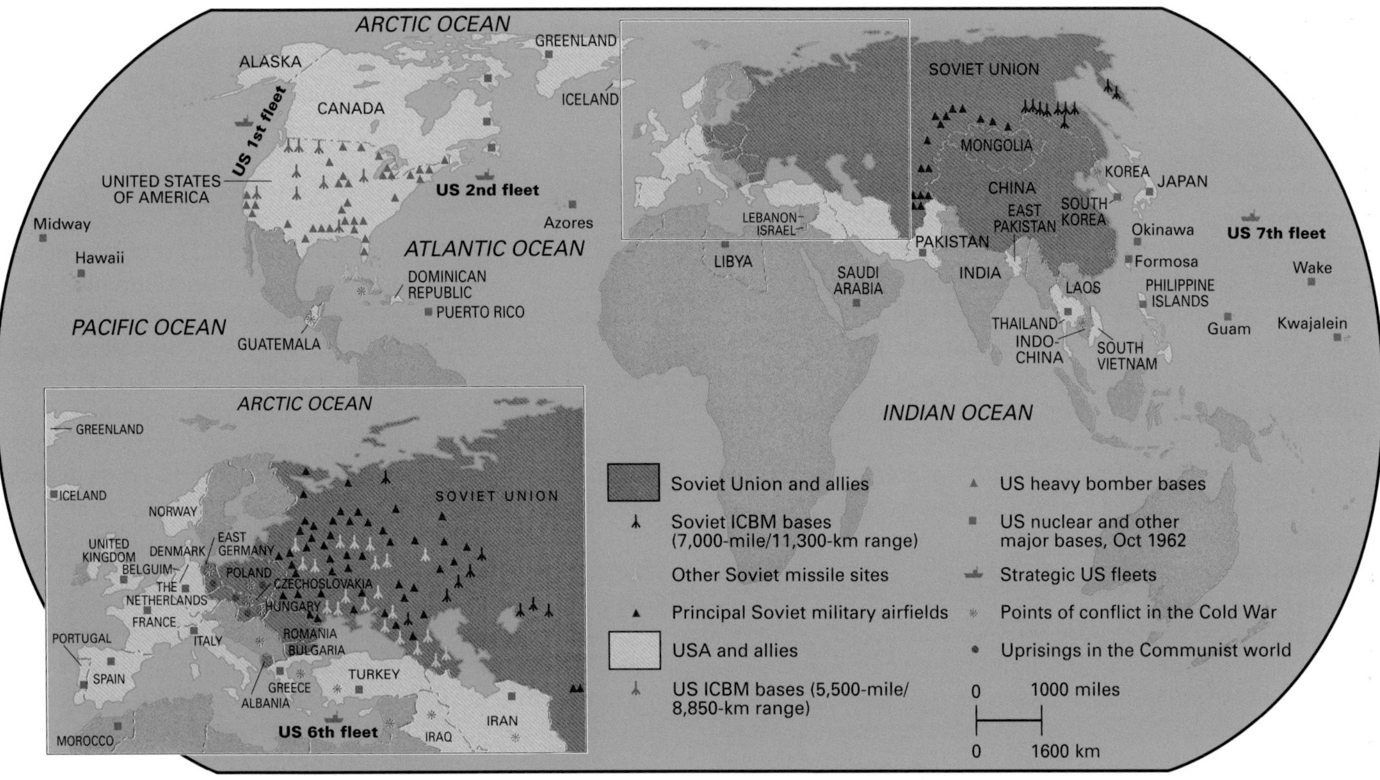

Map 27.1 The Cold War.

Søren Kierkegaard, 1813–55

A melancholy and lonely Dane, Kierkegaard (KEER-kuh-gard) was almost totally unnoticed in his own time. Kierkegaard's concern was with the individual, whom he saw as an actor on the stage of life. For each individual there was, according to Kierkegaard, the possibility of three ascending levels of existence along life's way: aesthetic, ethical, and religious. The aesthetic level was that of the pleasure-seeker, and the only goals were newer pleasant sensations. Eventually, the futile pursuit of pleasure ends in despair and life is absurd. The only way to rise above the aesthetic level is to recognize the reality of choice.

The second level is that of the ethical, which does not eliminate the aesthetic mode but rises above it. The ethical life is not, however, the same as advocating abstract ethical theories; one can know about ethical theories and still be an unethical slob. The ethical person, for Kierkegaard, is actively committed to long-range purposes, dedicated to the continuity of life, free to choose and be bound to a commitment. Choice is a necessity in the ethical life and, Kierkegaard says, the only absolutely ethical choice is between good and evil. But this is not enough. We are virtually helpless in facing the evils and injustices of everyday life; these evils can be overcome only by an outpouring of love and generosity beyond human justice and human powers. Such love and generosity is possible only if something transcending us breaks into history and works in our lives. Kierkegaard believed that the breakthrough of the eternal into history was the birth of Christ.

ECOLOGICAL SUICIDE

One of today's most serious concerns is the worldwide abuse of natural resources. This is not, however, a recent problem. The past is replete with chilling examples of cultures who, in effect, committed ecological suicide. A case in point are the Maya of Central America. This civilization can be traced back to around 2000 BC with a classic period (ca. AD 300–900) more advanced than European civilization in the same era, especially their mathematics and calendar. Equally notable were Maya achievements in astronomy, historical writing, architecture, and sculpture.

Numbering over 2,000,000 people at the height of their civilization, the Maya went into a long decline after 900 and, beginning around 1542, finally succumbed to Spanish conquest. Some archaeologists have theorized that this deterioration was caused by a combination of overpopulation and the devastation of natural resources through slash-and-burn agriculture. Widespread famine led to interminable civil wars over dwindling agricultural lands. The Maya left today still live in virtually the same geographical area, much of which is once again tropical jungle. Only haunting vestiges of their high culture remain.

To recapitulate: after the vain pursuit of pleasure we feel despair; through choice we can raise ourselves to the ethical level and become committed to our responsibilities, but this eventually proves insufficient; each of us becomes a "knight of infinite resignation." At this point we can choose to leap beyond reason to the religious mode of existence using the passion called faith ("where reason ends there begins faith").

Faith, for Kierkegaard, means total commitment to the inner personality of God. We cannot cleverly argue our way to God; we either accept God completely or reject him completely. The second and final leap of faith is into the arms of Jesus. However, Kierkegaard says, this leap to the God-man of Christian history is conceptually absurd. The intensity of the leap of faith to God is vastly increased by the second venture to the level of Christianity, which is unintelligible. As Kierkegaard wrote, "in an unpermissible and unlawful way people have become knowing about Christ, for the only permissible way is to be believing."

These absolute ventures are personal decisions taken in absolute loneliness with the utmost responsibility. The isolation of the individual in such a decision is absolute and this, says Kierkegaard, is what it means to be a human being. These leaps of faith make an existing individual. Speculative philosophy, according to Kierkegaard, plus the Christian establishment and the press had confused basic facts: "Christendom has done away with Christianity without being quite aware of it."

Values, for Kierkegaard, were not esoteric essences: "Good and evil are ways of existing and the human good is to exist authentically." Conversely, evil is an unauthentic, ungenuine existence. Authentic existence is a matter of choice and the existing person knows the risk and feels the dread of individual responsibility. But, as Kierkegaard observed, "dread is the possibility of freedom" and "man is condemned to freedom."

Friedrich Nietzsche, 1844–1900

Nietzsche (NEE-chuh) stressed the absurdity of human existence and the inability of our reason to understand the world. A passionate individualist, he proclaimed the will to power as the only value in a meaningless world. Nietzsche rejected any ideas or system that would limit the freedom of the individual, particularly Christianity, which taught, he contended, a "slave morality" of sympathy, kindness, humility, and pity, qualities beneficial only to the weak and the helpless. His "noble" man was a superman, an incarnate will to power, who would rise above the herd (the "bungled and the botched") to establish a "master morality" of the "aristocratic" qualities of strength, nobility, pride, and power. "God is dead," Nietzsche proclaimed, meaning that all absolute systems from Plato onward had died with the God of the Judeo-Christian tradition.

A fervent admirer of the culture of ancient Greece, Nietzsche evolved an influential aesthetic theory of the Apollonian and Dionysian modes. The Apollonian mode is intellectual. It draws an aesthetic veil over reality, creating an ideal world of form and beauty. The Apollonian attitude found expression in Greek mythology, in Homer's epic poems, in sculpture, painting, architecture, and Greek vases.

The Dionysian mode, somewhat like Freud's *id*, is the dark, turgid, and formless torrent of instinct, impulse, and passion that tends to sweep aside everything in its path. Tragedy and music are typical Dionysian art forms: they transmute existence into aesthetic phenomena without, however, drawing a veil over authentic existence. The Dionysian represents existence in aesthetic form and affirms this, says Nietzsche, in the human condition. True culture, for Nietzsche, is a unity of life forces, the dark Dionysian element combined with the love of form and beauty that characterizes the Apollonian. The highest product of this balanced culture is the creative genius, the superman.

Adolf Hitler drew on Nietzsche's purported work, *The Will to Power*, for key ideas about German superiority, the Master Race (Nietzsche's superman), and anti-Semitism. Scholars finally proved, by 1958, that Nietzsche did not write *The Will to Power*. After his death, Nietzsche's proto-Nazi sister combined his notebook jottings with thirty forged letters and other fabrications to publish the volume in her brother's name. Actually, Nietzsche was more anti- than pro-German, referring to Germans as "blond beasts of prey" and casting scorn on "their repulsive habit of stimulating themselves with alcohol." Far from a racist, Nietzsche saw all the races on the globe blending into a uniform color of beige and he called anti-Semites "another name for failures."

The basic theme of Nietzsche's life and thought was the antipolitical individual who sought self-perfection far from the modern world. His desire was "to live for one's education free from politics, nationality, and newspapers." For him, knowledge was power and the will to power was the use of education for the betterment of humankind. "Above all," he said, "become who you are!"

Kierkegaard and Nietzsche represent the two extremes of theistic and atheistic existentialism with Feodor Dostoevsky somewhere in between. In the Grand Inquisitor section of *The Brothers Karamazov* the latter denies all authority (symbolized by the Church of Rome) in favor of the individual search for faith, spirit, and redemption.

Jean-Paul Sartre, 1905–80

Sartre (sar-tru), an atheistic existentialist quite unlike Nietzsche, arrived at his conclusions using logic. Sartre contended that the idea of God was self-contradictory, that the man called Christ could not be both divine and human because the terms are mutually exclusive. In other words, said Sartre, divine means non-human and human means that which is not divine. You cannot draw a circular square or a square circle. And, if there is no God, there are no fixed values, no absolute right or wrong, no good or bad. In *The Brothers Karamazov* Dostoevsky has one of his characters say, "But you see, if there were no God, everything would be possible." And that is precisely Sartre's point, that human beings are the sole source of values and anything is possible.

Sartre's basic premise was that existence precedes essence. First, a person is; what he or she becomes is settled in the course of existence. For the existentialist things in the world just are; only human beings can create themselves. Liberty is unrestricted, our capacity for choice is absolute, and making choices is what makes us human. The only meaning that life has is in the significance of the values that we choose. Values are not waiting to be discovered; we invent values. To the question, "What meaning is there in life?", the existentialist replies, "only what you put into life." But, as Sartre warns, the exercise of freedom is inseparably linked with responsibility: "Man is condemned to be free; because once thrown into the world, man is responsible for everything he does."

You can never choose anything, wrote Sartre, without realizing that this is the choice you wish all humankind to make. If you choose truth then you want everyone to be truthful; if you choose to steal then you are willing that everyone should be a thief. In every choice you have chosen for all humankind, a crushing responsibility, a condition that Sartre calls "anguish."

What are the values for which the existentialist is willing to assume responsibility? The answer has a curiously old-fashioned ring: the values are those of individualism; value is in the individual; value is the individual. The supreme virtue is responsible choice, what we call integrity, and the ultimate vice is self-deception. "Know thyself," said the Greeks and the existentialist fervently agrees. What you choose determines what you will become but, Sartre emphasizes, you can change, you can redirect your steps. What gives meaning to life is not what happens to us but what we ourselves do. We are actors on the stage of life. As Sartre said: "Man is encompassed by his own existence and there is no exit." In 1947 Sartre wrote in *Existentialism:*

> Existentialism is nothing less than an attempt to draw all the consequences of a coherent atheistic position. It isn't trying to plunge man into despair at all. But if one calls every attitude of unbelief despair, like the Christian, then the word is not being used in its original sense. Existentialism isn't so atheistic that it wears itself out showing that God doesn't exist. Rather, it declares that even if God did exist, that would change nothing. There you've got our point of view. Not that we believe that God exists, but we think the problem of his existence is not the issue. In this sense existentialism is optimistic, a doctrine of action, and it is plain dishonesty for Christians to make no distinction between their own despair and ours and then to call us despairing.

Existentialism owes its popularity in no small part to repeated failures in politics, economics, and social organizations that have scarred our century. Whatever shortcomings the movement may have, it is not just a body of philosophical speculations, but an attitude that still helps a great many people in this muddled world to pursue a personal freedom, a way of life that ranks quality over quantity.

LITERARY SELECTION 89

The Myth of Sisyphus

Albert Camus, 1913–66

Both Sartre and Albert Camus were active in the French Resistance and both won the Nobel Prize for literature. Camus' brilliant novel, *The Stranger,* superbly delineates the existential themes of absurdity, anguish, despair, and alienation, but Camus always denied that he was an existentialist. He claimed instead that the world was so absurd that the philosopher should logically contemplate suicide. The alternative, for Camus, was to dismiss the world and lead an active, heroic life. The hero of ordinary life is the person who resolutely shoulders the responsibilities that life imposes, knowing that all is futile and meaningless, an attitude that is exemplified in the essay, "The Myth of Sisyphus," given here in a translation by J. O'Brien. In Greek mythology Sisyphus was a rogue-hero who delighted in tricking the gods. The gods were so furious that, through all eternity, they devised a divine plan that would keep Sisyphus too busy to plan another escape but, as Camus concludes, "one must imagine Sisyphus happy" in the act of doing.

The gods had condemned Sisyphus to ceaselessly rolling a rock to the top of a mountain, whence the stone would fall back of its own weight. They had thought with some reason that there is no more dreadful punishment than futile and hopeless labor.

If one believes Homer, Sisyphus was the wisest and most prudent of mortals. According to another tradition, however, he was disposed to practice the profession of highwayman. I see no contradiction in this. Opinions differ as to the reasons why he became the futile laborer of the underworld. To begin with, he is accused of a certain levity in regard to the gods. He stole their secrets. Aegina, the daughter of Aesopus, was carried off by Jupiter. The father was shocked by that disappearance and complained to Sisyphus. He, who knew of the abduction, offered to tell about it on condition that Aesopus would give water to the citadel of Corinth. To the celestial thunderbolts he preferred the benediction of water. He was punished for this in the underworld. Homer tells us also that Sisyphus had put Death in chains. Pluto could not endure the sight of his deserted, silent empire. He dispatched the god of war, who liberated Death from the hands of her conqueror.

It is said also that Sisyphus, being near to death, rashly

wanted to test his wife's love. He ordered her to cast his unburied body into the middle of the public square. Sisyphus woke up in the underworld. And there, annoyed by an obedience so contrary to human love, he obtained from Pluto permission to return to earth in order to chastise his wife. But when he had seen again the face of this world, enjoyed water and sun, warm stones and the sea, he no longer wanted to go back to the infernal darkness. Recalls, signs of anger, warnings were of no avail. Many years more he lived facing the curve of the gulf, the sparkling sea, and the smiles of earth. A decree of the gods was necessary. Mercury came and seized the impudent man by the collar and, snatching him from his joys, led him forcibly back to the underworld, where his rock was ready for him.

You have already grasped that Sisyphus is the absurd hero. He *is,* as much through his passions as through his torture. His scorn of the gods, his hatred of death, and his passion for life won him that unspeakable penalty in which the whole being is exerted toward accomplishing nothing. This is the price that must be paid for the passions of this earth. Nothing is told us about Sisyphus in the underworld. Myths are made for the imagination to breathe life into them. As for this myth, one sees merely the whole effort of a body straining to raise the huge stone, to roll it and push it up a slope a hundred times over; one sees the face screwed up, the cheek tight against the stone, the shoulder bracing the clay-covered mass, the foot wedging it, the fresh start with arms outstretched, the wholly human security of two earth-clotted hands. At the very end of his long effort measured by skyless space and time without depth, the purpose is achieved. Then Sisyphus watches the stone rush down in a few moments toward that lower world whence he will have to push it up again toward the summit. He goes back down to the plain.

It is during that return, that pause, that Sisyphus interests me. A face that toils so close to stones is already stone itself! I see that man going back down with a heavy yet measured step toward the torment of which he will never know the end. That hour like a breathing-space which returns as surely as his suffering, that is the hour of consciousness. At each of those moments when he leaves the heights and gradually sinks toward the lairs of the gods, he is superior to his fate. He is stronger than his rock.

If this myth is tragic, that is because its hero is conscious. Where would his torture be, indeed, if at every step the hope of succeeding upheld him? The workman of today works every day in his life at the same tasks, and this fate is no less absurd. But it is tragic only at the rare moments when it becomes conscious. Sisyphus, proletarian of the gods, powerless and rebellious, knows the whole extent of his wretched condition: it is what he thinks of during his descent. The lucidity that was to constitute his torture at the same time crowns his victory. There is no fate that cannot be surmounted by scorn.

If the descent is thus sometimes performed in sorrow, it can also take place in joy. This word is not too much. Again I fancy Sisyphus returning toward his rock, and the sorrow was in the beginning. When the images of earth cling too tightly to memory, when the call of happiness becomes too insistent, it happens that melancholy rises in man's heart: this is the rock's victory, this is the rock itself. The boundless grief is too heavy to bear. These are our nights of Gethsemane. But crushing truths perish from being acknowledged. Thus, Oedipus at the outset obeys fate without knowing it. But from the moment he knows, his tragedy begins. Yet at the same moment, blind and desperate, he realizes that the only bond linking him to the world is the cool hand of a girl. Then a tremendous remark rings out: "Despite so many ordeals, my advanced age and the nobility of my soul make me conclude that all is well." Sophocles' Oedipus, like Dostoevsky's Kirilov, thus gives the recipe for the absurd victory. Ancient wisdom confirms modern heroism.

One does not discover the absurd without being tempted to write a manual of happiness. "What! by such narrow ways—?" There is but one world, however. Happiness and the absurd are two sons of the same earth. They are inseparable. It would be a mistake to say that happiness necessarily springs from the absurd discovery. It happens as well that the feeling of the absurd springs from happiness. "I conclude that all is well," says Oedipus, and that remark is sacred. It echoes in the wild and limited universe of man. It teaches that all is not, has not been, exhausted. It drives out of this world a god who had come into it with dissatisfaction and a preference for futile sufferings. It makes of fate a human matter, which must be settled among men.

All Sisyphus' silent joy is contained therein. His fate belongs to him. His rock is his thing. Likewise, the absurd man, when he contemplates his torment, silences all the idols. In the universe suddenly restored to its silence, the myriad wondering little voices of the earth rise up. Unconscious, secret calls, invitations from all the faces, they are the necessary reverse and price of victory. There is no sun without shadow, and it is essential to know the night. The absurd man says yes and his effort will henceforth be unceasing. If there is a personal fate, there is no higher destiny, or at least there is but one which he concludes is inevitable and despicable. For the rest, he knows himself to be the master of his days. At that subtle moment when man glances backward over his life, Sisyphus returning toward his rock, in that slight pivoting he contemplates that series of unrelated actions which becomes his fate, created by him, combined under his memory's eye and soon sealed by his death. Thus, convinced of the wholly human origin of all that is human, a blind man eager to see who knows that the night has no end, he is still on the go. The rock is still rolling.

I leave Sisyphus at the foot of the mountain! One always finds one's burden again. But Sisyphus teaches the higher fidelity that negates the gods and raises rocks. He too concludes that all is well. This universe henceforth without a master seems to him neither sterile nor futile. Each atom of that stone, each mineral flake of that night-filled mountain, in itself forms a world. The struggle itself toward the heights is enough to fill a man's heart. One must imagine Sisyphus happy.

STUDY QUESTIONS

1. Imagine several children on a sandy beach busily constructing a large sand castle. A passerby maliciously stomps on a tower, providing a brief but violent confrontation. Finally the builders complete their elaborate fairy-tale structure just as the encroaching tide tentatively laps at the outer walls. The construction crew observes attentively as the noble turrets subside into the swirling water and then, losing interest, pick up their things and set off for the beach house. Why was there a fight over the mutilated tower but only calm acceptance of the watery demise of the castle? How is all of this analogous to Sisyphus and his rock?
2. Consider the millionaire who feels that he must aim for a hundred million, then a billion, or more. How much money will be enough, or is money even the main focus? How does this relate to Sisyphus?
3. Let us say that the gods have relented and that, as Sisyphus muscles the rock into place, it teeters for a moment and then remains firmly in place. Describe Sisyphus' feelings. Have the gods indeed relented or have they devised a more fiendish form of punishment?

Existentialism: Postscript

Some existentialists, particularly Christian existentialists, imagine that a person can become a sort of superhero when he or she infuses pointless life with meaning and thereby creates meaning in the universe. Some Christian existentialists believe that Christ was such a figure; and that, if the actuality for such being exists within one individual, then it is also a potentiality for all humanity.

A large number of philosophers and Christian theologians have advanced and developed this Christian existentialist point of view. Among them are Ernst Block and the Dutch Roman Catholic theologian Edward Schillebeeckx. Oversimplifying greatly, they view God as the Creative Purpose of the world; the End toward which the world is moving. Block has referred to him as "the God who is not yet"; Schillebeeckx as the God who is "wholly new." This concept is a far cry from the standard view of a God who is complete and whole from the beginning of time and who rules the world either as loving Father or as Great Engineer. Instead, he is constantly inventing himself or being invented here on earth, exactly as the existentialist person, moment by moment, invents himself or herself.

RELIGIONS

The continuing influx of new citizens from Asia and the Middle East simply adds to the multiculturalism of the United States. Though there have always been religions in addition to Judaism and Christianity in this country, the numbers are now changing rather significantly. Throughout the country there are new mosques, Buddhist and Hindu temples, and one can study with a Zen master in any major city. Islam was discussed at length in volume 1, chapter 12, but attention must be given to Hinduism, Buddhism, and Zen Buddhism.

Hinduism

The oldest of all world religions, Hinduism dates back to about 1500 BC. The word "Hindu" is derived from the Sanskrit word *sindhu*, meaning "river," specifically the Indus, where the earliest Indian civilization developed. Unlike any other religion, Hinduism's origins are unknown. It has no founder, it has more than one sacred book, and there is no single body of doctrine. Remarkably inclusive rather than exclusive, Hinduism is a blanket term for a wide diversity of beliefs and practices that do not, however, cause any conflicts or problems. Hindus worship many gods while also holding to the view that there is only one god, called Brahman, with all other divinities aspects of the unknowable Brahman.

A distinctive feature is the belief in the transmigration of souls and the idea that all living things are part of the same essence. An individual human soul may return many times in human, animal, or vegetable form. What a person does in a present life will affect the next life, which is the doctrine of *karma*, the law of cause and effect. The individual's goal is to escape the cycle of birth and death so that the soul, Atman, may become part of Brahman, the absolute soul.

India's caste system is a historic characteristic of Hinduism that originally divided all human beings into four classes: priests (or Brahmins), warriors, merchants, and servants. In today's India there are many castes, from the Brahmins at the top to the Untouchables (now outlawed as a caste) at the bottom. Adherents of Hinduism can be found around the globe but the caste system is confined to India.

Hindus regard many animals and plants as sacred, most notably the cow; beef is not eaten even among castes that are not vegetarian. Monkeys, tree squirrels, trees, and some snakes are also considered holy, as are some rivers, especially the Ganges. People are also sacred according to their position in life; thus parents are holy to their children, teachers to their students, and so on. It is estimated that there are more than 700,000,000 Hindus with 90 percent of them residing in India.

Buddhism

The religion of about one-eighth of all the people in the world, Buddhism is a complex set of beliefs built around the teaching of a single man. It was founded in northeast India in the fifth century BC by Siddhartha Gautama, known as the Buddha (the "Enlightened One"). Having lived a self-indulgent life and then one of bitter denial, Siddhartha sat for forty-nine days under a tree, where he was awakened to the truth about life. For many years he taught the Four Noble Truths and the Eightfold Path.

The first truth is that all life is suffering, pain, and misery. The second is that this suffering is caused by selfish craving and personal desire. But this selfishness can be overcome, which is the third truth. The fourth truth is that people can overcome this misery through the Eightfold Path. All Buddhists believe that people should not identify too strongly with their own personal existence in any one life. The cycle of reincarnation condemns the person to the suffering associated with being alive and striving. The goal, according the Buddha, is to escape from being born as a suffering person—to attain Nirvana, the highest bliss. This is what he experienced under the tree.

The Buddha called his Eightfold Path the Middle Way between a luxurious life and one of unnecessary poverty. Not everyone can attain Nirvana, of course, but everyone can at least start down the road. But first they must take a basic step that precedes the Middle Way. Buddhists are supposed to follow Right Association, that is, to associate only with other seekers of truth in a spirit of love.

The Eightfold Path

1. Right Knowledge of life is revealed in the Four Noble Truths.
2. Right Aspiration means being committed on the Path toward Enlightenment.
3. Right Speech is speaking with clarity and always kindly.
4. Right Behavior means paying attention to one's behavior and to the five basic laws of behavior: not to kill, steal, lie, drink intoxicants, or commit sexual offenses.
5. Right Livelihood means choosing a career that promotes life and good will rather than trying to make a lot of money.
6. Right Effort means learning to curb all selfish concerns.
7. Right Mindfulness is continual self-examination and awareness; as Socrates said, the unexamined life is not worth living.
8. Right Concentration is the final goal of being absorbed into a state of Nirvana.

The Eightfold Path, in reduced form, becomes the Threefold Learning: Discipline on Morality, Meditation, and Wisdom.

Schism

Two major traditions of Buddhism emerged early on and continue to this day. The older tradition, known as the Way of the Elders, is also called the Little Raft and also Theravada Buddhism. This is still the main tradition in Sri Lanka, Myanmar (Burma), Thailand, Laos, and Cambodia. The Greater Vehicle, Mahayana Buddhism, is the dominant form of Buddhism in Mongolia, Tibet, China, Taiwan, Japan, Korea, Vietnam, and Nepal. In all its forms Buddhism has three unchanging cornerstones, which are the Three Jewels: *Buddha*, the teacher; *Dharma*, the teachings or laws; and *Sangha*, the community of believers.

Zen (or Ch'an)

This is a Buddhist school that developed in China and later in Japan as a result of the fusion of Mahayana Buddhism with the Chinese philosophy of Taoism. Zen and Ch'an are the Japanese and Chinese ways of pronouncing the Sanskrit term *dhyana*, which connotes a state of mind roughly corresponding to contemplation or meditation. Zen is the peculiarly Chinese way of seeing the world just as it is, with a mind that neither grasps nor feels; it just contemplates. This is called "no-mind." Zen maintains that gradual practice cannot produce such freedom of the mind; it must come through insight. The world, according to Zen, is not many things; it is one reality. When reason analyzes the diversity of the world it obscures this oneness. But it can be apprehended by the non-rational part of the mind: intuition. Zen is fond of asking questions such as, "what is the sound of one hand clapping?", or, when asked about the Way of Zen, of replying "a cloud in the sky and water in the pail."

Zen has strongly influenced Eastern arts and crafts because it is concerned with acting rather than theorizing and because of its direct vision of nature rather than relying on interpretation. It has also appealed to many Western artists, philosophers, and psychologists. It has a special appeal for non-objective painters and sculptors. Philosophers have noted its similarities with the ideas of Ludwig Wittgenstein, the Austrian philosopher, and, to some extent, with existentialism as propounded by German philosopher Martin Heidegger.

CIVIL RIGHTS

Since World War II the United States has become more democratic, but it hasn't been easy. The so-called Second Reconstruction in American history began in the late 1940s with presidential decrees that banned discrimination in federal jobs and ordered desegregation of the armed forces. The target of the first stage of the civil rights movement, segregation in public education, was struck down by the landmark Supreme Court decision of 1954, Brown versus the Board of Education (Topeka). Despite sometimes violent opposition, the nation's schools were gradually integrated while, at the same time, other forms of discrimination were challenged with boycotts, sit-ins, and "freedom rides." Congress enacted, in 1957, the first civil rights legislation—to safeguard voting rights—since 1865, followed by voting legislation in 1960, and, in 1964, by a comprehensive Civil Rights Act that banned discrimination on the basis of race, sex, nationality, or religion in public places, employment, and unions.

The most powerful moving force behind the Civil Rights Movement was the Reverend Martin Luther King, Jr., the president of the Southern Christian Leadership Conference. He helped organize a coherent program of nonviolent resistance to networks of segregation laws, a program best described in his famous "Letter from Birmingham Jail." Written on 16 April 1963 while he was confined for parading without a permit, the letter was addressed to certain Protestant ministers, Catholic priests, and a rabbi.

LITERARY SELECTION 90

Letter from Birmingham Jail

Martin Luther King, Jr., 1929–68

My dear Fellow Clergymen,

While confined here in the Birmingham City Jail, I came across your recent statement calling our present activities "unwise and untimely." Seldom, if ever, do I pause to answer criticism of my work and ideas. But since I feel that you are men of genuine goodwill and your criticisms are sincerely set forth, I would like to answer your statement in what I hope will be patient and reasonable terms.

I think I should give the reason for my being in Birmingham, since you have been influenced by the argument of "outsiders coming in." Several months ago our local affiliate here in Birmingham invited us to be on call to engage in a nonviolent direct action program if such were deemed necessary. We readily consented and when the hour came we lived up to our promises. So I am here, along with several members of my staff, because we were invited here. Beyond this, I am in Birmingham because injustice is here.

Moreover, I am cognizant of the interrelatedness of all communities and states. I cannot sit idly by in Atlanta and not be concerned about what happens in Birmingham. Injustice anywhere is a threat to justice everywhere. We are caught in an inescapable network of mutuality tied in a single garment of destiny. Never again can we afford to live with the narrow, provincial "outsider agitator" idea. Anyone who lives inside the United States can never be considered an outsider anywhere in this country.

You deplore the demonstrations that are presently taking place in Birmingham. But I am sorry that your statement did not express a similar concern for the conditions that brought the demonstrations into being. I would not hesitate to say that it is unfortunate that so-called demonstrations are taking place in Birmingham at this time, but I would say in more emphatic terms that it is even more unfortunate that the white power structure of this city left the Negro community with no other alternative.

In any nonviolent campaign there are four basic steps:

1. collection of the facts to determine whether injustices are alive;
2. negotiation;
3. self-purification; and
4. direct action.

You may well ask, "Why direct action? Why sit-ins, marches, etc.? Isn't negotiation a better path?" You are exactly right in your call for negotiation. Indeed, this is the purpose of direct action. Nonviolent direct action seeks to create such a crisis and establish such creative tension that a community that has constantly refused to negotiate is forced to confront the issue. So the purpose of the direct action is to create a situation so crisis-packed that it will inevitably open the door to negotiation.

My friends, I must say to you that we have not made a single gain in civil rights without determined legal and nonviolent pressure. History is the long and tragic story of the fact that privileged groups seldom give up their privileges voluntarily. Individuals may see the moral light and voluntarily give up their unjust posture; but as Reinhold Niebuhr has reminded us, groups are more immoral than individuals.

We know through painful experience that freedom is never voluntarily given by the oppressor; it must be demanded by the oppressed. For years now I have heard the word "Wait!" It rings in the ear of every Negro with a piercing familiarity. This "wait" has almost always meant "never." We must come to see with the distinguished jurist of yesterday that "justice too long delayed is justice denied." We have waited for more than three hundred and forty years for our constitutional and God-given rights.

You express a great deal of anxiety over our willingness to break laws. This is certainly a legitimate concern. Since we so diligently urge people to obey the Supreme Court's decision of 1954 outlawing segregation in the public schools, it is rather strange and paradoxical to find us consciously breaking laws. One may well ask, "How can you advocate breaking some laws and obeying others?" The answer is found in the fact that there are two types of laws. There are *just* laws and there are *unjust* laws. One has not only a legal but a moral responsibility to obey just laws. Conversely, one has a moral responsibility to disobey unjust laws.

Now what is the difference between the two? A just law is a man-made code that squares with the moral law or the law of God. An unjust law is a code that is out of harmony with the moral law. Any law that degrades human personality is unjust. All segregation statutes are unjust because segregation distorts the soul and damages the personality. It gives the segregator a false sense of superiority and the segregated a false sense of inferiority.

Let us turn to a more concrete example of just and unjust laws. An unjust law is a code that a majority inflicts on a minority that is not binding on itself. This is *difference* made legal. On the other hand a just law is a code that a majority compels a minority to follow that is willing to follow itself. This is *sameness* made legal.

I hope you can see the distinction I am trying to point out. In no sense do I advocate evading or defying the law as the rabid segregationist would do. This would lead to anarchy. One who breaks an unjust law *openly, lovingly,* and with a willingness to accept the penalty by staying in jail to arouse the conscience of the community over its injustice, is in reality expressing the very highest respect for law.

Of course there is nothing new about this kind of civil disobedience. It was seen sublimely in the refusal of Shadrach, Meshach, and Abednego to obey the laws of Nebuchadnezzar because a higher moral law was involved. It was practiced superbly by the early Christians.

We can never forget that everything Hitler did in Germany was "legal" and everything the Hungarian freedom fighters did in Hungary was "illegal." It was "illegal" to aid and comfort a Jew in Hitler's Germany.

In your statement you asserted that our actions, even though peaceful, must be condemned because they precipitate violence. But can this assertion be logically made? Isn't this like condemning the robbed man because his possession of money precipitated the evil act of robbery? We must come to see, as federal courts have consistently affirmed, that it is immoral to urge an individual to withdraw his efforts to gain his basic constitutional rights because the quest precipitates violence. Society must protect the robbed and punish the robber.

Over the last few years I have consistently preached that nonviolence demands that the means we use must be as pure as the ends we seek. So I have tried to make it clear that it is wrong to use immoral means to gain moral ends. But now I must affirm that it is just as wrong, or even more so, to use moral means to preserve immoral ends. T. S. Eliot has said that there is no greater treason than to do the right deed for the wrong reason.

I wish you had commended the Negro sit-inners and demonstrators of Birmingham for their sublime courage, their willingness to suffer, and their amazing discipline in the midst of the most inhuman provocation. One day the South will recognize its real heroes. They will include old, oppressed, battered Negro women, symbolized in a seventy-two-year-old woman of Montgomery, Alabama, who rose up with a sense of dignity and with her people decided not to ride the segregated buses, and responded to one who inquired about her tiredness with ungrammatical profundity: "My feets is tired, but my soul is rested." One day the South will know that when these disinherited children of God sat down at the lunch counters they were in reality standing up for the best in the American dream and the most sacred values in our Judeo-Christian heritage, and thus carrying our whole nation back to great wells of democracy which were dug deep by the founding fathers in the formulation of the Constitution and the Declaration of Independence.

I hope this letter finds you strong in the faith. I also hope that circumstances will soon make it possible for me to meet each of you, not as an integrationist or a civil rights leader, but as a fellow clergyman and a Christian brother. Let us hope that the dark clouds of racial prejudice will soon pass away and the deep fog of misunderstanding will be lifted from our fear-drenched communities and in some not too distant tomorrow the radiant stars of love and brotherhood will shine over our great nation with all of their scintillating beauty.

Yours for the cause of Peace and Brotherhood

Martin Luther King, Jr.

By 1965 the attack on segregation was essentially completed and stage two of the civil rights movement had begun. The rising demand was for equal opportunity, not only for jobs but in every area in American life. Mounting dissatisfaction with ghetto life, *de facto* segregation, and deteriorating urban environments fueled frustrations that writers such as Langston Hughes early saw as unbearable. Hughes, the leading writer of the Harlem Renaissance, summed up the smoldering situation in 1951 with a prophetic eleven-line poem.

LITERARY SELECTION 91

Harlem

Langston Hughes, 1902–67

What happens to a dream deferred?
Does it dry up
like a raisin in the sun?
Or fester like a sore—
And then run?
Does it stink like rotten meat?
Or crust and sugar over—
like a syrupy sweet?

Maybe it just sags
like a heavy load.

Or *does it explode?*

Harlem, Detroit, Watts, and other urban centers erupted in the 1960s and extreme violence did not subside until after 1969. Equal opportunity for many African Americans, Hispanics, Native Americans, and other minorities remains a "dream deferred."

LITERARY SELECTION 92

The Transport of Slaves From Maryland to Mississippi

Rita Dove, b. 1952

U. S. Poet Laureate Rita Dove uses much historical material in her poetry, including some powerful poetry about slavery, which is not that far in the past. Her Pulitzer Prize-winning *Thomas and Beulah* (1993) consists of linked poems that pay homage to her grandparents as they migrated north. Her verse play, *The Darker Face of the Earth* (1994), is based on the story of Oedipus but the setting is slaveholding antebellum South Carolina. The following poem is from her book of poetry entitled *The Yellow House on the Corner* (1993).

[On August 22, 1839, a wagonload of slaves broke their chains, killed two white men, and would have escaped, had not a slave woman helped the Negro driver mount his horse and ride for help.]

I don't know if I helped him up
because I thought he was our salvation
or not. Left for dead in the middle
of the road, dust hovering around the body
like a screen of mosquitoes
shimmering in the hushed light.
The skin across his cheekbones
burst open like baked yams—
deliberate, the eyelids came apart—
his eyes were my eyes in a yellower face.
Death and salvation—one accommodates the other.
I am no brute, I got feelings.
He might have been a son of mine.

"The Negro Gordon, barely escaping with his life, rode
into the plantation just as his pursuers came into sight.
The neighborhood was rallied and a search begun.
Some of the Negroes had taken to the woods but
were routed, ending this most shocking affray and murder."

Eight miles south of Portsmouth, the last handcuff
broke clean from the skin. The last thing
the driver saw were the trees, improbable as broccoli,
before he was clubbed from behind. Sixty slaves
poured off the wagon, smelly, half-numb, free.

Baggage man Petit rushed in with his whip.
Some nigger's laid on another one's leg, he thought
before he saw they were loose. Hold it! he yelled;
but not even the wenches stopped. To his right
Atkins dropped under a crown of clubs. They didn't
even flinch. Wait. You ain't supposed to act this way.

STUDY QUESTION

If the slaves ain't supposed to act this way, how are they supposed to act?

GENDER ISSUES

> No man can make you feel inferior without your consent.
>
> Eleanor Roosevelt, 1884–1962

A roll call of influential women in Western culture can be impressive—at first glance. Cleopatra, Eleanor of Aquitaine, Queen Elizabeth I, Queen Victoria, and Margaret Thatcher certainly made their mark. What of the rest of the feminine half of the human race? With the exception of women such as those cited above, human history has been, until recently, an uninterrupted saga of male domination of the subordinate "inferior sex." Perhaps the first feminist to protest against such treatment in print was Christine de Pisan in her *Book of the City of Ladies,*[4] published in 1405. Not

THE RIGHTS OF WOMAN

Dedication: To M. Talleyrand-Perigord, Late Bishop of Autun

Sir, Having read with great pleasure a pamphlet which you have lately published, I dedicate this volume to you; to induce you to reconsider the subject and maturely weigh what I have advanced respecting the rights of woman and national education: and I call with the firm tone of humanity; for my arguments, Sir, are dictated by a disinterested spirit—I plead for my sex—not for myself. Independence I have long considered as the grand blessing of life, the basis of every virtue and independence I will ever secure by contracting my wants, though I were to live on a barren heath.

It is thus an affection for the whole human race that makes my pen dart rapidly along to support what I believe to be the cause of virtue: and the same motive leads me earnestly to wish to see woman placed in a station in which she would advance, instead of retarding, the progress of those glorious principles that give a substance to morality. My opinion, indeed, respecting the rights and duties of woman, seems to flow so naturally from these simple principles, that I think it scarcely possible, but that some of the enlarged minds who formed your admirable constitution, will coincide with me.

From Mary Wollstonecraft (1759–97), *A Vindication of the Rights of Woman*, 1792

4. Published in English in 1982 by Persea Books of New York.

27.3 Jacob Lawrence, *Harriet Tubman Series, No. 7.* 1939–40. Casein tempera on hardboard, $17\frac{1}{8}$ × 12" (43.5 × 30.5 cm). Hampton University Museum, Hampton, Virginia.

surprisingly, there was no reaction from either sex. It was not until Mary Wollstonecraft (1759–97) published *Vindication of the Rights of Woman* (1792) that there began a feminist movement, though it was barely a ripple across the broad waters of male dominance. John Stuart Mill helped change that; drawing on ideas supplied by his wife, Harriet Taylor Mill, he wrote an essay, *The Subjection of Women* (1869), that had considerable impact, particularly on those in England who were pressing for democratic reforms. Reform moved faster in New Zealand, the first nation to give women the vote (in 1893), with the British following suit in 1918 (for some women) and 1928 (for all women).

As in other Western democracies, the initial target of the American feminist movement was suffrage. Reasoning that voting rights would lead to equal rights, Susan B. Anthony (1820–1906) spent most of her life campaigning for women's suffrage. Not until 1920 was that particular fight won with the passage and ratification of the Nineteenth Amendment.

The right to vote changed virtually nothing for American women. Males continued their domination in government, politics, the professions, business, and unions, thus provoking increasingly militant reactions. The latest, most powerful, and most effective feminist movement began in the 1960s in the general context of a push for equal rights for all Americans regardless of race, creed, sex, age, or national origin. A key work for the movement was *The Second Sex* (1949) by the French writer and lover of Jean Paul Sartre, Simone de Beauvoir (1908–86). It was a brilliant exposition of misconceptions regarding women and their place in the world. But it was chiefly *The Feminine Mystique* (1963) by Betty Friedan (b. 1921) that sparked a wide popular reaction. Friedan analyzed the social and psychological pressures on women who were supposed to remain in the home and effectively attacked persistent stereotypes of feminine intellect and behavior.

By no means limited to women, the feminist movement includes many men who see the liberation of women as a necessary condition of freeing men from *their* traditional stereotypes. In fact, the proposed Equal Rights Amendment makes no reference to either sex.

LITERARY SELECTION 93

I Like to Think of Harriet Tubman

Susan Griffin, b. 1943

The women's movement toward equality in all areas of American life is far from over. Some say it has only begun. In this militant poem Susan Griffin cites Harriet Tubman as a heroic symbol of activism and freedom (fig. 27.3). Tubman (ca. 1820–1913) was an Abolitionist, an escaped slave who, before the Civil War, freed over 300 slaves through the Underground Railroad. During the Civil War she was a Union nurse, laundress, and spy.

I like to think of Harriet Tubman.
Harriet Tubman who carried a revolver,
who had a scar on her head from a rock thrown
by a slave-master (because she
talked back), and who
had a ransom on her head
of thousands of dollars and who
was never caught, and who
had no use for the law
when the law was wrong,
who defied the law. I like
to think of her.
I like to think of her especially
when I think of the problem of
feeding children.
The legal answer
to the problem of feeding children
is ten free lunches every month,

being equal, in the child's real life,
to eating lunch every other day.
Monday but not Tuesday.
I like to think of the President
eating lunch Monday, but not
Tuesday.
And when I think of the President
and the law, and the problem of
feeding children, I like to
think of Harriet Tubman
and her revolver.
And then sometimes
I think of the President
and other men,
men who practice the law,
who revere the law,
who make the law,
who enforce the law
who live behind
and operate through
and feed themselves
at the expense of
starving children
because of the law,
men who sit in paneled offices
and think about vacations
and tell women
whose care it is
to feed children
not to be hysterical
not to be hysterical as in the word
hysterikos, the Greek for
womb suffering,
not to suffer in their
wombs,
not to care,
not to bother the men
because they want to think
of other things
and do not want
to take the women seriously.
I want them
to take women seriously.
I want them to think about Harriet Tubman,
and remember,
remember she was beat by a white man
and she lived
and she lived to redress her grievances,
and she lived in swamps
and wore the clothes of a man
bringing hundreds of fugitives from
slavery, and was never caught,
and led an army,
and won a battle,
and defied the laws
because the laws were wrong, I want men
to take us seriously.
I am tired wanting them to think
about right and wrong.
I want them to fear.
I want them to feel fear now
as I have felt suffering in the womb, and
I want them
to know
that there is always a time
there is always a time to make right
what is wrong,
there is always a time
for retribution
and that time
is beginning.

STUDY QUESTIONS

1. You will note that the poem consists mostly of one-and two-syllable words with an occasional three-syllable word. There are only five different four-syllable words in the entire poem and two of these are related. What are the words? Is this a coincidence? What does the poet seem to have in mind?
2. What does Tubman's revolver signify?
3. What does Tubman herself symbolize?

LITERARY SELECTION 94

A Room of One's Own (1929)

If Shakespeare Had a Sister

Virginia Woolf, 1882–1941

Virginia Woolf, one of the most gifted writers of this century, often wondered why men had always had power, influence, wealth, and fame, while women had nothing but children. She reasoned that there would be female Shakespeares in the future provided women found the first two keys to freedom: independent incomes and rooms of their own. (The second key was a metaphor for women having access to their own private space.) When *A Room of One's Own* was first published it was considered both radical and revolutionary. Most people—including many women—did not talk about or even think about women's liberation and certainly no one was writing about it, let alone as persuasively as Virginia Woolf. Her essay became a classic, a landmark in the movement toward equality.

It was disappointing not to have brought back in the evening some important statement, some authentic fact. Women are poorer than men because—this or that. Perhaps now it would be better to give up seeking for the truth, and receiving on one's head an avalanche of opinion hot as lava, discoloured as dish-water. It would be better to draw the curtains; to shut out distractions; to light the lamp; to narrow the enquiry and to ask the historian, who records not opinions but facts, to describe under what conditions women lived, not throughout the ages, but in England, say in the time of Elizabeth.

For it is a perennial puzzle why no woman wrote a word of that extraordinary literature when every other man, it seemed, was capable of song or sonnet. What were the conditions in which women lived, I asked myself; for fiction, imaginative work that is, is not dropped like a pebble upon the ground, as science may be; fiction is like a spider's web, attached ever so lightly perhaps, but still attached to life at all four corners. Often the attachment is scarcely perceptible; Shakespeare's plays, for instance, seem to hang there complete by themselves. But when the web is pulled askew, hooked up at the edge, torn in the middle, one remembers that these webs are not spun in mid-air by incorporeal creatures, but are the work of suffering human beings, and are attached to grossly material things, like health and money and the houses we live in.

I went, therefore, to the shelf where the histories stand and took down one of the latest, Professor Trevelyan's *History of England*. Once more I looked up Women, found "position of", and turned to the pages indicated. "Wife-beating," I read, "was a recognised right of man, and was practised without shame by high as well as low . . . Similarly," the historian goes on, "the daughter who refused to marry the gentleman of her parents' choice was liable to be locked up, beaten and flung about the room, without any shock being inflicted on public opinion. Marriage was not an affair of personal affection, but of family avarice, particularly in the 'chivalrous' upper classes . . . Betrothal often took place while one or both of the parties was in the cradle, and marriage when they were scarcely out of the nurses' charge." That was about 1470, soon after Chaucer's time. The next reference to the position of women is some two hundred years later, in the time of the Stuarts. "It was still the exception for women of the upper and middle class to choose their own husbands, and when the husband had been assigned, he was lord and master, so far at least as law and custom could make him. Yet even so," Professor Trevelyan concludes, "neither Shakespeare's women nor those of authentic seventeenth-century memoirs, like the Verneys and the Hutchinsons, seem wanting in personality and character". Certainly, if we consider it, Cleopatra must have had a way with her; Lady Macbeth, one would suppose, had a will of her own; Rosalind, one might conclude, was an attractive girl. Professor Trevelyan is speaking no more than the truth when he remarks that Shakespeare's women do not seem wanting in personality and character. Not being a historian, one might go even further and say that women have burnt like beacons in all the works of all the poets from the beginning of time—Clytemnestra, Antigone, Cleopatra, Lady Macbeth, Phèdre, Cressida, Rosalind, Desdemona, the Duchess of Malfi, among the dramatists; then among the prose writers: Millamant, Clarissa, Becky Sharp, Anna Karenina, Emma Bovary, Madame de Guermantes—the names flock to mind, nor do they recall women "lacking in personality and character". Indeed, if woman had no existence save in the fiction written by men, one would imagine her a person of the utmost importance; very various; heroic and mean; splendid and sordid; infinitely beautiful and hideous in the extreme; as great as a man, some think even greater. But this is woman in fiction. In fact, as Professor Trevelyan points out, she was locked up, beaten and flung about the room.

A very queer, composite being thus emerges. Imaginatively she is of the highest importance; practically she is completely insignificant. She pervades poetry from cover to cover; she is all but absent from history. She dominates the lives of kings and conquerors in fiction; in fact she was the slave of any boy whose parents forced a ring upon her finger. Some of the most inspired words, some of the most profound thoughts in literature fall from her lips; in real life she could hardly read, could scarcely spell, and was the property of her husband.

It was certainly an odd monster that one made up by reading the historians first and the poets afterwards—a worm winged like an eagle; the spirit of life and beauty in a kitchen chopping up suet. But these monsters, however amusing to the imagination, have no existence in fact. What one must do to bring her to life was to think poetically and prosaically at one and the same moment, thus keeping in touch with fact—that she is Mrs. Martin, aged thirty-six, dressed in blue, wearing a black hat and brown shoes; but not losing sight of fiction either—that she is a vessel in which all sorts of spirits and forces are coursing and flashing perpetually. The moment, however, that one tries this method with the Elizabethan woman, one branch of illumination fails; one is held up by the scarcity of facts. One knows nothing detailed, nothing perfectly true and substantial about her. History scarcely mentions her. And I turned to Professor Trevelyan again to see what history meant to him. I found by looking at his chapter headings that it meant—"The Manor Court and the Methods of Open-field Agriculture . . . The Cistercians and Sheep-farming . . . The Crusades . . . The University . . . The House of Commons . . . The Hundred Years' War . . . The Wars of the Roses . . . The Renaissance Scholars . . . The Dissolution of the Monasteries . . . Agrarian and Religious Strife . . . The Origin of English Sea-power . . . The Armada . . ." and so on. Occasionally an individual woman is mentioned, an Elizabeth, or a Mary; a queen or a great lady. But by no possible means could middle-class women with nothing but brains and character at their command have taken part in any one of the great movements which, brought together, constitute the historian's view of the past. Nor shall we find her in any collection of anecdotes. Aubrey hardly mentions her. She never writes her own life and scarcely keeps a diary; there are only a handful of her letters in existence. She left no plays or poems by which we can judge her. What one wants, I thought—and why does not some brilliant student at Newnham or Girton supply it?—is a mass of information; at what age did she marry; how many children had she as a rule; what was her house like; had she a room to herself; did she do the cooking; would she be likely to have a servant? All these facts lie somewhere, presumably, in parish registers and account books; the life of the average Elizabethan woman must be scattered about somewhere, could one collect it and make a book of it. It would be ambitious beyond my daring, I thought, looking about the shelves for books that were not there, to suggest to the students of those famous colleges that they should re-write history, though I own that it often seems a little queer as it is, unreal, lop-sided; but why should they not add a supplement to history? calling it, of course, by some inconspicuous name so that women might figure there without impropriety? For one often catches a glimpse of them in the lives of the great, whisking away into the background, concealing, I sometimes think, a wink, a laugh, perhaps a tear. But what I find deplorable, I continued, looking about the bookshelves again, is that nothing is known about women before the eighteenth century. I have no model in my mind to turn about this way and that. Here am I asking why women did not write poetry in the Elizabethan age, and I am not sure how they were educated; whether they were taught to write; whether they had sitting-rooms to themselves; how many women had children before they were twenty-one; what, in short, they did from eight in the morning till eight at night. They had no money evidently; according to Professor Trevelyan they were married whether they liked it or not before they were out of the nursery, at fifteen or sixteen very likely. It would have been extremely odd, even upon this showing, had one of them suddenly written the plays of Shakespeare, I concluded, and I thought of that old gentleman, who is dead now, but was a bishop, I think, who declared that it was impossible for any woman, past, present, or to come, to have the genius of Shakespeare. He wrote to the papers about it. He also told a lady who applied to him for information that cats do not as a matter of fact go to heaven, though they have, he added, souls of a sort. How much thinking those old gentlemen used to save one! How the borders of ignorance shrank back at their approach! Cats do not go to heaven. Women cannot write the plays of Shakespeare.

Be that as it may, I could not help thinking, as I looked at the works of Shakespeare on the shelf, that the bishop was right at least in this; it would have been impossible, completely and entirely, for any woman to have written the plays of Shakespeare in the age of Shakespeare. Let me imagine, since facts are so hard to come by, what would have happened had Shakespeare had a wonderfully gifted sister, called Judith, let us say. Shakespeare himself went, very probably—his mother was an heiress—to the grammar school, where he may have learnt Latin—Ovid, Virgil and Horace—and the elements of grammar and logic. He was, it is well known, a wild boy who poached rabbits, perhaps shot a deer, and had, rather sooner than he should have done, to marry a woman in the neighbourhood, who bore him a child rather quicker than was right. That escapade sent him to seek his fortune in London. He had, it seemed, a taste for the theatre; he began by holding horses at the stage door. Very soon he got work in the theatre, became a successful actor, and lived at the hub of the universe, meeting everybody, knowing everybody, practising his art on the boards, exercising his wits in the streets, and even getting access to the palace of the queen. Meanwhile his extraordinarily gifted sister, let us suppose, remained at home. She was as adventurous, as imaginative, as agog to see the world as he was. But she was not sent to school. She had no chance of learning grammar and logic, let alone of reading Horace and Virgil. She picked up a book now and then, one of her brother's perhaps, and read a few pages. But then her parents came in and told her to mend the stockings or mind the stew and not moon about with books and papers. They would have spoken sharply but kindly, for they were substantial people who knew the conditions of life for a woman and loved their daughter—indeed, more likely than not she was the apple of her father's eye. Perhaps she scribbled some pages up in an apple loft on the sly, but was careful to hide them or set fire to them. Soon, however, before she was out of her teens, she was to be betrothed to the son of a neighbouring wool-stapler. She cried out that marriage was hateful to her, and for that she was severely beaten by her father. Then he ceased to scold her. He begged her instead not to hurt him, not to shame him in this matter of her marriage. He would give her a chain of beads or a fine petticoat, he said; and there were tears in his eyes. How could she disobey him? How could she break his heart? The force of her own gift alone drove her to it. She made up a small parcel of her belongings, let herself down by a rope one summer's night and took the road to London. She was not seventeen. The birds that sang in the hedge were not more musical than she was. She had the quickest fancy, a gift like her brother's, for the tune of words. Like him, she had a taste for the theatre. She stood at the stage door; she wanted to act, she said. Men laughed in her face. The manager—a fat, loose-lipped man—guffawed. He bellowed something about poodles dancing and women acting—no woman, he said, could possibly be an actress. He hinted—you can imagine what. She could get no training in her craft. Could she even seek her dinner in a tavern or roam the streets at midnight? Yet her genius was for fiction and lusted to feed abundantly upon the lives of men and women and the study of their ways. At last—for she was very young, oddly like Shakespeare the poet in her face, with the same grey eyes and rounded brows—at last Nick Greene the actor-manager took pity on her; she found herself with child by that gentleman and so—who shall measure the heat and violence of the poet's heart when caught and tangled in a woman's body?—killed herself one winter's night and lies buried at some cross-roads where the omnibuses now stop outside the Elephant and Castle.

That, more or less, is how the story would run, I think, if a woman in Shakespeare's day had had Shakespeare's genius. But for my part, I agree with the deceased bishop, if such he was—it is unthinkable that any woman in Shakespeare's day should have had Shakespeare's genius. For genius like Shakespeare's is not born among labouring, uneducated, servile people. It was not born in England among the Saxons and the Britons. It is not born today among the working classes. How, then, could it have been born among women whose work began, according to Professor Trevelyan, almost before they were out of the nursery, who were forced to it by their parents and held to it by all the power of law and custom? Yet genius of a sort must have existed among women as it must have existed among the working classes. Now and again an Emily Brontë or a Robert Burns blazes out and proves its presence. But certainly it never got itself on to paper. When, however, one reads of a witch being ducked, of a woman possessed by devils, of a wise woman selling herbs, or even of a very remarkable man who had a mother, then I think we are on the track of a lost novelist, a suppressed poet, of some mute and inglorious Jane Austen, some Emily Brontë who dashed her brains out on the moor or mopped and mowed about the highways crazed with the torture that her gift had put her to. Indeed, I would venture to guess that Anon, who wrote so many poems without signing them, was often a woman. It was a woman Edward Fitzgerald, I think, suggested who made the ballads and the folk-songs, crooning them to her children, beguiling her spinning with them, or the length of the winter's night.

This may be true or it may be false—who can say?—but what is true in it, so it seemed to me, reviewing the story of Shakespeare's sister as I had made it, is that any woman born with a great gift in the sixteenth century would certainly have gone crazed, shot herself, or ended her days in some lonely cottage outside the village, half witch, half wizard, feared and mocked at. For it needs little skill in psychology to be sure that a highly gifted girl who had tried to use her gift for poetry would have been so thwarted and hindered by other people, so tortured and pulled asunder by her own contrary instincts, that she must have lost her health and sanity to a certainty. No girl could have walked to London and stood at a stage door and forced her way into the presence of actor-managers without doing herself a violence and suffering an anguish which may have been irrational—for chastity may be a fetish invented by certain societies for unknown reasons—but were none the less inevitable. Chastity had then, it has even now, a religious importance in a woman's life, and has so wrapped itself round with nerves and instincts that to cut it free and bring it to the light of day demands courage of the rarest. To have lived a free life in London in the sixteenth century would have meant for a woman who was poet and playwright a nervous stress and dilemma which might well have killed her. Had she survived, whatever she had written would have been twisted and deformed, issuing from a strained and morbid imagination. And undoubtedly, I thought, looking at the shelf where there are no plays by women, her work would have gone unsigned. That refuge she would have sought certainly. It was the relic of the sense of chastity that dictated anonymity to women even so late as the nineteenth century. Currer Bell, George Eliot, George Sand, all the victims of inner strife as their writings prove, sought ineffectively to veil themselves by using the name of a man. Thus they did homage to the convention, which if not implanted by the other sex was liberally encouraged by them (the chief glory of a woman is not to be talked of, said Pericles, himself a much-talked-of man), that publicity in women is detestable. Anonymity runs in their blood. The desire to be veiled still possesses them. They are not even now as concerned about the health of their fame as men are, and, speaking generally, will pass a tombstone or a signpost without feeling an irresistible desire to cut their names on it, as Alf, Bert or Chas. must do in obedience to their instinct, which murmurs if it sees a fine woman go by, or even a dog, *Ce chien est à moi.* And, of course, it may not be a dog, I thought, remembering Parliament Square, the Sieges Allee and other avenues; it may be a piece of land or a man with curly black hair. It is one of the great advantages of being a woman that one can pass even a very fine negress without wishing to make an Englishwoman of her.

That woman, then, who was born with a gift of poetry in the sixteenth century, was an unhappy woman, a woman at strife against herself. All the conditions of her life, all her own instincts, were hostile to the state of mind which is needed to set free whatever is in the brain. But what is the state of mind that is most propitious to the act of creation, I asked. Can one come by any notion of the state that furthers and makes possible that strange activity? Here I opened the volume containing the Tragedies of Shakespeare. What was Shakespeare's state of mind, for instance, when he wrote *Lear* and *Antony and Cleopatra?* It was certainly the state of mind most favourable to poetry that there has ever existed. But Shakespeare himself said nothing about it. We only know casually and by chance that he "never blotted a line". Nothing indeed was ever said by the artist himself about his state of mind until the eighteenth century perhaps. Rousseau perhaps began it. At any rate, by the nineteenth century self-consciousness had developed so far that it was the habit for men of letters to describe their minds in confessions and autobiographies. Their lives also were written, and their letters were printed after their deaths. Thus, though we do not know what Shakespeare went through when he wrote *Lear,* we do know what Carlyle went through when he wrote the *French Revolution;* what Flaubert went through when he wrote *Madame Bovary;* what Keats was going through when he tried to write poetry against the coming of death and the indifference of the world.

And one gathers from this enormous modern literature of confession and self-analysis that to write a work of genius is almost always a feat of prodigious difficulty. Everything is against the likelihood that it will come from the writer's mind whole and entire. Generally material circumstances are against it. Dogs will bark; people will interrupt; money must be made; health will break down. Further, accentuating all these difficulties and making them harder to bear is the world's notorious indifference. It does not ask people to write poems and novels and histories; it does not need them. It does not care whether Flaubert finds the right word or whether Carlyle scrupulously verifies this or that fact. Naturally, it will not pay for what it does not want. And so the writer, Keats, Flaubert, Carlyle, suffers, especially in the creative years of youth, every form of distraction and discouragement. A curse, a cry of agony, rises from those books of analysis and confession. "Mighty poets in their misery dead"—that is the burden of their song. If anything comes through in spite of all this, it is a miracle, and probably no book is born entire and uncrippled as it was conceived.

But for women, I thought, looking at the empty shelves, these difficulties were infinitely more formidable. In the first place, to have a room of her own, let alone a quiet room or a sound-proof room, was out of the question, unless her parents were exceptionally rich or very noble, even up to the beginning of the nineteenth century. Since her pin money, which depended on the good will of her father, was only enough to keep her clothed, she was debarred from such alleviations as came even to Keats or Tennyson or Carlyle, all poor men, from a walking tour, a little journey to France, from the separate lodging which, even if it were miserable enough, sheltered them from the claims and tyrannies of their families. Such material difficulties were formidable; but much worse were the immaterial. The indifference of the world which Keats and Flaubert and other men of genius have found so hard to bear was in her case not indifference but hostility. The world did not say to her as it said to them, Write if you choose; it makes no difference to me. The world said with a guffaw, Write? What's the good of your writing? Here the psychologists of Newnham and Girton might come to our help, I thought, looking again at the blank spaces on the shelves. For surely it is time that the effect of discouragement upon the mind of the artist should be measured, as I have seen a dairy company measure the effect of ordinary milk and Grade A milk upon the body of the rat. They set two rats in cages side by side, and of the two one was furtive, timid and small, and the other was glossy, bold and big. Now what food do we feed women as artists upon? I asked, remembering, I suppose, that dinner of prunes and custard. To answer that question I had only to open the evening paper and to read that Lord Birkenhead is of opinion—but really I am not going to trouble to copy out Lord Birkenhead's opinion upon the writing of women. What Dean Inge says I will leave in peace. The Harley Street specialist may be allowed to rouse the echoes of Harley Street with his vociferations without raising a hair on my head. I will quote, however, Mr. Oscar Browning, because Mr. Oscar Browning was a great figure in Cambridge at one time, and used to examine the students at Girton and Newnham. Mr. Oscar Browning was wont to declare "that the impression left on his mind, after looking over any set of examination papers, was that, irrespective of the marks he might give, the best woman was intellectually the inferior of the worst man". After saying that Mr. Browning went back to his rooms—and it is this sequel that endears him and makes him a human figure of some bulk and majesty—he went back to his rooms and found a stable-boy lying on the sofa—"a mere skeleton, his cheeks were cavernous and sallow, his teeth were black, and he did not appear to have the full use of his limbs . . . 'That's Arthur' [said Mr. Browning]. 'He's a dear boy really and most high-minded.' " The two pictures always seem to me to complete each other. And happily in this age of biography the two pictures often do complete each other, so that we are able to interpret the opinions of great men not only by what they say, but by what they do.

But though this is possible now, such opinions coming from the lips of important people must have been formidable enough even fifty years ago. Let us suppose that a father from the highest motives did not wish his daughter to leave home and become writer, painter or scholar. "See what Mr. Oscar Browning says," he would say; and there was not only Mr. Oscar Browning; there was the *Saturday Review;* there was Mr. Greg—the "essentials of a woman's being," said Mr. Greg emphatically, "are that *they are supported by, and they minister to, men"*—there was an enormous body of masculine opinion to the effect that nothing could be expected of women intellectually. Even if her father did not read out loud these opinions, any girl could read them for herself; and the reading, even in the nineteenth century, must have lowered her vitality, and told profoundly upon her work. There would always have been that assertion—you cannot do this, you are incapable of doing that—to protest against, to overcome. Probably for a novelist this germ is no longer of much effect; for there have been women novelists of merit. But for painters it must still have some sting in it; and for musicians, I imagine, is even now active and poisonous in the extreme. The woman composer stands where the actress stood in the time of Shakespeare. Nick Greene, I thought, remembering the story I had made about Shakespeare's sister, said that a woman acting put him in mind of a dog dancing. Johnson repeated the phrase two hundred years later of women preaching. And here, I said, opening a book about music, we have the very words used again in this year of grace, 1928, of women who try to write music. "Of Mlle. Germaine Tailleferre one can only repeat Dr. Johnson's dictum concerning a woman preacher, transposed into terms of music. 'Sir, a woman's composing is like a dog's walking on his hind legs. It is not done well, but you are surprised to find it done at all.' " So accurately does history repeat itself.

Thus, I concluded, shutting Mr. Oscar Browning's life and pushing away the rest, it is fairly evident that even in the nineteenth century a woman was not encouraged to be an artist. On the contrary, she was snubbed, slapped, lectured and exhorted. Her mind must have been strained and her vitality lowered by the need of opposing this, of disproving that. For here again we come within range of that very interesting and obscure masculine complex which has had so much influence upon the woman's movement; that deep-seated desire, not so much that *she* shall be inferior as that *he* shall be superior, which plants him wherever one looks, not only in front of the arts, but barring the way to politics too, even when the risk to himself seems infinitesimal and the suppliant humble and devoted. Even Lady Bessborough, I remembered, with all her passion for politics, must humbly bow herself and write to Lord Granville Leveson-Gower: " . . . notwithstanding all my violence in politics and talking so much on that subject, I perfectly agree with you that no woman has any business to meddle with that or any other serious business, farther than giving her opinion (if she is ask'd)". And so she goes on to spend her enthusiasm where it meets with no obstacle whatsoever upon that immensely important subject, Lord Granville's maiden speech in the House of Commons. The spectacle is certainly a strange one, I thought. The history of men's opposition to women's emancipation is more interesting perhaps than the story of that emancipation itself. An amusing book might be made of it if some young student at Girton or Newnham would collect examples and deduce a theory—but she would need thick gloves on her hands, and bars to protect her of solid gold.

But what is amusing now, I recollected, shutting Lady Bessborough, had to be taken in desperate earnest once. Opinions that one now pastes in a book labelled cock-a-doodle-dum and keeps for reading to select audiences on summer nights once drew tears, I can assure you. Among your grandmothers and great-grandmothers there were many that wept their eyes out. Florence Nightingale shrieked aloud in her agony. Moreover, it is all very well for you, who have got yourselves to college and enjoy sitting-rooms—or is it only bed-sitting-rooms?—of your own to say that genius should disregard such opinions; that genius should be above caring what is said of it. Unfortunately, it is precisely the men or women of genius who mind most what is said of them. Remember Keats. Remember the words he had cut on his tombstone. Think of Tennyson; think—but I need hardly multiply instances of the undeniable, if very unfortunate, fact that it is the nature of the artist to mind excessively what is said about him. Literature is strewn with the wreckage of men who have minded beyond reason the opinions of others.

And this susceptibility of theirs is doubly unfortunate, I thought, returning again to my original enquiry into what state of mind is most propitious for creative work, because the mind of an artist, in order to achieve the prodigious effort of freeing whole and entire the work that is in him, must be incandescent, like Shakespeare's mind, I conjectured, looking at the book which lay open at *Antony and Cleopatra*. There must be no obstacle in it, no foreign matter unconsumed.

For though we say that we know nothing about Shakespeare's state of mind, even as we say that, we are saying something about Shakespeare's state of mind. The reason perhaps why we know so little of Shakespeare—compared with Donne or Ben Jonson or Milton—is that his grudges and spites and antipathies are hidden from us. We are not held up by some "revelation" which reminds us of the writer. All desire to protest, to preach, to proclaim an injury, to pay off a score, to make the world the witness of some hardship or grievance was fired out of him and consumed. Therefore his poetry flows from him free and unimpeded. If ever a human being got his work expressed completely, it was Shakespeare. If ever a mind was incandescent, unimpeded, I thought, turning again to the bookcase, it was Shakespeare's mind.

Afterword

Shakespeare's sister was fictional, but Wolfgang Amadeus Mozart did have a sister: Maria Anna (called Nannerl; 1751–1829). Performing as child prodigies, she and her younger brother astonished and delighted audiences all over Europe. She "showed an early talent scarcely inferior to her brother's,"[5] and he was probably the greatest musical genius who ever lived. Though Wolfgang was extremely critical of other people's music he did approve of Nannerl's compositions; none have survived. Because women did not perform in public, her musical gifts were strictly confined to her home after she turned eighteen. For many years after her husband's death she gave piano lessons in Salzburg; she was blind, alone, and living in wretched poverty when she died.

RACISM

No one needs to be reminded that racism has always been a problem for the human race. There seems to be a fairly general human failing that compels one race or nation or society to feel and act superior to another. Whether this attitude is based on ignorance or arrogance, or both, there seems to be no limit to the amount of destruction inflicted on human potential and on human life itself. No nation or group of people is immune to the blight of bigotry and intolerance but that does not mean that the problem can ever be ignored.

The destructive effects of racism can be seen around the globe. In the United States there has been a shift from fighting for civil rights to combating racism as such. The Civil Rights Acts of 1964 and 1965 were positive steps that eliminated racial segregation in public places and established equal access to the voting booth. During the 1980s there was a shift from the quest for constitutional guarantees to a focus on changing attitudes; the effect of this thrust was to contend that the opinions, feelings, and prejudices of private individuals were legitimate targets for political action.

Many political leaders see this drive as not only inappropriate but dangerous. It is divisive because it divides humanity into "them" and "us." A member of "us" can see the self as victim; as a self-styled victim the person has endless opportunities for self-pity and self-righteous anger. This can lead to a society at war with itself because there is no constitutional right to be free from racism, anti-Semitism, or sexism. The legal principles of freedom and justice for all are established though certainly less than fully accomplished. The negative movement against racism can never accomplish its objective of eliminating prejudices held by individuals. What, then, is the solution to the abiding affliction of racism?

5. Stanley Sadie (ed)., *The New Grove Dictionary of Music and Musicians* (London: Macmillan, 1980), vol. 12, p. 680.

THE INFORMATION SOCIETY AND THE GLOBAL VILLAGE

During the several decades of civil rights and gender issues other fundamental changes were quietly transforming American life. Once a nation of farmers, the Industrial Revolution made laborers the dominant work force. By the mid-1950s, however, white-collar workers outnumbered blue-collar laborers; by the early 1990s the manufacturing work force had dwindled to about 13 percent and farmers to less than 3 percent of the working population. The United States and Canada had shifted from an industrial society to an information society based on high technology; computers, communication satellites, fax machines, modems, robots, and other electronic marvels herald what has been called, variously, the Age of Information, the Computer Age, or the Communications Age. By the early 1990s over 75 percent of all jobs were involved with high tech and the products of high tech. Smokestack industries such as steel, textiles, and shipbuilding will probably continue to decline in the Western world as heavy industry expands in Third World countries that have large pools of cheap labor.

Not too many years ago children lived in a world not very different from that of their parents or grandparents. Information about the rest of the globe was confined to the printed word and technology was not even a word. The velocity of change was, metaphorically speaking, about ten miles an hour—the speed of a horse and buggy. In a society that was evolving almost imperceptibly, children tended to adopt the values, religion, and politics of their parents.

Today's world is so vastly different that comparisons boggle the mind. It has been estimated, for example, that human society has experienced more change during the past half-century than in all the preceding years of its history. The acceleration of change appears to be the single most important influence on our lives. We can choose a philosophical, religious, or humanistic point of view (probably very different from that of our parents), but we can neither avoid nor deny the reality of a future that so insistently crowds upon the present.

During the late 1960s Alvin Toffler wrote a book whose title, *Future Shock,* became a metaphor for the frustrations and anxieties thrust on us by the onslaught of rapid and relentless change. Toffler described the understandable reluctance of people to recognize and accept the existence of what he called the "accelerative thrust." The pace of change keeps quickening, keeps forcing people to cope with ever faster acceleration and still more future shock. Toffler's thesis was that the shock of change can be replaced by the recognition of change as the new reality of the late twentieth century. Change can be seen as proper and necessary in an age when process is reality. Children and young adults have made the transition with relative ease because rapid change is all that younger Americans have ever known. But many of those who once played 78 rpm records, placed phone calls through an operator, and are intimidated by computers have had their difficulties.

The magnitude of accelerating change can be comprehended by comparing the evolution of computers with the evolution of the automobile. If cars had progressed as rapidly as computers, a Rolls Royce today would:

1. cost $2.75
2. get 3 million miles per gallon
3. have enough power to propel the Queen Elizabeth II
4. fit six on the head of a pin.[6]

In a later book, *The Third Wave* (1980), Toffler predicted that individualized entertainment and information services would become readily available, and that there would be a whole new range of social, political, psychological, and religious adaptations throughout the Western world and around the Pacific Basin: Japan, Korea, Hong Kong, Singapore, Taiwan, New Zealand, and Australia. No one is predicting any drastic changes (in the near future) for Third-World countries, especially those in sub-Saharan Africa, but some countries have managed to leapfrog over older technology—such as railroads—to land in the middle of the high-tech revolution.

Developing technology tends to follow the line of least resistance. The first book printed with movable type, the Gutenberg Bible, looked like a handwritten manuscript. The first automobiles were called "horseless carriages" because they were indeed motorized carriages. Early steamships were sailing ships outfitted with paddle wheels. Much computer usage has been concerned with improving older technology: faster computations, quicker information retrieval, and improved typewriting in the form of a word processor, and so on. No one can predict the different directions computers will take except to say that, inevitably, there will be startling new applications of computer technology.

Einstein gave us new conceptions of space, and the age of computers and telecommunications has forced us to recognize space as a concept connected by electronics and not just as a physical reality linked by interstate highways. International television with worldwide viewers, fax machines, modems, and other forms of rapidly evolving telecommunications have shrunk our earth to a Global Village. The late 1990s will see a fully operational commercial telephone network that will enable subscribers to phone absolutely anywhere in the world. All of Antarctica, New Guinea, and the backwaters of the Amazon will be as immediately accessible as our next-door neighbor. Moreover, the telephone connection will enable the caller to fax or transmit computerized material throughout the world. One important effect of electronic communications is to open all societies to the world outside despite the efforts of tyrants to control what their subjects can see and hear.

What will life be like in the Global Village? No one can predict what the globalization of culture will lead to,

6. Paul Johnson, *Modern Times: The World from the Twenties to the Eighties* (New York: Harper & Row, 1983), pp. 128–9.

but the prognosis can be optimistic. The possibility of instantaneous close contact with people and their institutions can lead to closer human ties than at any time in human history.

SUMMARY

The long-awaited era of peace and prosperity that was supposed to follow World War II ended abruptly in 1949 when the Soviet Union joined the United States as a nuclear superpower. The next four decades saw a Cold War between the two powers highlighted by two very hot wars. Communist aggression was successfully resisted in South Korea, but not in Vietnam.

The widespread and surprisingly sudden collapse of Communist governments that began in 1989 was, of course, the most important series of events in the late twentieth century. Though much has already been revealed, it may take years before the extent and degree of the damage to people, societies, and the environment will be fully known. The world has yet to recover fully from the Hitler years; the Lenin legacy will undoubtedly plague civilization for decades to come.

> The central tragedy of modern world history is that both the Russian and the German republics, in turn, found in Lenin and Hitler adversaries of quite exceptional calibre, who embodied the will to power to a degree unique in our time.[7]

Existentialism as developed by Kierkegaard, Nietzsche, and Jean-Paul Sartre is discussed as a significant postwar movement and illustrated, in part, with "The Myth of Sisyphus" by Albert Camus.

Martin Luther King's "Letter from Birmingham Jail" outlines the strategy of non-violent resistance that helped make the Civil Rights movement effective in overcoming some barriers to equal opportunity. The poem "Harlem" by Langston Hughes predicted the racial violence that erupted in major American cities, violence that was precipitated by the realization that equal opportunity regardless of race still had a long way to go.

Susan Griffin's poem "I Like to Think of Harriet Tubman" stresses the anger and frustration of women who deeply resent their position as the subordinate sex. Virginia Woolf creates a suicidal sister for Shakespeare to emphasize the need and the right of all women to have the freedom to be individuals in their own right, to have a "room of their own."

CULTURE AND HUMAN VALUES

The themes discussed and illustrated in this chapter were chosen to delineate some of the problems of our era. Though far from definitive, these are some of the important issues: civil rights, gender issues, violence, and racism. If there were a universal, overwhelming concern for human values and human rights, these problems would not exist—and we would be living in Utopia.

Violence seems to be a fact of human existence but there is no logical reason why a society cannot end overt discrimination and guarantee civil rights for everyone. This is no pipe dream but a goal that can be reached. Why, in the affluent world we are fortunate to inhabit, hasn't some kind of humane society come into being? Has there been enough time? Has there been enough effort?

There is another way to approach the problem. There have been three great technological revolutions in the history of humankind, all of which are still in progress:

1. Agricultural, 10,000 years ago;
2. Industrial, eighteenth and nineteenth centuries;
3. Information, late nineteenth and twentieth centuries.

New discoveries are still being made in agriculture, robotics in home and industry is in its infancy, and who knows where the knowledge explosion will lead? If virtue is knowledge and ignorance is vice, as Aristotle, Socrates, and other Greeks contended, then perhaps the knowledge eruption can eventually lead the peoples of the world to form more rational and humane societies. Rapidly increasing scientific and technological knowledge can certainly improve our material existence; one must always consider the impact of technology on all of us.

> The universalizing imperative of technology is irresistible . . . it will continue to shape both modern culture and the consciousness of those who inhabit that culture.[8]

Moreover, knowledge tends to lead to greater tolerance of the differences between individuals and between the varieties of cultures, an acceptance of diversity that can help offset the bane of intolerance and its spin-offs of prejudice, bigotry, sexism, and racism. More than at any time in human history, we seem to be acquiring the means to make this a better world for all humankind.

7. Christopher Evans, *The Micro Millennium* (New York: The Viking Press, 1980), p. 4.

8. O. B. Hardison, Jr., *Disappearing through the Skylight: Culture and Technology in the Twentieth Century* (New York: Viking Penguin, 1989), p. 144.

Noted futurist Peter Drucker says that we are already deep in a new and vastly different century and living in what he calls a post-business society. The business values of enterprise and profit, according to Drucker, have receded before the growth of such values as knowledge and fuller development of human potential. That we are living in a knowledge society should be apparent to everyone. We already have the technology for self-teaching that will enable everyone to learn subjects while teachers are freed to teach people. Consequently, we can expect an acceleration in the rate of change in our educational system, particularly in light of the changes taking place in the rival trading nations in Europe and Asia.

Other authorities feel that we are living in what they call the post-modern world. In the modern movement in art, for example, artists sought originality and novelty and denied virtually the whole of the past. The postmodern movement in architecture (see p. 401) appears to reflect a general proclivity to depart from the *avant-garde* tendencies of most of this century, a desire to integrate much of the recent past with contemporary Western culture and, to some extent, non-Western cultures. There is a search for human values in the context of a global civilization. This movement seems to be, in part, a reaction to the speedily evolving Information Age and the growing realization that our world is becoming a Global Village. Another factor is the recognition that a mind-set that denies the past is severely hampered when trying to confront the complexities of contemporary life. Many feel that we have lost our way in this bewildering world and that we can improve our lives by incorporating elements from the Enlightenment, the Renaissance, the Middle Ages, even the Greek and Roman worlds. The previous values of novelty, originality, of being different have little appeal when we are constantly reminded that people of any age are no different from men and women of today. The world is changing rapidly but people haven't changed at all. Progress, success, invention, and innovation may be false gods that have nothing to do with such human values as truth, justice, love, family, fidelity, integrity, and honor. "Value education" is a buzz phrase in public education but one wonders how values are "taught." Values are learned from families, institutions, artists, philosophers, writers.

Finally, we should always keep in mind the profound question posed by philosopher William Barrett:

> What shall it profit a whole civilization, or culture, if it gains knowledge and power over the material world, but loses any adequate idea of the conscious mind, the human self, at the center of all that power?[9]

9. William Barrett, *Death of the Soul: From Descartes to the Computer* (Garden City, N.Y.: Anchor Press/Doubleday, 1986), p. 56.

Chagall.
1911. Paris.

CHAPTER 28

Art in the Twentieth Century: Shock Waves and Reactions

Art is either a plagiarist or a revolutionist.

Paul Gauguin

Would you realize what Revolution is, call it Progress; and would you realize what Progress is, call it Tomorrow.

Victor Hugo

PRELUDE

The beginnings of modern art can be traced back to the revolutionary innovations of Edouard Manet, especially as exemplified in his *Olympia* (see fig. 25.27). Manet insisted that the actual subject matter was "light," but the artist's response to the rapidly changing world about him was visible on the canvas. *Olympia* was a naked prostitute from Manet's contemporary world. She gazed unconcernedly at a shocked public that still expected art to be an academic enterprise, drawing its subject matter from myths and legends and instructing the viewer in the beauty of color and line. This was, however, the Age of Progress, the industrial era of cities, factories, slums, trains, Marx, Darwin, and Bismarck. The Renaissance tradition was no longer adequate or even appropriate. The Impressionists did paint from nature but even Monet painted many views of a Parisian train station crowded with powerful locomotives emitting clouds of steam. Gauguin fled to Polynesia to escape a civilization that he saw as corrupt and diseased. Cézanne's sources were nature, people, and objects of the world in which he lived, not stories and myths of the past. The contemporary world was the basis for the new reality of painting. The stage was set for the advent of modernism.

Opposite Marc Chagall, *I and the Village*. 1911. Oil on canvas, 6' 3⅝" × 4' 11⅝" (1.92 × 1.51 m). The Museum of Modern Art, New York (Mrs. Simon Guggenheim Fund). Photo: © 1996 The Museum of Modern Art, New York, © ADAGP, Paris and DACS, London 1995.

ARTISTIC STYLES TO 1945

Fauvism and Expressionism

Henri Matisse, 1869–1954

Modern art was in the air in 1905, especially in Collioure, a fishing port on the French Mediterranean coast a few miles from the Spanish border. Summering there with his family and a fellow artist, Matisse (ma-teess) saw some Tahitian paintings by Gauguin and was forcibly reminded of Gauguin's contention that color was whatever the artist perceived it to be. Still searching for a style, Matisse had become dissatisfied with copying nature as an Impressionist and he refused to even consider the dots-of-color technique of Seurat. At age thirty-six he found his style in Collioure. In the sparkling southern light he began painting in bold colors with broad and exuberant brushstrokes; he would delight in color for the rest of a long and marvelously productive career. When he displayed some of his Collioure pictures in Paris at the 1905 **Salon d'Automne**, critics were outraged, claiming that the "blotches of barbaric color" bore no relationship to real painting. There was, in fact, a whole room full of wildly colorful paintings by Matisse, his Collioure colleague, André Derain, and other French artists. Perhaps seeking to localize the repercussions, the judges assigned all their paintings to Room VII, leading the horrified public to believe that this was an organized school with Matisse, the eldest, as its leader. A critic's remark about a room full of *fauves* (Fr., "wild beasts")[1] gave the group a name, and critical and public hostility helped create a movement. For a public still unfamiliar with the works of van Gogh and Gauguin, Fauve paintings were shocking. Color was, after all, *true;* apples were red and trees were green. In *The Blue Window* (fig. 28.1) Matisse painted a landscape that is also a still life. The lampshade is green but the beautifully rounded trees in the background are blue. They are, nevertheless, still perceived as trees in an elegantly cool and decorative composition of curving shapes within a series of carefully proportioned rectangles. Color has been freed to become whatever the artist wants it to be.

1. Though commonly translated as "wild beasts," *fauves* actually means "deer"; the French call wild beasts *les grands fauves.*

28.1 Henri Matisse, *The Blue Window (Summer 1913).* Oil on canvas, 51½ × 35⅜" (130.8 × 87.7 cm). The Museum of Modern Art, New York (Abby Aldrich Rockefeller Fund). Photo: © 1996 The Museum of Modern Art, New York, © Succession H. Matisse/DACS 1995.

28.2 Henri Matisse, *Odalisque with Tambourine: Harmony in Blue.* 1926. Oil on canvas, 36 × 25½" (91.4 × 64.8 cm). Norton Simon Foundation, Pasadena, California. Photo: © Succession H. Matisse/DACS 1995.

In his *Odalisque with Tambourine: Harmony in Blue* (fig. 28.2) Matisse surrounded the harem girl with a variety of blues punctuated by spots of red and supported by a rich and colorful carpet. The color scheme in *The Blue Window* is cool and elegant. This painting is warmer and more emotional, representing the artist's reaction to an exotic African culture. (See figure 25.3 for a Neoclassical reaction to similar subject matter.) Matisse expressed himself through vivid color somewhat in the manner of van Gogh and Gauguin, but he was not a tortured creator like the two lonely Post-impressionists. Throughout his sixty-year career he was a hard-working, consistently cheerful painter and sculptor who seemingly paid not the slightest attention to the woes of the world, not even to the two terrible wars that his country endured. He was neither insensitive nor indifferent; his concern was with the creation of beauty in a world that had become most unbeautiful.

28.3 Georges Rouault, *Christ Mocked by Soldiers*. 1932. Oil on canvas, 36¼ × 28½" (92.1 × 72.3 cm). The Museum of Modern Art, New York (Given anonymously). Photo: © 1996 The Museum of Modern Art, New York © ADAGP, Paris and DACS, London 1995.

Georges Rouault, 1871–1958

Rouault (roo-oh) was, on the other hand, obsessed with the plight of humankind in the twentieth century. Deeply religious, unlike most modern artists, he was unable to accept the joyful hedonism of Matisse or the relaxed styles of other Fauves. His sympathies lay with clowns and other circus performers, whom he saw as symbols for the tragic victims

of society; he despised soldiers, corrupt judges, and the demimonde of prostitutes and criminals. His *Christ Mocked by Soldiers* (fig. 28.3) shows a tortured Christ at the mercy of brutal soldiers, a pathetic figure who also symbolizes the victims of the ruthless modern world. At one time a worker

28.4 Marguerite Thompson Zorach, *Man Among the Redwoods*. 1912. Oil on canvas, 25¾ × 20¼" (65.4 × 51.4 cm). Private collection, Hockessin, Delaware.

in stained glass, Rouault uses heavy black lines similar to the lead contours that frame the pieces of stained glass. The reds, greens, and blues are themselves the standard colors of medieval stained glass. Matisse and Rouault are both French and Fauves, that is, Expressionists, but there is no further similarity between them in their art or their lives.

Marguerite Thompson Zorach, 1887–1968

American artist Thompson went to Paris in 1908 to study in the academic tradition at the Ecole des Beaux-Arts but her visit to the Salon d'Automne, where she saw the new art of Matisse and other Fauvists, changed everything. Entirely captivated by the new style, she became an active participant in the *avant-garde* intellectual life and a noted Fauvist in her own right. Her *Man Among the Redwoods* (fig. 28.4) is a richly decorated California landscape done with strong, pure colors and lavish brushwork. She later established her studio in New York, where she married the modern sculptor William Zorach.

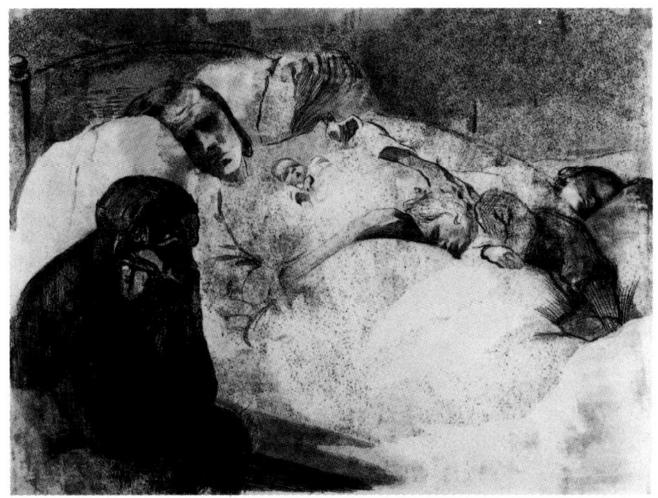

28.5 Käthe Kollwitz, *Unemployment*. 1909. Print, 7 × 5" (17.8 × 12.7 cm). Preussischer Kulturbesitz, Kupferstichkabinett, Staatliche Museen, Berlin. Photo: © DACS 1995.

German Expressionism

Käthe Kollwitz, 1867–1945

German artists were more concerned with political and social conditions before and after World War I than were the French, and none more so than Kollwitz. Both a sculptor and a graphic artist, Kollwitz became, in 1918, the first woman to be elected to a professorship in the Prussian Academy of Arts and, later, the first woman to head a department there. A socialist and a feminist, she concentrated on themes of poverty and injustice, and the difficulty of being a woman and mother in militaristic Prussia. Her *Raped* from her "Peasants' War" series is an early depiction of the criminal violation from a woman's point of view. In *Unemployment* (fig. 28.5) the exhausted mother stares numbly at the viewer, her newborn baby on her chest, her other child nestled down in the bed. The baby is presumably a girl. When first published the print's caption read: "If they are not used as soldiers they at least deserve to be treated as children." Kollwitz's lifelong campaign against German militarism began well before her personal tragedies. Her son was killed in combat in World War I and her grandson met the same fate in World War II.

28.6 George Grosz, *I Am Glad I Came Back*. 1943. Oil on masonite, 28 × 20" (71.1 × 50.8 cm). University Art Collections, Arizona State University (Gift of Oliver B. James). Photo: © DACS 1995.

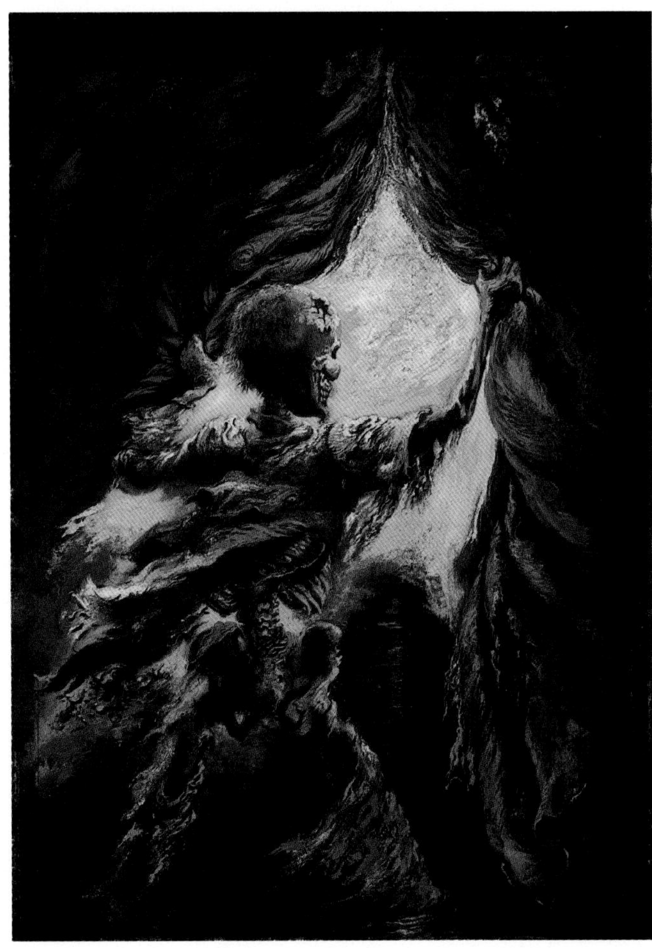

George Grosz, 1893–1959

Grosz became, with his satirical drawings, a prominent spokesman for the antiwar movement in Germany during the 1920s. At first identified with the Berlin Dadaists (see p. 377), Grosz developed a pessimistic Expressionist style influenced by the powerful imagery of Grünewald and Bosch (see fig. 17.26). His opposition to the Nazis forced him to flee Germany in 1932 for the United States, where he realized his dream of becoming an American citizen. Painted during the horror of a war that he, among many, had foreseen, *I Am Glad I Came Back* (fig. 28.6) depicts a grinning skeleton peering through parted draperies at the

28.7 Wassily Kandinsky, *Painting Number 198*. 1914. Oil on canvas, 64 × 36½" (162.5 × 92.1 cm). The Museum of Modern Art, New York (Mrs. Simon Guggenheim Fund). Photo: © 1996 The Museum of Modern Art, New York.

28.8 Pablo Picasso, *The Tragedy*. 1903. Oil on wood, 41½ × 27⅛" (105.4 × 69 cm). National Gallery of Art, Washington, D.C. (Chester Dale Collection). Photo: © DACS 1995.

inferno of World War II. Symbolically, the work is a vision of the rebirth of the Four Horsemen of the Apocalypse: War, Famine, Pestilence, and Death.

Wassily Kandinsky, 1866–1944

The expressive qualities of strong color also impressed some Russian artists, especially Kandinsky. Russia had a long history of robust colors derived from its Byzantine tradition, which Kandinsky realized as he studied the intense colors of richly decorated peasant clothing, furniture, and houses. After moving to Munich he began painting in the German Expressionist style. It was not until about 1908 that he discovered, apparently accidentally, that color could operate independently of subjects. Red, for example, need not be on an apple nor green on a tree; colors could function in expressive compositions without representing specific objects. Called the first Abstract Expressionist as early as 1919, Kandinsky developed theories about the spiritual qualities of colors and the interrelationship of music and art. As with many of his contemporaries, Kandinsky felt that the world was headed for disaster and that there was a real need for a spiritual rebirth in art and in life. He equated representational art with the materialism that appeared to be corrupting society, and thus removed all objective references from his paintings in an attempt to return to spiritual values. In *Painting Number 198* (also known as *Panel 3* or *Summer*; fig. 28.7) he created what can be described as "visual poetry" or "visual music," a celebration of the warmth and brightness of summer. That this work was completed in the year in which the Great War engulfed most of Europe may or may not be coincidental.

Cubism and Other Abstractions

Pablo Picasso, 1881–1973

The most famous and successful artist of this century, Picasso was a one-man art movement whose innovations throughout a long and enormously productive career make him impossible to classify or categorize. He is discussed under this heading because he, along with Georges Braque (brack; 1882–1963), invented Cubism. Working in his native Spain after a discouraging first attempt at a career in Paris, Picasso painted *The Tragedy* (fig. 28.8) as a somber monochromatic study, in blue, of sorrowing figures in a timeless setting by an unknown sea. There have been numerous explanations for the artist's brief Blue Period (ca. 1903–4), but the likeliest appears to be his prolonged melancholy at this stage of his career.

Picasso decided, in 1904, to live permanently in Paris. He was still poverty-stricken, but his first mistress helped to brighten his life and his style. The last of the circus-theme paintings of his Rose Period (ca. 1904–5), the *Family of Saltimbanques* (fig. 28.9) was his first large painting, a kind of summary that concluded the period. The Jester stands between Harlequin at the left along with two boy acrobats.

28.9 Pablo Picasso, *Family of Saltimbanques*. 1905. Oil on canvas, 6' 11¾" × 7' 6⅜" (2.13 × 2.29 m). National Gallery of Art, Washington, D.C. (Chester Dale Collection). Photo: © DACS 1995.

28.10 Pablo Picasso, *Les Demoiselles d'Avignon*. Paris, June to July 1907. Oil on canvas, 8' × 7' 8" (2.44 × 2.34 m). The Museum of Modern Art, New York (Acquired through the Lillie P. Bliss Bequest). Photo: © 1996 The Museum of Modern Art, New York, © DACS 1995.

Like objects in a still life, the figures are expressionless and motionless. As was his custom, Picasso has portrayed some members of his "gang," including himself as Harlequin, but there is no explanation for the isolated woman at the right.

Picasso could have painted indefinitely in the lyrical Rose-Period style. His works were selling so well that he had become, next to Matisse, perhaps the best-known painter in Paris. However, having mastered the technique, he changed his style. His studies of ancient Iberian sculptures and African masks led him to produce a painting of five nude women that astonished and horrified art dealers, and even his friends. Unlike anything ever seen in art, *Les Demoiselles d'Avignon* (fig. 28.10) represented a breakthrough as epochal as Masaccio's *Tribute Money* (see fig. 17.10) at the beginning of the Italian Renaissance. Masaccio established Renaissance perspective; Picasso destroyed it with this painting. Just about all the rules were broken by his innovations: flat picture plane with no single point of perspective; angular and fragmented bodies; distorted faces with enormous eyes; two figures wearing grotesque African-like masks. With a remarkable economy of means Picasso created tense and massive figures whose heads and facial features are seen simultaneously in full-face and profile, marking a great step forward in the evolution of Cubism. A friend of the artist added the title later, a reference to a brothel on Avignon Street in Barcelona. About this painting Picasso remarked that "nature has to exist so that we may rape it!" Braque commented that it made him feel "that someone was drinking gasoline and spitting fire."

Picasso and Braque took Cubism through several phases, from a faceting of three-dimensional figures to flattened images and rearranged forms. In *Still Life* (fig. 28.11) Picasso uses forms from the "real" world to confuse reality and illusion. All is two-dimensional, and shadows cast by objects on the tilted tabletop further add to the confusion. What is reality here? Actually, colors and forms on canvas. Inspired in part by Cézanne's compressed forms (see fig. 25.36), Cubism was a refutation of the Mediterranean classical heritage as the sole model for creating and viewing art.

Inspired by a new German mistress with blond hair and high-bridged nose, Picasso painted her in a number of colorful works. His personal favorite was *Girl Before a Mirror* (fig. 28.12). Standing nude in front of a mirror, she is young and innocent, but the mirror-image is older and darker, mysterious and sultry. The wide range of vivid colors set off by heavy dark lines is reminiscent of medieval stained glass, perhaps indicating that Picasso had in mind Eve the Temptress or even a modern-day version of the Madonna.

During the afternoon of 26 April 1937 the Spanish Civil War came home to the Spanish artist living in Paris. German bombers of the Condor Legion destroyed over 70 percent of the Basque town of Guernica and, twenty-five sketches and one month later, Picasso had completed his anguished protest against the brutal destruction of a

28.11 Pablo Picasso, *Still Life*. 1918. Oil on canvas, 38¼ × 51¼" (97.2 × 130.2 cm). National Gallery of Art, Washington, D.C. (Chester Dale Collection). Photo: © DACS 1995.

28.12 Pablo Picasso, *Girl Before a Mirror*. Boisgeloup, March 1932. Oil on canvas, 5' 4" × 4' 3¼" (1.62 × 1.3 m). The Museum of Modern Art, New York (Gift of Mrs. Simon Guggenheim). Photo: © 1996 The Museum of Modern Art, New York, © DACS 1995.

28.13 Pablo Picasso, *Guernica*. 1937. Oil on canvas, 25' 5¾" × 11' 5½" (7.77 × 3.49 m). Museo del Prado, Madrid. Photo: © DACS 1995.

defenseless town (fig. 28.13). The central figure is a wounded horse that, according to the artist, represents the people, whereas the bull symbolizes the pitiless brutality of fascism. Possibly representing the threatened Light of Reason, a light bulb is superimposed on the blazing sun. Painted on an enormous scale in a stark black, white, and gray, the work is a monumental protest against the impersonal cruelty of modern warfare. At the bottom center is one small symbol of life, a fragile flower above the broken sword. Picasso decreed that the work would remain on loan to the Museum of Modern Art in New York until democracy was restored in Spain. After difficult negotiations with heirs, politicians, and two art museums, the painting was officially inaugurated in Madrid on 24 October 1981.

American Modernists

Georgia O'Keeffe, 1887–1986

Undoubtedly reflecting her American training, O'Keeffe applied abstract concepts to American themes. She took special delight in painting organic forms found in the Southwest, to which she moved permanently after the death of her husband, the celebrated photographer Alfred Stieglitz. *Jack-in-the-Pulpit, No. 5* (fig. 28.14) is from the numerous series of floral images that she painted for over forty years, steering a middle path between nature and abstraction. Her imagery is a unique combination of graceful representation and elegant geometry.

28.14 Georgia O'Keeffe, *Jack-in-the-Pulpit, No. 5*. 1930. Oil on canvas, 48 × 30" (121.9 × 76.2 cm). National Gallery of Art, Washington, D.C. (Alfred Stieglitz Collection, Bequest of Georgia O'Keeffe). Photo: © ARS, New York and DACS, London 1995.

Alfred Stieglitz, 1864–1946

O'Keeffe and her husband operated the Little Gallery of the Photo-Secession that Stieglitz had earlier opened at 291 Fifth Avenue in New York. At "291," as the art world called it, the arts of photography and painting coexisted. Advocating "straight photography," Stieglitz used no gimmicks, relying instead on his eye, his camera, and his lens. Lonely in New York after nine years of study abroad, he came upon *The Terminal* (fig. 28.15), and captured a moment in a world of horse-drawn streetcars, quaint streetlamps, and men in bowler hats. In this photograph we share a personal instant in the life of the photographer.

Stieglitz was the strongest and most persuasive advocate of photography as an art form, but he was even more dedicated to the promotion of modern painting. His gallery showed, for the first time in America, works by Cézanne, Picasso, Toulouse-Lautrec, Rodin, Matisse, Brancusi, and Henri Rousseau.

28.15 Alfred Stieglitz, *The Terminal*. Ca. 1890. Photograph. Art Institute of Chicago (Alfred Stieglitz Collection).

The Armory Show

Early American abstract artists, like their European counterparts, had to combat the hostility of a public accustomed to representational art and the opposition of academicians and the Ash Can school (see p. 379). The modernists of "291" ended the internecine warfare by inducing academicians and Ash Can artists to form, in 1911, the Association of American Artists and Painters. An exhibition

28.16 Stuart Davis, *Radio Tubes*. 1940. Gouache, 22 × 14" (55.9 × 35.6 cm). University Art Collections, Arizona State University (Gift of Oliver B. James). Photo: © Estate of Stuart Davis/DACS, London/VAGA, New York 1995.

28.17 Piet Mondrian, *Composition with Red, Blue, Yellow, Black, and Gray*. 1936. Oil on canvas, 16½ × 19" (41.9 × 48.3 cm). Toledo Museum of Art, Toledo, Ohio (Purchased with funds from the Libbey Endowment; Gift of Edward Drummond Libbey, 1978).

of contemporary American art was to be the first project, but the end result was the epochal New York Armory Show of 1913, still the most controversial exhibition ever staged in the United States. Convinced that the public was ready for new ideas, the organizers included European modernists in what was officially termed the International Exhibition of Modern Art. Works by Cézanne, Rousseau, Gauguin, van Gogh, Matisse, Duchamp, and Picasso astounded and infuriated artists, critics, and most of all the public. The shocked organizers dismissed the public reaction as militant ignorance, which it was, but American modernists were dismayed to see how far behind they themselves were. The Armory Show was "the greatest single influence that I have experienced," said Stuart Davis (1894–1964) as he altered his style and, like many other American artists, sailed to Paris. His Cubistic *Radio Tubes* (fig. 28.16) is a characteristically whimsical celebration of American technology at a time when advanced technology was naively thought to be uniquely American. Contending that the camera was the proper instrument for recording facts, Davis believed, as did most modernists, that his function was to make new statements. Though influenced by European Cubism, *Radio Tubes* is, in its own way, as American as the work of Georgia O'Keeffe.

Piet Mondrian, 1872–1944

Though he was attracted to the work of the French Cubists, the Dutch artist Mondrian felt that their art did not express what he called "pure reality." He sought "plastic expression" in a basic reality made up solely of colors and forms that had their own spiritual values. *Composition with Red, Blue, Yellow, Black, and Gray* (fig. 28.17) is a precisely balanced work in a style generally called Geometric Abstraction. No two of the rectangles are of the same size or shape nor are all the heavy black lines the same width. The poised serenity of Mondrian's "composition" is as classical as a Greek temple. His ideas influenced many artists but they have also been popularized, in simplified and sometimes distorted versions, in fashion, interior, and advertising design.

Constantin Brancusi, 1876–1957

The Romanian sculptor Brancusi (bran-KOOSH) was first influenced by Rodin when studying in Paris, but developed an abstract style that influenced many artists. His *Bird in Space* (fig. 28.18) conveys, in an elegantly swelling shape, the soaring spirit of flight. It is a magnificent work of transcendental beauty that epitomizes the sculptor's statement: "I bring you pure joy."

Fantasy

Marc Chagall, 1889–1985

Fantasy plays a large part in twentieth-century art, with the Russian artist Chagall (shah-GALL) a leading exponent. Chagall combines Fauve color and Cubist forms with a personal vision of his early life in a Russian village. In *I and the*

Village (see p. 364) cow and peasant speak to each other; a peasant marches up the street after his wife, who floats upside down; and a magic tree grows out of a hand. Chagall's paintings are meant to be enjoyed as enchanting pictorial arrangements of images that fascinated the artist.

Paul Klee, 1879–1940

The German-Swiss artist Klee (klay) was a master of fantasy. Through his teaching at the Bauhaus (see fig. 28.34) and his painting, Klee was one of the most influential artists of the century. Rejecting illusionistic art as obsolete, he turned to the art of children and primitives as inspiration for his paintings. *Twittering Machine* (fig. 28.19) is a whimsical fantasy of stick-figure birds twittering soundlessly in an unknown language. The "machine" is apparently an industrial concoction of no conceivable use.

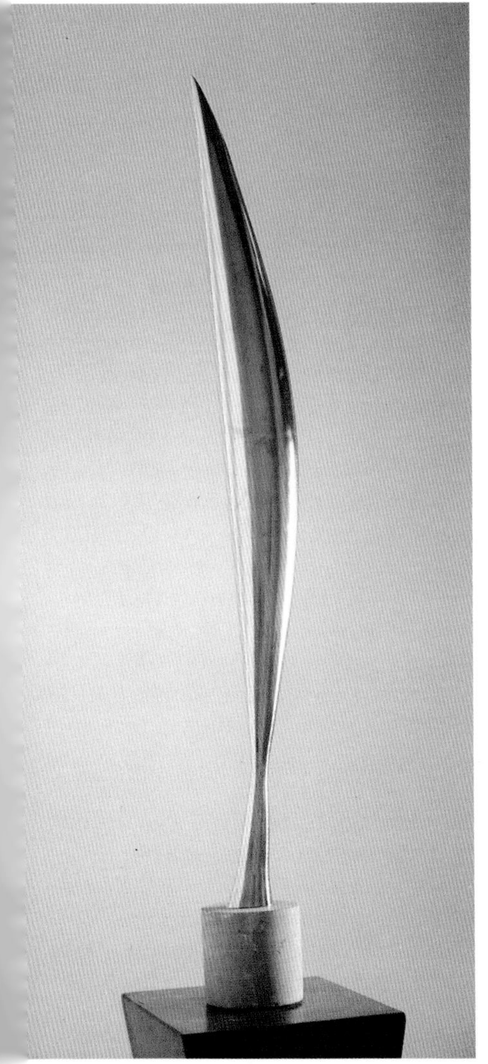

28.18 Constantin Brancusi, *Bird in Space*. Ca. 1928. Polished bronze, unique cast, 54 × 8½ × 6½" (137.2 × 21.6 × 16.5 cm). The Museum of Modern Art, New York (Given anonymously). Photo: © 1996 The Museum of Modern Art, New York, © ADAGP, Paris and DACS, London, 1995.

28.19 Paul Klee, *Twittering Machine*. 1922. Watercolor, pen, and ink on oil transfer drawing on paper, mounted on cardboard, 25¼ × 19" (64.1 × 48.3 cm). The Museum of Modern Art, New York (Purchase). Photo: © 1996 The Museum of Modern Art, New York.

28.20 *Above* Giorgio de Chirico, *The Nostalgia of the Infinite*. Ca. 1913–14 (?), dated 1911 on the painting. Oil on canvas, 53¼ × 25½" (135.3 × 64.8 cm). The Museum of Modern Art, New York (Purchase). Photo: © 1996 The Museum of Modern Art, New York, © DACS 1995.

Giorgio de Chirico, 1888–1979

The fantasies of de Chirico (day KEE-re-ko) were as subjective as those of Chagall but infused with pessimism and melancholy. Like Kandinsky and other intellectuals, de Chirico perceived a sick society defiled by materialism. Born in Greece of Italian parents, he studied in Athens and, like many other artists of the time, wound up in Paris, where he studied the Old Masters in the Louvre. Strongly influenced by the German philosopher Nietzsche (see p. 346), de Chirico looked on himself as a metaphysical painter who explored the mysteries of life. In *The Nostalgia of the Infinite* (fig. 28.20) he employed a distorted Renaissance perspective in a characteristic dreamlike cityscape in which everything is real, except that it isn't. Pennants are flying vigorously from a sinister and threatening tower in front of which two minuscule figures cast disproportionately long shadows. Like most of his images, this building actually exists (in Turin), but the strange juxtaposition creates another reality that is not of the waking world.

Dada

Marcel Duchamp, 1887–1968

As early as 1914 it had become obvious to some artists that World War I marked the low point of a bankrupt Western culture. In February of 1916 some exiles from the war that was consuming Europe formed, in neutral Switzerland, the Cabaret Voltaire, a loose-knit and contentious group devoted to attacking everything that Western civilization held dear. These writers, artists, musicians, and poets chose the word *Dada* to identify their iconoclastic movement, a word intended as nonsense but immediately adopted by acclamation. Dada was an idea whose time had come, for it had happened even earlier in New York with the arrival, in 1915, of Marcel Duchamp (due-shã). Duchamp was the greatest exponent of the "anti-art" movement known as Dada, having already turned "found" objects into art by, for example, hanging a snow shovel on a gallery wall and labelling it *In Advance of a Broken Arm*. He made the first mobile in 1913 by fastening an inverted bicycle wheel to the top of a stool and presenting it as a sculpture with moving parts. Typical of his assault on the citadel of art was a reproduction of the *Mona Lisa* to which he added a mustache and a goatee and the title of *L.H.O.O.Q.* that, when pronounced letter by letter in French, means "She's got a hot ass."

Duchamp found a congenial home in Stieglitz's "291" and began work on what turned out to be his greatest Dada work, the enigmatically titled *The Bride Stripped Bare by Her*

28.21 *Left* Marcel Duchamp, *The Large Glass; The Bride Stripped Bare by Her Bachelors, Even*. 1915–23. Oil, lead wire and foil, and dust and varnish on plate glass (in two parts), front 9' 1¼" × 5' 9⅛" (2.77 × 1.76 m). Philadelphia Museum of Art (Bequest of Katherine S. Dreier). Photo: © ADAGP, Paris and DACS, London 1995.

Bachelors, Even, commonly referred to as *The Large Glass* (fig. 28.21). The following analysis is based on Duchamp's notes that, given the artist's proclivity for paradox and irony, may be accepted, modified, or rejected. According to Duchamp, this is the story of a bride, located in the upper section and symbolized by an internal combustion engine with a reservoir of love gasoline and a magneto of desire. She is lusted after by the nine bachelors in the left lower section: the reddish-brown molds resembling chessmen. Each bachelor is a stereotype of what were, at the time, masculine occupations: priest, delivery boy, policeman, warrior, gendarme, undertaker's assistant, busboy, stationmaster, and flunky. Capillary tubes carry gas from each bachelor mold to the center of the glass and to one of seven funnels, where the gas solidifies into large needles. These needles, in turn, break into spangles of frosty gas and then into liquid drops of semen that splash into the bride's domain. At the moment depicted in the glass the bride is stripped but she remains undefiled; bride and bachelors are caught between desire and possession/surrender. Duchamp intended the work to be humorous and sexual, satirizing machines, people, and social conventions.

Kurt Schwitters, 1887–1948

The leading German Dadaist, Schwitters collected trash from wastebaskets and gutters to compose collages of the detritus of civilization. When once asked what art was, Schwitters responded with, "What isn't?" *Sichtbar* (fig. 28.22), meaning "visible," proves that an artist can arrange the unlikeliest materials into a meaningful statement. Like so many of his constructions, this work visualizes the modern city as a compressor and energizer of life, constantly changing, leaving behind the rubbish of yesterday.

28.22 Kurt Schwitters, *Sichtbar*. 1923. Collage, ca. 7 × 5" (17.8 × 12.7 cm). Estate of Kurt Schwitters. Photo: Marlborough Gallery, New York, © DACS 1995.

Surrealism

Though Schwitters continued to collect and arrange his Dada collages, completely filling several three-story houses in the process, the movement was generally absorbed by the Surrealists, who coalesced around the Manifesto of Surrealism issued in 1924 by the writer André Breton, a disciple of Sigmund Freud. Surrealism in art is, briefly stated, the theory that dreams, and those waking moments when subconscious images overwhelm our intellect, furnish us with material far more relevant to our lives than traditional subject matter. The world of psychic experience, as explored by Freud and others, was to be combined with consciousness to create a super-reality called Surrealism.

Joan Miró, 1893–1983

Surrealism was an organized movement in revolt against conventional art and society, but there was no single style. Artists like Miró (ME-row) drew on their personal dream-worlds. In *Person Throwing a Stone at a Bird* (fig. 28.23) Miró does not abstract the human image but seems, instead, to humanize abstractions. In a witty and

28.23 Joan Miró, *Person Throwing a Stone at a Bird*. 1926. Oil on canvas, 29 × 36¼" (73.7 × 92.1 cm). The Museum of Modern Art, New York (Purchase). Photo: © 1996 The Museum of Modern Art, New York, © ADAGP, Paris and DACS, London 1995.

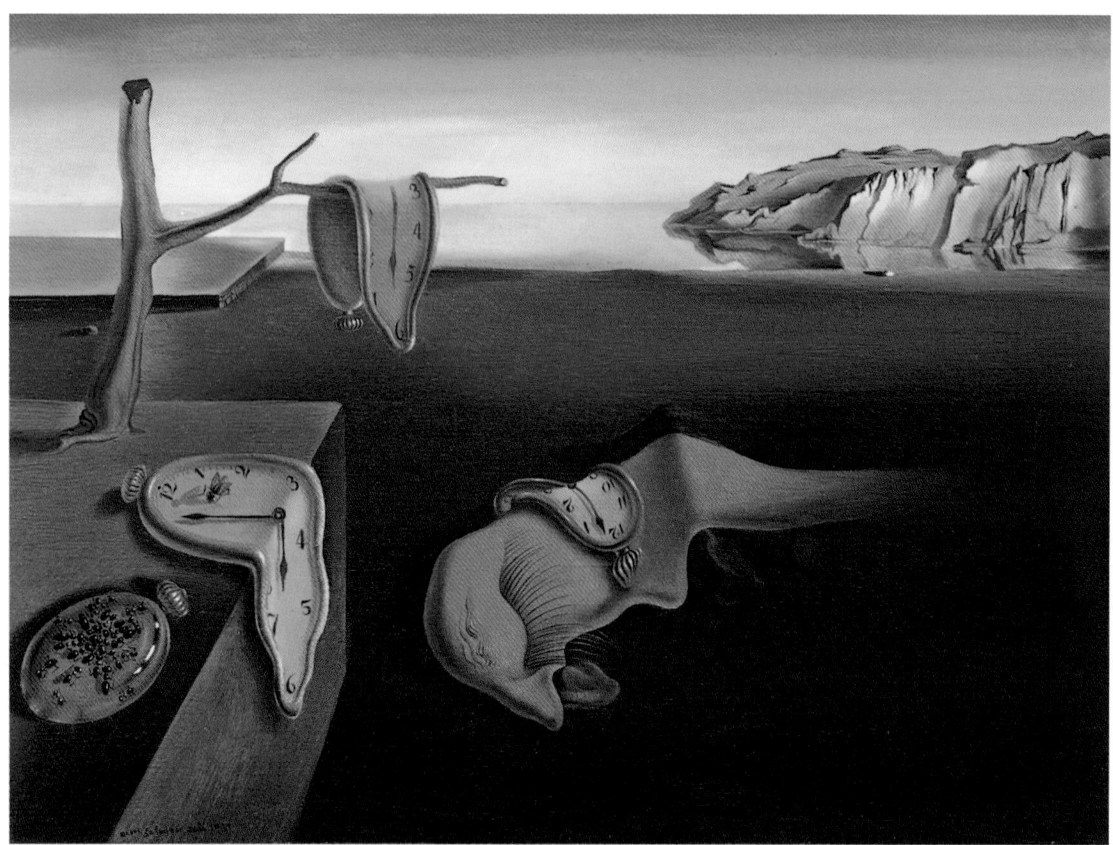

28.24 Salvador Dali, *The Persistence of Memory (Persistance de la mémoire)*. 1931. Oil on canvas, 9½ × 13" (24.1 × 33 cm). The Museum of Modern Art, New York (Purchase). Photo: © 1996 The Museum of Modern Art, New York, © DEMART PRO ARTE BV/DACS 1995.

28.25 Meret Oppenheim, *Object*. 1936. Fur-covered cup, saucer, and spoon; diameter of cup 4¾" (12.1 cm); diameter of saucer 9⅜" (23.7 cm); length of spoon 8" (20.3 cm); overall height 2⅞" (7.3 cm). The Museum of Modern Art, New York (Purchase). Photo: © 1996 The Museum of Modern Art, New York, © DACS 1995.

humorous style, sometimes called Biomorphic Abstraction, he creates an amoebic person with one huge foot, bulbous body, and orange and yellow eye. This being seems to fall back in wonder as an oblong stone falls toward an appealing bird with a crescent torso from which a longline neck projects to a lavender head topped by a flaming cock's comb. This is super-reality. "Everything in my pictures exists," stated Miró; "there is nothing abstract in my pictures."

Salvador Dali, 1904–89

The self-appointed spokesman of the Surrealist movement, Dali (DAH-lee) stressed paradox, disease, decay, and eroticism. *The Persistence of Memory* (fig. 28.24) is a tiny painting of a vast landscape in which watches hang limply and dejectedly. A strange chinless creature with protruding tongue (alive? dead?) lies in the foreground of a Renaissance perspective construction lit by an eerie glow. A dead tree grows out of a table (?) on which the only flat watch lies, a metal timepiece infested with sinister-looking bugs. Anything is possible in dreams.

Meret Oppenheim, 1913–85

Startling distortions or juxtapositions are basic to Surrealism, as Oppenheim's *Object* (fig. 28.25) demonstrates. The absurdity of a fur-lined teacup has become a symbol of Surrealism. Her now familiar but bizarre ensemble is typical of the push-pull effect of many Surrealist works. Our intellect is titillated, but our senses of touch and taste are outraged.

René Magritte, 1898–1967

Belgian Surrealist Magritte was a witty, even mischievous, painter who consistently questioned the nature of reality by representing ordinary images in a strange and extraordinary manner. *The False Mirror* (fig. 28.26) portrays a huge but recognizable human eye with an iris of fluffy clouds in a blue sky. Are we looking into someone's eye while viewing the world from within that other organ? Or?

28.26 René Magritte, *The False Mirror (Le Faux miroir)*. 1928. Oil on canvas, 21¼ × 31⅞" (54 × 81 cm). The Museum of Modern Art, New York (Purchase). Photo: © 1996 The Museum of Modern Art, New York, © ADAGP, Paris and DACS, London 1995.

Frida Kahlo, 1910–54

Mexican artist Kahlo is usually identified as a Surrealist because of the intensity of her paintings, her depiction of inner life and thought, and her unexpected, even strange arrangement of images. Kahlo, however, saw Surrealism as inherently misogynistic with women treated as objects of male fantasies. Further, she disavowed Surrealism because she claimed to be painting her own reality. *The Two Fridas* (fig. 28.27) depicts the reality of her divorce from Mexican muralist Diego Rivera. Dressed in a traditional Mexican wedding dress, the Frida on the left is the woman Rivera loved. The other Frida is the modern and independent feminist whom he abandoned. The Fridas hold hands but the artery joining them has been ruptured. The divorced Frida uses forceps but cannot stop the flow of blood. In constant pain because she was injured for life by a streetcar accident, Kahlo painted her uncompromising works from a wheelchair.

28.27 Frida Kahlo, *The Two Fridas*. 1939. Oil on canvas, 5' 9" × 5' 9" (1.75 × 1.75 m). Museum of Modern Art, Mexico City.

Realism in America: The Ash Can School

From the early days of the Republic there has always been a strain of realism on the American scene, a tradition separate from European realists like Courbet and Millet. While European artists were experimenting with Impressionism, Americans such as Winslow Homer and Thomas Eakins (see figs. 25.21 and 25.22) continued to paint reality as they perceived it.

At the beginning of this century Robert Henri (hen-RYE; 1865–1929) founded a new school of realism called The Eight. Working almost entirely in New York, the followers of Henri painted city scenes of tenement life and everyday activities, mainly of the working class. A derogatory remark by a critic gave still another new style a label. After the caustic comment that they "even painted ash cans," The Eight proudly bore the label of Ash Can school.

John Sloan, 1871–1951

Sloan painted *Roof Gossips* (fig. 28.28) as if the three women on the tenement roof were the subject of a casual snapshot. Actually, the work is an artful composition of lines and forms. Reminiscent of the high viewpoint of Mary Cassatt's *The Bath* (see fig. 25.32), we witness an intimate and relaxed scene but are not a part of it. Academicians were critical of the gritty realism of Sloan and the Ash Can school but

28.28 John Sloan, *Roof Gossips*. Ca. 1912. Oil on canvas, 24 × 20" (60 × 50.8 cm). University Art Collections, Arizona State University (Gift of Oliver B. James).

they collaborated with them and the *avant-garde* of "291" to present the Armory Show the year after this work was painted.

Edward Hopper, 1882–1967

A student of Henri's in the early 1900s, Hopper was more concerned with formal design than were his Ash Can colleagues. He was fascinated with lonely people isolated in the urban landscape, with empty streets, with windows looking on vacant streets and the like. His *Nighthawks* (fig. 28.29) has a typical broad horizontal base and a scene starkly free of details, with a sharp contrast between the subdued buildings in the background and the garish lighting in the all-night café. Sitting speechless in isolated loneliness at the counter, the three figures convey both a melancholy mood and the aching anonymity so characteristic of urban life. The signs and advertising symbols present in many of Hopper's works may be a wry commentary on his other career as a commercial artist.

Horace Pippin, 1888–1946

A notable artist in the manner of colonial artisan-painters, Pippin was a self-taught painter whose style can be

28.29 Edward Hopper, *Nighthawks*. 1942. Oil on canvas, 33 × 60" (83.8 × 152.4 cm). Art Institute of Chicago.

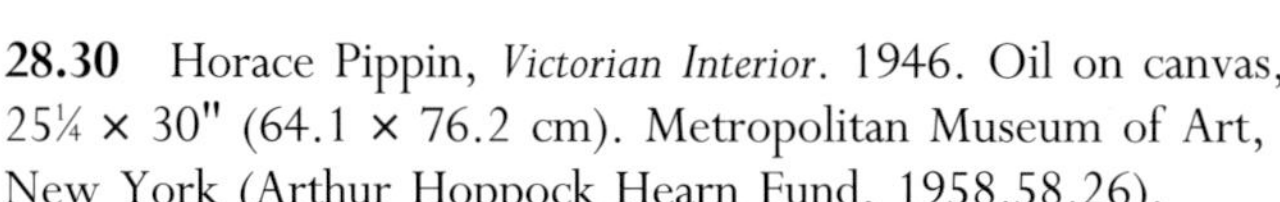

28.30 Horace Pippin, *Victorian Interior*. 1946. Oil on canvas, 25¼ × 30" (64.1 × 76.2 cm). Metropolitan Museum of Art, New York (Arthur Hoppock Hearn Fund, 1958.58.26).

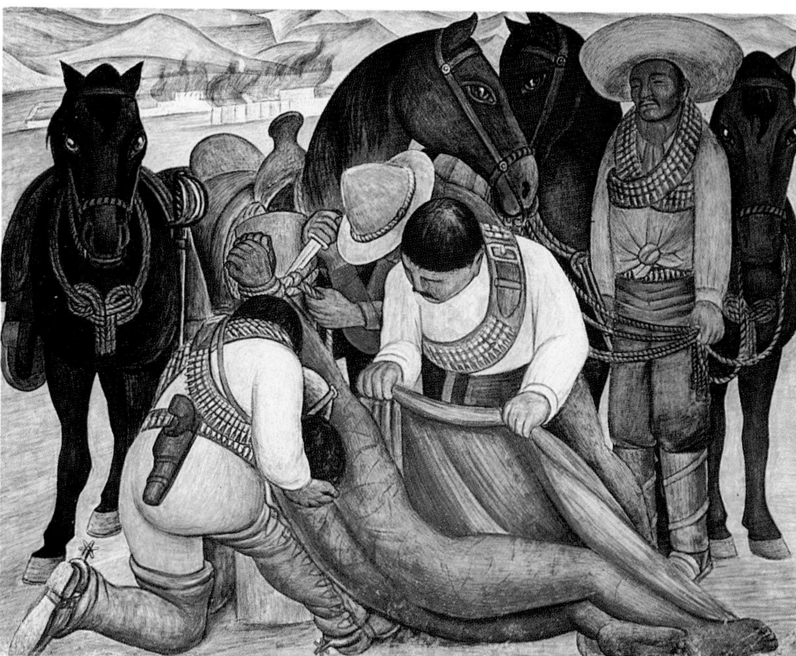

28.31 Diego Rivera, *The Liberation of the Peon*. 1931. Fresco, 6' 2" × 7' 11" (1.88 × 2.41 m). Philadelphia Museum of Art (Gift of Mr. and Mrs Herbert Cameron Morris).

described as modernized abstractions of folk art traditions. Unlike the French primitive, Henri Rousseau, Pippin was acclaimed in his lifetime and his works were acquired by major American museums. One of his most elegant paintings is *Victorian Interior* (fig. 28.30). At first glance the painting appears closely related to simple folk art, but further study reveals a complex arrangement of strong color and selected areas of intricate linear designs. The end result is a happy medium between primitive folk art and modernism. Pippin was not a member of the Ash Can school, but his wry and unique style adds another dimension to realism.

Mexican Social Realists

Diego Rivera, 1886–1957

Though he lived and studied in Europe for many years, Rivera disavowed modernism in his zeal to create a distinctly Mexican style in the socialist spirit of the protracted Mexican revolution (1910–40). Rivera's statements were usually political and consistently on the side of the vast Mexican underclass. In *The Liberation of the Peon* (fig. 28.31) he shows revolutionary soldiers tenderly wrapping the body of a peon, or worker, who has been tortured and then murdered. The victim's bound hands are being "liberated," echoing the only freedom that a peasant could expect: death that freed him from a life of grinding poverty and ceaseless toil.

José Clemente Orozco, 1883–1949

Orozco was even more strongly influenced by Mexican Indian traditions than was Rivera, perhaps because he received much of his training in Mexico City. Like Rivera, his teacher and collaborator, he was deeply committed to the revolution. His *Zapatistas* (fig. 28.32) is a prime example of the painterly illusion of rhythm. Moving from right to left, the Zapatistas set up a kind of beat in a pattern of continuous movement that symbolizes the ongoing revolution. Along with Pancho Villa, Emiliano Zapata (ca. 1879–1919) was one of the leaders of the revolution; the representation here is of some of his loyal Indian followers.

28.32 José Orozco, *Zapatistas*. 1931. Oil on canvas, 3' 9" × 4' 7" (1.14 × 1.4 m). The Museum of Modern Art, New York (Given anonymously). Photo: © 1996 The Museum of Modern Art, New York.

28.33 *Above* David Alfaro Siqueiros, *Echo of a Scream*. 1937. Enamel on wood, 48 × 36" (121.9 × 91.4 cm). The Museum of Modern Art, New York (Gift of Edward M. M. Warburg). Photo: © 1996 The Museum of Modern Art, New York.

David Alfaro Siqueiros, 1896–1974

Siqueiros (see-KEER-ohs) was a most politically active artist, who served a prison term for his leftist views. Though his early painting was heavy on Marxist ideology, his later work was directed more to humanistic concerns and universal problems. His *Echo of a Scream* (fig. 28.33) is a dramatic protest against the insanity of war. Set in the midst of a wasteland of debris, the enlarged head of the screaming child is the overwhelming center of attention. Forced to concentrate on the child's agonized face, we are confronted with the artist's passionate indictment of the madness called war. Edvard Munch's *The Scream* (see fig. 25.44) expressed the artist's reaction to critical tensions of the modern world: alienation, desperation, terror. In his painting Siqueiros has particularized the tensions into a single issue, an anti-war statement that appeared just two years before Hitler invaded Poland to launch World War II.

Architecture

The International Style

Walter Gropius, 1883–1969

The design school called the Bauhaus (BOUGH-house; fig. 28.34) was built expressly to exploit modern technology. As director of the Bauhaus, Gropius promoted instruction in painting, sculpture, architecture, and the crafts, with everything oriented toward the latest in technology and industrial design. As he wrote in 1919: "The separate arts must be brought back into intimate contact, under the wings of a great architecture." The workshop is a four-story box with an interior steel skeleton enclosed by window walls of glass, the latter a Gropius invention. The design established the principles of the International Style that was to dominate architectural design until the 1970s. Expensive to heat and to cool, not to mention washing the windows, many International Style buildings appear as anomalies in the energy-conscious 1990s. For half a century, however, they were the essence of modernity.

Le Corbusier (Charles-Edouard Jeanneret), 1887–1965

The International Style was brilliantly developed by the Swiss painter-architect Le Corbusier (luh core-boos-iay). For Le Corbusier, houses were "machines for living," as efficient as airplanes were for flying. Totally devoid of ornament, his Villa Savoye (fig. 28.35) is partially supported by slender columns but rests mostly on a recessed unit containing service functions, servants' quarters, entrance hall, and staircase to the living quarters on the second level. The living room is separated from an open interior terrace by floor-to-ceiling panes of glass, making the terrace a basic part of living arrangements.

28.34 *Left* Walter Gropius, The Bauhaus, Dessau, Germany. 1925–6. Photo: Esto, New York (Wayne Andrews).

28.35 Le Corbusier, Villa Savoye, Poissy-sur-Seine, France. 1929.

Organic Architecture

Frank Lloyd Wright, 1867–1959

International Style buildings are, in effect, disdainful of their environment, thrusting away from the earth to create their own space. America's greatest architect disagreed totally with this concept. Wright's buildings are generally organic, seemingly a natural consequence of their environment. One of his most imaginative designs is the Kaufmann House (fig. 28.36). Built on a site that would challenge any architect and which obviously inspired Wright, the house is situated on a steep and rocky hillside over a waterfall. Combining native rock construction with daring cantilevers colored beige to blend with the environment, the structure cannot be imagined on any other site. The Villa Savoye and "Falling Water" (as the Kaufmann House is known) represent, between them, opposite theories of modern design. Subsequent developments tended to fall somewhere between the two extremes.

28.36 Frank Lloyd Wright, Kaufmann House ("Falling Water"), Bear Run, Pennsylvania. 1936. Photo: Ralph Lieberman, North Adams, Massachusetts/Calmann & King Ltd., London.

ARTISTIC STYLES SINCE 1945

Action Painting: Abstract Expressionism

Jackson Pollock, 1912–56

The new style of Abstract Expressionism developed in New York, which, after World War II, replaced Paris as the artistic capital of the Western world. Once a Social Realist in the manner of Rivera, Pollock became the acknowledged leader of the new movement. His personal style of Abstract Expressionism began to bloom when he quit easel painting and, instead, tacked a large, unstretched canvas to the floor. Walking all around the canvas he became completely absorbed as he dropped, dripped, poured, and spattered paint on the canvas. Though he had no preconceived ideas when he began a canvas he could, as he said, "control the

28.37 Jackson Pollock, *Autumn Rhythm, No. 30, 1950*. 1950. Oil on canvas, 8' 9" × 17' 3" (2.67 × 5.26 m). Metropolitan Museum of Art, New York. Photo: © ARS, New York and DACS, London 1995.

28.38 Willem de Kooning, *Woman I*. 1950–2. Oil on canvas, 6' 3⅞" × 4' 10" (1.93 × 1.47 m). The Museum of Modern Art, New York (Purchase). Photo: © 1996 The Museum of Modern Art, New York, © Willem de Kooning/ARS, New York and DACS, London 1995.

28.39 Mark Rothko, *Number 10*. 1950. Oil on canvas, 7' 6⅜" × 4' 9⅛" (2.29 × 1.45 m). The Museum of Modern Art, New York (Gift of Philip Johnson). Photo: © 1996 The Museum of Modern Art, New York, © ARS, New York and DACS, London 1995.

flow of the paint," and he did complete works with brushstrokes as needed. His *Autumn Rhythm* (fig. 28.37) is an intricate and complex interplay of curvilinear lines and controlled spatters illustrating, as he remarked, "energy made visible." Pollock's energetic involvement in the act of painting led to the term "action painting" as a general description of the movement.

Willem de Kooning, b. 1904

The Dutch-American artist works in violent motions using a large brush heavy with paint. His favorite theme is that of the eternal woman: earth mother and fertility goddess. *Woman I* (fig. 28.38) is a giant, earthy figure of a woman painted in slashing brushstrokes. An energetic portrayal of a goddess-cum-movie queen and sex symbol, this is one man's view of the other half of the human race.

Mark Rothko, 1903–70

In his mature style Rothko covered large canvases with luminous, softly bleeding rectangles of color. *Number 10* (fig. 28.39) is an extremely subtle combination of softly glowing colors separated by ragged, foggy edges. Compared with the dynamics of Pollock and de Kooning, this is Abstract Expressionism in a gentle and meditative mood—in a style frequently called "color field."

Jacob Lawrence, b. 1917

Lawrence uses vigorous silhouetted patterns and narrative subject matter in his unique abstract style. Deeply committed to African-American history in America, Lawrence is perhaps best known for the series *The Migration of the Negro* (1940–41) and his *Harlem* series of 1943. *Daybreak—A Time to Rest* (fig. 28.40) is related, like much of his work, to the life of an African-American hero, Harriet Tubman, a famed conductor of slaves to freedom on the Underground Railway. This is from a children's book entitled *Harriet and the Promised Land,* which he illustrated. The work is balanced between a dream-world and reality, an artful juxtaposition of identifiable images and abstractions. The huge feet are pointed north but, even when traveling the route to freedom, there must be a time to rest and to dream of the promised land.

28.40 Jacob Lawrence, *Daybreak—A Time to Rest*. 1967. Tempera on hardboard, 30 × 24" (76.2 × 61 cm). National Gallery of Art, Washington, D.C. (Anonymous gift).

Reaction Against Action: Pop Art

The emotional fervor of Abstract Expressionism burned itself out in about fifteen years, to be superseded by a Dada-type reaction. The self-confidence of America after World War II was jolted by the Korean conflict, the Cold War, and the military build-up in Vietnam. A new breed of artists was skeptical of American accomplishments and chose the banalities of American life to satirize the superficiality of American culture. First called Neo-Dadaists, these artists used recognizable subject matter from American popular culture: soup cans, comic strips, road signs, and cult figures from rock music and commercial Hollywood movies.

Pop Art was the label applied to what seemed to be a uniquely American reaction to the numbing vulgarity of much of popular culture. Actually, the label and the movement had surfaced in England in the mid-1950s. English images tended, however, to be romantic and sentimental commentaries on popular idols, comic strips, and American movies; American reactions were much more aggressive, perhaps because the media hype in the United States was so blatant and all-pervasive.

Robert Rauschenberg, b. 1925

The movement burst on to the American scene in 1962, but Rauschenberg had been working his way from Abstract Expressionism to Pop Art since the mid-1950s. In his *Monogram* (fig. 28.41) he combined an old tire, a stuffed Angora goat, and pieces of stenciled signs into a wry and witty commentary on American life. The goat and tire are waste that has been recycled, so to speak. Paradoxically, they are still distasteful objects, retaining their identity and creating a tension between themselves and the total work. They should not be there but they are, undeniably there, forever and ever. Rauschenberg has stated that painting is related to art and to life and that his function is to "act in the gap between the two."

28.41 Robert Rauschenberg, *Monogram*. 1959. Construction, 4 × 6 × 6' (1.2 × 1.83 × 1.83 m). Moderna Museet, Stockholm, Sweden. Photo: Per-Anders Allsten, © Robert Rauschenberg/DACS, London/VAGA, New York, 1995.

28.42 Roy Lichtenstein, *Drowning Girl*. 1963. Oil and synthetic polymer on canvas, 5' 7⅝" × 5' 6¾" (1.72 × 1.69 m). The Museum of Modern Art, New York (Philip Johnson Fund and gift of Mrs. and Mrs. Bagley Wright). Photo: © 1996 The Museum of Modern Art, New York, © Roy Lichtenstein/DACS 1995.

Roy Lichtenstein, b. 1923

Rauschenberg generally retains the painterly quality of Abstract Expressionism but Lichtenstein adopted the mechanical techniques and imagery of comic strips, including the Benday dots used in newspaper reproductions of the comics. He also used the hard lines of comic strips but his paintings are monumental in scale. His cold and impersonal portrayal of a *Drowning Girl* (fig. 28.42) is an indictment of the casual and callous attitudes of many Americans toward violence in comic strips, in the streets, in Africa or the Middle East. The technique is that of the "low art" of the comics, but the result is a potent artistic statement. Lichtenstein, for obvious reasons, selected nothing from comic strips like *Peanuts* or *Doonesbury*.

Edward Kienholz, 1927–94

The sculptures of Kienholz have been called Pop but his work is also expressionistic and surreal. He combines painting, sculpture, collage, and the stage to depict some of the shabbiness, stupidity, and cruelty of modern urban life. In

28.43 Edward Kienholz, *The State Hospital*. 1966. Mixed media, 8 × 12 × 10' (2.4 × 3.6 × 8.5 m). Moderna Museet, Stockholm, Sweden. © Edward Kienholz.

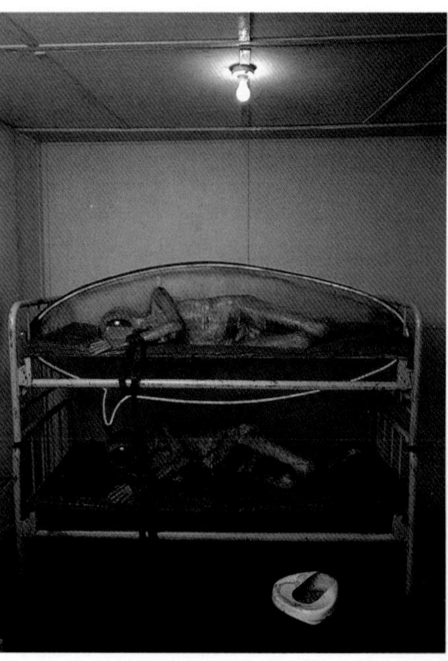

The State Hospital (fig. 28.43) he confronts us with an elderly patient—someone's father, someone's grandfather—who has been chained to a cot in a state facility. In the upper cot, encased in what appears to be a comic-strip balloon, is the same figure, possibly representing the patient's vision of himself: chained, caged, and abandoned. Is this how life should end?

Marisol, b. 1930

Marisol's work is lighter in spirit than that of Kienholz but with oblique social commentaries that are sophisticated, witty, ironic, and often sardonic. A Venezuelan born in Paris and living in the United States, Marisol (Escobar is her unused surname) creates her own world with assemblages of wood, plaster, paint, and assorted objects. In *Women and Dog* (fig. 28.44) she uses painting, drawing, stencil, relief, collage, carving, and assemblage to present the somewhat Cubist and Surrealist tableau. As is her custom, all the faces are of Marisol herself, giving the scene an introspective dimension. She has created a world without men in which the feminine gender is the self-contained reality. (We may safely assume that the dog is female.) Rather than an anti-male work, this is an assemblage of self-reliant females.

28.44 Marisol, *Women and Dog*. 1964. Wood, plaster, synthetic polymer, and miscellaneous items, 72¼ × 73 × 30$^{15}/_{16}$" (183.5 × 185.4 × 78.6 cm). Whitney Museum of American Art (Purchase, with funds from the Friends of the Whitney Museum of American Art). Photo: Robert E. Mates, New Jersey, © Marisol/DACS, London/VAGA, New York 1995.

28.45 Josef Albers, *1. Homage to the Square: Star Blue*. 1957. Oil on board, 29⅞ × 29⅞" (75.9 × 75.9 cm). Cleveland Museum of Art, Cleveland, Ohio (Contemporary Collection, 65.1). Photo: © DACS 1995.

Color, Geometry, and Optics

Josef Albers, 1888–1976

One of the first graduates of the Bauhaus, Albers emigrated from Nazi Germany in 1933 to the United States, where his work influenced the development of Abstract Geometric painting and Op Art. His *Homage to the Square* paintings were a serialization similar to Monet's paintings of haystacks and lily ponds, a process, not a solution. Working with three or four squares of different colors, Albers explored, in hundreds of paintings, the interaction of colors and straight lines. *Homage to the Square: Star Blue* (fig. 28.45) has an intensity based not on the squares themselves but on the relationship of the colors.

Helen Frankenthaler, b. 1928

Working against the currents of Abstract Expressionism and Geometric Abstraction, Frankenthaler stained the raw canvas to achieve a limpid freshness not seen in the work of any other artist. In *Interior Landscape* (fig. 28.46) the paint is applied in thin washes so integrated with the canvas that there is no illusion of either foreground or background. Like Pollock, she creates an open composition out of abstract shapes manipulated into patterns of color. In this sense she is an action painter. She begins with no preconceived idea; rather, the painting evolves as she interacts with her washes and the canvas. In another sense she is a color-field artist, in that she creates abstract landscapes of color that can be interpreted in many different ways.

28.46 Helen Frankenthaler, *Interior Landscape*. 1964. Acrylic on canvas, 8' 8⅞" × 7' 8⅝" (2.66 × 2.35 m). San Francisco Museum of Modern Art (Gift of the Women's Board).

28.47 Louise Nevelson, *Illumination—Dark*. 1961. Bronze, dimensions variable: 10'5" × 9'½" (3.18 × 2.76 m). Whitney Museum of American Art, New York (Gift of the artist, dedicated to the Whitney Museum of American Art). Photo: Geoffrey Clements, New York.

28.48 Bridget Riley, *Crest*. 1964. Emulsion on board, 5' 5½" × 5' 5½" (1.66 × 1.66 m). Private collection. Photo: Juda Rowan Gallery, London.

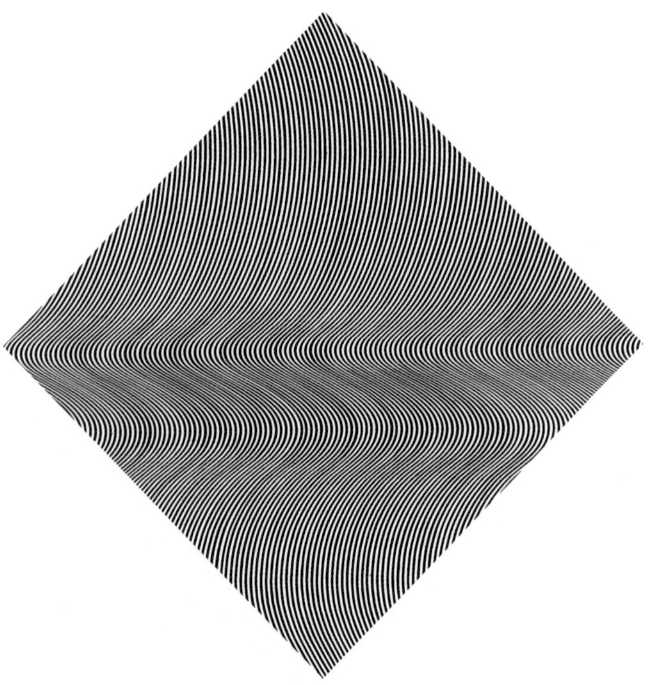

Louise Nevelson, 1900–88

Nevelson's assemblage of sculptures reflects the geometric forms of pre-Columbian sculpture, but her overriding interest in working with wood can be traced to her father's career as a cabinetmaker and her involvement with the wood in his shop. *Illumination—Dark* (fig. 28.47) is a large wooden wall on which the artist has arranged selected pieces of wood (culled from old houses) to form a three-dimensional geometric abstraction. With bronze-painted shapes against the flat black background of the wall, the piece resembles both a cupboard and a cityscape like the artist's native New York. As Nevelson has said, she "putters endlessly" with the design until she gets it right. The result here is a subtle blend of delicacy, mystery, and strength.

Bridget Riley, b. 1931

American painters like Albers were concerned with straight lines, but British artist Riley worked with the possibilities inherent in curved lines. *Crest* (fig. 28.48) is a large, complex composition that communicates directly with the eye and the optic nerve. Though she has been called an Op Artist (from "optical art"), Riley's style goes beyond merely confusing or tricking the eye. What we have here is a new way of perceiving and experiencing motion.

28.49 Jean Dubuffet, *Portrait of Henri Michaux*, from *More Beautiful Than They Think: Portraits* series. 1947. Oil on canvas, 51½ × 38⅜" (130.7 × 97.3 cm). The Museum of Modern Art, New York (Sidney and Harriet Janis Collection). Photo: © 1996 The Museum of Modern Art, New York, © ADAGP, Paris and DACS, London 1995.

28.50 Francis Bacon, *Number VII from Eight Studies for a Portrait*. 1953. Oil on linen, 5' × 3' 10⅛" (1.52 × 1.17 m). The Museum of Modern Art, New York (Gift of Mr. and Mrs. William A. M. Burden). Photo: © 1996 The Museum of Modern Art, New York.

Fantasy and Expressionism

Jean Dubuffet, 1901–85

Dubuffet (due-boo-fay), the most notable French artist since World War II, found some of his inspiration in strangely different areas: art of the insane, children's art, and graffiti. Contending that there should be no essential division between the art of amateurs, children, psychotics, and artists, Dubuffet described his collection of non-professional art as *art brut*. Dubuffet's art could not be called *art brut* because he was neither untrained nor psychotic; he painted intuitively, somewhat like the Abstract Expressionists, but his subjects were fantastic figures and landscapes. He combined pigments with different mixtures of plaster, sand, or twigs to make a thick **impasto** that he scratched and scored to make grotesque figures such as his *Portrait of Henri Michaux* (fig. 28.49). Like much of his work, this painting has a powerful primordial quality that both attracts and repels.

Francis Bacon, 1909–92

The Irish-born Bacon painted tormented visions distorted to the point of insanity. Preoccupied with deformity and disease, he selected works by Old Masters and restated them as anguished symbols of contemporary life. *Number VII from Eight Studies for a Portrait* (fig. 28.50) is based on the portrait of Pope Innocent X (reigned 1644–55) by Velasquez, who depicted the pope as a powerful, intelligent, and coolly confident pontiff. Bacon used Renaissance perspective but placed the pope in an isolation booth where his anguished screams tear his head asunder.

Fritz Scholder, b. 1937

The best-known Native-American artist, Scholder shows the influence of Expressionism and Pop Art, but his subject matter sets him apart from both styles. Scholder uses serialism to portray the paradoxical position of Native Americans in everyday life. With a poignant irony he has depicted stereotypes: a Super Chief eating an ice cream cone; a drunken Indian clutching a can of beer like a tomahawk; a Hollywood Indian and his captive "Anglo" maiden. Scholder's work is satirical and searching, depicting both the nobility and the degradation of his people. *Waiting Indian No. 4* (fig. 28.51) stands majestically in a barren landscape. In his awesome dignity he refuses to accept any part of a stereotype in the Anglo world.

28.51 Fritz Scholder, *Waiting Indian No. 4*. 1970. Oil on canvas, 5' 10" × 5' 4" (1.78 × 1.63 m). University Art Collections, Arizona State University.

28.52 Alexander Calder, *Many Pierced Discs*. 1950. Metal, 5' 5" × 4' 1" (1.65 × 1.25 m). University Art Collections, Arizona State University. Photo: © ADAGP, Paris and DACS, London 1995.

Alexander Calder, 1898–1976

For centuries sculptors have labored to give their works the illusion of movement. Calder invented abstract works that actually moved. Influenced by Surrealism and Geometric Abstraction, Calder created the true mobile. *Many Pierced Discs* (fig. 28.52) is a fantasy of abstract shapes wired together and delicately balanced so that it can respond to the slightest breeze. An indoor mobile, this work rests on its pedestal in an art gallery where it can gently gyrate and bow to museum visitors.

Henry Moore, 1898–1986

Moore was the most important English artist of his time in any medium. Like Calder, he was influenced by Surrealism but went on to develop his unique abstract figural style. In *Family Group* (fig. 28.53) the figures are recognizable but abstracted into curving, rather primitive shapes that emphasize the unity and stability of a family.

Minimal Art

Tony DeLap, b. 1927

Minimal Art began in the 1960s as a movement to reduce art to basics: one shape or one color or one idea. Also called primary structures or primary art, the style is easier to observe than to discuss. *Sentaro* (fig. 28.54) by DeLap is a sculpture/painting reduced to a basic shape and a single color. This is a beautiful hunk of a bright red rectangular box that seemingly floats within its plastic case. DeLap used commercial staining and spraying techniques so that the saturated painting/sculpture is a solid color field with no trace of brushwork or other manipulation by the artist. The

28.53 Henry Moore, *Family Group*. 1948–9. Bronze (cast 1950), 59¼ × 46½ × 29⅞" (150.5 × 118 × 75.9 cm), including base. The Museum of Modern Art, New York (A. Conger Goodyear Fund). Photo: © 1996 The Museum of Modern Art, New York.

28.54 Tony DeLap, *Sentaro*. 1967. Aluminum, wood, plexiglass, and lacquer, 16 × 16 × 5" (40.6 × 40.6 × 12.7 cm). University Art Collections, Arizona State University (American Art Heritage Fund).

vitality and spontaneity of Abstract Expressionism has given way to a laid-back restraint comparable to Cool Jazz (see pp. 420–1).

David Smith, 1906–65

American sculptor Smith applied his experience of working in an automotive plant and locomotive factory to sculpting with steel—something that, as he said, "had little art history." His *Cubi XV* (fig. 28.55) is a gravity-defying combination of simple geometric components that set up a lively interplay of forms and space. The stainless steel is highly polished, with controlled light patterns that make the metal surface as sensual as works by Brancusi (see fig. 28.18) or Verrocchio (see fig. 17.14).

Varieties of Realism

Though never absent from the American scene, realism has again become a major factor in a variety of styles called New Realism, Magic Realism, or Photorealism. The sculptor Duane Hanson (b. 1925) makes casts of living people and paints the resulting figures to look completely lifelike, including real clothing and accessories. Richard Estes (b. 1936) projects a slide directly onto canvas and makes a precise copy with an airbrush. Hanson selects subjects like gaudily dressed tourists, junkies, and overweight shoppers, whereas Estes paints banal cityscapes totally devoid of people.

28.55 David Smith, *Cubi XV*. 1963–4. Stainless steel, 10' 5⅛" × 4' 10½" (3.23 × 1.49 m). San Diego Museum of Art, California (Gift of Mr. and Mrs. Norton W. Walbridge). Photo: © Estate of David Smith/DACS, London/VAGA, New York, 1995.

28.56 Audrey Flack, *World War II (Vanitas), April 1945*; detail on p. 340. 1976–7. Oil over acrylic on canvas, 8 × 8' (2.44 × 2.44 m). Incorporating a portion of Margaret Bourke-White's photograph "Buchenwald, April 1945." © Time, Inc. Photo: Louis K. Meisel Gallery, New York.

28.57 Otto Duecker, *Russell, Terry, J. T., and a Levi Jacket*. 1979. Oil on masonite cutouts within a photograph. Elaine Horwitch Galleries, Scottsdale, Arizona. Photo: Don Wheeler, Tulsa, Oklahoma.

Audrey Flack, b. 1931

In their subject matter Hanson and Estes follow the orientation of Pop Art, but that Photorealism can pursue other paths has been illustrated by the work of Flack, the first Photorealist to have a painting purchased by the Museum of Modern Art in New York. Like others in the movement, she projects color slides onto a canvas and paints with an airbrush. Her subject matter, however, is a kind of collage, a still-life arrangement that conveys a specific idea or message. *World War II (Vanitas), April 1945* (fig. 28.56 and p. 340) refers to the liberation of the Nazi concentration camp at Buchenwald. Flack's painting, based on Margaret Bourke-White's famous photograph, is a tribute to the survivors of the death camps and a memorial to the 12,000,000—including about 6,000,000 Jews—who perished there. The rose, burning candle, pear, watch, butterfly, and black border are all symbols of mortality or the commemoration of the dead. The printed statement is a rabbinical quotation affirming belief in God and concluding: "You can take everything from me—the pillow from under my head, my house—but you cannot take God from my heart." The various objects are so much larger than life-size that they appear not to be "real." The basic reality is, of course, the haunted faces of the survivors of Buchenwald.

Otto Duecker, b. 1948

Our society has apparently learned to accept many real/unreal mystifications of the everyday world such as, for example, twelve-foot cowboys on a giant movie screen or six-inch football players on TV. Indeed, when Duecker paints larger-than-life figures, cuts them out, and arranges them in galleries, homes, and warehouses, we are inclined to accept them as "real." In *Russell, Terry, J. T., and a Levi Jacket* (fig. 28.57) we see the artist posed in front of his four cutouts and appearing, in this photograph, somehow less real than his creations.

If each generation develops its own concepts of reality, then what is real now? For the present century—sometimes called the Age of Uncertainty—it might be accurate to say that several concepts of reality are acceptable, or tolerable, given the scientific environment of relativity, quantum, chaos, and complex theories.

Environmental Art

There are two basic kinds of Environmental Art: art that creates an artificial environment that one can enter and art that alters the natural or constructed environment. The latter type will be considered here in the work of three notable artists.

Robert Smithson, 1938–73

Smithson chose Rozel Point in the Great Salt Lake for his *Spiral Jetty* (fig. 28.58) because it was remote and because algae colored the water pink. The spiral design was suggested, he said, by the intense light radiating from the pinkish water. A dedicated environmentalist with a special interest in land-reclamation, Smithson was always intent on integrating his works with their natural setting. This was particularly successful with *Spiral Jetty* because the work and the environment have indeed become accepted as one. Tragically, this was one of the artist's last works; he was killed in a plane crash while scouting a new site.

Christo and Jeanne-Claude (Christo and Jeanne-Claude Javacheff), both born 1935

These environmental artists have wrapped everything from a woman, a bicycle, and a machine, to a bridge in Paris. One of their largest projects was the arrangement of 1,000,000 square feet (92,900 m^2) of fabric on an Australian coastline. One of their most successful and best-known works is probably the *Running Fence* (fig. 28.60). Laid across the rolling countryside north of San Francisco, the fence celebrated the landscape in a manner somehow comparable to the work of landscape painters. Running from a major highway down to the Pacific Ocean, the fence was in place for two weeks during September 1976. Though viewed by many, it caused thousands more to become aware of the beauty of the countryside through the two books and the movie about the project.

None of the Christos' projects remains in place for very long, which is a deliberate aesthetic decision on their part. Just as each stage of life is temporary—childhood, maturity, old age—they feel that each project is best appreciated knowing that it is momentary, possessing what Jeanne-Claude has described as the "lovely quality of impermanence."

Architecture: The International Style

Before World War II skyscraper designs were generally eclectic, clothing steel skeletons with older styles. The innovations of Louis Sullivan (1856–1924) and Frank Lloyd Wright were more influential in Europe than at home and the International Style had yet to make much of an impression outside Europe. Until the 1950s New York skyscrapers were circumscribed by the demands of clients and rigid zoning restrictions. Buildings were designed to occupy every square foot of expensive real estate but zoning ordinances required that some sunlight had to fall into manmade canyons. The result was the so-called ziggurat, a setback design with upper floors terraced back from the street.

Beginning an international renaissance in architecture, the International Style appeared in New York with the design of the United Nations complex. Because modern buildings were so complicated, most were designed by a group of architects and engineers. Wallace K. Harrison (1895–1981) headed an international team that designed the Secretariat Building (fig. 28.59) in the shape of a giant slab,

28.59 *Right* Wallace K. Harrison and Associates, Secretariat Building of the United Nations, New York. 1947–50. Photo: United Nations, New York.

28.58 Robert Smithson, *Spiral Jetty*, Great Salt Lake, Utah. 1970. Rock, salt crystals, earth, algae; coil 1,500' (457 m). John Weber Gallery, New York. Photo: Gianfranco Gorgoni/Dawn Gallery, New York.

28.60 *Below* Christo and Jeanne-Claude (Christo and Jean-Claude Javacheff), *Running Fence, Sonoma and Marin Counties, California*. 1972–6. Fabric fence, height 18' (5.49 m), length 24½ miles (39.4 km). Photo: Jeanne-Claude. © Christo, 1976.

28.61 Ludwig Mies van der Rohe, Seagram Building, New York. 1958. Photo: Ezra Stoller/Esto, New York. Courtesy Joseph E. Seagram & Sons, Inc.

28.62 Le Corbusier, Notre-Dame-du-Haut, Ronchamp, France. 1950–5. Photo: Ralph Lieberman, North Adams, Massachusetts.

as suggested by Le Corbusier. Clothed on the sides in glass and on the ends in marble, the structure was the first American building to embody the Bauhaus tradition. Because it occupied only a portion of the riverfront site, it avoided the setback restrictions imposed on other high-rise structures.

Ludwig Mies van der Rohe, 1886–1969

The German architect Mies van der Rohe was initially influenced by Gropius but developed his own Minimalist version of the International Style. Illustrating his motto that "less is more," his Seagram Building (fig. 28.61) is a model of simplicity and elegance, a classic among glass skyscrapers.

Le Corbusier

Though he was an influential pioneer of the International Style, Le Corbusier later abandoned his boxes on stilts (see fig. 28.35) for a more sculptural style. His design for the pilgrimage chapel of Notre-Dame-du-Haut (fig. 28.62) was revolutionary, unlike any other building. The plan is irregular in every respect. Thick, curving white walls are topped by a heavy overhanging roof and flanked by a tall white tower on the left and a shorter tower on the right. The towers are decorative but they also transmit natural light to the two altars within. Window openings are cut through the massive walls to make tunnels of light. Randomly placed, the windows are of different sizes and cut through the walls in a variety of angles. Stained glass is used but each window has a different design and color scheme. The overall effect is intimate and magical.

Organic Architecture

Frank Lloyd Wright

Wright designed many buildings based on the circle but none as dramatic as the Solomon R. Guggenheim Museum in New York (fig. 28.63). The front circle is the administrative unit, with the gallery behind. The structure is essentially a cylinder rising in expanding circles. This is the antithesis, in every respect, of the International Style. Inside the building (fig. 28.64) a circular ramp rises to the top in six complete turns around a 90-foot (27-m) well that climaxes in a skylight dome. Visitors are taken to the top in an elevator, permitting them to walk on a continuous downhill grade while inspecting art works placed on the outside wall. The design necessarily limits how art is displayed but the Guggenheim interior is one of Wright's boldest concepts.

Eero Saarinen, 1910–61

New York's JFK International Airport is an uninspired collection of architectural clichés with the sole exception of the TWA Terminal (fig. 28.65). Designed by Saarinen, the structure is a triumph, a curvilinear enclosure of space that actually looks like an air terminal. Built of reinforced concrete, the continuously curving surfaces symbolize flight in a manner reminiscent of Brancusi's *Bird in Space* (see fig. 28.18).

28.63 Frank Lloyd Wright, Solomon R. Guggenheim Museum, New York. 1943–59. Photo: Robert E. Mates.

28.64 Solomon R. Guggenheim Museum, interior. Photo: Robert E. Mates.

Joern Utzon, b. 1918

The design competition for the new opera house in Sydney, Australia, was won by Danish architect Utzon in 1956, but it took thirteen years and several more architects to figure out how to build the unique concept (fig. 28.66). It is a cultural center that includes an opera house, exhibition hall, theatre, and other facilities, and the soaring gull-wing design—executed with a facing of brilliant white ceramic tiles—is a visual triumph, thanks in part to its location on one of the world's great harbors.

28.65 Eero Saarinen, TWA Terminal, JFK International Airport, New York. 1959–62. Photo: Ezra Stoller/Esto, New York.

28.66 Utzon, Hall, Todd, and Littleton, Sydney Opera House, Bennelong Point, Sydney, Australia. 1959–72. Photo: Associated Press/Topham, Edenbridge, U.K.

28.67 Ansel Adams, *Moonrise, Hernandez, New Mexico.* 1944. Photograph, 15½ × 19" (39.4 × 48.3 cm). Photo: by Ansel Adams. Copyright © 1995 by the Trustees of The Ansel Adams Publishing Rights Trust. All Rights Reserved.

28.68 W. Eugene Smith, *Spanish Wake*, from Spanish Village series. 1951. Photograph. © W. Eugene Smith Estate/Black. Photo: Center for Creative Photography, University of Arizona.

The Art of Photography

Anyone can take photographs, but there are few artists behind the camera. Mastering the technical aspects of photography is one thing, producing an artistic image quite another. Unlike painting or sculpture, there is no gradual build-up to a completed work, no chance to add, delete, modify, rework. The image can be altered after the fact, but the shot still begins with what the camera "sees" when the shutter is opened.

What is a good photograph? For that matter, what is a good painting? Like all art, photography is communication, a personal statement that the artist is making. Moreover, the work of a good photographer has a recognizable style just as, for example, paintings by Monet are stylistically consistent.

Portrait photographers have a special talent, an ability to reveal the nature and character of their subjects. Few were as accomplished as Matthew Brady (1823–96). Brady took so many photographs of Abraham Lincoln that the latter is reputed to have said that his Cooper Union speech and Brady's photos put him in the White House. But it was quality, not quantity, that accounted for the fame of Brady's portraits of Lincoln. Even the calling-card photo (see fig. 23.5) clearly shows the strength, dignity, and nobility of the future president.[2]

Like many painters, photographers tend to concentrate on specializations such as portraiture, landscape, cityscape, sports, combat photography, and so forth. Landscape photographer Ansel Adams (1902–84) was one of the charter members of the photographic society named "Group f/64." This optical term was chosen because the group generally set their lenses to the smallest aperture to

2. Brady also produced a remarkable photographic record of the Civil War.

secure the greatest depth of field: maximum sharpness from foreground to background. For most of his career Adams produced very sharp photos of the landscape of the American West. His *Moonrise, Hernandez, New Mexico* (fig. 28.67) magically conveys the immensity of the landscape as it and the night sky tower over the isolation of the few inhabitants.

Photo-journalist W. Eugene Smith (1918–78), on assignment for *Life* magazine, did a memorable photo-essay on life in a Spanish village. His *Spanish Wake* (fig. 28.68) from that series has characteristics comparable to a fine oil painting. The dramatic chiaroscuro and powerful composition add to the impact of the range of grief.

Also a photo-journalist for *Life,* Margaret Bourke-White (1904–71) photographed everything from industry and cities to natural disasters and World War II combat. It was her photograph of concentration camp survivors that inspired Photorealist painter Audrey Flack to create her memorial to the Holocaust (see fig. 28.56). Bourke-White's *Two Women, Lansdale, Arkansas* (fig. 28.69) is a serene study, taken during the Great Depression, of two companionable women who are totally at ease with themselves and with each other.

There is no more telling image of the Great Depression than the *Migrant Mother, Nipomo, California* (fig. 28.70 and p. 422) (by Dorothea Lange (1895–1965). Lange's compassion and respect for the farmers who migrated from the Midwest Dust Bowl to California in search of a better life are clearly revealed. This single photograph sums up the unflinching determination of thousands of homeless, rootless farmers to survive. The subject matter is comparable to John Steinbeck's novel *The Grapes of Wrath,* in which the Joad family migrated from Oklahoma to California.

Photography's strong points include its immediacy and ease of replication. The earlier question about what makes a good photograph is answered by the examples printed in this volume (see figs. 23.4, 23.5, 27.1, 28.15, and 28.67–70). Each picture communicates more than the sum of its parts; each image is unique; and the personal communication from the artist is just as apparent in these works as in paintings by Rembrandt, Monet, or van Gogh.

Painting and Sculpture: Postmodernism

Art was self-consciously "modern" from around 1910 to about 1970. Artists viewed themselves as *avant-garde* creators who denied the past as they searched for new means of expression. Abstraction or a renunciation of representation, a taste for novelty that affirmed originality and denied tradition (no more imitations of the world or of earlier artists) were characteristics of Modernism. Beginning around 1970 or so, however, there was a general shift to a reweaving of the recent past and Western culture, a search for human values in the context of a world civilization. Representation and history were reintroduced, though

28.69 Margaret Bourke-White, *Two Women, Lansdale, Arkansas.* 1936. Gelatin-silver print. George Arents Research Library, Syracuse University, Syracuse, New York.

28.70 Dorothea Lange, *Migrant Mother, Nipomo, California.* 1936. Gelatin-silver print, 12½ × 9⅞" (31.8 × 25.1 cm).

28.71 Gerhard Richter, *Vase*. 1984. Oil on canvas, 7' 4½" × 6' 6¾" (2.25 × 2 m). Museum of Fine Arts, Boston (Juliana Cheney Edwards Collection).

28.72 Sylvia Plimack Mangold, *Schunnemunk Mountain*. 1979. Oil on canvas, 5' ¼" × 6' 8⅛" (1.53 × 2.04 m). Dallas Museum of Art (General Acquisitions Fund and a gift of the 500, Inc. 1980.7).

without reverting to graphic realism. This was, of course, a reaction to the rapidly evolving Electronic/Information Age and the idea that the world was becoming a Global Village. For want of a better term this movement is called "post-modernism."

Postmodernism uses representation where appropriate and revives the connection with tradition by deliberately choosing between several traditions or by making explicit reference to tradition as such, which is anything but a traditional attitude. It recognizes the plurality of autonomous cultures within a world civilization.

Contemporary artistic styles are therefore wildly pluralistic. No one style predominates. A renewed interest in figurative painting called, for want of a better term, New Painting, seems to be significant, but some older styles persist and innovations abound. One of the newer innovations is Neo-Expressionism, which emerged in Germany in the 1980s, much as its ancestor surfaced some seven decades earlier. This is an authentic style practiced by a number of successful artists, notably Gerhard Richter (b. 1932). His *Vase* (fig. 28.71 and p. 323) is a vibrant abstraction achieved by superimposing many layers of pigment with a variety of brushes, including the wide brushes used by house painters. This is a very large work that exudes vigorous emotion.

There are literally thousands of artists hard at work turning out untold numbers of art works. In the absence, at present, of any towering figures, we have selected three artists to represent the many who have yet to be recognized.

Sylvia Mangold, b. 1938

Mangold lives and works in upstate New York. Her *Schunnemunk Mountain* (fig. 28.72) is a night landscape framed by larger painted rectangles and strips of applied masking tape. The country scene viewed from her studio is representational but the added rectangles, stripe, and masking tape make the illusion ambiguous; perhaps the painting is not a landscape but a commentary on how art is constructed. This is thus a poetic image that is "presented" to the viewer.

Jennifer Bartlett, b. 1941

Contrasting sharply with the hushed image of the New York mountain, Bartlett's art is consistently cheerful and often exuberant, as in *Sad and Happy Tidal Wave* (fig. 28.74). This is a diptych with a left panel of Bartlett's distinctive painted steel tiles and the right panel a two-piece canvas. Both panels focus on the abstract figure of a swimmer, composed of oval shapes. Though color and design are similar the two panels are sharply different: gleaming brilliance on the left and a softer, almost pastel quality on the right. The artist is playing not only with color and shapes, but with the characteristics of different media as well.

Robert Colescott, b. 1925

Colescott has been among the leaders in a Postmodern movement that is reexamining the whole range of the Western pictorial tradition. His *Les Demoiselles d'Alabama: Vestidas* (fig. 28.73) is a delightful and wickedly witty

28.73 *Above* Robert Colescott, *Les Demoiselles d'Alabama: Vestidas*. 1985. Acrylic on canvas, 8' × 7' 8" (2.44 × 2.37 m). Phyllis Kind Gallery, New York, Chicago.

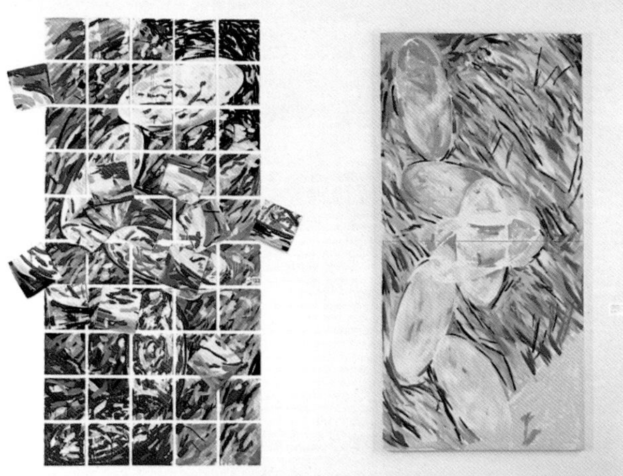

28.74 Jennifer Bartlett, *Sad and Happy Tidal Wave*. 1978. Enamel, silkscreen on steel plate (62 plates); oil on canvas (2 panels), 10' 9½" × 14' 4" (3.29 × 4.37 m). Dallas Museum of Art (Foundation for the Arts Collection, gift of Susan and Robert K. Hoffman).

"quotation" of Picasso's *Les Demoiselles d'Avignon* (see fig. 28.10), which was such a crucial step in modern art. Despite the many close similarities, this work is highly original, especially in the totally different mood the artist has given to his work as compared with the Picasso.

28.75 Michael Graves, Portland Public Services Building, Portland, Oregon, view from Fifth Avenue. 1980–2. Photo: Paschall/Taylor.

Outlook

Art in the 1990s is, in general, no longer a Bohemian activity and New York is no longer the primary center of artistic activity. Faced with a declining art market, some New York promoters seized on Neo-Expressionism as the new American style and then "discovered" artists who were working in the style, most of whom turned out to be Europeans. Happily discovered while working in Europe, Julian Schnabel is actually a Texan. He, along with Laurie Anderson and David Salle, is making a living out of Neo-Expressionism by promoting a "fast track" art market rivaling the hyped success of rock stars and soap-opera personalities. The marketing of art and "art stars" has become another American enterprise with the implication that "success" is more important than aesthetics. Where this will lead is anybody's guess, but the prognosis does not favor artistic integrity. Art critic Robert Hughes has called the 1980s probably the worst decade in the history of American art, a nadir that will likely continue through the 1990s because the social conditions that fostered the era's cultural traits give no evidence of changing.

Following is a selective listing of styles, attitudes, and movements that indicate the wide range of contemporary artistic activity.

New Painting	Primitivism
Neo-Expressionism	Naives
French Nouveau Réalisme	Abstractionists
Italian Arte Povera	Nul/Zero
Pop and Post-Pop	Computer Art
Fluxus	Holograhic Art
Conceptual Art	Performance Art
Minimalism	Body Art
Earth Art	Vague Art
Noise or Sound Art	Light Art
Site Sculpture	Bad Painting
Postmodern Art	

Whether any one style will predominate in the manner of Impressionism or Cubism is unlikely, given the rapid interactions of our Global Village in the Communications Age. Artistic influences are international but artists are individuals. They will pursue their own goals, creating art works faster than critics can conjure up labels. This is as it should be. Works of art are always best judged on their own merits regardless of style, school, or movement.

Architecture: Postmodernism

The most important architectural movement since the Bauhaus, Postmodernism has developed—since about 1970—into a worldwide phenomenon. Strictly urban in orientation, the style has appeared in New York, Paris, Hong Kong, Tokyo, Portland, Los Angeles, and many cities in between. In fact, the rise of Postmodern design has coincided with the increasing emphasis on city-based identities as opposed to traditional national boundaries. At the same time, these urban centers, with instant worldwide communications, are clearly part of the international community and the rapid evolution of the Global Village.

How can modernity be spoken of in the past tense? What is meant by *post*modern? During the middle segment of this century Modernism usually meant the *avant-garde*, unadorned geometry of the International Style. By the 1970s the stark boxes and towers that had long dominated cityscapes were increasingly viewed as cold and impersonal at best and, at worst, as profoundly anti-human. Not many buildings had the elegant proportions of the Seagram Building (see fig. 28.61).

Architectural critics and historians sometimes refer to the "coding" of a building. The Seagram Building, for example, is immediately recognizable as an office building; its code (design) reads "office building." But there is no other code or message, no reference to local or historical traditions. Postmodern design, on the other hand, is characterized by a double coding: the function of the structure coupled with architectural references to local and/or historical elements. The AT&T Building (fig. 28.76) by Philip Johnson (b. 1906) is a hotly debated example of Postmodernist dual coding. Basically a glass-and-steel skyscraper, it has an entrance that is reminiscent of Brunelleschi's Pazzi Chapel (see fig. 17.4) but the pediment resembles eighteenth-century furniture designed in England by Thomas Chippendale (1718–79). According to some detractors, this so-called Chippendale skyscraper looks very much like a grandfather clock. The design is both modern and traditional (Renaissance and Neoclassic) and the overall effect, according to some, is a welcome step away from the impersonal uniformity of the International Style.

The current architectural controversy is between latter-day Modernists and Postmodernists. The former, unrepentant adherents of Modernism and the International Style, remain committed to advanced technology, efficiency, and austerity. The latter emphasize the city context of each building, the needs and values of the users, and the appropriate ornamentation for each structure. Postmodernism does not, however, take a backseat to Late-Modernism in the use of the latest technology.

The first significant competition for Postmodernism took place in Portland, Oregon, where Michael Graves (b. 1934) competed against a Late-Modernist firm. Graves won the competition (twice) and built a structure now known as The Portland (fig. 28.75). This, the first major monument of Postmodernism, has a clear three-part division: a broad green base, a buff-colored shaft, and a brown keystone resting atop brown pilasters that indicate interior elevator cores. Though still a rather heavy high-rise structure, it has been generally accepted by the citizens as an attractive public building that is comfortably at home in the city of Portland.

28.76 Philip Johnson and John Burgee, with Simmons Architects, AT&T Building, New York. 1978. Photo: Peter Mauss/Esto, New York.

SUMMARY

The multiplicity of styles and the sheer number of artists of the present century cannot be adequately covered in a chapter or even in a set of books. The discussion of most major styles and some of the important artists should be considered as a preamble to continuing studies of what today's artists are creating. Twentieth-century art is as accessible in this country as Renaissance art is in Italy and can be viewed in any good-sized American city. Most of the illustrations for this chapter, for example, were drawn from the collections of American museums and galleries from New York to the West Coast. Following is a summary in outline form, providing both a review of the chapter and a framework for personal initiative.

I. Artistic Styles to 1945

A. Painting and Sculpture

1. Prelude
   a. Edouard Manet
   b. Impressionism: Monet et al.
   b. Postimpressionism: Cézanne et al.
2. Fauvism
   a. Henri Matisse
   b. Georges Rouault
3. Expressionism
   a. Wassily Kandinsky
   b. Käthe Kollwitz
   c. George Grosz
4. Cubism
   a. Pablo Picasso (but including Blue and Rose Periods and Neoclassicism)
   b. Stuart Davis
5. Abstractionists
   a. Georgia O'Keeffe
   b. Piet Mondrian (Geometric Abstraction)
   c. Constantin Brancusi
6. Fantasy
   a. Marc Chagall
   b. Paul Klee
   c. Giorgio de Chirico
7. Dada
   a. Marcel Duchamp
   b. Kurt Schwitters
8. Surrealism
   a. Joan Miró
   b. Salvador Dali
   c. Meret Oppenheim
   d. Alberto Giacometti
   e. René Magritte
9. Realism in America
   a. John Sloan (Ash Can school)
   b. Edward Hopper
   c. Horace Pippin
   d. Diego Rivera (Social Realism)
   e. José Clemente Orozco (Social Realism)
   f. David Alfaro Siqueiros (Social Realism)

B. Architecture

1. Walter Gropius (International Style)
2. Le Corbusier (International Style)
3. Frank Lloyd Wright (organic architecture)

II. Artistic Styles Since 1945

A. Painting and Sculpture

1. Abstract Expressionism
   a. Jackson Pollock
   b. Willem de Kooning
   c. Mark Rothko (color field)
   d. Jacob Lawrence
2. Pop Art
   a. Robert Rauschenberg
   b. Roy Lichtenstein
   c. Edward Kienholz
   d. Marisol
3. Color, Geometry, and Optics
   a. Josef Albers (Geometric Abstraction)
   b. Helen Frankenthaler
   c. Louise Nevelson (Geometric Abstraction)
   d. Bridget Riley (Op Art)
4. Fantasy and Expressionism
   a. Jean Dubuffet
   b. Francis Bacon (fantasy/expressionism)
   c. Fritz Scholder (Pop Art/Expressionism)
   d. Alexander Calder (abstract fantasy/kinetic)
   e. Mark di Suvero (abstract fantasy/kinetic)
   f. Henry Moore (abstract figurative)
   g. Gerhard Richter (Neo-expressionism)
   h. Jennifer Bartlett (mixed media)
   i. Robert Colescott
5. Minimal Art
   a. Tony DeLap
   b. David Smith
   c. Sylvia Mangold
6. Varieties of Realism
   a. Audrey Flack (Photorealism)
   b. Otto Duecker (Photorealism cutouts)
7. Environmental Art
   a. Robert Smithson
   b. Christo and Jeanne-Claude
8. African-American Artists
   a. Joshua Johnson
   b Robert Duncanson (Hudson River tradition)
   c. Horace Pippin (naive)
   d. Jacob Lawrence (image/abstraction)
   e. Robert Colescott
9. Photography
   a. Matthew Brady
   b. Alfred Stieglitz
   c. Ansel Adams
   d. W. Eugene Smith
   e. Margaret Bourke-White
   f. Dorothea Lange

B. Architecture

1. Wallace Harrison (International Style)
2. Ludwig Mies van der Rohe (Minimalist International Style)
3. Le Corbusier (sculptural architecture)
4. Frank Lloyd Wright (functional/organic)
5. Eero Saarinen (functional/expressionism)
6. Joern Utzon (Expressionism)
7. Philip Johnson (Postmodernism)
8. Michael Graves (Postmodernism)

WARNING: The outline on page 402 with artists placed neatly in pigeonholes is a generalized approximation and guide and only that. Artists, as stated before, are individuals and their works are unique. Treat the text and outline as points of departure, keeping in mind that artists do change their styles and that, art critics notwithstanding, we are still too close in time to many styles to make valid judgments. Mozart, for example, had no idea he was a Classical composer; he was criticized in his day as an *avant-garde* composer.

Finally, consider art as what anyone elects to present to us as art, as evidence of human creativity. If we do not like an art work, perhaps it communicates something we already know but refuse to acknowledge. Paradoxically, a work of art that tells us something we know and understand can leave us dissatisfied. We do want the artist to challenge our emotions, our intellect, our knowledge. The more we study art the more likely we are to respond to it and to seek out challenges.

CULTURE AND HUMAN VALUES

Philosopher William Barrett wryly remarked that "modern art tells us most, if we have but eyes to see, about the nature of the modern age which we have traversed or which has almost finished us."[3] Certainly some artistic values changed—at least in emphasis—during the century, notably the long-held belief that art existed to communicate beauty and give pleasure. Beauty and pleasure have not been entirely abandoned, but art as the communication of unpleasant and even terrible truths has been prominent in many artistic movements. Consider, for example, Picasso's *Les Demoiselles d'Avignon* (see fig. 28.10) and its portrayal of the darker aspects of human nature. His *Tragedy* (see fig. 28.8) could stand for all the suffering of the working class, but *Guernica* works in even broader terms (see fig. 28.13). The bombs are not only destroying a defenseless Basque village, but tearing at the very fabric of civilization itself.

Kollwitz (see fig. 28.5) depicts common people at the mercy of a militaristic state while George Grosz reveals the horror of Nazi Germany and of all totalitarian states (see fig. 28.6).

On a smaller scale, most of the work of Pop Artists portrays the tacky, tawdry, and banal American materialism (see fig. 28.42). For a statement on the care and treatment of the elderly, Kienholz gives us *The State Hospital* (see fig. 28.43). The Mexican Social Realists have pictured the plight of peasants, not just in Mexico, but in all Third-World countries (see figs. 28.31–33).

Consider also the sickness and terror communicated by the works of Dubuffet (see fig. 28.49) and Bacon (see fig. 28.50), and the horror depicted by Flack (see fig. 28.56). Whether institutionalized insanity or the madness of Nazi extermination camps, this is all part of the twentieth century.

Has modern art portrayed the twentieth century as thoroughly violent and hopeless beyond recall? Not at all. Some of the works of Brancusi (see fig. 28.18), Chagall (see chapter opener on p. 364), Le Corbusier (see fig. 28.35), Christo and Jeanne-Claude (see fig. 28.60), and Bartlett (see fig. 28.74) present a more positive image. In the final analysis, perhaps the best way to look at modern art is to recognize the truth, the beauty, the love, the faith, and the justice that artists have presented to all of us.

STUDY QUESTIONS

1. Divide the art in this chapter into four categories:
   - **a.** What you like
   - **b.** What you dislike
   - **c.** What you feel is or will become important
   - **d.** What you feel is not or will not become important

   Draw conclusions about yourself and about twentieth-century art.
2. In the last section of this chapter, Culture and Human Values, the discussion centered on modern art as exemplifying the twentieth century in its ugliness, violence, and despair. From other sources select works that, in your opinion, communicate something of the dark side of the century, then balance this with six works that present a brighter side. Which examples were harder to find?

3. *Death of the Soul: From Descartes to the Computer* (Garden City, N.Y.: Anchor Press/Doubleday, 1986), p. 56.

CHAPTER 29

Modern Music

MODERNISM

Twentieth-century music has developed in what have been essentially two phases. Phase one has been a continuation and development of instruments, forms, and styles inherited from the rich tradition represented by Bach, Beethoven, and Brahms. Phase two began in the 1950s with the electronic age. Though the past is still fundamental, an exciting new world of music has burst upon the scene, providing a dazzling display of electronic sounds and instruments, synthesizers, and computer composition and performance, and the innovations continue to proliferate.

Igor Stravinsky, 1882–1971

Stravinsky (fig. 29.1) is perhaps the modern composer whose career best summarizes the ceaseless experimentation and multiplicity of styles of this century. He exploited all the "neo" styles from neo-Gothic to Neoromantic, pausing along the way to try his hand at modern jazz. Thoroughly grounded in the music of the past—he admired the music of Bach above all—he was a superb musical craftsman as well as a bold and daring innovator. Always associated with the European *avant-garde,* he influenced Diaghilev, Cocteau, Picasso, and Matisse and was, in turn, influenced by all of them.

The first and perhaps strongest impetus came from Diaghilev, who commissioned several ballet scores for the Ballet Russe de Monte Carlo of which the first was *The Firebird.* Following the success of *The Firebird,* Stravinsky produced the popular *Petrouchka* ballet and then turned his attention to *The Rite of Spring.*

Success was not immediate for this daringly original work. The 1913 premiere in Paris set off a full-scale riot between Stravinsky's *avant-garde* partisans and his far more numerous detractors. The audience was restless even before the music began; the two camps of "liberal artist" and "conservative establishment" had, in effect, already taken sides. The liberals were as determined to relish the music and the ballet as the conservatives were bent on open hostility.

Opposite Memorial Sculpture, Dachau, Germany, detail of fig. 27.2. Photo: Ullstein, Berlin (Rudolf Dietrich).

29.1 Igor Stravinsky. Photo: Viollet, Paris.

Conservatives viewed the work as an assault on cherished values of Western culture; liberals regarded it as a metaphor for the vulgar materialism and decadence of the age.

The high-**register** bassoon solo at the very beginning of the piece provoked sneers and audible laughs from the conservative camp and the evening went downhill from there. By the time the police arrived things had gotten totally out of hand and the premiere performance was history. On a television program aired many years later Stravinsky sat in that Parisian hall in the same seat that he had occupied in 1913. When asked what he did during the riot, Stravinsky replied, "I just stood up, told all of them to go to hell and walked out."

The Rite of Spring, subtitled *Pictures of Pagan Russia,* exploits a very large symphony orchestra and uses many unique instrumental effects to portray the primitive ceremonies. Built around spring fertility rites of ancient Russia, the scenes include the coming of spring, various dances, games of rival tribes, and the selection of the sacrificial

29.2 *The Rite of Spring*, performance in New York. 1983–4. Photo: Winnie Klotz, New York.

virgin. The ballet concludes with the Sacrificial Dance: frenzied convolutions by the Chosen One until she collapses and dies, after which her body is solemnly placed on the sacred mound as an offering to the fertility gods (fig. 29.2).

Listening Example 39

BALLET MUSIC

Stravinsky, *The Rite of Spring*, Last scene, Sacrificial Dance
1913

Time: 4:37
Cassette 2, track 31[1]

Atonality

Atonality was a musical idea whose time had come. Strictly speaking, atonality was a twentieth-century technique that arbitrarily declared the twelve different notes in an octave to be created free and equal. No one tone would predominate; there would be no tonal center, no tonic, no tonality. Curiously symptomatic of the twentieth century, the new system was closely associated with mathematics.

Some modern composers developed what might be called mathematical music. Though atonal composers used no more than simple arithmetic, this was quite sufficient for their manipulations of notes, rhythm, and texture. Following is a brief description of the process of change from tonal to **atonal** music, a development that, in retrospect, was inevitable. Also included are some games that people can play with twelve-tone arithmetic.

The tonal music that had superseded the modes during the seventeenth century was based on the idea that the seven tones of a diatonic scale belonged to a key and that the other five tones were outside the key.[2] Composers relied increasingly on the five tones outside the key to give color and variety to their music. By the end of the nineteenth century musicians such as Wagner and Brahms were regularly using all of the tones as a twelve-tone system of tonality revolving around a central pitch called the tonic, or tonal center.

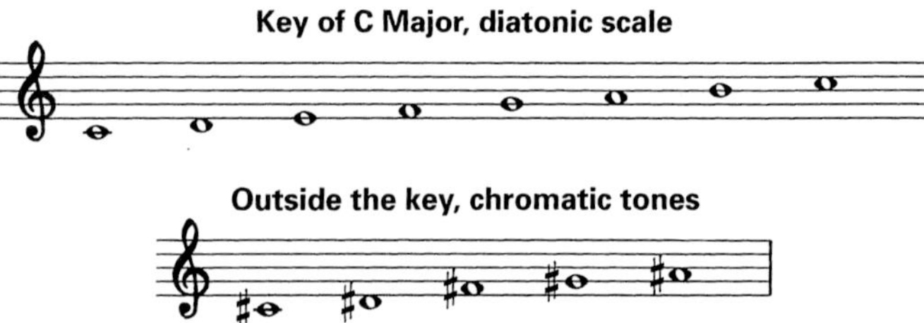

Arnold Schoenberg, 1874–1951

After World War I, Schoenberg (SHURN-burg; fig. 29.3) developed a system in which all twelve tones were considered exactly equal with no tonal center. There would be no dissonance or consonance as such because all the pitches could be used in any combination and without reference to the centrality of any single pitch. This system of twelve equal musical pitches is called atonality, or the dodecaphonic (twelve-tone) system.

Without a tonic pitch to give the music some sort of unity, it was necessary to devise another kind of unifying system. This new device was called a tone row, or basic set. Composers invented melodic sequences of the twelve tones, using each tone only once and refraining from using any sequence of notes that would imply a key (tonality). Since it is neither necessary nor desirable to limit the twelve dif-

1. CD 3, track 6.
2. In the key of C major, for example, the white notes belong to the key and the black notes are outside the key.

ferent tones to one octave, a basic set (tone row) could look like this:

Tone row

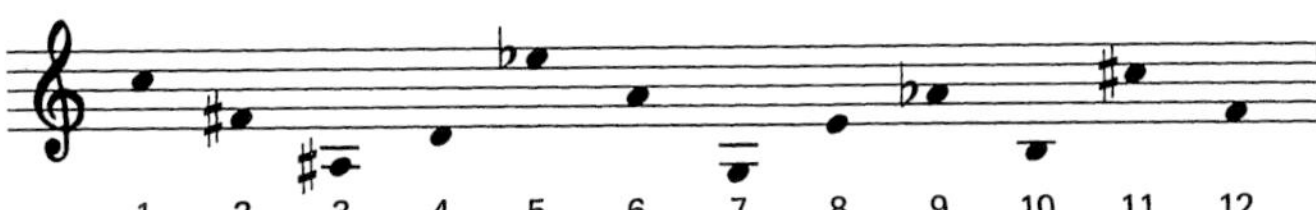

Basically, the twelve-tone system lends itself to polyphonic rather than homophonic writing, although almost anyone can devise and use a mixture of polyphonic and homophonic techniques. Because of the infinite possibilities of manipulating the row, the problem becomes one of selectivity, choosing those possibilities that make musical sense.

Twelve-tone composition is both a musical process and a mathematical or mechanical procedure. The finished composition might be very different and original in sound (and it might not). Whether it is good music or bad music still remains the province of the composer, who makes up one or more tone rows, manipulating, selecting, and modifying until he gets the musical results he wants. Neither a virtue nor a vice, twelve-tone technique is merely a means to an end. It may assist the composer to discover new melodic, rhythmic, and harmonic ideas and different combinations of these ideas, but it will not do a thing for the finished product; that's up to the creator.

29.3 Arnold Schoenberg, *Self-Portrait*. 1910. Arnold Schoenberg Institute, Los Angeles. Photo: Allan Dean Walker, Santa Monica, California.

29.4 Alban Berg. Photo: Range/Bettmann, London.

Alban Berg, 1885–1935

Berg (fig. 29.4) was one of the most musically creative of the twelve-tone composers. His style is also notable for clear, clean orchestral writing. For his Violin Concerto he used a small, versatile orchestra with a delicate contrapuntal texture.

Berg's tone row was not a mechanical contrivance but a point of departure for some lyrical music. He deliberately constructed a row with clear tonal implications, mixing G minor, A minor, and a portion of the whole-tone scale.

Listening Example 40

VIOLIN CONCERTO

Berg, Violin Concerto, 1st movement
1935; excerpt

Time: 2:12
Cassette 2, track 32

Violin Concerto, First movement **Berg (1885–1935)**

Theme A (tone row)

Andante
Solo violin
pp
1 2 3 4 5 6 7 8 9 10 11 12

NEOCLASSICISM, EXPRESSIONISM, AND NEOROMANTICISM

The styles of twentieth-century music are many and varied, as befits a dynamic art in a rapidly changing age. The vogue of neoprimitivism (*The Rite of Spring* and other similar compositions) had its day; Romanticism, whether called Neoromantic or Postromantic, continues to have some influence; nationalism is once again a characteristic of the works of some composers. One trend has been toward Classicism, as in the works of the twelve-tone school and, among many others, the music of the Hungarian composer Béla Bartók.

Béla Bartók, 1881–1945

Bartók was one of the outstanding composers of the century. Born in Hungary, he escaped the Nazi terror and settled in New York City where he made a meager living as a piano teacher and concert pianist. Only after his death was there any significant recognition of the consistently high quality of his music. The shy, soft-spoken Hungarian refugee wrote some powerful music characterized by great intensity and depth of feeling.

His style was an amalgam of Hungarian folk music, great rhythmic ingenuity, and a fundamental allegiance to Classical forms. He delighted in the folk music of southeastern Europe because it helped free him from the tyranny of the major-minor system and provided him with rhythmic conceptions. His preoccupation with formal unity and coherence led him to a unique style of continuous variations, a dynamic and thoroughly modern style of relentless tension and growth.

Bartók's Piano Concerto No. 3 has become a concert favorite. The third movement is in five-part rondo form: ABACA.

Listening Example 41

PIANO CONCERTO

Bartók, Piano Concerto No. 3, 3rd movement
1945

Time: 7:20[3]

Charles Ives, 1874–1954

The startling innovations of Charles Ives (fig. 29.5) anticipated just about every important development of the first half-century: serial and aleatory music,[4] mixed meters and tempos, blocks of sound, free forms, the possibilities of accidental or chance acoustical experiences, assemblages, collages, and even early manifestations of Pop Art. However, despite an impressive array of *avant-garde* techniques, Ives was still a traditional New Englander who wanted to maintain his philosophical relationship with the recent literary past. His important *Concord Sonata* for piano has four movements named after five Transcendentalists: Emerson, Hawthorne, the Alcotts, and Thoreau.

To understand what Ives is getting at in his music one must recognize the music that he quotes—the church hymns, dance music, and military band music. These quotes are comments on life in the small towns and rural areas of America. His nostalgic *Three Places in New England,* for orchestra, is replete with quotations from Americana and illustrates a concern for the American heritage as profound as that of Walt Whitman.

Listening Example 42

ORCHESTRAL MUSIC

Ives, *Three Places in New England*, 2nd movement, "Putnam's Camp, Redding, Connecticut"
1903–11; excerpt

Time: 3:05
Cassette 2, track 33[5]

29.5 *Right* Charles Ives. Photo: Omikron Photo Researchers, New York.

3. CD 3, track 12.
4. Aleatory (AY-lee-uh-tore-e) means "depending on chance, or luck: hence aleatory music allows for random choice in its composition.
5. CD 3, track 7.

> Near Redding Center is a small park preserved as a Revolutionary Memorial; for here General Israel Putnam's soldiers had their winter quarters in 1778–9. Long rows of stone camp fireplaces still remain to stir a child's imagination. The scene is a "4th of July" picnic held under the auspices of the First Church and the Village Cornet Band. The child wanders into the woods and dreams of the old soldiers, of the hardships they endured, their desire to break camp and abandon their cause, and of how they returned when Putnam came over the hills to lead them. The little boy awakes, he hears the children's songs and runs down past the monument to "listen to the band" and join in the games and dances.
>
> Charles Ives

Atonality: Postscript

The twelve-tone system of the Viennese School of Schoenberg, Berg, and Anton Webern (VAY-burn; 1883–1945) went into temporary decline in the 1930s and 1940s. Berg died in 1935 and many composers fled for their lives from totalitarian states that demanded simplistic music in a national style. Schoenberg emigrated to the United States. Webern, however, stayed on in Vienna, quietly creating rigorous twelve-tone music that was to captivate postwar composers. Ironically, Webern survived tyranny and the war only to be accidentally killed by an American soldier shortly after the end of the war.

The music of Webern (fig. 29.6) is difficult to characterize apart from the sound: a kind of Cubist pointillism with meaningful breathing spaces. Webern wrote some of the most beautiful rests—the sounds of silence—in music. He used few notes in a short space of time, manipulating isolated, contrasted tone colors in a space-time continuum. All is rigorous, precise, twelve-tone mathematics, but Webern combined the isolation of single tones with the dissociation of sequential events to make up a total musical interrelationship. The contrasting tone colors in his *Three Songs* are soprano voice, clarinet, and guitar.

Listening Example 43

SONGS WITH INSTRUMENTAL ACCOMPANIMENT

Webern, *Three Songs,* Op. 18, 1. "Schatzerl klein" ("Sweetheart, Dear"); 2 "Erlösung" ("Redemption"; 3. "Ave, Regina" ("Hail, Queen")
1925

Times: 1:01, 1:05, 1:22
Cassette 2, track 34 ("Schatzerl klein")[6]

6. CD 3, track 9 ("Schatzerl klein"); CD 3, track 10 ("Erlösung"); CD 3, track 11 ("Ave, Regina").

29.6 Anton Webern. Photo: Range/Bettmann, London.

Serial Technique and Electronic Music

Partly because of the presence of Schoenberg, twelve-tone composition in the United States flourished during the war. After 1945 it was again prominent in western Europe. Eastern-Bloc countries, however, condemned its dissonant complexities as "bourgeois decadence." Some composers expanded twelve-tone writing from a method into an elaborate system called serial technique or serial composition. Although the old method was never a matter of simply arranging the twelve pitches into a row, the new procedure systematized other elements of music such as rhythm, harmony, tempo, dynamics, **timbre**, and so forth. For example, a serial composition could contain mathematical permutations of twelve pitches, a sixteen-unit rhythmic organization, a sequence of twenty-nine chords, and fourteen timbres (tone colors). When one considers that there are approximately half a billion ways of arranging just the twelve pitches, the mathematical possibilities of serial technique systems approach infinity. Whether these combined mathematical procedures produce music worth listening to is strictly up to the composer.

While the serialists pursue the manifold possibilities of their systems, other composers have concentrated on the exploitation of noise and timbre. Traditionally, tone color has been more ornamental than essential to Western music and the incorporation of "noise" was unthinkable. But musical sounds as such are only a minuscule part of the modern world of acoustical phenomena. We are surrounded and often engulfed by noise ranging from city traffic, electrical appliances, and factory din to the "noises" of nature: sounds of the animal world, thunder, rain, hail, seasounds, windsounds, and so forth.

The Electronic Revolution

Much of the experimentation with timbre and noise has been incorporated into the several varieties of electronic music. In fact, electronic music appears to be a natural stage in the evolution of Western music. In the early, predominantly vocal, era, the singer was his or her own instrument. During the Baroque period there was a general parity between vocal and instrumental music, after which instrumental music clearly dominated vocal music. Musicians began to use what amounted to mechanical extensions for music-making, with varying degrees of dissociation between performer and instrument. Wind players, for example, are in close contact with their instruments, string players have some direct control, but keyboard instruments, especially the pipe organ, are quite mechanical. The evolution from a personal instrument (the voice) to an instrument once-removed (for example, the trumpet) has now progressed to the introduction of instruments twice-removed, that is, wholly the product of technology and entirely removed from direct human contact.

This instrumental evolution seems to reflect the condition of contemporary culture, in which so many activities are carried on untouched by human hands. Computers are talking to computers whereas many people find it ever more difficult to communicate with each other. One might argue that the exclusion of human beings from the production of musical sounds spells the death of art and the triumph of technology. On the other hand, there is evidence that the electronic manipulations of sound can open up a whole new era of musical forms, while simultaneously stimulating new vitality in vocal and instrumental music. If this optimistic view proves to be the correct one, it will bear out the thesis emphasized throughout this book: that the ferment and rapid change in contemporary life are apparently a necessary prelude to a more humane society that may already be taking form. In any event, electronic music, along with all our highly developed technology, is here to stay.

The age of electronic music began in 1951 when Cologne Radio opened the first electronic studio. Other studios were subsequently opened in Paris, Milan, Tokyo, and at Columbia University and the Bell Laboratories in the United States—and many more are now in operation. Milton Babbitt began working in electronic music with the R.C.A. Electronic Sound Synthesizer. His *Ensembles for Synthesizer* uses a wide variety of tone colors and complex rhythms at tempos faster than human performers can hope to reproduce.

Listening Example 44

ELECTRONIC MUSIC

Babbitt, *Ensembles for Synthesizer*
1962–4; excerpt

Time: 1:05
Cassette 2, track 35

Barton McLean (b. 1938) composed the following composition at the Electronic Music Center of the University of Texas in Austin. He used a Fairlight Computer Musical Instrument (CMI). Computer-generated sounds are used exclusively. The title refers to the tunefulness of the composition and its étude-like character.

Listening Example 45

ELECTRONIC MUSIC

McLean, *Etunytude*
1982

Time: 5:28[7]

Chance Music

After the mid-1950s, the nature of *avant-garde* music began to change. Total serialism grew into new materials based on the many ways of transforming textures, colors, and sound densities. From the earlier "controlled chance" compositions, with some options controlled by the composer and others by the performer, the movement shifted to multiple forms of control and chance and to so-called "open forms" in which chance was the major factor. Aleatory music (Lat., *alea*; "dice") is a general term describing various kinds of music in which chance, unpredictability, ambiguity, and even sheer chaos are realized in performance. If strict serial music represents a kind of Newtonian, mathematical determinism, then aleatory music represents its exact opposite: a symbolic rolling of musical dice just to see what will happen.

This conflict between calculation and chance is a musical equivalent to the current situation in science. The precision of the Newtonian world machine has been supplanted by a modern science that is forced to settle for contingent proofs, complementary truths, and/or mathematical

7. CD 4, track 1.

concepts of uncertainty. Quantum theory recognizes the element of chance and its language has been carried over, however ineffectively, into aesthetic theories. Strict mathematical concepts (except for "pure" mathematics), whether in science or art, can lead only to dead ends: scientific "truths" that are jarred by further gains in knowledge and strict mathematics in music that lead to the sterility of non-art. Chance music is therefore a corollary of modern science, and a reflection of both the profundity and absurdity of contemporary life.

John Cage, 1912–92

John Cage (fig. 29.7) was one of the first American composers to experiment with chance music. In the late 1930s he worked with a "prepared piano" that was designed to produce percussive sounds and noises that were unrelated to its traditional sound. From the early 1950s on, he produced works of indeterminate length, of chance operations, of chance media (a concert of a group of radios tuned to different stations), and similar techniques. One of his most widely discussed compositions is a piano solo titled *4'33"* during which the pianist merely sits quietly at the piano for this period of time, after which he or she bows and leaves the stage. Obviously the composition "sounds" different at each performance because of the variance in noise from the audience. This composition would have to be considered the ultimate in Minimal art as well as an achievement somewhat comparable to the "non-wheat" that a farmer produces in exchange for government money. The logical conclusion might be to have the government pay artists for non-poetry, non-novels, and non-paintings. At that point the ultimate absurdity would have been reached and Dada would reign supreme.

And Dada is related to chance music, or vice versa, just as are Cage's ideas of the Chinese chance technique of coin-throwing from the *I Ching* and his fascination with Zen Buddhism. Chance music may include instructions on manuscripts such as: "Start when you like and repeat as often as necessary"; "Hold this note as long as you like and then go on to the next one"; "Wait till the spirit moves you and then make up your own piece." Performers may also be instructed to destroy their instruments, stare at the audience, propel vehicles about the stage, blow sirens, flash lights, and perform other stimulating activities. The result might be called Aimless Theatre rather than theatre of the absurd, although there appear to be common elements.

29.7 John Cage "preparing" a piano. Photo: New York Times.

Functional Music

Not all contemporary music is of the *avant-garde* variety. Paul Hindemith (1895–1963) was a Neoclassicist in his retention of tonal writing and his devotion to the style of J. S. Bach. He also advocated *Gebrauchmusik* (Ger., "useful music," that is, functional) and wrote music for all ages and degrees of musical skills and for numerous special events that called for appropriate music. One of his best works is the symphonic version of *Mathis der Maler,* a moving depiction in sound of the *Isenheim Altarpiece* by Matthias Grünewald (1480–1528). The form of the second movement is ABA'Coda.

Listening Example 46

ORCHESTRAL MUSIC

Hindemith, *Mathis der Maler*, 2nd movement, Grablegung (Entombment)
1934

Time: 4:08[8]

American Musical Theatre

After meeting the playwright Bertolt Brecht, Kurt Weill (1900–50) deliberately rejected the complexities of modern music. In conjunction with Brecht he wrote *The Threepenny Opera* and *The Fall of the House of Mahagony. Threepenny* and *Mahagony* were partly responsible for the blossoming

8. CD 3, track 13.

of musical theatre in America, which began with Rodgers and Hammerstein's *Oklahoma!* and continued through their *South Pacific, Carousel,* and *The Sound of Music.* Bernstein's *West Side Story* and Lerner and Loewe's *My Fair Lady* and *Camelot* are notable contributions to the musical theatre. The finest talent in contemporary music theatre is unquestionably Stephen Sondheim (b. 1930), who writes both words and music. His musicals include *West Side Story* (lyrics), *A Funny Thing Happened on the Way to the Forum, A Little Night Music, Pacific Overtures, Sweeney Todd, Passion*, and, based on Seurat's painting, *Sunday in the Park with George.*

George Gershwin (1898–1937) may be one of America's best composers. Criticized by musical snobs as "popular" and thus, for some strange reason, beyond the pale, his music has endured and much of it has become a part of the standard repertory. *Rhapsody in Blue, An American in Paris,* and the Concerto in F have all become known throughout the world as truly representative of American music. *Of Thee I Sing* is now recognized as musical theatre at its satirical best and *Porgy and Bess* is perhaps America's finest opera.

Minimalism

Philip Glass, b. 1937

Some critics claim that Glass is, after Gershwin, America's best composer. Certainly one of the most provocative of contemporary composers, Glass has developed his own unique style of Minimalism. He combines Hindu rhythmic cycles and other devices of non-Western music with some Rock plus Western-style intervals and harmonies that have been reduced to the barest essentials. The result—sometimes called "solid state music"—is not so austere as it sounds, for Glass is not afraid to use elements from the classical tradition. On the other hand, he is just as likely to use the synthesis of Jazz and Rock styles called "New Age" Fusion.

One of his first major successes was *Einstein on the Beach* (1976), a 4½-hour multi-media production that has been billed as an opera, but which is actually a series of events. His first true opera was *Satyagrapha* (1980), a complex work based on the *Bhagavad Gita,* sung entirely in Sanskrit. This was followed by *Akhenaton* (1984), an opera about the pharaoh who introduced monotheism to ancient Egypt.

JAZZ IN AMERICA

Jazz is a uniquely different style of music, the result of a fusion—collision might be a better word—of certain elements of African and American musical cultures. Aside from Native American music, music in the United States and the rest of the New World was of European origin and influenced by European styles. Given the European heritage and the presence of African slaves and freedmen throughout the United States, the islands of the Caribbean, and Central and South America, the singular and significant fact remains that jazz originated solely in the United States. By the turn of the century, African-American spirituals, ragtime, blues, and jazz were established types or styles of music, none of which existed anywhere else in the Western Hemisphere.

The French, Spanish, Portuguese, Dutch, and even English cultures of the West Indies and Central and South America apparently provided a climate in which African arts, crafts, customs, and religious beliefs could coexist with their European counterparts. For whatever reasons, and there appear to be many, the dominant white culture of the American South was not as tolerant of African customs as were the transplanted European cultures south of the United States. There existed a strong conflict between white and black Americans in almost every area of life: religion, folklore, music, art, dance, and social and political customs.

In summary, jazz is a musical style that evolved out of three centuries of cultural and racial conflict, a clash between an inflexible dominant culture and a powerful and persistent subculture with its own age-old beliefs and customs. Jazz continues to evolve, of course, including even a change in name. A number of jazz musicians now refer to their music as African-American classical music.

The Elements of Jazz

The elements of jazz are those of any music: melody, harmony, rhythm, and tone color. The African-American mixture makes the difference. The development of any style of music normally follows an evolutionary process within a single culture. Outside influences, when they appear, tend to be transformed and absorbed into the stylistic development. The Viennese waltz, for example, is a modified, speeded-up version of an old Austrian folk dance called a *Ländler.* The *Ländler* was Austrian; the changes were compatible with Austrian concepts of melody, harmony, rhythm, and tone color. The finished product was in all respects the result of Austrian culture and the musical genius of one Johann Strauss, Jr. It would be ludicrous to remove a Strauss melody and insert a Russian boat song, an Irish jig, or a Hopi rain dance. Scale, harmony, rhythm, and tone color would be all wrong because an incompatible melody was introduced into a foreign context.

Jazz sounds the way it does because it *is* a compound of several different and even opposing concepts of melody, rhythm, and tone color. In very general terms, jazz is a musical style consisting of African-European melody, European harmony, African rhythm, and African-European tone color. A built-in conflict of musical styles lies at the root of jazz and probably accounts, at least in part, for the feelings of dislocation and sometimes anguish and even pain on the part of performers and listeners.

The fundamental conflict in the materials of jazz occurs in scale and tuning. Equal temperament, with its twelve equal semitones in each octave, is the tuning standard for Western music. On the other hand, African melody was and is based on the tones present in the overtone series. The distances between pitches range from whole steps and half steps, similar to those in the tempered scale, to other intervals between half steps, including quarter-tones. African harmony is quite rudimentary; melody, rhythm, and tone color are far more important.

African melodies, with their different-sized intervals, were, when transported to America, sung in a culture that did not use such a variety of intervals, that built musical instruments in equal temperament. In that culture African songs were often characterized as out of tune, primitive, or a poor imitation of "proper" singing.

Scale

The combining of African scales with the European diatonic scale produced a hybrid called the blues scale.[9] In terms of the equal-tempered piano the blues scale can be described as a diatonic scale plus three blue notes: flatted 3rd, 5th, and 7th.

Blues scale

Rhythm

Rhythm is the main ingredient in African music: highly developed, intricate, complex, as sophisticated in its own way as the harmonic system of Western culture. The African rhythms that have crossed over into jazz and into much of our modern music are but a relatively simple portion of a whole world of elaborate percussion music.

There are two interrelated fundamental characteristics of African rhythm: beat and syncopation. Emerging from the simultaneous rhythm patterns is a subjective beat, a rhythmic pulsation that is not necessarily played by any one drummer but which results from the combination of the whole. The beat is implicit. This beat (whether explicit or implicit) is so much a part of jazz that it can be called its heartbeat or pulse. Jazz can thus be defined as the "beauty of the beat."

Syncopation is a displacement or shifting of accents so that they disagree with natural metrical accents. It has the effect of tugging at the beat, a dynamic process that emphasizes the existence of the basic pulse by setting up a conflict with that pulse. The pull of syncopation against the ongoing beat gives a swing to the music, a buoyant resilience that is a fundamental characteristic of jazz.

9. The blues scale is not African in itself although its origins necessarily lie in African music. Rather it is an African-American scale, and it is the elemental component out of which jazz is made.

Tone Color

The story is told of a World War II air base in Africa that stockpiled aviation gasoline in steel drums. The drums were unloaded and stacked by native laborers, one of whom accidentally dropped a drum and noticed a booming, reverberant tone as it hit the ground. His neighbor immediately dropped his drum to discover its tone color. Within a very few minutes, in their delight at discovering new tone colors, the entire crew was enthusiastically engaged in dropping, hitting, and scraping gasoline drums.

Beating on logs, sticks, bones, metal, or drums, scratching gourds, shaking rattles—all are activities designed to exploit tone colors within a rhythmic framework. An African drummer can obtain several dozen different timbres by using his thumbs, fingers, flat of the hand, or fist on various areas of a drumhead. All that is necessary for a percussion instrument is a distinctive sound and virtually no limit to the number and variety of possible tone colors.

Distinctive tone color in jazz is not confined to the drums. It extends to the colors obtained by using mutes, hats, plungers, handkerchiefs, or anything else that will give variety to the timbre of instruments such as trumpet and trombone. Instrumentalists also use growls, slurs, and slides to broaden their expressive range and impart a personal quality to their music. The colors may be cool or hot or anything in between; in any event, jazz musicians are concerned with their sound, the distinctive coloration of their performance.

Harmony

Harmony, one of the most highly developed elements of Western culture, is of only slight importance in African music. Consequently, the fusion of African and American music was essentially a combining of African melody, rhythm, and tone color with an established harmonic system. The result, as stated before, was a synthesis of conflicting stylistic elements and the beginning of a new style of music called jazz.

Pre-Jazz Styles (African-American Folk Music)

Some of the many types of folk music date back to the arrival of the first indentured workers and slaves in the seventeenth century; other music developed in response to—or despite—the American environment. The African vocal tradition survived as it adjusted to the strange servile conditions and the new religion of Christianity. The instrumental tradition, especially drums, was rigorously suppressed by the slaveholders, who suspected, and rightly so, that African drums could communicate such terrifying possibilities as slave rebellions. The planters were thus inadvertently successful in their drive to break up tribal units and destroy their traditions. They did not know that tribal histories were entirely oral and perpetuated by the drummers and the language of the drum script.[10] The **banjo** (African, *banjar*) did manage to survive, but European instruments were gradually taken up by African-American musicians. Out of this mélange of African and American cultures emerged a remarkably rich tradition of folk music, much of which is still performed today.

Secular Music

The work song is closely related to an African tradition of rhythmic songs that have the effect of making hard work a bit easier. They are usually unaccompanied, but sometimes have a guitar or banjo accompaniment. They are associated with manual labor that has a rhythmic regularity: chopping wood, rowing a boat, driving railroad spikes.

Example: "Juliana Johnson"[11]

Hollers (field hollers) are sung during non-rhythmic fieldwork such as picking cotton or hoeing corn. Unaccompanied and with an irregular beat, they frequently use narration mixed with singsong chants.

Example: "Old Hannah"

The street cry is sung by street-sellers of fruit, vegetables, fish, and so forth. Unaccompanied, with constant repetition of the name of the product, the seller maintains interest with continuous changes in pitch and tone quality.

Examples: "Crab Man" and "Strawberry Woman" from Porgy and Bess *(George Gershwin)*

Narrative songs with numerous verses, **ballads** were originally African heroic songs of kings, warriors, and hunters. American versions are about folk heroes such as John Henry, the steel-driving man.

Example: "John Henry"

Blues

The blues are the most important single influence in the development of jazz. There are two basic kinds of blues: folk blues (rural blues) and urban blues (true jazz blues). They reflect African customs and musical traditions, but they are native to America. The blues are personal, subjective, introspective, a way of protesting misfortune and identifying trouble. Singing the blues is a survival technique for counteracting bad times, loneliness, and despair.

Blues lyrics usually consist of three lines of poetry. The first line is repeated (possibly with a slight variation) followed by a third line that completes the thought. Because blues are usually improvised, the repeating of the second line gives the singer more time to make up the last line. There may be only one verse or there may be many verses in a narrative blues. Favorite subjects are love, traveling, and trouble, but almost anything makes a fit subject, as shown by the following blues poems.

Love:
Love is like a faucet, you can turn it off or on, [twice]
But when you think you've got it, it's done turned off and gone.

Traveling:
I went to the deepot, an' looked upon de boa'd. [twice]
It say: dere's good times here, dey's better down de road.

Proverbs:
My momma tole me, my daddy tole me too: [twice]
Everybody grin in yo' face, ain't no friend to you.

Images:
Ef blues was whiskey, I'd stay drunk all de time. [twice]
Blues ain't nothin' but a po'man's heart disease.

Comedy:
Want to lay my head on de railroad line, [twice]
Let the train come along and pacify my mind.

Tragedy:
[one line images]
Got the blues but too damn mean to cry.
Standin' here lookin' one thousand miles away.
I hate to see the evenin' sun go down.
Been down so long, Lawd, down don't worry me.

Sacred Music

Most spirituals are derived from Protestant hymns, but with significant changes in text, melody, and rhythm (usually syncopated). Frequently improvised, especially during church services and prayer meetings, they use texts that are variations on existing hymns or paraphrases of biblical verses and stories. They are notable for vividness of imagery, the relating of biblical stories with direct and telling simplicity, and a strong concern for the sounds and rhythms of words.

Example: "Swing Low, Sweet Chariot"

The ring shout is similar to African circle dances in form and character. Usually performed outdoors after a church service, the worshipers form a ring while singing a spiritual to start the ring slowly revolving. Accompanied by hand claps and foot stomping, the spiritual is sung over and over until the accumulative effect is hypnotic.

Example: "Come and Go with Me"

A jubilee is a particular kind of spiritual that sings

10. Some African languages, especially the varieties of Bantu, used different pitch-levels of vowel sounds for different word-meanings. Tribal historians were highly select drummers who were trained to play the talking drum by beating out the word rhythms while at the same time varying the pitch by means of a stretched membrane. The drum script was virtually a vocal sound that could be transmitted over considerable distances with the aid of relay drummers.

11. Titles and/or performers are sometimes given rather than specific recordings, which may or may not be available given the vagaries of the recording industry.

triumphantly of the Year of Jubilee, as "When the Saints Go Marching In."

Gospel songs differ from hymns and spirituals mostly in the texts, which are more personal and subjective. "I," "me," "my" are the key words in songs that tend to reduce religious experience to a personal viewpoint.

Example: "My God Is Real"

The song-sermon is delivered from the pulpit, usually beginning with a scriptural quotation. The vocal delivery of the minister moves gradually from the spoken word to a kind of intoned chant, culminating in ringing declamation and vocalized phrases on higher and higher pitches. The African custom of responding verbally to important personages, such as tribal chieftains, is reflected in the congregational response to the song-sermon. There are shouts of "amen," "yes sir," "hallelujah," and impromptu wordless crooning.

Example: "Dry Bones"

Voodoo (*vodun*) is the name given to the combination of African and Catholic religious rites and beliefs that was developed in Haiti by the Dahomeans of West Africa and that still exists in the West Indies and in portions of the United States, particularly Louisiana. Voodoo rites took place in Congo Square in New Orleans before being driven underground. Voodoo helped perpetuate African customs and music and made significant contributions to African-American folk music and to the development of jazz.

Example: "Drums of Haiti"

Entertainment

Dating from about the middle of the nineteenth century, minstrel shows were sentimentalized "scenes of plantation life" performed by an all-male, all-white cast. Characteristic African-American elements were present in some of the group dances, the use of rhythmic "bones," tambourine, and banjo, the soft-shoe dances and the cakewalk finale. Stephen Collins Foster's songs (many of them based on African-American folk music) were a popular staple. Minstrelsy dealt with stereotypes that no longer exist, if they ever did, but it can be credited with disseminating a portion of African-American musical culture throughout the United States and Europe and preparing the way for the more authentic music of a later period.

Ragtime

Ragtime is a written-down style of music originally composed for the piano and featuring syncopated rhythmic patterns over a regular left-hand accompaniment in **duple meter**. The essentials of ragtime probably were in existence prior to the Civil War, although Scott Joplin (fig. 29.8) is formally credited as the first to write ragtime in the mid-1890s. Slaves in their quarters liked to imitate, even parody, the fancy balls in the plantation house by staging a cakewalking contest. The highest-stepping couple "took the cake." The basic cakewalk patterns consisted of duple meter plus two kinds of melodic syncopations:

Kinds of melodic syncopation

There is a considerable body of ragtime piano literature, but, since most of it is too difficult for the average pianist to play, there is also much watered-down semi-ragtime popular music from the period 1900–20. Almost any piece of music can be "ragged" by changing the meter to duple, if necessary, and converting the rhythms into ragtime patterns. In developed ragtime these syncopations would include the two patterns illustrated above plus the more difficult pattern of four-note groups in which every third note is accented:

Further ragtime pattern of syncopation

Examples: "The Entertainer" and "Maple Leaf Rag" by Scott Joplin

29.8 Scott Joplin. Cover of *The Entertainer*.

THE STYLES OF JAZZ

New Orleans Style

Jazz began at one or more places in the American South sometime between the end of the Civil War and the last decade of the nineteenth century. New Orleans may or may not be the birthplace of jazz, but it certainly figured prominently in the promulgation of the new music. Jazz, New Orleans style, began in the 1890s as brass-band performances of spirituals and gospel songs, and ragtime versions of standard band marches. This is the so-called traditional jazz that, in a more discreet version played by white musicians, became known as Dixieland jazz. The original New Orleans style, however, still exists and is normally referred to as such.

Brass bands secured many of their instruments from pawn shops, where they had been deposited after the Civil War by returning military bandsmen. The instrumentation was typical of marching bands: trumpets, trombones, tuba, snare drum, bass drum, and usually one clarinet. The bands played and paraded for all special functions but especially for funeral processions. According to a long-standing tradition they played spirituals and dirges on the way to the cemetery and some of the same music in a jazz idiom on the way back.

New Orleans jazz is ensemble jazz; everyone plays all the time. In general, the first trumpet has the melody, the clarinet a moving **obbligato** above the trumpet, and the trombone a contrapuntal bass below the lead trumpet. The material is normally gospel songs, spirituals, and marches, and the meter invariably duple. ("In the churches they sang the spirituals. In the bright New Orleans sun, marching down the street, they played them.") Needless to say, all the music was played by ear and everyone was free to improvise a suitable part for himself. ("You play your part and I play mine. You don't tell me what you want and I don't tell you. We will all variate on the theme.") The texture was polyphonic, a crude but dynamic grouping of musical voices improvising simultaneously on the melodic and harmonic framework of preexisting music. One word that best describes New Orleans jazz is "exuberant."

In the following example New Orleans jazz has moved indoors and added vocal and instrumental solos—plus a piano (fig. 29.9).

29.9 Louis Armstrong's Hot Five. Photo: Range/Bettmann, London.

Listening Example 47

NEW ORLEANS JAZZ

Hardin-Armstrong, *Hotter than That*
1927

Time: 3:02
Cassette 2, track 36[12]

Urban Blues

Urban blues are the heart of the true jazz idiom. The accompaniment has changed from the folk (or country) blues guitar to piano or jazz band. The subject matter revolves around the problems of urban (ghetto) life. The feeling is still bittersweet, and the form has crystallized into the classic twelve-bar blues accompanying the rhymed couplet in iambic pentameter. The blues may be sung or played by any instrument. Recorded in 1925, the following urban blues stars Bessie Smith as the blues singer with Louis Armstrong playing cornet.

Listening Example 48

BLUES

Handy, *St. Louis Blues*
1914

Time: 3:08[13]

12. CD 4, track 3.
13. CD 4, track 2.

Chicago Style

With the closing of Storyville, the legal red-light district of New Orleans (1897–1917), jazz musicians began moving north in increasing numbers. Prohibition and the rise of bootlegging in the Roaring Twenties helped make Chicago the home for unemployed musicians playing the new and exciting sounds of jazz. Briefly stated, Chicago jazz is New Orleans jazz moved indoors. The ensemble used on the march in the New Orleans sun now played in crowded speakeasies for such dances as the Fox Trot, Shimmy, Black Bottom, and Charleston.

Some of the simultaneous improvising remains, but bands are playing many popular songs in a more homophonic, though still lively and swinging, style. The meter is mostly duple, but the instrumentation has changed. The piano, a newcomer to jazz, furnishes the rhythmic harmonic background; drums, guitar or banjo, tuba, or string bass provide the rhythm. Varying combinations of trumpet, clarinet, trombone, and saxophone (another newcomer) play the melody and harmony. March tempos have been superseded by a range of tempos suitable for the various dances. The one word for Chicago style would be "frenetic."

Examples: Recordings made in the 1920s (and later): Jelly Roll Morton; Bix Beiderbecke

Swing

The Swing era began during the Depression years, the so-called Dancing Thirties. After the repeal of Prohibition in 1933 the speakeasies closed down, leaving many jazz musicians again out of work. The musical migration turned in the direction of New York City, with its radio stations, large ballrooms, and crowds of young dancers seeking cheap entertainment. (The usual cost of a dancing date was 25¢–30¢ admission plus two soft drinks.)

The six- or eight-piece bands of the Chicago era were large enough for the tiny speakeasies (with minuscule dance floors) but too small for the spacious ballrooms. More musicians had to be added and stylistic changes were made to accommodate them. The individuality of the New Orleans and Chicago styles was subordinated to ensemble playing mixed with improvised solo performances; Big Band jazz was born. Divided into three units of brass (two trumpets, two trombones), four saxophones, and a solid rhythm base (piano, drums, guitar, string bass), the swing band launched what is now recognized as the classic era of jazz. Swing was by far the dominant style of the Depression years through to the end of World War II.

Listening Example 49

BIG BAND SWING

Duke Ellington, *Old King Dooji*
1938

Time: 2:29[14]

Listening Example 50

JAZZ QUARTET

Benny Goodman, *Dizzy Spells*
1938

Time: 5:47[15]

After the Bop Revolution that followed World War II (see below) Big Band jazz surfaced again as Progressive jazz, a modern version of the basic swing style. By the 1970s the term was Mainstream jazz because the Big Band sound was once again in the mainstream of American jazz.

Examples: Recordings of the 1930s and 1940s (Swing) and 1970s, 1980s, and 1990s (Mainstream): Count Basie; Duke Ellington (fig. 29.10); *Benny Goodman* (fig. 29.11); *Glenn Miller; Woody Herman; Stan Kenton; Don Ellis*

29.10 *Right* Duke Ellington. Photo: Redferns, London (David Redfern).

14. CD 4, track 4.
15. CD 4, track 5.

29.11 Benny Goodman and His Orchestra. Photo: Range/Bettmann, London.

New Orleans Revival

The revival of Swing was preceded by an even more basic revival, that of traditional New Orleans jazz. Some white San Francisco musicians took the first steps, in 1939, to save what was left of the original jazz style. First-generation jazz musicians were brought out of retirement and old records collected and studied. Some revivalists used the ragtime piano, banjo, tuba, clarinet, trumpet, trombone, and drums in the authentic two-beat New Orleans style. Others mixed New Orleans with the four-beat characteristics of Swing to create Dixieland. Typical Dixieland jazz uses the "front line" of obbligato clarinet, lead trumpet, and fluid trombone (tailgate trombone) backed by drums, bass, and piano.

Listening Example 51
NEW ORLEANS REVIVAL

Steele, *High Society*
1955

Time: 3:03
Cassette 2, track 37[16]

Other Examples: Preservation Hall Jazz Band; Pete Fountain; Al Hirt

The Bop Revolution

During the long musicians' recording and broadcast strike midway through World War II, an entirely new style of jazz was developing. On the resumption of recording and broadcasting the unsuspecting public heard, in the style known as Bop (or Rebop or Bebop), the startling sounds of the beginning of modern jazz. The increasingly regimented swing style had stifled most creative activity. Bop took musical control away from the arranger and returned it to the performing musician. The domination of Swing was not the only issue, for the emergence of Bop was much more of a revolution than most people realized at the time. The radical change in jazz was, it might be said, the first wave of the Civil Rights movement that began with full force in the mid-1950s. Led by African-American jazz musicians, the Bop movement was opposed to all aspects of the white establishment, especially the white swing bands that had a near-monopoly of the commercial market of records, radio, and television.

Bop groups were small combos of six or seven instruments who played jazz for listening rather than for dancing. With fast, often frenetic, tempos, highly elaborated

16. CD 4, track 6.

melodic and rhythmic patterns, and modern dissonant harmonies, the Bop combo actually played chamber-music jazz. No longer confined to maintaining the beat, the piano and guitar were played much more melodically. The beat was lighter because it was laid down by the string bass rather than the Swing-style percussion of guitar, piano, and drums. The drummer was freed from the basic beat to become a more versatile percussionist.

Bop combos consistently improvised but they usually avoided the conventional pattern of paraphrasing an existing melody while "playing the changes" (improvising on the harmonies). They preferred to create new melodic lines out of existing harmonies. In this way, for example, Dizzy Gillespie (fig. 29.12) and Charlie Parker converted a popular romantic ballad named "Whispering" into an uptempo Bop version called "Groovin' High."

Combining a new melody with the existing harmonies of a popular song had a critical extra-musical function: it enabled musicians to avoid what many truly detested—audience requests for specific titles. This was the primary reason for performing "Whispering" as "Groovin' High." Technically, the request of the bewildered customer/listener was granted, but only on terms that the performer could accept. The problem was not a basic antagonism between musicians and the public but different perceptions of jazz itself.

29.12 Dizzy Gillespie. Photo: Institute of Jazz Studies Collection, Rutgers University.

Modern Jazz

Shortly after Bop arrived on the scene (during the late 1940s) jazz passed almost imperceptibly from a form of entertainment (dancing and listening) to an art form in its own right. Assimilated Bop techniques made important contributions but the significant factor was the change in attitude: music-making that had no other purpose or function than aesthetic communication between performers and their listening audience. The performance of "requests" would henceforth have about as much validity as asking the Philadelphia Orchestra to play "When the Saints Go Marching In."

The leaders of modern jazz included Dizzy Gillespie, Charlie Parker, Bud Powell, Miles Davis, and the big bands of Count Basie, Duke Ellington, Woody Herman, and Stan Kenton. It was Kenton who used the term "progressive jazz" to describe what he and some others saw as consistent advances in contemporary jazz. It is only in retrospect that we can see "progress" in jazz as the shift from mere entertainment for a dancing public to the only totally new art form the United States has yet produced.

Listening Example 52
MODERN JAZZ

Kooper, *House in the Country*
1969

Time: 2:46[17]

Third-Stream Jazz

Flowing between the parallel streams of classical music and jazz, Third-Stream jazz borrows techniques from both while attempting to remain in the jazz idiom. There had been earlier confrontations with classical music in the eras of ragtime ("ragging the classics") and swing ("swinging the classics"). Later jazz styles adopted instrumental, melodic, and harmonic techniques and musical forms from contemporary concert music. Third-Stream went a step further with combinations of jazz and string quartets, and jazz combos combined with symphony orchestras. In particular, the Dave Brubeck Quartet and the Modern Jazz Quartet have made interesting Third-Stream recordings.

29.13 Chick Corea in a jazz parade at the Royal Festival Hall, London. 21 July 1987. Photo: Dat's Jazz Picture Library, Harrow, U.K. (Derick A. Thomas).

The Listening Example is a modern cool version of a Gershwin song from *Girl Crazy* (1930), which was revived in 1993 as *Crazy for You*.

Listening Example 53
COOL JAZZ

Gershwin, *But Not for Me*
1965

Time: 3:46[18]

Liturgical Jazz

Liturgical jazz has met with considerably more success. Jazz has been a long-accepted practice in many African-American revivals and tent-meetings, but not until the 1960s did it begin to appear in the church services of major Protestant denominations. The prime moving force was the intent to update the liturgy by using more contemporary modes of thought and expression. (The basic thrust was, of course, the youth revolt against the Establishment and the war in Vietnam.) Though Liturgical jazz was generally accepted by liberal mainline churches there were those who opposed admitting a new art form to church. Some opponents confused jazz with popular music; others reasoned that music formerly associated with New Orleans bordellos, Chicago speakeasies, dance halls, and night clubs was obviously not good enough for church. The fact is, however, that much of the music presently used in churches has similar humble origins. Moreover, there is no such thing as "sacred music"; there is only music used with sacred services. Duke Ellington's recordings of sacred concerts performed in church are interesting, valid modes of jazz used for religious purposes.

Crossover and Fusion

Current jazz styles range from traditional jazz in the New Orleans manner to ragtime, Dixieland, Chicago, Bop, and Mainstream. Added to this mélange are the eclectic styles called *Crossover* and *Fusion*. Crossover combines some jazz and rock with popular songs in a style that downplays the drive of both jazz and rock. Fusion is much closer to the jazz tradition; it is defined by *Downbeat* magazine as "an agreement between jazz, rock, and funk (soul)." Fusion generally uses mixtures of electronic instruments and acoustic instruments.

Examples: Recent recordings by Miles Davis and Chick Corea (fig. 29.13)

17. CD 4, track 8.
18. CD 4, track 7.

But the latest and more authentic jazz style, called acoustic jazz or straight-ahead jazz, is successfully promoted by exceptionally talented musicians such as Wynton Marsalis (b. 1961). Trumpeter Marsalis refers to himself as a neo-traditionalist who has studied such jazz immortals as Louis Armstrong, Duke Ellington, and Charlie Parker as he forges ahead in what has become a renaissance of African-American jazz. Marsalis, like many of his colleagues, is accomplished in both classical music and jazz, having won Grammies in both types of music, from Bach to the blues. The movement is little concerned with electronic instruments—hence the occasional label of acoustic jazz. The Listening Example is a modern cool jazz original in quintuple meter (five beats per bar) by alto saxophonist Paul Desmond.

Listening Example 54

COOL JAZZ

Paul Desmond, *Take Five*

Time: 2:05
Cassette 2, track 38

SUMMARY

This chapter has dealt with only a few highlights selected from the bewildering complexities of modern music. Of course, twentieth-century music, like the music of any age, effectively mirrors the prevailing patterns of the age. The impending catastrophe of World War I was forecast in the primitive barbarity of Stravinsky's *The Rite of Spring*. Reflecting the rational, intellectual aspects of the Age of Analysis were the serial techniques of Alban Berg as he exploited the tone row to compose his Violin Concerto. Charles Ives anticipated many of the innovations of *avant-garde* twelve-tone composers such as Schoenberg, Berg, and Webern and, after World War II, the *avant-garde* developed the twelve-tone method into complete serial systems.

Electronic music in various forms exerted an ever-growing influence as reflected in much or all the work of McLean, Boulez, Stockhausen, and Cage. Aleatory music, with or without electronic assistance, is not dominating the musical scene but it is certainly making waves.

The essence of much of this century's music can be summarized in Yeats' phrase, "Things fall apart: the centre cannot hold." The old musical centers of clear-cut keys, major-minor tonality, and traditional musical instruments are no longer apropos. Composers have been trying to find new centers, new ways of relating to a rapidly changing world.

The search for new musical values has used mathematics (twelve-tone and serial techniques), technology (electronic media), the sounds of people, and the sounds of nature. Traditional music has been bent, borrowed, violated, and ignored. The search goes on and not until well into the the next century will people be able to see clearly where the search led and what twentieth-century music was all about.

The many faces of contemporary jazz and the infinite variety of the jazz-rock-pop scene seem to span the spectrum of twentieth-century life and thought.

New Orleans	basically the street band sounds of original jazz
Dixieland	a combination of New Orleans jazz and Swing for an exuberant, happy sound
Cool	romantic impressionism, always keeping its cool
Mainstream	a bit of Swing plus a bit more of Progressive and steering down the middle of the road
Hard Bop	uncompromising, blowing hard and hot
Soul	return to the roots, to unabashed emotion, to wholehearted involvement
Liturgical jazz	revitalization of the music of established churches
Crossover	some jazz with a little rock and much pop
Fusion	synthesis of jazz, rock, and funk
Straight-ahead jazz	a revival of traditional jazz combined with great technical virtuosity.

CULTURE AND HUMAN VALUES

It is generally agreed that music is the closest thing to an international language the world has. Some Western classical music has been performed around the world but classical music has not had nearly the international impact that jazz has had. As early as the 1920s, jazz was more popular in France than in its country of origin. After World War II, jazz became a worldwide phenomenon and continues to be widely popular around the globe.

The U.S. Department of State has consistently sent jazz groups as goodwill ambassadors to foreign countries. Considering the lingering after-effects of Western imperialism, and of international tensions in general, it appears that American jazz is a valuable American export and one that better exemplifies American values than, for example, the exportation of violent TV programs. Whether as a very personal and direct form of communication or as a universally admired art form, jazz sounds a positive note in a world that needs all the help it can get.

CHAPTER 30

Twentieth-Century Literature

The analogy of the broken center certainly applies to contemporary literature. Amid the wreckage of old values today's authors search for fresh meanings, new forms, and a revitalized sense of personal identity and community.

Almost any thesis about contemporary literature can be proposed and supported with a large body of writing, for ceaseless experimentation has produced many types, moods, and themes. Following are some generalizations about twentieth-century literature leading to comments on specific literary works. The reader is free to agree or disagree with any or all comments.

CONVENTIONS AND REVOLTS

Many writers of our century have violated most or all of the restrictions on form and idea that were characteristic of most nineteenth-century writing. There are at least two "literatures of the twentieth century," one before, the other after World War II. The two types are related because they are in revolt against both the literary tradition of the nineteenth century and the rigidity of Victorian mores. The literatures differ because early twentieth-century writers recognized a common core against which they might voice their protest; the writers since World War II are cast adrift, with little unifying force and few webs of connection, and with the urge, almost the necessity, to create anew the meanings and values of life.

The "conventional" revolt early in the century was predictable, as described by John Livingston Lowes: "The ceaseless swing of the artistic pendulum is from the convention of a former age to the revolt of a new day, which in its turn becomes a convention from which still newer artists will in their turn revolt."[1]

The poetic conventions of the nineteenth century generally favored the tight-knit structure of recognizable stanza form: blank verse or couplet, tercet or quatrain, or other nameable unit. There were exceptions of course, but in general a poem *looked* like a poem, because that was the way poems looked! The order and pattern and design appealed to an audience that liked design, approved of pattern, and believed in order.

But, in about 1914, the Imagist poets challenged the convention with *vers libre* (Fr., "free verse")—lines unrhymed and unmetrical. Not only is the form of T. S. Eliot's poem, "The Love Song of J. Alfred Prufrock" (see pp. 333–5), different from that of the past, but the meaning of the poem represents a revolt against the predominant nineteenth-century optimism (or even the pessimism). Yet, with all the innovations of form and meaning, Eliot works within a recognizable tradition. The poem is not only to be felt and experienced, it must be thought out as an intellectual poem within the rational tradition of European culture. Eliot expects his readers to share a common background of knowledge about Hesiod, Dante, and Shakespeare.

At about the same time, Aldous Huxley was writing *Brave New World,* a novel that portrayed a society pursuing its values until it had destroyed nearly everything of worth. The novel attacked entrenched and accepted values, but it followed the patterned, chronologically structured form of the plotted novel, and made certain assumptions about the common center of meanings that were held by both the author and the reader. Huxley assumed, for instance, a knowledge of Shakespeare, and he presumed that the reader shared a value system that accepted Shakespeare as good. The great body of literature since World War II cannot make these assumptions. What has happened?

Because World War II involved the obvious choice between freedom or submission to inhuman systems ruled by power-mad dictators, the emotions and rituals of patriotism seemed appropriate, even noble. Yet, when the conflict ended, the world went back to its old ways, with the victors seeming to take more of a beating than the vanquished. An introspective United States focused on its shortcomings and the hollowness of much of its way of life. The old materialistic values, as opposed to standards involving the quality of life itself, seemed no longer appropriate. The wars in Korea, Vietnam, even in the Persian Gulf, challenged much of the enthusiasm for the "rightness" of our value system.

Opposite Dorothea Lange, *Migrant Mother, Nipomo, California*, detail of fig. 28.70. 1936. Gelatin-silver print, full print 12½ × 9⅞" (31.8 × 25.1 cm).

1. John Livingston Lowes. *Convention and Revolt in Poetry,* New York, Gordon Press, n.d.

At the same time, the Western world was introduced to philosophies of existentialism that denied inherent intelligence and purpose in the universe, or intrinsic meaning in individual life. The effect on an ever-growing number of thoughtful individuals has been to destroy the old center of certainty: to force them to peer over the brink of life and discover nothing but senseless void beyond. Thus, for many, old values have been seriously questioned or destroyed completely.

None of these literary developments is entirely new. Pessimism was not invented in the twentieth century; existentialism had its immediate source in Kierkegaard and Nietzsche in the nineteenth century and can be traced as far back as the ancient Greek philosopher Democritos; new forms for literature (black humor, science fiction) have antecedents. Whatever writers have done in the recent and distant past appears to have all flowed together to become a rich reservoir available for literary creation.

Taboos

Previous restrictions about ethics, language, and structure have been relaxed or even swept away, profoundly affecting present-day writing.

Ethics

Social taboos about ethics in general and sexual ethics in particular are much more lax. Not too long ago it was difficult to buy Henry Miller's novels or D. H. Lawrence's *Lady Chatterley's Lover* in the United States, since they supposedly shocked the general public's idea of "proper" literature. Social restrictions have now become so relaxed that these particular books are not even very exciting in terms of raw sex. There are still restrictions, of course, on so-called hard-core pornography, but any work that has artistic value is protected by the Constitution, thus guaranteeing society's right to know. The maturation of the public in terms of the freedom to explore the whole range of human experience has stimulated all who create and all who enjoy art works in any medium.

Language

"Polite" language, was the norm in most nineteenth-century literature, with the other words appearing in the underground erotic literature of the Victorian era. That taboo has vanished. Words found on the walls and stalls of restrooms appear regularly in our "better" magazines—in fiction, poetry, and non-fiction. This is freedom of expression as guaranteed by the Bill of Rights. By the time any boy or girl has reached junior high school, he or she is familiar with all the four-letter words; intrinsically, the word "excrement" is neither better nor worse than its four-letter synonym. Not surprisingly, many writers, especially screenwriters, jumped on the bandwagon and used so many expletives in one form or another that the intended shock values were dissipated in the murk of monotonous obscenities. People do use these words in everyday life but does art have to become a Xerox machine in the pursuit of the "real" world? Writers who feel compelled to use the short Anglo-Saxon words may find a true freedom by choosing, from the whole range of language, whatever words are best suited to the purpose of their art work. That is, in fact, precisely what many contemporary writers are doing.

The freedom to choose from all the words in the language has certainly helped recent translations of ancient, medieval, and modern foreign language literature. Generations of students have assumed that the classics of ancient Greece and Rome, for example, were written in the stilted, sanitary language adopted by earlier translators. Not so! Greek and Roman writers used the full range of their languages, including as many explicit words and phrases as found in languages throughout the world. All the works of Aristophanes, Ovid, Catullus, and Juvenal, to name a few, are now available in translations that do justice to their lustily explicit vocabulary. These writers selected their words from the entire realm of their richly expressive languages, which helps explain their lofty rank in the world's literature.

Structure

A third restriction was the apparent necessity for rational or chronological structure in prose, and for traditional "sense" in poetry. The expectation that a literary work have a beginning, a middle, and an end has vanished except for the requirements imposed by the printed page. Present-day writers need not string their words on a "plot." (Plot may be defined as the working out of a theme, usually clearly stated, which is developed in chronological order by the confrontation of two "sides" in opposition, with the ultimate victory of one side over the other.) Until the last generation or so, this has been (with notable exceptions) the standard structure for most fiction and drama. It is, of course, still used, but structure is not necessary, and many important writers have discarded the flow-of-time convention and the idea of opposing forces. Many playwrights have discarded logical development in an attempt to achieve immediate and direct feeling that does not fit Aristotelian concepts of either thought or dramatic art. With the old structures no longer required, writers are free to seek truth in many different ways. Experimentalism in form, sometimes successful, sometimes merely confusing, has become a commonplace in the writer's art.

POETRY

Experiments in Form, Subject, and Language

Form, subject, and language are three aspects of poetry that are so closely united as to be inseparable in total effect. However, poetry can be analyzed by arbitrarily considering each aspect separately.

The free verse in Eliot's "The Love Song of J. Alfred Prufrock" is an excellent example of formal innovation. Robinson Jeffers' "Shine, Perishing Republic," with its long, flowing lines, is another instance of free verse (see p. 336). The poem has rhythmic effects—with phrases often indicated by punctuation—but not conventional poetic meter.

A strikingly different experiment is the following poem by e e cummings. The poet delights in typographical eccentricity—lack of capitals or punctuation, frequent parentheses—and the example below is mild in comparison with others among his poems. A notable characteristic is his use, avoidance, and distortion of rhyme: "town-down," "winter-did," "same-rain." Innovation in subject matter and form almost necessarily demands a difference in language. This does not simply mean that the modern poet talks about the artifacts of our culture—computers or space travel, for example—but that he or she uses a deliberately distorted grammar, syntax, and logic. Consider "anyone lived in a pretty how town." One must untangle the phrase, to find in it perhaps a sardonic amusement at a gushing cliché—"How pretty this little town is!" When the poet wishes to point out the passage of time, he does not say "time after time, as trees come out leaf by leaf"; he telescopes it to "when by now and tree by leaf," and the apparent nonsense suddenly becomes new sense.

LITERARY SELECTION 95

anyone lived in a pretty how town

e e cummings, 1894–1962

anyone lived in a pretty how town
(with up so floating many bells down)
spring summer autumn winter
he sang his didn't he danced his did.

Women and men (both little and small)
cared for anyone not at all
they sowed their isn't they reaped their same
sun moon stars rain

children guessed (but only a few
and down they forgot as up they grew
autumn winter spring summer)
that no one loved him more by more

when by now and tree by leaf
she laughed his joy she cried his grief
bird by snow and stir by still
anyone's any was all to her

someones married their everyones
laughed their cryings and did their dance
(sleep wake hope and then) they
said their nevers they slept their dream

stars rain sun moon
(and only the snow can begin to explain
how children are apt to forget to remember
with up so floating many bells down)

one day anyone died i guess
(and noone stooped to kiss his face)
busy folk buried them side by side
little by little and was by was

all by all and deep by deep
and more by more they dream their sleep
noone and anyone earth by april
wish by spirit and if by yes.

Women and men (both dong and ding)
summer autumn winter spring
reaped their sowing and went their came
sun moon stars rain

STUDY QUESTIONS

1. Much of the poetry of cummings is very rhythmic with considerable use of what is called the "variable foot." In stanza 1, for example, the variation occurs in the third line. Try reading the poem aloud to hear how the variations set off the nimble words in the other lines.
2. Many of the phrases are dissociated from expected relationships. Try rephrasing some of these to see what happens to the rhythm. Do the conventional versions become commonplace?

LITERARY SELECTION 96

When All My Five and Country Senses See

Dylan Thomas, 1914–53

When all my five and country senses see,
The fingers will forget green thumbs and mark
How, through the halfmoon's vegetable eye,
Husk of young stars and handful zodiac,
Love in the frost is pared and wintered by.
The whispering ears will watch love drummed away
Down breeze and shell to a discordant beach,
And, lashed to syllables, the lynx tongue cry
That her fond wounds are mended bitterly,
My nostrils see her breath burn like a bush.
My one and noble heart has witnesses
In all love's countries, that will grope awake:
And when blind sleep drops on the spying senses,
The heart is sensual, though five eyes break.

The language of Dylan Thomas is so unusual as to seem baffling at first reading. How can "fingers forget green thumbs" and what is the half-moon's "vegetable eye"? Certainly the poet is not talking with simple directness; his words do not "mean" with a single, unchanging meaning, but seem to move in several directions at once. Suppose we try to paraphrase in this fashion: "If all my five natural senses could perceive clearly, see—like my eyes—then even the sense of touch, that helped love grow, would 'see' with the passage of time how love grows old and is laid by, like fruit after harvest; the sense of hearing would 'see' love finished, driven away, ending in discord; the tongue, which is both taste and talk, would 'see' love's pains reluctantly ended; the sense of smell would 'see' love consumed as in a fire. But my heart has other means of perception of love, and these will go on beyond the decaying senses, so that my heart will still know love."

LITERARY SELECTION 97

Helen

George Seferis, 1900–71

The first Greek to win the Nobel Prize for literature (1963), Seferis is renowned for introducing modernist forms and techniques into Greek writing. Much of his own writing has been based on ancient Greek myths and history and critics have compared his philosophy, ethics, and sense of justice with those of Anaximander and Aeschylus. This selection is translated by Edmund Keeley and Philip Sherrard.

TEUCER: . . . *in sea-girt Cyprus, where it was decreed by*
Apollo that I should live, giving the city the name
of Salamis in memory of my island home.

. . . . . .

HELEN: *I never went to Troy; it was a phantom.*

. . . . . .

SERVANT: *What? You mean it was only for a cloud that*
we struggled so much?

HELEN by Euripides[2]

"The nightingales won't let you sleep in Platres."[3]

Shy nightingale, in the breathing of the leaves,
you who bestow the forest's musical coolness
on the parted bodies, on the souls
of those who know they will not return.
Blind voice, you who grope in the darkness of memory
for footsteps and gestures—I wouldn't dare say kisses—
and the bitter raging of the slavewoman grown wild.

"The nightingales won't let you sleep in Platres."

Platres: where is Platres? And this island: who knows it?
I've lived my life hearing names I've never heard before:
new countries, new idiocies of men
or of the gods;
my fate, which wavers
between the last sword of some Ajax
and another Salamis,[4]
brought me here to this shore.
The moon
rose from the sea like Aphrodite,
covered the Archer's stars, now moves to find
the heart of Scorpio, and changes everything.
Truth, where's the truth?
I too was an archer in the war;
my fate: that of a man who missed his target.

Lyric nightingale,
on a night like this, by the shore of Proteus,
the Spartan slave girls heard you and began their lament,
and among them—who would have believed it?—Helen!
She whom we hunted so many years by the banks of the Scamander.
She was there, at the desert's lip; I touched her; she spoke to me:
"It isn't true, it isn't true," she cried.
"I didn't board the blue-bowed ship.
I never went to valiant Troy."

High-girdled, the sun in her hair, and that stature
shadows and smiles everywhere,
on shoulders, thighs, and knees;
the skin alive, and her eyes
with the large eyelids,
she was there, on the banks of a Delta.
And at Troy?
At Troy, nothing: just a phantom image.
The gods wanted it so.
And Paris, Paris lay with a shadow as though it were a solid being;
and for ten whole years we slaughtered ourselves for Helen.

Great suffering descended on Greece.
So many bodies thrown
into the jaws of the sea, the jaws of the earth
so many souls
fed to the millstones like grain.
And the rivers swelling, blood in their silt,
all for a linen undulation, a bit of cloud,

2. Euripides' play assumes that only a phantom of Helen went with Paris to Troy. Helen herself was carried by Hermes to the Egyptian court of Proteus, where she was eventually reunited with her husband Menelaos long after the Trojan war ended.
3. Platres is a summer resort on the slopes of Mt. Troödos in Cyprus.
4. Where the Greeks defeated the Persian fleet in 480 BC.

a butterfly flicker, a swan's down,
an empty tunic—all for a Helen.
And my brother?
Nightingale, nightingale, nightingale,
what is a god? What is not a god? And what is there
between them?

"The nightingales won't let you sleep in Platres."

Tearful bird,
on sea-kissed Cyprus
consecrated to remind me of my country,
I moored alone with this fable,
if it's true that it is a fable,
if it's true that mortals will not again take up
the old deceit of the gods;
if it's true
that in future years some other Teucer,
or some Ajax or Priam or Hecuba,
or someone unknown and nameless who nevertheless
saw
a Scamander overflow with corpses,
isn't fated to hear
newsbearers coming to tell him
that so much suffering, so much life,
went into the abyss
all for an empty tunic, for a Helen.

STUDY QUESTIONS

1. Describe the poet's feeling about war, any war. Is there anger here? Remember that Italy and Germany invaded Greece in World War II and that there was a brutal civil war after the Allies drove the Germans out. Communists kidnapped thousands of Greek children, who were never seen again.
2. What does the nightingale symbolize? Why won't it let you sleep in a summer resort?

   Obviously these and the other poems in this chapter (and chapters 26 and 27) cannot do justice to the range and variety of contemporary poetry, but there is enough to demonstrate some of the ideas presented here.

DRAMA

Realistic Theatre

Modern drama is called "realistic" when its theatrical conventions generally reflect or represent the world in which we live. Actors look, act, and talk like people that any of us might know. The sets usually give the illusion of actual rooms, lawns, or gardens. No one on stage speaks in rhymed couplets; the medium is prose, not poetry. Actors do not regularly talk to ghosts, play to the audience, or meditate in blank verse on an empty stage. The characters are, in the main, men and women in all walks of life rather than kings and queens, knights and fair ladies.

Some realistic elements appeared in theatre shortly after the Renaissance, but the main development came after the middle of the nineteenth century. Realist dramatists (and representative plays) include Henrik Ibsen (1828–1906), *Hedda Gabler*; George Bernard Shaw (1856–1950), *Pygmalion*; Anton Chekhov (1864–1904), *The Cherry Orchard*; and, later, Arthur Miller (b. 1915), *Death of a Salesman*. The emergence of realistic drama paralleled a comparable development in the painting of Daumier, Courbet, and Winslow Homer (see figs. 25.19–25.21).

Theatre of the Absurd

The other major kind of modern theatre is generally called, for want of a better term, "unrealistic drama." Of the several varieties of "unreality" the most significant is Theatre of the Absurd, a movement that grew in response to existentialism as it affected, and was affected by, the status of society following World War II. Absurdist playwrights do not necessarily subscribe totally to the philosophy of existentialism, but they do share certain existential ideas: human life appears to have no meaning or purpose; we invent ourselves as we live our lives; our actions are either erratic or they respond to rules that make no sense; all we have in common with anyone else is certain death. Human existence is seen, therefore, as absurd.

The originator of Theatre of the Absurd was Samuel Beckett (1906–89; 1969 Nobel Prize for literature). A Protestant Irishman who once served as James Joyce's secretary (and as a spy for the French underground during World War II), Beckett preferred to live in Paris and compose his novels and plays in French. His play *Endgame* sums up human life with a blind, paralyzed protagonist who has bottled up his parents in a trash can. In *Krapp's Last Tape* a single actor sits at a tape recorder playing back a tape of a long-ago love affair. *Happy Days* stars a married couple—with the wife babbling incessantly about her possessions. She is buried up to the waist in the first act and up to her neck in the second act.

Beckett's first performed play, *Waiting for Godot*[5] (1953), remains one of the finest—and best known—of all absurdist dramas. Displaying what have become the most

5. At this time, the copyright holder does not allow this play to be anthologized, which explains its absence from this chapter. Reading it in its authorized version is strongly recommended.

familiar qualities of absurdist theatre, the drama takes place, not in sequential time, but in a timeless present. Two main characters, who may or may not be two different aspects of the same person, are waiting for Godot, who never comes, but who may or may not already be on stage as one of the players. All is ambiguity. Such drama substitutes "tension" for the "conflict" of traditional plot, but the tension is in the mind and emotions of the spectator. Since the tension is usually left unresolved, in marked distinction to the logical endings of conventional plays, the spectator is left with questions that he or she alone can resolve. Theatre that, in itself, appears to be unrealistic and illogical turns out to pose the greatest intellectual questions precisely where they should be raised—in the mind of the beholder. A questioning remains rather than the **catharsis** of the Aristotelian definition of tragedy. Indeed, Euripides anticipated this type of drama in the choral speeches with which he completes both *The Bacchae* and *Alcestis*:

Gods manifest themselves in many forms,
Bring many matters to surprising ends;
The things we thought would happen do not happen;
The unexpected, god makes possible:
And that is what has happened here today.

Shepard, Wilson, and Wasserstein

More recently, Sam Shepard, August Wilson, and Wendy Wasserstein have emerged as leading American playwrights. Shepard (b. 1943) writes in a hyperrealistic mode comparable to the Photorealism of artists such as Richard Estes and Audrey Flack (see pp. 391–2). But Shepard's realism is illusory; the facts are there, it seems, but where reality begins and ends borders on a fifth dimension. Shepard's dramas—like *Buried Child* (1979 Pulitzer Prize), *Curse of the Starving Class*, *Fool for Love*, and *A Lie of the Mind*—involve lower-middle-class families contending with hate, incest, murder, and love. Shepard's symbols are derived from junk-food and rock music, from movie, TV, and auto mystiques that represent all that is tawdry and tacky in American life. In *True West* (1980) he extols the mythic West, the Old West that is fast succumbing to bulldozers and cement mixers. In this and many more of his forty-plus plays, Shepard poses a basic question: must this New World become like the Old World just because so much of the Old World is becoming like us?

A poet turned playwright, August Wilson (b. 1945) uses a hyperrealistic style that examines issues of primary concern to the underclass in a society in which racism is still omnipresent. In particular, he writes of individual African Americans as they seek human dignity in such plays as *Ma Rainy's Black Bottom, Joe Turner's Come and Gone, Fences* (1987 Pulitzer Prize), *The Piano Lesson* (1990 Pulitzer Prize), and *Two Trains Running*. Though some critics fault Wilson for limiting his subject matter, his response is confident: "I write about the Black experience in America and try to explore in terms of the life I know best those things which are common to all cultures."

Wendy Wasserstein (b. 1950) writes from the feminist perspective in *Uncommon Women and Others*, *Isn't It Romantic*, *Happy Birthday, Montpelier, Pizz-zazz, The Heidi Chronicles* (1989 Pulitzer Prize), *Bachelor Girls*, and *The Sisters Rosensweig*. Using both absurdist and realist techniques, she displays an unerring ability to see the humorous aspects of human existence, particularly in the lives of modern women. A witty and cheerful optimist, she explores the comic spheres of women who strike out for themselves and who make a real difference in the world of men and women.

MODERN PROSE FICTION

Everything that has been said about modern literature applies also to the novel and short story. As in poetry and drama, prose writers are concerned with new forms, fresh methods of penetrating into the truths of human experience. Black humor and science fiction are two forms that writers have explored in considerable depth and with a great range of subject matter.

Black Humor

Catch-22 by Joseph Heller is perhaps the best known and one of the finest examples of black humor. Black humor *is* funny, but with a bitterness that stings. Basically it is satire, an attack on established ways of thought and action, but a satire that uses surrealistic techniques to achieve its purposes. The typical novel of this sort uses scenes that are sharply etched, with almost photographic naturalism. Yet the scenes and events exist in a bizarre juxtaposition—as in a Dali painting—so that all ordinary sense is lost, and a mind accustomed to logical relationships is utterly confounded. The reader is left with the sense of living through a comical nightmare in which time is compressed or expanded, in which space is purely relative and which may change without warning. A novel such as *Catch-22* reveals a crazy world that would amuse only the insane—and then the reverse: maybe the world of the novel is sane and we, with our conventional, Aristotelian minds, are the crazy ones.

A brief discussion of *Catch-22* (the novel, not the movie) can illustrate the nature of black humor. The central object of ridicule throughout the novel is rational thought that goes around in a circle until it ends in total absurdity. The novel takes place during World War II on an Air Force base off the coast of Italy. It seems to satirize military life, but a closer scrutiny reveals that it is an attack on much of twentieth-century society and its values. The "catch" is first unveiled when Yossarian, a bombardier and the protagonist of the novel, objects to flying more missions and pleads insanity with the medical officer in the expectation of a medical discharge (Section 8). The doctor explains that anyone who expresses fear in a dangerous situation is obviously sane and cannot be discharged. Yossarian asks about the men who are flying missions without protest. The doctor's explanation is simple: those men are insane, but since they aren't asking to be relieved of duty he can't send them home. If they asked, they, like Yossarian, would demonstrate they were sane and be immediately returned to duty. This is "Catch-22": perfectly logical, totally absurd, allowing no hope. Repeated use of this circular logic confirms the novel's hopeless, helpless mood.

Heller satirizes other fallacies of our way of life, such as our dependency on paperwork rather than facts in making judgments. Indeed, ex-P.F.C. Wintergreen, a mail clerk, handles and scrambles messages, directing military actions more completely than the generals. Another case in point is the suicidal mission to bomb the city of Bologna, when Yossarian sneaks down to the central map at headquarters and moves the ribbon showing the Allied ground position above the city. Word flies from one level of command to the next: Bologna has been taken and the bombing mission is scrubbed. Finally, inevitably, the truth is known and the mission rescheduled.

Free enterprise and the profit system are attacked unmercifully in the person of supply officer Milo Minderbinder and his M and M Enterprises. Starting with simple trading for supplies, he finally deals with both the enemy and his own side; at one point he directs the enemy bombing of his own airbase, at another he arranges a total battle, having charge of both sides. He reaps enormous profits, of course, though he constantly reminds each investor that he "has a share" in M and M Enterprises. "Having a share" is one of the great double-meanings of the book.

The first two-thirds of the book are timeless, shifting from one incident to another with no regard for chronology. For Yossarian, however, the central incident is the fate of his crewmate, Snowden. Yossarian attempts to treat the wounded gunner but, when he zips open the flak suit, Snowden's guts spill out on the floor of the plane. Yossarian suddenly realizes that the world, friend or enemy, is really divided into two groups, the killers and the victims, and that he, as bombardier, is a killer. He refuses this role and for a time goes naked (even when the general is pinning a medal on him) rather than wear the uniform. Referred to throughout the early part of the novel, the Snowden incident is not fully explained until two-thirds of the way through, at which point the story moves on in chronological time. The Snowden incident leads to the first explanation of "Catch-22" and the hopelessness of the situation.

One pilot, Yossarian's tentmate, Orr, has seemed crazier than all the others. His planes keep having engine trouble or are shot down over the sea. Orr ditches his bombers in the water from which everyone is always rescued. The last time Orr ditches his plane his crew is rescued but he is never found. It appears that he has drowned.

The novel ends with a hospital scene with Yossarian and other officers complaining that there is no hope at all. When they hear that Orr has successfully paddled his life raft to neutral Sweden (from the Mediterranean!) the mood changes. Yossarian flees to Rome, intending, somehow, to reach Sweden. The other men, bound by various obligations, will not run for it, but now there is some hope. Man may not conquer, but he can refuse to be conquered. In spite of "Catch-22," the individual can assert himself.

Science Fiction

Science fiction is not really new, for most utopian literature shares in its fantasy and Jules Verne and H. G. Wells wrote science fiction in the past century. What is new is its renewed status as a serious genre; what had degenerated into comic-strip stuff in the 1930s is now widely accepted. The difference lies in the reasons for writing science fiction. Utopians used it to show that things could be better; Jules Verne wrote literate, highly popular adventure tales containing some amazingly accurate predictions about the future. At the present time numerous writers are jolting our minds from ordinary channels and enlarging our concepts of what is possible, or what is not impossible. As we are transported through space, time, or time-warps we begin to inhabit a world in which A may not be A; in which not-A can very well be A. Writers have to work to stay ahead of developments in science and technology; advanced technology has already made some of the ideas and devices of earlier science fiction come true and more wonders are certain to come.

Flourishing Literary Arts

In an age when print media are eyeing the relentless onslaught of computer technology, more books (poetry, short stories, novels, biographies, drama, essays) are being published than at any time in history. No one can reasonably predict what the coming century holds, but the literary arts are currently flourishing as perhaps never before. Momentous changes, however, are even now waiting impatiently in the wings:

> We are coming to the end of the culture of the book. Books are still produced and read in prodigious numbers, and they will continue to be as far into the future as one can imagine. However, they do not command the center of the cultural stage. Modern culture is taking shapes that are more various and more complicated than the book-centered culture it is succeeding.[6]

Many of us have difficulty facing up to the waning centrality of the printed book; it has been, after all, basic to Western civilization for five centuries. On the other hand, what is a mere five centuries in the thousands of years of

6. O. B. Hardison, Jr. *Disappearing Through the Skylight: Culture and Technology in the Twentieth Century* (New York: Viking Penguin, 1989), p. 264.

human history? We must remember that the incredible pace of computer evolution is still accelerating. If, for example, "the cost of transportation had fallen as dramatically since 1950 as the cost of computing power, today's traveler would be able to buy a round-trip ticket to Mars for $12.50."[7]

LITERARY SELECTION 98

The Other Wife

Sidonie Gabrielle Colette, 1873–1954

One of the outstanding French writers of the century, Colette is known for her insight into human psychology, especially her vivid portrayals of a wide variety of women. Her novels include *Chéri, The Last of Chéri, The Cat,* and *Gigi*. In this very short story notice how adroitly she communicates key information with a remarkable economy of means; the translation is by Margaret Crosland.

"For two? This way, Monsieur and Madame, there's still a table by the bay window, if Madame and Monsieur would like to enjoy the view?"

Alice followed the *maître d'hôtel.*

"Oh, yes, come on Marc, we'll feel we're having lunch on a boat at sea. . . ."

Her husband restrained her, passing his arm through hers.

"We'll be more comfortable there."

"There? In the middle of all those people? I'd much prefer . . ."

"Please, Alice."

He tightened his grip in so emphatic a way that she turned round.

"What's the matter with you?"

He said "sh" very quietly, looking at her intently, and drew her towards the table in the middle.

"What is it Marc?"

"I'll tell you, darling. Let me order lunch. Would you like shrimps? Or eggs in aspic?"

"Whatever you like, as you know."

They smiled at each other, wasting the precious moments of an overworked, perspiring *maître d'hôtel* who stood near to them, suffering from a kind of St. Vitus's dance.

"Shrimps," ordered Marc. "And then eggs and bacon. And cold chicken with cos lettuce salad. Cream cheese? *Spécialité de la maison*? We'll settle for the *spécialité*. Two very strong coffees. Please give lunch to my chauffeur, we'll be leaving again at two o'clock. Cider? I don't trust it. . . . Dry champagne."

He sighed as though he had been moving a wardrobe, gazed at the pale noonday sea, the nearly white sky, then at his wife, finding her pretty in her little Mercury-type hat with its long veil.

"You're looking well, darling. And all this sea-blue colour gives you green eyes, just imagine! And you put on weight when you travel . . . It's nice, up to a point, but only up to a point!"

Her rounded bosom swelled proudly as she leant over the table.

"Why did you stop me taking that place by the bay window?"

It did not occur to Marc Séguy to tell a lie.

"Because you'd have sat next to someone I know."

"And whom I don't know?"

"My ex-wife."

She could not find a word to say and opened her blue eyes wider.

"What of it, darling? It'll happen again. It's not important."

Alice found her tongue again and asked the inevitable questions in their logical sequence.

"Did she see you? Did she know that you'd seen her? Point her out to me."

"Don't turn round at once, I beg you, she must be looking at us. A lady with dark hair, without a hat, she must be staying at this hotel . . . On her own, behind those children in red . . . "

"Yes, I see . . ."

Sheltered behind broad-brimmed seaside hats Alice was able to look at the woman who fifteen months earlier had still been her husband's wife. "Incompatibility," Marc told her. "Oh, it was total incompatibility! We divorced like well-brought-up people, almost like friends, quietly and quickly. And I began to love you, and you were able to be happy with me. How lucky we are that in our happiness there haven't been any guilty parties or victims!"

The woman in white, with her smooth, lustrous hair over which the seaside light played in blue patches, was smoking a cigarette, her eyes half-closed. Alice turned back to her husband, took some shrimps and butter and ate composedly.

"Why didn't you ever tell me," she said after a moment's silence, "that she had blue eyes too?"

"But I'd never thought about it!"

He kissed the hand that she stretched out to the bread basket and she blushed with pleasure. Dark-skinned and plump, she might have seemed slightly earthy, but the changing blue of her eyes, and her wavy golden hair, disguised her as a fragile and soulful blonde. She showed overwhelming gratitude to her husband. She was immodest without knowing it and her entire person revealed overconspicuous signs of extreme happiness.

They ate and drank with good appetite and each thought that the other had forgotten the woman in white. However, Alice sometimes laughed too loudly and Marc was careful of his posture, putting his shoulders back and holding his head up. They waited some time for coffee, in silence. An incandescent stream, a narrow reflection of the high and invisible sun, moved slowly over the sea and shone with unbearable brilliance.

"She's still there, you know," Alice whispered suddenly.

"Does she embarrass you? Would you like to have

7. *Ibid.*, p. 270.

coffee somewhere else?"

"Not at all! It's she who ought to be embarrassed! And she doesn't look as though she's having a madly gay time, if you could see her . . . "

"It's not necessary. I know that look of hers."

"Oh, was she like that?"

He breathed smoke through his nostrils and wrinkled his brows.

"Was she like that? No. To be frank, she wasn't happy with me."

"Well, my goodness."

"You're delightfully generous, darling, madly generous. . . . You're an angel, you're. . . . You love me . . . I'm so proud, when I see that look in your eyes . . . yes, the look you have now. . . . She. . . . No doubt I didn't succeed in making her happy. That's all there is to it, I didn't succeed."

"She's hard to please—"

Alice fanned herself irritably, and cast brief glances at the woman in white who was smoking, her head leaning against the back of the cane chair, her eyes closed with an expression of satisfied lassitude.

Marc shrugged his shoulders modestly.

"That's it," he admitted. "What can one do? We have to be sorry for people who are never happy. As for us, we're so happy. . . . Aren't we, darling?"

She didn't reply. She was looking with furtive attention at her husband's face, with its good colour and regular shape, at his thick hair, with its occasional thread of white silk, at his small, well-cared-for hands. She felt dubious for the first time and asked herself: "What more did she want, then?"

And until they left, while Marc was paying the bill, asking about the chauffeur and the route, she continued to watch, with envious curiosity, the lady in white, that discontented, hard-to-please, superior woman.

STUDY QUESTIONS

1. How does Colette use light to create feelings of ambiguity?
2. What is implied in the physical description of Marc and the fact that he has a chauffeur?
3. What is implied by a "woman in white"?
4. Explain how Alice's feelings for Marc change from beginning to end.

LITERARY SELECTION 99

The Distinterested Killer Bill Harrigan

Jorge Luis Borges, 1899–1986

The great Argentine master of short prose-forms is represented by a selection from his collection of essays called *A Universal History of Infamy* (1930s), here in a translation by Norman Thomas di Giovanni. This is a partly fictional story of Billy the Kid written in what Borges called "baroque," in which his writing "borders on its own parody." The style is deliberately cinematic and the ending becomes a playful parody on the tendency of writers to mythologize criminals and readers to venerate them—from a safe distance.

An image of the desert wilds of Arizona, first and foremost, an image of the desert wilds of Arizona and New Mexico—a country famous for its silver and gold camps, a country of breathtaking open spaces, a country of monumental mesas and soft colors, a country of bleached skeletons picked clean by buzzards. Over this whole country, another image—that of Billy the Kid, the hard rider firm on his horse, the young man with the relentless six-shooters, sending out invisible bullets which (like magic) kill at a distance.

The desert veined with precious metals, arid and blinding-bright. The near child who on dying at the age of twenty-one owed to the justice of grown men twenty-one deaths—"not counting Mexicans."

The Larval Stage

Along about 1859, the man who would become known to terror and glory as Billy the Kid was born in a cellar room of a New York City tenement. It is said that he was spawned by a tired-out Irish womb but was brought up among Negroes. In this tumult of lowly smells and wooly heads, he enjoyed a superiority that stemmed from having freckles and a mop of red hair. He took pride in being white; he was also scrawny, wild, and coarse. At the age of twelve, he fought in the gang of the Swamp Angels, that branch of divinities who operated among the neighborhood sewers. On nights redolent of burnt fog, they would clamber out of the foul-smelling labyrinth, trail some German sailor, do him in with a knock on the head, strip him to his underwear, and afterward sneak back to the filth of their starting place. Their leader was a gray-haired Negro, Gas House Jonas, who was also celebrated as a poisoner of horses.

Sometimes, from the upper window of a waterfront dive, a woman would dump a bucket of ashes upon the head of a prospective victim. As he gasped and choked, Swamp Angels would swarm him, rush him into a cellar, and plunder him.

Such were the apprentice years of Billy Harrigan, the future Billy the Kid. Nor did he scorn the offerings of Bowery playhouses, enjoying in particular (perhaps without an inkling that they were signs and symbols of his destiny) cowboy melodramas.

Go West!

If the jammed Bowery theatres (whose top-gallery riffraff shouted "Hoist that rag!" when the curtain failed to rise promptly on schedule) abounded in these blood and thunder productions, the simple explanation is that America was then experiencing the lure of the Far West. Beyond the sunset lay the goldfields of Nevada and California. Beyond the sunset were the redwoods, going down before the ax; the buffalo's huge Babylonian face; Brigham Young's beaver hat and plural bed; the red man's ceremonies and his rampages; the clear air of the deserts; endless-stretching range land; and the earth itself, whose nearness quickens the heart like the nearness of the sea. The West beckoned. A slow, steady rumor populated those years—that of thousands of Americans taking possession of the West. On that march, around 1872, was Bill Harrigan, treacherous as a bull rattler, in flight from a rectangular cell.

The Demolition of a Mexican

History (which, like certain film directors, proceeds by a series of abrupt images) now puts forward the image of a danger-filled saloon, located—as if on the high seas—out in the heart of the all-powerful desert. The time, a blustery night of the year 1873; the place, the Staked Plains of New Mexico. All around, the land is almost uncannily flat and bare, but the sky, with its storm-piled clouds and moon, is full of fissured cavities and mountains. There are a cow's skull, the howl and the eyes of coyotes in the shadows, trim horses, and from the saloon an elongated patch of light. Inside, leaning over the bar, a group of strapping but tired men drink a liquor that warms them for a fight; at the same time, they make a great show of large silver coins bearing a serpent and an eagle. A drunk croons to himself, poker-faced. Among the men are several who speak a language with many s's, which must be Spanish, for those who speak it are looked down on. Bill Harrigan, the red-topped tenement rat, stands among the drinkers. He has downed a couple of *aguardientes* and thinks of asking for one more, maybe because he hasn't a cent left. He is somewhat overwhelmed by these men of the desert. He sees them as imposing, boisterous, happy, and hatefully wise in the handling of wild cattle and big horses. All at once there is dead silence, ignored only by the voice of the drunk, singing out of tune. Someone has come in—a big, burly Mexican, with the face of an old Indian squaw. He is endowed with an immense sombrero and with a pair of six-guns at his side. In awkward English, he wishes a good evening to all the gringo sons of bitches who are drinking. Nobody takes up the challenge. Bill asks who he is, and they whisper to him, in fear, that the Dago—that is the Diego—is Belisario Villagrán, from Chihuahua. At once there is a resounding blast. Sheltered by that wall of tall men, Bill has fired at the intruder. The glass drops from Villagrán's hand; then the man himself drops. He does not need another bullet. Without deigning to glance to the showy dead man, Bill picks up his end of the conversation. "Is that so?" he drawled. "Well, I'm Billy the Kid, from New York." The drunk goes on singing unheeded.

One may easily guess the apotheosis. Bill gives out handshakes all around and accepts praises, cheers, and whiskies. Someone notices that there are no notches on the handle of his revolver and offers to cut one to stand for Villagrán's death. Billy the Kid keeps this someone's razor, though he says that "It's hardly worthwhile noting down Mexicans." This, perhaps, is not quite enough. That night, Bill lays out his blanket beside the corpse and—with great show—sleeps till daybreak.

Deaths for Deaths' Sake

Out of that lucky blast (at the age of fourteen), Billy the Kid the hero was born, and the furtive Bill Harrigan died. The boy of the sewer and the knock on the head rose to become a man of the frontier. He made a horseman of himself, learning to ride straight in the saddle—Wyoming- or Texas-style—and not with his body thrown back, the way they rode in Oregon and California. He never completely matched his legend, but he kept getting closer and closer to it. Something of the New York hooligan lived on in the cowboy; he transferred to Mexicans the hate that had previously been inspired in him by Negroes, but the last words he ever spoke were (swear) words in Spanish. He learned the art of the cowpuncher's life. He learned another, more difficult art—how to lead men. Both helped to make him a good cattle rustler. From time to time, Old Mexico's guitars and whorehouses pulled on him.

With the haunting lucidity of insomnia, he organized populous orgies that often lasted four days and four nights. In the end, glutted, he settled accounts with bullets. While his trigger finger was unfailing, he was the most feared man (and perhaps the most anonymous and most lonely) of that whole frontier. Pat Garrett, his friend, the sheriff who later killed him, once told him, "I've had a lot of practice with the rifle shooting buffalo."

"I've had plenty with the six-shooter," Billy replied modestly. "Shooting tin cans and men."

The details can never be recovered, but it is known that he was credited with up to twenty-one killings—"not counting Mexicans." For seven desperate years, he practiced the extravagance of utter recklessness.

The night of the twenty-fifth of July 1880, Billy the Kid came galloping on his piebald down the main, or only, street of Fort Sumner. The heat was oppressive and the lamps had not been lighted; Sheriff Garrett, seated on a porch in a rocking chair, drew his revolver and sent a bullet through the Kid's belly. The horse kept on; the rider tumbled into the dust of the road. Garrett got off a second shot. The townspeople (knowing the wounded man was Billy the Kid) locked their window shutters tight. The agony was long and blasphemous. In the morning, the sun by then high overhead, they began drawing near, and they disarmed him. The man was gone. They could see in his face the used-up look of the dead.

He was shaved, sheathed in ready-made clothes, and displayed to awe and ridicule in the window of Fort Sumner's biggest store, Men on horseback and in buckboards gathered for miles and miles around. On the third day, they had to use make-up on him. On the fourth day, he was buried with rejoicing.

STUDY QUESTIONS

1. How does the meaning of "disinterested" differ from that of "uninterested"? Does the style of the writing agree with the meaning of the text? How is this accomplished?
2. Borges consistently evokes "images," which are a major factor in his cinematic style. Does the style seem less or more serious than that of a standard biography? What does this style allow him to do that more ordinary biographies cannot accomplish?
3. What did the author accomplish by fictionalizing the display and disposal of the outlaw's body?
4. As related by Borges, does this disinterested killer possess any virtues? What did he value and what was of little or no interest? Listing these items should provide a rounded picture of Billy the Kid that was accomplished by a gifted writer in a few pungent paragraphs.

LITERARY SELECTION 100

The Happy Man

Naguib Mahfouz, b. 1911

Winner of the 1988 Nobel Prize for literature, Mahfouz is the most famous writer of fiction in Egypt and throughout the Arab world. His Cairo Trilogy (*Palace Walk, Palace of Desire, Sugar Street*) has been compared with the best of Dickens and Dostoevsky. Because he was a vocal supporter of Anwar Sadat's 1979 peace treaty with Israel, some of his novels are banned in Arabic-speaking countries. This translation is by Saad el-Gabalawy.

When he woke, he found himself happy. That was most strange compared with his habitual state of mind in the early morning. For he usually got up with a terrible headache from working late hours in his office at the newspaper, or with a hangover from too much eating and drinking at some wild party. The worries of the day before and the problems of the present day usually assailed him then, so that he dragged himself out of bed with great difficulty, trying to muster all his energy and face the troubles of life. But today he was unquestionably happy, overflowing with happiness. The feeling was so clear and intense that it imposed itself on his mind and senses. Yes, he was happy. If this was not happiness, what was it then? He felt all his organs were functioning in perfect harmony with each other and with the whole world around him. Inside him there was infinite energy and a tremendous capacity to achieve anything with great skill and confidence. And his heart was brimming with love for people, animals and things, with an overwhelming feeling of optimism, as if he had finally defeated fear, anxiety, sickness and death. Above all, there was the incomprehensible sensation which penetrated his body and soul, playing a delightful tune of joy, contentment and peace.

Intoxicated with this ecstasy, he savored it slowly and with a deep sense of wonder about its mysterious source. There was nothing in his past to explain it or in his future to justify it. How did it come? How long would it last? Oh no, this must be just a fleeting mood which could never be permanent. For if it lasted forever, man would become an angel and reach the world beyond. Let him enjoy it now, live with it, treasure it, before it became a vague memory in the distant horizon.

He ate his breakfast with great appetite, looking from time to time with a bright, smiling face at Am Beshir who was serving the food. The old man became increasingly surprised and anxious, because his master did not normally look in his direction except to give orders or ask questions. Then he said to him:

"Tell me, Am Beshir, am I a happy man?"

The man was embarrassed, since the master was for the first time addressing him as a companion or friend. After moments of uneasy silence, he replied:

"My master is happy with God's gifts and blessings."

"Do you mean that I must be happy with my excellent position, beautiful apartment and good health? Is this what you mean? But do you really think I am a happy man?"

"My master exerts himself beyond human endurance and often gets angry in heated discussions with other people."

He interrupted him with a loud laugh and asked:

"What about you? Don't you have any worries?"

"Of course. Nobody lives without worries."

"Do you mean that perfect happiness is impossible?"

"Well, this is the nature of life."

How could Beshir, or anybody else, imagine his wonderful state of happiness? It was something strange and unique, as if it were his own private secret of all people on earth.

In the conference room at the newspaper, he saw his greatest rival in the world turning the pages of a magazine. The man heard his footsteps but did not raise his eyes. No doubt he somehow glanced quickly but tried to ignore him for his own peace of mind. In regular meetings they often disagreed violently and exchanged the harshest words until they were on the verge of fighting. And only last week he was shamefully defeated by his rival in the union elections, which was a terrible blow to his pride that filled him with bitterness and darkened his vision. But here he was now approaching his enemy with a pure and carefree heart, intoxicated with that wonderful happiness, overflowing with tolerance and forgiveness, as if he were another man who conveyed the promise of a new friendship. And without feeling awkward, he smilingly greeted him. Taken by surprise, the man raised his eyes in wonder and for moments remained silent until he could collect himself and answer the greeting briefly, as if he did not believe his eyes and ears. He sat close to him, saying:

"The weather is gorgeous today."

"Oh yes."

"It's the kind of weather that fills the heart with deep happiness."

The man looked at him cautiously and intently, then mumbled:

"I am glad that you're happy."

He said laughingly:

"It's happiness beyond comprehension."

The other replied hesitantly:

"I hope that I will not spoil your mood at the meeting of the editorial board today."

"Oh, never. My opinion is well known to everybody. But I don't mind if the members accept your view. This will not spoil my happiness at all."

"You have changed considerably overnight."

"In fact, I am happy beyond comprehension."

"I bet your son has changed his mind about staying in Canada for good."

He chuckled and said:

"No, my friend, he has not changed his decision."

"But that was your greatest source of grief."

"Oh, yes. I have pleaded with him again and again to come back in order to relieve my loneliness and serve his country. But he told me that he intended to start an engineering business with a Canadian partner, and even invited me to join him there. Let him live where he likes. But here I am—as you see—happy, unbelievably happy."

"This is unique courage on your part."

"I don't know what it is, but I am happy in the full sense of the word."

Yes, this was happiness, rich and touchable, firm like absolute power, free as the air, violent as a flame, fascinating as the scent of flowers. Yet this unnatural feeling could not last forever.

The other man, attracted by his friendliness, said amicably:

"In fact, I always regarded you as a man with a violent nature that caused you a great deal of suffering."

"Really?"

"You don't know the meaning of compromise. You live intensely with your nerves, with your whole being, fighting fiercely as if any problem were a matter of life or death."

"Yes, that's true."

He accepted this criticism tolerantly, as though it were a little wave in his infinite ocean of happiness, and with a bright smile on his face, asked:

"Then, you believe that there should be some balance in my approach to events?"

"Certainly. Take, for example, our discussion yesterday about racism. We share the same opinion, and the issue is worthy of enthusiasm to the point of anger. But what kind of anger? It should, in a sense, be intellectual, abstract anger. Not the anger that would fray the nerves, cause indigestion and raise blood pressure. Right?"

"That is very clear to me now."

His heart would not release a single drop of its joys. Racism, Vietnam, Angola, Palestine . . . no problem could invade the fortress of happiness which surrounded his heart. Whenever he remembered a problem, his heart chuckled joyfully. It was, so to speak, a gigantic happiness, indifferent to any misery, always smiling in the face of suffering. He wished to laugh, to dance, to sing, spreading his infinite mirth over problems of the world.

Suddenly he felt that the office was too small for him; he had no desire to work. The mere thought of his daily work was treated with absolute indifference and contempt, and he failed completely to bring his mind down from the heaven of bliss. How could he write about the trolley bus which sank in the Nile, when he was intoxicated with all this terrifying happiness. Yes, it was terrifying, coming as it did from nowhere, violent to the point of exhaustion and paralyzing his will. Besides, it was now midday and the feeling still possessed him without any sign of diminishing at all. He left his papers blank on his desk and started pacing his room, laughing and snapping his fingers.

He had a moment of anxiety which did not sink deeply inside him, but floated as an abstract thought on the surface of the mind. It occurred to him to recall deliberately the tragedies of his life in order to test their effect on his present mood, hoping they might help him regain some equanimity or at least reassure him that this happiness might eventually fade away. He recreated in his memory, for example, the death of his wife with all its tragic circumstances. But the event seemed to him as a series of movements without meaning or effect, as if it happened to another woman, the wife of another man, in a remote age of ancient history. The recollection even had a pleasant effect on him so that he smiled and could not help laughing loudly.

The same thing happened when he remembered the first letter he received from his son, declaring his intention to emigrate to Canada. And when he started to review mentally the bloody tragedies of the world, his chuckles became so loud they might have been heard in the other offices or even in the street. Nothing could touch his happiness. The memories of grief floated softly like gentle waves touching the sands of the shore. Then he left his office and the whole building, without a note of apology for not attending the editorial meeting. After lunch, he went to bed for the usual nap, but felt that sleep was impossible. There was no sign of its approach in this bright, boisterous world of joy that kept him wide awake. He must have some rest and tranquility, some inertia, some numbness in his senses. But how? Finally he left his bed and started humming a tune while pacing his apartment back and forth. And he said to himself that if this state of mind and feeling lasted longer, he would become totally incapable of sleep or work or grief. It was time to go to the club, but he did not feel like meeting any of his friends. There was no sense in these endless talks about public affairs or private worries. And what would his friends think of him if they found him laughing at the most serious matters? No, he did not need anybody; he had no desire for conversation. It was essential for him to sit by himself or walk for miles to release some of this tremendous energy. He must think deeply of what happened to him. How did this fabulous happiness assault him? For how long could he carry this intolerable burden? Will this feeling deprive him forever of his work and friends, of his sleep and peace of mind? Should he yield to it and drift with the current? Or should he seek an outlet, through mental effort, strenuous work or professional advice?

He felt a little awkward when he was called to the examination room in the office of his friend, the eminent doctor. The physician looked at him smilingly and said:

"You don't seem to have any sickness."

"I didn't come to you because I am ill but because I am happy. Yes, I am extremely happy," he replied hesitantly.

There was a moment of silence charged with anxiety and surprise.

"It's a very strange sensation which I cannot define in words. But it's quite serious."

The doctor laughed and said jokingly:

"I wish your disease would be infectious."

"Oh, don't take the matter lightly. As I told you, it's very serious."

Then he started to tell the story of his happiness from the moment he got up in the morning until this visit for advice.

"Did you take any liquor or drugs or tranquilizers?"

"No, nothing of this sort at all."

"Maybe you have achieved something valuable in terms of work, love or money?"

"No, nothing of this sort either. Actually, in my life there is much more cause for sadness than happiness."

The doctor examined him very carefully, then said, shrugging his shoulders in wonder:

"You are in perfect health. I can give you some sleeping pills, but you must consult a neurologist."

The same thorough examination was carried out by the other specialist, who then said to him:

"Your nerves are in perfect shape."

"Don't you have any convincing explanation for my condition?"

"I'm sorry, there is absolutely nothing wrong with your nerves."

Whenever he heard the same reply from other specialists, he laughed, then apologized laughingly for his laughter, as if that was his way to express anxiety and despair. He felt very lonely in the company of this overwhelming happiness, without a friend or guide to help him. Suddenly he remembered there was the office of a psychiatrist across the street. But he did not trust these psychiatrists, in spite of his knowledge of the nature of psychoanalysis. Besides, he knew quite well that their treatment extended over long periods of time, so that they became almost constant companions of their patients. And he laughed when he remembered their method of treatment by free association to reveal the neuroses buried in the subconscious mind. While his feet were leading him to the doctor's office, he was still laughing, especially as he visualized the man listening to his strange complaint of happiness, when he usually listened to people complaining of hysteria, depression, anxiety or schizophrenia.

"To tell you the truth, doctor, I came to you because I am happy beyond comprehension."

And he looked at his face to see the effect of his words, but the doctor kept his calm. Hardly had he started to tell his story when the man stopped him with a gesture of his hand, and asked quietly:

"It is an overwhelming, strange, exhausting sort of happiness?"

He looked at him in amazement and was about to say something when the doctor resumed:

"It's happiness that would make you incapable of work, tired of friends and unable to sleep. And whenever you face any suffering you burst out laughing."

"You must be a mind reader."

"Oh no, nothing of this sort, but I see similar cases at least once a week."

"Is it an epidemic?"

"I didn't say that. I don't even claim that I have been able, so far, to trace a single case to its original cause."

"But it's a disease?"

"All the cases are still under treatment."

"But you are undoubtedly convinced they are all abnormal?"

"Well, in our field this is a necessary hypothesis."

"Did you observe a sign of insanity or emotional disturbance in any of them?" he asked anxiously. And he pointed to his head in fear, but the doctor said with certainty:

"No. I assure you they are all sane in the proper sense of the word. But you will need two sessions every week. You shouldn't worry or grieve . . . "

Worry, grief? He smiled and the smile widened on his face until he burst out laughing. Then his resistance collapsed completely and he could not control his tears.

STUDY QUESTIONS

1. Consider first how the protagonist usually got up in the morning. Then consider the servant's attitude toward his master, how his adversary described him, his own detached feelings about his wife, and his apparent relationship with his only child. What do all of these tell you about this man's character flaws?
2. The first doctor asked him if he had achieved something valuable. Had he? Why not? How did he feel about his newspaper job?

3. Consider the progression from family doctor to neurologist, other specialists, and, finally, the psychiatrist. What does this tell you about the man's condition? Did the man delay consulting the psychiatrist because he knew what the trouble was? What was the trouble?

LITERARY SELECTION 101

Invisible Man

Chapter 1

Ralph Ellison, b. 1914

A searing novel about black America and white America, Ralph Ellison's *Invisible Man,* winner of the 1952 National Book Award, is both a folk novel and a polished work in the American literary tradition. Opening with a bizarre boxing match in a white man's "smoker" and culminating in an explosive race riot, this is the epic tale of one man's voyage to self-discovery, a man who is "invisible simply because people refuse to see me." Appearing originally as a short story and then as chapter 1, the following selection gives something of the flavor of a book that everyone should read.

It goes a long way back, some twenty years. All my life I had been looking for something, and everywhere I turned someone tried to tell me what it was. I accepted their answers too, though they were often in contradiction and even self-contradictory. I was naïve. I was looking for myself and asking everyone except myself questions which I, and only I, could answer. It took me a long time and much painful boomeranging of my expectations to achieve a realization everyone else appears to have been born with: That I am nobody but myself. But first I had to discover that I am an invisible man!

And yet I am no freak of nature, nor of history. I was in the cards, other things having been equal (or unequal) eighty-five years ago. I am not ashamed of my grandparents for having been slaves. I am only ashamed of myself for having at one time been ashamed. About eighty-five years ago they were told that they were free, united with others of our country in everything pertaining to the common good, and, in everything social, separate like the fingers of the hand. And they believed it. They exulted in it. They stayed in their place, worked hard, and brought up my father to do the same. But my grandfather is the one. He was an odd old guy, my grandfather, and I am told I take after him. It was he who caused the trouble. On his deathbed he called my father to him and said, "Son, after I'm gone I want you to keep up the good fight. I never told you, but our life is a war and I have been a traitor all my born days, a spy in the enemy's country ever since I give up my gun back in the Reconstruction. Live with your head in the lion's mouth. I want you to overcome 'em with yeses, undermine 'em with grins, agree 'em to death and destruction, let 'em swoller you till they vomit or bust wide open." They thought the old man had gone out of his mind. He had been the meekest of men. The younger children were rushed from the room, the shades drawn and the flame of the lamp turned so low that it sputtered on the wick like the old man's breathing. "Learn it to the younguns," he whispered fiercely; then he died.

But my folks were more alarmed over his last words than over his dying. It was as though he had not died at all, his words caused so much anxiety. I was warned emphatically to forget what he had said and, indeed, this is the first time it has been mentioned outside the family circle. It had a tremendous effect upon me, however. I could never be sure of what he meant. Grandfather had been a quiet old man who never made any trouble, yet on his deathbed he had called himself a traitor and a spy, and he had spoken of his meekness as a dangerous activity. It became a constant puzzle which lay unanswered in the back of my mind. And whenever things went well for me I remembered my grandfather and felt guilty and uncomfortable. It was as though I was carrying out his advice in spite of myself. And to make it worse, everyone loved me for it. I was praised by the most lily-white men of the town. I was considered an example of desirable conduct—just as my grandfather had been. And what puzzled me was that the old man had defined it as *treachery.* When I was praised for my conduct I felt a guilt that in some way I was doing something that was really against the wishes of the white folks, that if they had understood they would have desired me to act just the opposite, that I should have been sulky and mean, and that really would have been what they wanted, even though they were fooled and thought they wanted me to act as I did. It made me afraid that some day they would look upon me as a traitor and I would be lost. Still I was more afraid to act any other way because they didn't like that at all. The old man's words were like a curse. On my graduation day I delivered an oration in which I showed that humility was the secret, indeed, the very essence of progress. (Not that I believed this—how could I, remembering my grandfather?—I only believed that it worked.) It was a great success. Everyone praised me and I was invited to give the speech at a gathering of the town's leading white citizens. It was a triumph for our whole community.

It was in the main ballroom of the leading hotel. When I got there I discovered that it was on the occasion of a smoker, and I was told that since I was to be there anyway I might as well take part in the battle royal to be fought by some of my schoolmates as part of the entertainment. The battle royal came first.

All of the town's big shots were there in their tuxedos, wolfing down the buffet foods, drinking beer and whiskey and smoking black cigars. It was a large room with a high ceiling. Chairs were arranged in neat rows around three sides of a portable boxing ring. The fourth side was clear, revealing a gleaming space of polished floor. I had some misgivings over the battle royal, by the way. Not from a distaste for fighting, but because I didn't care too much for the other fellows who were to take part. They were tough guys who seemed to have no grandfather's curse worrying their minds. No one could mistake their toughness. And besides, I suspected that fighting a battle royal might detract from the dignity of my speech. In those pre-invisible days I visualized myself as a potential Booker T. Washington. But the other fellows didn't care too much for me either, and there were nine of them. I felt superior to them in my way, and I didn't like the manner in which we were all crowded together into the servants' elevator. Nor did they like my being there. In fact, as the warmly lighted floors flashed past the elevator we had words over the fact that I, by taking part in the fight, had knocked one of their friends out of a night's work.

We were led out of the elevator through a rococo hall into an anteroom and told to get into our fighting togs. Each of us was issued a pair of boxing gloves and ushered out into the big mirrored hall, which we entered looking cautiously about us and whispering, lest we might accidentally be heard above the noise of the room. It was foggy with cigar smoke. And already the whiskey was taking effect. I was shocked to see some of the most important men of the town quite tipsy. They were all there—bankers, lawyers, judges, doctors, fire chiefs, teachers, merchants. Even one of the more fashionable pastors. Something we could not see was going on up front. A clarinet was vibrating sensuously and the men were standing up and moving eagerly forward. We were a small tight group, clustered together, our bare upper bodies touching and shining with anticipatory sweat; while up front the big shots were becoming increasingly excited over something we still could not see. Suddenly I heard the school superintendent, who had told me to come, yell, "Bring up the shines, gentlemen! Bring up the little shines!"

We were rushed up to the front of the ballroom, where it smelled even more strongly of tobacco and whiskey. Then we were pushed into place. I almost wet my pants. A sea of faces, some hostile, some amused, ringed around us, and in the center, facing us, stood a magnificent blonde—stark naked. There was dead silence. I felt a blast of cold air chill me. I tried to back away, but they were behind me and around me. Some of the boys stood with lowered heads, trembling. I felt a wave of irrational guilt and fear. My teeth chattered, my skin turned to goose flesh, my knees knocked. Yet I was strongly attracted and looked in spite of myself. Had the price of looking been blindness, I would have looked. The hair was yellow like that of a circus kewpie doll, the face heavily powdered and rouged, as though to form an abstract mask, the eyes hollow and smeared a cool blue, the color of a baboon's butt. I felt a desire to spit upon her as my eyes brushed slowly over her body. Her breasts were firm and round as the domes of East Indian temples, and I stood so close as to see the fine skin texture and beads of pearly perspiration glistening like dew around the pink and erected buds of her nipples. I wanted at one and the same time to run from the room, to sink through the floor, or go to her and cover her from my eyes and the eyes of the others with my body; to feel the soft thighs, to caress her and destroy her, to love her and murder her, to hide from her, and yet to stroke where below the small American flag tattooed upon her belly her thighs formed a capital V. I had a notion that of all in the room she saw only me with her impersonal eyes.

And then she began to dance, a slow sensuous movement, the smoke of a hundred cigars clinging to her like the thinnest of veils. She seemed like a fair bird-girl girdled in veils calling to me from the angry surface of some gray and threatening sea. I was transported. Then I became aware of the clarinet playing and the big shots yelling at us. Some threatened us if we looked and others if we did not. On my right I saw one boy faint. And now a man grabbed a silver pitcher from a table and stepped close as he dashed ice water upon him and stood him up and forced two of us to support him as his head hung and moans issued from his thick bluish lips. Another boy began to plead to go home. He was the largest of the group, wearing dark red fighting trunks much too small to conceal the erection which projected from him as though in answer to the insinuating low-registered moaning of the clarinet. He tried to hide himself with his boxing gloves.

And all the while the blonde continued dancing, smiling faintly at the big shots who watched her with fascination, and faintly smiling at our fear. I noticed a certain merchant who followed her hungrily, his lips loose and drooling. He was a large man who wore diamond studs in a shirtfront which swelled with the ample paunch underneath, and each time the blonde swayed her undulating hips he ran his hand through the thin hair of his bald head and, with his arms upheld, his posture clumsy like that of an intoxicated panda, wound his belly in a slow and obscene grind. This creature was completely hypnotized. The music had quickened. As the dancer flung herself about with a detached expression on her face, the men began reaching out to touch her. I could see their beefy fingers sink into the soft flesh. Some of the others tried to stop them and she began to move around the floor in graceful circles, as they gave chase, slipping and sliding over the polished floor. It was mad. Chairs went crashing, drinks were spilt, as they ran laughing and howling after her. They caught her just as she reached a door, raised her from the floor, and tossed her as college boys are tossed at a hazing, and above her red, fixed-smiling lips I saw the terror and disgust in her eyes, almost like my own terror and that which I saw in some of the other boys. As I watched, they tossed her twice and her soft breasts seemed to flatten against the air and her legs flung wildly as she spun. Some of the more sober ones helped her to escape. And I started off the floor, heading for the anteroom with the rest of the boys.

Some were still crying and in hysteria. But as we tried to leave we were stopped and ordered to get into the ring. There was nothing to do but what we were told. All ten of us climbed under the ropes and allowed ourselves to be blindfolded with broad bands of white cloth. One of the men seemed to feel a bit sympathetic and tried to cheer us up as we stood with our backs against the ropes. Some of us tried to grin. "See that boy over there?" one of the men said. "I want you to run across at the bell and give it to him right in the belly. If you don't get him, I'm going to get you. I don't like his looks." Each of us was told the same. The blindfolds were put on. Yet even then I had been going over my speech. In my mind each word was as bright as flame. I felt the cloth pressed into place, and frowned so that it would be loosened when I relaxed.

But now I felt a sudden fit of blind terror. I was unused to darkness. It was as though I had suddenly found myself in a dark room filled with poisonous cottonmouths. I could hear the bleary voices yelling insistently for the battle royal to begin.

"Get going in there!"

"Let me at that big nigger!"

I strained to pick up the school superintendent's voice, as though to squeeze some security out of that slightly more familiar sound.

"Let me at those black sonsabitches!" someone yelled.

"No, Jackson, no!" another voice yelled. "Here, somebody, help me hold Jack."

"I want to get at that ginger-colored nigger. Tear him limb from limb," the first voice yelled.

I stood against the ropes trembling. For in those days I was what they called ginger-colored, and he sounded as though he might crunch me between his teeth like a crisp ginger cookie.

Quite a struggle was going on. Chairs were being kicked about and I could hear voices grunting as with a terrific effort. I wanted to see, to see more desperately than ever before. But the blindfold was tight as a thick skin-puckering scab and when I raised my gloved hands to push the layers of white aside a voice yelled, "Oh, no you don't, black bastard! Leave that alone!"

"Ring the bell before Jackson kills him a coon!" someone boomed in the sudden silence. And I heard the bell clang and the sound of the feet scuffling forward.

A glove smacked against my head. I pivoted, striking out stiffly as someone went past, and felt the jar ripple along the length of my arm to my shoulder. Then it seemed as though all nine of the boys had turned upon me at once. Blows pounded me from all sides while I struck out as best I could. So many blows landed upon me that I wondered if I were not the only blindfolded fighter in the ring, or if the man called Jackson hadn't succeeded in getting me after all.

Blindfolded, I could no longer control my motions. I had no dignity. I stumbled about like a baby or a drunken man. The smoke had become thicker and with each new blow it seemed to sear and further restrict my lungs. My saliva became like hot bitter glue. A glove connected with my head, filling my mouth with warm blood. It was everywhere. I could not tell if the moisture I felt upon my body was sweat or blood. A blow landed hard against the nape of my neck. I felt myself going over, my head hitting the floor. Streaks of blue light filled the black world behind the blindfold. I lay prone, pretending that I was knocked out, but felt myself seized by hands and yanked to my feet. "Get going, black boy! Mix it up!" My arms were like lead, my head smarting from blows. I managed to feel my way to the ropes and held on, trying to catch my breath. A glove landed in my mid-section and I went over again, feeling as though the smoke had become a knife jabbed into my guts. Pushed this way and that by the legs milling around me, I finally pulled erect and discovered that I could see the black, sweat-washed forms weaving in the smoky-blue atmosphere like drunken dancers weaving to the rapid drum-like thuds of blows.

Everyone fought hysterically. It was complete anarchy. Everybody fought everybody else. No group fought together for long. Two, three, four, fought one, then turned to fight each other, were themselves attacked. Blows landed below the belt and in the kidney, with the gloves open as well as closed, and with my eye partly opened now there was not so much terror. I moved carefully, avoiding blows, although not too many to attract attention, fighting from group to group. The boys groped about like blind, cautious crabs crouching to protect their mid-sections, their heads pulled in short against their shoulders, their arms stretched nervously before them, with their fists testing the smoke-filled air like the knobbed feelers of hypersensitive snails. In one corner I glimpsed a boy violently punching the air and heard him scream in pain as he smashed his hand against a ring post. For a second I saw him bent over holding his hand, then going down as a blow caught his unprotected head. I played one group against the other, slipping in and throwing a punch then stepping out of range while pushing the others into the melee to take the blows blindly aimed at me. The smoke was agonizing and there were no rounds, no bells at three minute intervals to relieve our exhaustion. The room spun round me, a swirl of lights, smoke, sweating bodies surrounded by tense white faces. I bled from both nose and mouth, the blood spattering upon my chest.

The men kept yelling, "Slug him, black boy! Knock his guts out!"

"Uppercut him! Kill him! Kill that big boy!"

Taking a fake fall, I saw a boy going down heavily beside me as though we were felled by a single blow, saw a sneaker-clad foot shoot into his groin as the two who had knocked him down stumbled upon him. I rolled out of range, feeling a twinge of nausea.

The harder we fought the more threatening the men became. And yet, I had begun to worry about my speech again. How would it go? Would they recognize my ability? What would they give me?

I was fighting automatically when suddenly I noticed that one after another of the boys was leaving the ring. I was surprised, filled with panic, as though I had been left alone with an unknown danger. Then I understood. The boys had arranged it among themselves. It was the custom for the two men left in the ring to slug it out for the winner's place. I discovered this too late. When the bell sounded two men in tuxedos leaped into the ring and removed the blindfold. I found myself facing Tatlock, the biggest of the gang. I felt sick at my stomach. Hardly had the bell stopped ringing in my ears than it clanged again and I saw him moving swiftly toward me. Thinking of nothing else to do I hit him smash on the nose. He kept coming, bringing the rank sharp violence of stale sweat. His face was a black blank of a face, only his eyes alive—with hate of me and aglow with a feverish terror from what had happened to us all. I became anxious. I wanted to deliver my speech and he came at me as though he meant to beat it out of me. I smashed him again and again, taking his blows as they came. Then on a sudden impulse I struck him lightly and as we clinched, I whispered, "Fake like I knocked you out, you can have the prize."

"I'll break your behind," he whispered hoarsely.

"For *them*?"

"For *me*, sonofabitch!"

They were yelling for us to break it up and Tatlock spun me half around with a blow, and as a joggled camera sweeps in a reeling scene, I saw the howling red faces crouching tense beneath the cloud of blue-gray smoke. For a moment the world wavered, unraveled, flowed, then my head cleared and Tatlock bounced before me. That fluttering shadow before my eyes was his jabbing left hand. Then falling forward, my head against his damp shoulder, I whispered,

"I'll make it five dollars more."

"Go to hell!"

But his muscles relaxed a trifle beneath my pressure and I breathed, "Seven?"

"Give it to your ma," he said, ripping me beneath the heart.

And while I still held him I butted him and moved away. I felt myself bombarded with punches. I fought back with hopeless desperation. I wanted to deliver my speech more than anything else in the world, because I felt that only these men could judge truly my ability, and now this stupid clown was ruining my chances. I began fighting carefully now, moving in to punch him and out again with my greater speed. A lucky blow to his chin and I had him going too—until I heard a loud voice yell, "I got my money on the big boy."

Hearing this, I almost dropped my guard. I was confused: Should I try to win against the voice out there? Would not this go against my speech, and was not this a moment for humility, for nonresistance? A blow to my head as I danced about sent my right eye popping like a jack-in-the-box and settled my dilemma. The room went red as I fell. It was a dream fall, my body languid and fastidious as to where to land, until the floor became impatient and smashed up to meet me. A moment later I came to. A hypnotic voice said FIVE emphatically. And I lay there, hazily watching a dark red spot of my own blood shaping itself into a butterfly, glistening and soaking into the soiled gray world of the canvas.

When the voice drawled TEN I was lifted up and dragged to a chair. I sat dazed. My eye pained and swelled with each throb of my pounding heart and I wondered if now I would be allowed to speak. I was wringing wet, my mouth still bleeding. We were grouped along the wall now. The other boys ignored me as they congratulated Tatlock and speculated as to how much they would be paid. One boy whimpered over his smashed hand. Looking up front, I saw attendants in white jackets rolling the portable ring away and placing a small square rug in the vacant space surrounded by chairs. Perhaps, I thought, I will stand on the rug to deliver my speech.

Then the M.C. called us, "Come on up here boys and get your money."

We ran forward to where the men laughed and talked in their chairs, waiting. Everyone seemed friendly now.

"There it is on the rug," the man said. I saw the rug covered with coins of all dimensions and a few crumpled bills. But what excited me, scattered here and there, were the gold pieces.

"Boys, it's all yours," the man said. "You get all you grab."

"That's right, Sambo," a blond man said, winking at me confidentially.

I trembled with excitement, forgetting my pain. I would get the gold and the bills, I thought. I would use both hands. I would throw my body against the boys nearest me to block them from the gold.

"Get down around the rug now," the man commanded, "and don't anyone touch it until I give the signal."

"This ought to be good," I heard.

As told, we got around the square rug on our knees. Slowly the man raised his freckled hand as we followed it upward with our eyes.

I heard, "These niggers look like they're about to pray!"

Then, "Ready," the man said. "Go!"

I lunged for a yellow coin lying on the blue design of the carpet, touching it and sending a surprised shriek to join those rising around me. I tried frantically to remove my hand but could not let go. A hot, violent force tore through my body, shaking me like a wet rat. The rug was electrified. The hair bristled up on my head as I shook myself free. My muscles jumped, my nerves jangled, writhed. But I saw that this was not stopping the other boys. Laughing in fear and embarrassment, some were holding back and scooping up the coins knocked off by the painful contortions of the others. The men roared above us as we struggled.

"Pick it up, goddamnit, pick it up!" someone called like a bass-voiced parrot. "Go on, get it!"

I crawled rapidly around the floor, picking up the coins, trying to avoid the coppers and to get greenbacks and the gold. Ignoring the shock by laughing, as I brushed the coins off quickly, I discovered that I could contain the electricity—a contradiction, but it works. Then the men began to push us onto the rug. Laughing embarrassedly, we struggled out of their hands and kept after the coins. We were all wet and slippery and hard to hold. Suddenly I saw a boy lifted into the air, glistening with sweat like a circus seal, and dropped, his wet back landing flush upon the charged rug, heard him yell and saw him literally dance upon his back, his elbows beating a frenzied tattoo upon the floor, his muscles twitching like the flesh of a horse stung by many flies. When he finally rolled off, his face was gray and no one stopped him when he ran from the floor amid booming laughter.

"Get the money," the M.C. called. "That's good hard American cash!"

And we snatched and grabbed, snatched and grabbed. I was careful not to come too close to the rug now, and when I felt the hot whiskey breath descend upon me like a cloud of foul air I reached out and grabbed the leg of a chair. It was occupied and I held on desperately.

"Leggo, nigger! Leggo!"

The huge face wavered down to mine as he tried to push me free. But my body was slippery and he was too drunk. It was Mr. Colcord, who owned a chain of movie houses and "entertainment palaces." Each time he grabbed me I slipped out of his hands. It became a real struggle. I feared the rug more than I did the drunk, so I held on, surprising myself for a moment by trying to topple *him* upon the rug. It was such an enormous idea that I found myself actually carrying it out. I tried not to be obvious, yet when I grabbed his leg, trying to tumble him out of the chair, he raised up roaring with laughter, and, looking at me with soberness dead in the eye, kicked me viciously in the chest. The chair leg flew out of my hand and I felt myself going and rolled. It was as though I had rolled through a bed of hot coals. It seemed a whole century would pass before I would roll free, a century in which I was seared through the deepest levels of my body to the fearful breath within me and the breath seared and heated to the point of explosion. It'll all be over in a flash, I thought as I rolled clear. It'll all be over in a flash.

But not yet, the men on the other side were waiting, red faces swollen as though from apoplexy as they bent forward in their chairs. Seeing their fingers coming toward me I rolled away as a fumbled football rolls off the receiver's fingertips, back into the coals. That time I luckily sent the rug sliding out of place and heard the coins ringing against the floor and the boys scuffling to pick them up and the M.C. calling, "All right, boys, that's all. Go get dressed and get your money."

I was limp as a dish rag. My back felt as though it had been beaten with wires.

When we had dressed the M.C. came in and gave us each five dollars, except Tatlock, who got ten for being last in the ring. Then he told us to leave. I was not to get a chance to deliver my speech, I thought. I was going out into the dim alley in despair when I was stopped and told to go back. I returned to the ballroom, where the men were pushing back their chairs and gathering in groups to talk.

The M.C. knocked on a table for quiet. "Gentlemen," he said "we almost forgot an important part of the program. A most serious part, gentlemen. This boy was brought here to deliver a speech which he made at his graduation yesterday . . ."

"Bravo!"

"I'm told that he is the smartest boy we've got out there in Greenwood. I'm told that he knows more big words than a pocket-sized dictionary."

Much applause and laughter.

"So now, gentlemen, I want you to give him your attention."

There was still laughter as I faced them, my mouth dry, my eye throbbing. I began slowly, but evidently my throat was tense, because they began shouting, "Louder! Louder!"

"We of the younger generation extol the wisdom of that great leader and educator," I shouted, "who first spoke these flaming words of wisdom: 'A ship lost at sea for many days suddenly sighted a friendly vessel. From the mast of the unfortunate vessel was seen a signal: "Water, water; we die of thirst!" The answer from the friendly vessel came back: "Cast down your bucket where you are." The captain of the distressed vessel, at last heeding the injunction, cast down his bucket, and it came up full of fresh sparkling water from the mouth of the Amazon River.' And like him I say, and in his words, 'To those of my race who depend upon bettering their condition in a foreign land, or who underestimate the importance of cultivating friendly relations with the Southern white man, who is his next-door neighbor, I would say: "Cast down your bucket where you are"—cast it down in making friends in every manly way of the people of all races by whom we are surrounded . . .'"

I spoke automatically and with such fervor that I did not realize that the men were still talking and laughing until my dry mouth, filling up with blood from the cut, almost strangled me. I coughed, wanted to stop and go to one of the tall brass, sand-filled spittoons to relieve myself, but a few of the men, especially the superintendent, were listening and I was afraid. So I gulped it down, blood, saliva and all, and continued. (What powers of endurance I had during those days! What enthusiasm! What a belief in the rightness of things!) I spoke even louder in spite of the pain. But still they talked and still they laughed, as though deaf with cotton in dirty ears. So I spoke with greater emotional emphasis. I closed my ears and swallowed blood until I was nauseated. The speech seemed a hundred times as long as before, but I could not leave out a single word. All had to be said, each memorized nuance considered, rendered. Nor was that all. Whenever I uttered a word of three or more syllables a group of voices would yell for me to repeat it. I used the phrase "social responsibility" and they yelled:

"What's that word you say, boy?"

"Social responsibility," I said.

"What?"

"Social . . ."

"Louder."

". . . responsibility."

"More!"

"Respon—"

"Repeat!"

"—sibility."

The room filled with the uproar of laughter until, no doubt, distracted by having to gulp down my blood, I made a mistake and yelled a phrase I had often seen denounced in newspaper editorials, heard debated in private.

"Social . . . ."

"What?" they yelled.

". . . equality—'"

The laughter hung smokelike in the sudden stillness. I opened my eyes, puzzled. Sounds of displeasure filled the room. The M.C. rushed forward. They shouted hostile phrases at me. But I did not understand.

A small dry mustached man in the front row blared out, "Say that slowly, son!"

"What, sir?"

"What you just said!"

"Social responsibility, sir," I said.

"You weren't being smart, were you, boy?" he said, not unkindly.

"No, sir!"

"You sure that about 'equality' was a mistake?"

"Oh, yes, sir," I said. "I was swallowing blood."

"Well, you had better speak more slowly so we can understand. We mean to do right by you, but you've got to know your place at all times. All right, now, go on with your speech."

I was afraid. I wanted to leave but I wanted also to speak and I was afraid they'd snatch me down.

"Thank you, sir," I said, beginning where I had left off, and having them ignore me as before.

Yet when I finished there was a thunderous applause. I was surprised to see the superintendent come forth with a package wrapped in white tissue paper, and, gesturing for quiet, address the men.

"Gentlemen, you see that I did not overpraise this boy. He makes a good speech and some day he'll lead his people in the proper paths. And I don't have to tell you that this is important in these days and times. This is a good, smart boy, and so to encourage him in the right direction, in the name of the Board of Education I wish to present him a prize in the form of this . . ."

He paused, removing the tissue paper and revealing a gleaming calfskin brief case.

". . . in the form of this first-class article from Shad Witmore's shop."

"Boy," he said, addressing me, "take this prize and keep it well. Consider it a badge of office. Prize it. Keep developing as you are and some day it will be filled with important papers that will help shape the destiny of your people."

I was so moved that I could hardly express my thanks. A rope of bloody saliva forming a shape like an undiscovered continent drooled upon the leather and I wiped it quickly away. I felt an importance that I had never dreamed.

"Open it and see what's inside," I was told.

My fingers a-tremble, I complied, smelling the fresh leather and finding an official-looking document inside. It was a scholarship to the state college for Negroes. My eyes filled with tears and I ran awkwardly off the floor.

I was overjoyed; I did not even mind when I discovered that the gold pieces I had scrambled for were brass pocket tokens advertising a certain make of automobile.

When I reached home everyone was excited. Next day the neighbors came to congratulate me. I even felt safe from grandfather, whose deathbed curse usually spoiled my triumphs. I stood beneath his photograph with my brief case in hand and smiled triumphantly into his stolid black peasant's face. It was a face that fascinated me. The eyes seemed to follow everywhere I went.

That night I dreamed I was at a circus with him and that he refused to laugh at the clowns no matter what they did. Then later he told me to open my brief case and read what was inside and I did, finding an official envelope stamped with the state seal; and inside the envelope I found another and another, endlessly, and I thought I would fall of weariness. "Them's years," he said. "Now open that one." And I did and in it I found an engraved document containing a short message in letters of gold. "Read it," my grandfather said. "Out loud!"

"To Whom It May Concern," I intoned. "Keep This Nigger-Boy Running."

I awoke with the old man's laughter ringing in my ears.

(It was a dream I was to remember and dream again for many years after. But at that time I had no insight into its meaning. First I had to attend college.)

STUDY QUESTIONS

1. Why did the protagonist say that his grandfather's dying words "acted like a curse"?
2. Was the true function of the "battle royal" solely entertainment? Explain your answer.
3. What was implied in the way white males treated the naked blonde dancer? Was this at all comparable to the attitude toward blacks? In what ways?
4. The electrified rug was a metaphor for what?
5. Do you feel that the all-pervasive brutality in this story was exaggerated? If your answer was "yes" you might want to look much deeper into the history of race relations in this country and then examine your own attitude.

LITERARY SELECTION 102

The Bean Eaters

Gwendolyn Brooks, b. 1917

Brooks uses everyday language somewhat like Wordsworth, but her economic use of words and her vivid images mark her as one of the most effective of today's poets.

They eat beans mostly, this old yellow pair.
Dinner is a casual affair.
Plain chipware on a plain and creaking wood,
Tin flatware.

Two who are Mostly Good.
Two who have lived their day,
But keep on putting on their clothes
And putting things away.

And remembering . . .
Remembering, with twinklings and twinges,

As they lean over the beans in their rented back room that
is full of beads and receipts and dolls and cloths,
tobacco crumbs, vases and fringes.

STUDY QUESTIONS

1. What is this couple living on and why aren't their children helping them?
2. Are they living on something special in addition to food and money? What might that be?

We Real Cool

The Pool Players
Seven at the Golden Shovel

Gwendolyn Brooks

We real cool. We
Left school. We
Lurk late. We
Strike straight. We
Sing sin. We
Thin gin. We
Jazz June. We
Die soon.

LITERARY SELECTION 103

Adultery

James Dickey, b. 1923

Sex in all its manifestations is a basic theme in all literature. The following poem extols the mystery and excitement of an adulterous affair for, as Dickey has written, "adultery seems to me to be the most potentially beautiful and fruitful relationship between men and women, and also the most calamitous and destructive." He cites the "paradox in the relationship of men and women: the more used to each other they are, the less exciting they are to each other." He feels this is a terrible problem and things shouldn't be that way but, he concludes, "there *isn't* any justice in the world in that sense, and things *are* that way."

We have all been in rooms
We cannot die in, and they are odd places, and sad.
Often Indians are standing eagle-armed on hills

In the sunrise open wide to the Great Spirit
Or gliding in canoes or cattle are browsing on the walls
Far away gazing down with the eyes of our children

Not far away or there are men driving
The last railspike, which has turned
Gold in their hands. Gigantic forepleasure lives

Among such scenes, and we are alone with it
At last. There is always some weeping
Between us and someone is always checking

A wrist watch by the bed to see how much
Longer we have left. Nothing can come
Of this nothing can come

Of us: of me with my grim techniques
Or you who have sealed your womb
With a ring of convulsive rubber:

Although we come together,
Nothing will come of us. But we would not give
It up, for death is beaten

By praying Indians by distant cows historical
Hammers by hazardous meetings that bridge
A continent. One could never die here

Never die never die
While crying. My lover, my dear one
I will see you next week

When I'm in town. I will call you
If I can. Please get hold of please don't
Oh God. Please don't any more I can't bear . . . Listen:

We have done it again we are
Still living. Sit up and smile,
God bless you. Guilt is magical.

STUDY QUESTIONS

1. Describe a room "we cannot die in."
2. Why does the poet use images of Indians "gliding in canoes" and cattle "browsing on the walls"?
3. Dickey refers to a railspike that has "turned gold" and later speaks of "historical hammers" and of bridging a continent. What actual event does he have in mind and what does this imply in the poem? Is there a double meaning here?
4. What is meant by the phrase "guilt is magical"?

LITERARY SELECTION 104

Jews in the Land of Israel

Yehuda Amichai, b. 1924

Perhaps the best known contemporary Israeli poet, Amichai was born in Germany and emigrated to Israel in 1936. He has long struggled with the horrendous Jewish past and the problems of identity in what remains a strange and sunlit land. The translation here is by Assia Gutmann and Harold Schimmer.

We forget where we came from. Our Jewish
Names from the exile reveal us,
Bring up the memory of flower and fruit, medieval cities,
Metals, knights that became stone, roses mostly,
Spices whose smells dispersed, precious stones,
much red,
Trades gone from the world.
(The hands, gone too.)

The circumcision does it to us,
Like in the Bible story of Shechem and the sons
of Jacob,
With pain all our life.

What are we doing here on our return with this pain?
The longings dried up with the swampland,
The desert flowers for us and our children are lovely.
Even fragments of ships, that sunk on the way,
Reached this shore,
Even winds reached. Not all the sails.

What are we doing
In this dark land that casts
Yellow shadows, cutting at the eyes?
(Sometimes, one says even after forty
Years or fifty: "The sun is killing me.")

What are we doing with souls of mist, with the names,
With forest eyes, with our lovely children, with
swift blood?

Spilt blood isn't roots of trees,
But it's the closest to them
That man has.

LITERARY SELECTION 105

Two Songs

Adrienne Rich, b. 1929

In the following poem, reminiscent of the enthusiastic attitude of the ancient Greeks, Adrienne Rich speaks of lust that "too is a jewel."

1

Sex, as they harshly call it,
I fell into this morning
at ten o'clock, a drizzling hour
of traffic and wet newspapers.
I thought of him who yesterday
clearly didn't
turn me to a hot field
ready for plowing,
and longing for that young man
pierced me to the roots
bathing every vein, etc.
All day he appears to me
touchingly desirable,
a prize one could wreck one's peace for.
I'd call it love if love
didn't take so many years
but lust too is a jewel
a sweet flower and what
pure happiness to know
all our high-toned questions
breed in a lively animal.

2

That "old last act"!
And yet sometimes
all seems post coitum triste
and I a mere bystander.
Somebody else is going off,
getting shot to the moon.
Or, a moon-race!
Split seconds after
my opposite number lands
I make it—
we lie fainting together
at a crater-edge
heavy as mercury in our moonsuits
till he speaks—
in a different language
yet one I've picked up
through cultural exchanges . . .
we murmur the first moonwords:
Spasibo. Thanks. O.K.

STUDY QUESTIONS

1. Why does the poet use the phrase "as they harshly call it"?
2. Discuss the images evoked by "a drizzling hour of traffic and wet newspapers."
3. Why does line 11 end with "etc."?
4. Describe the distinction made between love and lust.
5. What are "moonwords"? Are there several levels of meaning?

LITERARY SELECTION 106

House Made of Dawn

Flight on the Wind

N. Scott Momaday, b. 1934

In *House Made of Dawn* (1969 Pulitzer Prize), young Abel returns to tribal life, wondering if he can resume the ancient ways after living like an Anglo in the Army. The seemingly endless conflict of Anglo and tribal customs is symbolized by the excerpt given below in which the captured, shivering eagle represents a Native American view of life in America.

He had seen a strange thing, an eagle overhead with its talons closed upon a snake. It was an awful, holy sight, full of magic and meaning.

The Eagle Watchers Society was the sixth to go into the kiva at the summer and autumn rain retreats. It was an important society, and it stood apart from the others in a certain way. This difference—this superiority—had come about a long time ago. Before the middle of the last century there was received into the population of the town a small group of immigrants from the Tanoan city of Bahkyula, a distance of seventy or eighty miles to the east. These immigrants were a wretched people, for they had experienced great suffering. Their land bordered upon the Southern Plains, and for many years they had been an easy mark for marauding bands of buffalo hunters and thieves. They had endured every kind of persecution until one day they could stand no more and their spirit broke. They gave themselves up to despair and were then at the mercy of the first alien wind. But it was not a human enemy that overcame them at last; it was a plague. They were struck down by so deadly a disease that, when the epidemic abated, there were fewer than twenty survivors in all. And this remainder, too, should surely have perished among the ruins of Bahkyula had it not been for these *patrones,* these distant relatives who took them in at the certain risk of their own lives and the lives of their children and grandchildren. It is said that the cacique himself went out to welcome and escort the visitors in. The people of the town must have looked narrowly at those stricken souls who walked slowly towards them, wild in their eyes with grief and desperation. The Bahkyush immigrants brought with them little more than the clothes on their backs, but even in this moment of deep hurt and humiliation, they thought of themselves as a people. They carried three things that should serve thereafter to signal who they were: a sacred flute; the bull mask of Pecos; and the little wooden statue of their patroness *Maria de los Angeles,* whom they called Porcingula. Now, after the intervening years and generations, the ancient blood of this forgotten tribe still ran in the veins of men.

The Eagle Watchers Society was the principal ceremonial organization of the Bahkyush. Its chief, Patiestewa, and all its members were direct descendants of those old men and women who had made that journey along the edge of oblivion. There was a look about these men, even now. It was as if, conscious of having come so close to extinction, they had got a keener sense of humility than their benefactors, and paradoxically a greater sense of pride. Both attributes could be seen in such a man as old Patiestewa. He was hard, and he appeared to have seen more of life than had other men. In their uttermost peril long ago, the Bahkyush had been fashioned into seers and soothsayers. They had acquired a tragic sense, which gave to them as a race so much dignity and bearing. They were medicine men; they were rainmakers and eagle hunters.

He was not thinking of the eagles. He had been walking since daybreak down from the mountain where that year he had broken a horse for the rancher John Raymond. By the middle of the morning he was on the rim of the Valle Grande, a great volcanic crater that lay high up on the western slope of the range. It was the right eye of the earth, held open to the sun. Of all the places that he knew, this valley alone could reflect the great spatial majesty of the sky. It was scooped out of the dark peaks like the well of a great, gathering storm, deep umber and blue and smoke-colored. The view across the diameter was magnificent; it was an unbelievably great expanse. As many times as he had been there in the past, each first new sight of it always brought him up short, and he had to catch his breath. Just there, it seemed, a strange and brilliant light lay upon the world, and all the objects in the landscape were washed clean and set away in the distance. In the morning sunlight the Valle Grande was dappled with the shadows of clouds and vibrant with rolling winter grass. The clouds were always there, huge, sharply described, and shining in the pure air. But the great feature of the valley was its size. It was too great for the eye to hold, strangely beautiful and full of distance. Such vastness makes for illusion, a kind of illusion that comprehends reality, and where it exists there is always wonder and exhilaration. He looked at the facets of a boulder that lay balanced on the edge of the land, and the first thing beyond, the vague, misty field out of which it stood, was the floor of the valley itself, pale and blue-green, miles away. He shifted the focus of his gaze, and he could just make out the clusters of dots that were cattle grazing along the river in the faraway plain.

Then he saw the eagles across the distance, two of them, riding low in the depths and rising diagonally towards him. He did not know what they were at first, and he stood watching them, their far, silent flight erratic and wild in the bright morning. They rose and swung across the skyline, veering close at last, and he knelt down behind the rock, dumb with pleasure and excitement, holding on to them with his eyes.

They were golden eagles, a male and a female, in their mating flight. They were cavorting, spinning and spiralling on the cold, clear columns of air, and they were beautiful. They swooped and hovered, leaning on the air, and swung close together, feinting and screaming with delight. The female was full-grown, and the span of her broad wings was greater than any man's height. There was a fine flourish to her motion: she was deceptively, incredibly fast, and her pivots and wheels were wide and full-blown. But her great weight was streamlined, perfectly controlled. She carried a rattlesnake; it hung shining from her feet, limp and curving out in the trail of her flight. Suddenly her wings and tail fanned, catching full on the wind, and for an instant she was still, widespread and spectral in the blue, while her mate flared past and away, turning round in the distance to look for her. Then she began to beat upward at an angle from the rim until she was small in the sky, and she let go of the snake. It fell, slowly, writhing and rolling, floating out like a bit of silver thread against the wide backdrop of the land. She held still above, buoyed up on the cold current, her crop and hackles gleaming like copper in the sun. The male swerved and sailed. He was younger than she and a little more than half as large. He was quicker, tighter in his moves. He let the carrion drift by; then suddenly he gathered himself and stooped, sliding down in a blur of motion to the strike. He hit the snake in the head, with not the slightest deflection of his course or speed, cracking its long body like a whip. Then he rolled and swung upward in a great pendulum arc, riding out his momentum. At the top of his glide he let go of the snake in turn, but the female did not go for it. Instead she soared out over the plain, nearly out of sight, like a mote receding into the haze of the far mountain. The male followed, and he watched them go, straining to see, saw them veer once, dip and disappear.

Now there was the business of the society. It was getting on towards the end of November, and the eagle hunters were getting ready to set forth to the mountains. He brooded for a time, full of a strange longing; then one day he went to old Patiestewa and told him of what he had seen. "I think you had better let me go," he said. The old chief closed his eyes and thought about it for a long time. Then he answered: "Yes, I had better let you go."

The next day the Bahkyush eagle watchers started out on foot, he among them, northward through the canyon and into the high timber beyond. They were gone for days, holding up here and there at the holy places where they must pray and make their offerings. Early in the morning they came out of the trees on the edge of the Valle Grande. The land fell and reached away in the early light as far as the eye could see, the hills folding together and the gray grass rolling in the plain, and they began the descent. At midmorning they came to the lower meadows in the basin. It was clear and cold, and the air was thin and sharp like a shard of glass. They needed bait, and they circled out and apart, forming a ring. When the circle was formed, they converged slowly towards the center, clapping and calling out in a high, flat voice that carried only a little way. And as they closed, rabbits began to jump up from the grass and bound. They got away at first, many of them, while the men were still a distance apart, but gradually the ring grew small and the rabbits crept to the center and hid away in the brush. Now and then one of them tried to break away, and the nearest man threw his stick after it. These weapons were small curved clubs, and they were thrown with deadly accuracy by the eagle hunters, so that when the ring was of a certain size and the men only a few feet apart, very few of the animals got away.

He bent close to the ground, his arm cocked and shaking with tension. A great jackrabbit buck bounded from the grass, straight past him. It struck the ground beyond and sprang again, nearly thirty feet through the air. He spun round and hurled the stick. It struck the jackrabbit a glancing blow just as it bounded again, and it slumped in the air and fell heavily to the ground.

The clapping and calling had stopped. He could feel his heart beating and the sweat growing cold on his skin. There was something like remorse or disappointment now that the rabbits were still and strewn about on the ground. He picked one of the dead animals from the brush—it was warm and soft, its eyes shining like porcelain, full of the dull lustre of death—then the great buck, which was not dead but only stunned and frozen with fear. He felt the warm living weight of it in his hands; it was brittle with life, taut with hard, sinewy strength.

When he had bound the bait together and placed it in the sack, he gathered bunches of tall grass and cut a number of evergreen boughs from a thicket in the plain; these he tied in a bundle and carried in a sling on his back. He went to the river and washed his head in order to purify himself. When all was ready, he waved to the others and started off alone to the cliffs. When he came to the first plateau he rested and looked across the valley. The sun was high, and all around there was a pale, dry uniformity of light, a winter glare on the clouds and peaks. He could see a crow circling low in the distance. Higher on the land, where a great slab of white rock protruded from the mountain, he saw the eagle-hunt house; he headed for it. The house was a small tower of stone, built round a pit, hollow and open at the top. Near it was a shrine, a stone shelf in which there was a slight depression. There he placed a prayer offering. He got into the house, and with boughs he made a latticework of beams across the top and covered it with grass. When it was finished there was a small opening at the center. Through it he raised the rabbits and laid them down on the boughs. He could see here and there through the screen, but his line of vision was vertical, or nearly so, and his quarry would come from the sun. He began to sing, now and then calling out, low in his throat.

The eagles soared southward, high above the Valle Grande. They were almost too high to be seen. From their vantage point the land below reached away on either side to the long, crooked tributaries of the range; down the great open corridor to the south were the wooded slopes and the canyon, the desert and the far end of the earth bending on the sky. They caught sight of the rabbits and were deflected. They veered and banked, lowering themselves into the crater, gathering speed. By the time he knew of their presence, they were low and coming fast on either side of the pit, swooping with blinding speed. The male caught hold of the air and fell off, touching upon the face of the cliff in order to flush the rabbits, while the female hurtled in to take her prey on the run. Nothing happened; the rabbits did not move. She overshot the trap and screamed. She was enraged and she hurled herself around in the air. She swung back with a great clamor of her wings and fell with fury on the bait. He saw her the instant she struck. Her foot flashed out and one of her talons laid the jackrabbit open the length of its body. It stiffened and jerked, and her other foot took hold of its skull and crushed it. In that split second when the center of her weight touched down upon the trap he reached for her. His hands closed upon her legs and he drew her down with all of his strength. For one instant only did she recoil, splashing her great wings down upon the beams and boughs—and she very nearly broke from his grasp; but then she was down in the darkness of the well, hooded, and she was still.

At dusk he met with the other hunters in the plain. San Juanito, too, had got an eagle, but it was an aged male and poor by comparison. They gathered round the old eagle and spoke to it, bidding it return with their good will and sorrow to the eagles of the crags. They fixed a prayer plume to its leg and let it go. He watched it back away and crouch on the ground, glaring, full of fear and suspicion. Then it took leave of the ground and beat upward, clattering through the still shadows of the valley. It gathered speed, driving higher and higher until it reached the shafts of reddish-gold final light that lay like bars across the crater. The light caught it up and set a dark blaze upon it. It levelled off and sailed. Then it was gone from sight, but he looked after it for a time. He could see it still in the mind's eye and hear in his memory the awful whisper of its flight on the wind. He felt the great weight of the bird which he held in the sack. The dusk was fading quickly into night, and the others could not see that his eyes were filled with tears.

That night, while the others ate by the fire, he stole away to look at the great bird. He drew the sack open; the bird shivered, he thought, and drew itself up. Bound and helpless, his eagle seemed drab and shapeless in the moonlight, too large and ungainly for flight. The sight of it filled him with shame and disgust. He took hold of its throat in the darkness and cut off its breath.

STUDY QUESTIONS

1. What is symbolized by the image of an eagle holding a snake?
2. Consider the first full paragraph. Could this be a capsule history of what happened to Native Americans?
3. What kinds of feelings are invoked by the descriptions of the land? Can cities be described in this general manner?
4. Consider the mating flight of the two eagles and what this symbolizes.
5. Why was the old eagle freed? Why was the female killed?

LITERARY SELECTION 107

Night of My Blood

Kofi Awoonor, b. 1935

Considered one of the finest English-language poets in Africa, Awoonor was educated in Ghana, England, and the United States. He taught at several American universities and at Ghana's University of Gold Coast before being appointed Ghana's ambassador to Brazil. His poetry draws on the structure and images of traditional African oral verse.

Did they whisper to us the miracle of time
Telling us over the dark waters
Where we came from? Did they
Call us unto themselves
With the story of time and beginning?
We sat in the shadow of our ancient trees
While the waters of the land washed
Washed against our hearts,
Cleansing, cleansing.
The purifier sat among us
In sackcloth and ashes,
Bearing on himself the burdens
of these people. He touched our
foreheads with the wine of sour corn
and sprinkled our feet
with the blood of the sacred ram
Whilst the baobab rained dew on our heads.
Comforter, where is your comforting?
With all our woes and our sins,
We walked from the beginning
towards the land of sunset.
We were a band of malefactors
and saints.
The purifier walked in our shadow
bearing the fly-whisk of his ancestors
for his task is not finished.
We stumbled through the briar bush
Consoling us, moved against the
passion of rest forever.
The touchstone of our journey
was the silent prayers of the purifier.
Then they asked whether the harvest
should be gathered. Who sowed the crops?
We do not know; the harvesters
We know them,
Them that howl at night in the lanes
returning every night from funerals
officiating at a million wakes.
Comforter, where is your comfort?
Gather us, gather us unto yourselves our fathers
Though we may bear the terror of this journey.
Through the briar we stumble
bearing the million crucifixes of time.
Save us the terror of our burden
Cleanse us,
The desert trees howl with wind blows
for the waters had washed
The sand which tossed in eyes
that opened wide in night's darkness
and there was no light
save the silent prayers of the purifier
As we bore the million crosses
across the vastness of time.
Then they appeared, the owners of the land
Among them were the silent lovers
of night's long harmattans;[8] questioners
at the fathers' weary court.
The girls bearing the flowers of the desert
Cinnamon and smeared with yellow pollen of the palm
Swaying through the earth beaten path fingers
pointed
singing songs we could not hear,
Tearing down the glories of a thousand shrines
and dancing.

8. Dry, dusty winds that blow from the Sahara.

Muddying the paved paths of the fathers
anointed, and the offering
they bore on the wooden plates
eyes glued on the offering plates
asking for the glory of the fathers' rebirth,
Their penance-prayer voicing
unto the fathers
Not asking for forgiveness.
We sat among the thistles of the desert
chewing the cactus freshened
by the tear-drops of long-ago.
Revelling howlers in time's garden
entering the forbidden grounds
stirring us from that sleep of time,
the bearers' head turned to sunset
trampling through desert sand
sang a song we could not
hear the music of.
It was the season of dry wind.
We are the sons of the land
hearing the terror of this journey
carrying the million crucifixes of time
Then we arrived by the river Mono.[9]
There we planted our bean plants
not to wait for the season of rain
We then were the harvesters
As we filled our barns
With the crops of the land
the strange land that gave us food to eat.
We opened wide our hearts
washed by the desert wind
for cleansing in the sacred river.
Our dreams were of a homeland
forever;
of a happier world.

Then we moved one day at dawn
carrying with us the remnants
of the feast of the passover
stumbling through dusk dawn faded
daylight making for the forests of the south.
We marched through marsh and marsh
retrieving acres of white sand
inhabitants sea-crabs and the
nocturnal wail of the bull frog.
One day at noon[10] we arrived;
my people, we arrived.
The shiny shingles washed white
glistening like the sacred ram
sacrifice awaiting; the dart of surf thrusts
into the sides of the glistening ram
The drums beat that day and many days
and still beat for the deliverance
from the terror of the burden of that journey.

STUDY QUESTIONS

1. How is the narrator's initiation or induction described?
2. How is the community experience reenacted?
3. Describe the obstacles that the narrator must overcome to achieve knowledge.

LITERARY SELECTION 108

A Sorrowful Woman

Gail Godwin, b. 1937

The following short story is a study of the gradual disintegration of a human personality. In keeping with the "once upon a time" lead, the style is similar to a fairy tale but no one lives "happily ever after." The reader should consider the monotonously repetitive tasks taken over by the husband and later shared with the live-in girl, and compare these with the various responsibilities of men in their jobs at the office or wherever. Then, decide how all of this relates to the final "legacy" of food, laundry, and, most importantly, sonnets.

Once upon a time there was a wife and mother one too many times.

One winter evening she looked at them: the husband durable, receptive, gentle; the child a tender golden three. The sight of them made her so sad and sick she did not want to see them ever again.

She told the husband these thoughts. He was attuned to her; he understood such things. He said he understood. What would she like him to do? "If you could put the boy to bed and read him the story about the monkey who ate too many bananas, I would be grateful." "Of course," he said. "Why, that's a pleasure." And he sent her off to bed.

The next night it happened again. Putting the warm dishes away in the cupboard, she turned and saw the child's gray eyes approving her movements. In the next room was the man, his chin sunk in the open collar of his favorite wool shirt. He was dozing after her good supper. The shirt was the gray of the child's trusting gaze. She began yelping without tears, retching in between. The man woke in alarm and carried her in his arms to bed. The boy followed them up the stairs, saying, "It's all right, Mommy," but this made her scream. "Mommy is sick," the father said, "go and wait for me in your room."

The husband undressed her, abandoning her only long enough to root beneath the eiderdown for her flannel

9. The Mono River in Dahomey marks an important state in the migratory journeys of the Ewes to their present homes from the upper regions of the Niger River. As a people the Ewes cover the territory that stretched from the Volta River in Ghana to the Mono in Dahomey.

10. This refers to the arrival of the Togbui Wenya and Anlo wings of Ewes at their present home on the sea coast in the southeastern corner of Ghana. This all occurred, possibly, during the thirteenth century, but maybe earlier.

gown. She stood naked except for her bra, which hung by one strap down the side of her body; she had not the impetus to shrug it off. She looked down at the right nipple, shriveled with chill, and thought, How absurd, a vertical bra. "If only there were instant sleep," she said, hiccuping, and the husband bundled her into the gown and went out and came back with a sleeping draught guaranteed swift. She was to drink a little glass of cognac followed by a big glass of dark liquid and afterwards there was just time to say Thank you and could you get him a clean pair of pajamas out of the laundry, it came back today.

The next day was Sunday and the husband brought her breakfast in bed and let her sleep until it grew dark again. He took the child for a walk, and when they returned, red-cheeked and boisterous, the father made supper. She heard them laughing in the kitchen. He brought her up a tray of buttered toast, celery sticks and black bean soup. "I am the luckiest woman," she said, crying real tears. "Nonsense," he said. "You need a rest from us," and went to prepare the sleeping draught, find the child's pajamas, select the story for the night.

She got up on Monday and moved about the house till noon. The boy, delighted to have her back, pretended he was a vicious tiger and followed her from room to room, growling and scratching. Whenever she came close, he would growl and scratch at her. One of his sharp little claws ripped her flesh, just above the wrist, and together they paused to watch a thin red line materialize on the inside of her pale arm and spill over in little beads. "Go away," she said. She got herself upstairs and locked the door. She called the husband's office and said, "I've locked myself away from him. I'm afraid." The husband told her in his richest voice to lie down, take it easy, and he was already on the phone to call one of the baby-sitters they often employed. Shortly after, she heard the girl let herself in, heard the girl coaxing the frightened child to come and play.

After supper several nights later, she hit the child. She had known she was going to do it when the father would see. "I'm sorry," she said, collapsing on the floor. The weeping child had run to hide. "What has happened to me, I'm not myself anymore." The man picked her tenderly from the floor and looked at her with much concern. "Would it help if we got, you know, a girl in? We could fix the room downstairs. I want you to feel freer," he said, understanding these things. "We have the money for a girl. I want you to think about it."

And now the sleeping draught was a nightly thing, she did not have to ask. He went down to the kitchen to mix it, he set it nightly beside her bed. The little glass and the big one, amber and deep rich brown, the flannel gown and the eiderdown.

The man put out the word and found the perfect girl. She was young, dynamic and not pretty. "Don't bother with the room, I'll fix it up myself." Laughing, she employed her thousand energies. She painted the room white, fed the child lunch, read edifying books, raced the boy to the mailbox, hung her own watercolors on the fresh-painted walls, made spinach soufflé, cleaned a spot from the mother's coat, made them all laugh, danced in stocking feet to music in the white room after reading the child to sleep. She knitted dresses for herself and played chess with the husband. She washed and set the mother's soft ash-blonde hair and gave her neck rubs, offered to.

The woman now spent her winter afternoons in the big bedroom. She made a fire in the hearth and put on slacks and an old sweater she had loved at school, and sat in the big chair and stared out the window at snow-ridden branches, or went away into long novels about other people moving through other winters.

The girl brought the child in twice a day, once in the later afternoon when he would tell of his day, all of it tumbling out quickly because there was not much time, and before he went to bed. Often now, the man took his wife to dinner. He made a courtship ceremony of it, inviting her beforehand so she could get used to the idea. They dressed and were beautiful together again and went out into the frosty night. Over candlelight he would say, "I think you are better, you know." "Perhaps I am," she would murmur. "You look . . . like a cloistered queen," he said once, his voice breaking curiously.

One afternoon the girl brought the child into the bedroom. "We've been out playing in the park. He found something he wants to give you, a surprise." The little boy approached her, smiling mysteriously. He placed his cupped hands in hers and left a live dry thing that spat brown juice in her palm and leapt away. She screamed and wrung her hands to be rid of the brown juice. "Oh, it was only a grasshopper," said the girl. Nimbly she crept to the edge of a curtain, did a quick knee bend and reclaimed the creature, led the boy competently from the room.

So the husband came alone. "I have explained to the boy," he said. "And we are doing fine. We are managing." He squeezed his wife's pale arm and put the two glasses on her table. After he had gone, she sat looking at the arm.

"I'm afraid it's come to that," she said. "Just push the notes under the door; I'll read them. And don't forget to leave the draught outside."

The man sat for a long time with his head in his hands. Then he rose and went away from her. She heard him in the kitchen where he mixed the draught in batches now to last a week at a time, storing it in a corner of the cupboard. She heard him come back, leave the big glass and the little one outside on the floor.

Outside her window the snow was melting from the branches, there were more people on the streets. She brushed her hair a lot and seldom read anymore. She sat in her window and brushed her hair for hours, and saw a boy fall off his new bicycle again and again, a dog chasing a squirrel, an old woman peek slyly over her shoulder and then extract a parcel from a garbage can.

In the evening she read the notes they slipped under her door. The child could not write, so he drew and sometimes painted his. The notes were painstaking at first; the man and boy offering the final strength of their day to her. But sometimes, when they seemed to have had a bad day, there were only hurried scrawls.

One night, when the husband's note had been extremely short, loving but short, and there had been nothing from the boy, she stole out of her room as she often did to get more supplies, but crept upstairs instead and stood outside their doors, listening to the regular breathing of the man and boy asleep. She hurried back to her room and drank the draught.

She woke earlier now. It was spring, there were birds. She listened for sounds of the man and the boy eating breakfast; she listened for the roar of the motor when they drove away. One beautiful noon, she went out to look at her kitchen in the daylight. Things were changed. He had bought some new dish towels. Had the old ones worn out? The canisters seemed closer to the sink. She inspected the cupboard and saw new things among the old. She got out flour, baking powder, salt, milk (he bought a different brand of butter), and baked a loaf of bread and left it cooling on the table.

The force of the two joyful notes slipped under her door that evening pressed her into the corner of the little room; she had hardly space to breathe. As soon as possible, she drank the draught.

Now the days were too short. She was always busy. She woke with the first bird. Worked till the sun set. No time for hair brushing. Her fingers raced the hours.

Finally, in the nick of time, it was finished one late afternoon. Her veins pumped and her forehead sparkled. She went to the cupboard, took what was hers, closed herself into the little white room and brushed her hair for a while.

"The girl upsets me," said the woman to her husband. He sat frowning on the side of the bed he had not entered for so long. "I'm sorry, but there it is." The husband stroked his creased brow and said he was sorry too. He really did not know what they would do without that treasure of a girl. "Why don't you stay here with me in bed," the woman said.

Next morning she fired the girl who cried and said, "I loved the little boy, what will become of him now?" But the mother turned away her face and the girl took down the watercolors from the walls, sheathed the records she had danced to and went away.

"I don't know what we'll do. It's all my fault, I know. I'm such a burden, I know that."

"Let me think. I'll think of something." (Still understanding these things.)

"I know you will. You always do," she said.

With great care he rearranged his life. He got up hours early, did the shopping, cooked the breakfast, took the boy to nursery school. "We will manage," he said, "until you're better, however long that is." He did his work, collected the boy from the school, came home and made the supper, washed the dishes, got the child to bed. He managed everything. One evening, just as she was on the verge of swallowing her draught, there was a timid knock on her door. The little boy came in wearing his pajamas. "Daddy has fallen asleep on my bed and I can't get in. There's not room."

Very sedately she left her bed and went to the child's room. Things were much changed. Books were rearranged, toys. He'd done some new drawings. She came as a visitor to her son's room, wakened the father and helped him to bed. "Ah, he shouldn't have bothered you," said the man, leaning on his wife. "I've told him not to." He dropped into his own bed and fell asleep with a moan. Meticulously she undressed him. She folded and hung his clothes. She covered his body with the bedclothes. She flicked off the light that shone in his face.

The next day she moved her things into the girl's white room. She put her hairbrush on the dresser; she put a note pad and pen beside the bed. She stocked the little room with cigarettes, books, bread and cheese. She didn't need much.

At first the husband was dismayed. But he was receptive to her needs. He understood these things. "Perhaps the best thing is for you to follow it through," he said. "I want to be big enough to contain whatever you must do."

All day long she stayed in the white room. She was a young queen, a virgin in a tower; she was the previous inhabitant, the girl with all the energies. She tried these personalities on like costumes, then discarded them. The room had a new view of streets she'd never seen that way before. The sun hit the room in late afternoon and she took to brushing her hair in the sun. One day she decided to write a poem. "Perhaps a sonnet." She took up her pen and pad and began working from words that had lately lain in her mind. She had choices for the sonnet, ABAB or ABBA for a start. She pondered these possibilities until she tottered into a larger choice: she did not have to write a sonnet. Her poem could be six, eight, ten, thirteen lines, it could be any number of lines, and it did not even have to rhyme.

She put down the pen on top of the pad.

In the evenings, very briefly, she saw the two of them. They knocked on her door, a big knock and a little, and she would call Come in, and the husband would smile though he looked a bit tired, yet somehow this tiredness suited him. He would put her sleeping draught on the bedside table and say, "The boy and I have done all right today," and the child would kiss her. One night she tasted for the first time the power of his baby spit.

"I don't think I can see him anymore," she whispered sadly to the man. And the husband turned away, but recovered admirably and said, "Of course, I see."

The man and boy came home and found: five loaves of warm bread, a roast stuffed turkey, a glazed ham, three pies of different fillings, eight molds of the boy's favorite custard, two weeks' supply of fresh-laundered sheets and shirts and towels, two hand-knitted sweaters (both of the same gray color), a sheath of marvelous watercolor beasts accompanied by mad and fanciful stories nobody could ever make up again, and a tablet full of love sonnets addressed to the man. The house smelled redolently of renewal and spring. The man ran to the little room, could not contain himself to knock, flung back the door.

"Look, Mommy is sleeping," said the boy. "She's tired from doing all our things again." He dawdled in a stream of the last sun for that day and watched his father roll tenderly back her eyelids, lay his ear softly to her breast, test the delicate bones of her wrist. The father put down his face into her fresh-washed hair.

"Can we eat the turkey for supper?" the boy asked.

STUDY QUESTIONS

1. Itemize the steps in the "abnormal" behavior of the wife from the opening paragraph on. Does this progression appear to be inevitable? What might the husband have done to stop this deterioration?
2. Consider the husband's solution of a live-in girl. What does this tell us about the husband and about his attitude toward his wife?
3. What is the significance of each of the gifts that the wife left for her son and her husband?
4. Why was it necessary for the child to be a boy? Why not a girl? Consider the implications of the final sentence.

LITERARY SELECTION 109

Catch-22

Chapter 39 The Eternal City

Joseph Heller, b. 1923

Before starting this excerpt the reader should review the discussion of *Catch-22* given earlier in this chapter.

By the end of chapter 38, Nately, one of Yossarian's companions, has been killed, and Nately's girlfriend, named only "Nately's whore," is pursuing Yossarian relentlessly in an effort to kill him. (Can she represent the Furies?) Yossarian has simply refused to fly any more missions, but for various reasons he cannot be court-martialed. His commanding officers simply do not know what to do with him. If he can get away with it, the other men will refuse to fly, too.

Chapter 39 is written in a surrealistic style with the added ironies of black humor: the M.P.s do not arrest Aarfy, the super-conformist, although he has just raped and killed a woman; when Yossarian is returned to the airbase he discovers that his commanding officers have decided to send him home.

This chapter, however, represents much more than technique in writing. The title has a double meaning. Rome has always been called "the eternal city," but in this chapter it seems to represent Hell on earth, its eternity a bitter comment on life in general. The events within the chapter deal with a descent into the underworld in the classic pattern of Virgil's and Dante's descent. Another interesting parallel can be drawn. Milo Minderbinder, who represents the profit motive in society, can here be compared to Mephistopheles in Goethe's *Faust*. As Faust makes his journey into the classical underworld he is accompanied by Mephistopheles until they encounter the "evil Phorkyads." At that point Mephistopheles deserts Faust exactly as Milo deserts Yossarian to pursue his profits.

After the journey to Rome, the scene starts in the comparative innocence of the brothel, now destroyed by the military police, and continues through the depths of human misery and cruelty, finally ending at the apartment reserved for officers-on-leave, and ends with the return to the airbase.

Yossarian was going absent without official leave with Milo, who, as the plane cruised toward Rome, shook his head reproachfully and, with pious lips pursed, informed Yossarian in ecclesiastical tones that he was ashamed of him. Yossarian nodded. Yossarian was making an uncouth spectacle of himself by walking around backward with his gun on his hip and refusing to fly more combat missions, Milo said. Yossarian nodded. It was disloyal to his squadron and embarrassing to his superiors. He was placing Milo in a very uncomfortable position, too. Yossarian nodded again. The men were starting to grumble. It was not fair for Yossarian to think only of his own safety while men like Milo, Colonel Cathcart, Colonel Korn and ex-P.F.C. Wintergreen were willing to do everything they could to win the war. The men with seventy missions were starting to grumble because they had to fly eighty, and there was a danger some of them might put on guns and begin walking around backward, too. Morale was deteriorating and it was all Yossarian's fault. The country was in peril; he was jeopardizing his traditional rights of freedom and independence by daring to exercise them.

Yossarian kept nodding in the co-pilot's seat and tried not to listen as Milo prattled on. Nately's whore was on his mind, as were Kraft and Orr and Nately and Dunbar, and Kid Sampson and McWatt, and all the poor and stupid and diseased people he had seen in Italy, Egypt and North Africa and knew about in other areas of the world, and Snowden and Nately's whore's kid sister were on his conscience, too. Yossarian thought he knew why Nately's whore held him responsible for Nately's death and wanted to kill him. Why the hell shouldn't she? It was a man's world, and she and everyone younger had every right to blame him and everyone older for every unnatural tragedy that befell them; just as she, even in her grief, was to blame for every man-made misery that landed on her kid sister and on all other children behind her. Someone had to do something sometime. Every victim was a culprit, every culprit a victim, and somebody had to stand up sometime to try to break the lousy chain of inherited habit that was imperiling them all. In parts of Africa little boys were still stolen away by adult slave traders and sold for money to men who disemboweled them and ate them. Yossarian marveled that children could suffer such barbaric sacrifice without evincing the slightest hint of fear or pain. He took it for granted that they did submit so stoically. If not, he reasoned, the custom would certainly have died, for no craving for wealth or immortality could be so great, he felt, as to subsist on the sorrow of children.

He was rocking the boat, Milo said, and Yossarian nodded once more. He was not a good member of the team, Milo said. Yossarian nodded and listened to Milo tell him that the decent thing to do if he did not like the way Colonel Cathcart and Colonel Korn were running the group was go to Russia, instead of stirring up trouble.

Yossarian refrained from pointing out that Colonel Cathcart, Colonel Korn and Milo could all go to Russia if they did not like the way he was stirring up trouble. Colonel Cathcart and Colonel Korn had both been very good to Yossarian, Milo said; hadn't they given him a medal after the last mission to Ferrara and promoted him to captain? Yossarian nodded. Didn't they feed him and give him his pay every month? Yossarian nodded again. Milo was sure they would be charitable if he went to them to apologize and recant and promised to fly eighty missions. Yossarian said he would think it over, and held his breath and prayed for a safe landing as Milo dropped his wheels and glided in toward the runway. It was funny how he had really come to detest flying.

Rome was in ruins, he saw, when the plane was down. The airdrome had been bombed eight months before, and knobby slabs of white stone rubble had been bulldozed into flat-topped heaps on both sides of the entrance through the wire fence surrounding the field. The Colosseum was a dilapidated shell, and the Arch of Constantine had fallen. Nately's whore's apartment was a shambles. The girls were gone, and the only one there was the old woman. The windows in the apartment had been smashed. She was bundled up in sweaters and skirts and wore a dark shawl about her head. She sat on a wooden chair near an electric hot plate, her arms folded, boiling water in a battered aluminum pot. She was talking aloud to herself when Yossarian entered and began moaning as soon as she saw him.

"Gone," she moaned before he could even inquire. Holding her elbows, she rocked back and forth mournfully on her creaking chair. "Gone."

"Who?"

"All. All the poor young girls."

"Where?"

"Away. Chased away into the street. All of them gone. All the poor young girls."

"Chased away by who? Who did it?"

"The mean tall soldiers with the hard white hats and clubs. And by our *carabinieri*. They came with their clubs and chased them away. They would not even let them take their coats. The poor things. They just chased them away into the cold."

"Did they arrest them?"

"They chased them away. They just chased them away."

"Then why did they do it if they didn't arrest them?"

"I don't know," sobbed the old woman. "I don't know. Who will take care of me? Who will take care of me now that the poor young girls are gone? Who will take care of me?"

"There must have been a reason," Yossarian persisted, pounding his fist into his hand. "They couldn't just barge in here and chase everyone out."

"No reason," wailed the old woman. "No reason."

"What right did they have?"

"Catch-22."

"*What?*" Yossarian froze in his tracks with fear and alarm and felt his whole body begin to tingle. "*What* did you say?"

"Catch-22," the old woman repeated, rocking her head up and down. "Catch-22. Catch-22 says they have a right to do anything we can't stop them from doing."

"What the hell are you talking about?" Yossarian shouted at her in bewildered, furious protest. "How did you know it was Catch-22? Who the hell told you it was Catch-22?"

"The soldiers with the hard white hats and clubs. The girls were crying. 'Did we do anything wrong?' they said. The men said no and pushed them away out the door with the ends of their clubs. 'Then why are you chasing us out?' the girls said. 'Catch-22,' the men said. 'What right do you have?' the girls said. 'Catch-22,' the men said. All they kept saying was 'Catch-22, Catch-22.' What does it mean, Catch-22? What is Catch-22?"

"Didn't they show it to you?" Yossarian demanded, stamping about in anger and distress. "Didn't you even make them read it?"

"They don't have to show us Catch-22," the old woman answered. "The law says they don't have to."

"What law says they don't have to?"

"Catch-22."

"Oh, God damn!" Yossarian exclaimed bitterly. "I bet it wasn't even really there." He stopped walking and glanced about the room disconsolately. "Where's the old man?"

"Gone," mourned the old woman.

"Gone?"

"Dead," the old woman told him, nodding in emphatic lament, pointing to her head with the flat of her hand. "Something broke in here. One minute he was living, one minute he was dead."

"But he can't be dead!" Yossarian cried, ready to argue insistently. But of course he knew it was true, knew it was logical and true: once again the old man had marched along with the majority.

Yossarian turned away and trudged through the apartment with a gloomy scowl, peering with pessimistic curiosity into all the rooms. Everything made of glass had been smashed by the men with the clubs. Torn drapes and bedding lay dumped on the floor. Chairs, tables and dressers had been overturned. Everything breakable had been broken. The destruction was total. No wild vandals could have been more thorough. Every window was smashed, and darkness poured like inky clouds into each room through the shattered panes. Yossarian could imagine the heavy, crashing footfalls of the tall M.P.s in the hard white hats. He could picture the fiery and malicious exhilaration with which they had made their wreckage, and their sanctimonious, ruthless sense of right and dedication. All the poor young girls were gone. Everyone was gone but the weeping old woman in the bulky brown and gray sweaters and black head shawl, and soon she too would be gone.

"Gone," she grieved, when he walked back in, before he could even speak. "Who will take care of me now?"

Yossarian ignored the question. "Nately's girlfriend—did anyone hear from her?" he asked.

"Gone."

"I know she's gone. But did anyone hear from her? Does anyone know where she is?"

"Gone."

"The little sister. What happened to her?"

"Gone." The old woman's tone had not changed.

"Do you know what I'm talking about?" Yossarian asked sharply, staring into her eyes to see if she were not speaking to him from a coma. He raised his voice. "What happened to the kid sister, to the little girl?"

"Gone, gone," the old woman replied with a crabby shrug, irritated by his persistence, her low wail growing louder. "Chased away with the rest, chased away into the street. They would not even let her take her coat."

"Where did she go?"

"I don't know. I don't know."

"Who will take care of her?"

"Who will take care of me?"

"She doesn't know anybody else, does she?"

"Who will take care of me?"

Yossarian left money in the old woman's lap—it was odd how many wrongs leaving money seemed to right—and strode out of the apartment, cursing Catch-22 vehemently as he descended the stairs, even though he knew there was no such thing. Catch-22 did not exist, he was positive of that, but it made no difference. What did matter was that everyone thought it existed, and that was much worse, for there was no object or text to ridicule or refute, to accuse, criticize, attack, amend, hate, revile, spit at, rip to shreds, trample upon or burn up.

It was cold outside, and dark, and a leaky, insipid mist lay swollen in the air and trickled down the large, unpolished stone blocks of the houses and the pedestals of monuments. Yossarian hurried back to Milo and recanted. He said he was sorry and, knowing he was lying, promised to fly as many more missions as Colonel Cathcart wanted if Milo would only use all his influence in Rome to help him locate Nately's whore's kid sister.

"She's just a twelve-year-old virgin, Milo," he explained anxiously, "and I want to find her before it's too late."

Milo responded to his request with a benign smile. "I've got just the twelve-year-old virgin you're looking for," he announced jubilantly. "This twelve-year-old virgin is really only thirty-four, but she was brought up on a low-protein diet by very strict parents and didn't start sleeping with men until—"

"Milo, I'm talking about a little girl!" Yossarian interrupted him with desperate impatience. "Don't you understand? I don't want to sleep with her. I want to help her. You've got daughters. She's just a little kid, and she's all alone in this city with no one to take care of her. I want to protect her from harm. Don't you know what I'm talking about?"

Milo did understand and was deeply touched. "Yossarian, I'm proud of you," he exclaimed with profound emotion. "I really am. You don't know how glad I am to see that everything isn't always just sex with you. You've got principles. Certainly I've got daughters, and I know exactly what you're talking about. We'll find that girl. Don't you worry. You come with me and we'll find that girl if we have to turn this whole city upside down. Come along."

Yossarian went along in Milo Minderbinder's speeding M & M staff car to police headquarters to meet a swarthy, untidy police commissioner with a narrow black mustache and unbuttoned tunic who was fiddling with a stout woman with warts and two chins when they entered his office and who greeted Milo with warm surprise and bowed and scraped in obscene servility as though Milo were some elegant marquis.

"Ah, Marchese Milo," he declared with effusive pleasure, pushing the fat, disgruntled woman out the door without even looking toward her. "Why didn't you tell me you were coming? I would have a big party for you. Come in, come in, Marchese. You almost never visit us any more."

Milo knew that there was not one moment to waste. "Hello, Luigi," he said, nodding so briskly that he almost seemed rude. "Luigi, I need your help. My friend here wants to find a girl."

"A girl, Marchese?" said Luigi, scratching his face pensively. "There are lots of girls in Rome. For an American officer, a girl should not be too difficult."

"No, Luigi, you don't understand. This is a twelve-year-old virgin that he has to find right away."

"Ah, yes, now I understand," Luigi said sagaciously. "A virgin might take a little time. But if he waits at the bus terminal where the young farm girls looking for work arrive, I—"

"Luigi, you still don't understand," Milo snapped with such brusque impatience that the police commissioner's face flushed and he jumped to attention and began buttoning his uniform in confusion. "This girl is a friend, an old friend of the family, and we want to help her. She's only a child. She's all alone in this city somewhere, and we have to find her before somebody harms her. Now do you understand? Luigi, this is very important to me. I have a daughter the same age as that little girl, and nothing in the world means more to me right now than saving that poor child before it's too late. Will you help?"

"*Si,* Marchese, now I understand," said Luigi. "And I will do everything in my power to find her. But tonight I have almost no men. Tonight all my men are busy trying to break up the traffic in illegal tobacco."

"Illegal tobacco?" asked Milo.

"Milo," Yossarian bleated faintly with a sinking heart, sensing at once that all was lost.

"*Si,* Marchese," said Luigi. "The profit in illegal tobacco is so high that the smuggling is almost impossible to control."

"Is there really that much profit in illegal tobacco?" Milo inquired with keen interest, his rust-colored eyebrows arching avidly and his nostrils sniffing.

"Milo," Yossarian called to him. "Pay attention to *me,* will you?"

"*Si,* Marchese," Luigi answered. "The profit in illegal tobacco is very high. The smuggling is a national scandal, Marchese, truly a national disgrace."

"Is that a fact?" Milo observed with a preoccupied smile and started toward the door as though in a spell.

"Milo!" Yossarian yelled, and bounded forward impulsively to intercept him. "Milo, you've got to help me."

"Illegal tobacco," Milo explained to him with a look of epileptic lust, struggling doggedly to get by. "Let me go.

I've got to smuggle illegal tobacco."

"Stay here and help me find her," pleaded Yossarian. "You can smuggle illegal tobacco tomorrow."

But Milo was deaf and kept pushing forward, nonviolently but irresistibly, sweating, his eyes, as though he were in the grip of a blind fixation, burning feverishly, and his twitching mouth slavering. He moaned calmly as though in remote, instinctive distress and kept repeating, "Illegal tobacco, illegal tobacco." Yossarian stepped out of the way with resignation finally when he saw it was hopeless to try to reason with him. Milo was gone like a shot. The commissioner of police unbuttoned his tunic again and looked at Yossarian with contempt.

"What do you want here?" he asked coldly. "Do you want me to arrest you?"

Yossarian walked out of the office and down the stairs into the dark, tomblike street, passing in the hall the stout woman with warts and two chins, who was already on her way back in. There was no sign of Milo outside. There were no lights in any of the windows. The deserted sidewalk rose steeply and continuously for several blocks. He could see the glare of a broad avenue at the top of the long cobblestone incline. The police station was almost at the bottom: the yellow bulbs at the entrance sizzled in the dampness like wet torches. A frigid, fine rain was falling. He began walking slowly, pushing uphill. Soon he came to a quiet, cozy, inviting restaurant with red velvet drapes in the windows and a blue neon sign near the door that said: TONY'S RESTAURANT. FINE FOOD AND DRINK. KEEP OUT. The words on the blue neon sign surprised him mildly for only an instant. Nothing warped seemed bizarre any more in his strange, distorted surroundings. The tops of the sheer buildings slanted in weird, surrealistic perspective, and the street seemed tilted. He raised the collar of his warm woolen coat and hugged it around him. The night was raw. A boy in a thin shirt and thin tattered trousers walked out of the darkness on bare feet. The boy had black hair and needed a haircut and shoes and socks. His sickly face was pale and sad. His feet made grisly, soft, sucking sounds in the rain puddles on the wet pavement as he passed, and Yossarian was moved by such intense pity for his poverty that he wanted to smash his pale, sad, sickly face with his fist and knock him out of existence because he brought to mind *all* the pale, sad, sickly children in Italy that same night who needed haircuts and needed shoes and socks. He made Yossarian think of cripples and of cold and hungry men and women, and of all the dumb, passive, devout mothers with catatonic eyes nursing infants outdoors that same night with chilled animal udders bared insensibly to that same raw rain. Cows. Almost on cue, a nursing mother padded past holding an infant in black rags, and Yossarian wanted to smash her too, because she reminded him of the barefoot boy in the thin shirt and thin, tattered trousers and of all the shivering, stupefying misery in a world that never yet had provided enough heat and food and justice for all but an ingenious and unscrupulous handful. What a lousy earth! He wondered how many people were destitute that same night even in his own prosperous country, how many homes were shanties, how many husbands were drunk and wives socked, and how many children were bullied, abused or abandoned. How many families hungered for food they could not afford to buy? How many hearts were broken? How many suicides would take place that same night, how many people would go insane? How many cockroaches and landlords would triumph? How many winners were losers, successes failures, rich men poor men? How many wise guys were stupid? How many happy endings were unhappy endings? How many honest men were liars, brave men cowards, loyal men traitors, how many sainted men were corrupt, how many people in positions of trust had sold their souls to blackguards for petty cash, how many had never had souls? How many straight-and-narrow paths were crooked paths? How many best families were worst families and how many good people were bad people? When you added them all up and then subtracted, you might be left with only the children, and perhaps with Albert Einstein and an old violinist or sculptor somewhere. Yossarian walked in lonely torture, feeling estranged, and could not wipe from his mind the excruciating image of the barefoot boy with sickly cheeks until he turned the corner into the avenue finally and came upon an Allied soldier having convulsions on the ground, a young lieutenant with a small, pale, boyish face. Six other soldiers from different countries wrestled with different parts of him, striving to help him and hold him still. He yelped and groaned unintelligibly through clenched teeth, his eyes rolling up into his head. "Don't let him bite his tongue off," a short sergeant near Yossarian advised shrewdly, and a seventh man threw himself into the fray to wrestle with the ill lieutenant's face. All at once the wrestlers won and turned to each other undecidedly, for now that they held the young lieutenant rigid they did not know what to do with him. A quiver of moronic panic spread from one straining brute face to another. "Why don't you lift him and put him on the hood of that car?" a corporal standing in back of Yossarian drawled. That seemed to make sense, so the seven men lifted the young lieutenant up and stretched him out carefully on the hood of a parked car, still pinning each struggling part of him down. Once they had him stretched out on the hood of the parked car, they stared at each other uneasily again, for they had no idea what to do with him next. "Why don't you lift him up off the hood of that car and lay him down on the ground?" drawled the same corporal behind Yossarian. That seemed like a good idea, too, and they began to move him back to the sidewalk, but before they could finish, a jeep raced up with a flashing red spotlight at the side and two military policemen in the front seat.

"What's going on?" the driver yelled.

"He's having convulsions," one of the men grappling with one of the young lieutenant's limbs answered. "We're holding him still."

"That's good. He's under arrest."

"What should we do with him?"

"Keep him under arrest!" the M.P. shouted, doubling over with raucous laughter at his jest, and sped away in his jeep.

Yossarian recalled that he had no leave papers and

moved prudently past the strange group toward the sound of muffled voices emanating from a distance inside the murky darkness ahead. The broad, rain-blotched boulevard was illuminated every half-block by short, curling lampposts with eerie, shimmering glares surrounded by smoky brown mist. From a window overhead he heard an unhappy female voice pleading, "Please don't. Please don't." A despondent young woman in a black raincoat with much black hair on her face passed with her eyes lowered. At the Ministry of Public Affairs on the next block, a drunken lady was backed up against one of the fluted Corinthian columns by a drunken young soldier, while three drunken comrades in arms sat watching nearby on the steps with wine bottles standing between their legs. "Pleeshe don't," begged the drunken lady. "I want to go home now. Pleeshe don't." One of the three sitting men cursed pugnaciously and hurled a wine bottle down at Yossarian when he turned to look up. The bottle shattered harmlessly far away with a brief and muted noise. Yossarian continued walking away at the same listless, unhurried pace, hands buried in his pockets. "Come on, baby," he heard the drunken soldier urge determinedly. "It's my turn now." "Pleeshe don't," begged the drunken lady. "Pleeshe don't." At the very next corner, deep inside the dense impenetrable shadows of a narrow, winding side street, he heard the mysterious, unmistakable sound of someone shoveling snow. The measured, labored, evocative scrape of iron shovel against concrete made his flesh crawl with terror as he stepped from the curb to cross the ominous alley and hurried onward until the haunting, incongruous noise had been left behind. Now he knew where he was; soon, if he continued without turning, he would come to the dry fountain in the middle of the boulevard, then to the officers' apartment seven blocks beyond. He heard snarling, inhuman voices cutting through the ghostly blackness in front suddenly. The bulb on the corner lamppost had died, spilling gloom over half the street, throwing everything visible off balance. On the other side of the intersection, a man was beating a dog with a stick like the man who was beating the horse with a whip in Raskolnikov's dream. Yossarian strained helplessly not to see or hear. The dog whimpered and squealed in brute, dumbfounded hysteria at the end of an old Manila rope and groveled and crawled on its belly without resisting, but the man beat it and beat it anyway with his heavy, flat stick. A small crowd watched. A squat woman stepped out and asked him please to stop. "Mind your own business," the man barked gruffly, lifting his stick as though he might beat her too, and the woman retreated sheepishly with an abject and humiliated air. Yossarian quickened his pace to get away, almost ran. The night was filled with horrors, and he thought he knew how Christ must have felt as he walked through the world, like a psychiatrist through a ward full of nuts, like a victim through a prison full of thieves. What a welcome sight a leper must have been! At the next corner a man was beating a small boy brutally in the midst of an immobile crowd of adult spectators who made no effort to intervene. Yossarian recoiled with sickening recognition. He was certain he had witnessed that same horrible scene sometime before. *Déja vu?* The sinister coincidence shook him and filled him with doubt and dread. It was the same scene he had witnessed a block before, although everything in it seemed quite different. What in the world was happening? Would a squat woman step out and ask the man to please stop? Would he raise his hand to strike her and would she retreat? Nobody moved. The child cried steadily as though in drugged misery. The man kept knocking him down with hard, resounding open-palm blows to the head, then jerking him up to his feet in order to knock him down again. No one in the sullen, cowering crowd seemed to care enough about the stunned and beaten boy to interfere. The child was no more than nine. One drab woman was weeping silently into a dirty dish towel. The boy was emaciated and needed a haircut. Bright-red blood was streaming from both ears. Yossarian crossed quickly to the other side of the immense avenue to escape the nauseating sight and found himself walking on human teeth lying on the drenched, glistening pavement near splotches of blood kept sticky by the pelting raindrops poking each one like sharp fingernails. Molars and broken incisors lay scattered everywhere. He circled on tiptoe the grotesque debris and came near a doorway containing a crying soldier holding a saturated handkerchief to his mouth, supported as he sagged by two other soldiers waiting in grave impatience for the military ambulance that finally came clanging up with amber fog lights on and passed them by for an altercation on the next block between a single civilian Italian with books and a slew of civilian policemen with armlocks and clubs. The screaming, struggling civilian was a dark man with a face white as flour from fear. His eyes were pulsating in hectic desperation, flapping like bat's wings, as the many tall policemen seized him by arms and legs and lifted him up. His books were spilled on the ground. "Help!" he shrieked shrilly in a voice strangling in its own emotion as the policemen carried him to the open doors in the rear of the ambulance and threw him inside. "Police! Help! Police!" the doors were shut and bolted, and the ambulance raced away. There was a humorless irony in the ludicrous panic of the man screaming for help to the police while policemen were all around him. Yossarian smiled wryly at the futile and ridiculous cry for aid, then saw with a start that the words were ambiguous, realized with alarm that they were not, perhaps, intended as a call for police but as a heroic warning from the grave by a doomed friend to everyone who was *not* a policeman with a club and a gun and a mob of other policemen with clubs and guns to back him up. "Help! Police!" the man had cried, and he could have been shouting of danger. Yossarian responded to the thought by slipping away stealthily from the police and almost tripped over the feet of a burly woman of forty hastening across the intersection guiltily, darting furtive, vindictive glances behind her toward a woman of eighty with thick, bandaged ankles doddering after her in a losing pursuit. The old woman was gasping for breath as she minced along and muttering to herself in distracted agitation. There was no mistaking the nature of the scene; it was a chase. The triumphant first woman was halfway across the wide avenue before the second woman reached the curb. The nasty, small, gloating smile with which she glanced back at the laboring old woman was both wicked and apprehensive. Yossarian knew he could help the troubled old woman if she would only cry out, knew he could spring forward and capture the sturdy first woman and hold her for the mob of policemen nearby if the second woman would only give him license with a shriek of distress. But the old woman passed by without even seeing him, mumbling in terrible, tragic vexation, and soon the first woman had vanished into the deepening layers of darkness and the old woman was left standing helplessly in the center of the thoroughfare, dazed, uncertain which way to proceed, alone. Yossarian tore his eyes from her and hurried away in shame because he had done nothing to assist her. He darted furtive, guilty glances back as he fled in defeat, afraid the old woman might now start following him, and he welcomed the concealing shelter of the drizzling, drifting, lightless, nearly opaque gloom. Mobs . . . mobs of policemen—everything but England was in the hands of mobs, mobs, mobs. Mobs with clubs were in control everywhere.

The surface of the collar and shoulders of Yossarian's coat was soaked. His socks were wet and cold. The light on the next lamppost was out, too, the glass globe broken. Buildings and featureless shapes flowed by him noiselessly as though borne past immutably on the surface of some rank and timeless tide. A tall monk passed, his face buried entirely inside a coarse gray cowl, even the eyes hidden. Footsteps sloshed toward him steadily through a puddle, and he feared it would be another barefoot child. He brushed by a gaunt, cadaverous, tristful man in a black raincoat with a star-shaped scar in his cheek and a glossy mutilated depression the size of an egg in one temple. On squishing straw sandals, a young woman materialized with her whole face disfigured by a God-awful pink and piebald burn that started on her neck and stretched in a raw, corrugated mass up both cheeks past her eyes! Yossarian could not bear to look, and shuddered. No one would ever love her. His spirit was sick; he longed to lie down with some girl he could love who would soothe and excite him and put him to sleep. A mob with a club was waiting for him in Pianosa. The girls were all gone. The countess and her daughter-in-law were no longer good enough; he had grown too old for fun, he no longer had the time. Luciana was gone, dead, probably; if not yet then soon enough. Aarfy's buxom trollop had vanished with her smutty cameo ring, and Nurse Duckett was ashamed of him because he had refused to fly more combat missions and would cause a scandal. The only girl he knew nearby was the plain maid in the officers' apartment, whom none of the men had ever slept with. Her name was Michaela, but the men called her filthy things in dulcet, ingratiating voices, and she giggled with childish joy because she understood no English and thought they were flattering her and making harmless jokes. Everything wild she watched them do filled her with enchanted delight. She was a happy, simple-minded, hard-working girl who could not read and was barely able to write her name. Her straight hair was the color of rotting straw. She had sallow skin and myopic eyes, and none of the men had ever slept with her because none of the men had ever wanted to, none but Aarfy, who had raped her once that same evening and had then held her prisoner in a clothes closet for almost two hours with his hand over her mouth until the civilian curfew sirens sounded and it was unlawful for her to be outside.

Then he threw her out the window. Her dead body was still lying on the pavement when Yossarian arrived and pushed his way politely through the circle of solemn neighbors with dim lanterns, who glared with venom as they shrank away from him and pointed up bitterly toward the second-floor windows in their private, grim, accusing conversations. Yossarian's heart pounded with fright and horror at the pitiful, ominous, gory spectacle of the broken corpse. He ducked into the hallway and bolted up the stairs into the apartment, where he found Aarfy pacing about uneasily with a pompous, slightly uncomfortable smile. Aarfy seemed a bit unsettled as he fidgeted with his pipe and assured Yossarian that everything was going to be all right. There was nothing to worry about.

"I only raped her once," he explained.

Yossarian was aghast. "But you killed her, Aarfy! You killed her!"

"Oh, I had to do that after I raped her," Aarfy replied in his most condescending manner. "I couldn't very well let her go around saying bad things about us, could I?"

"But why did you have to touch her at all, you dumb bastard?" Yossarian shouted. "Why couldn't you get yourself a girl off the street if you wanted one? This city is full of prostitutes."

"Oh, no, not me," Aarfy bragged. "I never paid for it in my life."

"Aarfy, are you insane?" Yossarian was almost speechless. "You *killed* a girl. They're going to put you in jail!"

"Oh, no," Aarfy answered with a forced smile. "Not me. They aren't going to put good old Aarfy in jail. Not for killing *her.*"

"But you threw her out the window. She's lying there dead in the street."

"She has no right to be there," Aarfy answered. "It's after curfew."

"Stupid! Don't you realize what you've done?" Yossarian wanted to grab Aarfy by his well-fed, caterpillar-soft shoulders and shake some sense into him. "You've murdered a human being. They *are* going to put you in jail. They might even *hang* you!"

"Oh, I hardly think they'll do that," Aarfy replied with a jovial chuckle, although his symptoms of nervousness increased. He spilled tobacco crumbs unconsciously as his short fingers fumbled with the bowl of his pipe. "No, sirree. Not to good old Aarfy." He chortled again. "She was only a servant girl. I hardly think they're going to make too much of a fuss over one poor Italian servant girl when so many thousands of lives are being lost every day. Do you?"

"Listen!" Yossarian cried, almost in joy. He pricked up his ears and watched the blood drain from Aarfy's face as sirens mourned far away, police sirens, and then ascended almost instantaneously to a howling, strident, onrushing cacophony of overwhelming sound that seemed to crash into the room around them from every side. "Aarfy, they're coming for you," he said in a flood of compassion, shouting to be heard above the noise. "They're coming to arrest you. Aarfy, don't you understand? You can't take the life of another human being and get away with it, even if she is just a poor servant girl. Don't you see? Can't you understand?"

"Oh, no," Aarfy insisted with a lame laugh and a weak smile. "They're not coming to arrest me. Not good old Aarfy."

All at once he looked sick. He sank down on a chair in a trembling stupor, his stumpy, lax hands quaking in his lap. Cars skidded to a stop outside. Spotlights hit the windows immediately. Car doors slammed and police whistles screeched. Voices rose harshly. Aarfy was green. He kept shaking his head mechanically with a queer, numb smile and repeating in a weak, hollow monotone that they were not coming for him, not for good old Aarfy, no sirree, striving to convince himself that this was so even as heavy footsteps raced up the stairs and pounded across the landing, even as fists beat on the door four times with a deafening, inexorable force. Then the door to the apartment flew open, and two large, tough, brawny M.P.s with icy eyes and firm, sinewy, unsmiling jaws entered quickly, strode across the room, and arrested Yossarian.

They arrested Yossarian for being in Rome without a pass.

They apologized to Aarfy for intruding and led Yossarian away between them, gripping him under each arm with fingers as hard as steel manacles. They said nothing at all to him on the way down. Two more tall M.P.s with clubs and hard white helmets were waiting outside at a closed car. They marched Yossarian into the back seat, and the car roared away and weaved through the rain and muddy fog to a police station. The M.P.s locked him up for the night in a cell with four stone walls. At dawn they gave him a pail for a latrine and drove him to the airport, where two more giant M.P.s with clubs and white helmets were waiting at a transport plane whose engines were already warming up when they arrived, the cylindrical green cowlings oozing quivering beads of condensation. None of the M.P.s said anything to each other either. They did not even nod. Yossarian had never seen such granite faces. The plane flew to Pianosa. Two more silent M.P.s were waiting at the landing strip. There were now eight, and they filed with precise, wordless discipline into two cars and sped on humming tires past the four squadron areas to the Group Headquarters building, where still two more M.P.s were waiting at the parking area. All ten tall, strong, purposeful, silent men towered around him as they turned toward the entrance. Their footsteps crunched in loud unison on the cindered ground. He had an impression of accelerating haste. He was terrified. Every one of the ten M.P.s seemed powerful enough to bash him to death with a single blow. They had only to press their massive, toughened, boulderous shoulders against him to crush all life from his body. There was nothing he could do to save himself. He could not even see which two were gripping him under the arms as they marched him rapidly between the two tight single-file columns they had formed. Their pace quickened, and he felt as though he were flying along with his feet off the ground as they trotted in resolute cadence up the wide marble staircase to the upper landing, where still two more inscrutable military policemen with hard faces were waiting to lead them all at an even faster pace down the long, cantilevered balcony overhanging the immense lobby. Their marching footsteps on the dull tile floor thundered like an awesome, quickening drum roll through the vacant center of the building as they moved with even greater speed and precision toward Colonel Cathcart's office, and violent winds of panic began blowing in Yossarian's ears when they turned him toward his doom inside the office, where Colonel Korn, his rump spreading comfortably on a corner of Colonel Cathcart's desk, sat waiting to greet him with a genial smile and said,

"We're sending you home."

STUDY QUESTIONS

1. What, exactly, is Catch-22? Why is this so absurd?
2. Why did MPs smash *everything* in the whorehouse?
3. What is symbolized by "Nately's whore's kid sister" and the search for her?
4. Assuming that all of the events that Yossarian observes on his nighttime stroll are metaphors for the war, select several events and discuss what they represent.
5. How much of what happens in this chapter can be considered rational and reasonable? Irrational and unreasonable? Give some examples.

THE LITERATURE OF MOVING IMAGES

Motion pictures were developed long before anyone realized their artistic or, especially, commercial possibilities. In 1824 Peter Mark Roget, an English scholar, published a paper entitled "The Persistence of Vision with Regard to Moving Objects." The thesis is that the human eye retains an image slightly longer than the image is actually present. Specifically, if sixteen pictures are made of one second of movement, the persistence of vision puts them together to give the illusion of movement. This is the basis of all motion pictures.

Generally considered the dominant medium of this century, motion pictures display interesting paradoxes inherent in the medium. Film uses machines to record images of reality and it combines still photographs to give the illusion of continuous motion. It therefore seems to present images of life itself but it is also used to portray unrealities unapproached even by anyone's wildest dreams.

Film can and should be studied as an art form, but it is a medium that must be experienced, preferably in a theatre with an audience. With very few exceptions movies are made to make money in public showings before a mass audience. "Motion picture industry" is the term generally used to describe corporate enterprises that use a large number of highly skilled people: screenwriter, director, actors, cinematographer, film editor, film scorer, set and costume designers, and many others. Unlike a novel, a film cannot be credited to a single creator. Critics tend to lavish credit on the director as the person in charge but this is only a convention that tends to slight everyone else. One cannot, for example, think of director Elia Kazan's *On the Waterfront* without recalling Marlon Brando's masterful performance. In the final analysis no film is better than its literary base, the screenplay itself, for this is where virtually all movies begin.

Movies are a prime mass-entertainment medium the world over and, as commercial enterprises, about 99 percent of them are eminently forgettable. But from the beginning of motion pictures, there have been exceptions, movies that have made an artistic impact and that have withstood the test of time. Usually referred to as film classics, these are works of art that effectively synthesized the efforts of many creators. Following is a list of movies that are generally regarded as true classics. Some, perhaps, are not to everyone's taste, but all are notable works of art and all should be seen, preferably more than once. They are among the best of a new literature that began in this century. Following the standard procedure, credit for the movies is assigned to the directors but, in every case, the viewer should give due credit to all participants, both on and off camera.

Antonioni, Michelangelo. *L'Avventura.* Italy, 1959.
Bergman, Ingmar. *The Seventh Seal.* Sweden, 1956.
——.*Wild Strawberries.* Sweden, 1957.
——.*Fanny and Alexander.* Sweden, 1985.
Buñuel, Luis. *Belle de Jour.* France, 1968.
Chaplin, Charles. *The Gold Rush.* U.S., 1925.
Cocteau, Jean. *Beauty and the Beast.* France, 1947.
DeSica, Vittorio. *The Bicycle Thief.* Italy, 1948.
Eisenstein, Serge. *Potemkin.* Russia, 1925.
Fellini, Federico. *La Strada.* Italy, 1954.
——.*La Dolce Vita.* Italy, 1959.
Gance, Abel. *Napoleon.* France, 1925, 1982.
Griffith, David W. *Intolerance.* U.S., 1916.
Hitchcock, Alfred. *Vertigo.* U.S., 1958.
Kazan, Elia. *On the Waterfront.* U.S., 1954.
Kurosawa, Akira. *Roshomon.* Japan, 1950.
——.*Ikiru.* Japan, 1952.
——.*Seven Samurai.* Japan, 1954.
——.*Ran.* Japan, 1986.
Lang, Fritz. *M.* Germany, 1931.
Penn, Arthur. *Bonnie and Clyde.* U.S., 1967.
Renoir, Jean. *La Grande Illusion.* France, 1938.
——.*Rules of the Game.* France, 1939, 1965.
Truffaut, François. *The 400 Blows.* France, 1959.
——.*Jules and Jim.* France, 1961.
Welles, Orson. *Citizen Kane.* U.S., 1941.
Wiene, Robert. *The Cabinet of Dr. Caligari.* Germany, 1919.
Wilder, Billy. *Some Like It Hot.* U.S., 1959.

SUMMARY

The time chart for the twentieth century on page 324 provides an overview of our bewildering century of violence and invention. The century has been one of interminable warfare, including the two most destructive wars in human history, but there have also been remarkable technological developments. Consider transportation, for example. The Wright brothers flew the first heavier-than-air flying machine in 1903. Thirty-one years later the jet engine was invented and, eighteen years after that, commercial jets were making the world much smaller. Goddard invented the liquid-fuel rocket in 1926, the Russians put Sputnik into orbit thirty-one years later and, twelve years after that, an American astronaut walked on the moon, just sixty-six years after the Wright brothers' flying machine.

Communications technology also developed in a rush. Twelve years after the beginning of commercial television transcontinental television became a reality; a decade later communication satellites were starting to beam television to the entire world. We do indeed live in a Global Community with the possibility, no matter how faint, of evolving into a peaceful community in which human values will be more important than material possessions and national rivalries. High-tech makes this possible, but only human beings can make it a reality.

CULTURE AND HUMAN VALUES

Does literature really matter? Further, are those who read and write morally or ethically superior to those who neither read nor write?

Literature has been manifestly important in every literate culture known to humankind; but whether or not literature makes anyone superior in any way seems to be an arbitrary, even artificial, issue. Non-literate societies are not necessarily morally or ethically inferior to any other culture regardless of the literacy rate.

If literature does not make us better human beings, then what does it do? Does it, as so often stated, conserve the past? The literature of past cultures is, of course, our heritage; but, as is amply demonstrated in this chapter, literature consumes the past as it seeks its own ways to expose and confront the foibles, vanities, and shenanigans of humankind.

The plays of Shakespeare, for example, were subversive; in effect they were dangerous to every aspect of English civilization that had a formal existence: government, religion, societal conventions, and so on. *Waiting for Godot,* in turn, is clearly hostile to every Shakespearean dramatic convention: chronology, character development, and logical plot construction. *Godot* is absurd because it violates all accepted dramatic conventions and, most importantly, because it directly confronts the absurdities seemingly inherent in the human condition.

Catch-22 attacks traditional attitudes about the necessity of warfare. Those who see war as insane can logically refuse to become involved. Anyone, however, who recognizes the insanity of war can still be ordered to fight because he is sane enough to know that warfare is madness—and *that* is Catch-22. Joseph Heller's novel is subversive literature; it challenges the whole concept of war as a necessary and proper instrument of national policy.

Similarly, literature such as Ellison's *Invisible Man* confronts a basic problem in American society. This and other selections in this unit attack the sickness of racism, whereas works such as Virginia Woolf's "If Shakespeare Had a Sister" are directed at chauvinism and a male-dominated society.

Most of the literary selections in this unit have targeted war, bigotry, and chauvinism, but what of the rest? Consider again the remarks on page 403 about modern art reflecting the twentieth century. The same statement can be made about modern literature and, to one extent or another, about all the arts.

Artists seem to be more sensitive and articulate (in their medium) than the average person and, one way or another, their era is reflected in their creative output. Though all art is concerned with truth as perceived by the artist, that truth is not always nor necessarily the ugliness of bigotry or war. Literature—and the other arts—can be concerned with such themes as beauty, love, faith, and justice. Our society may be neither better nor worse than a non-literate culture, but our literature certainly helps make it more articulate and much more interesting.

APPENDIX

Music Listening and Notation

Music listening is always enriched by a basic knowledge of how it is constructed. This appendix aims to provide such knowledge. It should, ideally, be studied for content and used, along with the glossary, as often as necessary in conjunction with the material on music.

CHARACTERISTICS OF MUSICAL SOUNDS

Musical tones are sounds of definite pitch and duration, as distinct from noises and other less identifiable sounds. Musical tones have the four characteristics of pitch, intensity, tone color, and duration, which may be described as follows:

Pitch The location of musical sound from low to high or high to low.

Intensity Relative degree of softness or loudness.

Tone color The quality of a sound that distinguishes it from other musical sounds of the same pitch and intensity; for example, the different tone quality of a flute as contrasted with a clarinet. Also called timbre.

Duration The length of time a tone is audible.

THE FOUR ELEMENTS OF MUSIC

Rhythm, melody, harmony, and tone color are the essential elements of music. Composers and performers are concerned with each, while for the listener, they are experienced as a web of sound that often makes it difficult to single out any one element. Each can, however, be considered in isolation as a guide to understanding.

Rhythm

There is rhythm in the universe: our heartbeat, the alternation of day and night, the progression of the seasons, waves crashing on a beach. Artificially produced rhythm can be heard in train wheels clicking on rails, a ping-pong game, or the clacking castanets of a Spanish dancer. Although little is known about prehistoric music, the earliest music was probably the beating out of rhythms long before the existence of either melody or speech.

Essentially, rhythm is the organization of musical time—that is, everything that takes place in terms of sound and silence, accent and non-accent, tension and relaxation. Rhythm can also be defined as the "melody of a monotone"; music can often be recognized just by hearing its rhythm. For example, tapping out the rhythmic patterns of "Dixie" can bring that familiar melody to mind.

Rhythm is not to be confused with beat, which results from a certain regularity of the rhythmic patterns. Beat, or pulse, can be compared with the heartbeat or the pulse rate. The beat will usually be steady, but it may temporarily speed up or slow down. It may be explicit (the uniform thump of a bass drum in a marching band) or implicit (resulting from combinations of rhythmic patterns). As soon as one note follows another, there will be rhythm but not necessarily beat. Certain types of music (such as Gregorian chant) do not produce the regular pulsation called beat.

When beats are produced by the music in a repeating pattern of accents, the result is meter. Metered music is measured music, with groupings of two, three, or four beats (or combinations of these) in each measure, or bar.

Time Signatures

When there is a regular pattern of accented and unaccented beats, it is customary to use a time signature. This looks like a fraction, in which the upper figure indicates the number of beats in a measure and the lower figure the unit of beat; that is, the note value the composer has selected to symbolize one beat. For example:

2 = two beats per measure (duple meter)
4 = ♩ unit of beat (quarter note receives one beat)

3 = three beats per measure (triple meter)
8 = ♪ unit of beat (eighth note receives one beat)

Melody and Harmony

A melody is a horizontal organization of pitches or, simply, a succession of musical tones. Harmony is a vertical organization of pitches in which two or more tones are sounded together. The following example illustrates melody on the upper staff and harmony on the lower staff.

"Old Folks at Home"

Tone Color

Sometimes called timbre (TAM-ber), tone color is to music what color is to the painter. It is tone color that enables us to distinguish between a flute, a clarinet, and an oboe. A soprano voice differs from a bass voice not only by its higher pitch, but also by its different tone color. Through experience, people learn to recognize the unique colors of many instruments. Further study leads to finer discriminations between similar instruments such as violin and viola, oboe and English horn, and so on. Composers select instruments for expressive purposes based largely on their coloration, whether singly or in combination. The full sound of a Beethoven symphony differs from a work by Richard Strauss, for example, because Strauss uses a wider range of instrumental colors.

MUSICAL LITERACY

The most abstract of the arts, music is sound moving in time. Factual information about music certainly helps the listener, but all the facts in the world can only assist the listening process; information can never replace the sound of music. One extremely useful method of learning to understand music is to study major themes and ideas in musical notation while listening to the music itself.

A practical approach to intelligent listening must include some instruction in musical literacy sufficient to read a single line of music. This is a simple process that can be quickly learned by young children and can be taught to an adult in a few minutes. The strangely prevalent attitude that musical notation is "too hard" or "too technical" has no foundation in fact, and probably refers to reading music as a performer—a very different matter that need not concern us here. As basic to music as the ABC's of written language, musical notation is an indispensable guide for music listeners.

Learning to pick out musical themes will turn abstract sounds into intelligible tunes, thus giving oneself an opportunity to anticipate the themes as they emerge in the music. Equally valuable is the repetition of themes after the listening experience. To summarize, picking out melodies on the page is an aid to understanding, a helpful preview of music to be listened to, and a reminder of music already heard.

Try to approach the following material not with apprehension but with anticipation. Master the principles of musical notation with the positive attitude that this not only will materially assist in a better understanding of the music in this text but also lead, in time, to a lifetime of pleasurable listening.

MUSICAL NOTATION

Pitch

The essential elements of our notational system were devised some ten centuries ago and subsequently altered and augmented to become a reasonably efficient means of communicating the composer's intentions to a performer. The system is based on the first seven letters of the alphabet and can best be illustrated on a piano keyboard. The pitches range from low to high, from A through G in a repeating A–G pattern.

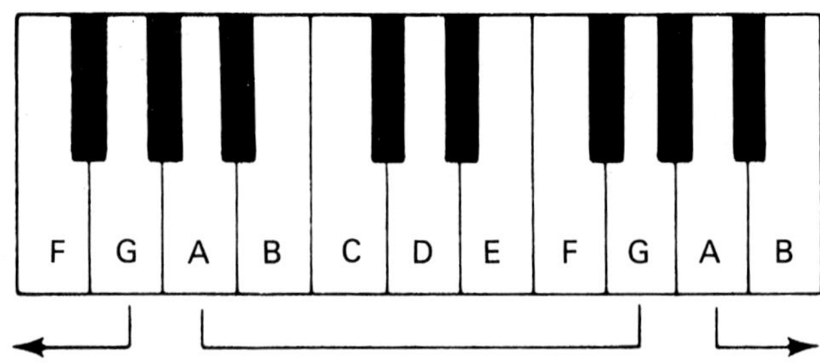

In order to know which of the eight A's available on the piano is the intended note, you will need to do the following:

5 4 3 2 1 (lines)
4 3 2 1 (spaces)

1. Use a musical staff (also called a stave) of five lines and four spaces.
2. Use a symbol for a musical pitch, i.e., a note.

3. Place the notes on the lines or in the spaces of the staff.

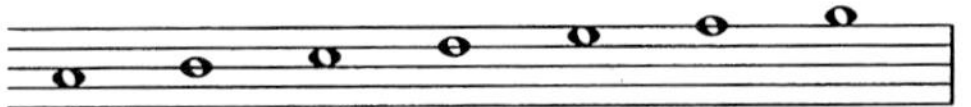

4. Indicate by means of a clef sign the names of the notes.

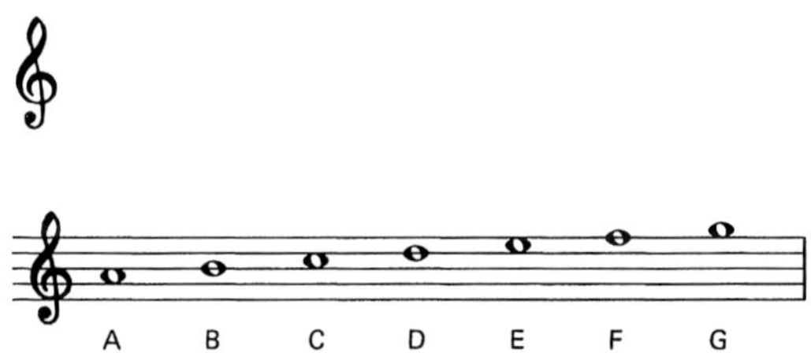

The word "clef" (French, "key") implies that the key to precise placement of the notes is the establishment of the letter name of one of the lines or spaces of the staff. There are two clefs in common use. Both are ornamental symbols, one derived from the letter G and one from F. The solid lines below are the present clef signs and the dotted lines their original form:

The clefs are placed on the staff to indicate the location of the letters they represent. The spiral portion of the G clef curls around the second line to fix the location of G; the two dots of the F clef are placed above and below the fourth line to show that this is the F line.

Once the five-line staff has received its pitch designation of G or F, the staff is subsequently identified as a treble or a bass staff.

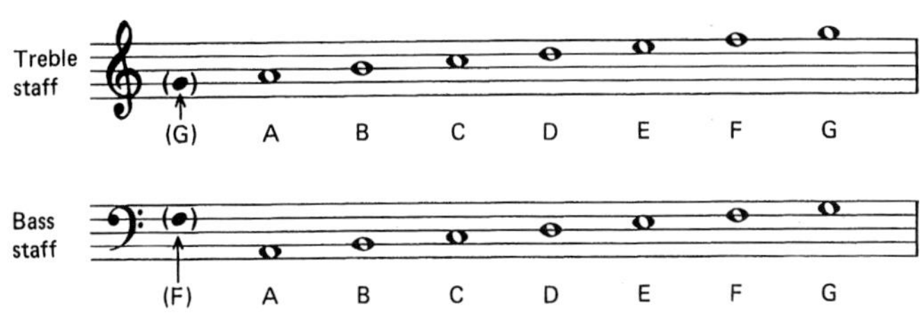

You will see that the staff just given has an added short line, a ledger line, used to accommodate the last two notes.

On a piano keyboard the black keys are grouped in alternating sets of two and three. The white note, or key, immediately to the left of the two black keys is always C. There are eight C's; the C closest to the center is called middle C. It is from this C that you can locate the notes of the themes.

Not all melodies are composed so that they can be played on the white notes only of the piano. Sometimes another key, or different set of pitches, is used, as demonstrated in the following examples:

"Joy to the World" **Handel (1685–1759)**

Key of C

In the second version, below, the key signature indicates that all the F's and C's have been raised a half step to the next closest note—on a piano the adjacent black keys to the right. A symbol called a sharp (#) indicates raised notes.

"Joy to the World" **Handel**

Key of D

The other common symbol that changes a note is the flat (♭), which lowers a note a half step to the next closest note. Following is the same melody written in the key of B♭. As indicated by the key signature, all the B's and E's have been lowered to B♭ and E♭. Key signatures can include up to seven sharps or flats.

"Joy to the World" **Handel**

Key of B♭

Below is a guide to the chromatic scale, which includes all the black and white keys, twelve in all, in one octave.

Duration

The notation of the length of time of musical sounds (and silences) was developed, more or less, in conjunction with the notation of pitch. The modern note-value system consists of fractional parts of a whole unit, or whole note (𝅝), expressed in mathematical terms as 1/1. A half note (𝅗𝅥) is one-half the whole unit, or 1/2; a quarter note (♩) is one-quarter the unit, or 1/4; and so on.

The name of the note value indicates the number of notes in the whole-note unit. There are four quarter notes (4 × 1/4 = 1/1), eight eighth notes (8 × 1/8 = 1/1), etc.

With note values smaller than the whole note, the relationships remain constant. There are two quarter notes in a half note (2 × 1/4 = 1/2), two eighth notes in a quarter note (2 × 1/8 = 1/4), etc.

Rhythmic notation is both relative and fixed. The duration of a whole note is dependent on the tempo (speed) and notation of music. It may have a duration of one second, eight seconds, or something in between. The interior relationships, however, never vary.

A whole note has the same duration as two half notes, four quarter notes, and so forth. The mathematical relationship is fixed and precise. See table A.1 for an outline of the system.

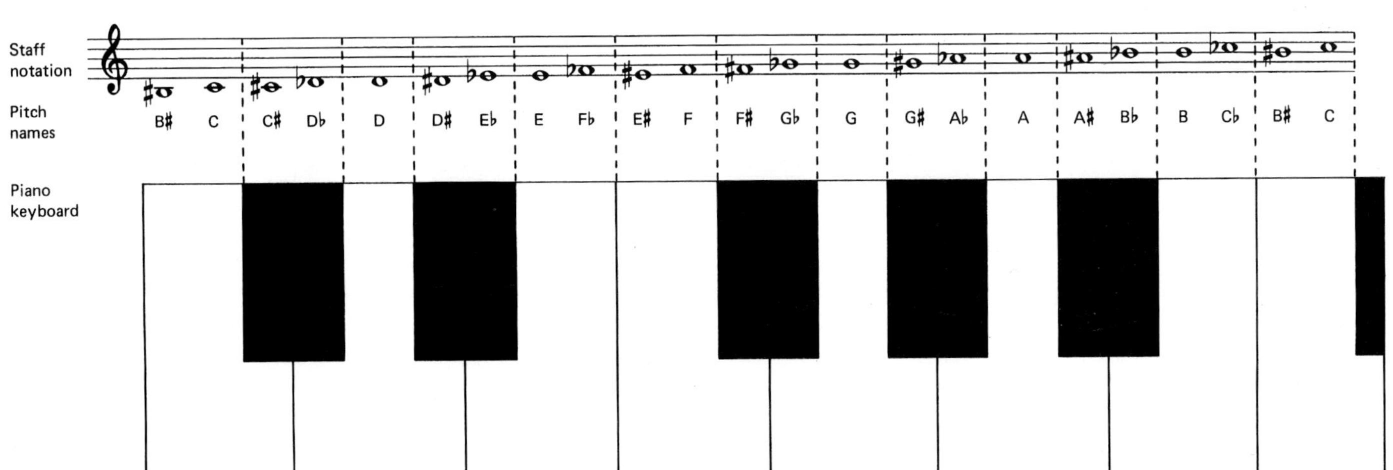

VOICES AND INSTRUMENTS

Choral ensembles are usually divided into four voice parts ranging from high to low: soprano and alto (women) and tenor and bass (men).

TABLE A.1 NOTE AND REST VALUES

Note value	Symbol
Whole note (basic unit)	𝅝
Half note	𝅗𝅥
Quarter note	♩
Eighth note	♪
Sixteenth note	𝅘𝅥𝅯

Rest value	Symbol
Whole (note) rest	𝄻
Half rest	𝄼
Quarter rest	𝄽
Eighth rest	𝄾
Sixteenth rest	𝄿

Instruments of the symphony orchestra and other ensembles are grouped by family, from highest pitch to lowest:

Strings	Woodwinds	Brass	Percussion
violin	piccolo	trumpet (and cornet)	snare drum
viola	flute	French horn	timpani
cello	oboe	trombone	bass drum
bass	clarinet	tuba	cymbals
	bassoon		(many others)

Keyboard instruments include piano, harpsichord, and organ. The piano, originally called *pianoforte* (It., "soft" "loud"), is based on the principle of hammers striking the strings; the harpsichord has a mechanism that plucks the strings. Organs are built with two or more keyboards called manuals. The traditional organ uses forced air to activate the pipes; some modern organs use an electronic reproduction of sound.

MUSICAL TEXTURE

The words for the three kinds of musical texture are derived from Greek and are virtually self-explanatory:

monophonic (one sound)
homophonic (same sound)
polyphonic (many sounds)

Monophonic music has a single unaccompanied melodic line. Much of the world's music—including Chinese and Hindu music and, in Western civilization, Gregorian chant and troubadour songs—is monophonic. Homophonic music has a principal melodic line accompanied by harmony, sometimes referred to as chordal accompaniment. Although homophony is relatively unknown outside Western culture, it comprises the bulk of our music, including nearly all popular music. Polyphonic music has two or more melodies sounding simultaneously. Familiar rounds such as "Three Blind Mice" and "Row, Row, Row Your Boat" are polyphonic, as is most Renaissance music. The music of Baroque composers such as Bach, Handel, and others is basically polyphonic too.

MUSICAL FORM

Briefly stated, form in music is a balance of unity and variety. Too much unity becomes boring, whereas excessive variety leads to fragmentation and even chaos. Understanding form in music is essential to its appreciation. As German composer Robert Schumann remarked, "Only when the form is quite clear to you will the spirit become clear to you."

The smallest unit of form is the motive. This is a recurring combination of at least two notes with an identifiable rhythmic pattern. The principal motive in the first movement of Beethoven's Fifth Symphony has two different pitches in a four-note rhythmic pattern:

Symphony No. 5, First movement — **Beethoven (1770–1827)**

A musical phrase is a coherent group of notes roughly comparable to a literary phrase and having about the same function. Two related phrases form a period, analogous to a sentence. In the period illustrated below, the first phrase has a transitional ending called a half cadence, and the second phrase ends solidly with a full cadence. Note also the extreme unity; the first three measures of each phrase are identical.

"Ode to Joy" — **Beethoven**

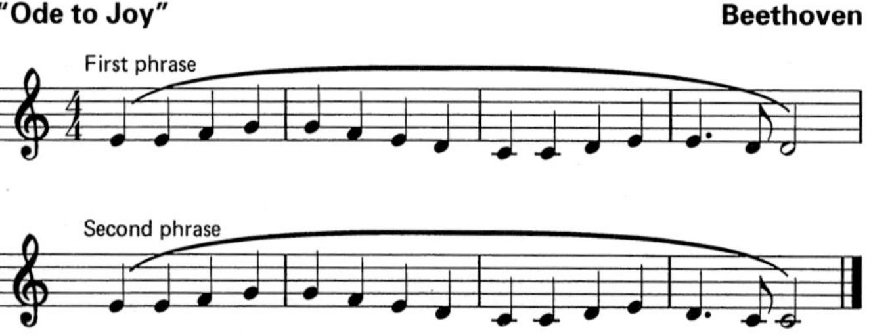

In large works the musical periods are used in various combinations to expand the material into sections comparable to paragraphs, and these are then combined to make still larger units.

Musical structure can be comprehended only after the music has arrived at wherever the composer intends it to go. Look again at "Ode to Joy" (from Beethoven's Ninth Symphony). You can "see" its form only because the music is notated, which is why learning some notation is so important. When the music is played, your ear follows the line to the half cadence, which is then heard as a statement that demands completion. As the second phrase begins, there is aural recognition of its relationship to the first phrase. When the second phrase concludes with a gratifying full cadence, there is a kind of flashback to the memory of the first phrase. In other words, the conclusion of the second phrase is satisfying because it completes the thought of the still-remembered first phrase. The music conforms to its own inner logic; that is, the second phrase is a logical consequence of the first.

As a general rule, most music is constructed around two different but logically related musical ideas. We can call one idea A and the other B. One common musical form is two-part (binary), or simply AB. An even more common form is three-part (ternary), or ABA. In two-part form the composer makes a musical statement (A), which is followed by a new section (B), which is sufficiently different to provide variety but not so different as to destroy the balance. The following hymn tune is a complete composition in two-part form, with two phrases in each section. Section B has the same rhythm as Section A, but the melody is a kind of inversion of the melody in A. The inner logic is maintained through the similarities.

"St. Anne"

The following complete hymn tune has a form related to two-part form: AA'B, called A, A prime, B. Part A is followed by another A that is varied going into the cadence. Part B is properly different but related to A and A' by the similarity of measures 2, 6, and 10. In terms of measures, the structure of the piece can be diagrammed as:

A	A'	B
2 + 2	2 + 2	2 + 2

"Regent Square"

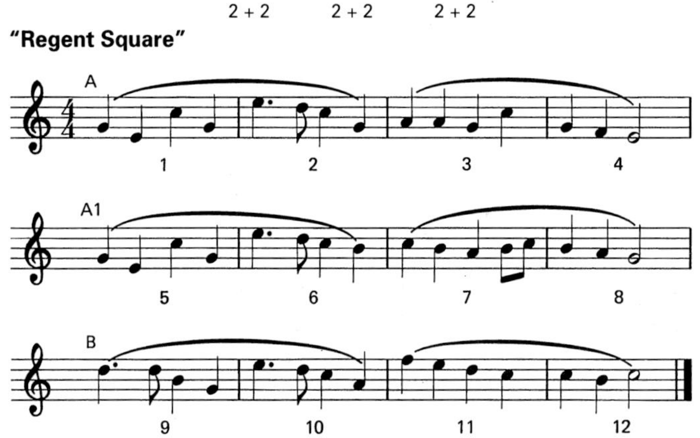

Three-part form operates on the principle of closing with the melody that began the piece, a rounding off of the material: ABA. The following example can be analyzed as AA'BA' and diagrammed as:

A	A'	B	A'
4 + 4	4 + 4	4 + 4	4 + 4

This is the thirty-two-measure form most commonly used for popular songs.

"In the Gloaming"

There are, of course, other variants of AB and ABA forms, as well as several other structures. However, the examples given illustrate the principle of a balance between unity and variety, of which unity is paramount. Perhaps because of its fluid nature, music, more than any other art, emphasizes repetition, restating the material again and again, but mixing it with enough variety to maintain interest. The forms illustrated can also be heard in the larger context of longer compositions. For example, "In the Gloaming" has thirty-two measures in a basic ABA form; a large symphonic work could have, say, 200 measures and be diagrammed as follows:

A	B	A		A	B	A'		A	B	A'
aba	aba	aba	*or*	aba'	aba	a'ba'	*or*	aa'ba	aba	aa'ba'

THE LISTENING EXPERIENCE

Listening to music begins with the question, *What do you hear?* This is an objective question that has nothing whatever to do with a story you may imagine the music is telling, random associations the music happens to trigger, or any meaning that may be attributed to the music. The idea, rather, is to objectively identify the sounds to determine how the sounds are produced, and to try to determine how the sounds are organized.

Composers do not pour out notes as if emptying a can of beans on a tabletop. They arrange their sounds in a sort of container in a manner that molds the receptacle to the material it holds. Learning to comprehend the musical structure leads to the ability to anticipate the next melody, cadence, section, or other development. Being able to anticipate what is to happen next means that you are tuned in to the web of sound, listening along with the pace of the music. Almost everyone has already acquired the ability to follow the progress of popular music and to anticipate what comes next in favorite recordings. The larger world of classical music lies only a step beyond this level of listening ability. It is an inspiring and enriching stride into one of the greatest achievements of Western civilization.

Glossary

Pronunciation: Approximations are given where necessary. The syllables are to be read as English words and with the capital letters accented.

Abbreviations: Lat., Latin; Fr., French; Ger., German; Gk., Greek; It., Italian.

Asterisks: An asterisk preceding a word or phrase indicates that a definition and/or illustration can be found under that heading.

A

Abacus The flat slab on top of a *capital.
Abstract Art Term covers many kinds of non representational art, e.g., action painting, works by Kandinsky. All art is abstracted to some degree.
A cappella (Lat., ah ka-PELL-ah) Originally unaccompanied music sung "in the chapel." Term now applies to choral music without instrumental accompaniment.
Acoustics The science of sound. Important in architectural design and city planning as well as music.
Aerial perspective See *perspective.
Aesthetic Concerned with a sensitivity to the pleasurable and the beautiful; the opposite of anaesthetic.
Aesthetics The study or philosophy of beauty; theory of the fine arts and human responses.
Allegory A literary mode with a literal level of meanings plus a set of meanings above and beyond themselves. This second level may be religious, social, political, or philosophical, e.g., *The Faerie Queen* by Spenser is an allegory about Christian virtues.
Alleluia Latinization of the Hebrew *Halleluyah* ("Praise ye the Lord"). Third item of the Proper of the *Mass.
Altarpiece A painted (or sculptured) panel placed over or behind an altar.
Ambulatory A passageway around the *apse of a church.
Apocalypse Prophetic revelation; the Book of Revelation in the New Testament.
Apse A recess, usually semicircular, in the east wall of a Christian church or, in a Roman *basilica, at the wall opposite to the general entrance way.
Arcade A series of connected *arches resting on columns.
Arch A curved structure (semicircular or pointed) spanning a space, usually made of wedge-shaped blocks. Known to the Greeks, who preferred a post and lintel system, but exploited by the Romans.
Architrave The lowest part of an entablature, a horizontal beam or *lintel directly above the *capital.
Aria (It., AHR-eeah, "air") Solo song (sometimes duet) in *operas, *oratorios, *cantatas.
Art Nouveau A style of architecture, crafts, and design of the 1890s and a bit later characterized by curvilinear patterns. Examples include Tiffany lamps and the work of Beardsley and Klimt.
Art song Song intending an artistic combination of words and music, as distinct from popular song or folk song.
Astrolabe An instrument formerly used to determine positions of heavenly bodies. It had a suspended disk with degrees marked on the circumference and a movable pointer at the center. It was succeeded in the eighteenth century by the sextant.
Atonal Music that has no tonal center, in which all notes are of relatively equal importance. In a composition in C major, on the other hand, C is the most important note. Almost all popular music is written in keys such as C major, D major and so on. Most compositions by Schoenberg are atonal.
Augustinian Roman Catholic monastic order that uses the old rule of St. Augustine.
Avant-garde (a-vã-gard) A French term meaning, literally, "advanced guard," used to designate innovators and experimentalists in the various arts.

B

Baldachino (ball-da-KEEN-o) A canopy over a tomb or altar of which the most famous is that over the tomb of St. Peter in St. Peter's, Rome, designed by Bernini.
Ballad (Lat., *ballare*, "to dance") Originally a dancing song. A narrative song, usually folk song but term also applied to popular songs.
Ballade Medieval trouvère song. In the nineteenth and twentieth centuries dramatic piano pieces, frequently inspired by romantic poetry.
Balustrade A railing plus a supporting row of posts.
Banjo Instrument of the *guitar family, probably introduced into Africa by Arab traders and brought to America on the slave ships. The body consists of a shallow, hollow metal drum with a drumhead on top and open at the bottom. It has four or more strings and is played with fingers or plectrum.
Baptistery Originally a separate building, later a part of the church containing the baptismal font.
Barrel vault See *vault.
Basilica In Roman architecture, a rectangular public building used for business or as a tribunal. Christian churches that use a *cruciform plan are patterned after Roman basilicas. Though basilica is an architectural style, the Church of Rome designates a church a basilica if it contains the bones of a saint.
Behaviorism School of psychology that restricts both animal and human psychology to the study of behavior; stresses the role of the environment and conditioned responses to exterior stimuli.
Blank verse Unrhymed *iambic pentameter* (see *meter) in the English language, much used in Elizabethan drama.
Bourgeoisie The middle class; in Marxist theory, the capitalist class, which is opposed to the proletariat, the lower or industrial working class.
Buttress Exterior support used to counter the lateral thrust of an *arch or *vault. A *pier buttress* is a solid mass of masonry added to the wall; a *flying buttress* is typically a pier standing away from the wall from which an arch "flies" from the pier to connect with the wall at the point of outward thrust.

C

Cadence Term in music applied to the concluding portion of a phrase (temporary cadence) or composition (permanent cadence).
Campanile Italian for bell tower, usually freestanding. The Leaning Tower of Pisa is a campanile.
Canon (Gk., "law, rule") 1. A body of principles, rules, standards, or norms. 2. In art and architecture, a criterion for establishing proportion, measure, or scale. 3. In music, in which a melody is imitated strictly and in its entirety by another voice. Canons that have no specified way to end but keep going around are called "rounds," e.g., "Three Blind Mice."
Cantata (It., *cantare*, "to sing") A "sung" piece as opposed to a "sound"

(instrumental) piece, e.g., *sonata. The term is now generally used for secular or sacred choral works with orchestral accompaniment, which are on a smaller scale than *oratorios.

Cantilever A self-supporting projection that needs no exterior bracing; e.g., a balcony or porch can be cantilevered.

Cantus firmus (Lat., "fixed song") A preexisting melody used as the foundation for a *polyphonic composition. *Plainsong melodies were used for this purpose, but other sources included secular songs, Lutheran *chorales, and *scales. Any pre-existing melody may serve as a cantus firmus.

Capital The top or crown of a *column.

Cartoon A full-size preliminary drawing for a pictorial work, usually a large work such as a *mural, *fresco, or tapestry. Also a humorous drawing.

Caryatid (care-ee-AT-id) A female figure that functions as a supporting *column; male figures that function in a like manner are called *atlantes* (at-LAN-tees; plural of Atlas).

Catharsis (Gk., "purge, purify") Purification, purging of emotions effected by tragedy (Aristotle).

Chamber music Term now restricted to instrumental music written for a limited number of players in which there is only one player to each part, as opposed to orchestral music, which has two or more players to some parts, e.g., sixteen or more players on the first violin part. True chamber music emphasizes ensemble rather than solo playing.

Chanson (Fr., "song") A major part of the troubadour-trouvère tradition, dating from the eleventh through the fourteenth centuries. Also a generic term for any song with a French text.

Chiaroscuro (kee-ar-oh-SKOOR-oh; It., "light-dark") In the visual arts the use of gradations of light and dark to represent natural light and shadows.

Chinoiserie (she-nwaz-eh-ree; Fr.) Chinese motifs as decorative elements for craft objects, screens, wallpaper, and furniture; prominent in eighteenth-century rococo style.

Choir That part of the church where the singers and clergy are normally accommodated; usually between the *transept and the *apse; also called chancel.

Chorale A *hymn tune of the German Protestant (Lutheran) church.

Chord In music the simultaneous sounding of two or more tones.

Chromatic (Gk., *chroma*, "color") The use of notes that are foreign to the musical *scale and have to be indicated by a sharp, flat, natural, etc. The *chromatic* scale is involved in these alterations. It consists of twelve tones to an octave, each a semitone apart.

Clavier Generic term for any instrument of the stringed keyboard family: clavichord, harpsichord, and piano.

Clef (Fr., "key") In music a symbol placed on the staff to indicate the pitches of the lines and spaces. There are three clefs in use today: G, F, and C. The G clef is used to indicate that the note on the second line is G (treble clef). The F clef is usually used to indicate that F is on the fourth line (bass clef).

Cloisonné (Fr., "partition") An enameling technique. Raised fences of metal ribbon are soldered to a plane surface and the little enclosures filled with colored enamels and fired.

Collage (Fr., "pasting") Paper and other materials pasted on a two-dimensional surface.

Colonnade A series of spaced *columns, usually connected by *lintels.

Column A vertical support, usually circular, which has a base (except in *Doric style), shaft, and *capital.

Comedy A play or other literary work in which all ends well, properly, or happily. Opposite of *tragedy.

Concerto (con-CHAIR-toe) A musical work for one or two solo instruments with orchestral accompaniment.

Concerto grosso A musical work for a small group of instruments (usually three or four) with orchestral accompaniment.

Corinthian The most ornate style of Greek architecture, little used by the Greeks but preferred by the Romans; tall, slender, channeled *columns topped by an elaborate *capital decorated with stylized acanthus leaves.

Cornice The horizontal, projecting member crowning an entablature.

Cosmology Philosophic study of the origin and nature of the universe.

Counterpoint In music, the art of combining melodies.

Couplet In poetry two successive lines in the same *meter; if rhymed, called a rhyming couplet.

Crocket In Gothic architecture an ornamental device shaped like a curling leaf and placed on the outer angles of *gables and pinnacles.

Cruciform The floor plan of a church in the shape of a Latin cross.

D

Daguerrotype Photograph made on a silver-coated glass plate; after L. J. M. Daguerre (1789–1851), the inventor.

Determinism (Lat., *de*, "from," and *terminus*, "end") The doctrine that all events are conditioned by their causes and that people are mechanical expressions of heredity and environment; in short, we are at the mercy of blind, unknowing natural laws in an indifferent universe.

Deus ex machina (DAY-oos ex ma-KEE-na; Lat.) In Greek and Roman drama a deity who was brought in by stage machinery to resolve a difficult situation; hence any unexpected or bizarre device or event introduced to untangle a plot.

Dialectic Associated with Plato as the art of debate by question and answer. Also dialectical reasoning using syllogisms (Aristotle) or, according to Hegel, the distinctive characteristic of speculative thought.

Didactic Intended to instruct or teach.

Dome A hemispherical vault; may be viewed as an *arch rotated on its vertical axis.

Dominican Roman Catholic monastic order founded by St. Dominic in 1216. More officially, the Order of Preachers (O.P.).

Doric The oldest of Greek temple styles, characterized by sturdy *columns with no base and unornamented cushionlike *capitals.

Dormer A window set vertically in a small gable projecting from a sloping roof.

Drums Percussion musical instruments having a skin stretched over one or both ends of a frame.

Dualism In *metaphysics, a theory that admits two independent substances, e.g., Plato's dualism of the sensible and intelligible worlds, Cartesian dualism of thinking and extended subjects, Kant's dualism of the noumenal and the phenomenal.

Duple meter In music, two beats per measure. Most marches and ragtime music are in duple meter.

Dynamics In music, the degrees of loudness and softness.

E

Empiricism System of thought in which the sole source of knowledge is held to be experience; no knowledge is possible independent of experience.

Enamel A vitreous, usually opaque, protective or decorative coating baked on metal, glass, or ceramic ware. A paint that dries to a hard, glossy surface. Any glossy, hard coating resembling enamel, such as nail enamel.

Engraving The process of using a sharp instrument to cut a design into a metal plate, usually copper; also the print that is made from the plate after ink has been added.

Etching A kind of *engraving in which the design is incised into a wax-covered metal plate, after which the exposed metal is etched by a corrosive acid; the print made from the plate is also called an etching.

Euphemism An innocuous term substituted for one considered to be offensive or socially unacceptable, e.g., "passing away" for "dying."

F

Facade In architecture the face of a building; one or more of the exterior walls of a building, especially the one containing the main entrance.

Fiddle Colloquialism for the violin. Also used to designate the bowed ancestors of the violin, particularly the medieval instrument used to accompany dances (see *viol).

Flute A woodwind instrument made of wood (originally), silver, gold, or preferably platinum. It is essentially a straight pipe with keys, which is held horizontally and played by blowing across a mouthpiece.

Fluting The vertical grooves, usually semicircular, in the shaft of a *column or *pilaster.

Foot A metrical unit in poetry such as the iamb (˘—) (see *meter).

Foreshortening Creating the illusion in

painting or drawing that the subject is projecting out of or into the frontal plane of a two-dimensional surface.

Free verse Verse that uses parallelism and sound effects rather than *meter and rhyme.

Fresco (It., "fresh") Painting on plaster, usually wet plaster, into which the colors sink as the plaster dries so that the fresco becomes part of the wall.

Frieze In architecture, a decorated horizontal band, often embellished with carved figures and molding; the portion of an entablature between the *architrave and the *cornice above.

Fugue *Polyphonic musical composition in which a single theme is developed by the different musical voices in succession. A favorite style of Baroque composers such as Bach and Handel.

G

Gable In architecture, the triangular section at the end of a pitched roof, frequently with a window below.

Genre (zhan-re) In the pictorial arts, a depiction of scenes of everyday life. In literature, the type of work—epic, novel, and so on.

Gesso White chalky pigment bound in a water and glue medium, used as a ground on wood and other supports in painting and gilding.

Gouache (Fr., gwahsh) Watercolor made opaque by adding zinc white.

Graphic arts Visual arts that are linear in character: drawing, engraving, printing, printmaking, typography, and advertising design.

Great Schism Rival popes of the Church of Rome in Rome, Avignon, and Pisa, 1378–1417.

Greek cross A cross in which the four arms are of equal length.

Gregorian chant See *plainsong.

Guild An association of persons of the same trade, pursuits or interests, formed for their mutual aid and protection and the maintenance of standards; they flourished during the Middle Ages and into the Renaissance.

Guitar A plucked string instrument with a flat body and six strings (modern guitar). Brought into Europe during the Middle Ages by the Moorish conquest of Spain.

H

Harpsichord Actually a harp turned on its side and played by means of quills or leather tongues operated by a keyboard. It was the most common keyboard instrument of the sixteenth to eighteenth centuries and is again being built today in increasing numbers.

Heroic couplet Two successive lines of rhymed iambic pentameter, used e.g., in Pope's *Essay on Man*.

Holy Roman Empire Political body embracing most of central Europe from 962 to 1806. "Roman" because it claimed succession to imperial Rome. "Holy" because it originally claimed supremacy over Christendom.

Homophonic (Gk., "same sound") Music in which a single melodic line is supported by chords or other subordinate material (percussion instruments).

Hubris (HU-bris) Tragic flaw, i.e., excessive pride or arrogance that harms other people and brings about the downfall of the person with the flaw.

Hue The attribute of a color. The chief colors of the spectrum are: red, yellow, blue (primary); green, orange, violet (secondary).

Humanism "Man is the measure of all things" (Protagoras) and "Many are the wonders of the world, and none so wonderful as man" (Sophocles) give the essence of humanism. The Greeks conceived their gods as perfect human beings, free from infirmities and immortal, but subject to human passions and ambitions. The Renaissance conception of man as the potential master of all things arose out of the awakening to the glories of Greece and Rome.

Hymn A poem of praise; usually, but not necessarily, sacred. The music accompanying a hymn is called the hymn tune.

I

Iconography Visual imagery used to convey concepts in the visual arts; the study of symbolic meanings in the pictorial arts.

Illumination Decorative illustrations or designs, associated primarily with medieval illuminated manuscripts.

Impasto (It., "paste") A painting style in which the pigment is laid on thickly, as in many of van Gogh's paintings.

Intaglio (in-TAL-yo) A graphic technique in which the design is incised; used on seals, gems, and dies for coins and also for the kinds of printing and printmaking that have a depressed ink-bearing surface.

Inductive method The process of arriving at a general conclusion from a set of particular facts.

Ionic A style of Greek classical architecture using slender, *fluted *columns and *capitals decorated with scrolls and *volutes.

J

Jamb figure Sculpted figure flanking the portal of a Gothic church.

K

Keystone The central wedge-shaped stone in an *arch; the last stone put in place, it makes the arch stable.

L

Lantern In architecture, a small decorative structure that crowns a *dome or roof.

Libretto (It., "little book") The text or words of an *opera, *oratorio, or other extended choral work.

Lied, Lieder (Ger., leet, LEE-der; "song, songs"). Term usually applied to the German Romantic *art songs of Schubert, Schumann, Brahms, Wolf, and others.

Lintel In architecture, a horizontal crosspiece over an open space, which carries the weight of some of the superstructure.

Lithography A printmaking process that uses a polished stone (or metal plate) on which the design is drawn with a crayon or greasy ink. Ink is chemically attracted only to the lines of the drawing, with a print made by applying paper to the inked stone.

Liturgical Pertaining to public worship, specifically to the organized worship patterns of Christian churches.

Lute Plucked string instrument with a pear-shaped body and a fingerboard with frets. It had eleven strings tuned to six notes (five sets of double strings plus a single string for the highest note). It was the most popular instrument of the Middle Ages and Renaissance. Lutes are again being made, mainly for present-day performances of Renaissance music.

Lyric Poetry sung to the accompaniment of a lyre (Greek); short poems with musical elements.

M

Madrigal Name of uncertain origin that refers to fourteenth-century vocal music or, more usually, to the popular sixteenth-century type. Renaissance madrigals were free-form vocal pieces (usually set to love lyrics) in a *polyphonic style with intermixed *homophonic sections. Flemish, Italian, and English composers brought the madrigal to a high level of expressiveness in word painting and imagery. Madrigals were sometimes accompanied but mostly *a cappella.

Manifest Destiny The belief that the United States was destined to extend from sea to sea so that it could bring the blessings of liberty to the entire continent. The westward expansion was also seen as a moral obligation to enlarge the area of freedom, thereby keeping the lands from falling to a tyrant.

Mass The central service of public worship of some Christian churches, principally the Church of Rome.

Materialism The doctrine that the only reality is matter; that the universe is not governed by intelligence or purpose but only by mechanical cause and effect.

Metaphor A form of figurative language that compares dissimilar objects (e.g., publicity is a two-edged sword).

Metaphysics Philosophic inquiry into the ultimate and fundamental reality; "the science of being as such."

Meter In music, a grouping of beats into patterns of two, three, or four beats or combinations thereof; in English poetry the basic rhythmic pattern of stressed (—) and unstressed (⌣) syllables. Metrical patterns include: *iambic* (⌣ —), *trochaic* (— ⌣), *anapestic* (⌣ ⌣ —), and *dactylic* (— ⌣ ⌣).

Metope (MET-o-pay) In classical architecture, the panel between two *triglyphs in a *Doric *frieze; may be plain or carved. The Parthenon metopes are all carved.

Monophonic (Gk., "one sound") A single line of music without accompaniment or additional parts, as in *plainsong, and some folk songs, hollers, street cries, and blues.

Montage (mon-tahzh) A composition made of existing photographs, paintings, or drawings; in cinematography the effects achieved by superimposing images or using rapid sequences.

Mosaic The technique of embedding bits of stone, colored glass, or marble in wet concrete to make designs or pictures for walls or floors. To achieve a complex interplay of light and shadows, the bits are set in the holding material with minute differences in the angles, as in the mosaics of San Vitale in Ravenna.

Motet (from Fr., *mot*, "word") The most important form of early *polyphonic music (ca. thirteenth to seventeenth centuries). Renaissance motet (fifteenth to sixteenth centuries): a four- or five-part composition, *a cappella, generally *polyphonic, with a single Latin text; a serious vocal piece intended for use in sacred services. There are also Baroque motets (e.g., by J. S. Bach) for mixed chorus and orchestra (German text) and some Romantic motets (e.g., by Brahms), again in the *a cappella style.

Mural A painting on a wall; a *fresco is a type of mural.

Mythology Collection of stories explaining natural phenomena, customs, institutions, religious beliefs, and so forth of a people. Usually concerned with the supernatural, gods, goddesses, heroic exploits, and the like.

N

Naturalism The view that the universe requires no supernatural cause or government, that it is self-existent, self-explanatory, self-operating, and self-directing, and that it is purposeless, deterministic, and only incidentally productive of humankind. In relation to literature sometimes defined as "realism on all fours." The dominant traits of literary naturalism are biological determinism (people are what they must be because of their genes) and environmental determinism (people are what they are because of how they are brought up).

Nave The main central space of a church running from the entrance to the crossing of the *transepts; typically flanked by one or two side aisles. Name derived from "naval" because the barrel *vault ceiling has the appearance of the inside hull of a ship.

Neoplatonists The Florentine Neoplatonists derived some of their ideas from Plotinus, the founder of Neoplatonism, from Plato, and from Christian mysticism.

O

Obbligato In music, an essential instrumental part, second in importance only to the principal melody.

Oboe (From Fr., *haut bois*, "high wind," i.e., high-pitched) A double-reeded, soprano-range instrument with a conical bore (slightly expanding diameter from reed to bell). It has a nasal but mellow and poignant tone.

Odalisque (oh-da-leesk) French word for a harem slave or concubine but used more broadly to refer to a reclining female figure, a favorite subject of such painters as Ingres and Matisse.

Ode A formal lyric usually on a dignified theme, in exalted language, e.g., works by Horace.

Office hours In the Church of Rome, the services (usually observed only in monastic churches) that take place eight times a day (every three hours): Matins, Lauds, Prime, Terce, Sext, None, Vespers, and Compline. Musically the important services are Matins, Vespers, and Compline.

Onomatopoeia A word that sounds like its referent, e.g., the bee buzzes.

Ontology (Gk., *on*, "being," and *logos*, "logic") Philosophic inquiry into the ultimate nature of things, what it means to be.

Opera (From It., *opera in musica*, "work in music") A play in which the text is generally sung throughout to the accompaniment of an orchestra. Modern opera had its beginnings in Florence in the late sixteenth century when some musicians, poets, and scholars attempted a revival of Greek drama, which they assumed to have been sung throughout.

Oratorio A musical setting of a religious or epic theme for performance by soloists, chorus, and orchestra in a church or concert hall. Originally (early seventeenth century) it was similar to an *opera (sacred opera) with staging, costumes, and scenery. It is now usually presented in concert form, e.g., *The Messiah*, by G. F. Handel.

Orchestra (From Gk., *orkheisthai*, "to dance") In ancient Greek theatres the circular or semicircular space in front of the stage used by the chorus; group of instrumentalists performing ensemble music, e.g., symphony orchestra.

Organ, pipe organ An instrument of ancient origin consisting of from two to seven keyboards (manuals) and a set of pedals (usually thirty-two notes) for the feet.

Organum (OR-ga-num; Lat.) The name given to the earliest types of *polyphonic music.

Ornamentation In music, the added trills and turns that make lines, usually the melodic lines, more elaborate.

P

Pediment In classical architecture, a triangular space at the end of a building framed by the *cornice and the ends of the sloping roof.

Pendentive In architecture, a concave triangular piece of masonry, four of which form a transition from a square base to support the circular rim of a *dome.

Percussion Instruments that are played by striking, shaking, scraping, etc.

Peristyle A series of *columns that surround the exterior of a building or the interior of a court; the Parthenon, e.g., has a peristyle.

Perspective The illusion of a three-dimensional world on a two-dimensional surface. *Linear perspective* uses lines of projection converging on a vanishing-point, with objects appearing smaller the further from the viewer. *Aerial (atmospheric) perspective* uses diminished color intensity and blurred contours for objects apparently deeper in space.

Pier A mass of masonry, usually large, used to support *arches or *lintels; more massive than a *column and with a shape other than circular.

Pietà (pyay-TA; It., "pity, compassion") Representations of the Virgin mourning the body of her Son.

Pilaster A flat* column projecting from the wall of a building; usually furnished with a base and *capital in the manner of an engaged column, which is rounded rather than rectangular like the pilaster.

Plainsong The term generally used for the large body of nonmetrical, *monophonic, *liturgical music of the Church of Rome; also called Gregorian chant.

Polyphony (po-LIF-o-nee) *Polyphonic* (pol-ly-PHON-ik), i.e., "many-voiced" music, having melodic interest in two or more simultaneous melodic lines. Examples of polyphonic music would be *canons and *rounds.

Positivism Philosophic inquiry limited to problems open to scientific investigation. Traditional subjects such as *aesthetics and *metaphysics are dismissed as "meaningless" because their content cannot be subjected to verification.

Pragmatism (Gk., *pragma*, "things done") Philosophic doctrine that the meaning of a proposition or course of action lies in its observable consequences and that its meaning is the sum of its consequences. In everyday life the favoring of practical means over theory; if something works, it's good; if not, it's bad.

Primary colors The *hues of red, yellow, and blue with which the colors of the spectrum can be produced. Primary colors cannot be produced by mixing.

Program music Music intended to depict ideas, scenes, or other extramusical concepts.

Psalm A sacred song, poem, or *hymn; the songs in the Old Testament book of Psalms.

Psalter Vernacular name for the book of Psalms.

Purgatory In the teaching of the Church of Rome, the state after death in which the soul destined for heaven is purged of all taint of unpunished or unrepented minor sins.

Q

Quatrain A poetic stanza of four lines, either rhymed or unrhymed.

R

Refrain Recurring section of text (and usually music), e.g., verse-refrain.

Register In music, the range of an instrument or voice, described as high, middle, or low.

Relief In sculpture, carvings projecting from a background that is a part of the whole. Reliefs may be high (almost disengaged from the background) or low (*bas relief*, slightly raised above the background).

Round In music, a commonly used name for a circle *canon. At the conclusion of a melody the singer returns to the beginning, repeating the melody as often as desired. Examples: "Brother James," "Dona Nobis Pacem," and "Row, Row, Row Your Boat."

S

Sacrament In Christianity, one of certain ceremonial observances held to be instituted by Christ when on earth.

Salon The French equivalent and precursor of the Royal Academy exhibitions. It derived its name from the *Salon d'Apollon* in the Louvre. It became a biennial feature in 1737 and annual after the Revolution. In the nineteenth century the admissions system was so exclusive that the *Salon des Refusés* arose as a short-lived alternative.

Salon d'Automne In Paris, the annual fall exhibition of contemporary art.

Satire An indictment of human foibles using humor as a weapon, e.g., the relatively mild satires of Horace and the bitter ones of Juvenal and Jonathan Swift.

Scale (Lat., "ladder") The tonal material of music arranged in a series of rising or falling pitches. Because of the variety in the world's music there are many different scales. The basic scale of European music is the diatonic scale (C-D-E-F-G-A-B-C), i.e., the white keys of the piano. This arrangement of tones is also called a major scale or, in the example given, a C major scale.

Scherzo In music, a lively symphonic movement, usually in 3/4 time.

Secondary colors Those *hues located between the *primary colors on a traditional color wheel: orange, green, and violet.

Seven liberal arts Term originally used to mean studies suited to freemen and consisting of *trivium* (grammar, logic, rhetoric) and *quadrivium* (arithmetic, geometry, astronomy, music).

Sfumato (foo-MAH-toe) A hazy, smoky blending of color tones in a painting to create ambiguities of line and shape, as in Leonardo's *Mona Lisa*.

Silk screen Stencil process. Closely woven silk is tacked tightly over a frame; areas on the silk not to be printed are "stopped out" before paint is squeezed through the silk mesh onto cloth or paper underneath.

Simile A comparison between two quite different things, usually using "like" or "as."

Sonata (From It., *sonare*, "to sound") A musical composition, usually in three or four movements (sections) for a piano or organ or a solo instrument (violin, trumpet, etc.) with keyboard accompaniment.

Sonnet A fourteen-line poem in iambic pentameter (see *meter). Petrarch, the fourteenth-century Italian poet, used a rhyming scheme of *abbaabba* followed by *cde cde* or variants thereof. Shakespeare used a rhyming scheme of *abab cdcd efef gg*, or four *quatrains followed by a rhymed couplet.

Still life In pictorial arts, inanimate objects used as subject matter.

Stucco A durable finish for exterior walls, applied wet and usually composed of cement, sand, and lime.

Symphony A long composition for orchestra, consisting of related movements, usually four in number.

T

Teleology (Gk., *telos*, "end, completion") The theory of purpose, ends, goals, final cause; opposite of materialism.

Tempera A painting technique using pigment suspended in egg yolk.

Tenor (Lat., *tenere*, "to hold") 1. Originally the part that "held" the melody on which early sacred *polyphonic music was based. 2. The highest male voice (SA*T*B). 3. Prefix to the name of an instrument, e.g., tenor saxophone.

Thrust The outward force caused by the weight and design of an *arch or *vault, a thrust that must be countered by a *buttress.

Timbre The quality of a sound that distinguishes it from other sounds of the same pitch and volume; especially the distinctive tone color of a musical instrument or voice.

Tragedy A serious play or other literary work with an unhappy or disastrous ending caused, in Greek drama, by *hubris on the part of the protagonist.

Transcendental Beyond the realm of the senses; rising above common thought or ideas; exalted.

Transept That part of a *cruciform-plan church whose axis intersects at right angles the long axis of the cross running from the entrance through the *nave to the *apse; the cross-arm of the cross.

Triglyph Projecting block with vertical channels that alternates with *metopes in a *Dorian *frieze of a Greek temple. The ends of the marble beams are stylized versions of the wooden beams used in early temples.

Tuscan order Simplified form of the Doric order.

V

Vanishing point In linear *perspective the point at which parallel lines converge on the horizon.

Vault A masonry ceiling constructed on the principle of the *arch. A *barrel vault* is an uninterrupted series of arches amounting to a very deep arch.

Viol Family of bowed string instruments. Developed in the fifteenth century and popular until supplanted in the eighteenth century by the violin family.

Virginal A *harpsichord used mainly in England and supposedly played by young ladies.

Volute The spiral scrolls of an *Ionic *capital.

W

Woodcut A wood block that has been carved so that the design stands out slightly from the block, comparable to printing type.

Annotated Bibliography

Prologue An Introduction to Integrated Humanities

Bennett, William J. *To Reclaim a Legacy: A Report on the Humanities in Higher Education.* Washington, D.C.: Government Printing Office, 1984. Bennett bewails the current lack of emphasis on our past cultural creations and argues for their centrality in education and for understanding our own civilization.

Boorstein, Daniel J. *The Discoverers: A History of Man's Search to Know His World and Himself.* New York: Random House, 1983. An exciting introduction to cultural and intellectual history. Very highly recommended.

Hassan, Ihab, and Sally Hassan, eds. *Innovation/Renovation: New Perspectives on the Humanities.* Madison: University of Wisconsin Press, 1982. Innovative approaches to furthering our understanding of the humanities.

Munro, Thomas. *The Arts— Their Interrelations.* Western Reserve University Press, 1967. An unusual and fascinating approach to comparative aesthetics by a man who is both a professor of philosophy and professor of art.

Post, Gaines, Jr. *The Humanities in American Life.* Berkeley: University of California Press, 1980. Supported by the Rockefeller Foundation, this report of a special commission notes deficiencies in current education and recommends a better integration of the humanities into the curriculum.

Rader, Melvin, and Bertram Jessup. *Art and Human Values.* Englewood Cliffs, N.J.: Prentice Hall, 1976. The role of art in formulating and communicating values.

Read, Herbert. *Education Through Art.* New York: Pantheon Books, 1974. The author bases his approach to aesthetic education on Plato's thesis that art should be the basis of education.

Toynbee, Arnold. *A Study of History.* In several editions (preferably the one-volume abridgement). This classic study articulates and documents one of the most impressive culture-epoch theories of the rise and fall of civilizations.

16 A New Way of Looking at the World

Bainton, Roland H. *Here I Stand: A Life of Martin Luther.* Nashville: Abingdon Press, 1978. Acclaimed as the best introductory biography in English.

———. *Women of the Reformation: In Germany and Italy.* Minneapolis: Augsburg Publishing, 1971. Explores a dimension too often neglected.

Burckhardt, Jacob C. *The Civilization of the Renaissance in Italy.* In any edition. The 19th-century classic that formulated, in part, the modern view of a golden age.

Dickens, A. G. *The Counter-Reformation.* New York: W. W. Norton, 1969. The Roman Catholic response to the Reformation.

Gilmore, Myron P. *The World of Humanism, 1453–1517.* New York: Greenwood, 1983. A well-written survey.

Grimm, Harold J. *The Reformation Era: 1500–1650.* New York: Macmillan, 1973. Fine overview.

Hale, John R. *Renaissance Exploration.* New York: W. W. Norton, 1972. Splendid introduction.

Morison, Samuel E. *Christopher Columbus, Mariner.* New York: New American Library, 1983. A fine, shorter version of this superb storyteller's definitive *Admiral of the Open Sea.*

Rachum, Ilan. *The Renaissance: An Illustrated Encyclopedia.* New York: W. W. Smith, 1980. Exceptionally useful.

Simon, Edith. *The Reformation.* Alexandria, Va.: Time-Life Books, 1966. Another excellent work in the *Great Ages of Man* series.

Weber, Max. *The Protestant Ethic and the Spirit of Capitalism.* New York: Charles Scribner's Sons, 1977. The classic study arguing that Calvinism led to the triumph of capitalism.

17 Renaissance Art: A New Golden Age

Ackerman, James S. *Palladio.* New York: Penguin, 1977. Fine study of a very influential architect.

Andres, Glenn, and others. *The Art of Florence.* 2 vols. New York: Abbeville, 1989. Florence from 1200 to 1600 is given a social and historical context in an excellent new study.

Berenson, Bernard. *The Italian Painters of the Renaissance.* Ithaca: Cornell University Press, 1980. A classic study, still influential.

Bramly, Serge, trans. Sian Reynolds. *Discovering the Life of Leonardo da Vinci.* New York: HarperCollins, 1991. An excellent new study.

Clark, Kenneth. *The Art of Humanism.* New York: Harper & Row, 1983. An urbane art historian presents his sophisticated analysis of Renaissance works.

———. *Civilisation: A Personal View.* New York: Harper & Row, 1970. Excellent chapters on the Renaissance in a work that was the basis for a notable television series.

———. *Leonardo da Vinci.* New York: Penguin, 1976. The dean of art historians takes on the fabulous genius of Leonardo.

Coulas, Ivan. *The Borgias.* New York: Franklin Watts, 1989. A readable scholarly study of an infamous but fascinating family.

De Tolnay, Charles. *Michelangelo: Sculptor, Painter, Architect.* Princeton: Princeton University Press, 1982. A condensation of the author's magisterial six-volume study.

Fine, Elsa Honig. *Women and Art; A History of Women Painters and Sculptors from the Renaissance to the 20th Century.* Montclair/London: Allanheld & Schram/Prior, 1978.

Fuller, Edmund, ed. *Vasari's Lives of the Painters, Sculptors, and Architects.* New York: Dell Publishing, 1963. The most pertinent selections from the Renaissance classic.

MacCurdy, Edward, trans. *The Notebooks of Leonardo da Vinci.* 2 vols. London: Chatto Bodley Jonathan, 1978. Only in the notebooks can one begin to appreciate the range and richness of one of the greatest minds in history.

Martineau, Jane, and Charles Hope, eds. *The Genius of Venice.* New York: Abrams, 1984. Art in the unique city.

Panofsky, Erwin. *The Life and Art of Albrecht Dürer.* Princeton: Princeton University Press, 1955. Probably the finest single work in English on the German genius.

Snyder, James. *Northern Renaissance Art.* New York: Abrams, 1985. Excellent coverage.

18 Renaissance Music: Court and Church

Dolmetsch, Mabel. *Dances of England and France from 1450–1600: With Their Music and Authentic Manner of Performance.* New York: Da Capo Press, 1975.

Lincoln, Harry B., ed. *Madrigal Collection L'amorosa Ero* (Brescia, 1588). Albany, N.Y.: State University of New York Press, 1968.

Scott, Charles K., ed. *Madrigal Singing.* Westport, Conn: Greenwood, n.d.

19 Shadow and Substance: Literary Insights into the Renaissance

Chute, Marchette. *Shakespeare of London.* New York: E. P. Dutton, 1950. One of the best popular biographies.

Montaigne, Michel de. *Essays.* Trans. J. M. Cohen. New York: Penguin, 1959. Recommended translation of fascinating essays by the inventor of the form.

More, Thomas. *UTOPIA and Other Writings.* James Green and John Dolan, eds. New York: New American Library, 1984. Excellent edition.

Phillips, Margaret M. *Erasmus and the Northern Renaissance.* New York: Rowman, 1981. Explores the central role of Erasmus.

Rabelais, François. *Gargantua and Pantagruel.* Trans. John M. Cohen. New York: Penguin, 1955. Excellent translation of the ribald classic.

Ross, James Bruce, and Mary Martin McLaughlin, eds. *The Portable Renaissance Reader.* New York: Viking, 1968. Excellent collection of writings of acknowledged masters.

20 Science, Reason, and Absolutism

Historical Background

Blitzer, Charles. *Age of Kings.* New York: Time, Inc., 1967. Every volume in the *Great Ages of Man* series is interesting and informative.

Lefebvre, Georges. *The French Revolution: Vol. I From Its Origins to 1793.* Trans. John H. Stewart. New York: Columbia University Press, 1962. By the greatest modern scholar of the French revolt.

Stone, Laurence. *The Causes of the English Revolution, 1529–1642.* New York: Harper & Row, 1972. How clashes between Puritans and monarchs led to the Cromwell commonwealth experiment.

Cultural Developments

Bennet, Jonathan. *Locke, Berkeley, Hume: Central Themes.* New York: Oxford University Press, 1971. Three of the most influential thinkers of the time.

Burke, Peter. *Popular Culture in Early Modern Europe.* New York: New York University Press, 1978. A fascinating account of the period 1500–1800.

Gay, Peter. *The Enlightenment: An Interpretation.* 2 vols. New York: W. W. Norton, 1977. A remarkable work by a noted authority.

Hall, A. Rupert. *The Revolution in Science: 1500–1750.* New York: Longman, 1983. From Copernicus and Galileo to Newton and the foundation of the modern scientific outlook.

Santillana, Giorgio de. *The Crime of Galileo.* New York: Time Inc., 1962. A devastating analysis of what a powerful institution can do to an innocent victim.

Original Materials

Brady, Frank, ed. *Boswell's Life of Samuel Johnson.* New York: New American Library, 1981. An abridged version of this mammoth biographical masterpiece.

Montesquieu, Charles de. *The Spirit of the Laws.* Ed. David W. Carrithers. Berkeley: University of California Press, 1978. Influential in several revolutions.

Peterson, Merrill D., ed. *The Portable Thomas Jefferson.* New York: Penguin, 1979. Ample collection of writings by the Yankee genius, including correspondence with prominent people.

21 Art: Baroque, Rococo, and Neoclassic

Bazin, Germain. *Baroque and Rococo Art.* New York: Oxford University Press, 1964. Good survey by a noted authority.

———. *The Baroque: Principles, Styles, Modes, Themes.* New York: W. W. Norton, 1978. A comprehensive analysis of general features.

Brown, Dale. *The World of Velasquez, 1599–1660.* New York: Time-Life Books, 1969. A thorough study in the very fine *Library of Art* series. This series is valuable and rewarding for critics and laymen alike. One wonders why the former have not given them the time and appraisal they so clearly deserve. No matter—don't miss any volume in this extensive series.

Clark, Kenneth. *An Introduction to Rembrandt.* New York: Harper & Row, 1978. A fine art historian on one of the most famous painters.

Schneider, Pierre. *The World of Watteau, 1684–1721.* New York: Time-Life Books, 1967. A delightful volume in the *Library of Art* series, as charming as the artists, works, and society it presents.

Wallace, Robert. *The World of Bernini, 1598–1680.* New York: Time-Life Books, 1970. Superb, as usual for the *Library of Art* series.

Wright, Christopher. *The Dutch Painters: One Hundred Seventeenth-Century Masters.* Woodbury, N.Y.: Barron, 1978.

22 Music: Baroque, Rococo, and Classical

Pauly, Reinhard. *Music in the Classic Period.* Englewood Cliffs, N.J.: Prentice Hall, 1965. Survey of the style with a minimum of technical obstacles.

Rosen, Charles. *The Classical Style: Haydn, Mozart, Beethoven.* New York: W. W. Norton, 1972. Winner of the 1972 National Book Award for Arts and Letters.

23 Revolution, Romanticism, Realism

Historical Background

Arendt, Hannah. *On Revolution.* New York: Penguin, 1977. A noted political analyst examines what the American and French revolutions mean to people living today.

Burchell, Samuel C. *The Age of Progress.* New York: Time-Life Books, 1966. Excellent.

Fieldhouse, D. K. *Colonialism, 1870–1945: An Introduction.* New York: St. Martin's Press, 1981. Today's world, especially the Third World, cannot be fully understood without constant reference to colonialism and its aftermath.

Schama, Simon. *Citizens: A Chronicle of the French Revolution.* New York: Knopf, 1989. A revisionist theory claiming that the *ancien régime* was itself the catalyst of the political and social changes. Historians have attacked the theory as irresponsible nonsense.

Tuchman, Barbara. *The Guns of August.* New York: Macmillan, 1962. A vivid account of the Great War's outbreak. Her *The Proud Tower* is an equally riveting study of the two decades leading to the war.

Cultural Developments

Eiseley, Loren C. *Darwin's Century: Evolution and the Men Who Discovered It.* Garden City, N.Y.: Doubleday, 1958. A beautifully written account.

———. *The Immense Journey.* New York: Random House, 1957. A classic account of evolution and the story of humankind.

Literature and Criticism

Bloom, Harold, and Lionel Trilling, eds. *Romantic Prose and Poetry.* New York: Oxford University Press, 1973. An excellent anthology.

Rozanov, Vasily. *Dostoevsky and the Legend of the Grand Inquisitor.* Ithaca, N.Y.: Cornell University Press, 1972. The origins of Dostoevsky's ideas.

Sandor, Ellis. *Political Apocalypse: A Study of Dostoevsky's Grand Inquisitor.* Baton Rouge: Louisiana State University Press, 1971.

Trilling, Lionel, and Harold Bloom, eds. *Victorian Prose and Poetry.* New York: Oxford University Press, 1973. A fine companion volume to their anthology of Romantic works.

Videotape

Burns, Ken. *The Civil War.* First aired in 1990 on PBS, this is a stunning 13-hour series. Richmond, Va., Time-Life Video.

24 Romanticism in Music

Dannreuther, E. *The Romantic Period.* New York: Cooper Square, 1973. Quite a thorough exposition of the varieties of Romantic expression.

Holoman, D. Kern. *Berlioz: A Musical Biography of the Creative Genius of the Romantic Era.* Cambridge, Mass.: Harvard University Press, 1990. By far the most intellectual of the great composers, Berlioz is also honored in French literature as a writer and a critic.

Plantinga, Leon. *Romantic Music.* New York: W. W. Norton, 1982. Introductory text.

25 Nineteenth-Century Art: Conflict and Diversity

Herbert, Robert L. *Impressionism.* New Haven: Yale University Press, 1988. A major new interpretation of the style in its social/cultural context. Strongly recommended.

Prather, Marla, and Charles F. Stuckey, eds. *Gauguin: A Retrospective.* New York: Hugh Lauter Levin Associates, 1987. Outstanding text and illustrations.

Prideaux, Tom, et al. *The World of Delacroix.* New York: Time-Life Books, 1966. The focus is on Delacroix, but his important contemporaries are also included.

———. *The World of Whistler, 1834–1903.* New York: Time-Life Books, 1970. Still more in the fine *Library of Art* series.

Rewald, John. *The History of Impressionism.* New York: New York Graphic Society Books, 1980. Any book by Rewald on Impressionism or Postimpressionism is highly recommended.

———. *Post-Impressionism: From van Gogh to Gauguin.* New York: New York Graphic Society Books, 1979.

Schneider, Pierre. *The World of Manet, 1832–1883.* New York: Time-Life Books,

1968. Scholarly, clear, concise, and beautiful.
Shapiro, Meyer. *Van Gogh.* New York: Abrams, 1984. One of the few objective studies. Highly recommended.
Simpson, Marc, and others. *Winslow Homer: Paintings of the Civil War.* Fine Arts Museum of San Francisco and Bedford Arts Publications, 1988. A unique visual overview of the conflict. Poignant.
Wallace, Robert, et al. *The World of van Gogh, 1853–1890.* New York: Time-Life Books, 1969. Concise biographies of van Gogh and other artists who have been romanticized in literature and in the movies.

26 Things Fall Apart: The Center Cannot Hold

Historical Background

Galbraith, John Kenneth. *The Great Crash, 1929.* Boston: Houghton Mifflin, 1979. The celebrated economist on the catastrophe that ushered in the Great Depression.
Mitchell, Broadus. *Depression Decade: From New Era through New Deal, 1929–1941.* Arnmonk, N.Y.: M. E. Sharpe, 1977. New York: Newsweek Books, 1970. Fine review of significant developments.
Taylor, A. J. P. *The Origins of the Second World War.* New York: Atheneum, 1983. A respected historian reviews the evidence.
———. *This Fabulous Century: Sixty Years of American Life.* New York: Time-Life Books, 1969–70. From 1870 to 1970 in eight volumes. A vivid overview.

Cultural and Scientific Developments

Abraham, N. B., ed. *Complexity and chaos: proceedings of the second Bryn Mahr Workshop on Measures on Complexity and Chaos*, Bryn Mahr, Pa., 13–15 August 1992. Riveredge, N.J., 1992.
Calder, Nigel. *Einstein's Universe.* New York: Greenwich House, 1982. Einstein explained for the general reader.
Dawkins, Richard. *The Blind Watchmaker: Why the Evidence of Evolution Reveals a Universe Without Design.* New York: W. W. Norton, 1986. The author's thesis is that the Darwinian worldview could, in principle, help solve the mystery of our existence.
Edelson, Marshall. *Hypothesis and Evidence in Psychoanalysis.* Chicago: University of Chicago Press, 1984.
Gell-Mann, Murray. *The Quark and the Jaguar: Adventures in the Simple and Complex.* New York: W. H. Freeman, 1994.
Gleick, James. *Chaos: Making a New Science.* New York: Viking, 1887. As a physicist put it, "relativity eliminated the Newtonian illusion of absolute space and time; quantum theory eliminated the Newtonian dream of a controllable measurement process; and chaos eliminated the Laplacian fantasy of deterministic predictability."
Grünbaum, Adolf. *The Foundations of Psychoanalysis: A Philosophical Critique.* Berkeley: University of California Press, 1984.
Hitler, Adolf. *Mein Kampf.* Boston: Houghton Mifflin, 1962. Hitler's self-serving autobiography of 1925 with his version of history and vision of the future.
Lewin, Roger. *Complexity: Life at the Edge of Chaos.* New York: Macmillan, 1992.
Noakes, Jeremy, and Geoffrey Pridham, eds. *Documents on Nazism, 1919–1945.* New York: Viking, 1975. A revealing collection, to say the least.
Pipes, Richard. *The Russian Revolution.* New York: Knopf, 1990. The thesis that the February Revolution was a military rebellion (not a workers' revolt) and the Bolshevik takeover in October a *coup d'état.* Further, that when Stalin came to power in 1924 Lenin had all the totalitarian controls firmly in place.
Waldrop, M. Mitchell. *Complexity: The Emerging Science at the Edge of Chaos.* New York: Simon & Schuster, 1992.

Historical Fiction

Pasternak, Boris. *Dr. Zhivago.* New York: Ballantine Books, 1981. The Nobel Laureate's portrait of the Russian Revolution and its aftermath as seen from the inside.
Steinbeck, John. *The Grapes of Wrath.* New York: Penguin, 1977. An indelible picture of the Great Depression as experienced by the Joad family from Oklahoma.

27 Ideas and Conflicts that Motivate the Twentieth Century

Historical Background

Capute, Philip. *A Rumor of War.* New York: Ballantine Books, 1978. Acclaimed the best memoir of the American experience in Vietnam.
Hilberg, Raul. *The Destruction of European Jews.* New York: Harper & Row, 1979. A study of Nazi genocide.
Johnson, Paul. *Modern Times: The World from the Twenties to the Eighties.* New York: Harper & Row, 1983. Highly recommended.
Knox, Bernard. *The Oldest Dead White European Males and Other Reflections on the Classics.* New York: W. W. Norton, 1993. Despite all the sound and fury about being "politically correct," the title of this latest book by a noted classicist states what cannot be denied: this is where, for the most part, Western civilization came from.
Lerner, Gerda. *Women and History. Volume One: The Creation of Patrimony.* New York: Oxford University Press, 1986. Excellent.
Wiesel, Elie. *Night.* Trans. Stella Rodway. New York: Bantam Books, 1982. The celebrated writer and Nobel Laureate describes his experiences in Hitler's death camps.
Taplin, Oliver. *Greek Fire: The Influence of Ancient Greece on the Modern World.* New York: Atheneum, 1990. Fascinating. The opening line foretells the contents: "Not back to the Greeks, but forward with the Greeks."

Cultural Developments

Baruch, Grace, Rosalind Barnett, and Caryl Rivers. *Life Prints: New Patterns of Love and Work for Today's Women.* New York: McGraw-Hill, 1983. Important study.
Blashfield, Jean F. *Hellraisers, Heroines, and Holy Women: Women's Most Remarkable Contributions to History.* New York: St. Martin's Press, 1981. Just about everything from the "Astronomer to Classify the Most Stars" (Annie Jump Cannon) to the "First Woman to be Kicked Out of Harvard" (Harriet Hunt, 1859).
Bullock, Alan, and R. B. Woodings, eds. *Modern Culture: A Biographical Companion.* New York: Harper & Row, 1984. Articles on key figures in 20th-century culture.
Greer, Germaine. *Sex and Destiny: The Politics of Human Fertility.* New York: Harper & Row, 1984. An analysis of gender relations in contemporary society.
Herbert, Nick. *Quantum Reality: Beyond the New Physics.* Garden City, N.Y.: Anchor Press/Doubleday, 1985. A popular exposition of six emergent models of the ultimate nature of atomic reality based on post–Einsteinian physics.
Littwin, Susan. *The Postponed Generation: Why American Youth Are Growing Up Later.* New York: William Morrow and Company, 1986. An intriguing analysis of diminished expectations.
Mosse, George L. *Nazi Culture.* New York: Schocken Books, 1981. A noted historian analyzes the vulgarity of Hitler's Germany.

28 Art in the Twentieth Century: Shock Waves and Reactions

Arnason, H. Hovard. *History of Modern Art: Painting, Sculpture, and Architecture.* New York: Abrams, 1986. Excellent general study with an exhaustive bibliography.
Bearden, Romare, and Harry Henderson. *Six Black Masters of American Art.* New York: Doubleday, 1972. Includes Johnson, Duncanson, Pippin, and Lawrence.
———. *A History of African-American Artists: From 1792 to the Present.* New York: Pantheon, 1993.
Billington, David P. *The Tower and the Bridge: The New Art of Structural Engineering.* New York: Basic Books, Publishers, 1983. The efficiency, economy, and elegance of structural engineering.
Broude, Norma, and Mary D. Garrard, eds. *Feminism and Art History: Questioning the Litany.* New York: Harper & Row, 1982. Essays toward revising the history of art.
Chipp, Herschel. *Picasso's Guernica: History, Transformations, Meanings.* Berkeley: University of California Press, 1988.
Connor, Steven. *Postmodernist Culture: An Introduction to Theories of the Contemporary.* New York: Blackwell, 1990.
Fine, Elsa Honig. *The Afro-American Artist: A Search for Identity.* Reprint. New York: Hacker, 1982. Twenty important artists.

Goodman, Cynthia. *Digital Visions: Computers and Art.* New York: Abrams, 1987. Computer-generated art.

Huffington, Arianna Stassinopoulos, "Picasso: Creator and Destroyer." *The Atlantic*, June 1988, Vol. 261, No. 6, pp. 37–78. Controversial and highly critical biography of Picasso the man.

Hughes, Robert. *The Shock of the New: Art and the Century of Change.* New York: Knopf, 2nd ed., 1990. This fascinating work grew out of the TV series for BBC and, later, PBS.

Hutcheon, Linda. *A Poetics of Postmodernism: History, Theory, Fiction.* New York: Routledge, 1990. Primary focus on literature.

Jencks, Charles. *Architecture Today.* New York: Abrams, 1988. Significant trends in Late-Modern and Postmodern architecture.

Newhall, Beaumont. *The History of Photography: From 1839 to the Present.* Completely revised and enlarged edition. New York: The Museum of Modern Art, 1982. Hailed as a classic work on the subject.

Normand-Romain, Antoinette Le. *Sculpture: The Adventure of Modern Sculpture in the Nineteenth and Twentieth Centuries.* New York: Rizzoli, 1986. Fine overview and beautifully illustrated.

Parker, Rozsica, and Griselda Pollock. *Old Mistresses: Women, Art, and Ideology.* New York: Pantheon, 1982. A reexamination not merely of women artists, but of art history in general.

Quirarte, Jacinto. *Mexican American Artists.* Austin: University of Texas Press, 1973. A good overview with an extensive bibliography.

Rosen, Randy, and Catherine Brewer. *Making Their Mark: Women Artists Move into the Mainstream.* New York: Abbeville, 1989. The prominent role of women: 1970–85.

Rubinstein, Charlotte Streifer. *American Women Artists: From Early Indian Times to the Present.* Boston: G. K. Hall, 1982. The first comprehensive survey of American women artists.

Russell, John. *The Meaning of Modern Art.* New York: Harper & Row, 1981. Outstanding interpretation. Invaluable.

Slatkin, Wendy. *Women Artists in History: From Antiquity to the 20th Century.* Englewood Cliffs, N.J.: Prentice Hall, 2nd ed., 1990. Good overview. Recorded names of women artists dating back to the 3rd century BC (updated 31 July, 1992).

Tomkins, Calvin, et al. *The World of Marcel Duchamp.* New York: Time-Life Books, 1966. One of the most informative and enjoyable (at times hilarious) studies in art literature.

Toulmin, Stephen. *Cosmopolis: The Hidden Agenda of Modernity.* New York: Free Press, 1990. Primary focus on philosophy.

29 Modern Music

Classical Music

Hamm, Charles. *Music in the New World.* New York: W. W. Norton, 1983. Good overview of American music.

Morgan, Robert P. *Twentieth-Century Music.* New York: W. W. Norton, 1987. From the Norton Introduction to Music Series.

Zaimont, Judith Lang, and Karen Famera, eds. *Contemporary Concert Music by Women: A Directory of the Composers and Their Works.* Westport, Conn.: Greenwood, 1981.

Jazz

Berendt, Joachim. *The Jazz Book: From Ragtime to Fusion and Beyond.* Westport, Conn.: Hill, Lawrence, 1982. Excellent work by a recognized authority.

Booth, Mark W. *American Popular Music: A Reference Guide.* Westport, Conn.: Greenwood, 1983. Valuable resource for ragtime, jazz, Tin Pan Alley, Broadway, Hollywood, Nashville, and so on.

Oliver, Paul. *The Meaning of the Blues.* New York: Macmillan, 1963. Probably the best single book on the blues.

Placksin, Sally. *American Women in Jazz: 1900 to the Present.* New York: Seaview Books, 1982. Overdue recognition of some fine jazz musicians.

Tanner, Paul, et al. *Jazz.* 6th ed. Dubuque, Ia.: Wm. C. Brown, 1988. Good general text.

Credits

Every effort has been made to contact the copyright holders of literary extracts within this book, but should there by any errors or omissions, the publisher would be pleased to insert the appropriate credit in any subsequent edition.

CHAPTER 19
Page 84: © Peter Bondanella and Mark Musa 1979. Reprinted from *The Prince* by Niccolo Machiavelli trans. Peter Bondanella and Mark Musa (1984) by permission of Oxford University Press.

Page 99: "Second Book, Chapter Eight" from *The Works of François Rabelais*, Volume I, by Alfred J. Nock, C. R. Wilson, trans. Urguhart-Lemontteux, copyright 1931 by Harcourt Brace Jovanovich, Inc. and renewed 1959 by Catherine Rose Wilson and S. Nock, reprinted by permission of the publisher.

CHAPTER 20
Page 146: *Tartuffe* by Moliére, translation copyright © 1963, 1961 and renewed 1991, 1990, 1989 by Richard Wilbur, reprinted by permission of Harcourt Brace & Company. CAUTION: Professionals and amateurs are hereby warned that this translation, being fully protected under the copyright laws of the United States of America, the British Empire, including the Dominion of Canada, and all other countries which are signatories to the Universal Copyright Convention and the International Copyright Union, is subject to royalty. All rights, including professional, amateur, motion picture, recitation, lecturing, public reading, radio broadcasting, and television are strictly reserved. Particular emphasis is laid on the question of readings, permission for which must be secured from the author's agent in writing. Inquiries on professional rights (except for amateur rights) should be addressed to Curtis Brown, 10 Astor Place, New York, N.Y. 10003; inquiries on translation rights should be addressed to Harcourt Brace & Company, Permissions Department, Orlando, Fla. 32887.

CHAPTER 23
Page 258: Reprinted from *The Brothers Karamazov* by Fyodor Dostoevsky, trans. from the German by Constance Garnett, rev. and ed. Ralph E. Matlaw, with the permission of W. W. Norton & Company, Inc. Copyright © 1976 by W. W. Norton & Company, Inc.

CHAPTER 26
Page 333: "The Love Song of J. Alfred Prufrock" from *Collected Poems 1909–1962*, copyright 1936 by Harcourt Brace Jovanovich. Inc., copyright © 1964, 1963 by T. S. Eliot, reprinted by permission of Harcourt Brace Jovanovich, Inc., and Faber & Faber Limited, London.

Page 335: "Dulce et Decorum Est" from *Complete Poems and Fragments of Wilfred Owen,* ed. Jon Stallworthy, © Chatto & Windus and Wilfred Owen: *Collected Poems of Wilfred Owen*. Copyright © 1963 by Chatto & Windus, Ltd. Reprinted by permission of New Directions Publishing Corporation.

Page 335: "The Second Coming" reprinted with permission of Macmillan Publishing Company from *The Poems of W. B. Yeats: A New Edition,* ed. Richard J. Finneran. Copyright © 1924 by Macmillan Publishing Company, renewed 1952 by Bertha Georgie Yeats.

Page 336: From the *Selected Poetry of Robinson Jeffers* by Robinson Jeffers. Copyright © 1925 and renewed 1953 by Robinson Jeffers. Reprinted by permission of Random House, Inc.

Page 336: Reprinted by permission of GRM Associates, Inc., Agents for the Estate of Ida M. Cullen, from the book *Color* by Countee Cullen. Copyright © 1925 by Harper & Brothers; copyright renewed 1953 by Ida M. Cullen.

CHAPTER 27
Page 341: From *Collected Poems 1930–1976* by Richard Eberhart. Copyright © 1988 by Richard Eberhart. Reprinted by permission of Oxford University Press, Inc.

Page 347: From *The Myth of Sisyphus and Other Essays* by Albert Camus, trans. J. O'Brien. Copyright © 1955 by Alfred A. Knopf, Inc. Reprinted by permission of Alfred A. Knopf, Inc., New York, N.Y., and Hamish Hamilton Ltd., London.

Page 351: Letter from Birmingham Jail, April 16th 1963 from Martin Luther King, Jr., *Why We Can't Wait*, reprinted by arrangement with The Heirs to the Estate of Martin Luther King, Jr., c/o Joan Daves Agency as agent for the proprietor. Copyright 1963 by Martin Luther King, Jr., copyright renewed 1991 by Coretta Scott King.

Page 352: From *The Panther and the Lash* by Langston Hughes. Copyright © 1951 by Langston Hughes. Reprinted by permission of Alfred A. Knopf, Inc. and Harold Ober Associates Incorporated.

Page 354: "I Like to Think of Harriet Tubman" from *Like the Iris of an Eye* by Susan Griffin. Copyright Susan Griffin. Reprinted by permission.

Page 355: "If Shakespeare Had A Sister" from *A Room of One's Own* by Virginia Woolf, copyright 1929 by Harcourt Brace Jovanovich, Inc. and renewed 1957 by Leonard Woolf, reprinted by permission of the publisher.

CHAPTER 30
Page 425: "anyone lived in a pretty how town" is reprinted from *Complete Poems, 1904–1962*, by e e cummings, ed. George J. Firmage, by permission of Liveright Publishing Corporation. Copyright © 1940, 1968, 1991 by the Trustees for the E. E. Cummings Trust.

Page 425: "When all My Five and Country Senses See" from Dylan Thomas: *Poems of Dylan Thomas*. Copyright 1939 by new Directions Publishing Corporation. First printed in "Poetry."

Page 431: "The Disinterested Killer Bill Harrigan," from *A Universal History of Infamy* by Jorge Luis Borges, trans. Norman Thomas di Giovanni. Translation copyright © 1970, 1971, 1972 by Emece Editores, S. A. and Norman Thomas di Giovanni. Used by permission of Dutton Signet a division of Penguin Books USA Inc.

Page 436: From *Invisible Man* by Ralph Ellison. Copyright © 1948 by Ralph Ellison. Reprinted by permission of Random House, Inc.

Page 441: Gwendolyn Brooks, "The Bean Eaters" and "We Real Cool" from *Black* © 1991, published by Third World Press, P.O. Box 19730, Chicago, Ill. 60619.

Page 442: "Adultery" Reprinted from *Poems, 1957–1967*. © 1967 by James Dickey, Wesleyan University Press. Reprinted by permission of University Press of New England.

Page 443: "Two Songs" is reprinted from *The Face of a Doorframe,* Poems Selected and New, 1950–1984, by Adrienne Rich, by permission of W. W. Norton & Company, Inc. Copyright © 1984 by Adrienne Rich, Copyright © 1975, 1978 by W. W. Norton & Company, Inc. Copyright © 1981 by Adrienne Rich.

Page 443: "Flight on the Wind" from *House Made of Dawn* by N. Scott Momaday. Copyright © 1966, 1967, 1968 by N. Scott Momaday. Reprinted by permission of HarperCollins Publishers.

Page 447: From *Dream Children* by Gail Godwin. Copyright © 1976 by Gail Godwin. Reprinted by permission of Alfred A. Knopf, inc.

Page 450: From *Catch-22* by Joseph Heller. Copyright © 1955, 1961, 1989 by Joseph Heller. Reprinted by permission of Simon & Schuster, Inc.

Index